HANDBOOK OF TEMPERAMENT

Edited by
**Marcel Zentner
Rebecca L. Shiner**

THE GUILFORD PRESS
New York   London

© 2012 The Guilford Press
A Division of Guilford Publications, Inc.
72 Spring Street, New York, NY 10012
www.guilford.com

All rights reserved

No part of this book may be reproduced, translated, stored in a retrieval system, or transmitted, in any form or by any means, electronic, mechanical, photocopying, microfilming, recording, or otherwise, without written permission from the publisher.

Printed in the United States of America

This book is printed on acid-free paper.

Last digit is print number: 9 8 7 6 5 4 3 2 1

Library of Congress Cataloging-in-Publication Data

Handbook of temperament / edited by Marcel Zentner, Rebecca L. Shiner.
    p. cm.
  Includes bibliographical references and index.
  ISBN 978-1-4625-0648-4 (hardcover)
  1. Temperament. 2. Temperament—Handbooks, manuals, etc. I. Zentner, Marcel. II. Shiner, Rebecca L.
  BF798.H36 2012
  152.4—dc23
                                                         2012003562

About the Editors

Marcel Zentner, PhD, is Senior Lecturer in Psychology at the University of York, United Kingdom. Dr. Zentner serves as an associate editor of *Frontiers in Personality Science and Individual Differences*. His main areas of research are personality, temperament, emotion, test development, and music perception.

Rebecca L. Shiner, PhD, is Associate Professor, Presidential Scholar, and Chair of Psychology at Colgate University, Hamilton, New York. Dr. Shiner's research focuses on temperament and personality development in childhood and adolescence, with a particular interest in the pathways through which personality traits contribute to the development of personality disorders and other forms of psychopathology.

Contributors

Kelly M. Allred, BA, Department of Psychology, University of Pennsylvania, Philadelphia, Pennsylvania

Elaine N. Aron, PhD, Department of Psychology, Stony Brook University, Stony Brook, New York

Marian J. Bakermans-Kranenburg, PhD, Centre for Child and Family Studies, Department of Education and Child Studies, Leiden University, Leiden, The Netherlands

Christina S. Barr, VMD, PhD, Section of Comparative Behavioral Genomics, Laboratory of Neurogenetics, National Institute on Alcohol Abuse and Alcoholism, National Institutes of Health, Rockville, Maryland

John E. Bates, PhD, Department of Psychological and Brain Sciences, Indiana University, Bloomington, Indiana

David J. Bridgett, PhD, Department of Psychology, Northern Illinois University, DeKalb, Illinois

Amanda Bullock, MA, Department of Psychology, Carleton University, Ottawa, Ontario, Canada

Susan D. Calkins, PhD, Department of Human Development and Family Studies and Department of Psychology, University of North Carolina at Greensboro, Greensboro, North Carolina

Avshalom Caspi, PhD, Department of Psychology and Neuroscience, Duke University, Durham, North Carolina

Xinyin Chen, PhD, Applied Psychology and Human Development Division, Graduate School of Education, University of Pennsylvania, Philadelphia, Pennsylvania

Ashleigh Collins, MEd, Department of Teaching and Learning, Steinhardt School of Culture, Education, and Human Development, New York University, New York, New York

Robert J. Coplan, PhD, Department of Psychology, Carleton University, Ottawa, Ontario, Canada

Kirby Deater-Deckard, PhD, Department of Psychology, Virginia Polytechnic Institute and State University, Blacksburg, Virginia

Sarah S. W. De Pauw, PhD, Department of Developmental, Personality and Social Psychology, Ghent University, Ghent, Belgium

Richard A. Depue, PhD, Laboratory of Neurobiology of Personality, Department of Human Development, Cornell University, Ithaca, New York

Angela Lee Duckworth, PhD, Department of Psychology, University of Pennsylvania, Philadelphia, Pennsylvania

Margaret W. Dyson, MA, Department of Psychology, Stony Brook University, Stony Brook, New York

Nicole M. Else-Quest, PhD, Department of Psychology, University of Maryland, Baltimore County, Baltimore, Maryland

Nathan A. Fox, PhD, Department of Human Development, University of Maryland, College Park, Maryland

Rui Fu, MA, Applied Psychology and Human Development Division, Graduate School of Education, University of Pennsylvania, Philadelphia, Pennsylvania

Yu Fu, MS, Laboratory of Neurobiology of Personality, Department of Human Development, Cornell University, Ithaca, New York

Jeffrey R. Gagne, PhD, Department of Psychology, University of Texas at Arlington, Arlington, Texas

Maria A. Gartstein, PhD, Department of Psychology, Washington State University, Pullman, Washington

H. Hill Goldsmith, PhD, Department of Psychology, University of Wisconsin–Madison, Madison, Wisconsin

Sarah E. Hampson, PhD, Oregon Research Institute, Eugene, Oregon

Sarah M. Helfinstein, PhD, Department of Psychology, University of Texas at Austin, Austin, Texas

Anja C. Huizink, PhD, Department of Developmental Psychology, Faculty of Psychology and Education, VU University Amsterdam, Amsterdam, The Netherlands

Salomon Israel, MA, Department of Psychology, The Hebrew University, Jerusalem, Israel

Jerome Kagan, PhD, Department of Psychology, Harvard University, Cambridge, Massachusetts

Daniel N. Klein, PhD, Department of Psychology, Stony Brook University, Stony Brook, New York

Ariel Knafo, PhD, Department of Psychology, The Hebrew University, Jerusalem, Israel

Roman Kotov, PhD, Department of Psychiatry and Behavioral Science, Stony Brook University, Stony Brook, New York

Autumn J. Kujawa, BA, Department of Psychology, Stony Brook University, Stony Brook, New York

Shauna C. Kushner, MA, Department of Psychology, University of Toronto, Toronto, Ontario, Canada

Connie Lamm, PhD, Child Development Laboratory, Department of Human Development, University of Maryland, College Park, Maryland

Liliana J. Lengua, PhD, Department of Psychology, University of Washington, Seattle, Washington

Christina M. Low, BA, Department of Psychology, Washington State University, Pullman, Washington

Kevin B. MacDonald, PhD, Department of Psychology, California State University, Long Beach, Long Beach, California

Michelle M. Martel, PhD, Department of Psychology, University of New Orleans, New Orleans, Louisiana

Sandee Graham McClowry, PhD, RN, FAAN, Department of Counseling Psychology and Department of Teaching and Learning, Steinhardt School of Culture, Education, and Human Development, New York University, New York, New York

Ivan Mervielde, PhD (deceased), Department of Developmental, Personality and Social Psychology, Ghent University, Ghent, Belgium

Isaac T. Petersen, BA, Department of Psychological and Brain Sciences, Indiana University, Bloomington, Indiana

Samuel P. Putnam, PhD, Department of Psychology, Bowdoin College, Brunswick, Maine

Mary K. Rothbart, PhD, Department of Psychology, University of Oregon, Eugene, Oregon

M. Rosario Rueda, PhD, Department of Experimental Psychology, Faculty of Psychology, University of Granada, Granada, Spain

Kimberly J. Saudino, PhD, Department of Psychology, Boston University, Boston, Massachusetts

Alice C. Schermerhorn, PhD, Department of Psychological and Brain Sciences, Indiana University, Bloomington, Indiana

Rebecca L. Shiner, PhD, Department of Psychology, Colgate University, Hamilton, New York

Jan Strelau, PhD, Faculty of Psychology, University of Social Sciences and Humanities, Warsaw, Poland

Margaret M. Swingler, PhD, Department of Human Development and Family Studies, University of North Carolina at Greensboro, Greensboro, North Carolina

Jennifer L. Tackett, PhD, Department of Psychology, University of Houston, Houston, Texas

Marinus H. van IJzendoorn, PhD, Centre for Child and Family Studies, Rommert Casimir Institute of Developmental Psychopathology, Institute of Education and Child Studies, Leiden University, Leiden, The Netherlands

Margarete E. Vollrath, PhD, Department of Psychosomatics and Health Behavior, Norwegian Institute of Public Health, Oslo, Norway

Theodore D. Wachs, PhD, Department of Psychological Sciences, Purdue University, West Lafayette, Indiana

Manjie Wang, MA, Department of Psychology, Boston University, Boston, Massachusetts

Zhe Wang, MS, Department of Psychology, Virginia Polytechnic Institute and State University, Blacksburg, Virginia

Lauren K. White, MS, Child Development Laboratory, Department of Human Development, University of Maryland, College Park, Maryland

Fan Yang, MEd, Applied Psychology and Human Development Division, Graduate School of Education, University of Pennsylvania, Philadelphia, Pennsylvania

Bogdan Zawadzki, PhD, Faculty of Psychology, University of Warsaw, Warsaw, Poland

Marcel Zentner, PhD, Department of Psychology, University of York, York, United Kingdom

Marvin Zuckerman, PhD, Department of Psychology, University of Delaware, Newark, Delaware

Preface

During the last decades, temperament research has undergone a momentous transformation. Formerly a small area nested within personality research, it has grown into a cross-disciplinary field investigating individual differences at the interface of brain and behavior. Today, temperament research examines the neurogenetics, early appearance, life-course patterns, and clinical implications of complex traits, including anxiety, anger proneness, or impulse control. Such a research endeavor goes far beyond the domain of personality, requiring an integration of knowledge from various disciplines, notably genetics, neuroscience, biological psychiatry, psychopathology, perinatology, pediatrics, developmental psychology, prevention, and intervention. Blending perspectives and findings from all these areas, temperament has become a veritable new synthesis of research into the neuroaffective core of human individuality.

Three developments contributed to this remarkable growth of temperament research. The identity of temperament research, as known from Galen to Sheldon, was drastically altered when, in 1963, Thomas and colleagues reported the findings of their research into infants' temperamental characteristics and the impact of these characteristics on psychological development (Thomas, Chess, Birch, Hertzig, & Korn, 1963). Subsequent developmental research has identified key features of early-appearing temperament traits and has generated ever more refined tools to measure them. Most important, this work has demonstrated the pivotal role that child temperament plays in shaping later outcomes, including adolescent and adult personality and psychopathology, parent–child interaction, attachment, relationship with peers, health, and scholastic and occupational achievement.

Second, since antiquity, temperament has been seen as representing the biological or constitutional core of personality. But decoding this biological basis proved elusive. The lack of methods to measure brain processes constrained researchers to rely on morphology as a proxy for the biology of temperament, earning the field a somewhat dubious reputation. Over the past 20 years, startling advances in brain-imaging techniques and molecular genetics have led to breakthroughs in our understanding of the biological underpinnings of such complex behavioral traits as anxiety, impulsivity, exuberance, and willpower.

Finally, new approaches to treatment and prevention are being developed from these strands of basic research. Because research on child temperament offers unprecedented insights into very early childhood risk factors for the development of behavior disorders and school failure, tools for their assessment and screening, as well as innovative forms of intervention, are being developed. In addition, the rapidly growing understanding of the neurogenetic foundations of temperament traits and risk factors holds promise for advances in biological psychiatry and neuropsychopharmacology.

This handbook is the first to capture all of these exciting developments in a single volume. However, our aim was not only to assemble these areas but also to promote a certain degree of integration of the developments through several means. One first step we took toward this goal was to organize the various strands of research on temperament in a way that promotes coherence and facilitates recognition of connections and interrelationships across various research areas. Second, we strove for integration by means of extensive cross-referencing across chapters. Third, we provide an integrative chapter at the end of the volume that pulls the various threads of the volume together and takes stock of 50 years of progress in research on temperament. This chapter offers the reader wishing to get an overview of some of the main themes and findings covered in the handbook a way to do so relatively quickly. Despite the emphasis on integration, we felt that readers should be able to read a given chapter without having to read all of the others as well. Thus, each chapter can stand on its own. The price to pay for this autonomy is a certain degree of overlap across some of the chapters.

The volume is organized in eight parts. Part I opens the book by addressing issues related to the meaning and structure of temperament. Part II expands this information on temperament structure through a set of chapters focusing in depth on particular temperament traits. Part III then reviews self- and other-report, behavioral, and psychobiological methodologies for assessing temperament. Part IV addresses the biological underpinnings of temperament from comparative, evolutionary, prenatal, genetic, and neurobiological perspectives. The chapters in Part V explore the interplay between context and temperament traits in shaping development from the early days of attachment through the adult development of personality; the contexts range from those more proximal to the individual (e.g., the parent–child relationship, peers) to broader contexts (e.g., culture). Part VI brings together research initiatives that examine how temperament dispositions are involved in the emergence of clinically relevant outcomes such as resilience, psychopathology, and health. Part VII offers reviews of innovative applications of temperament findings in the context of the classroom, prevention programs, and therapy. The final chapter, in Part VIII, tracks the progress in temperament research in the past 50 years.

Though relatively comprehensive, not every domain of research in temperament could be covered as extensively as it might have been. In some instances, it proved impossible to find authors prepared to cover a given area. In others, we felt that a given domain had not matured enough to warrant a dedicated chapter. The final chapter points to such additional areas and findings whose inclusion would have undoubtedly enriched the volume. It should be seen as a sign of the vitality of the temperament field that even a volume as thick as this one still leaves much to be covered.

MARCEL ZENTNER
REBECCA L. SHINER

Reference

Thomas, A., Chess, S., Birch, H., Hertzig, M., & Korn, S. (1963). *Behavioral individuality in early childhood*. New York: New York University Press.

Acknowledgments

A number of people contributed their time and experience to this volume. First of all, this handbook would not exist without the contributors, who devoted themselves with great enthusiasm and professionalism to this project. We would like to express our gratitude for their unwavering commitment to this volume. Our thanks extend also to all those who participated in the review process of the chapters, providing our contributors with detailed comments and constructive critical feedback. Specifically, we thank Jonathan Adler, Gerianne Alexander, Jay Belsky, Sheri Berenbaum, John Capitanio, Susan Crockenberg, Elysia Davis, Kate Degnan, Colin de Young, Emily Durbin, Heidi Gazelle, Megan Gunnar, Amie Hane, Michel Hansenne, Claire Haworth, James Higley, Barbara Keogh, Grazyna Kochanska, Robert Latzman, Dan Mroczek, Janae Neiderhiser, Petra Netter, Joel Nigg, Michael Posner, Michael Potegal, Ronald Rapee, Frances Rice, Randall Salekin, David Schwebel, Lani Shiota, David Sinn, Tracy Spinrad, Marion Underwood, Carlos Valiente, Kees van Oers, Carolyn Zahn-Waxler, and Qing Zhou.

In addition to this large number of external referees, we are also grateful to many of the contributors to this volume who participated in the review process. Annelies Vredeveldt read through many chapters and made valuable editing suggestions. We would also like to acknowledge everyone at The Guilford Press who helped us with this project, especially Kristal Hawkins, Judith Grauman, and Laura Specht Patchkofsky, who were highly supportive of the project at various stages.

Work on this book was supported by grants from the Colgate Research Council and from a Presidential Scholar award from Colgate University to Rebecca L. Shiner.

Contents

Part I. Foundations of Temperament

1. Advances in Temperament: History, Concepts, and Measures   3
   Mary K. Rothbart

2. Models of Child Temperament   21
   Ivan Mervielde and Sarah S. W. De Pauw

3. Models of Adult Temperament   41
   Marvin Zuckerman

Part II. Basic Temperament Traits

4. The Biography of Behavioral Inhibition   69
   Jerome Kagan

5. Activity as a Temperament Trait   83
   Jan Strelau and Bogdan Zawadzki

6. Positive Emotionality   105
   Samuel P. Putnam

7. Anger and Irritability   124
   Kirby Deater-Deckard and Zhe Wang

8. Effortful Control   145
   M. Rosario Rueda

9. Empathy, Prosocial Behavior, and Other Aspects of Kindness   168
   Ariel Knafo and Salomon Israel

Part III. Measures of Temperament

10. Asking Questions about Temperament: Self- and Other-Report Measures across the Lifespan — 183
    Maria A. Gartstein, David J. Bridgett, and Christina M. Low

11. Behavioral Assessment of Temperament — 209
    H. Hill Goldsmith and Jeffrey R. Gagne

12. Psychobiological Measures of Temperament in Childhood — 229
    Susan D. Calkins and Margaret M. Swingler

Part IV. Biological Perspectives on Temperament

13. Temperament in Animals — 251
    Christina S. Barr

14. Temperament and Evolution — 273
    Kevin B. MacDonald

15. Prenatal Factors in Temperament: The Role of Prenatal Stress and Substance Use Exposure — 297
    Anja C. Huizink

16. Quantitative and Molecular Genetic Studies of Temperament — 315
    Kimberly J. Saudino and Manjie Wang

17. Neurobiology and Neurochemistry of Temperament in Children — 347
    Lauren K. White, Connie Lamm, Sarah M. Helfinstein, and Nathan A. Fox

18. Neurobiology and Neurochemistry of Temperament in Adults — 368
    Richard A. Depue and Yu Fu

Part V. Temperament in Context

19. Integrating Temperament and Attachment: The Differential Susceptibility Paradigm — 403
    Marinus H. van IJzendoorn and Marian J. Bakermans-Kranenburg

20. Temperament and Parenting in Developmental Perspective — 425
    John E. Bates, Alice C. Schermerhorn, and Isaac T. Petersen

21. Temperament and Peer Relationships — 442
    Robert J. Coplan and Amanda Bullock

22. Culture and Temperament — 462
    Xinyin Chen, Fan Yang, and Rui Fu

23. Gender Differences in Temperament — 479
    Nicole M. Else-Quest

24. Temperament and the Development of Personality Traits, Adaptations, and Narratives — 497
    Rebecca L. Shiner and Avshalom Caspi

Part VI. Clinical Perspectives on Temperament

25. Temperament and Risk: Resilient and Vulnerable Responses to Adversity — 519
    Liliana J. Lengua and Theodore D. Wachs

26. Temperament and Internalizing Disorders — 541
    Daniel N. Klein, Margaret W. Dyson, Autumn J. Kujawa, and Roman Kotov

27. Temperament, Externalizing Disorders, and Attention-Deficit/Hyperactivity Disorder — 562
    Jennifer L. Tackett, Michelle M. Martel, and Shauna C. Kushner

28. Temperament and Physical Health over the Lifespan — 581
    Sarah E. Hampson and Margarete E. Vollrath

Part VII. Applied Perspectives on Temperament

29. Temperament-Based Intervention: Reconceptualized from a Response-to-Intervention Framework — 607
    Sandee Graham McClowry and Ashleigh Collins

30. Temperament in the Classroom — 627
    Angela Lee Duckworth and Kelly M. Allred

31. Temperament in Psychotherapy: Reflections on Clinical Practice with the Trait of Sensitivity — 645
    Elaine N. Aron

Part VIII. Integration and Outlook

32. Fifty Years of Progress in Temperament Research: A Synthesis of Major Themes, Findings, and Challenges and a Look Forward — 673
    Marcel Zentner and Rebecca L. Shiner

Author Index — 701

Subject Index — 727

Part I

Foundations of Temperament

CHAPTER 1

Advances in Temperament
History, Concepts, and Measures

Mary K. Rothbart

This new *Handbook of Temperament*, organized and edited by Marcel Zentner and Rebecca L. Shiner, reflects the rapid growth of temperament research and application during the last 40 years (see Zentner & Shiner, Chapter 32, this volume). The influence of temperament concepts and research on related areas has also expanded to include general development, education, personality, psychopathology, and the neurosciences (Caspi & Shiner, 2006; Kagan & Fox, 2006; Posner & Rothbart, 2007a; Rothbart & Bates, 2006). For psychologists, clinicians, and teachers, temperament provides an introduction to individual differences in the infant and young child. Concepts of temperament also introduce us to basic processes of social and personality development, psychopathology, and adjustment. Finally, temperament provides links between our understanding of infants and young children and our understanding of older children and adults, including ourselves (Rothbart, 2011).

Temperament and Personality

Temperamental tendencies form building blocks that underlie development of individual differences in personality (see Shiner & Caspi, Chapter 24, this volume). Allport (1937) defined *personality* as the organization of the "systems that determine [the person's] unique adjustment to his environment" (p. 48). One level of personality organization is the *trait*, defined as a pattern of thoughts, emotions, and behavior that show consistency over situations and stability over time. Temperament traits, a subset of personality traits, include the emotional, motor, and attentional reactive tendencies and regulative capacities seen early in development. These tend to show consistency across situations and stability over time, although they also may be altered in development (Rothbart & Bates, 2006) and applied in different ways to specific persons and situations (Rothbart, 2011).

In infancy, temperament is the predominant influence on the child's reactions and adjustments to a given environment. In adulthood, there remain close links between the broad factors used to describe personality (the Big Five, the Five-Factor Model [FFM]) and the broad factors found within the temperament domain in children and adults (Evans & Rothbart, 2007; McCrae et al., 2000). The most recently discovered of these are the links between temperamental perceptual sensitivity and Big Five Openness. These links suggest that temperament dispositions developing early in life may form the basis of the adult structure of broad personality traits (Rothbart, 2011; Zentner & Bates, 2008).

It is important to remember, however, that the personality domain extends considerably beyond traits. In addition to temperament and personality traits, personality includes one's interpretations, attitudes, identifications, goals, specific adaptations, defenses, values, and ideas about general and more specific events and situations, including concepts of the self and others (Rothbart, 2011). Because personality includes cognitive as well as behavioral adjustments, and because some of the most important aspects of our adjustment include ideas and behaviors specific to a particular person or situation, a trait-limited view is inadequate to describe the developing personality (also see Zentner & Bates, 2008). General context and indeed specific situations and people also need to be taken into account (see chapters in Part V, this volume).

Temperament, Evolution, and Development

We all inherit adaptations that are general to our species, genetically based processes geared to the "environment of evolutionary adaptiveness" in Bowlby's (1971) terms. These processes support the basic emotions and related motivations, such as approach and fear, and individuals differ in their propensities toward these reactions. Our genetic inheritance also supports the individual's response to change via shifting and focusing attention and the development of expectations. Allport (1937) would call these "nomothetic" processes, general to humans. When we consider the individual person, however, we see adaptations to a specific life history and to specific others that can be applied uniquely to the person through "idiographic" processes, and ultimately describe the development of a single person. The person adapts to other people and situations but can also select a range of environments and persons with whom to interact, and can influence the physical and social environment. Thus, both change and an inflexibility of thought and behavior are possible consequences of the person's history.

Temperament reflects individual information processing through the emotions, motivation, and attention networks. By identifying the basic dimensions of temperament, we can study temperament's influence on the development of behavioral strategies and cognition (Rothbart, 2011). We can also clarify the role of life experiences, recent events, identifications, and other influences on individual development. We share a number of temperamental processes with nonhuman animals; others, such as propositional concepts of self and others, we do not (see Barr, Chapter 13, and MacDonald, Chapter 14, this volume). The child's developing concepts of the self and the social and physical environment go beyond temperament to provide another level of information processing that influences the expression of temperament, and vice versa.

This volume provides detailed reviews of the field, offering support for future research and applications of temperament as a science of development. It lets us build a model of the developing person based on children's temperament and their adaptations to environmental challenges. At the same time it links temperament to our understanding of biology and the neurosciences. This handbook thus provides a unique basis for studying the development of human coping, psychopathology, and competence, including an exploration of the range of individual differences that the child brings to school and the adult brings to the workplace and family settings. As neuroscience methods and findings proliferate, our understanding of temperament processes will be further extended and clarified.

In this introductory chapter, I offer a brief historical introduction to temperament concepts. I then put forward a definition of temperament that we and others have found useful, noting that alternative definitions are to be found in later chapters of the book. I then describe a hierarchical model of development first proposed by Robert Hinde (1998) and discussed in greater depth in Rothbart (2011). Hinde's model gives us a systematic way to think about contributions to this volume and to develop new directions for research and strategies for intervention.

Throughout this chapter, suggestions are offered as to how this handbook can be used to generate ideas and research.

Ancient Historical Roots

Temperament concepts have a truly ancient past—as early as the Hindu Rig Vedas (approximately 1500–1000 B.C.E.) and the Bhagavad Gita (500–200 B.C.E.). For example, concepts of the *gunas* described basic qualities of the material world, including the human body, that were seen to contribute to mind and behavior (Larson, 1979; Needham, 1973). The *gunas* were seen as supporting the experience of pleasure, pain, and related approach and inhibition, as well as cognitively based detachment from the sources of pleasure and pain. They included *rajas* (desire and the anger and other suffering that result when we do not get what we want), related to approach and reactivity to incentives; *tamas* (restraint and inertia), related to behavioral inhibition; and *sattwa* (clear thinking and detachment), related to attention and self-regulation. These were seen as processes of nature that could activate or support each other, dominate or interact with each other (Larson, 1979). *Rajas*, as evidenced in the desire for clarity, for example, helps to support *sattwa*, clear thinking, although desire and clear thinking may at times conflict. *Tamas* may also follow the loss of *rajasic* desired objects. The *gunas* were reflected in the emotions and related motivations, and in the qualities of attention and regulation. They were also represented in the moods that could vary within a day.

Ancient Chinese approaches to what we would call temperament were based on the concept of energy, or *chi* (Yosida, 1973). The movement and fluctuation of *chi* was seen as the basis for individual differences in emotion and behavior, with the more active force of *yang* and the more passive force of *yin* acting to oppose and to complement each other, just as the *gunas* opposed and complemented each other in the Hindu model. Neither the Hindu nor the Chinese tradition put forward typologies but rather described dynamic interactions of human qualities or tendencies.

In the Western tradition, Galen (second century C.E.) is usually given credit for putting forward the fourfold typology of temperament (e.g., Carey, 1997; Kagan, 1994). However, parts of the typology were anticipated in Hellenistic medicine and cosmology, and the fourfold typology itself did not emerge until the fourth century C.E. with Vindician (Diamond, 1974). The word *temperament* was derived from the Latin *temperamentum*, meaning to "mingle in due proportion." The typology was thus based on the relative strength of temperament components we all share.

The Greco-Roman physicians foreshadowed modern research by linking temperament to physiology. In present-day research, we investigate the genetics and biochemistry of individual differences in temperament, a currently flourishing area of research. In the Greco-Roman fourfold typology, temperament was linked to the bodily humors, so that the *melancholic* person was seen as moody, with a tendency to fear and sadness, and a predominance of black bile (Diamond, 1974). The *choleric* person was touchy, aggressive and active, with a predominance of yellow bile. The *sanguine* person, sociable and easygoing, was seen to have a predominance of blood; the *phlegmatic* individual was calm, even-tempered, and slow to emotion, with a predominance of phlegm. The typology was further linked to aspects of psychopathology, with the choleric person likely to show problems with aggression, and the melancholic person to show problems with sadness and depression. The typology was applied throughout the Middle Ages, and into the 18th to 20th centuries.

In his 18th-century treatise titled *Anthropology from a Pragmatic Point of View*, for example, Immanuel Kant (1789/2006) discussed the ancient typology with the aim of distinguishing temperament from character or moral action. He described *temperament* as "what nature makes of the human being" (p. 192), whereas *character* refers to "what the person makes of himself" (p. 192) through willful thought and action and the application of virtue. While virtues themselves represented moral ideals, character referred to moral behavior and thought as expressed and observed in the person. Kant's argument relates in interesting ways to recent progress in the study of temperament, and I return to it later in this chapter.

In the early years of psychology as a science, a shift was made from positing typologies to talking about dimensions of individual variability. Kant's (1789/2006) typology of temperament had been based on dimensions that included activity–passivity and emotionality, and Wundt (1903) proposed the temperament dimensions of strength and speed of change of emotions. Ebbinghaus (1911), on the other hand, proposed the dimensions of optimism–pessimism and emotionality (H. J. Eysenck & M. Eysenck, 1985). Each of these sets of two dimensions could be used to generate four quadrants corresponding to the fourfold typology. Although typological approaches to temperament continue to play a role in the field (see Kagan, Chapter 4, this volume), most research today focuses on temperament dimensions rather than types.

Constitutional Psychology

An early approach to temperament called *constitutional psychology* is little studied today. This approach linked body types first identified by Hippocrates and linked to health (fifth century B.C.E.) and later to mental illness (Kretschmer, 1925). Kretschmer's work was followed by applications of his constitutional approach to the study of temperament and behavior in children, but these developments were hardly noted outside German-speaking countries (see Zentner, 1998). Sheldon and Stevens (1942) measured *endomorphic* (soft, rounded), *mesomorphic* (hard, rectangular), and *ectomorphic* (linear, fragile) components of five different body areas (measures were refined by Sheldon, Lewis, & Tenney, 1969). These components were then linked to temperament clusters of *viscerotonia* (sociable, gluttonous, appreciative of comfort and affection, even tempered, slow, relaxed, tolerant), *somatotonia* (need for vigorous activity, risk taking and adventure seeking, courage, aggression and callousness toward others), and *cerebretonia* (restraint, inhibition, fearfulness, self-consciousness, need to be alone, secretiveness), respectively.

In applications to children, moderate correlations were found between somatotype and teachers' ratings of 2- to 4-year-olds' behavior patterns (Hanley, 1951; Walker, 1962), and adolescents' self-reports (Cortes & Gatti, 1965). These findings may be influenced by the child's activity level and by the strong stereotypes that raters have of body types (Lerner, 1969), but studies have also linked delinquency to greater mesomorphy and lower ectomorphy (Cortes & Gatti, 1972; Glueck & Glueck, 1950, 1956). Greater longitudinal stability has been found for mesomorphy and ectomorphy than for endomorphy (Walker & Tennes, 1980), but recent increases in obesity in children may influence the stability of endomorphy. Although constitutional psychology appears to have died out, the connections between temperament and health continue to be exciting ones, as described by Hampson and Vollrath (Chapter 28, this volume).

Pavlov and the Eastern to Middle European Schools

Pavlov's model of temperament was based on his observations of dogs during conditioning, and linked to his ideas about the nervous system (Gray, 1979; Rothbart, 2011; Strelau, 1983). Russian temperament research was originally based in the laboratory, where properties such as nervous system strength of excitation were assessed. Individuals who continued to function under high-intensity or prolonged exposure to stimulation before the onset of inhibition of responses were described as having "strong" nervous systems, and those with low thresholds for inhibition as having "weak" nervous systems. Additional nervous system properties were labeled *strength of inhibition*, *balance between excitation and inhibition*, and *mobility* (speed of responding to changes in the signal value of a stimulus). Later, *lability* and *dynamism* were added to this list (see review by Strelau, 1983; Teplov, 1964).

Nebylitsyn (1972) and his followers reported that individuals with weak nervous systems demonstrated lower sensory thresholds. However, problems developed for the Russian School when the laboratory measures of general nervous system properties proved to be highly dependent on the nature of the stimulus and the modality of the response. Thus, sensitivity varied from one sensory system to another, for example, from audition to vision, and the properties did not appear to be general ones (a phenomenon called *partiality*; Strelau, 1983). One result of partiality was that researchers moved out of the laboratory and into the development of questionnaire measures (Rusalov, 1987; Rusalov & Trofimova, 2007; Strelau, Angleitner, & Newberry, 1999; see also Strelau & Zawadzki, Chapter 5, this volume, for more recent developments).

Temperament in Western Europe

During the early 20th century, the Dutch researchers Heymans and Wiersma (1906) began a pioneering psychometric study by collecting questionnaire data from doctors concerning their patients, including both parents and children. They then applied an early form of factor analysis to the data, yielding three broad factors: (1) *Activity*, the tendency to express or act out what is thought or desired; (2) *Emotionality*, the tendency to show body symptoms and to be fearful and shy; and (3) *Primary vs. Secondary Function*, the tendency to react immediately rather than in a postponed and more organized way. These factors foreshadowed three of the broad factors of temperament we study today: Extraversion, Negative Emotionality, and Effortful Control (Rothbart, 2011). Heymans and Wiersma also crossed each of these three factors with interpretable cells seen as forming eight types, labeled Passionate, Choleric, Phlegmatic, Apathetic, Sentimental, Nervous, Sanguine, and Amorphous, that were particularly influential in the French school of *caractérologie* (Le Senne, 1945). A manual written for teachers and parents explained childrearing practices that would work best for each of the types (Le Gall, 1950).

Other French researchers (Wallon, 1925, 1934) carried out longitudinal studies of infant characteristics and their role in later development (see review by Balleyguier, 1989). Beginning in 1950, Meili in Switzerland studied 3- to 4-month-old infants' responses to unfamiliar stimuli, such as a black ball descending into the infant's visual field. Meili was among the first to code infants' reactions from filmed recordings that have just recently been digitized and catalogued. The authors found that the 3- to 4-month-old infants' muscle tension and emotional distress in response to the unfamiliar objects predicted later behavioral inhibition or shyness at 7 and 14 years (Meili-Dworetzki & Meili, 1972). The Swiss work and findings showed a number of similarities to the more recent work of Kagan and his colleagues (Zentner, 2008; also see Kagan, Chapter 4, this volume).

The British Psychometric Tradition

Whereas in Eastern Europe research moved from the laboratory to questionnaires, in Great Britain the order was reversed. There, temperament and personality factors were derived from self-report measures and only later related to the nervous system. Webb (1915), a student of Spearman, and Cyril Burt (1915) each carried out factor analyses of temperament-related items early in the 20th century. Webb analyzed items assessing emotionality, activity, self-qualities, and intellect, identifying a factor defined as "consistency of action resulting from deliberate volition or will" (p. 34).

Burt (1915) identified a factor he labeled Emotionality or Emotional Stability–Instability, which was later called Neuroticism by Eysenck (1947). (This habit of renaming constructs has been widely used in the field). Burt also identified the factor of Introversion–Extraversion and generated the fourfold typology by crossing the dimensions of Emotionality (Neuroticism) and Introversion–Extraversion. In addition, he discovered secondary dimensions of negative emotionality: "a general trait or tendency which, when positive, predisposes people towards assertive angry, sociable and inquisitive behavior, in short towards active or aggressive conduct, and when negative towards submissiveness, fear, sorrow, tenderness and disgust, in a word, towards repressive or inhibitive emotions" (Burt, 1937, p. 182). This factor foreshadows later externalizing and internalizing factors in behavior problems (see Lengua & Wachs, Chapter 25; Klein, Dyson, Kujawa, & Kotov, Chapter 26; Tackett, Martel, & Kushner, Chapter 27, this volume), and the two kinds of negative emotionality found in temperament in adults (Evans & Rothbart, 2007) and children (Rothbart, 2011).

Eysenck (1967) and later Gray (1971, 1982) posited biological bases for temperament dimensions. Eysenck's theory was based on cortical arousal, whereas Gray rotated the axes of Eysenck's model 45 degrees, making anxiety the behavioral inhibition system (or BIS) and impulsivity the behavioral activation system (or BAS) the basic dimensions of temperament. Eysenck (1947) also identified the dimension of Psychoticism, associated with hostile and aggressive behavior. The 20th century showed extensive development of psychobiological models of adult temperament by Eysenck and Gray in Britain, and Cloninger, Zuckerman, Depue, Panksepp, and others in the United States (see Zuckerman, Chapter 3, this volume).

U.S. Research on Temperament in Childhood

The influential normative child psychologists in the 1920s and 1930s observed children in order to establish the normal sequences of motor and mental development, using both large samples and more intensively studied small samples of children. In doing so, they noted striking temperamental variability among the children they observed (Gesell, 1928, as cited in Kessen, 1965; Shirley, 1933). Mary Shirley's intensive longitudinal study of motor development during the first 2 years of life led her to observe the infant's "core of personality." She noted that, developmentally, "both constancy and change characterize the personality of the baby. Traits are constant enough to make it plausible that a nucleus of personality exists at birth and that this nucleus persists and grows and determines to a certain degree the relative importance of (other) traits" (Shirley, 1933, p. 56). She devoted a full volume to these traits, even though she had originally intended to study only motor and intellectual development.

Gesell (1928, as cited in Kessen, 1965) identified the critical importance of temperament in development and illustrated it with the example of CD, a child closely observed over early development who showed "a striking degree of amenability, sociality and good nature as early as the age of nine months. . . . In spite of a varied experience in boarding homes and institutions she has not lost these engaging characteristics" (p. 223). Gesell pointed out that there may be some stability of early temperament, but that "more than this cannot be predicted in the field of personality. For whether she (CD) becomes a delinquent, and she is potentially one, will depend upon her subsequent training, conditioning, and supervision. She is potentially also a willing, helpful, productive worker. Environment retains a critical role even though heredity sets metes and bounds" (p. 223).

Shirley (1933) and Gesell (1928, as cited in Kessen, 1965) argued that temperament traits are constitutionally based characteristics that provide the core of personality and influence directions for development. They also argued that although some stability is expected, outcomes also strongly depend on the child's experience in the social context. Finally, a given set of temperament characteristics will allow for multiple possible outcomes. Different trajectories and outcomes may occur for children with similar temperamental traits, and children differing in temperament may come to similar developmental outcomes via different pathways (Kochanska, 1997). In addition, specific life histories will influence the person's idiographic adaptations to life.

The next major line of research on temperament in childhood following the normative psychologists came from biologically oriented clinicians. Bergman and Escalona (1949) identified children who were particularly reactive to low intensities of stimulation in one or more sensory modalities. Escalona (1968) proposed the concept of *effective experience*, the idea that events in children's lives are experienced only as they are filtered through the individual child's nervous system. A given event will thus differ in its effects for children who differ in temperament. An adult's vigorous play, for example, may lead to pleasure in one child and distress in another.

Given individual differences in temperament, the objective coding of environmental events will not capture essential information about the individual child's reaction to that event, that is, the child's experience (see also Wachs, 2000). Research on temperament thus introduced the idea that in addition to individual differences in thoughts and motor patterns, individual differences in children's *emotional* processing could bias their reactions and representations of experience, with important implications for their development. In other studies, Fries and Woolf (1954) identified and studied congenital activity type, Korner (1964) studied neonatal individuality and developed an extensive assessment schedule for the newborn, and Birns, Barten, and Bridger (1969) developed and implemented some of the earliest standardized assessments of temperament.

Among clinical investigators, Thomas, Chess, Birch, Hertzig, and Korn (1963) published the first of their volumes on the extremely influential New York Longitudinal Study (NYLS). Chess and Thomas studied individual differences in what they called "primary reaction patterns," collecting interviews from parents of infants on repeated occasions. Beginning when their initial sample of 22 infants was 3–6 months of age, parents were interviewed about their infants' behavior in varying contexts. Each infant reaction and its context was then typed on a separate sheet of paper, and Birch inductively sorted the descriptions into categories that came to represent the nine NYLS temperament dimensions (Chess & Thomas, personal communication, May 1992; Thomas et al., 1963): activity level, approach–withdrawal, adaptability, mood, threshold, intensity, distractibility, rhythmicity, and attention span/persistence. Later, Michael Rutter suggested the term *temperament* to describe their area of study, and this term was adopted by the NYLS group (Chess & Thomas, personal communication, May 1992). The NYLS is further discussed by Mervielde and De Pauw (Chapter 2, this volume).

In recent years, concepts of temperament and personality in adulthood and childhood have increasingly come together (Halverson, Kohnstamm, & Martin, 1994; Rothbart & Derryberry, 1981), and their joint influence is seen in many chapters of this volume. Nevertheless, more integrated work is needed. For example, one can compare and contrast concepts and methods in the two review chapters on adult temperament (see Zuckerman, Chapter 3, and Depue & Fu, Chapter 18, this volume) and the two chapters on child temperament (see Mervielde & De Pauw, Chapter 2, and White, Lamm, Helfinstein, & Fox, Chapter 17, this volume), leading to hypotheses for future integrative developmental research.

Defining Temperament

My coauthor and I (Rothbart & Derryberry, 1981) have defined *temperament* as constitutionally based individual differences in reactivity and self-regulation, influenced over time by genes, maturation, and experience. The term *constitutional* refers to the biological bases of temperament. By *reactivity*, we mean dispositions toward emotional, motor, and orienting reactions (these are sometimes referred to as the three A's: affect, activity, and attention). By temperamental *self-regulation*, we refer to processes that regulate our reactivity. Self-regulatory dispositions include our motivational tendencies to approach or withdraw from a stimulus, to direct our attention toward or away from it, and the effortful attentional control that serves to regulate our thoughts and emotions. These tendencies form the basis for early coping with challenges presented by others and the environment.

Temperamental reactivity can be measured by the latency, intensity, peak rise time, and recovery of the person's reaction (Rothbart & Derryberry, 1981). For example, how rapidly do we become fearful, inhibited, withdrawing, or self-protective in a potentially fear-inducing situation? How rapidly do we approach a novel or threatening object, or become frustrated when we are prevented from achieving our goals, and become sad when we experience loss? How intense are our reactions, and how long does it take to recover from the reaction? Reactivity can be measured broadly, as in Kagan's (1994; Chapter 4, this volume) observations of the development of behavioral inhibition, and it can be also be measured more specifically in terms of emotional systems and components of those systems (e.g., in links between behavioral inhibition and amygdala function; see, in this volume, Kagan, Chapter 4; White et al., Chapter 17, and Depue & Fu, Chapter 18; and Zentner & Shiner, Chapter 32).

Approach and inhibitory or withdrawal tendencies can oppose one another (Gray, 1971; Rothbart & Sheese, 2007), and regulatory tendencies can moderate reactive ones. Thus, approach and impulsivity are opposed by reactive fear, and by effortful self-regulatory control. Both reactivity and self-regulation are adaptive processes, and they form the basis for the child's earliest patterns of evaluating and coping with the environment. Temperament supports individual differences in infancy and shapes the personality adaptations that develop out of our initial dispositions and our history of life experiences. Our life experiences also shape our reactivity by influencing our emotional evaluations, experience of stress, and strategies for coping with situations and people (Rothbart, 2011).

Temperament develops, as can be seen throughout this volume. Not all aspects of temperament are observable in the newborn, but rapid development occurs over the first years of life in both temperament and in the mental capacities that allow us to move beyond temperament traits to the wider domain of personality. Early in development, emotional reactivity and relatively unregulated approach (impulsivity) characterize the infant, but as motivational and attentional systems develop, greater individual control over emotion, thought, and action becomes available. In fact, the regulation of temperament tendencies can be seen as a major aim of the child's socialization into a society or culture (Olson & Sameroff, 2009; Vohs & Baumeister, 2011).

The Structure of Temperament

One of the major advances in temperament over the past four decades has been our increased understanding of the basic dimensions of temperament and their relation to each other. Factor-analytic work with parent-report and self-report questionnaires has strongly contributed to this effort (Rothbart & Bates, 2006). As mentioned earlier, Thomas and Chess (1977) originally offered nine dimensions of temperament based on a content analysis of infant reaction patterns in their NYLS. More recently, their list of dimensions has been revised and supplemented as research on temperament has progressed (Rothbart & Bates, 2006). This handbook reflects many of the dimensions of temperament studied today, including behavioral inhibition, activity, anger/irritability, positive emotionality, effortful control, and candidate dimensions of empathy/agreeableness and sensory sensitivity (see,

in this volume, Kagan, Chapter 4; Strelau & Zawadzki, Chapter 5; Putnam, Chapter 6; Deater-Deckard & Wang, Chapter 7; Rueda, Chapter 8; Knafo & Israel, Chapter 9; see also Aron, Chapter 31).

Research reported in this handbook depends heavily on our understanding of temperamental dimensions and components. An understanding of the structure of temperament allows us to explore links between temperament in children and temperament in adults integrating the contributions to Part I. In addition, this understanding furthers improvement in measurement (Part II), allows us to make links between temperament and biology (Part IV), relate temperament to the development of psychopathology and physical health (Part VI), and study contextual influences on temperament (Part V). Part VII, on applications, is particularly dependent on the prior chapters and on how we see the structure of temperament. As McClowry and Collins argue in their chapter on prevention and intervention, in order to instruct children and parents about temperament, we need a solid understanding of temperament itself (Chapter 29, this volume).

A General Model for Thinking about Temperament and Development

Recent advances in neuroscience, including research on brain imaging and the genome, and our progress in understanding temperament at multiple levels, has allowed us to study a number of bidirectional influences on the development of individual differences. Hinde's (1998) model of human development allows us to take these influences into account (see Figure 1.1). He argues that thought, emotion, and action will be influenced by both the dispositions of the individual and the influence of the environment at any point in development. At the same time, each person will see others and the physical environment based on his or her specific past history of experiences and goals for the future. As Hinde puts it, "Individuals respond selectively to the environment, assign meanings to it, change it, and are changed by it" (p. 166).

The point where the person and the perceived environment most dramatically come

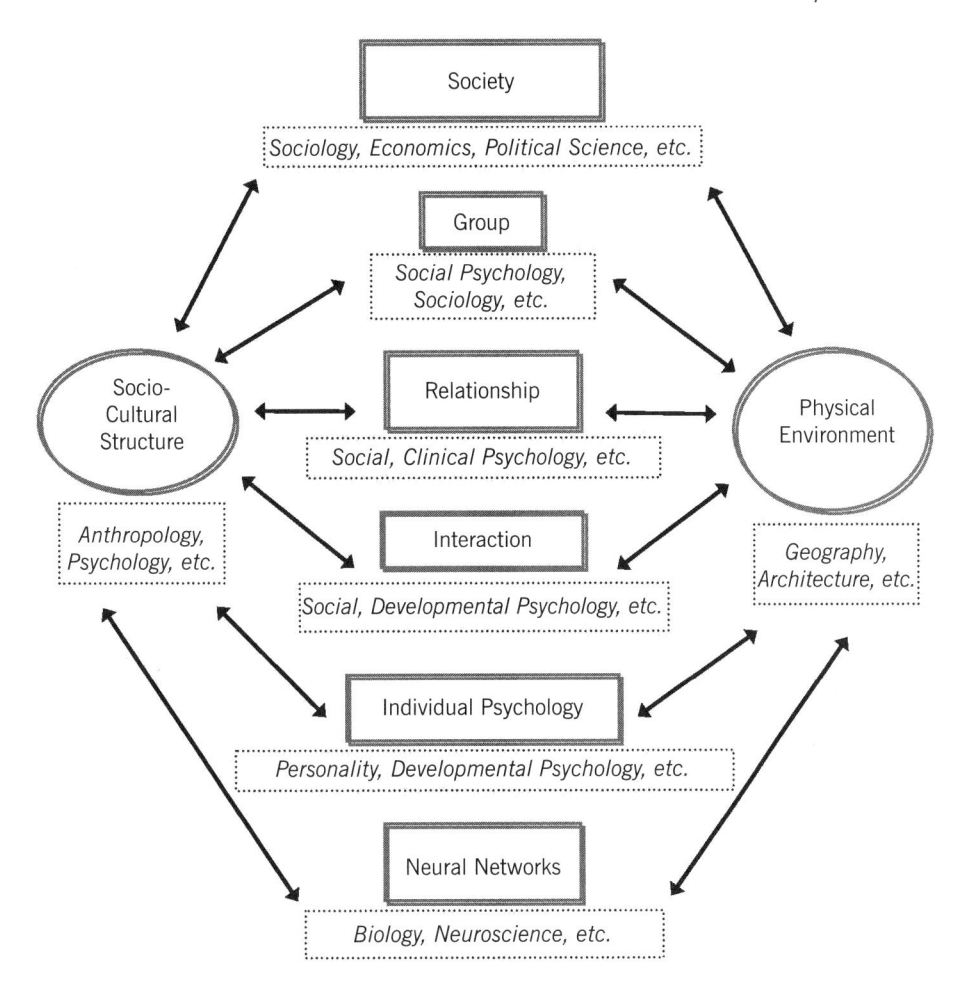

FIGURE 1.1. An adaptation of Hinde's (1998) framework for study in the human sciences. The levels of influence are listed within solid rectangles and circles; below, in dashed rectangles, are areas of study related to these influences.

together is in one's experiences with others over a life history, played out in social relationships. Temperament, especially early in life, makes basic contributions to the person's interpretations, actions, and relationships, while, at the same time, interpretations, actions, and relationships make basic contributions to the expressions of temperament (Rothbart, 2011).

To study multiple levels of influence, we need to explore biological, physical, social, and cultural influences on the individual and vice versa, along with the usual psychological level of analysis. This requires the study of "physiology, individual psychology, social psychology, sociology, anthropology, political science, and economics, among others" (Hinde, 1998, p. 166). Different explanatory concepts and methods apply at different levels of analysis, and a full understanding of development requires making connections between levels (Hinde, 1998; Figure 1.1). One level of the hierarchy can influence a quite distant level, and influences are bidirectional.

The downturn of an economy, for example, may create the threat or actuality of unemployment, increasing stress levels and marital conflict in parents. Marital conflict in turn affects the child's stress levels at the biological and individual levels, and the child's social behavior (Cummings, Papp, & Kouros, 2009). The child also develops adaptive strategies for coping with parental conflict (e.g., playing the role of the peacemaker or the distracting troublemaker, or withdrawing from interaction), which can then feed back to influence marital conflict. These strategies can also be carried forward to other situations, interactions, and relationships, affecting the child's overall adjustment (Cummings et al., 2009). Throughout his analysis, Hinde (1998) emphasizes the importance of relationships in the home, the workplace, and the social world. Each partner to a relationship contributes to the experience of the other and to the constructions each partner comes to hold about the other and the self. The child's relationships in the family can easily be carried forward to influence other relationships, and vice versa. Each level of analysis is also related to what Hinde calls the *sociocultural structure*, that is, the norms, values, beliefs, and institutional roles of a culture.

Societal policies can have strong influences on the relationship, interaction, individual, and biological levels. The one-child policy in China, for example, instituted as a corrective for a high birthrate, affected individuals, family groups, interactions, and relationships. The policy in turn influenced not only the size of families but also the gender distribution of children, through a selection against girl babies (Hesketh, Liu, & Xing, 2005). The family unit is clearly affected by the policy, as is the child's relation to other family members. The differences in gender distribution are also related to the health of mothers and female children, and to the mental and physical health of young adults (Hesketh et al., 2005).

Numerous other applications of Hinde's (1998) framework are possible, and one of their major benefits is in thinking about the implications of change at the level of societies and economies, as well as the influences of roles, relationships, and individual psychology and biology on other levels of the hierarchy. For example, an economic factor closely related to many levels of bidirectional influence is whether the child is raised in poverty, and this is a worldwide problem subject to remediation at a number of levels (Lipina & Colombo, 2009).

Temperament, Socialization, and Culture

Many interactions within and between levels of analysis are observed as we study temperament "in context." This can be in the context of the neighborhood, the culture, the family, the parents' relationship with each other and with the child (see, in this volume, van IJzendoorn & Bakermans-Kranenburg, Chapter 19; Bates, Schermerhorn, & Petersen, Chapter 20; Coplan & Bullock, Chapter 21; Chen, Yang, & Fu, Chapter 22), and in the classroom (see, in this volume, Rueda, Chapter 8, and Duckworth & Allred, Chapter 30). In Hinde's (1998) framework, culture and the physical environment show a bidirectional influence across different levels of analysis, and in the study of temperament we have become increasingly concerned with issues of temperament and culture (Chen et al., Chapter 22, this volume).

Culture among humans is defined by Mascolo (2004) as "a dynamic distribution of meanings, practices, and artifacts throughout a linguistic community" (p. 83). Reasons for studying culture in relation to temperament are clear, although at times concerns about political correctness have led temperament researchers to avoid cultural issues. Research in differing cultures gives us a real-world laboratory for testing similarities in the structure of temperament even if childrearing strategies and cultural values vary (Rothbart, 2011). Because temperament includes emotional reactivity, and the primary emotions are similarly displayed and understood in different cultures (Ekman, Sorenson, & Friesen, 1969), we have had reason to expect that the structure of temperament would also be universal. This is not to say that levels of reactivity and self-regulation are identical across cultures, but that the dimensions of temperament are similar across cultures. The values of the culture can then act upon temperament to influence both how we act and how we think about ourselves and others.

It is likely that the brain's basic networks for attention are similar across cultures, with details depending on social and individual experience, including training (Rueda, Chapter 8, this volume; see also Diamond & Lee, 2011). Studies using the Children's Behavior Questionnaire (CBQ; Rothbart, Ahadi, Hershey, & Fisher, 2001) and other temperament scales in the United States and other cultures have replicated the structure of temperament across cultural boundaries (Ahadi, Rothbart, & Ye, 1993; Rothbart, 2011). Finally, to the extent that the Big Five and FFM measures reflect the structure of temperament, they have also proven to be consistent across numerous cultures (McCrae et al., 2000).

As psychologists, we are interested in how the expression of temperament can be shaped by culture and how individuals shape their culture. Temperamental qualities seen as "difficult" in children, for example, have been found to vary across cultures (Super et al., 2008). If we adopt Mascolo's (2004) definition, we realize that each of us belongs to a number of different cultures, such as our family of origin, nuclear family, work group, religion, gender, and political party. These different cultures yield overlapping and sometimes conflicting meanings, practices, and artifacts, and our temperaments will influence our adaptations to both cultures and culture conflicts.

Goodenough (1981) has identified a number of ways in which culture affects personality that clearly go beyond traits to describe how individuals develop in context. In our family, school, neighborhood, or work setting, for example, we

1. Assimilate the language categories and explicit knowledge that we will use to represent events.
2. Develop *beliefs* (propositions for which we do not have satisfactory evidence, but which we believe to be true), values and goals, and awareness of cultural rules and values (including the aspects of temperament that are valued or not valued by the culture).
3. Are influenced by the scripts, routines, and standards of behavior we follow and the skills we practice.
4. Are influenced by the books, television, tools, Internet, and networking websites we use.

Culture also contributes to

5. The narratives we use to describe events and our role in them, including family stories.
6. The models of self and others and the relationships we develop. The individual and groups of individuals can in turn influence the culture, especially when a subgroup or individual holds power over others.

Temperament, as noted earlier, is seen in our patterns of reactivity and in the coping methods we use in adapting to situations and people. The reactivity we express and the coping measures we use will in turn be affected by the values that the culture places on a given temperament characteristic. Temperamental shyness is particularly interesting in this regard, in that it varies in acceptability not only from culture to culture (Kerr, 2001) but also from girls to boys within a culture (Chen et al., Chapter 22, and Else-Quest, Chapter 23, this volume). Culture will in turn be shaped by the temperament of the group members who share it, and as a group's membership and leadership change, the culture may also change, sometimes in dramatic ways.

Hinde's (1998) framework helps us to pose many additional cross-cultural research questions. Studies of shyness have identified links between shyness and the values of a culture (Kerr, 2001; see review by Rothbart, 2011), but how does culture influence the development of warm intimate relationships, security, argumentativeness, leadership qualities, and political values? Studies of genetic contributions to development will be important in investigating the effect of interactions between genes, environment, and sociocultural values on temperament and personality outcomes. As a final example of the application of multiple levels of analysis, and a way of returning to Kant's (1789/2006) argument, I now consider research that we and others have conducted at multiple levels of analysis.

Exploring Multiple Levels

Chapters by many of the contributors to this handbook show how temperament has been studied at multiple levels, and I present here a brief review of our work on effortful control and executive attention as an example. In our work at Oregon, we have studied the development of attentional self-regulation and effortful control at many levels. We first identified Effortful Control (EC) in factor analyses of the CBQ (Ahadi et al., 1993; Rothbart et al., 2001). Analyses of scale scores in this research yielded commonly found broad factors of Surgency/Extraversion (Putnam, Chapter 6, this volume), Negative Affectivity (Deater-Deckard & Wang, Chapter 7, this volume), Behavioral Inhibition (Kagan, Chapter 4, this volume), and Effortful Control (Rueda, Chapter 8, this volume). In research ranging from parent's report of toddlers' behavior to adults' self-report of temperament, we have reliably extracted an EC factor that includes some combination of attentional focusing, attentional shifting, and inhibitory and activational control (Derryberry & Rothbart, 1988; Ellis, Rothbart, & Posner, 2004; Evans & Rothbart, 2007; Putnam, Ellis, & Rothbart, 2001; Putnam, Gartstein, & Rothbart, 2006). Persons high in EC also tend to be low in negative emotionality, in agreement with the idea that attention can be used to regulate emotion, and vice versa (Rothbart & Sheese, 2007).

EC falls under the umbrella constructs of self-control, willpower, self-regulation, and executive functions. These general constructs have been used to designate processes that do not seem to be externally driven, and include, but are not limited to, working memory, planning, problem solving, and future-oriented activities The construct of EC refers more specifically to the ability to resolve conflict by inhibiting a dominant response in order to perform a nondominant response. The EC measure has been related to a brain network of executive attention involving the anterior cingulate, anterior insula, and basal ganglia (Posner, 2012; Posner & Rothbart, 2007a, 2009; Rothbart, Sheese, Rueda, & Posner, 2011). Correlations between EC and the ability to resolve conflict in cognitive tasks such as the Attention Network Test or Stroop effect have been shown from ages 3–4 to adulthood (Rothbart, 2011).

EC questionnaire measures are also directly linked to the activation of the executive attention brain areas involved in self-regulation (Kanske, 2008; Whittle et al., 2008). Individual differences in the function of this brain network have been related to genetic polymorphisms in the dopamine and serotonin system (Posner, Rothbart, & Sheese, 2007). In this way EC has become more than a measure of parent-reported differences in behavior and is a way of understanding the dramatic changes in self-control that occur early in childhood. Together EC and the underlying executive attention network allow connecting societal influences (Moffitt et al., 2011) to brain networks, genetic and experiential influences (Rothbart, 2011).

The Interaction of Genes and Experience to Predict Outcomes

In recent years, measurement of the genome has allowed us to study interactions between the genome and environmental factors in development. In a longitudinal study, we found that the 7-repeat allele of the dopamine D4 receptor (*DRD4*) gene interacted with quality of parenting to influence surgent temperamental variables of activity level, sensation seeking, and impulsivity (Sheese, Voelker, Rothbart, & Posner, 2007). With high-quality parenting, 18- to 20-month-old children with the 7-repeat allele showed average levels of these sensation-seeking scales, and those with poorer quality parenting showed much higher levels; children without the 7-repeat allele were not influenced by parenting. We also found that, at 3–4 years, the *DRD4* 7-repeat allele interacted with parenting to influence parent-reported EC (Sheese, Voelker, Rothbart, & Posner, in press), with higher-quality parenting related to greater EC for children with the 7-repeat allele, but not for those without the 7-repeat variation. In accord with these findings, a recent study showed that only those children with the 7-repeat variant of the *DRD4* gene showed the influence of a parent training intervention (Bakermans-Kranenburg, van IJzendoorn, Pijlman, Mesman, & Juffer, 2008; see also Depue & Fu, Chapter 18, and van IJzendoorn & Bakermans-Kranenburg, Chapter 19). Extensive reviews of interactions among genes, temperament, and the environment are provided in this volume (Saudino & Wang, Chapter 16; White et al., Chapter 17; Depue & Fu, Chapter 18; van IJzendoorn & Bakermans-Kranenburg, Chapter 19; Bates et al., Chapter 20).

EC and Moral Development

In our laboratory and others, EC has been found to undergo rapid development in children between the ages of 2 and 7 years, especially during the preschool years (Gerardi-Caulton, 2000; Kochanska, Murray, & Harlan, 2000; Rothbart, Ellis, Rueda, & Posner, 2003). Kochanska and her colleagues studied the development of EC in two studies that followed children from ages 2 to 5 years and from 9 to 45 months of age (Kochanska, Murray, & Coy, 1997; Kochanska et al., 2000; Kochanska, Murray, Jacques, Koenig, & Vandegeest, 1996). They behaviorally measured five skills involving the ability to suppress a dominant response in order to perform a subdominant response, including both delay and conflict tasks. Beginning at age 2½ years (30 months), children's performance became highly consistent across these tasks, suggesting that an underlying quality of EC was developing. Children were also remarkably stable across age in their performance on the behavioral EC tasks, and stability correlations were consistently high, as high as those for the stability of intelligence (Kochanska et al., 2000). Guerin, Gottfried, Oliver, and Thomas (2003) have also reported that toddler persistence, an aspect of EC, predicts adolescent task orientation in parent-reports.

The construct of EC has important theoretical implications. Early theoretical models of temperament stressed how our actions are driven by our level of arousal, or by our positive and negative emotions. The control of approach by fear and the control of fear by strong approach or impulsivity tendencies fit with this kind of model (Gray, 1982). EC, however, means we are not always at the mercy of emotion. With EC, we can choose to approach situations we fear and inhibit actions we desire, giving a strong self-regulatory basis for socialized action, conscience, and self-control (Eisenberg, Smith, Sadovsky, & Spinrad, 2004).

EC also brings with it the possibility of the person changing his or her own thoughts and behavior. With the development of executive attention and EC, we can observe our own actions and select other actions based on our values and goals. Although the effectiveness of EC depends on the strength of the emotional and motivational processes against which it is exerted, it provides the possibility for true flexibility of thought, emotion, and action, and the volitional development of virtue.

This provides a link to Kant's (1789/2006) ideas about how we can influence ourselves through willed action. EC allows us to use self-regulatory attention systems to shape our own character. While our character reflects our use of attention in conflict situations, as well as other self-regulative functions, the development of moral character also reflects our motivation to do the right thing. EC measured in both questionnaires and in the laboratory predicts the development of conscience (Kochanska, 1997; Kochanska & Aksan, 2007), but EC, as expressed in daily life, is also linked to social and moral motivation. I suspect that children's affiliative tendencies and desire to please others (and perhaps gender; see Else-Quest, Chapter 23, this volume) are also involved in whether a child desires to comply with an adult's requests or orders.

Measurement of Temperament and Future Directions

How then do we measure temperament? It should be clear that there are many approaches to the measurement of temperament and related variables, depending on the question of interest and our level, or levels, of analysis (in this volume, see Gartstein, Bridgett, & Low, Chapter 10; Goldsmith & Gagne, Chapter 11; Calkins & Swingler, Chapter 12; see also Strelau & Zawadzki, Chapter 5; Huizink, Chapter 15; Saudino & Wang, Chapter 16). Aspects of temperament in the individual can be measured at the molecular genetic (genome) level, as well as at levels of everyday interaction. In the past, our view of the measurement of temperament was much more limited, including chiefly questionnaires, laboratory observations, measures, and behavioral home observations (reviewed by Rothbart & Goldsmith, 1985). Our review noted that each measure is associated with both advantages and potential sources of error (see also Rothbart & Bates, 2006). Because each method has both advantages and disadvantages, it is preferable to look for convergence of findings across measures, or to compare and combine measures of the same construct, rather than to dismiss any one measure (see, in this volume, Gartstein et al., Chapter 10; Goldsmith & Gagne, Chapter 11; Calkins & Swingler, Chapter 12).

We have also argued that contributions of questionnaires to our understanding of both temperament and personality have been substantial (Rothbart & Bates, 2006), as can be seen in a number of contributions to this volume beginning with Mervielde and De Pauw (Chapter 2). Although Kagan (1994, 1998) earlier argued against the use of questionnaire measures, there is also evidence for convergence of questionnaire, observational, and laboratory measures of temperament (Rothbart & Bates, 2006). Questionnaire scores are also directly linked to measures of brain structure and function (Kanske, 2008; Whittle et al., 2008).

There are now measures at the molecular genetic, genetic imaging, neurochemical, neuroimaging, and behavioral levels that allow us to study relations within and between different levels of temperament-related variables. Two important issues for future behavioral measurement arise. The first concerns the identification of narrower individual differences contributing to broader assessments, and their study within and across levels. The second concerns the relation of temperament to broader biological tendencies that can be studied in the laboratory and with nonhuman animals. Expanding the possibilities of temperament measurement allows us to study temperament in a way that is appropriate to the question we are addressing. We have already learned that fear and anger tendencies (subconstructs of Negative Affectivity) are likely to set up different routes or trajectories for the development of behavior problems (see Rothbart, 2011; Rothbart & Bates, 2006; see also, in this volume, Lengua & Wachs, Chapter 25, and Klein et al., Chapter 26). Furthermore, greater differentiation within both negative and positive emotions, and within different reward- and punishment-related sensitivities, will likely be possible in the future.

How, for example, does a broad temperament dimension, such as Surgency/Extraversion or Positive Emotionality break down into component processes such as reward sensitivity and pleasure, and how are these related to individual biology (see Putnam, Chapter 6, this volume)? What are the links between social fear (shyness), nonsocial fear, and cognition at different points in development (see Kagan, Chapter 4, this volume)? To what degree can EC be broken down into components of executive attention and motivation? How do children's structures of meaning, especially cognitions about the self and others, affect the expression of temperament, and how does temperament affect children's structures of meaning? How are both broad and differentiated measures of temperament related to genetic structure, and how do environmental events interact with effects of genes to predict developmental outcomes (see Saudino & Wang, Chapter 16, this volume)? As temperament is increasingly linked to brain structure and function, our understanding of both temperament and neuroscience will be enriched.

Another important research question is how social and nonsocial temperament reactions can be differentiated at different ages. When, for example, is social fear (shyness) first differentiated from fear of objects? How does the developing concept of self affect social and nonsocial fear? Aksan and Kochanska (2004) have distinguished between the joy expressed toward objects and toward people in infancy, and more differentiated measures related to surgency and affiliation will be helpful in addressing these research questions in the future.

In summary, our understanding of temperament has progressed rapidly (Rothbart, 2011), making use of new methods and linking genes to environments. These methods allow us to take a much broader view of temperament, and studies of molecular and imaging genetics of temperament are currently being published at an explosive rate (e.g., Hariri & Weinberger, 2003). At the same time, research using our earlier methods has continued to yield fruitful results. This recent rapid growth allows for greater understanding at the multiple levels proposed by psychobiological researchers and Robert Hinde (1998), as well as Posner and Rothbart (2007b). In the future, this handbook will provide the basis for a multilevel perspective on the study and application of temperament concepts and measures. There will clearly be many questions to for us to address and answer.

Acknowledgment

I am very appreciative of the contributions to this chapter by Michael I. Posner.

Further Reading

Hinde, R. A. (1998). Integrating across levels of complexity. In D. M. Hann, L. C. Huffman, I. I. Lederhendler, & D. Meineke (Eds.), *Advancing research on developmental plasticity* (pp. 165–173). Bethesda, MD: National Institute of Mental Health.

Kochanska, G., Murray, K. T., & Harlan, E. T. (2000). Effortful control in early childhood: Continuity and change, antecedents, and implications for social development. *Developmental Psychology, 36*(2), 220–232.

Rothbart, M. K. (2011). *Becoming who we are: Temperament and personality in development.* New York: Guilford Press.

Rothbart, M. K., & Bates, J. E. (2006). Temperament. In W. Damon, R. Lerner, & N. Eisenberg (Eds.), *Handbook of child psychology, Vol. 3: Social, emotional, and personality development* (6th ed., pp. 99–106). New York: Wiley.

References

Ahadi, S. A., Rothbart, M. K., & Ye, R. (1993). Children's temperament in the U.S. and China: Similarities and differences. *European Journal of Personality, 7,* 359–378.

Aksan, N., & Kochanska, G. (2004). Links between systems of inhibition from infancy to preschool years. *Child Development, 75,* 1477–1490.

Allport, G. W. (1937). *Personality: A psychological interpretation.* New York: Holt.

Bakermans-Kranenburg, M. J., van IJzendoorn, M. H., Pijlman, F. T. A., Mesman, J., & Juffer, F. (2008). Differential susceptibility to intervention: Dopamine D4 receptor polymorphism (DRD4 VNTR) moderates effects on toddlers' externalizing behavior in a randomized control trial. *Developmental Psychology, 44,* 293–300.

Balleyguier, G. (1989). Temperament and character: The French school. In G. A. Kohnstamm, J. E. Bates, & M. K. Rothbart (Eds.), *Temperament in childhood* (pp. 597–606). Chichester, UK: Wiley.

Bergman, D., & Escalona, S. K. (1949). Unusual sensitivities in very young children. *Psychoanalytic Study of the Child, 3/4,* 333–352.

Birns, B., Barten, S., & Bridger, W. (1969). Individual differences in temperamental characteristics of infants. *Transactions of the New York Academy of Sciences, 31,* 1071–1082.

Bowlby, J. (1971). *Attachment and loss: Vol. 1. Attachment.* New York: Basic Books.

Burt, C. L. (1915). General and specific factors underlying the primary emotions. *British Association Annual Report, 84,* 694–696.

Burt, C. L. (1937). The analysis of temperament. *British Journal of Medical Psychology, 17,* 158–188.

Carey, W. B. (1997). *Understanding your child's temperament.* New York: Macmillan.

Caspi, A., & Shiner, R. L. (2006). Personality development. In W. Damon & R. Lerner (Series Eds.) & N. Eisenberg (Vol. Ed.), *Handbook of child psychology: Vol. 3. Social, emotional, and personality development* (6th ed., pp. 300–365). New York: Wiley.

Cortes, J. B., & Gatti, F. M. (1965). Physique and self-descriptions of temperament. *Journal of Consulting Psychology, 29,* 432–439.

Cortes, J. B., & Gatti, F. M. (1972). *Delinquency and crime: A biopsychosocial approach.* New York: Seminar Press.

Cummings, E. M., Papp, L. M., & Kouros, C. D. (2009). Regulatory processes in children's coping with exposure to mental conflict. In S. L. Olson & A. J. Sameroff (Eds.), *Biopsychosocial regulatory processes in the development of childhood behavior problems* (pp. 212–237). New York: Cambridge University Press.

Derryberry, D., & Rothbart, M. K. (1988). Arousal, affect, and attention as components of temperament. *Journal of Personality and Social Psychology, 55*(6), 958–966.

Diamond, A., & Lee, L. (2011). Interventions shown to aid executive function development in children 4 to 12 years old. *Science, 33,* 959–964.

Diamond, S. (1974). *The roots of psychology: A sourcebook in the history of ideas.* New York: Basic Books.

Ebbinghaus, H. (1911). *Psychology: An elementary textbook.* Boston: Heath.

Eisenberg, N., Smith, C. L., Sadovsky, A., & Spinrad, T. (2004). Effortful control: Relations with emotion regulation, adjustment, and socialization in childhood. In R. F. Baumeister & K. D. Vohs (Eds.), *Handbook of self regulation: Research, theory, and applications* (pp. 259–282). New York: Guilford Press.

Ekman, P., Sorenson, E. R., & Friesen, W. V. (1969). Pan-cultural elements in facial displays of emotion. *Science, 164,* 86–88.

Ellis, L. K., Rothbart, M. K., & Posner, M. I. (2004). Individual differences in executive attention predict self-regulation and adolescent psychosocial behaviors. *Annals of the New York Academy of Sciences, 1021,* 337–340.

Escalona, S. (1968). *The roots of individuality: Normal patterns of development in infancy.* Chicago: Aldine.

Evans, D., & Rothbart, M. K. (2007). Developing a model for adult temperament. *Journal of Research in Personality, 41,* 868–888.

Eysenck, H. J. (1947). *Dimensions of personality.* London: Routledge & Kegan Paul.

Eysenck, H. J. (1967). *The biological basis of personality.* Springfield, IL: Thomas.

Eysenck, H. J., & Eysenck, M. W. (1985). *Personality and individual differences: A natural science approach.* New York: Plenum Press.

Fries, M. E., & Woolf, P. (1954). Some hypotheses on the role of congenital activity type in personality development. *Psychoanalytic Study of the Child, 8,* 48–64.

Gerardi-Caulton, G. (2000). Sensitivity to spatial conflict and the development of self-regulation in children 24–36 months of age. *Developmental Science, 3*(4), 397–404.

Gesell, A. (1928). *Infancy and human growth.* New York: Macmillan.

Glueck, S., & Glueck, E. (1950). *Unraveling juvenile delinquency.* New York: Commonwealth Fund.

Glueck, S., & Glueck, E. (1956). *Physique and delinquency.* New York: Harper.

Goodenough, W. H. (1981). *Culture, language, and society.* Menlo Park, CA: Benjamin.

Gray, J. (1979). *Ivan Pavlov.* New York: Penguin.

Gray, J. A. (1971). *The psychology of fear and stress.* New York: McGraw-Hill.

Gray, J. A. (1982). *The neuropsychology of anxiety: An enquiry into the functions of the septohippocampal system.* London: Oxford University Press.

Guerin, C. W., Gottfried, A. W., Oliver, P. H., & Thomas, C. (2003). *Temperament: Infancy through adolescence.* New York: Kluwer Adademic/Plenum Press.

Halverson, C. F., Jr., Kohnstamm, G. A., & Martin, R. P. (1994). *The developing structure of temperament and personality from infancy to adulthood.* Hillsdale, NJ: Erlbaum.

Hanley, C. (1951). Physique and reputation of junior high school boys. *Child Development, 22,* 247–260.

Hariri, A., & Weinberger, D. R. (2003). Imaging genomics. *British Medical Bulletin, 65,* 259–270.

Hesketh, T., Liu, L., & Xing, Z. W. (2005). The effect of China's one-child family policy after 25 years. *New England Journal of Medicine, 353,* 1171–1176.

Heymans, G., & Wiersma, E. D. (1906). Beiträge zur speziellen psychologie auf Grund einer Messenuntersuchungung. *Zeitschrift für Psychologie, 42,* 81–127, 258–301.

Hinde, R. A. (1998). Integrating across levels of complexity. In D. M. Hann, L. C. Huffman, I. I. Lederhendler, & D. Meineke (Eds.), *Advancing research on developmental plasticity* (pp. 165–173). Bethesda, MD: National Institute of Mental Health.

Kagan, J. (1994). *Galen's prophecy: Temperament in human nature.* New York: Basic Books.

Kagan, J. (1998). Biology and the child. In W. S. E. Damon & N. V. E. Eisenberg (Eds.), *Handbook of child psychology: Vol. 3. Social, emotional and personality development* (5th ed., pp. 177–235). New York: Wiley.

Kagan, J., & Fox, N. (2006). Biology, culture, and temperamental biases. In W. Damon & R. Lerner (Series Eds.), & N. Eisenberg (Vol. Ed.), *Handbook of child psychology: Vol. 3. Social, emotional, and personality development* (6th ed., pp. 99–166). New York: Wiley.

Kanske, P. (2008). *Exploring executive attention in emotion: ERP and fMRI evidence. MPI series in human cognitive and brain sciences: Vol. 106.* Leipzig, Germany: Max Planck Institute for Human Cognitive and Brain Sciences, University of Leipzig.

Kant, I. (2006). *Anthropology from a pragmatic point of view* (R. B. Louden, Trans. & Ed.). Cambridge, UK: Cambridge University Press. (Original work published 1789)

Kerr, M. (2001). Culture as a context for temperament: Suggestion from the life courses of shy Swedes and Americans. In T. D. Wachs & G. A. Kohnstamm (Eds.), *Temperament in context* (pp. 139–152). Mahwah, NJ: Erlbaum.

Kessen, W. (1965). *The child.* New York: Wiley.

Kochanska, G. (1997). Multiple pathways to conscience for children with different temperaments: From toddlerhood to age 5. *Developmental Psychology, 33,* 228–240.

Kochanska, G., & Aksan, N. (2007). Conscience in childhood: Past, present, and future. In G. W. Ladd (Ed.), *Appraising the human developmental sciences: Essays in honor of Merrill–Palmer Quarterly* (pp. 238–249). Detroit, MI: Wayne State University Press.

Kochanska, G., Murray, K. T., & Coy, K. C. (1997). Inhibitory control as a contributor to conscience in childhood: From toddler to early school age. *Child Development, 68,* 263–277.

Kochanska, G., Murray, K. T., & Harlan, E. T. (2000). Effortful control in early childhood: Continuity and change, antecedents, and implications for social development. *Developmental Psychology, 36*(2), 220–232.

Kochanska, G., Murray, K. T., Jacques, T. Y., Koenig, A. L., & Vandegeest, K. A. (1996). Inhibitory control in young children and its role in emerging internalization. *Child Development, 67,* 490–507.

Korner, A. (1964). Some hypotheses regarding the significance of individual differences at birth for later development. *Psychoanalytic Study of the Child, 19,* 58–72.

Kretschmer, E. (1925). *Physique and character.* New York: Harcourt Brace.

Larson, G. J. (1979). *Classical Samkhya.* Delhi: Motilal Banarsidass.

Le Gall, A. (1950). *Caractérologie des enfants et des adolescents, à l'usage des parents et des éducateurs.* Paris: PUF.

Lerner, R. (1969). The development of stereotyped expectancies of body build–behavior relations. *Child Development, 40,* 137–141.

Le Senne, R. (1945). *Traité de Caractérologie.* Paris: PUF.

Lipina, S. J., & Colombo, J. A. (2009). *Poverty and brain development during childhood: An approach from cognitive psychology and neuroscience.* Washington, DC: American Psychological Association.

Mascolo, M. F. (2004). The coactive construction of selves in cultures. *New Directions for Child and Adolescent Development, 104,* 79–90.

McCrae, R. R., Costa, P. T., Jr., Ostendorf, F., Angleitner, A., Hrebícková, M., Avia, M. D., et al. (2000). Nature over nurture: Temperament, personality, and life span development. *Journal of Personality and Social Psychology, 78*(1), 173–186.

Meili-Dworetzki, G., & Meili, R. (1972). *Grundlagen individueller Persönlichkeitsunterschiede: Ergebnisse einer Längsschnittuntersuchung mit zwei Gruppen von der Geburt bis zum 8. und 16. Altersjahr* [Foundations of individual personality differences: Results of a longitudinal study with two cohorts from birth to the 8th and 16th year of age]. Berne: Huber.

Moffitt, T. E., Arsenault, L., Belsky, D., Dickson, N., Hancox, R. J., Harrington, H., et al. (2011). A gradient of childhood self-control predicts health, wealth and public safety. *Proceedings of the National Academy of Sciences USA, 108,* 2693–2698.

Nebylitsyn, V. D. (1972). *Fundamental properties of the human nervous system.* New York: Plenum Press.

Needham, J. (1973). *Chinese science.* Cambridge, MA: MIT Press.

Olson, S. L., & Sameroff, A. J. (Eds.). (2009). *Regulatory processes in the development of behavior problems: Biological, behavioral, and social-ecological perspectives.* Cambridge, UK: Cambridge University Press.

Posner, M. I. (2012). *Attention in a social world.* New York: Oxford University Press.

Posner, M. I., & Rothbart, M. K. (2007a). *Educating the human brain.* Washington, DC: American Psychological Association.

Posner, M. I., & Rothbart, M. K. (2007b). Research on attention networks as a model for the integration of psychological science. *Annual Review of Psychology, 58,* 1–23.

Posner, M. I., & Rothbart, M. K. (2009). Toward a physical basis of attention and self-regulation. *Physics of Life Reviews, 6/2,* 103–120.

Posner, M. I., Rothbart, M. K., & Sheese, B. E. (2007). Attention genes. *Developmental Science, 10*(1), 24–29.

Putnam, S. P., Ellis, L. K., & Rothbart, M. K. (2001). The structure of temperament from infancy through adolescence. In A. Eliasz & A. Angleitner (Eds.), *Advances in research on temperament* (pp. 165–182). Lengerich, Germany: Pabst Science.

Putnam, S. P., Gartstein, M. A., & Rothbart, M. K. (2006). Fine-grained assessment of toddler temperament. *Infant Behavior and Development, 29,* 386–401.

Rothbart, M. K. (2011). *Becoming who we are: Temperament and personality in development.* New York: Guilford Press.

Rothbart, M. K., Ahadi, S. A., Hershey, K., & Fisher, P. (2001). Investigations of temperament at three to seven years: The Children's Behavior Questionnaire. *Child Development, 72*(5), 1394–1408.

Rothbart, M. K., & Bates, J. E. (2006). Temperament. In W. Damon, R. Lerner, & N. Eisenberg (Eds.), *Handbook of child psychology: Social, emotional, and personality development* (6th ed., Vol. 3, pp. 99–106). New York: Wiley.

Rothbart, M. K., & Derryberry, D. (1981). Development of individual differences in temperament. In M. E. Lamb & A. L. Brown (Eds.), *Advances in developmental psychology* (Vol. 1, pp. 37–86). Hillsdale, NJ: Erlbaum.

Rothbart, M. K., Ellis, L. K., Rueda, M. R., & Posner, M. I. (2003). Developing mechanisms of temperamental effortful control. *Journal of Personality, 71,* 1113–1143.

Rothbart, M. K., & Goldsmith, H. H. (1985). Three approaches to the study of infant temperament. *Developmental Review, 5,* 237–260.

Rothbart, M. K., & Rueda, M. R. (2005). The development of effortful control. In U. Mayr, E. Awh, & S. W. Keele (Eds.), *Developing individuality in the human brain: A festschrift honoring Michael I. Posner—May 2003* (pp. 167–188). Washington, DC: American Psychological Association.

Rothbart, M. K., & Sheese, B. E. (2007). Temperament and emotion regulation. In J. J. Gross (Ed.), *Handbook of emotion regulation* (pp. 331–350). New York: Guilford Press.

Rothbart, M. K., Sheese, B., & Posner, M. I. (2007). Executive attention and effortful control: Linking temperament, brain networks, and genes. *Child Development Perspectives, 1*(1), 2–7.

Rothbart, M. K., Sheese, B., Rueda, M. R., & Posner, M. I. (2011). Developing mechanisms of self regulation in early life. *Emotion Review, 3,* 207–213.

Rusalov, V. M. (1987). *Questionnaire for the measurement of the structure of temperament (QST), short manual*. Moscow: Moscow University.

Rusalov, V. M., & Trofimova, I. (2007). *Structure of temperament and its measurement*. Toronto: Psychological Services Press.

Sheese, B. E., Voelker, P. M., Rothbart, M. K., & Posner, M. I. (2007). Parenting quality interacts with genetic variation in dopamine receptor DRD4 to influence temperament in early childhood. *Development and Psychopathology, 19*, 1039–1046.

Sheese, B. E., Voelker, P. M., Rothbart, M. K., & Posner, M. I. (in press). Parenting quality and DRD4: Attention and temperament at four years of age. *Child Development Research*.

Sheldon, W. H., Lewis, N. K. C., & Tenney, A. (1969). Psycholtic patterns and physical constitution. In D. V. Siva Sanker (Ed.), *Schizophrenia: Current concepts and research*. Hillsdale, NJ: PJD Publications.

Sheldon, W. H., & Stevens, S. S. (1942). *The varieties of human temperament*. New York: Harper & Row.

Shirley, M. (1933). *The first two years: Vol. III. Personality manifestations*. Minneapolis: University of Minnesota Press.

Strelau, J. (1983). *Temperament personality activity*. New York: Academic Press.

Strelau, J., Angleitner, A., & Newberry, B. H. (1999). *The Pavlovian Temperament Survey (PTS): An international handbook*. Göttingen, Germany: Hogrefe & Huber.

Super, C. M., Axia, G., Harkness, S., Welles-Nystrom, B., Zylicz, P. O., Parminder, P., et al. (2008). Culture, temperament, and the "difficult child": A study in seven Western cultures. *European Journal of Developmental Science, 2*(1/2), 136–157.

Teplov, B. M. (1964). Problems in the study of general types of higher nervous activity in man and animals. In J. A. Gray (Ed.), *Pavlov's typology* (pp. 3–156). Oxford, UK: Pergamon Press.

Thomas, A., & Chess, S. (1977). *Temperament and development*. New York: Brunner/Mazel.

Thomas, A., Chess, S., Birch, H. G., Hertzig, M. E., & Korn, S. (1963). *Behavioral individuality in early childhood*. New York: New York University.

Vohs, K. D., & Baumeister, R. F. (Eds.). (2011). *Handbook of self-regulation: Research, theory, and applications* (2nd ed.). New York: Guilford Press.

Wachs, T. D. (2000). *Necessary but not sufficient: The respective roles of single and multiple influences on individual development*. Washington, DC: American Psychological Association.

Walker, R. N. (1962). Body build and behavior in young children: I. Body build and nursery school teachers' ratings. *Monographs of the Society for Research in Child Development, 27*(3, Serial No. 84).

Walker, R. N., & Tennes, J. M. (1980). Prediction of adult Sheldon somatotypes I and II from rankings and measurements at childhood ages. *Annals of Human Biology, 7*, 1–8.

Wallon, H. (1925). *L'enfant turbulent*. Paris: Alcan.

Wallon, H. (1934). *Les origins du caractere chez l'enfant*. Paris: Boivin.

Webb, E. (1915). Character and intelligence. *British Journal of Psychology Monographs, 1*(3), 1–99.

Whittle, S., Yücel, M., Fornito, A., Barrett, A., Wood, S., Lubman, D., et al. (2008). Neuroanatomical correlates of temperament in early adolescents. *Journal of the American Academy of Child and Adolescent Psychiatry, 47*(6), 682–693.

Wundt, W. (1903). *Grundzuge der physiologischen psychologie* (5th ed., Vol. 3). Leipzig, Germany: W. Engelmann.

Yosida, M. (1973). The Chinese concept of nature. In S. Nakayama & N. Sivin (Eds.), *Chinese science* (pp. 71–90). Cambridge, MA: MIT Press.

Zentner, M. (1998). *Die Wiederentdeckung des Temperaments. Eine Einführung in die Kinder-Temperamentforschung [The rediscovery of temperament. An introduction to research on child temperament]*. Frankfurt: Fischer Verlag.

Zentner, M. (2008). Current trends in the study of child temperament (Editorial). *European Journal of Developmental Science, 2*, 2–6.

Zentner, M., & Bates, J. E. (2008). Child temperament: An integrative review of concepts, research programs, and measures. *European Journal of Developmental Science, 2*, 7–37.

CHAPTER 2

Models of Child Temperament

Ivan Mervielde
Sarah S. W. De Pauw

What Is Temperament?

The notion of temperament originated with the Greek physician Galen (second century A.D.), who developed it from the physiological theory of the four basic body fluids: blood, phlegm, black bile, and yellow bile. According to their relative predominance in the individual, these fluids were supposed to produce the temperaments (literally referring to "mixtures" of humors) designated as sanguine (warm), phlegmatic (apathetic), melancholic (sad) and choleric (easily angered). Most contemporary researchers studying differences among children, and especially among young children, still conceive these differences in terms of "temperament," but without referring to the theory of the four basic "humors."

Although a consensus on the nature of temperament has not yet been reached, Rothbart and Bates (1998) provide a useful qualification of temperamental individual differences among children in terms of the "three A's": individual differences in the affective, activational, and attentional core of personality. Temperament is traditionally distinguished from personality—another popular concept to denote individual differences—because it refers to stable individual differences that appear from birth onward and that presumably have a strong genetic and neurobiological basis. Theorists differ in the emphasis they put on the role of emotional processes, stylistic components, and attentional processes as the core of temperament. Following Darwin, Goldsmith and Campos (1982) define temperamental categories as basic emotions, while others go beyond emotions and include processes such as attentional self-regulation (Rothbart, 1981) and activity (Buss & Plomin, 1984). The emphasis on the formal or stylistic characteristics of behavior as the core of temperament is particularly well articulated in the work of Strelau (1996, 2008) on the regulative theory of temperament.

Although developmental psychologists studying individual differences invested a great deal of effort to discover the structure and meaning of temperamental differences in children, there is still considerable discussion on a precise definition and model of temperament and the best way to measure it (Goldsmith et al., 1987; Rothbart & Bates, 2006; Tackett, 2006). Based on their review of several approaches to temperament, Zentner and Bates (2008) propose the following set of inclusion criteria (Table 2.1) regarding the origin, stylistic aspects, biological

TABLE 2.1. Inclusion Criteria for Child Temperament

1. Individual differences in normal behaviors pertaining to the domains of affect, activity, attention, and sensory sensitivity
2. Typically expressed in formal characteristics such as response intensities, latencies, durations, thresholds, and recovery times
3. Appearance in the first few years of life
4. Counterpart exists in primates as well as in certain social mammals
5. Closely, if complexly linked to biological mechanisms
6. Relatively enduring and predictive of conceptually coherent outcomes

Note. Based on Zentner and Bates (2008).

basis and the content or type of behaviors. Although these criteria are primarily tailored toward assessment of temperament in young children, they also appear to be applicable to adults.

Over the last 15 years, the debate on the structure of individual differences in children and adolescents has become even more complex because of the proposition that *personality*—a term historically reserved to qualify individual differences in adults—can be used to describe behavioral individuality in youngsters (Caspi & Shiner, 2006). During the last 25 years, the Five-Factor Model of personality has become the leading model, capturing personality traits as part of five bipolar dimensions referred to as Extraversion (vs. introversion), Agreeableness (vs. antagonism), Neuroticism (vs. emotional stability), Conscientiousness (vs. negligence), and Openness (vs. closedness) to Experience. These five factors have emerged from lexical approaches examining the structure of everyday, natural language used to describe personality (Goldberg, 1990), as well as from factor-analytic studies of personality measures (McCrae & Costa, 1987) and the analysis of free parental descriptions of children (Kohnstamm, Halverson, Mervielde, & Havill, 1998; Kohnstamm, Mervielde, Besevegis, & Halverson, 1995). To date, a growing number of research groups demonstrate that the Five-Factor Model of personality is also relevant to classify individual differences in childhood (for a review, see Mervielde, De Clercq, De Fruyt, & Van Leeuwen, 2005, 2006).

The Structure of Temperament

Although the empirical structure of most temperament scales has been demonstrated as part of the construction process, very few published studies demonstrate the replicability of the original structure with different samples. Furthermore, only a few studies attempted to recover the original structure from foreign-language versions of these instruments. Therefore, in this chapter we assess the replicability, within a Dutch-speaking Flemish sample, of the structure of four temperament scales at three different nonoverlapping age levels.

Several recent narrative reviews of research on individual differences point toward the common traits assessed by temperament and personality questionnaires, and propose a common taxonomy covering both systems (Caspi & Shiner, 2006; Shiner, 1998; Shiner & Caspi, 2003). However, the systematic integration of this exponentially growing literature is complicated because the traits evaluated in various studies are assessed with instruments based on diverse models. As of yet, there have been only a few empirical attempts (e.g., Gibbs, Reeves, & Cunningham, 1987; Goldsmith, Rieser-Danner, & Briggs, 1991) to compare the convergence among several temperament models in childhood. However, these studies typically relied on very small samples and reported major psychometric weaknesses of the temperament scales precluding the evaluation of the latent structure. Although some information has become available on the links between temperament and five-factor personality in adults (e.g., Angleitner & Ostendorf, 1994; Evans & Rothbart, 2007; McCrae & Costa, 1985), the empirical convergence across temperament and personality models in childhood remains largely unknown. Hence, it is not clear how the dimensions measured by these different instruments empirically map onto each other, and how the lower-order scales should be aggregated in broader domains (De Pauw & Mervielde, 2010; De Pauw, Mervielde, & Van Leeuwen, 2009; Mervielde & Asendorpf, 2000).

Besides describing five different models of childhood temperament, this chapter provides empirical evidence on the structure of the major questionnaires measuring temperament in early, middle, and late childhood, and—in addition—reports on the empirical relations among the dimensions of temperament derived from the questionnaire measures at the three age levels.

The structure of the instruments developed to measure temperament in accordance with the four models is determined by extracting orthogonal principal components from the covariation among the scales proposed by each model. Given that the content of some of the temperament measures is tied to a specific age level, the higher structure is assessed in three large samples of Flemish children rated by a parent or caregiver: an early childhood sample of 449 children ages 1½–3 years; a middle childhood sample of 626–668 children ages 4–7 years; and a late childhood sample of 570–578 children ages 8–14 years (De Pauw, 2010). The relations between the temperament models are assessed at each age level by correlating the scores on the principal components extracted as part of the analysis of the structure of the instruments.

Five Models of Temperament

We focus on five models of temperament that have attracted the attention of many temperament researchers: the behavioral styles approach of Thomas and Chess, the criterial approach of Buss and Plomin, the psychobiological approach of Rothbart, the emotion regulation model of Goldsmith and Campos, and the behavioral inhibition model of Kagan. (In addition to these desriptions, see also, in this volume, Rothbart, Chapter 1; Kagah, Chapter 4; Strelau & Zwadzki, Chapter 5; and Goldsmith & Gagne, Chapter 11.) With the exception of the Kagan model, these models were developed to capture multiple dimensions of infant temperament but were later expanded by adding and adapting items to describe temperament in older children until early adolescence and even beyond. Moreover, the trait dimensions postulated by these models are primarily operationalized by questionnaire measures, although some studies also included observational assessment procedures (Goldsmith, Reilly, Lemery, Longley, & Prescott, 1993; Majdandzic & van den Boom, 2007).

The Behavioral Styles Approach of Thomas and Chess

The New York Longitudinal Study

The New York Longitudinal Study (NYLS) was a milestone for introducing the concept of individual differences in developmental psychology and pediatrics (Chess & Thomas, 1966; Thomas & Chess, 1977). This work announced a paradigmatic shift from the prevailing psychodynamic and behaviorist focus on external forces to the internal forces leading to early-appearing individual differences in behavior and reaction patterns. Inspired by the differences they observed between their own children, Stella Chess and Alexander Thomas assessed on a regular basis the development of 141 infants by conducting interviews with their parents. Based on inductive content analyses of the first 22 of these interviews, they identified nine categories of behaviors they considered to be relevant for child development and that refer to basic psychological mechanisms of behavioral functioning: activity level (i.e., physical activity), regularity or rhythmicity (i.e., predictability of behavior), adaptability (i.e., response to changes in the environment), approach–withdrawal (i.e., responses to novelty), threshold of responsiveness (i.e., amount of stimulation necessary to evoke reaction), intensity of reaction (i.e., the energy level of a response), quality of mood (i.e., amount of positive and negative feelings), distractibility (i.e., effectiveness of external stimuli in altering the child's behavior), and attention span/task persistence (i.e., length of time and maintenance of activity pursued by the child).

Thomas and Chess (1977) confined temperament to the how of behavior (i.e., how intensely a child cries), rather than to content (i.e., what a child does during crying) or the motivation of behavior (i.e., why is the child crying), hence emphasizing the stylistic aspects of behavior. Their theory further emphasized that reciprocal interactions between the child and his or her environment influence the adjustment of the child. In this regard, they postulated the "goodness-of-fit" concept, suggesting that to ensure a healthy psychological development, parenting should be tailored to a child's unique temperament. They also introduced three types of children based on temperamental characteristics and described them as the *difficult, the slow to warm up*, and the *easy* child. This typology has been instrumental in linking temperament to behavioral problems (Carey, 1998).

The Thomas and Chess theory was further operationalized in several questionnaires and rating forms to be used by parents, caregivers, or teachers of infants, preschoolers, and school-age children (Presley & Martin, 1994). Although standard psychometric criteria were used to construct these instruments, small samples and the limited number of items prohibited a thorough analysis of the alleged nine-dimensional structure proposed by Thomas and Chess. A dozen item-level factor analyses of behavioral styles instruments, reviewed by Martin, Wisenbaker, and Huttunen (1994) and Presley and Martin (1994), provided little support for the postulated nine-dimensional structure but revealed that four rather than nine factors are sufficient to categorize the items.

The Structure of Behavioral Styles in Childhood

Three widely used questionnaires measure the nine Thomas and Chess dimensions in three age groups. In early childhood, the Toddler Temperament Scale (TTS; Fullard, McDevitt, & Carey, 1984; Dutch version by Hermanns, Leenders, van Tijen, van der Vlugt, & Super, 1992) targets temperament in children ages 1 to 3. In middle childhood, the Behavioral Style Questionnaire (BSQ; McDevitt & Carey, 1978; Dutch version by Leenders, van Tijen, van der Vlugt, & Super, 1992) originally targeted children ages 3 to 7. In late childhood, we administered our Dutch translation of the Middle Childhood Temperament Questionnaire (MCTQ; Hegvik, McDevitt, & Carey, 1982).

The TTS, BSQ and MCTQ comprise 97, 100, and 99 items, respectively, rated on a 6-point scale (1 = *almost never* to 6 = *almost always*), on which parents indicate how often the child exhibits a given behavior. Eight of the nine postulated dimensions have identical labels in the TTS, BSQ, and MCTQ: Activity, Adaptability, Approach–Withdrawal, Threshold of Response, Intensity of Reaction, Quality of Mood, Distractibility, and Task Persistence. The ninth dimension indicates Regularity, but in the TTS and BSQ, it primarily targets biological rhytmicity of bodily functions (e.g., regularity in sleeping, eating) and hence is labeled as Rhythmicity. The equivalent MCTQ scale captures the overall predictability of children's social behaviors, as well as task performance, and is labeled as Predictability/Quality of organization (Hegvik et al., 1982).

The TTS, BSQ, and MCTQ were administered respectively to three age-appropriate samples of Flemish children: an early childhood group of 449 toddlers ages 1½–3 years, a middle childhood group of 626 children ages 4–7 years, and a late childhood group of 570 children ages 8–14 years. Principal component analysis indicated that extracting three components accounts for 62% of the TTS variance, 63% of BSQ variance, and 70% of the variance of the MCTQ. Table 2.2 lists the loadings of the nine Thomas and Chess scales in the three age groups.

In early childhood, the nine Thomas and Chess TTS scales group in three orthogonal components. The first component is primarily marked by Activity, Persistence/Attention and Intensity of Reaction. The second component combines Quality of Mood, Approach–Withdrawal, Adaptability, and Regularity/Predictability. The third independent component is exclusively defined by Threshold of Responsiveness and Distractibility. A similar Activity/Persistence component coupled with Regularity/Predictability emerges from the BSQ for middle childhood. Three of the four scales loading on the Adaptability/Mood component in the youngest age group also load on this component in middle childhood. The third Threshold/Distractibility component is also marked by the Threshold of Responsiveness and Distractibility scales in middle and late childhood. In late childhood, the separate Activity/Persistence and Adaptability/Mood components extracted in early and middle childhood merge into one big component. Although Thomas and Chess postulate nine different categories, the current principal component analyses of the scales in three age groups indicate substantial correlations among some of the categories. Activity and Persistence/Attention Span consistently load the same component in each age group. Threshold of Responsiveness and Distractibility also consistently load on the same component. Quality of Mood, Approach–Withdrawal, and Adaptability load the same component in early and

TABLE 2.2. Principal Component Analysis of the Thomas and Chess Scales in Three Age Groups

	TTS: 1½–3 years			BSQ: 4–7 years			MCTQ: 8–14 years		
	AP	AM	TD	AP	AM	TD	APAM	TD	App
Activity level	**.82**	.07	–.11	**.76**	–.05	.29	**.78**	.16	–.24
Persistence/attention span	**.75**	.10	.02	**.78**	.13	–.07	**.81**	–.14	.11
Intensity of reaction	.47	.42	.04	.14	.35	**.69**	**.68**	.36	–.13
Quality of mood	.30	**.81**	.12	.16	**.75**	.36	**.76**	.09	.35
Approach–withdrawal	–.25	**.71**	.32	–.19	**.79**	–.16	.14	–.01	**.86**
Adaptability	.57	**.62**	–.16	.32	**.81**	.03	**.80**	.07	.34
Regularity/predictability	.05	**.52**	–.16	**.46**	.14	–.42	**.79**	–.10	.09
Threshold of responsiveness	–.12	.10	**.85**	–.12	.15	**.76**	–.01	**.87**	.25
Distractibility	.57	–.26	**.57**	.13	–.22	**.69**	.07	**.69**	–.40
% Explained variance	25.2	23.1	13.6	17.9	23.1	21.9	40.0	15.9	14.4

Note. TTS, Toddler Temperament Scale; BSQ, Behavioral Styles Questionnaire; MCTQ, Middle Childhood Temperament Questionnaire. AP, Activity/Persistence; AM, Adaptability/Mood; TD, Threshold/Distractibility; App, Approach. Early childhood: $N = 449$ (152 imputed); middle childhood: $N = 626$; late childhood: $N = 570$. Primary loadings are in **bold print**.

middle childhood but merge into one component in late childhood MCTQ, without Approach–Withdrawal that separates into a distinct component. Although the structure varies with age level, it is not entirely clear whether this is due to age-related processes or to differential item content or differences in the distribution of items in the three questionnaires. Most remarkable is the across-age consistency of the typical Thomas and Chess component combining Threshold of Responsiveness and Distractibility.

The Criterial Approach of Buss and Plomin

Emotionality, Activity, and Sociability

According to Buss and Plomin (1975), a trait could only be considered as temperamental if it satisfied five criteria: it should be "inherited," relatively stable during childhood, retained into adulthood, evolutionary adaptive, and present in our phylogenetic relatives. Initially, they distinguished four temperamental dimensions within their EASI model: Emotionality, Activity, Sociability, and Impulsivity. Emotionality is roughly equivalent to distress; it varies from stoic lack of reaction to extreme emotional reactions, such as crying and tantrums. It involves intense activation of the sympathetic nervous system, hence high emotional arousal. By the second year of life, Emotionality comprises three components: distress, fear, and anger. Activity, the second temperamental dimension, has two major components: tempo and vigor. It is best measured by the rate and amplitude of speech and movement, displacement of body movements, and duration of energetic behavior. Sociability is described as the preference for being with others, and the need to share activities and to receive rewarding attention as the result of social interaction. Typical measures for Sociability are the frequency of attempts to initiate social contacts, the number of affiliations, the amount of time spent with others, and reactions to isolation. In accordance with the research on "inhibition" by Kagan, Reznick, and Snidman (1987, 1988), later researchers proposed to split the Sociability dimension into Sociability (i.e., preference to be with others) and Shyness (i.e., feelings of tension and distress in social situations, and a tendency to escape from social interactions with strangers). This distinction is supported by the differential relation of shyness and sociability to fear and anxiety and the development of anxiety disorders (Cheek & Buss, 1981; Kagan et al., 1987). More recent research has questioned the cross-cultural generalizability of the EAS structure (Boer

& Westenberg, 1994; Gasman et al., 2002; Mathiesen & Tambs, 1999).

Because Buss and Plomin explicitly refer to "inherited personality traits" as defining characteristics of temperamental traits, various questionnaires based on the EAS model have been used in behavior genetic studies, providing evidence for not only the heritability of the EAS dimensions but also contrast effects in twin ratings (Goldsmith, Buss, & Lemery, 1997; Saudino, McGuire, Reiss, Hetherington, & Plomin, 1995; Spinath & Angleitner, 1998).

The Structure of the EAS Temperament Survey in Childhood

The EAS Temperament Survey (EAS; Buss & Plomin, 1984) is a concise instrument (only 20 items) that probes four dimensions: Emotionality, Activity, Sociability, and Shyness. All items refer to behaviors that are observable in children as young as 1 year of age, as well as in adolescents. The Dutch translation of the EAS Temperament Survey (Boer & Westenberg, 1994) assesses the four postulated dimensions, with five items per dimension rated on a 5-point Likert scale.

Given that the authors of the EAS postulate three dimensions measured by four scales, we extracted three principal components from the covariance matrix and rotated them according to the Varimax criterion. The loading matrix resulting from this principal component analysis is reported in Table 2.3. A clear and convincing three-component structure emerges for the analysis of the early (1½–3 years), middle (4–7 years) and late (8–14 years) childhood. The variance accounted for by the three components varies from 88.9% for late childhood to 89.3% for early childhood to 89.6% for middle childhood. The analysis shows that Sociability and Shyness combine into one component, with somewhat lower primary loadings for Shyness than for Sociability. Moreover, Shyness tends to have decreasing secondary loadings on Emotionality with increasing age level. Finally, Activity has consistent but low to modest secondary loadings on Sociability with increasing age, perhaps foreshadowing a blend of Activity with Sociability in adolescence and adulthood, as suggested by Digman and Inouye (1986) and Eaton (1994).

The Psychobiological Approach of Rothbart

The Psychobiological Basis of Temperament

The theoretical model developed by Rothbart and colleagues (Rothbart, 1981; Rothbart & Ahadi, 1994) delineates temperament as constitutionally based individual differences in reactivity and self-regulation, and expands the original "stylistic" temperament construct to incorporate emotion, motivation, and attention-related processes. Fundamental is the assumption that temperamental differences are largely determined by the responsiveness of underlying psychobiological processes. In this regard, *reactivity* refers to physiological excitability of neural systems, whereas *self-regulation* refers to the processes enabling the modula-

TABLE 2.3. Principal Component Analysis of the Buss and Plomin EAS Scales in Three Age Groups

	EAS: 1½–3 years			EAS: 4–7 years			EAS: 8–14 years		
	SS	EMO	ACT	SS	EMO	ACT	SS	EMO	ACT
Sociability	**.94**	.08	.07	**.86**	.20	.21	**.83**	.15	.26
Shyness	**−.72**	.39	−.30	**−.83**	.33	−.12	**−.88**	.19	−.09
Emotionality	−.05	**.97**	.07	−.04	**.97**	.02	−.03	**.99**	.05
Activity	.16	.06	**.97**	.20	.01	**.98**	.22	.04	**.97**
% Explained variance	35.5	27.6	26.2	36.8	27.4	25.4	37.5	25.8	25.6

Note. SS, Sociability/Shyness; EMO, Emotionality; ACT, Activity. Early childhood: $N = 449$ (152 imputed); middle childhood: $N = 659$; late childhood: $N = 573$. Primary loadings are in **bold print**.

tion of this automatic, involuntary reactivity. Behaviorally, temperament can be observed across all ages as differences in patterns of emotionality, activity and attention. Motivational as well as attentional systems are considered to provide the link relating specific neural systems to the major dimensions of personality.

Derryberry and Rothbart (1997) discuss four motivational and three attentional systems. Each of the motivational systems is related not only to specific neural structures, mainly located in the limbic system, but also to emotional states and major personality dimensions. As a first motivational system, they distinguish the *appetitive system*, mobilizing approach behavior to stimuli that predict rewards and hence related to Gray's (1987) "behavioral activation system." The second system is called the *defensive or fearful motivational system*, responding to novel stimuli, biologically prepared fear signals, and signals predicting punishment and non-reward. This system is explicitly related to Gray's "behavioral inhibition system." The third, the *frustrative and aggressive behavior system*, encompasses defensive aggressive responses that are explicitly linked to Gray's fight–flight system. This system also includes irritative aggressive responses aimed at actively removing the undesired obstacle and that are also closely related to Gray's behavioral activation system. The fourth system, serving affliative nurturant needs and regulating social behaviors, is called the *affiliative* or *nurturant system*.

The first attentional system discussed by Derryberry and Rothbart (1997) is a *vigilance system*, thought to regulate tonic maintenance and phasic adjustments of alertness. The *posterior attentional system* involves components that allow a flexible shift of attention from one location to another. "Effortful control" of behavior is supposed to be regulated by the *anterior attentional system*, which is viewed as an executive system that regulates the posterior attentional system, as well as attention to semantic information (Posner & Rothbart, 1992). This last system is believed to be related to the adult personality factor Conscientiousness (Ahadi & Rothbart, 1994; Evans & Rothbart, 2007; Putnam, Ellis, & Rothbart, 2001).

The Structure of the Rothbart Temperament Questionnaires

The Rothbart model originally described temperament during the first year of life but was later on expanded to include older age groups, such as preschool (Rothbart, Ahadi, Hershey, & Fisher, 2001), primary school and early adolescent children (Ellis & Rothbart, 2001), and recently also toddlers (Putnam, Gartstein, & Rothbart, 2006) and adults (Evans & Rothbart, 2007). For each age group, specific behavioral and emotional descriptors are itemized to assess the underlying neural processes of Rothbart's theoretical model. Factor analyses of these age-specific instruments provide noteworthy evidence that the structure of temperament in any age group can be covered by at least three broad dimensions: Negative Affect, Surgency, and Effortful Control (Rothbart & Bates, 2006). Negative Affect and Surgency incorporate most aspects of the assumed reactivity processes, while Effortful Control subsumes the proposed regulation processes.

The lower-order structures depend on the behavioral indicators included in the age-adapted instruments. The Children's Behavior Questionnaire (CBQ; Putnam et al., 2006; Rothbart et al., 2001) assesses 15 scales, combined into three factors. The first factor, Surgency, refers to social orientation and combines aspects of motor activity and the experience of positive emotion. This factor encompasses the traits of positive anticipation, high-intensity pleasure, smiling/laughter, activity level, impulsivity, and low levels of shyness. The second factor, Negative Affect, indicates a general tendency to experience negative emotions and is captured by the scales Discomfort, Fear or Distress to Novelty, Anger/Frustration, Sadness, and Low Soothability. The third factor, Effortful Control, includes inhibitory control and attentional focusing, but also perceptual sensitivity and taking pleasure from low intensity (quiet, or routine) activities.

The three-dimensional structure is supported by cross-sectional research, but the age-specific instruments comprise only partially overlapping sets of scales. This heterogeneous content poses problems for longitudinal and cross-sectional comparison of different age groups (Putnam, Rothbart, & Gartstein, 2008). Moreover, some lower-order scales appear to have inconsistent primary factor loadings or weaker psychometric properties (De Pauw et al., 2009; Muris & Meesters, 2009).

THE CBQ

The Dutch translation (Majdandzic & van den Boom, 2007) of the CBQ–Short Form (Putnam & Rothbart, 2006) is a parent-report measure that contains 94 statements designed for rating children ages 3 to 7 years, on a 7-point scale.

The CBQ measures 15 primary temperamental traits, assigned to three higher-order dimensions: Negative Affect (Anger/Frustration, Discomfort, Fear, Sadness, and Soothability), Surgency (Activity Level, Impulsivity, High-Intensity Pleasure, and Shyness), and Effortful Control (Attentional Focusing, Inhibitory Control, Low-Intensity Pleasure, and Perceptual Sensitivity). Two additional scales, Positive Anticipation/Approach and Smiling/Laughter, were not allocated to a higher-order dimension because of inconsistent patterns of loadings (Rothbart et al., 2001).

To assess its structure, the CBQ was completed by 668 parents of 4- to 7-year-olds attending the second or third class of kindergarten or the first or second class of primary education in the Flemish-speaking community of Belgium. The loading matrix after extraction and Varimax rotation of three principal components is reported in Table 2.4.

Twelve of the theoretically assigned CBQ scales have their highest loading on the expected three factors: Surgency, Negative Affect, and Effortful Control. The three components explain almost 54% of the variance of the scales. The additional scale,

TABLE 2.4. Principal Component Analysis of the Rothbart Scales in Two Age Groups

	CBQ: 4–7 years			EATQ-R: 8–14 years		
	SU	NA	EC	SU	NA	EC
SU: Activity Level	.82	–.05	–.14			
SU: High-Intensity Pleasure	.79	–.09	–.09	.74	–.15	–.16
SU: Impulsivity	.76	–.31	.11			
APPROACH	.65	.28	.23			
NA: Sadness	.00	.71	.08			
NA: Soothability	–.08	–.66	.29			
NA: Discomfort	–.15	.64	.09			
NA: Anger/Frustration	.32	.63	–.18	.04	.69	–.37
NA: Fear	–.17	.60	.08	–.19	.87	–.07
SU: Shyness	–.39	.49	–.08	–.81	.15	–.04
EC: Low-Intensity Pleasure	.09	.10	.75			
EC: Perceptual Sensitivity	.01	.15	.73			
EC: Attention Focusing	–.20	–.19	.61	.04	–.11	.86
EC: Inhibitory Control	–.52	–.11	.60	–.08	–.40	.70
SMILING/LAUGHTER	.35	–.19	.59			
EC: Activation Control				.08	–.05	.86
AFFILIATION				.70	.34	.29
% Explained variance	20.3	17.6	16.0	21.7	19.5	27.9

Note. SU, Surgency; NA, Negative Affect; EC, Effortful Control. Middle childhood: $N = 668$; late childhood: $N = 578$. Primary loadings are in **bold print**.

Approach, primarily loads Surgency with moderate loadings on Negative Affect and Effortful Control. The Smiling/Laughter scale loads primarily on Effortful Control and moderately on Surgency, as is the case for the U.S. sample (Rothbart et al., 2001). The principal component analysis largely confirms the expected CBQ structure with one notable exception: Shyness is not a pure marker for Surgency but moderately (.49) loads Negative Affect and Surgency (–.39). The link between Shyness and Negative affect is not uncommon and presumably is age-dependent because Shyness emerges as a rather pure Surgency marker in the analysis of the Early Adolescent Temperament Questionnaire—Revised (EATQ-R), targeting 8- to 14-year-olds. The analysis of the Buss and Plomin EAS reported in Table 2.3 also shows important age-dependent declining secondary loadings on Emotionality. The analysis of the Toddler Behavior Assessment Questionnaire, to be reported further on in Table 2.5, also confirms the early childhood Shyness–Negative Affect link showing important loadings on the component combining Social Fearfulness (.88) and Pleasure/Positive Affect (–.80) in the early childhood sample.

THE EATQ-R

The Dutch version (Hartman, 2000) of the EATQ-R (Ellis, 2002; Ellis & Rothbart, 2001) assesses temperament in children and adolescents between 8 and 16 years of age. This 62-item parent-report measure includes two behavioral scales, Depression and Aggression (not included in this research), and seven temperament traits representing Negative Affect (combining the subscales Fear, Frustration), Surgency (High-Intensity Pleasure, Shyness), and Effortful Control (Activation Control, Attention, Inhibitory Control). In addition, the EATQ-R assesses Need for Affiliation, the desire for warmth and closeness to others. This trait is hypothesized to emerge in early adolescence and to relate to adult Agreeableness. Items are rated on a 5-point Likert scale.

The structure of the EATQ-R was assessed with parental ratings of 578 children ages 8–14 years. The expected structure for the seven indigenous EATQ-R scales was clearly replicated with the Flemish translation and sample. Three principal components account for 69% of the variance of the EATQ-R scales. Both Shyness and High-Intensity Pleasure have high primary loadings on the Surgency component. The Negative affect component is primarily defined by the Anger/Frustration and the Fear scales. The Effortful Control scales, Attention Focusing, Activation Control, and Inhibitory control, act as the primary EATQ-R markers for Effortful Control. The additional Affiliation scale primarily loads on Surgency, with a moderate loading on Negative Affect and Effortful Control.

Although the EATQ-R, compared to the CBQ, targets the three Rothbart factors with about half the number of scales, its empirical structure completely confirms the expectations. Moreover, the loading pattern of the six scales common to both the CBQ and the EATQ-R is remarkably stable given the substantial difference in the number of scales included in both instruments. As we noted in discussing the CBQ, only the Shyness scale behaves differently in both instruments, loading primarily Negative Affect in the middle childhood CBQ but acting as a rather pure marker of Surgency in the late childhood EATQ-R. Hence, we can conclude that the structure of both the CBQ and the EATQ-R is very stable because the structure of the U.S. version is recovered with a different language version administered to a large representative Flemish sample.

TABLE 2.5. Principal Component Analysis of the Goldsmith–Campos TBAQ Scales in Early Childhood

	TBAQ: 1½–3 years		
	AnA	SoP	IP
Anger Proneness	**.90**	.23	.04
Activity Level	**.81**	–.22	–.35
Social Fearfulness	.13	**.88**	.15
Pleasure/Positive Affect	.10	**–.80**	.39
Interest/Persistence	–.16	–.07	**.93**
% Explained variance	30.3	30.2	23.4

Note. AnA, Anger Proneness/Activity Level; SoP, Social Fearfulness/Pleasure; IP, Interest/Persistence. N = 449 (imputed N = 152). Primary loadings are in **bold print**.

The Emotion Regulation Model of Goldsmith and Campos

Temperament as Emotion Regulation

Goldsmith and Campos define *temperament* as individual differences in the probability of experiencing and expressing primary emotions and arousal (Goldsmith et al., 1987; Goldsmith & Campos, 1982). They specify as inclusion criteria for temperament that it is emotional in nature, pertains to individual differences, refers to behavioral tendencies, and is indexed by expressive acts of emotion, excluding cognitive and perceptual factors, as well as transitory states. *Emotions* are defined in terms of four characteristics: (1) emotions regulate internal psychological processes; (2) emotions crucially regulate social and interpersonal behaviors; (3) basic emotions can be specified by unique patterns of facial, vocal, or gestural expressions; and (4) basic emotions use a noncodified communication process that has an innate basis. The basic emotions that form the content dimensions of this model are those considered to be universal by Ekman and Friesen (1971): anger, sadness, fear, joy and pleasure, disgust, interest, and surprise.

The basic components of temperament, as defined in the Goldsmith–Campos model, can be assessed not only with a questionnaire to be used by parents or a caregiver to rate children on a set of more than 100 items (Goldsmith, 1996) but also by observing the behavior of preschoolers in a laboratory setting while they perform a number of laboratory tasks included in the Preschool Laboratory Temperament Assessment Battery (PS Lab-TAB; Goldsmith et al., 1993). Recent research on the Goldsmith and Campos model is mainly confined to behavior genetic analyses (Goldsmith et al., 1997; Goldsmith, Lemery, Buss, & Campos, 1999; Lemery, Essex, & Smider, 2002). Goldsmith and colleagues (1997) show that there is clear evidence for moderate genetic effects on Activity Level, Social Fearfulness, Anger Proneness, and Interest/Persistence (h^2 ranging from .26 to .78). However, Social Fearfulness and Anger Proneness also exhibited moderate shared environmental effects (c^2 ranging from .28 to .63). Most interesting was the fact that the Pleasure scale, referring to positive emotions, showed the strongest evidence for exclusive shared environmental effects (c^2 of .50 or .66).

Continuity across age levels is traditionally viewed as one of the defining characteristics of temperament. Lemery, Goldsmith, Klinnert, and Mrazek (1999) concluded from a review of longitudinal studies of early temperament that there is evidence for stability, at least within a given research tradition based on the same or highly similar instruments. The same research group has also played a significant role in demonstrating that childhood temperament is linked to symptomatology and problem behavior, and to temperament scales targeting other age levels (Goldsmith & Lemery, 2000; Lemery et al., 2002).

The Structure of the Toddler Behavior Assessment Questionnaire

Goldsmith (1996) constructed the Toddler Behavior Assessment Questionnaire (TBAQ), a caregiver report with acceptable psychometric properties, including reasonable convergent and discriminant validity (Goldsmith et al., 1997; Lemery et al., 1999). The TBAQ includes five fairly independent scales: Activity Level, Pleasure/Positive Affect, Social Fearfulness, Anger Proneness, and Interest/Persistence. The TBAQ is longitudinally related to Rothbart's CBQ, whereas 13 CBQ scales correlate from .34 to .68 with one of the five TBAQ scales (Goldsmith et al., 1997).

The 108-item Dutch version (Van Bakel & Riksen-Walraven, 2004) of the TBAQ (Goldsmith, 1996) was used to assess temperament in 449 Flemish children ages 1½ to 3 years. The TBAQ was developed within the psychobiological tradition, emphasizing the emotional aspects of behavior. It measures Activity Level, Pleasure, Social Fearfulness, Anger Proneness, and Interest/Persistence on a 7-point rating scale (1 = *never*, 4 = *about half the time*, 7 = *always*), indicating the frequency of behaviors tailored to the toddler period during the past month.

The higher-order structure of the TBAQ scales was assessed for the Flemish sample of 449 children ages 1½–3 years with partial data (*N* = 152) imputation for randomly selected cases. To facilitate comparing the TBAQ structure to that of the other temperament measures, we extracted three orthogonal principal components from the covariance among the five scales (see Table 2.5 on page 29). The three components accounted jointly for almost 84% of the variance. Although the five scales were conceived as relatively independent, the principal component analysis shows some interesting clustering. The first component is highly defined by Anger Proneness and Activity Level, whereas the second component combines Social Fearfulness with Pleasure/Positive Affect. Again, we notice that a Shyness indicator (Social Fearfulness) is combined with a reversed indicator for Negative Affect (Pleasure/Positive Affect), confirming the linkage between Shyness and Negative Affect in early childhood temperament scales. The Interest/Persistence scale emerges as a separate component that is moderately defined (−.35) by Activity Level and Pleasure/Positive Affect (.39). Moreover, the three extracted components appear to be related to symptomatology of problem behavior (Lemery et al., 2002). Although this should be further tested empirically, the first and third components might be considered as indicators for externalizing behavior, whereas the second component might denote a marker for internalizing (De Pauw et al., 2009).

Kagan's Behavioral Inhibition Model

The Role of Behavioral Inhibition in Temperament

Kagan (1994) puts "behavioral inhibition" center stage in his biotypological approach to temperament. According to Kagan (2003, pp. 8–9),

> Healthy middle-class Caucasian four-month-old infants who show vigorous motor activity and distress in response to unfamiliar visual, auditory, and olfactory stimuli are called high-reactive and comprise about 20% of similar samples. High-reactive infants tend to become shy, timid, and fearful in response to unfamiliar events in the second year (Kagan, 1994). One third of the high-reactive infants become very fearful and are called inhibited. By contrast, infants who display low levels of motor activity and minimal irritability in response to the same stimuli (about 40% of most samples and called low-reactive) are biased to become sociable, relatively fearless children. One third of the low-reactive infants become minimally fearful and are called uninhibited.

The confirmation of Kagan's theory of temperament requires longitudinal research. Mullen, Snidman, and Kagan (1993) reported that 4-month-old infants classified as high reactive, based on motor activity and frequency of crying to visual and auditory stimuli, had higher inhibition scores when observed at 14 months during a free-play period. Two longitudinal studies of 2-year-old children who displayed extreme behavioral restraint or spontaneity in unfamiliar contexts revealed that by 7 years of age, a majority of members of the restrained group were quiet and socially avoidant with unfamiliar children and adults, whereas a majority of the more spontaneous children were talkative and interactive (Kagan et al., 1988). Children who were inhibited or uninhibited at 21 months were observed at 4 years of age in situations designed to evaluate behavior with an unfamiliar peer, heart rate, and heart rate variability in response to various challenging tasks. At age 4, the 22 formerly inhibited children, compared with the 21 uninhibited children, were socially inhibited with the other child, displayed a higher and more stable heart rate, were more reluctant to guess at difficult problems, and preferentially fixated the passive figure (Kagan, Reznick, Clarke, Snidman, & Garcia-Coll, 1984). Follow-up of inhibited and uninhibited children at 7½ years showed that a majority of the formerly shy, timid children became quiet and socially avoidant in unfamiliar social situations, while a majority of the formerly sociable children became talkative and interactive with peers and adults. However, absolute heart rate and cortisol level at 7½ years were not as discriminating of the two behavioral groups as they had been 2 years earlier. This longitudinal research was further extended to adolescents, showing a significant association between earlier classifications of a child as inhibited and generalized social anxiety in adolescence (Schwartz, Snidman, & Kagan, 1999). Kagan and colleagues (1984) also documented that behavioral inhibition in infancy predicts higher likelihood of various forms of psychological disorder (Biederman et al., 1990, 1993; Kagan, 2003; Kagan, Snidman, Zentner, & Peterson, 1999).

Measurement of Inhibition

Kagan (2003) believes scientists should recognize that the meaning of a scientific construct cannot be separated from its source of evidence. He argues that the single use of questionnaires and interviews as the sole basis for inferring psychological constructs is problematic because (1) each semantic representation of a trait is related to other categories; (2) some traits are not represented in the semantic network of layman raters; (3) few individuals have conscious access to bodily events, and children and adults therefore cannot be asked about them on questionnaires; and (4) children described similarly by a parent can be very different biologically, which can lead to conclusions that violate both biology and common sense.

Although Kagan is not an advocate of questionnaires, he often uses them as a device for prescreening large samples to detect potentially inhibited children. Garcia-Coll, Kagan, and Reznick (1984) used the TTS (Fullard et al., 1984) to prescreen 305 children and to identify 56 inhibited and 104 uninhibited children who were invited to the laboratory for an extended series of behavioral assessments targeting the children's behavioral inhibition (e.g., observing them in free play, confronting them with unfamiliar persons and objects, and separating the child from the mother). Two coders independently coded the videotape records of the sessions, and continuous variables were divided at the median, leading to classification of 33 children as inhibited and 38 as uninhibited.

In contrast to most of the other temperament theories, Kagan refers to high- versus low-reactive and inhibited versus uninhibited children as belonging to distinctive and discrete categories produced by different biological factors. This choice is based on his conviction that different phenotypes are often the result of distinct genotypes (Kagan, 2008).

The Biological Basis of Behavioral Inhibition

Kagan and colleagues (1988) noted that variation in behavioral withdrawal in rats, cats, and monkeys is often related to physiological reactions that imply greater arousal, particularly in the amygdala. Therefore, in inhibited infants, they expected higher sympathetic reactivity indicated by high and minimally variable heart rate, heart rate acceleration, pupillary dilatation, and higher norepinephrine level to psychological stress and challenge. Several studies by the Kagan group confirmed these expected differences in sympathetic reactivity between children identified as inhibited and noninhibited by means of laboratory behavior assessments (Kagan et al., 1984, 1987, 1988, 1999).

In his *Annual Review of Psychology* article, Kagan (2003) reiterated that each temperamental type inherits a distinct neurochemistry that affects the excitability of the amygdala and/or the bed nucleus of the stria terminalis and their projections. He added that neurochemical profiles might involve variation in the concentration of, or distribution of receptors for, dopamine, norepinephrine, corticotropin-releasing hormone, opioids, or gamma-aminobutyric acid (GABA). Because one function of GABA is to inhibit neural activation, newborns who cannot regulate their distress may possess compromised GABA function. Given the tremendous surge of neuropsychological research in the last decade, it is likely that our knowledge of the biological and neurological basis of temperament is bound to take a great leap forward, further elucidating the important links between neurobiology and phenotypical temperamental differences in childhood.

Similarities and Differences among the Temperament Models

Early Childhood

To substantiate the various narrative and partial empirical accounts of the relationships between the typical temperament measures administered in early childhood, we correlated the scores on the principal components extracted from the Thomas and Chess TTS, the Buss and Plomin EAS Temperament Survey, and the Goldsmith and Campos TBAQ based on the data from the Flemish sample of 1½- to 3-year-old children. As is evident from the top panel of Table 2.6, there is no clear-cut one-to-one relationship between the first or second TTS

2. Models of Child Temperament 33

TABLE 2.6. Bivariate Correlations between Temperament Components in Each Age Group

Early childhood (N = 449)	EAS SS	EAS EMO	EAS ACT	TBAQ AnA	TBAQ SoP	TBAQ IP
TTS AP	.25***	.25***	.42***	.57***	−.09	−.67***
TTS AM	−.39***	.60***	−.12**	.43***	.64***	.20***
TTS TD	.04	.18***	−.19***	−.08	.10*	.13**
EAS SS				.08	−.50***	−.10*
EAS EMO				.35***	.33***	−.03
EAS ACT				.48***	−.31***	−.20***

Middle childhood (N = 557–564)	EAS SS	EAS EMO	EAS ACT	CBQ SU	CBQ NA	CBQ EC
BSQ AP	.25***	.03	.43***	.49***	−.01	−.22***
BSQ AM	−.36***	.48***	−.16***	−.18***	.53***	−.08
BSQ TD	.13**	.29***	.19***	.18***	.22***	.19***
EAS SS				.32***	−.21***	.12**
EAS EMO				.05	.54***	.00
EAS ACT				.60***	−.09*	−.10*

Late childhood (N = 561–565)	EAS SS	EAS EMO	EAS ACT	EATQ-R SU	EATQ-R NA	EATQ-R EC
MCTQ APAM	−.01	.35***	.16***	.03	.10*	−.55***
MCTQ TD	.09*	.14***	.12**	.08	.15***	.07
MCTQ App	−.50***	.11**	−.36***	−.51***	.06	.04
EAS SS				.56***	.03	.08
EAS EMO				−.12	.37***	−.23***
EAS ACT				.25***	.05	−.08*

Note. AP, Activity/Persistence; AM, Adaptability/Mood; TD, Threshold/Distractibility; App, Approach; AnA, Anger Proneness/Activity Level; SoP, Social Fearfulness/Pleasure; IP, Interest/Persistence; SU, Surgency; NA, Negative Affect; EC, Effortful Control. Higher scores on the components of the TTS, BSQ and MCTQ refer to more maladaptive behaviors. Correlations ≥ |.40| are listed in **bold print**.
***p < .001; **p < .01; *p < .05.

component and the components of either the EAS and the TBAQ. TTS Activity/Persistence is moderately related to the three EAS components, but primarily to Activity (r = .42). It is also substantially (r = .57) related to TBAQ Anger Proneness/Activity, but primarily (r = −.67) to TBAQ Interest/Persistence. Apparently, the TTS combines scale content in a different manner than the EAS and the TBAQ do.

The third TTS component, Threshold/Distractibility, is only weakly related to both the EAS and the TBAQ components. Hence, Threshold/Distractibility is a rather unique component assessing perceptual sensitivity and distractibility, capturing variance among toddlers that is barely picked up by the two other temperament measures.

The relationships between the EAS and the TBAQ are more distinctive than the links between the TTS on the one hand and both the EAS and the TBAQ on the other. The EAS Sociability/Shyness component is uniquely (r = .50) tied to TBAQ Social Fearfulness/Pleasure, and EAS Activity is, as expected, primarily linked to TBAQ Anger Proneness/Activity but also moderately correlated with the two remaining TBAQ components. EAS Emotionality is only moderately linked to more specific emotions captured by TBAQ Anger Proneness/Activity Level and Social Fearfulness/Pleasure.

The third TBAQ component, Interest/Persistence, is not represented in the EAS, but it is a prominent correlate of the TTS Activity/Persistence component.

As we concluded in our narrative reviews of childhood temperament models (De Pauw & Mervielde, 2010; Mervielde & Asendorpf, 2000), *Activity* is clearly represented in each of the early childhood temperament measures, and this analysis confirms that the components capturing Activity content in the three instruments are substantially correlated with each other. *Emotionality* in early childhood, as captured by the TTS Adaptability/Mood and the EAS Emotionality components are also highly correlated (*r* = .60). However, the TBAQ Social Fearfulness/Pleasure component is primarily linked to TTS Adaptability/Mood, but only moderately to EAS Emotionality. Hence, emotionality is also captured by two of the three early childhood measures of temperament. *Sociability/Shyness* (SS) emerges from two of the three models: as the separate SS component in the EAS, whereas in the TBAQ Social Fearfulness is combined with Pleasure. *Persistence* is captured by both TBAQ Interest/Persistence and TTS Activity/Persistence components, but not by the Buss and Plomin EAS. Finally, Thomas and Chess's *Threshold/Distractibility* is a unique component that is not captured by the two other temperament questionnaires.

Eight out of the 27 correlations between the components extracted from the three models are ≥ |.40|, suggesting that the three models share a substantial amount of variance, but there are also some important missing links. The Thomas and Chess model, as specified by the TTS, lacks a pure Sociability/Shyness component. The EAS does not have a scale targeting Interest/Persistence and does not capture TTS Threshold/Distractibility content. The TBAQ targets several specific emotions, such as Social Fearfulness, Anger, and Pleasure, but lacks a general Emotionality component and also misses content related to Threshold/Distractibility.

Middle Childhood

The scores on the principal components extracted from the BSQ, the EAS Temperament Survey, and the CBQ–Short Form were based on data from the Flemish sample of 4- to 7-year-old children. The middle panel of Table 2.6 shows slightly more specificity in the relationships between the components of the three instruments than the top panel because 6 of the 27 correlations are ≥ |.40|. The BSQ Activity/Persistence component is primarily related to EAS Activity and to CBQ Surgency, with secondary links to EAS Sociability/Shyness and to CBQ Effortful Control. The BSQ Adaptability/Mood component is primarily associated with EAS Emotionality (*r* = .48) and CBQ Negative Affect. The Adaptability/Mood component emerges in middle childhood as clearly related to Emotionality and Negative Affect. The third BSQ Threshold/Distractibility component is, again, not clearly linked to any of the other components and hence is unique for the measure of the Thomas and Chess model.

The links between the EAS and the CBQ components are also quite distinct. EAS Emotionality is firmly associated with CBQ Negative Affect, and EAS Activity is an important and unique correlate of CBQ Surgency. EAS Shyness/Sociability is modestly correlated with the three CBQ components. Finally, CBQ Effortful Control seems to share little variance with the EAS and the BSQ components.

Interestingly, *Activity* is also clearly present in each of the questionnaires targeted toward middle childhood. The pattern of mutual correlations indicates that Activity is a common and important component in middle childhood. It should be noted, however, that activity level is not a higher-order factor in the CBQ, but it is the best marker for the Surgency component (see Table 2.4). In middle childhood, there is also evidence for an *Emotionality* triad: BSQ Adaptability/Mood, EAS Emotionality, and BSQ Negative Affect. As was the case for early childhood, *Sociability/Shyness* is not well represented in the Thomas and Chess model. Although the EAS has a separate SS component, it is only moderately correlated with CBQ Surgency, which is in turn strongly related to EAS Activity. This suggests that CBQ Surgency is more related to Activity than to Sociability. This was already evident from Table 2.4, reporting a higher loading of CBQ Shyness on Negative Affect than on the Surgency component. *Effortful Control*, the middle childhood successor of early childhood Persistence, is apparently not substantially related to any other component because it only correlates −.22 with BSQ Activity/Persistence and .19 with Threshold/Distractibility. Finally, *Threshold/Distractibility* is also a unique component in middle childhood. Besides documenting the links between the instruments representing the three models, this analysis also shows some noteworthy omissions. The BSQ has neither a clear SS component nor content related to Effortful Control, as measured by the CBQ. The EAS also lacks scales capturing Effortful Control and Threshold/Distractibility. The CBQ lacks Threshold/Distractibility and its Surgency component is more related to Activity than to SS.

Late Childhood

The correlations between the principal components extracted from the MCTQ, the EAS, and the EATQ-R—administered to the late childhood Flemish sample of 8- to 14-year-olds—are reported in the bottom panel of Table 2.6.

The bottom panel has only four correlations ≥ |.40|, indicating that the three late childhood temperament questionnaires are less related to each other than those administered in middle and early childhood. The principal component analysis of the MCTQ reported in Table 2.2 showed that the separate Activity/Persistence and Adaptability/Mood (APAM) components—which emerged in early and middle childhood—merge into one large component in late childhood. The APAM component is only substantially related to EATQ-R Effortful Control. The only clear link between the three late childhood models is a *Sociability* triad formed by mutual high correlations between MCTQ Approach, EATQ-R Surgency and EAS SS. *Activity*, measured by the EAS, has no obvious counterpart in either the MCTQ or the EATQ-R. Activity is no longer included as a subscale in the EATQ-R and has become a small part of the large first MCTQ component. *Effortful Control* is now substantially related to the large MCTQ APAM component. The *Emotionality* links detected in early and middle childhood are now replaced by a moderate correlation between EAS Emotionality and EATQ-R Negative Affect ($r = .37$) and the MCTQ APAM component ($r = −.35$). Finally, once again, the *Threshold/Distractibility* component is unique for the Thomas and Chess model. The instruments representing the three temperament models in late childhood seem to have far less common content than was the case for early and middle childhood. With the exception of the Sociability triad and the link between EATQ-R Effortful Control and MCTQ APAM, each instrument captures content that is hardly correlated with any of the components extracted from the other instruments. Notice also that similar labels do not always refer to similar content. Negative Affect measured by the CBQ in middle childhood has a quite different pattern of correlates than Negative Affect as measured by the EATQ-R in late childhood. The gradual drifting apart of the temperament measures in late childhood hinders the progress of temperament research because it impedes generalization of research outcomes over questionnaires and longitudinal, as well as cross-sectional, comparisons of findings across age levels.

Discussion and Conclusions

The study of individual differences in temperament is alive and well. Several theories, based on diverging core assumptions, compete for the attention of the researcher and the practitioner. These "customers" are often confused by the varying theoretical foundations, numerous constructs, the choice of instruments, the shifts of scope and content from one age level to another, and the lack of communality between the various approaches to temperament. This chapter succinctly describes five temperament models and attempts to provide a map of the empirical relations between three major models at three consecutive age levels: early (1½–3 years); middle (4–7 years) and late (8–14 years) childhood. Constructing a readable map requires a convincing strategy to discover common ground and to eliminate excessive specificity. This was accomplished by extracting three principal components from the correlations between the scales of three popular temperament questionnaires at three age levels. We opted for analysis of average scale scores instead of item-level analysis in order to increase the stability of the results and to avoid idiosyncratic effects due to the translation of the items into Dutch, necessary to administer the questionnaires to the large Flemish samples.

The extracted principal components were rotated, according to the Varimax procedure, to obtain orthogonal solutions and hence to avoid any correlation between the components extracted from the same instrument. This strategy produces a clearer picture of the relations between components extracted from the different instruments. The nine sets of triple components extracted from the questionnaires representing three temperament models at three age levels explained, on average, 74% of the variance, ranging from 54% (CBQ, 4–7 years) to 89% (EAS, 4–7 years).

The analysis of the structure of the temperament questionnaires largely confirms the proposed or expected structure. The nine "dimensions" of the age-specific temperament measures based on the Thomas and Chess model are grouped into rather similar components for the early and middle childhood sample: Activity/Persistence, Adaptability/Mood, and Threshold/Distractibility. In late childhood, the first two merge into one large component, accompanied by a Threshold/Distractibility and an Approach–Withdrawal component. The four traditional EAS scales are regrouped in the components: Sociability/Shyness, Emotionality, and Activity. The structure of the CBQ tapping the Rothbart temperament model in middle childhood and that of the EATQ-R in late childhood correspond to the expected three-factor structure proposed by Rothbart. The five scales included in the TBAQ targeting the Goldsmith and Campos model in early childhood are grouped in three components: Anger Proneness/Activity Level, Social Fearfulness/Pleasure, and Interest/Persistence.

Given that these structural analyses were based on translated (Dutch) versions of the instruments administered to large Flemish samples, the adequate replication of the initial structure derived from American samples is remarkable. It suggests that, at least at the scale level, the temperament questionnaires capture similar content in both cultures and languages; hence, U.S. and Flemish parents or caregivers assign similar meaning to the constructs targeted by these questionnaires. Although both the United States and Flanders are typical, affluent Western societies, and Dutch and English are both Germanic languages, the present analysis at least confirms the stability of the structure across two regions on both sides of the Atlantic, and this should further encourage others to translate temperament questionnaires into various languages.

Although the principal component analysis of the temperament questionnaires largely confirms the expected structures, the analysis of the relationships among the instruments targeting temperament at the three age levels is less clear-cut. In *early childhood*, we noticed corresponding components extracted from the TTS, the EAS, and the TBAQ targeting Activity and to a lesser extent Emotionality. Besides these triadic relationships, we also noticed clear bivariate relationships between (1) EAS Sociability/Shyness and TBAQ Social Fearfulness/Pleasure, and (2) TTS Activity/Persistence and TBAQ Interest/Persistence. The Thomas and Chess Threshold/Distractibility component has no counterpart in the other models.

In *middle childhood*, the convergence between the different instruments drops compared to the early childhood sample. Also in middle childhood, there is an Activity triad linking BSQ Activity/Persistence, EAS Activity, and CBQ Surgency. There is also a clear correspondence between the Emotionality components BSQ Adaptability/Mood, EAS Emotionality, and CBQ Negative Affect. The remaining components are unique to one model: CBQ Effortful Control, EAS Sociability/Shyness and, once again, BSQ Threshold/Distractibility.

The correspondence between the components extracted from the *late childhood* temperament questionnaires is even lower than for the younger samples. The EAS, MCTQ, and EATQ-R have strongly correlated Sociability components: MCTQ Approach–Withdrawal, EAS Sociability/Shyness, and EATQ-R Surgency. In contrast to middle childhood, where Effortful Control emerges as a unique component, EATQ-R Effortful Control is now strongly related to the large MCTQ APAM component. All other components have no clear counterparts in any of the other two instruments and hence should be considered as tied to one model. This is the case for EAS Activity and Emotionality; EATQ-R Negative Affect; and, of course, MCTQ Threshold/Distractibility.

The declining convergence between temperament models with increasing age is an intriguing finding that emerges from comparison of the age-specific analyses. Although this decline may be explained by differences in item content or distribution over scales, such an explanation does not account for the systematic and gradual nature of the decline. The age-related decline in convergence between temperament models can also be attributed to the age-related expansion of the child's behavioral repertoire. The larger the behavioral repertoire, the more likely it becomes that the behaviors selected by the authors of the questionnaires will diverge. A corollary of the expanded behavioral repertoire is that parents and caregivers who rate the child have to cope with and to ponder a larger set of behaviors before they can confidently rate each item, and this, with increasing age, may in turn introduce an additional source of divergence between instruments.

The flagships of the temperament flotilla are in good shape and are navigating the world seas to other continents. Their impact is likely to increase if they do not drift further away from each other, and if they continue to perceive each other as members of one family.

Author Note

Ivan Mervielde, PhD, was a leading professor in personality and social psychology at Ghent University, Belgium, before his untimely passing in August 2011. Ivan's research was largely dedicated to the measurement and the broader significance of temperament and personality characteristics in children and adolescents, addressing both typical and maladaptive trait development. He was one of the pioneers identifying developmental antecedents of the Five-Factor Model of personality and the founding father of the Hierarchical Personality Inventory for Children (HiPIC), a comprehensive trait measure constructed from parents' free descriptions of their children's personality. Ivan Mervielde is remembered by his colleagues as a brilliant and creative scholar, thorough and persistent, with a broad view on the discipline of psychology, and a prolific and witty speaker and writer. He is greatly missed.

Further Reading

Caspi, A., & Shiner, R. L. (2006). Personality development. In W. Damon, R. Lerner, & N. Eisenberg (Eds.), *Handbook of child psychology: Vol. 3. Social, emotional, and personality development* (6th ed., pp. 300–364). New York: Wiley.

De Pauw, S. S. W., & Mervielde, I. (2010). Temperament, personality and developmental psychopathology: A review based on the conceptual dimensions underlying childhood traits. *Child Psychiatry and Human Development*, 41(3), 313–329.

De Pauw, S. S. W., Mervielde, I., & Van Leeuwen, K. G. (2009). How are traits related to problem behavior in preschoolers?: Similarities and contrasts between temperament and personality. *Journal of Abnormal Child Psychology*, 37(3), 309–325.

Zentner, M., & Bates, J. E. (2008). Child temperament: An integrative review of concepts, research programs, and measures. *European Journal of Developmental Science*, 2(1/2), 7–37.

References

Ahadi, S. A., & Rothbart, M. K. (1994). Temperament, development, and the Big Five. In C. F. Halverson, G. A. Kohnstamm, & R. F. Martin (Eds.), *The developing structure of temperament and personality from infancy to adulthood* (pp. 189–207). Hillsdale, NJ: Erlbaum.

Angleitner, A., & Ostendorf, F. (1994). Temperament and the Big Five factors of personality. In C. F. Halverson, G. A. Kohnstamm, & R. P. Martin (Eds.), *The developing structure of temperament and personality from infancy to adulthood* (pp. 69–90). Hillsdale, NJ: Erlbaum.

Biederman, J., Rosenbaum, J. F., Bolduc-Murphy, E. A., Faraone, S. V., Chaloff, J., Hirshfeld, D. R., et al. (1993). A 3-year follow-up of children with and without behavioral inhibition. *Journal of the American Academy of Child and Adolescent Psychiatry*, 32(4), 814–821.

Biederman, J., Rosenbaum, J. F., Hirshfeld, D. R., Faraone, S. V., Bolduc, E. A., Gersten, M., et al. (1990). Psychiatric correlates of behavioral inhibition in young children of parents with and without psychiatric disorders. *Archives of General Psychiatry*, 47(1), 21–26.

Boer, F., & Westenberg, P. M. (1994). The factor structure of the Buss and Plomin EAS Temperament Survey (parental ratings) in a Dutch Sample of elementary school children. *Journal of Personality Assessment*, 62(3), 537–551.

Buss, A. H., & Plomin, R. (1975). *A temperament theory of personality development*. New York: Wiley.

Buss, A. H., & Plomin, R. (1984). *Temperament: Early developing personality traits.* Hillsdale, NJ: Erlbaum.

Carey, W. B. (1998). Temperament and behavior problems in the classroom. *School Psychology Review, 27*(4), 522–534.

Caspi, A., & Shiner, R. L. (2006). Personality development. In W. Damon, R. Lerner, & N. Eisenberg (Eds.), *Handbook of child psychology: Vol. 3. Social, emotional, and personality development* (6th ed., pp. 300–364). New York: Wiley.

Cheek, J. M., & Buss, A. H. (1981). Shyness and sociability. *Journal of Personality and Social Psychology, 41*(2), 330–339.

Chess, S., & Thomas, A. (1966). *Temperament: Theory and practice.* Yonkers, NY: World Book.

De Pauw, S. S. W. (2010). *The contribution of temperament versus personality to problem behavior in children and adolescents.* Doctoral dissertation, Ghent University, Ghent, Belgium.

De Pauw, S. S. W., & Mervielde, I. (2010). Temperament, personality and developmental psychopathology: A review based on the conceptual dimensions underlying childhood traits. *Child Psychiatry and Human Development, 41*(3), 313–329.

De Pauw, S. S. W., Mervielde, I., & Van Leeuwen, K. G. (2009). How are traits related to problem behavior in preschoolers?: Similarities and contrasts between temperament and personality. *Journal of Abnormal Child Psychology, 37*(3), 309–325.

Derryberry, D., & Rothbart, M. K. (1997). Reactive and effortful processes in the organization of temperament. *Development and Psychopathology, 9*(4), 633–652.

Digman, J. M., & Inouye, J. (1986). Further specification of the 5 robust factors of personality. *Journal of Personality and Social Psychology, 50*(1), 116–123.

Eaton, W. (1994). Temperament, development, and the five-factor model: Lessons from activity level. In C. F. Halverson, G. A. Kohnstamm, & R. P. Martin (Eds.), *The developing structure of temperament and personality from infancy to adulthood* (pp. 173–188). Hillsdale, NJ: Erlbaum.

Ekman, P., & Friesen, W. V. (1971). Constants across cultures in face and emotion. *Journal of Personality and Social Psychology, 17*(2), 124–129.

Ellis, L. K. (2002). *Individual differences and adolescent psychosocial development.* Unpublished doctoral dissertation, University of Oregon, Eugene.

Ellis, L. K., & Rothbart, M. K. (2001, April). *Revision of the Early Adolescent Temperament Questionnaire.* Paper presented at the biennial meeting of the Society for Research in Child Development, Minneapolis, MN.

Evans, D. E., & Rothbart, M. K. (2007). Developing a model for adult temperament. *Journal of Research in Personality, 41*(4), 868–888.

Fullard, W., McDevitt, S. C., & Carey, W. B. (1984). Assessing temperament in one-year-old to 3-year-old children. *Journal of Pediatric Psychology, 9*(2), 205–217.

Garcia-Coll, C. G., Kagan, J., & Reznick, J. S. (1984). Behavioral inhibition in young children. *Child Development, 55*(3), 1005–1019.

Gasman, I., Purper-Ouakil, D., Michel, G., Mouren-Simeoni, M. C., Bouvard, M., Perez-Diaz, F., et al. (2002). Cross-cultural assessment of childhood temperament—a confirmatory factor analysis of the French Emotionality Activity and Sociability (EAS) Questionnaire. *European Child and Adolescent Psychiatry, 11*(3), 101–107.

Gibbs, M. V., Reeves, D., & Cunningham, C. C. (1987). The application of temperament questionnaires to a British sample—issues of reliability and validity. *Journal of Child Psychology and Psychiatry and Allied Disciplines, 28*(1), 61–77.

Goldberg, L. R. (1990). An alternative description of personality—the Big-5 factor structure. *Journal of Personality and Social Psychology, 59*(6), 1216–1229.

Goldsmith, H. H. (1996). Studying temperament via construction of the toddler behavior assessment questionnaire. *Child Development, 67*(1), 218–235.

Goldsmith, H. H., Buss, A. H., Plomin, R., Rothbart, M. K., Thomas, A., Chess, S., et al. (1987). Round table: What is temperament: Four approaches. *Child Development, 58*(2), 505–529.

Goldsmith, H. H., Buss, K. A., & Lemery, K. S. (1997). Toddler and childhood temperament: Expanded content, stronger genetic evidence, new evidence for the importance of environment. *Developmental Psychology, 33*(6), 891–905.

Goldsmith, H. H., & Campos, J. J. (1982). Toward a theory of infant temperament. In R. N. Emde & R. J. Harmon (Eds.), *The development of attachment and affiliative systems* (pp. 161–193). New York: Plenum Press.

Goldsmith, H. H., & Lemery, K. S. (2000). Linking temperamental fearfulness and anxiety symptoms: A behavior-genetic perspective. *Biological Psychiatry, 48*(12), 1199–1209.

Goldsmith, H. H., Lemery, K. S., Buss, K. A., & Campos, J. J. (1999). Genetic analyses of focal aspects of infant temperament. *Developmental Psychology, 35*(4), 972–985.

Goldsmith, H. H., Reilly, J., Lemery, K. S., Longley, S., & Prescott, A. (1993). *Preschool Laboratory Temperament Assessment Battery (PS Lab-TAB; Version 1.0).* Technical Report, Department of Psychology, University of Wisconsin–Madison.

Goldsmith, H. H., Rieser-Danner, L. A., & Briggs,

S. (1991). Evaluating convergent and discriminant validity of temperament questionnaires for preschoolers, toddlers, and infants. *Developmental Psychology, 27*(4), 566–579.

Gray, J. A. (1987). *The psychology of fear and stress* (2nd ed.). Cambridge, UK: Cambridge University Press.

Hartman, C. A. (2000). *Dutch translation of the Early Adolescent Temperament Questionnaire* (Internal report). Department of Psychiatry, University of Groningen, The Netherlands.

Hegvik, R. L., McDevitt, S. C., & Carey, W. B. (1982). The Middle Childhood Temperament Questionnaire. *Journal of Developmental and Behavioral Pediatrics, 3*(4), 197–200.

Hermanns, J. M. A., Leenders, F., van Tijen, N., van der Vlugt, E., & Super, C. M. (1992). *Dutch translation of the Toddler Temperament Survey for children aged 1 to 3 years* (Internal report). Department of Pedagogical and Educational Sciences, University of Amsterdam, The Netherlands.

Kagan, J. (1994). *Galen's prophecy: Temperament in human nature*. New York: Basic Books.

Kagan, J. (2003). Biology, context, and developmental inquiry. *Annual Review of Psychology, 54*, 1–23.

Kagan, J. (2008). The biological contributions to temperaments and emotions. *European Journal of Developmental Science, 2*, 38–51.

Kagan, J., Reznick, J. S., Clarke, C., Snidman, N., & Garcia-Coll, C. (1984). Behavioral inhibition to the unfamiliar. *Child Development, 55*(6), 2212–2225.

Kagan, J., Reznick, J. S., & Snidman, N. (1987). The physiology and psychology of behavioral inhibition in children. *Child Development, 58*(6), 1459–1473.

Kagan, J., Reznick, J. S., & Snidman, N. (1988). Biological bases of childhood shyness. *Science, 240*, 167–171.

Kagan, J., Snidman, N., Zentner, M., & Peterson, E. (1999). Infant temperament and anxious symptoms in school age children. *Development and Psychopathology, 11*(2), 209–224.

Kohnstamm, G. A., Halverson, C. F., Jr., Mervielde, I., & Havill, V. L. (Eds.). (1998). *Parental descriptions of child personality: Developmental antecedents of the Big Five?* Mahwah, NJ: Erlbaum.

Kohnstamm, G. A., Mervielde, I., Besevegis, E., & Halverson, C. F. (1995). Tracing the Big 5 in parents' free descriptions of their children. *European Journal of Personality, 9*(4), 283–304.

Leenders, F., van Tijen, N., van der Vlugt, E., & Super, C. M. (1992). *Dutch translation of the Behavior Styles Questionnaire for children aged 3 to 7* (Internal report). Department of Pedagogical and Educational Sciences, University of Amsterdam, The Netherlands.

Lemery, K. S., Essex, M. J., & Smider, N. A. (2002). Revealing the relation between temperament and behavior problem symptoms by eliminating measurement confounding: Expert ratings and factor analyses. *Child Development, 73*(3), 867–882.

Lemery, K. S., Goldsmith, H. H., Klinnert, M. D., & Mrazek, D. A. (1999). Developmental models of infant and childhood temperament. *Developmental Psychology, 35*(1), 189–204.

Majdandzic, M., & van den Boom, D. C. (2007). Multimethod longitudinal assessment of temperament in early childhood. *Journal of Personality, 75*(1), 121–167.

Martin, R. P., Wisenbaker, J., & Huttunen, M. (1994). Review of factor analytic studies of temperament measures based on the Thomas–Chess structural model: Implications for the Big Five. In C. F. Halverson, G. A. Kohnstamm, & R. P. Martin (Eds.), *The developing structure of temperament and personality from infancy to adulthood* (pp. 157–172). Hillsdale, NJ: Erlbaum.

Mathiesen, K. S., & Tambs, K. (1999). The EAS Temperament questionnaire: Factor structure, age trends, reliability, and stability in a Norwegian sample. *Journal of Child Psychology and Psychiatry and Allied Disciplines, 40*(3), 431–439.

McCrae, R. R., & Costa, P. T. (1985). Openness to experience. In R. Hogan & W. H. Johnson (Eds.), *Perspectives in personality* (Vol. 1, pp. 145–172). Greenwich, CT: JAI Press.

McCrae, R. R., & Costa, P. T. (1987). Validation of the 5-factor model of personality across instruments and observers. *Journal of Personality and Social Psychology, 52*(1), 81–90.

McDevitt, S. C., & Carey, W. B. (1978). Measurement of temperament in 3–7 year old children. *Journal of Child Psychology and Psychiatry and Allied Disciplines, 19*(3), 245–253.

Mervielde, I., & Asendorpf, J. B. (2000). Variable-centered versus person-centered approaches to childhood personality. In S. E. Hampson (Ed.), *Advances in personality psychology* (Vol. 1, pp. 37–76). Philadelphia: Taylor & Francis.

Mervielde, I., De Clercq, B., De Fruyt, F., & Van Leeuwen, K. (2005). Temperament, personality, and developmental psychopathology as childhood antecedents of personality disorders. *Journal of Personality Disorders, 19*(2), 171–201.

Mervielde, I., De Clercq, B., De Fruyt, F., & Van Leeuwen, K. (2006). Temperament and personality as broad-spectrum antecedents of psychopathology in childhood and adolescence. In T. A. Widiger, E. Simonsen, P. J. Sirovatka, & D. A. Regier (Eds.), *Dimensional models of personality disorders: Refining the research agenda for DSM-V* (pp. 85–109). Washington, DC: American Psychiatric Association.

Mullen, M., Snidman, N., & Kagan, J. (1993). Brief report free-play behavior in inhibited and uninhibited children. *Infant Behavior and Development, 16*(3), 383–389.

Muris, P., & Meesters, C. (2009). Reactive and regulative temperament in youths: Psychometric evaluation of the Early Adolescent Temperament Questionnaire—Revised. *Journal of Psychopathology and Behavioral Assessment*, 31(1), 7–19.

Posner, M. I., & Rothbart, M. K. (1992). Attentional mechanism and conscious experience. In D. Milner & M. Rugg (Eds.), *The neuropsychology of consciousness* (pp. 91–111). San Diego, CA: Academic Press.

Presley, R., & Martin, R. P. (1994). Toward a structure of preschool temperament: Factor structure of the Temperament Assessment Battery for Children. *Journal of Personality*, 62(3), 415–448.

Putnam, S. P., Ellis, L. K., & Rothbart, M. K. (2001). The structure of temperament from infancy through adolescence. In A. Eliasz & A. Angleitner (Eds.), *Advances in research on temperament* (pp. 165–182). Lengerich, Germany: Pabst Science.

Putnam, S. P., Gartstein, M. A., & Rothbart, M. K. (2006). Measurement of fine-grained aspects of toddler temperament: The early childhood behavior questionnaire. *Infant Behavior and Development*, 29(3), 386–401.

Putnam, S. P., & Rothbart, M. K. (2006). Development of short and very short forms of the Children's Behavior Questionnaire. *Journal of Personality Assessment*, 87(1), 102–112.

Putnam, S. P., Rothbart, M. K., & Gartstein, M. A. (2008). Homotypic and heterotypic continuity of fine-grained temperament during infancy, toddlerhood, and early childhood. *Infant and Child Development*, 17(4), 387–405.

Rothbart, M. K. (1981). Measurement of temperament in infancy. *Child Development*, 52(2), 569–578.

Rothbart, M. K., & Ahadi, S. A. (1994). Temperament and the development of personality. *Journal of Abnormal Psychology*, 103(1), 55–66.

Rothbart, M. K., Ahadi, S. A., Hershey, K. L., & Fisher, P. (2001). Investigations of temperament at three to seven years: The Children's Behavior Questionnaire. *Child Development*, 72(5), 1394–1408.

Rothbart, M. K., & Bates, J. E. (1998). Temperament. In W. Damon & N. Eisenberg (Eds.), *Handbook of child psychology: Vol. 3. Social, emotional and personality development* (5th ed., pp. 37–86). New York: Wiley.

Rothbart, M. K., & Bates, J. E. (2006). Temperament. In W. Damon, R. Lerner, & N. Eisenberg (Eds.), *Handbook of child psychology: Vol. 3. Social, emotional, and personality development* (6th ed., pp. 99–166). New York: Wiley.

Saudino, K. J., McGuire, S. M., Reiss, D., Hetherington, E. M., & Plomin, R. (1995). Parent ratings of EAS temperaments in twins, full siblings, half siblings, and step siblings. *Journal of Personality and Social Psychology*, 68(4), 723–733.

Schwartz, C. E., Snidman, N., & Kagan, J. (1999). Adolescent social anxiety as an outcome of inhibited temperament in childhood. *Journal of the American Academy of Child and Adolescent Psychiatry*, 38(8), 1008–1015.

Shiner, R. (1998). How shall we speak of children's personalities in middle childhood?: A preliminary taxonomy. *Psychological Bulletin*, 124(3), 308–332.

Shiner, R., & Caspi, A. (2003). Personality differences in childhood and adolescence: Measurement, development, and consequences. *Journal of Child Psychology and Psychiatry and Allied Disciplines*, 44(1), 2–32.

Spinath, F. M., & Angleitner, A. (1998). Contrast effects in Buss and Plomin's EAS questionnaire: A behavioral-genetic study on early developing personality traits assessed through parental ratings. *Personality and Individual Differences*, 25(5), 947–963.

Strelau, J. (1996). The regulative theory of temperament: Current status. *Personality and Individual Differences*, 20(2), 131–142.

Strelau, J. (2008). *Temperament as a regulator of behavior*. New York: Eliot Werner Publications.

Tackett, J. L. (2006). Evaluating models of the personality–psychopathology relationship in children and adolescents. *Clinical Psychology Review*, 26(5), 584–599.

Thomas, A., & Chess, S. (1977). *Temperament and development*. New York: Brunner/Mazel.

Van Bakel, H. J. A., & Riksen-Walraven, J. M. (2004). AQS security scores: What do they represent?: A study in construct validation. *Infant Mental Health Journal*, 25(3), 175–193.

Zentner, M., & Bates, J. E. (2008). Child temperament: An integrative review of concepts, research programs, and measures. *European Journal of Developmental Science*, 2(1/2), 7–37.

CHAPTER 3

Models of Adult Temperament

Marvin Zuckerman

Early appearing behavioral traits in infants and young children are called *temperament*, but in adults these individual differences are called *personality*. Is there any distinction between adult temperament and personality traits? One of Strelau's (2008) distinctions is that personality traits that are temperamental are present from infancy. However, it is conceivable that some adult temperament traits depend on a certain level of maturation for clear expression. For instance, the trait of sociability may not be obvious until children reach an age at which there is the opportunity to interact with different peers. Another possibility is that sociability is expressed in a different form in infants than in adults. Sociability in infants may be expressed in positive emotional responses to adults, whereas in adults it may be expressed in positive interactions with many friends. Activity in children may be primarily expressed in gross motor form, whereas in adults it may be expressed in the need for variety of mental activities rather than just physical ones.

Temperament in Childhood and Adult Life: Comparisons of Traits

The comparative psychologist T. C. Schneirla (1959) defined a basic trait in all organisms: *approach* (A) versus *withdrawal* (W). He did not define these as a source of individual differences in temperament but emphasized the intensity of stimulation as a source of A or W responses (low intensities eliciting A responses, and high intensities of stimulation eliciting W responses). A and W are more reflexive, tropistic, and instinctive reactions. In more developed organisms under the influence of learning, A becomes a "seeking" and W an "avoidance" response.

Nearly all child temperament systems include an approach factor; however, this factor is reflective of the reactions to novel stimuli or persons rather than to stimulus intensity. One must be cautious in using just the labels of factors in personality psychology because investigators sometimes use different names for the same construct or the same name for different constructs. Approach is labeled as such in the child temperament theories of Rothbart, Derryberry, and Posner (1994) and Thomas and Chess (1977), but it is called "sensation seeking" by Buss and Plomin (1975) and "activity" by Strelau and Zawadzki (1993). The latter is somewhat misleading because it suggests general activity, which is called "briskness" by Strelau (2008). Zuckerman (1994, 2002, 2008) has defined sensation seeking (or "impulsive sensation seeking") as one of his five major traits, and Cloninger (1987) describes a major trait of "novelty seeking" that is highly correlated with impulsive sensation seeking (Zuckerman & Cloninger, 1996). Costa and McCrae (1992) list a similar trait of "excitement seeking." S. B. G. Eysenck and H. J. Eysenck (1977) also describe a similar trait that they call "venturesomeness" as a subtrait of Impulsivity and Extraversion.

General physical activity is a trait described as such in nearly all child temperament theorists (Buss & Plomin, 1975; Goldsmith & Campos, 1986; Rothbart et al., 1994; Strelau & Zawadzki, 1993; Thomas & Chess, 1977). It is described as a subtrait of Extraversion in some adult personality systems (Costa & McCrae, 1992; H. J. Eysenck & M. W. Eysenck, 1985), but as one of the five major factors in the Alternative Five system (Zuckerman, 1994, 2002, 2008; Zuckerman, Kuhlman, & Camac, 1988; Zuckerman, Kuhlman, Joireman, Teta, & Craft, 1993; Zuckerman, Kuhlman, Thornquist, & Kiers, 1991). Negative emotionality, fearfulness, or general emotionality is used to describe a temperament in all child temperament systems. It corresponds to the basic personality trait of Neuroticism found in all adult personality trait systems, although it is called "negative emotionality" in the Tellegen (1985) model and "harm avoidance" in the Cloninger (1987) model. Extraversion is a major factor in nearly every adult personality trait system beginning with Eysenck, but in child temperament systems it is only found in Buss and Plomin (1975) and Rothbart and colleagues (1994) in the forms of "sociability" and "affiliation." In contrast, persistence or perseverance is a factor in nearly every child temperament system but is only given a factor status in Cloninger's (1987) model. A number of child temperament factors observed in infants (distractibility, rhythmicity, and adaptability) by Thomas and Chess (1977) are not listed in other child or adult temperament or personality scales, perhaps because they represent characteristics of early infancy and are not salient as traits in later maturation.

Kagan (1989) is known for his study of a behaviorally defined trait of inhibition. *Inhibition* was first defined as infant and child reactions to novel stimuli, situations, or strangers and assessed by approach, withdrawal, or physiological reactions. As such it might represent the low end of the approach dimension, but in fact it measures a fearful type of inhibition more related to anxiety and neuroticism. The uninhibited child was regarded as normal rather than impulsive or uncontrolled. Caspi (2000) classified children at age 3 into three types: inhibited, undercontrolled, and well adjusted. The inhibited type resembles the children described as such by Kagan. In a longitudinal study of the children from ages 3 to 21, the inhibited type was more likely to develop depression, whereas the undercontrolled type was more likely to develop an antisocial personality (Caspi, Moffitt, Newman, & Silva, 1996). A *behavioral inhibition system* was described by Gray (1991) in terms of neuropsychological and behavioral characteristics and identified most closely with H. J. Eysenck's N (Neuroticism) trait of personality. The undercontrolled temperament has been linked to impulsivity as a component of ImpSS (Impulsive Sensation Seeking) in Zuckerman's Alternative Five, P (Psychoticism) in Eysenck's Big Three system, and the inverse of Conscientiousness in Costa and McCrae's Big Five.

Anger, as a temperament trait, has been differentiated from negative mood (fearfulness or depression) in the temperament systems of Buss and Plomin (1975) and Rothbart and colleagues (1994). In the Big Five, "angry hostility" is a subtrait of N, but in the Alternative Five "Aggression–Hostility" is one of the five major factors.

There is obviously some similarity in at least five of the temperament factors identified in children. Of course, only longitudinal studies can reveal whether the child temperament factors are consistent over the long span from infancy and early childhood to adult life. The expressions of child temperament in adult personality are bound to change. Traits such as approach, activity, and aggression may be less physically expressed than they were in childhood. In the next sections, particular adult personality systems are examined to see how well they fit the definition of temperament as genetic, biologically influenced traits with expressions in animal behavior, as well as infancy and childhood.

Hans J. Eysenck's Big Three

Personality theorists before Eysenck had referred to biological bases of temperament and personality, but Hans Eysenck was the first to build a theoretical model and conduct a research program based on that model. Appointed to head a Department of Experimental Psychology at the Mill Hill Emergency Center during World War II, he developed a battery of test ratings and experimental methods described in his first book, *Dimensions of Personality* (1947). At this time he described only two major dimensions of personality: Extraversion–Introversion (E) and Neuroticism (N). He referred to these broad supertraits as "types" (although normally distributed in the population) at the apex of a hierarchal organization. Each subsumed narrower traits, which in turn subsumed certain behavioral habits or physiological responses. Finally, habits comprised specific responses in certain classes of situations.

Psychoticism (P), the third type dimension, emerged from factor and discriminant analyses of symptoms and clinical diagnoses of psychiatric patients in the 1950s (H. J. Eysenck & S. B. G. Eysenck, 1976). The question addressed by Hans and Sybil Eysenck was whether neurosis and psychosis could be considered as points on a single dimension or constituted extremes of two separate dimensions of personality. The results of their analyses supported the latter conclusion. However, for nearly two decades, their primary focus of research was E and N. Much of it used assessment based on a questionnaire, the Eysenck Personality Inventory (EPI; H. J. Eysenck & S. B. G. Eysenck, 1964; S. B. G. Eysenck, 1956). Finally, a questionnaire scale for P was developed and incorporated into the three-factor Eysenck Personality Questionnaire (EPQ; H. J. Eysenck & S. B. G. Eysenck, 1975).

Under one name or another, E and N remain part of nearly every system of multitrait assessment. The only question for dispute is "What lies beyond E and N?" (Zuckerman et al., 1988), in terms of additional basic personality or temperament traits. In subsequent sections each conception of E and N within different models is discussed in terms of subtraits and biological bases. In terms of actual factorial similarity, based on correlations of E and N questionnaire scales across methods, there is near identity, or convergent and divergent validity, despite variations in item content (Zuckerman et al., 1993). The P scale turns out to be a major marker for a third dimension of personality, with somewhat different characteristics than those proposed by the Eysencks (Zuckerman, 1989).

Extraversion

Trait systems differ somewhat in terms of which subtraits, or facets, are included in the broader traits. The earlier form of the E scale included two primary kinds of items: sociability and impulsivity. Carrigan (1960) and Guilford (1975) viewed these as two independent dimensions, but the Eysencks defended their conception of these as correlated subtraits within E. More recently, Depue and Collins (1999) distinguished two types of E: "interpersonal engagement," including affiliation or warmth, and "agency," including dominance, exhibitionism, and achievement. The first has also been called "affiliation" and the second "impulsivity." According to Depue and Collins, the two E subtraits may have different biological substrates (see also Depue & Fu, Chapter 18, this volume).

H. J. Eysenck and M. W. Eysenck (1985) listed the subtraits of E as sociable, lively, active, assertive, sensation seeking, carefree, dominant, surgent, and venturesome. Some of these subtraits, such as sensation seeking and venturesomeness, are virtually synonymous. However, the facets were not used to modify the EPQ. H. J. Eysenck and Wilson (1991) finally developed a factor/facet test with seven subfactors for E: activity, sociability, expressiveness, assertiveness, ambition, dogmatism, and aggressiveness. One of the changes is that sensation seeking, formerly included as a subtrait of E, became part of the P dimension, along with impulsivity. The new P resembles the ImpSS factor of (Zuckerman, Kuhlman, et al., 1988; Zuckerman et al., 1991, 1993), for which P is one of the best markers.

Behavioral Genetics of Extraversion

Many behavioral genetic studies have been done using E as defined by either the EPQ or Costa and McCrae's (1985) NEO Personality Inventory. A meta-analysis by Johnson, Vernon, and Feiler (2008) identified 35 twin studies contrasting identical and fraternal twin correlations on E, in order to derive estimates of the proportions of variance due to genetics (heritability), shared environment, and nonshared environment (including error of measurement). The mean of the heritability estimates was .54; that for the shared environment was .05, and that for the nonshared environment, .45. In other words, half of the variance of E is due to genetic factors and a little less than half to nonshared environment, with a trivial 5% due to shared environment. The heritability of E is higher but not by much compared to other personality traits. The mean correlations are .50 for identical twins raised together and .42 for adopted identical twins raised in different families, again indicating little influence of shared environment. Correlations between biological siblings and between biological parent and child on E are .14 and .19, respectively, whereas those for adopted siblings and parent–child are close to zero.

Psychophysiology of Extraversion

H. J. Eysenck's (1957) early biological theory of E was based on Pavlov's (1927/1960) theory of individual differences in cortical excitation and inhibition. Extraverts were thought to be less reactive to cortical excitation and more susceptible to cortical inhibition than introverts, and therefore were less likely to develop stable conditioned responses and tended to be impulsive and less able to learn from punishment. The theory was based on hypothetical physiological traits. H. J. Eysenck (1967) later based the E model on findings that the reticular activating system (RAS) regulated cortical arousal as a function of level of stimulation. The cortex, in turn, regulated the RAS through a descending branch, inhibiting input in a kind of homeostatic function. These findings were put into a psychological context by Hebb (1955), who proposed *optimal levels of arousal* as a function of stimulus intensity and task complexity. Eysenck suggested that introverts had a low optimal level of arousal at which they functioned and felt best. Extraverts functioned and felt best at higher levels of stimulation. This difference in brain thresholds for excitation and inhibition could explain some of the behavioral preferences and social styles of extraverts and introverts. Eysenck based his theory on intensity rather than other properties of stimulation, such as novelty and valence (positive or negative). Later theories have stressed novelty as a reward for sensation seeking (Zuckerman, 1969, 1979, 1994, 2007) and valence (associations of stimuli with reward or punishment; Gray, 1971, 1973).

The first psychophysiological tests of Eysenck's theory defined cortical arousal by the electroencephalographic (EEG) wave patterns, such as alpha rhythm. Gale (1983) and O'Gorman (1984) reviewed these earlier studies and concluded that the findings were inconclusive, perhaps due to differences in methodology. There was little consistent evidence of differences between high and low E participants in basal conditions with no variation in stimulation. Reviews of the arousal hypothesis for E two decades later had the advantage of larger studies with more varied methodology beyond the crude EEG band method (De Pascalis, 2004; Stelmack & Rammsayer, 2008; Zuckerman, 2007). As in previous reviews, there was still no consistent evidence to support the hypothesis of lower arousal in high E participants in basal, unstimulated conditions. Studies using event-related potential (ERP), a measure of cortical reactivity to stimuli, show some relationships with E, but these are influenced by the novelty, in addition to the intensity, of the stimulus (Brocke, Tasche, & Beauducel, 1997). At lower intensities of background auditory stimulation, introverts had larger ERPs than extraverts, but at higher noise intensity, extraverts had larger ERPs. This is suggestive of the "cocktail party effect" (Cherry, 1953), which may make it more difficult for introverts to focus on a conversation. While this would seem contradictory to the arousal hypothesis of E, H. J. Eysenck (1967) did allow for the greater effect of a protective mechanism, transmarginal inhibition, in introverts at high intensities of stimulation.

H. J. Eysenck's arousal hypothesis of E referred to response at the cortical level of the nervous system, but a study by Stelmack and Wilson (1982) measured evoked potentials (EPs) of the auditory brainstem and found that extraverts had longer latencies than introverts. This study was replicated by Stelmack, Campbell, and Bell (1993) and Cox-Fuenzalida, Gilliland, and Swickert (2001), and could account for the greater sensitivity of introverts to sensory stimulation. Studies on extraversion using brain imaging methods have yielded inconsistent results (Haier, 2004; Zuckerman, 2005), but several have shown relationships between E and subcortical nuclei, such as the caudate and putamen, dopaminergic rich areas. Since Eysenck did not predict neurotransmitter bases for E, these are discussed later in the context of other theories.

Neuroticism

H. J. Eysenck's trait concept of neuroticism (N) emerged from his first job in a clinical setting. Unlike psychiatrists, however, he conceived of N as a major dimension of personality, with clinical cases at the extreme of the dimension. Psychiatrists at that time conceived of neuroses as specific clinical syndromes rather than dimensions ranging from normal to pathological. The ancient Greeks thought of N as a type they called the "melancholic" disposition. N itself comprised correlated traits of negative emotionality, such as anxiety, depression, guilt, tension, and moodiness, plus some cognitive traits, such as low self-esteem and irrationality (H. J. Eysenck & M. W. Eysenck, 1985). H. J. Eysenck (1957) also distinguished between two subtypes, dependent on the combination of high N with introversion (anxiety) or extraversion (hysteria). The core of the N trait consists of emotional traits, such as anxiety and depression, which may take the form of states, or reactions to contemporary negative events or transient clinical disorders; therefore, there may be an inherent instability of the trait. However, 6-year retest studies show equal retest reliabilities for E and N for both total scores and subtraits (Costa & McCrae, 1988). Emotional states may vary from one day to the next or one month to another, depending on changing experiences, but the average level of states correlates highly with single trait measures (Zuckerman, 1976).

Behavioral Genetics of Neuroticism

The Johnson and colleagues (2008) meta-analysis of twin studies for N gives a mean heritability of .43, shared environment proportion of variance of .06, and nonshared environment of .40. The mean correlations are .43 for twins raised together and .29 for twins raised apart. The last finding could indicate some influence of shared environment, although the overall proportion is only 6%.

Psychophysiology of Neuroticism

H. J. Eysenck's theory attributes N to sensitivity of the autonomic nervous system and limbic centers of emotional arousal. Peripheral measures of autonomic arousal such as blood pressure, heart and respiratory rates, and skin conductance are elevated in persons with anxiety disorders. However, large-scale studies of such measures have found no correlations with N under either basal or stressful conditions (Fahrenberg, 1987; Myrtek, 1984).

The startle response (SR) in humans is often measured by the amplitude of the electromyogram (EMG) eyeblink response to a sudden intense auditory stimulus. When the tone is presented with a visual stimulus, the SR may be augmented or attenuated by the characteristics of the stimulus. Several studies have shown that the SR is augmented by negative but not by positive visual stimuli in individuals scoring high on a measure of N (Corr et al., 1995; Corr, Kumari, Wilson, Checkley, & Gray, 1997; Wilson, Kumari, Gray, & Corr, 2000). EEG investigations of N have not revealed many consistent findings (Stelmack & Rammsayer, 2008), nor would one expect such findings considering Eysenck's localization of N-related arousal to subcortical areas. However, fast wave activity (beta) in frontal and temporal cortical areas in participants with high N has been found in several studies (Ivashenko, Berus, & Zhuravlev, & Myamlin, 1999; Knyazev, Slobodskaya, & Wilson, 2002; Matthews & Amelang, 1993).

Psychoticism

Psychoticism as a trait of personality was developed later than E and N. Its name derived from the early studies of the Eysencks (e.g., S. B. G. Eysenck, 1956) distinguishing separate clinical dimensions of symptoms for neurosis and psychosis. A few items were suggestive of delusional thinking in the first version of the P scale, but most of these were dropped from a revised

P scale. H. J. Eysenck and M. W. Eysenck (1985) described the narrower component traits as aggressive, cold, egocentric, impersonal, impulsive, antisocial, unempathic, tough-minded, and creative. Except for the last of these, any clinician would identify the complex as descriptive of the antisocial personality disorder. The highest scoring group on the P scale is not psychotics but prison inmates. This has led to the suggestion that "psychopathy" might be a better description of the dimension and scale than "psychoticism" (Zuckerman, 1989). In factor analyses of personality scales, the P scale emerged as the best marker for a factor described as "Impulsive Unsocialized Sensation Seeking" (Zuckerman et al., 1991, 1993). Scales of sensation seeking, aggression, and impulsivity defined the positive pole, and scales for socialization, restraint, and responsibility described the negative pole.

Behavioral Genetics of Psychoticism

Twin studies of the P scale itself have generally shown heritabilities of about .50 (Eaves, Eysenck, & Martin, 1989; Zuckerman, 2005), and studies of related scales such as impulsivity and conscientiousness have averaged about the same (Zuckerman, 2005). As in E and N, there is little indication of a shared environment effect, but there is a nonshared environment effect for the remainder. Studies show a relationship of antisocial behavior in children with antisocial and substance abuse disorders in parents, and with harsh disciplinary practices of parents (e.g., Ge et al., 1996). The former may represent a genetic effect, and the latter a reactive effect to the negative behavior in the children. The results suggest a gene–environment interaction effect on antisocial behavior. Such an effect has been found by Caspi and colleagues (2002).

Monoamine oxidase type A (MAO-A) is involved in the oxidation and regulation of the neurotransmitters norepinephrine and serotonin in the brain. An absence of the gene form producing MAO-A is related to aggressive behavior in mice and men (Shih, Chen, & Ridd, 1999). A form of the gene promoter producing low MAO-A was found with greater frequency in alcoholics with antisocial personality disorder than in alcoholics without this disorder and nonalcoholic controls (Samochowiez et al., 1999). Caspi and colleagues (2002) did a longitudinal study of males from ages 3 to 26 and found that parental maltreatment during childhood increased the frequency of conduct disorder in children and antisocial disorder by age 26, *but only in those who had the gene form producing low MAO-A activity.* In other words, childhood maltreatment affected only those with a genetic vulnerability. Such interactions probably affect other personality traits as well.

Paul T. Costa and Robert R. McCrae's Big Five

The Big Five started with a Big Three. Costa and McCrae (1976), who were engaged in a longitudinal study of personality using the Sixteen Personality Factor (16PF) test of Cattell, Eber, and Tatsuoko (1970), substituted three broad dimensions in place of Cattell and colleagues' 16: E, N, and Openness to Experience (Costa, McCrae, & Arenberg, 1980). The first two were equated with Eysenck's E and N, but the only facet the third had in common with P was creativity or a capacity for divergent thinking. Impressed by the lexical studies of personality-relevant adjectives by Norman (1963) and Goldberg (1990), Costa and MacCrae (1985) decided to add scales for Agreeableness (A) and Conscientiousness (C) to their three-factor questionnaire. Openness was equated with the intellect or culture factor in the lexical analyses. Finally, they developed a factor/facet measure in which each of the five major traits comprise six narrower subtraits or facets. The model is a hierarchal one, with each major trait defined by the addition of the six facets (Costa & McCrae, 1992). The model is described below in terms of the facets:

- Neuroticism (N): (1) anxiety, (2) angry hostility, (3) depression, (4) self-consciousness, (5) impulsiveness, (6) vulnerability.
- Extraversion (E): (1) warmth, (2) gregariousness, (3) assertiveness, (4) activity, (5) excitement seeking, (6) positive emotions.
- Openness (O): (1) fantasy, (2) aesthetics, (3) feelings, (4) actions, (5) ideas, (6) values.

- Agreeableness (A): (1) trust, (2) straightforwardness, (3) altruism, (4) compliance, (5) modesty, (6) tender-mindedness.
- Conscientiousness (C): (1) competence, (2) order, (3) dutifulness, (4) achievement striving, (5) self-discipline, (6) deliberation.

McCrae and Costa claim that their Five-Factor Model is the only one that accurately portrays human (and animal!) basic personality and that all other trait systems should be defined in terms of their five factors (McCrae & Costa, 2008; McCrae et al., 2000): "Just as any place on Earth can be specified by the three dimensions of latitude, longitude, and altitude, so anyone's personality can be characterized in terms of the five dimensions of the FFM [Five-Factor Model]" (McCrae & Costa, 2008, p. 274). This claim is partly based on the cross-cultural results and consistency of the scores over long periods of the lifespan. Variations in individual results on scales such as N are temporary adaptations to life changes. The distinction between "basic tendencies" and characteristic life adaptations is important. The Big Five are regarded as temperaments due only to biological bases in genetics and those environmental influences that can cause brain changes, such as prenatal hormone influences. McCrae and Costa (2008) stated that "FFT asserts that traits are influenced only by biology. . . . Neither life experiences nor culture are supposed to affect traits" (p. 279). They acknowledge that this is a radical position, especially in view of the fact that behavior genetic studies show that heritability accounts for half or less of the variance for most personality traits. They contend that the remainder is primarily error or limitation of trait measurement. Gene–environment interactions such as the one already described between *MAO-A* gene and harsh parental practices (Caspi et al., 2002) would be presumably explained by "dynamic processes" affecting characteristic adaptations. But perhaps the "characteristic adaptations are part of the trait.

The fact, however, is that we do not inherit personality traits as such, but only differences in our biological makeup. McCrae and Costa do not specify the biological processes we inherit that influence their five temperaments. Some of these may be directly influenced by prolonged stress during the formative years when the brain is maturing (see also Depue & Fu, Chapter 18, and van IJzendoorn & Bakermans-Kranenburg, Chapter 19, this volume), but the influences may be in the limitations of early capacities for behavior control or later opportunities for expression.

Genetics of Conscientiousness, Agreeableness, and Openness

The genetics of E and N, the first two major traits in the Costa and McCrae model, have already been discussed in the previous sections on H. J. Eysenck. Measures of E and N in the questionnaires developed by Eysenck and Costa and McCrae are highly correlated. This section focuses on the genetics of the three other major factors in the Big Five.

The mean heritabilities for C, A, and O are .47, .49, and .48, respectively (Johnson et al., 2008). Shared environment proportions are .12, .18, and .14, respectively. Those for nonshared environment (and error of measurement) are .49, .57, and .48, respectively. The results are similar to what was found for E and N. About half of the variance is due to genetic factors, with small contributions from shared environment and major contributions from nonshared environment. Even if we discount the error involved in the last source, the total environmental contribution to the Big Five cannot be easily dismissed. Since the authors of the Big Five are largely silent about the biological factors other than genetics involved in their five basic traits, I do not discuss the psychophysiology, psychopharmacology, and neuropsychology here but these topics are deferred to later sections on theories in which they are relevant.

Marvin Zuckerman and D. Michael Kuhlman's Alternative Five

The Alternative Five developed from a search for biologically relevant factors using tests being used in psychobiological research in the 1980s, before the Big Five emerged from Costa and McCrae's original three (N, E, and O). However, unlike their approach based on the lexical analyses of previous adjective studies, ours was based on factor analyses of a sampling of questionnaire scales using several subscales for each hypothesized factor (Zuckerman, Kuhlman, et al., 1988, 1991). Five factors replicable across gender and samples were found: Impulsive Sensation Seeking (ImpSS), Neuroticism–Anxiety (N-Anx), Aggression–Hostility (Agg-Host), Sociability (Sy), and Activity (Act). These factors were confirmed in factor analyses of items selected from the high-loading scales, and a scale was constructed from these: the Zuckerman–Kuhlman Personality Questionnaire (ZKPQ; Zuckerman, 2002, 2008; Zuckerman et al., 1993). Four of the five scales developed from these items were later found to be substantially related to factors in H. J. Eysenck's Big Three, and Costa and McCrae's Big Five (Zuckerman et al., 1993).

Aluja, Kuhlman, and Zuckerman (2010) conceived of new items to construct a factor/facet version of the ZKPQ. The facets broadened the scope of the scales. In terms of their component subscales, they are named and described as follows:

- Extraversion: (1) positive emotions, (2) social warmth, (3) exhibitionism, (4) sociability.
- Neuroticism: (1) anxiety, (2) depression, (3) dependency, (4) low self-esteem.
- Sensation seeking: (1) thrill and adventure seeking, (2) experience seeking, (3) disinhibition, (4) boredom susceptibility/impulsivity.
- Aggression: (1) physical aggression, (2) verbal aggression, (3) anger, (4) hostility.
- Activity: (1) work compulsion, (2) general activity, (3) restlessness, (4) work energy.

A comparison of the Alternative Five with the Big Five in terms of their facets shows some similarities and some differences. Both the Zuckerman–Kuhlman–Aluja Personality Questionnaire (ZKA-PQ) and NEO include facets for positive emotions, social warmth, and sociability in the E factor. The NEO also includes activity and sensation ("excitement") seeking as facets of E, whereas they are independent factors in the Alternative Five. Both the ZKA-PQ and NEO include anxiety and depression as facets of N. The NEO also includes angry hostility as a facet of N, whereas anger and hostility are facets of a broader Aggression factor in the ZKA-PQ. The E factor on the two tests correlates .62. Even though they share no facets, Agreeableness on the NEO and Aggression on the ZKA correlate negatively (–.53). The Sensation Seeking (SS) factor on the ZKA-PQ correlates negatively with the Conscientiousness factor (–.36) and there is a somewhat lower positive correlation (.27) with the Openness factor of the NEO. The ImpSS factor of the ZKPQ, however, correlated –.51 with Conscientiousness and zero with Openness (Zuckerman, 2008). Factor-analytic studies show that four factors have similar factor content in H. J. Eysenck's Big Three, Costa and McCrae's Big Five, and Zuckerman and Kuhlman's Alternative Five: E, N, P (P with ImpSS and Conscientiousness) and Aggression (with low Agreeableness; Zuckerman et al., 1993).

Sensation Seeking

Behavioral Genetics of Sensation Seeking

The genetics of E, N, C, and A of the Big Three and Big Five, and P of the Big Three, have been discussed previously. Genetic studies of sensation seeking predated the studies of the Big Five and Alternative Five and used the SSS Form V. Fulker, Eysenck, and Zuckerman (1980), examining a sample of English twins, found a heritability of .58. Hur and Bouchard (1997; also see discussion of their results in Zuckerman, 2007) examined a sample of twins separated at birth and raised in different families without contact during their formative years. The combined heritabilities, estimated from both separated identicals and fraternals, was .59. The data from both studies show heritability near the maximal range for twin studies, and both studies show little or no effect of shared environment. This conclusion is challenged by the results of a study in the Netherlands that examined the effect of a religious versus nonreligious family background on the Disinhibition subscale of the SSS (Boomsma, de Geus, van Baal, & Koopmans, 1999). These investigators found that for the total sample, and for the subsample of twins raised in a nonreligious home, the results were similar to other studies with a major effect of genetics (heritability; .5 to .6) and little or no effect of shared environment. However, for those raised in religious homes there was little or no effect of genetics and a substantial effect of shared environment, particularly in males (.62). Most biometric twin studies do not analyze the shared environment effect as an independent variable. In this case it was crucial. In presumably more permissive homes, the disinhibition factor was free to vary with genetic predisposition, but in more restricted homes, the environmental effects were stronger for fraternal twins, overriding the genetic effect.

Molecular Genetics of Sensation Seeking

The discovery of the structure of the DNA molecule in mid-20th century, and the more recent decoding of the DNA, created a scientific revolution with important implications for personality research. Behavior genetics tells us the relative role of genetic and environmental factors in a personality trait, but not the particular genes involved and the biological factors they shape and regulate. Biological scientists have been successful in discovering genes and gene regulators ("switches") that account for differences between species and for abnormal variants in the human species, but the search for the genetic sources of continuously distributed individual differences within our species, such as personality, is only beginning. Behavior genetics studies suggest an additive genetic model for most personality traits, with many genes of small effect summating to produce the trait or its predisposition. Many of the genes may be difficult to identify. However, the search for some genes that may have major effects has begun. All genes involved may be equal, "but some may be more equal than others."

The first major gene to be identified with a personality trait was that for the dopamine D4 receptor (*DRD4*) (Ebstein et al., 1996). This gene was associated with the trait of novelty seeking, a strong correlate ($r = .68$) of impulsive sensation seeking (Zuckerman & Cloninger, 1996). There are a number of forms of the gene, ranging from 2 to 10 repeats of the base sequence, but the more common forms in Western and Israeli populations are the short form, with 4 repeats, and the long form, with 7 repeats of the base sequence. In the original and subsequent studies the long repeat forms are associated with high sensation or novelty seeking, and the short forms with low to medium scores (Ebstein, Benjamin, & Belmaker, 2003; Schinka, Letsch, & Crawford, 2002). In other species, the gene is associated with exploration, curiosity, and aggression (Ebstein, 2006). In humans, the long forms are associated with heroin and alcohol use, pathological gambling, and attention-deficit/hyperactivity disorder. The gene is also associated with sexual desire, function, and arousal, which are correlates of sensation seeking and indications of its evolutionary fitness (Ben-Zion et al., 2006).

Other genes have also been associated with novelty or sensation seeking in isolated and often unreplicated studies. Derringer and colleagues (2010) used such evidence to see whether an aggregation of multiple single-nucleotide polymorphisms (SNPs) within candidate genes related to dopamine production, degradation (catabolism), or whether receptors could predict sensation seeking (Total SSS). Twelve SNPs were significantly related to the SSS Total score. Of these, eight were from the dopa decarboxylase gene, which codes a protein that converts L-dihydroxyphenylalanine (L-dopa) to dopamine. None were from the *DRD4* or any of the other dopamine receptors. This could indicate that the genetic variation is largely a function of the regulation of dopamine production. However, the correlation between the aggregated genetic risk score and the SSS ($r = .20$) indicates that even a multiple-gene approach accounts for only 4% of the trait variance and 7% of the genetic variance in the trait. While comparable to other genetic effects found in medicine, the results indicate that many other genes are involved. Perhaps some of these are from non-dopaminergic-related genes, such as those regulating serotonin. (See, in this volume, Saudino & Wang, Chapter 16; Depue & Fu, Chapter 18; and Zentner & Shiner, Chapter 32.)

Psychophysiology of Sensation Seeking

Sensation seeking is defined as the seeking of novel and intense stimulation. The *orienting response* (OR) is an index of arousal in response to novel stimulation. ORs can be expressed in skin conductance and heart rate responses to first (novel) presentations of stimuli, that rapidly habituate when the stimulus is repeated. Such responses are stronger in high than in low sensation seekers (Orlebeke & Feij, 1979; Zuckerman, 1990; Zuckerman, Simons, & Como, 1988), particularly when the stimulus has a meaningful relationship to sensation seeking (Smith, Perlstein, Davidson, & Michael, 1986).

Augmenting versus reducing of the cortical evoked potential (EP) describes individual differences in the amplitude of EP responses to intensity of stimulation. *Augmenting* describes a pattern of EP increases in amplitude in direct relationships to intensity of stimuli. *Reducing* is a pattern of little increase in EP and sometimes a significant decrease in response to the higher intensities of stimulation. Although described in terms of extremes, the EP stimulus intensity slope is normally distributed. Zuckerman, Murtaugh, and Siegel (1974) first reported a positive relationship between the Disinhibition subscale of the SSS and the slope of the visual EP. High disinhibiters tend to be augmenters, whereas low disinhibiters tend to be reducers. The difference in response has been attributed to a trait of cortical inhibition. Since then, the basic finding has been frequently replicated for visual and auditory EPs (Brocke, 2004; Zuckerman, 1990) and impulsivity, as well as sensation seeking (Barratt, Pritchard, Faulk, & Brandt, 1987).

Of interest from the view of temperament and evolutionary selection is that the augmenting–reducing pattern has been related to inhibitory versus impulsive behavior in cats (Saxton, Siegel, & Lukas, 1987), and to an exploratory and aggressive strain of rats versus a more inhibited and fearful one (Siegel, Sisson, & Driscoll, 1993). The augmenting strain of rats responded to stress by increased release of the neurotransmitter dopamine in the prefrontal cortex, whereas the reducer strain responded with increased serotonin and corticotropin-releasing factor in the hypothalamus and increased adrenocorticotropic hormone in the pituitary gland.

Biochemistry of Sensation Seeking

Zuckerman (1995) outlined a general biochemical model for ImpSS, suggesting that the neurotransmitter dopamine regulates the temperament factor called *approach*, common to both extraversion and sensation seeking, and serotonin regulates the inhibition factor related negatively to ImpSS (see Figure 3.1). However, the effects of a neurotransmitter depend on where it is located in the central nervous system (CNS), as shown in a study comparing two strains of rats, one selected for novelty-seeking behavior and the other for novelty-avoidance behavior (Dellu, Piazza, Mayo, Le Moal, & Simon, 1996). Autopsy revealed that that basal dopaminergic activity was higher in the nucleus accumbens (NA), a primary reward center, in the novelty-seeking rats, but higher in the prefrontal cortex in the novelty-avoiding rats. The level of dopamine in the NA correlated positively with approach response to novelty, whereas the dopamine response in the prefrontal cortex correlated negatively with reactivity to novelty. When a rat voluntarily enters the novel arm of a maze, there is a surge of dopamine in the NA, confirming

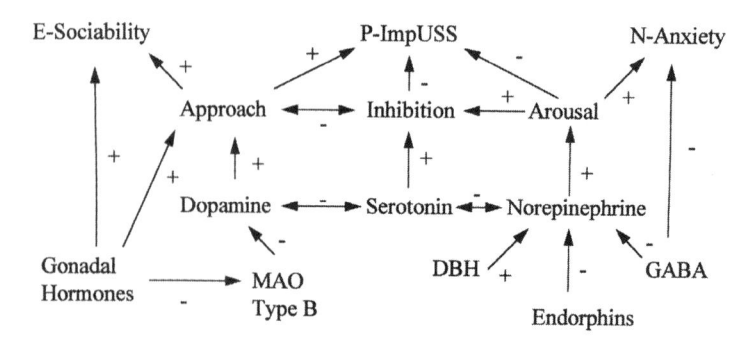

FIGURE 3.1. Psychopharmacological model for extraversion, neuroticism, and impulsive sensation seeking. E, Extraversion; P-ImpUSS, Psychoticism–Impulsive Unsocialized Sensation Seeking; N, Neuroticism; MAO, monoamine oxidase; DBH, dopamine-beta-hydroxylase; GABA, gamma-aminobutyric acid. From Zuckerman (1995). Copyright 1995 by Cambridge University Press. Reprinted by permission.

the theory that dopamine release stimulated by novelty constitutes a reward for novelty-seeking organisms (Bardo, Donohew, & Harrington, 1996). This is also the effect of stimulant drugs such as cocaine in rats and humans. A dopamine antagonist reduces or eliminates novelty seeking in rats.

The role of dopamine in personality could depend on not only levels of the neurotransmitter itself but also enzymes that regulate its production or catabolism. MAO type B in the brain regulates the monoamines, particularly dopamine, by breaking them down before they are stored after reuptake. The enzyme, as measured from blood platelets, is low in high sensation seekers and high in low sensation seekers. The correlation is low but fairly replicable in many studies (Zuckerman, 1994, 2005, 2007). In humans it is also low in various types of disorders involving a lack of impulse control, such as criminality, antisocial and borderline personality disorders, alcoholism, drug abuse, pathological gambling, and bipolar disorder. MAO is low in EP augmenters and high in reducers. Monkeys with low MAO are observed to be sociable, playful, and dominant.

Serotonin is associated with behavioral inhibition and is antagonistic to dopamine in many brain areas, particularly in the limbic system (Soubrie, 1986). Sensation seeking is negatively related to response to serotonin stimulants, indicating a lack of inhibitory capacity, one basis of risky sensation seeking (Depue, 1995; Netter, Hennig, & Roed, 1996).

Gonadal hormones, particularly testosterone, have been associated with sensation seeking (particularly disinhibition) and impulsivity, as well as extraversion-related traits such as sociability, activity, and assertiveness (Aluja & Torrubia, 2004; Daitzman & Zuckerman, 1980). This association may account in part for effect of sex and age differences on sensation seeking. The hormone is also related to number of sexual partners, as is sensation seeking. Handgrip strength, a measure of overall muscle strength, has been found to be related to sensation seeking, particularly to the subscale of Thrill and Adventure Seeking (Fink, Hamdaoui, Wenig, & Neave, 2010). Some studies show muscle strength to be related to testosterone. Testosterone mediates the growth of muscle in males during puberty. The authors speculate that overall muscle strength and risk taking are attractive to women in evolutionary selection.

The convergent evidence from genetic research, biological trait research, and comparative studies of other species suggest that sensation seeking is a primary temperamental trait expressive of the approach motive. Its evolutionary significance is obvious in its links with exploration and sexual behavior. Enjoyment of risky behavior, rather than mere tolerance or fear of risk, may account for the success of our species in the fight for survival and sexual selection. However, another trait, aggressiveness (not mere "agreeableness") may have been another factor in the evolutionary success of *Homo sapiens*.

Aggression

Behavioral Genetics of Aggression

The genetics of Agreeableness, one of the five major traits of the Big Five, has already been discussed. Agreeableness is moderately and negatively related to Aggression/Hostility in the Alternative Five, but aggression is more than the absence of agreeableness and is more important in other species as a method of dominance. In the Big Five, Angry Hostility is a subtrait of Neuroticism, not Agreeableness. Studies of this subscale in three countries yielded heritabilities of .40 to .52 (Jang et al., 2001). Research using the Buss–Durkee (1957) Hostility Inventory found heritabilities ranging from zero to .50 for the subscales in males and females, respectively. The two extreme correlations were found for the subscale of direct assault: zero heritability for females and .50 for males. Heritabilities for the other subscales—Indirect Assault, Verbal Hostility, and Irritability—were intermediate.

In the previous section on H. J. Eysenck's P factor, the study of Caspi and colleagues (2002) was described in reference to antisocial personality. The gene for MAO-A was also related to a disposition toward violence and convictions for violent offenses, but only in those adults who had experienced severe maltreatment as children. Conversely, maltreatment during childhood was associated with violent disposition and convictions for violent offenses, only in those with the form of the gene associated with aggression, a good example of gene–environment interaction.

Psychophysiology of Aggression

Whereas tonic levels of arousal played little or no role in extraversion or sensation seeking, underarousal seems to be an important factor in aggression. Low heart rate in childhood is a well-replicated predictor of aggression in adolescent and adult samples (Raine, 2002). Studies of cortical arousal using EEG in violent criminals show a high frequency of diffused or focal slowing (Volavka, 1995; Wong, Lumsden, Fenton, & Fenwick, 1994). Positron emission tomographic (PET) studies of violent criminals also show hypoarousability, particularly in prefrontal cortex, temporal lobe, and subcortical structures such as the amygdala. The amplitude of the P300 EP is diminished in impulsive aggressive college students (Gerstle, Mathias, & Stanford, 1998). Hypoarousability is related to weakened control of angry aggression. The weakness of inhibition may also be related to the neurotransmitter serotonin.

Biochemistry of Aggression

Testosterone is related to several approach traits, such as extraversion and sensation seeking. Within normal populations, testosterone is less consistently related to questionnaire measures than to behavioral ratings of observers (Archer, Birring, & Wu, 1998). Prison inmates and delinquents with a history of violent crimes have higher testosterone than nonviolent controls from the same populations (Dabbs, Carr, Frady, & Riad, 1995).

The most consistent and strongest correlate of aggression in humans is the serotonin metabolite 5-hydroxyindoleacetic acid (5-HIAA). In 20 studies, two-thirds showed a significant negative correlation between 5-HIAA and aggression, or reduced levels of the metabolite in aggressive persons (Coccaro, 1998; Zalsman & Apter, 2002). Low levels of the metabolite are found in impulsive and violent murderers. In a study of free-ranging monkeys, ratings for aggression were strongly negatively correlated with 5-HIAA in the cerebrospinal fluid (CSF) (Higley, Suomi, & Linnoila, 1992). These investigators also found strong positive correlations between aggression and a norepinephrine metabolite. As postulated with respect to impulsive sensation seeking, serotonin plays a behavioral inhibitory role, and the lack of inhibition affects the likelihood of aggressive behavior as an impulsive reaction to frustrating or socially challenging situations.

Interactions between Pregnancy and Birth Complications and Parental Treatment

As noted previously, there is an interaction between genetic disposition in the *MAO-A* gene and childhood maltreatment in producing violent behavior in adult life (Caspi et al., 2002). Similar interactions with genetic factors have been found for pregnancy and birth complications and maternal rejection in infancy (Raine, Brennan, & Mednick, 1997), or poor parenting (Piquero & Tibbetts, 1999). In all of these studies, the combination of genetic or biological and social environmental ones predicted later violent behavior, whereas the presence of either factor alone was not sufficient to increase the risk for adult aggression.

Jeffrey A. Gray

The theoretical models of adult temperament discussed thus far might be called "top-down" models because they start with traits derived in studies of humans and then try to find their biological bases in humans or in other species (most often rats). The advantage in using nonhuman species is that it is possible to conduct experiments to examine brain function. Gray started his work in the animal laboratories of the Maudsley Hospital, where Hans Eysenck was the director of the entire Psychology Unit. Gray (1964) translated the neo-Pavlovian theory of Teplov and interpreted it in terms of the optimal level of arousal. Eysenck adapted this theory to a biological basis for introversion–extraversion. Gray then turned to a pure "bottom-up" approach, starting with neurobiological models developed from studies of rats and extended by analogy to humans.

Gray (1971, 1982) started with the study of fear and stress using rats, and tried to define the brain systems mediating fear and anxiety. Using learning theory, he defined a behavioral inhibition system (BIS) associated with sensitivity to signals or cues for punishment (or anxiety), and a behavioral approach system (BAS, or impulsivity) associated with sensitivity to signals of reward (Gray, 1971, 1987, 1991). A third system called "fight–flight" (FF; aggression or active avoidance) was associated with unconditioned responses to pain or punishment. Although not precisely aligned with Eysenck's three dimensions but rather with combinations of them, the BAS was closest to E, the BIS to N, and the FF to P. However, the bottom-up nature of Gray's systems constituted a primary difference with Eysenck's model.

Eysenck based his concept of E on the optimal level of arousal in response to intensity of stimulation. To Gray, however, it was the arousal produced by valence or affective associations of stimuli conditioned by reward or punishment that underlay E and N, respectively. Extraverts were primarily responsive to signals of reward, whereas introverts, particularly those who were also high on N, were primarily responsive to signals of punishment. Behaviorally, extraverts had a strong BAS and introverts, a strong BIS. The Extraversion–Introversion (E-I) dimension depended on the balance between reward and punishment sensitivities, whereas the N dimension was associated with the summed arousability from both. Actually, this would lead to the N dimension being closer to what Eysenck called the E dimension because it was closer to the intensity (arousability) of stimuli in general.

Investigators of what has come to be called reinforcement sensitivity theory (RST) soon recognized that it would be useful to translate Gray's theory to the personality trait level by developing questionnaires based on the theory. The first test, developed by Wilson, Barrett, and Gray (1989), was too literally based on animal behavior, and the subscales did not correlate as they should have within the Gray model. Torrubia and Tobena (1984) developed a Sensitivity to Punishment (SP) scale, which was subsequently revised to become the Sensitivity to Punishment and Sensitivity to Reward Questionnaire (SPSRQ; Torrubia, Avila, Molto, & Caserás, 2001). Carver and White (1994) developed a BIS–BAS Scale in which there is one subscale for BIS but three for BAS: Drive, Reward Responsiveness, and Fun Seeking. The last of these closely resembles sensation seeking.

These questionnaire scales were correlated with established scales for E, N, P, sensation seeking, anxiety, and impulsivity. Torrubia and colleagues (2001) and Zuckerman, Joireman, Kraft, and Kuhlman (1999) compared the SPSRQ with Eysenck's E, N, and P scales. SP and SR scales were uncorrelated. SP correlated strongly positively with N and weakly positively with SR. SR correlated positively with E but also weakly positively with N, as would be predicted by Gray's theory. In the study by Zuckerman and colleagues (1999), E correlated positively with SR and negatively with SP, but N correlated only with SP. Carver and White (1994) used different temperament scales than Eysenck's. They found that an E scale correlated only with their BAS scales, highest with the BAS subscale Fun Seeking (sensation seeking), whereas the BIS scale correlated only with N-type scales, including Negative Temperament, Negative Affectivity, and Harm Avoidance. The highest and most specific correlations were between N and BIS.

Performance and Conditioning Studies

Gray's theory would predict that those with a strong BIS or SP system would do better in aversive conditioning experiments than those with a weaker BIS or SP system, whereas those with a strong BAS or SR system would be superior in appetitive conditioning. Many studies tend to support the former prediction with BIS and trait anxiety measures and the latter prediction using BAS and impulsivity trait measures (e.g., Ávila & Torrubia, 2008; Leue & Beauducel, 2008). However, as Corr and McNaughton (2008) point out, impulsive behavior may result from either an underactive BIS or an overactive BAS, or a combination of the two. A weak BIS may play a role in appetitive learning in conflict situations. The interaction of the two systems is the basis of Zuckerman's (1995) psychobiological theory of impulsive sensation seeking (ImpSS). In the early revised RST, Pickering (2004) believed that an "impulsive antisocial sensation seeking" factor was the more direct expression of a dopaminergic system underlying the BAS. Pickering and Smillie (2008) describe the BAS system falling between the E and P axes of Eysenck's primary dimensions. ImpSS falls between these axes, but is much closer to P than to E. The area between E and P has been called "agentic extraversion" by Depue and Collins (1999), and is their trait candidate for the dopaminergic BAS system.

Revised Reinforcement Sensitivity Theory

Changes in a scientist's theory are usually made to reconcile the theory with research results that do not fit. There is a risk in premature changes in a well-developed theory. The discrepancies between data may be due to methodological issues rather than to basic failures of the theoretical postulates. Researchers may continue to address their hypotheses to the old theory, particularly if the new theory is more complex. Changes in a theory take some time for researchers to assimilate and apply to their research hypotheses. Gray's revisions occurred in the last few years of his life (Corr, 2008; Gray & McNaughton, 2000). In 2008, Corr complained that most empirical studies continue to test the unrevised earlier theory.

The major changes were made in the FF system and BIS (Corr, 2008) (see Figure 3.2). The concept of the BAS remained virtually unchanged. The FF system, which previously referred to tendencies to fight or flee in response to unconditioned stimuli such as pain, now also included fight–flight–freezing (FFF) in response to conditioned *or* unconditioned stimuli. Inhibition in response to aversive conditioned stimuli was considered a BIS response. In the revised version, the BIS is only activated in conflict situations, where it results in a slowed, cautious, or defensive approach. The conflict in response is between the BAS and the BIS. Punishment sensitivity represents individual differences in both FF and BIS. The distinction between FF and BIS is made in the clinical literature as that between *fear* and *anxiety* or between panic or phobic reactions and generalized anxiety disorder. The former (FF) is based on the strength of immediate reactions to threatening stimuli or situations, whereas the latter (BIS) is based on general anticipations of threat in future situations.

The BAS construct was changed only in the addition of some cognitive elements in reaction to anticipations of appetitive stimuli. Associated traits include optimism, as well as impulsivity, with clinical expressions in addiction and mania. The behavioral and clinical aspects of BAS sound very much like ImpSS (Zuckerman, 1994, 2005, 2007).

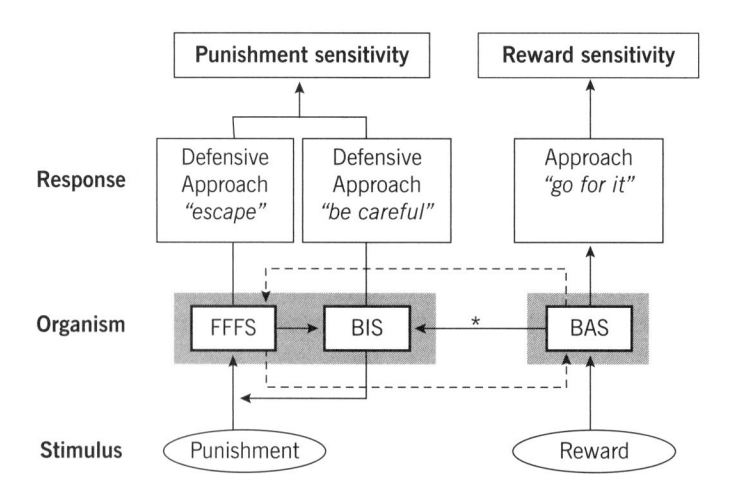

FIGURE 3.2. Biobehavioral architecture comprising reinforcement sensitivity as understood from the perspective of reinforcement sensitivity theory. The behavioral inhibition system (BIS) is activated only if the fight–flight–freeze system (FFFS) and behavioral approach system are jointly activated, signaling goal conflict (e.g., approach–avoidance). Punishment sensitivity is represented by both FFFS and BIS variation. Reward sensitivity is represented by individual variation in BAS functioning. From Smillie (2008, p. 362). Copyright 2008 by Wiley. Reprinted by permission.

However, ImpSS is conceptualized as the balance between approach and inhibition rather than just approach (Figure 3.2). The questionnaire correlations of sensation seeking and sensitivity scales show positive correlations with reward (SR) and negative correlations with punishment (SP) sensitivities (Torrubia et al., 2001; Zuckerman, 2005).

Comparisons of Adult Models of Temperament

Even though the adult models of temperament have some factors with different names and different content, there are substantial similarities revealed by factor analysis. Table 3.1 shows the results of a factor analysis of H. J. Eysenck's (1967) Big Three (EPQ), Costa and McCrae's (1992) Big Five (NEO), and Zuckerman and Kuhlman's Alternative Five (ZKPQ; Zuckerman et al., 1993). Four factors accounted for 74% of the variance, and additional factors added little more. The first three factors contain scales from each of the tests. Using Eysenck's labels, the first factor is clearly E, the second is N, and the third factor is P. The fourth factor is ZKPQ Aggression–Hostility versus NEO Agreeableness, with a secondary loading from NEO Openness. Loadings on the primary factors are high and there are few secondary factor loadings, indicating excellent convergent validity and good discriminant validity.

Auke Tellegen

Tellegen (1985; Tellegen & Waller, 2008) devised a three-factor model with 11 facet scales:

- Positive Emotionality: well-being, social potency, social closeness
- Negative Emotionality: stress reaction, alienation, aggression
- Constraint: control, harm avoidance, traditionalist

Tellegen and Waller (2008) more recently proposed that Positive Emotionality could be divided into two types: Agentic (active) and Communal (sociable). Depue and Collins (1999) found this a useful distinction in that the agentic but not the communal type was related to dopaminergic activity in the brain.

The model shows good convergence and discriminant validity in relation to Eysenck's major dimensions: Positive Emotionality with Extraversion; Negative Emotional-

TABLE 3.1. Four-Factor Analysis of NEO, ZKPQ, and EPQ Personality Scales

| | Factor loadings ||||
Scale	Factor 1	Factor 2	Factor 3	Factor 4
NEO Extraversion	**.88**	−.14	−.05	.17
EPQ Extraversion	**.79**	−.32	.17	−.08
ZKPQ Sociability	**.76**	−.16	.10	−.07
ZKPQ Activity	**.60**	.01	−.18	.02
ZKPQ N-Anxiety	−.13	**.92**	−.01	.08
NEO Neuroticism	−.15	**.90**	.10	−.11
EPQ Neuroticism	−.16	**.91**	−.04	−.08
NEO Conscientious	.15	−.07	**−.86**	−.02
EPQ Psychoticism	−.09	−.08	**.80**	−.28
ZKPQ ImpSS	.48	.08	**.74**	−.02
NEO Agreeableness	−.04	−.07	−.31	**.81**
ZKPQ Agg-Host	.35	.34	.24	**−.72**
NEO Openness	.27	.14	.18	**.67**

Note. From Zuckerman, Kuhlman, Joireman, Teta, and Kraft (1993). Copyright 1993 by the American Psychological Association. Reprinted by permission.
[a]Loadings for defining scales are in **boldface**.

ity with Neuroticism; and Constraint with Psychoticism (reversed). The correspondence of the model with the McCrae and Costa (2008) Big Five model is more complex depending on particular subscales within the Multidimensional Personality Questionnaire (MPQ). Within the Positive Emotion factor, social potency and well-being are only weakly related to E, but the social closeness facet is highly related to E. Within the Negative Emotionality factor, aggression is negatively related to Agreeableness, whereas stress reaction is highly related to Neuroticism. In the Zuckerman (2008) and the Big Five model aggression (or Agreeableness) is a distinct factor that is not part of neuroticism/anxiety factor. Within the Constraint factor, control is most highly related to Conscientiousness and achievement is second. McCrae and Costa's fifth factor, Openness, is weakly related to three of the four Positive Emotionality scales but also to harm avoidance and absorption.

The Tellegen and Waller model is also important because of its use in the Minnesota Separated Twin Studies (Bouchard, Lykken, McGue, Siegel, & Tellegen, 1990) and the New Zealand Longitudinal Study (Caspi, 2000). Bouchard (2007) recently summarized the results in studies of twins separated at birth and raised in different families using the MPQ (Tellegen & Waller, 2008). The correlations of identical twins raised separately is a direct measure of heritability. The average correlation of these twins was .46. The average correlation of identical twins raised together was exactly the same, indicating no detectable effect of shared environment on these traits.

C. Robert Cloninger

Cloninger (1987; Cloninger, Svrakic, & Przybeck, 1993) originally devised a rational three-factor model, without use of factor analysis, then extended it to seven factors with facets described below:

- Novelty Seeking: exploratory excitability versus rigidity; impulsivity versus reflection; extravagance versus reserve; and disorder versus regimentation.
- Harm Avoidance: worry versus optimism; fear of uncertainty versus confidence; shyness versus gregariousness; and fatigueability versus vigor. [*Note*: The first two facets suggest N, and the second two resemble E facets.]
- Reward Dependence: sentimentality versus insensitivity, persistence versus irresoluteness, attachment versus detachment, and dependence versus independence. [*Note*: Although the factor name suggests a relation to Gray's BAS or sensitivity to cues for reward, the content suggests social dependency.]
- Persistence: perseverance despite frustration and fatigue
- Self-Directiveness: responsibility versus blaming, purposeful versus goal undirected, resourcefulness versus apathy, and self-acceptance versus self-striving.
- Cooperativeness: social acceptance versus intolerance, empathy versus social disinterest, helpfulness versus unhelpfulness, compassion versus revengefulness, and pure-hearted versus self-serving.
- Self-Transcendence: self-forgetful versus self-conscious, transpersonal identification, and spiritual acceptance versus materialism.

Despite its psychometric problems the scale has found widespread use in the psychiatric literature, particularly in the psychobiology of clinical disorders. Conspicuous in the system is the lack of a specific factor for extraversion. The Harm Avoidance factor correlates with both E and N, representing introverted neuroticism at the high end.

Cloninger (1987) initially described a general theory of personality that included three basic and genetically independent dimensions of personality: novelty seeking (NS), harm avoidance (HA), and reward dependence (RD). The first of these, NS, was conceptualized as a heritable tendency toward the seeking of arousing, intense, and novel stimuli. Note the similarity to the definitions of sensation seeking (Zuckerman, 1979, 1994). There is a high correlation between NS and sensation seeking (Zuckerman & Cloninger, 1996). The NS definition also includes a sensitization to cues for reward and relief of punishment, suggestive of Gray's (1973, 1991, 2000) BAS. Like Gray and Zuckerman, Cloninger suggested that the neurotransmitter dopamine in the midbrain is a major underlying biological basis for this trait because of its involvement in activation of the higher forebrain centers in response to stimuli associated with reward. They all suggest that this system is involved in the trait of exploration in humans and other species.

HA is described as a BIS in much the same terms as Gray's (1982) BIS. The underlying neurobiology is said to include the septohippocampal system and serotonergic tracts from the raphe nuclei projecting to limbic centers and the precentral cortex. Cloninger accepts Gray's conception of the septohippocampal system as a "comparator" checking expected stimuli or events against actual incoming stimuli and interrupting or inhibiting ongoing behavior in the event of novel, punishment, or nonreward signals. The HA subscale of the Temperament and Character Inventory (TCI) correlates highly with anxiety and Neuroticism and negatively with Extraversion in Zuckerman and Eysenck scales (Zuckerman & Cloninger, 1996).

RD in Cloninger's model is actually specific to social RD rather than a general RS, as in Gray's theory. Individuals who are high in this trait are described as sympathetic, sensitive to social cues, and eager to help and please others. The trait is biologically based in ascending noradrenergic pathways from the locus coeruleus to the hypothalamus, amygdala, and hippocampus, and arising further to innervate the entire neocortex. Other theories (Gray, 1982; Redmond, 1977; Zuckerman, 1995) regard the ascending noradrenergic system as a general arousal system associated with anxiety, fear, and neuroticism, although Gray and Zuckerman believe that other neurotransmitters, such as serotonin, are also involved in this trait. At the trait level the strongest correlation is a negative one with Eysenck's P scale (Zuckerman & Cloninger, 1996), which makes sense in that Cloninger describes the person scoring low on RD as detached, emotionally cool, independent, and tough-minded. The latter term has been used by H. J. Eysenck and S. G. B. Eysenck (1976) as a descriptor for the P dimension.

Persistence (Per) was originally thought to be a facet of RD but later analyses showed it to be an independent fourth dimension of personality (Cloninger et al., 1993), resembling a factor found in many studies of temperament in children. Its highest correlate in Zuckerman's dimensions is with Activity (Zuckerman & Cloninger, 1996).

The four basic personality traits, NS, HA, RD, and Per, are regarded as temperament traits because they are heritable, appear early in life, and involve preconscious or unconscious biases in learning. Cloninger and colleagues (1993) distinguished them from character traits based on insight learning and later-developing self-concepts. Unlike the automatic mechanisms of temperament, characterological traits are based on abstract concepts related to different concepts of self. The three character traits are self-directedness (SD), cooperativeness (C), and self-transcendence (ST).

Cloninger identifies SD with the old concept of "willpower" or the ability of individuals to control and regulate their behavior in a situation to conform to individual goals and values. Many anxious and neurotic persons feel driven by impulses and emotions that they cannot consciously control. SD is the opposite of this kind of helpless feeling. SD is usually related to high self-esteem and capacity to delay gratification. Low SD is associated with depression, dependence on approval of others, and blaming others for perceived imperfections of self. SD is moderately and negatively correlated with Neuroticism and Anxiety in the ZKPQ and EPQ (Zuckerman & Cloninger, 1996).

The second character dimension, C, is positively related to agreeability and negatively related to aggression. High cooperators are described as socially tolerant, empathic, and helpful, whereas those low on the trait are intolerant of others, disinterested in others, and revengeful. Low cooperativeness is related to all categories of personality disorder. C is highly and negatively correlated with aggression in the ZKPQ and moderately and negatively correlated with Psychoticism in the EPQ (Zuckerman & Cloninger, 1996).

The third character dimension, ST, is rarely found in other personality measures. It is a spirituality rather than a religiosity measure and reflects a union with nature, as well as purely spiritual feelings of identification with other persons or higher powers. It has low correlations with other primary personality factors.

Although there is little correlation among the four personality/temperament traits, SD and RD are highly correlated with C, and SD is negatively correlated with HA (Cloninger et al., 1993). Some factor-analytic studies suggest that the seven factors of the TCI can be reduced to five in view of correlations between HA and SD, and between RD and C (Herbst, Zonderman, McCrae, & Costa, 2000). Of course, this would eliminate most of the distinction between temperament and character scales. Supporting the idea that character traits mature with age is the finding that all facets of SD and C increase from age 15 to middle age (35–40), then remain level to age 60 (Cloninger et al., 1993). However, only the spiritual facet of ST increases to age 40, while the self-forgetful and transpersonal facets actually decrease from ages 15 to 35.

Cloninger and colleagues (1993) seem ambivalent about the distinction between environment and genetic influences in character development. Although they say it is likely that genetic factors are as important for character development as for temperament, they also suggest that environmental effects in family and cultures are more important in character development. If families were more important in character development, we would expect that the shared environment in biometric genetic studies would reflect this difference. A large study of Australian twins showed no significant effects of shared environment in either type of scale, and about the same effects of additive genetic factors in the four temperament scales (30–41%) and the three character scales (27–44%) (Gillespie, Cloninger, Heath, & Martin, 2003).

Jan Strelau

Strelau's (1998, 2008) regulative theory of temperament differs from the preceding personality theories in that temperament not only appears early in development but is also distinguished from personality in that it is expressed in the formal or expressive characteristics of behavior, such as energy and sensitivity to stimulation, rather than the later developing social traits, such as extraversion and agreeableness. This distinction is important in theories of childhood temperament (see Mervielde & De Pauw, Chapter 2, this volume). However, Strelau has always been primarily an adult temperament theorist, and he was the first to develop questionnaire measures based on Pavlovian constructs.

His first questionnaire, the Strelau Temperament Inventory (STI; 1983), contained three scales directly corresponding to three Pavlovian constructs based on hypothetical differences in brain reactive characteristics:

- Strength of Excitation, or the ability to work in intense, distracting, or disturbing conditions. This characteristic was also called "strength of the nervous system." Persons with a strong nervous system were also called "low reactives," and those with a weak nervous system were called "high reactives."
- Strength of Inhibition, or the ability to exert behavioral restraint and to remain calm under provocation. This characteristic is presumably related to emotional reactivity.
- Mobility of Nervous Processes, or the ability to shift from states of excitation to inhibition or back again.

The scales were rationally derived and as a consequence there were high correlations between the subscales and poor correspondence between item assignment to scales and the actual factorial dimensions emerging from factor analyses of items. Some of these psychometric deficiencies were corrected in a revised STI, although the direct Pavlovian constructs were retained (Strelau, Angleitner, Bantelmann, & Ruch, 1980). However, the subsequent developments of Strelau's theory led to more distance from the old Pavlovian theory and the construction of a new scale more closely resembling childhood temperament rating scales in the West (Strelau & Zawadzki, 1993). The new questionnaire was called Formal Characteristics of Behavior—Temperament Inventory (FCB-TI) and included six subscales:

- Briskness: a tendency to rapid reaction with a high tempo of activity, and ease in shifting from one behavior to another, representing the energetic aspect of behavior. Although the nature of activity is not specified, it most closely resembles activity in other systems.
- Perseveration: a tendency to persevere in

behavior even when the situation or stimuli eliciting the behavior have ceased.
- Sensory Sensitivity: ability to react to stimuli of low intensity.
- Emotional Reactivity: tendency to react intensively to emotional stimuli; high emotional sensitivity and low emotional endurance. Although the types of emotions are not specified, there is the suggestion that this pertains to negative emotions and thus resembles neuroticism in other questionnaires.
- Endurance: adequate response to persisting situations of high intensity.
- Activity (see Strelau & Zawadzki, Chapter 5, this volume): a construct that originated from the ideas of neo-Pavlovians, representing the idea of a preference for or selection of stimuli of high stimulative value, or taking actions to intensify stimulation from the environment. It resembles the concept of active sensation seeking, but, as with other Pavlovian constructs, the reference is to intensity rather than novelty of stimulation. Novelty could be subsumed under the idea of "stimulative value," although the experimental definitions are largely in terms of stimulus intensity.

A central postulate of the theory is the contrast between low and high reactives as a function of intensity of reaction in response to different intensities of stimulation. Remember that low reactives are those with a strong nervous system and high reactives have a weak nervous system in Pavlovian terms. High reactives have high sensitivity to low stimulus intensities but low endurance to high intensities. Conversely, low reactives have low sensory sensitivity at low stimulus intensities and high endurance to high external stimulation.

Nothing is said about the qualities of the stimulus other than intensity, and the types of reaction are not defined. In other theories the stimulus characteristics of novelty (Zuckerman and Cloninger) or valence (cues for reward or punishment; Gray) are also important sources of individual differences. In terms of reaction, the main distinctions in these theories are among approach, inhibition, and avoidance or withdrawal.

As one might expect, the correlations between temperament and personality tests are low. Strelau and Zawadzki (2008) reported on a factor analysis of a number of temperament and personality scales that included the Eysenck EPQ. They reported that most of the temperament scales loaded on the first two major factors identifiable as Emotionality–Neuroticism and Extraversion–Activity. The temperamental scales were not the best markers for the two factors. This challenges the idea that personality factors emerge from temperament factors.

Most concepts of temperament suggest that it is influenced more strongly genetically than are personality traits. Strelau (1998) reported on the genetic–environmental analysis of results on the FCB-TI, and on other temperament scales. Actually the FCB-TI had higher heritabilities than the other temperament scales, with an average .44 for the six scales. This is similar to the heritabilities reported for most personality scales. Peer report data yielded a lower heritability for the FCB-TI, with only 32% of the variance accounted for by genetics. Only the emotional reactivity factor reached a heritability of .50 for the questionnaire scales. Strelau and Zawadzki (2008) concluded that the hypothesis of greater genetic determination of temperament measures is not supported in many studies.

In contrast to previously discussed theorists such as Cloninger, H. J. Eysenck, Gray, and Zuckerman, Strelau (1998) does not believe in the value of looking for specific neurochemical or neurological bases of temperament, since the entire brain and all neurotransmitters are involved in any specific type of reaction. Of course, the psychobiological connections are complex but not impenetrable to science, with new methods such as functional magnetic resonance imaging and molecular genetics. Also, good animal models may be used to experiment with the brain or its pharmacology, and observations of animal behavior, such as those of Gray and others, have yielded evidence and new hypotheses to be applied to humans. Actually, Strelau describes broad arousal systems such as corticoreticular arousal for activity-oriented systems and sensory sensitivity, and the "limbic system" and autonomic nervous system for emotional reactivity. These old hypotheses by H. J. Eysenck, largely originating in the 1950s, are out of date with more specific neurobiological findings in the last 50 years, and had little predictive power even when they were current. However, Strelau is correct in that models postulating single neurotransmitters or brain loci for each trait are unlikely to be correct because behavior in situations is often the outcome of conflict between two or more systems, such as the relative strength of approach and inhibition behavioral systems or reactivity of dopaminergic and serotonergic neurotransmission systems. Such interactions among biological systems, situations, and behavior can be studied.

Conclusions

Obviously there is considerable overlap between most systems of temperament or basic personality discussed in this chapter. Although the constructs vary and the content is different, there are three or four basic traits or temperaments, as indicated by correlations and factor analyses of scales within the different systems. Differences mainly concern which are basic traits and which are subtraits or facets of the basic traits within hierarchal models. Table 3.2 attempts to define some of the similarities across factor scales based on empirical correlations and inspection of content. Strelau's model is not included because terms in his six basic traits are different than those of personality theorists and represent regulative mechanisms rather than social or motivational expressions of traits.

Are these all temperaments rather than acquired characteristics? All seem to have the same degree of heritability, usually ranging from about 40–50% to about 50–60% at the maximum. Most have significant biological correlates in humans and expressions in animal behavior, suggesting an evolutionary origin (in this volume, see MacDonald, Chapter 14; White, Lamm, Helfinstein, & Fox, Chapter 17; Depue & Fu, Chapter 18). At the root of temperament are individual differences in approach (sociability and sensation seeking), inhibition (fear and anxiety), and aggression (see Barr, Chapter 13, this volume). Some of the prototypes for these inherited predispositions are apparent in early childhood, whereas others appear in later development. Accounts of the interactions between genetic or prenatal biological factors and early experience are beginning to appear in the literature, particularly in longitudinal studies (in this volume, see Huizink, Chapter 15; Depue & Fu, Chapter 18; van IJzendoorn & Bakermans-Kranenburg, Chapter 19). What we are or will be is not set solely in our genes, brain, parental treatment, or life events. Rather, it is the interactions of all of these that determine our adult temperament or personality.

TABLE 3.2. A Comparative Overview of Adult Temperament Models and Traits Comparisons of Similar Factors and Facets across Systems

Eysenck	Gray[a]	Big Five	Alternative Five	Tellegen	Cloninger
Extraversion	Behavioral Approach	E-Gregarious E-Assertive	Sociability	PE-Communal PE-Agentic	—
Neuroticism	Behavioral Inhibition	Neuroticism	N-Anxiety	NE: Stress Reaction	Harm Avoidance
Psychoticism	Fight–Flight	Conscientiousness	Impulsive Sensation Seeking	Constraint: Control Harm Avoidance	Novelty Seeking
		Agreeableness	Aggression–Hostility	NE: Aggression	Cooperativeness

Note. E, Extraversion; N, Neuroticism; PE, Positive Emotionality; NE, Negative Emotionality. From Zuckerman (2011). Copyright 2011 by the American Psychological Association. Adapted by permission.
[a]Based on Gray's earlier three-dimensional model.

Further Reading

Carr, P. J. (Ed.). (2008). *The reinforcement sensitivity theory of personality*. Cambridge, UK: Cambridge University Press.

Strelau, J. (2008). *Temperament as a regulator of behavior*. Clinton Corners, NY: Eliot Werner Publications.

Zuckerman, M. (2005). *Psychology of personality* (2nd ed., rev. and updated). New York: Cambridge University Press.

Zuckerman, M. (2011). *Personality science: Three approaches and their applications to the causes and treatment of depression*. Washington, DC: American Psychological Association.

References

Aluja, A., Kuhlman, M., & Zuckerman, M. (2010). Development of the Zuckerman–Kuhlman–Aluja Personality Questionnaire (ZKA-PQ): A factor/facet version of the Zuckerman–Kuhlman Personality Questionnaire (ZKPQ). *Journal of Personality Assessment, 92*, 416–431.

Aluja, A., & Torrubia, R. (2004). Hostility–aggressiveness, sensation seeking, and sexual hormones in men: Reexploring their relationship. *Neuropsychobiology, 50*, 102–107.

Archer, J., Birring, S. S., & Wu, F. C. W. (1998). The association between testosterone and aggression in young men: Empirical findings and a meta-analysis. *Aggressive Behavior, 24*, 411–420.

Ávila, C., & Torrubia, R. (2008). Performance and conditioning studies. In P. J. Corr (Ed.), *The reinforcement sensitivity theory of personality* (pp. 228–260). New York: Cambridge University Press.

Bardo, M. T., Donohew, R. L., & Harrington, N. G. (1996). Psychobiology of novelty seeking and drug seeking behavior. *Behavioural Brain Research, 77*, 23–43.

Barratt, E. S., Pritchard, W. S., Faulk, D. M., & Brandt, M. E. (1987). The relationship between impulsiveness subtrait, trait anxiety, and visual augmenting–reducing: A topographic analysis. *Personality and Individual Differences, 8*, 43–51.

Ben-Zion, I. Z., Tessler, R., Cohen, L., Lerer, E., Bachner-Melman, R., Gritsenko, I., et al. (2006). Polymorphisms in the dopamine D4 receptor gene (DRD4) contribute to individual differences in human sexual behavior: Desire, arousal and sexual function. *Molecular Psychiatry, 11*(8), 782–786.

Boomsma, D. I., de Geus, E. J. C., van Baal, G. C. M., & Koopmans, J. R. (1999). A religious upbringing reduces the influence of genetic factors on disinhibition: Evidence for interaction between genotypes and environment on personality. *Twin Research, 2*, 115–125.

Bouchard, T. J., Jr. (2007). Genes and human psychological traits. In P. Carruthers, S. Laurence, & S. Stich (Eds.), *The innate mind: Foundations for the future* (Vol. 3, pp. 69–89). Oxford, UK: Oxford University Press.

Bouchard, T. J., Jr., Lykken, D. T., McGue, M., Segal, N. L., & Tellegen, A. (1990). Sources of human psychological differences: The Minnesota study of twins reared apart. *Science, 250*, 223–228.

Brocke, B. (2004). The multilevel approach in sensation seeking: Potentials and findings of a four-level research program. In R. M. Stelmack (Ed.), *On the psychobiology of personality: Essays in honor of Marvin Zuckerman* (pp. 267–293). Amsterdam: Elsevier.

Brocke, B., Tasche, K. G., & Beauducel, A. (1997). Biopsychological foundations of extraversion: Differential effort reactivity and state control. *Personality and Individual Differences, 22*, 447–458.

Buss, A. H., & Durkee, A. (1957). An inventory for assessing different kinds of hostility. *Journal of Consulting Psychology, 21*, 343–349.

Buss, A. H., & Plomin, R. (1975). *A temperament theory of personality development*. New York: Wiley.

Carrigan, P. M. (1960). Extraversion–introversion as a dimension of personality: A reappraisal. *Psychological Bulletin, 57*, 329–360.

Carver, C. S., & White, T. L. (1994). Behavioral inhibition, behavioral activation, and affective responses to impending reward and punishments: The BIS/BAS scales. *Journal of Personality and Social Psychology, 67*, 319–333.

Caspi, A. (2000). The child is father of the man: Personality continuities from childhood to adulthood. *Journal of Personality and Social Psychology, 78*, 158–172.

Caspi, A., McClay, J., Moffitt, T. E., Mill, J., Martin, J., Craig, I. W., et al. (2002). Role of genotype in the cycle of violence in maltreated children. *Science, 297*, 851–854.

Caspi, A., Moffitt, T. E., Newman, D. L., & Silva, P. A. (1996). Behavioral observations at age 3 predict adult psychiatric disorders: Longitudinal evidence for a birth cohort. *Archives of General Psychiatry, 53*, 1033–1039.

Cattell, E. B., Eber, H. W., & Tatsuoko, M. M. (1970). *The handbook for the Sixteen Personality Factor Questionnaire*. Champaign, IL: Institute for Personality and Ability Testing.

Cherry, E. C. (1953). The cocktail party effect. *Journal of the Acoustical Society of America, 25*, 975.

Cloninger, C. R. (1987). A systematic method for clinical description and classification of personality variants. *Archives of General Psychiatry, 44*, 573–588.

Cloninger, C. R., Svrakic, D. M., & Przybeck, T. R. (1993). A psychobiological model of temperament and character. *Archives of General Psychiatry, 50*, 975–990.

Coccaro, E. F. (1998). Central neurotransmitter function in human aggression and impulsivity. In M. Maes & E. F. Coccaro (Eds.), *Neurobiology and clinical views on aggression and impulsivity* (pp. 143–168). Chichester, UK: Wiley.

Corr, P. J. (2008). Reinforcement sensitivity theory (RST): Introduction. In P. J. Corr (Ed.), *The reinforcement sensitivity theory of personality* (pp. 1–43). New York: Cambridge University Press.

Corr, P. J., Kumari, V., Wilson, G. D., Checkley, S., & Gray, J. A. (1997). Harm avoidance and affective modulation of the startle reflex: A replication. *Personality and Individual Differences, 22*, 591–593.

Corr, P. J., & McNaughton, N. (2008). Reinforcement sensitivity theory and personality. In P. J. Corr (Ed.), *The reinforcement sensitivity theory of personality* (pp. 155–187). New York: Cambridge University Press.

Corr, P. J., Wilson, G. D., Fotiadou, M., Kumari, V., Gray, N. S., Checkley, S., et al. (1995). Personality and affective modulation of the startle reflex. *Personality and Individual Differences, 19*, 543–553.

Costa, P. T., Jr., & McCrae, R. R. (1976). Age differences in personality structure: A cluster analytic approach. *Journal of Gerontology, 31*, 564–570.

Costa, P. T., Jr., & McCrae, R. R. (1985). *The NEO Personality Inventory manual*. Odessa, FL: Psychological Assessment Resources.

Costa, P. T., Jr., & McCrae, R. R. (1988). Personality in adulthood: A six-year longitudinal study of self-reports and spouse ratings on the NEO Personality Inventory. *Journal of Personality and Social Psychology, 54*, 853–843.

Costa, P. T., Jr., & McCrae, R. R. (1992). *Revised NEO Personality Inventory (NEO-PI-R)*. Odessa, FL: Psychological Assessment Resources.

Costa, P. T., Jr., McCrae, R. R., & Arenberg, D. (1980). Enduring dispositions in adult males. *Personality and Social Psychology, 38*, 793–800.

Cox-Fuenzalida, L.-E., Gilliland, F., & Swickert, R. J. (2001). Congruency of the relationship between extraversion and the brainstem evoked response based on the EPI versus the EPQ. *Journal of Research in Personality, 35*, 117–126.

Dabbs, J. M., Jr., Carr, T. S., Frady, R. I., & Riad, J. F. (1995). Testosterone, crime, and misbehavior among 692 prison inmates. *Personality and Individual Differences, 18*, 627–633.

Daitzman, R. J., & Zuckerman, M. (1980). Disinhibitory sensation seeking, personality and gonadal hormones. *Personality and Individual Differences, 1*, 103–110.

Dellu, F., Piazza, P. V., Mayo, W., Le Moal, M., & Simon, H. (1996). Novelty-seeking in rats: Biobehavioral characteristics and possible relationship with the sensation seeking trait in man. *Neuropsychobiology, 34*, 136–145.

De Pascalis, V. (2004). On the psychophysiology of extraversion. In R. M. Stelmack (Ed.), *On the psychobiology of personality: Essays in honor of Marvin Zuckerman* (pp. 205–327). Oxford, UK: Elsevier.

Depue, R. A. (1995). Neurobiological factors in personality and depression. *European Journal of Personality, 9*, 413–439.

Depue, R. A., & Collins, P. F. (1999). Neurobiology of the structure of personality: Dopamine facilitation of incentive motivation and extraversion. *Behavioral and Brain Sciences, 22*, 491–569.

Derringer, J., Krueger, R. F., Dick, D. M., Saccone, S., Grucza, R. A., Agrawal, A., et al. (2010). Predicting sensation seeking from dopamine genes: A candidate-system approach. *Psychological Science, 21*, 1282–1290.

Eaves, L. J., Eysenck, H. J., & Martin, N. G. (1989). *Genes, culture, and personality*. London: Academic Press.

Ebstein, R. P. (2006). The molecular genetic architecture of human personality. *Molecular Psychiatry, 11*(5), 427–445.

Ebstein, R. P., Benjamin, J., & Belmaker, R. H. (2003). Behavioral genetics, genomics, and personality. In R. Plomin, J. C. DeFries, I. W. Craig, & P. McGuffin (Eds.), *Behavioral genetics in the postgenomic era* (pp. 365–388). Washington, DC: American Psychological Association.

Ebstein, R. P., Novick, O., Umansky, R., Priel, B., Osher, Y., Blaine, D., et al. (1996). Dopamine D4 receptor (D4DR) exon III polymorphism associated with the human personality trait of novelty seeking. *Nature Genetics, 12*, 78–80.

Eysenck, H. J. (1947). *Dimensions of personality*. New York: Praeger.

Eysenck, H. J. (1957). *The dynamics of anxiety and hysteria*. New York: Praeger.

Eysenck, H. J. (1967). *The biological basis of personality*. Springfield, IL: Thomas.

Eysenck, H. J., & Eysenck, M. W. (1985). *Personality and individual differences: A natural science approach*. New York: Plenum Press.

Eysenck, H. J., & Eysenck, S. B. G. (1964). *The Eysenck Personality Inventory*. London: Hodder & Stoughton.

Eysenck, H. J., & Eysenck, S. B. G. (1975). *Manual of the Eysenck Personality Questionnaire*. London: Hodder & Stoughton.

Eysenck, H. J., & Eysenck, S. B. G. (1976). *Psychoticism as a dimension of personality*. New York: Crane, Russak, & Company.

Eysenck, H. J., & Wilson, G. D. (1991). *The Eysenck Personality Profiler.* London: Corporate Assessment Network.

Eysenck, S. B. G. (1956). Neurosis and psychosis: An experimental analysis. *Journal of Mental Science, 102,* 206–220.

Eysenck, S. B. G., & Eysenck, H. J. (1977). The place of impulsiveness in a dimensional system of personality. *British Journal of Social and Clinical Psychology, 16,* 57–68.

Fahrenberg, J. (1987). Concepts of activation and arousal in the theory of emotionality (neuroticism): A multivariate conceptualization. In J. Strelau & H. J. Eysenck (Eds.), *Personality dimensions and arousal* (pp. 99–120). New York: Plenum Press.

Fink, B., Hamdaoui, A., Wenig, F., & Neave, N. (2010). Handgrip strength and sensation seeking. *Personality and Individual Differences, 49,* 789–793.

Fulker, D. W., Eysenck, S. B. G., & Zuckerman, M. (1980). A genetic and environmental analysis of sensation seeking. *Journal of Research in Personality, 14,* 261–281.

Gale, A. (1983). Electroencephalographic studies of extraversion–introversion: A case study in the psychophysiology of individual differences. *Personality and Individual Differences, 4,* 371–380.

Ge, X., Cadoret, R. J., Conger, R. D., Neiderhiser, J. M., Yates, W., Troughton, E., et al. (1996). The developmental interface between nature and nurture: A mutual influence model of child antisocial behavior and parent behaviors. *Developmental Psychology, 32,* 574–589.

Gerstle, J. E., Mathias, C. W., & Stanford, M. S. (1998). Auditory P300 and self-reported impulsive aggression. *Progress in Neuropsychopharmacology and Biological Psychiatry, 22,* 575–583.

Gillespie, N. A., Cloninger, C. R., Heath, A. C., & Martin, N. G. (2003). The genetic and environmental relationship between Cloninger's dimensions of temperament and character. *Personality and Individual Differences, 35,* 1931–1946.

Goldberg, L. R. (1990). An alternative description of personality: The Big-Five factor structure. *Journal of Personality and Social Psychology, 59,* 1216–1229.

Goldsmith, H. H., & Campos, J. J. (1986). Fundamental issues in the study of early temperament. The Denver Twin Temperament Study. In M. E. Lamb, A. L. Brown, & B. Rogoff (Eds.), *Advances in developmental psychology* (Vol. 4, pp. 231–283). Hillsdale, NJ: Erlbaum.

Gray, J. A. (1964). *Pavlov's typology: Recent theoretical and experimental developments from the laboratory of B. M. Teplov.* New York: Macmillan.

Gray, J. A. (1971). *The psychology of fear and stress.* New York: McGraw-Hill.

Gray, J. A. (1973). Causal theories of personality and how to test them. In J. R. Royce (Ed.), *Multivariate analysis and psychological theory* (pp. 409–463). New York: Academic Press.

Gray, J. A. (1982). *The neuropsychology of anxiety: An enquiry into the function of the septohippocampal system.* New York: Oxford University Press.

Gray, J. A. (1991). The neuropsychology of temperament. In J. Strelau & A. Angleitner (Eds.), *Explorations in temperament: International perspectives on theory and measurement* (pp. 105–128). New York: Plenum Press.

Gray, J. A. (1987). The neuropsychology of emotion and personality. In S. M. Stahl, S. D. Iverson, & E. C. Goodman (Eds.), *Cognitive neurochemistry* (pp. 171–190). Oxford, UK: Oxford University Press.

Gray, J. A. (2000). *The neuropsychology of anxiety* (2nd ed.). Oxford, UK: Oxford University Press.

Gray, J., & McNaughton. N. (2000). *The neuropsychology of anxiety* (2nd ed.). Oxford, UK: Oxford University Press.

Guilford, J. P. (1975). Factors and factors of personality. *Psychological Bulletin, 82,* 802–814.

Haier, R. J. (2004). Brain imaging studies of personality: The slow revolution. In R. M. Stelmack (Ed.), *On the psychobiology of personality: Essays in honor of Marvin Zuckerman* (pp. 329–340). New York: Elsevier.

Hebb, D. O. (1955). Drives and the C.N.S. (conceptual nervous system). *Psychological Review, 62,* 243–254.

Herbst, J. H., Zonderman, A. B., McCrae, R. R., & Costa, P. T. (2000). Do the dimensions of the Temperament and Character Inventory map a simple genetic architecture?: Evidence from molecular genetics and factor analysis. *American Journal of Psychiatry, 157,* 1285–1290.

Higley, J. D., Suomi, S. J., & Linnoila, M. (1992). A longitudinal study of CSF monoamine metabolite and plasma cortisol concentration in young rhesus monkeys. *Biological Psychiatry, 32,* 127–145.

Hur, Y.-M., & Bouchard, T. J., Jr. (1997). The genetic correlation between impulsivity and sensation seeking traits. *Behavior Genetics, 27,* 455–463.

Ivashenko, O. V., Berus, A. V., Zhuravlev, A. B., & Myamlin, V. V. (1999). Individual and typological features of basic personality traits in normals and their EEG correlates. *Human Physiology, 25,* 152–170.

Jang, K. L., Hu, S., Livesley, W. J., Angleitner, A., Riemann, R., Ando, J., et al. (2001). Covariance structure of neuroticism and agreeableness: A twin and molecular genetic analysis of the role

of the serotonin transporter gene. *Journal of Personality and Social Psychology, 81,* 295–304.
Johnson, A. M., Vernon, P. A., & Feiler, A. R. (2008). Behavior genetic studies of personality: An introduction and review of the results of 50+ years of research. In G. J. Boyle, G. Matthews, & D. H. Saklofske (Eds.), *Personality theory and assessment* (Vol. 1, pp. 145–173). Los Angeles: Sage.
Kagan, J. (1989). Temperamental contributions to social behavior. *American Psychologist, 44,* 668–674.
Knyazev, G. G., Slobodskaya, H. R., & Wilson, G. D. (2002). Psychophysiological correlates of behavioural inhibition and activation. *Personality and Individual Differences, 33,* 647–660.
Leue, A., & Beauducel, A. (2008). A meta-analysis of reinforcement sensitivity theory: On performance parameters. *Personality and Social Psychology Review, 12,* 353–369.
Matthews, G., & Amelang, M. (1993). Extraversion, arousal theory and performance: A study of individual differences in EEG. *Personality and Individual Differences, 14,* 347–363.
McCrae, R. R., & Costa, P. T., Jr. (2008). Empirical and theoretical status of the five-factor model of personality. In G. J. Boyle, G. Matthews, & D. H. Saklofske (Eds.), *Personality theory and assessment* (Vol. 1, pp. 273–294). Los Angeles: Sage.
McCrae, R. R., Costa, P. T., Jr., Ostendorf, E., Angleton, A., Hrebick, M., Avia, M.D., et al. (2000). Nature over nurture: Temperament, personality and lifespan development. *Journal of Personality and Social Psychology, 78,* 173–186.
Myrtek, M. (1984). *Constitutional psychophysiology.* London: Academic Press.
Netter, P., Hennig, J., & Roed, I. S. (1996). Serotonin and dopamine as mediators of sensation seeking behavior. *Neuropsychobiology, 34,* 155–165.
Norman, W. T. (1963). Toward an adequate taxonomy of personality attributes: Replicated factor structure. *Journal of Abnormal and Social Psychology, 66,* 574–583.
O'Gorman, J. G. (1984). Extraversion and the EEG I: An evaluation of Gale's hypothesis. *Biological Psychology, 19,* 95–112.
Orlebeke, J. F., & Feij, J. A. (1979). The orienting reflex as a personality correlate. In E. H. van Holst & J. F. Orlebeke (Eds.), *The orienting reflex in humans* (pp. 567–585). Hillsdale, NJ: Erlbaum.
Pavlov, I. P. (1960). *Conditioned reflexes: An investigation of the physiological activity of the cerebral cortex* (G. V. Anrep, Trans. & Ed.). New York: Dover. (Original work published 1927)
Pickering, A. D. (2004). The neuropsychology of impulsive antisocial sensation seeking personality traits: From dopamine to hippocampal function? In R. M. Stelmack (Ed.), *On the psychobiology of personality: Essays in honor of Marvin Zuckerman* (pp. 453–476). New York: Elsevier.
Pickering, A. D., & Smillie, L. D. (2008). *The reinforcement sensitivity of personality* (pp. 120–154). New York: Cambridge University Press.
Piquero, A., & Tibbetts, S. (1999). The impact of pre/perinatal disturbances and disadvantaged familial environment in predicting criminal offending. *Studies on Crime and Crime Prevention, 8,* 52–70.
Raine, A. (2002). Biosocial studies of antisocial and violent behavior in children and adults: A review. *Journal of Abnormal Child Psychology, 30,* 311–326.
Raine, A., Brennan, P., & Mednick, S. A. (1997). Interaction between birth complications and early maternal rejection in predisposing individuals to adult violence: Specificity to serious, early-onset violence. *American Journal of Psychiatry, 154,* 1265–1271.
Redmond, D. E., Jr. (1977). Alterations in the function of the nucleus locus coeruleus: A possible model for studies of anxiety. In J. Hanin & E. Usdin (Eds.), *Animal models in psychiatry and neurology* (pp. 293–305). New York: Pergamon.
Rothbart, M. K., Derryberry, D., & Posner, M. I. (1994). A psychobiological approach to the development of temperament. In J. E. Bates & T. D. Wachs (Eds.), *Temperament: Individual differences at the interface of biology and behavior* (pp. 83–116). Washington, DC: American Psychological Association.
Samochowiez, J., Lesch, K.-P., Rottmann, M., Smolka, M., Syagailo, Y. V., Okladnova, O., et al. (1999). Association of a regulatory polymorphism in the promoter region of the monoamine oxidase A gene with antisocial alcoholism. *Psychiatry Research, 86,* 67–72.
Saxton, P. M., Siegel, J., & Lukas, J. H. (1987). Visual evoked potential augmenting/reducing slopes in cats–2. Correlations with behavior. *Personality and Individual Differences, 8,* 511–519.
Schinka, J. A., Letsch, E. A., & Crawford, F. C. (2002). DRD4 and novelty seeking: Results of meta-analyses. *American Journal of Medical Genetics, 114,* 643–648.
Schneirla, T. C. (1959). An evolutionary and developmental theory of biphasics processes underlying approach and withdrawal. In M. J. Jones (Ed.), *Nebraska Symposium on Motivation* (Vol. 7). Lincoln: University of Nebraska Press.
Shih, J. C., Chen, K., & Ridd, M. J. (1999). Monoamine oxidase: From genes to behavior. *Annual Review of Neuroscience, 22,* 197–217.
Siegel, J., Sisson, D. F., & Driscoll, P. (1993). Augmenting and reducing of visual evoked potentials

in Roman high- and low-avoidance rats. *Physiology and Behavior, 54*, 707–711.
Smillie, L. D. (2008). What is reinforcement sensitivity?: Neuroscience paradigms for approach-avoidance process theories of personality. *European Journal of Personality, 22*, 359–384.
Smith, B. D., Perlstein, W. M., Davidson, R. A., & Michael, K. (1986). Sensation seeking: Differential effects of relevant novel stimulation on electrodermal activity. *Personality and Individual Differences, 4*, 445–452.
Soubrie, P. (1986). Reconciling the role of central serotonin neurons in human and animal behavior. *Behavioral and Brain Sciences, 9*, 319–364.
Stelmack, R. M., Campbell, K. B., & Bell, I. (1993). Extraversion and brainstem auditory evoked potentials. *Personality and Individual Differences, 14*, 447–453.
Stelmack, R. M., & Rammsayer, T. H. (2008). Psychophysiological and biochemical correlates of personality. In G. J. Boyle, G. Matthews, & D. H. Saklofske (Eds.), *The Sage handbook of personality and assessment* (Vol. 1, pp. 33–55). Los Angeles: Sage.
Stelmack, R. M., & Wilson, K. G. (1982). Extraversion and the effects of frequency and intensity on the auditory brainstem evoked response. *Personality and Individual Differences, 3*, 373–380.
Strelau, J. (1983). *Temperament, personality, activity*. London: Academic Press.
Strelau, J. (1998). *Temperament: A psychological perspective.*. New York: Plenum Press.
Strelau, J. (2008). *Temperament as a regulator of behavior: After 50 years of research*. Clifton Corners, NY: Werner.
Strelau, J., Angleitner, A., Bantelmann, J., & Ruch, W. (1990). The Strelau Temperament Inventory Revised (STI-R): Theoretical considerations and scale development. *European Journal of Personality, 4*, 209–235.
Strelau, J., & Zawadzki, B. (1993). The Formal Characteristics of Behavior—Temperament Inventory (FCB-TI): Theoretical assumptions and scale construction. *European Journal of Personality, 7*, 313–336.
Strelau, J., & Zawadzki, B. (2008). Temperament from a psychometric perspective. In G. J. Boyle, G. Matthews, & D. H. Saklofske (Eds.), *The Sage handbook of personality theory and assessment* (pp. 352–373). Los Angeles: Sage.
Tellegen, A. (1985). Structures of mood and personality and their relevance to assessing anxiety, with an emphasis on self-report. In A. H. Tuma & J. D. Maser (Eds.), *Anxiety and the anxiety disorders* (pp. 681–706). Hillsdale, NJ: Erlbaum.
Tellegen, A., & Waller, N. G. (2008). Exploring personality through test construction: Development of the Multidimensional Personality Questionnaire. In G. J. Boyle, G. Matthews, & D. H. Saklofske (Eds.), *The Sage handbook of personality theory and assessment* (Vol. 2, pp. 261–292). Los Angeles: Sage.
Thomas, A., & Chess, S. (1977). *Temperament and development*. New York: Brunner/Mazel.
Torrubia, R., Ávila, C., Molto, J., & Caserás, X. (2001). The Sensitivity to Punishment and Sensitivity to Reward Questionnaire (SPSRQ) as a measure of Gray's anxiety and impulsivity dimensions. *Personality and Individual Differences, 15*, 837–862.
Torrubia, R., & Tobena, A. (1984). A scale for the assessment of susceptibility to punishment as a measure of anxiety: Preliminary results. *Personality and Individual Differences, 5*, 371–375.
Volavka, J. (1995). *Neurobiology of violence*. Washington, DC: American Psychiatric Press.
Wilson, G. D., Barrett, P. T., & Gray, J. A. (1989). Human reactions to reward and punishment: A questionnaire examination of Gray's personality theory. *British Journal of Psychology, 80*, 509–515.
Wilson, G. D., Kumari, V., Gray, J. A., & Corr, P. J. (2000). The role of neuroticism in startle reactions to fearful and disgusting stimuli. *Personality and Individual Differences, 29*, 1077–1082.
Wong, M. T. H., Lumsden, J., Fenton, G. W., & Fenwick, B. B. C. (1994). Electroencephalography, computed tomography and violence ratings of male patients in a maximum security hospital. *Acta Psychiatrica Scandinavica, 90*, 97–101.
Zalsman, G., & Apter, A. (2002). Serotonergic metabolism and violence/aggression. In J. Glicksohn (Ed.), *Neurobiology of criminal behavior* (pp. 231–250). Boston: Kluwer.
Zuckerman, M. (1969). Theoretical formulations: I. In J. P. Zubek (Ed.), *Sensory deprivation: Fifteen years of research* (pp. 407–432). New York: Appleton–Century–Crofts.
Zuckerman, M. (1976). General and situation specific traits and states: New approaches to assessment of anxiety and other constructs. In M. Zuckerman & C. D. Spielberger (Eds.), *Emotions and anxiety: New concepts, methods, and applications* (pp. 133–174). Hillsdale, NJ: Erlbaum.
Zuckerman, M. (1979). *Sensation seeking: Beyond the optimal level of arousal*. Hillsdale, NJ: Erlbaum.
Zuckerman, M. (1989). Personality in the third dimension: A psychobiological approach. *Personality and Individual Differences, 10*, 391–418.
Zuckerman, M. (1990). The psychophysiology of sensation seeking. *Journal of Personality, 58*, 313–345.
Zuckerman, M. (1994). *Behavioral expressions and biosocial bases of sensation seeking*. New York: Cambridge University Press.
Zuckerman, M. (1995). Good and bad humors: Biochemical bases of personality and its disorders. *Psychological Science, 6*, 325–332.
Zuckerman, M. (2002). Zuckerman–Kuhlman Per-

sonality Questionnaire (ZKPQ): An alternative five-factorial model. In B. De Raad & M. Perugini (Eds.), *Big Five assessment* (pp. 377–396). Seattle, WA: Hogrefe & Huber.

Zuckerman, M. (2005). *Psychobiology of personality* (2nd ed., rev. & updated). New York: Cambridge University Press.

Zuckerman, M. (2007). *Sensation seeking and risky behavior.* Washington, DC: American Psychological Association.

Zuckerman, M. (2008). Zuckerman–Kuhlman Personality Questionnaire: An operational definition of the alternative five factorial model of personality. In G. J. Boyle, G. Matthews, & D. H. Saklofske (Eds.), *Personality theory and assessment* (Vol. 2, pp. 219–238). Los Angeles: Sage.

Zuckerman, M. (2011). *Personality science: Three approaches and their applications to the causes and treatment of depression.* Washington, DC: American Psychological Association.

Zuckerman, M., & Cloninger, C. R. (1996). Relationships between Cloninger's, Zuckerman's and Eysenck's dimensions of personality. *Personality and Individual Differences, 21,* 283–285.

Zuckerman, M., Joireman, J., Kraft, M., & Kuhlman, D. M. (1999). Where do motivational and motivational traits fit within three factor models of personality? *Personality and Individual Differences, 26,* 487–504.

Zuckerman, M., Kuhlman, D. M., & Camac, C. (1988). What lies beyond E and N?: Factor analyses of scales believed to measure basic dimensions of personality. *Journal of Personality and Social Psychology, 54,* 96–107.

Zuckerman, M., Kuhlman, D. M., Joireman, J., Teta, P., & Kraft, M. (1993). A comparison of three structural models for personality: The Big Three, the Big Five, and the Alternative Five. *Journal of Personality and Social Psychology, 65,* 757–768.

Zuckerman, M., Kuhlman, D., Thornquist, M., & Kiers, H. (1991). Five (or three) robust questionnaire scale factors of personality without culture. *Personality and Individual Differences, 12,* 929–941.

Zuckerman, M., Murtaugh, T. T., & Siegel, J. (1974). Sensation seeking and cortical augmenting–reducing. *Psychophysiology, 11,* 535–542.

Zuckerman, M., Simons, R. F., & Como, P. G. (1988). Sensation seeking and stimulus intensity as modulators of cortical, cardiovascular, and electrodermal response: A cross-modality study. *Personality and Individual Differences, 9,* 361–372.

Part II

Basic Temperament Traits

Chapter 4

The Biography of Behavioral Inhibition

Jerome Kagan

Many scholars have noted that the meaning of a word, like New England weather, is vulnerable to change over time. The pace of change can be unusually rapid in science because investigators frequently alter the meaning of the name applied to an initial observation following further study of an original discovery, even though many continue to use the same term for the new referents. The concept of *gene* provides an example from biology. The concept of *arousal* supplies an equally persuasive example from psychology and neuroscience because the original meaning of *arousal*, which was based on subjective reports, differs from the later meaning that refers to the profile of power bands in the electroencephalogram (EEG). Unfortunately, some scientists use the same concept for these distinctive sources of evidence.

Many psychologists belong to one of two distinct camps that follow different strategies of inquiry. Most investigators studying human personality, psychopathology, and attitudes begin with words and assume they refer to real phenomena, which they try to detect in settings designed to affirm, rather than refute, the validity of the favored semantic concept. Three obvious examples are regulation, stress, and fear. Some scientists who attribute fear to animals base their inference on behaviors, such as freezing or startling, to a cue associated with an aversive event rather than on a person's interpretation of their feeling in a threatening situation.

Other investigators begin with reliable observations, rather than a priori concepts, and design experiments intended to illuminate the observation rather than to affirm the validity of a favorite concept. The surprising observation that rat pups who experienced a great deal of maternal licking developed reactions to threat that differed from those of minimally licked pups eventually led to the discovery of the epigenetic consequences of the maternal stimulation.

The history of the natural sciences implies that when a domain is immature, which is true of psychology, it is more useful to begin with reliable facts than with an a priori concept. Garcia-Coll, Kagan, and Reznick (1984) invented the concept of behavioral inhibition (BI) to describe the directly observed behaviors of a small group of middle-class, European American 2-year-olds, who were consistently shy, timid, or avoidant when they encountered unfamiliar people, rooms, or objects. The concept of BI is similar to the notion of reticence posited by Coplan, Rubin, Fox, Calkins, and Stewart (1994). The term BI does not refer to displays of distress when exposed to pain or dangerous events, only to timidity in unexpected or unfamiliar experiences. We did not initiate this research by assuming that some children were especially fearful and look for an experimental design that might prove that premise.

Donald Hebb anticipated, over 60 years ago, the power of novel or unexpected events to produce behaviors in primates that resemble BI (Hebb, 1946), and Thomas, Chess, Birch, and Hertzig (1960) nominated withdrawal to new experiences as one of their nine infant temperamental dimensions. Although we (Garcia-Coll et al., 1984) believed that the behavioral profile we called BI had a biological foundation in a temperamental bias, we intended BI to refer to behaviors and not to the underlying, but unknown, biological processes. We were also certain that our meaning of BI was not synonymous with the neurobiological concept of *behavioral inhibition system* (BIS) posited by Gray (1982), which refers to a brain circuit in animals that responds to signs of threat with freezing or avoidance.

The meaning of a scientific concept acquires richer theoretical significance when scientists gather information on the origins, intrinsic features, and consequences of a set of reliable observations. The concept *malaria* meets these criteria. However, we (Garcia-Coll et al., 1984) knew only the extrinsic features of the BI profile and did not yet possess a grasp of its origins, intrinsic features, or consequences. The task of elaborating the theoretical network of BI has occupied my colleagues and myself for close to three decades.

The First Studies

The initial work attempted to illuminate the consequences of BI by following children who displayed this profile. After demonstrating that the profile had modest stability over a 5-year interval, we sought to detect its origins and intrinsic features by observing a large sample of 16-week-old European American infants and following them through their 18th birthday. The narratives that describe this extended corpus appear in many places, but especially in the books *Galen's Prophecy* (Kagan, 1994), *The Long Shadow of Temperament* (Kagan & Snidman, 2004), *The Temperamental Thread* (Kagan, 2010); the monograph, *The Preservation of Two Infant Temperaments into Adolescence* (Kagan, Snidman, Kahn, & Towsley, 2007); and a chapter by Kagan and Fox (2006) in the sixth edition of the *Handbook of Child Psychology*. Nathan Fox and his colleagues at the University of Maryland had implemented a similar set of longitudinal studies. Their observations have generally affirmed our conclusions and contributed to the depth of our mutual understanding of the origins, consequences, and intrinsic features of BI (Fox, Henderson, Rubin, Calkins, & Schmidt, 2001; see also White, Lamm, Helfinstein, & Fox, Chapter 17, this volume).

Our Current Understanding

My colleagues and I now recognize that the 21-month-old children we labeled BI over 25 years ago comprise a heterogeneous category. Some of these children possessed an inherited temperamental bias that predisposed them to display this persona; others acquired this profile as a result of prior experiences. Therefore, BI names a set of behaviors in response to unfamiliar events usually observed after the first birthday. But this concept does not name a unitary phenomenon because only some children who display BI behavior possess an inherited set of biological features. Thus, the concept BI shares features with the terms *headache*, *autism*, and *depression*, which also refer to phenomena with different origins, consequences, and intrinsic features.

Unfortunately, some investigators assume that all children (or animals) who consistently show an avoidant profile in response to unfamiliar events possess the same temperamental bias or have the same life history. However, investigators should not assume that any class of behavior has the same origin in a temperamental bias or experience because every temperament with a biological basis can lead to a variety of possible behaviors and moods. The individual's life history selects particular members from the larger set of possibilities. Investigators must gather some biological evidence, along with the behavioral data, if they wish to generate inferences about a specific temperamental bias. They cannot rely on behavior alone because almost every behavioral profile can be actualized through distinctive mechanisms that originate in different conditions.

This last claim rests on the critical premise that the meaning of every scientific concept is affected by its source of evidence. If the sources are different, their meanings are not always similar. At present, BI is measured by behavioral observations of children. However, some psychologists use the same term for children who have been described by parents, teachers, or peers as shy or fearful. Unfortunately, many parental descriptions of children are subject to distortion because parents usually pay attention to deviant behaviors and often ignore actions and moods that are more frequent (Hane, Fox, Polak-Toste, Ghera, & Guner, 2006). Some investigators who asked adolescents or adults to recall their level of childhood timidity or shyness classified those who reported being unusually shy or avoidant as BI children (Reznick, Hegeman, Kaufman, Woods, & Jacobs, 1992). However, recollections of earlier behaviors or stressful experiences can be serious distortions of the past (Kieling et al., 2010). For example, a meta-analysis of studies evaluating the possibility of an interaction between an allele of the serotonin transporter gene and number of life stressors revealed inconsistent support for an interaction when questionnaires were used, but modest support when objective indices of adversity were gathered (Uher & McGuffin, 2010).

A large sample of Norwegians who experienced the 2004 tsunami in Southeast Asia reported their feelings 6 and 24 months after the disaster. Their subjective judgments of the intensity of distress they felt increased over time, but this increase was not related to the severity of their exposure or immediate stress response (Heir, Piatigorsky, & Weisaeth, 2009). Rather, the later reports of their original level of stress were affected more by their current feeling than by their emotions at the time of the disaster. Thus, the meaning of BI based on direct observations of children is not identical with the meaning that originates in self-reports or descriptions by informants, although the two meanings might share some features.

Rothbart's (1989) temperamental dimensions of reactivity, based primarily on parental report, share some features (but are not synonymous) with the concept of BI based on direct behavioral observations. Questionnaire evidence can, on occasion, generate inferences that violate biology and common sense. The replies of 794 pairs of adult identical and fraternal twins to questions about both self-esteem and physical health revealed that the heritability values were equivalent for both concepts (Kendler, Myers, & Neale, 2000). Had the investigators gathered x-rays and blood and urine samples I suspect the results would have been very different. If troubled adults seeking help from a psychotherapist often distort, or openly lie when describing past events or emotions, it seems unreasonable to assume that ordinary adults, who are not spending valuable resources, usually provide accurate accounts (Kottler, 2010).

High- and Low-Reactive Infants

We now believe that between 15 and 20% of healthy, middle-class, 4-month-old, European American infants born at term possess a temperamental bias to react to unexpected or unfamiliar events that pose no objective threat with vigorous motor activity and distress. These events include moving mobiles composed of colorful toys, recorded human speech without an obvious human source, and the smell of dilute alcohol. The infants who display frequent thrashing of limbs, motor tension in the arms and legs, occasional arching of the back, and frequent crying in response to these events are called high-reactive by Kagan (1994) and high-negative by Fox and colleagues (2001). These infants are biased to display BI behavior in the second year in response to unfamiliar objects or settings.

Our working hypothesis is that high-reactive infants inherited a particular neurochemistry, neuroanatomy, or both, that created a hyperexcitable amygdala and, as a result, a susceptibility to overreact to unexpected or unfamiliar events. Unpublished data, gathered in collaboration with Kevin Nugent and Nancy Snidman, revealed that the small proportion of sleeping newborns who cried so intensely when their swaddling blanket was removed that they could not be soothed, were classified as high-reactive when they were 4 months old. As with BI, we assume that the concept of a high-reactive temperament that originates in an inherited neural profile involving the amygdala is not equivalent in meaning to a concept based on similar behaviors that originated either in nonheritable prenatal events or in early postnatal experiences. Preschool children who displayed BI because they were conceived during the Fall months when the pregnant mother was secreting high levels of melatonin belong to a different category than those whose BI profile was the product of an inherited neurochemistry that altered the excitability of the amygdala, even though the behaviors of the two groups are similar (Gortmaker, Kagan, Caspi, & Silva, 1997). The origin of a behavioral profile is an important feature of the category to which it belongs. An institutionalized 5-year-old with retarded language does not belong to the category of autistic children with Rett syndrome who have the same level of language compromise.

The Amygdala

There is a great deal of research with animals and humans affirming that almost all unexpected events activate the amygdala, and often the prefrontal cortex. Inbred mice strains, for example, differ in their reactions to unfamiliar objects and settings as a function of their genomes (Lad et al., 2010). The primary function of the amygdala is to respond to any unexpected event, especially if it is unfamiliar, independent of its valence. When the individual anticipates an unfamiliar event there is less activation of the amygdala than if the same event were unexpected (Gundersen, Specht, Gruner, Ersland, & Hugdahl, 2008; Herry et al., 2007; Lang & Kotchoubey, 2002). Unexpected or unfamiliar events also provoke the secretion of dopamine, which in turn affects the excitability of the amygdala (Dommett et al., 2005). Adults with a high density of dopamine receptors (D2/D3) in the prefrontal cortex available for activation showed the largest increase in blood flow to the amygdala when they were looking at unpleasant pictures that were not anticipated (Kobiella et al., 2010).

The amygdala consists of three major neuronal clusters, each with a distinct profile of connectivity, neurochemistry, and function. The *basolateral area* receives information from the thalamus, sensory cortices, and parahippocampal region, and registers whether a visual, auditory, somatosensory, or gustatory event deviates from the expectations generated by the immediate past or the agent's long-term knowledge. The *corticomedial nucleus* does the same for olfactory events. When the event violates an expectation, neurons in the basolateral area transmit their excited state to the central nucleus, which in turn sends projections to a variety of targets that can produce immobility, defensive behavior, sympathetic activity, and/or activation of the HPA axis depending on the context. Once an event has become a conditioned cue for an avoidant reaction, the amygdala is no longer needed for the expression of an avoidant response. The amygdala is required, however, to acquire the conditioned avoidant reaction to an unexpected or unfamiliar event (Machado, Kazama, & Bachevalier, 2009).

A set of cells called the *intercalated mass*, lying between the basolateral and central nucleus of the amygdala, modulates the central nucleus. This means that the detection of an unexpected event does not guarantee a change in motor or autonomic activity in all individuals because of the potential inhibitory activity of the intercalated cells. As a result, not all infants become distressed or highly active in response to violations of their expectancies. Those who do probably possess a special neurochemistry that renders either the intercalated cells less effective or the basolateral or central nucleus more excitable. High-reactive infants with a neurochemistry that produces a lower threshold of excitability in either or both the basolateral and central areas of the amygdala should show vigorous limb movements, arching of the back, and crying in response to unexpected events.

The assumption that infants with an excitable amygdala are biased to display BI as toddlers finds support in the fact that newborns whose rate of sucking increased dramatically following an unexpected change in taste sensation from water to a sweet liquid displayed more BI behavior in their second year than newborns who showed a minimal increase in sucking rate following the same change in taste (La Gasse, Gruber, & Lipsitt, 1989). It is likely that the unexpected change in taste sensation activated the amygdala and led to activation of the motor centers that control sucking.

Observations of kittens affirm this conclusion. About 1 in 7 house cats resemble BI children, for these animals fail to explore unfamiliar places, withdraw from unfamiliar objects, and are reluctant to attack rats. This behavioral profile, which appears at about 30 days of age, becomes a relatively stable trait 1 month later, when the kitten's amygdala gains control of the circuits that mediate avoidant behavior. The inhibited kittens show a larger rise in amygdalar activation than other kittens when they hear sounds resembling the threat howl of an adult cat (Adamec, 1991). Most animal species contain a small group of individuals who are more avoidant to novel events than the majority in that species (Fox, Shelton, Oakes, Davidson, & Kalin, 2008; Nelson, Shelton, & Kalin, 2003; Saetre et al., 2006).

Because psychologists do not possess a standard metric for most behaviors, it is necessary to compare children who show high reactivity as an infant or BI as a toddler with one or more comparison groups in order to arrive at inferences about the former. Physicists do not compare the mass or velocity of a falling apple with that of a raindrop in order to give meaning to the concepts *mass* and *velocity*. The usual comparisons for high-reactive (or high-negative) infants are the *low-reactives*, who show the opposite profile, namely, low motor activity and minimal crying in response to the same set of unexpected events. Fox and colleagues (2008) detected a third group of 4-month-olds, characterized by high motor activity, and frequent smiling and babbling, but minimal fretting or crying; they called these infants *high-positive*.

The Development of High-Reactives

The longitudinal studies at Harvard University and the University of Maryland found that high-reactive infants are more likely than low-reactives to become shy, avoidant preschool or kindergarten children (Coplan, Rubin, Fox, Calkins, & Stewart, 1994; Fox et al., 2001; Rimm-Kaufman, Rosenstock, & Arcus, 1996). Although BI has modest heritabilities during the second year (Robinson, Kagan, Reznick, & Corley, 1992), by 4 or 5 years, the differences in BI behavior between those who had been high-reactive infants and those who were not become smaller and, in some samples, of marginal statistical significance. However, more children who had been low-reactive or high-positive as infants retained their expected profile of high sociability and low timidity through school entrance because these child behaviors are not subject to disapproval by adults or peers. The high- and low-reactives assessed at 7½ years were classified as possessing, or not possessing, signs of anxiety in response to unfamiliar or threatening events, based on interviews with each child's mother and teacher. Forty-five percent of the high-reactive 7-year-olds, but only 15% of the low-reactives, displayed several signs of anxiety. These signs were more frequent among the high-reactives who had displayed the most BI behavior at 21 months of age (Kagan, Snidman, Zentner, & Peterson, 1999). However, some high-reactives can learn to suppress avoidant behaviors because they recognize that these actions violate the American cultural ideal. Fox's high-negative infants who preserved their BI profile were more often raised under sole parental care; whereas those who showed a decrease in BI had spent some time in surrogate care (Fox et al., 2001; see also Asendorpf, 1991; Coplan, DeBow, Schneider, & Graham, 2009; Rubin & Coplan, 2010).

All of the evidence implies that the most accurate prediction of the later development of high-reactive infants is that they will not display a consistently fearless, sociable, uninhibited profile. This prediction holds for over 80% of high-reactive (or high-negative) infants. However, the prediction that a high-reactive infant will become an extremely shy, timid, anxious adolescent is only correct for 20–30% of these infants (see Essex, Klein, Slattery, Goldsmith, & Kalin, 2010, for a similar result with a different sample and different methods).

Although the BI profile is susceptible to suppression as children mature and become acquainted with a greater number of settings (Laptook, Klein, Olino, Dyson, & Carlson, 2010), the behavioral changes do not necessarily imply that the biological foundations for the temperamental bias have also been altered. The claim that the biological foundations of a temperamental bias, or its consequences in private feelings, are less susceptible to change than the behavioral persona is based on a number of facts. First, many 15-year-olds who were high-reactive infants and displayed BI during the second year were not exceptionally shy as adolescents. But many of these adolescents told the woman who interviewed them in their home that they often felt tense, uneasy, or anxious when they met strangers, visited new places, or had to deal with novel challenges. A large proportion admitted to worrying excessively about the future. About two of every three adolescents who had been high-reactive infants reported intense uncertainty over one or more unrealistic sources of worry, compared with only one in four adolescents who had been either low-reactive or a member of neither temperamental group (Kagan et al., 2007). However, many of these adolescents were not excessively shy.

The distinction between realistic worries over inadequate grades or poor athletic performance on the one hand, and worries over meeting strangers or visiting new places on the other, resembles Freud's contrast between realistic and neurotic anxiety. Unrealistic worries among monozygotic twins were more heritable than more realistic fears of illness or an automobile accident (Sundet, Skre, Okkenhaug, & Tambs, 2003).

Some 15-year-old high-reactives, but no low-reactives, frequently looked away from the interviewer during the 3-hour interview in their home. The tendency to avoid looking at the eyes of another is characteristic of social phobics (Moukheiber et al., 2010). At the end of the home interview, the 15-year-olds ranked 20 traits in accord with the degree to which they applied to the self. Four items in the set were as follows: "I am pretty serious"; "I think too much before deciding what to do"; "I wish I were more relaxed"; and "I'm easygoing." The ranks each youth assigned to each of these items (reversing the item "I'm easygoing") were averaged to create an index of a dour, serious mood. The high-reactives were significantly more dour than others, whether or not they were shy or timid during the home interview.

This evidence implies that the high-reactives retain a bias for uncomfortable feelings when they are unable to predict or control potential sources of uncertainty, even though they might not be exceptionally shy or avoidant in their behavior. The following verbatim excerpts from interviews with high-reactives are illustrative. "In a crowd I feel isolated and left out; I don't know what to pay attention to because it is all so ambiguous"; "I worry about the future, over not knowing what will happen next"; "I wanted to be a doctor but decided against it because I felt it would be too much of a strain"; "I like being alone and, therefore, horses are my hobby; I don't have to worry about fitting in with others when I am with my horses"; and "I get nervous before every vacation because I don't know what will happen." The critical feature of these worries is the inability to predict what might happen in the future or to know which behaviors are most appropriate in a certain context. (For a discussion of the clinical implications of BI, see Klein, Dyson, Kujawa, & Kotov, Chapter 26, this volume.)

College students reporting high levels of social anxiety, compared with those reporting low levels, showed significantly greater coupling in the right prefrontal cortex between power in the delta band of the EEG (1–3 Hz, which originates mainly in subcortical centers) and power in the beta band (13–30 Hz, which originates in the cortex) while preparing to give a speech to a stranger (Miskovic et al., 2010). This finding implies that individuals who are especially prone to salient feelings of uncertainty in unfamiliar social situations experience a particular brain state when they are unsure of what they will do.

Sexton and Dugas (2009) developed a scale that presumably measures the tendency to experience uncertainty over future actions. The scores on the scale are correlated with standard scales for state and trait anxiety. Two of the most sensitive items are "When it is time to act, uncertainty paralyzes me" and "I always want to know what the future has in store for me." Everyone experiences uncertainty over the future, but only some individuals experience salient, uncomfortable feelings and a response paralysis. It is likely that these individuals were born with an excitable amygdala that generated bodily sensations demanding an interpretation (Sarinopolous et al., 2010). It is possible that an adolescent's realization that he or she does not know what might happen in a future encounter can function as a conditioned stimulus that generates a conditioned amygdalar reaction, leading to the uncomfortable sensations that motivate avoidance. This conditioned association could have been established in childhood when high-reactives experienced these feelings with strangers, in crowds, or in unfamiliar settings.

Because all children and adolescents meet new people and visit unfamiliar places, we have to ask why high-reactive adolescents were most likely to name these experiences as primary sources of worry. One contribution to this vulnerability is frequent, spontaneous visceral feedback from the autonomic nervous system to the brain. When this unpredictable sensory feedback pierces consciousness it creates a state of uncertainty because it is ambiguous in origin, and the person searches for an interpretation. The setting and the individual's history influence the interpretation that will be imposed on these sensations. A meta-analysis of 117 studies using the anxiety sensitivity scale with American or European adults revealed that individuals susceptible to experiencing the uncomfortable sensations resulting from autonomic lability were especially vulnerable to panic attacks, general anxiety disorder, posttraumatic stress disorder (PTSD), or social phobia (Naragon-Gainey, 2010).

High-reactive youth in America and Europe are biased by their culture to interpret these changes in feeling as implying that they are probably anxious or guilty because of the folk theory to which they were exposed. However, members of other cultures experiencing the same feelings might impose a different interpretation on this state. Cambodian refugees living in Massachusetts interpreted an unexpected racing of the heart to mean that they had lost energy because of insufficient sleep or a diminished appetite, and they did not assume that they were anxious (Hinton & Hinton, 2002). The Saulteaux Indians of Manitoba concluded that they were coming down with an illness because they violated an ethical norm on sexual, aggressive, or sharing behavior (Hallowell, 1941). Social anxiety is more frequent in those societies in which encounters with strangers occur frequently, social acceptability and an easy style with others are desirable, and anxiety about future encounters with strangers is high in the hierarchy of possible events. It is estimated that about 8% of American adults suffer from social phobia (El-Gabalawy, Cox, Clara, & Mackenzie, 2010).

Shyness and social reticence are not regarded as maladaptive in all cultures. This is especially true in Asian societies (Chen, Chen, Li, & Wang, 2009). Two-year-old Chinese children who displayed high levels of BI were judged by peers as more cooperative and better adjusted than children who were less avoidant. A temperamental bias favoring high reactivity renders a child vulnerable to a family of feelings, behaviors, and emotions; life history and culture select the specific members of that family of feelings that will be actualized. Put plainly, a cascade of psychological processes occurs between the brain's initial reaction to a thought or situation and the final interpretation of that reaction and subsequent behavior. The varied forms that water vapor can assume provide an analogy. Depending on conditions, it can become a storm cloud, mackerel sky, rain, snow, or dense fog.

Biological Measures

I noted earlier that investigators who wish to infer temperamental biases should gather biological information that is theoretically related to the temperamental construct. One promising variable measured in the Fox and Kagan laboratories is hemisphere asymmetry in alpha power in the EEG. The EEG represents synchronized activity of large numbers of cortical pyramidal neurons, which have a dominant frequency of oscillation at a particular site depending on the immediate demands. When adults are relaxed, maximal power is usually in the alpha range of 8–13 Hz, and about 50–60% of most samples display less alpha power in the left than in the right frontal area (usually EEG leads F3 vs. F4), implying greater cortical activation in the left frontal lobe, due perhaps to greater input from the left amygdala to the left prefrontal cortex. About 25% of most samples show less alpha power and, therefore, greater activation in the right frontal area, which might be due to greater input to this area from the right amygdala (Davidson, 2003; Fox et al., 1995). Depressed patients who showed improvement following administration of an antidepressant drug were likely to display left-hemisphere activation;

those who were not helped by the same drug were typically right-hemisphere dominant (Bruder et al., 2008).

The Kagan and Fox laboratories have reported that older children who had been high-reactive infants and displayed BI in the second year had the highest probability of showing greater cortical activation in the right rather than the left frontal area. The psychological correlates of right or left frontal activation, however, always depend on the temperament, age, ethnicity, and gender of the individual. Adolescent males with left frontal activation who had been low-reactive infants often had lower heart rates and had been less inhibited in the second year than high-reactives with equivalent levels of left frontal activation. Of course, many individuals with right frontal activation show no obvious signs of anxiety (Smit, Posthuma, Boomsma, & De Geus, 2007), and the stability correlations for right or left frontal activation over a 3-year period hover around a value of 0.5 (Vuga et al., 2006). Thus, left or right frontal activation should be treated as only one feature in a pattern.

A second biological measure that differentiated high- and low-reactive youth was the fifth wave form in the brainstem auditory evoked potential, originating in the inferior colliculus, evoked by a series of click sounds. Because the amygdala projects to the inferior colliculus, individuals with an excitable amygdala should have an enhanced fifth wave form. Adults who believed that they might receive an electric shock showed an enhanced fifth wave compared with a condition in which they were certain that no shock would be delivered (Baas, Milstin, Donlevy, & Grillon, 2006). High-reactive 11- and 15-year-olds had a larger fifth wave form than other children. Four of the five high-reactive adolescent females in the original Harvard sample who received a clinical diagnosis of depression had a larger wave form than the remaining high-reactive girls (Kagan et al., 2007). It is relevant that the inferior colliculus of rats is regarded as part of a "fear circuit" responsible for freezing or defensive aggression, although high levels of mu-opioids in the colliculus can modulate the excitability of this circuit (De Ross et al., 2009).

A third sensitive variable was the magnitude of the event-related potential (ERP) in frontal central sites in response to unfamiliar visual scenes. The magnitude of this ERP wave form is influenced by a circuit that usually includes the hippocampus, parahippocampal gyrus, amygdala, and prefrontal cortex. A more excitable amygdala should be accompanied by stronger projections from this structure to the prefrontal cortex, resulting in a larger ERP wave form. About one-half of the 11- and 15-year-olds who had been high-reactives displayed a large ERP to unfamiliar, discrepant pictures, compared with less than 20% of other adolescents. In addition, a group of 10- to 14-year-olds who reported high levels of anxiety had a larger N100 wave form in response to an unexpected event than low-anxious adolescents (Hogan, Butterfield, Phillips, & Hadwin, 2007).

Because the amygdala also projects to the cardiovascular system we would expect high-reactives to show greater sympathetic tone on the heart. A spectral analysis of supine heart rate separates the power in the lower frequency band of the spectrum, reflecting both sympathetic and parasympathetic activity, from power in the higher frequency band, predominantly reflecting parasympathetic (vagal) activity. When this measure was combined with resting heart rate at age 11 years, one of every three high-reactives, but only one of five low-reactives, combined greater power in the lower frequency band with a high resting heart rate. Children with high vagal tone are more resilient when asked to speak in front of strangers than those with high sympathetic tone (Souza et al., 2007). The 11-year-old low-reactive boys who smiled frequently in the laboratory had a lower baseline heart rate than the low-reactive boys who smiled less often (Kagan & Snidman, 2004). Individuals who combined high sympathetic tone in the cardiovascular system with right frontal activation in the EEG were the most vigilant to faces displaying angry expressions (Miskovic & Schmidt, 2010).

In addition, the 11-year-old high-reactives were somewhat more likely than low-reactives to possess light blue eyes, a smaller body size or an ectomorphic body build, and a narrower face, all of which are heritable. An ectomorphic body build is associated with panic attacks in adults (Bulbena et al., 1996) and is more characteristic of social phobics who did not profit from social skills training than those who did (Kellett, Marzillier, & Lambert, 1981). Several studies have affirmed that blue eyes are more common than brown eyes among extremely shy, European American, school-age children (Coplan, Coleman, & Rubin, 1998; Rosenberg & Kagan, 1987; Rubin & Both, 1989). Most observers are probably unaware of the association between blue eyes and shyness. Arcus (1989) examined an archive containing illustrations of the eye color that cartoonists gave to the characters in the most famous Disney movies. The characters whose personalities were marked by emotional vulnerability or extreme shyness were given blue eyes (Dopey, Alice, and Cinderella), whereas those who were invulnerable to threat or unusually aggressive, such as the evil queen, Grumpy, the Mad Hatter, Captain Hook, and Cinderella's stepsisters, were given dark eyes. This observation suggests that the artists were responding, probably unconsciously, to a real-life correlation between eye color and personality in European American adults.

This result is consistent with the biological changes that accompany the domestication of mammals, such as foxes, mink, and cattle. Untamed, nondomesticated foxes have hairs that are black at the base and silver white at the outer edge, stiff-erect ears, and a tail that turns down. However, when the small proportion of tame male foxes were bred with equally tame females, the offspring of 40 generations of selective breeding displayed white spots in their coat that were free of melanin pigmentation, floppy rather than stiff ears, a shorter snout, and a lower level of cortisol (Trut, 1999). In 36 vertebrate species, including mammals, fish, birds, and reptiles, members of the species with darker skin coloration were more active and aggressive than those with lighter skin (Ducrest, Keller, & Roulin, 2008). Salmonid fish who had higher concentrations of melanin in their skin showed a smaller rise in cortisol to an administered stress than those with less melanin (Kittilsen et al., 2009). In summary, lighter pigmentation of the eyes in humans or the fur in animals tends to be associated with higher levels of the avoidant behavior characteristic of BI children.

Measures of the Brain

Carl Schwartz of the Massachusetts General Hospital gathered information on some of the structural and functional brain properties of a large group of the 18-year-olds that Kagan and colleagues had classified as high- or low-reactive as infants. This evidence supports the hypothesis that adolescents who had been high-reactives possess a brain profile characterized by greater amygdalar excitability and might have possessed these properties as infants. One intriguing difference between the adolescents who were formerly high- or low-reactive involves the thickness of an area (169 mm^2) in the ventromedial prefrontal cortex of the right hemisphere (Schwartz et al., 2010). Cortical thickness in this area is moderately heritable but does not necessarily imply more gray matter (Lenroot et al., 2008; Winkler et al., 2010). This site projects to the amygdala, sympathetic nervous system, hypothalamus, and central gray, and contributes to excessive rumination and brooding (Koenigs et al., 2008), as well as the state accompanying the recall of emotional memories (Oddo et al., 2010). High-reactives had significantly thicker cortical values in this area than low-reactives. It is relevant that this area projects to the ventrolateral area of the central gray, which mediates arching of the back, a reaction that high-reactive infants showed in excess in response to the unfamiliar events presented to them at 4 months. The high-reactive girls who displayed the largest number of arches of the back at 4 months had the highest level of BI behavior in the second year.

Extremely impulsive boys (7 to 17 years), whose behavioral profile is the opposite of BI children, had a significantly smaller volume in an area of the right ventromedial prefrontal cortex that overlaps with the area for which high-reactives had a thicker cortex (Boes et al., 2009). This observation supports the speculation that the thicker cortex in high-reactives may have contributed to their more cautious and less impulsive behavior. Adults who reported high levels of social anxiety displayed a strong coupling in the right prefrontal cortex between the low frequency power (3–4 Hz) originating in limbic sites and the high frequency power (13–30 Hz) that typically originates in the cortex (Miskovic et al., 2010). This fact implies that socially anxious individuals are especially vulnerable to arousal in the circuit linking limbic and prefrontal sites when they are in an unfamiliar setting.

A second feature distinguishing the 18-year-olds who had been high- or low-reactive was the magnitude of increased blood flow (blood oxygenation level–dependent [BOLD] signal) to the right amygdala in response to an unexpected change in the identities of six different faces with neutral expressions (Schwartz et al., in press). Schwartz, Wright, Shin, Kagan, and Rauch (2003) had reported a similar result in adults who had been classified as BI at age 2. A different sample of adults who reported being BI when younger also showed the largest surge of blood flow to the right amygdala when presented with a set of faces they did not expect to see (Blackford & Zald, 2010).

The third episode presented to these 18-year-olds comprised four pairs of alternating blocks of ecologically valid and invalid scenes, none of which was symbolic of fear, anger, or disgust (e.g., a typical chair or an infant's head on a puppy's body). More high- than low-reactives showed a shallower habituation of the BOLD signal to the amygdala across the eight blocks of pictures, together with thicker values in the right ventromedial prefrontal cortex (Schwartz et al., in press). Moreover, over 90% of the high-reactives who, at 4 months, displayed a very large number of arches of the back, an intense cry in response to the first presentation of a taped human voice speaking a sentence without a human present, or a face marked by wariness or grimaces during most of the battery (these were uncommon reactions) had the shallowest slopes of habituation of the BOLD signal to the amygdala. In addition, the adolescents from this sample classified as high-reactive who reported unusual anxieties or depression at age 15 years also showed shallow habituation of blood flow to the amygdala across the eight blocks of scenes at age 18. One of these girls had panic attacks, another had frequent nightmares, still another felt anxious when she had to sit next to a stranger on a bus, and three had a psychiatric diagnosis of clinical depression. One girl said that she did not like Spring because she could not predict the weather, and one high-reactive adolescent boy with a shallow slope of habituation did not look at the interviewer for over two-thirds of the 3-hour interview in his home. These unusual traits imply that these children retained a more excitable amygdala in response to novel or unexpected events since their infancy.

The 18-year-old boys who had been low-reactive were relatively unique. One-fourth of this group had very steep slopes of habituation of BOLD to the amygdala to both the faces and pictures, as well as thin values in the right ventromedial cortex. Thus, the combination of a low-reactive temperament and a male biology created a distinctive profile.

The complete corpus of evidence supports (but does not prove) that high-reactive (and Fox's high-negative) infants possess a distinct profile in the amygdala that supports the assumption that these youth possess, and may have retained since childhood, a more excitable amygdala and, perhaps, greater excitability in the circuit connecting the amygdala with the ventromedial prefrontal cortex. The small number of high-reactives who combined thick cortical values for the right ventromedial cortex and a large BOLD signal to the amygdala in response to changes in the identity of the neutral faces displayed the highest levels of motor arousal at 4 months, frequent BI behavior in the second year, and were most likely to report serious anxiety over meeting strangers or entering crowds at age 15. Should future research affirm these results and interpretations, scientists will be a trifle closer to possessing a biological profile characteristic of the children whose BI behavior originated in a temperamental bias rather than in experience alone. (For more information on the neurobiology of BI, see White, Lamm, Helfinstein, & Fox, Chapter 17, this volume.)

Patterns

A serious problem with contemporary research is that many investigators compare two or more groups on one measure and pool the groups if they have the same average scores, even though the patterns of relations on a large number of variables are often dissimilar for the two groups. This result is most common when the groups are males and females (Kagan, 1994). This is why investigators might benefit from examining their data for patterns of measures rather than performing regressions or analyses of variance on single variables, under the assumption that the meaning of a variable remains the same across all values or types of participants.

The blood flow data gathered on the 18-year-olds provides an example. Some low-reactive boys showed shallow habituation of the blood flow signal to the amygdala across the eight blocks of pictures, compared with other low-reactive boys who showed steep habituation. However, the former group of low-reactive boys with a shallow habituation were significantly more likely than high-reactives with shallow habituation to possess a large body build (top quintile for height and weight at age 11 years), a thinner cortex in the right ventromedial area, less cortical arousal in the EEG, and less sympathetic arousal in the cardiovascular system at age 11 years. These low-reactive boys displayed a distinctive pattern of measures that clearly separated them from the high-reactives with similar slopes of habituation of the BOLD signal across the blocks of pictures.

No biologist would classify a mammal into a species category based on a single measure, such as body weight, rise in glucocorticoids in response to stress, or posture with an intruder. The adult psychological phenotypes displayed by large, representative samples of high- or low-reactive infants are likely to be a function of at least four relatively independent factors that form a variety of patterns. These factors include social class of the family, the child's ordinal position, size of the community where the first 15 years were spent, and the values of the local culture. These conditions, acting on a temperamental bias over time, can create a number of possible personality profiles.

Two Final Points

It is important to recognize the serious dissociation that can occur between a measured brain state and a psychological outcome, be it a behavior, feeling, memory, or emotion. There are at least two reasons for this dissociation. First, the local context selects one outcome from a number of possibilities. Second, similar brain profiles can originate in different conditions. This suggestion is supported by many studies in both humans and animals (e.g., Belova, Paton, Morrison, & Salzman, 2007; Herry et al., 2007; Hsu, Bhatt, Adolphs, Tranel, & Camerer, 2005).

A second point concerns the relevance of the behaviors of mice or rats encountering novel open fields or the lit alleys of the elevated maze to BI in children or social anxiety in adults. Rodents have unique behavioral and brain reactions to brightly lit areas; humans, too, have species-specific reactions when they anticipate that another person might evaluate their behavior in an undesirable light. Thus, we cannot be certain that the mechanisms that provoke a rat to avoid the lit areas of an elevated maze or the center of an open field, which some investigators treat as a sign of anxiety, are similar to the mechanisms that create social anxiety in children or adults. These reactions might be examples of *phenocopies*, in which two behaviors that appear to serve similar functions rest on distinctive origins. The investigators who assume that the mechanisms that lead mice to bite an intruder animal resemble those that cause adolescents to bully another child may be making this error (Nelson & Chiavegatto, 2001).

Summary

This chapter makes two central points. First, BI refers to a behavioral profile in children that is observed soon after the first birthday and is marked by avoidance and timidity in response to unfamiliar people, events, and objects. However, this profile can originate in different conditions; therefore, BI is not a unitary theoretical construct, but a name for a family of phenomena. Investigators working in this domain should try to gather information on the social class and ethnicity of their participants and record their hair and eye color; height; weight; body mass; and, if possible, baseline heart rate, blood pressure, and EEG asymmetry. These variables are easy to gather and will help investigators distinguish between children whose BI profile has a temperamental contribution and those whose behavior is primarily due to life history.

Second, BI behaviors are vulnerable to change over time, even though the biology that is the foundation of the temperamental bias appears to be preserved to a greater degree. Over 80% of high-reactives will not maintain a consistently exuberant, fearless profile, but only 20% will preserve a behavioral pattern marked by extreme timidity, shyness, and avoidance. Thus, knowledge of a child's temperamental bias allows one to predict with some confidence what the child will *not* become. This information is less predictive of what the child *will* become.

Further Reading

Kagan, J. (2010). *The temperamental thread*, New York: Dana Press.
Ledoux, J. E. (2000). Emotion circuits in the brain. *Annual Review of Neuroscience, 23*, 155–184.
Rothbart, M. K., Ellis, L. K., Rueda, M. R., & Posner, M. I. (2003). Developing mechanisms of temperamental effortful control. *Journal of Personality, 71*, 1113–1143.

References

Adamec, R. E. (1991). Individual differences in temporal lobe sensory processing of threatening stimuli in the cat. *Physiology and Behavior, 49*, 455–464.
Arcus, D. (1989). Vulnerability and eye color in Disney cartoon characters. In J. S. Reznick (Ed.), *Perspectives on behavioral inhibition* (pp. 291–297). Chicago: University of Chicago Press.
Asendorpf, J. B. (1991). Development of inhibited children's coping with unfamiliarity. *Child Development, 62*, 1460–1474.
Baas, J. M., Milstin, J., Donlevy, M., & Grillon, C. (2006). Brain stem correlates of defensive states in humans. *Biological Psychiatry, 59*, 588–593.
Belova, M. A., Paton, J. J., Morrison, S. E., & Salzman, C. D. (2007). Expectation modulates neural responses to pleasant and aversive stimuli in the primate amygdala. *Neuron, 55*, 970–984.
Blackford, J. U., & Zald, P. H. (2010). *Amygdala response to familiar, not novel, faces characterizes inhibited temperament*. Unpublished manuscript, Vanderbilt University, Nashville, TN.
Boes, A. D., Bechara, A., Tranel, D., Anderson, S. W., Richman, L., & Nopoulos, P. (2009). Right ventromedial prefrontal cortex: A neuroanatomical correlate of impulse control in boys. *Social, Cognitive, and Affective Neuroscience, 4*, 1–9.
Bruder, G. E., Sedoruk, J. P., Stewart, J. W., McGrath, P. J., Quitkin, F. M., & Tenke, C. E. (2008). Electroencephalographic alpha measures predict therapeutic response to a selective serotonin reuptake inhibitor antidepressant: Pre- and post-treatment findings. *Biological Psychiatry, 63*, 1171–1177.
Bulbena, A., Martin-Santos, R., Porta, M., Buro, K. C., Gago, J., Sangorrin, J., et al. (1996). Somatotype in panic patients. *Anxiety, 2*, 80–85.
Chen, X., Chen, H., Li, D., & Wang, L. (2009). Early childhood behavioral inhibition and social and school adjustment in Chinese children: A 5-year longitudinal study. *Child Development, 80*, 1692–1704.
Coplan, R. J., Coleman, B., & Rubin, K. H. (1998). Shyness and Little Boy Blue: Iris pigmentation, gender, and social wariness in preschoolers. *Developmental Psychobiology, 32*, 37–44.
Coplan, R. J., DeBow, A., Schneider, B. H., & Graham, A. A. (2009). The social behaviors of extremely inhibited children in and out of preschool. *British Journal of Developmental Psychology, 27*, 891–905.
Coplan, R. J., Rubin, K. H., Fox, N. A., Calkins, S. D., & Stewart, S. L. (1994). Being alone, playing alone, and acting alone. *Child Development, 65*, 129–137.
Davidson, R. J. (2003). Affective neuroscience and psychophysiology. *Psychophysiology, 4*, 655–665.
De Ross, J., Avila, M. A., Ruggiero, R. N., Nobre, M. J., Brandao, M. L., & Castiho, V. M. (2009). The unconditioned fear produced by morphine withdrawal is regulated by mu- and kappa-opioid receptors in the midbrain tectum. *Behavioural Brain Research, 204*, 140–146.
Dommett, E., Coizet, V., Blaha, C. D., Martindale, J., Lefebvre, V., Walton, N., et al. (2005). How visual stimuli activate dopaminergic neurons at short latency. *Science, 307*, 1476–1479.
Ducrest, A. L., Keller, L., & Roulin, A. (2008). Pleiotropy in the melanocortin system, coloration, and behavioural syndromes. *Trends in Ecological Evolution, 23*, 502–510.
El-Gabalawy, R., Cox, B., Clara, I., & Mackenzie, C. (2010). Assessing the validity of social anxiety disorder subtypes using a nationally representative sample. *Journal of Anxiety Disorders, 24*, 244–249.
Essex, M. J., Klein, M. H., Slattery, M. J., Goldsmith, H., & Kalin, N. H. (2010). Early risk factors and developmental pathways to chronic high inhibition and social anxiety disorder in adolescence. *American Journal of Psychiatry, 167*, 40–46.
Fox, A. S., Shelton, S. E., Oakes, T. R., Davidson, R. J., & Kalin, N. H. (2008). Trait-like brain activity during adolescence predicts anxious temperament in primates. *PloS ONE, 3*(7), e2570.
Fox, N. A., Henderson, H. A., Rubin, K. H., Calkins, S. D., & Schmidt, L. A. (2001). Continuity and discontinuity of behavioral inhibition and exuberance. *Child Development, 72*, 1–21.
Fox, N. A., Rubin, K. H., Calkins, S. B., Marshall, J. R., Coplan, R. J., Porgess, W., et al. (1995). Frontal activation asymmetry and social competence at 4 years of age. *Child Development, 60*, 1770–1784.
Garcia-Coll, C., Kagan, J., & Reznick, J. S. (1984). Behavioral inhibition in children. *Child Development, 55*, 1005–1009.
Gortmaker, S. L., Kagan, J., Caspi, A., & Silva, P. A. (1997). Daylength during pregnancy and shyness in children. *Developmental Psychobiology, 31*, 107–114.
Gray, J. (1982). *The neuropsychology of anxiety*. New York: Oxford University Press.
Gundersen, H., Specht, K., Gruner, R., Ersland, L.,

& Hugdahl, K. (2008). Separating the effects of alcohol and expectancy on brain activation: An fMRI working memory study. *NeuroImage*, 42, 1587–1596.

Hallowell, A. I. (1941). The social function of anxiety in a primitive society. *American Sociological Review*, 6, 869–891.

Hane, A. A., Fox, N. A., Polak-Toste, C., Ghera, M. M., & Guner, B. M. (2006). Contextual basis of maternal perceptions of infant temperament. *Developmental Psychology*, 42, 1077–1088.

Hebb, D. O. (1946). On the nature of fear. *Psychological Review*, 53, 259–276.

Heir, T., Piatigorsky, A., & Weisaeth, L. (2009). Longitudinal changes in recalled perceived life threat after a natural disaster. *British Journal of Psychiatry*, 194, 510–514.

Herry, C., Bach, D. R., Esposito, F., Di Salle, F., Perrig, W. J., Scheffler, K., et al. (2007). Processing of temporal unpredictability in human and animal amygdala. *Journal of Neuroscience*, 27, 5958–5966.

Hinton, D., & Hinton, S. (2002). Panic disorder, somatization, and the new cross-cultural psychiatry. *Culture, Medicine, and Psychiatry*, 26, 155–178.

Hogan, A. M., Butterfield, E. L., Phillips, L., & Hadwin, J. A. (2007). Brain response to novel noises in children with low and high trait anxiety. *Journal of Cognitive Neuroscience*, 19, 25–31.

Hsu, M., Bhatt, M., Adolphs, R., Tranel, D., & Camerer, C. F. (2005). Neural systems respond to degrees of uncertainty in human decision-making. *Science*, 310, 1680–1683.

Kagan, J. (1994). *Galen's prophecy*. New York: Basic Books.

Kagan, J. (2010). *The temperamental thread*. Washington, DC: Dana Press.

Kagan, J., & Fox, N. A. (2006). Biology, culture and temperamental biases. In N. Eisenberg (Vol. Ed.) & W. Damon & R. M. Lerner (Series Eds.), *Handbook of child psychology* (6th ed., pp. 167–225). New York: Wiley.

Kagan, J., & Snidman, N. (2004). *The long shadow of temperament*. Cambridge, MA: Harvard University Press.

Kagan, J., Snidman, N., Kahn, V., & Towsley, S. (2007). The preservation of two infant temperaments into adolescence. *Monographs of the Society for Research in Child Development*, 72(Serial No. 287).

Kagan, J., Snidman, N., Zentner, M., & Peterson, E. (1999). Infant temperament and anxious symptoms in school age children. *Development and Psychopathology*, 11, 209–224.

Kellett, J., Marzillier, J. S., & Lambert, C. (1981). Social skill and somatotype. *British Journal of Medical Psychology*, 54, 149–155.

Kendler, K. S., Myers, J. M., & Neale, M. C. (2000). A multi-dimensional twin study of mental health in women. *American Journal of Psychiatry*, 157, 506–517.

Kieling, C., Kieling, R. R., Rohde, L. A., Frick, P. J., Moffitt, T., Nigg, J. T., et al. (2010). The age of onset of attention deficit hyperactivity disorder. *American Journal of Psychiatry*, 167, 14–16.

Kittilsen, S., Schjolden, J., Beitnes-Johansen, I., Shaw, J. C., Pottinger, T. G., Sorensen, C., et al. (2009). Melanin-based skin spots reflect stress responsiveness in salmonid fish. *Hormones and Behavior*, 56, 292–296.

Kobiella, A., Volstadt-Klein, S., Buhler, M., Graf, C., Buchholz, H. G., Bernow, N., et al. (2010). Human dopamine receptor D2/D3 availability predicts amygdala reactivity to unpleasant stimuli. *Human Brain Mapping*, 31, 716–726.

Koenigs, M., Huey, E. D., Calamia, M., Raymont, C., Tranel, D., & Grafman, J. (2008). Distinct regions of prefrontal cortex mediate resistance and vulnerability to depression. *Journal of Neuroscience*, 28, 12341–12348.

Kottler, J. (2010). *The assassin and the therapist*. New York: Routledge.

Lad, H. V., Liu, L., Paya-Cono, L. L., Parsons, M. J., Kember, R., Fernandes, C., et al. (2010). Behavioral battery testing. *Physiology and Behavior*, 99, 301–316.

La Gasse, L., Gruber, C., & Lipsitt, L. P. (1989). The infantile expression of avidity in relation to later assessment. In J. S. Reznick (Ed.), *Perspectives on behavioral inhibition* (pp. 159–176). Chicago: University of Chicago Press.

Lang, S., & Kotchoubey, B. (2002). Brain responses to number sequences with and without active task requirement. *Clinical Neurophysiology*, 113, 1734–1741.

Laptook, R. S., Klein, D. N., Olino, T. M., Dyson, M. W., & Carlson, G. (2010). Low positive affectivity and behavioral inhibition in preschool-age children. *Personality and Individual Differences*, 48, 547–551.

Lenroot, R. K., Schmitt, J. E., Ordaz, S. J., Wallace, G. L., Neale, M. C., Lerch, J. P., et al. (2008). Differences in genetic and environmental influences on the human cerebral cortex associated with development during childhood and adolescence. *Human Brain Mapping*, 30, 163–174.

Machado, C. J., Kazama, A. M., & Bachevalier, J. (2009). Impact of amygdala, orbital frontal, or hippocampal lesions on threat avoidance and emotional reactivity in nonhuman primates. *Emotion*, 9, 127–163.

Miskovic, V., Ashbaugh, A. R., Santesso, D. L., McCabe, R. E., Antony, M. M., & Schmidt, L. A. (2010). Frontal brain oscillations and social anxiety: A cross-frequency spectral analysis during baseline and speech anticipation. *Biological Psychology*, 83, 125–132.

Miskovic, V., & Schmidt, L. (2010). Frontal brain electrical asymmetry and cardiac vagal tone

predict biased attention to social threat. *International Journal of Psychophysiology, 75,* 332–338.
Moukheiber, A., Rautureau, G., Perez-Diaz, F., Soussignan, R., Dubal, S., Jouvent, R., et al. (2010). Gaze avoidance in social phobia. *Behaviour Research and Therapy, 46,* 147–151.
Naragon-Gainey, K. (2010). Meta-analysis of the relations of anxiety sensitivity to the depression and anxiety disorders. *Psychological Bulletin, 136,* 128–150.
Nelson, E. E., Shelton, S. E., & Kalin, N. H. (2003). Individual differences in the responses of naive rhesus monkeys to snakes. *Emotion, 3,* 3–11.
Nelson, R. J., & Chiavegatto, S. (2001). Molecular basis of aggression. *Trends in Neuroscience, 24,* 713–718.
Oddo, S., Lux, S., Weiss, P. H., Schwab, A., Welzer, H., Markowitsch, H. J., et al. (2010). Specific role of medial prefrontal cortex in retrieving recent autobiographical memories: An fMRI study of young female subjects. *Cortex, 46,* 29–39.
Reznick, J. S., Hegeman, I. M., Kaufman, E., Woods, S. W., & Jacobs, M. (1992). Retrospective and concurrent self-report of behavioral inhibition and their relations to mental health. *Development and Psychopathology, 4,* 301–321.
Rimm-Kaufman, S. E., Rosenstock, E. G., & Arcus, D. (1996, April). *Developmental outcomes of behavioral inhibition in infancy: How do inhibited and uninhibited children differ in their behavioral reactions to entrance into kindergarten?* Paper presented at the International Conference on Infant Studies, Providence, RI.
Robinson, J. L., Kagan, J., Reznick, J. S., & Corley, R. (1992). The heritability of inhibited and uninhibited behavior. *Developmental Psychology, 28,* 1030–1037.
Rosenberg, A., & Kagan, J. (1987). Iris pigmentation and behavioral inhibition. *Developmental Psychobiology, 20,* 377–392.
Rothbart, M. K. (1989). Temperament in childhood. In G. A. Kohnstamm, J. E. Bates, & M. K. Rothbart (Eds.), *Temperament in childhood* (pp. 59–73). New York: Wiley.
Rubin, K. H., & Both, L. (1989). Iris pigmentation and sociability in childhood. *Developmental Psychobiology, 22,* 1–9.
Rubin, K. H., & Coplan, R. J. (2010). *The development of shyness and social withdrawal.* New York: Guilford Press.
Saetre, P., Strandberg, E., Sundgren, P. E., Pettersson, U., Jazin, E., & Bergstrom, T. F. (2006). The genetic contribution to canine personality. *Genes, Brain, and Behavior, 5,* 240–248.
Sarinopolous, I., Grupe, D. W., Mackiewicz, K. L., Herrington, J. D., Lor, M., Steege, E. E., et al. (2010). Uncertainty during anticipation modulates neural responses to aversion in human insula and amygdala. *Cerebral Cortex, 20,* 929–940.
Schwartz, C. E., Kunwar, P. S., Greve, D. N., Kagan, J., Snidman, N. C., & Bloch, R. B. (in press). A phenotype of early infancy predicts reactivity of the amygdala in male adults. *Molecular Psychiatry.*
Schwartz, C. E., Kunwar, P. S., Greve, D. N., Moran, L. R., Viner, J. C., Covino, J. M., et al. (2010). Structural differences in adult orbital and ventromedial prefrontal cortex predicted by infant temperament at four months of age. *Archives of General Psychiatry, 67,* 78–84.
Schwartz, C. E., Wright, C. E., Shin, L. M., Kagan, J., & Rauch, S. L. (2003). Inhibited and uninhibited infants grown up: Adult amygdalar response to novelty. *Science, 300,* 1952–1953.
Sexton, K. A., & Dugas, M. J. (2009). Defining distinct negative beliefs about uncertainty: Validating the factor structure of the Intolerance of Uncertainty Scale. *Psychological Assessment, 21,* 176–186.
Smit, D. J. A., Posthuma, D., Boomsma, D. I., & De Geus, E. J. C. (2007). The relation between frontal EEG asymmetry and the risk for anxiety and depression. *Biological Psychology, 74,* 26–33.
Souza, G. G., Medonca-de-Souza, A. C., Barros, E. M., Coutinho, E. F., Oliveira, L., Mendiowicz, M. V., et al. (2007). Resilience and vagal tone predict cardiac recovery from acute social stress. *Stress, 10,* 368–374.
Sundet, J. M., Skre, I., Okkenhaug, J. J., & Tambs, K. (2003). Genetic and environmental causes of the inter-relationships between self-reported fears. *Scandinavian Journal of Psychology, 44,* 97–106.
Thomas, A., Chess, S., Birch, H., & Hertzig, M. E. (1960). A longitudinal study of primary reaction patterns in children. *Comprehensive Psychiatry, 1,* 103–112.
Trut, L. M. (1999). Early canid domestication. *American Scientist, 87,* 160–169.
Uher, R., & McGuffin, P. (2010). The moderation by the serotonin transporter gene of environmental adversity in the etiology of depression: 2009 update. *Molecular Psychiatry, 15,* 18–22.
Vuga, M., Fox, N. A., Cohn, J. F., George, C. J., Levenstein, R. M., & Kovacs, M. (2006). Long-term stability of frontal electroencephalographic asymmetry in adults with a history of depression and controls. *International Journal of Psychophysiology, 59,* 107–115.
Winkler, A. M., Kochunov, P., Blangero, J., Almasy, L., Zilles, K., Fox, P. T., et al. (2010). Cortical thickness or grey matter volume?: The importance of selecting the phenotype for imaging genetic studies. *NeuroImage, 53,* 1135–1156.

CHAPTER 5

Activity as a Temperament Trait

Jan Strelau
Bogdan Zawadzki

Since the first pioneering studies on temperament, activity has been regarded as one of the primary traits by means of which individual differences of behavior have been described. It is present in animal behavior and may be observed in people. Motor activity expressed in behavior became an attractive object to study temperament in neonates. Even trails have been undertaken to assess temperament in advanced developmental stages of fetal life. The frequency and intensity of fetal movements, identified as motor activity, is the initial temperament trait to be recorded in humans (Eaton & Saudino, 1992).

At the beginning of the 20th century Dutch psychiatrists Heymans and Wiersma described the structure of temperament composed of three traits—activity, emotionality, and primary/secondary function (also called perseveration). These traits have been separated on the basis of an inventory study of 400 families, comprising over 2,000 subjects. The project has to be regarded as the first psychometric approach to temperament/personality (Heymans, 1908; see also Strelau, 1998). The construct of *activity*, constituting the core of this chapter, according to Heymans (1908) refers to goal-directed, operant behavior, and is characterized by the amount of time a person spends performing given kinds of action.

Our aim in this chapter is to present the mainstream of studies centered on activity that is understood as a temperamental trait present in children and adults, the methods (procedures) applied to measure individual differences in activity, and the functional role of activity, especially as expressed in the process of adaptation. A separate section is devoted to our research on activity less known in Western countries.

Activity as One of the Basic Temperament Traits Present in Infants and Children

Basic Child-Oriented Theories in Which Activity Plays an Essential Role

In the second half of the 1950s, child psychiatrists Thomas and Chess (1977), as a result of observations conducted during their psychiatric practice, arrived at the conclusion that individual differences in children's temperament play an important role in normal and deviant development. One of the nine traits composing the structure of children's temperament according to Thomas and

83

Chess is activity. *Activity level* refers to "the motor component present in a given child's functioning and the diurnal proportion of active and inactive periods" (p. 21).

Under the influence of Thomas and Chess (1977), studies on temperament, including trait activity, mostly understood in a manner similar to that defined by the two prominent scholars, gained high popularity among researchers interested in early stages of human development, especially in the United States (see Zentner & Bates, 2008). Mervielde and De Pauw (Chapter 2, this volume) devote much space to activity present in models of child temperament, underlining that "activity is clearly represented in each of the early childhood temperament measures" (p. 34), and it is also a "common and important component of middle childhood" (p. 34). As mentioned by Goldsmith and Gagne (Chapter 11, this volume; also see Gagne, Vendlinski, & Goldsmith, 2009), beside dimensions such as anger/frustration, behavioral inhibition/fear, effortful control, and positive affect, activity is currently among the most commonly examined temperament dimensions.

In studying activity and its adaptive role of special importance was the concept of temperament presented by Buss and Plomin (1975, 1984). According to them, temperament, which is present from early childhood and essentially influenced by the genetic factor, has a structure composed of three basic traits—emotionality, activity, and sociability (EAS). *Activity* has two components, vigor and tempo, related to each other; "the twin aspects of activity—vigor and tempo—are best seen in *how* a response is delivered (style)" (Buss & Plomin, 1975, p. 33). A very active person is strongly motivated to be energetic (i.e., he or she expends energy in vigorous activity performed with rapid tempo).

Activity occupies a special place among the three traits composing the structure of temperament. Every response is accompanied by expended energy, and thus varies in vigor (intensity) and tempo. This means that activity has a more diffuse character and so may be considered a *stylistic* trait (Buss & Plomin, 1984).

Buss and Plomin (1984) reviewed several studies investigating the heritability of the EAS traits. Reports from monozygotic (MZ) and dizygotic (DZ) twins ages 43 months to 7 years, 6 months, have shown that the correlations between MZ twins are without exception essentially higher compared to DZ twin. These data support their view on the significant role of genes in determining individual differences in activity.

Activity is also a factor in other developmental theories of temperament, although the status of this trait is not as strongly evident as it is in Buss and Plomin's EAS theory. For example, in the developmental model of temperament by Rothbart and Derryberry (1981), and further extended by Rothbart and her associates (e.g., Rothbart & Ahadi, 1994; Rothbart & Posner, 1985), in which reactivity and self-regulation play the essential role, activity is seen as a trait involved in self-regulation processes. This means that activity takes part in processes that facilitate or inhibit *reactivity*, which refers to arousability of the physiological and behavioral systems. Temperamental traits are expressed in such behaviors as attentional, emotional, and motor activity; however, these behaviors have a developmentally specific organization (Rothbart & Ahadi, 1994).

Activity is also present as a temperament trait in the emotion-centered theory of temperament developed by Goldsmith and Campos (1982). According to the authors, individual differences in primary emotions (positive and negative), such as disgust, distress, fear or pleasure, joy, and surprise are considered as content dimensions of temperament. In this theory, activity as a temperament trait plays a non-content-oriented role. Goldsmith and Campos (1990) consider activity as an *expressional component* of all emotions. Thus, the main argument in this theory is based on the assumption that activity is related to a general level of emotional arousal (Goldsmith & Campos, 1990) and genes contribute essentially to individual differences in activity, as measured by means of inventories (Goldsmith, Buss, & Lemery, 1997). This view has its roots in the Wundtian tradition. According to Wundt (1887) temperament is a disposition that applies exclusively to emotions, and the four classic temperaments distinguished by Hippocrates and Galen are characterized by Wundt on the basis of two non-content-related dimensions—intensity and speed of changes in emotions.

De Pauw, Mervielde, and Van Leeuwen (2009), in a study of 443 preschoolers, demonstrated that a joint principal component analysis of 28 temperament scales and 18 personality scales measured by the Hierarchical Personality Inventory for Children (Mervielde & De Fruyt, 2002) resulted in a six-factor solution, with activity being one of them. The temperamental scales were representative for the theories of temperament by Thomas and Chess (Behavioral Styles Activity Questionnaire; BSQ), Buss and Plomin (EAS Temperament Survey; EAS-TS), and Rothbart (Children's Behavior Questionnaire; CBQ) presented below.

The theories of temperament provoked many developmental-oriented researchers to construct different instruments aimed at assessing temperament in children.

Temperament Instruments Aimed at Measuring Activity

As mentioned earlier, temperament is present already in neonates and develops until adolescence in respect to behavioral expressions and number of traits being age-specific. This explains the extensive development of techniques aimed at assessing temperament. Most of them stem directly from the discussed theories or take them as a starting point for constructing instruments aimed at measuring traits that comprise alternative structures of temperament. In this chapter we refer to those in which activity is present as one of the traits in the structure of temperament or to instruments aimed exclusively at assessing observed motor activity.

Most of the instruments measure temperament traits, as assessed by parents, teachers or caregivers, and only exceptionally at later stages of development are applied in self-report form. Our aim in this chapter is not to go into the particulars of the specific inventories (for a detailed description, see Joyce, 2010; Strelau, 1998) but to present the most important inventories (English language) in which the scale Activity occurs (see Table 5.1).

Activity based on the theory of temperament by Thomas and Chess (1977) may be measured by the following inventories (see Table 5.1): Parent Temperament Questionnaire (PTQ) and Teacher Temperament Questionnaire (TTQ) developed by Thomas and Chess, and the Baby Behavior Questionnaire (BBQ), BSQ, Early Infancy Temperament Questionnaire (EITQ), Middle Childhood Temperament Questionnaire (MCTQ), Revised Dimensions of Temperament Questionnaire (DOTS-R), Revised Infant Temperament Questionnaire (RITQ), Revised Infant Temperament Questionnaire—Short Form (SITQ), Temperament Assessment Battery (TAB) and Toddler Temperament Scale (TTS) by their followers and other researchers. For the assessment of activity based on the EAS theory developed by Buss and Plomin the following inventories are available: Colorado Childhood Temperament Inventory (CCTI) and EAS-TS. Rothbart's developmental model of temperament offers the following questionnaires for measuring activity: Children's Behavior Questionnaire (CBQ), Infant Behavior Questionnaire (IBQ), and Infant Behavior Questionnaire—Revised (IBQ-R). But also the School-Age Temperament Inventory (SATI) has its roots in her theory. Finally, for measuring activity as understood by Goldsmith and Campos the Toddler Behavior Assessment Questionnaire (TBAQ) is appropriate. As seen in Table 5.1 the separate inventories are age-specific and allow assessment of activity within the age range from 1 month to 12 years.

A meta-analysis by Else-Quest, Hyde, Goldsmith, and Van Hulle (2006) has shown that temperament activity is higher in boys compared to girls; however, the gender difference is rather small ($d = 0.15–0.30$). The analysis comprised data from 80 studies in which activity was measured in children from infancy to school age by 17 inventories representing the Thomas and Chess, Buss and Plomin, and Rothbart approaches to temperament.

It was Goldsmith (1983) who asked the question about genetic influences on temperament, including activity, depending on age. Analysis of data comprising over a dozen temperament traits and stemming from twin, adoption, and family designs collected on samples from infancy to adolescence, brought him to the conclusion that the genetic evidence is perhaps the weakest at young ages (the first half-year of life in twin studies, childhood in adoption studies).

Analysis of data stemming from studies covering birth to old age, in which activity was included among other personality/

TABLE 5.1. Questionnaires Aimed at Assessing Temperament in Children

Instrument name	Activity scale
Baby Behavior Questionnaire (BBQ; Bohlin, Hagekull, & Lindhagen, 1981)[a]	3–7 months, 54 items, 5-point scales, parents
Behavioral Style Activity Questionnaire (BSQ; McDevitt & Carey, 1978)[a]	3–7 years, 100 items, 6-point scale, parents
Children's Behavior Questionnaire (CBQ; Rothbart, Ahadi, Hershey, & Fisher, 2001; see also Putnam, & Rothbart, 2006)[c]	3–7 years, 195 items, 7-point scale, caregivers
Colorado Childhood Temperament Inventory (CCTI; Rowe & Plomin, 1977)[b]	1–6 years, 74 items, 5-point scale, parents
Early Infancy Temperament Questionnaire (EITQ; Medoff-Cooper, Carey, & McDevitt, 1993)[a]	1–4 months, 76 items, 6-point scale, parents
EAS Temperament Survey for children (EAS-TS; Buss & Plomin, 1984)[b]	1–12 years, 20 items, 5-point scale, parents
Infant Behavior Questionnaire (IBQ; Rothbart, 1981)[c]	3–12 months, 87 items, 7-point scale, parents
Infant Behavior Questionnaire—Revised (IBQ-R; Gartstein & Rothbart, 2003)[c]	3–12 months, 184 items, 7-point scale, parents
Middle Childhood Temperament Questionnaire (MCTQ; Hegvik, McDevitt, & Carey, 1982)[a]	8–12 years, 99 items, 6-point scale, parents
Parent Temperament Questionnaire (PTQ; Thomas & Chess, 1977)[a]	3–7 years, 72 items, 7-point scale, parents
Revised Dimensions of Temperament Survey (DOTS-R; Windle & Lerner, 1986)[a]	Pre- and elementary school, 54 items, 4-point scale, parents
Revised Infant Temperament Questionnaire (RITQ; Carey & McDevitt, 1978)[a]	4–8 months, 95 items, 6-point scale, parents
Revised Infant Temperament Questionnaire—Short Form (SITQ; Sanson, Prior, Garino, Oberklaid, & Sewell, 1987)[a]	4–8 months, 30 items, 6-point scale, parents
School-Age Temperament Inventory (SATI; McClowry, 1995)[c]	8–11 years, 38 items, 5-point scale, parents
Teacher Temperament Questionnaire (TTQ; Thomas & Chess, 1977)[a]	3–7 years, 64 items, 7-point scale, teachers
Temperament Assessment Battery (TAB; Martin, 1988a)[a]	3–7 years, 48 items, 7-point scale, parents and teachers; 24 items, clinicians
Temperament Assessment Battery—Revised (TAB-R; Martin & Bridger, 1999)[a]	3–7 years, 48 items, 7-point scale, parents and teachers; 24 items, clinicians
Temperament Inventory for Children (TIC; Oniszczenko & Radomska, 2002)[e]	6–12 years, 30 items, 2-point scale, parents and teachers
Toddler Behavior Assessment Questionnaire (TBAQ; Goldsmith, 1996)[d]	18 months–4 years, 108 items, 7-point scale, parents
Toddler Temperament Scale (TTS; Fullard, McDevitt, & Carey, 1984)[a]	1–3 years, 97 items, 6-point scale, parents

Note. The inventories are in alphabetic order according to their names. Inventories have been developed within the following theories: [a]theory of temperament by Thomas and Chess, [b]EAS theory by Buss and Plomin, [c]Rothbart's developmental model of temperament, [d]Goldsmith and Campos's theory, [e]Strelau's RTT theory. See Strelau (1998) for a complete list of references for all inventories.

temperament traits, brought Loehlin (1992, p. 103) to a similar conclusion: There is "little evidence for heritability of temperament at birth, evidence of some but not much heritability during the first year, and heritabilities . . . increasing toward levels characteristic of the major portion of the life-span, with perhaps a slight decrease in old age."

Apart from psychometric instruments for assessing activity, methods such as mechanical measures, experimental indices, and locomotion in open field have been applied. As the best example for an experimental approach to the assessment of temperamental traits, including activity, the so-called Laboratory Temperament Assessment Battery (Lab-TAB) elaborated by Goldsmith and Rothbart (1996), should be mentioned here. Among other traits Lab-TAB allows assessment of activity in 6-month-old infants (prelocomotor version) and in 12- to 18-month-old infants (locomotor version). These batteries describe in detail the standardized episodes presumed to evoke behaviors typical of the temperamental traits under study. An adaptation of the Lab-TAB that presented episodes in a way that is consistent with aspects of temperament in the IBQ-R resulted in development of the Temperament Laboratory Assessment (TLA; Gonzalez, Gartstein, Carranza, & Rothbart, 2003; after Gartstein & Marmion, 2008). The TLA allows assessment of temperament, including motor activity, in children ages 6–12 months.

For instruments assessing motor activity, watch terms such as actometer, actigraph, accelometers, or fidgetometer have been applied. The different measures of motor activity are not entirely the same. This chapter concentrates mainly on actometer measures, mostly applied in measuring motor activity. The actometer allows researchers to register the number, frequency, or magnitude of body movements recorded from the waist or limbs, as well as a composite score from the separate measures. Reliability and validity across different actometer measures of motor activity mostly recorded during free play and home settings show high consistency and moderate stability (see Eaton, 1983; Eaton, McKeen, & Saudino, 1996).

Several studies have examined the extent to which genes are responsible for individual differences in mechanical measures of activity. When measuring motor activity in 463 MZ and DZ pairs of twins ages 7–9 years, Wood, Saudino, Rogers, Asherson, and Kuntsi (2007) demonstrated that the additive genetic component explains 36% of the actometer variance expressing individual differences in activity. A study of infants and older children by Eaton and Enns (1986) has shown that motor activity is essentially higher in boys; however, the difference was smaller in infants and increased with age. In turn, to examine the genetic influence on motor activity, Saudino and Zapfe (2008) studied 314 twin pairs (including 144 MZ twin pairs) at age 2 in three different situations—at home, in the laboratory, and play situation. Motor activity was assessed with actigraph. Results of this study have shown that (1) scores on motor activity correlated significantly across situations; (2) the genetic variance that explained individual differences in motor activity was significant for all three situations; (3) situational differences in motor activity resulted from shared environmental and nonshared environmental influences; and (4) the genetic factor explained observed cross-situational continuity in motor activity.

The Functional Significance of Trait Activity in Children

Measures of activity, whether recorded by means of inventories or based on objective records, are meaningful if there is evidence that temperament activity plays an essential role in human behavior.

It is impossible to present in this chapter all essential results showing the significance of activity in human adaptation processes. Only selected examples are given to show that activity, mostly present with other temperament traits, plays an important role in adaptation processes. In respect to activity, Thomas and Chess (1977) were the first researchers to show that activity is related to behavior disorders. In a working-class Puerto Rican sample living in New York, high activity became a temperamental trait, resulting in some individuals' behavioral disorders expressed in excessive motor activity, which was almost absent in the New York Longitudinal Study sample of children living in upper-middle-class families. This study demonstrates the essence of the "goodness-of-fit" construct introduced by Thomas and Chess to studies on temperament. It implies that the adequacy of the individual's functioning is dependent on the degree to which environmental demands are in accord with the individual's own characteristics.

Activity and Attention-Deficit/Hyperactivity Disorder

A study by Foley, McClowry, and Castellanos (2008) has shown that two samples of 6- to 11-year-old children, with symptoms of attention-deficit/hyperactivity disorder (ADHD) and with no symptoms present, differed essentially in activity level measured by means of the SATI. The correlations between activity and ADHD symptoms such as hyperactivity, impulsivity, and inattention were significant and high (.83, .60, .67, respectively). McIntosh and Cole-Love (1996) demonstrated that a sample of 5- to 11-year-old boys diagnosed with ADHD scored significantly higher in level of activity compared to a sample of boys comparable in age but without ADHD. Activity was assessed by parents and teachers by means of the Temperament Assessment Battery for Children (TABC). As underlined by White (1999) in a review of the literature regarding the relationship between personality, including temperament traits, and ADHD, this disorder shows close association with activity.

> The relationship between temperament and ADHD is well established. Perhaps the most obvious related temperament characteristic is activity level. Children with unusually high activity levels may also be more distractible and more impulsive and are frequently diagnosed with ADHD. (p. 592)

Activity and Adjustment

In a study taking a multimethod approach in assessing activity only, Schaughency and Fagot (1993) measured activity in 5-year-old children by means of inventory scores, home observation, play sessions, and an actometer. Adjustment was assessed 2 years later by means of the Child Behavior Checklist (Achenbach & Edelbrock, 1981) and a self-report adjustment measure. The results showed that the relationship between temperament activity and adjustment scores is strong but mainly when both variables were measured by inventory techniques. Activity at age 5 was related to parents' ratings of aggression and hyperactivity, and to learning problems (but only in girls) at age 7. In turn, in a study searching for the relationship between activity and adjustment, Teglasi and coworkers (2009) have shown that two samples of siblings—Sample 1 identified with emotional disability (ED; 5 to 13 years) and Sample 2 without ED (9 to 17 years)—differed significantly in the level of activity as measured by the DOTS-R and the Structured Temperament Interview (STI; Teglasi, 1998), with the level of activity higher in Sample 1. Most important, however, when two factors of activity—Modulation and Vigor—were taken into account, it was mainly Modulation—the *regulatory component* of activity that correlated essentially with adjustment, as measured by the Behavior Assessment System for Children (BASC; Reynolds & Kamphaus, 1992), which comprises scales such as Externalizing and Internalizing composites. Also a study of preschoolers by De Pauw and coauthors (2009) has shown that problem behavior (a total score), but especially externalizing, as measured by the preschool version of the Child Behavior Checklist, is significantly related to high activity scores.

Activity and Substance Use

Several studies have investigated the relationship between temperament, including activity level, and substance use (cigarettes, alcohol, or marijuana). Wills, DuHamel, and Vaccaro (1995) studied almost 2,000 seventh-grade male and female students to determine whether Tarter's (1988) statement based on a series of studies, that excessively high activity level constitutes a risk factor for alcoholism, could be confirmed when extending this relationship to other substances. In their study, substance use was measured with three items referring to the typical frequency of cigarette, alcohol, and marijuana use. Participants assessed themselves and their friends. The DOTS-R was administered to assess level of general activity, which "corresponds to a behavioral domain involving more pervasive movement and high energy expenditure" (Windle &

Lerner, 1986, p. 225). Also, other inventories were applied to mediate the effect of the relationship: "activity–substance use." As mediators over 20 variables were taken into account; among them were self-control, behavioral competence, coping, novelty seeking, friends' substance use, and parent support. The results show that activity level correlated significantly with the adolescent's total substance use score. However, structural equation modeling has shown no significant direct effect of activity on the adolescent's total substance use. The relationship of activity to substance use is "mediated through self-control, maladaptive coping, and novelty seeking, with affiliation with nonnormative (substance-using) peers indicated as a proximal factor for involvement in substance use" (Wills et al., 1995, p. 909).

Activity Trait as a Component of Difficult Temperament

In several studies activity is present in the so-called "difficult temperament," as postulated by Thomas and Chess (1977).

Maziade, Boutin, Cote, and Thivierge (1986), on the basis of studies of thousands of normal children from Quebec City, ages 7–12 years, obtained a consistent structure of temperament in which the first factor was regarded as a pattern typical for the easy–difficult temperament. Referring to this factor, children judged by parents as difficult to manage were characterized by high activity, low predictability, low adaptability, high intensity, negative mood, and low persistence. In turn, a study by Maziade, Caron, Cote, Boutin, and Thivierge (1990) on more than five hundred 3- to 7-year-old children and over three hundred 8- to 12-year-olds with psychiatric problems demonstrated that it was not the structure of temperament but the larger number of cases with difficult temperament that distinguished these two groups from the general population. In this study two factors of difficult temperament were distinguished. Among them, one of the factors comprised low persistence, high sensory threshold, and high activity level. This factor correlated with developmental delay in children.

Brody, Stoneman, and Burke (1988) have demonstrated that in families with two children of the same gender (brother pairs and sister pairs), one 4.5 to 6.6 years old, and the other 7 to 9 years old, fathers and mothers perceived a consistent relationship between difficult temperament and level of adjustment. Children assessed as having high levels of persistence, activity, and emotional intensity were perceived as less well adjusted in comparison to children with low temperament scores on these dimensions. This finding also occurred when temperament was measured by one of the parents, and adjustment by the other.

Studies have also shown that difficult temperament, combined with activity traits, influences school achievement. Most of the studies in this domain have been conducted by Martin and his coworkers (Martin, 1988a, 1989; Martin, Drew, Gaddis, & Moseley, 1988). Data obtained from these studies have shown that three of the six temperament dimensions measured by the TAB—Activity, Distractibility, and Persistence, which comprise one factor labeled by Martin (1989) as Task Attention—permit prediction of scholastic achievement as measured by standardized methods and teachers' grades. With few exceptions, the correlations are statistically significant and vary from .24 to .72, depending on the achievement criterion taken into account. The median correlation between temperament characteristics—Persistence (positive), Distractibility and Activity (both negative)—and standardized scholastic achievement tests, as rated by teachers, is .45 for reading and .39 for mathematics. In a more recent study in which Martin's Task Attention factor was taken into account in relation to science achievements, Li, Onaga, Shen, and Chiou (2009) demonstrated that the simple effect of activity level on science achievement was not significant. However, of significance was the interaction effect of activity level and persistence. Activity has negative effects on high persistence, and the interaction effect increases with age.

A longitudinal investigation by Martin, Olejnik, and Gaddis (1994) of over 100 pupils from first to fifth grades has shown that the factor Task Orientation (tendency to be active, distractible, and nonpersistent) had a stronger impact on mathematics and reading performance than did scholastic ability. According to the authors the result is not surprising if we consider that at least one-third of the variance in academic achievement depends on temperament/personality factors.

Summary

Selected studies in which activity understood as one of the basic temperamental traits was related to behavior or behavior disorders in children have demonstrated the functional significance of this trait. The adaptive role of children's level of activity comes out, whether activity occurs as an independent variable alone or in composition with other traits, as well as when this trait has been given the status of a moderator or predictor.

Activity as One of the Temperament Traits Present in Adults

The specificity of activity, as defined by Heymans and Wiersma (Heymans, 1908), involves treating this trait as expressed in goal-directed, operant behavior, without necessarily referring to motor behavior, as is the case in studies on children. Activity as an object of study in older adolescents, but especially in adults (the term *adults* will be applied when we refer to both), did not gain as much popularity as it did in research on children. Probably one of the reasons is that motor activity, present since birth, may be observed and assessed by parents, caregivers, and teachers. The literature on the relationship between activity that is understood as a temperament trait and adaptive behavior, including behavior disorders, is almost lacking in empirical data, but rich evidence has been collected in studies based on the regulative theory of temperament (see Strelau, 2008).

The Place of Activity in Research on Adults

In research on adults it is not uncommon that the notion "temperament" was treated as a synonym of the construct "personality." Two citations taken from leaders in personality research illustrate this tendency. According to Eysenck (H. J. Eysenck & M. W. Eysenck, 1985), "Personality as we look at it, has two major aspects: temperament and intelligence. Most textbooks of personality deal with temperament only" (p. vii). More recently, Costa and McCrae (2001), in the paper "A Theoretical Context for Adult Temperament," stated that the Big Five factors have a status of temperament. Probably under the influence of Buss and Plomin's (1984) definition, which says that *temperament* is equal to personality in early childhood, researchers dealing with the same constructs (e.g., traits) often refer to temperament when studying children, and to personality when investigating adults (Strelau, 1998; see also De Pauw et al., 2009; Zentner & Bates, 2008).

In research on adults, activity is rarely represented as one of the basic traits in the structure of temperament. Almost a half-century after Heymans and Wiersma designated activity as one of the three basic temperament traits, Guilford and Zimmerman (1949) proposed Activity as one of the traits represented as a separate scale in the Guilford–Zimmerman Temperament Survey (GZTS). Almost three decades later, a revised form of the GZTS was published (Guilford, Zimmerman, & Guilford, 1976) with 13 scales, among them was a more elaborated Activity scale identified as *General Activity*. So-called positive qualities of General Activity include rapid pace activities, energy, vitality, keeping in motion, production, efficiency, liking for speed, hurrying, quickness of action, enthusiasm, and liveliness. Understood in this way, *General Activity* has a much broader meaning than the term *activity* when applied to research on children.

Two years later, Thurstone (1951) distinguished seven temperamental traits described in terms of adjectives, such as *active, vigorous, impulsive, dominant, emotionally stable, sociable,* and *reflective*. They are represented as scales in the inventory known as the Thurstone Temperament Schedule (Thurstone, 1953).

Some of the many inventories developed by child-oriented psychologists were adapted in such a way as to allow temperament measurement, with the Activity scale present also in measures for adults. Thus, Thomas, Mittelman, Chess, Korn, and Cohen (1982) developed the Early Adult Temperament Questionnaire with the same scales, including Activity, as is the case in the Parent Temperament Questionnaire (PTQ; Thomas & Chess, 1977). Also the EAS-TS

(Buss & Plomin, 1984) and the DOTS-R (Windle & Lerner, 1986) were adapted in order to measure, among other traits, activity in adults.

Zuckerman (2002), most known from his pioneering studies on sensation seeking (see Zuckerman, 1994), developed the Zuckerman–Kuhlman Personality Questionnaire (ZKPQ), representing an alternative five-factorial model in which activity is present as a trait representing one of the Big Five factors. According to Zuckerman (2002, p. 383) the factor Activity has two components: "need for general activity and need for work activity." In a revised version of the ZKPQ, the scale Activity comprises the four following subscales: Work Compulsion, General Activity, Restlessness, and Work Energy (Aluja, Kuhlman, & Zuckerman, 2010; see also Zuckerman, Chapter 3). Again, general activity defined in a way that underlines approach or avoidance of behaviors characterized by level of stimulation supply has not much in common with temperament activity as a subject of study in children.

Finally, in the 1990s, Strelau and Zawadzki (1993, 1995) constructed the Formal Characteristics of Behavior—Temperament Inventory (FCB-TI), in which Activity is one of the six scales representing the structure of temperament. As explained below, Activity as measured by FCB-TI is not limited to motor activity.

Activity, spectacularly present since early infancy, has not been singled out as one of the major factors by the most distinguished authors, represented by the psychometric approach to the Three Giant Factors introduced by H. J. Eysenck and the Big Five factors, as adapted from the lexical project by Costa and McCrae. This, however, does not mean that activity as a temperament trait is not present in the structure of temperament (identified with personality) postulated by these scientists. The Eysenck (H. J. Eysenck & M. W. Eysenck, 1985) hierarchical structure of temperament/personality comprised on the highest level three factors—Psychoticism, Extraversion, and Neuroticism (the so-called PEN theory)—and included activity with Extraversion as one of its nine lower-order components. As a consequence, his most known inventory, the Eysenck Personality Questionnaire—Revised (EPQ-R; S. B. G. Eysenck, Eysenck, & Barrett, 1985) does not allow measurement of activity. Similarly, Costa and McCrae's (1992) Revised NEO Personality Inventory (NEO-PI-R) comprises scales representing the Big Five factors; however, distinct from the EPQ-R, the Extraversion scale has six subscales, and among them is Activity. This means that this trait can be assessed separately; however, there are few, if any, studies centered separately on activity.

Mechanical measures, as well as observed behavior during experimentally arranged sessions, have been applied very rarely to measure motor activity in adults. One of the most spectacular studies on adults' temperament activity, in which not only actometer but also inventories were applied, was by Spinath, Wolf, Angleitner, Borkenau, and Riemann (2002). Apart from actometer measures when subjects perform a variety of tasks for a period of 6 hours, among others, inventories such as DOTS-R, EAS, and FCB-TI were applied to measure activity (via self- and peer reports). The study comprised a sample of 300 MZ and DZ twin pairs (from ages 18 to 70 years), and included men and women. The results have shown that there was almost no correlation (from .02 to .11) between psychometric scores and actometer data. The essential lack of concordance suggests that objectively measured activity does not correspond with subjective assessments based on retrospection, or that activity scales present in inventories applied in this study refer to a different understanding of this construct. Additional information from this study indicates that the composite actometer score on motor activity has shown moderate genetic influence (42%). This result suggests that the contribution of genes to individual differences in motor activity is comparable across age (compare the 36% genetic contribution obtained in children by Wood et al., 2007).

The number of projects in which the role of activity is understood as a temperament trait has demonstrated that the functional significance of this trait in adult behavior is much less than that in children. Two studies on adults, one in the 1970s and another 30 years later, illustrate that activity plays an essential adaptive role.

Guilford and coworkers (1976) have drawn profiles of temperamental characteristics based on GZTS scores that are typical for dozens of samples representing different populations. By limiting the characteristics to the General Activity scale, some examples show the location of activity for selected samples: Male dental students occupy rank 3 on the C-score scale (from 0 to 10); male college students, rank 4; police officers, rank 5; male salesmen, rank 6; male employees with general management potential, rank 7; and top male managers, rank 8. These data show that different levels of General Activity are adaptive depending on the kind of professional activity represented by the selected samples. The growing activity scores in adults compared to students are contradictory to findings on motor activity, and may be explained by the fact that general activity, as understood by Guilford and coworkers, is not limited to motor activity (e.g., efficiency and productivity are components of activity).

A 9-year follow-up study by Hintsanen and coworkers (2009) examined whether the EAS traits predict unemployment status and duration of unemployment. Participants were ages 24 to 39 years. Duration of unemployment was reported by 1,893 participants, and 1,493 of them reported unemployment during the last 12 months. Activity (as well as Emotionality and Sociability) was self-reported three times—1992, 1997, and 2001. At the end of this study, the year of unemployment or loss of job (layoffs) was self-reported as well. All required demographic variables were under control. Regression analysis has shown that activity assessed in three time periods predicts unemployment during the past 12 months, and unemployment and layoffs during last 10 years. Significant correlations between temperament traits and unemployment during the last 12 months and the last 10 years were obtained when EAS traits measured in 1992, 1997, or 2001 were simultaneously entered into the regression model. The data show that low activity (and high negative emotionality) predict later unemployment over 9 years, irrespective of educational level and parental education. Low activity was associated with higher total unemployment during the last 10 years. The data were taken from a population-based sample in 2001 representing Finns of the age cohort 24 to 39 years. "It seams plausible that high activity employees are valued as they are likely to perform their tasks faster" (Hintsanen et al., 2009, p. 622). By the way, activity measured across 9 years has shown essential stability: Activity assessed in 1992 correlated significantly with measures taken in 1997 (.66) and in 2001 (.62).

Summary

Studies on trait activity in adults are not as spectacular as the ones conducted in children. Probably one of the reasons is the scarcity of instruments to measure activity in adults. However, the few examples mentioned in this section demonstrate that this temperament trait plays an important role as one of the many factors influencing adaptive behavior. It is also possible that motor activity does not play as important a role in adults as in children. However, in children, motor activity serves not solely to perform movements but as one of the methods used to explore surroundings, to approach relatives and friends or to avoid strangers, to satisfy curiosity, and so forth—a way of thinking that reminds us of Zuckerman's understanding of the General Activity factor. As underlined by Teglasi and coauthors (2009), activity in children serves, among other factors, to satisfy "preferences for activities that are low key versus exciting" (p. 506), and to increase or decrease the level of arousal expressed in reactivity[1] by seeking or avoiding certain types of stimuli. Such an interpretation of the construct *activity*, which, according to Teglasi (1998), refers to the regulatory component she identified as modulation of activity, serves as a kind of gateway to the understanding of activity as proposed by the regulative theory of temperament, which is less known in the West.

Activity as the Core Construct in the Regulative Theory of Temperament

The development of the regulative theory of temperament (RTT) has a long history (see Strelau, 1983, 1998, 2008), but in this chapter presenting studies devoted to trait activity mainly in adults and its role in human behavior, the data are limited to the last two decades. For a better understanding of the construct activity within the structure of temperament, the definition of this personality component is given below.

> Temperament refers to basic, relatively stable, personality traits expressed mainly in the formal (energetic and temporal) characteristics of reactions and behavior. These traits are present from early childhood and they have their counterpart in animals. Primarily determined by inborn biological mechanisms, temperament is subject to changes caused by maturation and individual–specific genotype–environment interplay. (Strelau, 1998, p. 165)

According to RTT the structure of temperament comprises six traits—briskness (BR), perseveration (PE), sensory sensitivity (SS), emotional reactivity (ER), endurance (EN), and activity (AC). BR and PE represent the temporal features of behavior, whereas the four remaining traits represent the energetic characteristics of behavior. In the RTT, *activity* is defined as "the tendency to undertake highly stimulating behaviors or behaviors providing intensive external (environmental) stimulation" (Strelau, 2008, p. 95). Individuals low in activity have a tendency to avoid behaviors or situations of high stimulative value. Activity in RTT plays a regulative function and goes beyond understanding of motor activity. It reminds us that the concept of activity as understood by the pioneers in psychometric studies on temperament—Heymans and Wiersma—and as noted by Rothbart (1989, p. 59), shows some similarities with self-regulation.

Temperament traits belonging to the energetic and temporal characteristics have different adaptive functions, although they are based on similar neurobiochemical mechanisms responsible for regulating the level of arousal. Individual differences in the reactivity of these mechanisms determine the tendency toward chronically elevated or suppressed level of arousal. Therefore the construct of arousability introduced by Gray (1964) is essential for RTT. Temperament traits, determined by the individual-specific level of arousability, are the principal moderator of the stimulating and temporal value of behaviors. Drawing on the concepts of augmentation–reduction of stimulation, we may say that individuals who have temperament traits typically associated with a high level of arousability have a stimulation-augmenting mechanism. As illustrated in Figure 5.1, stimulation (sensory, motor, emotional, cognitive) of a given (constant) intensity (S_C) leads to a higher level of arousal than that intensity of stimulation would imply (A_{C+X}). Individuals

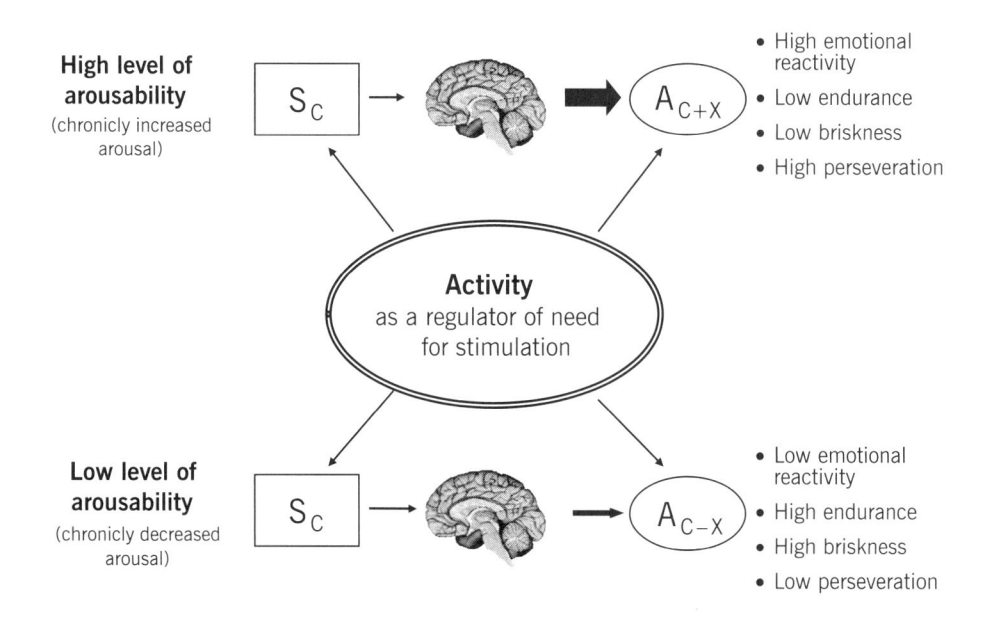

FIGURE 5.1. Activity as a regulator of stimulation need. S, stimulus; A, level of arousal; C, constant intensity; ± X, increased/decreased level of arousal.

who have temperament traits typically associated with a low level of arousability have a stimulation-reducing mechanism; stimulation of the same intensity leads to a lower level of arousal than that intensity of stimulation would imply (A_{C-X}). In the regulation of the level of arousal in such a way as to achieve or maintain the individual's optimal level of arousal, trait activity plays the most essential role.

Activity is related to other temperamental traits postulated by RTT, mostly to endurance and briskness (about .20), and emotional reactivity (around −.30). Among other relations, it means that the role of activity may itself be concerned, but first of all in configuration or interaction with other traits. As our studies have shown, the configuration of AC and ER plays a special role in adaptive behavior. Therefore, in presenting our data, we also take into account how emotional reactivity is understood as a "tendency to react intensively to emotion-generating stimuli, expressed in high emotional sensitivity and low emotional endurance" (Strelau, 2008, p. 95).

Strelau and Zawadzki (2008), summarizing studies on temperament, formulated 10 particular postulates characterizing temperamental traits. They refer to such issues as: assessment, cultural universality, genetic and environmental origin, the moderating role of reactions to stress, and pathogenesis of psychiatric and somatic illnesses. In this section we present some assessment issues (including the location among personality dimensions), studies on genetic and environmental factors, and the functional role of activity.

Assessment of Activity and of Activity in the Context of Demographic and Non-RTT Temperament/Personality Traits

According to RTT, *activity* is described as a temporally stable, homogenous trait, which is identified in all age and gender groups, as well as in different cultures, indicating its cultural universality.

Assessment

For measuring temperamental traits in adults and adolescents (age 14 or older), according to RTT, the FCB-TI was developed (Strelau & Zawadzki, 1993, 1995). It contains 120 items, keyed on "yes" or "no"; every trait is described by 20 items. In the construction sample (N = 2,023: 1,166 females/857 males, ages 15–80) the Activity scale demonstrated high internal consistency (Cronbach's alpha = .83), fully congruent with results obtained in a "normative" sample (N = 4,041: 2,123 females/1,918 males, ages 15–77, alpha = .84; Zawadzki & Strelau, 1997). Among other characteristics, temporal stability of activity was assessed in two groups of flood survivors (N = 267: 158 females/109 males, ages 14–75; N = 413: 210 females/203 males, ages 14–74) and one group of home-fire victims (N = 234: 128 females/106 males, ages 14–85), investigated 1 year after the first study—the correlations were .66, .67, and .68 (p < .01), respectively. In the first sample the third assessment was also done after 2 years, and correlation of .63 (p < .01) was obtained, which indicates rather high temporal stability of activity assessment. Finally, we should also mention that high consistency between self-report and averaged peer rating (two independent peers) was found (.62; p < .001) in a sample of 1,092 subjects (664 females/428 males, ages 17–64), indicating high "observability" of activity. For other countries a cross-cultural version of the FCB-TI inventory was developed (Zawadzki, Van de Vijver et al., 2001). The cross-cultural sample consisted of 3,723 subjects (including 2,295 females) from eight countries (Germany, Italy, The Netherlands, Poland, Russia, South Korea, Ukraine, and the United States), ages 14–85 years (Zawadzki, 2002). For the Activity scale, high congruence among items' factor loadings was obtained (mean of Tucker's phi = .985; range from .960 to .995), as well as reliability (mean of Cronbach's alphas = .78; differences of reliability coefficient among eight samples were not significant).

For measuring temperamental traits in older children (ages 6–13), according to RTT, the Temperament Inventory for Children (TIC) was developed by Oniszczenko and Radomska (2002). It contains 30 items, keyed on "yes" or "no," and five items in each of the six scales: Briskness, Perseveration, Sensory Sensitivity, Endurance, Emotional Reactivity, and Activity. In the Polish construction sample (N = 278: 157 females/132 males, ages 7–12) the Activity scale demonstrated sufficient internal consistency (Cronbach's alpha = .66), fully congruent with results obtained in the next study on flood survivors (N = 124: 65 females/59 males, ages 8–13; alpha = .66; Kaczmarek & Zawadzki, 2006). Test–retest reliability after two weeks in the construction sample was equal to .73 ($p < .05$) and after nine months, .72 ($p < .05$). Temporal stability was also assessed in one group of young flood survivors (N = 58: 34 females/24 males, ages 6–12), investigated 1 year after the first study; the correlation was .47 ($p < .05$). Finally, we should mention that TIC was developed in the form designed for parent rating; studies on flood survivors demonstrated rather high congruence between mother's and father's rating: .69 ($p < .05$; N = 124), .57 and .76 (N = 58), the first and second assessments, respectively. TIC was used only in Poland, mostly in behavior genetic and clinical studies (Kaczmarek & Zawadzki, 2006), and has no cross-cultural version.

Gender and Age

Intensity of activity, although common to all humans, differs for gender and age cohorts. In the two basic Polish samples (construction sample, N = 2,023; normative sample, N = 4,041), females demonstrated lower activity level than males, which was also confirmed in the cross-cultural study (N = 3,723). However, the significant differences were found only for adults and adolescents; in the case of children, the correlation of gender and activity was not significant. Activity also almost linearly decreases with age: The correlation was equal to $-.37$ ($p < .05$) and $-.35$ ($p < .05$, Polish construction and normative sample; Zawadzki & Strelau, 1997), and $-.20$ ($p < .05$, cross-cultural sample; Zawadzki, 2002). The result demonstrating that there is no difference in activity between boys and girls, which is contradictory to most data in which activity was measured as a trait referring to motor activity, may be explained by the fact that in the RTT, *activity*, as mentioned earlier, has a different meaning.

RTT Activity in the Context of Personality/Temperament Traits

Although defined differently than in other models, activity as documented in former studies (Strelau, 2008; Zawadzki & Strelau, 1997) has much in common with extraversion, Pavlovian strength of excitation and mobility of nervous processes, Zuckerman's sensation seeking, Windle and Lerner's general activity level, approach–withdrawal and mood quality, Buss and Plomin's sociability and activity, and Cloninger's harm avoidance (low pole), as well as novelty seeking. Figure 5.2 presents the correlations between the FCB-TI Activity scale and selected scales from the Pavlovian Temperament Survey (PTS; Strelau, Angleitner, & Newberry, 1999), EPQ-R, NEO Five-Factor Inventory (NEO-FFI), DOTS-R, EAS-TS, and the Temperament and Character Inventory (TCI; Cloninger, Przybeck, Svrakic, & Wetzel, 1994). These results were fully confirmed in other countries.

In the factor analysis rotated to the five factors, corresponding to the Big Five model, one of the factors came out as Activity saturated with the activity scales or scales sharing common variance with Activity from the aforementioned inventories—a result very similar to that obtained with preschoolers by De Pauw and coauthors (2009). A recent analysis (Zawadzki & Strelau, 2010) based on the temperament/personality inventories presented earlier demonstrated that Activity, together with Emotional Reactivity, are the two crucial dimensions contributing to the statistically generated construct known as general factor of personality (GFP).

Genes and Environment Contributing to Individual Differences in Activity

Based on the assumption of biological roots of activity, several behavior genetic studies were undertaken. The most extended studies were conducted within the Bielefeld–Warsaw Twin Project, in which the impact of genetic and environmental factors on several temperamental dimensions, including activity, was analyzed. The study comprised 1,555 pairs of German and Polish twins (1,049 MZ and 456 one-sex DZ twins reared together, ages 14–80 years) who completed the FCB-TI inventory in self-report format, and were assessed additionally by two independent peers (Oniszczenko et al., 2003; Zawadzki, Strelau, Oniszczenko, Riemann, & Angleitner, 2001). The analysis indicated that heritability of activity was .47 for self-report and .38 for averaged peer ratings. The remaining

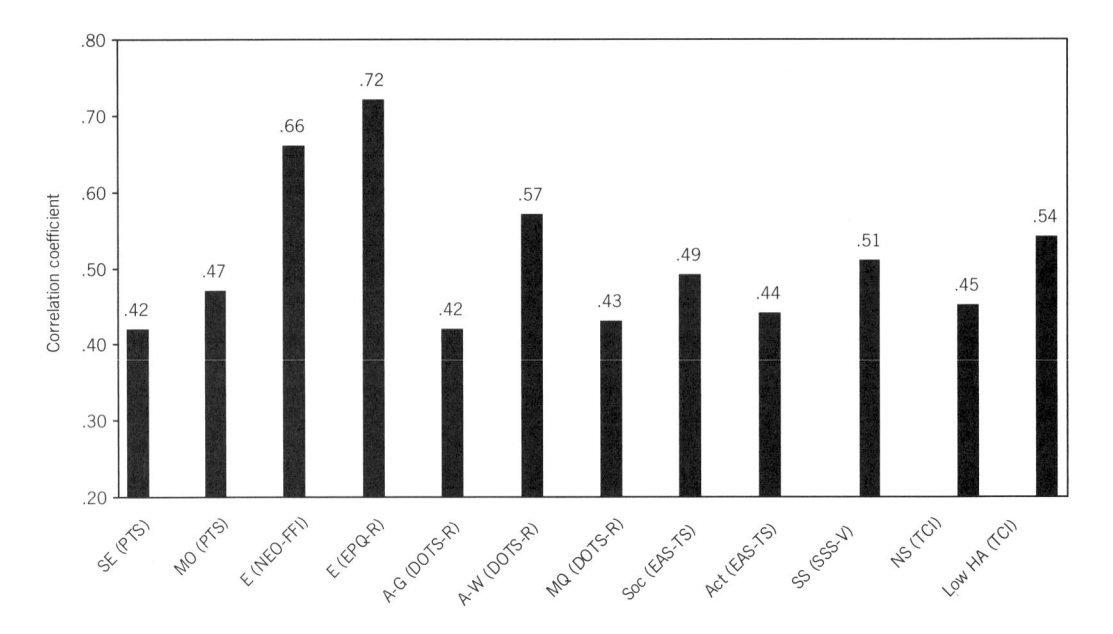

FIGURE 5.2. Correlation coefficients between activity and personality/temperament dimensions. Correlations with PTS, NEO-FFI, EPQ-R, DOTS-R, and EAS-TS were averaged across samples for self-report and peer rating: $N = 919$, 443 females/476 males, ages 16–77; $N = 1,092$, 664 females/428 males, ages 17–64; peers: $N = 2,184$, 1,282 females/ 716 males, lack information about gender for 186, ages 14–87, mostly family members or friends; SSS-V: $N = 534$: 324 females/210 males, ages 15–69 (Zawadzki & Strelau, 1997). TCI: $N = 382$, 245 females/137 males, ages 18–83 (Hornowska, 2003). SSS-V, Sensation Seeking Scale—Form V; SE, Strength of Excitation; MO, Mobility of Nervous Processes; E, Extraversion; A-G, Activity Level—General; A-W, Approach–Withdrawal; MQ, Mood Quality; Soc, Sociability; Act, Activity; HA, Harm Avoidance; NS, Novelty Seeking. Abbreviations are explained in the text.

53 and 62% of activity variance was attributed to nonshared environmental sources, with no significant differences between Polish and German samples. However, when a joint analysis of self-report and averaged peer ratings was conducted, the heritability score increased to .63 (Zawadzki, Strelau, et al., 2001). These findings indicate that heritability is higher when the valid variance of activity is being analyzed. Similar results were obtained in the Polish study of children, in which activity of 166 twins (60 MZ and 100 DZ, ages 6–11) was assessed by parent TIC ratings; the heritability estimate for activity was .45 (Oniszczenko, 2005). These results indicate the genetic roots of activity and at the same time underline the role of nonshared environmental factors. However, it is much more difficult to demonstrate the impact of particular environmental factors on activity.

Activity and Health

Although activity may play important role in academic and job surroundings, its role is especially evident when somatic and mental health are analyzed. RTT underlines that not only may activity by itself be an important predictor of health status, but also in interaction with other temperamental traits, mainly with emotional reactivity. High level of activity when associated with high emotional reactivity may be a risk factor for diseases. This idea was reflected in the concept of temperament risk factor (TRF), adapted from Carey (1986) to studies on adults in which TRF refers to "any temperament trait or configuration of traits, that in interaction with other factors acting excessively, persistently or recurrently . . . increases the risk of developing behavior disorders or pathology, or that favors the shaping of a maladjusted personality" (Strelau, 1998, p. 376).

Activity and Somatic Diseases

The hypothesis linking temperament and somatic diseases is probably the oldest one in the history of mankind. The correlations between emotional reactivity and activity regarded as TRFs and somatic diseases, such as Type A, Type 1 (cancer-prone), and Type 2 (coronary heart disease [CHD]–prone type of personality) as well as depressiveness, hostility, and submissiveness (Strelau & Zawadzki, 2005), and results of regression analysis are presented in Table 5.2.

Although high emotional reactivity is associated with all personality risk factors, as was shown in regression analyses, high activity level characterizes specific personality risk factors for CHD: Type A and hostility (but not Type 2). In opposition the specific personality risk factors for Type 1 cancer and submissiveness is characterized by low activity level. Low activity is also the main predictor of lung cancer (see note to Table 5.2). The interaction of both temperamental traits—activity and emotional reactivity—was found only in Type 1 cancer and depressiveness, which is a common risk factor for both diseases (Strelau & Zawadzki, 2005), showing that high emotional reactivity level associated with low activity enables prediction of Type 1 cancer and depressiveness.

Activity as Related to Mental and Personality Disorders

Similar results were found for mental and personality disorders, according to the Axis I and Axis II in DSM-IV. For assessment of

TABLE 5.2. Regression Analysis of Temperamental Traits: Activity and Emotional Reactivity as Predictors of Personality Risk Factors of Somatic Diseases

Dependent variables	Predictor	Zero-order correlation	Model $R(R^2)$	Semipartial correlation
Type A	Emotional reactivity	.01	.30* (.09)	.13#
	Activity	.27*		.30*
Type 1	Emotional reactivity	.32*	.42* (.18)	.21*
	Activity	−.34*		−.17*
	Interaction	—		−.14*
Type 2	Emotional reactivity	.25	.25* (.06)	.25*
	Activity	−.19*		X
Depressiveness	Emotional reactivity	.68*	.72* (.52)	.58*
	Activity	−.42*		−.24*
	Interaction	—		−.10*
Hostility	Emotional reactivity	.46*	.47* (.23)	.48*
	Activity	−.01		.14*
Submissiveness	Emotional reactivity	.18*	.24* (.06)	.12*
	Activity	−.21*		−.16*

Note. R, multiple correlation; R^2, variance explained by the model; X, variable not introduced to the final model of regression; —, zero-order correlations were not calculated for interactions; Type A and Type 1 and 2, Type A Inventory and Short Interpersonal Reactions Inventory: N = 200, 99 females/101 males, ages 20–25; Depressiveness, Hostility, Submissiveness, Inventory of Personality Patterns and health status: N = 366, 148 females/218 males, ages 27–77, 135 healthy subjects, 135 patients with lung cancer and 96 patients with CHD. The eta correlation with health status (patients with lung cancer or CHD vs. healthy subjects) was equal to .10 for emotional reactivity, −.14* for activity in the case of patients with lung cancer and healthy subjects, .18* for emotional reactivity, and −.07 for activity in the case of patients with CHD and healthy subjects (sign of the correlation was added after analysis of direction of difference in FCB-TI scores between groups).
*$p < .05$; #$p < .10$.

disorders in a sample of 227 subjects (143 females/84 males, ages 20–80) the Polish version of the Test for Axial Evaluation and Interview Applications (TALEIA-400A) was used (Boncori, 2007). It contains eight scales that refer to mental disorders (Axis I) and 10 to personality disorders (Axis II) (Strelau & Zawadzki, 2011). The correlations and results of the regression analysis are presented in Table 5.3.

The high level of emotional reactivity and low activity level was found for almost all mental disorders (except mania), in congruence with findings of a meta-analysis for Extraversion and Neuroticism within the Big Five model (Malouff, Thorsteinsson, & Schutte, 2005). The regression analysis shows that low activity is associated with depression, phobias, and eating disorders, and high activity level, with manic tendencies. Interactions between both temperamental traits are significant for depression, acute anxiety, phobias, and generalized anxiety disorder (GAD)—all indicating that high emotional reactivity level associated with low activity predicts mental disorders.

The role of activity is more evident in the case of personality disorders: The results are fully congruent with findings of a meta-analysis for extraversion (Saulsman & Page, 2004); what is not surprising is the high correlation between both temperamental dimensions (see bottom part of Table 5.3).

The lowest activity level was found for avoidant, schizoid, and schizotypal disorders, but the highest was for histrionic and narcissistic personality disorders. With some exceptions, high emotional reactivity and low activity level characterize personality disorders from Clusters A and C (paranoid, schizoid, schizotypal avoidant, and dependent disorders; except for obsessive–compulsive disorder, which was not significantly related to both temperamental traits), while high emotional reactivity and high activity characterize personality disorders from Cluster B (antisocial, borderline, histrionic and narcissistic). No interaction of temperamental traits was found for personality disorders.

The results indicate that although low activity in general characterizes most of the pathological tendencies, its role depends on emotional reactivity. In line with the TRF concept, the configuration or interaction of high emotional reactivity with low–high activity level seems to be a risk factor for several mental or somatic diseases.

Summary

The central place of activity among temperamental traits is especially underlined by RTT. The presented results indicate that activity also fulfills criteria for basic personality dimensions—it is demographically and culturally universal, highly inherited, and demonstrates high adaptative value. Activity may be one of the best indicators of mental and somatic health; however, according to RTT, its functional significance is especially evident when it is analyzed in configuration with other temperamental traits, especially with emotional reactivity.

Final Remarks

Activity as a temperament trait in humans and animals may be observed from the first stages of life. It is expressed in neonates' motor activity and may be measured objectively and by means of inventories. However, when both methods are compared, the estimation of activity may essentially differ. This is due to the differences in methods by means of which this trait has been assessed (see Saudino, 2009), as well as distinctions in the understanding of the construct *activity*. In developmental-oriented research—since the pioneering studies by Thomas and Chess—activity has been regarded as one of the most essential temperament traits, and dozens of instruments allow us to assess this trait from a lifespan perspective and under a variety of conditions.

Whereas there is more or less agreement about understanding of the construct *activity* among developmental researchers, who refer almost without exception to motor activity or to general activity expressed in motor behavior, this term—from the very beginning in temperament studies on adults—has different meanings. Researchers with a developmental background who conduct studies on adult temperament concentrate on motor activity mostly expressed in energy expenditure. Some adult-oriented researchers consider the trait activity as a component of a broader dimension—mostly extraversion, as exemplified in the Giant Three or

TABLE 5.3. Regression Analysis of Temperamental Traits: Activity and Emotional Reactivity as Predictors of Mental and Personality Disorders

	Predictor	Zero-order correlation	Model R(R²)	Semipartial correlation
	TALEIA scales assessing mental disorders			
Schizophrenia	Emotional reactivity	.31*	.31* (.10)	.31*
	Activity	−.03		X
Depression and dysthymia	Emotional reactivity	.65*	.67* (.45)	.55*
	Activity	.38*		−.17*
	Interaction	X		−.09#
Mania and hypomania	Emotional reactivity	−.17*	.49* (.24)	X
	Activity	.49*		.49*
Acute anxiety–panic attacks	Emotional reactivity	.52*	.54* (.29)	.50*
	Activity	−.12#		.06
	Interaction	X		−.12*
Phobias	Emotional reactivity	.58*	.64* (.41)	.45*
	Activity	−.44*		−.26*
	Interaction	X		−.10#
Generalized anxiety disorder	Emotional reactivity	.60*	.61* (.37)	.57*
	Activity	−.17*		.03
	Interaction	X		−.09#
Obsessive–compulsive disorder	Emotional reactivity	.42*	.42* (.18)	.42*
	Activity	−.05		X
Eating disorders	Emotional reactivity	.53*	.57* (.33)	.42*
	Activity	.39*		−.22*
	TALEIA scales assessing personality disorders			
Paranoid	Emotional reactivity	.36*	.37* (.13)	.37*
	Activity	−.07		X
Schizoid	Emotional reactivity	.16*	.32* (.11)	X
	Activity	−.32*		−.32*
Schizotypal	Emotional reactivity	.48*	.49* (.24)	.41*
	Activity	−.27*		−.11#
Antisocial	Emotional reactivity	.24*	.34* (.11)	.31*
	Activity	.13*		.23*
Borderline	Emotional reactivity	.27	.35* (.12)	.33*
	Activity	.12#		.23*
Histrionic	Emotional reactivity	.02	.46* (.21)	.17*
	Activity	.42*		.46*

(cont.)

TABLE 5.3. *(cont.)*

	Predictor	Zero-order correlation	Model $R(R^2)$	Semipartial correlation
Narcissistic	Emotional reactivity	–.11	.41 (.17)	X
	Activity	.41*		.41*
Avoidant	Emotional reactivity	.58*	.68* (.47)	.42*
	Activity	–.54*		–.36*
Dependent	Emotional reactivity	.39*	.39* (.15)	.39*
	Activity	–.16*		X
Obsessive–compulsive	Emotional reactivity	.07	X	X
	Activity	–.07		X

Note. Mental and personality disorders were assessed by the TALEIA-400A (Boncori, 2007). R, multiple correlation; R^2, variance explained by the model; X, variable not introduced to the final model of regression or the multiple correlation was not significant.
*$p < .05$; #$p < .10$.

the Big Five traditions. Other researchers centered on adults ascribe to the term *activity* a broader meaning, mostly related to stimulation seeking/avoiding not necessarily expressed only in motor behavior. Such an understanding of trait activity has a 100-year tradition—since the pioneering studies on temperament by Heymans and Wiersma.

Whatever the understanding of activity as a temperament trait, studies have demonstrated the functional significance of activity, and this is especially evident in studies on children. The adaptive role of children's level of activity comes out in behavior or behavior disorders, whether activity is present as an independent variable alone or in combination with other traits, or when the status of a moderator or predictor has been given to this trait. Studies on adults have also demonstrated the significance of activity as a personal variable playing an essential role in adaptive behavior, although the evidence is not as rich when compared to research on children. The functional role of activity in adults differs depending on what meaning researchers ascribe to the term *activity*, as demonstrated by data collected within the RTT.

Note

1. Reactivity regarded as a temperamental trait was introduced by Strelau (1974) in the early 1970s and understood in a similar way as incorporated a decade later to the developmental model of temperament by Rothbart (Rothbart & Derryberry, 1981).

Further Reading

Bates, J. E., & Wachs, T. D. (Eds.). (2002). *Temperament: Individual differences at the interface of biology and behavior.* Washington, DC: American Psychological Association.

Graziano, W. G., Jensen-Campbell, L. A., & Sullivan-Logan, G. M. (1998). Temperament, activity, and expectations for later personality development. *Journal of Personality and Social Psychology, 74,* 1266–1277.

Strelau, J. (1998). *Temperament: A psychological perspective.* New York: Plenum Press.

Teglasi, H., French, M., Lohr, L., Miller, K. J., Erwin, H. D., Rothman, L., et al. (2009). Dimensions of temperamental activity level and adjustment. *Journal of Applied Developmental Psychology, 30,* 505–514.

References

Achenbach, T. M., & Edelbrock, C. S. (1981). Behavioral problems and competencies reported by parents of normal and disturbed children aged four through sixteen. *Monographs of the Society for Research in Child Development, 46* (No. 188).

Aluja, A., Kuhlman, M., & Zuckerman, M. (2010). Development of the Zuckerman–Kuhlman–Aluja Personality Questionnaire (ZKA-PQ): A factor/

facet version of the Zuckerman–Kuhlman Personality Questionnaire (ZKPQ). *Journal of Personality Assessment, 92*, 416–431.

Bohlin, G., Hagekull, B., & Lindhagen, K. (1981). Dimensions of infant behavior. *Infant Behavior and Development, 4*, 83–96.

Boncori, L. (2007). *TALEIA-400A: Test for Axial Evaluation and Interview for clinical, personnel, and guidance Applications—manual.* Trento, Italy: Erickson.

Brody, G. H., Stoneman, Z., & Burke, M. (1988). Child temperament and parental perceptions of individual child adjustment: An intrafamilial analysis. *American Journal of Orthopsychiatry, 58*, 532–542.

Buss, A. H., & Plomin, R. (1975). *A temperament theory of personality development.* New York: Wiley.

Buss, A. H., & Plomin, R. (1984). *Temperament: Early developing personality traits.* Hillsdale, NJ: Erlbaum.

Carey, W. B. (1986). The difficult child. *Pediatrics in Review, 8*, 39–45.

Carey, W. B., & McDevitt, S. C. (1978). Revision of the Infant Temperament Questionnaire. *Pediatrics, 61*, 735–739.

Cloninger, C. R., Przybeck, T. R., Svrakic, D. M., & Wetzel, R. D.(1994). *The Temperament and Character Inventory (TCI): A guide to its development and use.* St. Louis, MO: Center for Psychobiology of Personality.

Costa, P. T., Jr., & McCrae, R. R. (1992). *Revised NEO Personality Inventory (NEO-PI-R) and NEO Five Factor Inventory (NEO-FFI): Professional manual.* Odessa FL: Psychological Assessment Resources.

Costa, P. T., Jr., & McCrae, R. R. (2001). A theoretical context for adult temperament. In T. D. Wachs & G. A. Kohnstamm (Eds.), *Temperament in context* (pp. 1–21). Mahwah, NJ: Erlbaum.

De Pauw, S. S. W., Mervielde, I., & Van Leeuwen, K. G. (2009). How are traits related to problem behavior in preschoolers?: Similarities and contrasts between temperament and personality. *Journal of Abnormal Child Psychology, 37*, 309–325.

Eaton, W. O. (1983). Measuring activity level with actometers: Reliability, validity, and arm length. *Child Development, 54*, 720–726.

Eaton, W. O., & Enns, L. R. (1986). Sex differences in human motor activity level. *Psychological Bulletin, 100*, 19–28.

Eaton, W. O., McKeen, N. A., & Saudino, K. J. (1996). Measuring human individual differences in general motor activity with actometers. In K.-P. Ossenkopp, M. Kavaliers, & P. R. Sanrates (Eds.), *Measuring movement and locomotion: From invertebrates to humans* (pp. 79–92). New York: Springer.

Eaton, W. O., & Saudino, K. J. (1992). Prenatal activity level as a temperament dimension?: Individual differences and developmental functions in fetal movement. *Infant Behavior and Development, 15*, 57–70.

Else-Quest, N. M., Hyde, J. S., Goldsmith, H. H., & Van Hulle, C. A. (2006). Gender differences in temperament: A meta-analysis. *Psychological Bulletin, 132*, 33–72.

Eysenck, H. J., & Eysenck, M. W. (1985). *Personality and individual differences: A natural science approach.* New York: Plenum Press.

Eysenck, S. B. G., Eysenck, H. J., & Barrett, P. (1985). A revised version of the Psychoticism scale. *Personality and Individual Differences, 6*, 21–29.

Foley, M., McClowry, S. G., & Castellanos, F. X. (2008). The relationship between attention deficit hyperactivity disorder and child temperament. *Journal of Applied Developmental Psychology, 29*, 157–169.

Fullard, W., McDevitt, S. C., & Carey, W. B. (1984). Assessing temperament in one-to-three-year-old children. *Journal of Pediatric Psychology, 9*, 205–216.

Gagne, J. R., Vendlinski, M. K., & Goldsmith, H. H. (2009). The genetics of childhood temperament. In Y.-K. Kim (Ed.), *Handbook of behavioral genetics* (pp. 251–267). New York: Springer.

Gartstein, M. A., & Marmion, J. (2008). Fear and positive affectivity in infancy: Convergence/discrepancy between parent-report and laboratory-based indicators. *Infant Behavior and Development, 31*, 227–238.

Gartstein, M. A., & Rothbart, M. K. (2003). Studying infant temperament via the Revised Infant Behavior Questionnaire. *Infant Behavior Development, 26*, 64–86.

Goldsmith, H. H. (1983). Genetic influences on personality from infancy. *Child Development, 54*, 331–355.

Goldsmith, H. H. (1996). Studying temperament via construction of the Toddler Behavior Assessment Questionnaire. *Child Development, 67*, 218–235.

Goldsmith, H. H., Buss, K. A., & Lemery, K. S. (1997). Toddler and childhood temperament: Expanded content, stronger genetic evidence, new evidence for the importance of environment. *Developmental Psychology, 33*, 891–905.

Goldsmith, H. H., & Campos, J. J. (1982). Toward a theory of infant temperament. In R. N. Emde & R. J. Harmon (Eds.), *The development of attachment and affiliative systems* (pp. 161–193). New York: Plenum Press.

Goldsmith, H. H., & Campos, J. J. (1990). The structure of temperamental fear and pleasure in infants: A psychometric perspective. *Child Development, 61*, 1944–1964.

Goldsmith, H. H., & Rothbart, M. K. (1996). *Prelocomotor and locomotor Laboratory Temperament Assessment Battery (Lab-TAB; version 3.0, Technical manual)*. Madison: University of Wisconsin, Department of Psychology.

Gonzalez, C., Gartstein, M. A., Carranza, J. A., & Rothbart, M. K. (2003). *Temperament laboratory assessment: Procedures parallel to the Infant Behavior Questionnaire—Revised*. Department of Psychology. Pullman: Washington State University.

Gray, J. A. (1964). Strength of the nervous system and levels of arousal: A reinterpretation. In J. A. Gray (Ed.), *Pavlov's typology* (pp. 289–364). Oxford, UK: Pergamon Press.

Guilford, J. P., & Zimmerman, W. S. (1949). *Manual of instructions and interpretations: The Guilford–Zimmerman Temperament Survey*. Beverly Hills, CA: Sheridan Supply Co.

Guilford, J. S., Zimmerman, W. S., & Guilford, J. P. (1976). *The Guilford–Zimmerman Temperament Survey handbook: Twenty-five years of research and application*. San Diego, CA: EdITS.

Hegvik, R., McDevitt, S. C., & Carey, W. (1982). The Middle Childhood Temperament Questionnaire. *Developmental and Behavioral Pediatrics, 3*, 197–200.

Heymans, G. (1908). Über einige psychische Korrelationen [About some psychological correlations]. *Zeitschrift für Angewandte Psychologie, 1*, 313–381.

Hintsanen, M., Lipsanen, J., Pulkki-Raback, L., Kivimäki, M., Hintsa, T., & Keltikangas-Järvinen, L. (2009). EAS temperaments as predictors of unemployment in young adults: A 9-year follow-up of the Cardiovascular Risk in Young Finns Study. *Journal of Research in Personality, 43*, 618–623.

Hornowska, E. (2003). *Temperamentalne uwarunkowania zachowania. Badania z wykorzystaniem kwestionariusza TCI R. C. Cloningera* [Temperamental influences on behavior. Studies with TCI R. C. Cloninger's inventory]. Poznań, Poland: Bogucki Wydawnictwo Naukowe.

Joyce, D. (2010). *Essentials of temperament assessment*. Hoboken, NJ: Wiley.

Kaczmarek, M., & Zawadzki, B. (2006). Temperamental and environmental determinants of the intensity of PTSD symptoms in children two years after a flood. In J. Strelau & T. Klonowicz (Eds.), *People under extreme stress* (pp. 49–66). New York: Nova Science.

Li, I., Onaga, E., Shen, P.-S., & Chiou, H.-H. (2009). Temperament Characteristics and Science Achievement: A longitudinal study of elementary students in Taiwan. *International Journal of Science Education, 31*, 1175–1185.

Loehlin, J. C. (1992). *Genes and environment in personality development*. Newbury Park, CA: Sage.

Malouff, J. M., Thorsteinsson, E. B., & Schutte, N. S. (2005). The relationship between the five-factor model of personality and symptoms of clinical disorders: A meta-analysis. *Journal of Psychopathology and Behavioral Assessment, 27*, 101–114.

Martin, R. P. (1988a). Child temperament and educational outcomes. In A. D. Pellegrini (Ed.), *Psychological bases for early education* (pp. 185–205). Chichester, UK: Wiley.

Martin, R. P. (1988b). *The Temperament Assessment Battery for Children: Manual*. Brandon, VT: Clinical Psychology Press.

Martin, R. P. (1989). Activity level, distractibility, and persistence: Critical characteristics in early schooling. In G. A. Kohnstamm, J. E. Bates, & M. K. Rothbart (Eds.), *Temperament in childhood* (pp. 451–461). New York: Wiley.

Martin, R. P., & Bridger, R. (1999). *The Temperament Assessment Battery for Children—Revised*. Athens: University of Georgia.

Martin, R. P., Drew, D., Gaddis, L., & Moseley, M. (1988). Prediction of elementary school achievement from preschool temperament: Three studies. *School Psychology Review, 17*, 125–137.

Martin, R. P., Olejnik, S., & Gaddis, L. (1994). Is temperament an important contributor to schooling outcomes in elementary school?: Modeling effects of temperament and scholastic ability on academic achievement. In W. B. Carey & S. C. McDevitt (Eds.), *Prevention and early intervention: Individual differences as risk factors for the mental health of children* (pp. 59–68). New York: Brunner/Mazel.

Maziade, M., Boutin, P., Cote, R., & Thivierge, J. (1986). Empirical characteristics of the NYLS temperament in middle childhood: Congruities and incongruities with other studies. *Child Psychiatry and Human Development, 17*, 38–52.

Maziade, M., Caron, C., Cote, R., Boutin, P., & Thivierge, J. (1990). Extreme temperament and diagnosis. *Archives of General Psychiatry, 47*, 447–484.

McClowry, S. G. (1995). The development of the School-Age Temperament Inventory. *Merrill–Palmer Quarterly, 41*, 271–285.

McDevitt, S. C., & Carey, W. B. (1978). The measurement of temperament in 3–7 year old children. *Journal of Child Psychology and Psychiatry and Allied Disciplines, 19*, 245–253.

McIntosh, D. E., & Cole-Love, A. S. (1996). Profile comparisons between ADHD and non-ADHD children on the temperament assessment battery for children. *Journal of Psychoeducational Assessment, 14*, 362–372.

Medoff-Cooper, B., Carey, W. B., & McDevitt, S. C. (1993). The Early Infancy Temperament Questionnaire. *Journal of Developmental and Behavioral Pediatrics, 14*, 230–235.

Mervielde, I., & De Fruyt, F. (2002). Assessing

children's traits with the hierarchical personality inventory for children. In B. De Raad & M. Perugini (Eds.), *Big Five assessment* (pp. 129–146). Seattle, WA: Hogrefe & Huber.

Oniszczenko, W. (2005). *Genetyczne podstawy ludzkich zachowań. Przegląd badań w populacji polskiej* [Genetic foundations of human behavior: An overview of studies in Polish samples]. Gdańsk: Gdańskie Wydawnictwo Psychologiczne.

Oniszczenko, W., & Radomska, A. (2002). Kwestionariusz Temperamentu dla Dzieci (KTD) oparty na Regulacyjnej Teorii Temperamentu—wersja eksperymentalna [Temperament Inventory for Children based on the Regulative Theory of Temperament—experimental version]. *Psychologia–Etologia–Genetyka, 5*, 85–98.

Oniszczenko, W., Zawadzki, B., Strelau, J., Riemann, R., Angleitner, A., & Spinath, F. M. (2003). Genetic and environmental determinants of temperament: A comparative study based on Polish and German samples. *European Journal of Personality, 17*, 207–220.

Putnam, S. P., & Rothbart, M. K. (2006). Development of short and very short forms of the Children's Behavior Questionnaire. *Journal of Personality Assessment, 81*, 102–112.

Reynolds, C. R., & Kamphaus, R. W. (1992). *Behavior Assessment System for Children*. Circle Pines: MN: American Guidance Service.

Rothbart, M. K. (1981). Measurement of temperament in infancy. *Child Development, 52*, 569–578.

Rothbart, M. K. (1989). Temperament in childhood: A framework. In G. A. Kohnstamm, J. E. Bates, & M. K. Rothbart (Eds.), *Temperament in childhood* (pp. 59–73). Chichester, UK: Wiley.

Rothbart, M. K., & Ahadi, S. A. (1994). Temperament and the development of personality. *Journal of Abnormal Psychology, 103*, 55–66.

Rothbart, M. K., Ahadi, S. A., Hershey, K. L., & Fisher, P. (2001). Investigations of temperament at three to seven years: The Children's Behavior Questionnaire. *Child Development, 72*, 1394–1408.

Rothbart, M. K., & Derryberry, D. (1981). Development of individual differences in temperament. In M. E. Lamb & A. L. Brown (Eds.), *Advances in developmental psychology* (Vol. 1, pp. 37–86). Hillsdale, NJ: Erlbaum.

Rothbart, M. K., & Posner, M. I. (1985). Temperament and the development of self-regulation. In L. C. Hartlage & C. F. Telzrow (Eds.), *The neuropsychology of individual differences: A developmental perspective* (pp. 93–123). New York: Plenum Press.

Rowe, D. C., & Plomin, R. (1977). Temperament in early childhood. *Journal of Personality Assessment, 41*, 150–156.

Sanson, A., Prior, M., Garino, E., Oberklaid, F., & Sewell, J. (1987). The structure of infant temperament. Factor analysis of the Revised Infant Temperament Questionnaire. *Infant Behavior and Development, 10*, 97–104.

Saudino, K. J. (2009). Do different measures tap the same genetic influences?: A multi-method study of activity level in young twins. *Developmental Science, 12*, 626–633.

Saudino, K. J., & Zapfe, J. A. (2008). Genetic influences on activity level in early childhood: Do situations matter? *Child Development, 79*, 930–943.

Saulsman, L. M., & Page, A. C. (2004). The five-factor model and personality disorder empirical literature: A meta-analytic review. *Clinical Psychology Review, 23*, 1055–1085.

Schaughency, E. A., & Fagot, B. I. (1993). The prediction of adjustment at age 7 from activity at age 5. *Journal of Abnormal Child Psychology, 21*, 29–50.

Spinath, F. M., Wolf, H., Angleitner, A., Borkenau, P., & Riemann, R. (2002). Genetic and environmental influences on objectively assessed activity in adults. *Personality and Individual Differences, 33*, 633–645.

Strelau, J. (1974). Temperament as an expression of energy level and temporal features of behavior. *Polish Psychological Bulletin, 5*, 119–127.

Strelau, J. (1983). *Temperament, personality, activity*. London: Academic Press.

Strelau, J. (1998). *Temperament: A psychological perspective*. New York: Plenum Press.

Strelau, J. (2008). *Temperament as a regulator of behavior: After fifty years of research*. Clinton Corners, NY: Eliot Werner.

Strelau, J., Angleitner, A., & Newberry, B. H. (1999). *The Pavlovian Temperament Survey (PTS): An international handbook*. Göttingen, Germany: Hogrefe & Huber.

Strelau, J., & Zawadzki, B. (1993). The Formal Characteristics of Behaviour—Temperament Inventory (FCB-TI): Theoretical assumptions and scale construction. *European Journal of Personality, 7*, 313–336.

Strelau, J., & Zawadzki, B. (1995). The Formal Characteristics of Behavior—Temperament Inventory (FCB-TI): Validity studies. *European Journal of Personality, 9*, 207–229.

Strelau, J., & Zawadzki, B. (2005). The functional significance of temperament empirically tested: Data based on hypotheses derived from the regulative theory of temperament. In A. Eliasz, S. Hampson, & B. De Raad (Eds.), *Advances in personality psychology* (Vol. 2, pp. 19–46). Hove, UK: Psychology Press.

Strelau, J., & Zawadzki, B. (2008). Temperament from a psychometric perspective: Theory and measurement. In G. J. Boyle, G. Matthews, & D. H. Saklofske (Eds.), *Handbook of personality theory and assessment: Personality measure-*

ment and assessment (Vol. 2, pp. 347–368). Los Angeles: Sage.

Strelau, J., & Zawadzki, B. (2011). Fearfulness and anxiety in research on temperament: Temperamental traits are related to anxiety disorders. *Personality and Individual Differences, 50*, 907–915.

Tarter, R. E. (1988). Are there inherited behavioral traits that predispose to substance abuse? *Journal of Consulting and Clinical Psychology, 56*, 189–196.

Teglasi, H. (1998). Temperament constructs and measures. *School Psychology Review, 27*, 564–585.

Teglasi, H., French, M., Lohr, L., Miller, K. J., Erwin, H. D., Rothman, L., et al. (2009). Dimensions of temperamental activity level and adjustment. *Journal of Applied Developmental Psychology, 30*, 505–514.

Thomas, A., & Chess, S. (1977). *Temperament and development*. New York: Brunner/Mazel.

Thomas, A., Mittelman, M., Chess, S., Korn, S. J., & Cohen, J. (1982). A temperament questionnaire for early adult life. *Educational and Psychological Measurement, 42*, 593–600.

Thurstone, L. L. (1951). The dimensions of temperament. *Psychometrica, 16*, 11–20.

Thurstone, L. L. (1953). *Examiner manual for the Thurstone Temperament Schedule* (2nd ed.). Chicago: Science Research Associates.

White, J. D. (1999). Personality, temperament, and ADHD: A review of the literature. *Personality and Individual Differences, 27*, 589–598.

Wills, T. A., DuHamel, K., & Vaccaro, D. (1995). Activity and mood temperament as predictors of adolescent substance use: Test of a self-regulation mediational model. *Journal of Personality and Social Psychology, 68*, 901–916.

Windle, M., & Lerner, R. M. (1986). Reassessing the dimensions of temperamental individuality across the life-span: The Revised Dimensions of Temperament Survey (DOTS-R). *Journal of Adolescent Research, 1*, 213–230.

Wood, A. C., Saudino, K. J., Rogers, H., Asherson, P., & Kuntsi, J. (2007). Genetic influences on mechanically-assessed activity level in children. *Journal of Child Psychology and Psychiatry, 48*, 695–702.

Wundt, W. (1887). *Grundzüge der physiologischen Psychologie* [Outlines of physiological psychology] (3rd ed., Vol. 2). Leipzig, Germany: Verlag von Wilhelm Engelmann.

Zawadzki, B. (2002). *Temperament—geny i środowisko. Porównania wewnątrz- i międzypopulacyjne* [Temperament—genes and environment: Intra- and cross-populations comparisons]. Gdańsk, Poland: Gdańskie Wydawnictwo Psychologiczne.

Zawadzki B., & Strelau J. (1997). *Formalna Charakterystyka Zachowania—Kwestionariusz Temperamentu (FCZ-KT). Podręcznik* [Formal Characteristics of Behaviour—Temperament Inventory (FCB-TI): Manual]. Warszawa, Poland: Pracownia Testów Psychologicznych PTP.

Zawadzki, B., & Strelau, J. (2010). Structure of personality: Search for a general factor viewed from a temperament perspective. *Personality and Individual Differences, 49*, 77–82.

Zawadzki, B., Strelau, J., Oniszczenko, W., Riemann, R., & Angleitner, A. (2001). Genetic and environmental influences on temperament: The Polish–German twin study, based on self-report and peer-rating. *European Psychologist, 6*, 272–286.

Zawadzki, B., Van de Vijver, F. J. R., Angleitner, A., De Pascalis, V., Newberry, B., Clark, W., et al. (2001). The comparison of two basic approaches of cross-cultural assessment of Strelau's temperament dimensions in eight countries. *Polish Psychological Bulletin, 33*, 133–141.

Zentner, M., & Bates, J. E. (2008). Child temperament: An integrative review of concepts, research programs, and measures. *European Journal of Developmental Science, 2*, 7–37.

Zuckerman, M. (1994). *Behavioral expressions and biosocial bases of sensation seeking*. New York: Cambridge University Press.

Zuckerman, M. (2002). Zuckerman–Kuhlman Personality Questionnaire (ZKPQ): An alternative five-factorial model. In B. De Raad & M. Perugini (Eds.), *Big Five assessment* (pp. 377–396). Göttingen, Germany: Hogrefe & Huber.

CHAPTER 6

Positive Emotionality

Samuel P. Putnam

Until recently, psychology as a discipline had largely disregarded positive emotions (Cohn & Fredrickson, 2009), and the temperament subfield is no exception. Although the pioneering analyses of Thomas and Chess (1977) identified mood as a salient aspect of temperament, their dimensional rubric emphasized negativity, and their three categories (difficult, slow-to-warm, easy) largely described patterns of adaptability rather than displays of positive affect. Similarly, Buss and Plomin's (1984) emotionality dimension considered behaviors such as crying but not expressions of pleasure.

Other early research took positivity into account, but only as a corollary to negativity. For instance, measures based in the Thomas and Chess tradition (e.g., Fullard, McDevitt, & Carey, 1984) included mood scales containing both positive and negative emotions. Kagan included lack of positive affect as a marker of behavioral inhibition in some assessments (e.g., Kagan, Reznick, Snidman, Gibbons, & Johnson, 1988; also see Kagan, Chapter 4, this volume), but the mechanisms under investigation were those associated with restraint, rather than positive emotions themselves. In developing a measure of difficultness, Bates, Freeland, and Lounsbury (1979) focused only implicitly on positivity, discerning a "Dull" dimension defined by low levels of smiling and excitement during play.

There are, however, exceptions to this early relative disregard of temperamental positive affect. Rothbart (1981) included a Smiling and Laughter scale on the Infant Behavior Questionnaire, which has been combined with scales indexing vocalizations and activity level to form a higher-order positive reactivity factor (Rothbart, 1986). Goldsmith and Campos (1990) and Belsky, Hsieh, and Crnic (1996) demonstrated relative independence of temperamental pleasure and negative emotionality in laboratory and parent-report data. Calkins, Fox, and Marshall (1996) also coded positive affect, assigning the label of "exuberant" to babies demonstrating elevated positivity and activity in response to novel stimuli.

Building on the promise of these early efforts, the new millennium has seen an exponential increase in temperament studies focusing explicitly on positive affect. These studies have yielded insight into the place of positive affect in hierarchical models of temperament and have been interpreted within models of neural activity. Furthermore, recent theory and research have increased understanding of the role of positive emotionality in a variety of developmental outcomes. Figure 6.1 provides a graphic summary of the biological mechanisms, temperamental correlates, and outcomes that have been associated with positive affectivity to date. Because temperament scholars have only recently begun to focus on positive emotionality, substantial questions and potential directions for investigation remain.

Temperamental Correlates of Positive Affectivity

Broad Approach-Based Constructs Involving Positivity

The structural model identified by Watson and Tellegen (1985) has strongly influenced thinking with regard to temperament and provides a valuable starting point for a discussion of positive emotionality. Earlier factor analyses of mood words and facial expressions had described mood in terms of two orthogonal dimensions of "Pleasantness–Unpleasantness" (anchored by terms such as *happy* and *content*, as opposed to *sad* and *lonely*) and "Engagement–Disengagement" (with terms such as *aroused* and *astonished* vs. *quiet* and *still*). Analyses of data from several studies (Watson & Tellegen, 1985), however, consistently identified dimensions representing a 45-degree shift of this structure; that is, one dimension, labeled "Positive Affect," included mood terms referring to pleasant engagement, such as *enthusiastic* and *excited* at the high end, and *drowsy* and *dull* at the low end; a second dimension, "Negative Affect," involved terms such as *distressed* and *fearful* at one end, and *calm* and *relaxed* at the other. Tellegen (1985)

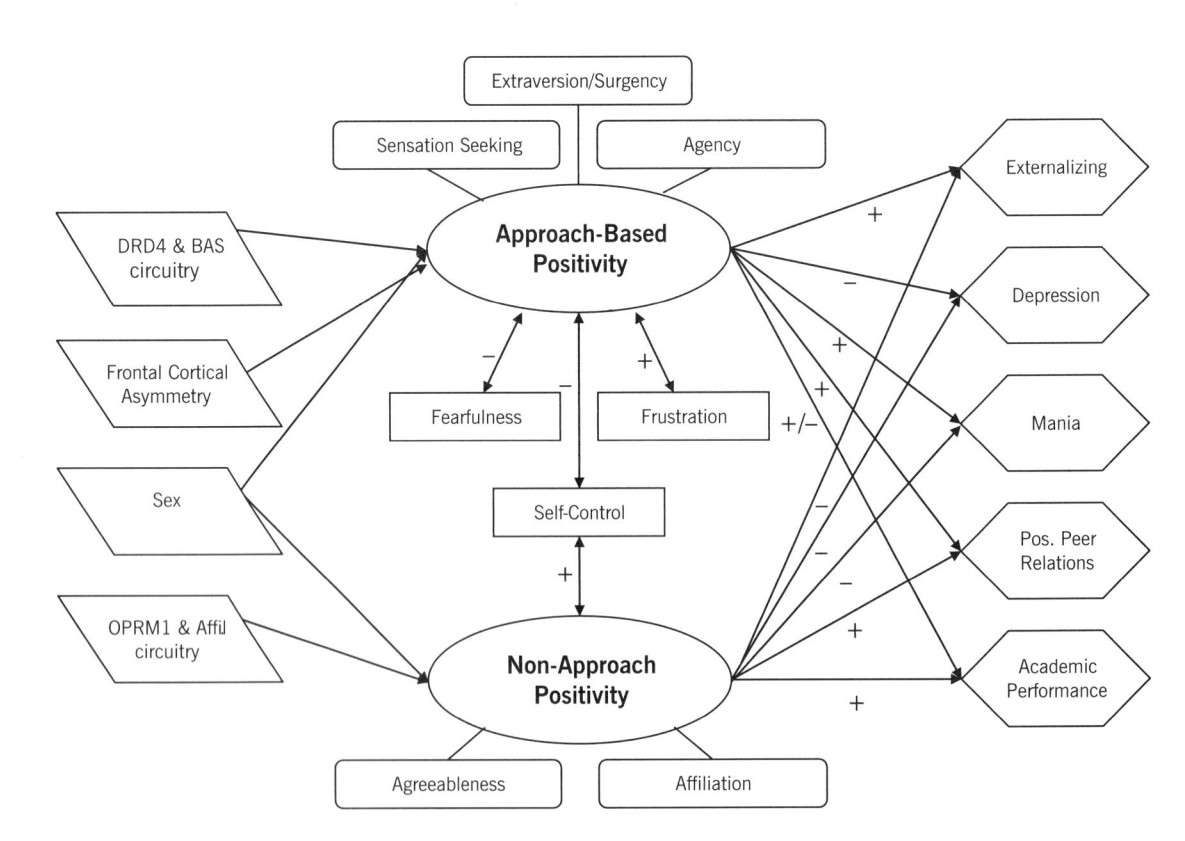

FIGURE 6.1. Conceptual model of biological underpinnings (represented by parallelograms), temperament/personality correlates (represented by rectangles), and outcomes (represented by hexagons) associated with two forms of positive emotionality. Rounded rectangles represent broad constructs involving positivity, whereas angular rectangles represent traits that do not themselves involve positive affect.

asserted that, in addition to more accurately representing the organization of mood, their model was preferable to previous models because it corresponded more clearly to factors that had emerged from analyses of personality inventories. As acknowledged by Caspi (1998), all structural models of personality include factors marking a tendency toward positive engagement. The most well known of these is Extraversion, identified first by Burt (1937; as cited in Rothbart & Bates, 2006) and found in models identified throughout the lifespan (e.g., Digman, 1997; Halverson et al., 2003). The centrality of affect in definitions of Extraversion is clear. Costa and McCrae (1980) contended that propensities to experience positive emotions represented a core feature of Extraversion, and Lucas, Le, and Dyrenforth (2008) recently summarized several studies showing that extraverts experience greater amounts of positive affect across multiple contexts.

In analyses of fine-grained parent-report measures of temperament in infants, toddlers, children, adolescents, and adults, Rothbart and colleagues have consistently derived a Surgency factor bearing considerable similarity to Extraversion (Evans & Rothbart, 2007; Putnam, Ellis, & Rothbart, 2001). In all age groups, scales indicating enjoyment of high-intensity activities load highly on this factor. Other scales defining Surgency at several different ages include those assessing activity level, vocal reactivity, smiling and laughter, rapid approach, positive anticipation, impulsivity, and sociability. These factors share attributes with those that have emerged in other studies of childhood temperament structure (e.g., Presley & Martin, 1994; Sanson, Smart, Prior, Oberklaid, & Pedlow, 1994). Strong correlations obtained by Rothbart, Ahadi, and Evans (2000) confirmed the relation between Surgency, as measured in temperament questionnaires, and Big Five Extraversion.

Positive affect is also implicated in theory and research surrounding the behavioral activation system (BAS) proposed by Gray (e.g., 1991), which is based in sensitivity to reward and the pleasurable emotions accompanying the seeking and acquisition of goals. The BAS and Extraversion constructs are somewhat distinct, in that Gray considers Extraversion as representing a ratio of BAS to a complementary behavioral inhibition system (BIS), such that high Extraversion is due to high BAS and low BIS. In addition, typical measures of Extraversion are largely based in sociability, which is not prominent in Gray's model. Carver and White (1994) found that the BAS scales of Drive, Fun Seeking, and Reward Responsiveness each correlated moderately with scales assessing Extraversion and Positive Affectivity, confirming that the BAS construct was related, but not identical, to these other constructs. Similar findings were more recently reported by Elliot and Thrash (2002).

Another relevant construct, identified originally in adults but also examined in children, is Sensation Seeking (e.g., Kafry, 1982; Zuckerman, 1994). Comprised of dimensions involving desire for thrills and novel experiences, social disinhibition, and boredom susceptibility, this trait does not explicitly include positive affect. It is slightly correlated with Extraversion, but more closely connected with Big Five Openness to Experience, and correlates negatively with Agreeableness and Conscientiousness. Sensation Seeking is, however, relevant to Positive Affectivity. Individuals high in Sensation Seeking exhibit a strong desire for hedonic pursuits likely to lead to positive affect, and sensation seekers have reported greater frequency of positive mood in daily life (see Zuckerman, 1994). Similar dimensions have emerged from behavioral observation. For example, explicitly connecting approach tendencies to Positive Affectivity, Rothbart (1988; Rothbart, Derryberry, & Hershey, 2000) found that, in comparison to infants who reached more slowly, infants who reached quickly for objects demonstrated more smiling and laughter, and showed greater impulsivity and positive anticipation as 7-year-olds. Activity level in the laboratory also predicted aspects of Surgency at the later assessment. As discussed in a later section, observational studies of behavioral inhibition have also revealed connections between positivity and approach.

The work described in this section speaks to the prominence of models that link positive affect to a behavioral approach system. This connection is demonstrated in classic and contemporary research on transitory mood, the structure of personality, childhood temperament, and neurobiological models of motivation. There are, however, qualifications to this broad model. Positive affect is sometimes expressed in the absence of approach tendencies and in contexts that are relatively low in hedonic value. In addition, the role of inhibition as a complement to approach in relation to positive affect is ambiguous. Finally, approach tendencies are associated with certain emotions that are typically considered to be negative. In the following sections, these caveats to the dominant model are discussed.

Broad Non-Approach-Based Constructs Involving Positivity

Not all positive emotions activate approach behaviors (Carver & Harmon-Jones, 2009; Gruber & Johnson, 2009; Nigg, Goldsmith, & Sachek, 2004; Watson, Wiese, Vaidya, & Tellegen, 1999). As such, not all traits involving positive emotions should concern strong approach tendencies or responses to high-intensity stimuli. Pfeifer, Goldsmith, Davidson, and Rickman (2002) argued that exuberance consists of intense positivity, not calm satisfaction, and suggested that Depue's (Depue & Morrone-Strupinsky, 2005; Depue & Fu, Chapter 18, this volume) separation of Positive Emotionality into affiliation and agency subcomponents represents the two types of pleasant emotion systems. Examinations of the higher-order factor structure of temperament and consideration of temperament factors other than Surgency–Extraversion are informative in understanding these distinct forms of positivity.

Prior to the prominence of the Big Five, researchers had noted the multifaceted nature of Extraversion, commonly finding affiliative and agentic subcomponents (Dupue & Morrone-Strupinsky, 2005). The common element of these subcomponents seems to be positive emotion: When positive emotion is partialled out, relations between agency and affiliation scales become nonsignificant (Watson & Clark, 1997a). Relating these dimensions to temperament, Caspi (1998) hypothesized that childhood positive affectivity should predict Big Five traits of both Extraversion and Agreeableness, with the latter also associated with high persistence and low activity level. Consistent with this proposition, second-order factor analyses of the Adult Temperament Questionnaire (ATQ) have revealed a factor containing aspects of Extraversion–Surgency, including Positive Emotionality and Affiliativeness.

In an earlier study, Evans and Rothbart (2007) found ATQ Affiliativeness to be related to Big Five Agreeableness, with both the Extraversion–Surgency and Affiliativeness scales of the ATQ related to measures of cooperation. Taken together, these findings suggest that positivity contributes to a prosocial orientation toward others. Graziano and Tobin (2009) cite several findings that support this suggestion, arguing that Agreeableness "plays an important role in the experience of positive emotions within the context of interpersonal relations" (p. 47). For instance, individuals high in Agreeableness tend to report greater enjoyment of interaction partners, and Agreeableness is moderately correlated with self-reported happiness. Also consistent with this idea are data from Krueger, Hicks, and McGue (2001) showing correlations between Positive Emotionality and altruism. The contribution of early positivity to later Agreeableness is still largely speculative, however, and Shiner and Caspi (2003) have noted that traits reflecting Agreeableness are not included in most temperament questionnaires.

Graziano and Tobin (2009) have suggested that Agreeableness is closely related to Conscientiousness, a contention consistent with second-order factor analyses of the Big Five (Digman, 1997), and that both of these personality traits have roots in temperamental Effortful Control. Conceptually, Effortful Control concerns successful management of one's conduct, and scales measuring attentional and behavioral control load on factors measuring Effortful Control or an analogous Regulatory Capacity factor in infants (Putnam et al., 2001). Less attention has been paid to the emotional components of this factor. In infants, toddlers, and children, scales measuring pleasure in low-intensity situations and cuddliness (including apparent enjoyment when being held) load on Regulatory Capacity/Effortful Control. Also, a Smiling and Laughter scale not specific to stimulus intensity loads primarily on Surgency in samples of Chinese children, but on Effortful Control in U.S. children (Ahadi, Rothbart, & Ye, 1993). These results suggest that a capacity for pleasure in nonarousing contexts may facilitate the ability to focus attention in infancy and inhibit prohibited activities thereafter, and that displays of positive affect more generally are bound to cultural expectations regarding emotion expression.

Self-Control

The complementary relationship between positivity and effortful control described in the preceding section contrasts with studies documenting inverse relations between approach-based positivity and constraint. Rothbart, Derryberry, and Hershey (2000) found that strong approach tendencies in infancy predicted low childhood inhibitory control and high impulsivity, and Caspi and colleagues (2003) found that 3-year-olds described as "confident" were low on self-reported control as adults. Polak-Toste and Gunnar (2006) cite several other studies suggesting that exuberant children will experience difficulties in appropriate regulation of conduct. Rothbart (Derryberry & Rothbart, 1997; Rothbart, Derryberry, & Hershey, 2000) has utilized a metaphor of brakes and accelerators in explaining these findings, suggesting that a strong approach drive may overwhelm attempts at self-control. Consistent with this idea, Rydell, Berlin, and Bohlin (2003) and Dennis, Hong, and Solomon (2010) found exuberance to be negatively associated with scales assessing regulation of positivity.

The relation between positive affect and effortful control may be influenced by age. Factors representing Surgency and Regulatory Capacity are positively correlated on infant measures, but Surgency and Effortful Control are uncorrelated or slightly negatively correlated thereafter (Gartstein & Rothbart, 2003; Putnam, Gartstein, & Rothbart, 2006; Rothbart, Ahadi, Hershey, & Fisher, 2001). Longitudinally, Komsi and colleagues (2006, 2008) found that infant Positive Affectivity was positively predictive of Effortful Control in preschoolers. Similarly, Putnam, Rothbart, and Gartstein (2008) reported positive correlations between infant Surgency and toddler Effortful Control. Conversely, these researchers found a negative correlation between toddler Surgency and preschool Effortful Control. It may be that positivity during infancy, when few external demands are placed on conduct, facilitates searching behaviors that lead individuals to encounter mild threat, necessitating exercise of effortful constraint. As expectations for control increase throughout early childhood, however, an excess of surgent activation exceeds inhibitory control.

An important advance in understanding the two faces of positivity was recently made by Kochanska, Aksan, Penney, and Doobay (2007). These authors noted that observational measures of positivity take two forms. One utilizes situations designed to provoke exuberance, such as popping bubbles or playing a practical joke. The other comprises observations of unscripted interaction, typically with parents. Whereas the former are expected to evoke responses involving approach systems, the latter may provide a marker of positivity related to affiliativeness. Although measures of these two types of positivity were correlated with one another from infancy through preschool age, they were differentially related to self-regulation. Whereas positivity in mother–child interactions predicted rule-compatible conduct and effortful control, Laboratory Temperament Assessment Battery (Lab-TAB) positivity correlated negatively with self-control (Kochanska et al., 2007). This connection between effortful control and positive affect expressed in partnership with a significant other may reflect a control system based in children's desires to maintain relationships (MacDonald, 1992; Rothbart & Bates, 2006).

A final observation regarding the place of positive emotionality in models of self-control is that these two forms of positivity may interact with one another. As stated by Kochanska and colleagues "Early experience of pleasure in interactions with parents is likely to evolve into future high Agreeableness and well-modulated impulse control and Conscientiousness; such a social relationship-based form of (Positive Emotionality) may in fact serve as a 'brake' on a surgent, impulsive approach and on the pursuit of immediate gratification" (2007, p. 1064). These complex relations between positive reactivity and regulation represent a rich source of questions for future exploration.

Fear and Inhibition

The role of positive emotionality in the etiology of behavioral inhibition has been addressed in a number of studies. As described earlier, Calkins and colleagues identified a group of "exuberant" infants who were positive and active. These infants were found to be very low on inhibition as toddlers and preschoolers (Calkins et al., 1996; Fox, Henderson, Rubin, Calkins, & Schmidt, 2001). Similarly, Park, Belsky, Putnam, and Crnic (1997) found that negativity in infancy only forecast inhibition in 3-year-old boys when temperamental positivity was low. Pfeifer and colleagues (2002) found that uninhibited toddlers demonstrated high exuberance in Lab-TAB episodes as 7-year-olds. A slightly different strategy was employed by Putnam and Stifter (2005), who measured positive affect, negative affect, and behavioral approach–inhibition in 2-year-olds placed in both low-intensity contexts (e.g., play with "boring" toys) and high-intensity situations (e.g., request to jump to a mattress from a series of steps). Consistent with the propositions that approach tendencies should predominate in low-intensity situations, whereas both approach and inhibition should govern behavior in high-intensity contexts, only positivity related to low-intensity approach, whereas positivity and negativity were both associated with approach in more intense contexts. Laptook and colleagues (2008) and Laptook, Klein, Olino, Dyson, and Carlson (2010) obtained analogous results. In other publications (e.g., Hayden, Klein, Durbin, & Olino, 2006), this group has combined positive affect scores with behavioral approach variables to create a construct bearing similarity to the Watson and Tellegen (1985) dimension.

This interaction between forces of approach and inhibition is evident elsewhere. In some of the earliest writings on personality, descriptions of a prototypical extraverted child indicated that "shyness in regard to objects is very slight" (Jung, 1928, p. 303; as cited by Rothbart & Hwang, 2005). Similarly, Zuckerman's (1994, p. 27) Sensation Seeking construct is defined as not only "a trait defined by the seeking of varied, novel, complex, and intense sensations and experiences" (approach), but also "the willingness to take physical, social, legal, and financial risks for the sake of such experience" (reversed inhibition). Indeed, Zuckerman has suggested that temperamental Approach–Withdrawal or (reversed) behavioral inhibition appear to be early manifestations of sensation seeking. Investigations of temperament structure also reveal a role of fear in dimensions associated with Positive Affect–Approach. Although nonsocial fear scales load primarily on Negative Affect in toddlers and children, Shyness scales hold strong (negative) loadings on Surgency in these age groups, and both Fear and Shyness load primarily on Surgency in adolescents (Putnam et al., 2001). Similarly, laboratory fear in infants is negatively correlated with parent-reported impulsivity, activity, and positive anticipation (Rothbart, Derryberry, & Hershey, 2000).

Some researchers have successfully distinguished children who fail to approach due to low sociability from those whose withdrawal is due to shyness (see Coplan, Prakash, O'Neil, & Armer, 2004), but the large majority of research on behavioral inhibition confounds these two forces. The inhibition literature is described thoroughly by Kagan (see Chapter 4, this volume). Scholars interested in either positive affectivity or inhibition should interpret findings involving either construct with an eye on the other.

Frustration

Although factor-analytic exercises typically place anger or frustration within Negative Emotionality or Neuroticism factors, this emotional proclivity has connections with systems implicated in Positive Affect. Close examination of correlation matrices of finegrained temperament reveals positive associations between frustration and aspects of Surgency such as activity level and approach (e.g., Gartstein & Rothbart, 2003). Frustration often exhibits high secondary loadings on Surgency, and scales assessing positive emotions expressed in anticipation of upcoming activities load on the Negative Affectivity factor in childhood (Rothbart et al., 2001). Because of the importance of reward systems in conceptualizations of positive emotion, it is not surprising that *anger*, frequently defined as a response to a blocking of reward-salient goals, would be expressed most emphatically by individuals high in positivity.

Concurrent relations between anger and positivity are seen even in infancy. Infants who showed the most joy and interest in activities were those who became most frustrated when prevented from playing (He et al., 2010; Lewis, Sullivan, Ramsey, & Alessandri, 1992; Stifter & Grant, 1993). In preschool-age children, teacher-rated Extraversion predicted tendencies to express anger upon losing a game (Donzella, Gunnar, Krueger, & Alwin, 2000), and observed approach reactivity was associated with demonstrations of frustration when asked to wait for a prize (Dennis, 2006). In slightly older children, parent ratings of exuberance were related to scales measuring anger (Rydell et al., 2003). Relations between anger and positive approach have also been demonstrated longitudinally. Rothbart and colleagues (Putnam et al., 2008; Rothbart, Ahadi, & Hershey, 1994; Rothbart, Derryberry, & Hershey, 2000) have demonstrated connections between frustration and components of Surgency such as activity level, impulsivity, positive anticipation, rapid approach, and high-intensity pleasure from infancy through childhood.

The evidence establishing a relationship between anger and positive affect, especially as expressed in circumstances of high intensity and potential for reward, is compelling. Carver and Harmon-Jones (2009) have been particularly critical of models associating approach motivation solely with positive affect, suggesting an alternative two-dimensional model, in which either approach or inhibition can result in positive or negative emotions (i.e., successful approach and rewards inspire elation; unsuccessful approach leads to anger; successful avoidance or nonpunishment results in relief or contentment; and unsuccessful avoidance of punishment leads to fear). In defense of the positive and negative emotionality model, Watson (2009) noted the frequent co-occurrence of anger, anxiety, and other negative affects in transitory state and trait measures, suggesting that anger involves components of both approach and inhibition. Temperament scholars are advised to heed Watson's recommendation to "decouple these two models rather than attempting to create a simple, neat structure that integrates both the motivational and psychometric evidence into a single overall scheme" (p. 208).

Conclusion

Understanding positive affectivity requires consideration of how positivity interacts with other aspects of behavior and emotion. It can be argued that the most basic element of behavioral tendencies is approach. Because emotions are frequently defined as reactions to changes in the environment (Ekman, 1993), and temperament as individual differences in proclivities to experience emotion (Goldsmith & Campos, 1990), it is worth considering whether approach tendencies represent the most basic dimension of individual differences. The broad dimension of Positive Affectivity as conceptualized by Watson and Tellegen (1985), revealed in Extraversion and Surgency (e.g., Digman, 1997; Rothbart et al., 2001), and connected to neural models of motivation (e.g., Gray, 1991) are rooted in this elementary distinction.

The union of approach and positive affectivity, however, is an imperfect one. Approach tendencies can lead to anger, and persistent seeking of stimulation is associated with unpleasant sensations reflected in the susceptibility to boredom experienced by sensation seekers (Zuckerman, 1994). Meanwhile, some individuals derive pleasure from a variety of low-intensity stimuli. A focus on pleasantness as a defining feature of positive emotions brings the issue back to dimensional models common before Watson and Tellegen's seminal work, and those reflected in classic perspectives such as Meehl's (1975) and more recent models proposed by Carver and Harmon-Jones (2009). Measures of low- and high-intensity pleasure are correlated in infancy and early childhood (Gartstein & Rothbart, 2003; Kochanska et al., 2007), suggesting that reward sensitivity to *all* levels of intensity is the most basic underpinning of positive emotionality.

Perhaps researchers have focused almost exclusively on approach-based exuberance because of the observability of this type of positivity. Tellegen (1985) noted that factor rotations lead to alignment with spaces characterized by high density, such that a lexical approach to personality will be influenced by the number of terms denoting similar behaviors. Because expressions of laughter and excitement are readily experienced by others, there are more words for these emotions (e.g., *enthusiasm*, *delight*) than for low-intensity pleasant affect (e.g., *contented*), leading to a lack of emphasis on the latter in Positive Emotionality factors. Also, logistic constraints require that observational data collected in the laboratory or home rely on brief episodes; therefore, displays of temperament are typically provoked by tasks involving changes in stimulation that will elicit codable joy from at least some children (Polak-Toste & Gunnar, 2006).

Because pleasure in low-intensity situations is linked to important regulatory capacities, measurement of such pleasure seems to be a valuable direction for future studies. Interactions with parents, as utilized by Kochanska and colleagues (2007) or tasks involving "boring" toys, as used by Putnam and Stifter (2005), may be useful in these endeavors. In a time of limited funding, it should be recognized that many existing recordings of laboratory and home visits contain transition moments of low intensity. Such recordings may allow opportunity for generating new perspectives from existing datasets. Also worth considering are elicitors associated with distinct types of positive emotion not linked to agentic activity. For instance, compassion and awe are experienced during care for others and during moments of rapid but insufficient shifts in understanding, respectively (Shiota, Keltner, & John, 2006). Thus, compassion might be reliably observed in children's behavior with vulnerable others, and awe in response to exposure to "magical" events.

Biological Systems Implicated in Positive Affectivity

Multiple biological systems have been implicated as constitutional bases of positive affect. Behavior genetic studies of heritability have recently been complemented by molecular assays. The genes suspected of influencing positive affectivity are associated with dopamine regulation, as are the systems proposed in neural models of approach motivation, including those involving hemispheric balance. The vast majority of research in this area concerns positivity as connected with approach tendencies and exuberance, whereas sedate forms of positive affect have received less attention (cf. Depue & Morrone-Strupinsky, 2005).

Genetic Underpinnings

Although Positive Affectivity and Extraversion generate heritability estimates similar in magnitude to other dimensions of temperament, shared environment components are substantially larger for Positive Affectivity than for Negative Affectivity across multiple age groups and methodologies (Goldsmith, Lemery, Buss, & Campos, 1999; Tellegen et al., 1988; Wachs & Bates, 2010). Goldsmith and colleagues (1999) have speculated that twin similarities in attachment security or parental extraversion promoting positive affect may play a role in shaping these tendencies. Nonfamilial aspects of the environment may play increasingly important roles later in life, as Positive Affectivity, but not Negative Affectivity, shows large increases in variance associated with unshared environment during early adulthood (Clark & Watson, 1999).

South, Krueger, Johnson, and Iacono (2008) suggest that Positive Affectivity may actually shape the degree to which environments influence genes. These authors found that Positive Emotionality in adolescents moderated the heritability of parent–child relationships, such that the genetic variance associated with parental regard was greatest when offspring were high in Positive Emotionality. South and colleagues proposed that tendencies toward positive emotions result in interactions with parents that support expression of a child's genotype, whereas less positive adolescents may elicit parental treatment that promotes change in child personality in ways counter to their genotype.

The molecular genetic research most relevant to Positive Affectivity has concerned the dopamine D4 receptor (*DRD4*; see White, Lamm, Helfinstein, & Fox, Chapter 17, and Depue & Fu, Chapter 18, this volume, for additional discussion). The 7-repeat allele of this gene has been associated with novelty seeking in adult humans and animals, and Auerbach and colleagues (1999) found that infants who possessed the long form of *DRD4* expressed less distress in response to novel stimuli, a precursor to behavioral inhibition. Also suggestive are relations between *DRD4* alleles and externalizing problems and attention-deficit/hyperactivity disorder (ADHD) (see Rothbart & Bates, 2006), outcomes frequently associated with high levels of approach. Occasional failure to replicate may suggest that *DRD4* interacts with the environment in development of approach tendencies. Consistent with this proposal, Sheese, Voelker, Rothbart, and Posner (2007) found that toddlers with the 7-repeat allele were high in components of Surgency (activity level, impulsivity, and high-intensity pleasure) when parenting was low in quality, whereas this same allele was linked to low Surgency when parenting was supportive and stimulating. Depue and Fu (Chapter 18, this volume) have additionally discussed the gene *OPRM1* as implicated in affiliative forms of positivity.

Motivational System Models

The importance of distinguishing between differing forms of positive affectivity is suggested by contemporary models of neurobiology and neurochemistry relevant to positive affectivity. Depue and Fu (Chapter 18, this volume; see also Depue & Morrone-Strupinsky, 2005) describe a behavioral approach system implicated in Extraversion that is largely based in dopamine circuits involving the nucleus accubens and ventral tegmental areas associated with goal-directed behavior and related anticipatory emotions such as excitement and enthusiasm. A separate opiate system projecting from the medial basal arcuate nucleus of the hypothalamus plays a primary role in consummatory processes associated with quiescent positive emotions, and may interact with dopamine and oxytocin systems to form the basis for individual differences in the capacity for affiliation.

Cortical Asymmetry

A large body of research has connected emotionality to differential activity of cortical hemispheres, particularly in frontal areas (cf. Hayden et al., 2008). Readers are directed to a special issue of *Biological Psychology* (e.g., Allen & Kline, 2004) for a thorough consideration of this literature. The general interpretation of these studies holds that left frontal activity is associated with positive emotions and approach, whereas right frontal activity is associated with negative emotions and withdrawal. These findings and interpretations are consistent with neural models presented in the previous section, as indicated by differential dopamine release in the right and left nucleus accumbens and ventromedial areas (Besson & Louilot, 1997). An area of recent controversy concerns whether anterior cortical asymmetry is more relevant to approach–withdrawal or to emotion valence. Carver and Harmon-Jones (2009) are strong proponents of the motivational approach, and summarize several studies linking transitory and trait anger, but not sadness, to left frontal activation.

Studies relating electroencephalographic (EEG) asymmetry to temperament have largely focused on inhibition, and a review by Polak-Toste and Gunnar (2006) indicates that no studies have examined this biological variable in relation to exuberance. Papers by Fox and colleagues (Calkins et al., 1996; Fox et al., 2001), however, warrant consideration. Calkins and colleagues (1996) found that infants who demonstrated high positivity and activity level in response to novelty at 4 months demonstrated greater relative left-hemispheric activation at 9 months than those who had been negative and active in early infancy. In a follow-up study, children who were continuously uninhibited through early childhood had greater left frontal activation than did consistently inhibited children (Fox et al., 2001). Recent analyses of this sample focus more clearly on approach tendencies. Hane, Fox, Henderson, and Marshall (2008) found that infants who had been positively reactive at 4 months demonstrated greater left-hemispheric activity and joy and approach to Lab-TAB exuberance tasks at 9 months than other infants, and He and colleagues (2010) found that infants most prone to anger at 4 months of age were more likely than other infants to evince exuberance at 9 months only if they also exhibited left frontal asymmetry.

Sex

Findings regarding sex differences in positive emotionality have been mixed. For instance, Zhou, Lengua, and Wang (2009) and Dougherty, Klein, Durbin, Hayden, and Olino (2010) found higher positivity in girls than in boys, and Majdandzic and van den Boom (2007) reported greater Lab-TAB exuberance among boys. A meta-analysis by Else-Quest, Hyde, Goldsmith, and Van Hulle (2006; see also Else-Quest, Chapter 23, this volume) sheds light on this inconsistency, showing higher positive mood among females but greater high-intensity pleasure in males. The adult personality literature similarly demonstrates higher levels of Sensation Seeking in males and greater Agreeableness in females (Graziano & Tobin, 2009; Zuckerman, 1994). These relations are surely impacted by social expectations, and Graziano and Tobin (2009) note that Agreeableness is more strongly linked to psychological femininity than biological sex, but hormonal factors presumably contribute as well. Zuckerman (1994) reviewed several studies showing associations between sensation seeking and testosterone. Similarly, oxytocin function is implicated in sex differences in nurturing behavior (Taylor et al., 2000), suggesting that gender differences in aspects of positivity associated with affiliation may be influenced by oxytocin systems.

Outcomes Associated with Positive Affectivity

Propensities for experiencing and expressing positive affect are associated with both strengths and difficulties. Positivity can attract and retain social partners and protect against depression, but a strong focus on rewards can challenge self-regulatory capacities and result in externalizing behaviors based in frustration. The type of positive affect considered is important: Positivity involving strong approach tendencies or expressed in highly stimulating contexts is more likely to be associated with problematic conduct, whereas pleasant emotional tone in low-intensity situations and interpersonal interactions is more closely associated with desirable behaviors (Dennis et al., 2010; Kochanska et al., 2007).

Connections between positive emotionality and outcomes are both direct and indirect. For example, low positive affect is directly implicated in depression, both in the sense that ahedonia is a symptom of depression and because the biological systems relevant to normative variation in positivity constitute predisposing factors to pathological depression. Low positivity may also lead to environmental factors that present risk for depression, such as deficits in parental support, acceptance, and involvement (Branje, van Lieshout, & van Aken, 2005; Lengua & Kovacs, 2005). Positive affectivity tends to be less longitudinally stable than negativity (Wachs & Bates, 2010), and environmental variables have been shown to shape developmental trajectories of positive affectivity. For instance, maternal contingent responding and involvement have been linked to increased levels of positive emotionality and oxytocin levels in infants (Belsky, Fish, & Isabella, 1991; Feldman, Gordon, & Zagoory-Sharon, 2010). As discussed by Lengua and Wachs (Chapter 25, this volume), positive affectivity may promote resilience and active coping styles, buffering the harmful effects aversive environments. Effects of positivity moderate and are moderated by other traits as well. For instance, Dennis and colleagues (2010) found that effortful control was associated with on-task behavior only among children low in exuberance.

Externalizing

Theory suggests that aggressive and destructive behaviors should be associated with excessive activity in approach systems, especially when approach tendencies are not countered by adequate inhibitory input (Quay, 1993). These expectations have been confirmed across the lifespan, in multiple contexts, and in relation to a variety of externalizing behaviors. Concurrent relations between exuberant positive affectivity and externalizing behaviors including aggression and conduct disorder have been documented in toddlers (Gartstein, Putnam, & Rothbart, 2012; Putnam & Stifter, 2005), elementary schoolchildren (Oldehinkel, Hartman, deWinter, Veenstra, & Ormel, 2004; Rothbart, Ahadi, & Hershey, 1994), adolescents (Muris, Meesters, & Blijlevens, 2007), and adults (see Zuckerman, 1994). Longitudinal associations have been established as well. Rothbart and colleagues (1994) found that activity level and smiling and laughter in infants were related to parent reports of high aggression at ages 6 and 7, and exuberant toddlers identified by Stifter, Putnam, and Jahromi (2008) demonstrated high externalizing at 4½ years. Once initiated, externalizing behavior can lead to self-maintaining environmental factors. For instance, Gunnar, Sebanc, Tout, Donzella, and van Dulman (2003) found that a combination of surgency and low control led to externalizing, which in turn predicted aggression in the classroom.

The degree to which approachful positivity translates to externalizing problems may differ in relation to cultural and gender expectations. For instance, Berdan, Keane, and Calkins (2008) reported relations between Surgency and "wild" behavior among kindergarten girls, but not boys, and also found that Surgency most strongly predicted aspects of externalizing among girls who perceived themselves as socially accepted but actually scored low on peer-rated social preference. Zhou and colleagues (2009) reported lower levels of smiling and laughter in parent reports of Chinese than U.S. schoolchildren, and also found scores on this scale to be linked to teacher reports of externalizing in China, but not the United States. The authors suggested that, in comparison to Western culture, Chinese society encourages the inhibition of emotional displays, particularly those indicating pride or intense pleasure. Children who violate these cultural expectations may jeopardize social relationships, placing them at risk for externalizing problems.

Temperamental exuberance may be particularly troublesome when combined with low capabilities for control. Rubin, Coplan, Fox, and Calkins (1995) indicated poor peer relations and high externalizing in preschoolers who were high in exuberance and low in emotion regulation. More recently, Stifter and colleagues (2008) found exuberant children to be high in internalizing and externalizing only when they were low in emotion regulation. Rydell and colleagues (2003) explicitly examined the ability of children to control inappropriate positive emotions. In their initial report, they demonstrated moderate correlations between exuberance at age 5 years and externalizing demonstrated in preschool, home, and elementary school at later ages. However, a scale indexing problems with becoming calm in rewarding situations (e.g., "When my child wins a game or contest, he or she has difficulties quieting down") predicted externalizing over and above the positive emotionality variable. Interaction effects indicated that the regulatory variable only predicted school externalizing for children high in positivity. A second report (Rydell, Thorell, & Bohlin, 2007) replicated some of these findings, also showing that the role of exuberance regulation in preventing externalizing was independent of anger regulation.

Some studies, however, have found positive affectivity to be associated with low externalizing. Lengua, West, and Sandler (1998; Lengua, Wolchik, Sandler, & West, 2000) reported negative correlations between conduct problems and both parent- and child-reported positive mood in adolescents, and also found that positive emotionality buffered the effect of parental rejection. Kim, Walden, Harris, Karrass, and Catron (2006) found that frequent self-reported experience of happiness in late childhood and early adolescence was modestly associated with low externalizing. In contrast to investigations utilizing positivity measures reflecting strong approach tendencies, the operationalizations used by these authors may be more reflective of low-intensity or socially motivated positivity relevant to Agreeableness, which is inversely related to aggression (Graziano & Tobin, 2009).

Attention-Deficit/Hyperactivity Disorder

Expectations of links between positive emotionality and ADHD are based in proposals that a strong approach system may compromise the development and/or demonstration of effortful control (e.g., Derryberry & Rothbart, 1997). Although the literature is inconsistent (Nigg et al., 2004), some researchers have demonstrated relations between Extraversion or reward sensitivity and ADHD (e.g., Mitchell, 2010; Parker, Majeski, & Collin, 2003; also see Klein, Dyson, Kujawa, & Kotov, Chapter 26, this volume). Also suggestive are findings of positive affectivity as a concurrent and longitudinal correlate of impulsivity (Kochanska et al., 2007; Putnam et al., 2008). No studies to date, however, have empirically supported a connection between positivity-bound temperament traits and ADHD. This may be due to the tendency for developmentalists to subsume attention problems in broader dimensions of externalizing. Mitchell (2010), however, has recently shown that approach tendencies contribute to ADHD symptomology, after accounting for comorbidity with psychopathy symptoms, highlighting the value of separating attentional from other aspects of externalizing in future studies. In addition, because Agreeableness is associated with low levels of ADHD (Parker et al., 2003), explorations of low-intensity positive affectivity may be productive in explaining the temperamental origins of this disorder.

Depression and Mania

As reviewed by Watson (2000), low levels of Positive Affectivity have been related to several internalizing problems, including social phobia, agoraphobia, posttraumatic stress disorder, and eating disorders. These findings are echoed by studies of children and adolescents in which low positive affect or approach is associated with anxiety problems or internalizing, measured broadly (Putnam & Stifter, 2005; Zhou et al., 2009). Examinations of more discrete components of problem behavior provide support for models in which aspects of internalizing associated with anxiety are closely connected to negativity, whereas deficits in positive affect are most relevant to depressive forms of internalizing in children, adolescents, and adults (Brown, Chorpita, & Barlow, 1998; Lonigan, Phillips, & Hooe, 2003; Watson, Clark, & Carey, 1988). As early as 1975, Meehl suggested the importance of capacity for pleasure as a factor in depression, and concurrent relationships between positive emotionality and depression have been demonstrated among children and adolescents in both community and clinical samples; and in longitudinal as well as cross-sectional designs (see review in Dougherty et al., 2010). Complementing these findings, Dougherty and colleagues (2010) found that low Positive Affectivity at age 3 predicted depressive symptoms at age 10, even after controlling for negativity and depressive behaviors at age 3. They also reported an interactive effect, such that negativity only predicted depression when positivity was low.

These associations appear to be mediated by both cognitive and environmental factors. Nusslock, Abramson, Harmon-Jones, Alloy, and Coan (2009) reviewed adult literature implicating BAS deactivation with decreased self-esteem, lack of responsivity to positive cues, and low expectancies for success and goal-directed activity. Adding a developmental perspective to this phenomenon, Hayden and colleagues (2006) found that low Positive Emotionality in toddlerhood predicted interpersonal helplessness and decreased recall of positive self-descriptors. These cognitive styles, in addition to directly presenting risk factors for depression, may lead to behaviors that diminish the likelihood of beneficial social relationships. Consistent with this suggestion, Wetter and Hankin (2009) found the relationship between Positive Emotionality and depression in early adolescence to be partially mediated by a lack of social support. They also reported a moderation effect, in which the implications of low Positive Emotionality for depression were most pronounced among youth with low social support. Similarly, Lengua and colleagues (2000) found that parental rejection was more strongly related to depression and aggressive symptoms among children low in Positive Affectivity than among their high-positivity peers.

Relatively fewer investigations have concerned dysregulated positive affect in association with mania. Gruber and Johnson (2009) recently reviewed the literature relating high BAS scores to mania risk or symptomology. These authors highlighted the importance of considering specific types of positive emotions, and found reward and achievement-focused positive emotions such as joy and pride to be more profoundly implicated as risk factors for mania than prosocial emotions such as love or compassion. Similarly, joy and amusement predicted increased mania levels over the subsequent 6 months in patients with bipolar disorder, whereas compassion was associated with decreased mania severity over this period (Gruber et al., 2009).

Peer Relationships

A number of studies are consistent with Wetter and Hankin (2009) in showing positive social outcomes associated with positive emotionality. High levels of sociability associated with exuberance motivate children to greater levels of social engagement, and frequent expressions of joy can make children more attractive social partners. As described by Denham, McKinley, Couchoud, and Holt (1990, p. 1145), "Peers find it easier and more pleasant to interact with emotionally positive children." Large amounts of time spent in the company of other children may in turn enhance social skills. Both approach-centered and more sedate aspects of positivity are relevant, as both Agreeableness and Extraversion are linked to social competence (Jensen-Campbell & Graziano, 2001; Shiner, 2000). A variety of different prosocial tendencies are associated with positivity. In addition to exhibiting confidence in the form of high self-esteem and social potency, positive children are adept at recognizing and reacting with sympathy to others' emotion displays, and show better organized regulation of their own emotion (Davey, Eaker, & Walters, 2003; Dennis et al., 2010; Eisenberg, Wentzel, & Harris, 1998; Shiner & Masten, 2002). These attributes constitute important pathways from temperament to relationships: Denham and colleagues (1990) found that prosocial behavior mediated the relation of expressed emotion to peers' ratings of preschoolers' likability.

Associations between positivity and social connections continue into adulthood. Watson and Clark (1997b) found trait Positive Affectivity to be linked to more hours spent with friends and to a greater number of close friends. Relatedly, Positive Affectivity in adulthood is associated both concurrently and longitudinally with a variety of social and romantic competencies (Harker & Keltner, 2001; Shiner & Caspi, 2003). The social support derived from these relationships may provide an explanation for links between positive emotionality, physical health, and longevity (Danner, Snowdon, & Friesen, 2001; Shiner & Caspi, 2003).

Academic Motivation and Performance

Although unregulated activity level may present problems for surgent children in traditional classroom settings, approach systems implicated in positive affectivity may also confer benefits for academic pursuits. Shiner (1998) suggested that mastery motivation, reflecting an intrinsic drive to engage in challenging tasks, could be conceived as a component or outcome of Tellegen's (1985) positive emotionality construct. Elliot and Thrash (2002) provided empirical support for this notion, demonstrating links between mastery and multiple operationalizations of approach-based temperament. Longitudinally, Shiner and Masten (2002) found that mastery motivation and self-assurance in middle school predicted positive emotionality in adulthood. Rothbart and Hwang (2005) elaborated on the relationship between motivational style and Surgency, reviewing literature connecting positive affect in children and adults to sustained engagement and expectations for success. Parenting and other aspects of temperament may enhance or detract from these relationships. The implications of positive emotionality may extend beyond motivation to cognitive style: Gable and Harmon-Jones (2010) have proposed a model in which approach-based positive emotions narrow perception, enhancing strong attentional focus, whereas non-approachful forms of positivity (e.g., contentment) allow for broader thinking associated with creativity.

The implications of positive affect and related behaviors for academic performance may differ across the lifespan. Whereas Martin, Drew, Gaddis, and Mosley (1988; Martin & Holbrook, 1985) found activity level to be associated with poor concurrent academic achievement in elementary school, Rudasill, Gallagher, and White (2010) found activity level at age 4 years to predict better academic performance at ages 8 and 9 years. The authors suggested that activity level in earlier years may primarily reflect energy and motivation to learn, in contrast to measurements at older ages, when children are increasingly expected to dampen their activity level to conform to classroom settings. Shiner (2000) proposed a similar process to explain positive correlations between Extraversion and academic achievement in childhood, but negative correlations between these variables in high school and college.

Conclusion

Increased recognition of positive affectivity as a characteristic of temperament that is separate from the absence of negativity represents an important advance in the field. Tendencies to experience and express positive emotions are associated with both beneficial and detrimental outcomes. Promotion of the former and prevention or amelioration of the latter are enhanced by greater understanding of the biological and social forces underlying proclivities toward positivity. Nusslock and colleagues (2009) have recently proposed guidelines for psychosocial interventions for bipolar disorder that take into account dysregulation of the behavioral approach system. Future intervention and therapeutic steps can build upon perspectives such as these.

A critical consideration for basic and applied work concerns differentiation of the various facets of positive affectivity. To date, most research and theory in this area has addressed aspects of positivity revealed through exuberant behaviors, especially those expressed in highly intense contexts. Conceptualized as under the influence of motivational behavioral approach systems, these forms of positivity are those most closely linked to externalizing problems and deficits in attentional and behavioral control. Deserving increased focus are contented and affiliative types of positivity expressed in low-intensity situations, which reflect capacities for satisfaction and close social bonds that represent protective factors for maladaptive patterns of behavior and cognition. Within these two broad distinctions, however, is room for finer differentiation. Explorations of high-intensity pleasure have largely confounded the intensity of the situation and magnitude of the affective display. This need not be the case, as boisterous enthusiasm is frequently expressed in the absence of thrill seeking, and enjoyment of extreme activities often is not accompanied by smiling and laughter. Another distinction concerns social and nonsocial forms of positive affectivity, a clarification that has proven valuable in the study of fearfulness (e.g., Kochanska, 1991). Resolution of methodological challenges in making these distinctions, and in the measurement of sedate aspects of positivity, is important.

Appreciation of the temperamental origins of positive emotionality may have broader societal benefits as well. Greater understanding of developmental trajectories of positivity may allow for insights that increase the likelihood of pleasant emotions among the world's population. Such a goal, however, involves an important caveat. Held (2004) has argued that societies such as the United States are characterized by a "tyranny" of positive affect, such that individuals are made to feel inadequate if they do not conform to expectations for expressing positive affect. It is hoped that awareness of constitutional constraints on individual differences in the likelihood of these emotions might facilitate acceptance of those who demonstrate either high or low levels of positive emotionality.

Acknowledgments

I would like to express my appreciation to Louisa Slowiaczek for helpful comments on an early draft of this chapter, and to Anna Wright for assistance with editing.

Further Reading

Depue, R. A., & Morrone-Strupinsky, J. V. (2005). A neurobehavioral model of affiliative bonding: Implications for conceptualizing a human trait of affiliation. *Behavioral and Brain Sciences*, 28, 313–395.

Polak-Toste, C. P., & Gunnar, M. R. (2006). Temperamental exuberance: Correlates and consequences. In P. J. Marshall & N. A. Fox (Eds.), *The development of social engagement: Neurobiological perspectives* (pp. 19–45). New York: Oxford University Press.

Watson, D., Wiese, D., Vaidya, J., & Tellegen, A. (1999). The two general activation systems of affect: Structural findings, evolutionary considerations, and psychobiological evidence. *Journal of Personality and Social Psychology*, 76, 820–838.

References

Ahadi, S. A., Rothbart, M. K., & Ye, R. M. (1993). Child temperament in the U.S. and China: Similarities and differences. *European Journal of Personality*, 7, 359–378.

Allen, J. J. B., & Kline, J. P. (2004). Frontal EEG asymmetry, emotion, and psychopathology: The first, and the next 25 years. *Biological Psychology*, 67, 1–5.

Auerbach, J., Geller, V., Letzer, S., Shinwell, E., Levine, J., Belmaker, R., et al. (1999). Dopamine D4 receptor (DRD4) and serotonin transporter promoter (5-HTTLPR) polymorphisms in the

determination of temperament in 2-month-old infants. *Molecular Psychiatry, 4,* 369–374.
Bates, J. E., Freeland, C. A. B., & Lounsbury, M. L. (1979). Measurement of infant difficultness. *Child Development, 50,* 794–803.
Belsky, J., Fish, M., & Isabella, R. (1991). Continuity and discontinuity in infant negative and positive emotionality: Family antecedents and attachment consequences. *Developmental Psychology, 27,* 421–431.
Belsky, J., Hsieh, K., & Crnic, K. (1996). Infant positive and negative emotionality: One dimension or two? *Developmental Psychology, 32,* 289–298.
Berdan, L., Keane, S., & Calkins, S. (2008). Temperament and externalizing behavior: Social preference and perceived acceptance as protective factors. *Developmental Psychology, 44,* 957–968.
Besson, C., & Louilot, A. (1997). Striatal dopaminergic changes depend on the attractive or aversive value of stimulus. *NeuroReport, 8,* 3523–3526.
Branje, S., van Lieshout, C., & van Aken, M. (2005). Relations between Agreeableness and perceived support in family relationships: Why nice people are not always supportive. *International Journal of Behavioral Development, 29,* 120–128.
Brown, T., Chorpita, B., & Barlow, D. (1998). Structural relationships among dimensions of the DSM-IV anxiety and mood disorders and dimensions of negative affect, positive affect, and autonomic arousal. *Journal of Abnormal Psychology, 107,* 179–192.
Burt, C. (1937). The analysis of temperament. *British Journal of Medical Psychology, 3,* 281–291.
Buss, A. H., & Plomin, R. (1984). *Temperament: Early developing personality traits.* Hillsdale, NJ: Erlbaum.
Calkins, S. D., Fox, N. A., & Marshall, T. R. (1996). Behavioral and psychological antecedents of inhibition in infancy. *Child Development, 67,* 523–540.
Carver, C. S., & Harmon-Jones, E. (2009). Anger is an approach-related affect: Evidence and implications. *Psychological Bulletin, 135,* 183–204.
Carver, C. S., & White, T. L. (1994). Behavioral inhibition, behavioral activation, and affective responses to impending reward and punishment: The BIS/BAS scales. *Journal of Personality and Social Psychology, 67,* 319–333.
Caspi, A. (1998). Personality development across the life course. In W. Damon & N. Eisenberg (Eds.), *Handbook of child psychology: Vol. 3. Social, emotional, and personality development* (pp. 311–388). New York: Wiley.
Caspi, A., Harrington, H., Milne, B., Amell, J. W., Theodore, R. F., & Moffitt, T. E. (2003). Children's behavioral styles at age 3 are linked to their adult personality traits at age 26. *Journal of Personality, 71,* 495–513.

Clark, L. A., & Watson, D. (1999). Temperament: A new paradigm for trait psychology. In L. A. Pervin & O. P. John (Eds.), *Handbook of personality* (2nd ed., pp. 399–423). New York: Guilford Press.
Cohn, M. A., & Fredrickson, B. L. (2009). Positive emotions. In S. Lopez & C. R. Snyder (Eds.), *Oxford handbook of positive psychology* (2nd ed., pp. 13–24). New York: Oxford University Press.
Coplan, R. J., Prakash, K., O'Neil, K., & Armer, M. (2004). Do you "want" to play?: Distinguishing between conflicted shyness and social disinterest in early childhood. *Developmental Psychology, 40,* 244–258.
Costa, P. T., & McCrae, R. R. (1980). Influence of Extraversion and Neuroticism on subjective well-being: Happy and unhappy people. *Journal of Personality and Social Psychology, 38,* 668–678.
Danner, D. D., Snowdon, D. A., & Friesen, W. V. (2001). Positive emotions in early life and longevity: Findings from the nun study. *Journal of Personality and Social Psychology, 80,* 804–813.
Davey, M., Eaker, D. G., & Walters, L. H. (2003). Resilience processes in adolescents: Personality profiles, self-worth, and coping. *Journal of Adolescent Research, 18,* 347–362.
Denham, S. A., McKinley, M., Couchoud, E. A., & Holt, R. (1990). Emotional and behavioral predictors of preschool per ratings. *Child Development, 61,* 1145–1152.
Dennis, T. (2006). Emotional self-regulation in preschoolers: The interplay of child approach reactivity, parenting, and control capacities. *Developmental Psychology, 42,* 84–97.
Dennis, T. A., Hong, M., & Solomon, B. (2010). Do the associations between exuberance and emotion regulation depend on effortful control? *International Journal of Behavioral Development, 34*(5), 462–472.
Depue, R. A., & Morrone-Strupinsky, J. V. (2005). A neurobehavioral model of affiliative bonding: Implications for conceptualizing a human trait of affiliation. *Behavioral and Brain Sciences, 28,* 313–395.
Derryberry, D., & Rothbart, M. K. (1997). Reactive and effortful processes in the organization of temperament. *Development and Psychopathology, 9,* 633–652.
Digman, J. M. (1997). Higher-order factors of the Big Five. *Journal of Personality and Social Psychology, 73,* 1246–1256.
Donzella, B., Gunnar, M. R., Krueger, W. K., & Alwin, J. (2000). Cortical and vagal tone response to competitive challenge in preschoolers: Associations with temperament. *Developmental Psychobiology, 37,* 209–220.
Dougherty, L. R., Klein, D. N., Durbin, C. E., Hayden, E. P., & Olino, T. M. (2010). Tempera-

mental positive and negative emotionality and children's depressive symptoms: A longitudinal prospective study from age three to age ten. *Journal of Social and Clinical Psychology, 29,* 462–488.
Eisenberg, N. A., Wentzel, M. N., & Harris, D. (1998). The role of emotionality and regulation in empathy-related responding. *School Psychology Review, 27,* 506–522.
Ekman, P. (1993). Moods, emotions, and traits. In P. Ekman & R. J. Davidson (Eds.), *The nature of emotion* (pp. 56–58). New York: Oxford University Press.
Elliot, A. J., & Thrash, T. M. (2002). Approach–avoidance motivation in personality: Approach and avoidance temperaments and goals. *Journal of Personality and Social Psychology, 82,* 804–818.
Else-Quest, N., Hyde, J., Goldsmith, H., & Van Hulle, C. (2006). Gender differences in temperament: A meta-analysis. *Psychological Bulletin, 132,* 33–72.
Evans, D. E., & Rothbart, M. K. (2007). Developing a model for adult temperament. *Journal of Research in Personality, 41,* 868–888.
Evans, D. E., & Rothbart, M. K. (2009). A two-factor model of temperament. *Personality and Individual Differences, 47,* 565–570.
Feldman, R., Gordon, I., & Zagoory-Sharon, O. (2010). The cross-generation transmission of oxytocin in humans. *Hormones and Behavior, 58,* 669–676.
Fox, N. A., Henderson, H. A., Rubin, K. H., Calkins, S. D., & Schmidt, L. A. (2001). Continuity and discontinuity of behavioral inhibition and exuberance: Psychophysiological and behavioral influences across the first four years of life. *Child Development, 72,* 1–21.
Fullard, W., McDevitt, S., & Carey, W. (1984). Assessing temperament in one- to three-year-old children. *Journal of Pediatric Psychology, 9*(2), 205–217.
Gable, P., & Harmon-Jones, E. (2010). The motivational dimensional model of affect: Implications for breadth of attention, memory, and cognitive categorization. *Cognition and Emotion, 24,* 322–337.
Gartstein, M. A., Putnam, S. P., & Rothbart, M. K. (2012). Etiology of preschool behavior problems: Contributions of temperament attributes in early childhood. *Infant Mental Health Journal, 33,* 197–211.
Gartstein, M. A., & Rothbart, M. K. (2003). Studying infant temperament via a revision of the Infant Behavior Questionnaire. *Infant Behavior and Development, 26,* 64–86.
Goldsmith, H., & Campos, J. (1990). The structure of temperamental fear and pleasure in infants: A psychometric perspective. *Child Development, 61,* 1944–1964.
Goldsmith, H. H., Lemery, K. S., Buss, K. A., & Campos, J. J. (1999). Genetic analysis of focal aspects of infant temperament. *Developmental Psychology, 35,* 972–985.
Gray, J. A. (1991). The neuropsychology of temperament. In J. Strelau & A. Angleitner (Eds.), *Explorations in temperament: International perspectives on theory and measurement* (pp. 105–128). New York: Plenum Press.
Graziano, W. G., & Tobin, R. M. (2009). Agreeableness. In M. R. Leary & R. H. Hoyle (Eds.), *Handbook of individual differences in social behavior* (pp. 46–61). New York: Guilford Press.
Gruber, J., Culver, J. L., Johnson, S. L., Nam, J. Y., Keller, K. L., & Ketter, T. A. (2009). Do positive emotions predict symptomatic change in bipolar disorder? *Bipolar Disorders, 11,* 330–336.
Gruber, J., & Johnson, S. L. (2009). Positive emotional traits and ambitious goals among people at risk for mania: The need for specificity. *International Journal of Cognitive Therapy, 2,* 176–187.
Gunnar, M. R., Sebanc, A. M., Tout, K., Donzella, B., & van Dulman, M. M. H. (2003). Peer rejection, temperament, and cortical activity in preschoolers. *Developmental Psychobiology, 43,* 346–358.
Halverson, C., Havill, V., Deal, J., Baker, S., Victor, J., Pavlopoulous, V., et al. (2003). Personality structure as derived from parental ratings of free descriptions of children: The Inventory of Child Individual Differences. *Journal of Personality, 71,* 995–1026.
Hane, A. A., Fox, N. A., Henderson, H. A., & Marshall, P. J. (2008). Early behavioral reactivity and approach–withdrawal in infancy. *Developmental Psychology, 44,* 1491–1496.
Harker, L., & Keltner, D. (2001). Expressions of positive emotion in women's college yearbook pictures and their relationship to personality and life outcomes across adulthood. *Journal of Personality and Social Psychology, 80,* 112–124.
Hayden, E. P., Klein, D. N., Durbin, C. E., & Olino, T. M. (2006). Low positive emotionality at age three predicts depressotypic cognitions in seven-year-old children. *Development and Psychopathology, 18,* 409–423.
Hayden, E. P., Shankman, S. A., Olino, T. M., Durbin, C. E., Tenke, C. E., Bruder, G. E., et al. (2008). Cognitive and temperamental vulnerability to depression: Longitudinal associations with regional cortical activity. *Cognition and Emotion, 22,* 1415–1428.
He, J., Degnan, K. A., McDermott, J. M., Henderson, H. A., Hane, A. A., Xu, Q., et al. (2010). Anger and approach motivation in infancy: Relations to early childhood inhibitory control and behavior problems. *Infancy, 15,* 246–269.

Held, B. S. (2004). The negative side of positive psychology. *Journal of Humanistic Psychology, 44,* 9–46.

Jensen-Campbell, L. A., & Graziano, W. G. (2001). Agreeableness as a moderator of interpersonal conflict. *Journal of Personality, 69,* 323–362.

Jung, C. G. (1928). *Contributions to analytic psychology.* New York: Wiley.

Kafry, D. (1982). Sensation seeking of young children. *Personality and Individual Differences, 3,* 161–166.

Kagan, J., Reznick, J. S., Snidman, N., Gibbons, J., & Johnson, M. O. (1988). Childhood derivatives of inhibition and lack of inhibition to the unfamiliar. *Child Development, 59,* 1580–1589.

Kim, G., Walden, T., Harris, V., Karrass, J., & Catron, T. (2006). Positive emotion, negative emotion, and emotion control in externalizing problems of school age children. *Child Psychiatry and Human Development, 37,* 221–239.

Kochanska, G. (1991). Patterns of inhibition to the unfamiliar in children of normal and affectively ill mothers. *Child Development, 62,* 250–263.

Kochanska, G., Aksan, N., Penney, S. J., & Doobay, A. F. (2007). Early positive emotionality as a heterogeneous trait: Implications for children's self-regulation. *Journal of Personality and Social Psychology, 93,* 1054–1066.

Komsi, N., Raikkonen, K., Heinonen, K., Pesonen, A.-K., Keskivaara, P., Jarvenpaa, A.-L., et al. (2006). Continuity of temperament from infancy to middle childhood. *Infant Behavior and Development, 29,* 494–508.

Komsi, N., Raikkonen, K., Heinonen, K., Pesonen, A.-K., Keskivaara, P., Jarvenpaa, A.-L., et al. (2008). Continuity of father-rated temperament from infancy to middle childhood. *Infant Behavior and Development, 31,* 239–254.

Krueger, R. F., Hicks, B. M., & McGue, M. (2001). Altruism and antisocial behavior: Independent tendencies, unique personality correlates, distinct etiologies. *Psychological Science, 12,* 397–402.

Laptook, R. S., Klein, D. N., Durbin, C. E., Hayden, E. P., Olino, T. M., & Carlson, G. (2008). Differentiation between low positive affectivity and behavioral inhibition in preschool-age children: A comparison of behavioral approach in novel and non-novel contexts. *Journal of Personality and Individual Differences, 44,* 758–767.

Laptook, R. S., Klein, D. N., Olino, T. M., Dyson, M. W., & Carlson, G. (2010). Low positive affectivity and behavioral inhibition in preschool-age children: A replication and extension of previous findings. *Personality and Individual Differences, 48,* 547–551.

Lengua, L. J., & Kovacs, E. A. (2005). Bidirectional associations between temperament and parenting and the prediction of adjustment problems in middle childhood. *Applied Developmental Psychology, 26,* 21–38.

Lengua, L. J., West, S. G., & Sandler, I. N. (1998). Temperament as a predictor of symptomology in children: Addressing contamination of measures. *Child Development, 69,* 164–181.

Lengua, L. J., Wolchik, S. A., Sandler, I. N., & West, S. G. (2000). The additive and interactive effects of parenting and temperament in predicting adjustment problems of children of divorce. *Journal of Clinical Child Psychology, 29,* 232–244.

Lewis, M., Sullivan, M. W., Ramsay, D. S., & Alessandri, S. M. (1992). Violation of expectancy, loss of control, and anger expressions in young infants. *Developmental Psychology, 26,* 745–751.

Lonigan, C. J., Phillips, B. M., & Hooe, E. S. (2003). Relations of positive and negative affectivity to anxiety and depression in children: Evidence from a latent variable longitudinal study. *Journal of Consulting and Clinical Psychology, 71,* 465–481.

Lucas, R. E., Le, K., & Dyrenforth, P. S. (2008). Explaining the Extraversion/positive affect relation: Sociability cannot account for extraverts' greater happiness. *Journal of Personality, 76,* 385–414.

MacDonald, K. (1992). Warmth as a developmental construct: An evolutionary analysis. *Child Development, 63,* 753–773.

Majdandzic, M., & van den Boom, D. (2007). Multimethod longitudinal assessment of temperament in early childhood. *Journal of Personality, 75,* 121–167.

Martin, R. P., Drew, K. D., Gaddis, L. R., & Mosley, M. (1988). Prediction of elementary school achievement from preschool temperament: Three studies. *School Psychology Review, 17,* 125–137.

Martin, R. P., & Holbrook, J. (1985). Relationship of temperament characteristics to the academic achievement of first-grade children. *Journal of Psychoeducational Assessment, 3,* 131–140.

Meehl, P. E. (1975). Hedonic capacity: Some conjectures. *Bulletin of the Menninger Clinic, 39,* 295–306.

Mitchell, J. T. (2010). Behavioral approach in ADHD: Testing a motivational dysfunction hypothesis. *Journal of Attention Disorders, 13,* 609–617.

Muris, P., Meesters, C., & Blijlevens, P. (2007). Self-reported reactive and regulative temperament in early adolescence: Relations to internalizing and externalizing problem behavior and "Big Three" personality factors. *Journal of Adolescence, 30,* 1035–1049.

Nigg, J. T., Goldsmith, H. H., & Sachek, J. (2004). Temperament and attention deficit hyperactivity disorder: The development of a multiple pathway model. *Journal of Clinical Child and Adolescent Psychology, 33,* 42–53.

Nusslock, R., Abramson, L., Harmon-Jones, E., Alloy, L., & Coan, J. (2009). Psychosocial interventions for bipolar disorder: Perspective from the behavioral approach system (BAS) dysregulation theory. *Clinical Psychology: Science and Practice, 16,* 449–469.

Oldehinkel, A. J., Hartman, C. A., de Winter, A. F., Veenstra, R., & Ormel, J. (2004). Temperamental profiles associated with internalizing and externalizing problems in preadolescence. *Development and Psychopathology, 16,* 421–440.

Park, S. Y., Belsky, J., Putnam, S. P., & Crnic, K. (1997). Infant emotionality, parenting, and 3-year inhibition: Exploring stability and lawful discontinuity in a male sample. *Developmental Psychology, 33,* 218–227.

Parker, J. D. A., Majeski, S. A., & Collin, V. T. (2003). ADHD symptoms and personality: Relationships with the five-factor model. *Personality and Individual Differences, 36,* 977–987.

Pfeifer, M., Goldsmith, H. H., Davidson, R. J., & Rickman, M. (2002). Continuity and change in inhibited and uninhibited children. *Child Development, 73,* 1474–1488.

Polak-Toste, C. P., & Gunnar, M. R. (2006). Temperamental exuberance: Correlates and consequences. In P. J. Marshall & N. A. Fox (Eds.), *The development of social engagement: Neurobiological perspectives* (pp. 19–45). New York: Oxford University Press.

Presley, R., & Martin, R. P. (1994). Toward a structure of preschool temperament: Factor structure of the Temperament Assessment Battery for Children. *Journal of Personality, 62,* 415–448.

Putnam, S. P., Ellis, L. K., & Rothbart, M. K. (2001). The structure of temperament from infancy through adolescence. In A. Eliasz & A. Angleitner (Eds.), *Advances/proceedings in research on temperament* (pp. 165–182). Lengerich, Germany: Pabst Science.

Putnam, S. P., Gartstein, M. A., & Rothbart, M. K. (2006). Measurement of fine-grained aspects of toddler temperament: The Early Childhood Behavior Questionnaire. *Infant Behavior and Development, 29,* 386–401.

Putnam, S. P., Rothbart, M. K., & Gartstein, M. A. (2008). Homotypic and heterotypic continuity of fine-grained temperament during infancy, toddlerhood, and early childhood. *Infant and Child Development, 17,* 387–405.

Putnam, S. P., & Stifter, C. A. (2005). Behavioral approach–inhibition in toddlers: Prediction from infancy, positive and negative affective components, and relations with behavior problems. *Child Development, 76,* 212–226.

Quay, H. C. (1993). The psychobiology of undersocialized aggressive conduct disorder: A theoretical perspective. *Development and Psychopathology, 5,* 165–180.

Rothbart, M. K. (1981). Measurement of temperament in infancy. *Child Development, 52,* 569–578.

Rothbart, M. K. (1986). Longitudinal observation of infant temperament. *Developmental Psychology, 22,* 356–365.

Rothbart, M. K. (1988). Temperament and the development of inhibited approach. *Child Development, 59,* 1241–1250.

Rothbart, M. K., Ahadi, S. A., & Evans, D. E. (2000). Temperament and personality: Origins and outcomes. *Journal of Personality and Social Psychology, 78,* 122–135.

Rothbart, M. K., Ahadi, S. A., & Hershey, K. L. (1994). Temperament and social behavior in childhood. *Merrill–Palmer Quarterly, 40,* 21–39.

Rothbart, M. K., Ahadi, S. A., Hershey, K. L., & Fisher, P. (2001). Investigation of temperament at three to seven years: The Children's Behavior Questionnaire. *Child Development, 72,* 1394–1408.

Rothbart, M. K., & Bates, J. E. (2006). Temperament. In N. Eisenberg, W. Damon, & R. M. Lerner (Eds.), *Handbook of child psychology* (6th ed., Vol. 3, pp. 99–166). Hoboken, NJ: Wiley.

Rothbart, M. K., Derryberry, D., & Hershey, K. L. (2000). Stability of temperament in childhood: Laboratory infant assessment to parent report at seven years. In V. J. Molfese & D. L. Molfese (Eds.), *Temperament and personality development across the life span* (pp. 85–119). Hillsdale, NJ: Erlbaum.

Rothbart, M. K., & Hwang, J. (2005). Temperament and the development of competence and motivation. In A. J. Elliot & C. S. Dweck (Eds.), *Handbook of competence and motivation* (pp. 167–184). New York: Guilford Press.

Rubin, K. H., Coplan, R. J., Fox, N. A., & Calkins, S. D. (1995). Emotionality, emotion regulation, and preschoolers' social adaptation. *Development and Psychopathology, 7,* 49–62.

Rudasill, K. M., Gallagher, K. C., & White, J. M. (2010). Temperamental attention and activity, classroom emotional support, and academic achievement in third grade. *Journal of School Psychology, 48,* 113–134.

Rydell, A., Berlin, L., & Bohlin, G. (2003). Emotionality, emotion regulation, and adaptation among 5- to 8-year-old children. *Emotion, 3,* 30–47.

Rydell, A., Thorell, L. B., & Bohlin, G. (2007). Emotion regulation in relation to social functioning: An investigation of child self-reports. *European Journal of Developmental Psychology 4,* 293–313.

Sanson, A. V., Smart, D. F., Prior, M., Oberklaid,

F., & Pedlow, R. (1994). The structure of temperament from three to seven years: Age, sex and sociodemographic influences. *Merrill–Palmer Quarterly, 40,* 233–252.

Sheese, B. E., Voelker, P. M., Rothbart, M. K., & Posner, M. I. (2007). Parenting quality interacts with genetic variation in dopamine receptor D4 to influence temperament in early childhood. *Development and Psychopathology, 19,* 1039–1046.

Shiota, M. N., Keltner, D., & John, O. P. (2006). Positive emotion dispositions differentially associated with Big Five personality and attachment style. *Journal of Positive Psychology, 1,* 61–71.

Shiner, R. L. (1998). How shall we speak of children's personalities in middle childhood?: A preliminary taxonomy. *Psychological Bulletin, 124,* 308–332.

Shiner, R. L. (2000). Linking childhood personality with adaptation: Evidence for continuity and change across time into late adolescence. *Journal of Personality and Social Psychology, 78,* 310–325.

Shiner, R. L., & Caspi, A. (2003). Personality differences in childhood and adolescence: Measurement, development, and consequences. *Journal of Child Psychology and Psychiatry, 44,* 2–32.

Shiner, R. L., & Masten, A. S. (2002). Transactional links between personality and adaptation from childhood through adulthood. *Journal of Research in Personality, 36,* 580–588.

South, S. C., Krueger, R. F., Johnson, W., & Iacono, W. G. (2008). Adolescent personality moderates genetic and environmental influences on relationships with parents. *Journal of Personality and Social Psychology, 94,* 899–912.

Stifter, C. A., & Grant, W. (1993). Infant responses to frustration: Individual differences in the expression of negative affect. *Journal of Nonverbal Behavior, 17,* 187–204.

Stifter, C. A., Putnam, S. P., & Jahromi, L. (2008). Exuberant and inhibited toddlers: Stability of temperament and risk for problem behavior. *Developmental Psychopathology, 20,* 401–421.

Taylor, S. E., Klein, L. C., Lewis, B. P., Gruenewald, T. L., Gurung, R. A. R., & Updegraff, J. A. (2000). Biobehavioral responses to stress in females: Tend-and-befriend, not fight-or-flight. *Psychological Review, 107*(3), 411–429.

Tellegen, A. (1985). Structures of mood and personality and their relevance to assessing anxiety, with an emphasis on self-report. In A. H. Tuma & J. Maser (Eds.), *Anxiety and the anxiety disorders* (pp. 681–706). Hillsdale, NJ: Erlbaum.

Tellegen, A., Lykken, D. T., Bouchard, T. J., Jr., Wilcox, K. J., Segal, N. L., & Rich, S. (1988). Personality similarity in twins reared apart and together. *Journal of Personality and Social Psychology, 54,* 1031–1039.

Thomas, A., & Chess, S. (1977). *Temperament and development.* New York: Brunner/Mazel.

Wachs, T. D., & Bates, J. (2010). Temperament. In J. G. Bremner & T. D. Wachs (Eds.), *Wiley Blackwell handbook of infant development: Vol. 1. Basic research* (2nd ed., pp. 592–622). Malden, MA: Wiley Blackwell.

Watson, D. (2000). *Mood and temperament.* New York: Guilford Press.

Watson, D. (2009). Locating anger in the hierarchical structure of affect: Comment on Carver and Harmon-Jones (2009). *Psychological Bulletin, 135,* 205–208.

Watson, D., & Clark, L. A. (1997a). Extraversion and its positive emotional core. In S. Briggs, W. Jones, & R. Hogan (Eds.), *Handbook of personality psychology* (pp. 767–793). San Diego, CA: Academic Press.

Watson, D., & Clark, L. A. (1997b). The measurement and mismeasurement of mood: Recurrent and emergent issues. *Journal of Personality Assessment, 68,* 267–296.

Watson, D., Clark, L. A., & Carey, G. (1988). Positive and negative affectivity and their relation to anxiety and depressive disorders. *Journal of Abnormal Psychology, 97,* 346–353.

Watson, D., & Tellegen, A. (1985). Toward a consentual structure of mood. *Psychological Bulletin, 98,* 219–235.

Watson, D., Wiese, D., Vaidya, J., & Tellegen, A. (1999). The two general activation systems of affect: Structural findings, evolutionary considerations, and psychobiological evidence. *Journal of Personality and Social Psychology, 76,* 820–838.

Wetter, E. K., & Hankin, B. L. (2009). Mediational pathways through which positive and negative emotionality contribute to anhedonic symptoms of depression: A prospective study of adolescents. *Journal of Abnormal Child Psychology, 37,* 507–520.

Zhou, Q., Lengua, L. J., & Wang, Y. (2009). The relations of temperament reactivity and effortful control to children's adjustment problems in China and the United States. *Developmental Psychology, 45,* 724–739.

Zuckerman, M. (1994). *Behavioral expressions and biosocial bases of sensation seeking.* Cambridge, UK: Cambridge University Press.

CHAPTER 7

Anger and Irritability

Kirby Deater-Deckard
Zhe Wang

Some people are usually "hotheaded" and irritable, but others hardly ever get frustrated. Can this wide variation in people be attributed in part to an underlying disposition for thinking angry thoughts, and experiencing and expressing angry feelings? The short answer is "yes," but the long answer is more complex and interesting. Addressing this question requires consideration of a large body of research that points to complex systems of biological and environmental influences in development that produce individual differences in anger and irritability over the lifespan.

Constructs and Measurement

Anger and irritability are closely interrelated unpleasant emotions that are part of a broader negative affectivity construct. *Anger* is a universal basic negative emotion that is unpleasant to the person experiencing it and to those who witness it. It has distinct motor features (e.g., facial expressions, body movements, and vocalization patterns), body sensations rooted in physiology (e.g., increased heart rate, blood pressure, and muscle tension), and cognitive attributes involving perception and appraisal (Novaco, 2000). Like other negative emotions, anger is critical to adaptation and survival through its role in motivation and social signaling of preemptive or retaliatory reward-seeking and harm-avoiding behavior (Darwin, 1872). However, if experienced and expressed frequently and intensely, it has serious deleterious consequences for health and social functioning.

Irritability is a related unpleasant emotional experience that has many of the same objective and subjective features as anger. Irritability involves aversive sensations arising in response to different kinds of stimulation and can precede or follow an angry episode. It can be thought of as general reactivity, quick temperedness, and rudeness (Buss & Durkee, 1957). *Frustration*, yet another unpleasant emotional experience closely related to anger and irritability, arises from perceived threats to resources or rewards, or barriers to pursuit of a goal. Frustration and anger motivate the individual to take preemptive or retaliatory action when such threats or barriers are perceived, while also communicating to others his or her potential to act in a way that may damage objects or harm people (Kennedy, 1992; Lewis, 2010). These various concepts, definitions, and examples of measures are summarized in Table 7.1. Given the conceptual

TABLE 7.1. Concepts, Definitions, and Examples of Measures

Concept	Definition	Examples of measures
Anger	An unpleasant negative emotion accompanied by behaviors, sensations, and cognitions that motivate preemptive or retaliatory action	• Observed response to stimuli (Alessandri, Sullivan, & Lewis, 1990; Calkins & Johnson, 1998; LAB-TAB: Goldsmith & Rothbart, 1988) • Toddler Behavior Assessment Questionnaire: Anger Proneness (Goldsmith, 1996) • Children's Behavior Questionnaire: Frustration/Anger (Putnam & Rothbart, 2006) • EASI Questionnaire: Emotionality (Buss & Plomin, 1975) • Hostility Inventory (Buss & Durkee, 1957)
Irritability	Unpleasant sensations and accompanying behavioral expressions of quick temper and rudeness that arise from reactivity to stimulation	• Irritability and Emotional Susceptibility Scales (Caprara et al., 1985) • Neonatal Behavioral Assessment Scale (Brazelton & Nugent, 2011)
Frustration	Unpleasant cognitive–affective experience arising from appraisal of impeded goal pursuit or threat to resource	• Observed response to stimuli (Alessandri et al., 1990; Calkins & Johnson, 1998; Goldsmith & Rothbart, 1988) • Child Behavior Questionnaire: Frustration/Anger (Putnam & Rothbart, 2006)
Aggression	Physical, verbal, or relational behavior directed at objects or people with intent to damage or harm, for self-protection or enhancement goal pursuit	• Observed response to modeled aggression (Bandura, Ross, & Ross, 1963) • Aggression Scale: Relational, Reactive, Instrumental (Little, Jones, Henrich, & Hawley, 2003) • Reactive–Proactive Aggression Questionnaire (Raine et al., 2006)
Difficult temperament	Broad affective–behavioral construct comprised of variety of behaviors that are challenging to others, including anger and irritability	• Infant Characteristics Questionnaire (Bates, Freeland, & Lounsbury, 1979) • Observed undercontrolled behavior (Caspi et al., 2003)

overlap in anger, irritability and frustration, we refer generally to *anger* throughout the chapter except when addressing research that has examined irritability or frustration specifically.

Disposition and Temperament

Anger, irritability, and frustration are closely related aspects of negative emotion that are experienced and expressed by nearly everyone at one time or another. They function as emotion or mood states elicited by situational factors that change over time, so they occur rapidly and without effort, often outside of awareness (Ruys & Stapel, 2008). They also are expressed at different frequencies and levels of intensity across a variety of situations, depending on the individuals in question. This has led to the idea that there is an underlying disposition for experiencing and expressing anger that is part of temperament.

Temperament represents biologically influenced individual differences in affective and behavioral reactivity, and self-regulation that provide the foundation for personality and other domains of individuality (Rothbart & Bates, 1998; also see, this volume, Rothbart, Chapter 1; Mervielde & De Pauw, Chapter 2; Zuckerman, Chapter 3). It comprises emotions and behaviors that vary across individuals from infancy and onward, show moderate to substantial stability or test–retest correlations (i.e., $r > .3$) across contexts and over time, and are influenced by genetic and other biological factors (Caspi & Shiner, 2006; Zentner & Bates, 2008).

According to Strelau (2001), temperament traits or dispositions arise from genetic and nongenetic factors that influence neurological and biochemical mechanisms and in turn produce variability in behaviors (including expression of emotions) and internal states (including subjective experiences of emotion). These behaviors and internal states are the situation-by-situation manifestations of the underlying dispositions, as well as the influences of situational factors and prior behaviors and states. Thus, the observed behaviors that define dispositions reflect neural activity involved in energy, motivation, and responses to perceived changes in the environment, as well as mechanisms of self-regulation (Posner & Rothbart, 2007).

Like all other emotions, anger is socially embedded. Dispositional anger depends in part on cognitive and affective appraisal mechanisms involving attention and interpretation of the social environment, as well as one's own thoughts and body sensations (Lemerise & Arsenio, 2000; Wranik & Scherer, 2010). Three prominent cognitive aspects of dispositional anger include the tendency to attribute hostile intent in others' actions, to perceive frustration in a variety of situations, and to engage in continuous conscious pondering and rumination over one's own anger, as well as the perceived provocations of others (Kuppens, Mechelen, & Rjimen, 2008; Wilkowski & Robinson, 2010).

Individuals who are hostile and argumentative tend to be vigilant for potential provocation from others, to initiate and sustain arguments when provocation is perceived, and to react angrily when others' behaviors are viewed as hostile or rejecting (Romero-Canyas, Downey, Berenson, Ayduk, & Kang, 2010). The likelihood of this pattern of emotion in social interaction is enhanced by arousal during potential conflict. Unlike chronically hostile individuals, nonargumentative individuals typically experience a rapid decline in negative emotion when a potential conflict is averted—an affective experience that is strongly self-reinforcing because the feelings and social consequences of irritability and anger are so unpleasant (Moskowitz, 2010). Individual differences in these kinds of cognitive–affective features are associated with anger, as well as aggressive behavior problems, and are evident even in young children (Dodge, Bates, & Pettit, 1990). Such social-cognitive processes increase the likelihood of anger and irritability, while other cognitive features such as effortful control of attention and working memory serve to dampen and reduce anger (Bell & Deater-Deckard, 2007; Deffenbacher, 1992; Posner & Rothbart, 2007; Spielberger, Krasner, & Solomon, 1988; Wilkowski & Robinson, 2007).

Methods and Measurement

The experiential and expressive features of anger and irritability can be reliably measured using questionnaires and observations, and the latent structure of the underlying dispositional components can be quantified using exploratory and confirmatory factor analysis (in this volume, see Mervielde & De Pauw, Chapter 2; Zuckerman, Chapter 3; Gartstein, Bridgett, & Low, Chapter 10). Psychometric studies have demonstrated the reliability and validity of dimensional scales at different ages and for different informants. These scales capture the emotional, behavioral, and cognitive components of dispositional anger, irritability, and frustration (Martin, Watson, & Wan, 2000). As shown in Table 7.1, a variety of questionnaire and observational measurement tools have been developed to measure anger, irritability, and frustration in children and adults. The laboratory-based measures use observers' ratings of child behavior in situations in which anticipated interesting events do not occur, the body is physically restrained, or access to toys or treats is blocked or impeded. Computerized tasks also can be used (see Goldsmith & Gagne, Chapter 11, this volume). The questionnaire measures use parents' reports and self-reports of perceived behavior. A number of studies also incorporate physiological measurements to capture aspects of nervous system activity and regulation (Engebretson, Sirota, Niaura, Edwards, & Brown, 1999; Lewis, 2010; see Calkins & Swingler, Chapter 12, this volume).

Individual differences in dispositional anger, irritability, and frustration covary and are used interchangeably to refer to the various common aspects they share (Leon, 1992; Siegman & Smith, 1994; Stringaris, Cohen, Pine, & Leibenluft, 2009). As a result, many of the measures in this literature combine indicators pertaining to anger, frustration, and irritability within the same scale. This mixing of indicators reflects changes over time in theories about the constructs, as well as the substantial covariation between the constructs that make it difficult to distinguish them in psychometric analyses. On a more substantive note, the overlap may represent a broader dimension of *difficult temperament* that has been identified by some theorists (Bates, Freeland, & Lounsbury, 1979; Chess & Thomas, 1984). Furthermore, these constructs can co-occur in different ways with each other and other negative emotions and behaviors to form clusters of qualitatively distinct subgroups of individuals. Clustering approaches have been the basis for defining a temperamentally *difficult* subgroup of young children (Thomas & Chess, 1977), as well as a subgroup of *undercontrolled* children who are at greater risk for maladaptive outcomes in adolescence and adulthood (Caspi & Silva, 1995).

Anger also is part of a higher-order dimension of negative affectivity that includes other negative emotions (e.g., fear and sadness), as measured in instruments such as the Children's Behavior Questionnaire and Adult Temperament Questionnaire (Evans & Rothbart, 2007; Putnam & Rothbart, 2006). Figure 7.1 illustrates this higher-order latent variable structure using data from parents' ratings on the Children's Behavior Questionnaire of their firstborn (Twin 1) and secondborn (Twin 2) 6- to 10-year-old twins (Mullineaux, Deater-Deckard, Petrill, Thompson,

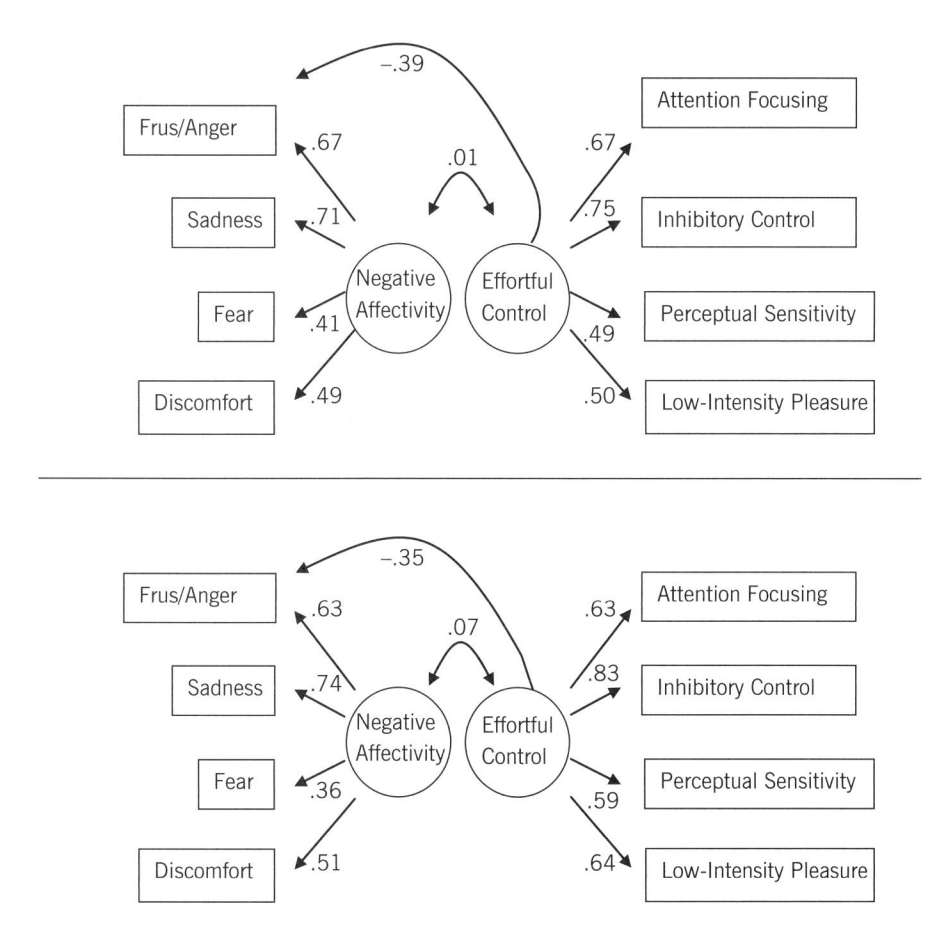

FIGURE 7.1. Factor analysis model. Principal axis factor analysis results (pattern matrix values) based on data from Mullineaux et al. (2009). At the top are data for Twin 1, and at the bottom, data for Twin 2.

& DeThorne, 2009). Figure 7.1 shows on the left the pattern matrix values from a principal axis factor analysis representing the facets of a general negative affectivity (NA) factor. The magnitude and pattern of the factor loadings provide clear evidence of the NA factor—a structure that is replicated across the Twin 1 and Twin 2 subsamples. However, anger is also negatively related to the effortful control (EC) construct on the right—an aspect of emotion regulation that we return to later (also see Rueda, Chapter 8, this volume).

In summary, dispositional anger and irritability are important facets of temperament from early in life. Once a measure has been established and tested for reliability and validity it can be used for self-reporting; reporting by knowledgeable informants, such as parents and peers; and reporting by strangers who observe individuals' behaviors. As one would expect for any dispositional construct, individual differences in anger and irritability are correlated across informants and contexts (Kerr, 2008; Tangney, 1996). However, there also are systematic perceiver effects that lead to informant bias, as well as systematic context effects due to situational features of particular settings (i.e., laboratory, home, school, and workplace). These nondispositional factors also predict some of the individual-difference variability in anger and should not be ignored (Kim, Mullineaux, Allen, & Deater-Deckard, 2010). Likewise, physiological, behavioral, and questionnaire measures of anger tend to correlate, but each type of measure also has its own systematic method variance that does not correlate with the others (Hubbard, Parker, & Ramsden, 2004). Informant, context, and method effects certainly complicate measurement and hypothesis testing. However, their presence is not inconsistent with theories of temperament defining underlying dispositions that are neither expressed in all situations nor perceived in the same way by all people (Strelau, 2001; Wood, Harms, & Vazire, 2010).

Development

If individual differences in anger and irritability are part of temperament, how does this dimension of negative affectivity develop? To answer this question, examination of two aspects of development can be helpful: increases and decreases in the average levels of anger at different points in the lifespan, and stability versus change in individual differences in anger over the lifespan.

Change and Stability of Average Levels

Humans are capable of displaying signs of distress and irritability in their facial expressions, vocalizations, and body movements from the time they are born. Behavioral states (including emotion expressions) in newborns are not well organized, but this changes rapidly over the first 4 to 5 months of life as infants' emotional and behavioral states coalesce into distinguishable patterns of the universal basic or primary emotions of anger, fear, sadness, joy, surprise, disgust, and interest (Lewis, 2010). By 5 or 6 months of age infants show wide-ranging individual differences in the frequency and intensity of angry responses to frustrating circumstances when anticipated environmental contingencies are disrupted (Rothbart, 1986). Infants of this age can be reliably distinguished in their level of irritability and frustration tolerance, typically measured as the latency to respond to a mildly irritating or painful stimulus, the magnitude of the response, and the time it takes for the negative emotional state to subside (Posner & Rothbart, 2007).

Over the first 2 to 3 years of life, the average level of dispositional anger gradually increases (Braungart-Rieker, Hill-Soderlund, & Karrass, 2010; Putnam, Gartstein, & Rothbart, 2006), then from age 3 to 6 declines and levels off (Rothbart, Ahadi, Hershey, & Fisher, 2001). Over middle childhood, the average level of anger does not change (Deater-Deckard et al., 2010; Kim et al., 2010). Anger again increases in the transition into and through adolescence (Larson & Asmussen, 1991), but again gradually decreases over the transition to and through adulthood (Blonigen, Carlson, Hicks, Krueger, & Iacono, 2008; Caspi & Roberts, 2001; Galambos & Krahn, 2008). The gradual decrease in anger continues through middle and old age (Charles, Mather, & Carstensen, 2003; Phillips, Henry, Hosie, & Milne, 2006), although the magnitude of change over adulthood is modest.

Change and Stability of Individual Differences

The second aspect of development to consider is whether there are changes over time between individuals when compared to each other. For this comparison, longitudinal data are used to compute "test–retest" or "stability" correlations. These correlations represent the degree to which individuals' rank at a given age correlates with their rank at a subsequent point in development. The more substantial the stability correlation, the less change there is in relative rank order between individuals over time. For the vast majority of longitudinal studies, stability correlations have been based on parents' ratings from infancy through childhood, and self-reports from adolescence through adulthood.

It takes the first 4–5 months of postnatal life for anger, irritability, and frustration to cohere into organized affective–behavioral states (Lewis, 2010). As infants rapidly develop the capacity to express and regulate anger, they can change markedly and unpredictably from one month to the next in their levels of anger and irritability—a developmental pattern that is reflected in modest stability correlations up to and through 9 months of age (Rothbart, 1981, 1986). As infants become toddlers, then move through the preschool years, the stability correlation increases into the .3 to .6 range (Putnam & Rothbart, 2006; Putnam et al., 2006). Over middle childhood and the transition to early adolescence, the typical stability correlation is in the .5 to .7 range (Kim et al., 2010; Rothbart et al., 2001). A similar range of stability correlations is found in adolescence and adulthood (Cole, Peeke, Dolezal, Murray, & Canzoniero, 1999; McCrae & Costa, 1994).

Development and Self-Regulation

A temperament perspective on dispositional anger also includes consideration of the regulatory aspects of negative emotionality and behavior more broadly (Block & Block, 1980; Rothbart & Bates, 1998). Data from many studies show that children and adults who have the highest levels of anger also have the lowest levels of cognitive self-regulation (Wilkowski & Robinson, 2010).

Consistent with this are the data in Figure 7.1 for 6- to 10-year-old children. The dispositional anger variable loads on the higher-order effortful control (EC) self-regulation factor, as well as the higher-order negative affect (NA) factor. More generally, individual differences in self-regulation in childhood predict a wide range of positive and negative outcomes over adolescence and into adulthood (Moffitt et al., 2011).

Developmental changes in anger and irritability over the lifespan can be attributed in part to developmental changes in self-regulation (Halverson, Kohnstamm, Martin, & Martin, 1994; see Rueda, Chapter 8, this volume). Self-regulation includes cognitive control of attention and working memory, as well as other aspects of executive function that involve neural activity in the brain's orbitofrontal cortex (Ochsner & Gross, 2005; Posner & Rothbart, 2007; Rueda, Posner, & Rothbart, 2005, see also White et al., Chapter 17, this volume). Cognitive regulation of attention and memory improves dramatically from 2 to 5 years of age, then more gradually over childhood and adolescence (Posner & Rothbart, 2007). In those periods in development such as early childhood and early adolescence, when there are bursts of autonomy but lagging cognitive self-regulation capacity, there is growth in the average level of anger. By adulthood, gradual improvement in the capacity to regulate negative emotions continues into middle age and beyond (Blonigen et al., 2008; Phillips et al., 2006), and may arise from developmental changes in contexts, as well as cognitive regulation mechanisms (Blanchard-Fields, 2008).

In summary, there are clear patterns of lifespan developmental change in the average level and stability correlation for anger. This includes a gradually increasing stability correlation for dispositional anger that mirrors the pattern found for broader measures of negative affectivity and trait Neuroticism (Roberts & DelVecchio, 2000)—a finding that is interesting but not surprising, given that anger is a major facet of the higher-order Negative Affectivity/Neuroticism factor (see Figure 7.1). Although the developmental literature clearly points to continuity in individual rank order over time, even the most substantial stability correlation explains only about half of the individual difference variation. The other half or more of the variance at any point in development may be difficult to predict, in part because it includes measurement error. Nevertheless, this serves as a reminder that individuals do change relative to each other, particularly in early childhood when stability correlations are modest.

Biological Factors

A temperament perspective on dispositional anger stipulates that biological influences contribute to individual differences (Rothbart & Bates, 1998; Strelau, 2001). This has fueled a great deal of research on neurobiological and genetic factors. There is extensive animal and human research examining the anatomical and functional components of the central nervous system (CNS) that account for dispositional anger and irritability. Dispositional anger and aggressive behavior involve a CNS hierarchy of neural systems, hormones, and neurotransmitters (Sander, Grandjean, Pourtois, Schwartz, & Seghier, 2005). This literature has shown that the amygdala and superior temporal sulcus regions of the brain are involved in processing information pertaining to anger, with dorsal anterior cingulate cortex and prefrontal cortex being involved in the elicitation, experience, rumination, expression, and cognitive control of anger. These cortical systems do this by initiating, integrating, and regulating activities in the subcortical limbic system involved in perception, memory, affect, and motivation (Denson, Pedersen, Ronquillo, & Nandy, 2008; Potegal & Stemmler, 2010; see also White et al., Chapter 17, and Depue & Fu, Chapter 18, this volume). As regulatory cognitive processes develop and become more habitual and automatic, the neurocognitive resources for appraisal and problem solving in anger-inducing situations become more readily available and effective (Mauss, Cook, & Gross, 2007; Wilkowski & Robinson, 2007).

Anger, irritability, and frustration may be distinct from other negative emotions through the role they play in appetitive reward-seeking approach behaviors (Williams et al., 2005). Relative activation of left frontal cortex and deactivation of right frontal cortex is indicative of anger and behavioral approach motivation (Eddie, 2007; Harmon-Jones & Sigelman, 2001; van Honk, Harmon-Jones, Morgan, & Schutter, 2010). Behavioral approach enhances detection and monitoring of potential rewards, and involves dopamine neurons and changes in activation in ventral striatum. At the same time, monitoring and detection of perceived impediments to attaining a reward and motivation to overcome those impediments (i.e., frustration) involves serotonin neurons, changes in activation in anterior insula and prefrontal cortex brain regions (Abler, Walter, & Erk, 2005). Correlational and experimental psychopharmacological studies also have implicated low levels of serotonin in the etiology of poor emotion regulation and chronic anger (Bond & Wingrove, 2010; van Honk et al., 2010).

Genetic Factors

There is clear evidence of genetic contributions to individual differences in anger and irritability from childhood through adulthood (see Saudino & Wang, Chapter 16, this volume). Most of the evidence comes from behavioral genetic studies involving twins and adoptees, showing that 40–70% of the variance in dispositional anger is heritable (Coccaro, Bergeman, Kavoussi, & Seroczynski, 1997; Gagne, Vendlinski, & Goldsmith, 2009; Saudino, 2005). In the data on school-age twins shown in Figure 7.1, two-thirds of the variance in parent-reported child frustration and anger was heritable, an effect size that is consistent with prior studies of children and adolescents (Mullineaux et al., 2009). Other studies have found additional nonadditive genetic dominance variance that may differ for males and females (Hur, 2006; Rebollo & Boomsma, 2006). The genetic variance tends to be consistent over time, accounting for the majority of the stability correlations for dispositional anger, fear, and sadness (Blonigen et al., 2008). There also is a moderate degree of nongenetic variance that does not contribute to family member similarity (i.e., nonshared environment and random measurement error), with some studies finding that some of this nongenetic variance also contributes to family member similarity (i.e., shared environment; e.g., Wang, Trivedi, Treiber, & Snieder, 2005).

Unlike behavioral genetic methods, molecular genetic methods examine statistical effects of measured structural variants in the DNA molecule. The most obvious of these variants is chromosomal sex, defined by the presence of "XX" or "XY" sex chromosomes (although typically its measurement is based on parent- or self-report). Overall, there is little evidence of a temporally and situationally stable sex difference in dispositional anger in community studies of children and adolescents (e.g., Aldrich & Tenenbaum, 2006; Deater-Deckard et al., 2010; Mullineaux et al., 2009). Some studies of adolescents and adults indicate that males express more anger than females (Potegal & Archer, 2004) but the literature is mixed, and when a difference is found, it tends to be a small effect (Deffenbacher, 1992; Newman, Fuqua, Gray, & Simpson, 2006).

There also is little evidence of a robust and consistent sex difference in physiological indicators of negative emotions, including anger (Kelly, 2008). Although testosterone levels during and after puberty are heritable for males and females alike, this genetic variance for testosterone probably does not overlap with any of the genetic variance in dispositional anger (Hoekstra, Bartels, & Boomsma, 2006; Sluyter et al., 2000). Thus, when a sex difference is found (i.e., males > females), it may reflect a gender difference rather than a biological sex difference in anger (Milovchevich, Howells, Drew, & Day, 2001). Overall, most of the variation in dispositional anger between people is within male and female groups, a pattern that is found for most complex human attributes (Hyde, 2005; see Else-Quest, Chapter 23, this volume).

Moving beyond sex chromosomes, molecular genetic research has focused on functional candidate genes that are involved in the production, metabolization, and regulation of serotonin, dopamine, and testosterone (Reuter, 2010). Serotonin plays a critical role in negative affectivity, including anger and irritability (Moskowitz, 2010; van Honk et al., 2010; Depue & Fu, Chapter 18, this volume). Several candidate genes involved in serotonin regulation have been identified as potential predictors of individual differences in anger. For instance, structural variations in the serotonin 1b receptor gene (*HTR1B*) statistically predict anger in young European American adult males (Conner et al., 2009), and variants of the tryptophan hydroxylase genes statistically predict anger in German (Rujescu et al., 2002) and Korean samples (Yang et al., 2010). Overall, dysregulation of serotonergic activity has been implicated in the biology of anger and aggression (Virkkeuen et al., 1994) and may function differently for males and females (Suarez & Krishnan, 2006).

The dopamine D4 receptor (*DRD4*) gene also has been implicated as a candidate gene for multiple facets of temperament, including anger (Saudino, 2005). Its link with dispositional anger has been found for different structural variants of the gene in Korean (Kang, Namkoong, & Kim, 2007) and Jewish samples (Auerbach, Faroy, Ebstein, Kahana, & Levine, 2001). The *DARPP-32* gene involved in the modulation of dopamine has been implicated in a German sample (Reuter, Weber, Fiebach, Elger, & Montag, 2009), and the *COMT* gene involved in the inactivation of dopamine also has been implicated (Baud et al., 2007; Rujescu, Giegling, Gietl, Hartmann, & Moller, 2003; but see Kang et al., 2007, for an example of a nonreplication). The monoamine oxidase Type A gene involved in the metabolizing of dopamine and serotonin has been implicated in a sample of Korean women (Yang et al., 2007). Still other candidate genes for dispositional anger include the norepinephrine system receptor gene *ADRA2A* (Comings et al., 2000), the *TBX 19* gene (Wasserman, Geijer, Sokolowski, Rozanov, & Wasserman, 2007), and the Huntington's disease gene (Kloppel, Stonnington, Petrovic, Mobbs, & Tuscher, 2010).

Candidate gene studies permit tests of hypotheses about specific genetic factors that might account for the heritability in dispositional anger and irritability. However, the samples and effect sizes in these studies tend to be small and specific to particular populations and measures. As a result, candidate gene effects have been hard to replicate. More recently, researchers have been exploring large swaths of the DNA molecule (i.e., genomewide association, or GWAS) using very large samples. However, the first published GWAS study for personality traits did not identify a replicated genetic marker for any personality dimension, including trait Neuroticism or Negativity Affectivity and its facets (Verweij et al., 2010).

In summary, understanding about the biological bases of anger and irritability has improved over the past few decades with the advent of animal and human neuroscience, and genetic methods that can be used even with very young children. Dispositional anger is moderately to substantially heritable, but identification of specific genes that account for the genetic variance has proven difficult. One explanation is that DNA-based factors interact with each other (i.e., gene × gene interaction) and with nongenetic factors (i.e., gene × environment interaction) to cause individual differences (see van IJzendoorn & Bakermans-Kranenburg, Chapter 19, this volume). For example, the statistical association between the *COMT* gene and dispositional anger may depend on exposure to abuse in childhood (Perroud et al., 2010), and the statistical association between the *DRD4* gene, anger, and aggression may depend on prior exposure to antisocial violence and deviance (Dmitrieva, Chen, Greenberger, Ogunseitan, & Ding, 2011). However, it remains to be seen whether these or other interactive effects replicate (Zammit, Owen, & Lewis, 2010). Even if all of the effects of additive and interactive genetic factors are detected, the typical effect sizes will be small. This is because the variance in complex attributes such as dispositional anger and irritability may reflect a number of individually rare structural DNA variants that nevertheless may be functionally equivalent in their effects on neural systems, sensations, and behaviors (McClellan & King, 2010).

Socialization and the Environment

Although biological factors are important in the etiology of dispositional anger, a temperament perspective also stipulates that these factors work in transaction with environmental factors (Rothbart & Bates, 1998; Strelau, 2001). This has motivated researchers to examine different aspects of the environment to understand how socialization, learning, and other contextual factors contribute to the development of dispositional anger.

Socialization of Emotion

In childhood, much of the socialization of emotion occurs in the family context by parents who redirect their children's expressions of anger and irritability (van IJzendoorn & Bakermans-Kranenburg, Chapter 19, and Bates, Schermerhorn, & Petersen, Chapter 20, this volume). These parenting behaviors include planned and reactive responses to child anger that instruct children about ways to understand and express anger that are deemed appropriate for their family and cultural context (Halberstadt & Eaton, 2002). From early childhood, most children are aware and make use of socialized emotion display rules regarding situational constraints on when and how anger is to be expressed, although there are individual differences (Shipman, Zeman, Nesin, & Fitzgerald, 2003; Underwood, Coie, & Herbsman, 1992).

Harsh home environments model and reinforce anger. Parents who are less responsive and sensitive to their children's social bids from late infancy through adolescence have youth with higher levels of dispositional anger and poorer self-regulation of negative emotions (Campbell, 2010; Snyder, Stoolmiller, Wilson, & Yamamoto, 2003). Authoritarian parenting that emphasizes punishment when children express anger actually promotes expression of anger, while affording the child fewer opportunities to learn emotion regulation strategies (Zhou, Eisenberg, Wang, & Reiser, 2004)—influences that may persist into adulthood (Burrowes & Halberstadt, 1987). Thus, children and adolescents who grow up in high-conflict environments develop higher levels of anger themselves, in part because the socialization that occurs in these contexts reinforces physiological processes that heighten arousal via chronic vigilance for hostile social cues (El-Sheikh, 2005; Jenkins, 2000; Jenkins, Shapka, & Sorenson, 2006; Radke-Yarrow & Kochanska, 1990). These social and biological processes operate in transaction to account for parent–child and sibling similarities and differences in dispositional anger and interpersonal negativity in the family (Deater-Deckard, 2009).

Socialization of emotion can happen because humans notice and appraise social information that is relevant to emotion expression and regulation (Sander et al., 2005). The appraisal of socially embedded emotion requires norms that are learned through experience and stored semantically as schemas in long-term memory (Lemerise & Arsenio, 2000). Ultimately, the socialization challenge for caregivers is to help children and adolescents learn how to modulate the inward experiences and outward behaviors, so that they can express anger and other emotions in ways that are appropriate and interpersonally adaptive rather than maladaptive (Nugier, 2007; see Lengua & Wachs, Chapter 25, this volume). Environments in which anger and hostility are frequent and normative teach and support the expression of these and other negative emotions, as seen in contexts that include high levels of harsh and rejecting interactions between peers or friends (Leary, 2006), parents and children (Chang, Schwartz, Dodge, & McBride-Chang, 2003), and bosses and coworkers (Fox & Spector, 1999). Thus, caregivers and peers play a critical role in socializing the regulation and expression of anger. To make use of these important social resources, individuals also must develop strategies for noticing and eliciting support when it is needed—interpersonal skills that are part of a broader set of emotion and social competencies that are critical to healthy emotional development (Dahlen & Martin, 2005; see Coplan & Bullock, Chapter 21, this volume).

Different norms are established in regard to when and how anger should be expressed, depending on the type of social relationship and context in question. This can be seen in the distinctions people make in expressing anger toward peers versus more powerful individuals, such as their parents or their bosses (Allan & Gilbert, 2002). Culture also influences these norms. Cultural differences reflect broad distinctions in individualism and collectivism (Eid & Diener, 2009), as well as specific distinctions in the value placed on self-control of emotion (Mauss, Butler, Roberts, & Chu, 2010; see Chen, Yang, & Fu, Chapter 22, this volume). Although there is cross-cultural variability in norms, the psychometric measurement structures and physiological patterns of anger, irritability, and other negative and positive emotions tend to be similar across cultures (Elfenbein & Ambady, 2002; Kovecses, 2000; Levenson, Ekman, Heider, & Friesen, 1992). This suggests that there are universally consistent underlying processes of emotion but culturally distinct display rules with regard to frequency and intensity of emotion expression.

Other Environmental Factors

Interpersonal and cultural contexts are critical in the socialization of emotion experience and expression, but other kinds of environmental factors matter, too. The prenatal environment of the womb plays a role in the development of dispositional irritability, anger, and difficult temperament (see Huizink, Chapter 15, this volume). The prenatal environment conveys maternal physical and psychological factors during fetal development that influence temperament. Prenatal exposure to cocaine, tobacco, and alcohol may cause higher levels of reactive negative affect and irritability in newborns (Eiden et al., 2009; Herrmann, King, & Weitzman, 2008; Lemola, Stadlmayr, & Grob, 2009). Mothers who experience high levels of negative affect and stress during pregnancy tend to have infants who are more irritable and emotionally reactive—effects that may operate through disruptions in the development of the fetal neuroendocrine system (Field, Diego, & Hernandez-Reif, 2002; Lemola et al., 2009). Maternal negative affect and birthing complications just prior to and during labor and delivery also have been implicated as possible causes of elevated fetal and infant irritability over the birth transition (DiPietro, Ghera, & Costigan, 2008; Weerth & Buitelaar, 2007). Overall, this literature on prenatal and perinatal risk factors suggests that these influences on infant negative affectivity may be enhanced by the presence of postnatal risk factors such as postpartum distress, depression, and malnourishment.

There is further evidence of the importance of diet beyond the prenatal and early childhood periods. Correlational and experimental studies have converged to show that low levels of certain fatty acids that are normally acquired in a healthy diet can contribute to dispositional negative affect such as anger (Buydens-Branchey, Branchey, & Hibbeln, 2007). Clinical interventions in which nutrition is improved have resulted in improvements in well-being and reductions in anger and irritability (Stanga et al., 2007). Other examples of environmental influences include air and noise pollution, which have been implicated as causes of irritability and anger (Melamed & Bruhis, 1996; Zeidner & Shechter, 1988).

In summary, many of the general environmental and specific situational cues that elicit anger, irritability, and frustration are embedded in social relationships and contexts. Relationship partners such as parents and peers play a prominent socializing role in the individual's development of dispositional anger and irritability. Through these social processes, individuals acquire knowledge about when and how to express anger in ways that are considered appropriate and normative for their family, peer, and cultural groups.

Anger, Health, and Functioning

If anger and irritability arise in part from an underlying disposition, what are the effects of this dispositional trait on health and functioning? This turns out to be a heavily studied question in research on emotions and health. The intense interest is merited given that anger and irritability are risk factors for psychopathological disorders, spanning personality and mood disorders to psychoses (Novaco, 2010), as well as physical illness, chronic and acute cardiovascular pathology, and mortality (Friedman, Kern, & Reynolds, 2010).

Aggression and Psychopathology

Perhaps the most obvious and direct connection between anger and maladaptive functioning is the development of overt verbal and nonverbal physical aggression (see Table 7.1). Individual differences in aggressive behavior are moderately stable over time and across contexts, due in part to continuities in contextual, cognitive, affective, and behavioral causes of dispositional anger (Olweus, 1979; see Tackett, Martel, & Kushner, Chapter 27, this volume). Chronic angriness, particularly if it co-occurs with poor self-regulation and frequent exposure to hostile social environments, contributes to growth in aggressive and nonaggressive antisocial behavior problems from childhood to adulthood (Brook, Whiteman, Cohen, Shapiro, & Balka, 1995; Caprara, Paciello, Gerbion, & Cugini, 2007; Dodge, Coie, & Lynam, 2006; Peled & Moretti, 2007).

Figure 7.2 shows a conceptual model that summarizes our research on the connection between dispositional anger and aggressive behavior problems in children from 5–11 years of age. Children who are high in dispositional behavioral approach (i.e., anticipation and enjoyment of potential reward) are more likely to exhibit aggressive behavior problems, a link that is mediated by dispositional anger, as shown in pathway 1 in Figure 7.2 (Deater-Deckard et al., 2010). Furthermore, children with higher levels of dispositional anger are more likely to be aggressive, a link that is mediated by poorer regulation of sustained attentive behavior, as shown in pathway 2 in Figure 7.2 (Deater-Deckard, Petrill, & Thompson, 2007). In addition, sustained attentive behavior operates as a moderator, with better attention regulation dampening the link between dispositional anger and aggressive behavior problems, as shown in pathway 3 in Figure 7.2 (Kim & Deater-Deckard, 2011). The behavioral genetic analyses in these studies have implicated an underlying genetic correlation that accounts for much of the covariation between approach, anger, and aggression. Likewise, other research suggests that anger and aggression probably involve the same neural circuits in medial orbitofrontal cortex and amygdala (Coccaro, McCloskey, Fitzgerald, & Phan, 2007). Nevertheless, the neural circuitry and genetic influences are complex, particularly when considering their interactions with nonbiological factors—not to mention the role of hormones, such as testosterone, that have been implicated in the etiology of anger and aggression (Archer, Birring, & Wu, 1998; Book, Starzyk, & Quinsey, 2001). From this complexity arises patterns of regulatory, social-cognitive, affective, and physiological functions that distinguish strategic proactive aggression from hotheaded reactive aggression (Hubbard, McAuliffe, Morrow, & Romano, 2010; van Honk et al., 2010).

Individuals who experience chronically high levels of anger and irritability also are at risk for mood and substance abuse dis-

```
                    ┌─────────────────────┐
                    │ Attention regulation│
                    └─────────────────────┘
                      2↗      ⋮3       ↘2
                              ▼
┌──────────────┐    ┌──────────────┐    ┌──────────────┐
│  Approach/   │ →  │ Dispositional│ →  │  Aggressive  │
│  Activation  │    │    Anger     │    │   Behavior   │
│              │  1 │              │  1 │   Problems   │
└──────────────┘    └──────────────┘    └──────────────┘
```

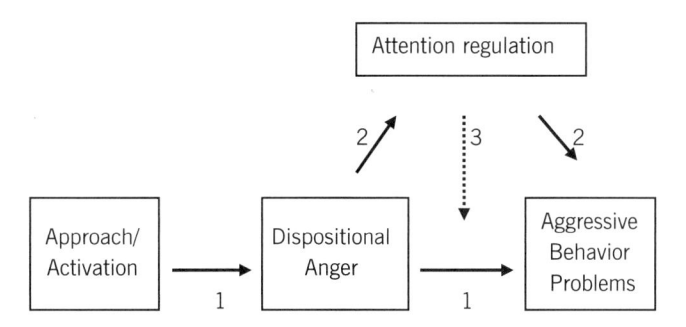

FIGURE 7.2. A conceptual model of anger and aggression. The figure is a synopsis of our correlational and quasi-experimental behavioral genetic studies on the connections between dispositional behavioral approach, dispositional anger, attention regulation, and aggressive behavior problems in middle childhood. Numbers for paths refer to three sets of interrelated processes. (1) Children who are high in approach/activation tendencies are more prone to aggressive behavior, a link that is accounted for by dispositional anger (Deater-Deckard et al., 2010). (2) Higher levels of dispositional anger are linked with aggressive conduct problems, in part through lower levels of cognitive regulation of attention span and persistence (Deater-Deckard et al., 2007). (3) Attention span also modulates the connection between anger and aggressive behavior problems, with the link enhanced for those with poor attention spans but attenuated for those with good attention regulation (Kim & Deater-Deckard, 2011). Behavioral genetic analyses implicate a common core of genetic influences accounting for substantial portions of the covariation between approach, anger, and aggressive behavior problems.

orders (see Klein, Dyson, Kujawa, & Kotov, Chapter 26, this volume). Anger and irritability contribute to the etiology of depression and anxiety disorders among adolescents and adults (Leibenluft, Cohen, Gorrindo, Brook, & Pine, 2006; Riley, Treiber, & Woods, 1989), with longitudinal predictive effects possibly sustained over decades (Stringaris et al., 2009). Higher levels of anger and irritability intensify symptoms of depression and anxiety, including increased likelihood of suicide (Perlis, Fava, Trivedi, Alpert, & Luther, 2009). This enhancement effect probably derives from inward-looking cognitive features, such as rumination, that increase the somatic and psychological symptoms of mood disturbance and in turn reinforce the maintenance of anger and irritability (Miers, Rieffe, Terwogt, Cowan, & Linden, 2007; Orth, Cahill, Foa, & Maercker, 2008). Dispositional anger also is related to chronic use of legal and illicit substances. Substance abuse for chronically angry individuals may reflect an attempt to cope with highly aversive negative emotions and social problems by minimizing psychological impact through the alteration of physiology, body sensations, and consciousness (Nichols, Mahadeo, Bryant, & Botvin, 2008; Tarter, Blackson, Brigham, Moss, & Caprara, 1994).

Physical Illness and Mortality

When chronic anger persists it has implications for not only mental and behavioral health but also physical health. There is a well-established connection between poorer physical health and chronic anger, as well as other facets of negative affectivity over the lifespan (Friedman et al., 2010; see Hampson & Vollrath, Chapter 28, this volume). Chronic anger increases risk of mortality through its role in substance abuse (as just described) and other risk-taking behaviors. For instance, hostile aggressive driving is a common individual and public health risk that contributes to traffic fatalities (Deffenbacher, Lynch, Oetting, & Yingling, 2001).

Even more substantial is the impact of chronic anger and hostility on cardiovascular system pathophysiology in adolescence and adulthood, and possibly childhood (Kerr, 2008). The illnesses of greatest concern are cardiovascular disease, coronary heart disease, and stroke—all of which increase risk of mortality (Smith, Glazer, Ruiz, & Gallo, 2004; Williams, Nieto, Sanford,

Couper, & Tyroler, 2002). The largest and longest standing line of relevant research is on coronary heart disease and its connection to "Type A" behavioral style or personality profile—a pattern of behavior characterized by a loud voice, facial muscle tension, anger and irritability, intense involvement in work, and competitiveness (Friedman & Rosenman, 1974). Research suggests that it is the angry and irritable emotion components of Type A behavior that increase risk of heart disease, through their substantial deleterious alterations of physiology (Palmero, Diez, & Asensio, 2001; Siegman & Smith, 1994). Like the link between anger and psychopathology, the link between anger and coronary heart disease is enhanced by cognitive processes, such as rumination, that maintain and increase discomfort, pain, and hypertension (Markovitz, Matthews, Wing, Kuller, & Meilahn, 1991; Miers et al., 2007; Schneider, Egan, Johnson, Drobny, & Julius, 1996). However, the health risk is evident only if anger is chronic. Expressing anger infrequently and in socially appropriate ways may reduce risk for cardiovascular disease (Eng, Fitzmaurice, Kubzansky, Rimm, & Kawachi, 2003).

Intervention

To summarize up to this point, dispositional anger is an important correlate and an early-emerging predictor of a variety of maladaptive physical and mental health outcomes. Furthermore, the expression of anger involves self-regulation of emotion that is influenced through socialization and contextual reinforcement. Does this mean that chronic anger and irritability can be reduced through intervention, to improve health outcomes (see McClowry & Collins, Chapter 29, this volume)?

Anger management interventions with adults can effectively produce lasting change in the affective, cognitive, behavioral, and physiological features of anger and aggression (Digiuseppe & Tafrate, 2003). Anger management treatments apply a variety of methods, such as cognitive-behavioral training, progressive relaxation, teaching of social and coping skills, and psychotherapy (Glancy & Saini, 2005). These types of interventions have been used to address broad chronic patterns of hostility, as well as context-specific anger problems such as hostile and aggressive driving (Deffenbacher et al., 2001; Vecchio & O'Leary, 2004; see also McClowry & Collins, Chapter 29, this volume).

For interventions with children, there is growing interest in using classmates to deliver targeted group or schoolwide programs that teach and encourage more effective coping with anger and aggression (Puskar, Stark, Northcut, Williams, & Haley, 2011). These types of programs often have multiple components that use didactic and participatory cognitive-behavioral treatment methods. School-based and individual treatment modes have been shown to be effective at reducing anger and related behavioral and emotional problems among high-risk children and adolescents (Blake & Hamrin, 2007; Gansle, 2005; Sukhodolsky, Kassinove, & Gorman, 2004; Sukhodolsky, Solomon, & Perine, 2000; Duckworth & Allred, Chapter 30, this volume).

In summary, the dispositional nature of anger and irritability does not imply that these emotional experiences and behaviors cannot be modified. To the contrary, the intervention literature suggests that the effective management of emotions—particularly for those who are prone to chronic and intense anger and irritability—has become an important target for intervention and prevention efforts. As a result, the future looks promising for effective evidence-based treatments that reduce chronic anger and irritability, and improve the lives of children and adults alike (see Duckworth & Allred, Chapter 30, this volume).

Conclusions and Future Directions

Temperament research is well positioned to produce innovative science on the causes and consequences of individual differences in anger and irritability. In addition to growth in consensus about what constitutes temperament (Zentner & Bates, 2008), the ongoing scientific revolutions in neuroimaging and neurophysiology, neuroendocrinology, and molecular genetics will provide increasingly useful tools for integrating behavioral and biological approaches. As this happens, it will become more feasible for scientists to assess individual differences in structures and functions across many levels of analysis (e.g., molecular, neural, thoughts and beliefs, emotions, behavior of individual and groups). The challenge will be to sort out how to use these methods to improve theories and the efficacy of applications.

To this end, we offer several areas of inquiry that could be fruitful. One direction is to explore the distinctions between anger, irritability, and frustration. Is the difference between these highly interrelated aspects largely semantic, or are there qualitative differences in their construct and predictive validity that cut across methods and levels of measurement and analysis? And how can we best use the answer to that question to advance our understanding of the inner states and outward expressions of anger that have deleterious effects on individuals and the people who are close to them?

A second, related direction is to integrate better the empirical investigation of biology–environment interplay with theories of temperament. Correlational and quasi-experimental designs involving neuroimaging and genetic methods will continue to build our understanding of stable individual differences and their correlates. Can we also design experiments with children, as well as adults, that identify the genetic and neural functions—along with the experiential and expressive aspects of anger and irritability—that will inform us about underlying traits?

A third and final suggested direction is to build lifespan models of individual differences in dispositional anger and irritability. The research literature on anger and irritability and their chronic (trait) and transient (state) presentation already is vast. Most theories of temperament assume that temporally and situationally stable individual differences in anger and irritability are caused by the same underlying causal processes from childhood through old age. Presumably, the same assumption holds regarding developmental continuity in the causes of transient angry states. However, these assumptions are rarely tested, in part because most of the research is based either in childhood (in the developmental psychology literature) or young adulthood (in the social and personality psychology literature). There is too little longitudinal research spanning childhood and adolescence, and less still spanning the transition to and through middle and old age. As a result, drawing solid conclusions about developmental continuities and discontinuities in processes has proven difficult. The field will be well served if temperament researchers build a developmentally informed knowledge base using rigorous longitudinal designs that represent the lifespan.

Acknowledgments

During the preparation of this chapter we were supported by Grant Nos. HD38075, HD54481, and HD60110 from the National Institute of Child Health and Human Development. We wish to thank Anarkali Morrill, who assisted with library research. The content is solely the responsibility of the authors and does not necessarily represent the official views of the National Institute of Child Health and Human Development or the National Institutes of Health.

Further Reading

Gagne, J., Vendlinski, M., & Goldsmith, H. (2009). The genetics of childhood temperament. In Y.-K. Kim (Ed.), *Handbook of behavioral genetics* (pp. 251–267). New York: Springer.

Potegal, M., Stemmler, G., & Spielberger, C. (Eds.). (2010). *International handbook of anger*. New York: Springer.

Kim, J., & Deater-Deckard, K. (2011). Dynamic changes in anger, externalizing and internalizing problems: Attention and regulation. *Journal of Child Psychology and Psychiatry, 52*, 156–166.

References

Abler, B., Walter, H., & Erk, S. (2005). Neural correlates of frustration. *NeuroReport, 16*, 669–672.

Aldrich, N., & Tenenbaum, H. (2006). Sadness, anger, and frustration: Gendered patterns in early adolescents' and their parents' emotion talk. *Sex Roles, 55*, 11–12.

Alessandri, S. M., Sullivan, M. W., & Lewis, M. W. (1990). Violation of expectancy and frustration in early infancy. *Developmental Psychology, 26*, 738–744.

Allan, S., & Gilbert, P. (2002). Anger and anger expression in relation to perceptions of social rank, entrapment and depressive symptoms. *Personality and Individual Differences, 3*, 551–565.

Archer, J., Birring, S. S., & Wu, F. C. W. (1998). The association between testosterone and aggression among young men: Empirical findings and a meta-analysis. *Aggressive Behavior*, 24, 411–420.

Auerbach, J. G., Faroy, M., Ebstein, R., Kahana, M., & Levine, J. (2001). The association of the dopamine D4 receptor gene (DRD4) and the serotonin transporter promoter gene (5-HTTLPR) with temperament in 12-month-old infants. *Journal of Child Psychology and Psychiatry*, 42, 777–783.

Bandura, A., Ross, D., & Ross, S. A. (1963). Imitation of film-mediated aggressive models. *Journal of Abnormal and Social Psychology*, 66(1), 3–11.

Bates, J. E., Freeland, C. A. B., & Lounsbury, M. L. (1979). Measurement of infant difficultness. *Child Development*, 50, 794–803.

Baud, P., Courtet, P., Perroud, N., Jollant, F., Buresi, C., & Malafosse, A. (2007). Catechol-O-methyltransferase polymorphism (COMT) in suicide attempters: A possible gender effect on anger traits. *American Journal of Medical Genetics*, 144B, 1042–1047.

Bell, M. A., & Deater-Deckard, K. (2007). Biological systems and the development of self-regulation: Integrating behavior, genetics, and psychophysiology. *Journal of Development and Behavioral Pediatrics*, 28(5), 409–420.

Blake, C. S., & Hamrin, V. (2007). Current approaches to the assessment and management of anger and aggression in youth: A review. *Journal of Child and Adolescent Psychiatric Nursing*, 20, 209–221.

Blanchard-Fields, F. (2008). The experience of anger and sadness in everyday problems impacts age differences in emotion regulation. *Developmental Psychology*, 44, 1547–1556.

Block, J. H., & Block, J. (1980). The role of ego-control and ego-resiliency in the organization of behavior. In W. A. Collins (Ed.), *Minnesota Symposium on Child Psychology* (Vol. 13, pp. 39–101). Hillsdale, NJ: Erlbaum.

Blonigen, D. M., Carlson, M. D., Hicks, B. M., Krueger, R. F., & Iacono, W. G. (2008). Stability and change in personality traits from later adolescence to early adulthood: A longitudinal twin study. *Journal of Personality*, 76, 229–266.

Bond, A., & Wingrove, J. (2010). The neurochemistry and psychopharmacology of anger. In M. Potegal, G. Stemmler, & C. Spielberger (Eds.), *International handbook of anger* (pp. 79–102). New York: Springer.

Book, A. S., Starzyk, K. B., & Quinsey, V. L. (2001). The relationship between testosterone and aggression: A meta-analysis. *Aggression and Violent Behavior*, 6, 579–599.

Braungart-Rieker, J. M., Hill-Soderlund, A. L., & Karrass, J. (2010). Fear and anger reactivity trajectories from 4 to 16 months: The role of temperament, regulation, and maternal sensitivity. *Developmental Psychology*, 46, 791–804.

Brazelton, T., & Nugent, K. (2011). *Neonatal behavioral assessment scale* (4th ed.). New York: Wiley.

Brook, J. S., Whiteman, M., Cohen, P., Shapiro, J., & Balka, E. (1995). Longitudinally predicting late adolescent and young adult drug use: Childhood and adolescent precursors. *Journal of the American Academy of Child and Adolescent Psychiatry*, 34, 1230–1238.

Burrowes, B. D., & Halberstadt, A. G. (1987). Self- and family-expressiveness in styles in the experience and expression of anger. *Journal of Nonverbal Behavior*, 11, 254–268.

Buss, A., & Durkee, A. (1957). An inventory for assessing different kinds of hostility. *Journal of Consulting Psychology*, 21(4), 343–349.

Buss, A. H., & Plomin, R. A. (1975). *A temperament theory of personality development*. New York: Wiley.

Buydens-Branchey, L., Branchey, M., & Hibbeln, J. R. (2007). Associations between increases in plasma n-3 polyunsaturated fatty acids following supplementation and decreases in anger and anxiety in substance abusers. *Progress in Neuropsychopharmacology and Biological Psychiatry*, 32, 568–575.

Calkins, S. D., & Johnson, M. C. (1998). Toddler regulation of distress to frustrating events: Temperamental and maternal correlates. *Infant Behavior and Development*, 21, 379–395.

Campbell, S. (2010). Maternal depression and children's adjustment in early childhood. In R. E. Tremblay, R. G. Barr, R. V. Peters, & M. Boivin (Eds.), *Encyclopedia on early childhood development* (pp. 1–5). Montreal: Centre of Excellence for Early Childhood Development.

Caprara, G. V., Cinanni, G., D'Imperio, G., Passerini, S., Renzi, P., & Travaglia, G. (1985). Indicators of impulsive aggression: Present status of research on irritability and emotional susceptibility scales. *Personality and Individual Differences*, 6, 665–674.

Caprara, G. V., Paciello, M., Gerbion, M., & Cugini, C. (2007). Individual differences conducive to aggression and violence: Trajectories and correlates of irritability and hostile rumination through adolescence. *Aggressive Behavior*, 33, 359–374.

Caspi, A., Harrington, H., Milne, B., Amell, J. W., Theodore, R. F., & Moffitt, T. E. (2003). Children's behavioral styles at age 3 are linked to their adult personality traits at age 26. *Journal of Personality*, 71, 495–514.

Caspi, A., & Roberts, B. W. (2001). Personality development across the life course: The argument for change and continuity. *Psychological Inquiry*, 12, 49–66.

Caspi, A., & Shiner, R. L. (2006). Personality development. In W. Damon & R. Lerner (Series Eds.), & N. Eisenberg (Vol. Ed.), *Handbook of child psychology: Vol. 3. Social, emotional, and personality development* (6th ed., pp. 300–365). New York: Wiley.

Caspi, A., & Silva, P. A. (1995). Temperamental qualities at age three predict personality traits in young adulthood: Longitudinal evidence from a birth cohort. *Child Development, 66,* 486–498.

Chang, L., Schwartz, D., Dodge, K. A., & McBride-Chang, C. (2003). Harsh parenting in relation to child emotion regulation and aggression. *Journal of Family Psychology, 17,* 598–606.

Charles, S. T., Mather, M., & Carstensen, L. L. (2003). Aging and emotional memory: The forgettable nature of negative images for older adults. *Journal of Experimental Psychology, 132,* 310–324.

Chess, S., & Thomas, A. (1984). *Origins and evolution of behavior disorders.* New York: Brunner/Mazel.

Coccaro, E., Bergeman, C., Kavoussi, R., & Seroczynski, A. (1997). Heritability of aggression and irritability: A twin study of the Buss–Durkee aggression scales in adult male subjects. *Biological Psychiatry, 41,* 273–284.

Coccaro, E. F., McCloskey, M. S., Fitzgerald, D. A., & Phan, L. (2007). Amygdala and orbitofrontal reactivity to social threat in individuals with impulsive aggression. *Biological Psychiatry, 62,* 168–178.

Cole, D. A., Peeke, L., Dolezal, S., Murray, N., & Canzoniero, A. (1999). A longitudinal study of negative affect and self-perceived competence in young adolescents. *Journal of Personality and Social Psychology, 77,* 851–862.

Comings, D. E., Johnson, J. P., Gonzalez, N. S., Huss, M., Saucier, G., McGue, M., et al. (2000). Association between the adrenergic alpha 2A receptor gene (ADRA2A) and measures of irritability, hostility, impulsivity and memory in normal subjects. *Psychiatric Genetics, 10,* 39–42.

Conner, T. S., Jensen, K. P., Tennen, H., Furneaux, H. M., Kranzler, H. R., & Covault, J. (2009). Functional polymorphisms in the serotonin 1B receptor gene (HTR1B) predict self-reported anger and hostility among young men. *American Journal of Medical Genetics, 153B,* 67–78.

Dahlen, E. R., & Martin, R. C. (2005). The experience, expression, and control of anger in perceived social support. *Personality and Individual Differences, 39,* 391–401.

Darwin, C. R. (1872). *The expression of the emotions in man and animals.* Chicago: University of Illinois Press.

Deater-Deckard, K. (2009). Parenting the genotype. In K. McCartney & R. Weinberg (Eds.), *Experience and development: A festschrift in honor of Sandra Wood Scarr* (pp. 141–161). New York: Taylor & Francis.

Deater-Deckard, K., Beekman, C., Wang, Z., Kim, J., Petrill, S. A., Thompson, L. A., et al. (2010). Approach/positive anticipation, frustration/anger, and overt aggression in childhood. *Journal of Personality, 78,* 991–1010.

Deater-Deckard, K., Petrill, S. A., & Thompson, L. A. (2007). Anger/frustration, task persistence, and conduct problems in childhood: A behavioral genetic analysis. *Journal of Child Psychology and Psychiatry, 48,* 80–87.

Deffenbacher, J. (1992). Trait anger: Theory, findings, and implications. In C. D. Spielberger & J. N. Butcher (Eds.), *Advances in personality assessment* (Vol. 9, pp. 177–201). Hillsdale, NJ: Erlbaum.

Deffenbacher, J., Lynch, R., Oetting, E., & Yingling, D. (2001). Driving anger: Correlates and a test of state–trait theory. *Personality and Individual Differences, 31,* 1321–1331.

Denson, T. F., Pedersen, W. C., Ronquillo, J., & Nandy, A. S. (2008). The angry brain: Neural correlates of anger, angry rumination, and aggressive personality. *Journal of Cognitive Neuroscience, 21,* 734–744.

Digiuseppe, R., & Tafrate, R. C. (2003). Anger treatment for adults: A meta-analytic review. *Clinical Psychology: Science and Practice, 10,* 70–84.

DiPietro, J., Ghera, M., & Costigan, K. (2008). Prenatal origins of temperamental reactivity. *Early Human Development, 84,* 569–575.

Dmitrieva, J., Chen, C., Greenberger, E., Ogunseitan, O., & Ding, Y.-C. (2011). Gender-specific expression of the DRD4 gene on adolescent delinquency, anger and thrill seeking. *Social Cognitive and Affective Neuroscience, 6*(1), 82–89.

Dodge, K., Bates, J. E., & Pettit, G. S. (1990). Mechanisms in the cycle of violence. *Science, 250,* 1678–1683.

Dodge, K., Coie, J. D., & Lynam, D. (2006). Aggression and antisocial behavior in youth. In W. Damon, R. Lerner, & N. Eisenberg (Eds.), *Handbook of child psychology* (pp. 719–788). New York: Wiley.

Eddie, H. J. (2007). Trait anger predicts relative left frontal cortical activation to anger-inducing stimuli. *International Journal of Psychophysiology, 66,* 154–160.

Eid, M., & Diener, E. (2009). Norms for experiencing emotions in different cultures: Inter- and intranational differences. *Social Indicators Research Series, 38,* 169–202.

Eiden, R. D., McAuliffe, S., Kachadourian, L., Coles, C., Colder, C., & Schuetze, P. (2009). Effects of prenatal cocaine exposure on infant reactivity and regulation. *Neurotoxicology and Teratology, 31,* 60–68.

Elfenbein, H. A., & Ambady, N. (2002). On the universality and cultural specificity of emotion recognition: A meta-analysis. *Psychological Bulletin, 128,* 203–235.

El-Sheikh, M. (2005). The role of emotional responses and physiological reactivity in the marital conflict–child functioning link. *Journal of Child Psychology and Psychiatry, 46*, 1191–1199.

Eng, P. M., Fitzmaurice, G., Kubzansky, L. D., Rimm, E., & Kawachi, I. (2003). Anger expression and risk of stroke and coronary heart disease among male health professionals. *Psychosomatic Medicine, 65*, 100–110.

Engebretson, T. O., Sirota, A. D., Niaura, R. S., Edwards, K., & Brown, W. A. (1999). A simple laboratory method for inducing anger: A preliminary investigation. *Journal of Psychosomatic Research, 47*, 13–26.

Evans, D. E., & Rothbart, M. K. (2007). Developing a model for adult temperament. *Journal of Research in Personality, 41*(4), 868–888.

Field, T., Diego, M., & Hernandez-Reif, M. (2002). Prenatal anger effects on the fetus and neonate. *Journal of Obstetrics and Gynaecology, 22*, 260–266.

Fox, S., & Spector, P. E. (1999). A model of work frustration–aggression. *Journal of Organizational Behavior, 20*, 915–931.

Friedman, H. S., Kern, M. L., & Reynolds, C. A. (2010). Personality and health, subjective well-being, and longevity. *Journal of Personality, 78*, 179–216.

Friedman, M., & Rosenman, R. (1974). *Type A behavior and your heart.* New York: Knopf.

Gagne, J., Vendlinski, M., & Goldsmith, H. (2009). The genetics of childhood temperament. In Y.-K. Kim (Ed.), *Handbook of behavioral genetics* (pp. 251–267). New York: Springer.

Galambos, N. L., & Krahn, H. J. (2008). Depression and anger trajectories during the transition to adulthood. *Journal of Marriage and Family, 70*, 15–27.

Gansle, K. A. (2005). The effectiveness of school-based anger interventions and programs: A meta-analysis. *Journal of School Psychology, 43*, 321–341.

Glancy, G., & Saini, M. A. (2005). An evidence-based review of psychological treatments of anger and aggression. *Brief Treatment and Crisis Intervention, 5*, 229–248.

Goldsmith, H. H. (1996). Studying temperament via construction of the Toddler Behavior Assessment Questionnaire. *Child Development, 67*, 218–235.

Goldsmith, H. H., & Rothbart, M. K. (1988). *The Laboratory Temperament Assessment Battery (LAB-TAB): Locomotor Version* (Technical Report No. 88-01). Eugene, OR: Center for the Study of Emotion.

Halberstadt, A. G., & Eaton, K. L. (2002). A meta-analysis of family expressiveness and children's emotion expressiveness and understanding. *Marriage and Family Review, 34*, 35–62.

Halverson, C. F., Kohnstamm, G. A., Martin, R. P., & Martin, R. (1994). *The developing structure of temperament and personality from infancy to adulthood.* Hillsdale, NJ: Erlbaum.

Harmon-Jones, E., & Sigelman, J. (2001). State anger and prefrontal brain activity: Evidence that insult-related relative left-prefrontal activation is associated with experienced anger and aggression. *Journal of Personality and Social Psychology, 80*, 797–803.

Herrmann, M., King, K., & Weitzman, M. (2008). Prenatal tobacco smoke and postnatal secondhand smoke exposure and child neurodevelopment. *Current Opinion in Pediatrics, 20*, 184–190.

Hoekstra, R. A., Bartels, M., & Boomsma, D. I. (2006). Heritability of testosterone levels in 12-year-old twins and its relation to pubertal development. *Twin Research and Human Genetics, 9*, 558–565.

Hubbard, J. A., McAuliffe, M. D., Morrow, M. T., & Romano, L. J. (2010). Reactive and proactive aggression in childhood and adolescence: Precursors, outcomes, processes, experiences, and measurement. *Journal of Personality, 78*, 95–118.

Hubbard, J. A., Parker, E. H., & Ramsden, S. R. (2004). The relations among observational, physiological, and self-report measures of children's anger. *Social Development, 13*, 15–39.

Hur, Y. (2006). Nonadditive genetic effects on hostility in South Korean adolescent and young adult twins. *Twin Research and Human Genetics, 9*, 637–641.

Hyde, J. S. (2005). The gender similarities hypothesis. *American Psychologist, 60*, 581–592.

Jenkins, J. M. (2000). Marital conflict and children's emotions: The development of an anger organization. *Journal of Marriage and the Family, 62*, 723–736.

Jenkins, J., Shapka, J., & Sorenson, A. M. (2006). Teenager mothers' anger over twelve years: Partner conflict, partner transitions and children's anger. *Journal of Child Psychology and Psychiatry, 47*, 775–782.

Kang, J. I., Namkoong, K., & Kim, S. J. (2007). Association of DRD4 and COMT polymorphisms with anger and forgiveness traits in healthy volunteers. *Neuroscience Letters, 430*, 252–257.

Kelly, M. (2008). Sex differences in emotional and physiological responses to the Trier Social Stress Test. *Journal of Behavior Therapy and Experimental Psychiatry, 39*(1), 87–98.

Kennedy, H. G. (1992). Anger and irritability. *British Journal of Psychiatry, 161*, 145–153.

Kerr, M. (2008). Anger expression in children and adolescents: A review of the empirical literature. *Clinical Psychology Review, 28*, 559–577.

Kim, J., & Deater-Deckard, K. (2011). Dynamic changes in anger, externalizing and internalizing problems: Attention and regulation. *Journal of Child Psychology and Psychiatry, 52,* 156–166.

Kim, J., Mullineaux, P. Y., Allen, B., & Deater-Deckard, K. (2010). Longitudinal studies of stability in attention span and anger: Context and informant effects. *Journal of Personality, 78,* 419–440.

Kloppel, S., Stonnington, C., Petrovic, P., Mobbs, D., & Tuscher, O. (2010). Irritability in preclinical Huntington's disease. *Neuropsychologia, 48,* 549–557.

Kovecses, Z. (2000). The concept of anger: Universal or culture specific? *Psychopathology, 33,* 159–170.

Kuppens, P., Mechelen, I., & Rjimen, F. (2008). Toward disentangling sources of individual differences in appraisal and anger. *Journal of Personality, 76,* 969–1000.

Larson, R., & Asmussen, L. (1991). Anger, worry, and hurt in early adolescence: An enlarging world of negative emotions. In M. E. Colten & S. Gore (Eds.), *Adolescent stress: Causes and consequences* (pp. 21–41). New York: Aldine de Gruyter.

Leary, M. (2006). Interpersonal rejection as a determinant of anger and aggression. *Personality and Social Psychology Review, 10,* 111–132.

Leibenluft, E., Cohen, P., Gorrindo, T., Brook, J., & Pine, D. (2006). Chronic versus episodic irritability in youth: A community-based longitudinal study of clinical and diagnostic associations. *Journal of Child and Adolescent Psychopharmacology, 16,* 456–466.

Lemerise, E., & Arsenio, W. (2000). An integrated model of emotion processes and cognition in social information processing. *Child Development, 71,* 107–118.

Lemola, S., Stadlmayr, W., & Grob, A. (2009). Infant irritability: The impact of fetal alcohol exposure, maternal depressive symptoms, and low emotional support from the husband. *Infant Mental Health Journal, 30,* 57–81.

Leon, C. F. M. (1992). Anger and impatience/irritability in patients of low socioeconomic status with acute coronary heart disease. *Journal of Behavioral Medicine, 15,* 273–284.

Levenson, R. W., Ekman, P., Heider, K., & Friesen, W. V. (1992). Emotion and autonomic nervous system activity in the Minangkabau of West Sumatra. *Journal of Personality and Social Psychology, 62,* 972–988.

Lewis, M. (2010). The development of anger. In M. Potegal, G. Stemmler, & C. Spielberger (Eds.), *International handbook of anger* (pp. 177–191). New York: Springer.

Little, T., Jones, S., Henrich, C., & Hawley, P. (2003). Disentangling the "whys" from the "whats" of aggressive behaviour. *International Journal of Behavioral Development, 27,* 122–133.

Markovitz, J., Matthews, K. A., Wing, R. R., Kuller, L. H., & Meilahn, E. M. (1991). Psychological, biological, and health behavior predictors of blood pressure changes in middle-aged women. *Journal of Hypertension, 9,* 399–406.

Martin, R., Watson, D., & Wan, C. K. (2000). A three-factor model of trait anger: Dimensions of affect, behavior, and cognition. *Journal of Personality, 68,* 869–897.

Mauss, I., Butler, E., Roberts, N., & Chu, A. (2010). Emotion control values and responding to an anger provocation in Asian-American and European-American individuals. *Cognition and Emotion, 24,* 1026–1043.

Mauss, I. B., Cook, C. L., & Gross, J. J. (2007). Automatic emotion regulation during anger provocation. *Journal of Experimental Social Psychology, 43,* 698–711.

McClellan, J., & King, M. (2010). Genetic heterogeneity in human disease. *Cell, 141,* 210–217.

McCrae, R. R., & Costa, P. T., Jr. (1994). The stability of personality: Observations and evaluations. *Current Directions in Psychological Science, 3,* 173–175.

Melamed, S., & Bruhis, S. (1996). The effects of chronic industrial noise exposure on urinary cortisol, fatigue, and irritability: A controlled field experiment. *Journal of Occupational and Environmental Medicine, 38,* 252–256.

Miers, A., Rieffe, C., Terwogt, M., Cowan, R., & Linden, W. (2007). The relation between anger coping strategies, anger mood, and somatic complaints in children and adolescents. *Journal of Abnormal Child Psychology, 35*(4), 653–664.

Milovchevich, D., Howells, K., Drew, N., & Day, A. (2001). Sex and gender role differences in anger: An Australian community study. *Personality and Individual Differences, 31,* 117–127.

Moffitt, T. E., Arseneault, L., Belsky, D., Dickson, N., Hancox, R. J., Harrington, H., et al. (2011). A gradient of childhood self control predicts health, wealth and public safety. *Proceedings of the National Academy of Sciences USA, 108*(7), 2693–2698.

Moskowitz, D. S. (2010). Quarrelsomeness in daily life. *Journal of Personality, 78,* 39–66.

Mullineaux, P. Y., Deater-Deckard, K., Petrill, S. A., Thompson, L. A., & DeThorne, L. S. (2009). Temperament in middle childhood: A behavioral genetic analysis of mothers' and fathers' reports. *Journal of Research in Personality, 43,* 737–746.

Newman, J. L., Fuqua, D. R., Gray, E. A., & Simpson, D. B. (2006). Gender differences in the relationship of anger and depression in a clinical sample. *Journal of Counseling and Development, 84,* 157–162.

Nichols, T. R., Mahadeo, M., Bryant, K., & Botvin, G. J. (2008). Examining anger as a predictor of drug use among multiethnic middle school students. *Journal of School Health*, 78, 480–486.

Novaco, R. W. (2000). Anger. In A. E. Kazdin (Ed.), *Encyclopedia of psychology* (pp. 170–174). Washington, DC: American Psychological Association and Oxford University Press.

Novaco, R. (2010). Anger and psychopathology. In M. Potegal, G. Stemmler, & C. Spielberger (Eds.), *International handbook of anger* (pp. 465–497). New York: Springer.

Nugier, A. (2007). Moral and angry emotions provoked by informal social control. *Cognition and Emotion*, 21(8), 1699–1720.

Ochsner, K. N., & Gross, J. J. (2005). The cognitive control of emotion. *Trends in Cognitive Sciences*, 9, 242–249.

Olweus, D. (1979). Stability of aggressive reaction patterns in males: A review. *Psychological Bulletin*, 86(4), 852–875.

Orth, U., Cahill, S. P., Foa, E. B., & Maercker, A. (2008). Anger and posttraumatic stress disorder symptoms in crime victims: A longitudinal analysis. *Journal of Consulting and Clinical Psychology*, 76, 208–218.

Palmero, F., Diez, J. L., & Asensio, A. B. (2001). Type A behavior pattern today: Relevance of the JAS-S factor to predict heart rate reactivity. *Behavioral Medicine*, 27, 28–36.

Peled, M., & Moretti, M. (2007). Rumination on anger and sadness in adolescence: Fueling of fury and deepening of despair. *Journal of Clinical Child and Adolescent Psychology*, 36(1), 66–75.

Perlis, R., Fava, M., Trivedi, M., Alpert, J., & Luther, J. (2009). Irritability is associated with anxiety and greater severity, but not bipolar spectrum features, in major depressive disorder. *Acta Psychiatrica Scandinavica*, 119, 282–289.

Perroud, N., Jaussent, I., Guillaume, S., Bellivier, F., Baud, P., Jollant, F., et al. (2010). COMT but not serotonin-related genes modulates the influence of childhood abuse on anger traits. *Genes, Brain and Behavior*, 9, 193–202.

Phillips, L. H., Henry, J. D., Hosie, J. A., & Milne, A. B. (2006). Age, anger regulation and well-being. *Aging and Mental Health*, 10, 250–256.

Posner, M. I., & Rothbart, M. K. (2007). *Educating the human brain*. Washington, DC: American Psychological Association.

Potegal, M., & Archer, J. (2004). Sex differences in childhood anger and aggression. *Child and Adolescent Psychiatric Clinics of North America*, 13, 513–528.

Potegal, M., & Stemmler, G. (2010). Constructing a neurology of anger. In M. Potegal, G. Stemmler, & C. Spielberger (Eds.), *International handbook of anger* (pp. 39–59). New York: Springer.

Puskar, K. R., Stark, K. H., Northcut, T., Williams, R., & Haley, T. (2011). Teaching kids to cope with anger: Peer education. *Journal of Child Health Care*, 15(1), 5–13.

Putnam, S. P., Gartstein, M. A., & Rothbart, M. K. (2006). Measurement of fine-grained aspects of toddler temperament: The Early Childhood Behavior Questionnaire. *Infant Behavior and Development*, 29, 386–401.

Putnam, S. P., & Rothbart, M. K. (2006). Development of short and very short forms of the Children's Behavior Questionnaire. *Journal of Personality Assessment*, 87, 102–112.

Radke-Yarrow, M., & Kochanska, G. (1990). Anger in young children. In N. L. Stein, B. Leventhal, & T. Trabasso (Eds.), *Psychological and biological approaches to emotion* (pp. 297–310). Hillsdale, NJ: Erlbaum.

Raine, A., Dodge, K., Loeber, R., Gatzke-Kopp, L., Lynam, D., Reynolds, C., et al. (2006). The Reactive–Proactive Aggression Questionnaire: Differential correlates of reactive and proactive aggression in adolescent boys. *Aggressive Behavior*, 32(2), 159–171.

Rebollo, I., & Boomsma, D. (2006). Genetic analysis of anger: Genetic dominance or competitive sibling interaction. *Behavior Genetics*, 36(2), 216–228.

Reuter, M. (2010). Population and molecular genetics of anger and aggression: Current state of the art. In M. Potegal, G. Stemmler, & C. Spielberger (Eds.), *International handbook of anger* (pp. 27–37). New York: Springer.

Reuter, M., Weber, B., Fiebach, C. J., Elger, C., & Montag, C. (2009). The biological basis of anger: Associations with the gene coding for DARPP-32 (PPP1R1B) and with amygdale volume. *Behavioural Brain Research*, 202, 179–183.

Riley, W. T., Treiber, F. A., & Woods, M. G. (1989). Anger and hostility in depression. *Journal of Nervous and Mental Disease*, 177, 668–674.

Roberts, B. W., & DelVecchio, W. F. (2000). The rank-order consistency of personality traits from childhood to old age: A quantitative review of longitudinal studies. *Psychological Bulletin*, 126, 3–25.

Romero-Canyas, R., Downey, G., Berenson, K., Ayduk, O., & Kang, N. J. (2010). Rejection sensitivity and the rejection–hostility link in romantic relationships. *Journal of Personality*, 78, 119–148.

Rothbart, M. K. (1981). Measurement of temperament in infancy. *Child Development*, 52, 569–578.

Rothbart, M. K. (1986). Longitudinal observation of infant temperament. *Developmental Psychology*, 22, 356–365.

Rothbart, M. K., Ahadi, S. A., Hershey, K. L., & Fisher, P. (2001). Investigation of temperament at three to seven years: The Children's Behavior Questionnaire. *Child Development*, 72, 1394–1408.

Rothbart, M. K., & Bates, J. E. (1998). Temperament. In W. Damon & N. Eisenberg (Eds.),

Handbook of child psychology (Vol. 3, pp. 105–176). New York: Wiley.

Rueda, M. R., Posner, M. I., & Rothbart, M. K. (2005). The development of executive attention: Contributions to the emergence of self-regulation. *Developmental Neuropsychology, 28,* 573–549.

Rujescu, D., Giegling, I., Bondy, B., Gietl, A., Zill, P., & Moller, H.-J. (2002). Association of anger-related traits with SNPs in the TPH gene. *Molecular Psychiatry, 7,* 1023–1029.

Rujescu, D., Giegling, I., Gietl, A., Hartmann, A. M., & Moller, H. J. (2003). A functional single nucleotide polymorphism (V158M) in the COMT gene is associated with aggressive personality traits. *Biological Psychiatry, 54*(1), 34–39.

Ruys, K., & Stapel, D. (2008). The secret life of emotions. *Psychological Science, 9*(4), 385–391.

Sander, D., Grandjean, D., Pourtois, G., Schwartz, S., & Seghier, M. (2005). Emotion and attention interactions in social cognition: Brain regions involved in processing anger prosody. *NeuroImage, 28,* 848–858.

Saudino, K. J. (2005). Behavioral genetics and child temperament. *Journal of Developmental and Behavioral Pediatrics, 26,* 214–223.

Schneider, R. H., Egan, B. M., Johnson, E. H., Drobny, H., & Julius, S. (1996). Anger and anxiety in borderline hypertension. *Psychosomatic Medicine, 48,* 242–248.

Shipman, K. L., Zeman, J., Nesin, A. E., & Fitzgerald, M. (2003). Children's strategies for displaying anger and sadness: What works with whom? *Merrill–Palmer Quarterly, 49,* 100–122.

Siegman, A. W., & Smith, T. W. (Eds.). (1994). *Anger, hostility, and the heart.* Hillsdale, NJ: Erlbaum.

Sluyter, F., Keijser, J. N., Boomsma, D. I., van Doornen, L. J. P., van den Oord, E. J. C. G., & Snieder, H. (2000). Genetics of testosterone and the aggression–hostility–anger (AHA) syndrome: A study of middle-aged male twins. *Twin Research, 3,* 266–276.

Smith, T. W., Glazer, K., Ruiz, J. M., & Gallo, L. C. (2004). Hostility, anger, aggressiveness, and coronary heart disease: An interpersonal perspective on personality, emotion, and health. *Journal of Personality, 72,* 1217–1270.

Snyder, J., Stoolmiller, M., Wilson, M., & Yamamoto, M. (2003). Child anger regulation, parental responses to children's anger displays, and early child antisocial behavior. *Social Development, 12,* 335–360.

Spielberger, C. D., Krasner, S., & Solomon, E. (1988). The experience, expression, and control of anger. In M. P. Janisse (Ed.), *Health psychology: Individual differences and stress* (pp. 89–108). New York: Springer-Verlag.

Stanga, Z., Field, J., Iff, S., Stucki, A., Lobo, D., & Allison, S. (2007). The effect of nutritional management on the mood of malnourished patients. *Clinical Nutrition, 26*(3), 379–382.

Strelau, J. (2001). The concept and status of trait in research on temperament. *European Journal of Personality, 15,* 311–325.

Stringaris, A., Cohen, P., Pine, D. S., & Leibenluft, E. (2009). Adult outcomes of youth irritability: A 20-year prospective community-based study. *American Journal of Psychiatry, 166,* 1048–1054.

Suarez, E. C., & Krishnan, R. R. (2006). The relation of free plasma tryptophan to anger, hostility, and aggression in a nonpatient sample of adult men and women. *Annals of Behavioral Medicine, 31,* 254–260.

Sukhodolsky, D. G., Kassinove, H., & Gorman, B. S. (2004). Cognitive-behavioral therapy for anger in children and adolescents: A meta-analysis. *Aggression and Violent Behavior, 9,* 247–269.

Sukhodolsky, D. G., Solomon, R. M., & Perine, J. (2000). Cognitive-behavioral anger control intervention for elementary school children: A treatment-outcome study. *Journal of Child and Adolescent Group Therapy, 10,* 159–170.

Tangney, J. (1996). Assessing individual differences in constructive versus destructive responses to anger across the lifespan. *Journal of Personality and Social Psychology, 70,* 780–796.

Tarter, R. E., Blackson, T., Brigham, J., Moss, H., & Caprara, G. V. (1994). The association between childhood irritability and liability to substance use in early adolescence: A 2-year follow-up study of boys at risk for substance abuse. *Drug and Alcohol Dependence, 39,* 253–261.

Thomas, A., & Chess, S. (1977). *Temperament and development.* New York: Brunner/Mazel.

Underwood, M. K., Coie, J. D., & Herbsman, C. R. (1992). Display rules for anger and aggression in school-age children. *Child Development, 63,* 366–380.

van Honk, J., Harmon-Jones, E., Morgan, B. E., & Schutter, D. J. L. G. (2010). Socially explosive minds: The triple imbalance hypothesis of reactive aggression. *Journal of Personality, 78,* 67–94.

Vecchio, T. D., & O'Leary, K. D. (2004). Effectiveness of anger treatments for specific anger problems: A meta-analytic review. *Clinical Psychology Review, 24,* 15–34.

Verweij, K. J. H., Zietsch, B. P., Medland, S. E., Gordon, S. D., Banyamin, B., Nyholt, D. R., et al. (2010). A genome-wide association study of Cloninger's temperament scales: Implications for the evolutionary genetics of personality. *Biological Psychology, 85,* 306–317.

Virkkunen, M., Kallio, E., Rawlings, R., Rokola, R., Poland, R., & Guidotti, A. (1994). Personality profiles and state aggressiveness in Finnish alcoholic, violent offenders, fire setters, and healthy volunteers. *Archives of General Psychiatry, 51,* 28–33.

Wang, X., Trivedi, R., Treiber, F., & Snieder, H.

(2005). Genetic and environmental influences on anger expression, John Henryism, and stressful life events: The Georgia cardiovascular twin study. *Psychosomatic Medicine, 67,* 16–23.

Wasserman, D., Geijer, T., Sokolowski, M., Rozanov, V., & Wasserman, J. (2007). Genetic variation in the hypothalamic–pituitary–adrenocortical axis regulatory factor, T-box 19, and the angry/hostility personality trait. *Genes, Brain, and Behavior, 6,* 321–328.

Weerth, C., & Buitelaar, J. (2007). Childbirth complications affect young infants' behavior. *European Child and Adolescent Psychiatry, 16,* 379–388.

Wilkowski, B. M., & Robinson, M. (2007). Keeping one's cool: Trait anger, hostile thoughts, and the recruitment of limited capacity control. *Personality and Social Psychology Bulletin, 33,* 1201–1213.

Wilkowski, B. M., & Robinson, M. D. (2010). The anatomy of anger: An integrative cognitive model of trait anger and reactive aggression. *Journal of Personality, 78,* 9–38.

Williams, J. E., Nieto, F. J., Sanford, C. P., Couper, D. J., & Tyroler, H. A. (2002). The association between trait anger and incident stroke risk the atherosclerosis risk in communities study. *Stroke, 33,* 13–20.

Williams, L. M., Das, P., Liddell, B., Olivieri, G., Peduto, A., Brammer, M. J., et al. (2005). BOLD, sweat, and fears: FMRI and skin conductance distinguish facial fear signals. *NeuroReport, 16,* 49–52.

Wood, D., Harms, P., & Vazire, S. (2010). Perceiver effects as projective tests: What your perceptions of others say about you. *Journal of Personality and Social Psychology, 99,* 174–190.

Wranik, T., & Scherer, K. (2010). Why do I get angry?: A componential appraisal approach. In M. Potegal, G. Stemmler, & C. Spielberger (Eds.), *International handbook of anger* (pp. 243–266). New York: Springer.

Yang, J. W., Lee, M. S., Lee, S. H., Lee, B. C., Kim, S. H., Joe S. H., et al. (2010). Association between tryptophan hydroxylase 2 polymorphism and anger-related personality traits among young Korean women. *Neuropsychobiology, 62,* 158–163.

Yang, J. W., Lee, S. H., Ryu, S. H., Lee, B. C., Kim, S. H., Joe, S. H., et al. (2007). Association between monoamine oxidase A polymorphisms and anger-related personality traits in Korean women. *Neuropsychobiology, 56,* 19–23.

Zammit, S., Owen, M. J., & Lewis, G. (2010). Misconceptions about gene–environment interactions in psychiatry. *Evidence-Based Mental Health, 13,* 65–68.

Zeidner, M., & Shechter, M. (1988). Psychological responses to air pollutions: Some personality and demographic correlates. *Journal of Environmental Psychology, 8,* 191–208.

Zentner, M., & Bates, J. E. (2008). Child temperament: An integrative review of concepts, research programs, and measures. *European Journal of Developmental Science, 2,* 7–37.

Zhou, Q., Eisenberg, N., Wang Y., & Reiser, M. (2004). Chinese children's effortful control and dispositional anger/frustration: Relations to parenting styles and children's social functioning. *Developmental Psychology, 40,* 352–366.

CHAPTER 8

Effortful Control

M. Rosario Rueda

From early infancy, children differ from one another in their reactions to the environment. Over many years of research, scientists have tried to identify and characterize patterns in these differences. Building on the pioneering work of Thomas and Chess (1977), recent research on human infants has identified dimensions of temperament showing large similarities to those of nonhuman animals. These include the defensive reactions of fear and anger, approach reactions involving positive affect and activity, and duration of attentional orienting and voluntary control (Rothbart, 2011; Rothbart & Bates, 2006). The reactivity–regulation framework for temperament developed initially by Rothbart and Derryberry (1981) has been used to develop methods for measuring temperament across the lifespan (see Table 8.1).

This chapter focuses on the attention-related temperament dimension called effortful control (EC). Unlike early theoretical models of temperament that emphasized how people are moved by the positive and negative emotions or level of arousal, people are not always at the mercy of affect. EC is the temperamental dimension that captures individual differences in the ability to regulate emotions and actions in an internally guided or voluntary mode. The construct of EC is akin to many other concepts in the literature that also emphasize regulation of reactivity (see Kochanska, Murray, & Harlan, 2000). The chapter begins by defining EC as an important regulatory component of temperament and establishing its connections to attention. In successive sections I present a set of methods used for measuring EC and discuss research on the biological and experiential basis of this temperamental dimension, its developmental course during childhood, and the important role that EC plays in the socialization of the child.

Definition of EC

The EC construct emerged initially from psychometric studies of temperament questionnaires. Factor analyses of large datasets involving descriptions of individuals' behavior in a variety of dimensions have yielded three broad temperamental factors that are fairly consistent in studies of infants, children, and adults (Rothbart & Bates, 2006). The first two factors are related to emotional reactivity and describe 1) positive/approaching and 2) negative/avoiding response tendencies. The third factor captures individual differences in self-regulation and the control of reactivity. These factors map both conceptually and empirically onto the Extra-

TABLE 8.1. Dimensions Loading onto the EC Factor in the Various Rothbart Temperament Questionnaires

Questionnaire	Age	Dimensions loading into the EC factor[a]	Reference
Infant Behavior Questionnaire (IBQ)	3 to 12 months	• Low-intensity Pleasure • Duration of Orienting • Cuddliness • Soothability	Rothbart (1981); Gartstein & Rothbart (2003)
Early Childhood Behavior Questionnaire (ECBQ)	18 to 36 months	• Inhibitory Control • Attention Shifting • Low-Intensity Pleasure • Cuddliness • Attention Focusing	Putnam, Gartstein, & Rothbart (2006)
Children's Behavior Questionnaire (CBQ)	3 to 7 years	• Inhibitory Control • Attention Focusing • Low-Intensity Pleasure • Perceptual Sensitivity • Smiling and Laughter	Rothbart et al. (2001)
Temperament in Middle Childhood Questionnaire (TMCQ)	7 to 10 years	• Inhibitory Control • Activation Control • Attention Focusing • Low-Intensity Pleasure • Perceptual Sensitivity	Simonds & Rothbart (2004)
Early Adolescence Temperament Questionnaire—Revised (EATQ-R)	9 to 15 years	• Attention • Inhibitory Control • Activation Control	Ellis & Rothbart (2001)
Adult Temperament Questionnaire (ATQ)	Adults	• Attentional Control • Inhibitory Control • Activation Control	Evans & Rothbart (2007)

[a] For the IBQ, the factor is named Orienting/Regulation instead of EC.

version/Positive Emotionality, Neuroticism/Negative Emotionality, and Conscientiousness/Constraint dimensions found in Big Five and Big Three studies of adult personality (Ahadi & Rothbart, 1994; Evans & Rothbart, 2007; Rothbart, Ahadi, & Evans, 2000). This general structure suggests that temperament goes beyond generalized characteristics of positive and negative emotionality, found in early definitions of temperament (Allport, 1961; Eysenck, 1990). Instead, a more complete account of temperament takes into account the individual's motivational impulses linked to reactive emotion, as well as his or her ability to control them. The temperament construct that captures individual differences in the ability to control the influence of reactive systems on behavior is what is called EC.

The term *effortful control* (EC) was introduced by Rothbart and colleagues (Rothbart, 1989; Rothbart & Ahadi, 1994; Rothbart & Bates, 1998) to describe the self-regulatory aspect of temperament. It is defined as the ability to inhibit a dominant response in order to perform a subdominant response, to detect errors, and to engage in planning (Rothbart & Bates, 2006; Rothbart & Rueda, 2005). The concept includes aspects related to *attention*, as the ability to move, focus, and sustain attention as needed, and *behavioral regulation*, which includes both inhibitory control (the ability to effortfully inhibit behavior when appropriate; e.g., as when talking to a classmate must be avoided in the classroom) and activation control (the capacity to perform an action when there is a strong tendency to avoid it; e.g., as when one must smile upon reception of an undesired gift).

During early infancy, when voluntary and effortful forms of self-regulation are not yet available, temperamental regulation is for the most part linked to attentional orientation. For instance, in the Infant Behavior Questionnaire the so-called *Orienting/Regulation* factor is defined from scales of Duration of Orienting, Soothability, Cuddliness, and Low-Intensity Pleasure (Gartstein & Rothbart, 2003). As more voluntary forms of control progressively develop around the end of the first year of life, individual differences in EC can be observed. In childhood studies, a broad EC/Self-Regulation factor is consistently found across measurement instruments and cultures (Ahadi, Rothbart, & Ye, 1993; Rothbart, Ahadi, Hersey, & Fisher, 2001; Sanson, Smart, Prior, Oberklaid, & Pedlow, 1994). The behavioral dimensions included in this factor are Inhibitory Control, Attentional Focusing, Persistence, Low-Intensity Pleasure, and Perceptual Sensitivity. Intercorrelations among measures of attentional focusing, attentional shifting, and inhibitory control are also found in adults (Derryberry & Rothbart, 1988; Evans & Rothbart, 2007), and significant correlations are obtained between the resulting EC factor and the Big Five measure of Conscientiousness (Evans & Rothbart, 2007).

It is important to emphasize the effortful and volitional nature embedded in the concept of EC, and to differentiate it from more reactive forms of regulation (Derryberry & Rothbart, 1997; see also Eisenberg & Morris, 2002). Behavioral inhibition, when associated with anxiety or fear, reflects a passive form of control. At the opposite extreme, impulsive approach tendencies also constitute a form of behavioral control that is not voluntarily determined. These forms of involuntary regulation may lead to excessively rigid response patterns of over- or underregulation that may in turn lead to pathological behavior. On the contrary, EC constitutes a voluntary mode of control that allows the individual to display a much more flexible repertoire of responses according to his or her own goals and the particular requirements of the situation. Using EC, we can more flexibly approach situations we fear and inhibit actions we desire. The efficiency of control, however, will at least partially depend on the strength of the emotional processes against which effort is exerted (Rothbart, Derryberry, & Hershey, 2000).

The control of thoughts, emotions, and responses has been linked to mechanisms of attention from the earliest theoretical models (James, 1890). In the past decades, Posner and colleagues have developed a neurocognitive model of attention (Posner & Fan, 2008; Posner & Petersen, 1990; Posner, Rueda, & Kanske, 2007). In this model, attentional control is attributed to the executive attention network, a neurocognitive system that becomes activated in situations requiring action coordination in novel or dangerous situations, detection and correction of errors, or overcoming habitual (or automatic) responses (Posner & DiGirolamo, 1998).

Based on the strong conceptual link between the two constructs, Posner and Rothbart have argued that the executive attention network is the neural substrate supporting EC (Posner & Rothbart, 1998; 2007; Rothbart, Sheese, & Posner, 2007). The conceptual link is strengthened by empirical results showing that measures of efficiency of the executive attention network in the laboratory are related to parental and self-reported ratings of temperamental effortful control (Gerardi-Caulton, 2000; Rothbart, Ellis, Rueda, & Posner, 2003; Simonds, Kieras, Rueda, & Rothbart, 2007). Individual variability in EC is also related to structural and functional differences in brain regions considered to be part of the executive attention network (Whittle et al., 2008, 2009), as I discuss later. Thus, Executive Attention and EC are viewed as concepts representing different levels of analysis of the ability to exercise control over one's behavior (Rothbart & Rueda, 2005; Rueda, Posner, & Rothbart, 2011). Executive Attention, a construct emerging from the neurocognitive literature, is linked to the control of cognition and cognitive flexibility, whereas EC has been developed in the field of temperament as a concept capturing individual differences in the regulation of emotional reactivity.

Measures of EC

Approaches to measuring temperament have included the use of caregivers and self-report questionnaires, laboratory tasks providing situations designed to elicit temperament-related reactions, and direct observations in naturalistic settings (Rothbart & Goldsmith, 1985). Each approach offers advantages and also entails potential sources of errors, which have been extensively discussed elsewhere (see, e.g., Bates, 1989; Rothbart & Bates, 2006). By extension, the tools developed within each of these approaches can be used to measure EC. In addition, given the link that has been established between EC and Executive Attention, understanding of EC can also benefit from experimental paradigms and measures developed in the field of cognitive psychology to examine processes and mechanisms underlying individuals' efficiency in the control of cognition and action (Rothbart et al., 2003; Rueda, Posner, & Rothbart, 2005).

Questionnaires

During the past few decades, Mary Rothbart and her colleagues have developed a battery of questionnaires to measure temperament across the lifespan. Her effort began with the development of the Infant Behavior Questionnaire in the early 1980s (Rothbart, 1981), which soon became a widely used instrument to measure infants' temperament. In the past decade, her collaborative work with graduate and postdoctoral students has provided a complete set of questionnaires, each suitable for a particular age range, covering infancy, toddlerhood, early and middle childhood, adolescence and adulthood (see Table 8.1). The instruments consist of a number of questions grouped into scales designed specifically to tap temperamental domains that are common to individuals of a particular age range. Nowadays, Dr. Rothbart's temperament questionnaires have been translated into many different languages (Spanish, Norwegian, Chinese, Arabic, Japanese, French, Dutch, Hebrew, etc.) and are widely used in temperament research around the world. Information on these temperament questionnaires is easily accessed on the Internet (*www.bowdoin.edu/~sputnam/rothbart-temperament-questionnaires*) and instruments are available upon request.

The factors reliably retrieved from the Rothbart temperament questionnaires follow three general, broad temperament system structures of Negative Affectivity, Extraversion/Surgency, and EC. This three-factor structure is complemented in some of the instruments by additional scales relevant to a particular developmental period. For instance, the Middle-Childhood and Early-Adolescence Temperament Questionnaires include a Sociability/Affiliation factor assessing the individual's desire for warmth and closeness with others that is independent of extraversion or shyness. As a result of this factor structure, each questionnaire contains a number of questions that provide a measure of the construct of EC. Table 8.1 summarizes the various instruments developed by Rothbart and colleagues for different ages, as well as information about each of the scales that load into the EC factor.

Behavioral Tasks

A number of researchers have developed batteries of laboratory tasks to measure various domains of children's temperament, including regulation and/or EC. Most of the laboratory batteries have been designed for developmental periods ranging from late infancy and toddlerhood to preschool years. In the early 1990s, Goldsmith and Rothbart (1992) developed a number of tasks to evaluate temperament in toddlers, the Laboratory Temperament Assessment Battery (Lab-TAB). In the following years, this battery has been extended both in number of tasks and the age range of its application (Goldsmith, Reilly, Lemery, Longley, & Prescott, 1993; see also *www.waisman.wisc.edu/twinresearch/researchers/instruments.shtml*). The battery consists of a number of episodes designed to elicit measurable reactions in the children. It includes several episodes designed to tap the constructs of Interest/Persistence and Inhibitory Control as part of the broader factor of EC.

Kochanska and her colleagues (Kochanska, Murray, Jacques, Koenig, & Vandegeest, 1996; Kochanska et al., 2000) also developed a battery of laboratory tasks intended to measure EC. Their battery assesses different skills, including delay (e.g., waiting for candy displayed under a transparent cup), slowing motor activity (e.g., drawing a line slowly), suppressing and initiating responses to changing signals, effortful attention (e.g., recognizing small shapes hidden within a dominant large shape), and lowering the voice. In two large longitudinal studies (with children ages 32 to 66 months and 9 to 45 months, respectively), Kochanska and her associates have shown that beginning at age 2½, children's performance is highly consistent across tasks, indicating that the tasks all appeared to measure a common underlying quality that has developed over time. Measures also showed stability for children across time, with correlations across repeated assessments ranging from .44 for the youngest children (ages 22 to 33 months) to .59 for ages 32 to 46 months, and to .65 for ages 46 to 66 months (Kochanska et al., 2000).

Table 8.2 provides information on laboratory tasks used to evaluate the various temperamental dimensions that have been included in the EC factor in childhood (Rothbart & Bates, 2006). These include tasks designed to observe (1) children's ability to delay immediate gratification in order to comply with instructions or get a larger reward after a period of waiting; (2) duration of engagement or persistence on performing a mundane task, such as passively watching a set of slides projected on a screen or sorting beads according to their color; (3) individuals' ability to control behavior by either suppressing or initiating activity to a signal; and (4) the capacity to focus attention as needed and/or resolve conflict by ignoring or suppressing a dominant stimulus or response in favor of a subdominant one.

The fact that tasks targeting multiple behavioral dimensions are generally used to assess EC raises the question of whether all these tasks load into a single factor, or whether the construct of EC has a latent multidimensional structure. In a recent study with a large sample of over 850 preschoolers, seven laboratory tasks (knock tap, rabbit/turtle, two versions of gift delay, bear/dragon, yarn tangle, and a child-friendly version of the continuous performance task) and an aggregated score of the Inhibitory Control and Attention Focusing scales of the Children's Behavior Questionnaire (CBQ) reported by teachers were used to assess EC (Sulik et al., 2010). Exploratory factor analyses indicated that a one-factor structure was the most appropriate solution across sex and ethnic groups. This result supports the use of diverse behavioral measures as indicators of a single latent construct of EC.

The one-factor structure of EC was also supported by data obtained in the Konchanska and colleagues (2000) longitudinal study. However, using principal components analyses in other studies, either two (Delay/Gross Motor Activity, and Inhibitory/Activation Control) or four (Delay, Fine Motor, Gross Motor, and Inhibition/Activation Control) grouping components were found, depending on the age of the subjects and the number of tasks included in the analyses (Murray & Kochanska, 2002). Importantly, when using tasks assessing impulsivity and approach reactivity together with EC tasks, factors analyses produce two clusters of measures, clearly differentiating between reactive and effortful forms of control (Olson, Schilling, & Bates, 1999). The two-factors structure differentiates between tasks involving inhibitory control (e.g., performance on Stroop-like and go/no-go tasks, and the ability to inhibit motor behavior on command or in the face of a strong competing response tendency) and those reflecting behavioral regulation in tasks involving rewards (i.e., gift delay and other tasks involving motivationally salient stimuli, such as earning money or points). This differentiation is in consonance with the distinction made between "cool" (emotionally neutral) and "hot" (reward-related or motivationally salient) aspects of executive function, which appear to be associated with distinct brain regions. The "cool" aspect has been associated with dorsolateral prefrontal regions whereas the "hot" system involves ventral and medial frontal regions (Hongwanishkul, Happaney, Lee, & Zelazo, 2005).

Marker Tasks

The study of EC has largely benefited from interdisciplinary research that has helped to connect different levels of analysis related to attention and self-regulation (Posner & Rothbart, 2007; Rothbart & Rueda, 2005; Rueda, Posner, & Rothbart, 2011). Cognitive tasks involving conflict between stimuli and/or responses have been extensively used in the fields of cognitive psychology and cognitive neuroscience to measure attentional control (Botvinick, Braver, Barch, Carter, & Cohen, 2001). Reasons for utilizing cognitive tasks in an effort to further understand individual differences in EC are strength-

TABLE 8.2. Examples of Laboratory Tasks Used to Measure Dimensions of Temperament Included in the EC Construct

Temperamental dimension	Task name	Brief task description	Age range	Reference
Persistence	• Slides	Viewing series of projected slides	Infants/toddlers	Goldsmith & Rothbart (1992)
	• Blocks	Manipulating a set of block during a period of time	Toddlers/preschoolers	Goldsmith & Rothbart (1992)
	• Bead sorting	Sorting color beads into different containers	Toddlers/preschoolers	Goldsmith et al. (1993)
	• Yarn tangle	Untangle a ball of yarn	Preschoolers	Goldsmith et al. (1993)
Inhibition/Activation Control	• Rabbit/turtle	Maneuvering a turtle (slowly) and a rabbit (fast) along a curved path	Preschoolers	Kochanska et al. (2000)
	• Bear/dragon	Performing commands of bear/suppressing commands of dragon	Preschoolers	Reed et al. (1984)
	• Tower	Taking turns building a tower with experimenter	Toddlers/preschoolers	Kochanska et al. (1996)
	• Dinky toys	Choosing a prize from a box filled with small toys without touching or pointing at it	Toddlers/preschoolers	Kochanska et al. (2000)
	• Whisper	Whisper names of popular cartoon characters	Preschoolers	Kochanska et al. (1996)
Focused Attention/Conflict	• Shapes	Pointing to small pictures embedded in larger (dominant) pictures of fruit	Toddlers/preschoolers	Kochanska et al. (2000)
	• Knock tap	Reverse experimenter actions of tapping and knocking on a table	Preschoolers	Sulik et al. (2010)
	• Day–night	Say "day" to pictures of the moon/starts and "night" to pictures of the sun	Preschoolers	Gerstadt et al. (1994)
Delay	• Snack delay	Waiting for a candy displayed under a transparent box	Preschoolers	Kochanska et al. (2000)
	• Gift delay	Waiting for experimenter to return with a bow before opening a gift	Toddlers/preschoolers	Kochanska et al. (1996)
	• Delay of gratification	Choosing between getting an immediate reward or waiting in order to get double amount	Preschoolers	Mischel et al. (1989)
	• Tongue	Competing with experimenter to keep a candy on the tongue without chewing at it	Preschoolers	Kochanska et al. (2000)

ened because performance on such tasks in the laboratory has been linked to aspects of children's EC in naturalistic settings. Children who are relatively less affected by conflict also receive higher parental ratings of temperamental EC and higher scores on laboratory measures of inhibitory control (Checa, Rodriguez-Bailon, & Rueda, 2008; Gerardi-Caulton, 2000; Gonzalez, Fuentes, Carranza, & Estevez, 2001; Rothbart et al., 2003; Simonds et al., 2007).

Another important reason for using cognitive tasks is that they provide valuable information in neuroimaging studies of the neural anatomy and mechanisms underlying task performance. Thus, the performance of theoretically grounded and appropriately designed cognitive tasks can be considered as a marker of the efficiency of neural systems subserving a particular psychological function, such as EC. In turn, knowing the neural substrates for EC allows us to examine the aspects of this form of self-regulation that are subject to genetic influence, as well as how the functioning of this system may be influenced by experience.

A basic measure of conflict interference is provided by the Stroop task (Stroop, 1935). The original form of this task required subjects to look at words denoting colors and to report the color of ink in which the words were written instead of reading them. Presenting incongruent perceptual and semantic information (e.g., the word *blue* written with red ink) induces conflict and produces a delay in reaction time (RT) compared to when the two sources of information match. The flanker task is another widely used method to study conflict resolution. In this task, a target stimulus is surrounded by irrelevant stimulation that can either match or conflict with the response required by the target (Eriksen & Eriksen, 1974). As with the Stroop task, resolving interference from distracting incongruent stimulation delays RTs. In both tasks, the amount of delay in the conflict condition is compared with no conflict. This *conflict effect* is indicative of the efficiency with which interference from irrelevant stimulation is overcome. The larger the conflict scores, the poorer the efficiency overcoming interference.

With young children, somewhat easier versions of adult conflict tasks must be used. In one example of these, the spatial conflict task (Gerardi-Caulton, 2000), children sit in front of two response buttons, one located to the left and one to the right. Each button displays a picture, and on every trial a picture identical to one member of the pair appears on either the left or right side of a computer screen (see Figure 8.1a). The child's job is to press the button corresponding to the identity of the stimulus regardless of its spatial location on the screen. Conflict trials are those in which the location of the picture is opposite to that of the matching response button. This spatial incompatibility induces conflict and delays RT compared to when the picture is presented on the same side as the corresponding response button.

Several years ago I helped developing a child-friendly version of the flanker task in which stimuli were rows of fish pointing left and right (Rueda, Fan, et al., 2004; Rueda, Posner, Rothbart, & Davis-Stober, 2004). Instructions were for children to help feed the fish in the middle, or simply make it happy, by pressing a key corresponding to the direction it points. In each trial, fish point in either the same direction as the middle fish (congruent trials) or the opposite direction (incongruent trials) (see Figure 8.1b). The task also involves postresponse feedback as the fish becomes animated, which is intended to help maintain the child's engagement with the task.

Marker tasks have been useful to trace the development of the executive attention network, as well as to explore the biological basis of this function. These two aspects are discussed in the next sections of the chapter.

Biology of EC

From the earlier conceptualizations, temperament has been regarded as dependent upon constitutional makeup (Allport, 1961). In the past, studies with nonhuman animals served to elaborate neural models of temperament, particularly related to reactivity systems of approach and avoidance (Gray, 1991). The biological bases of EC have for the most part been related to neural models of executive attention and the regulation of emotional reactivity (Rothbart et al., 2007). Two major advances in the last decades have exponentially increased the prospect of integrating individual differences in tempera-

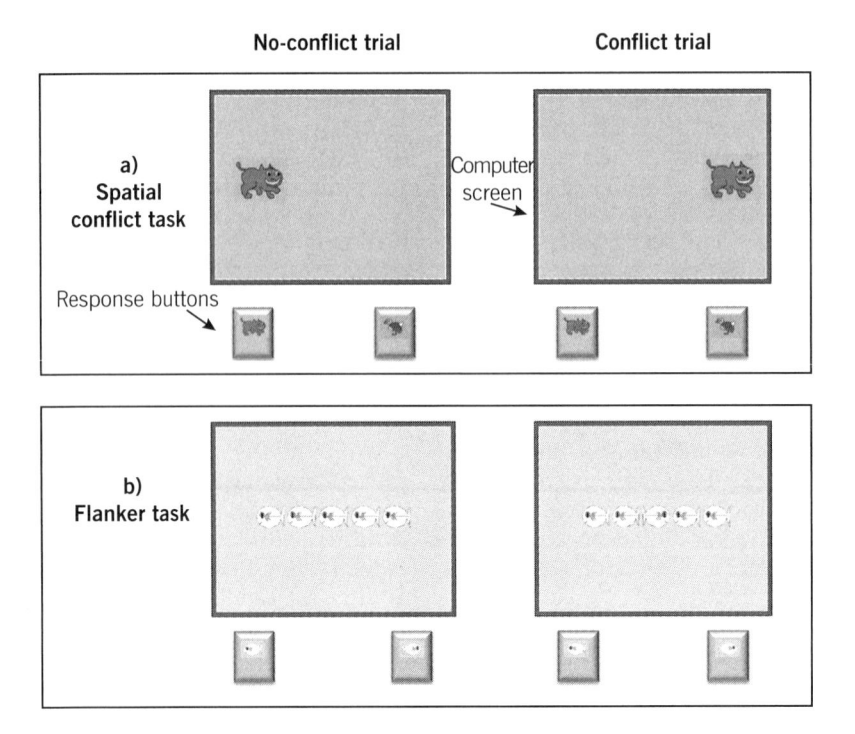

FIGURE 8.1. Example of conflict tasks used to measure executive attention with young children. In the spatial conflict task (a), the child is asked to press the button corresponding to the identity of the picture presented on the screen. In the flanker task (b), the child's job is to indicate the direction of the fish in the middle by pressing the corresponding button.

ment and personality and the study of the human brain. The first, the development of neuroimaging, allows the online examination of the neural circuits activated during performance of particular tasks (Posner & Raichle, 1994). The second, the sequencing of the human genome (Venter et al., 2001), has made it possible to study how genetic differences might lead to individual variations in the potential to use these neural circuits to acquire and perform skills.

In relation to EC, the use of marker tasks of the executive attention network has allowed analysis of the brain circuitry and neuromodulators involved in attentional control and self-regulation, as well as candidate genes that might be related to the efficiency of the network (Posner & Rothbart, 2009; Rueda, Posner, & Rothbart, 2011).

Neural Network

According to Posner's model of attention, a frontal neural network involving the anterior cingulate cortex (ACC) and lateral prefrontal areas subserves the function of controlling thoughts, emotions, and responses (Posner & Petersen, 1990; Posner et al., 2007). Adult imaging studies have shown that conflict tasks activate the ACC (Fan, Flombaum, McCandliss, Thomas, & Posner, 2003). A meta-analysis of imaging studies indicated that the dorsal section of the ACC was activated in response to cognitive conflict tasks, such as variants of the Stroop task, whereas the ventral section appeared to be mostly activated by emotional tasks and emotional states (Bush, Luu, & Posner, 2000). The two divisions of the ACC also seem to interact in a mutually exclusive way. When the cognitive division is activated, the affective division tends to be deactivated, and vice versa, suggesting the possibility of reciprocal effortful and emotional controls of attention (Drevets & Raichle, 1998). Also, resolving conflict from incongruent stimulation in the flanker task activates the dorsal portion of the ACC, together with other regions of the lateral prefrontal cortex (Botvinick, Nystrom, Fissell, Carter, & Cohen, 1999; Fan, Flombaum, et al., 2003).

EC has been directly linked to the executive attention network in imaging studies. Whittle and colleagues (2008) found a positive correlation between the size of several brain regions, including the dorsal division of the ACC, left orbitofrontal cortex, and hippocampus, and the EC score in self-report questionnaires. Interestingly, the correlation with the ventral portion of the ACC was negative, which is consistent with the reciprocal relation between the dorsal and ventral portions of the ACC observed in other studies. Also, a leftward asymmetric pattern of cortical folding of the ACC was associated with higher EC and lower negative affectivity, particularly in males (Whittle et al., 2009).

Different parts of the ACC appear to be well connected to a variety of other brain regions, including limbic structures and parietal and frontal areas (Posner, Sheese, Odludas, & Tang, 2006). Furthermore, the ACC appears to be functionally connected to those areas involved in processing information that is relevant in a particular situation. For example, the instruction to avoid arousal during processing of erotic events (Beauregard, Levesque, & Bourgouin, 2001) or to ward off emotion when looking at negative pictures (Ochsner, Bunge, Gross, & Gabrieli, 2002) produces a locus of activation in midfrontal and cingulate areas. In addition, if people are required to select an input modality, the ACC shows functional connectivity to the selected sensory system (Crottaz-Herbette & Menon, 2006). Similarly, when involved with emotional processing, the cingulate shows a functional connection to limbic areas (Etkin, Egner, Peraza, Kandel, & Hirsch, 2006). These findings support the role of the ACC in the control of cognition and emotion.

Additionally, pharmacological studies with monkeys and rats have aided understanding of the neurochemical mechanisms that affect efficiency of the executive attention network. Data suggest that dopamine (DA) is an important neurotransmitter for executive control. Blocking DA in the dorsolateral prefrontal cortex (DLPFC) of rhesus monkeys causes deficits on tasks involving inhibitory control (Brozoski, Brown, Rosvold, & Goldman, 1979). Additionally, activation of mesocortical dopaminergic neurons in rats enhances activity in the prefrontal cortex (McCulloch, Savaki, McCulloch, Jehle, & Sokoloff, 1982), as well as expression of dopamine receptors in the ACC (Stanwood, Washington, Shumsky, & Levitt, 2001).

Genes

Twin studies have provided evidence that reports of EC (Lemery-Chalfant, Doelger, & Goldsmith, 2008), as well as conflict scores obtained with the Attention Network Task (ANT; Fan, Wu, Fossella, & Posner, 2001), show significant indices of heritability. Findings like these have encouraged identification of genes related to individual differences in EC. Given the association between the neuromodulator DA and the functioning of the executive attention network, DA-related genes constitute a list of candidate genes that are likely to play a part in the development of regulatory skills.

Using indices of performance in conflict tasks as phenotypes, an increasing number of studies has shown that efficiency of the executive attention network is related to variation in several DA-related genes. In a study with adults, Fossella and colleagues (2002) showed that two genes related to the synthesis of DA and norepinephrine (NE), the dopamine receptor D4 (*DRD4*) and monoanime oxidase type A (*MAOA*) genes, were related to executive attention. Individuals carrying the more common 4-repeat allele on the *DRD4* gene have higher conflict scores compared to those without the 4-repeat allele (mainly 7-repeat carriers), as well as those carrying the 3-repeat allele on the *MAOA* gene. In a subsequent imaging study by the same group, these polymorphisms also were related to differences in brain activation in the ACC (Fan, Fossella, Sommer, Wu, & Posner, 2003).

Additionally, the dopamine transporter 1 (*DAT1*) gene appears to be related to efficiency of attentional regulation as measured at various levels of analysis, including temperament questionnaires, interference scores in the flanker task, and electrophysiological patterns of brain activation during task performance in a group of preschoolers (Rueda, Rothbart, McCandliss, Saccomanno, & Posner, 2005). The 10-repeat polymorphism in this gene is linked to attention-deficit/hyperactivity disorder (ADHD) (Swanson et al., 2001), along with poorer performance in tasks requiring sustained attention (Bellgrove et al., 2005). The catechol-O-methyltransferase (*COMT*) gene also influences the brain level of several neuromodulators, including DA and NE. Diamond, Briand, Fossella, and Gehlbach (2004) reported that children homozygous for the Met/Met allele at the Val-158Met polymorphism performed better on a version of the spatial conflict task. Also, Blasi and colleagues (2005), in a functional magnetic resonance imaging study with adults, found that presence of the Met variation is associated with better performance and lower ACC activation during an attentional control task, which can be interpreted as increased relative efficiency of the executive attention network (see also White, Lamm, Helfinstein, & Fox, Chapter 17, this volume).

The relation of genetic factors to attentional control does not mean that the system cannot be influenced by experience. Rather, it appears that some genetic variations allow for additional influence from parenting and other experiences. For instance, it has been found that the 7-repeat allele of the *DRD4* gene interacts with the quality of parenting to influence temperamental variables in the child, such as activity level, sensation seeking, and impulsivity (Sheese, Voelker, Rothbart, & Posner, 2007). Similarly, Kochanska, Philibert, and Barry (2009) have found that variation of the serotonin transporter (*5-HTTPR*) gene interacts with early mother–child attachment in predicting later development of regulatory skills. Among children who carried the short (ss/sl) variation of the gene, associated with risk for poor regulatory control, only those who were insecurely attached developed poor regulatory abilities. Other research has shown similar findings for externalizing behavior of the child, as rated by parents (Bakermans-Kranenburg & van IJzendoorn, 2006). More recently, a similar gene × parenting interaction has been observed with the *COMT* gene for 2-year-old children's performance of a visual sequence task thought to involve attention (Voelker, Sheese, Rothbart, & Posner, 2009).

The frequency of genetic alleles changes during human evolution, and there is evidence that the 7-repeat allele of the *DRD4* gene is under positive selective pressure (Ding et al., 2002). The fact that presence of the 7-repeat allele is associated with risk of attentional disorders such as ADHD is certainly puzzling. A plausible interpretation is that genetic variations that make individuals more susceptible to being influenced by their culture (e.g., through parenting style) have more potential to promote adaptation to the environment and thus are positively selected (Posner & Rothbart, 2009). The more negative side of this hypothesis is that this type of genetic disposition combined with an unfavorable environment would make individuals more vulnerable to developing pathologies.

Development of EC

During the first months of life, caregivers provide much of control over babies' behavior. For example, soothing the baby by holding and rocking or calling his or her attention away from the source of distress are common practices for controlling negative reactions (Harman, Rothbart & Posner, 1997). Likewise, adults help babies focus attention on relevant external events and exert much control over the sensory stimulation that reaches them. With maturation, the child will be more able to regulate his or her emotional and behavioral reactions, and control progressively becomes internalized.

At about the end of the first year of life, some aspects of EC begin to emerge. By this time, executive attention-related frontal structures come into play. The maturation of the frontal lobe and its connection with parietal structures involved in the orientation of attention allow for a progressive increase in the duration of attentional orientation based on goals and intentions (Ruff & Rothbart, 1996). This also allows the child to display some forms of executive control.

Perhaps the earliest evidence of activation of the executive attention network is at about 7 to 9 months of age. The ability to detect errors is an important form of self-regulation that has been linked to activation of the ACC (Dehaene, Posner, & Tucker, 1994). Berger, Tzur, and Posner (2006) examined the ability of infants ages 7 to 9 months to detect errors. In their study, infants observed a scenario in which one or two puppets were hidden behind a screen. A hand was seen to reach behind the screen and either add or remove a puppet. When the screen was removed, there was either the correct number of puppets or an incorrect number. Wynn (1992) found that infants of 7 months looked longer when the number was in error that when it was correct. More recently, Berger and colleagues replicated the Wynn study using event-related potentials (ERPs) to examine infant's brain reactions. They found that infants show a similar brain response to the error-related negativity shown by adults, which suggests that even very early in life the anatomy of the executive attention system begins to be functional.

Adele Diamond's work using the "A not B" and the reaching tasks also provides evidence of the emergence of executive control in late infancy, and its dependence upon maturation of prefrontal cortex. These two marker tasks involve inhibition of an action that is strongly elicited by the situation, such as retrieving an object from a previously reinforced location (A not B) or reaching for a toy through the line of sight. Important changes in the performance of these tasks are observed in infants between 6 and 12 months of age, and maturation of the prefrontal cortex seems to be critical for the development of this form of inhibition (Diamond, 2006).

Another task that has proven useful for studying the early development of voluntary attention in infants and toddlers involves anticipatory looking in a visual sequence of stimuli. It has been shown that infants as young as 3½ to 4 months are able to look ahead to locations when sequences of stimuli are presented in a predictable order (Clohessy, Posner, & Rothbart, 2001). However, learning more complex sequences of stimuli, such as those in which a location is followed by one of two or more different locations, with the particular location depending on the location of the previous stimulus within the sequence (location 1, then location 2, then location 1, then location 3, etc.), requires the monitoring of context and, in adult studies, has been shown to depend on the lateral prefrontal cortex (Keele, Ivry, Mayr, Hazeltine, & Heuer, 2003). The ability to respond when such conflict occurs is not present until ages 18–24 months (Clohessy et al., 2001). Altogether, data suggest a slow development of the executive attention network during the first and second year of life.

The visual sequence task is related to other features that reflect executive attention. One of these is the cautious reach toward novel toys. Rothbart and colleagues (2001) found that the slow, cautious reach of infants of 10 months predicted higher levels of EC, as measured at 7 years of age by parent report. Infants age 7 months who show higher levels of correct anticipatory looking in the visual sequence task also show longer inspection before reaching toward novel objects and slower reaching toward the object (Sheese, Rothbart, Posner, Fraundorf, & White, 2008). This suggests that successful anticipatory looking at 7 months is one feature of self-regulation. In addition, infants with higher levels of correct anticipatory looking also showed evidence of higher levels of emotionality in a distressing task and more evidence of efforts to self-regulate their emotional reactions.

Using behavioral tasks of the type presented at Table 8.2, a number of studies indicate considerable development of EC during toddlerhood and the preschool years. In one such study, Kochanska and colleagues (2000) reported a significant increase in indices of performance of all the EC tasks included in their battery in children between 22 and 33 months of age. Also, better EC during toddlerhood was predicted by focused attention at 9 months and was positively linked to regulation of both negative and positive reactivity. Carlson (2005) has examined developmental changes occurring in children between 2 and 6 years of age in a large number of tasks, including inhibitory control, conflict, and working memory tasks. She provided a scale of task difficulty for each age group included in her study (2, 3, 4, and 5–6 years) based on children's probability of passing each task. This information can be very useful for selecting those tasks most sensitive to individual differences for a particular age during the preschool period.

From about age 3 on, children are able to perform simple tasks that require voluntary key press responses, in which their ability to resolve conflict can be measured through RT and response accuracy. When used online with registration of brain activity, these tasks offer an opportunity to examine changes in brain processes underlying the development of EC. Examples of these are the spatial conflict and flanker tasks (see Figure 8.1), mentioned earlier as an example of marker tasks of the executive attention network. Performance on the spatial conflict task strongly develops between 2 and 3 years of age (Rothbart et al., 2003). Also, larger conflict scores (greater RT or percentage of errors in conflict compared to nonconflict trials) in this study were related to poorer EC, as reported by parents. Moreover, at 30 months, the ability to resolve conflict was positively related to the percentage of correct anticipations in ambiguous sequences of the visual sequence task.

Using the child version of the flanker task (Figure 8.1b), we have also reported a steady increase in children's efficiency in resolving conflict between 4 and 7 years of age (Rueda, Posner, et al., 2005), and we have examined the neural mechanisms underlying this maturation with ERPs. When a response is required to the presentation of a target stimulus, a negative ERP component is observed over frontal channels around 200–300 milliseconds after presentation of the target (N200). The amplitude of the N200 is modulated by conflict, indicating greater activation of frontal structures, such as the ACC, in conditions involving conflict (van Veen & Carter, 2002). In preschool children, the presence of conflict produces larger N200 effects compared to adults; also, the effect appears later, and it is sustained over a longer period and has a more anterior distribution compared to that of adults (Rueda, Posner, Rothbart, et al., 2004; Rueda, Rothbart, et al., 2005). Studies with older children have shown that the progressive decrease in the amplitude and latency of the N200 effect with age continues during middle and late childhood (Davis, Bruce, Snyder, & Nelson, 2004; Jonkman, 2006). The reduction of the amplitude appears to relate to the increase in efficiency of the system, and not to the overall amplitude decrease in ERPs observed with age (Lamm, Zelazo, & Lewis, 2006). The fact that the N200 conflict effect is more widely distributed for young children and becomes more focalized with age (Jonkman, 2006; Rueda, Posner, Rothbart, & Davis-Stober, 2004) suggests that, compared to adults, children need to engage additional frontal structures over longer time to resolve conflict.

The focalization of signals in adults, compared to children, is consistent with neuroimaging studies. It has been shown that children activate similar brain regions as adults when performing the same task, but with remarkably larger volume of activation (Casey, Thomas, Davidson, Kunz, & Franzen, 2002; Durston et al., 2002). Altogether, these data suggest that the brain circuitry underlying executive functions becomes more focal and refined as it gains efficiency. This maturational process may involve not only greater anatomical specialization but also a reduction of the time neural systems need to be engaged in order to resolve the task. This is consistent with recent data showing that the network of brain areas involved in attentional control shows increased segregation of short-range connections but increased integration of long-range connections with maturation (Fair et al., 2007). Segregation of short-range connectivity may be responsible for greater local specialization, whereas integration of long-range connectivity likely increases efficiency by improving coordinated responses between different processing networks.

EC and Self-Regulation

Self-regulation is a broad concept that refers to the many processes by which individuals exert control over their behavior, including actions, as well as inner states and cognition (see Vohs & Baumeister, 2011). As stated at the beginning of the chapter, EC relates to self-regulation because it captures individual differences in the ability to self-regulate emotions and actions. So far, I have discussed the constitutional basis of EC and the average developmental course of this function during childhood. However, it is evident to parents and educators that, over and above the general evolution shown during maturation, children differ greatly in their ability to regulate behavior. Individual differences in this skill are likely to affect children's daily lives and social success. In recent years, a growing amount of literature has emphasized the key role of EC and self-regulation in aspects of the social and emotional development of children, as well as their success in school.

Socioemotional Development

What is considered moral or socially acceptable greatly depends on the cultural context and needs to be learned during development. Throughout childhood, caretakers help children to learn what is socially acceptable and to accommodate to it by showing the appropriate controls. Success in the development of self-regulation has many advantages for the child's socialization process. In a study at the University of Oregon, we observed that in the course of development, children are increasingly able to accommodate to social norms, and that this capacity is related to the efficiency of attentional mechanisms. In this study, children were given an undesired gift while their emotional reactions were videotaped. The amount of smiling in response to the undesired gift increased with age. However, greater accommodation to the social norm of smiling when receiving an undesired gift was related to less interference due to distracting stimulation while performing the child version of the flanker task (Simonds et al., 2007). This suggests that greater efficiency of executive attention is likely to provide the attentional flexibility required to link negative affect (feelings of disappointment), internalized social norms (smiling when receiving a gift), and action in everyday life situations.

Children high in EC also appear to be high in empathy and guilt/shame, and low in aggressiveness (Rothbart, Ahadi, & Hershey, 1994). Eisenberg, Fabes, Nyman, Bernzweig, and Pinuelas (1994) also found that 4- to 6-year-old boys with good attentional control tend to deal with anger by using nonhostile verbal methods rather than overt aggressive methods. To display empathy toward others requires that we interpret their signals of distress or pleasure. EC may support empathy by allowing attention to the thoughts and feelings of others, and it may also help to regulate one's own distress and not become overwhelmed by it and enable helping behavior.

Similarly, guilt/shame in 6- to 7-year-olds is positively related to EC and to negative affectivity (Rothbart et al., 1994). Negative affectivity may contribute to guilt by providing strong internal cues of discomfort, increasing the likelihood that the cause of these feelings will be attributed to an internal conscience rather than external reward or coercion (Kochanska, Barry, Jimenez, Hollatz, & Woodard, 2009). Effortful control may contribute further by providing the attentional flexibility needed to notice these feelings and relate them to feelings of responsibility for one's own specific actions and their negative consequences for another person (Rothbart, Ellis, & Posner, 2004).

In turn, Kochanska and Aksan (2006) have shown that EC plays an important role in the development of conscience. The internalization of moral principles appears to be facilitated in fearful preschool-age children, especially when their mothers use gentle discipline (Kochanska, 1997), and internalized control is greater in children high in EC (Kochanska et al., 2000).

Individual differences in EC are also related to some aspects of metacognitive knowledge, such as theory of mind (i.e., knowing that people's behavior is guided by their beliefs, desires, and other mental states; Carlson & Moses, 2001). The relation between measures of inhibitory control and theory of mind holds after controlling for other executive functions such as working memory or planning (Carlson, Moses, & Claxton, 2004). Due to the importance of understanding the feelings and desires of others in the socialization process, this ability is likely to play a part in social–emotional development and the degree of successful socialization.

Evidence also show that during childhood EC is negatively related to the incidence of externalizing behavioral problems, characterized by high levels of aggression and impulsivity, after controlling for other cognitive and social risk factors (Olson, Sameroff, Kerr, Lopez, & Wellman, 2005; Valiente et al., 2003). Individuals who exhibit externalizing problems also show higher scores on Extraversion/Surgency and Frustration, and lower rates of EC, whereas individuals showing internalizing problems are high on Fear and Shyness and moderately low on EC (Oldehinkel, Hartman, De Winter, Veenstra, & Ormel, 2004). Other studies have also shown that both mother- and self-reported low EC, together with poor efficiency of executive attention, predict behavior problems during adolescence (Ellis, Rothbart, & Posner, 2004). We have also shown that larger flanker interference and lower EC is associated with greater incidence of disturbing behavior in the classroom and increased rates of peer rejection in a group of 12-year-old children (Checa et al., 2008).

Mechanisms related to the executive attention network are likely to play a role in the relation between low EC and poor socialization. As discussed earlier, error-related negativity (ERN) can be considered a brain index of the function of the executive attention system. The amplitude of ERN seems to reflect detection of errors, as well as the salience of the error for a particular individual in the context of the task. Generally, larger ERN amplitudes are associated with greater engagement in the task and/or greater efficiency of the error-detection system (Falkenstein, Hoormann, Christ, & Hohnsbein, 2000).

Developmentally, the amplitude of the ERN shows a progressive increase during childhood into late adolescence (Segalowitz & Davies, 2004), with young children (age 7–8 years) being less likely than older children and adults to exhibit ERN relative to self-committed errors. Supporting the role of error detection for self-regulation, we have found that the amplitude of ERN is positively related to the percentage of delay choices in a delay of gratification task and negatively related to impulsivity after controlling by age (Checa & Rueda, 2012). Also, it has been found that empathy shows a positive relation with amplitude of the ERN (Santesso & Segalowitz, 2009). Moreover, children who commit more errors on incongruent trials in a flanker task show smaller amplitudes in the ERN (Santesso, Segalowitz, & Schmidt, 2005). This result suggests less sensitivity of the brains of these children to the commission of errors. Moreover, the amplitude of the ERN is predicted by individual differences in social behavior. Children with poorer social sensitivity, as assessed by a self-report personality questionnaire, show ERNs of smaller amplitude (Santesso et al., 2005). These results are consistent with imaging studies in which adults with socialization abnormalities (e.g., psychopathy) have deficient activation of limbic structures, including the anterior and posterior cingulate cortex and amygdala, in response to affective stimulation (Kiehl et al., 2001). All these data suggest that relatively unsocialized individuals have greater difficulty experiencing or appreciating the emotional significance of errors and other unfavorable outcomes due to weaker responses of their limbic structures.

Imaging work with adults shows that human faces displaying negative affect (e.g., fear and sadness) activate the amygdala. When increasing the intensity of distress signals in the faces, the amygdala activation is accompanied by activity in the ACC as part of the executive attention network (Blair, Morris, Frith, Perrett, & Dolan, 1999). It seems likely that ACC activity represents the basis for our attention to the distress of others. In children, a strongly reactive amygdala would provide the signals of distress that would easily allow empathic feelings toward others, leading to children who might be relatively easy to socialize. In the absence of this form of control, development of the executive attention network would allow appropriate attention to signals of distress in others.

Altogether, these data suggest that more efficient mechanisms of executive attention, such as interference inhibition and conflict resolution, lead to greater ability to exert regulation at the cognitive, emotional, and behavioral levels, which in turn results in better chances of successful socialization.

School Achievement

I have just argued that variations in reactivity and attentional control affect children's socioemotional adjustment processes. These processes in turn influence aspects of social development, such as self-esteem and relationships with peers, parents and teachers (Sanson, Hemphill, & Smart, 2004). Moreover, socialization processes are very likely to affect children's adjustment to the requirements and challenges of the educational setting. As a matter of fact, there is evidence that peer rejection leads to decreases in classroom participation and to lower rates of achievement in childhood (Buhs, Ladd, & Herald, 2006).

There is evidence that children's regulatory strategies, such as self-distraction and attention, are associated with adjustment to the school context (Raver, Blackburn, Bancroft, & Torp, 1999; see also Duckworth & Allred, Chapter 30, this volume). Eisenberg and colleagues (1997) found an association between teachers' and parents' reports of elementary schoolchildren attentional control and peer nominations for social status. Negative emotionality and low EC also have been consistently linked to problems in adjustment at school from a young age (Nelson, Martin, Hodge, Havill, & Kamphaus, 1999). In a study in Spain with 12-year-olds, we found a consistent negative relation between peer social rejection and schooling competence, with better socially adjusted children obtaining higher grades and showing better schooling skills (Checa et al., 2008). Teacher-rated higher levels of aggression and anxiety in kindergarten are also related to poorer achievement through a lack of cognitive self-control in school tasks (Normandeau & Guay, 1998). The relationship between school maladjustment and poor academics thus seems to be found consistently across ages and cultures. Some authors have proposed that positive social relationships at school constitute the primary factor promoting school competence (Mashburn & Pianta, 2006). However, in the Spanish study, we found that individual differences in EC mediated the relationship between peer-reported rates of successful socialization at school. Both academic achievement and skills important for school success, such as rule following, tolerance to frustration and understanding the role of the student in the classroom, were predicted by EC (Checa et al., 2008).

Attentional control also appears to be an important skill for learning arithmetic (Fuchs et al., 2005). For instance, Passolunghi and colleagues have shown that children's arithmetic performance is related to the ability to control irrelevant information. In one of their studies, they selected fourth graders according to their ability to solve word problems in arithmetic and followed them longitudinally for a 2-years period. Despite the fact that poor problem-solvers were able to identify relevant information, they remembered less relevant but more irrelevant information about the arithmetic questions than good problem-solvers (Passolunghi, Cornoldi, & De Liberto, 1999). This finding indicates that children exhibiting poorer arithmetic performance have greater difficulty inhibiting irrelevant information compared to better performers. Other measures tapping the executive attention network, such as Stroop-like interference and performance on inhibitory control tasks, have shown a consistent relationship with arithmetic competency (Blair & Razza, 2007; Bull & Scerif, 2001). Using the arrow flanker task, we have also reported an association between degree of interference by distracting stimulation and lower grades in math (Checa et al., 2008), and we have found that the amplitude of the interference-related ERP component, together with parent-reported EC, significantly predicts grades in mathematics, as well as rule-following skills, after controlling for IQ (Checa & Rueda, 2011).

The role of attentional control in school performance and reasoning might also have to do with the anatomical overlap between the executive attention network and brain areas related to general intelligence and a wide range of cognitive demands related to the control of cognition. Lateral frontal regions of the brain considered to be part of the executive attention network are activated by marker tasks of general intelligence (Duncan et al., 2000). Efficiency of this brain network is very likely to result in more successful acquisition and application of knowledge taught in the school, especially in those subjects involving complex reasoning, such as mathematics.

Promoting EC

Temperament is thought to have a constitutional basis (Rothbart & Bates, 2006). However, this does not mean that it cannot be influenced by experience. The importance of parenting for the development of EC suggests that children's regulatory abilities may depend on the joint interaction of genes and environment. Aspects of parent–child relationship, such as attachment security, early positive mutuality, warmth, responsiveness, and discipline, have been shown to play a role in the development of regulatory abilities (see van IJzendoorn & Bakermans-Kranenburg, Chapter 19, and Bates, Schermerhorn, & Petersen, Chapter 20, this volume). Carlson (2003) has proposed three aspects of parenting that are likely to promote regulatory skills and executive functions: (1) maternal sensitivity (i.e., appropriate and consistent responses to children's signals); (2) scaffolding (i.e., offering children age-appropriate problem-solving strategies and providing opportunities to use them); and (3) mind-mindedness (i.e., the use of mental terms by parents when talking to the child). Although all three dimensions of parenting have been related to children's executive functioning, autonomy support seems to be the strongest predictor of children's performance on age-appropriate conflict tasks (Bernier, Carlson, & Whipple, 2010). Also, Cipriano and Stifter (2010) have shown that parents' educational style plays an important role in the development of EC during early childhood, particularly in children with exuberant temperament. In a longitudinal study, they found that children of parents who use gentle discipline (i.e., give commands and prohibitive statements in a positive tone) have greater EC 2 years later, whereas the use of reasoning explanations and redirections in a neutral tone was associated to poorer EC later on. In line with this, other studies have shown that positive parental control can buffer the risk of developing externalizing behavioral problems in children low in EC (Karreman, van Tuijl, van Aken, & Dekovic, 2009). A similar result is also found for teacher–child relationships. Supportive teaching appears to safeguard the risk of academic failure in children who are low in EC (Liew, Chen, & Hughes, 2010). Data of this sort indicate that temperament both *influences* and *is influenced* by experience.

Growing evidence points to the vulnerability of attention and self-regulation to environmental aspects such as parenting and socioeconomic status (Bornstein & Bradley, 2003; Hackman & Farah, 2009). For instance, children whose parents have lower levels of education have more difficulty selecting out irrelevant information, as shown by ERPs, than those with highly educated parents (Stevens, Lauinger, & Neville, 2009). Low income also appears to be associated with children's higher levels of fear and irritability and lower EC, as well as higher levels of rejection by parents and inconsistent discipline (Lengua, 2006).

To examine the role of experience in the executive attention network, we designed a set of computer exercises aimed at training attention and tested a 5-day training intervention with children between 4 and 6 years of age, a period of major development of executive attention. Before and after training, the children performed the fish flanker task while their brain activation was recorded with an EEG system. Children in the intervention group showed clear evidence of improvement in the executive attention network following training, in comparison with a control group that viewed interactive videos matched to the duration of the intervention (Rueda, Rothbart, et al., 2005). The frontal negative ERP typically observed in conflict tasks showed a more adult-like pattern (shorter delay and progressively more posterior scalp distribution) in trained children compared to controls, suggesting that the training altered the brain mechanisms of conflict resolution in a positive direction. The beneficial effect of training attention also generalized to nontrained measures of fluid intelligence. Recently, a replication of this study was carried out with a sample of 37 5-year-olds in a Spanish preschool. In this study, the benefits of training in brain activation and intelligence were replicated, and the trained group was shown to maintain these training effects 2 months after without further training (Rueda, Checa, & Cómbita, 2012). The training of attention also showed a modest positive effect on performance of affective regulation tasks, such as delay of gratification and the children's gambling task.

Consistent with our results, other studies have shown beneficial effects of cognitive training on attention and other forms of executive function during development. For instance, auditory selective attention was improved by training with a computerized program designed to promote oral language skills in both language-impaired and typically developing children (Stevens, Fanning, Coch, Sanders, & Neville, 2008). Klingberg and colleagues have shown that training can enhance working memory, and that the effect shows some degree of transfer to aspects of attention (Thorell, Lindqvist, Nutley, Bohlin, & Klingberg, 2009). This research group has also shown evidence that training produces changes at various levels of brain function, such as the activation (Olesen, Westerberg, & Klingberg, 2004) and density of dopamine receptors (McNab et al., 2009) in areas of the cerebral cortex involved in the trained function.

One study has also shown that the use of a specific curriculum in preschool classrooms can foster executive functions (Diamond,

Barnett, Thomas, & Munro, 2007). An important question is whether such training in childhood can lead to long-lasting changes in behavior or schooling. Some evidence on this question comes from efforts to evaluate early education programs, such as the Head Start program applied in the United States (Duncan et al., 2007). Although Head Start does not specifically involve attention training, the programs are likely to influence it through the forms of training provided. There is evidence that later school attendance and socioemotional adjustment is improved in children trained in Head Start, and it has been suggested that these improvements are based on changes in the ability to regulate thoughts and behavior through attention training (Ludwig & Phillips, 2008).

The study of attention training as a whole suggests that networks can be shaped both by informal ways and formal training. With the availability of imaging and related methods it should be possible to design appropriate methods with various forms of difficulty for children of different ages. The studies to date certainly support the importance of attention training as one tool for improving children's regulatory skills and their learning at school.

Summary and Conclusions

EC is viewed as a dynamic temperamental dimension determined by a multiplicity of factors, including both constitutional dispositions and experience. It captures individual differences in the voluntary and effortful regulation of thoughts, emotions, and responses. This capacity emerges around the end of the first year of life, along with the maturation of brain structures related to the executive attention network in Posner's model. There are strong increases in this function during early childhood, followed by a more progressive development during late childhood and adolescence, as brain processes related to executive control become progressively more refined and efficient. The connection between EC and executive control allows the examination of brain mechanisms underpinning differences in efficiency of this function. These differences are found between individuals and across development at multiple levels of analysis, including cognitive, neural, and molecular levels. Individual differences in EC are important for a broad range of behaviors that will significantly influence children's social adjustment and their success in school. In this chapter, I have presented timely research showing that the efficiency of systems of self-regulation appears to be partially determined by the genetic endowment of the individual and is also affected by environmental factors such as parenting and familial socioeconomic status. Susceptibility to experience provides an opportunity to promote EC by means of appropriate educational interventions. This effort may serve the purpose of helping children to become successful and happily adjusted members of the society.

Acknowledgments

This work was supported by Grant No. PSI2008.02955 from the Spanish Ministry of Science and Innovation. I am also grateful to Grazyna Kochanska and Mary Rothbart for their valuable comments on an earlier version of this chapter.

Further Reading

Posner, M. I., & Rothbart, M. K. (2009). Toward a physical basis of attention and self-regulation. *Physics of Life Reviews, 6*(2), 103–120.

Rothbart, M. K. (2011). *Becoming who we are: Temperament and personality in development*. New York: Guilford Press.

Rueda, M. R., Posner, M. I., & Rothbart, M. K. (2011). Attentional control and self-regulation. In K. D. Vohs & R. F. Baumeister (Eds.), *Handbook of self-regulation: Research, theory, and applications* (2nd ed., pp. 284–299). New York: Guilford Press.

References

Ahadi, S. A., & Rothbart, M. K. (1994). Temperament, development, and the Big Five. In C. F. Halverson, G. A. Kohnstamm, & R. P. Martin (Eds.), *The developing structure of temperament and personality from infancy to adulthood* (pp. 189–207). Hillsdale, NJ: Erlbaum.

Ahadi, S. A., Rothbart, M. K., & Ye, R. (1993). Children's temperament in the U.S. and China: Similarities and differences. *European Journal of Personality, 7*, 359–378.

Allport, G. W. (1961). *Pattern and growth in personality*. New York: Holt, Rinehart & Winston.

Bakermans-Kranenburg, M. J., & van IJzendoorn, M. H. (2006). Gene–environment interaction of the dopamine D4 receptor (DRD4) and observed maternal insensitivity predicting externalizing behavior in preschoolers. *Developmental Psychobiology, 48*(5), 406–409.

Bates, J. E. (1989). Concepts and measure of temperament. In J. E. Bates & M. K. Rothbart (Eds.), *Temperament in childhood* (pp. 3–26). Chichester, UK: Wiley.

Beauregard, M., Levesque, J., & Bourgouin, P. (2001). Neural correlates of conscious self-regulation of emotion. *Journal of Neuroscience, 21*(18), 6993–7000.

Bellgrove, M. A., Hawi, Z., Kirley, A., Gill, M., Robertson, I. H., & Fitzgerald, M. (2005). Association between dopamine transporter (DAT1) genotype, left-sided inattention, and an enhanced response to methylphenidate in attention-deficit hyperactivity disorder. *Neuropsychopharmacology, 30*, 2290–2297.

Berger, A., Tzur, G., & Posner, M. I. (2006). Infant brains detect arithmetic errors. *Proceedings of the National Academy of Sciences USA, 103*(33), 12649–12653.

Bernier, A., Carlson, S. M., & Whipple, N. (2010). From external regulation to self-regulation: Early parenting precursors of young children's executive functioning. *Child Development, 81*(1), 326–339.

Blair, C., & Razza, R. P. (2007). Relating effortful control, executive function, and false belief understanding to emerging math and literacy ability in kindergarten. *Child Development, 78*(2), 647–663.

Blair, R. J. R., Morris, J. S., Frith, C. C., Perrett, D. I., & Dolan, R. J. (1999). Dissociable neural responses to facial expressions of sadness and anger. *Brain: A Journal of Neurology, 122*(5), 883–893.

Blasi, G., Mattay, V. S., Bertolino, A. L., Elvevåg, G., Callicot, J. H., Das, S., et al. (2005). Effect of catechol-O-methyltransferase val158met genotype on attentional control. *Journal of Neuroscience, 25*, 5038–5045.

Bornstein, M. H., & Bradley, R. H. (2003). *Socioeconomic status, parenting, and child development*. Mahwah, NJ: Erlbaum.

Botvinick, M., Nystrom, L. E., Fissell, K., Carter, C. S., & Cohen, J. D. (1999). Conflict monitoring versus selection-for-action in anterior cingulate cortex. *Nature, 402*, 179–181.

Botvinick, M. M., Braver, T. S., Barch, D. M., Carter, C. S., & Cohen, J. D. (2001). Conflict monitoring and cognitive control. *Psychological Review, 108*(3), 624–652.

Brozoski, T. J., Brown, R. M., Rosvold, H. E., & Goldman, P. S. (1979). Cognitive deficit caused by regional depletion of dopamine in prefrontal cortex of rhesus monkey. *Science, 205*, 929–932.

Buhs, E. S., Ladd, G. W., & Herald, S. L. (2006). Peer exclusion and victimization: Processes that mediate the relation between peer group rejection and children's classroom engagement and achievement? *Journal of Educational Psychology, 98*(1), 1–13.

Bull, R., & Scerif, G. (2001). Executive functioning as a predictor of children's mathematics ability: Inhibition, switching, and working memory. *Developmental Neuropsychology, 19*(3), 273–293.

Bush, G., Luu, P., & Posner, M. I. (2000). Cognitive and emotional influences in anterior cingulate cortex. *Trends in Cognitive Sciences, 4*(6), 215–222.

Carlson, S. M. (2003). Executive function in context: Development, measurement, theory, and experience. *Monographs of the Society for Research in Child Development, 68*(Serial No. 274).

Carlson, S. M. (2005). Developmentally sensitive measures of executive function in preschool children. *Developmental Neuropsychology, 28*(2), 595–616.

Carlson, S. M., & Moses, L. J. (2001). Individual differences in inhibitory control and children's theory of mind. *Child Development, 72*(4), 1032–1053.

Carlson, S. M., Moses, L. J., & Claxton, L. J. (2004). Individual differences in executive functioning and theory of mind: An investigation of inhibitory control and planning ability. *Journal of Experimental Child Psychology, 87*(4), 299–319.

Casey, B., Thomas, K. M., Davidson, M. C., Kunz, K., & Franzen, P. L. (2002). Dissociating striatal and hippocampal function developmentally with a stimulus–response compatibility task. *Journal of Neuroscience, 22*(19), 8647–8652.

Checa, P., Rodriguez-Bailon, R., & Rueda, M. R. (2008). Neurocognitive and temperamental systems of self-regulation and early adolescents' school competence. *Mind, Brain and Education, 2*(4), 177–187.

Checa, P., & Rueda, M. R. (2011). Behavioral and brain measures of attention control predict schooling competence in early adolescence. *Developmental Neuropsychology, 36*(8), 1018–1032.

Checa, P., & Rueda, M. R. (2012). *Brain response to conflict and errors and the development of self-regulation*. Manuscript submitted for publication.

Cipriano, E. A., & Stifter, C. A. (2010). Predicting preschool effortful control from toddler temperament and parenting behavior. *Journal of Applied Developmental Psychology, 31*(3), 221–230.

Clohessy, A. B., Posner, M. I., & Rothbart, M. K.

(2001). Development of the functional visual field. *Acta Psychologica, 106*(1–2), 51–68.

Crottaz-Herbette, S., & Menon, V. (2006). Where and when the anterior cingulate cortex modulates attentional response: Combined fMRI and ERP evidence. *Journal of Cognitive Neuroscience, 18*(5), 766–780.

Davis, E. P., Bruce, J., Snyder, K., & Nelson, C. A. (2004). The X-trials: Neural correlates of an inhibitory control task in children and adults. *Journal of Cognitive Neuroscience, 15*, 532–443.

Dehaene, S., Posner, M. I., & Tucker, D. M. (1994). Localization of a neural system for error detection and compensation. *Psychological Science, 5*(5), 303–305.

Derryberry, D., & Rothbart, M. K. (1988). Arousal, affect, and attention as components of temperament. *Journal of Personality and Social Psychology, 55*(6), 958–966.

Derryberry, D., & Rothbart, M. K. (1997). Reactive and effortful processes in the organization of temperament. *Development and Psychopathology, 9*, 633–652.

Diamond, A. (2006). The early development of executive functions. In E. Bialystok & F. I. M. Craik (Eds.), *Lifespan cognition: Mechanisms of change* (pp. 70–95). New York: Oxford University Press.

Diamond, A., Barnett, W. S., Thomas, J., & Munro, S. (2007). Preschool program improves cognitive control. *Science, 318*, 1387–1388.

Diamond, A., Briand, L., Fossella, J., & Gehlbach, L. (2004). Genetic and neurochemical modulation of prefrontal cognitive functions in children. *American Journal of Psychiatry, 161*(1), 125–132.

Ding, Y. C., Chi, H. C., Grady, D. L., Morishima, A., Kidd, J. R., Kidd, K. K., et al. (2002). Evidence of positive selection acting at the human dopamine receptor D4 gene locus. *Proceedings of the National Academy of Sciences, 99*, 309–314.

Drevets, W. C., & Raichle, M. E. (1998). Reciprocal suppression of regional cerebral blood flow during emotional versus higher cognitive processes: Implications for interactions between emotion and cognition. *Cognition and Emotion, 12*(3), 353–385.

Duncan, G. J., Dowsett, C. J., Claessens, A., Magnuson, K., Huston, A. C., Klebanov, P., et al. (2007). School readiness and later achievement. *Developmental Psychology, 43*(6), 1428–1446.

Duncan, J., Seitz, R. J., Kolodny, J., Bor, D., Herzog, H., Ahmed, A., et al. (2000). A neural basis for general intelligence. *Science, 289*, 457–460.

Durston, S., Thomas, K. M., Yang, Y., Ulug, A. M., Zimmerman, R. D., & Casey, B. (2002). A neural basis for the development of inhibitory control. *Developmental Science, 5*(4), F9–F16.

Eisenberg, N., Fabes, R. A., Nyman, M., Bernzweig, J., & Pinuelas, A. (1994). The relations of emotionality and regulation to children's anger-related reactions. *Child Development, 65*(1), 109–128.

Eisenberg, N., Fabes, R. A., Shepard, S. A., Murphy, B. C., Guthrie, I. K., Jones, S., et al. (1997). Contemporaneous and longitudinal prediction of children's social functioning from regulation and emotionality. *Child Development, 68*(4), 642–664.

Eisenberg, N., & Morris, A. S. (2002). Children's emotion-related regulation. In R. V. Kail (Ed.), *Advances in child development and behavior* (Vol. 30, pp. 189–229). San Diego, CA: Academic Press.

Ellis, L. K., & Rothbart, M. K. (2001). *Revision of the Early Adolescent Temperament Questionnaire*. Poster presented at the Biennial Meeting of the Society for Research in Child Development, Minneapolis, MN.

Ellis, L. K., Rothbart, M. K., & Posner, M. I. (2004). Individual differences in executive attention predict self-regulation and adolescent psychosocial behaviors. In R. E. Dahl & L. P. Spear (Eds.), *Adolescent brain development: Vulnerabilities and opportunities* (pp. 337–340). New York: New York Academy of Sciences.

Eriksen, B. A., & Eriksen, C. W. (1974). Effects of noise letters upon the identification of a target letter in a nonsearch task. *Perception and Psychophysics, 16*(1), 143–149.

Etkin, A., Egner, T., Peraza, D. M., Kandel, E. R., & Hirsch, J. (2006). Resolving emotional conflict: A role for the rostral anterior cingulate cortex in modulating activity in the amygdala. *Neuron, 51*(6), 871–882.

Evans, D. E., & Rothbart, M. K. (2007). Developing a model for adult temperament. *Journal of Research in Personality, 41*(4), 868–888.

Eysenck, H. J. (1990). Biological dimensions of personality. In L. A. Pervin (Ed.), *Handbook of personality: Theory and research* (pp. 249–276). New York: Guilford Press.

Fair, D. A., Dosenbach, N. U. F., Church, J. A., Cohen, A. L., Brahmbhatt, S., Miezin, F. M., et al. (2007). Development of distinct control networks through segregation and integration. *Proceedings of the National Academy of Sciences USA, 104*(33), 13507–13512.

Falkenstein, M., Hoormann, J., Christ, S., & Hohnsbein, J. (2000). ERP components on reaction errors and their functional significance: A tutorial. *Biological Psychology, 51*, 87–107.

Fan, J., Flombaum, J. I., McCandliss, B. D., Thomas, K. M., & Posner, M. I. (2003). Cognitive and brain consequences of conflict. *NeuroImage, 18*(1), 42–57.

Fan, J., Fossella, J., Sommer, T., Wu, Y., & Posner, M. I. (2003). Mapping the genetic variation of executive attention onto brain activity. *Proceedings of the National Academy of Sciences USA*, *100*(12), 7406–7411.

Fan, J., Wu, Y., Fossella, J., & Posner, M. I. (2001). Assessing the heritability of attentional networks. *BMC Neuroscience*, *2*, 14.

Fossella, J., Sommer, T., Fan, J., Wu, Y., Swanson, J. M., Pfaff, D. W., et al. (2002). Assessing the molecular genetics of attention networks. *BMC Neuroscience*, *3*, 14.

Fuchs, L. S., Compton, D. L., Fuchs, D., Paulsen, K., Bryant, J. D., & Hamlett, C. L. (2005). The prevention, identification, and cognitive determinants of math difficulty. *Journal of Educational Psychology*, *97*, 493–513.

Gartstein, M. A., & Rothbart, M. K. (2003). Studying infant temperament via the Revised Infant Behavior Questionnaire. *Infant Behavior and Development*, *26*(1), 64–86.

Gerardi-Caulton, G. (2000). Sensitivity to spatial conflict and the development of self-regulation in children 24–36 months of age. *Developmental Science*, *3*(4), 397–404.

Gerstadt, C. L., Hong, Y. J., & Diamond, A. (1994). The relationship between cognition and action: Performance of children 3.5–7 years old on a Stroop-like day–night test. *Cognition*, *53*, 129–153.

Goldsmith, H. H., Reilly, J., Lemery, K. S., Longley, S., & Prescott, A. (1993). *Preschool Laboratory Temperament Assessment Battery (PS Lab-TAB; Version 1.0)* [Technical report]. Department of Psychology, University of Wisconsin–Madison.

Goldsmith, H. H., & Rothbart, M. K. (1992). *The Laboratory Temperament Assessment Battery (Lab-TAB): Locomotor version 3.0* [Technical manual]. Eugene: University of Oregon, Department of Psychology.

Gonzalez, C., Fuentes, L. J., Carranza, J. A., & Estevez, A. F. (2001). Temperament and attention in the self-regulation of 7-year-old children. *Personality and Individual Differences*, *30*(6), 931–946.

Gray, J. A. (1991). The neuropsychology of temperament. In J. Strelau & A. Angleitner (Eds.), *Explorations in temperament: International perspectives on theory and measurement* (pp. 105–128). New York: Plenum Press.

Hackman, D. A., & Farah, M. J. (2009). Socioeconomic status and the developing brain. *Trends in Cognitive Sciences*, *13*(2), 65–73.

Harman, C., Rothbart, M. K., & Posner, M. I. (1997). Distress and attention interactions in early infancy. *Motivation and Emotion*, *21*(1)m 27–43.

Hongwanishkul, D., Happaney, K. R., Lee, W. S., & Zelazo, P. D. (2005). Assessment of hot and cool executive function in young children: Age-related changes and individual differences. *Developmental Neuropsychology*, *28*(2), 617–644.

James, W. (1890). *The principles of psychology*. New York: Holt.

Jonkman, L. M. (2006). The development of preparation, conflict monitoring and inhibition from early childhood to young adulthood: A go/no-go ERP study. *Brain Research*, *1097*(1), 181–193.

Karreman, A., van Tuijl, C., van Aken, M. A., & Dekovic, M. (2009). Predicting young children's externalizing problems: Interactions among effortful control, parenting, and child gender. *Merrill–Palmer Quarterly*, *55*(2), 111–134.

Keele, S. W., Ivry, R. B., Mayr, U., Hazeltine, E., & Heuer, H. (2003). The cognitive and neural architecture of sequence representation. *Psychological Review*, *110*, 316–339.

Kiehl, K. A., Smith, A. M., Hare, R. D., Mendrek, A., Forster, B. B., Brink, J., et al. (2001). Limbic abnormalities in affective processing by criminal psychopaths as revealed by functional magnetic resonance imaging. *Biological Psychiatry*, *50*(9), 677–684.

Kochanska, G. (1997). Multiple pathways to conscience for children with different temperaments: From toddlerhood to age 5. *Developmental Psychology*, *33*, 228–240.

Kochanska, G., & Aksan, N. (2006). Children's conscience and self-regulation. *Journal of Personality*, *74*(6), 1587–1617.

Kochanska, G., Barry, R. A., Jimenez, N. B., Hollatz, A. L., & Woodard, J. (2009). Guilt and effortful control: Two mechanisms that prevent disruptive developmental trajectories. *Journal of Personality and Social Psychology*, *97*(2), 322–333.

Kochanska, G., Murray, K., Jacques, T. Y., Koenig, A. L., & Vandegeest, K. A. (1996). Inhibitory control in young children and its role in emerging internalization. *Child Development*, *67*, 490–507.

Kochanska, G., Murray, K. T., & Harlan, E. T. (2000). Effortful control in early childhood: Continuity and change, antecedents, and implications for social development. *Developmental Psychology*, *36*(2), 220–232.

Kochanska, G., Philibert, R. A., & Barry, R. A. (2009). Interplay of genes and early mother–child relationship in the development of self-regulation from toddler to preschool age. *Journal of Child and Psychology and Psychiatry and Allied Disciplines*, *50*(11), 1331–1338.

Lamm, C., Zelazo, P. D., & Lewis, M. D. (2006). Neural correlates of cognitive control in childhood and adolescence: Disentangling the contributions of age and executive function. *Neuropsychologia*, *44*(11), 2139–2148.

Lemery-Chalfant, K., Doelger, L., & Goldsmith, H. H. (2008). Genetic relations between effortful and attentional control and symptoms of psychopathology in middle childhood. *Infant and Child Development*, *17*(4), 364–385.

Lengua, L. J. (2006). Growth in temperament and parenting as predictors of adjustment during children's transition to adolescence. *Developmental Psychology, 42*(5), 819–832.

Liew, J., Chen, Q., & Hughes, J. N. (2010). Child effortful control, teacher–student relationships, and achievement in academically at-risk children: Additive and interactive effects. *Early Childhood Research Quarterly, 25*(1), 51–64.

Ludwig, J., & Phillips, D. A. (2008). The long term effects of head start on low-income children. *Annals of the New York Academy of Sciences, 40*, 1–12.

Mashburn, A. J., & Pianta, R. C. (2006). Social relationships and school readiness. *Early Education and Development, 17*(1), 151–176.

McCulloch, J., Savaki, H. E., McCulloch, M. C., Jehle, J., & Sokoloff, L. (1982). The distribution of alterations in energy metabolism in the rat brain produced by apomorphine. *Brain Research, 243*, 67–80.

McNab, F., Varrone, A., Farde, L., Jucaite, A., Bystritsky, P., Forssberg, H., et al. (2009). Changes in cortical dopamine D1 receptor binding associated with cognitive training. *Science, 323*, 800–802.

Mischel, W., Shoda, Y., & Rodriguez, M. L. (1989). Delay of gratification in children. *Science, 244*, 933–938.

Murray, K. T., & Kochanska, G. (2002). Effortful control: Factor structure and relation to externalizing and internalizing behaviors. *Journal of Abnormal Child Psychology, 30*(5), 503–514.

Nelson, B., Martin, R., Hodge, S., Havill, V., & Kamphaus, R. (1999). Modeling the prediction of elementary school adjustment from preschool temperament. *Personality and Individual Differences, 26*(4), 687–700.

Normandeau, S., & Guay, F. (1998). Preschool behavior and first-grade school achievement: The mediational role of cognitive self-control. *Journal of Educational Psychology, 90*(1), 111–121.

Ochsner, K. N., Bunge, S. A., Gross, J. J., & Gabrieli, J. D. (2002). Rethinking feelings: An fMRI study of the cognitive regulation of emotion. *Journal of Cognitive Neuroscience, 14*(8), 1215–1229.

Oldehinkel, A. J., Hartman, C. A., De Winter, A. F., Veenstra, R., & Ormel, J. (2004). Temperament profiles associated with internalizing and externalizing problems in preadolescence. *Development and Psychopathology, 16*(2), 421–440.

Olesen, P. J., Westerberg, H., & Klingberg, T. (2004). Increased prefrontal and parietal activity after training of working memory. *Nature Neuroscience, 7*(1), 75–79.

Olson, S. L., Sameroff, A. J., Kerr, D. C., Lopez, N. L., & Wellman, H. M. (2005). Developmental foundations of externalizing problems in young children: The role of effortful control. *Development and Psychopathology, 17*(1), 25–45.

Olson, S. L., Schilling, E. M., & Bates, J. E. (1999) Measurement of impulsivity: Construct coherence, longitudinal stability, and relationship with externalizing problems in middle childhood and adolescence. *Journal of Abnormal Child Psychology, 27*, 151–165.

Passolunghi, M. C., Cornoldi, C., & De Liberto, S. (1999). Working memory and intrusions of irrelevant information in a group of specific poor problem solvers. *Memory and Cognition, 27*(5), 779–790.

Posner, M. I., & DiGirolamo, G. J. (1998). Executive attention: Conflict, target detection, and cognitive control. In R. Parasuraman (Ed.), *The attentive brain* (pp. 401–423). Cambridge, MA: MIT Press.

Posner, M. I., & Fan, J. (2008). Attention as an organ system. In J. R. Pomerantz (Ed.), *Topics in integrative neuroscience* (pp. 31–61). New York: Cambridge University Press.

Posner, M. I., & Petersen, S. E. (1990). The attention system of human brain. *Annual Review of Neuroscience, 13*, 25–42.

Posner, M. I., & Raichle, M. E. (1994). *Images of mind*. New York: Scientific American Library.

Posner, M. I., & Rothbart, M. K. (1998). Attention, self-regulation and consciousness. *Philosophical Transactions of the Royal Society of London B, 353*, 1915–1927.

Posner, M. I., & Rothbart, M. K. (2007). Research on attention networks as a model for the integration of psychological science. *Annual Review of Psychology, 58*, 1–23.

Posner, M. I., & Rothbart, M. K. (2009). Toward a physical basis of attention and self-regulation. *Physics of Life Reviews, 6*(2), 103–120.

Posner, M. I., Rueda, M. R., & Kanske, P. (2007). Probing the mechanisms of attention. In J. T. Cacioppo, J. G. Tassinary, & G. G. Berntson (Eds.), *Handbook of psychophysiology* (3rd ed., pp. 410–432). Cambridge, UK: Cambridge University Press.

Posner, M. I., Sheese, B. E., Odludas, Y., & Tang, Y. (2006). Analyzing and shaping human attentional networks. *Neural Networks, 19*(9), 1422–1429.

Putnam, S. P., Gartstein, M. A., & Rothbart, M. K. (2006). Measurement of fine-grained aspects of toddler temperament: The Early Childhood Behavior Questionnaire. *Infant Behavior and Development, 29*(3), 386–401.

Raver, C., Blackburn, E. K., Bancroft, M., & Torp, N. (1999). Relations between effective emotional self-regulation, attentional control, and low-income preschoolers' social competence with peers. *Early Education and Development, 10*(3), 333–350.

Reed, M., Pien, D., & Rothbart, M. K. (1984).

Inhibitory self-control in preschool children. *Merrill–Palmer Quarterly, 30*, 131–148.
Rothbart, M. K. (1981). Measurement of temperament in infancy. *Child Development, 52*, 569–578.
Rothbart, M. K. (1989). Temperament and development. In G. A. Kohnstamm, J. A. Bates, & M. K. Rothbart (Eds.), *Temperament in childhood* (pp. 187–247). New York: Wiley.
Rothbart, M. K. (2011). *Becoming who we are: Temperament and personality in development.* New York: Guilford Press.
Rothbart, M. K., & Ahadi, S. A. (1994). Temperament and the development of personality. *Journal of Abnormal Psychology, 103*, 55–66.
Rothbart, M. K., Ahadi, S. A., & Evans, D. E. (2000). Temperament and personality: Origins and outcomes. *Journal of Personality and Social Psychology, 78*, 122–135.
Rothbart, M. K., Ahadi, S. A., & Hershey, K. L. (1994). Temperament and social behavior in childhood. *Merrill–Palmer Quarterly, 40*, 21–39.
Rothbart, M. K., Ahadi, S. A., Hersey, K. L., & Fisher, P. (2001). Investigations of temperament at three to seven years: The Children's Behavior Questionnaire. *Child Development, 72*(5), 1394–1408.
Rothbart, M. K., & Bates, J. A. (1998). Temperament. In N. Eisenberg (Ed.), *Handbook of child psychology: Vol. 3. Social, emotional and personality development* (5th ed., pp. 105–176). New York Wiley.
Rothbart, M. K., & Bates, J. A. (2006). Temperament. *Handbook of child psychology: Vol. 3. Social, emotional, and personality development* (6th ed., pp. 99–166). Hoboken, NJ: Wiley.
Rothbart, M. K., & Derryberry, D. (1981). Development of individual differences in temperament. In M. E. Lamb & A. L. Brown (Eds.), *Advances in developmental psychology* (Vol. 1, pp. 37–86). Hillsdale, NJ: Erlbaum.
Rothbart, M. K., Derryberry, D., & Hershey, K. (2000). Stability of temperament in childhood: Laboratory infant assessment to parent report at seven years. In V. J. Molfese & D. L. Molfese (Eds.), *Temperament and personality development across the life span* (pp. 85–119). Hillsdale, NJ: Erlbaum.
Rothbart, M. K., Ellis, L. K., & Posner, M. I. (2004). Temperament and self-regulation. In R. F. Baumeister & K. D. Vohs (Eds.), *Handbook of self-regulation: Research, theory, and applications* (pp. 357–370). New York: Guilford Press.
Rothbart, M. K., Ellis, L. K., Rueda, M., & Posner, M. I. (2003). Developing mechanisms of temperamental effortful control. *Journal of Personality, 71*(6), 1113–1143.
Rothbart, M. K., & Goldsmith, H. H. (1985). Three approaches to the study of infant temperament. *Developmental Review, 5*, 237–260.
Rothbart, M. K., & Rueda, M. R. (2005). The development of effortful control. In U. Mayr, E. Awh, & S. W. Keele (Eds.), *Developing individuality in the human brain. A tribute to Michael I. Posner* (pp. 167–188). Washington, DC: American Psychological Association.
Rothbart, M. K., Sheese, B. E., & Posner, M. I. (2007). Executive attention and effortful control: Linking temperament, brain networks, and genes. *Child Development Perspectives, 1*(1), 2–7.
Rueda, M., Fan, J., McCandliss, B. D., Halparin, J. D., Gruber, D. B., Lercari, L. P., et al. (2004). Development of attentional networks in childhood. *Neuropsychologia, 42*(8), 1029–1040.
Rueda, M., Posner, M. I., & Rothbart, M. K. (2005). The development of executive attention: Contributions to the emergence of self-regulation. *Developmental Neuropsychology, 28*(2), 573–594.
Rueda, M. R., Checa, P., & Cómbita, L. M. (2012). Enhanced efficiency of the executive attention network after training in preschool children: Immediate changes and affects after two months. *Developmental Cognitive Neuroscience, 2S*, S192–S204.
Rueda, M. R., Posner, M. I., & Rothbart, M. K. (2011). Attentional control and self-regulation. In K. D. Vohs & R. F. Baumeister (Eds.), *Handbook of self-regulation: Research, theory, and applications* (2nd ed., pp. 284–299). New York: Guilford Press.
Rueda, M. R., Posner, M. I., Rothbart, M. K., & Davis-Stober, C. P. (2004). Development of the time course for processing conflict: An event-related potentials study with 4 year olds and adults. *BMC Neuroscience, 5*(39), 1–13.
Rueda, M. R., Rothbart, M. K., McCandliss, B. D., Saccomanno, L., & Posner, M. I. (2005). Training, maturation, and genetic influences on the development of executive attention. *Proceedings of the National Academy of Sciences USA, 102*(41), 14931–14936.
Ruff, H. A., & Rothbart, M. K. (1996). *Attention in early development: Themes and variations.* New York: Oxford University Press.
Sanson, A., Hemphill, S. A., & Smart, D. (2004). Connections between temperament and social development: A review. *Social Development, 13*(1), 142–170.
Sanson, A. V., Smart, D. F., Prior, M., Oberklaid, F., & Pedlow, R. (1994). The structure of temperament from 3 to 7 years: Age, sex, and sociodemographic influences. *Merrill–Palmer Quarterly, 40*, 233–252.
Santesso, D. L., & Segalowitz, S. J. (2009). The error-related negativity is related to risk taking

and empathy in young men. *Psychophysiology, 46*(1), 143–152.

Santesso, D. L., Segalowitz, S. J., & Schmidt, L. A. (2005). ERP correlates of error monitoring in 10-year olds are related to socialization. *Biological Psychology, 70*(2), 79–87.

Segalowitz, S. J., & Davies, P. L. (2004). Charting the maturation of the frontal lobe: An electrophysiological strategy. *Brain and Cognition, 55*(1), 116–133.

Sheese, B. E., Rothbart, M. K., Posner, M. I., Fraundorf, S. H., & White, L. K. (2008). Executive attention and self-regulation in infancy. *Infant Behavior and Development, 31*(3), 501–510.

Sheese, B. E., Voelker, P. M., Rothbart, M. K., & Posner, M. I. (2007). Parenting quality interacts with genetic variation in dopamine receptor D4 to influence temperament in early childhood. *Development and Psychopathology, 19*(4), 1039–1046.

Simonds, J., Kieras, J. E., Rueda, M., & Rothbart, M. K. (2007). Effortful control, executive attention, and emotional regulation in 7-10-year-old children. *Cognitive Development, 22*(4), 474–488.

Simonds, J., & Rothbart, M. K. (2004, October). *The Temperament in Middle Childhood Questionnaire (TMCQ): A computerized self-report measure of temperament for ages 7–10.* Paper presented at the Occasional Temperament Conference, Athens, GA.

Stanwood, G. D., Washington, R. A., Shumsky, J. S., & Levitt, P. (2001). Prenatal cocaine exposure produces consistent developmental alteration in dopamine-rich regions of the cerebral cortex. *Neuroscience, 106,* 5–14.

Stevens, C., Fanning, J., Coch, D., Sanders, L., & Neville, H. (2008). Neural mechanisms of selective auditory attention are enhanced by computerized training: Electrophysiological evidence from language-impaired and typically developing children. *Brain Research, 1205,* 55–69.

Stevens, C., Lauinger, B., & Neville, H. (2009). Differences in the neural mechanisms of selective attention in children from different socioeconomic backgrounds: An event-related brain potential study. *Developmental Science, 12*(4), 634–646.

Stroop, J. R. (1935). Studies of interference in serial verbal reactions. *Journal of Experimental Psychology, 18,* 643–662.

Sulik, M. J., Huerta, S., Zerr, A. A., Eisenberg, N., Spinrad, T. L., Valiente, C., et al. (2010). The factor structure of effortful control and measurement invariance across ethnicity and sex in a high-risk sample. *Journal of Psychopathology and Behavioral Assessment, 32*(1), 8–22.

Swanson, J., Posner, M., Fusella, J., Wasdell, M., Sommer, T., & Fan, J. (2001). Genes and attention deficit hyperactivity disorder. *Current Psychiatry Reports, 3,* 92–100.

Thomas, A., & Chess, S. (1977). *Temperament and development.* New York: Brunner/Mazel.

Thorell, L. B., Lindqvist, S., Nutley, S. B., Bohlin, G., & Klingberg, T. (2009). Training and transfer effects of executive functions in preschool children. *Developmental Science, 12*(1), 106–113.

Valiente, C., Eisenberg, N., Smith, C. L., Reiser, M., Fabes, R. A., Losoya, S., et al. (2003). The relations of effortful control and reactive control to children's externalizing problems: A longitudinal assessment. *Journal of Personality, 71*(6), 1171–1196.

van Veen, V., & Carter, C. (2002). The timing of action-monitoring processes in the anterior cingulate cortex. *Journal of Cognitive Neuroscience, 14,* 593–602.

Venter, J. C., Adams, M. D., Myers, E. W., Li, P. W., Mural, R. J., Sutton, G. G., et al. (2001). The sequence of the human genome. *Science, 291,* 1304–1351.

Voelker, P., Sheese, B. E., Rothbart, M. K., & Posner, M. I. (2009). Variations in catechol-O-methyltransferase gene interact with parenting to influence attention in early development. *Neuroscience, 164*(1), 121–130.

Vohs, K. D., & Baumeister, R. F. (Eds.). (2011). *Handbook of self-regulation: Research, theory, and applications* (2nd ed.). New York: Guilford Press.

Whittle, S., Allen, N. B., Fornito, A., Lubman, D. I., Simmons, J. G., Pantelis, C., et al. (2009). Variations in cortical folding patterns are related to individual differences in temperament. *Psychiatry Research: Neuroimaging, 172*(1), 68–74.

Whittle, S., Yücel, M., Fornito, A., Barrett, A., Wood, S. J., Lubman, D. I., et al. (2008). Neuroanatomical correlates of temperament in early adolescents. *Journal of the American Academy of Child and Adolescent Psychiatry, 47*(6), 682–693.

Wynn, K. (1992). Addition and subtraction by human infants. *Nature, 358,* 749–750.

CHAPTER 9

Empathy, Prosocial Behavior, and Other Aspects of Kindness

Ariel Knafo
Salomon Israel

Kindness, broadly defined as a constellation of positive attitudes, feelings, and behaviors toward others (including variables such as empathy, prosocial behavior, generosity, and altruism) is so important to social functioning that it forms a core part of individuals' perceptions of others. For example, Osgood's (1952) early social-psychological account of person perception included three dimensions: power, activity, and evaluation (good–bad). At the evolutionary level, being prosocial, altruistic, and empathic—or not—may have profound implications for survival (de Waal, 2008; Nowak, 2006). Being able to tell whether another person is kind or not may also pay in the long run (Axelrod, 1984). And, as early as in the first year of life, infants show not only an ability to distinguish between "helpers" and "nonhelpers" (Hamlin, Wynn, & Bloom, 2007), but also a preference for "helpers." In summary, the kindness of individuals is a central dimension in person perception.

The possibility of an "altruistic personality" or a "prosocial personality" (i.e., a predisposition for kindness) has been discussed intensively in past research (Eisenberg et al., 1999; Penner, Fritzsche, Craiger, & Freifeld, 1995). There is enough evidence to view a prosocial tendency as a relatively enduring disposition (Eisenberg et al., 1999). However, kindness is rarely included in theories of childhood temperament, and in adults it is typically subsumed under the broader Big Five dimension of Agreeableness (Graziano, Habashi, Sheese, & Tobin, 2007). In this chapter, we investigate the possibility that kindness and other prosocial traits may represent an unjustly neglected temperament dimension that should be integrated into future conceptualizations of temperament.

Definitional Issues

This chapter deals with a multitude of dispositional variables, all interconnected by virtue of their focus on the benefit of others. We refer to them as the *network of kindness*. Baldwin and Baldwin (1970, p. 30) defined *kindness* as "a motivation that is sometimes inferred from the fact that one person benefits another, provided the circumstances are appropriate." Thus, kindness involves both the prosocial acts and the underlying motivations. This leads to an important distinction between empathy and prosocial behavior. *Empathy* is an other-oriented tendency to comprehend and share the (in most definitions, emotional) states of others. *Sympathy* and *compassion* that involve concern for others are related constructs (Eisenberg et al., 1999). *Prosocial behavior* is voluntary behavior (e.g., volunteering, sharing personal resources, providing instrumental help, and supporting others emotionally in times of distress) enacted with the intent of benefiting others (e.g., Eisenberg, Fabes, & Spinrad, 2006).

The distinctions and relationships among components of the network of kindness (e.g., altruism and prosocial behavior) have yielded very rich discussions in the literature that are beyond the scope of this chapter. In some cases prosocial behavior involves *generosity*, a behavior intended to benefit others beyond normative standards of giving, and sometimes it involves *altruism*, a behavior intended to benefit others at expense to the self.[1] It is virtually impossible to measure reliably prosocial behaviors that are purely altruistic because even the sense of doing good can be rewarding to the self (Andreoni, 1990). Therefore, prosocial behavior is often measured without strong evidence for the underlying motivation behind it (Eisenberg et al., 1999). Importantly, evolutionary reasoning (de Waal, 2008) and social-psychological research (Batson, 2009; Hoffman, 1988; Van Lange, 2008) both suggest that empathy may in many cases provide the underlying motivation for behaving prosocially.

Is Kindness a Temperamental Dimension?

Different approaches to temperament vary greatly in their theoretical premises and in the dimensions of temperament they cover (Goldsmith et al., 1987). Nevertheless, some common characteristics can be seen across theories. Zentner and Bates (2008) provided six criteria that we discuss with regards to different aspects of kindness. The first three of these criteria deals with the essence of temperament—what it includes, how it is expressed, and whether it is a stable individual characteristic. The other three criteria deal with the biological, evolutionary, and ontogenetic origins of temperament.

Individual Differences in Normal Behaviors

Individual differences in kindness can be observed, for example, while watching children play or adults interact (Eisenberg, Cameron, & Tryon, 1984; Knafo, Israel, et al., 2008; Light et al., 2009). Experimental studies, which provide individuals with situational cues that enable them either to show kindness or not, are especially suitable for showing this variation. For example, the observation of a mother or an examiner in (simulated) pain elicits behaviors in children that range from no reaction, to some interest, to sustained facial and vocal expressions of concern for the other (Zahn-Waxler, Robinson, & Emde, 1992). A study in which children were given 10 stickers, then asked whether they wanted to donate them to another child, found children willing to donate none, all, or any number in between (Benenson, Pascoe, & Radmore, 2007).

The extremes of the distribution of the kindness dimension are also interesting. Very low levels of certain aspects of kindness are often observed in diverse conditions of psychopathology, such as impaired empathy in psychopathy and autism (Baron-Cohen & Wheelwright, 2004; Viding, 2004). However, there can also be too much of a good thing, and a new field of inquiry shows how the high end of the distribution of kindness can be associated with extreme, emotionally exhausting empathy, or what has been called "pathological altruism" (Klimecki & Singer, 2012; Lowe, Edmundson, & Widiger, 2009; O'Connor, Berry, Lewis, & Stiver, 2012; Zahn-Waxler & Van Hulle, 2012).

Expression in Formal, Measurable Characteristics

Although most studies of kindness involve questionnaire methods, observations regarding behaviors such as spontaneous helping, volunteerism, and blood donations, as well as experimental measures such as behavior in resource allocation tasks, have been shown to indicate individual differences in empathy and prosocial behavior (Piliavin & Charng, 1990). Although it is hard to know whether prosocial behavior is guided by a prosocial motivation, the behaviors themselves can be observed reliably in the laboratory by providing individuals with the opportunity to donate or help. Observing children's reaction to a busy examiner dropping a bunch of pencils may include measures such as latency to help, duration of helping, and number of pencils recovered in a minute. Similarly, it is difficult to observe empathy directly, but children's facial and vocal expressions in response to another person's suffering have been reliably coded to indicate an empathic response (Zahn-Waxler et al., 1992).

Stability and Consistency

Modest cross-situational consistency has been observed for empathy and prosocial behavior. In response to critics who have noted that no two behavioral measures of prosocial behavior correlate above .30, Rushton (1984) argued that, when aggregated, behaviors did correlate across tasks. Prosocial behaviors, at least in children, may represent more than one dimension. Recently, Knafo, Israel, and Ebstein (2011) reported no correlation between children's compliant (following a request) and self-initiated (without direct request) prosocial behavior, each measured with three behavioral tasks. These results echo those found in past studies (Eisenberg et al., 1984). Finally, using questionnaire measures at 7 years of age, teacher and parent reports correlated only modestly (< .20), a substantially weaker correlation than that found for conduct problems or hyperactivity (Saudino, Ronald, & Plomin, 2005).

Higher consistency has been observed for empathy. Researchers in a twin study that observed children's reactions at 14, 20, 24, and 36 months, in response to their mothers' and an examiner's simulated pain, measured children's empathic concern (the more affective component of empathy) and the more cognitive component of empathy, so-called "hypothesis testing" (inquisitiveness). The two components of empathy intercorrelated substantially ($r = .28–.52$, depending on age). Moreover, the correlations between behavior toward the mother and the examiner averaged .36 (empathic concern) and .43 (hypothesis testing) across the four age groups (Knafo, Zahn-Waxler, Van Hulle, Robinson, & Rhee, 2008). In a rare study, children's *positive empathy* (i.e., a vicarious pleasure in response to another person's positive emotion) correlated positively (.30–.38) with empathic concern (Light et al., 2009). These results support the idea of an overall empathy disposition.

Both empathy and prosocial behavior show substantial longitudinal stability. In the empathy twin study of children ages 14, 20, 24, and 36 months, an empathy factor correlated substantially across ages (.57 to .76 between two consecutive time points; Knafo, Zahn-Waxler, Van Hulle, Robinson, & Rhee, 2008). A study with older children (second to fifth grade, with an average age of 9 years, 3 months) also found substantial stability in self-reported as well as observed empathy across a 2-year lag (Zhou et al., 2002). In a sample of British twins, children's parent-reported prosocial behavior at age 2 years correlated strongly ($r > .50$) with their behavior 1 year later. Naturally, behavior at age 2 correlated much less strongly with parent-reported behavior reported at age 7 ($r < .20$; Knafo & Plomin, 2006a), indicating that stability is also accompanied by change. In adolescence, substantial stability was found (Carlo, Crockett, Randall, & Roesch, 2007). A unique study that followed 32 children from ages 4–5 years into early adulthood found that spontaneous prosocial behaviors observed in preschool predicted prosocial behavior in early adulthood (Eisenberg et al., 1999). Importantly, these authors noted that some prosocial behaviors (low-cost helping and compliant prosocial behavior) did not predict later prosocial behaviors, again casting doubts on prosocial behavior as a unitary construct with a common developmental pattern.

The preceding three criteria implicate kindness as a set of observable and measurable responses that vary meaningfully in the normal population and show consistency and stability. This would be expected of a dimension of temperament (Zentner & Bates, 2008).

Phylogenetic Origins

Diamond (1957) argued that observations of temperament in humans are clouded by cultural factors that may contribute to individual differences beyond innate differences; thus, he argued that the study of human temperament should focus only on dimensions applicable to other primates (see Zentner & Bates, 2008, for a discussion). This position is debatable; whereas existence across species can be used as evidence for the innate nature of a trait, the lack thereof cannot be used to prove there is no innate nature (e.g., language abilities).

Although altruism exists widely across the animal kingdom, it is often performed toward genetically related conspecifics (Hamilton, 1964). Mechanisms such as reciprocity and reputation have been proposed as accounting for non-kin altruism (Nowak, 2006; Trivers, 1971), but their occurrence outside of humans is considered rare (Stephens, McLinn, & Stevens, 2002). Other-oriented altruism, with no reciprocity considerations, is often regarded as uniquely human (Fehr & Fischbacher, 2003). A review of personality in nonhuman animals found an Agreeableness dimension in 10 mammal (primate and nonprimate) species (Gosling & John, 1999), but this dimension did not include altruism or concern for others, in contrast with Agreeableness among humans (Graziano & Eisenberg, 1997). However, there is evidence for a rudimentary sort of empathy in diverse mammals, ranging from rodents (Chen, Panksepp, & Lahvis, 2009; Langford et al., 2006) to chimpanzees (Anderson, Myowa-Yamakoshi, & Matsuzawa, 2004; O'Connell, 1995; Romero, Castellanos, & de Waal, 2010), and for altruistic helping in captive chimpanzees (Warneken & Tomasello, 2006). de Waal (2008) proposed that empathy has evolved through a mechanism whose function is to help parents attend to their children's needs. Once the capacity for empathy developed, it could be applied outside the rearing context and play a role in wider networks of social relationships. The existence of this ability enables an extension of empathy to non-kin.

Appearance in the First Few Years of Life

Infants (only several days old) often cry in response to the cry of other infants (Sagi & Hoffman, 1976). This affect sharing has been observed at 3, 6, and 9 months of age as well (Geangu, Benga, Stahl, & Striano, 2010). Empathy to others' suffering response has been observed in 8-month-old infants (Roth-Hanania, Davidov, & Zahn-Waxler, 2011). In contrast to these primarily reactive behaviors, prosocial behaviors require some skills in order for the child to understand the needs of others and prepare an appropriate reaction; 18-month-olds have been observed readily to help unknown adults in a laboratory setting (Warneken & Tomasello, 2006). Thus, a preliminary form of kindness can be observed very early on.

As children mature cognitively and increase their social involvement, their levels of cognitive empathy (though not affective empathy; Knafo, Zahn-Waxler, et al., 2008; Roth-Hanania et al., 2011) and prosocial behavior tend to increase as well (Benenson et al., 2007; Roth-Hanania et al., 2011; see Eisenberg & Fabes, 1998, for a meta-analysis). Nevertheless, there might be a decline during adolescence (Carlo et al., 2007), and the increase with age has been debated (Hay, Castle, Davies, Demetriou, & Stimson, 1999). The abstractness and complexity of prosocial behavior increase with age (Bar-Tal, Raviv, & Leiser, 1980; Eisenberg et al., 2006), as does children's sensitivity to reciprocity and to other social rules and cues governing prosocial behavior (Hay, 1994). These changes may represent an ontogenetic growth due to maturation, the learning of societal norms, and major shifts in children's social worlds (e.g., the increasing relevance of the peer group). Despite these developmental changes in the extent and quality of prosocial behavior, the early emergence of aspects of kindness is supportive of its classification as a temperamental dimension.

Relation to Biological Mechanisms

Neuroscience has accumulated an impressive yet preliminary body of evidence for the brain processes underlying empathy and prosocial behavior. Reviewing this evidence is beyond the scope of this chapter (for reviews, see Decety, 2010; Mayr, Harbaugh, & Tankersley, 2008; Singer, 2006; see Light & Zahn-Waxler, 2011, for a discussion of possible brain processes associated with very early empathy; for a review of the neurobiology and neurochemistry of agreeableness, see Depue & Fu, Chapter 18, this volume). These brain processes may not be unique for kindness; for example, empathy in response to others' pain uses parts of the "pain matrix"; thus, understanding and sharing others' pain involves the brain areas involved in experiencing pain (Lamm, Batson, & Decety, 2007; Singer, Kiebel, Winston, Dolan, & Frith, 2004). As another example, activation of the ventral striatum, which increases when individuals get rewarding stimuli, also increases when they observe money being donated to a favorite charity (Mayr et al., 2008). Although discussion of this is beyond the scope of this chapter, it is important to note that while the neural circuits underlying different forms of empathy overlap, there is also evidence for the involvement of specific brain areas for cognitive and affective empathy (e.g., ventromedial prefrontal cortex vs. the anterior insula and midcingulate cortex, among other regions; Walter, 2012; see also Singer, 2006).

Importantly, individual differences in changes in activity of specific brain regions upon observation of a loved person in pain were associated with self-reported trait empathy (Singer et al., 2004). In addition, individual differences in Agreeableness (a trait involving, among other things, altruism) covaried with volume in brain regions that process information about the intentions and mental states of other individuals (DeYoung et al., 2010). Thus, brain processes observed with imaging techniques may reflect stable individual differences.

The stable differences in behavior and feeling, which may reflect individual differences in certain brain mechanisms, are in part heritable. Most studies of genetic and environmental contributions to individual differences in prosocial behavior and empathy have used the twin design, which compares monozygotic (MZ) twins, who share all of their genetic sequence, with dizygotic (DZ) twins, who share on average half of their genes (see Knafo & Israel, 2009, for a review). Assuming that MZ and DZ twins growing up in their biological families share their environments to a similar degree, greater similarity of MZ twins than of DZ twins indicates genetic influence (*heritability*). Further similarity is attributed to the environment that twins share (*shared environment*), and further twin differences indicate an effect of the *nonshared environment* and error (for details, see Plomin, DeFries, McClearn, & McGuffin, 2001; see also Saudino & Wang, Chapter 16, this volume).

Genetic effects on observed empathy and change in empathy with age have been observed in the life period between 20 and 36 months (Knafo, Zahn-Waxler, et al., 2008). Individual differences in teacher-, mother-, or self-reported prosocial behavior have also been observed (Gregory, Light-Häusermann, Rijsdijk, & Eley, 2009; Hur & Rushton, 2007; Scourfield, John, Martin, & McGuffin, 2004). Recently, a study of observed prosocial behavior in laboratory experiments reported heritabilities of 34–43% (Knafo, Israel, & Ebstein, 2011). Importantly, whereas the heritability of empathy (Knafo, Zahn-Waxler, et al., 2008) and prosocial behavior has been observed to increase with age (Knafo & Plomin, 2006a), the effects of the shared environment on individual differences in kindness decrease with age, and most studies find that by adulthood, all of the environmental influence on aspects of kindness is of the nonshared kind (e.g., Rushton, Fulker, Neale, Nias, & Eysenck, 1986; but see Krueger, Hicks, & McGue, 2001, for an exception). The decrease in the importance of the shared environment may reflect, in part, children's exposure to social groups that become larger and more complex as they grow up (Knafo & Plomin, 2006a). The joint effects of genetics and the environment have also been observed, both with regard to gene–environment correlations in which children's prosocial behavior was genetically related to the parenting they received (Knafo & Plomin, 2006b), and in terms of gene–environment interactions in which genetic effects moderated the impact of parenting (Knafo, Israel, et al., 2011).

Specific genetic polymorphisms, mostly related to the regulation of the neurohormones vasopressin and oxytocin, have been shown to relate to individual differences in prosocial behavior and empathy (Chakrabarti et al., 2009; Israel et al., 2009; Knafo, Israel, et al., 2008). Furthermore, the homologues of these genes have been shown to relate to social behavior in other mammalian species, which is important to the earlier phylogenetic discussion (for reviews, see Donaldson & Young, 2008; Israel et al., 2008). It is important to note that vasopressin and oxytocin have been implicated in brain processes relevant to prosocial behavior and empathy—such as identification of others' emotions, trust, and prosociality—but also in ingroup preference (De Dreu et al., 2010; Kosfeld, Heinrichs, Zak, Fischbacher, &

Fehr, 2005; Tost et al., 2010). A fuller understanding of how the genes coding for these hormones (and neurotransmitters, e.g., dopamine; Bachner-Melman, Gritsenko, Nemanov, Zohar, & Ebstein, 2005) affect brain processes and thus account for the heritability of empathy and prosocial behavior is still needed, although recently some key advances have been made (e.g., Meyer-Lindenberg, 2008; Tost et al., 2010). The evidence from brain and genetic research provides strong evidence for the biological basis of empathy and prosocial behavior.

Overlap with Other Temperament Dimensions

To be regarded as another temperamental dimension, kindness should also appear as distinct from other temperamental dimensions, such as affect, attention, sensory sensitivity, and activity (see Kagan [Chapter 4], Strelau & Zawadzki [Chapter 5], Putnam, [Chapter 6], Deater-Deckard & Wang [Chapter 7], and Rueda [Chapter 8], this volume). By definition, *empathy* has a strong affective component, as it involves the ability to share others' affective states, while regulating the affective state of the self. Attention and sensory sensitivity may also be relevant to empathy because of the need to attend to others and to perceive their affective states correctly. Prosocial behaviors may also involve a degree of attention to social cues, especially when these behaviors occur without obvious cues from the social environment (Knafo, Steinberg, & Goldner, 2011).

Some research has examined the relationships between empathy and prosocial behavior, and other temperamental variables such as sociability and negative emotionality. Empathy at 2 years of age related positively to reactivity and to affect intensity, as observed at 4 months of age (Young, Fox, & Zahn-Waxler, 1999). Empathy has also been linked to behavioral inhibition (Young et al., 1999), positive affectivity (Volbrecht, Lemery-Chalfant, Aksan, Zahn-Waxler, & Goldsmith, 2007), and self-regulatory behaviors (Rothbart, Ahadi, & Hershey, 1994; Valiente et al., 2004). Increased ability to plan, focus, and control reactions may promote the ability to empathize by helping individuals focus on others' states of mind and by allowing children to regulate distress when encountering others' plight (see Rueda, Chapter 8, this volume). Another approach to temperament can focus on predicting kindness from children's temperamental profiles. There is new evidence for the relationship between prosociality and specific combinations of different temperament dimensions (Laible, Carlo, & Panfile, 2011).

In adults, the personality trait of Agreeableness has been shown to relate to prosociality (Graziano et al., 2007; Penner et al., 1995). Prosocial behavior has been associated with temperament (Russell, Hart, Robinson, & Olsen, 2003). For example, attentional regulation and low negative emotionality have been related to prosocial disposition (Eisenberg et al., 1996). However, these relationships are modest at best.

We are not aware of any study that jointly predicts empathy and prosociality with a broad set of temperamental measures. We therefore present illustrative evidence from a study of 3-year-old twins. We draw on data from a subsample of the Longitudinal Israeli Study of Twins (LIST; Knafo, 2006), previously described by Benish-Weisman, Steinberg, and Knafo (2010). Seven hundred fifty-nine mothers of 3-year-old twins rated their children's temperament using the EAS (Emotionality, Activity, Sociability, Shyness) Temperament Survey (Buss & Plomin, 1984) and children's prosocial behaviors using the Strengths and Difficulties Questionnaire (Goodman, 1997). Figure 9.1 presents the correlations between temperament and mother-rated prosocial behavior. Prosocial behavior correlated positively with sociability and to a smaller extent with activity, and negatively with shyness and with negative emotionality. These four dimensions of temperament, taken together, did not account for more than 7% of the variance in prosociality.

What is the underlying basis for these relationships? In the Benish-Weisman and colleagues (2010) sample, as in previous research, all temperament dimensions showed substantial heritabilities of 53–70% (an exception was negative emotionality, which showed no heritability for girls). Possibly, the same genetic factors relevant to temperament might overlap with those relevant to prosocial behavior. Bivariate genetic analysis, although based on results from both twins within a pair, can be used to estimate the contribution of genetics and the environment to correlations between variables across individuals. Thus, it is possible to partition the phenotypic relationship between prosocial behavior and temperament into *bivariate heritability* (the proportion of the phenotypic covariance attributed to genetic covariance between two variables); bivariate shared and bivariate nonshared environmental effects sum to the total phenotypic correlation (e.g., Knafo & Plomin, 2006b; see the caption to Figure 9.1 for some details on this analysis).

The modest negative correlations between negative emotionality and prosocial behavior were accounted for (in part for boys, fully for girls) by the bivariate nonshared environment, meaning that nonshared environmental factors made the same children relatively prosocial and relatively low in negative emotionality. In contrast, Figure 9.1 shows that for Shyness, Sociability, and Activity, genetic factors accounted for 100% of the correlation between temperament and prosocial behavior. For example, the –.27 correlation with Shyness is due to an overlap between the genetic factors that make children relatively prosocial and relatively low in shyness.

Taken together, current and past findings suggest a discriminant validity of the kindness concept. It is possible that other temperamental dimensions contribute to prosociality and empathy, but these contributions are limited. This pattern of results supports the consideration of kindness as a separate temperamental dimension.

Discussion

The broad construct of kindness largely stands up to the challenge of being considered a temperamental dimension. Of the six criteria described by Zentner and Bates (2008), prosociality and empathy fulfill five, as they show an early-appearing (yet further developing) meaningful and measurable

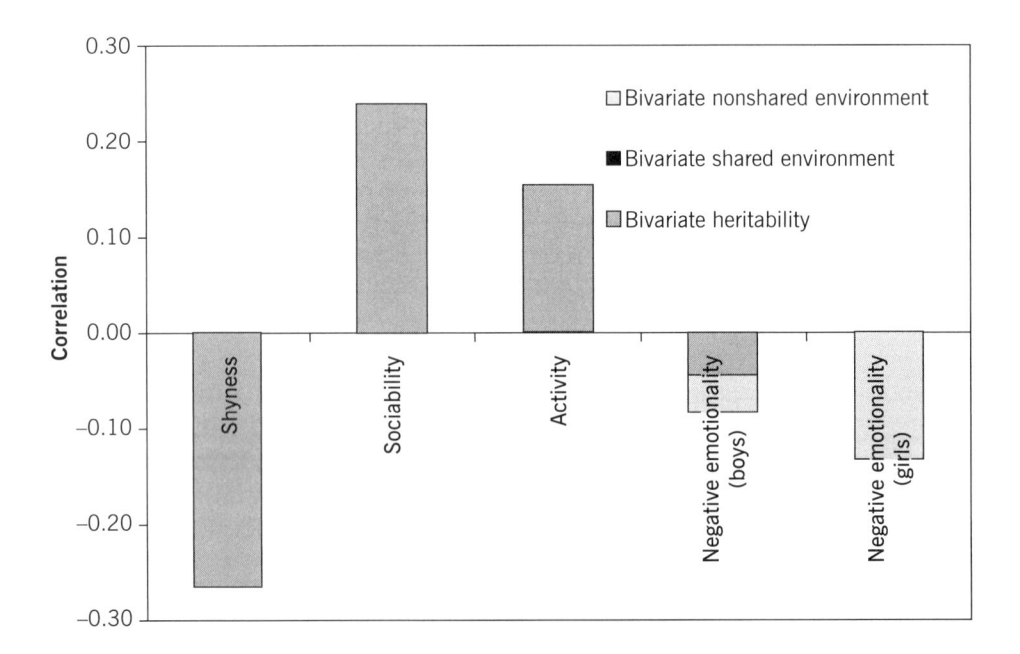

FIGURE 9.1. Correlations between temperament and prosocial behavior partitioned to their genetic and environmental components. Results of a bivariate (prosocial behavior and temperament) genetic model, using twins' variance–covariance matrices, in Mx (Neale, Boker, Xie, & Maes, 1999). Similar analyses from the same sample (with regard to children's temperament in relation to peer problems) are explicated elsewhere (Benish-Weisman et al., 2010), and further details can be obtained from the authors.

variation, which appears to generalize across time and contexts in the same individuals, and which seems to reflect partially heritable biological mechanisms. There is only partial evidence that empathy and prosociality have their homologues in other species, but this criterion may be less central for the definition of temperament. Kindness may be one dimension that does distinguish humans from other species.

While the evidence for empathy is quite strong, less consistent evidence was found for prosocial behaviors, especially with regard to cross-situational consistency. Mischel and Shoda (1995), for example, demonstrated how individual differences in prosociality are situation-dependent, so that some children are consistently more prosocial than others, depending on the contingencies of the situation (and some children are relatively prosocial across different situations). Although empathy is multifaceted (Light et al., 2009; Singer, 2006), it is a rather narrow construct when compared with prosocial behavior. For example, empathy always includes an other-oriented emotional response, whereas some prosocial behaviors may be self-interested (e.g., for tax benefits, or for avoiding negative feelings; Cialdini et al., 1987).

The feeling of empathy or sympathy can be activated automatically upon perception of another person's plight (Preston & de Waal, 2002), but acting prosocially upon the perception of need necessitates overcoming many situational barriers. For example, seeing the suffering victims of an earthquake is likely to elicit empathy in most of us—but due to lack of resources, ability, or perceived responsibility, not all of us would help, as detailed in the social psychological literature (Latané & Darley, 1970).

In summary, empathy may be a purer temperamental dimension, the core of the kindness dimension, whereas prosocial behavior may be the context-dependent behavioral manifestation of kindness. In Batson's (1981) carefully controlled experiments in adults, when all other obstacles to helping were removed, increased empathy predicted higher likelihood of help. If this is applied to individual differences, then environmental contingencies are more likely to affect prosocial behavior than to affect empathy. Similarly, other dimensions of temperament may moderate the link between empathy, or the motivation to behave prosocially, and prosocial behavior. For example, a high activity level can interact with empathy in increasing self-initiated prosocial behavior. Similarly, children's prosocial disposition is predicted by an interaction between their negative emotionality and their attentional regulation (Eisenberg et al., 1996).

It is important to note that one reason for the lesser consistency in prosocial behavior may be the breadth of this construct. Although sharing, helping, and providing emotional support all fall under the umbrella of "prosocial behavior," as they are behaviors intended to benefit others, they are qualitatively different behaviors with regard to their content (e.g., only sharing necessitates giving away resources).

While we have reviewed extensive evidence regarding the proposed temperamental dimension of kindness, many additional issues remain unanswered. Other constructs, which were not discussed here, such as mercifulness, respect for others, and forgiveness, may be part of the dimension or may result from an interaction between kindness and a third variable. The lower end of the kindness dimension is also interesting (Hastings, Zahn-Waxler, Robinson, Usher, & Bridges, 2000). Is this simply an absence of empathy and prosocial behavior, or does it translate into more harsh or offensive actions such as antisocial behavior or cruelty? The answer may be related to what aspect of kindness (e.g., empathy or prosocial behavior) is referred to, and perhaps also to the combination with other temperamental dimensions, such as aggression, sociability, and emotionality. We hope that this chapter will open a new line of inquiry into the origins and consequences of kindness.

Acknowledgments

Parts of this chapter were presented by Ariel Knafo in an invited address at the Society for Research in Child Development meetings, Denver, 2009. We are indebted to the parents and twins in the Longitudinal Israeli Study of Twins (LIST) for making the study possible. We thank Carolyn Zahn-Waxler, Ilanit Siman-Tov, and the members of the Social Development Lab at the Hebrew University for their insightful comments on parts of the chapter. LIST is supported by Grant No. 31/06 from the Israel Science Foundation to Ariel Knafo. Preparation of this chapter was supported by a grant from the Science of Generosity Initiative, Center for the Study of Religion and Society, University of Notre Dame, funded by the Templeton Foundation, to Ariel Knafo.

Note

1. It is important to note that the other-oriented focus of kindness excludes *cooperation* in this chapter (defined here as acting jointly with one or more other individuals to reach a shared goal, and not in the evolutionary psychology sense of prosocial behavior), since the motivation for cooperative behaviors can originate exclusively from selfish concerns.

Further Reading

de Waal, F. B. M. (2008). Putting the altruism back into altruism: The evolution of empathy. *Annual Review of Psychology, 59*, 279–300.

Knafo, A., Zahn-Waxler, C., Van Hulle, C., Robinson, J., & Rhee, S. H. (2008). The developmental origins of a disposition toward empathy: Genetic and environmental contributions. *Emotion, 8*, 737–752.

Penner, L. A., Dovidio, J. F., Piliavin, J. A., & Schroeder, D. A. (2005). Prosocial behavior: Multilevel perspectives. *Annual Review of Psychology, 56*, 365–392.

References

Anderson, J. R., Myowa-Yamakoshi, M., & Matsuzawa, T. (2004). Contagious yawning in chimpanzees. *Proceedings of the Royal Society of London B: Biological Sciences, 271*, S468–S470.

Andreoni, J. (1990). Impure altruism and donations to public-goods: A theory of warm-glow giving. *Economic Journal, 100*(401), 464–477.

Axelrod, R. (1984). *The evolution of cooperation.* New York: Basic Books.

Bachner-Melman, R., Gritsenko, I., Nemanov, L., Zohar, A. H., & Ebstein, R. P. (2005). Dopaminergic polymorphisms associated with self-report measures of human altruism: A fresh phenotype for the dopamine D4 receptor. *Molecular Psychiatry, 10*, 333–335.

Baldwin, C. P., & Baldwin, A. L. (1970). Children's judgments of kindness. *Child Development, 41*(1), 29–47.

Baron-Cohen, S., & Wheelwright, S. (2004). The empathy quotient: An investigation of adults with Asperger syndrome or high functioning autism, and normal sex differences. *Journal of Autism and Developmental Disorders, 34*, 163–175.

Bar-Tal, D., Raviv, A., & Leiser, T. (1980). The development of altruistic behavior: Empirical evidence. *Developmental Psychology, 16*, 516–524.

Batson, C. D. (1981). Is empathic emotion a source of altruistic motivation? *Journal of Personality and Social Psychology, 40*(2), 290–302.

Batson, C. D. (2009). Empathy-induced altruistic motivation. In P. R. Shaver & M. Mikulincer (Eds.), *Prosocial motives, emotions, and behavior* (pp. 15–34). Washington, DC: American Psychological Association.

Benenson, J. F., Pascoe, J., & Radmore, N. (2007). Children's altruistic behavior in the dictator game. *Evolution and Human Behavior, 28*, 168–175.

Benish-Weisman, M., Steinberg, T., & Knafo, A. (2010). Genetic and environmental links between children's temperament and their problems with peers. *Israel Journal of Psychiatry and Related Sciences, 47*(2), 144–151.

Buss, A. H., & Plomin, R. (1984). *Temperament: Early developing personality traits.* Hillsdale, NJ: Erlbaum.

Carlo, G., Crockett, L. J., Randall, B. A., & Roesch, S. C. (2007). Parent and peer correlates of prosocial development in rural adolescents: A longitudinal study. *Journal of Research on Adolescence, 17*, 301–324.

Chakrabarti, B., Dudbridge, F., Kent, L., Wheelwright, S., Hill-Cawthorne, G., Allison, C., et al. (2009). Genes related to sex steroids, neural growth, and social–emotional behavior are associated with autistic traits, empathy, and Asperger syndrome. *Autism Research, 2*(3), 157–177.

Chen, Q. L., Panksepp, J. B., & Lahvis, G. P. (2009). Empathy is moderated by genetic background in mice. *PLoS One, 4*(2), e4387.

Cialdini, R. B., Schaller, M., Houlihan, D., Arps, K., Fultz, J., & Beaman, A. L. (1987). Empathy-based helping: Is it selflessly or selfishly motivated? *Journal of Personality and Social Psychology, 52*, 749–758.

Decety, J. (2010). The neurodevelopment of empathy in humans. *Developmental Neuroscience, 32*, 257–267.

De Dreu, C. K. W., Greer, L. L., Handgraaf, M. J. J., Shalvi, S., Van Kleef, G. A., Baas, M., et al. (2010). The neuropeptide oxytocin regulates parochial altruism in intergroup conflict among humans. *Science, 328*, 1408–1411.

de Waal, F. B. M. (2008). Putting the altruism back into altruism: The evolution of empathy. *Annual Review of Psychology, 59*, 279–300.

DeYoung, C. G., Hirsh, J. B., Shane, M. S., Papademetris, X., Rajeevan, N., & Gray, J. R. (2010). Testing predictions from personality neuroscience: Brain structure and the Big Five. *Psychological Science, 21*, 820–828.

Diamond, S. (1957). *Personality and temperament.* New York: Harper.

Donaldson, Z. R., & Young, L. J. (2008). Oxytocin, vasopressin, and the neurogenetics of sociality. *Science, 322,* 900–904.

Eisenberg, N., Cameron, E., & Tryon, F. (1984). Prosocial behavior in the preschool years: Methodological and conceptual issues. In E. Staub, D. Bar-Tal, J. Karylowski, & J. Reykowski (Eds.), *The development and maintenance of prosocial behavior: International perspectives on positive development* (pp. 101–115). New York: Plenum Press.

Eisenberg, N., & Fabes, R. A. (1998). Pro-social development. In N. Eisenberg & W. Damon (Eds.), *Handbook of child psychology: Vol. 3. Social, emotional and personality development* (5th ed., pp. 701–778). New York: Wiley.

Eisenberg, N., Fabes, R. A., Karbon, M., Murphy, B. C., Wosinski, M., Polazzi, L., et al. (1996). The relations of children's dispositional prosocial behavior to emotionality, regulation, and social functioning. *Child Development, 67,* 974–992.

Eisenberg, N., Fabes, R. A., & Spinrad, T. (2006). Prosocial development. In N. Eisenberg (Vol. Ed.) & W. Damon & R. M. Lerner (Series Eds.), *Handbook of child psychology: Vol. 3. Social, emotional, and personality development* (6th ed., pp. 646–718). New York: Wiley.

Eisenberg, N., Guthrie, I. K., Murphy, B. C., Shepard, S. A., Cumberland, A., & Carlo, G. (1999). Consistency and development of prosocial dispositions: A longitudinal study. *Child Development, 70,* 1360–1372.

Fehr, E., & Fischbacher, U. (2003). The nature of human altruism. *Nature, 425,* 785–791.

Geangu, E., Benga, O., Stahl, D., & Striano, T. (2010). Contagious crying beyond the first days of life. *Infant Behavior and Development, 33*(3), 279–288.

Goldsmith, H. H., Buss, A. H., Plomin, R., Rothbart, M. K., Chess, S., Thomas, A., et al. (1987). Roundtable: What is temperament? Four approaches. *Child Development, 58,* 505–529.

Goodman, R. (1997). The Strengths and Difficulties Questionnaire: A research note. *Journal of Child Psychology and Psychiatry, 38,* 581–586.

Gosling, S. D., & John, O. P. (1999). Personality dimensions in nonhuman animals: A cross-species review. *Current Directions in Psychological Science, 8,* 69–75.

Graziano, W. G., & Eisenberg, N. (1997). Agreeableness: A dimension of personality. In W. G. Graziano, N. Eisenberg, R. Hogan, J. Johnson & S. Briggs (Eds.), *Handbook of personality psychology* (pp. 795–824). San Diego, CA: Academic Press.

Graziano, W. G., Habashi, M. M., Sheese, B. E., & Tobin, R. M. (2007). Agreeableness, empathy, and helping: A person × situation perspective. *Journal of Personality and Social Psychology, 93,* 583–599.

Gregory, A. M., Light Häusermann, J. H., Rijsdijk, F., & Eley, T. C. (2009). Behavioral genetic analyses of prosocial behavior in adolescents. *Developmental Science, 12,* 165–174.

Hamilton, W. D. (1964). The genetical evolution of social behaviour. *Journal of Theoretical Biology, 7,* 1–16.

Hamlin, J. K., Wynn, K., & Bloom, P. (2007). Social evaluation by preverbal infants. *Nature, 450,* 557–559.

Hastings, P. D., Zahn-Waxler, C., Robinson, J., Usher, B., & Bridges, D. (2000). The development of concern for others in children with behavior problems. *Developmental Psychology, 36,* 531–546.

Hay, D. F. (1994). Prosocial development. *Journal of Child Psychology and Psychiatry, 35,* 29–71

Hay, D. F., Castle, J., Davies, L., Demetriou, H., & Stimson, C. (1999). Prosocial action in very early childhood. *Journal of Child Psychology and Psychiatry, 40,* 905–916.

Hoffman, M. L. (1988). Moral development. In M. Bornstein & M. Lamb (Eds.), *Developmental psychology: An advanced textbook* (pp. 497–548). Hillsdale, NJ: Erlbaum.

Hur, Y. M., & Rushton, J. P. (2007). Genetic and environmental contributions to prosocial behaviour in 2- to 9-year-old South Korean twins. *Biology Letters, 3,* 664–666.

Israel, S., Lerer, E., Shalev, I., Uzefovsky, F., Reibold, M., Bachner-Melman, R., et al. (2008). Molecular genetic studies of the arginine vasopressin 1a receptor (AVPR1a) and the oxytocin receptor (OXTR) in human behavior: From autism to altruism with some notes in between. *Progress in Brain Research, 170,* 435–449.

Israel, S., Lerer, E., Shalev, I., Uzefovsky, F., Riebold, M., Laiba, E., et al. (2009). The oxytocin receptor (OXTR) contributes to prosocial fund allocations in the dictator game and the social value orientations task. *PLoS One, 4,* e5535.

Klimecki, O., & Singer, T. (2012). Empathic distress fatigue rather than compassion fatigue?: Integrating findings from empathy research in psychology and social neuroscience. In B. Oakley, A. Knafo, G. Madhavan, & D. S. Wilson (Eds.), *Pathological altruism* (pp. 368–382). New York: Oxford University Press.

Knafo, A. (2006). The Longitudinal Israeli Study of Twins (LIST): Children's social development as influenced by genetics, abilities, and socialization. *Twin Research and Human Genetics, 9,* 791–798.

Knafo, A., & Israel, S. (2009). Genetic and environmental influences on prosocial behavior. In M. Mikulincer & P. R. Shaver (Eds.), *Prosocial motives, emotions, and behavior: The better angels of our nature* (pp. 149–167). Washington, DC: American Psychological Association.

Knafo, A., Israel, S., & Ebstein, R. P. (2011). Heritability of children's prosocial behavior and differential susceptibility to parenting by variation in the dopamine D4 receptor (DRD4) gene. *Development and Psychopathology, 23,* 53–67.

Knafo, A., Israel, S., Darvasi, A., Bachner-Melman, R., Uzefovsky, F., Cohen, L., et al. (2008). Individual differences in allocation of funds in the Dictator Game and postmortem hippocampal mRNA levels are correlated with length of the arginine vasopressin 1a receptor (AVPR1a) RS3 promoter-region repeat. *Genes, Brain and Behavior, 7,* 266–275.

Knafo, A., & Plomin, R. (2006a). Parental discipline and affection, and children's prosocial behavior: Genetic and environmental links. *Journal of Personality and Social Psychology, 90,* 147–164.

Knafo, A., & Plomin, R. (2006b). Prosocial behavior from early to middle childhood: Genetic and environmental influences on stability and change. *Developmental Psychology, 42,* 771–786.

Knafo, A., Steinberg, T., & Goldner, I. (2011). Children's low affective perspective-taking ability is associated with low self-initiated prosociality, *Emotion, 11,* 194–198.

Knafo, A., Zahn-Waxler, C., Van Hulle, C., Robinson, J., & Rhee, S. H. (2008). The developmental origins of a disposition toward empathy: Genetic and environmental contributions. *Emotion, 8,* 737–752.

Kosfeld, M., Heinrichs, M., Zak, P. J., Fischbacher, U., & Fehr, E. (2005). Oxytocin increases trust in humans. *Nature, 435,* 673–676.

Krueger, R. F., Hicks, B. M., & McGue, M. (2001). Altruism and antisocial behavior: Independent tendencies, unique personality correlates, distinct etiologies. *Psychological Science, 12,* 397–402.

Laible, D. J., Carlo, G., & Panfile, T. M. (2011, April). *Predicting children's prosocial and cooperative behavior from temperamental profiles.* Paper presented at the biannual meetings of the Society for Research in Child Development, Montreal, Canada.

Lamm, C., Batson, C. D., & Decety, J. (2007). The neural substrate of human empathy: Effects of perspective-taking and cognitive appraisal. *Journal of Cognitive Neuroscience, 19*(1), 42–58.

Langford, D. J., Crager, S. E., Shehzad, Z., Smith, S. B., Sotocinal, S. G., Levenstadt, J. S., et al. (2006). Social modulation of pain as evidence for empathy in mice. *Science, 312,* 1967–1970.

Latané, B., & Darley, J. M. (1970). *The unresponsive bystander: Why doesn't he help?* New York: Appleton–Century–Crofts.

Light, S. N., Coan, J. A., Zahn-Waxler, C., Frye, C., Goldsmith, H. H., & Davidson, R. J. (2009). Empathy is associated with dynamic change in prefrontal brain electrical activity during positive emotion in children. *Child Development, 80*(4), 1210–1231.

Light, S. N., & Zahn-Waxler, C. (2011). The nature and forms of empathy in the first years of life. In J. Decety (Ed.), *Empathy: From bench to bedside* (pp. 109–130). Cambridge, MA: MIT Press.

Lowe, J. R., Edmundson, M., & Widiger, T. A. (2009). Assessment of dependency, agreeableness, and their relationship. *Psychological Assessment, 21,* 543–553.

Mayr, U., Harbaugh, W. T., & Tankersley, D. (2008). Neuroeconomics of charitable giving and philanthropy. In P. W. Glimcher, E. Fehr, R. A. Poldrack, & C. F. Camerer (Eds.), *Neuroeconomics: Decision making and the brain* (pp. 301–318). London: Academic Press.

Meyer-Lindenberg, A. (2008). Impact of prosocial neuropeptides on human brain function. *Progress in Brain Research, 170,* 463–470.

Mischel, W., & Shoda, Y. (1995). A cognitive–affective system theory of personality: Reconceptualizing situations, dispositions, dynamics, and invariance in personality structure. *Psychological Review, 102,* 246–268.

Neale, M., Boker, S., Xie, G., & Maes, H. (1999). *Mx: Statistical modeling.* (Available from Department of Psychiatry, Virginia Commonwealth University, Richmond, VA 23298)

Nowak, M. A. (2006). Five rules for the evolution of cooperation. *Science, 314,* 1560–1563.

O'Connell, S. M. (1995). Empathy in chimpanzees: Evidence for theory of mind? *Primates, 36*(3), 397–410.

O'Connor, L. E., Berry, J. W., Lewis, T., & Stiver, D. J. (2012). Empathy-based pathogenic guilt, pathological altruism, and psychopathology. In B. Oakley, A. Knafo, G. Madhavan, & D. S. Wilson (Eds.), *Pathological altruism* (pp. 10–30). New York: Oxford University Press.

Osgood, C. (1952). The nature and measurement of meaning. *Psychological Bulletin, 49*(3), 197–237.

Penner, L. A., Fritzsche, B. A., Craiger, J. P., & Freifeld, T. R. (1995) Measuring the prosocial personality. In J. Butcher & C. D. Spielberger (Eds.), *Advances in personality assessment* (Vol. 10, pp. 147–163). Hillsdale, NJ: Erlbaum.

Piliavin, J. A., & Charng, H. W. (1990). Altruism: A review of recent theory and research. *Annual Review of Sociology, 16,* 27–65.

Plomin, R., DeFries, J. C., McClearn, G. E., & McGuffin, P. (2001). *Behavioral genetics* (4th ed.). New York: Worth.

Preston, S. D., & de Waal, F. B. M. (2002). Empathy: Its ultimate and proximate bases. *Behavioral and Brain Sciences, 25,* 1–72.

Romero, T., Castellanos, M. A., & de Waal, F. B. M. (2010). Consolation as possible expression of sympathetic concern among chimpanzees. *Proceedings of the National Academy of Sciences, 107,* 12110–12115.

Rothbart, M. K., Ahadi, S. A., & Hershey, K. L. (1994). Temperament and social behavior in childhood. *Merrill–Palmer Quarterly, 40*, 21–39.

Roth-Hanania, R., Davidov, M., & Zahn-Waxler, C. (2011). Empathy development from 8 to 16 months: Early signs of concern for others. *Infant Behavior and Development, 34*(3), 447–458.

Rushton, J. P. (1984). The altruistic personality: Evidence from laboratory, naturalistic, and self-report perspectives. In E. Staub, D. Bar-Tal, J. Karylowski, & J. Reykowski (Eds.), *The development and maintenance of prosocial behavior: International perspectives on positive development* (pp. 271–290). New York: Plenum Press.

Rushton, J. P., Fulker, D. W., Neale, M. C., Nias, D. K. B., & Eysenck, H. J. (1986). Altruism and aggression: The heritability of individual differences. *Journal of Personality and Social Psychology, 50*, 1192–1198.

Russell, A., Hart, C. H., Robinson, C., & Olsen, S. F. (2003). Children's sociable and aggressive behavior with peers: A comparison of the U.S. and Australia, and contributions of temperament and parenting styles. *International Journal of Behavioral Development, 27*, 74–86.

Sagi, A., & Hoffman, M. (1976). Empathic distress in the newborn. *Developmental Psychology, 12*(2), 175–176.

Saudino, K., Ronald, A., & Plomin, R. (2005). Rater effects in the etiology of behavior problems in 7-year-old twins: Parent ratings and ratings by same and different teachers. *Journal of Abnormal Child Psychology, 33*, 113–130.

Scourfield, J., John, B., Martin, N., & McGuffin, P. (2004). The development of prosocial behaviour in children and adolescents: A twin study. *Journal of Child Psychology and Psychiatry, 45*, 927–935.

Singer, T. (2006). The neuronal basis and ontogeny of empathy and mind reading: Review of literature and implications for future research, *Neuroscience and Biobehavioral Reviews, 30*, 855–863.

Singer, T., Kiebel, S. J., Winston, J. S., Dolan, R. J., & Frith, C. D. (2004). Brain responses to the acquired moral status of faces. *Neuron, 41*, 653–662.

Stephens, D. W., McLinn, C. M., & Stevens, J. R. (2002). Discounting and reciprocity in an iterated prisoner's dilemma. *Science, 298*, 2216–2218.

Tost, H., Kolachana, B., Hakimi, S., Lemaitre, H., Verchinski, B. A., Mattay, V. S., et al. (2010). A common allele in the oxytocin receptor gene (OXTR) impacts prosocial temperament and human hypothalamic–limbic structure and function. *Proceedings of the National Academy of Sciences, 107*(31), 13936–13941.

Trivers, R. L. (1971). Evolution of reciprocal altruism. *Quarterly Review of Biology, 46*, 35–57.

Valiente, C., Eisenberg, N., Fabes, R. A., Shepard, S. A., Cumberland, A., & Losoya, S. H. (2004). Prediction of children's empathy-related responding from their effortful control and parents' expressivity. *Developmental Psychology, 40*, 911–926.

Van Lange, P. A. M. (2008). Does empathy trigger only altruistic motivation?: How about selflessness or justice? *Emotion, 8*, 766–774.

Viding, E. (2004). Annotation: Understanding the development of psychopathy. *Journal of Child Psychology and Psychiatry, 45*, 1329–1337.

Volbrecht, M. M., Lemery-Chalfant, K., Aksan, N., Zahn-Waxler, C., & Goldsmith, H. H. (2007). Examining the familial link between positive affect and empathy development in the second year. *Journal of Genetic Psychology, 168*, 105–129.

Walter, H. (2012). Social cognitive neuroscience of empathy—concepts, circuits and genes. *Emotion Review, 4*, 9–17.

Warneken, F., & Tomasello, M. (2006). Altruistic helping in human infants and young chimpanzees. *Science, 311*, 1301–1303.

Young, S. K., Fox, N. A., & Zahn-Waxler, C. (1999). The relations between temperament and empathy in 2-year-olds. *Developmental Psychology, 35*, 1189–1197.

Zahn-Waxler, C., Robinson, J., & Emde, R. N. (1992). The development of empathy in twins. *Developmental Psychology, 28*, 1038–1047.

Zahn-Waxler, C., & Van Hulle, C. (2012). Empathy, guilt, and depression: When caring for others becomes costly to children. In B. Oakley, A. Knafo, G. Madhavan, & D. S. Wilson (Eds.), *Pathological altruism* (pp. 321–344). New York: Oxford University Press.

Zentner, M., & Bates, J. E. (2008). Child temperament: An integrative review of concepts, research programs, and measures. *European Journal of Developmental Science, 1*(2), 7–37.

Zhou, Q., Eisenberg, N., Losoya, S., Fabes, R. A., Reiser, M., Guthrie, I. K., et al. (2002). The relations of parental warmth and positive expressiveness to children's empathy-related responding and social functioning: A longitudinal study. *Child Development, 73*, 893–915.

PART III

MEASURES OF TEMPERAMENT

CHAPTER 10

Asking Questions about Temperament
Self- and Other-Report Measures across the Lifespan

Maria A. Gartstein
David J. Bridgett
Christina M. Low

"How should we go about studying temperament?" is a question that has stirred much debate and has resulted in a number of different methods of evaluating temperament across the lifespan. Of particular importance to this chapter are self- and other-report measures of temperament, which have been widely developed and adapted. No single measurement approach can boast of being limitation-free, and self- and other-report instruments are no exception. Thus, in this chapter, important strengths are discussed alongside specific weaknesses (e.g., concerns voiced regarding bias/inaccuracies impacting parent-report questionnaires; Kagan, 1994, 1998). Individuals may be motivated to present their own or their children's temperament in a more positive/culturally appropriate manner. However, this possibility has generally not compromised the demonstration of validity for parent- and self-report instruments, or prevented researchers from relying on these approaches in their investigations (Rothbart & Bates, 2006). Minimizing the impact of potential bias on ratings of temperament is certainly important, and at the same time, strengths of parent report should be considered. For example, parents are in a unique position to provide information regarding their infant's temperament given that others do not have the necessary access to the babies to provide such descriptions. Furthermore, laboratory observations may not capture the full repertoire of the child's reactivity and regulation (Rothbart & Gartstein, 2008).

Given the importance of self- and other-report measures, separately and in conjunction with observational/laboratory methods, for understanding temperament, we hope to help guide readers toward self- and other-report measures that demonstrate qualities important for use in research. Unfortunately, given the abundance of measures available, we were not able to consider all of the possible instruments developed to capture individual differences in temperament, which necessitated careful selection of criteria for measures to be considered for inclusion. First, accessible (e.g., published) accounts of the psychometric properties (e.g., aspects of reliability and validity) of a given instrument were required. Briefly, indices of internal consistency were considered most important because the ability of the items to "hang together" has been deemed essential for measures comprising questions intended to form scales/factors. There has been some debate as to minimal standards for internal consistency; however, minimally adequate internal consistency estimates generally range between .60 and .70, with values higher than .70 considered satisfactory (Henson, 2001; Nunnally, 1967, 1978; Nunnally & Bernstein, 1994; Streiner, 2003). It should be noted that internal consistency varies from one sample to another, making it essential to examine reliability estimates for each sample, in addition to selecting instruments with previously demonstrated reliability and validity (Streiner, 2003). We also considered other psychometric properties, including interrater reliability (i.e., agreement across raters) and test–retest reliability (i.e., stability of a measure across time), exploratory and confirmatory factor-analytic work, and indices of convergent validity, in selecting instruments for this chapter.

Second, we focused on measures with explicit links to established theories of temperament. It is important to recognize that temperament constructs overlap to some extent with those prominent in the discussion of personality. Neuroticism and Extraversion (e.g., De Pauw, Mervielde, & Van Leeuwen, 2009; Mervielde & De Pauw, Chapter 2, this volume; Strelau, 1998) in particular demonstrate strong connections with Negative Emotionality and Positive Emotionality/Surgency. Although distinctions between temperament and personality are sometimes blurred in the context of a more general approach emphasizing "individual differences," these domains can be conceptually differentiated. Specifically, *personality* has been described as a more inclusive, broader construct (encompassing intelligence, self-reflection, etc.), that does not come online until later in childhood (Rothbart, Ahadi, & Evans, 2000), whereas *temperament* can be measured at birth and, some would argue, prenatally (DiPietro, Hodgson, Costigan, & Johnson, 1996; Snidman, Kagan, Riordan, & Shannon, 1995). Nevertheless, several measures of personality that encompass aspects closely linked with temperament (i.e., Extraversion and Neuroticism) are addressed in this chapter, along with a brief list of personality measures that demonstrate some conceptual overlap with temperament dimensions (Appendix 10.1).

Finally, conceptual/item overlap between domains of individual differences and other constructs (e.g., psychopathology) was considered because of our interest in discriminant validity of the measures discussed in this chapter. Concerns regarding this potential content overlap have been raised, with researchers going as far as attempting to eliminate questionable items from established questionnaires to ensure nonoverlapping item pools between measures of temperament and childhood psychopathology (Lemery, Essex, & Smider, 2002). Thus, we attended to discriminant validity considerations when selecting measures for review in this chapter, recognizing that temperament attributes are important to developmental outcomes, often examined as risk/protective factors in models of developmental psychopathology (e.g., Frick, 2004).

The structure of this methodological review follows the developmental sequence, starting with infancy, then addressing questionnaires available for toddler/preschool, school-age, adolescent, and adult age groups. Some instruments developed for an early developmental period were revised for use with older populations, and the latter versions are discussed together with the original instruments. In adulthood, individuals themselves are most frequently consulted as the best available source of information concerning their temperament, and during the years of formal education, other significant individuals (e.g., teachers) are able to provide such reports. However, in infancy and early childhood, parents are the most widely utilized informants.

Infancy

The New York Longitudinal Study (NYLS) and subsequent research have led to the development of a number of instruments designed to evaluate nine dimensions—Rhythmicity, Adaptability, Approach–Withdrawal, Attention Span/Persistence, Activity Level, Distractability, Quality of Mood, Intensity, and Sensory Threshold—along with the "difficultness" of temperament. Carey, McDevitt, and colleagues developed a number of instruments providing indices of the nine NYLS dimensions, as well as the overall "difficultness," in the infancy period (Table 10.1). The Infant Characteristic Questionnaire (ICQ; Bates, Freeland, & Lounsbury, 1979), also a NYLS-inspired measure, provides an indicator of "difficultness" based primarily on the infant's irritability and demandingness. NYLS dimensions also provided the foundation for the Baby Behavior Questionnaire (Bohlin, Hagekull, & Lindhagen, 1981), another parent-report instrument utilized in the first year of life.

Somewhat low estimates of internal consistency (Table 10.1) have been reported for the NYLS-inspired measures, especially for the early infancy instruments (Rothbart, Chew, & Gartstein, 2001). In addition, the Infant Temperament Questionnaire (ITQ) scores were criticized for reflecting maternal characteristics (e.g., anxiety, hostility) more than infant temperament attributes (Vaughn, Taraldson, Crichton, & Egeland, 1981). Nonetheless, NYLS-inspired questionnaires continue to enjoy widespread use in research and are utilized exclusively in clinical interventions involving temperament, in which temperament assessment is conducted to provide feedback to the caregivers concerning their children's attributes.

Contemporary temperament theory has also led to the development of a number of parent-report measures of child temperament, with the psychobiological approach described by Rothbart and Derryberry (1981) serving as a foundation for a number of these questionnaires. A key conceptual distinction between the parent-report questionnaires inspired by NYLS and those based on psychobiological accounts is that the former were designed to address "clinically meaningful" attributes in children (Carey & McDevitt, 1989), whereas the latter were developed to examine temperament factors and fine-grained dimensions related to underlying neurobehavioral systems, central to the emergence and development of temperament attributes (Rothbart & Bates, 2006). The original Infant Behavior Questionnaire (IBQ; Rothbart, 1981) and the revised version (IBQ-R; Gartstein & Rothbart, 2003) have been demonstrated as reliable in terms of internal consistency, with other satisfactory psychometric properties also noted for these instruments (Table 10.1). Whereas the IBQ included six fine-grained temperament scales, the IBQ-R comprises 14 scales, which in turn have been shown to cluster into three overarching temperament factors: Positive Affectivity/Surgency, Negative Emotionality, and Orienting/Regulatory Capacity.

The IBQ has been widely used in a variety of investigations since its introduction, receiving consistent support for different forms of reliability and validity (Rothbart, Chew, & Gartstein, 2001). In particular, both IBQ and IBQ-R have shown convergent validity with respect to laboratory-based indicators of temperament (Gartstein & Marmion, 2008; Kochanska, Coy, Tjebkes, & Husarek, 1998). Importantly, convergent validity has been established between scores based on observations of infant fearfulness in the laboratory, and mother and father reported fear scores on the IBQ-R (Parade & Leerkes, 2008). Contemporary theories and models of temperament emphasize that temperament changes over time as a function of biological and environmental influences (Rothbart & Bates, 2006); recent studies using growth modeling techniques have confirmed that the IBQ-R is sensitive to developmental changes in infancy (Bridgett et al., 2009, 2011; Gartstein et al., 2010), and that a number of contextual variables (e.g., maternal depression) contribute to these growth trajectories. Furthermore, these studies demonstrate that how temperament changes early in life has important implications for subsequent outcomes. These studies illustrate the use of this instrument in facilitating our understanding of change in temperament across time, as well as contextual influences that may contribute to such growth and outcomes that such changes predict.

Although teachers cannot be consulted about infants' temperament, care providers other than parents who interact with infants in various day care settings can report regarding early appearing characteristics. Goldsmith, Rieser-Danner, and Briggs (1991) administered eight widely used temperament measures to mothers and teachers/care providers of children spread across three age groups, including infancy. Analyses conducted with infancy measures (Revised ITQ [RITQ], IBQ, and ICQ) indicated generally adequate reliability (i.e., internal consistency) for care providers outside the home, as well as for primary caregivers.

(text resumes on page 190)

TABLE 10.1. Temperament Measures across the Lifespan

Measure	Author(s) and year of publication	Age range	Number of items	Internal consistency	Test–retest reliabilities
Infancy					
Infant Temperament Questionnaire (ITQ)	Carey (1973)	4–8 months	70 items	Ranges from .49 to .83	.84
Revised Infant Temperament Questionnaire (RITQ)	Carey & McDevitt (1978)	4–8 months	95 items	.49 to .71 for scales, .83 for composite	.66 to .81
Short Infant Temperament Questionnaire (SITQ)	Sanson, Prior, Garino, Oberklaid, & Sewell (1987)	4–8 months	30 items	.57 to .76	.77 to .90
Early Infancy Temperament Questionnaire (EITQ)	Medoff-Cooper, Carey, & McDevitt (1993)	1–4 months	76 items	.42 to .76, mean = .62	.43 to .87 (2–3 week follow-up)
Infant Characteristics Questionnaire (ICQ)	Bates, Freeland, & Lounsbury (1979)	4–6 months	24 items	.39 to .79	.47 to .70 for four factors
Baby Behavior Questionnaire (BBQ)	Bohlin, Hagekull, & Lindhagen (1981)	3–10 months	54 items	.51 to .71 for all scales	.63 to .93 for all scales
Infant Behavior Questionnaire (IBQ)	Rothbart (1981)	3–12 months	94 items	.67 to .85, mean = .77	
Infant Behavior Questionnaire—Revised (IBQ-R)	Rothbart & Gartstein (2003)	3–12 months	184 items	.77 to .87, mean =.81	
Toddler/preschool					
Toddler Behavior Questionnaire (TBQ)	Hagekull (1985)	11–15 months	54 items	.59 to .77 for all scales	.64 to .87 for all scales
Toddler Temperament Scale (TTS)	Fullard, McDevitt, & Carey (1984)	1–3 years	97 items	Median = 0.7	Median = .81
Early Childhood Behavior Questionnaire (ECBQ)	Putnam, Gartstein, & Rothbart (2006)	18–36 months	201 items	All scales above 0.7 except impulsivity (.58)	Ranges from .30 to .35 over 6 months; .26 to .73 over 18 months
Berkeley Puppet Interview (BPI)	Ablow & Measelle (1993)	4.5–7.5 years	60 self-perception items	Ranges from .63 to .77; Mean =.71	.51 for 1-year follow-up; .28 for 2-year

(cont.)

TABLE 10.1. *(cont.)*

Measure	Author(s) and year of publication	Age range	Number of items	Internal consistency	Test–retest reliabilities
Toddler Behavior Assessment Questionnaire (TBAQ)	Goldsmith (1996)	16–36 months	111 items	All scales above .80	.41 to .52
Parent Temperament Questionnaire (PTQ)	Thomas & Chess (1977)	3–7 years	72 items	.56 to .72	.48 to .92 over a 2-week period
Behavioral Style Questionnaire (BSQ)	McDevitt & Carey (1978)	3–7 years	100 items	.89	.84
Teacher Temperament Questionnaire (TTQ)	Thomas & Chess (1977)	3–6 years	64 items	.69 to .88, mean = .81	.69 to .88
Teacher Temperament Questionnaire Short Form (STTQ)	Keogh, Pullis, Cadwell (1982)	3–6 years	23 items	.62 to .94	
Temperament Assessment Battery for Children (TABC)—Parent Report version	Martin (1988)	3–7 years	48 items	.65 to .86	.43 to .70
Temperament Assessment Battery for Children (TABC)—Teacher Report version	Martin (1988)	3–7 years	48 items	>.80	.69 to .85
Behavioral Inhibition Questionnaire (BIQ)—Parent Report version	Bishop, Spence, & McDonald (2003)	2–6 years	30 items	.70	.49 to .79
Behavioral Inhibition Questionnaire (BIQ)—Teacher Report version	Bishop, Spence, & McDonald (2003)	2–6 years	28 items	.66 to .97 for scales	.42 to .58
EASI-III Questionnaire	Buss & Plomin (1975)	Toddlers and preschoolers	50 items	.79 to .92 toddlers; .68 to .82 preschoolers	
Colorado Childhood Temperament Inventory (CCTI)	Rowe & Plomin (1977)	1–6 years	30 items	.73 to .88	.43 to .80

(cont.)

TABLE 10.1. (cont.)

Measure	Author(s) and year of publication	Age range	Number of items	Internal consistency	Test–retest reliabilities
Preschool Temperament and Character Inventory (psTCI)	Constantion et al. (2002)	Toddlers and preschoolers	74 item	.79 to .82	.41 to .80
Middle Childhood Temperament Questionnaire (MCTQ)	Hegvik, McDevitt, & Carey (1982)	8–12 years	99 items	Mean = .81	Mean = .88
How I Feel (HIF)	Walden, Harris, & Catron (2003)	8–12 years (can likely be used with ages up to 15 years)	30 items	.84 to .90	.30 to .63
School Age Temperament Inventory (SATI)	McClowry (1995)	8–11 years	38 items	.85 to .90	.80 to .89
Adolescence					
Dimensions of Temperament Survey (DOTS)	Lerner et al. (1982)	Adolescents	42 items	Ranges from .39 to .84 for all factors	Ranges from .59 to .75 for all factors
Dimensions of Temperament Survey—Revised (DOTS-R)	Windle (1992), Windle & Lerner (1986)	Adolescents	54 items	.62 to .91 for scales and .82 to .86 for factors	Ranges .60 to .93
Early Adolescent Temperament Questionnaire—Revised (EATQ-R)	Ellis & Rothbart (2001)	9–15 years	92 items	Ranges from .65 to .82	.55 to .85; Muris & Meesters (2009)
Adolescent Temperament Questionnaire (ADTQ)	Scheier, Casten, & Fullard (1995)	12–18 years	70 items	No evidence of reliability provided	
Junior Temperament and Character Inventory (JTCI)	Luby et al. (1999)	9–13 years	108 items	.44 to .77; Luby et al. (1999)	.62 to .85 for temperament scales; 76 to .79 for character scales
Adults					
Early Adult Questionnaire (EAQ)	Thomas et al. (1982)	Adults	54 items	.72 or higher for all scales	

(cont.)

TABLE 10.1. (cont.)

Measure	Author(s) and year of publication	Age range	Number of items	Internal consistency	Test–retest reliabilities
Adult Temperament Questionnaire (ATQ)	Evans & Rothbart (2007)	Adults	Long form—177 items; Short form—77 items	Ranges from .66 to .90 for long form; .59 to .79 for short form	
Emotionality, Activity, and Sociability Temperament Survey for Adults (EAS)	Buss & Plomin (1984); Naerde et al. (2004)	Adults	20 items	Ranges from .53 to .75 Naerde et al. (2004)	.60 or higher for all scales
Temperament and Character Inventory (TCI)	Cloninger et al. (1993)	Adults	218 items	Ranges from .76 to .89 for broad scales	
Adult Measure of Behavioral Inhibition (AMBI)	Gladstone & Parker (2005)	Adults	16 items	Ranges from .52 to .86	Interclass correlation coefficients = .60 to .86 for all subscales
Retrospective Measure of Behavioral Inhibition (RMBI)	Gladstone & Parker (2005)	Adults	18 items	Ranges from .40 to .87	Interclass correlation coefficients = .56 to .77 for all subscales
Behavioral Inhibition Scale (BIS)	Carver & White (1994)	Adults	7 items	.74	.66
Behavioral Activation Scale (BAS)	Carver & White (1994)	Adults	3 scales; 13 items total	.66 to .76 for all scales	.59 to .69 for all scales
Positive and Negative Affect Schedule (PANAS)	Watson, Clark, & Tellegen (1988)	Adults	20 items	>.80 for both scales	.39 to .71 for all time intervals (follow-up 8 weeks)
NEO-Personality Inventory—Revised (NEO-PIR)	Costa, McCrae, & Dye (1992); Costa (1996)	17 years+	240 items	.86 to .92 for domain scales	.71 to .89; Trull, Useda, Costa, & McCrae (1995)
Temperament Evaluation of the Memphis, Pisa, Paris, and San Diego Autoquestionnaire (TEMPS-A)	Akiskal et al. (2005)	Adults	110 items: Long version; 50 items: Clinical version	Cyclothymic scale, 0.88; Irritable scale, 0.84; Hyperthymic scale, 0.81; Dysthymic scale, 0.76	Cyclothymic scale, 0.81; Irritable scale, 0.76; Hyperthymic scale, 0.93; Depressive scale, 0.91 (Vahip et al., 2005)

(cont.)

TABLE 10.1. *(cont.)*

Measure	Author(s) and year of publication	Age range	Number of items	Internal consistency	Test–retest reliabilities
Temperament Evaluation of the Memphis, Pisa, Paris, and San Diego Autoquestionnaire— Short Form (TEMPS-A Short)	Akiskal, Mendlowicz, et al. (2005)	Adults	39 items	Cyclothymic subscale, 0.91; Depressive subscale, 0.81; Irritable subscale, 0.77; Hyperthymic subscale, 0.76; Anxious subscale, 0.67	
Strelau Temperament Inventory—Revised (STI-R)	Strelau Angleitner, Bantelmann, & Ruch (1990)	Adults	166	.69 to .89 for scales (Ruch, Angleitner, & Strelau, 1991)	
Strelau Temperament Inventory—Revised Short Form (STI-RS)	Strelau Anglietner, Bantelmann, & Ruch (1990)	Adults	84	.69 to .88 for scales (Ruch, Angleitner, & Strelau, 1991)	
Formal Characteristics of Behavior— Temperament Inventory (FCB-TI)	Strelau & Zawadzki (1993)	Adults (some samples included ages 15 years +)	120	.73 to .85 for scales (Strelau & Zawadzki, 1995)	

Toddler/Preschool Age

A variety of toddler and preschool-age parent-report temperament instruments are available for use. For example, the Toddler Behavior Assessment Questionnaire (TBAQ; Goldsmith, 1996) was developed with the intent of constructing internally consistent and conceptually independent scales (possessing discriminant validity), focusing on "basic" emotions. The initial evaluation of the psychometric properties for the five TBAQ scales (Activity Level, Pleasure, Social Fearfulness, Anger Proneness, and Interest/Persistence) demonstrated satisfactory reliability (Table 10.1) and convergence with existing temperament measures (Goldsmith, 1996). Subsequent research further supported the utility of this instrument across a variety of applications. For instance, TBAQ temperament scales were shown to be predictive of child compliance, with less socially fearful and angry youngsters demonstrating greater cooperation (Lehman, Steier, Guidash, & Wanna, 2002). The TBAQ has been utilized in behavioral genetics research (Goldsmith, Buss, & Lemery, 1997) and successfully adapted for use with teachers (Goldsmith et al., 1991).

The Children's Behavior Questionnaire (CBQ; Rothbart, Ahadi, Hershey, & Fisher, 2001) was developed to be consistent with the psychobiological model of temperament proposed by Rothbart and Derryberry (1981). The CBQ has been widely utilized since its introduction, with a variety of research applications consistently supporting the reliability and validity of this parent-report questionnaire. Several studies have noted associations between CBQ factors/scales and temperament behavioral tasks administered during home or laboratory observations (Gerardi-Caulton, 2000; Kochanska, Murray, Jacques, Koenig, & Vandergeest, 1996; Schaughency & Fagot, 1993). The three-factor structure of the CBQ (Extraversion, Negative Emotionality, and Effortful Control) has been supported by cross-cultural evaluations, including factor analyses of temperament data from China and Japan (Ahadi, Rothbart, & Ye, 1993; Kusanagi, 1993; Rothbart et al., 2001). It should be noted that the IBQ-R regulation-related factor, Orienting/Regulatory Capacity differs considerably from the Effortful Control factor produced by the CBQ, as well as from the Early Childhood Behavior Questionnaire (ECBQ; Putnam, Gartstein, & Rothbart, 2006) (Table 10.1). This difference is developmental in nature, largely a result of the maturation of the executive attention network, which gives toddlers and preschoolers greater volitional control over their behaviors and emotions relative to infants, for whom regulation is often parent-facilitated.

In addition to the extensive use of the CBQ as a parent-report measure, the CBQ has been successfully adapted for use with teachers in several investigations, producing reliable estimates of temperament manifestations in the school setting that are valid with respect to convergent and predictive validity (Donzella, Gunnar, Krueger, & Alwin, 2000; Eisenberg et al., 2001, 2003). The use of teacher-report temperament questionnaires becomes more extensive in the preschool period, presumably because by 3–4 years of age the number of children attending day care/educational programs increases, with teacher-report techniques generally representing adaptations of the parent-report methods.

A self-report measure of temperament was also developed on the basis of items from the CBQ (Rothbart et al., 2001). Cognitive- and language-development considerations required an adaptation of the CBQ via the Berkeley Puppet Interview (BPI; Ablow & Measelle, 1993), utilizing a play-based methodology as an age-appropriate means of obtaining young children's self-reports. Specifically, puppets are used to present temperament items via a child-friendly script, ensuring comprehension of questions/items. An initial evaluation of this methodological approach produced promising results, with generally adequate psychometric properties (Hwang, 2004).

Several NYLS-inspired instruments have also been designed for the toddler/preschooler age group (e.g., Parent Temperament Questionnaire [PTQ]; Thomas & Chess, 1977). Generally adequate reliability has been reported for these instruments (Katz-Newman & Johnson, 1986; Sheeber & Johnson, 1992), with the PTQ scores linked to children's behavior problems and parent–child interactions (Earls, 1981; Gordon, 1983). The Teacher Temperament Questionnaire (TTQ; Thomas & Chess, 1977), and its short form (Keogh, Pullis, & Cadwell, 1982), derived from the PTQ, have also demonstrated satisfactory psychometric properties, as well as a consistent structure/item clustering (Keogh et al., 1982; Pullis, 1979). The TTQ has been successfully utilized to measure teacher perceptions of temperament for school-age children (Baker & Velicer, 1982).

The 100-item Behavioral Style Questionnaire (BSQ) is designed for use in primary pediatric practice, to be completed by a parent in about 25 minutes. Preliminary evidence of construct and external validity were reported by McDevitt and Carey (1978), along with the scale's psychometric properties (Table 10.1). Consistent with the intended use of the BSQ, a number of studies noted relationships between temperament scores derived from this measure and childhood conditions such as asthma (Sarafino, 2000), stuttering (Anderson, Pellowski, Conture, & Kelly, 2003), and fragile X syndrome (Hatton, Bailey, Hargett-Beck, Skinner, & Clark, 1999). The Toddler Temperament Scale (TTS) scores were shown to be associated with maternal ratings of overall child temperament difficulty (Fullard, McDevitt, & Carey, 1984). Although the TTS scores demonstrated considerable stability from 1 to 3 years of age, maternal general impressions of child temperament difficulty changed over time (McDevitt & Carey, 1981).

Similar to NYLS measures developed for use with infants, concerns have been raised about the reliability of several of the NYLS-based instruments noted earlier (the notable exception being the TTQ), with relatively low estimates of internal consistency noted in the literature (Gibbs, Cunningham, & Reeves, 1989; Prior, Sanson, Oberklaid, & Northam, 1987; Zhang, Xu, & Shen, 2000). Despite potential psychometric issues, these instruments continue to be widely used, especially in clinically relevant research, and have enabled scientists to address a number of important questions. Nevertheless, several NYLS-inspired measures appear to have overall improved psychometric properties and are reviewed below.

The Dimensions of Temperament Survey (DOTS; Lerner, Palermo, Spiro, & Nesselroade, 1982; Windle, 1992; Windle & Lerner, 1986) was developed to assess NYLS temperament dimensions, as well as the overall "difficult temperament" (Thomas & Chess, 1977) in childhood and adulthood, starting with the preschool period. Another goal of the DOTS developers was to include items that would lend themselves to self- as well as teacher-report for older children. The original DOTS items were developed via consultation with temperament experts, who selected from 400 questions identified as relevant to the NYLS conceptualization of temperament (Lerner et al., 1982). This selection resulted in a set of 89 items (agreed upon by at least eight or nine experts as belonging to one of the nine NYLS temperament dimensions) that were subsequently administered to children distributed across three age groups (mean ages of 3.97, 10.77, and 20.75 years, respectively), with youth in the latter two groups responding to self-report instruments. The 42 items remaining after this initial psychometric evaluation were subjected to factor analysis, producing a structure closely corresponding to five of the nine NYLS scales (Lerner et al., 1982).

The revised DOTS (DOTS-R; Windle, 1992; Windle & Lerner, 1986) was developed with adolescents, demonstrating satisfactory psychometric properties with this age group. The DOTS-R has been used extensively, especially in investigations of associations between temperament and symptom/psychopathology (e.g., Bell, Kellison, Garvan, & Bussing, 2010; Giancola & Mezzich, 2003), which have provided support for the validity of the measure. The self-report versions of the DOTS (e.g., Dimensions of Temperament Survey—Child Self-Report and Adult Self-Report, DOTS-CSR and -ASR; Lerner et al., 1982) should be noted. The DOTS-ASR was also adapted to obtain peer report of temperament, utilizing self- and peer-report of adult temperament in a cross-cultural twin study of individual differences, with data collected in Germany and Poland (Strelau, Zawadski, Oniszczenko, Angleitner, & Riemann, 2002). Thus, the DOTS questionnaires represent a system of measurement wherein a few items, not developmentally constrained to a particular age, are used throughout most of the lifespan to address NYLS-based temperament dimensions. This consistency across developmental periods may offer advantages in certain situations, whereas in others the potential limitations set on the ability to detect developmental differences may represent a concern. In addition, DOTS and DOTS-R generally have more favorable psychometric characteristics than other NYLS-inspired measures developed for this age group.

The Temperament Assessment Battery for Children (TABC), also based on the NYLS conceptualization of temperament, was developed by Martin (1988) in three versions: Parent, Teacher, and Clinician, with the first two receiving the most attention. The parent and teacher report items were derived primarily from the PTQ and TTQ (Thomas & Chess, 1977). Their purpose was to construct shorter scales than their predecessors and improve internal consistency. These measures were also intended to overcome criticisms aimed at the NYLS nine-dimensional model, primarily concerning conceptual overlap, or limited discriminant validity, and a lack of coherence for the dimensions. Factor-analytic studies conducted with the TABC produced a four-factor solution (Inhibition, Negative Emotionality, Activity Level, and Task Persistence); with three factors emerging for teacher report (Presley & Martin, 1994). Parent and Teacher versions of the TABC were used to compare children with and without attention-deficit/hyperactivity disorder (ADHD); parents and teachers indicated that children with this diagnosis displayed higher activity level and distractibility, and lower persistence (McIntosh & Cole-Love, 1996). Furthermore, kindergartners' persistence predicted higher school readiness scores (Shoen & Nagle, 1994). The Revised TABC (TABC-R) is also available (Martin & Bridger, 1999), and a number of studies support its reliability and validity (Healey, Brodzinsky, Bernstein, Rabinovitz, & Halperin, 2010; Mullola et al., 2010). For example, for school-age children, Activity, Persistence, Distractibility, Inhibition, and Negative Emotionality were significantly associated with language and math grades (Mullola et al., 2010). In the Healey and colleagues (2010) study, lower neuropsychological test scores, coupled with lower Task Persistence and higher Negative Emotionality (measured via TABC-R), emerged as significant predictors of overall child functioning. In addition, TABC-R scores can provide a categorical evaluation of temperament, via assigning children to different types (Martin & Bridger, 1999).

Two additional theories (i.e., Buss & Plomin, 1975; Garcia-Coll, Kagan, & Reznick, 1984) that have notably influenced the measurement of temperament during this developmental period are extensively described by Mervielde and De Pauw in Chapter 2, this volume. Namely, the work of Kagan and colleagues (e.g., Garcia-Coll, Kagan, & Reznick, 1984), on *behavioral inhibition* (defined in terms of hesitancy in one's approach of new/unfamiliar objects, people, and/or situations, and distress associated with exposure to unfamiliarity/unpredictability), and Buss and Plomin's temperament model (1975) encompassing early appearing characteristics that demonstrate stability, with an emphasis on genetic contributions to such characteristics, have led to the development of temperament-related measurement tools. The Behavioral Inhibition Questionnaire (BIQ; Bishop, Spence, & McDonald, 2003) assesses three domains: Social Novelty, Situational Novelty, and Physical Challenges, and was developed on the basis of Kagan's model of behavioral inhibition (Garcia-Coll et al., 1984; Kagan, 1994). Social Novelty is represented by three contexts: adults, peers, and performance situations. Situational Novelty addresses two contexts: preschool/separation and unfamiliar situations. The Physical Challenges domain, which lacks differentiation of contexts, contains four items (e.g., "Is cautious in activities that involve physical challenge"). This measure was developed by drawing from a number of existing parent and teacher temperament questionnaires, including the Parental Inhibition Questionnaire (Asendorpf, 1987), the California Child Q-Sort (Block, 1978; Block & Block, 1980), Preschool Characteristics Questionnaire (Finegan, Niccols, Zacher, & Hood, 1989), Middle Childhood Temperament Questionnaire (MCTQ; Hegvik, McDevitt, & Carey, 1982), Colorado Childhood Temperament Inventory (Rowe & Plomin, 1977), and the TTQ (Thomas & Chess, 1977).

Adequate psychometric properties have been demonstrated for the BIQ (Bishop, Spence, & McDonald, 2003), in both Parent and Teacher versions. Stability coefficients examined over a period of 12 months were somewhat lower for teacher-report than for parent-report; however, this is likely due to the fact that different teachers often provided ratings at baseline and during follow-up evaluations. Bishop and colleagues (2003) also conducted a confirmatory factor analysis of the BIQ, wherein a model comprising six correlated factors emerged, interpreted as reflecting the six contexts studied: Unfamiliar Peers, Unfamiliar Adults, Performing in Front of Others, Preschool, Unfamiliar Situations, and Novel Physical Activities Suggestive of Minor Risk. In addition, a single, second-order factor, thought to represent behavioral inhibition, explained the intercorrelations between the six lower-order factors. This instrument was also shown to be reliable and valid in measuring behavioral inhibition in older school-age children (Broeren & Muris, 2010).

Buss and Plomin's (1975) EASI-III Questionnaire, examining Emotionality, Activity Level, Sociability, and Impulsivity, has also enjoyed widespread use and has received support for its psychometric properties (Goldsmith et al., 1991). This instrument has been utilized extensively in behavioral genetics research, generally providing indices of heritability for monozygotic twins that double the values obtained for their dizygotic counterparts (Rothbart & Bates, 2006).

The Colorado Childhood Temperament Inventory (CCTI) was developed through a synthesis of two prominent models of temperament, namely, the NYLS conceptualization and the Buss and Plomin approach (Rowe & Plomin, 1977). That is, NYLS (Carey, 1972) and EASI items were combined in the context of the CCTI, which was derived on the basis of a factor-analytic procedure applied to the joint set of NYLS and EASI items. The CCTI scales (Sociability, Emotionality, Activity, Attention Span Persistence, and Soothability), with the exception of Reaction to Food, were shown to have a considerable genetic basis (Plomin & Rowe, 1977). Attention Span-Persistence and Soothability were also linked to academic achievement (Palisin, 1986). It should be noted that the CCTI and the EASI have been adapted for use with 4- to 18-month-old infants, demonstrating moderate reliability and associations with maternal temperament (Field, Vega-Lahr, Scafidi, & Goldstein, 1987). These infancy adaptations have some resemblance to the IBQ/IBQ-R, insofar as the modification of EASI includes an Activity scale, and the CCTI contains Activity, Soothability, and Attention Span-Persistence (similar to Duration of Orienting found in both IBQ and IBQ-R). However, significant differences exist as well, insofar as neither of these adapted instruments includes different forms of negative and positive emotionality, whereas the infancy instruments based on Rothbart's psychobiological model afford such distinctions.

In addition, the preschool Temperament and Character Inventory (psTCI; Constantion, Cloninger, Clarke, Hashemi, & Przybeck, 2002), based on the Cloninger, Svrakic, and Przybeck's (1993) model of temperament, is also available for use with preschool-age children. Cloninger (1984) developed a general model of temperament based on genetic, neurobiological, and neuropharmacological data. He first described three dimensions of temperament, thought to be independently inherited: Harm Avoidance (anxious, pessimistic vs. outgoing, optimistic), Novelty Seeking (impulsive, quick-tempered vs. rigid, slow-tempered), Reward Dependence (warm, approval-seeking vs. cold, aloof) and Persistence (diligent vs. undetermined) (Cloninger, 1986; Cloninger et al., 1993). Subsequently, a second domain of personality variables, reflecting the humanistic and transpersonal style of the individual, was developed, including Self-Directedness (reliable, purposeful vs. blaming, aimless), Cooperativeness (tolerant, helpful vs. prejudiced, revengeful), and Self-Transcendence (self-forgetful, spiritual vs. self-conscious, materialistic) (Cloninger et al., 1993). The original three and the subsequently proposed temperament dimensions have been associated with genetic influences, and demonstrated to contribute to personality dysfunction (Cloninger et al., 1993; Gillespie, Cloninger, Heath, & Martin, 2003). The psTCI represents a downward extension of the TCI (see "Adulthood" section) and the Junior Temperament and Character Inventory (JTCI; see "Adolescence" section) but has not been used as widely as its counterparts.

School Age

For school-age children, a number of choices for questionnaire assessment of temperament exist. For example, some of the parent-report preschool instruments continue to be of use for older children (e.g., CBQ: Rothbart at al., 2001; DOTS: Lerner et al., 1982; Windle, 1992; Windle & Lerner, 1986), and are not discussed further here. Others (e.g., Parent-Report MCTQ; Hegvik et al., 1982) were developed specifically with this age group in mind. The NYLS-inspired Parent-Report MCTQ was designed to accommodate this older age group, wherein the construct of Rhythmicity was replaced with a more age-appropriate temperament dimension labeled as Predictability. Satisfactory reliability estimates were reported for the measurement development sample (Hegvik et al.,); however, later work utilizing this instrument with a German sample has raised some questions about the structure and psychometric properties of the MCTQ (Czeschlik, 1992). Partial support was obtained for the previously proposed structure, with six of the nine original scales (Hegvik et al., 1982) emerging as appropriate for the data in the Czeschlik (1992) study.

In addition to the parent-report measures, self-report questionnaires can be utilized with school-age children, typically starting at 8 years of age. These have been designed to examine emotionality and regulation during this developmental period, albeit not always from the temperament perspective per se. How I Feel (HIF; Walden, Harris, & Catron, 2003) is a measure of emotion and control of emotion that comprises three broad factors: Positive Emotion (happiness and excitability), Negative Emotion (being mad, scared, and sad), and Emotion Control (control over positive and negative emotion). Each aspect of emotion is assessed by two questions on the dimensions of frequency and intensity. For example, happiness is assessed by the ratings of *feeling happy all the time*, *feeling happy often*, *having powerful happy feelings*, and *having strong happy feelings*. The authors report an extensive evaluation of the psychometric properties of the HIF with satisfactory results (Walden et al., 2003). Evidence of the validity of the HIF has also been provided, with Kim, Walden, Harris, Karrass, and Catron (2007) noting associations between HIF Anger and externalizing problems. Although the HIF was not conceptualized on the basis of a temperament theoretical framework, the content of the scales reflecting positive and negative emotionality, and to a certain extent, scales reflecting the control of positive and negative emotions appears to be consistent with contemporary definitions/models of temperament. For example, the higher-order factor structure of the HIF reported by Walden and colleagues (2003) closely resembles that of the psychobiological model of temperament (e.g., Rothbart & Bates, 2006).

Adolescence

Most temperament assessment tools for adolescents include self-reports. Some of the measures utilized earlier in childhood, and their adaptations, continue to be of use (e.g., DOTS-R; Windle, 1992; Windle & Lerner, 1986). Other instruments, such as the Early Adolescent Temperament Questionnaire—Revised (EATQ-R; Ellis & Rothbart, 2001; Muris & Meesters, 2009), were designed specifically for this developmental period. The EATQ-R represents a revision of the EATQ (Capaldi & Rothbart, 1992), developed on the basis of Rothbart's psychobiological theory for use in children/adolescents. Early development and factor-analytic work yielded four factors: Effortful Control, Negative Affectivity, Surgency, and Affiliativeness. Two additional scales, Aggression and Depressive Mood, were also included in the measure. Overall, research with the EATQ-R has demonstrated satisfactory reliability for this instrument (Ellis & Rothbart, 2001; Muris & Meesters, 2009). In addition, Muris and Meesters (2009) provided data demonstrating validity, reporting associations between EATQ-R scales and the Behavioral Inhibition Scale and the Behavioral Activation Scale (BIS/BAS; Carver & White, 1994), the Revised Child Anxiety and Depression Scale (Chorpita et al., 2000), the Strengths and Difficulties Questionnaire (Goodman, 2001) and the Child Rating Scale of Aggression (Brown, Atkins, Osborne, & Milnamow, 1996). Based on the significant associations between the EATQ-R scores and these established measures, the authors concluded that support has been obtained for the validity of the EATQ-R. Finally, the EATQ-R has been used in investigations examining associations between temperament and psychopathology (e.g., Bridgett, Valentino, & Hayden, in press), demonstrating the usefulness of this measure for such research.

The Adolescent Temperament Questionnaire (ADTQ; Scheier, Casten, & Fullard, 1995) includes items chosen to reflect the nine dimensions of temperament identified in the NYLS (Thomas & Chess, 1977). Factor-analytic work related to this measure identified three higher-order factors and 11 first-order factors. The second-order factor, Diligence, is comprised of loadings from the first-order factors of Distractibility, Threshold, and Persistence. Similarly, the higher-order factor, Vigor/Mobility, is comprised of loadings from three first-order factors: Activity, Intensity, and Rhythmicity. The third second-order factor comprises loadings from five first-order factors: Approach–Withdrawal, Ego Control, Negative Mood, Adaptable, and Positive Mood (Scheier et al., 1995). Despite its potential as an adolescent self-report measure of temperament, no evidence of ADTQ reliability was provided. Thus, additional studies of the ADTQ's psychometric properties should be conducted in the future.

The JTCI represents a downward extension of the Temperament and Character Inventory (TCI), which has been used extensively in adult studies and is discussed in the "Adulthood" section. Initial work on the JTCI resulted in seven scales (comprising 23 subscales): Harm Avoidance, Novelty Seeking, Persistence, Reward Dependence, Self-Directedness, Self-Transcendence, and

Cooperativeness (Luby, Svrakic, McCallum, Przybeck, & Cloninger, 1999). Subsequent work by Lyoo and colleagues (2004), using a Korean sample, confirmed the generally adequate psychometric properties of the JTCI. Since its initial development by Luby and colleagues (1999), the JTCI has been used extensively to evaluate theoretical and conceptual associations between temperament/character and symptoms of psychopathology (e.g., Rettew, Althoff, Dumenci, Ayer, & Hudziak, 2008). Caution should be exercised in using the JTCI, however, given difficulties observed with other measures based on Cloninger's model of temperament, calling into question the underlying theory (see Farmer & Goldberg, 2008, for discussion). Specifically, Farmer and Goldberg (2008) suggest that measurement-related problems observed for instruments based on Cloninger's model lead to questions concerning the viability of the underlying psychobiological model of personality. Indeed, these authors concluded that "there is not strong support for the main assumptions of Cloninger's theory, nor is there solid support for the hypothesized structure of personality traits, as measured in several versions of his inventory" (p. 289). An additional issue concerns the labels utilized to represent this measure. Although the instrument was named the Temperament and Character Inventory, and thus was included in this review, the underlying theory developed by Cloninger refers to personality traits. Given the potentially important distinctions between personality and temperament outlined earlier, the confounding of terms seems problematic and possibly misleading when it comes to decisions regarding the appropriate use of this measure. In summary, while the measure was initially promising and widely used, those considering self-report measures of temperament should use caution.

Adulthood

Self-report is the most prominent approach to gathering temperament-related information about adults. The NYLS Early Adult Questionnaire (Thomas, Mittelman, Chess, Korn, & Cohen, 1982) is a self-report instrument that represents the nine NYLS temperament categories—Rhythmicity, Adaptability, Approach–Withdrawal, Attention Span/Persistence, Activity Level, Distractibility, Quality of Mood, Intensity, and Sensory Threshold—based on the work of Thomas and Chess (1977). Thomas and colleagues (1982) reported adequate estimates of reliability and validity for this measure, with the latter derived on the basis of correlations between each scale and ratings by interviewers on the nine temperament dimensions.

The Adult Temperament Questionnaire (ATQ; Evans & Rothbart, 2007) represents one of the most recent additions to adult temperament measures, originating in the psychobiological model described by Rothbart and colleagues (e.g., Rothbart & Derryberry, 1981). Long and short forms of the ATQ are available, with factor-analytic studies yielding five factors (Effortful Control, Negative Affect, Orienting/Sensitivity, Affiliativeness, and Extraversion/Surgency). This structural model represents a departure from both the three-factor structure typically observed in early childhood (Gartstein & Rothbart, 2003) and for school-age children (Rothbart et al., 2001), and the four-factor model emerging in adolescence (Ellis & Rothbart, 2001), more closely resembling the Five-Factor Model of personality (e.g., McCrae & John, 1992). The reliability of individual scales has been demonstrated, and associations between the Big Five personality scales (McCrae & Costa, 1996) and the factor scores of the ATQ have been reported, supporting the validity of this instrument. Although continued research demonstrating the validity of this recently developed instrument is needed, in one recent study using the short form of the ATQ, positive associations between Negative Affect and anxiety, along with negative associations between Extraversion/Surgency and Effortful Control and anxiety, were reported (Clements & Bailey, 2010). In general, it appears that the ATQ is a promising self-report instrument for the assessment of temperament in adults.

The Emotionality, Activity, and Sociability Temperament Survey for Adults (EAS; Buss & Plomin, 1984; Naerde, Roysamb, & Tambs, 2004) is a short self-report measure originally developed by Buss and Plomin (1984) to correspond to their theoretical conceptualization of temperament. The most recent investigation of the psychometric properties of the EAS was conducted by

Naerde and colleagues (2004). Although support was generally obtained for the factor structure and stability of the EAS, the internal consistency estimates of all but one of the scales were below .70, with some lower than .60, which are less than ideal based on information outlined at the beginning of this chapter. One caveat regarding the study by Naerde and colleagues is that only data from adult women were obtained. To our knowledge, similar studies examining the psychometric properties of the instrument with men have not been reported.

The TCI (Cloninger et al., 1993), mentioned earlier, has been revised (TCI-R; Cloninger, 1999), with updated evaluations of the psychometric properties reported (e.g., Farmer & Goldberg, 2008). Although the TCI-R demonstrates adequate reliability across facet scales, concerns have been raised regarding the factorial validity of the TCI and the TCI-R. For example, Self-Directedness and Harm Avoidance could not be adequately differentiated on the basis of available factor analyses (e.g., Farmer & Goldberg, 2008; Herbst, Zonderman, McCrae, & Costa, 2000). It should be noted that the problems noted earlier for the JTCI apply to these adult versions as well.

The Adult Measure of Behavioral Inhibition (AMBI) and Retrospective Measure of Behavioral Inhibition (RMBI; Gladstone & Parker, 2005), developed from the conceptualizations of inhibited–uninhibited temperament by Kagan and colleagues (e.g., Garcia-Coll et al., 1984), are also self-report instruments. That is, the AMBI and RMBI are adult self-report measures of tendencies to be more or less inhibited at present and in childhood, respectively. Based on the results of factor-analytic studies, the AMBI includes 16 and the RMBI, 18 items, making these measures potentially useful when a more comprehensive temperament evaluation is not permitted due to the constraints of research (e.g., when a number of additional variables are being addressed and measures have to be brief), and/or when the research is focused specifically on behavioral inhibition. Whereas both measures have factors of Fearful Inhibition, Non-Approach, and Risk Avoidance, the AMBI has a Low Sociability factor and the RMBI has a factor labeled Shyness and Sensitivity. Mixed results have been obtained with regard to reliability, but the construct validity of both measures was supported by associations with measures of anxiety and introversion (Gladstone & Parker, 2005).

The BIS/BAS Scales (Carver & White, 1994) were developed in the tradition of Gray's (1972, 1981) physiological theory of personality to provide a short self-report measure of the physiologically based tendencies to be more fearful/hesitant and to engage in more approach behavior. Carver and White (1994) reported a four-factor structure (BIS, BAS Reward Responsiveness, BAS Drive, and BAS Fun Seeking) with adequate internal consistency. Subsequently, a number of studies that have used the BIS/BAS scales have found theoretically meaningful associations with important outcomes. For example, Kasch, Rottenberg, Arnow, and Gotlib (2002) found that depression in a sample of adults was associated with higher BIS and lower BAS.

The Positive and Negative Affect Schedule (PANAS) developed by Watson, Clark, and Tellegen (1988) is a brief self-report measure that comprises an equal number of Positive Affect (PA) and Negative Affect (NA) items. This questionnaire appears to reflect affective processes, consistent with most conceptualizations and operational definitions of temperament. The two-factor structure of the PANAS was supported with low, negative associations between the two factors, which indicate some independence of the two constructs (Watson et al., 1988). Numerous studies have used the PANAS, examining associations between PA and NA and internalizing types of symptoms. Low scores on the PA scale have consistently demonstrated associations with more frequent or intense symptoms of depression, while high scores on the NA scale have demonstrated positive associations with more frequent or intense symptoms of depression and anxiety (e.g., Crawford & Henry, 2004; Dyck, Jolly, & Kramer, 1994). A longer, 60-item version of the PANAS is also available (Watson & Clark, 1991), but it has been less frequently investigated. Furthermore, downward extensions of the PANAS for use with older children and adolescents have been developed with generally good psychometric properties (e.g., Laurent et al., 1999; Lonigan, Hooe, David, & Kistner, 1999). Overall, PANAS and its derivations appear to demonstrate adequate psychometric properties and represent an effective self-report measure of PA and NA, which are important components of several models of temperament (e.g., Rothbart & Bates, 2006) applicable across the lifespan.

Finally, the Revised NEO Personality Inventory (NEO-PI-R; Costa & McCrae, 1992; Costa, McCrae, & Dye, 1991) represents a prototypic Big Five measure, and is relevant given that the personality dimensions of Neuroticism and Extraversion reflect temperament characteristics associated with Negative and Positive Affect/Emotionality, measured from early infancy into adulthood (De Pauw et al., 2009; Mervielde & De Pauw, Chapter 2, this volume; Strelau, 1998), and Conscientiousness has some parallels with Effortful Control, which is measured reliably starting at 18 months of age (Evans & Rothbart, 2007). The NEO-PI-R is a widely used self-report instrument that includes Neuroticism, Extraversion, Conscientiousness, Openness to Experience, and Agreeableness, often thought of as the Big Five, with all scales demonstrating satisfactory psychometric properties (see Costa et al., 1991; Costa & McCrae, 1992); numerous studies report evidence for the validity of this measure (e.g., Costa, 1996).

Tellegen also has developed a measure of personality, the Multidimensional Personality Questionnaire (MPQ), which has ties to temperament and Big Five personality characteristics (Tellegen & Waller, 2008). The MPQ Positive Emotionality factor comprises the subscales Well-Being, Achievement, Social Potency, and Social Closeness, whereas Negative Emotionality comprises the subscales Aggression, Stress Reaction, and Alienation. A third factor, Constraint, comprises the subscales Traditionalism, Harm Avoidance, and Control. While the subscales of Traditionalism and Harm Avoidance are more consistent with conceptualizations of personality, Control is similar to temperamental Effortful Control and Conscientiousness in the traditional Big Five. Other examples of measures of personality containing factors/scales linked to temperament are presented in Appendix 10.1.

One additional approach to adult temperament deserves a mention because it represents a substantial departure from the literature discussed thus far. Akiskal, Akiskal, Haykal, Manning, and Conner (2005) developed the Temperament Evaluation of the Memphis, Pisa, Paris, and San Diego Autoquestionnaire (TEMPS-A) on the basis of a temperament conceptualization that stemmed from work with clinical populations, primarily with mood and personality disorder diagnoses. Briefly, Akiskal, Akiskal, and colleagues were interested in describing mood disorders in terms of underlying traits, as opposed to the framework outlined in the *Diagnostic and Statistical Manual of Mental Disorders*, fourth edition (DSM-IV; American Psychiatric Association, 1994), and the word "temperament" in this context was utilized in a manner more consistent with prior use of the "personality disorder" terminology (Akiskal, Akiskal, et al., 2005, pp. 4–5). The TEMPS-A semistructured interview yields Dysthymic, Cyclothymic, Irritable, and Hyperthymic temperament subscales (see Table 10.1 for psychometric properties). This approach to temperament shares some aspects with other temperament definitions (e.g., focus on positive, adaptive aspects of affective temperament attributes and traits serving an "evolutionary" function) (Akiskal, Mendlowicz, et al., 2005, p. 7); at the same time, the TEMPS-A is not representative of the mainstream temperament perspectives and research.

Summary and Future Directions

Our primary aim in this chapter was to outline available self- and other-report approaches, to facilitate making an appropriate choice with respect to temperament measurement. Navigating the many measurement tools may seem daunting, yet decisions can be made effectively by asking a few key questions. First, there is a question concerning the purpose of temperament assessment. On the one hand, the NYLS-inspired instruments have been relied on exclusively for the purposes of temperament-based clinical intervention. On the other hand, research applications have found some troubling properties (e.g., low internal consistency, unstable scale structure) for a number of these questionnaires. Future studies should examine the utility of more recently developed instruments, consistent with current temperament theories, in clinical interventions.

Second, the choice of instruments will be dictated by the age range of interest to the research and/or clinical project. Longitudinal projects pose special challenges, due to the need to provide continuity in the assessment of key variables. A series of questionnaires has been made available to address this issue. For example, Carey, McDevitt and colleagues, as well as Rothbart and her collaborators, constructed multiple developmentally appropriate questionnaires for use from infancy to adulthood, whereas the DOTS (Lerner et al., 1982; Windle, 1982) was constructed in such a way as to provide a universal set of items for use from the preschool period to adulthood.

A number of the instruments reviewed earlier have parent-, teacher-, as well as self-report versions, which brings up the third key question relating to the informant(s) of choice. This choice may not present itself equally across developmental periods (e.g., young infants may not be spending time outside the home). It may be tempting to assume that including more sources of information will always be advantageous; however, information from multiple sources inevitably presents its own challenges. That is, agreement between different sources of information is often low to moderate, complicating data reduction (i.e., forming constructs on the basis of information from multiple sources) and interpretation of results (e.g., different patterns of results emerge across informants). Nonetheless, obtaining data from multiple sources of information becomes essential given certain research goals, such as aims that involve measurement construction or refinement, and/or ascertaining temperament manifestations across settings. It has also been noted that aggregation across raters, settings, and/or occasions is essential if the goal is to increase reliability (which is generally the case) and should thus be attempted if there are significant associations between the various sources of information (Epstein, 1983).

In addition, measurement selection should take discriminant validity into account. Whereas some researchers have raised questions about the NYLS-inspired instruments in particular because of the apparent conceptual overlap between scales representing the nine dimensions (Czeschlik, 1992; Gibbs, Reeves, & Cunningham, 1987; Rothbart & Bates, 2006), others have argued that conceptual overlap is a non-issue when the instruments are used with clinical goals in mind, and that clinically utilized instruments should not be subjected to factor-analytic procedures as a test of their construct validity and utility (Carey & McDevitt, 1989). However, current psychometric theory, as it pertains to construct validity and scale construction in particular (Clark & Watson, 1995; Comrey, 1988; Floyd & Widaman, 1995; Messick, 1995; Simms, 2008), would suggest otherwise. In some respects, measures used in the clinical setting may have to meet even more stringent psychometric standards because diagnostic and treatment decisions are made on the basis of scores (Henson, 2001; Nunnally, 1967, 1978; Nunnally & Bernstein, 1994; Streiner, 2003).

Finally, it should be noted that research including a variety of measures of temperament has led to findings that demonstrate associations with important child outcomes, such as psychopathology/symptoms and academic achievement (e.g., Deater-Deckard, Mullineaux, Petrill, & Thompson, 2009; De Pauw & Mervielde, 2011; Gartstein et al., 2010; Mian, Wainwright, Briggs-Gowan, & Carter, 2011; Rudasill, Gallagher, & White, 2010). These studies illustrate the important role of temperament attributes, and suggest that temperament assessment can potentially play a part in the early identification of children at risk for adverse outcomes, as well as in the prevention and early intervention efforts. The relatively inexpensive and easy-to-administer questionnaire measures of temperament may have an important role to play in bridging the science of temperament with clinical practice. One obstacle to proliferation of such uses has to do with the fact that, to our knowledge, no measures of temperament have been subjected to a standardization process with large, representative, national samples in the United States or any other country, in a manner similar to the established measures of psychopathology (e.g., the Child Behavior Checklist [CBCL]; Achenbach & Rescorla, 2000). Thus, identification of individual children who may be exhibiting normatively high (e.g., frustration/anger) or low (e.g., effortful control) levels of temperament characteristics that would place them at significant risk for the subsequent emergence of a disruptive behavior or other difficulties is rendered more challenging. Given the potential benefits of standardizing contemporary measures of temperament, investigators should consider pursuing such an endeavor as one of the important next steps in the evolution of self- and other-report temperament measures.

In summary, although no single measure can be identified as representing the "gold standard" in temperament assessment, several criteria for selection of temperament questionnaires can be outlined: (1) theoretically grounded constructs; (2) satisfactory reliability estimates; and (3) evidence of construct validity. Depending on the nature of the study, developmental sensitivity of the instruments may also be important. Thus, the multitude of available measurement techniques does not imply that any measures of temperament are equally appropriate and can be selected in a haphazard manner. Rather, careful decisions about the most appropriate measurement tool(s) should be made on a case-by-case basis given the specific research/clinical needs of a project.

Finally, the continuing importance of development/refinement of self- and other-report measures of temperament should be noted. First, remaining concerns about questionnaire-based evaluations, and the use of parent-report in particular (e.g., Kagan, 1994, 1998) in examining temperament, should be addressed. Although superior predictive validity has been demonstrated for parent-report ratings relative to laboratory observation indices (Hart, Field, & Roitfarb, 1999; Pauli-Pott, Mertesacker, Bade, Haverkock, & Beckmann, 2003), more recently questions have been raised about the accuracy of parents' ratings in comparison to those of trained examiners. Specifically, Seifer, Sameroff, Dickstein, Schillera, and Hayden (2004) reported a lower correspondence between mothers' and observers' ratings for mothers' own children than for children with no relation to parents or trained raters. This pattern of results calls parents' accuracy regarding their own children's temperament into question given that the laboratory situation is thought to provide the "gold standard" of measurement.

However, the laboratory, while enabling high levels of experimental control, introduces its own challenges in terms of eliciting representative samples of children's behavior. In our own work, we have noted advantages of the laboratory setting in eliciting behavioral inhibition/fearfulness, in part because of the demand characteristics resulting from the child's lack of familiarity with this setting. On the other hand, eliciting positive emotionality is likely challenged by the unavoidable engagement of the behavioral inhibition system, the activity of which can be expected to dampen positive reactions. Thus, although it is possible that parents are not accurate with respect to their own children relative to observers, it is also conceivable that discrepant ratings are a reflection of their attempts to compensate for what they perceive as atypical behavior in their children.

Future research comparing different sources of information, and examining their complementary use, should continue in light of these lingering questions. In addition, temperament theories/models continue to be refined, and it is essential that the questionnaire techniques keep up with these developments, providing researchers with the tools necessary to measure new or revised constructs. Despite availability of other measurement approaches, self- and other-report of temperament continues to be one of the most prominent assessment tools because of the advantages these questionnaires offer in terms of their accessibility, costs, and time demands.

Further Reading

Goldsmith, H. H., Buss, A. H., Plomin, R., Rothbart, M. K., Thomas, A., & Chess, S. (1987). What is temperament?: Four approaches. *Child Development, 58,* 505–529.

Goldsmith, H. H., Rieser-Danner, L. A., & Briggs, S. (1994). Evaluating convergent and discriminant validity of temperament questionnaires for preschoolers, toddlers, and infants. *Journal of Developmental Psychology, 27*(4), 566–579.

Kagan, J. (1994). *Galen's prophecy: Temperament in human nature.* Cambridge, MA: Harvard University Press.

Rothbart, M. K., & Bates, J. E. (2006) Temperament. In W. Damon, R. Lerner, & N. Eisenberg (Eds.), *Handbook of child psychology: Vol. 3. Social, emotional, and personality development* (6th ed., pp. 99–166). New York: Wiley.

Thomas, A., & Chess, S. (1977). *Temperament and development.* New York: New York University Press.

Zentner, M., & Bates, J. E. (2008). Child temperament: An integrative review of concepts, research programs, and measures. *European Journal of Developmental Science, 2,* 7–37.

References

Ablow, J. C., & Measelle, J. R. (1993). *The Berkeley Puppet Interview: Administration and scoring system manuals.* Berkeley: University of California.

Achenbach, T. M., & Rescorla, L. A. (2000). *Manual for the ASEBA Preschool Forms and Profiles.* Burlington: University of Vermont, Research Center for Children, Youths, and Families.

Ahadi, S. A., Rothbart, M. K., & Ye, R. (1993). Children's temperament in the U.S. and China: Similarities and differences. *European Journal of Personality, 7,* 359–378.

Akiskal, H. S., Akiskal, K. K., Haykal, R. F., Manning, J. S., & Conner, P. D. (2005). TEMPS-A: Progress towards validation of a self-rated clinical version of the Temperament Evaluation of the Memphis, Pisa, Paris, and San Diego Autoquestionniare. *Journal of Affective Disorders, 85,* 3–16.

Akiskal, H. S., Mendlowicz, M. V., Jean-Louis, G., Rapaport, M. H., Kelsoe, J. R., Gillin J. C., et al. (2005). TEMPS-A: Validation of a short version of a self-rated instrument designed to measure variations in temperament. *Journal of Affective Disorders, 85,* 45–52.

American Psychiatric Association. (1994). *Diagnostic and statistical manual of mental disorders* (4th ed.). Washington, DC: American Psychiatric Association.

Anderson, J. D., Pellowski, M. W., Conture, E. G., & Kelly, E. M. (2003). Temperamental characteristics of young children who stutter. *Journal of Speech, Language, and Hearing Research, 46,* 1221–1233.

Asendorpf, J. B. (1987). Videotape reconstruction of emotions and cognitions related to shyness. *Journal of Personality and Social Psychology, 53,* 542–549.

Baker, E. H., & Velicer, W. F. (1982). The structure and reliability of the Teacher Temperament Questionnaire. *Journal of Abnormal Child Psychology, 10,* 531–546.

Barbaranelli, C., Caprara, G. V., Rabasca, A., & Pastorelli, C. (2003). A questionnaire for measuring the Big Five in late childhood. *Personality and Individual Differences, 34,* 645–664.

Bates, J., Freeland, C. A. B., & Lounsbury, M. L. (1979). Measurement of infant difficultness. *Child Development, 50,* 794–803.

Bell, L., Kellison, I., Garvan, C. W., & Bussing, R. (2010). Relationships between child-reported activity level and task orientation and parental attention-deficit/hyperactivity disorder symptom ratings. *Journal of Developmental Behavioral Pediatrics, 31,* 233–237.

Bishop, G., Spence, S. H., & McDonald, C. (2003). Can parents and teachers provide a reliable and valid report of behavioral inhibition? *Child Development, 74,* 1899–1917.

Block, J. (1978). *The Q-Sort Method in personality assessment and psychiatric research.* Mountain View, CA: Consulting Psychologists Press.

Block, J., & Block, J. H. (1980). *The California Child Q-Set.* Mountain View, CA: Consulting Psychologists Press.

Bohlin, G., Hagekull, B., & Lindhagen, K. (1981). Dimensions of infant behavior. *Infant Behavior and Development, 4,* 83–96.

Bridgett, D. J., Gartstein, M. A., Putnam, S., McKay, T., Iddins, E., Robertson, C., et al. (2009). Maternal and contextual influences and the effect of temperament development during infancy on parenting in toddlerhood. *Infant Behavior and Development, 32,* 103–116.

Bridgett, D. J., Gartstein, M. A., Putnam, S. P., Lance, K. O., Iddins, E., Waits, R., et al. (2011). Emerging effortful control in toddlerhood: The role of infant orienting/regulation, maternal effortful control, and maternal time spent in caregiving activities. *Infant Behavior and Development, 34,* 189–199.

Bridgett, D. J., Valentino, K., & Hayden, L. C. (in press). The contribution of children's temperament fear and effortful control to restraint and seclusion during inpatient treatment in a psychiatric hospital. *Child Psychiatry and Human Development.*

Broeren, S., & Muris, P. (2010). A psychometric evaluation of the Behavioral Inhibition Questionnaire in a non-clinical sample of Dutch children and adolescents. *Child Psychiatry and Human Development, 41,* 214–229.

Brown, K., Atkins, M. S., Osborne, M. L., & Milnamow, M. (1996). A revised teacher rating scale for reactive and proactive aggression. *Journal of Abnormal Child Psychology, 24,* 473–480.

Buss, A. H., & Plomin, R. (1975). *A temperament theory of personality development.* New York: Wiley.

Buss, A. H., & Plomin, R. (1984). *Temperament: Early developing personality traits.* Hillsdale, NJ: Erlbaum.

Capaldi, D. M., & Rothbart, M. K. (1992). Development and validation of an early adolescent temperament measure. *Journal of Early Adolescence, 12,* 153–173.

Carey, W. B. (1972). Clinical applications of infant temperament measures. *Journal of Pediatrics, 77,* 188–194.

Carey, W. B. (1973). Measurement of infant temperament in pediatric practice. In J. C. Westman (Ed.), *Individual differences in children* (pp. 293–305). New York: Wiley.

Carey, W. B., & McDevitt, S. C. (1978). Revision of the Infant Temperament Questionnaire. *Pediatrics, 61,* 735–739.

Carey, W. B., & McDevitt, S. C. (1989). Technical note: Comment on paper by Gibbs et al. *Journal of Child Psychiatry and Psychology, 30,* 639–641.

Carver, C. S., & White, T. L. (1994). Behavioral inhibition, behavioral activation, and the affective responses to impending reward and punishment: The BIS/BAS Scales. *Journal of Personality and Social Psychology, 67*(2), 319–333.

Chorpita, B. F., Yim, L., Moffitt, C., Umemoto, L. A., & Francis, S. E. (2000). Assessment of symptoms of DSM-IV anxiety and depression in children: A revised child anxiety and depression scale. *Behaviour Research and Therapy, 38,* 835–855.

Clark, L. A., & Watson, D. (1995). Constructing validity: Basic issues in objective scale development. *Psychological Assessment, 7,* 309–319.

Clements, A. D., & Bailey, B. A. (2010). The relationship between temperament and anxiety. *Journal of Health Psychology, 15,* 515–525.

Cloninger, C. R. (1984). A systematic method for clinical description and classification of personality variants. *Archives of General Psychiatry, 44,* 573–588.

Cloninger, C. R. (1986). A unified biosocial theory of personality and its role in the development of anxiety states. *Psychiatric Developments, 4,* 167–226.

Cloninger, C. R. (1999). *The Temperament and Character Inventory—Revised.* St. Louis, MO: Washington University, Center for Psychobiology of Personality. (Available from C. R. Cloninger, Washington University School of Medicine, Department of Psychiatry, P.O. Box 8134, St. Louis, MO 63110)

Cloninger, C. R., Svrakic, D. M., & Przybeck, T. R. (1993). A psychobiological model of temperament and character. *Archives of General Psychiatry, 50,* 975–990.

Comrey, A. L. (1988). Factor-analytic methods of scale development in personality and clinical psychology. *Journal of Consulting and Clinical Psychology, 56,* 754–761.

Constantion, J. N., Cloninger, C. R., Clarke, A. R., Hashemi, B., & Przybeck, T. (2002). Application of the seven-factor model of personality to early childhood. *Psychiatry Research, 109,* 229–243.

Costa, P. T., Jr. (1996). Work and personality: Use of the NEO-PI-R in industrial/organizational psychology. *Applied Psychology: An International Review, 45*(3), 225–241.

Costa, P. T., Jr., & McCrae, R. R. (1992). *Revised NEO Personality Inventory (NEO-PI-R) and NEO Five-Factor Inventory (NEO-FFI) professional manual.* Odessa, FL: Psychological Assessment Resources.

Costa, P. T., Jr., McCrae, R. R., & Dye, D. A. (1991). Facet scales for agreeableness and conscientiousness: A revision of the NEO Personality Inventory. *Personality and Individual Differences, 12*(9), 887–898.

Crawford, J. R., & Henry, J. D. (2004). The Positive and Negative Affect Schedule (PANAS): Construct validity, measurement properties and normative data in a large non-clinical sample. *British Journal of Clinical Psychology, 43,* 245–265.

Czeschlik, T. (1992). The Middle Childhood Temperament Questionnaire: Factor structure in a German sample. *Personality and Individual Differences, 13,* 205–210.

Deal, J. E., Halverson, C. F., Jr., Martin, R. P., Victor, J., & Baker, S. (2007). The Inventory of Children's Individual Differences: Development and validation of a short version. *Journal of Personality Assessment, 89*(2), 162–166.

Deater-Deckard, K., Mullineaux, P. Y., Petrill, S. A., & Thompson, L. A. (2009). Effortful control, surgency, and reading skills in middle childhood. *Reading and Writing, 22,* 107–116.

De Bolle, M., De Clercq, B., Van Leewen, K., Decuyper, M., Rosseel, Y., & De Fruyt, F. (2009). Personality and psychopathology in Flemish referred children: Five perspectives of continuity. *Child Psychiatry and Human Development, 40,* 269–285.

De Pauw, S. S. W., & Mervielde, I. (2011). The role of temperament and personality in problem behaviors of children with ADHD. *Journal of Abnormal Child Psychology, 39,* 377–291.

De Pauw, S. S. W., Mervielde, I., & Van Leeuwen, K. G. (2009). How are traits related to problem behavior in preschoolers?: Similarities and contrasts between temperament and personality. *Journal of Abnormal Child Psychology, 37*(3), 309–325.

DiPietro, J. A., Hodgson, D. M., Costigan, K. A., & Johnson, T. R. B. (1996). Fetal antecedents of infant temperament. *Child Development, 67,* 2568–2583.

Donzella, B., Gunnar, M. R., Krueger, W. K., & Alwin, J. (2000). Cortisol and vagal tone responses to competitive challenge in preschoolers: Associations with temperament. *Developmental Psychobiology, 37,* 209–220.

Dyck, M. J., Jolly, J. B., & Kramer, T. (1994). An evaluation of positive affectivity, negative affectivity, and hyperarousal as markers for assessing between syndrome relationships. *Personality and Individual Differences, 17,* 637–646.

Earls, F. (1981). Temperament characteristics and behavior problems in three-year-old children. *Journal of Nervous and Mental Disorders, 169,* 367–373.

Eisenberg, N., Cumberland, A., Spinrad, T. L., Fabes, R. A., Shepard, S. A., Reiser, M., et al. (2001). The relations of regulation and emotionality to children's externalizing and internalizing problem behavior. *Child Development, 72,* 1112–1134.

Eisenberg, N., Valiente, C., Fabes, R. A., Smith, C. L., Reiser, M., Shepard, S. A., et al. (2003). The relations of effortful control and ego control to children's resiliency and social functioning. *Developmental Psychology, 39,* 761–776.

Ellis, L. K., & Rothbart, M. K. (2001, April). *Revision of the Early Adolescent Temperament Questionnaire.* Poster presented at the biennial meeting of the Society for Research in Child Development, Minneapolis, MN.

Epstein, S. (1983). Aggregation and beyond: Some basic issues on the prediction of behavior. *Journal of Personality, 53,* 360–392.

Evans, D. E., & Rothbart, M. K. (2007). Developing a model of adult temperament. *Journal of Research in Personality, 41,* 868–888.

Farmer, R. F., & Goldberg, L. R. (2008). A psychometric evaluation of the Revised Temperament and Character Inventory (TCI-R) and the TCI-140. *Psychological Assessment, 20*(3), 281–291.

Field, T., Vega-Lahr, N., Scafidi, F., & Goldstein, S. (1987). Reliability, stability, and relationships between infant and parent temperament. *Infant Behavior and Development, 10,* 117–122.

Finegan, J. A., Niccols, A., Zacher, J., & Hood, J. (1989). Factor structure of the Preschool Characteristics Questionnaire. *Infant Behavior and Development, 12,* 221–227.

Floyd, F. J., & Widaman, K. F. (1995). Factor analysis in the development and refinement of clinical assessment instruments. *Psychological Assessment, 7,* 286–299.

Frick, P. J. (2004). Integrating research on temperament and childhood psychopathology: Its pitfalls and promise. *Journal of Clinical Child and Adolescent Psychology, 33,* 2–7.

Fullard, W., McDevitt, S. C., & Carey, W. B. (1984). Assessing temperament in one- to three-year-old children. *Journal of Pediatric Psychology, 9,* 205–217.

Garcia-Coll, C., Kagan, J., & Reznick, J. S. (1984). Behavioral inhibition in young children. *Child Development, 55,* 1005–1019.

Gartstein, M. A., Bridgett, D. J., Rothbart, M. K., Robertson, C., Iddins, E., Ramsay, K., et al. (2010). A latent growth examination of fear development in infancy: Contributions of maternal depression and the risk for toddler anxiety. *Developmental Psychology, 46*(3), 651–668.

Gartstein, M. A., & Marmion, J. (2008). Fear and positive affectivity in infancy: Convergence/discrepancy between parent-report and laboratory-based indicators. *Infant Behavior and Development, 31,* 227–238.

Gartstein, M. A., & Rothbart, M. K. (2003). Studying infant temperament via the Revised Infant Behavior Questionnaire. *Infant Behavior and Development, 26,* 64–86.

Gerardi-Caulton, G. (2000). Sensitivity to spatial conflict and the development of self-regulation in children 24–36 months of age. *Developmental Science, 3,* 397–404.

Giancola, P. R., & Mezzich, A. C. (2003). Executive functioning, temperament, and drug use involvement in adolescent females with a substance use disorder. *Journal of Child Psychology and Psychiatry, 44,* 857–866.

Gibbs, M. V., Cunningham, C. C., & Reeves, D. (1989). The application of temperament questionnaires scales to a British sample: Issues of reliability and validity: Reply. *Journal of Child Psychology and Psychiatry, 30*(4), 643–647.

Gibbs, M. V., Reeves, D., & Cunningham, C. C. (1987). The application of temperament questionnaires to a British sample: Issues of reliability and validity. *Journal of Child Psychology and Psychiatry, 28,* 61–77.

Gillespie, N. A., Cloninger, C. R., Heath, A. C., & Martin, N. G. (2003). The genetic and environmental relationship between Cloninger's dimensions of temperament and character. *Personality and Individual Differences, 35,* 1931–1946.

Gladstone, G., & Parker, G. (2005). Measuring a behaviorally inhibited temperament style: Development and initial validation of new self-report measures. *Psychiatry Research, 135,* 133–143.

Goldsmith, H. H. (1996). Studying temperament via the construction of the Toddler Behavior Assessment Questionnaire. *Child Development, 67,* 218–235.

Goldsmith, H. H., Buss, K. A., & Lemery, K. S. (1997). Toddler and childhood temperament: Expanded content, stronger genetic evidence, new evidence for the importance of environment. *Developmental Psychology, 33,* 891–905.

Goldsmith, H. H., Rieser-Danner, L. A., & Briggs, S. (1991). Evaluating convergent and discriminant validity of temperament questionnaires for preschoolers, toddlers, and infants. *Developmental Psychology, 27,* 566–579.

Goodman, R. (2001). Psychometric properties of the Strengths and Difficulties Questionnaire. *Journal of the American Academy of Child and Adolescent Psychiatry, 40,* 1337–1345.

Gordon, B. (1983). Maternal perception of child temperament and observed mother–child interaction. *Child Psychiatry and Human Development, 13,* 153–167.

Gray, J. A. (1972). The psychophysiological basis of Introversion–Extraversion: A modification of Eysenck's theory. In V. D. Nebylitsyn & J. A. Gray (Eds.), *The biological bases of individual behaviour* (pp. 182–205). San Diego, CA: Academic Press.

Gray, J. A. (1981). A critique of Eysenck's theory of personality. In H. J. Eysenck (Ed.), *A model for personality* (pp. 246–276). Berlin: Springer-Verlag.

Gustavsson, J. P., Jonsson, E. G., Linder, J., & Weinryb, R. M. (2003). The HP5 inventory: Definition and assessment of five health-relevant personality traits from a five-factor model perspective. *Personality and Individual Differences, 35*, 69–89.

Hagekull, B. (1985). The Baby and Toddler Behavior Questionnaire: Empirical studies and conceptual considerations. *Scandinavian Journal of Psychology, 26*, 110–122.

Halverson, C. F., Havill, V. L., Deal, J., Baker, S. R., Victor, J. B., Pavlopoulos, V., et al. (2003). Personality structure as derived from parental ratings of free descriptions of children: The Inventory of Child Individual Differences. *Journal of Personality, 71*(6), 996–1026.

Hart, S., Field, T., & Roitfarb, M. (1999). Depressed mothers' assessments of their neonates' behavior. *Infant Mental Health Journal, 20*, 200–210.

Hatton, D. D., Bailey, D. B., Hargett-Beck, M. Q., Skinner, M., & Clark, R. D. (1999). Behavioral style of young boys with fragile X syndrome. *Developmental Medicine and Child Neurology, 41*, 625–632.

Healey, D. M., Brozdinsky, L. K., Bernstein, M., Rabinovitz, B., & Halperin, J. M. (2010). Moderating effects of neurocognitive abilities on the relationship between temperament and global functioning. *Child Neuropsychology, 16*, 20–31.

Hegvik, R. L., McDevitt, S., & Carey, W. B. (1982). The Middle Childhood Temperament Questionnaire. *Developmental and Behavioral Pediatrics, 3*, 197–200.

Hendricks, A. A. J., Hofstee, W. K. B., & De Raad, B. (1999). The Five-Factor Personality Inventory. *Personality and Individual Differences, 27*, 307–325.

Henson, R. K. (2001). Understanding internal consistency reliability estimates: A conceptual primer on coefficient alpha. *Measurement and Evaluation in Counseling and Development, 34*, 177–189.

Herbst, J. H., Zonderman, A. B., McCrae, R. R., & Costa, P. T., Jr. (2000). Do the dimensions of the Temperament and Character Inventory map a simple genetic architecture?: Evidence from molecular genetics and factor analysis. *American Journal of Psychiatry, 157*, 1285–1290.

Hwang, J. (2004, April). *Development of a temperament self-report measure for young children.* Presentation at the biannual meeting of the Society for Research in Child Development, Boston.

Kagan, J. (1994). *Galen's prophecy.* New York: Basic Books.

Kagan, J. (1998). Biology and the child. In W. Damon & N. Eisenberg (Eds.), *Handbook of child psychology: Vol. 3. Social, emotional and personality development* (5th ed., pp. 177–235). New York: Wiley.

Kasch, K. L., Rottenberg, J., Arnow, B. A., & Gotlib, I. H. (2002). Behavioral activation and inhibition systems and the severity and course of depression. *Journal of Abnormal Psychology, 111*, 589–597.

Katz-Newman, R., & Johnson, J. H. (1986). Note on reliability of Parent Temperament Questionnaire. *Psychological Reports, 59*, 802.

Keogh, B. K., Pullis, M. E., & Cadwell, J. (1982). A short form of the Teacher Temperament Questionnaire. *Journal of Educational Measurement, 19*, 323–329.

Kim, G., Walden, T., Harris, V., Karrass, J., & Catron, T. (2007). Positive emotion, negative emotion, and emotion control in the externalizing problems of school-aged children. *Child Psychiatry and Human Development, 37*, 221–239.

Kochanska, G., Coy, K. C., Tjebkes, T. L., & Husarek, S. J. (1998). Individual differences in emotionality in infancy. *Child Development, 64*, 375–390.

Kochanska, G., Murray, K., Jacques, T. Y., Koenig, A. L., & Vandergeest, K. A. (1996). Inhibitory control in young children and its role in emerging internalization. *Child Development, 67*, 490–507.

Kusanagi, E. (1993). A psychometric examination of the Children's Behavior Questionnaire. *Annual Report of the Research and Clinical Center for Child Development, 15*, 25–33.

Laurent, J., Catanzaro, S., Joyner, T., Rudolph, K., Potter, K., Lambert, S., et al. (1999). A measure of positive and negative affect for children: Scale development and preliminary validation. *Psychological Assessment, 11*, 326–338.

Lehman, E. B., Steier, A., Guidash, K. M., & Wanna, S. Y. (2002). Predictors of compliance in toddlers: Child temperament, maternal personality, and emotional availability. *Early Child Development and Care, 172*, 301–310.

Lemery, K. S., Essex, M. J., & Smider, N. A. (2002). Revealing the relation between temperament and behavior problem symptoms by eliminating measurement confounding: Expert ratings and factor analysis. *Child Development, 73*, 867–882.

Lerner, R. M., Palermo, M., Spiro, A., & Nesselroade, J. R. (1982). Assessing dimensions of temperamental individuality across the life span: Dimensions of Temperament Survey (DOTS). *Child Development, 53*, 149–159.

Lonigan, C. J., Hooe, E. S., David, C. F., & Kistner, J. A. (1999). Positive and negative affectivity in children: Confirmatory factor analysis of a two-factor model and its relation to symptoms of anxiety and depression. *Journal of Consulting and Clinical Psychology, 67*(3), 374–386.

Lounsbury, J. W., Tatum, H., Gibson, L. W., Park, S., Sundstrom, E. D., Hamrick, F. L., et al. (2003). The development of a Big Five Adolescent Personality Inventory. *Journal of Psychoeducational Assessment, 21*, 111–133.

Luby, J. L., Svrakic, D. M., McCallum, K., Przybeck, T. R., & Cloninger, C. R. (1999). The Junior Temperament and Character Inventory: Preliminary validation of a child self-report measure. *Psychological Reports, 84*, 1127–1138.

Lyoo, I. K., Han, C. H., Lee, S. J., Yune, S. K., Ha, J. H., Chung, S. J., et al. (2004). The reliability and validity of the Junior Temperament and Character Inventory. *Comprehensive Psychiatry, 45*(2), 121–128.

Martin, R. P. (1988). *The Temperament Assessment Battery for Children.* Brandon, VT: Clinical Psychology Publishing.

Martin, R. P., & Bridger, R. (1999). *The Temperament Assessment Battery for Children—Revised (TABC-R).* Athens, GA: School Psychology Clinic.

McClowry, S. G. (1995). The development of the School-Age Temperament Inventory. *Merrill–Palmer Quarterly, 41*(3), 271–285.

McCrae, R. R., & Costa, P. T., Jr. (1996). Toward a new generation of personality theories: Theoretical contexts for the five factor model. In J. S. Wiggins (Ed.), *The five-factor model of personality: Theoretical perspectives* (pp. 51–87). New York: Guilford Press.

McCrae, R. R., & John, O. P. (1992). An introduction to the Five Factor Model and its applications. *Journal of Personality, 60*, 175–215.

McDevitt, S. C., & Carey, W. B. (1978). The measurement of temperament in 3–7 year old children. *Journal of Child Psychology and Psychiatry, 19*, 245–253.

McDevitt, S. C., & Carey, W. B. (1981). Stability of ratings vs. perceptions of temperament from early infancy to 1–3 years. *Journal of Orthopsychiatry, 51*, 342–345.

McIntosh, D. E., & Cole-Love, A. S. (1996). Profile comparisons between ADHD and non-ADHD children on the Temperament Assessment Battery for Children. *Journal of Psychoeducational Assessment, 14*, 362–372.

Medoff-Cooper, B., Carey, W. B., & McDevitt, S. (1993). The Early Infancy Temperament Questionnaire. *Developmental and Behavioral Pediatrics, 14*, 230–235.

Mervielde, I., & De Fruyt, F. (1999). Construction of the Hierarchical Personality Inventory for Children (HiPIC). In I. Mervielde, I. Deary, F. De Fruyt, & F. Ostendorf (Eds.), *Personality psychology in Europe* (pp. 107–127). Tilburg, the Netherlands: Tilburg University Press.

Messick, S. (1995). Validity of psychological assessment: Validation of inferences from persons' responses and performances as scientific inquiry into score meaning. *American Psychologist, 50*, 741–749.

Mian, N. D., Wainwright, L., Briggs-Gowan, M. J., & Carter, A. S. (2011). An ecological risk model for early childhood anxiety: The importance of early child symptoms and temperament. *Journal of Abnormal Child Psychology, 39*, 501–512.

Mullola, S., Ravaja, N., Lipsanen, J., Hirstiö-Snellman, P., Alatupa, S., & Keltikangas-Järvinen, L. (2010). Teacher-perceived temperament and educational competence as predictors of school grades. *Learning and Individual Differences, 20*, 209–214.

Muris, P., & Meesters, C. (2009). Reactive and regulative temperament in youths: Psychometric evaluation of the Early Adolescent Temperament Questionnaire—Revised. *Journal of Psychopathology and Behavioral Assessment, 31*, 7–19.

Naerde, A., Roysamb, E., & Tambs, K. (2004). Temperament in adults—reliability, stability, and factor structure of the EAS Temperament Survey. *Journal of Personality Assessment, 82*, 71–79.

Nunnally, J. C. (1967). *Psychometric theory.* New York: McGraw-Hill.

Nunnally, J. C. (1978). *Psychometric theory* (2nd ed.). New York: McGraw-Hill.

Nunnally, J. C., & Bernstein, I. H. (1994). *Psychometric theory* (3rd ed.). New York: McGraw-Hill.

Palisin, H. (1986). Preschool temperament and performance on achievement tests. *Developmental Psychology, 22*, 766–770.

Parade, S. H., & Leerkes, E. M. (2008). The reliability and validity of the Infant Behavior Questionnaire—Revised. *Infant Behavior and Development, 31*, 637–646.

Pauli-Pott, U., Mertesacker, B., Bade, U., Haverkock, A., & Beckmann, D. (2003). Parental perceptions and infant temperament development. *Infant Behavior and Development, 26*, 27–48.

Paunonen, S. V., Ashton, M. C., & Jackson, D. N. (2001). Nonverbal assessment of the Big Five personality factors. *European Journal of Personality, 15*, 3–18.

Plomin, R., & Rowe, D. C. (1977). A twin study of temperament in young children. *Journal of Psychology, 97*, 103–113.

Presley, R., & Martin, R. P. (1994). Toward a structure of preschool temperament: Factor structure of the Temperament Assessment Battery for Children. *Journal of Personality, 62*, 415–448.

Prior, M., Sanson, A., Oberklaid, F., & Northam, E. (1987). Measurement of temperament in one to three year old children. *International Journal of Behavioral Development, 10*, 121–132.

Pullis, M. E. (1979). *An investigation of the relationship between children's temperament and school adjustment.* Unpublished doctoral dissertation, University of California, Los Angeles.

Putnam, S. P., Gartstein, M. A., & Rothbart, M. K. (2006). Measurement of fine-grained aspects of toddler temperament: The Early Childhood Behavior Questionnaire. *Infant Behavior and Development, 29,* 386–401.

Rettew, D. C., Althoff, R. R., Dumenci, L., Ayer, L., & Hudziak, J. J. (2008). Latent profiles of temperament and their relations to psychopathology and wellness. *Journal of the American Academy of Child and Adolescent Psychiatry, 47,* 273–281.

Rothbart, M. K. (1981). Measurement of temperament in infancy. *Child Development, 52,* 569–578.

Rothbart, M. K., Ahadi, S. A., & Evans, D. E. (2000). Temperament and personality: Origins and outcomes. *Journal of Personality and Social Psychology, 78,* 122–135.

Rothbart, M. K., Ahadi, S. A., Hershey, K., & Fisher, P. (2001). Investigations of temperament at three to seven years: The Children's Behavior Questionnaire. *Child Development, 72,* 1394–1408.

Rothbart, M. K., & Bates, J. E. (2006). Temperament. In W. Damon, R. Lerner, & N. Eisenberg (Eds.), *Handbook of child psychology: Vol. 3. Social, emotional, and personality development* (6th ed., pp. 99–166). New York: Wiley.

Rothbart, M. K., Chew, K. H., & Gartstein, M. A. (2000). Assessment of temperament in early development. In L. T. Singer & P. S. Zeskind (Eds.), *Biobehavioral assessment of the infant* (pp. 190–208). New York: Guilford Press.

Rothbart, M. K., & Derryberry, D. (1981). Development of individual differences in temperament. In M. E. Lamb & A. L. Brown (Eds.), *Advances in developmental psychology* (Vol. 1, pp. 37–86). Hillsdale, NJ: Erlbaum.

Rothbart, M. K., & Gartstein, M. A. (2008). Temperament. In M. Haith & J. Benson (Eds.), *Encyclopedia of infant and early childhood development* (pp. 318–332). Oxford, UK: Elsevier.

Rowe, D. C., & Plomin, R. (1977). Temperament in early childhood. *Journal of Personality Assessment, 41,* 150–156.

Ruch, W., Angleitner, A., & Strelau, J. (1991). The Strelau Temperament Inventory—Revised (STI-R): Validity studies. *European Journal of Personality, 5,* 287–308.

Rudasill, K. M., Gallagher, K. C., & White, J. M. (2010). Temperamental attention and activity, classroom emotional support, and academic achievement in third grade. *Journal of School Psychology, 48,* 113–134.

Sanson, A. V., Prior, M., Garino, E., Oberklaid, F., & Sewell, J. (1987). The structure of infant temperament: Factor analysis of the Revised Infant Temperament Questionnaire. *Infant Behavior and Development, 10,* 97–104.

Sarafino, E. P. (2000). Tests of the relationship between children's temperament and asthma and of the reliability and validity of the Brief Scale of Temperament. *Journal of Genetic Psychology, 161,* 23–36.

Schaughency, E. A., & Fagot, B. I. (1993). The prediction of adjustment at age 7 from activity level at age 5. *Journal of Abnormal Child Psychology, 21,* 29–49.

Scheier, L. M., Casten, R. J., & Fullard, W. (1995). Latent-variable confirmatory factor analysis of the Adolescent Temperament Questionnaire. *Journal of Adolescent Research, 10,* 246–278.

Schoen, M. J., & Nagle, R. J. (1994). Prediction of school readiness from kindergarten temperament scores. *Journal of School Psychology, 32,* 135–147.

Seifer, R., Sameroff, A., Dickstein, S., Schillera, M., & Hayden, L. C. (2004). Your own children are special: Clues to the sources of reporting bias in temperament assessments. *Infant Behavior and Development, 27,* 323–341.

Sheeber, L. B., & Johnson, J. H. (1992). Child temperament, maternal adjustment, and changes in family life style. *American Journal of Orthopsychiatry, 62,* 178–185.

Simms, L. J. (2008). Classical and modern methods of psychological scale construction. *Social and Personality Psychology Compass, 2*(1), 414–433.

Snidman, N., Kagan, J., Riordan, L., & Shannon, D. (1995). Cardiac function and behavioral reactivity during infancy. *Psychophysiology, 32,* 199–207.

Streiner, D. L. (2003). Starting at the beginning: An introduction to coefficient alpha and internal consistency. *Journal of Personality Assessment, 80*(1), 99–103.

Strelau, J. (1998). *Temperament: A psychological perspective.* New York: Plenum Press.

Strelau, J., Angleitner, A., Bantelmann, J., & Ruch, W. (1990). The Strelau Temperament Inventory Revised (STI-R): Theoretical considerations and scale development. *European Journal of Personality, 4,* 209–235.

Strelau, J., & Zawadzki, B. (1993). The Formal Characteristics of Behavior—Temperament Inventory (FCB-TI): Theoretical assumptions and scale construction. *European Journal of Personality, 7,* 313–336.

Strelau, J., & Zawadzki, B. (1995). The Formal Characteristics of Behaviour—Temperament Inventory (FCB-TI): Validity studies. *European Journal of Personality, 9,* 207–229.

Strelau, J., Zawadzki, B., Oniszczenko, W., Angleitner, A., & Riemann, R. (2002). Genetic and environmental determinants of emotions: Data based on cross-country twin studies on temperament. *Polish Psychological Bulletin, 33,* 5–13.

Tellegen, A., & Waller, N. G. (2008). Exploring personality through test construction: Development of the Multidimensional Personality Questionnaire. In G. J. Boyle, G. Matthews, & D. H. Saklofske (Eds.), *The SAGE handbook of personality theory and assessment: Vol. 2. Personality measurement and testing* (pp. 261–292). Thousand Oaks, CA: Sage.

Thomas, A., & Chess, S. (1977). *Temperament and development.* New York: Brunner/Mazel.

Thomas, A., Mittelman, M., Chess, S., Korn, S. J., & Cohen, J. (1982). A temperament questionnaire for early adult life. *Educational and Psychological Measurement, 42,* 593–600.

Trull, T. J., Useda, J. D., Costa, P. T., & McCrae, R. R. (1995). Comparison of the MMPI-2 Personality Psychopathyology Five (PSY-5), the NEO-PI, and the NEO-PI-R. *Psychological Assessment, 7,* 508–516.

Vahip, S., Kesebir, S., Alkan, M., Yazici, O., Akiskal, K. K., & Akiskal, H. S. (2005). Affective temperaments in clinically-well subjects in Turkey: Initial psychometric data on the TEMPS-A. *Journal of Affective Disorders, 85,* 113–125.

Vaughn, B. E., Taraldson, B. J., Crichton, L., & Egeland, B. (1981). The assessment of infant temperament: A critique of the Carey Infant Temperament Questionnaire. *Infant Behavior and Development, 4,* 1–17.

Walden, T. A., Harris, V. S., & Catron, T. F. (2003). How I Feel: A self-report measure of emotional arousal and regulation for children. *Psychological Assessment, 15*(3), 399–412.

Watson, D., & Clark, L. A. (1991). *The PANAS-X: Preliminary manual for the Positive and Negative Affect Schedule—Expanded Form.* Dallas, TX: Authors.

Watson, D., Clark, L. A., & Tellegen, A. (1988). Development and validation of brief measures of positive and negative affect: The PANAS scales. *Journal of Personality and Social Psychology, 54,* 1063–1070.

Windle, M. (1992). Revised Dimensions of Temperament Survey (DOTS-R): Simultaneous group confirmatory factor analysis for adolescent gender groups. *Psychological Assessment, 4,* 228–234.

Windle, M., & Lerner, R. M. (1986). Reassessing the dimensions of temperamental individuality across the lifespan: The Revised Dimensions of Temperament Survey (DOTS-R). *Journal of Adolescent Research, 1,* 213–230.

Zhang, J., Xu, J., & Shen, L. (2000). The assessment of Carey's five temperament questionnaires. *Chinese Mental Health Journal, 14,* 153–156.

APPENDIX 10.1. Examples of Measures of Personality Containing Scales with Conceptual Overlap/Similarities to Temperament Characteristics

Measure	Total number of items in measure	Overlapping constructs (alpha)	Age group	First author (year of publication)
Big Five Questionnaire—Children	65	Extraversion (NR[a]) Emotional Instability (NR)	School age and early adolescent: 3–14 years	Barbaranelli et al. (2003)
Inventory of Children's Individual Differences	144	Extraversion (NR) *Positive Emotions*[b] (.83 to .86) *Sociability* (.84 to .88) *Activity Level* (.76 to .84) Neuroticism (NR) *Fearful/Insecure* (.73 to .79) *Shy* (.72 to .75) *Negative Affect* (.74 to .80)	3–14 years	Halverson et al. (2003)
Inventory of Children's Individual Differences—Short Version	45	Extraversion (NR) *Positive Emotions* (.85) *Sociability* (.81) *Activity Level* (.80) Neuroticism (NR) *Fearful/Insecure* (.71) *Shy* (.70) *Negative Affect* (.78)	3–14 years	Deal et al. (2007)
Adolescent Personal Style Inventory	55	Extraversion (.81 to .82) Neuroticism (.79 to .81)	11–18 years	Lounsbury et al. (2003)
Hierarchical Personality Inventory for Children	144	Extraversion (.79) Emotional Stability (NR)	6–12 years	Mervielde & De Fruyt (1999) De Bolle et al. (2009)
HP5 Inventory	20	Hedonic Capacity (NR) Negative Affectivity (NR)	Adults	Gustavsson et al. (2003)
Five Factor Nonverbal Personality Questionnaire	56	Extraversion (.75) Neuroticism (.64)	Adults	Paunonen et al. (2001)
Five-Factor Personality Inventory	100	Extraversion (.86) Emotional Stability (.85)	Adults	Hendricks et al. (1999)

[a]NR, not reported.
[b]Scales in *italics* are subscales, reflecting overlap with aspects of temperament, of the immediately preceding broad domain.

Chapter 11

Behavioral Assessment of Temperament

H. Hill Goldsmith
Jeffrey R. Gagne

Advances in temperament research are crucially dependent on the assessment methods available. In turn, the best methods for assessing temperament must be consonant with theoretical specifications and must change as temperament theory becomes more sophisticated and precise. In the simplest terms, temperament may be assessed via (1) self or others' perceptions and viewpoints, gleaned from questionnaires and, occasionally, interviews; (2) observed or recorded behavior, either extracted from a naturally occurring behavioral stream or elicited by specific incentives; or (3) recording of neurophysiological measures, again either naturally occurring or specifically elicited. Different temperament theories demand an emphasis on one of these three approaches or an integration of approaches. This chapter focuses on the second approach, behavioral assessment, as applied to infants and children. We argue that behavioral assessment should lie at the core of contemporary temperament research.

The field of temperament research overlaps with various disciplines of biobehavioral research (Gagne, Vendlinski, & Goldsmith, 2009), and each of these disciplines has favored assessment approaches to offer. Over the past two decades, connections between early temperament traits and later personality and psychopathology have assumed a central role in the field (e.g., Caspi, Roberts, & Shiner, 2005; Goldsmith, Lemery, & Essex, 2004). Personality research is dominated by questionnaire-based assessment approaches, and psychopathology research typically relies in part on structured interviews, as well as questionnaires. Thus, temperament assessment in the context of personality and psychopathology research often adopts the methods endemic to those contexts: questionnaires and interviews.

Although temperament theories have various emphases, all theories require close attention to specific facets of behavior. Unlike personality research, which typically employs questionnaire methods, temperament research, at least from the time of Pavlov, has been rooted in behavioral assessment techniques. Despite this history, most contemporary studies use parental rating scales as the primary means of assessing temperament. Typically, these studies do not include observational and laboratory-based assessments, even as a check on the validity of the questionnaire measures. Using parent ratings as the sole basis for assessment of child temperament introduces the potential for several biases, as detailed in a special section of *Infant Behavior and Development* in 2003 (Vol. 26, Issue 1).

Some researchers have honored the theoretical focus on constitutional origins of temperament by incorporating psychophysiological or neuroscience approaches into the study of temperament. Despite some promising efforts, including those reviewed by Rothbart (2007), a comprehensive delineation of temperament solely in terms of the structure and function of brain systems remains premature. Clearly, pathways involving dopamine and serotonin as neurotransmitters, limbic system function more generally, prefrontal inhibitory mechanisms, and attentional systems, including those instantiated in the anterior cingulate (Posner & Rothbart, 2007) will all play central roles in a comprehensive neuroscientific theory of temperament (see, in this volume, White, Lamm, Helfinstein, & Fox, Chapter 17; Depue & Fu, Chapter 18). The assessment of those systems will involve substantial instrumentation. However, without a comprehensive neuroscience-based conception of temperament, current temperament definitions and theory remain centered at the behavioral level.

Many researchers suggest that a multimethod perspective including behavioral assessments provides the best evidence for the significance of temperament to important developmental outcomes (Hwang & Rothbart, 2003). Relying on one method of temperament assessment (parent ratings, physiological approaches, or behavioral assessment) is likely an incomplete strategy, particularly if the method of assessment has demonstrable flaws. Therefore, the development of appropriate behavioral assessments is an important aspect of temperament research. The science of behavioral assessment has not converged on a consensus approach; instead, different approaches and protocols offer investigators a range of choices. Some tasks for the behavioral assessment of temperament are specific to a particular laboratory, investigator strategy, or domain/dimension of temperament. In addition, there are widely used computer-based measures, such as the stop-signal task for the assessment of inhibitory control, or mechanical assessments, such as motion recorders, that measure activity level. Finally, a few investigators have developed comprehensive behavioral assessment protocols that assess a wide range of temperament dimensions in the laboratory or home.

In this chapter, we first describe the historical and theoretical contexts for temperament assessment, with an emphasis on temperament theory and contemporary psychometrics. Then, we review temperament assessment research, focusing on the differences among behavioral assessment approaches, the pros and cons of behavioral assessment, and descriptions of selected single-domain and multidimensional approaches. We conclude the chapter with a description of current challenges for temperament assessment research. A guide to the terminology used in this chapter is provided in Table 11.1.

TABLE 11.1. Terminology Used in This Chapter

Temperament	used to refer collectively to sets of either dimensions or types that are specified by a theory or by general agreement among temperament researchers
Domain	used to refer to the "content" of either a dimension or type of temperament; for instance, "fearfulness" and "activity level" would be domains of temperament
Dimension	used to denote a continuously varying temperamental trait (contrasted to a dichotomous type)
Incentive	a simple or complex stimulus that typically evokes a reaction, usually of an affective nature
Episode	used generically to characterize structured events (situations, trials, vignettes) used in laboratory- or home-based assessment of temperament; episodes are distinguished by their incentive properties
Parameter	a measureable quantity of a response, such as latency, intensity, or duration

Historical and Theoretical Contexts for Behavioral Assessment of Temperament

Temperament concepts have been rooted in direct behavioral observations throughout most of the history of temperament research (see Chapter 4 by Kagan and Chapter 2 by Mervielde & De Pauw, this volume). For instance, Pavlov and his followers observed reactive and regulatory aspects of the canine nervous system, phenomena that correspond reasonably well with certain current temperament concepts (see Chapter 1 by Rothbart and Chapter 5 by Strelau & Zawadzki, this volume). In the late 1940s and 1950s, Escalona employed detailed and intensive observational methods to examine individual differences in personality development in healthy infants (Escalona & Leitch, 1952). Her observations of early emerging emotional and behavioral development laid some of the groundwork for contemporary temperament research. These and other early theorists all emphasized observed behavior as essential to the study of temperament.

Building on the work of these pioneers, Thomas and Chess began the classic New York Longitudinal Study (NYLS; Thomas, Chess, & Birch, 1968) of temperament in the early 1950s. They used parent interviews, school observations and teacher interviews, behavioral observations, clinical evaluations, and, later, interviews with the children to collect longitudinal behavioral data (Chess & Thomas, 1984). These data collection techniques focused on a wide range of daily activities assessed across several situations, and children were followed from birth until early adulthood. They rated children on nine temperament characteristics that they inferred from patterns of infant behavior: Activity, Regularity, Initial Reaction, Adaptability, Intensity, Mood, Distractibility, Persistence/Attention Span, and Sensitivity. Currently, the most commonly examined temperament dimensions are Activity Level, Anger/Frustration, Behavioral Inhibition/Fear, Effortful Control, and Positive Affect (Gagne et al., 2009; Zentner & Bates, 2008). Although these dimensions are not representative of any single theoretical framework, researchers have reached some consensus about their importance and have sometimes used observational measures to assess them.

Many theorists have conceptualized temperament categorically or typologically. Thomas and Chess discerned "easy," "difficult," and "slow-to-warm-up" patterns among their nine dimensions, and these three patterns constituted categories to complement the nine dimensions in their theory of temperament. Meehl (1992) and Kagan (1994), among others, emphasized that the issue of dimensions versus types is conceptually complex, and that types remain a viable yet understudied alternative to temperamental dimensions. Kagan's research focuses on the temperamental category of "reactivity" from an experimental child psychology perspective that relied on observational techniques. Kagan and his colleagues tested infants at several ages (4, 14, and 21 months) using behavioral assessments in the laboratory; for example, they presented novel stimuli and recorded infant behavioral reactions. Children who became aroused and distressed in the laboratory situation (in response to novel stimuli) at 4 months were categorized as highly reactive. Upon longitudinal follow-up, these children tended to develop fearfulness to unfamiliar events in the laboratory, and Kagan described them as behaviorally inhibited. By 4½ years of age, children assessed as inhibited in the laboratory at earlier ages were at higher risk for developing anxiety disorders. At 7 years of age, previously reactive infants were more behaviorally anxious than nonreactive infants and also showed distinct physiological reactions (Kagan, Snidman, Zentner, & Peterson, 1999). Thus, Kagan's approach (see Chapter 4, this volume) combined both the objective assessment strategy and the typological perspective. Although different implications follow from typological versus dimensional approaches, early innovators using both perspectives in temperament research emphasized the importance of behavioral assessment.

Objective behavioral approaches allow for the ability to capture very specific parameters and content of temperament that are largely inaccessible to questionnaire/interview or neuroscience-based approaches. Questionnaire and interview approaches generally inquire about more global behavioral patterns, and measures from neuroscience-based approaches seldom map to behavioral reactions in a one-to-one fashion. Many laboratory assessments are designed to elicit targeted behavioral reactions that occur in response to specific stimuli in the laboratory. Often, multiple parameters of response, such as latency, duration, and frequency of occurrence, are measured in the laboratory situation. Similarly, multiple response modalities (e.g., facial, gestural, vocal behaviors) can be captured in observational assessments. This microscopic level of assessment is not typically available outside of an observational setting; that is, asking a parent about a child's latency to express facial fear after the onset of a sudden and novel noise seems unlikely to result in a reliable answer. However, achieving this level of detail is a strength of behavioral assessment. These micro-level behavioral assessments also provide much richer, more nuanced illustrations of child behavior than responses to questionnaire/interview items or a single physiological assessment.

Because theories of temperament posit cross-situational consistency of temperament traits, investigators who employ behavioral assessments often average across contexts with related incentives before analyzing data. Similarly, temperament traits are generally viewed as extending across response modalities, such that facial, vocal, and instrumental reactions are often aggregated (Goldsmith & Campos, 1982). When aggregated, behavioral responses indicative of temperament may approach the generality characteristic of questionnaire assessment (although they differ in many other ways from parental report, of course). Importantly, we suggest that the individual questionnaire items do *not* approach the specificity of behavioral response parameters from laboratory-based assessments; instead, behavioral assessment captures parameters of response (usually affective response) that are largely inaccessible to questionnaires or interviews, or to neuroscience-inspired approaches. We believe that another advantage of behavioral assessment—one harder to support empirically—is that actual behavioral observations inspire theorizing in a way that parental questionnaire responses do not.

Selective Review of Temperament Assessment Research

Variation in Assessment Paradigms, Including Advantages and Pitfalls

The question of precisely *what* is assessed during behavioral assessment of temperament does not have a singular answer. Assessments may focus on one or several domains of temperament. Perhaps the most important distinction is between observations of naturally occurring behavior versus elicitation of targeted behavioral reactions. That is, a temperament researcher might unobtrusively observe children on a playground or in a classroom, much in the manner of an ethologist. This observer would use a coding system for the occurrence of behaviors thought to be indicative of temperament and would systematically sample the behavior of children. This observational approach effectively quantifies the frequencies and perhaps durations of target instrumental behaviors, although it may not be sensitive to nuances of facial and vocal affect or other subtle behaviors. Clearly, an advantage of this approach is ecological validity and lack of need for extensive instrumentation. On the other hand, observers need to be highly trained for real-time observation (although videotaping may also be feasible for observations of this sort).

The elicitation of specific behavioral responses is generally done in a laboratory context, or sometimes in other settings where a degree of standardization is possible. The key requirement for this type of assessment is that some theoretical orientation must guide the choice of eliciting stimuli. For example, if theory specifies that anger proneness is a domain of temperament, then stimuli that elicit anger should be used. Theory and prior empirical work must also guide the choice of what constitutes an incentive to anger (e.g., goal blockage, physical insult). The advantages of laboratory-based, objective, behavioral assessment of elicited behavior are familiar to any experimentalist (control of context, standardization of stimuli, use of instruments to present stimuli and record responses, etc.). A chief disadvantage is questionable ecological validity. Almost by definition, the laboratory context is novel, and interactions with an experimenter (who may be quite friendly but nevertheless is a stranger) are a prominent part of the assessment process. Thus, a child's reactions to novelty and strangers can conceivably color laboratory assessment of temperament domains that are ostensibly independent of fearfulness and shyness. Another problem with laboratory assessment is that children may become fatigued during the process, such that their reactions become unrepresentative of their everyday behavior. Yet another issue is that some temperament-related behaviors (e.g., sleep-related behaviors and soothability after becoming distressed) are difficult to assess within the confines of the laboratory. Similarly, crucial contexts, such as the presence of peers, are difficult to recreate in the laboratory. More generally, we worry that laboratory assessment is susceptible to "state" effects, whereas temperament is by definition a trait. This problem implies that multioccasion laboratory assessment is needed, at least for some research goals. Goldsmith and Rieser-Danner (1990), Rothbart and Goldsmith (1985), and Rothbart and Bates (1998) provide more detailed lists of advantages and pitfalls of different types of temperament assessment.

Descriptions of Selected Single-Domain Approaches

Several researchers have devised behavioral assessments that focus on a specific dimension or domain of temperament. For example, Kagan (1994) has developed extensive laboratory procedures to assess behavioral inhibition across ages. Infants' and toddlers' reactions to unfamiliar stimuli (both persons and objects) in several laboratory and home episodes are scored, as well as in episodes that involve separation from the mother. In longitudinal follow-up studies, older children were assessed for laboratory inhibition, peer play inhibition, and school inhibition. In general, behavioral inhibition is relatively stable across age using objective behavioral assessment. In addition, physiological measures, in combination with these behavioral assessments, have also been used to assess behavioral inhibition. Children who exhibit patterns of high- and low-reactive behaviors in the laboratory show differences in heart rate variability (Kagan, 1998; Kagan & Fox, 2006), and children who show greater right frontal activation on electroencephalographic (EEG) measures are more likely to react to these laboratory situations with avoidance and anxiety (Calkins, Fox, & Marshall, 1996; Kagan & Fox, 2006; also see Kagan, Chapter 4, this volume). Laboratory assessments have also been used to examine gene–environment interactions between the serotonin transporter promoter polymorphism and maternal social support, and behavioral inhibition (Fox et al., 2005; also see White et al., Chapter 17, this volume).

Eaton and Saudino examined early activity level using both objective mechanical measures and laboratory assessments, often in conjunction with parent and teacher ratings (Eaton, 1983; Saudino & Eaton, 1991, 1995; Saudino, Wertz, Gagne, & Chawla, 2004; Saudino & Zapfe, 2008). In earlier studies, analog actometers were worn on the dominant wrist of children, and scores composited across multiple assessments showed high reliability and significant agreement with parent and teacher ratings, even after accounting for age and gender effects (e.g., Eaton, 1983). In later investigations, similar actometers were attached to all four limbs, and composite scores were derived from the average of each child's limb scores (Saudino & Eaton, 1991, 1995). Composite reliability was high in infancy (7 months) and toddlerhood (35.4 months), and there was moderate convergence with parent ratings in infancy but not in toddlerhood. More recently, computerized actigraph motion recorders have been employed in related studies to similar effect (Saudino et al., 2004; Saudino & Zapfe, 2008; also see Saudino & Wang, Chapter 16, this volume). In general, correlations between actigraph scores and parent ratings were moderate or nonsignificant. Actigraph scores averaged across four limbs were also modestly associated with laboratory assessments of activity level (Saudino & Zapfe, 2008).

Kochanska's research on effortful control (EC) and inhibitory control (IC) also used laboratory-based assessments of temperament (Kochanska, Murray, & Coy, 1997;

Kochanska, Murray, & Harlan, 2000; Kochanska, Murray, Jacques, Koenig, & Vandegeest, 1996). Kochanska has typically employed a battery of laboratory episodes and computed composite variables of EC or IC based on aggregated scores from various intercorrelated behavioral indices. The laboratory tasks assess five components of EC/IC (Kochanska et al., 1996, 1997, 2000): delaying (e.g., waiting for a pleasant event), slowing down motor activity (e.g., walking or drawing), suppressing or initiating activity to a signal (e.g., games in which the child responds to one signal and inhibits to another signal), lowering one's voice (whispering), and effortful attention (Stroop-like paradigms). Children who are *unable* to delay gratification, to wait their turn, to slow down, to pay attention, or to modulate their speaking voice in the episodes receive lower EC/IC scores. In these studies, task reliability was generally high, and increased from 22 to 33 to 45 months of age. These EC assessments demonstrate substantial longitudinal stability (Kochanska & Knaack, 2003), and cross-method convergence with parent ratings, and longitudinal stability across methodologies are apparent in toddlers, preschoolers, and children at early school age (Kochanska et al., 1996, 1997, 2000). These studies show developmentally significant associations between EC/IC and ratings of conscience, emotion, and behavioral adjustment (Kochanska et al., 1996, 1997, 2000; Kochanska & Knaack, 2003). Spinrad, Eisenberg, and Gaertner (2007) review additional laboratory-based assessment approaches to regulatory features of temperament.

Computer-Based Assessments of Single Dimensions of Temperament

In addition to the aforementioned laboratory-based and mechanical assessments, many investigators employ computer-based tasks to assess single dimensions of temperament. These include assessments such as the continuous performance task (CPT; Dougherty, Marsh, & Mathias, 2002), the Attention Network Test (ANT; Fan, McCandliss, Sommer, Raz, & Posner, 2002), the stop-signal task (Logan, Schachar, & Tannock, 1997), go/no-go tasks (Barkley, 1991), and elements of the Cambridge Neuropsychological Test Automated Battery (CANTAB; Luciana & Nelson, 2002). Most of these assessments require participants to view nonverbal stimuli presented on a computer screen, to make decisions about these stimuli that require the activation or inhibition of cognitive processes; often, reaction times are measured. The CPT assesses attention and impulsivity; the ANT assesses alerting, orienting, and executive attention; the stop-signal and go/no-go tasks focus on participant response inhibition (sustained attention, goal orientation, and target detection); and the CANTAB includes assessments of attention, reaction time, decision making, and response control. These computer-based tasks are typically depicted as assessments of executive functioning and are more commonly employed by neuroscientists and psychopathology researchers than by temperament researchers (also see Rueda, Chapter 8, this volume). For example, although IC is often described as a temperament dimension, it can also be viewed as an executive function. Nevertheless, the assessed behavioral and cognitive domains are very similar, if not equivalent, to dimensions of temperament, including EC and IC, impulsivity, attention, and self-regulation. These computer-based assessments rarely focus on motor activity or emotional aspects of temperament.

Multidimensional Approaches

Assessing single dimensions of temperament allows researchers to be efficient and focused. However, there is a natural tradeoff between depth and breadth of measurement in observational research. For the field as a whole, narrower approaches need to be balanced by research programs that take a broader and more integrative view. Such broader approaches typically employ a multidimensional assessment that parallels multiscale temperament questionnaires. Although there are only a few multidimensional observational protocols that can be used to measure a range of temperament-related variables, this area of temperament assessment is active.

Multidimensional assessment can begin as early as the neonatal period. One prominent example, the Neonatal Behavioral Assessment Scale (NBAS; Brazelton, 1973;

Brazelton & Nugent, 1995), was often used to measure infant behavior in temperament investigations during the 1970s and early 1980s (Matheny, Riese, & Wilson, 1985). The NBAS includes several observationally assessed behavioral and reflex items that are used to construct a behavioral profile of the infant. Most studies that used NBAS factors to predict later temperament have yielded weak and inconsistent results, and it is well documented that the original goal of the NBAS was *not* to assess neonatal temperament (Goldsmith & Campos, 1982; Hubert, Wachs, Peters-Martin, & Gandour, 1982; Matheny et al., 1985; Sameroff, Krafchuk, & Bakow, 1978). The NBAS was designed to capture displays of complex social and emotional responses rather than specific dimensions of temperament (Matheny et al., 1985). Nevertheless, some temperament researchers continue to use it to assess infant irritability. A fourth edition of the NBAS was released as this chapter went to press (Brazelton & Nugent, 2011).

Many of the first researchers who adopted a multidimensional perspective used relatively free-flowing assessments in conjunction with cognitive and motor testing in early childhood. In the early stages of the Louisville Twin Study, Matheny (1980, 1983) used observational measures of child temperament based on the items from Bayley's Infant Behavior Record (IBR; Bayley, 1969). The IBR assesses a range of temperament-like infant behaviors that are observed in the cognitive testing situation of the Bayley Scales of Infant Development (Bayley, 1969). Factor analyses of the IBR yield Task Orientation, Affect–Extraversion, Activity, Auditory–Visual Awareness, and Motor Coordination dimensions of behavior. These assessments are not focused on eliciting specific temperament-related behavior; instead, observers provide global ratings based on their impressions of the child's behavior during the testing situations that target other characteristics. Although more fine-grained methods for measuring temperament in observational settings have been developed, the IBR is still used, often as part of a multimethod strategy. The most recent version of this instrument, the Bayley-III (Bayley, 2005), is often administered with an accompanying caregiver report, the Social–Emotional and Adaptive Behavior Questionnaire. The Social–Emotional part of this questionnaire taps social–emotional milestones that are typically achieved by certain ages, but it is not conceptualized within a temperamental framework.

In other Louisville Twin Study work (Matheny & Wilson, 1981; Wilson & Matheny, 1983), infants were confronted with a series of behavioral vignettes, with specific opportunities to interact with child testers and engage in play. One vignette was a standardized assessment of observed cuddling, and another employed a visible barrier task, behind which an attractive toy was placed. In these and other vignettes (i.e., puppet, and mechanical toy games), several behavioral categories were rated, leading to scores for emotional tone, activity, attentiveness, and social orientation, as judged by observers across all the episodes (Riese, 1998). Each behavioral dimension was rated every 2 minutes from videotapes, and acceptable interrater agreement was obtained. Summary scores reflecting both central tendency and variability across the rating intervals were then calculated. This approach was also extended for use with 36- and 48-month-olds in the same sample (Matheny, 1987). Although more sophisticated than those used with the IBR, these ratings and coding systems were not designed to elicit particular behaviors or to assess a specific structure of temperament.

Rothbart (1988) assessed the temperament dimensions of Activity Level, Smiling and Laughter, Distress to Limitations, and Fear in structured tasks in a laboratory setting. The frequency and intensity of target behaviors were assessed, and contextual information regarding the laboratory situations was obtained. These episodes were developed to elicit specific behavioral responses, and the dimensions assessed correspond to the prominent structure of Rothbart's questionnaires. In another study of infant temperament and emotion, Goldsmith and Campos (1990) assessed fearfulness and joy/pleasure using several laboratory vignettes. Fear was assessed in two visual cliff episodes and one stranger approach episode, and joy was assessed in a series of four game-like episodes. In the MacArthur Longitudinal Twin Study (Robinson, McGrath, & Corley, 2001), researchers included distinct episodes that elicit anger (restraint and toy removal), prohibition/inhibition (prohibition of touching an attractive toy), and behavioral inhibition (stranger approach) during laboratory visits with young children. The Rothbart (1988) and the Goldsmith and Campos (1986; 1990) studies were precursors of the approach used in the Laboratory Temperament Assessment Battery (Goldsmith & Rothbart, 1991).

The Laboratory Temperament Assessment Battery (Lab-TAB) is an objective, behaviorally based laboratory assessment battery for studying infant, toddler, and preschool temperament. The Lab-TAB uses standardized procedures intended to elicit and record targeted affective and behavioral reactions in the laboratory. One of the primary goals of the Lab-TAB is to provide a comprehensive standardized assessment, so that it will be unnecessary to develop new measures for each study, and so that results can be compared across laboratories. There are separate versions for prelocomotor infants who can reach (Goldsmith & Rothbart, 1991), locomotor infants and toddlers who can crawl or walk (Goldsmith & Rothbart, 1991), and preschoolers (Goldsmith, Reilly, Lemery, Longley, & Prescott, 1993). The Lab-TAB assessments yield scores for the following dimensions of temperament, depending on the age of the participant: Anger, Sadness, Fear, Shyness, Positive Affect, Approach, Activity Level, Persistence, and Inhibitory Control. Lab-TAB is designed to be used in a typical developmental research laboratory with experimental rooms and a control room with video equipment. Experimenters are trained to interact with the children and parents during a warm-up period, then administer the episodes. Lab-TAB episodes are designed to elicit reactions specific to various dimensions of temperament, and each dimension has multiple corresponding episodes, defined by conceptually similar incentives. For example, anger episodes include reactions to the following episodes: (1) gentle arm restraint by the parent; (2) attractive toy placed behind a barrier; (3) a brief separation from parents; and (4) confinement in a car seat. Depending on the Lab-TAB version, 20 or more episodes form the context for assessment. Research studies tend to use only a subset of the episodes.

Lab-TAB episodes contain multiple trials, and longer episodes are divided into shorter intervals or trials. Within each interval or trial, several child responses, such as smiling, reaching, or crying, are scored. In many cases, the presence or absence of a response is simply noted; however, typically, response parameters such as latency, duration, and intensity are coded. Data aggregation and composite formation strategies (see Figure 11.1) differ across studies that use the Lab-TAB. Often, correlated parameters of the same response within an episode (e.g., latency, mean level, and peak angry facial expression) are combined (Gagne, Van Hulle, Aksan, Essex, & Goldsmith, 2011). These response parameter–level composites are then examined for covariation with other response parameter–level composites, still within the episode (e.g., postural anger and facial anger). For example, "facial anger," "postural anger," and "protest" are lower-level composites that could be combined into an "anger" component within an episode with incentives such as blocked goals. These episode-level components can then be composited into higher-level "temperamental" composites that exhibit cross-situational consistency. The conceptual starting point for this strategy of data aggregation is the theoretical view of temperament as involving emotional and regulatory dimensions of behavior.

A recent investigation used a two-stage factor-analytic approach to explore the structure of preschool temperament as assessed with the Lab-TAB (Dyson, Olino, Durbin, Goldsmith, & Klein, 2012). The best-fitting model consisted of five dimensions of temperament (Sociability, Positive Affect/Interest, Dysphoria, Fear/Inhibition, and Constraint vs. Impulsivity) that overlap with the five-factor trait structure of adult personality, as well as with similar models derived from parent-report measures of temperament. Using Lab-TAB, researchers have the option to pursue more complex microanalytic data aggregation and reduction strategies such as these, or they can use a macro/global approach. Some researchers who find that a specific Lab-TAB episode captures a context that is crucial for evaluating a specific hypothesis thus use specific episode-based scores instead of aggregating across multiple episodes. Others prefer using a more global approach and use summary scores based on coding across all episodes. In

```
Discrete Trials or Episode Intervals

┌──────────┬──────────┬──────────┬──────────┐
│Transparent│Transparent│Transparent│Transparent│
│   Box    │   Box    │   Box    │   Box    │
│ Speed of │Mean Intensity│Speed of │Mean Intensity│
│Facial Anger│Facial Anger│Postural Anger│Postural Anger│
└──────────┴──────────┴──────────┴──────────┘
     ┌──────────┬──────────┬──────────┐
     │Transparent│Transparent│Transparent│
     │   Box    │   Box    │   Box    │
     │   Peak   │ Speed of │   Peak   │
     │Facial Anger│Frustration (3x)│Postural Anger│
     └──────────┴──────────┴──────────┘
```

Raw behavioral data: Transparent Box facial (scores range from 0-3), postural anger (scores range from 0-2) and presence of frustration variables across epochs.

Response parameter level: the mean, peak and speed of Transparent Box facial and postural anger, and the speed of frustration are calculated.

Episode level components: response parameters are averaged to form Transparent Box episode Anger score.

| Transparent Box Anger | End of Line Anger | Box Empty Anger |

Primary level temperament composite: episode level components averaged to form Anger composite.

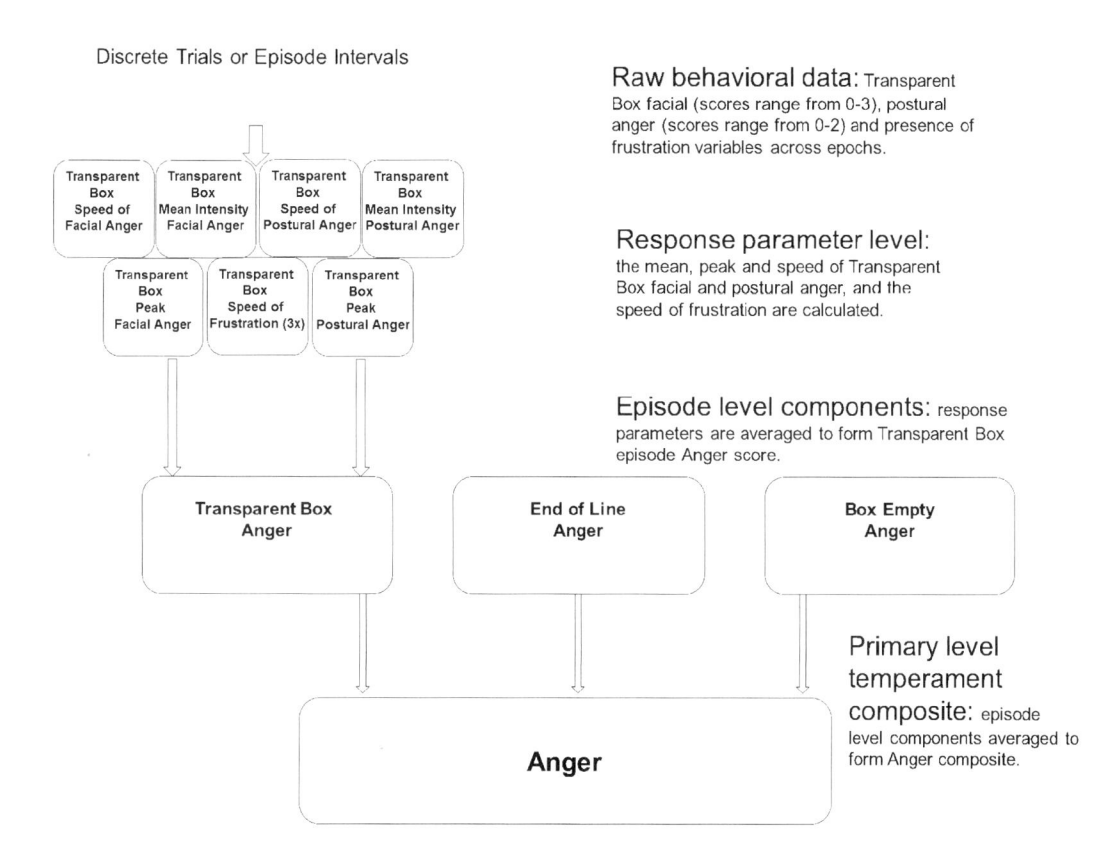

Anger

FIGURE 11.1. Depiction of the process of composite variable formation from a set of Lab-TAB episodes.

one recent study, micro-level and global coding schemes were developed for 12 Lab-TAB episodes (Hayden, Klein, & Durbin, 2005). Global coding involved raters watching an entire episode and making a rating based on all behaviors relevant to each dimension of temperament. Both the micro- and macro-level coding schemes were fairly equal in predictive power, and the global coding schemes were used in subsequent analyses (Durbin, Hayden, Klein, & Olino, 2007).

Once formed, Lab-TAB temperamental composites show low to moderate intercorrelations (e.g., Gagne et al., 2011; Gagne & Goldsmith, 2011; Pfeifer, Goldsmith, Davidson, & Rickman, 2002). Associations between dimensions within the Positive Affectivity domain and within the Behavioral Control–Regulation domain are significant, but Negative Affectivity dimensions show little correlation with one another, suggesting that negative emotions as assessed by the Lab-TAB are more distinct from one another in early childhood than positive emotions (Gagne et al., 2011). Generally, correlations between Lab-TAB dimensions and comparable questionnaire scales are lower than those between Lab-TAB and postvisit observer ratings. As Hane, Fox, Polak-Toste, Ghera, and Guner (2006) have shown, the convergence between Lab-TAB scores and maternal questionnaire report may depend on contextual factors, such as the affective quality of infant–mother interactive behavior in the home. Lab-TAB ratings of positive and negative emotionality at age 3 showed moderate to high levels of stability with matched laboratory assessments at 5–6 and 9 years (Durbin et al., 2007). These results were particularly robust, in that stability was high even though tasks were different across age. Laboratory temperament batteries that employ multiple, layered tasks not only provide a more nuanced measure of individual differences in emotional reactivity but also may offer more accurate estimates of change and stability (Durbin, 2010).

Home Observations of Naturally Occurring Behavior

Researchers have also used home observations of child behavior to assess temperament. Many of these investigators studied "naturally occurring" behavior, without eliciting specific reactions. This approach provides an assessment of behavior that occurs in a relatively natural context, although the presence of the observer in the home may alter the environment somewhat. Typically, these home observations last 1–3 hours, and one or more trained observers attempt to remain as unobtrusive as possible. Often, the observers apply the same rating scales that are used in parental questionnaires after an observation is over. In addition to the laboratory protocols described earlier, Rothbart (1986) also conducted home visits where she assessed activity level, positive affect, anger, fear, and vocal activity during bath, feeding, and play situations with infants at 3, 6, and 9 months of age. The dimensions corresponded to Infant Behavior Questionnaire (IBQ) scales. At each age, observations were conducted for 3 days, and the average score across all 3 days was used for each observational dimension score. Interrater correlations ranged from .56 to .90.

Bates, Freeland, and Lounsbury (1979) also collected home observation data on infants 5–7 months of age in validity studies of the Infant Characteristics Questionnaire (ICQ). Observers rated the frequency and duration of infant behaviors such as crying, and factor analyses yielded Fussiness, Negative versus Fun, and Soothability factors. In later studies, Bates and Bayles (1984) used trained observers both to make subjective ratings of child behavior and to record molecular events that took place during the observations with children at 6, 13, and 24 months of age. Different sets of factors were generated at each age based on the molecular data, and behavioral dimensions included social and motivational behavior, as well as temperament. Bornstein, Gaughan, and Homel (1986) combined data from maternal questionnaires with observer and maternal ratings of a 2-hour observation session. In all three domains of assessment, the same 62 behavioral items were used and items formed five dimensions: Positive Affect, Negative Affect, Persistence, Motor Responsivity, and Soothability. During the home observations, free-play periods and structured vignettes were alternated. Therefore, this approach preserves ecological validity, while also taking advantage of some of the strengths of laboratory-based protocols that use incentives to elicit temperamental reactions.

In addition to more free-flowing home observations, a few investigators have adopted laboratory-based protocols that elicit specific behavioral reactions for use in the home. Researchers often bring equipment and stimuli similar to those employed in laboratory episodes to the home, including video recording equipment. In the MacArthur Longitudinal Twin Study (Robinson et al., 2001), researchers included distinct episodes that elicited anger (restraint and toy removal), prohibition/inhibition (prohibition of touching an attractive toy), and behavioral inhibition (stranger approach) during home visits with young children. These home observations complemented their laboratory work. A home-based version of the Lab-TAB has also been developed and used on a community sample of 4½-year-old children (Gagne et al., 2011). In this study, the 12 Lab-TAB episodes yielded 24 within-episode temperament components that collapsed into nine higher-level dimensional composites.

Another version of the Lab-TAB was adapted for administration in a home setting and designed to assess dimensions of temperament potentially relevant to the development of psychopathology in school-age children (described in Gagne et al., 2011). The dimensions of temperament included in this assessment battery are Activity Level, Attention/Distractibility, Impulsivity, Inhibition, Persistence, Positive Affect, and Vulnerability to Negative Affect (and Regulation of Negative Affect). Given recent evidence for a possible temperamental basis to empathy and other prosocial behaviors (see Knafo & Israel, Chapter 9, this volume), we also included empathy and compliance in this protocol. For this home visit version of the Lab-TAB, 17 episodes that comprise the middle childhood version of Lab-TAB were used. Because home visits are often much more convenient for participants and may provide a more natural context for observing child behavior, we expect the use of home-based temperament assessment protocols to increase. The ease of administration of these assessments through the introduction of standardized stimuli and equipment into the home, video and computer technology advances, and no driving or parking issues for families, all contribute to the attractiveness of this approach.

Convergent and Discriminant Properties across Assessment Methods, and Their Interpretation

Although similar dimensions of temperament are often recovered from laboratory-based observational protocols and questionnaires, the literature on temperament clearly shows that observational measures and parental reports of the putatively "same" temperament trait often fail to show substantial agreement (Gagne et al., 2011; Goldsmith, Rieser-Danner, & Briggs, 1991; Mangelsdorf, Schoppe, & Buur, 2000; Saudino & Cherny, 2001; Seifer, Sameroff, Barrett, & Krafchuck, 1994). Typically, cross-method covariance is either low and nonsignificant or significant but relatively moderate; cross-method correlations of similarly named temperament measures often lie in the range of .10 to .40. In the Gagne and colleagues (2011) study that used the home-based Lab-TAB with 4½-year-olds, the nine dimensions of temperament (shown in Table 11.2) were similar to those found in questionnaire-based assessments. As was expected, agreement between Lab-TAB measures and postvisit observer ratings was stronger than agreement between the Lab-TAB and mother questionnaire. Similar findings of somewhat mixed or low agreement between temperament subscales or composites derived from observational approaches and parent reports occur in several studies.

Conceptually, this lack of agreement might result from (1) flaws in one or both of the assessment approaches or (2) fundamental differences in the features of temperament captured by the two approaches. Of course, the most obvious flaw would be that lack of agreement is mainly due to unreliability, as elaborated by Epstein (e.g., 1983, 1986). In short, validity (cross-method agreement, in this case) is limited by the degree of reliability. Reliability is improved by aggregation, and the ability to aggregate is more difficult for observational approaches than for questionnaires. A questionnaire can be lengthened or administered twice or more, with fewer conceptual and practical problems than would be associated with administering the same behavioral assessment twice or more.

The more fundamental difference that could account for lack of agreement is that the nature of, say, behavioral inhibition assessed by independent observers might differ from the nature of behavioral inhibition that parents report. Whereas careful scoring of videotaped behavior may capture flashes of fearful signals in the face and voice, parents may be more likely to miss these subtle signs and base their reports on withdrawal and distress that affect molar behavior and perhaps even interpersonal interaction.

Empirically, we noted that associations between Lab-TAB composites and corresponding postvisit observer rating variables were moderate and significant for all temperament dimensions in the study of 4½-year-olds (Gagne et al., 2011), providing evidence of convergent validity for the assessment, regardless of lower agreement with parent report. Recently, Saudino (2009) showed that parent-rated activity level in toddlers tapped different genetic and environmental factors than laboratory-based and mechanical ratings of activity level. Other studies have shown that parent and laboratory ratings have differential correlates to outcomes such as maternal depression (Gartstein & Marmion, 2008; Hayden et al., 2005). Using a multimethod perspective in temperament assessment is advantageous because multiple sources of information about participants' behavior allow for more general conclusions about the behavior being investigated. However, answers to substantive issues may differ depending on the methodology employed.

Lower covariance between observational assessments and parent ratings could be due to limited content overlap between the measures, despite similarities in how the dimensions are named. Postvisit observer ratings that show higher agreement with home/laboratory-based assessments are often conducted in the context of the laboratory or home visit. Therefore, the overlapping behavioral "content" being tapped by both

TABLE 11.2. Temperamental Traits Derived from a Home Administration of 12 Lab-TAB Episodes for 4½-Year-Olds

Temperament dimensions	Constituents of the episode-level components	Internal consistency (α)
Anger	• *Box Empty episode:* Anger component of mean, peak, speed of facial anger, postural anger, speed of frustration (9 items)	.93
	• *End of the Line episode:* Anger component of mean, peak, speed of facial anger, postural anger, speed of frustration (9 items)	.87
	• *Transparent Box episode:* Anger component of mean, peak, speed of facial anger, postural anger, speed of frustration (9 items)	.84
Sadness	• *Box Empty episode:* Sadness component of mean, peak, speed of facial sadness, postural sadness (6 items)	.87
	• *End of the Line episode:* Sadness component of mean, peak, speed of facial sadness, postural sadness (6 items)	.80
	• *Transparent Box episode:* Sadness component of mean, peak, speed of facial sadness, postural sadness (6 items)	.85
Fear	• *Spider episode:* Approach-related fear component of initial touch and peak wariness of approach (2 items)	($r = .77$)
	• *Spider episode:* Postapproach fear expression component of mean facial fear, bodily fear, vocal distress and withdrawal (4 items)	.87
Shyness	• *Stranger Approach episode:* Shyness component of approach and shyness ratings across two raters (4 items)	.90
Positive Expression	• *Bookmark episode:* Smiling component of mean, peak and speed of smiling (3 items)	.73
	• *Popping Bubbles episode, low-intensity trials:* Positive affect expression component of mean, peak and speed of smiling, % intervals laughter (6 items)	.78
	• *Popping Bubbles episode, high-intensity trials:* Positive affect expression component of mean, peak and speed of smiling, % intervals laughter (4 items)	.84
	• *Pop-Up Snakes episode:* Positive affect expression component of mean, peak and speed of smiling, % intervals laughter (14 items)	.88
Approach	• *Box Empty episode:* Anticipation component of mean, peak, speed of anticipatory behavior (3 items)	.94
	• *Perpetual Motion episode:* Approach component of mean and peak of active approach, mean frequency of touches, and speed of anticipatory behavior (4 items)	.86
	• *Popping Bubbles episode, low-intensity trials:* Approach component of mean, peak, speed of vigor of approach (3 items)	.76
	• *Popping Bubbles episode, high-intensity trials:* Approach component of mean, peak, speed of vigor of approach (2 items)	($r = .83$)
	• *Pop-Up Snakes episode:* Approach component of mean, peak, speed of vigor of approach (6 items)	.84
Active Engagement	• *Bookmark episode:* Active engagement component of mean, peak of active approach (2 items)	($r = .62$)
	• *Workbench episode:* Activity level component of mean, peak of play (2 items)	($r = .62$)
Persistence	• *Perpetual Motion episode:* Persistence component of % time on task and latency to off-task behavior (2 items)	($r = .52$)
	• *Transparent Box episode:* Persistence component of % time on task and latency to off-task behavior (2 items)	($r = .83$)
Inhibitory Control	• *Dinky Toys episode:* Inhibitory control component of mean and speed of impulsivity across trials (4 items)	.50
	• *Snack Delay episode:* Inhibitory control component of global inhibitory control across trials (4 items)	.75

Note. From Gagne, Van Hulle, Aksan, Essex, and Goldsmith (2011). Copyright 2011 by the American Psychological Association. Reprinted by permission.

the laboratory-based assessments and post-visit observer ratings probably contributes to their relatively high covariance, whereas parent questionnaires are based on parental impressions of child behavior in much broader contexts than a single assessment visit. Another element in interpreting findings of low agreement is that mothers probably view their children's behavior much more pragmatically than do researchers, who are trained to assess the subtleties of emotional reactions and changes. Mothers' concerns may be with the relative "success" of the child's behavior; that is, mothers may focus on the child's ability to negotiate a task or situation regardless of the affective quality of the child's engagement in the task. For example, if a child tolerates the presence of strangers with little intervention, and if these situations usually "work out" without disruption, mothers might be less inclined to rate the child as being fearful of strangers, regardless of fearful emotional expressions the child might show during interactions with strangers. Analogous laboratory-based assessments (e.g., stranger approach episodes) focus on the specific emotional reactions of the child rather than emphasizing the resolution of the episode.

A clear advantage of objective assessment of temperament is its flexibility. Different data reduction schemes allow temperament to be characterized in terms of specific reactions to specific eliciting stimuli, as well as in terms of more functional units of behavior, such as emotion–attention or emotion–action pairings that occur simultaneously. For example, in the Transparent Box episode of the Lab-TAB, the child is assessed for a range of anger and sadness reactions (e.g., facial, bodily, and vocal), persistence ("stops"), and attention (gaze shifts). Attending to this task and expressing anger simultaneously is qualitatively different from simply being rated "high" on questionnaire scales tapping attention and anger. Many objective assessments allow us to encapsulate situational expressions of emotion and attention–action across multiple episodes, with various target and secondary behaviors assessed. Depending on the coding and data reduction scheme, such episodes and coding systems can lend greater richness and flexibility to temperament assessment than standardized questionnaires or global observer ratings. The molecular view contributes to the work of researchers interested in the specificity of emotional expression in the context of individual tasks, multiple expressions of emotion within a situation (e.g., anger and sadness), and the stability of emotion and temperament across eliciting contexts. It is important to note that Lab-TAB episodes can also be coded from a global perspective (much like some parent and observer ratings), wherein coders view a range of videotaped episodes and rate their overall impression of the child's temperament. Thus, depending on the goals of a given study, objective assessments of temperament yield different types of data.

The data structure produced by nuanced objective assessments that use multiple elicited behavioral episodes also affords structural equation modeling and multilevel modeling (MLM) statistical approaches. Kiel and Buss (2006) applied MLM to Lab-TAB data collected in a toddler sample, and Durbin (2010) discussed the advantages of MLM approaches. In brief, MLM can be employed to model the temperamental reactivity for a particular emotion as a function of the "potency" of the task or situation. The specific emotion or temperament dimension is identified as the dependent variable, and the tasks are assigned a potency value indexing ability to elicit that variable. For example, a stranger approach laboratory task would have a high potency value for fear, but a low potency value for other aspects of temperament (Durbin, 2010). These analyses provide both overall emotion–temperament scores (the intercept) and the slope of the emotion variable across increasingly potent laboratory episodes. Slopes, which capture some of the dynamics of expression, may inform us of regulatory features of temperament that are risk factors for later psychopathology. Thus, MLM can improve the estimation of cross-contextual consistency and inconsistency, and suggest better strategies for relating temperament to functional outcomes.

Challenges to Temperament Assessment

The past 30 years have witnessed tremendous advances in temperament assessment, from rather casually constructed measures to measures that are comparable in quality to those used in personality research more generally. On the other hand, even the best contemporary temperament assessment falls far short of what would be optimal. Here, we mention key challenges facing the temperament assessment field. Temperament assessment in general, and behavioral assessment of temperament in particular, requires substantial development to reach its potential. Some of the challenges are psychometric in nature, whereas others require taking advantage of evolving technology.

Recognizing the Psychometric Features of Observed and Elicited Behavior

To date, the *measurement approach to behavioral assessment*—that is, the process of transforming scored behaviors into variables for analysis—has imitated the approach to questionnaire items. At the risk of oversimplifying, investigators who construct questionnaires tend to generate relevant items derived from their explicit or implicit theories of temperament. Then, using classical true and error score measurement theory, they form scales by some combination of (1) maximizing scale internal consistency; (2) minimizing items' correlations with scales to which they are not assigned; (3) factor-analyzing items using exploratory and/or confirmatory methods; then often (4) factor-analyzing scales to identify patterns of scale covariation. This approach is reasonable enough for questionnaire items. But should this approach be applied to objectively observed or elicited behavior? Not uncritically, in our opinion.

If we think of Lab-TAB episodes as used by many of the investigators we have cited, we must realize that many of the scored parameters of response do not meet the basic, required independence of variables for many multivariate approaches. When a mother answers, say, item 20 on a questionnaire, her response is not operationally constrained by her answer to item 19. However, a toddler who cries during a 5-second scoring interval of a Lab-TAB episode is likely constrained from smiling broadly in the next 5-second interval by the nature of his or her physiology. Similar constraints would apply to the behavior of children engaged in a dispute on the playground; that is, the structure of social interactions constrains the extent of second-by-second behavioral change of the participants in the interaction. More concretely, we suggest that the check marks, circles, and numbers on a typical behavioral coding sheet are generally *not* comparable data to the responses on a questionnaire answer sheet. What is the implication of this incomparability? We suggest that the main implication is a caution against factor-analyzing laboratory data gathered across episodes with different incentives. In a field in which temperament traits are the targeted source of variation among behaviors, laboratory episodes that strongly direct children's attention and constrain their behavior will be a potent competing source of variation.

Transitioning to Item Response Theory Approaches

Another challenge is more statistical in character. In the broader world of psychological and educational assessment, the state-of-the-art approach to scale construction and evaluation is item response theory (IRT). However, IRT approaches have yet to be applied to either questionnaire scale or behavioral composite construction in the temperament domain. An explication of IRT is beyond the scope of this chapter (see Embretson & Reise, 2000), but one element of the approach is an explicit modeling of an individual's trait level in the item-analytic process. Because most temperament assessment is essentially an effort to quantify trait levels, IRT would seem well suited as a method for constructing temperament scales. Careful attention to item difficulty within the classical approach to scale construction provides some of the advantages of the IRT approach, but a full IRT approach brings several other key advantages, including the possibility of more efficient testing. Given the extensive time required for behavioral assessment, any technique that allows tailoring the assessment to the individual's trait level is to be welcomed. Research reports suggesting initial directions for incorporating IRT approaches into the temperament field include Emons, Meijer, and Denollet (2007) and Gelhorn and colleagues (2009).

Distinguishing Reactivity and Regulation

Another major challenge to behavioral assessment of temperament is cleanly distinguishing reactive from regulatory features. At the outset, we suggest that attempts to achieve this distinction with behavioral approaches alone (i.e., without physiological measures) may be futile endeavors. Neuroscientific approaches that incorporate the time course of responses (*affective chronometry*; Davidson, Jackson, & Kalin, 2000) appear more promising (Goldsmith, Pollak, & Davidson, 2008).

We previously reported a lack of distinction among measures intended to tap inhibitory control, inattention, and impulsivity (Ruf, Goldsmith, Lemery-Chalfant, & Schmidt, 2008). In describing Eisenberg's puzzle box task, Spinrad and colleagues (2007) comment that the task "probably assesses a combination of attentional persistence, inhibitory control, and impulsivity" (p. 612). In other words, both reactive and regulatory processes influence the children's observed behavior; similarly, multiple features of reactive temperament can be elicited in a complex situation (Rothbart & Sheese, 2007). We suspect that this is often the case; that is, observed behavior is difficult to parse cleanly into reactive and regulatory features.

Emotion regulation—a topic closely related to regulatory features of temperament—has become a vast topic in developmental, personality, and social psychology. In fact, an entire recent handbook is devoted to emotion regulation (Gross, 2007). It is beyond the scope of this chapter to analyze or even enumerate the varieties of emotion regulation that have been theoretically specified. Regulatory processes can be automatic or strategic; they can precede or follow behavioral reactions; they can involve various attentional systems; and they can be general or emotion-specific—to mention only a few distinctions in the literature. Eisenberg, Champion, and Ma (2004) recount the history of emotion regulation constructs and mention some of the assessment quandaries that we treat here. Our point is that temperament assessment research has not kept pace with conceptual distinctions relating to emotional regulation, precluding quantification and comparison of individual differences in the family of regulatory constructs.

The Need for Fresh Thinking about the Domains of Temperament

Another challenge to temperament assessment research is exploring understudied domains of temperament. Thomas and Chess deserve great credit for educing nine domains of temperament that were not then commonly studied. Since then, however, many investigators have targeted the Thomas and Chess dimensions rather than testing other possibilities. The strongest recent tendencies in the field have been toward achieving a consensus on a few broad factors of temperament, under the influence of the Five-Factor Model described by Mervielde and De Pauw (Chapter 2, this volume), for instance. Thus, investigators have tried to match the Five-Factor Model of personality research with its temperamental counterparts. While such matching is clearly worthwhile and integrative, it may leave some of the territory of temperament unmapped. One early, welcome countertrend to premature constriction of the temperamental domain has been Rothbart's questionnaire-based temperament assessment program. Her revision of the Infant Behavior Questionnaire (IBQ-R) expanded the number of scales from six to 14, and her toddler questionnaire is similarly broad. We have revised and expanded our toddler questionnaire multiple times since its initial validation studies were published (e.g., Goldsmith, 2003). Examples of "unusual" scales from Rothbart's IBQ-R include Vocal Reactivity, Falling Reactivity/Rate of Recovery from Distress, Perceptual Sensitivity, and a distinction between scales that measure High- and Low-Intensity Pleasure. We view these and other expansions of content as healthy signs for the field. Moving to laboratory-based temperament assessment, we have recently derived nine primary temperament domains from a set of 12 episodes (Gagne et al., 2011), as described in Table 11.2. The implication is that with more episodes, our horizons for the number of primary temperament dimensions could expand.

We emphasize that narrower domains of temperament can be fully valid and may be more predictive of specific outcomes than broad domains such as negative emotionality. For instance, it seems curious that while individual differences in the hedonically negative affects of fear, sadness, and anger are often viewed as "temperamental" (e.g., anger proneness), another hedonically negative affect, disgust, is seldom viewed in that way. However, individual differences in disgust–sensitivity are apparent, and information about the neural signature of disgust is available (e.g., Adolphs, Tranel, & Damasio, 2003; Phan, Wager, Taylor, & Liberzon, 2002). Because of their phenomenological similarity and their overlapping neural circuitry, disgust and obsessive–compulsive disorder (OCD) are hypothesized to be related (Phillips, Senior, Fahy, & David, 1998). For these and several other reasons, disgust is a prime candidate for a "new" domain of temperament, one that is amenable to laboratory-based measurement.

Another need in temperament research is to parse the broad domain of positive emotionality. As noted earlier, Rothbart usefully distinguished high- from low-intensity positive affect, which was a crucial first step in this process. Phenomenologically, distinctions among positive affects include awe, anticipation, amusement, relief, sensory pleasure, pride in achievement, the thrill of excitement, satisfaction, and contentment (Ekman, 1992). We have demonstrated EEG patterns that dynamically change with a specific feature of positive emotionality, increasing positive anticipation (Light, Goldsmith, Coan, Frye, & Davidson, 2009). These and other lines of research suggest that an overarching concept of positive emotionality may obscure distinctions that biologically informed views of temperament will demand. The same might be claimed for other affective domains.

The Need for Fresh Thinking about Assessment Methods

The broad enterprise of measurement and assessment in any field involves tensions and compromises. On the one hand, pressure develops in a field to adopt a uniform set of instruments and to designate these instruments as the "gold standard." Unlike infant attachment research (the "Strange Situation"), adult personality research (the "Big Five"), and psychiatric diagnoses, temperament research has not yet experienced a strong press for uniformity in assessment. However, one can understand reasons for this pressure; on the one hand, uniform assessment practices lend coherence to a literature and allow more confident comparison of findings. On the other hand, many aspects of human behavior are poorly understood, and as understanding grows, improved assessments that incorporate these new insights are needed. Thus, we think that the field of temperament research will be well served by an attitude that current assessment is never "good enough." Witness the startling advances in DNA sequencing methods since the seminal work of Sanger and colleagues in the 1970s. The earliest methods of DNA sequencing were workable and accurate, but cheaper and faster methods that employ new bioengineering insights are being developed at an accelerating pace. The field of temperament research needs to encourage insights about assessment that are "outside the box."

One question requires fresh thinking: How can we formulate affordable assessment approaches for large samples (e.g., >1,000) that avoid the biases of questionnaires? Obviously, Internet-based protocols can be part of the answer to this question, but simply providing questionnaires via websites to respondents in a way that allows greater convenience to both investigator and respondent is only an initial step. More compellingly, capturing massive corpuses of behavioral data through Internet-based protocols that stream video from settings such as day care centers should be feasible. Algorithms that cull behavioral patterns indicative of temperament from such corpuses would be needed. It should also be feasible to blend interview and observational methods with clever use of videotaped exemplars of child behavior, an approach that we explored some years ago (Rothbart & Goldsmith, 1985) but did not exploit due to complexities such as dealing with the physical similarity of exemplars to children being assessed. Contemporary digital methods of rendering human likenesses might be capable of addressing this complexity. In any case, modern video techniques and computer technology have not been sufficiently exploited to improve temperament assessment; both technical expertise and outside-the-box thinking about assessment are needed for this exploitation.

Acknowledgments

Preparation of this chapter was supported by research grants from the National Institute of Mental Health (Nos. R01 MH59785 and R37 MH50560 to H. Hill Goldsmith) and the Wisconsin Center for Affective Science (No. P50 MH069315). Jeffrey R Gagne was supported by postdoctoral training grants (Nos. T32 MH75880 and T32 MH18931). Infrastructure support was provided by the Waisman Center via a core grant from the National Institute of Child Health and Human Development (No. P30 HD03352).

Further Reading

Durbin, C. E., Hayden, E. P., Klein, D. N., & Olino, T. M. (2007). Stability of laboratory assessed temperament traits from ages 3 to 7. *Emotion*, 7, 388–399.

Gagne, J. R., Van Hulle, C. A., Aksan, N., Essex, M. J., & Goldsmith, H. H. (2011). Deriving childhood temperament measures from emotion-eliciting behavioral episodes: Scale construction and initial validation. *Psychological Assessment*, 23, 337–353.

Saudino, K. J., Wertz, A. E., Gagne, J. R., & Chawla, S. (2004). Night and day: Are siblings as different in temperament as parents say they are? *Journal of Personality and Social Psychology*, 87, 698–706.

References

Adolphs, R., Tranel, D., & Damasio, A. R. (2003). Dissociable neural systems for recognizing emotions. *Brain and Cognition*, 52, 61–69.

Barkley, R. A. (1991). The ecological validity of laboratory and analogue assessments of ADHD symptoms. *Journal of Abnormal Child Psychology*, 19, 149–178.

Bates, J. E., & Bayles, K. (1984). Objective and subjective components in mothers' perceptions of their children from age 6 months to 3 years. *Merrill–Palmer Quarterly*, 30, 111–130.

Bates, J. E., Freeland, C. A. B., & Lounsbury, A. L. (1979). Measurement of infant difficultness. *Child Development*, 50, 794–803.

Bayley, N. (1969). *Bayley Scales of Infant Development*. New York: Psychological Corporation.

Bayley, N. (2005). *Bayley Scales of Infant and Toddler Development, Third Edition (Bayley-III)*. San Antonio, TX: Pearson.

Bornstein, M. H., Gaughan, J. M., & Homel, P. (1986). Infant temperament: Theory, tradition, critique, and new assessments. In C. E. Izard & P. B. Read (Eds.), *Measuring emotions in infants and children* (Vol. 2, pp. 172–199). New York: Cambridge University Press.

Brazelton, T. B. (1973). *Neonatal Behavioral Assessment Scale*. Philadelphia: Lippincott.

Brazelton, T. B., & Nugent, J. K. (1995). *The Neonatal Behavioral Assessment Scale*. London: Mac Keith Press.

Brazelton, T. B., & Nugent, J. K. (2011). *The Neonatal Behavioral Assessment Scale, Fourth Edition*. London: Mac Keith Press.

Calkins, S. D., Fox, N. A., & Marshall, T. R. (1996). Behavioral and physiological antecedents of inhibited and uninhibited behavior. *Child Development*, 67, 523–540.

Caspi, A., Roberts, B. W., & Shiner, R. L. (2005). Personality development: Stability and change. *Annual Review of Psychology*, 56, 453–484.

Chess, S., & Thomas, A. (1984). *Origins and evolution of behavior disorders: From infancy to early adult life*. Cambridge, MA: Harvard University Press.

Davidson, R. J., Jackson, D. C., & Kalin, N. H. (2000). Emotion, plasticity, context, and regulation: Perspectives from affective neuroscience. *Psychological Bulletin*, 126, 890–909.

Dougherty, D. M., Marsh, D. M., & Mathias, C. W. (2002). Immediate and delayed memory tasks: A computerized behavioral measure of memory, attention, and impulsivity. *Behavior Research Methods, Instruments and Computers*, 34, 391–398.

Durbin, C. E. (2010). Modeling temperamental risk for depression using developmentally sensitive laboratory paradigms. *Child Development Perspectives*, 4, 168–173.

Durbin, C. E., Hayden, E. P., Klein, D. N., & Olino, T. M. (2007). Stability of laboratory assessed temperament traits from ages 3 to 7. *Emotion*, 7, 388–399.

Dyson, M. W., Olino, T. M., Durbin, C. E., Goldsmith, H. H., & Klein, D. E. (2011). The structure of temperament in preschoolers: A two-stage factor analytic approach. *Emotion*, 12, 44–57.

Eaton, W. O. (1983). Measuring activity level with actometers: Reliability, validity, and arm length. *Child Development*, 54, 720–726.

Eisenberg, N., Champion, C., & Ma, Y. (2004). Emotion-related regulation: An emerging construct. *Merrill–Palmer Quarterly*, 50, 236–259.

Ekman, P. (1992). An argument for basic emotions. *Cognition and Emotion*, 6, 169–200.

Embretson, S. E., & Reise, S. P. (2000). *Item response theory for psychologists*. Mahwah, NJ: Erlbaum.

Emons, W. H., Meijer, R. R., & Denollet, J. (2007). Negative affectivity and social inhibition in cardiovascular disease: Evaluating type-D personality and its assessment using item response theory. *Journal of Psychosomatic Research, 63,* 27–39.

Epstein, S. (1983). Aggregation and beyond: Some basic issues on the prediction of behavior. *Journal of Personality, 51,* 360–392.

Epstein, S. (1986). Does aggregation produce spuriously high estimates of behavior stability? *Journal of Personality and Social Psychology, 50,* 1199–1210.

Escalona, S., & Leitch, M. (1952). Early phases of personality development: A non-normative study of infant behavior. *Monographs of the Society for Research in Child Development, 17*(1, Serial No. 54).

Fan, J., McCandliss, B. D., Sommer, T., Raz, A., & Posner, M. I. (2002). Testing the efficiency and independence of attentional networks. *Journal of Cognitive Neuroscience, 14,* 340–347.

Fox, N. A., Nichols, K. E., Henderson, H. A., Rubin, K., Schmidt, L., Hamer, D., et al. (2005). Evidence for a gene–environment interaction in predicting behavioral inhibition in middle childhood. *Psychological Science, 16,* 921–926.

Gagne, J. R., & Goldsmith, H. H. (2011). A longitudinal analysis of anger and inhibitory control in twins from 12 to 36 months of age. *Developmental Science, 14,* 112–124.

Gagne, J. R., Van Hulle, C. A., Aksan, N., Essex, M. J., & Goldsmith, H. H. (2011). Deriving childhood temperament measures from emotion-eliciting behavioral episodes: Scale construction and initial validation. *Psychological Assessment, 23,* 337–353.

Gagne, J. R., Vendlinski, M. K., & Goldsmith, H. H. (2009). The genetics of childhood temperament. In Y.-K. Kim (Ed.), *Handbook of behavioral genetics* (pp. 251–267). New York: Springer.

Gartstein, M. A., & Marmion, J. (2008). Fear and positive affectivity in infancy: Convergence/discrepancy between parent-report and laboratory-based indicators. *Infant Behavior and Development, 31,* 227–238.

Gelhorn, H., Hartman, C., Sakai, J., Mikulich-Gilbertson, S., Stallings, M., Young, S., et al. (2009). An item response theory analysis of DSM-IV conduct disorder. *Journal of the American Academy of Child and Adolescent Psychiatry, 48,* 42–50.

Goldsmith, H. H. (2003). The *Toddler Behavior Assessment Questionnaire—Revised.* Unpublished test, Waisman Center, University of Wisconsin–Madison, Madison.

Goldsmith, H. H., & Campos, J. J. (1982). Toward a theory of infant temperament. In R. N. Emde & R. J. Harmon (Eds.), *The development of attachment and affiliative systems* (pp. 161–193). New York: Plenum Press.

Goldsmith, H. H., & Campos, J. J. (1986). Fundamental issues in the study of early temperament: The Denver Twin Temperament Study. In M. E. Lamb, A. L. Brown, & B. Rogoff (Eds.), *Advances in developmental psychology* (Vol. 4, pp. 231–283). Hillsdale, NJ: Erlbaum.

Goldsmith, H. H., & Campos, J. J. (1990). The structure of temperamental fear and pleasure in infants: A psychometric perspective. *Child Development, 61,* 1944–1964.

Goldsmith, H. H., Lemery, K. S., & Essex, M. J. (2004). Temperament as a liability factor for childhood behavioral disorders: The concept of liability. In L. F. DiLalla (Ed.), *Behavior genetics principles: Perspectives in development, personality, and psychopathology* (pp. 19–39). Washington, DC: American Psychological Association.

Goldsmith, H. H., Pollak, S. D., & Davidson, R. J. (2008). Developmental neuroscience perspectives on emotion regulation. *Child Development Perspectives, 2,* 132–140.

Goldsmith, H. H., Reilly, J., Lemery, K. S., Longley, S., & Prescott, A. (1993). *Preliminary manual for the Preschool Laboratory Temperament Assessment Battery* (version 1.0). Technical Report, Department of Psychology, University of Wisconsin–Madison, Madison.

Goldsmith, H. H., & Rieser-Danner, L. (1990). Assessing early temperament. In C. R. Reynolds & R. W. Kamphaus (Eds.), *Handbook of psychological and educational assessment of children: Vol. 2. Personality, behavior, and context* (pp. 345–378). New York: Guilford Press.

Goldsmith, H. H., Rieser-Danner, L. A., & Briggs, S. (1991). Evaluating convergent and discriminant validity of temperament questionnaires for preschoolers, toddlers, and infants. *Developmental Psychology, 27,* 566–579.

Goldsmith, H. H., & Rothbart, M. K. (1991). Contemporary instruments for assessing early temperament by questionnaire and in the laboratory. In J. Strelau & A. Angleitner (Eds.), *Explorations in temperament* (pp. 249–272). New York: Plenum Press.

Gross, J. J. (Ed.). (2007). *Handbook of emotion regulation.* New York: Guilford Press.

Hane, A. A., Fox, N. A., Polak-Toste, C., Ghera, M. M., & Guner, B. (2006). Contextual basis of maternal perceptions of infant temperament. *Developmental Psychology, 42,* 1077–1088.

Hayden, E. P., Klein, D. N., & Durbin, C. E. (2005). Parent reports and laboratory assessments of child temperament: A comparison of their associations with risk for depression and externalizing disorders. *Journal of Psychopathology and Behavior Assessment, 27,* 89–100.

Hubert, N. C., Wachs, T. D., Peters-Martin, P., & Gandour, M. J. (1982). The study of early temperament: Measurement and conceptual issues. *Child Development, 53,* 571–600.

Hwang, J., & Rothbart, M. K. (2003). Behavior

genetics studies of infant temperament: Findings vary across parent-report instruments. *Infant Behavior and Development, 26,* 112–114.

Kagan, J. (1994). *Galen's prophecy: Temperament in human nature.* New York: Basic Books.

Kagan, J. (1998). Biology and the child. In W. Damon (Series Ed.) & N. Eisenberg (Vol. Ed.), *Handbook of child psychology: Vol. 3. Social, emotional, and personality development* (5th ed., pp. 177–235). New York: Wiley.

Kagan, J., & Fox, N. A. (2006). Biology, culture, and temperamental biases. In N. Eisenberg, W. Damon, & R. M. Lerner (Eds.), *Handbook of child psychology: Vol. 3. Social, emotional, and personality development* (6th ed., pp. 167–225). New York: Wiley.

Kagan, J., Snidman, N., Zentner, M., & Peterson, E. (1999). Infant temperament and anxious symptoms in school age children. *Development and Psychopathology, 11,* 209–224.

Kiel, E. J., & Buss, K. A. (2006). Maternal accuracy in predicting toddlers' behaviors and associations with toddlers' fearful temperament. *Child Development, 77,* 355–370.

Kochanska, G., & Knaack, A. (2003). Effortful control as a personality characteristic of young children: Antecedents, correlates, and consequences. *Journal of Personality, 71,* 1087–1112.

Kochanska, G., Murray, K. T., & Coy, K. C. (1997). Inhibitory control as a contributor to conscience in childhood: From toddler to early school age. *Child Development, 68,* 263–277.

Kochanska, G., Murray, K. T., & Harlan, E. T. (2000). Effortful control in early childhood: Continuity and change, antecedents, and implications for social development. *Developmental Psychology, 36,* 220–232.

Kochanska, G., Murray, K., Jacques, T. Y., Koenig, A. L., & Vandegeest, K. A. (1996). Inhibitory control in young children and its role in emerging internalization. *Child Development, 67,* 490–507.

Light, S. N., Goldsmith, H. H., Coan, J. A., Frye, C., & Davidson, R. J. (2009). Dynamic variation in pleasure in children predicts nonlinear change in lateral frontal brain electrical activity. *Developmental Psychology, 45,* 525–533.

Logan, G. D., Schachar, R. J., & Tannock, R. (1997). Impulsivity and inhibitory control. *Psychological Science, 8,* 60–64.

Luciana, M., & Nelson, C. (2002). Assessment of neuropsychological function through use of the Cambridge Neuropsychological Testing Automated Battery: Performance in 4- to 12-year-old children. *Developmental Neuropsychology, 22,* 595–624.

Mangelsdorf, S. C., Schoppe, S. J., & Buur, H. (2000). The meaning of parental reports: A contextual approach to the study of temperament and behavior problems in childhood. In V. J. Molfese & D. L. Molfese (Eds.), *Temperament and personality development across the life span* (pp. 121–140). Mahwah, NJ: Erlbaum.

Matheny, A. P., Jr. (1980). Bayley's Infant Behavior Record: Behavioral components and twin analyses. *Child Development, 51,* 1157–1167.

Matheny, A. P., Jr. (1983). A longitudinal twin study of stability of components from Bayley's Infant Behavior Record. *Child Development, 54,* 356–360.

Matheny, A. P., Jr. (1987). Psychological characteristics of childhood accidents. *Journal of Social Issues, 43,* 45–60.

Matheny, A. P., Jr., Riese, M. L., & Wilson, R. S. (1985). Rudiments of infant temperament: Newborn to 9 months. *Developmental Psychology, 21,* 486–494.

Matheny, A. P., Jr., & Wilson, R. S. (1981). Developmental tasks and rating scales for the laboratory assessment of infant temperament. *JSAS: Catalog of Selected Documents in Psychology, 11,* 81–82.

Meehl, P. E. (1992). Factors and taxa, traits and types, differences of degree and differences in kind. *Journal of Personality, 60,* 117–174.

Pfeifer, M., Goldsmith, H. H., Davidson, R. J., & Rickman, M. (2002). Continuity and change in inhibited and uninhibited children. *Child Development, 73,* 1474–1485.

Phan, K. L., Wager, T., Taylor, S. F., & Liberzon, I. (2002). Functional neuroanatomy of emotion: A meta-analysis of emotion activation studies in PET and fMRI. *NeuroImage, 16,* 331–348.

Phillips, M. L., Senior, C., Fahy, T., & David, A. S. (1998). Disgust—the forgotten emotion of psychiatry. *British Journal of Psychiatry, 172,* 373–375.

Posner, M. I., & Rothbart, M. K. (2007). *Educating the human brain.* Washington, DC: American Psychological Association.

Riese, M. L. (1998). Predicting infant temperament from neonatal reactivity for AGA/SGA twin pairs. *Twin Research, 1,* 65–70.

Robinson, J. L., McGrath, J., & Corley, R. P. (2001). The conduct of the study: Sample and procedures. In R. N. Emde & J. K. Hewitt (Eds.), *Infancy to early childhood: Genetic and environmental influences on developmental change* (pp. 23–41). New York: Oxford University Press.

Rothbart, M. K. (1986). Longitudinal observation of infant temperament. *Developmental Psychology, 22,* 356–365.

Rothbart, M. K. (1988). Temperament and the development of inhibited approach. *Child Development, 59,* 1241–1250.

Rothbart, M. K. (2007). Temperament, development, and personality. *Current Directions in Psychological Science, 16,* 207–212.

Rothbart, M. K., & Bates, J. E. (1998). Temperament. In W. Damon (Series Ed.) & N. Eisenberg (Vol. Ed.), *Handbook of child psychology: Vol.*

3. *Social, emotional, and personality development* (pp. 105–176). New York: Wiley.

Rothbart, M. K., & Goldsmith, H. H. (1985). Three approaches to the study of infant temperament. *Developmental Review, 5,* 237–250.

Rothbart, M. K., & Sheese, B. E. (2007). Temperament and emotion regulation. In J. J. Gross (Ed.), *Handbook of emotion regulation* (pp. 331–350). New York: Guilford Press.

Ruf, H. T., Goldsmith, H. H., Lemery-Chalfant, K., & Schmidt, N. L. (2008). Components of childhood impulsivity. *European Journal of Developmental Science, 2,* 52–76.

Sameroff, A. J., Krafchuk, E. E., & Bakow, H. A. (1978). Issues in grouping items from the Neonatal Behavioral Assessment Scale. *Monographs of the Society for Research in Child Development, 43,* 46–59.

Saudino, K. J. (2009). Do different measures tap the same genetic influences?: A multi-method study of activity level in young twins. *Developmental Science, 12,* 626–633.

Saudino, K. J., & Cherny, S. S. (2001). Parental ratings of temperament in twins. In R. N. Emde & J. K. Hewitt (Eds.), *Infancy and early childhood: Genetic and environmental influences on developmental change* (pp. 73–88). New York: Oxford University Press.

Saudino, K. J., & Eaton, W. O. (1991). Infant temperament and genetics: An objective twin study of motor activity level. *Child Development, 62,* 1167–1174.

Saudino, K. J., & Eaton, W. O. (1995). Continuity and change in objectively assessed temperament: A longitudinal twin study of activity level. *British Journal of Developmental Psychology, 13,* 81–95.

Saudino, K. J., Wertz, A. E., Gagne, J. R., & Chawla, S. (2004). Night and day: Are siblings as different in temperament as parents say they are? *Journal of Personality and Social Psychology, 87,* 698–706.

Saudino, K. J., & Zapfe, J. A. (2008). Genetic influences on activity level in early childhood: Do situations matter? *Child Development, 79,* 930–943.

Seifer, R., Sameroff, A. J., Barrett, L. C., & Krafchuck, E. (1994). Infant temperament measured by multiple observations and mother report. *Child Development, 65,* 1478–1490.

Spinrad, T. L., Eisenberg, N., & Gaertner, B. M. (2007). Measures of effortful regulation for young children. *Infant Mental Health Journal, 28,* 606–626.

Thomas, A., Chess, S., & Birch, H. G. (1968). *Temperament and behavior disorders in children.* New York: New York University Press.

Wilson, R. S., & Matheny, A. P., Jr. (1983). Assessment of temperament in infant twins. *Developmental Psychology, 19,* 172–183.

Zentner, M., & Bates, J. E. (2008). Child temperament: An integrative review of concepts, research programs, and measures. *European Journal of Developmental Science, 2,* 7–37.

CHAPTER 12

Psychobiological Measures of Temperament in Childhood

Susan D. Calkins
Margaret M. Swingler

Definitional Issues/Theoretical Approaches

We define the construct of *temperament* as the basic organization of personality that is observable as early as infancy, and that becomes elaborated over the course of development as the individual's skills, abilities, cognitions, and motivations become more sophisticated (Rothbart & Bates, 1998; Shiner & Caspi, 2003). Specifically, temperament refers to individual characteristics that are assumed to have a biological or genetic basis and to determine the individual's affective, attentional, and motoric responding cross-situationally, and that play a role in subsequent social interactions and social functioning. For the purposes of this chapter, we first provide a brief review of temperament theories that motivated much of the early research on physiology–behavior relations (see Mervielde & De Pauw, Chapter 2, this volume, for a comprehensive review of temperament theory). Contemporary temperament theory reflected in the current directions of physiologically based empirical studies are discussed later in the chapter.

Temperament is a focus of considerable developmental and clinical psychology research because it has the potential to capture important traits that are intrinsic to an individual and measureable at both a behavioral and physiological level, and that contribute to interactions with the environment to influence an individual's development processes and outcomes. Current theorizing about infant and child temperament and its role in emotional functioning and behavioral adjustment has its roots in the work of Thomas and Chess (Thomas, Birch, Chess, Hertzig, & Korn, 1964; Thomas & Chess, 1977; Thomas, Chess, & Birch, 1970), who described nine different behavioral dimensions that clustered into three temperament types. Children displaying these different temperament types exhibited characteristic patterns of responding across a variety of situations, suggesting a biological basis, at least in part, for these temperament profiles.

Although many theorists have built upon Thomas and Chess's foundational theory that intrinsic traits and external influences determine an individual's temperament, we focus on those who emphasize a biological basis for temperament. For example, Buss and Plomin (1975, 1984) specified that temperament traits must be apparent early in life and be highly heritable, an idea that has been repeated in more recent temperament theories (e.g., Ruf, Goldsmith, Lemery-Chalfant, & Schmidt, 2008). Buss and Plomin also required that temperament traits be continuous across development, with early traits being predictive of later development and functioning, thereby highlighting the strong influence of biological processes in the development and expression of temperament throughout the lifespan. Kagan and colleagues (e.g., Kagan, 1994; Kagan, Snidman, Kahn, & Towsley, 2007) also define *temperament* as biologically based, likely stemming from heritable neurochemical profiles, and resulting from a combination of personal history and a bias for specific traits. Much of this theory comes from empirical work that has focused on two extreme temperaments, inhibited and uninhibited, which Kagan suggests are defined by distinct biobehavioral profiles that underlie different patterns of characteristic behavioral responses present throughout the lifespan (Kagan et al., 2007).

Goldsmith and Campos have also placed a strong emphasis on the role of biological origins and processes in the expression of temperament, although their approach focuses heavily on early-developing individual differences in the experience, expression, and regulation of emotion (e.g., Goldsmith & Campos, 1990; Goldsmith, Lemery, Aksan, & Buss, 2000). Their inclusion of emotion regulation (ER) is significant because ER includes both extrinsic and intrinsic processes for monitoring, processing, evaluating, and modifying one's emotional responses (Thompson, 1994) and has therefore been argued to depend on preexisting regulatory processes rooted in an individual's neural and physiological experience of emotion (Zentner & Bates, 2008). Goldsmith and colleagues (2000) suggest that temperament traits are an initial substrate of temperament that are acted upon by biological and environmental influences to produce the behavioral manifestations of an individual's mature personality.

Perhaps the most influential theory that has emphasized the roles of physiology and biology in the emergence and development of temperament comes from the work of Rothbart and colleagues (Derryberry & Rothbart, 1997; Rothbart, 1981; Rothbart & Bates, 1998; Rothbart, Derryberry, & Hershey, 2000; Rothbart & Sheese, 2007).

Their model (covered in more detail by Rothbart, Chapter 1, this volume) also posits both a reactive and regulatory component to temperament, and assumes that both of these have an autonomic basis, with more reactive behaviors present as early as birth, and the emergence of new self-regulatory behaviors with development strongly linked to neurobehavioral processes and maturation of neural pathways and brain areas responsible for such behaviors (Calkins & Degnan, 2005; Rothbart et al., 2000).

One underlying point of agreement among all of these theories is the notion that temperament has both a biological basis and a continuous biological influence (i.e., measureable at the level of an individual's physiology) throughout the lifespan. In our work, and for the purposes of this chapter, we see an important role for physiological processes in understanding the *behavioral* aspects of temperament (Calkins & Mackler, 2011). That is, if, as temperament theorists propose, temperament traits or types reflect the behavioral manifestations of underlying biological processes, it is necessary to observe convergent validity of behavior and physiology (Calkins & Degnan, 2005), or at least explore the role of physiological processes in behavior. This is not a new idea, as is made clear by the fact that researchers increasingly include physiological measures in the study of temperament to provide a necessary complement to observation-based behavioral measures. Indeed, some researchers (e.g., Fox, 1989, 1991; Fox & Card, 1999; Kagan et al., 2007) have centered their research programs on the hypothesized underlying physiological basis for temperament as opposed to its more commonly studied behavioral manifestations. This chapter reviews the primary measures that have been used to investigate a physiological basis for temperament throughout the lifespan: heart rate, brain electrical and functional activity, and activity of the adrenocortical system.

Physiological Measures of Temperament

Cardiac Measures

Heart rate measures were among the first biological indicators applied to temperament work, especially in developmental studies, and have since provided information about significant physiology–temperament–behavior links. Early work by Kagan and colleagues (Garcia-Coll, Kagan, & Reznick, 1984; Kagan, 1982; Kagan, Reznick, Clarke, Snidman, & Garcia-Coll, 1984; Kagan, Reznick, & Snidman, 1987) indicated a relation between the pattern of heart rate observed in young children and their social behavior. Children with high and stable heart rates were more likely to display inhibited and fearful behaviors in social situations. These children, labeled *behaviorally inhibited* (Kagan et al., 1984), also appeared to be more anxious and distressed by mildly stressful events and engaged in less social interaction with their peers. The application of heart rate measures to emotion work was a logical choice because the experience of emotion for an individual is associated with varying degrees of physiological arousal (Levenson, 2003). Measures of self-control in infancy and early childhood point to a central role played by modulation of arousal for the control of emotion. Individual differences in arousal and reactivity that are present early in life have been suggested to be part of an individual's temperament system, and may underlie downstream development at the level of behavioral control of emotional experience and expression (Fox & Calkins, 2003).

Theories that focus on the underlying physiological components (arousal and reactivity) of temperament and its regulatory components highlight maturation of the central and autonomic nervous system (ANS) as the foundation for emotional and behavioral regulation (Santucci et al., 2008). The ANS is primarily responsible for the physiological arousal associated with the experience of emotion, which in turn is the result of input from both the excitatory sympathetic nervous system (SNS) and the inhibitory peripheral nervous system (PNS). The SNS and the PNS often interact antagonistically to produce varying levels of physiological arousal. The SNS is primarily dominant during periods of stress and produces heightened physiological arousal (i.e., higher heart rates) to respond to the increased demands of a challenge, while the PNS is primarily active during periods of relative calm and serves to maintain homeostasis for the individual. The ANS functions as a complex system of afferent and efferent feedback pathways that are integrated with other neurophysiological and neuroanatomical processes, to provide a reciprocal loop between cardiac activity and central nervous system processes (Chambers & Allen, 2007).

The sympathetic branch of the ANS has been the focus of normative changes in response to emotional stimuli, while the parasympathetic branch, as measured by vagal control of the heart, has been the primary focus of research on the individual differences in behavior- or temperament-based responding to the environment (Stifter & Jain, 1996). This is because pathways of the parasympathetic nervous system serve to modulate changes in sympathetic activity and therefore play a key role in the regulation of state, motor activity, emotion, and cognition (Porges, 2003). Specifically, the myelinated vagus nerve, originating in the brainstem nucleus ambiguous, provides input to the sinoatrial node of the heart, producing dynamic changes in cardiac activity that allow the organism to transition from sustaining metabolic processes to generating more complex behavioral responses to environmental events (Porges, 2007). This central-peripheral neural feedback loop is functional relatively early in development (Porges, 2007), though there is good evidence that individual differences in the integrity of these processes are a consequence of both organic characteristics of the individual and postnatal experiences (Calkins & Hill, 2007).

Parasympathetic influences on heart rate can be easily quantified by measuring heart rate variability (HRV). Variability in heart rate that occurs at the frequency of spontaneous respiration (respiratory sinus arrhythmia, RSA) can be measured noninvasively and is considered a good estimate of the parasympathetic influence on HRV via the vagus nerve. Based on this, Porges developed a method that measures the amplitude and period of HRV associated with inhalation and exhalation, referred to as vagal tone (Vna) (Porges, 1991, 1995; Porges & Byrne, 1992). Porges and others have found that parasympathetic nervous system functioning, as reflected in HRV influenced by the vagal system, is related to the control of attention, emotion, self-regulation, and motor behavior in development (Calkins,

1997; Calkins & Dedmon, 2000; DeGangi, DiPietro, Greenspan, & Porges, 1991; Huffman et al., 1998; Porges, Doussard-Roosevelt, Portales, & Greenspan, 1996).

Studies of Vna in children have primarily examined baseline (resting) Vna as a predictor of behavior or emotional health, and have found that high baseline Vna is associated with appropriate emotional reactivity, better regulation/soothability (Calkins, 1997; Calkins & Fox, 2002; Stifter & Fox, 1990), and good attentional ability in infants and children (Richards, 1985, 1987; Suess, Porges, & Plude, 1994). Several studies have linked high baseline Vna in newborns with good developmental outcomes, suggesting that it may be an important early physiological trait that promotes appropriate engagement and interaction with the environment (Hoffheimer, Wood, Porges, Pearson, & Lawson, 1995; Richards & Cameron, 1989). This research also suggests that children with a biological predisposition to low baseline Vna may be at risk for less optimal developmental outcomes due to difficulty attending to and using environmental cues to learn about their world (Porges, 1991; Wilson & Gottman, 1996). Individual differences in indices of baseline Vna (and vagal reactivity) have also been associated with differences in emotional expressiveness, temperamental reactivity, attentional capacity, behavioral inhibition, and aggression in infant and child samples (see Beauchaine, 2001, for a review).

Similarly, high baseline Vna in toddlers is associated with approach to strangers, high activity level, regulated distress in frustrating situations, and lower levels of aggression (Calkins & Dedmon, 2000; Porges et al., 1996; Stifter & Fox, 1990; Stifter, Fox, & Porges, 1989; Stifter & Jain, 1996). In young boys in particular, high baseline Vna has been found to be associated with greater empathy, social competence, and subjective feelings of sympathy, as well as teacher- and parent-reports of sociability and emotion regulation (Fabes, Eisenberg, & Eisenbud, 1993; Fabes, Eisenberg, Karbon, Troyer, & Switzer, 1994). One notable exception to this pattern of findings comes from a recent study of temperament and ANS activity in preschool-age children (Stifter, Dollar, & Cipriano, 2011). Contrary to the authors' expectations, low surgent children who exhibited higher baseline Vna demonstrated poorer emotion regulation skills than low surgent children with lower baseline Vna. However, the authors noted that their measure of surgency was a parent-report measure of temperament, which is known to have a subjective component (Stifter et al., 2011), and suggested that future work would benefit from multiple measures of temperament.

High baseline Vna has also been associated with greater self-reported emotion regulation and use of effective coping strategies in college students, although this relationship was mediated by negative emotional arousal (Fabes & Eisenberg, 1997). Individuals with lower baseline Vna experienced greater negative emotional arousal, which may have precluded them from implementing adaptive coping strategies. Indeed, in a recent study with adults, Miskovic and Schmidt (2010) found that undergraduates exhibiting low baseline Vna showed biased attention toward social threat in the form of angry faces. Other studies of adolescents and adults have linked atypical baseline Vna to a number of negative outcomes, such as hostility, aggression, anxiety, and panic (see Beauchaine, 2001). Therefore, the vast majority of work has shown that higher levels of baseline Vna in infancy, childhood, and early adulthood are associated with a greater capacity for regulated emotional responding and consequently are associated with better social and cognitive outcomes.

Of particular interest to researchers studying temperament and self-regulation are measures of cardiac activity related to the kinds of regulatory behaviors children begin to display in toddlerhood and early childhood that modulate temperamental reactivity. Such regulation is indexed by a decrease in Vna (vagal withdrawal) during situations in which coping or emotional and behavioral regulation is required (Porges, 2003, 2007). Vagal regulation in the form of decreases in Vna is often described as the functioning of "the vagal brake" because a decrease, or withdrawal, of vagal input to the heart has the effect of stimulating increases in heart rate (HR). Vagal withdrawal during demanding tasks has been suggested to reflect physiological processes that allow the individual to shift focus from internal homeostatic demands to demands that require deeper processing or the generation of coping strategies to control affective or behavioral arousal. Thus, vagal withdrawal is thought to be a physiological strategy that results in greater cardiac output in the form of HR acceleration, and that supports behaviors indicative of active coping (Calkins, Graziano, & Keane, 2007; El-Sheikh & Whitson, 2006; Porges, 1991, 1996; Propper & Moore, 2006; Wilson & Gottman, 1996).

Indeed, in a number of studies, greater vagal withdrawal in infants during challenging situations was related to better state regulation, which is behaviorally manifested as greater self-soothing and more attentional control. For example, Huffman and colleagues (1998) found that 3-month-olds who responded to a laboratory-administered assessment of temperament with higher Vna withdrawal were rated higher by their mothers on measures of soothability and duration of attentional orienting scales. DeGangi and colleagues (1991) found that 8- to 11-month-old infants with regulatory problems demonstrated lower Vna withdrawal during a challenge task than a control group of infants. In preschool-age children, greater vagal withdrawal during challenge has been associated with fewer behavior problems and more appropriate emotion regulation (Calkins, 1997; Calkins & Dedmon, 2000; Calkins & Keane, 2004; Porges et al., 1996). Similarly, in school-age children, greater vagal withdrawal has been predictive of greater effortful control of attention and sustained attention (Calkins et al., 2007; Suess et al., 1994). Importantly, this work highlights the necessity of considering how specific physiological indices, in this case, cardiac indices, of the broad construct of temperament map onto different dimensions that it encompasses, such as reactivity and regulation (Calkins, 1997).

Research involving measures of baseline Vna and vagal withdrawal have contributed important information regarding the relationship between an individual's temperament and activity of the parasympathetic branch of the ANS. However, Porges's influential polyvagal theory also proposed that conditions of perceived threat may also necessitate the mobilization of the sympathetic branch of the ANS (Porges, 1995, 2007). Individual differences in temperament likely result in individual differences in perceptions of threat; therefore, the activity of the sympathetic system may also be related to individual differences in temperament in children and adults (Beauchaine, 2001; Kagan, 1994). Historically, HR increases have been used as a proxy for sympathetic input to the heart. However, since HR is autonomically controlled by both the sympathetic and parasympathetic branches of the ANS, this measure does not allow for isolation of the activity of the sympathetic branch alone (Stifter et al., 2011). Instead, other physiological measures have been used to index sympathetic activity.

Preejection period (PEP), the sympathetically mediated time between the beat of the heart and ejection of blood into the aorta, provides a more direct measure of sympathetic activity that is independent of parasympathetic activity (Bernston et al., 1994). Cardiac impedance measures of PEP have been validated as a measure of sympathetic activity in adults (Bernston et al., 1994) and, more recently, have been shown to be highly correlated across time and tasks in developmental populations as well (Alkon et al., 2003; McGrath & O'Brien, 2001). Developmental work examining relations between PEP and behavioral outcomes have found that decreased sympathetic reactivity is associated with externalizing behaviors in children (Boyce et al., 2001) and the presence of conduct disorders in adolescents (Beauchaine, Katkin, Strassberg, & Snarr, 2001). In a sample of toddlers, Buss, Davidson, Kalin, and Goldsmith (2004) found that freezing behavior (a fear response often associated with inhibited temperament) during interaction with a stranger was associated with increased baseline sympathetic activity measured 1 week later.

Although little work has examined the relationship between PEP and behavior related to temperament dimensions in young children, the few studies reporting associations have not yielded strong findings (Talge, Donzella, & Gunnar, 2008). This has been especially true with regard to PEP reactivity measured in response to stress-inducing situations, and may be partly due to a number of studies reporting no change in PEP from baseline to task engagement, despite changes in HR and Vna (e.g., Buss et al., 2004). One exception to this is a recently published study directly examining a relationship between PEP and temperament, in which sympathetic reactivity measured by PEP interacted with a higher-order temperament factor that Ahadi, Rothbart, and Ye (1993) labeled "surgency" and Fox, Henderson, Rubin, Calkins, and Schmidt (2001) called "exuberant." This factor includes traits such as impulsivity, approach to novelty, activity level, and sensation seeking (high pleasure). Stifter and colleagues (2011) found that children rated as higher in surgency showed better emotion regulation when they had higher baseline PEP and higher PEP reactivity scores. There was no relationship between baseline PEP or PEP reactivity and emotion regulation for low-surgent children. These data extend previous work using HR that has demonstrated an association between low HR and negative outcomes (e.g., externalizing behavior) and provides preliminary support for an association between SNS activity and temperament-related behavioral outcomes for children. However, the lack of consistency in findings from the relatively few studies suggests a need for caution in interpretation of these results and more systematic study.

Electrical Brain Activity

Although the use of HR measures and assessment of ANS arousal have a long and productive history in the study of temperament, the application of measures of neural activation to the field has been more recent. The majority of this research has used electroencephalogram (EEG) methodology in research with infants (e.g., Davidson & Fox, 1982, 1989; Fox & Davidson, 1984, 1987, 1988, 1991), young children (Schmidt, Fox, Shulkin, & Gold, 1999), and adolescents (Kagan et al., 2007). The EEG is a measurement of scalp-recorded brain electrical activity that represents the synchronized activity of large numbers of cortical pyramidal neurons firing together. This synchronization of activity leads to a dominant frequency of oscillation that is measureable at electrode sites placed at specific scalp locations (e.g., Kagan et al., 2007). The EEG provides information about the presence of anatomical connections in the central nervous system, as well as the extent of cortical activity both at rest and in response to specific situations or stimuli (e.g., Coan & Allen, 2004; Nunez, 1981). For example, based on an early series of studies using EEG methodology, Fox (1989, 1994) and Davidson (1993) noted that the frontal lobes of the brain are differentially specialized for responses to situations involving approach versus avoidance, and that individual differences in frontal lobe activation in developmental populations are related to behaviors that children engage in when emotionally and behaviorally aroused.

In large part, these studies were based on the idea that baseline measures of prefrontal cortex (PFC) activity provide a relatively noninvasive way to gain insight about an individual's predisposition toward certain types or kinds of emotional expression, experience, and regulation (Davidson, 2000; see White, Lamm, Helfinstein, & Fox, Chapter 17, this volume, for links to other brain systems). Specifically, patterns of frontal EEG asymmetry are thought to relate to individual differences in the tendency to approach or withdraw from novel or stressful events, and in the experience and expression of emotion (Davidson, 1992; Davidson & Fox, 1982; Fox, 1991, 1994; Henderson, Fox, & Rubin, 2001). One way to quantify individual differences in frontal asymmetry is to measure the pattern of resting frontal EEG power in the alpha frequency; a frequency that is present throughout the lifespan, although its specific values have been shown to change with development. Difference scores are computed between homologous left- and right-hemisphere scalp electrodes such that frontal EEG asymmetry provides a measure of the difference in the degree of activation between left and right frontal regions (e.g., Henderson et al., 2001; Miskovic & Schmidt, 2010; Vuga, Fox, Cohn, Kovacs, & George, 2008).

Early studies indicated that left frontal activation is associated with behaviors facilitating approach, such as fine motor behavior, language, and the expression of certain positive emotions (Fox & Davidson, 1984). More recent work has shown that individuals with greater left frontal activation also more often report relaxed mood, are more likely to interpret neutral stimuli as positive, and show less anxiety both in everyday life and in response to stress-inducing situations than are individuals who show greater right frontal activation (e.g., Davidson, 2003; Davidson, Jackson, & Kalin, 2000; Fox, Calkins, & Bell, 1994; Fox et al., 2005; Schmidt et al., 1999). The right frontal area has been associated with behaviors facilitating withdrawal from novel or stressful stimuli, such as gross motor movement, autonomic reactivity, and the expression of negative affect (Fox & Davidson, 1984). One possible explanation proposed in the literature is that approach–withdrawal tendencies act as a potential bias for an individual's interactions with their environment, leading them preferentially to initiate or withdraw from stressful situations or unfamiliar social exchanges, for example (Henderson et al., 2001).

Indeed, a large body of research has established that resting levels of frontal EEG asymmetry explain important sources of variation in affective style, personality, and risk for psychopathology (Coan & Allen, 2004). The conclusion from a review of these studies is that asymmetries in frontal EEG activity—found during baseline periods, during task or state engagement, and when looking at differences between these two conditions—are consistently present and involved in both trait predispositions to respond to emotional stimuli and changes in emotional state (Coan & Allen, 2003). Resting asymmetric EEG activity has been shown to be stable across a wide range of contexts in infancy (Schmidt, 2008; Schmidt, Cote, Santesso, & Milner, 2003), across childhood (Vuga et al., 2008) and in adulthood (Vuga et al., 2006). This, in combination with its psychometric properties (Tomarken, Davidson, Wheeler, & Kinney, 1992) has led to the suggestion that EEG asymmetry in general, but especially resting asymmetry, functions as a trait-like construct that signifies a specific style of affective responding.

There is also evidence that the neurophysiological underpinnings for temperamental differences are present at almost every stage in development, show some consistency across time, and often interact with or are predictive of behavior. For example, Calkins and colleagues (1996) reported that infants displaying high motor arousal and negative affect at 4 months of age were more likely to display right frontal EEG activity at 9 months of age and behavioral inhibition at 14 months. Six-month-olds who showed greater right than left frontal activation in response to the introduction of an unfamiliar adult also displayed negative facial expressions in response to the stranger's approach (Buss et al., 2003). Interestingly, these infants also showed an increased cortisol (stress) response to the unfamiliar setting of the laboratory, a topic we return to in a later section. Similarly, Henderson and colleagues (2001) found that negative emotionality at 9 months was predictive of social wariness at 4 years for infants who also displayed a pattern of right frontal EEG asymmetry at 9 months, but not for infants who displayed a pattern of left frontal asymmetry. The authors of this study interpreted this as evidence that the presence of left frontal asymmetry at 9 months served as a protective factor and attenuated the relationship between negative reactivity and later social wariness.

Fox and others have also found relations between EEG asymmetry and shyness in adults and reticence in children. Preschool children who displayed elevated amounts of reticent and anxious behavior during interactions with unfamiliar peers exhibited increased electrical activity in the right frontal region (right frontal EEG asymmetry) compared with their more sociable peers (Fox et al., 1995). In contrast, young children who displayed consistently high levels of sociability across the toddler years were more likely to exhibit left frontal EEG asymmetry (Fox et al., 2001). In a sample of school-age children, increases in anxiety when placed in a situation designed to elicit social stress were paralleled by increases in right frontal EEG asymmetry in a group of shy children (Schmidt et al., 1999). In a longitudinal study of temperament, Kagan and colleagues (2007) found that 11-year-olds who were high (compared to low) reactive as infants and inhibited at 2 years also showed greater right- than left-hemisphere activation in both frontal and parietal scalp locations. Finally, adults who rated themselves as high in shyness also displayed right frontal EEG asymmetry during a baseline condition (Schmidt & Fox, 1994).

A novel paper involving an approach in which gene–*endo*environment interactions were examined found an association between the dopamine D4 receptor gene (*DRD4*; see Saudino & Wang, Chapter 16, this volume) and EEG asymmetry at 9 months to be a predictor of child temperament at 48 months (Schmidt, Fox, Pérez-Edgar, & Hamer, 2009). These authors showed that the *DRD4* gene moderated the relationship between resting frontal EEG asymmetry at 9 months and temperament at 48 months. Specifically, children who exhibited left frontal asymmetry at 9 months and possessed the *DRD4* long allele were significantly more soothable at 48 months than other children. Conversely, children who exhibited resting right frontal asymmetry at 9 months and had the *DRD4* long allele had significantly more difficulties focusing and sustaining attention at 48 months than those with resting right frontal asymmetry and the short allele. Therefore, while studies including a physiological basis for temperament have much to contribute to the study of temperament, there is clearly more to be learned from the inclusion of additional child variables.

Functional Brain Activity

While it is clear that EEG methodology has much to offer to the field of temperament, it is important to note that the EEG is only an indirect measure of brain functioning. Therefore, conclusions regarding localization of function are limited and should be regarded with caution. Two psychobiological measures that do have the potential to inform about localization of differences in neural activation, as well as brain structure, associated with differences in temperamental profiles are functional (fMRI) and structural magnetic resonance imaging (sMRI). sMRI provides a quantification of both gray and white matter volume, while fMRI provides brain maps with millimeter level spatial information about localized changes in blood oxygenation measured either at rest or in response to the introduction of stimuli or task demands. Both of these measures have a very recent history of application to the study of temperament profiles and specific temperament traits.

Reactive temperament, for example, has been related to neural function, especially to the functioning of the amygdala; and the trait of extraversion/surgency has been related to dopamine systems in the brain (Rothbart, 2007; also see White et al., Chapter 17, this volume, for a detailed discussion of the neurobiology and neurochemistry of temperament). Much of the research investigating a neural basis for reactive temperament has used measures of cortical attentional networks, which develop over time and are related to individual differences in other temperament constructs, such as effortful control. In addition, behaviors such as monitoring and resolving conflict between incompatible responses have been linked to specific executive attention networks in the brain (Rothbart, 2007). A basic measure of conflict resolution is provided by the Stroop task, in which the name of a word conflicts with the name of the color in which it is printed. Tasks such as the Attention Network Test (ANT) present flanking stimuli that distract one's attention from the task of responding to a central stimulus. In adult imaging work, Stroop and flanker tasks activate the anterior cingulate and lateral prefrontal areas of the brain, which are parts of the executive attention network (Posner & Rothbart, 2007; Rothbart, 2007). These tasks have been modified for use with toddlers and children as markers of executive attention development, allowing researchers an indirect measure of brain function through task performance. However, methodological limitations have mostly precluded these tasks being used in conjunction with fMRI and MRI measures in developmental populations. One solution to this problem is to combine early measures of temperament with later measures of neural activation and structure in a longitudinal framework (e.g., Kagan et al., 2007).

For example, new evidence has shown that adults categorized in infancy or toddlerhood as inhibited later showed differences in functional neural activation in the amygdala in response to novel social stimuli when compared to adults earlier categorized as uninhibited (Schwartz, Wright, Shin, Kagan, & Rauch, 2003). This result was seen as consistent with an account that emphasizes variation in the excitability of the amygdala and its projections to the ventral striatum, periaqueductal gray, and anterior cingulate as a potential underlying biological factor for behaviors associated with temperament, although this is perhaps most applicable to extreme temperament traits such as inhibition. Nonetheless, for these two temperament groups, the differences in amygdalar activation, as well as other physiological measures, were consistent with expected differences in activity in circuits that project from the amygdala to the sympathetic chain and suggest that the complex behavioral and physiological profiles of these two temperaments might reflect differential excitability of the amygdala. In addition, this was one of the first studies of its kind to provide evidence that some brain properties relating to temperament are preserved from infancy to adulthood (Schwartz et al., 2003).

Schwartz and colleagues (2010) provided another layer of evidence for this in a follow-up study with the same two groups of participants, in which they found that these early temperamental differences also had implications for the architecture of the development of cerebral cortex measured in adulthood. Specifically, they found that the adults with low-reactive infant temperament showed greater thickness in the left orbitofrontal cortex (OFC), while the participants categorized as high-reactive in infancy showed greater thickness in the right ventromedial prefrontal cortex. Results from previous fMRI work led these authors to suggest that low-reactive subjects are able to modulate their hedonic tone in a more positive direction more effectively than high-reactive subjects because of more robust pathways in this subregion of the OFC that suppress unpleasant feelings. In addition, taken in combination with the results from their fMRI study that suggested amygdala hyperreactivity in response to novelty in inhibited compared with uninhibited children, Schwartz and colleagues suggest that low-reactive subjects would be expected to be more effective than high-reactive subjects at inhibiting the amygdalar response to unfamiliarity through this neural circuitry.

With regard to right-hemisphere findings, the authors suggested that the thicker subregion of the right ventromedial cortex in high-reactive subjects might reflect increased connectivity with structures responsible for prototypical behavioral characteristics of high-reactive infants. For example, this subregion preferentially targets the periaqueductal gray, which is linked to defensive and somatovisceral responses, active avoidance, and defensive behaviors. These behaviors include a response they called "arching of the back," which is seen almost exclusively in 4-month-old high-reactive infants (Schwartz et al., 2010). In addition, direct projections to the hypothalamus from this subregion of the prefrontal cortex can activate the medulla and sympathetic chain, which may underlie the increases in blood pressure and HR seen in inhibited children in response to the unfamiliar (e.g., Kagan et al., 2007).

While these findings are novel and exciting, these authors do acknowledge the significant limitations to the results. For example, the variations in thickness of the cortex could be potentially related to variation in the size or density of neurons, inhibitory interneurons, glial cells, or the size and density of unmyelinated neuronal processes (dendrites, dendritic spines, and axons) referred to as *neuropil*. The current state of high-resolution MRI does not allow for research to address which of these components contributed to the cortical thickness differences observed. Furthermore, because imaging data were not collected in infancy, these findings cannot address the question of whether the reported structural differences were intrinsic and could be detected earlier, or whether they developed over time because of genetic factors, environmental influences, or some interaction of the two.

Hypothalamic–Pituitary–Adrenocortical Axis and Alpha-Amylase Activity

Another psychobiological measure that has been applied to the study of temperament is that of adrenocortical activity measured in plasma and salivary cortisol. Cortisol is a glucocorticoid (GC) and the primary hormonal product of the hypothalamic–pituitary–adrenocortical (HPA) axis of the neuroendocrine system, which is a stress-sensitive physiological system that includes a complex set of direct influences and feedback interactions among the hypothalamus, the pituitary gland, and the adrenal glands. Receptors for GCs reside in most tissues and organs of the body, including many structures in the brain (Lupien, McEwen, Gunnar, & Heim, 2009). The measurement of cortisol levels in saliva is simple and noninvasive, and has greatly facilitated the study of the interactions among the HPA axis, environmental events, and behavior in the context of the study of health and development across the lifespan, but particularly in work with infants and young children (Larson, Prudhomme-White, Cochran, Donzella, & Gunnar, 1998). The concentration of cortisol in saliva is only a small fraction of that in blood; therefore, when collecting salivary cortisol, methods are commonly used to increase the volume of saliva tested (i.e., a several-fold increase above that typically recommended for testing serum) to increase assay sensitivity (Larson et al., 1998). As part of the body's normal regulatory functions, cortisol production follows a circadian rhythm, with the highest level peaking around 30 minutes after wake-up, followed by a sharp decrease over the next 1–2 hours, then a more gradual decline over the remaining daytime and evening hours (Watamura, Donzella, Alwin, & Gunnar, 2003). An early morning peak and evening dip in cortisol levels can be observed at least as early as 3 months of age (Larson et al., 1998), although an adult-like pattern of production does not emerge until children are around 3 or 4 years of age and begin to give up their afternoon naps (Lane & Donzella, 1999).

Although cortisol production varies fairly rhythmically in the course of a 24-hour period, cortisol levels are also sensitive to both physiological and psychological elicitors (Calkins & Degnan, 2005). Stressors typically increase cortisol over basal levels for that time of day; therefore, cortisol is often described as a stress-sensitive hormone and has frequently been used as such in research (Watamura et al., 2003). Cortisol responses to stress serve an important function in adaptation to novel and stressful circumstances; however, there appears to be an optimal level of response to be adaptive for the individual. That is, while effective reactivity of the HPA system is adaptive, hyperreactivity of the system has been found to have negative effects on immune system activity (Coe, Rosenberg, & Levine, 1988), child health (Flinn & England, 1995), and cognitive and memory functioning (Heffelfinger & Newcomer, 2001). It is this model, based on administration of high levels of GC, that shapes most assumptions regarding the effects of GC on cognition. It has been well documented that the effects of GC on many cognitive processes follow a U-shaped curve, such that high levels have a detrimental effect on performance, but very low levels also are associated with impairments. It is moderate GC levels that seem to be associated with optimal performance on many cognitive tasks (Davis, Bruce, & Gunnar, 2001).

Based on the known neural circuitry involved in activating stress responses of both the HPA axis and the sympathetic adrenomedullary system, a number of researchers also hypothesized that shyness or behavioral inhibition would be associated with greater stress reactivity and cortisol production (e.g., Kagan, 1994; Rosen & Schulkin, 1998). Research examining a potential relationship between social behavior and salivary cortisol has generally found that a higher level of cortisol is, in fact, associated with shy, withdrawn behavior, although these results are vulnerable to a direction-of-effect debate. In addition, some studies have found that a higher level of cortisol within a moderate range is positively associated with approach behavior, social competence, and cognitive and behavioral inhibitory control in children and adults (Blair, Peters, & Granger, 2004; Davis et al., 2001). In addition, while shy, inhibited children have been found in a number of studies to have higher levels of cortisol than other children (e.g., de Haan, Gunnar, Tout, Hart, & Stansbury, 1998; Kagan et al., 1987; Watamura et al., 2003) it is also clear from this work that temperament–cortisol associations are sensitive to context. For example, in one study, cortisol and shy/anxious behavior were positively correlated when cortisol was sampled in the home, but not when sampled in preschool for the same children (de Haan et al., 1998).

Several other researchers have found positive associations between shyness and cortisol when cortisol was measured when children were at home (Kagan et al., 1987; Schmidt et al., 1997). Yet when cortisol is measured while children are in peer group settings, results have varied. Sometimes positive associations between shyness and cortisol production are present (e.g., Watamura et al., 2003), and sometimes dispositions that would seem to be the opposite of shyness relate positively to measures of HPA activity (see Gunnar, 2001, for a review). In particular, surgent or exuberant children have been found at times to have elevated cortisol levels (Davis, Donzella, Krueger, & Gunnar, 1999; Gunnar, Tout, de Haan, Pierce, & Stansbury, 1997) similar to withdrawn, anxious and shy children. However, Gunnar (1994) hypothesized that this might an unavoidable artifact of surgent, exuberant children being more likely to be involved in stressful encounters with peers and adults. In a yearlong systematic study of preschoolers in day care, Gunnar and colleagues found that high levels of cortisol in surgent children were attributable to discordant peer relations, and that when this aspect of behavior was controlled statistically, basal cortisol levels in children characterized by high levels of approach were lower rather than higher than those observed in temperamentally shy children (Gunnar, Sebanc, Tout, Donzella, & van Dulmen, 2003). This finding provided further support for the direction of the relationship between cortisol and temperament most commonly predicted (Kagan et al., 1987; Vanyukov et al., 1993) and fit with several studies of children at risk for conduct problems, which have found these children to have low cortisol levels, perhaps indicating underarousal (Vanyukov et al., 1993).

In a study with children in a similar age range, Blair and colleagues (2004) found that preschool children characterized by parental report as high-approach exhibited high levels of initial cortisol and decreasing cortisol across a testing session. However, children characterized as high on inhibition tended to exhibit lower initial cortisol and increasing cortisol across the assessment session. Taking the time course of the expression of cortisol in saliva into account, these authors suggested that levels of cortisol observed in saliva samples collected at the beginning their testing session represented child state prior to the time children were retrieved from the classroom to participate in the testing session. In addition, changes in cortisol seen across the testing session were likely due to the children's participation in the assessment and interaction with the examiner. Therefore, children characterized by higher behavioral inhibition entered the testing session with lower levels of cortisol, but interaction with the examiner seemed to be arousing and resulted in cortisol increase. In contrast, for children characterized by high-approach, interaction with the examiner in the testing session did not appear to be as arousing and, as a result, these children exhibited decreasing cortisol across the testing session.

Perhaps the most important contribution of these studies (Blair et al., 2004; Gunnar et al., 2003) and others like them (e.g., de Haan et al., 1998) is the idea that the specific direction of the relationship between cortisol levels and temperament traits is a dynamic process that is sensitive to child factors, as well as environmental cues. The range of these cues may be as fundamental as physical location of cortisol sampling to the more complicated intricacies of the child's relationships with peers and caregivers. This has led a number of researchers to suggest the importance of both context and reactivity in the examination of relations between neuroendocrine function and behavior (Blair et al., 2004; Davis, Parker, Tottenham, & Gunnar, 2003).

The study of cortisol has a long history of application to the study of temperament. More recently, salivary alpha-amylase (sAA) protein has emerged as a candidate for the measurement of SNS activity related to temperament. sAA production follows a circadian rhythm similar to the rhythmic changes in cortisol levels. Secretion of sAA has also been shown to increase in response to sympathetic stimulation, and these increases correlate with increases in the catecholamine norepinephrine (Rohleder, Nater, Wolf, Ehlert, & Kirschbaum, 2004), which is suggested to be critical for a number of temperament-related behaviors, including those underlying regulatory abilities (see Lisonbee, Pendry, Mize, & Gwynn, 2010). Indeed, higher reactive sAA levels have been found to correlate with lower levels of dispositional anger and impulsivity, and relatively higher levels of regulation, particularly for girls (Spinrad et al., 2009). In addition, increases in sAA from baseline to task were found to predict greater ability to delay gratification in preschool-age children (Lisonbee et al., 2010).

In addition to the findings in studies only examining sAA, a number of interesting results have emerged from work combining HPA and SNS measures, leading some to suggest that to examine psychobiological markers of stress reactivity more adequately, it is necessary to use multiple measures of biological processes (Spinrad et al., 2009). Several studies now have revealed that individual differences in sAA levels or reactivity moderate associations between cortisol and children's behavior. For instance, low levels of cortisol and high sAA were found to predict higher levels of aggression in young adolescents, while high cortisol and high sAA predicted internalizing difficulties (Gordis, Granger, Susman, & Trickett, 2006). This combination of high cortisol and sAA as predictors of internalizing difficulties was also found in school-age children (El-Sheikh, Erath, Buckhalt, Granger, & Mize, 2008). Finally, toddlers displaying higher sAA and lower cortisol were marginally less likely to show approach behaviors in a stranger interaction task (Fortunao, Dribin, Granger, & Buss, 2008). Taken together, these results suggest that sAA is a useful measure of reactivity in developmental populations, but the most complete picture of psychophysiological underpinnings of reactive behavior seems to come from combined measures of both SNS and HPA axis function.

Future Directions

Although the perception was that early temperament work focused on "innate traits" that were heritable and highly stable, longitudinal temperament research demonstrates that the environment has an important role to play in the equifinal and multifinal pathways that ultimately emerge in personality across the lifespan. Future directions for temperament research include possibilities for understanding how physiology plays a role in individual–environment transactions that alter the display of temperament. Here we offer suggestions for how these directions may be fruitfully explored.

Combining Psychobiological Measures and Environmental Variables

A common theme in this review of psychobiological measures of temperament is the need for assessing both intrinsic and extrinsic variables in research examining the origins, development, and outcomes of temperament. Indeed, the variability in outcomes for infants who are similar in temperament, even those in the extremes, suggest that other environmental factors, such as parent–child interactions and out-of-home care experiences, may moderate the link between early temperament and adjustment. As such, temperament may be linearly related to social outcomes, albeit through indirect processes, such that the relations are moderated by other variables (Rothbart & Bates, 1998). These variables may be some combination of factors intrinsic to the child, in the form of biologically based physiological differences, or factors external to child, in the form of environmental input (see Fox & Calkins, 2003). Therefore, temperament research involving the measurement of temperament traits, physiological functioning, and environmental variables may be important in forming a complete picture of the individual's current and future psychological state.

In effect, as Rothbart (2007) has suggested, temperament may function as the initial state from which personality develops and link individual differences in behavior to underlying neural networks. In Rothbart's words, temperament and experience together "grow" a personality that will include the child's developing cognitions about self, others, and the physical and social world, as well as his or her values, attitudes, and coping strategies. Following from this, Henderson and colleagues (2001) suggest that certain types of temperament, and even extreme temperament, may not reflect a direct risk for maladjustment, but rather act as a catalyst that, in combination with other factors, defines trajectories of social and emotional development. Physiological markers may provide an early measurement of risk for extreme temperament, but knowledge about the relationship between temperament and environment could inform options for potential methods of intervention to produce favorable outcomes. For example, a number of theorists have presented work proposing a moderational role for the caregiving environment on the relationship among temperament, social competence, and social functioning (see Bates & McFadyen-Ketchum, 2000, for a review). Work that considers both child intrinsic factors and extrinsic factors such as the quality of child–caregiver interactions has the potential to provide the most information about any bidirectional nature of these two factors on child development and later outcomes.

Although most of the emphasis in the empirical literature has been on the effects of caregiver behavior on behavioral manifestations of temperament and regulation, there is already some evidence that the caregiver–

child relationship has both a concurrent and lasting effect on child physiology as well. Our research group (Calkins, Graziano, Berdan, Keane, & Degnan, 2008) published a study that used measures of mother–child interaction quality to predict child cardiac vagal regulation in early childhood. Relationship quality was assessed using laboratory measures of hostility, positive guidance, and stress related to the quality of the relationship as reported by mothers. Cardiac vagal regulation at age 2 was assessed across six challenge tasks, three in which the child and mother worked together, and three in which the child worked independently, and was indexed by the magnitude of vagal withdrawal (decrease in Vna) to challenge. Children displayed greater cardiac vagal regulation and HR acceleration during collaborative tasks versus independent tasks. In addition, maternal–child relationship quality predicted the degree of vagal regulation in children at age 5, even after controlling for early and concurrent level of behavior problems, as well as 2-year cardiac vagal regulation. Specifically, children with poorer quality relationships displayed significantly poorer vagal regulation and lower HR acceleration.

A review by Propper and Moore (2006) attempted to clarify how early parent–infant interaction may play a role in shaping one aspect of temperamental development, emotion reactivity and emotion regulation, using multiple levels of analysis, including behavioral, physiological, and genetic methods. These authors note that although early experience and biology both contribute to behavioral outcomes, it is impossible to identify the separate contributions each make. Rather, they suggest that these factors should be viewed as probabilistically related to later outcomes resulting from the combination of biological, psychological, and environmental input. Their review of the literature showed that, in general, when the effects of early parenting experiences were taken into account, several consistent patterns emerged. First, there was a consistent effect of parenting influences on child Vna, such that dyadic synchrony and maternal responsiveness predicted differences in baseline levels of infant Vna. In addition, there were developmental differences in levels of Vna between infants of depressed and nondepressed mothers, and in infants from families with high levels of conflict between parents. Finally, in infants with very early behavioral and physiological markers for risk, appropriate parent responses to infant distress appeared to affect behavioral outcomes, so that several months later these infants showed more positive, sociable behaviors than other infants with less sensitive parents (Propper & Moore, 2006).

Integrating Measures of Caregiver and Child Psychobiology with Behavior

Although our review makes clear the importance of considering the effects of parenting behaviors and quality of parent–child interaction on child physiology and behavior, it may also be important to include measures of parent physiology in studies of child temperament. Recent work that has done so found valuable links between mothers' physiological responses to interactions with their children and maternal behavior during these interactions. Mills-Koonce and colleagues (2009) examined associations between maternal cortisol levels, Vna reduction, and parenting behaviors among mothers of young infants. Their results indicated a positive association between mothers' baseline cortisol levels and negative–intrusive caregiving behavior. However, this effect was attenuated when mothers displayed Vna reduction while soothing their infant following a face-to-face still face episode. Furthermore, lower levels of negative–intrusive behaviors were observed during the still face reunion as compared to free play for mothers with lower cortisol levels only. Finally, each of the physiological or contextual associations between maternal physiology and behavior was limited to maternal negative intrusiveness; there were no differences in positive engagement as a function of cortisol levels, Vna reduction, or context of observation.

The links between maternal physiology and sensitivity found in the work of Mills-Koonce and colleagues (2009) are striking and provide an important basis for including parent psychophysiology in studies of child development. Perhaps a next step in this work is illustrated in a study by Moore and colleagues (2009), in which they examined the effect of parents' physiology on infant physiology during normal and disrupted social interaction. These authors found evidence that maternal physiological regulation may have served to support infants' regulation. Specifically, mothers and infants showed opposite patterns of Vna change in response to disrupted interaction; mothers' Vna increased and infants' decreased, suggesting self-regulation of distress. During reunion, the typical pattern was for infants to return to baseline levels; however, sensitive mothers and their infants both showed a significant decrease in Vna from baseline. Therefore, these authors suggest that mothers' and infants' physiological responses may be a function of mutual responsiveness, especially during stressful or challenging situations. It is clear that examining synchrony between and among mothers' and infants' behavioral and physiological responses is an important direction for future research. To explore these constructs, measures, and methods that take into account and are sensitive to temporal, dynamic, and dyadic qualities of the interaction would need to be employed (Moore et al., 2009).

In summary, our view of temperament is that it is a consequence of a dynamic developmental process that can be observed across multiple levels of functioning. Measurement of the biological component of temperament can include a variety of indicators, but these indicators should be considered as part of a transactional process between the child and his or her environment, rather than as markers for static behavioral traits. Such a conceptualization creates obvious conceptual and empirical complexity but will likely yield a more accurate picture of the way in which early-appearing tendencies influence and are influenced by the developmental process over time.

Further Reading

Calkins, S. D., Graziano, P., Berdan, L., Keane, S. P., & Degnan, K. (2008). Predicting cardiac vagal regulation in early childhood from maternal–child relationship quality during toddlerhood. *Developmental Psychobiology, 50,* 751–766.

Propper, C., & Moore, G. (2006). The influence of parenting on infant emotionality: A multi-level psychobiological perspective. *Developmental Review, 26,* 427–460.

Rothbart, M. K. (2004). Temperament and the pursuit of an integrated developmental psychology. *Merrill–Palmer Quarterly, 50,* 492–505.

Rothbart, M. K. (2007). Temperament, development, and personality. *Current Directions in Psychological Science, 16,* 207–212.

References

Ahadi, S., Rothbart, M., & Ye, R. (1993). Children's temperament in the U.S. and China: Similarities and differences. *European Journal of Personality, 7,* 359–377.

Alkon, A., Goldstein, L. H., Smider, N., Essex, M. J., Kupfer, D. J., & Boyce, W. T. (2003). Developmental and contextual influences on autonomic reactivity in young children. *Developmental Psychobiology, 42,* 64–78.

Bates, J. E., & McFadyen-Ketchum, S. (2000). Temperament and parent–child relations as interacting factors in children's behavioral adjustment. In V. J. Molfese & D. L. Molfese (Eds.), *Temperament and personality development across the lifespan* (pp. 141–176). Mahwah, NJ: Erlbaum.

Beauchaine, T. (2001). Vagal tone, development, and Gray's motivational theory: Toward an integrated model of autonomic nervous system functioning in psychopathology. *Development and Psychopathology, 13,* 183–214.

Beauchaine, T., Katkin, E., Strassberg, Z., & Snarr, J. (2001). Disinhibitory psychopathology in male adolescents: Discriminating conduct disorder from attention-deficit/hyperactivity disorder through concurrent assessment of multiple autonomic states. *Journal of Abnormal Psychology, 110,* 610–624.

Bernston, G., Cacioppo, J., Binkley, P., Uchino, B., Quigley, K., & Fieldstone, A. (1994). Autonomic cardiac control: III. Psychological stress and cardiac response in autonomic space as revealed by pharmacological blockades. *Psychophysiology, 31,* 599–608.

Blair, C., Peters, R., & Granger, D. (2004). Physiological and neuropsychological correlates of approach/withdrawal tendencies in preschool: Further examination of the behavioral inhibition system/behavioral activation system scales for young children. *Developmental Psychobiology, 45,* 113–124.

Boyce, W. T., Quas, J., Alkon, A., Smider, N. A., Essex, M. J., & Kupfer, D. J. (2001). Autonomic reactivity and psychopathology in middle childhood. *British Journal of Psychology, 179,* 144–150.

Buss, A. H., & Plomin, R. (1975). *A temperament theory of personality development.* New York: Wiley.

Buss, A. H., & Plomin, R. (1984). *Temperament: Early developing personality traits.* Hillsdale, NJ: Erlbaum.

Buss, K. A., Davidson, R. J., Kalin, N. H., & Goldsmith, H. H. (2004). Context-specific freezing and associated physiological reactivity as a dysregulated fear response. *Developmental Psychology*, 40, 583–594.

Buss, K. A., Schumacher, J. R. M., Dolski, I., Kalin, N. H., Goldsmith, H. H., & Davidson, R. J. (2003). Right frontal brain activity, cortisol, and withdrawal behavior in 6-month-old infants. *Behavioral Neuroscience*, 117, 11–20.

Calkins, S. D. (1997). Cardiac vagal tone indices of temperamental reactivity and behavioral regulation in young children. *Developmental Psychology*, 31, 125–135.

Calkins, S. D., & Dedmon, S. E. (2000). Physiological and behavioral regulation in two-year-old children with aggressive/destructive behavior problems. *Journal of Abnormal Child Psychology*, 28, 103–118.

Calkins, S. D., & Degnan, K. A. (2005). Temperament in early development: Implications for childhood psychopathology. In R. Ammerman (Ed.), *The comprehensive handbook of childhood psychopathology* (pp. 64–84). New York: Guilford Press.

Calkins, S. D., & Fox, N. A. (2002). Self-regulatory processes in early personality development: A multilevel approach to the study of childhood social withdrawal and aggression. *Development and Psychopathology*, 14, 477–498.

Calkins, S. D., Fox, N. A., & Marshall, T. R. (1996). Behavioral and psychological antecedents of inhibition in infancy. *Child Development*, 67, 523–540.

Calkins, S. D., Graziano, P., Berdan, L., Keane, S. P., & Degnan, K. (2008). Predicting cardiac vagal regulation in early childhood from maternal–child relationship quality during toddlerhood. *Developmental Psychobiology*, 50, 751–766.

Calkins, S. D., Graziano, P. A., & Keane, S. P. (2007). Cardiac vagal regulation differentiates among children at risk for behavior problems. *Biological Psychology*, 74, 144–153.

Calkins, S. D., & Hill, A. (2007). Caregiver influences on emerging emotion regulation: Biological and environmental transactions in early development. In J. J. Gross (Ed.), *Handbook of emotion regulation* (pp. 229–248). New York: Guilford Press.

Calkins, S. D., & Keane, S. P. (2004). Cardiac vagal regulation across the preschool period: Stability, continuity, and implications for childhood adjustment. *Developmental Psychobiology*, 45, 101–112.

Calkins, S. D., & Mackler, J. S. (2011). Temperament, emotion regulation, and social development. In M. K. Underwood & L. H. Rosen (Eds.), *Social development: Relationships in infancy, childhood, and adolescence* (pp. 44–71). New York: Guilford Press.

Chambers, A., & Allen, J. (2007). Cardiac vagal control, emotion, psychopathology, and health. *Biological Psychology*, 74, 113–115.

Coan, J. A., & Allen, J. J. B. (2003). The state and trait nature of frontal EEG asymmetry in emotion. In K. Hugdahl & R. J. Davidson (Eds.), *The asymmetrical brain* (pp. 565–615). Cambridge, MA: MIT Press.

Coan, J. A., & Allen, J. J. B. (2004). Frontal EEG asymmetry as a moderator and mediator of emotion. *Biological Psychology*, 67, 7–49.

Coe, C. L., Rosenberg, L. T., & Levine, S. (1988). Immunological consequences of psychological disturbance and maternal loss in infancy. In C. Rovee-Collier & L. P. Lipsitt (Eds.), *Advances in infancy research* (Vol. 5, pp. 97–134). Norwood, NJ: Ablex.

Davidson, R. J. (1992). Anterior cerebral asymmetry and the nature of emotion. *Brain and Cognition*, 20, 125–151.

Davidson, R. J. (1993). Cerebral asymmetry and emotion: Conceptual and methodological conundrums. *Cognition and Emotion*, 7, 115–138.

Davidson, R. J. (2000). Affective style, psychopathology, and resilience: Brain mechanisms and plasticity. *American Psychologist*, 55, 1196–11214.

Davidson, R. J. (2003). Affective neuroscience and psychophysiology: Toward a synthesis. *Psychophysiology*, 40, 655–665.

Davidson, R. J., & Fox, N. A. (1982). Asymmetrical brain activity discriminates between positive and negative affective stimuli in human infants. *Science*, 218, 1235–1237.

Davidson, R. J., & Fox, N. A. (1989). Frontal brain asymmetry predicts infants' response to maternal separation. *Journal of Abnormal Psychology*, 98, 127–131.

Davidson, R. J., Jackson, D. C., & Kalin, N. H. (2000). Emotion, plasticity, context, and regulation: Perspectives from affective neuroscience. *Psychological Bulletin*, 126, 890–909.

Davis, E. P., Bruce, J., & Gunnar, M. R. (2001). The anterior attention network: Associations with temperament and neuroendocrine activity in 6-year-old children. *Developmental Psychobiology*, 40, 43–56.

Davis, E. P., Donzella, B., Krueger, W. K., & Gunnar, M. R. (1999). The start of a new school year: Individual differences in salivary cortisol response in relation to child temperament. *Developmental Psychobiology*, 35, 188–196.

Davis, E. P., Parker, S. W., Tottenham, N., & Gunnar, M. R. (2003). Emotion, cognition, and the hypothalamic–pituitary–adrenocortical axis: A developmental perspective. In M. de Haan & M. Johnson (Eds.), *The cognitive neuroscience of development* (pp. 181–206). New York: Psychology Press.

DeGangi, G., DiPietro, J., Greenspan, S., & Porges,

S. W. (1991). Psychophysiological characteristics of the regulatory disordered infant. *Infant Behavior and Development, 14,* 37–50.

de Haan, M., Gunnar, M. R., Tout, K., Hart, J., & Stansbury, K. (1998). Familiar and novel contexts yield different associates between cortisol and behavior among 2-year-olds. *Developmental Psychobiology, 31,* 93–101.

Derryberry, D., & Rothbart, M. K. (1997). Reactive and effortful processes in the organization of temperament. *Development and Psychopathology, 9,* 633–652.

El-Sheikh, M., Erath, S. A., Buckhalt, J. A., Granger, D. A., & Mize, J. (2008). Cortisol and children's adjustment: The moderating role of sympathetic nervous system activity. *Journal of Abnormal Child Psychology, 36,* 601–611.

El-Sheikh, M., & Whitson, S. (2006). Longitudinal relations between marital conflict and child adjustment: Vagal regulation as a protective factor. *Journal of Family Psychology, 20,* 30–39.

Fabes, R. A., & Eisenberg, N. (1997). Regulatory control and adults' stress-related responses to daily life events. *Journal of Personality and Social Psychology, 73,* 1107–1117.

Fabes, R. A., Eisenberg, N., & Eisenbud, L. (1993). Behavioral and physiological correlates of children's reactions to others in distress. *Developmental Psychology, 29,* 655–663.

Fabes, R. A., Eisenberg, N., Karbon, M., Troyer, D., & Switzer, G. (1994). The relations of children's emotion regulation to their vicarious emotional responses and comforting behaviors. *Child Development, 65,* 1678–1693.

Flinn, M. V., & England, B. G. (1995). Childhood stress and family environment. *Current Anthropology, 36,* 854–866.

Fortunao, C. K., Dribin, A. E., Granger, D. A., & Buss, K. A. (2008). Salivary alpha-amylase and cortisol in toddlers: Differential relations to affective behavior. *Developmental Psychobiology, 50,* 807–818.

Fox, N. A. (1989). Psychophysiological correlates of emotional reactivity during the first year of life. *Developmental Psychology, 25,* 364–372.

Fox, N. A. (1991). It's not left, it's right: Electroencephalogram asymmetry and the development of emotion. *American Psychologist, 46,* 863–872.

Fox, N. A. (1994). Dynamic cerebral process underlying emotion regulation. *Monographs of the Society for Research in Child Development, 59*(2–3, Serial No. 240), 152–166.

Fox, N. A., & Calkins, S. D. (2003). The development of self-control of emotion: Intrinsic and extrinsic influences. *Motivation and Emotion, 27,* 7–26.

Fox, N. A., Calkins, S. D., & Bell, M. A. (1994). Neural plasticity and development in the first year of life: Evidence from cognitive and socioemotional domains of research. *Development and Psychopathology, 6,* 677–696.

Fox, N. A., & Card, J. A. (1999). Psychophysiological measures in the study of attachment. In J. Cassidy & P. R. Shaver (Eds.), *Handbook of attachment: Theory, research, and clinical applications* (pp. 226–245). New York: Guilford Press.

Fox, N. A., & Davidson, R. J. (1984). Hemispheric substrates for affect: A developmental model. In N. A. Fox & R. J. Davidson (Eds.), *The psychobiology of affective development* (pp. 353–382). Hillsdale, NJ: Erlbaum.

Fox, N. A., & Davidson, R. J. (1987). Electroencephalogram asymmetry in response to the approach of a stranger and material separation in 10-month-old infants. *Developmental Psychology, 23,* 233–240.

Fox, N. A., & Davidson, R. J. (1988). Patterns of brain electrical activity during the expression of discrete emotions in ten month old infants. *Developmental Psychology, 24,* 230–236.

Fox, N. A., & Davidson, R. J. (1991). Hemispheric asymmetry and attachment behaviors: Developmental processes and individual differences in separation protest. In J. L. Gewirtz & W. M. Kurtines (Eds.), *Intersections with attachment* (pp. 147–164). Hillsdale, NJ: Erlbaum.

Fox, N. A., Henderson, H. A., Rubin, K., Calkins, S. D., & Schmidt, L. A. (2001). Continuity and discontinuity of behavioral inhibition and exuberance: Psychophysiological and behavioral influences across the first 4 years of life. *Child Development, 72,* 1–21.

Fox, N. A., Nichols, K. E., Henderson, H. A., Rubin, K. H., Schmidt, L. A., Hamer, D., et al. (2005). Evidence for a gene–environment interaction in predicting behavioral inhibition in middle childhood. *Psychological Science, 16,* 921–926.

Fox, N. A., Rubin, K. H., Calkins, C. D., Marshall, T. R., Coplan, R. J., Porges, S. W., et al. (1995). Frontal activation asymmetry and social competence at four years of age. *Child Development, 66,* 1770–1784.

Garcia-Coll, C., Kagan, J., & Reznick, J. S. (1984). Behavioral inhibition in young children. *Child Development, 55,* 1005–1019.

Goldsmith, H. H., & Campos, J. J. (1990). The structure of temperamental fear and pleasure in infants: A psychometric perspective. *Child Development, 61,* 1944–1964.

Goldsmith, H. H., Lemery, K. S., Aksan, N., & Buss, K. A. (2000). Temperamental substrates of personality. In V. J. Molfese & D. L. Molfese (Eds.), *Temperament and personality development across the life span* (pp. 1–32). Mahwah, NJ: Erlbaum.

Gordis, E. B., Granger, D. A., Susman, E. J., & Trickett, P. K. (2006). Asymmetry between salivary cortisol and α-amylase reactivity to stress:

Relation to aggressive behavior in adolescents. *Psychoneuroendocrinology, 31*, 976–987.

Gunnar, M. (1994). Psychoendocrine studies of temperament and stress in early childhood: Expanding current models. In J. E. Bates & T. D. Wachs (Eds.), *Temperament: Individual differences at the interface of biology and behavior* (pp. 175–198). Washington, DC: American Psychological Association.

Gunnar, M. R. (2001). The role of glucocorticoids in anxiety disorders: A critical analysis. In M. W. Vasey & M. R. Dadds (Eds.), *The developmental psychopathology of anxiety* (pp. 143–159). New York: Oxford University Press.

Gunnar, M. R., Sebanc, A. M., Tout, K., Donzella, B., & van Dulmen, M. M. H. (2003). Peer rejection, temperament and cortisol activity in preschoolers. *Developmental Psychobiology, 43*, 346–358.

Gunnar, M. R., Tout, K., de Haan, M., Pierce, S., & Stansbury, K. (1997). Temperament, social competence, and adrenocortical activity in preschoolers. *Developmental Psychobiology, 31*, 65–85.

Heffelfinger, A. K., & Newcomer, J. W. (2001). Glucocorticoid effects on memory function over the human life span. *Development and Psychopathology, 13*, 491–513.

Henderson, H. A., Fox, N. A., & Rubin, K. H. (2001). Temperamental contributions to social behavior: The moderating roles of frontal EEG asymmetry and gender. *Journal of the American Academy of Child and Adolescent Psychiatry, 40*, 68–74.

Hoffheimer, J. A., Wood, B. R., Porges, S. W., Pearson, E., & Lawson, E. (1995). Respiratory sinus arrhythmia and social interaction patterns in preterm newborns. *Infant Behavior and Development, 18*, 233–245.

Huffman, L. C., Bryan, Y., del Carmen, R., Pederson, F., Doussard-Roosevelt, J., & Porges, S. (1998). Infant temperament and cardiac vagal tone: Assessments at twelve weeks of age. *Child Development, 69*, 624–635.

Kagan, J. (1982). Heart rate and heart rate variability as signs of temperamental dimension in infants. In C. E. Izard (Ed.), *Measuring emotions in infants and children* (pp. 38–66). Cambridge, UK: Cambridge University Press.

Kagan, J. (1994). On the nature of emotion. *Monographs of the Society for Research in Child Development, 59*(2–3, Serial No. 240), 7–24.

Kagan, J., Reznick, J. S., Clarke, C., Snidman, N., & Garcia-Coll, C. (1984). Behavioral inhibition to the unfamiliar. *Child Development, 55*, 2212–2225.

Kagan, J., Reznick, J. S., & Snidman, N. (1987). The physiology and psychology of behavioral inhibition in children. *Child Development, 58*, 1459–1473.

Kagan, J., Snidman, N., Kahn, V., & Towsley, S. (2007). The preservation of two infant temperaments into adolescence. *Monographs of the Society for Research in Child Development, 72*, 1–95.

Lane, S. K., & Donzella, B. (1999, April). *The relationship between cortisol levels across the day, sleep/wake patterns, and temperament in 24 and 36 month olds*. Poster presented at the Society for Research in Child Development, Albuquerque, NM.

Larson, M. C., Prudhomme-White, B., Cochran, A., Donzella, B., & Gunnar, M. R. (1998). Dampening of the cortisol response to handling at 3 months in human infants and its relation to sleep, circadian cortisol activity, and behavioral distress. *Developmental Psychobiology, 33*, 327–337.

Levenson, R. W. (2003). Blood, sweat and fears: The autonomic architecture of emotion. *Annals of the New York Academy of Sciences, 1000*, 348–366.

Lisonbee, J. A., Pendry, P., Mize, J., & Gwynn, E. P. (2010). Hypothalamic–pituitary–adrenal and sympathetic nervous system activity and children's behavioral regulation. *Mind, Brain and Education, 4*, 171–181.

Lupien, S. J., McEwen, B. S., Gunnar, M. R., & Heim, C. (2009). Effects of stress throughout the lifespan on the brain, behaviour and cognition. *Nature Reviews Neuroscience, 10*, 434–445.

McGrath, J. J., & O'Brien, W. H. (2001). Pediatric impedance cardiography: Temporal stability and inter-task consistency. *Psychophysiology, 38*, 479–484.

Mills-Koonce, W. R., Propper, C. B., Barnett, M., Gariépy, J.-L., Moore, G., Calkins, S., et al. (2009). Psychophysiological correlates of parenting behavior in mothers of young children. *Developmental Psychobiology, 51*, 650–661.

Miskovic, V., & Schmidt, L. A. (2010). Frontal brain electrical asymmetry and cardiac vagal tone predict biased attention to social threat. *International Journal of Psychophysiology, 75*, 332–338.

Moore, G., Propper, C., Hill, A., Calkins, S. D., Mills-Koonce, R., & Cox, M. (2009). Mother–infant vagal regulation in the face-to-face still-face paradigm is moderated by maternal sensitivity. *Child Development, 80*, 209–223.

Nunez, P. L. (1981). *Electrical fields in the brain: The neophysics of EEG*. New York: Oxford University Press.

Porges, S. W. (1991). Vagal tone: An autonomic mediatory of affect. In J. A. Garber & K. A. Dodge (Eds.), *The development of affect regulation and dysregulation* (pp. 11–128). New York: Cambridge University Press.

Porges, S. W. (1995). Orienting in a defensive world: Mammalian modifications of our evolutionary heritage: A polyvagal theory. *Psychophysiology*, 32, 301–318.

Porges, S. W. (1996). Physiological regulation in high-risk infants: A model for assessment and potential intervention. *Development and Psychopathology*, 8, 43–58.

Porges, S. W. (2003). The polyvagal theory: Phylogenetic contributions to social behavior. *Physiology and Behavior*, 79, 503–513.

Porges, S. W. (2007). The polyvagal perspective. *Biological Psychology*, 74, 116–143.

Porges, S. W., & Byrne, E. A. (1992). Research methods for measurement of heart rate and respiration. *Biological Psychology*, 34, 93–130.

Porges, S. W., Doussard-Roosevelt, J. A., Portales, A. L., & Greenspan, S. I. (1996). Infant regulation of the vagal "brake" predicts child behavior problems: A psychobiological model of social behavior. *Developmental Psychobiology*, 29, 697–712.

Posner, M. I., & Rothbart, M. K. (2000). Developing mechanisms of self-regulation. *Development and Psychopathology*, 12, 427–441.

Posner, M. I., & Rothbart, M. K. (2007). *Educating the human brain*. Washington, DC: American Psychological Association.

Propper, C., & Moore, G. (2006). The influence of parenting on infant emotionality: A multi-level psychobiological perspective. *Developmental Review*, 26, 427–460.

Richards, J. E. (1985). Respiratory sinus arrhythmia predicts heart rate and visual responses during visual attention in 14- and 20-week-old infants. *Psychophysiology*, 22, 101–109.

Richards, J. E. (1987). Infant visual sustained attention and respiratory sinus arrhythmia. *Child Development*, 58, 488–496.

Richards, J. E., & Cameron, D. (1989). Infant heart rate variability and behavioral developmental status. *Infant Behavior and Development*, 12, 45–58.

Rohleder, N., Nater, U. M., Wolf, J. M., Ehlert, U., & Kirschbaum, C. (2004). Psychosocial stress-induced activation of salivary alpha-amylase: An indicator of sympathetic activity? *Annals of the New York Academy of Sciences*, 1032, 258–263.

Rosen, J. B., & Schulkin, J. (1998). From normal fear to pathological anxiety. *Psychological Review*, 105, 325–350.

Rothbart, M. K. (1981). Measurement of temperament in infancy. *Child Development*, 52, 569–578.

Rothbart, M. K. (1989). Temperament and development. In G. Kohnstamm, J. Bates, & M. K. Rothbart (Eds.), *Temperament in childhood* (pp. 187–248). Chichester, UK: Wiley.

Rothbart, M. K. (2007). Temperament, development, and personality. *Current Directions in Psychological Science*, 16, 207–212.

Rothbart, M. K., & Bates, J. E. (1998). Temperament. In W. Damon (Series Ed.) & N. Eisenberg (Vol. Ed.), *Handbook of child psychology: Vol. 4. Social, emotional, and personality development* (5th ed., pp. 105–176). New York: Wiley.

Rothbart, M. K., Derryberry, D., & Hershey, K. (2000). Stability of temperament in childhood: Laboratory infant assessment to parent report at seven years. In V. Molfese & D. Molfese (Eds.), *Temperament and personality development across the lifespan* (pp. 85–119). Mahwah, NJ: Erlbaum.

Rothbart, M. K., Posner, M. I., & Rosicky, J. (1994). Orienting in normal and pathological development. *Development and Psychopathology*, 6, 635–352.

Rothbart, M. K., & Sheese, B. E. (2007). Temperament and emotion regulation. In J. J. Gross (Ed.), *Handbook of emotion regulation* (pp. 331–350). New York: Guilford Press.

Ruf, H. T., Goldsmith, H. H., Lemery-Chalfant, K., & Schmidt, N. L. (2008). Components of childhood impulsivity. *European Journal of Developmental Science*, 2, 52–76.

Santucci, A. K., Silk, J. S., Shaw, D. S., Gentzler, A., Fox, N. A., & Kovacs, M. (2008). Vagal tone and temperament as predictors of emotion regulation strategies in young children. *Developmental Psychobiology*, 50, 205–216.

Schmidt, L. A. (2008). Patterns of second-by-second resting frontal brain (EEG) asymmetry and their relation to heart rate and temperament in 9-month-old human infants. *Journal of Personality and Individual Differences*, 44, 216–225.

Schmidt, L. A., Cote, K. A., Santesso, D. L., & Milner, C. E. (2003). Frontal electroencephalogram alpha asymmetry during sleep: Stability and its relation to affective style. *Emotion*, 3, 401–407.

Schmidt, L. A., & Fox, N. A. (1994). Patterns of cortical electrophysiology and autonomic activity in adults' shyness and sociability. *Biological Psychology*, 38, 183–198.

Schmidt, L. A., Fox, N. A., Pérez-Edgar, K., & Hamer, D. H. (2009). Linking gene, brain, and behavior: DRD4, frontal asymmetry, and temperament. *Psychological Science*, 20, 831–837.

Schmidt, L. A., Fox, N. A., Rubin, K. H., Sternberg, E. M., Gold, P. W., Smith, C. C., et al. (1997). Behavioral and neuroendocrine responses in shy children. *Developmental Psychobiology*, 30, 127–140.

Schmidt, L. A., Fox, N. A., Shulkin, J., & Gold, P. W. (1999). Behavioral and physiological correlates of self-presentation in temperamentally shy children. *Developmental Psychobiology*, 35, 119–135.

Schwartz, C. E., Kunwar, P. S., Greve, D. N., Moran, L. R., Viner, J. C., Covino, J. M., et al. (2010). Structural differences in adult orbital and ventromedial prefrontal cortex predicted by infant temperament at 4 months of age. *Archives of General Psychiatry, 67,* 78–84.

Schwartz, C. E., Wright, C. I., Shin, L. M., Kagan, J., & Rauch, S. L. (2003). Inhibited and uninhibited infants "grown up": Adult amygdalar response to novelty. *Science, 300,* 1952–1953.

Shiner, R. L., & Caspi, A. (2003). Personality differences in childhood and adolescence: Measurement, development, and consequences. *Journal of Child Psychology and Psychiatry and Allied Disciplines, 44,* 1–31.

Spinrad, T. L., Eisenberg, N., Granger, D. A., Eggum, N. D., Sallquist, J., Haugen, R. G., et al. (2009). Individual differences in preschoolers' salivary cortisol and alpha-amylase reactivity: Relations to temperament and maladjustment. *Hormones and Behavior, 56,* 133–139.

Stifter, C. A., Dollar, J. M., & Cipriano, E. A. (2011). Temperament and emotion regulation: The role of autonomic nervous system reactivity. *Developmental Psychobiology, 53,* 266–279.

Stifter, C. A., & Fox, N. A. (1990). Infant reactivity: Physiological correlates of newborn and 5-month temperament. *Developmental Psychology, 26,* 582–588.

Stifter, C. A., Fox, N. A., & Porges, S. W. (1989). Facial expressivity and vagal tone in five- and ten-month old infants. *Infant Behavior and Development, 12,* 127–137.

Stifter, C. A., & Jain, A. (1996). Psychophysiological correlates of infant temperament: Stability of behavior and autonomic patterning from 5 to 18 months. *Developmental Psychobiology, 29,* 379–391.

Suess, P. E., Porges, S. W., & Plude, D. J. (1994). Cardiac vagal tone and sustained attention in school-age children. *Psychophysiology, 31,* 17–22.

Talge, N. M., Donzella, B., & Gunnar, M. R. (2008). Fearful temperament and stress reactivity among preschool-aged children. *Infant and Child Development, 17,* 427–445.

Thomas, A., Birch, H., Chess, S., Hertzig, M., & Korn, S. (1964). *Behavioral individuality in early childhood.* New York: New York University Press.

Thomas, A., & Chess, S. (1977). *Temperament and development.* New York: Brunner/Mazel.

Thomas, A., Chess, S., & Birch, H. G. (1970). The origins of personality. *Scientific American, 223,* 102–109.

Thompson, R. A. (1994). Emotion regulation: A theme in search of definition. *Monographs of the Social for Research in Child Development, 59,* 250–283.

Tomarken, A. J., Davidson, R. J., Wheeler, R. F., & Kinney, L. (1992). Psychometric properties of resting anterior EEG asymmetry: temporal stability and internal consistency. *Psychophysiology, 29,* 576–592.

Vanyukov, M. M., Moss, H. B., Plial, J. A., Blackson, T., Mezzich, A. C., & Tarter, R. E. (1993). Antisocial symptoms in preadolescent boys and in their parents: Associations with cortisol. *Psychiatry Research, 46,* 9–17.

Vuga, M., Fox, N. A., Cohn, J. F., George, C. J., Levenstein, R. M., & Kovacs, M. (2006). Long-term stability of frontal electroencephalographic asymmetry in adults with a history of depression. *International Journal of Psychophysiology, 59,* 107–115.

Vuga, M., Fox, N. A., Cohn, J. F., Kovacs, M., & George, C. J. (2008). Long-term stability of electroencephalographic asymmetry and power in 3 to 9 year-old children. *International Journal of Psychophysiology, 67,* 70–77.

Watamura, S. E., Donzella, B., Alwin, J., & Gunnar, M. (2003). Morning to afternoon increases in cortisol concentrations for infants and toddlers at child care: Age differences and behavioral correlates. *Child Development, 74,* 1005–1020.

Wilson, B., & Gottman, J. (1996). Attention—the shuttle between emotion and cognition: Risk, resiliency, and physiological bases. In E. Hetherington & E. Blechman (Eds.), *Stress, coping and resiliency in children and families* (pp. 189–228). Mahwah, NJ: Erlbaum.

Zentner, M., & Bates, J. E. (2008). Child temperament: An integrative review of concepts, research programs, and measures. *European Journal of Developmental Science, 2,* 7–37.

PART IV

BIOLOGICAL PERSPECTIVES ON TEMPERAMENT

CHAPTER 13

Temperament in Animals

Christina S. Barr

> Our space will not permit us to recite in detail, as we are tempted to do, the peculiarities which these birds exhibited during a memorable summer. We must content ourselves with the simple statement that in reactions which may be designated as those of wildness, fear, timidity, curiosity, suspicion, initiative, sociability, the individuals differed most obviously and importantly. We hope sometime, in justice to the problem of crow temperament, to devote a summer to the intensive study of sex and individual differences in these extremely intelligent birds.
> —R. M. YERKES AND A. W. YERKES (1917, p. 3)

Even the many of us who perceive ourselves to be experts in the studies of animal behavior often marvel at the degree to which we can observe human-like temperament traits in other species. Aspects of *temperament*, defined as a constellation of heritable behavioral, personality and psychological dimensions, are trait-like and present from a time early in development. Much is known about the origins and potential outcomes of human temperament, for which various assessment tools have been developed and a range of dimensions have been described. Although they have evolved over time and are divergent in many ways, each approach—old and new—captures similar degrees of phenotypic variation among subjects that can reliably contribute to the accurate assessment of an individual's temperament.

Many psychologists have made enormous contributions to the field of developmental psychology. To name a few, Thomas and Chess (1977, 1986), Diamond (1957), Buss and Plomin (1984), Kagan (1984a, 1984b; Kagan, Resnick, & Snidman, 1988), Rothbart and Derryberry (1981), and Cloninger (1987) were major contributors, each devising assessment tools and/or behavioral/temperament inventories that contribute significantly to our ability to assess reliably and, therefore, understand the neurobiological underpinnings of human temperament (see Rothbart, Chapter 1, this volume, for a summary of this classic literature). The various tools and scales employed are somewhat diverse in complexity and scope, as reviewed by Zentner and Bates (2008), but the resultant dimensions show a certain degree of consistency or overlap across the various studies (see Mervielde & De Pauw, Chapter 2, and Zuckerman, Chapter 3, this volume). In this chapter, I first describe features of animal temperament as they relate to those that are present in humans. Subsequently, I introduce some of the neurobiological systems that contribute to behavior and temperament across animal species. Finally, I discuss how genetic variation that influences neurobiological function contributes to individual differences in temperament, with a focus on nonhuman primate species.

Looking to Animals in Order to Understand the Roots of Human "Temperament"

Since we commonly observe or cohabitate with animals because they are in our service and because animal models are commonly used in biomedical, psychological, and neuroscience research, the creation of tools that allow us to characterize animal temperament might not only help us to understand their behaviors better and facilitate increased cooperativity but may also provide constructs that reliably translate to the human condition.

Of particular relevance for this chapter might be an accounting of the early work of Diamond (1957), which describes some features of temperament in children (e.g., fearfulness and aggressiveness) as they relate to their likely phylogenetic underpinnings.

Though he is only one among many who have described animal behaviors in relation to those present in humans (predecessors include Lorenz and Darwin, to name two notable ones), Diamond's unique contribution was to be among the first to focus on describing features that were also observed in a variety of animal species and directly relating them to human *temperament*. The two basic dimensions on which Diamond initially focused were fearfulness and aggressiveness. He adroitly stated that these traits were more or less evident in some animal species, and that they also varied, perhaps to a lesser extent, among individuals within any given species. The species he referenced in this work included both laboratory (i.e., predominantly rodents but also nonhuman primates) and domestic animal species, notably, the cat and dog, with which many humans regularly interact and which they themselves could consider as subjects of their own behavioral observations (Table 13.1).

Though individual and breed-based differences in temperament have been studied in a variety of species, of particular relevance to

TABLE 13.1. Some Types of Tools Used for Assessment of Temperament in Animals

Assessment approach	Rodent	Dog	Horse	Monkey
Forced swim	BI, Act			
Open field	BI, Act		BI	
Open arm/bridge	BI, Act, Imp		BI	
Place preference	Rwd	Rwd		Rwd
Handling	BI, Agg		BI, Agg	
Focal scoring	BI, Act, Imp, Agg, Soc	BI, Act, Imp, Agg, Soc	BI, Act, Imp, Agg, Soc	BI, Act, Imp, Agg, Soc
Novelty challenge	BI, Act, Imp	BI, Act	BI, Act	BI, Act, Imp
Intruder challenge	BI, Act, Imp, Agg, Soc	BI, Act, Agg, Soc		BI, Act, Imp, Agg, Soc
Social separation	BI, Soc	BI, Soc	BI, Soc	BI, Soc
Startle	BI	BI, Agg	BI, Act	BI
Questionnaires	N/A	All	All	N/A

Note. This table lists approaches used (both inside and outside of the laboratory) and the species in which they are performed, in addition to the behavioral dimensions that are reliably accessed in their execution. BI, behavioral inhibition; Act, activity; Imp, impulsivity; Agg, aggression; Soc, sociability; Rwd, reward sensitivity.

the human condition may be those examined in nonhuman primates. Early studies of temperament differences in nonhuman primates indicated that rhesus macaques could be classified as being either "uptight" or "laid back" (Higley & Suomi, 1989). Vervet monkeys can be similarly characterized on the basis of behavior in the social group and responses to challenge (Bradwejn et al., 1992). In the social group, laid-back vervets are more active, are groomed more often, and compete more effectively for resources. Uptight monkeys, on the other hand, are more isolated and exhibit extremely submissive behaviors (cowering or crouching). When placed in a single cage, the uptight vervets exhibit stereotypical behaviors, whereas those that are laidback sit quietly, exploring their environment.

As is true in humans, multiple tools have been developed for assessment of temperament in animal species. In most cases, behavioral "probes" are used in the laboratory (i.e., open-field stress, social separation stress, intruder challenge test, novelty challenge, handling) in order to generate complex phenotypic characterization and to access behaviors that might not otherwise be assessable in the baseline state. All of these are performed in a variety of species, with the goal of dissecting out and determining contributions to stress reactivity or the various dimensions of temperament. Some of these tests have predefined criteria for describing a given "trait," while others use factor analysis of behavior collected to generate temperament traits or dimensions without any expectancies or predefinition involved (see Table 13.1). Though traits relating to fearfulness and aggressiveness are typically core dimensions found in these studies, it is safe to say that many other dimensions emerge from these studies. This demonstrates the potential relevance and richness of using animal species for determining genetic and neurobiological factors contributing to individual differences in temperament.

Given that many of us consider ourselves experts in animal behavior, it is not a surprise that the majority of assessments performed for domestic animal species depend on owner-informed questionnaires. These are available for a number of domestic animal species, including horses, dogs, and cats (Duberstein & Gilkeson, 2010; Lansade, Bouissou, & Erhard, 2008; Ley, McGreevy, & Bennett, 2009; McGrogan, Hutchison, & King, 2008; Van den Berg et al., 2010). Although these questionnaires are generally designed to minimize owner bias and maximize interrater reliability, several problems should be noted. First, particularly in species in which we see so much similarity to the human form (i.e., nonhuman primates) or in others that are artful interpreters and imitators of the human condition (i.e., dogs), the tendency to anthropomorphize might be difficult to avoid. Second, among most rodent neurobehaviorists, there has been set a precedent of caution in the use of certain terms that rely on inferences—for example, *anxious*—in describing rodent temperament or behavior. Instead, behaviors such as freezing, defecation in the open field, or rearing (all of which indicate reactivity to the environment and can be reflective of anxiety) should be termed *anxiety-like behavior*. This does not necessarily extend to other fields, in which evidence for a tendency to over-anthropomorphize can be suggested by the terminologies used. Veterinarians often hear owners refer to their animals as being "angry" or "jealous" (because a dog is agonistic or aggressive, does it necessarily mean that it is angry?).

Owners and investigators alike can fall prey to these inclinations. In assessment of dog and cat temperaments, there are cases in which investigators have created dimensions that involve the use of descriptors such as *arrogant*, *calculating*, *coldhearted*, and *ingenuous*. To think that we can not only observe the expression but also deeply understand the roots or motivation for animal behavior might be considered *arrogant* indeed. The (potentially) invalid characterizations of these behaviors might also lead to significant sources of error when one is attempting to characterize a complex phenomenon such as temperament and to retrieve information about its underlying neurobiology. Even Diamond (1957), who argued for the validity of using animals to describe or model human temperament, questioned whether there might be a tendency to over-anthropomorphize in his reference to descriptions provided for a captive male chimpanzee, in which he used terms such as *sanguine*, *mercurial*, and *good-natured* to describe the animal.

Fearfulness, Aggressiveness, and the "Other" Temperament Dimensions

We have seen many striking analogies between the behavior of rats and man, which encourage us in the view that there are variables of temperament which are common to both and that discovering these in rats may help us to discern them in men. It is clear that all rats and mice have innate dispositions to fearful and aggressive behavior. In the life of each rat, these original dispositions to fearful withdrawal from danger and to aggressive attack against victims or competition are often in conflict and undergo many modifying experiences.
—DIAMOND (1957, p. 49)

What might justify our tendencies to over-anthropomorphize is that these traits in animals seem to share the same neurobiological underpinnings as those similarly discussed in humans, some of which are described below. Diamond (1957) claimed that if a child psychologist were asked to describe behavioral variation among children, he or she would perhaps reduce the variation to four different types of individuals. The first (Type 1) would be described as exceptionally fearful, consistently apprehensive, and readily reactive. The second (Type 2) would be described as resistant to authority, combative, and sometimes cruel to animals. The third (Type 3) would be said to be constantly getting into trouble as a result of behavioral dyscontrol or impulsivity. And, finally, the last (Type 4) would be described as being apathetic or generally disinterested. In fact, not even in animals can temperament be reduced to the dimensions of fearfulness and aggressiveness. Such descriptions can be made not only for human subjects but also among individuals of various animal species (Overall, 1997).

In contemporary society, it is common to hear people refer to a certain personality or temperament type as it matches those of not only a certain species of animals but also within-species variation, for example, among various breeds of dogs. There are temperament traits and constellations of these traits observed in dogs, many of which are heritable and/or breed-specific (Saetre et al., 2006). For example, a dalmatian (Turcsán, Kubinyi, & Miklósi, 2011) is characterized by a small number of animal behaviorists as low in calmness, high in trainability, low in sociability, and low in boldness, and would likely match the individual temperament listed earlier for Type 1. On the other hand, the bull terrier is described as low in calmness, low in trainability and sociability, with increased boldness, indicating that it might be a good representation for the Type 2 individual. Similar temperament types are described among horses (Lesimple, Fureix, LeScolan, Richard-Yris, & Hausberger, 2011; Lloyd, Martin, Bornett-Gauci, & Wilkinson, 2008). Most importantly, and of most relevance to the discussion below, the fact that variation in temperament dimensions has been described across dog or horse breeds reinforces the fact that these are likely to be heritable traits within the breed with functional, neurogenetically based underpinnings (Hausberger, Bruderer, Le Scolan, & Pierre, 2004; Lesimple et al., 2011; Lloyd et al., 2008; Oki et al., 2007; Turscán et al., 2011; Van den Berg, Heuven, Van den Berg, Duffy, & Serpell, 2010; von Borstel, Duncan, Lundin, & Keeling, 2010).

Hawks, Doves, and the Maintenance of Variations in Temperament within and across Species

In 1984, Maynard Smith applied "game theory" to animal behavior and found that aggressivity and fearfulness are traits that tend to balance each other in any social population. He described the "hawk–dove game" in which "hawks" (aggressive individuals, who were proactive and adopted fight-or-flight responses to stress) and "doves" (who were fearful and cooperative and adopted a freeze-and-hide strategy with stress) were likely to co-occur in the same species. He determined that both hawk and dove strategies could potentially be adaptive, perhaps especially so in certain environmental contexts. While hawks would be predicted to do better when food is abundant and population density is high (i.e., they are better off fighting for access to mates than foraging), doves would likely outcompete hawks when the opposite is true (i.e., they would be better at getting food during periods of scarcity of resource and avoiding danger during times of increased conflict). The two types of temperaments must be balanced in any given population because in a population comprised completely of hawks, there would be an excessive level of aggressive encounters among members of the population, reducing the likelihood that any one individual would survive to reproduce successfully, and in one comprising only doves, they would be killed off by some other hawk species. It stands to reason, then, that the genetic factors that underlie these two alternative strategies would likely be subject to balancing selection and, as a result, both types of traits or strategies would be observed among individuals of many social species.

If one examines individual differences in avian behavior not only across but also within species, one sees that there are traits consistent with the hawk and dove classifications of temperament described earlier. Take, for example, the great tit (*Parus major*). It has been observed that there are two types of male "temperaments" present in this species. One type of individual has high levels of aggression and is a superficial, fast explorer, whereas the other is nonaggressive and explores its environment thoroughly and slowly. It has been suggested that the traits observed in these "temperaments" did not evolve in isolation but as a package, perhaps due to *haplotype structure* (gene linkage) or to *genetic pleiotropy* (when gene variants contribute to variation in multiple phenotypes) (Korte, Koolhaas, Wingfield, & McEwen, 2005). These findings translate to other species as well. In fact, these two basic temperament types—hawk versus dove—have been consistently described, though perhaps not in explicit terms, in the assessments of temperament of rodents, cats, dogs, horses, nonhuman primates, and humans.

Hawk, dove, or fowl? *Pecking order*, a term commonly used to describe an individual's dominance status, was derived from work based on domestic fowl behaviors (Schjerlderup-Ebbe, 1935). Dominance can result from the balance between anxiety and aggressivity, as stated earlier, but it is not a temperament trait per se, as it is actually a position of "status" awarded by another individual (of the same or another species), that has agreed to defer to the first. It is, therefore, a relative measure, such that one individual can be both dominant and submissive, depending on the relationship between members of the particular dyad being studied. Diamond stated that "it is only at the extremes of the hierarchic order that one can find consistently submissive or dominant behavior" (1957, p. 36).

In citing the importance of the effect of genetic selection on behavior, Diamond (1957) stated that an individual's relative dominance status is likely to result from the balance between two temperament dimensions—fearfulness and aggressiveness. *Dominance*, as described in wild or even some laboratory animals, is quite different from that described in domesticated species. Among members of most species own social group, dominance status is awarded, sometimes because of the family history of the dominant animal (i.e., in most Old World monkey species, females "inherit" dominance status along the matriline). In domestic animal species, although dominance status can be defined relative to other conspecifics in a home, herd, or paddock, often temperaments that are referred to as being *dominant* are those defined in terms of an individual's interactions with humans rather than among conspecifics. This is likely quite different than dominance among members of a social group (within species), as assertion of dominance toward humans may relate to "tameness"-like phenotypes (Albert et al., 2009) and the relative degree of an animal's willingness to accept a subordinate role and comply with human demands.

The Importance of Assessing Neurobiological Differences

Reward dependence, sensation seeking, extraversion, novelty seeking, empathy, activity, impulsivity, sociability—these are all temperament "traits" that have described humans but do not necessarily always relate to the core traits of fearfulness and aggressiveness. Rather, they may relate to traits such as impulse control and affiliativeness. For these ancillary traits, there is likely a great degree of variability in terms of their "causation." In other words, such traits can be driven by multiple motivational or behavioral systems and, thus, by a range of neurobiological mechanisms, theoretically resulting in both inaccurate calling and imprecise dissection. For example, an individual who is high in novelty seeking may be so assessed because he or she is impulsive, even if he or she is not seeking out novelty per se. On the one hand, these classifications could in some ways be overly simplistic for the purpose of identification of underlying neurobiological systems. An individual who rates high on affiliativeness may do so because he or she is novelty seeking (craving novelty and the unexpected nature of social interaction; Zuckerman, 1983). On the other hand, one who is sociable/affiliative may also be more anxious (needs the comfort of companionship). Finally, increased sociability and affiliativeness can also be attributed to enhanced reward sensitivity and/or stronger roots of social attachment (enjoying or depending more on social interaction).

Recent meta-analyses indicate that three temperament dimensions are universally, reliably, and consistently detected in rhesus macaques: Sociability, Confidence/Aggression, and Fearfulness (Freeman & Gosling, 2010). Although some of the same basic traits are being accessed, work on the rhesus macaque employs additional or different, more specific nomenclatures (e.g., see Capitanio & Widaman, 2005; Chamove, Eysenck, & Harlow, 1972). Some of the inconsistencies generated may also relate to interlaboratory differences in the behaviors assessed, the age at which animals are tested, the ethograms employed, or the stimulus probes used. In this sense, our own laboratory has been a contributor to the literature's internal inconsistencies, as we typically have considered not only context but also developmental stage in our "calling" of traits likely to be represented by behavioral factors generated in our analyses. By using factor analysis of homecage behavior for rhesus macaque infants, we generated dimensions that we attempted to ascribe to animals' internal states: We described these as "Anxious" (positive loading for locomotion, passive behavior, and mutual ventral contact with the mother), "Exploratory/Bold" (positive loadings for environmental exploration, infant leaving and approaching the mother, vocalization, and aggression) or "Attached" (positive loading for leaving and approaching the mother, social contact with the mother, and mutual break between mother and infant) (Barr, Dvoskin, et al., 2008; Barr, Schwandt, et al., 2008).

Factor analysis of behavior assessed in adolescent and adult animals during intruder challenge tests (in which an unfamiliar conspecific is used as a probe) generates a list of distinct and more extensive dimensions than do infant populations. These analyses generated factors termed "Agonistic/Highly Aggressive" (positive loading for approaching, maintaining proximity to, and exhibiting contact aggression toward the intruder), "Harm Avoidant" (maintenance of proximity to group members and passive behavior), "Curious/Bold" (positive loading for locomotion and approaching the intruder), "Threatening" (exhibiting noncontact aggression toward the intruder), and "Reactive" (exhibiting self-directed behavior) (Barr, Dvoskin, et al., 2008). These are provided as an example of investigator- or study-generated variability and, potentially, investigator bias in calling the dimensions, and it is clear in surveying the literature that similar levels and types of inconsistency are evident in assessments for other species (i.e., rodents, dogs, and horses). Though it is accepted that there is a need to excise the specific subdimensions of temperament and to track various subtleties, the inconsistencies observed across platforms for behaviors ascribed to any one temperament trait (both between and within species) call out for the identification of neurobiological substrates and, perhaps ultimately, reformed, biologically informed nomenclature (also see Kagan, Chapter 4, this volume).

There is ample evidence that both the intermediate phenotypes that predict temperament and temperament itself are linked to neurobiological substrates in animals. The Old World monkeys, which diverged from humans only 25 million years ago, give us evidence for these relationships. It has been shown that anxious macaques exhibit increased behavioral and endocrine responses to stress in the laboratory. Field studies show that, in addition to being inhibited, anxious animals have higher cerebrospinal fluid levels of corticotropin-releasing hormone (CRH) and a high degree of electroencephalographic (EEG) laterality (Kalin & Shelton, 2003; Kalin, Shelton, & Davidson, 2000), both of which have been documented in anxious or depressed human subjects (see White, Lamm, Helfinstein, & Fox, Chapter 17, and Depue & Fu, Chapter 18, this volume). Other field studies show that impulsive macaques engage in risky behaviors and aggressive encounters, and migrate from their natal troops at a younger age (Mehlman et al., 1994, 1995). They also have lower cerebrospinal fluid levels of the serotonin metabolite 5-hydroxyindoleacetic acid (5-HIAA) (Westergaard et al., 2003). In both instances, these traits appear to be fairly consistent across time and situations (Higley, Suomi, & Linnoila, 1996; Kalin & Shelton, 2003; Shannon et al., 2005). Using a tool that assesses individual responses to an unfamiliar conspecific, studies have shown that both anxious and impulsive behaviors appear to be heritable in vervet monkeys (Fairbanks et al., 2004). Other studies show anxiety to be heritable in rhesus monkeys (Williamson et al., 2003).

Heritable genetic factors that contribute to individual variation in neurotransmitter or neurohormonal function would be predicted to influence temperament and, therefore, behavioral strategies and fitness. It has been argued that the fact that characterization of many temperament traits in animals relies on making inferences about underlying motivations and emotions has restrained ethologists and evolutionary biologist from examining how an individual's temperament might impact fitness (Reale, Reader, Sol, McDouball, & Dingermanse, 2007). Reale and colleagues claim that the creation of definitions of the various traits using inference-free terminology would permit these types of investigations. It would also likely aid in more precise dissection of underlying mechanisms. The temperament trait categories that they described were shyness–boldness, exploration–avoidance, activity, sociability and aggressiveness. What follows is a discussion of some of the key neurobiological systems that contribute to individual differences in behavioral style and temperament. Rather than using the "inference-free" classifications put forth by Reale and colleagues (2007), I use the temperament dimensions described in independent sections presented earlier in this handbook (see Kagan, Chapter 4; Strelau & Zawadzki, Chapter 5; Putnam, Chapter 6; Deater-Deckard & Wang, Chapter 7; Rueda, Chapter 8; Knafo & Israel, Chapter 9). There is some overlap with the inference-free classifications, although there are some important differences as well (see Figure 13.1). My hope is that the context of the preceding chapters of the text will promote more facile navigation of this section.

These trait dimensions, relevance to the animal condition and/or limitations of their assessment/applicability, and a brief account of some of the neurobiological systems that are likely contributors to each, are introduced. Since some of the systems described can simultaneously contribute to multiple dimensions or traits, each neurotransmitter or neurohormonal system is then considered in turn, providing confirmation for the systems' roles in the development of temperament with data generated from behavioral genetic studies.

Potential Neurobiological Substrates

Behavioral Inhibition (Fearfulness)

Behavioral inhibition refers to a pattern of behavior involving avoidance, withdrawal, fearfulness in response to novelty, and overarousal of the sympathetic nervous system—a trait observed across all animal species, one that increases likelihood of survival of self and offspring and is therefore likely to be subject to intense selection. It also is a pattern that increases the risk for development of multiple neurobehavioral disorders in humans and animal species alike (e.g., generalized anxiety disorder, which is observed in both dogs and humans; compulsive, stereotypical behaviors in humans, dogs, and horses) (Overall, 1997). Some of the systems that contribute to behavioral inhibition are serotonin, gamma-aminobutyric acid (GABA), cannabinoids, and CRH (Dunn & Berridge, 1990; Koob & Le Moal, 2001; Lanfenêtre, Chaouloff, & Marsicano, 2009). Serotonin and GABA downmodulate, whereas CRH typically promotes anxiety-like behavior (though, depending on the receptor subtype and brain region, the opposite can be true). Therefore, compounds aimed and increasing serotonin and GABA neurotransmission or receptor binding can decrease fear and inhibition, while those that block the high-affinity receptor for CRH (CRHR1) can produce similar effects. Fearfulness may also influence other traits, such as novelty seeking, activity, or aggression, since it determines relative levels of shyness–boldness and may also enhance an individual's sensitivity to punishment. It is also likely to predict an individual's level

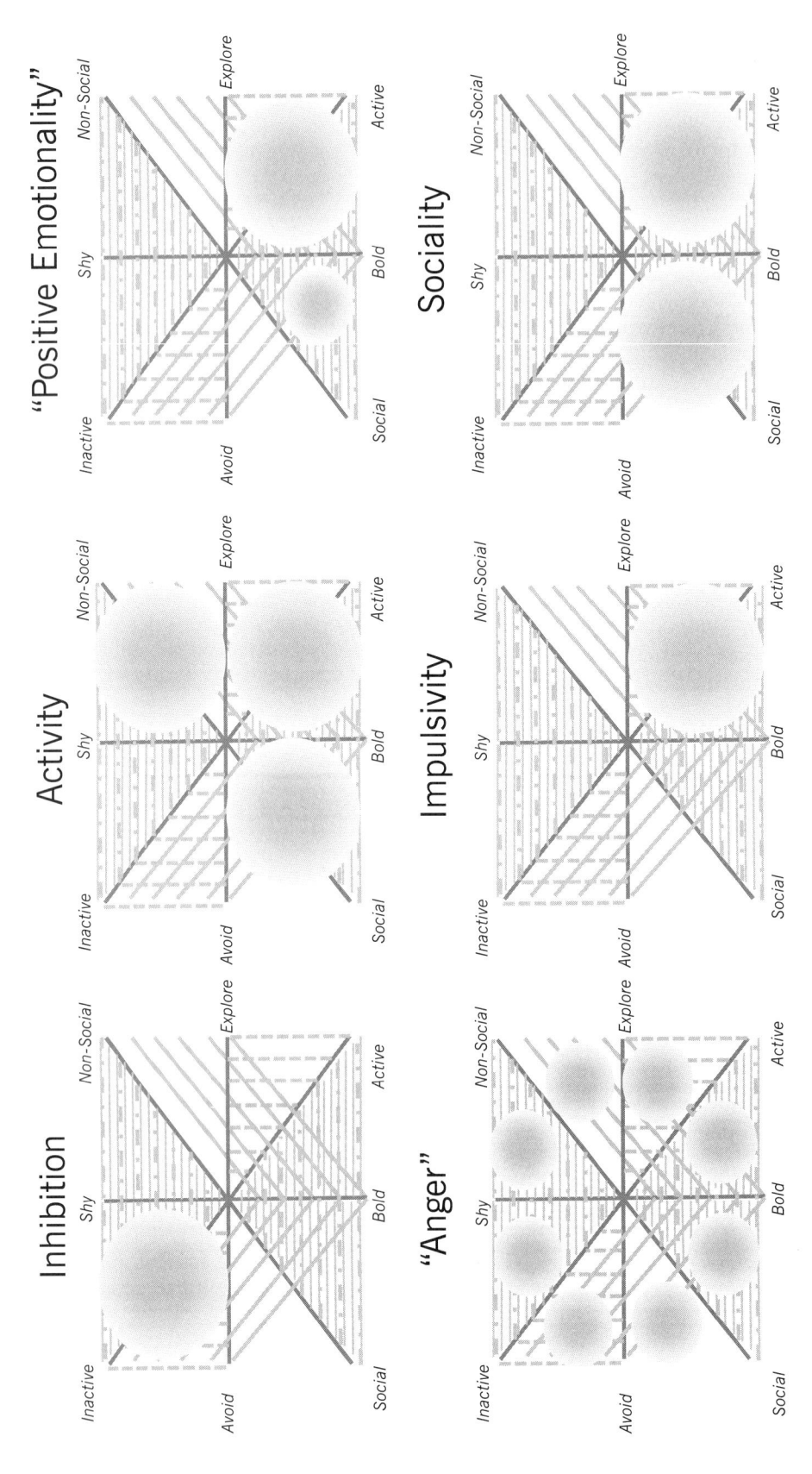

FIGURE 13.1. The human temperaments as they relate to traits that can be reliably described for various animal species. Shown are the inference-free dimensions or behaviors accessed in animals (indicated by circles) as they relate to each human temperament trait described in the text.

of dominance (see earlier discussion), which, for example, can be altered by the ratio of binding of serotonin to specific serotonin receptor subtypes (Yeh, Fricke, & Edwards, 1996).

Activity

Activity, like behavioral inhibition, can also be a manifestation of increased (or, paradoxically, decreased) levels of arousal, though its origins are not necessarily in fear or anxiety. Animals who maintain high levels of activity may also do so because they seek out stimulation (novelty seeking), are in a heightened state of stimulation, or to avoid excessive hypostimulation. The neurotransmitter systems most likely to moderate this trait are the dopamine and sympathetic nervous systems, though others are likely to be involved (Cabib, Puglisi-Allegra, & Ventura, 2002; Fan, Bruno, & Hess, 2012; Russell, 2011).

Activity resulting from increased arousal/stimulation is a trait that is likely under both natural and artificial selection. With regard to the latter, rodent lines selected for differences in drug response and sensation seeking show particularly marked differences in their levels of activity. The horse is also a species in which artificial selection has promoted differences in levels of activity. It is well known that horse breeds are loosely divided into three categories based on general temperament and activity: (1) "Hot bloods" are spirited breeds of horses, with high levels of speed and endurance (i.e., Arabians and thoroughbreds); (2) "cold bloods," for example, draft horses (i.e., Percherons), are more suitable for slow, heavy work; and (3) "warm bloods" (i.e., Hanoverians) exhibit an intermediate phenotype, are used in equitation, eventing and jumping, and were developed from crosses between hot bloods and cold bloods. Among very closely related dog breeds (i.e., the Alaskan malamute and the Siberian husky), a great deal of variation in activity is observed. This is likely attributable to the selection pressures on the respective breeds; whereas huskies are explorers and are built for speed, malamutes historically remain with the family as "nannies" and, when working, are used for slow, heavy work. It is likely that in all of these species, by selecting for levels of activity, other traits (notably, fearfulness or anxiety) were inadvertently selected as well. It is equally likely, therefore, that intrabreed variation is present.

Positive Emotionality

According to Depue (see Depue & Collins, 1999), "When our dopamine system is activated, we are more positive, excited, and eager to go after goals or rewards, such as food, sex, money, education, or professional achievements"; that is, when our dopamine system is activated, we are more extroverted, or exhibit more "positive emotionality."

Positive emotionality (and all that this term connotes) might be considered one of those traits that is somewhat difficult to evaluate in animals, especially if one is trying to avoid making inferences. This being said, dogs can be characterized by some as being "positive" or "extraverted" (picture, perhaps, a Labrador retriever that trots around the house wagging its tail, panting with excitement, hopping up and down whenever someone new comes into the room and taking a play-bow stance, even when another dog tries to engage it in an agonistic encounter). Since there has been little study with regard to this trait in animals, the neurobiological mechanisms are not known, but based on our knowledge of human temperament, it is probably safe to assume that the endogenous opioids (by producing comfort), dopamine (in driving reward), and serotonin (which influences anxiety and affect) are likely involved (see Depue & Fu, Chapter 18, this volume).

Anger/Irritability

When a dog approaches a strange dog or man in a savage or hostile frame of mind, he walks upright and very stiffly; his head is slightly raised; the tail is held erect and quite rigid; the hairs bristle, especially along the neck and back; his pricked ears are directed forwards, and the eyes have a fixed stare.
—DARWIN (1896, p. 50)

It is often easy for even the layperson to appreciate behaviors in animal species that predict the animal's intent or willingness to engage in an aggressive encounter. Dogs, as cited in the earlier example, use various forms of communication, including staring while maintaining an erect tail and forward ears. They may also approach one another at an angle (perpendicular to the shoulder), an action that invites a reaction to challenge. Increased arousal and sympathetic drive in an animal that is primed for an agonistic encounter also produces pupillary dilation and piloerection, which can be confined to the shoulders or, in a particularly aroused dog, extend down the ridge of its back (see Van den Berg et al., 2010). The result is that we, as humans, can with relative ease read both the relative level of arousal and the dog's intent to interact in aggressive manner.

However, "anger" is a trait that is difficult to assess in animals, since they cannot verbally communicate with us, and we are able truly to appreciate only overt expressions of their emotions. Many experts on animal behavior maintain that animals that experience anger as humans can (ruminating, lusting for revenge, etc.) are the exception rather than the rule, if they exist at all (Grandin, 2005). Perhaps the behavior that most likely matches that of human "anger" would be that referred to as "affective aggression," but even this is quite variable in its origins and expression (Grandin, 2005). In her book *Animals in Translation*, Temple Grandin (2005) lists the four core emotions in animals, one of which she terms *rage*. *Affective aggression* is aggression that she described as being driven by rage. This is in contrast to *predatory aggression*, which is driven by instinct and is actually likely to be rewarding for most predators (simply envision a cat toying with a mouse). Both types of aggression likely involve a degree of arousal, but the types of arousal (tense vs. energetic; K. MacDonald, 1988) differ.

There are various different forms of this type of aggression: dominance aggression, fear-induced aggression, intermale aggression, pain-induced aggression, and irritable or stress-induced aggression (e.g., redirected aggression). These forms are frequently observed among wild animals and in the domestic animal species with which we work or cohabitate, such as cats, dogs, and horses. In the domestic animals, these are also behaviors whose underlying neurobiology we know, since many therapeutic agents used for treatment of feline and canine aggression—for example, tricyclic antidepressants and selective serotonin reuptake inhibitors (SSRIs)—reduce their frequency and severity. The serotonin and norepinephrine systems are targets for ameliorating various forms of affective aggression (Overall, 1997). It is likely that, depending on the subtype, the dopamine, endogenous opioid, and CRH systems may also be involved (Barr, Dvoskin, et al., 2008; Barr, Schwandt, et al., 2008; Miller et al., 2004; Veenema & Neumann, 2007). The involvement of these systems in the expression of rage in animals may therefore give us clues about the underlying neurobiological factors controlling irritability and anger in humans.

Effortful Control/Impulsivity

Impulse control is a trait that has been extensively studied in a wide variety of animal species. Many tools can be used to assess inhibitory control, which generally involves assessment of risk-taking behavior in order to gain a reward or measurements of immediacy of response for reward at the expense of potential gain. These studies have been performed in a large number of laboratory studies, both in rodents and in nonhuman primates (e.g., Fairbanks et al., 2004; Olmstead, Ouagazzal, & Kieffer, 2009).

Although a number of systems are certainly involved (the endogenous opioids, dopamine, etc.), one of the most replicated findings in psychiatric research areas is that impaired or low central nervous system (CNS) serotonin results in impaired impulse control. There are many serotonin receptors at which both genetic manipulation and spontaneously occurring genetic variation produce impulsive behavior. In animals and humans alike, an intermediate phenotype observed in impulsively aggressive subjects is low cerebrospinal fluid levels of the major serotonin metabolite 5HIAA, which is said to be reflective of diminished central serotonin function among impulsive subjects. Among humans, these include impulsive alcoholics and fire-setters, suicide attempters, and violent offenders. Similar to what has been reported in humans, in dominantly aggressive dogs (dogs that have a type of "impulsive" aggression that is more common among males, involves uncontrolled aggression directed toward a human family member, and is worsened by punishment) the same neurochemical intermediate phenotype is observed (Reisner, Mann, Stanley, Huang, & Houpt, 1996). In highly impulsive and aggressive monkeys (both vervets and rhesus macaques), decreased serotonin system function is also observed (Barr et al., 2003). Rhesus macaques with low 5-HIAA are more likely to exhibit behaviors characteristic of impaired impulse control, such as spontaneous, long leaps at dangerous heights and repeated jumping into baited traps in which they have a prior history of having been captured and restrained (reviewed in Barr & Goldman, 2006; Barr, Schwandt, Newman, & Higley, 2004). In vervet monkeys and cynomolgus macaques, the latency to approach a potentially dangerous conspecific (intruder) correlates with 5-HIAA concentrations, and treatment with agents that modify serotonin transmission provide pharmacological validation of serotonin's role in this trait (Fairbanks, Melega, & Jorgensen, 2001; Manuck, Kaplan, & Rymeski, 2003). In the end, although there are certainly other systems whose dysregulations contribute to impairments in impulse control, the serotonin system is undeniably the most prominent among them (for other genetic studies performed in humans, see also Bevilacqua et al., 2010; Reist, Mazzanti, Vu, Fujimoto, & Goldman, 2004).

Empathy/Prosocial Behavior (Affiliativeness)

In discussing the role of the domestic dog, Diamond (1957) introduced the concept of attachment. He stated that

> the dog's relationship to man highlights another important temperamental characteristic, his readiness and even need to form dependent attachments. . . . This is not a uniquely canine characteristic, although it has undergone an extraordinary development in the dog, whose lasting attachments to humans may have become the very symbol of affectionate devotion. (p. 70)

It is difficult to discuss the use of animal models for learning about the development and expression of temperament in humans without discussing the work of John Bowlby (1969, 1973). Bowlby, a psychoanalyst and psychiatrist, was a great admirer of the work of ethologists such as Lorenz and Hinde. For this reason, he often discussed the findings from his own work (and others in the field) as they related to ancestral traits that would likely have conferred selective advantage in the early evolutionary history of humans. Most notable among these was his research on social attachment.

As stated earlier, affiliativeness may be driven by a diversity of traits relating to temperament (anxiety, reward sensitivity, etc.). Heightened affiliativeness can also be partially attributable to stronger roots of social attachment (enjoying or depending more on social interaction). Formation and maintenance of the mother–infant attachment bond is essential to infant survival not only for the provision of nourishment but also protection from injury and predation (Bowlby, 1969). In a wide variety of animal species, attachment increases the motivation of an infant to employ evolutionarily conserved behavioral strategies in order to maintain proximity to its mother and to gain her attention during periods of separation. Studies examining the role of the neurobiology of social attachment have pointed to several systems in particular: the endogenous opioid ß-endorphin, and the vasopressin and oxytocin systems (Burkett, Spiegel, Inoue, Murphy, & Young, 2011; Copeland et al., 2011; Kennedy, Panksepp, Wong, Krause, & Lahvis, 2011; Panksepp & Lahvis, 2011). All of these neuropeptides promote the development of attachment and, ultimately, general levels of sociality or social cognition. The potential genetic contributions and expression of individual differences in social attachment are addressed in more detail later in the chapter.

Looking to Behavioral Genetics as Experiments of Nature

The preceding discussion is about the various temperament dimensions described earlier in this handbook, their expression in animal species, and the neurobiological systems that might contribute to their expression. This discussion now shifts focus from behavior to genetic variation and molecular mechanisms. The genetics of temperament is discussed in several other chapters of this handbook (Saudino & Wang, Chapter 16; White et al., Chapter 17; Depue & Fu, Chapter 18). Research on genetics in animals casts an important light onto the genetics of human temperament. Below is a glimpse into the roles of some of the neuropeptide and neurotransmitter systems that contribute to the expression of temperament, as evidenced by the effects of functional genetic variation on relevant traits and behavior. It would be impossible to address all of the genetic variation that contributes to the traits or relevant systems in this format. Instead, genetic loci at which functional genetic variation is present and produces similar phenotypic effects across species are discussed, with a focus on data generated in the nonhuman primate. The inconsistencies in the depths of discussion for each gene relates not to relative importance of the various systems in contributing to variation in temperament, but rather, to their relative complexities, available information relating to the existence of spontaneously occurring genetic variation in animal species, and the abundance of descriptions of molecular effects and genotype–phenotype relationships. Those genes to be included in the discussion are *SLC6A4* (the serotonin transporter gene), *MAOA* (the monoamine oxidase A gene), *CRH* (the CRH gene), *DRD4* (the dopamine receptor D4 gene), and *OPRM1* (the mu-opioid receptor gene) (summarized in Figure 13.2).

SLC6A4

The serotonin transporter is a protein critical to regulating serotonin function in the brain, since serotonin's action in the synapse is terminated by reuptake. In mice, targeted disruption of the serotonin transporter gene results in increased adrenocorticotropic hormone (ACTH) and corticosterone responses to immobilization stress, as well as increased anxiety during the elevated plus maze and light–dark exploration tasks (Lanfumey, Mannoury La Cour, Froger, & Hamon, 2000; Li et al., 1999). Gene expression studies demonstrate that monkeys with high levels of stress reactivity have lower gene expression levels for the serotonin transporter (Bethea et al., 2005).

In humans, there is a variant in the regulatory region for *SLC6A4* that reduces levels of

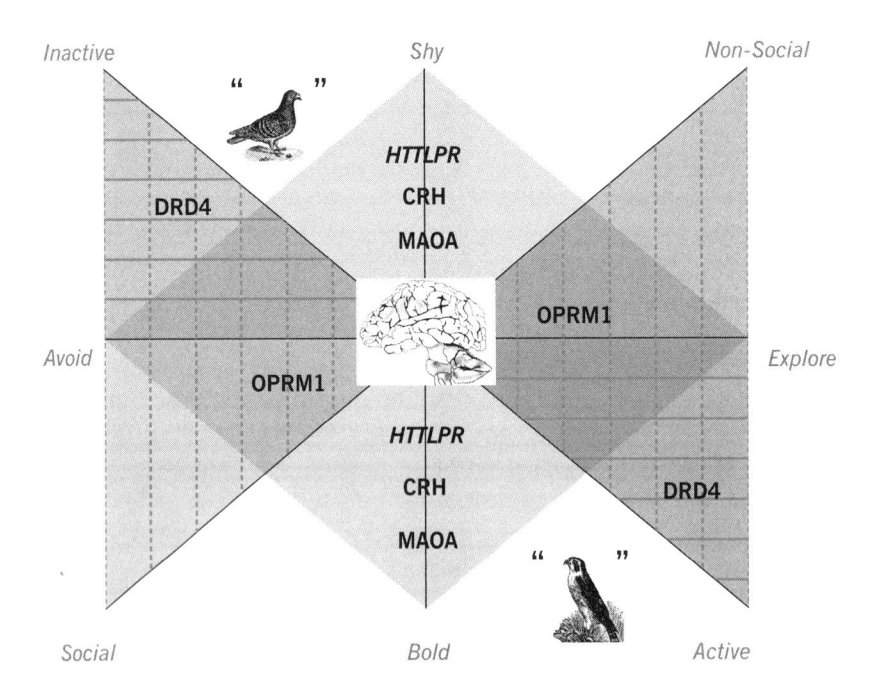

FIGURE 13.2. Functional genetic variants that predict individual differences in brain function and the behavioral traits that contribute to temperament. Known effects of functional variation at the serotonin transporter (*5-HTT*), *CRH*, and *MAOA* genes (central diamond), *DRD4* (horizontal lines), and *OPRM1* (hatched vertical lines) as they relate to traits associated with the hawk and dove types of temperament traits are indicated.

expression of *SLC6A4*, and variation of this serotonin-transporter-linked polymorphic region (*HTTLPR*) predicts certain temperament traits related to anxiety, depression, and aggression, such as neuroticism, harm avoidance, and disagreeableness (Lesch et al., 1997; Mazzanti et al., 1998). There is variation in the *SLC6A4* regulatory region in many nonhuman primate species (Lesch et al., 1997; Wendland et al., 2005). In the rhesus monkey, a similar polymorphism has been shown to alter transcriptional efficiency (Bennett et al., 2002), resulting in decreased serotonin transporter mRNA levels in brains of animals carrying the variant allele (Lopez & Higley, 2002), which may be further regulated by epigenetic mechanisms (Kinnally et al., 2010). Because it might predict alternative strategies, particularly in certain environmental contexts, the *HTTLPR* polymorphism has been studied extensively in both rhesus and human gene × environment interaction studies (Barr, Newman, Lindell, et al., 2004; Barr, Newman, Schwandt, et al., 2004; Barr, Newman, Shannon, et al., 2004).

Studies in multiple, independent laboratories demonstrate that the *HTTLPR* s allele predicts anxiety and responses to stress in rhesus macaques (Bethea et al., 2005; Champoux et al., 2002). Furthermore, these rhesus studies show that *HTTLPR* genotype can interact with controlled exposures to prenatal stress/alcohol or early life adversity to result in long-lasting differences in stress reactivity, sensation seeking, and aggression (Barr, Newman, Lindell, et al., 2004; Barr, Newman, Schwandt, et al., 2004; Barr, Newman, Shannon, et al., 2004; Barr, Schwandt, et al., 2004; Kraemer et al., 2008; Schneider et al., 2010; Schwandt et al., 2010; Spinelli et al., 2007). These rhesus studies have provided support for the notion that *HTTLPR* variation interacts with stressful life experiences to moderate temperament (Lesch et al., 1997) and risk for stress-related disorders in humans (Caspi et al., 2003; Caspi, Hariri, Holmes, Uher, & Moffitt, 2010).

CRH

CRH is critical to stress coping. Studies utilizing experimental manipulations of CRH system activity suggest that naturally occurring *CRH* gene variation may mediate individual variability in behavioral and physiological traits that are key to determining an individual's coping style. One of the most consistent behavioral correlates of stress reactivity common to taxa as phylogenetically diverse as humans, rhesus macaques, rodents, and great tits is the way an organism approaches (or avoids) novel objects and unfamiliar conspecifics (Kalin et al., 2000; Korte et al., 2005). Individuals that readily seek out and investigate novel stimuli are considered "exploratory" or "bold"; those more likely to show fear or withdrawal when confronted with new objects or individuals are described as more "inhibited" or "shy" (Kagan et al., 1988; also see Kagan, Chapter 4, this volume). Individuals show stable tendencies in their behavioral reactions, which are linked—in mice, humans, and nonhuman primates, among others—to biological traits such as heart rate variability, frontal brain electrical activity, and cortisol levels (Barr, Schwandt, et al., 2008; Barr et al., 2009).

Some of the strongest arguments for a genetic basis for CRH-regulated temperament have come from behaviorally polytypic rodents. Short-attack-latency (SAL) mice, which consistently attack a nonaggressive intruder in under 50 seconds, display what is called an "active" coping strategy, in contrast to the more "passive" long-attack-latency (LAL) mice that typically do not attack a stranger under the same circumstances. The genetic lines also show consistent differences in hypothalamic–pituitary–adrenocortical (HPA) axis activity, with SAL mice exhibiting higher basal ACTH levels (Korte et al., 2005; Veenema & Neumann, 2007).

In humans, the *CRH* haplotype has been shown to predict behavioral inhibition (Smoller et al., 2003), and studies in rhesus macaques suggest that human *CRH* variation may moderate risk for externalizing disorders, perhaps through the pathway of behavioral inhibition. In rhesus, genetic variation predicts multiple indices of reactivity and temperament. Infant macaques that are carriers of one type of *CRH* polymorphism are characterized as being more exploratory and bold (Barr, Schwandt, et al., 2008), and, following adolescence, males that are carriers exhibit a more bold and active response to an unfamiliar conspecific. They also had high baseline levels of ACTH (consistent with the endocrine endophenotype reported for SAL mice, Veenema & Neumann, 2007) and lower levels of cerebrospinal fluid (CSF) *5-HIAA*, a neurochemical endophenotype observed among impulsive and aggressive macaques, dogs, and humans.

However, the CRH system influences not only how individuals approach novel stimuli and conspecifics, but it is also absolutely critical for physiological and behavioral adaptation to stress. Despite its critical role, it is also known that chronic overactivity of this system can lead to persistent angst and stress-related pathologies, such as depression, posttraumatic stress disorder, heart disease, diabetes, and Cushing's disease (Gold & Chrousos, 2002; Goldman & Barr, 2002; Hundt, Zimmermann, Pottig, Spring, & Holsboer, 2001; Korte et al., 2005; McEwen, 2006; Sapolsky, 2001; Southwick, Vythilingam, & Charney, 2005), to which anxious and inhibited individuals are particularly vulnerable. Studies performed in animal models have shown that increased activity of the CRH system can produce anxiety- and/or depression-like phenotypes (Jaferi & Bhatnagar, 2007; Kalin et al., 2000; Strome et al., 2002). Increased activity and, in particular, reactivity of the CRH system to stress, is an intermediate phenotype observed in "dove"-like members of a wide variety of species (Korte et al., 2005). In addition to the variant discussed earlier, there is another CRH promoter single-nucleotide polymorphism (SNP) in rhesus macaques (Barr et al., 2009) that, given its molecular effects, would putatively results in augmented CRH expression and release when an animal carrying this allele was confronted with a stressful stimulus. For this genotype, the alternative allele predicted increased behavioral and endocrine responses to stress among monkeys with a history of early stress exposure. Here, note that genetic variation at a single gene can produce varied effects, whether under different environmental conditions (stress vs. nonstress) or, potentially, on different dimensions of temperament. It may be that in humans, genetic variation that altered CRH system function could influence multiple behavioral dimensions (i.e., both neuroticism and extraversion), and that variants that placed an individual at the extremes of these spectra (i.e., inhibited and anxious/stress reactive vs. bold/impulsive and novelty seeking) would drive certain temperament types. Together, these studies suggest that functional CRH variants could alter temperament through distinct, varied, and potentially interactive mechanisms—either by inducing a novelty-seeking/bold temperament or by enhancing stress reactivity.

DRD4

Dopamine neurotransmission underlies many reward-dependent and reinforcing processes. Repeat polymorphisms in this gene exist across a variety of animal species (humans, macaques, vervets, dogs, horses, and chimpanzees) and have in some instances been shown to predict behaviors related to altered sensitivity to reward (Bailey, Breidenthal, Jorgensen, McCracken, & Fairbanks, 2007; Benjamin et al., 1996; Hejjas et al., 2009; Wendland et al., 2006). Macaque species also exhibit variation at this gene (rhesus macaques, pigtail macaques and Tonkean macaques), which differ in frequencies across species (Wendland et al., 2006). One trait predicted by *DRD4* variation in humans is that of novelty seeking (Benjamin et al., 1996; Ebstein et al., 1996). This has been replicated in vervet monkeys, in which a *DRD4* length variant was also observed (Bailey et al., 2007). Of interest, in the dog, which has been subject to intense artificial selection, a repeat polymorphism predicts social impulsivity and activity-impulsivity endophenotypes (Hejjas et al., 2009).

MAOA

One gene at which variation is linked to impulsivity and impulsive aggression in both animal models and humans is *MAOA* (Caspi et al., 2002; Newman et al., 2005). *MAOA* degrades the monoamine transmitters (dopamine, norepinephrine, and serotonin), and, therefore can influence synaptic concentrations of these neurotransmitters. A *VNTR* (variable number of tandem repeats) polymorphism in the transcriptional control region for the human *MAOA* gene (*MAOA-LPR*) has been shown to produce differences in gene expression levels (Sabol, Hu, & Hamer, 1998). In humans, the *MAOA-LPR* low-activity alleles predict decreased prefrontocortical and increased amygdalar responses to emotional stimuli, suggesting impaired ability to control emotional responses during arousal (Buckholtz & Meyer-Lindenberg, 2008; Meyer-Lindenberg et al., 2006). The low-activity *MAOA-LPR* allele has also been associated with trait-like, alcohol-independent antisocial behavior in alcohol-dependent populations (Samochowiec et al., 1999; Tikkanen et al., 2009), and various studies have shown that early environmental factors interact with genotype to predict antisocial behavior, aggressiveness, and violence (Caspi et al., 2002; Sjoberg et al., 2008). Of interest, this polymorphism is present across macaque species but differs substantially in its frequency (Wendland et al., 2006). The low-activity allele of *MAOA-LPR* increases impulsivity and aggression among rhesus macaques, suggesting that serotonin, norepinephrine, and dopamine levels, as determined by genetic variation as this locus, can drive impulsivity and dyscontrol (Barr et al., 2003; Newman et al., 2005).

OPRM1

The endogenous opioid system is critically involved in driving the euphoric and stimulating effects of reward. Among the behaviors driven by reward are consumption, sexual activity, social interactions, exploration, and, in some cases, aggression, to name a few. Genetic variation that influences *OPRM1* affinity or signaling would therefore be expected to influence a diversity of traits dependent on reward processes. Studies of rodents indicate that there are effects of activation of this receptor on activation of brain reward circuits, impulsivity, consummatory behaviors (alcohol drinking and eating), attenuation of fear responses, alcohol-induced stimulation, and the development of social attachment (Moles, Kieffer, & D'Amato, 2004; Olmstead et al., 2009; Sanders, Kieffer, & Fanselow, 2005).

In both humans and rhesus macaques, polymorphisms in the *OPRM1* gene (*OPRM1 A118 G* and *C77G*, respectively) alter affinity for beta-endorphin *in vitro* (Bond et al., 1998; Miller et al., 2004). In both species, HPA responses to stress are blunted (Schwandt et al., 2011). A number of effects of *OPRM1* variation that might suggest a role for these variants in driving temperament have been reported. Miller and colleagues (2004) reported increased aggressivity as a function of this allele in macaques, and there is also evidence that it influences maternal behavior in macaques, the development of social attachment in both human and nonhuman primates (Barr, Schwandt, et al., 2008; Copeland et al., 2011; Higham et al., 2011), and sensitivity to social rejection in humans (Way, Taylor, & Eisenberger, 2009). Data obtained from rhesus macaques also suggest that it influences activity and/or novelty seeking, since carriers of the G allele exhibit increased locomotion and reactivity to novel environmental stimuli (Lindell et al., 2010).

The Role of Genetic Selection: Understanding the Origins of Alcohol Use Disorders in Modern Humans

In certain instances, genetic variants that are functionally similar or orthologous to those that moderate risk for human psychiatric disorders are maintained across primate species (Barr & Goldman, 2006). We have identified several examples of this phenomenon in rhesus macaques and have studied them in order to model how genetic variation moderates risk for developing psychopathology. Some of these studies have suggested the potential for convergent evolution or allelic variants being maintained by selection in both species (Barr, Schwandt, et al., 2008; Vallender et al., 2008). These findings reinforce the potential for comparative behavioral genomics studies to demonstrate how relatively common human genetic variants, which are linked to traits that may be adaptive in certain environmental contexts, can increase vulnerability to psychiatric disorders or alcohol problems.

While the field of behavioral genetics is growing rapidly, most of its research is concerned with the identification of "disease alleles" or gene variation underlying what is considered pathological behavior. Its methods and findings, however, can be applied to a long-standing goal of evolutionary anthropology, to understand how changes in allele frequency can affect divergences in primate behavior. Several studies have identified associations between specific alleles and natural features of behavior and life history strategies. For example, the loss-of-function short (s) allele of the serotonin transporter gene promoter length polymorphism (*5-HTTLPR*), which increases risk for developing depression in the face of adversity, has a functional equivalent in the rhesus macaque (see earlier discussion). In macaques, this allele is associated with increased endocrine and behavioral stress reactivity as a function of stress exposure, often in a sexually dichotomous manner (Barr, Newman, et al., 2004; Schwandt et al., 2010; Spinelli et al., 2007). Therefore, this variant appears to increase risk for developing psychopathology, particularly in the context of stress. Despite this, these variants have been maintained in both humans and in rhesus macaque (in addition to some other nonhuman primate species). Moreover, in human populations in which the s allele is rare, another loss-of-function variant on the L allele background (LA > LG) is present at a higher frequency (Hu et al., 2006). In humans, there is also a variable number of tandem repeats (VNTR) in the second intron, which appears to be functional (Fiskerstrand, Lovejoy, & Quinn, 1999). This VNTR is present in a number of primate and nonprimate species and is polymorphic in a number of hominoid species (Soeby, Larsen, Olsen, Rasmussen, & Werge, 2005).

Although SNPs are not necessarily conserved across species, there are instances in which functionally similar SNPs occur in the human and rhesus macaque (Barr, Dvoskin, et al., 2008; Barr, Schwandt, et al., 2008; Miller et al., 2004; Vallender et al., 2008). It has been demonstrated that gain-of-function *5-HTT SNPs* have arisen and been maintained in both rhesus and in humans, suggesting that both gain- and loss-of-function variants may be under selection in primates (Vallender et al., 2008). It is of interest that *5-HTT* variation not only predicts individual differences in impulse control and stress reactivity (Barr, Newman, Lindell, et al., 2004; Barr, Newman, Schwandt, et al., 2004; Barr, Newman, Shannon, et al., 2004; Barr, Schwandt, et al., 2004; Bennet et al., 2002; Champoux et al., 2002; Schwandt et al., 2010), but that it is also associated with adaptive traits in free-ranging macaques, such as earlier male dispersal (Trefilov, Berard, Krawczak, & Schmidtke, 2000) and male reproductive timing (Krawczak et al., 2005). Whether allelic variation at *5-HTT* predicts "adaptive" traits in humans has not been elucidated, though there is speculation that this is indeed the case (Homberg & Lesch, 2011).

As another example, in both the rhesus macaque and in humans, there are nonsynonymous SNPs in the portion of the *OPRM1* gene that encodes the N-terminal domain of the receptor (C77G in rhesus macaque and A118G in human), and these SNPs have been observed to confer similar functions *in vivo* (Barr et al., 2007; Chong et al., 2006; Ray & Hutchison, 2004). In humans, the 118G allele is suspected to increase the likelihood that an individual will abuse alcohol because it increases alcohol-induced euphoria (Ray & Hutchison, 2004). We have shown that rhesus carrying the 77G allele exhibit increased alcohol-induced stimulation (a marker for the euphorogenic effects of alcohol) and that G allele carriers also consume more alcohol in the laboratory (Barr et al., 2007). It would stand to reason that *OPRM1* variation might predict sensitivity to natural rewards as well. Based on the fact that these two variants confer similar functional effects, that both are observed at relatively high frequencies, and, furthermore, that there is an extended region of linkage disequilibrium (LD) with the A118G allele in humans (Luo et al., 2008; Pang, Wang, Wang, Goh, & Lee, 2009), it might be hypothesized that they have evolved as result of similar selective pressures in the two species. Data to directly address this hypothesis are presently not available. However, studies performed in the macaque demonstrate this variant to predict behaviors that could theoretically be under selection. The 77G allele predicts aggressive behavior (Miller et al., 2004), and G allele carriers form stronger attachment bonds with their mothers during infancy (Barr, Schwandt, Lindell, et al., 2008), especially as a function of repeated maternal separation. It is of interest that the effects reported to occur during repeated exposures to maternal separation and reunion are similar to those one might observe during periods of alcohol intake and withdrawal, and these types of findings have been shown to replicate in human studies (Copeland et al., 2011; Way et al., 2009). These types of studies highlight how traits that could have conferred selective advantage at some point in the evolutionary history of humans can increase risk for addictive disorders in modern society.

Animal Temperament as It Relates to Modeling Gene–Environment Interactions and Human Psychiatric Disorders

Animals share many behavioral and temperament traits with humans, making them both worthy adversaries and confident friends. Because of these similarities, they may also be useful for studying how genetic factors influence temperament. The fact that we can examine effects of genetic variation in these species in addition to gene × environment interactions (which may be less tractable in humans because of the degree of environmental heterogeneity) can potentially increase our understanding of how genetic variation predicts individual differences not only in temperament but also in vulnerability to psychiatric disorders.

Rhesus macaques are diverged from humans only 25 million years ago and, like humans, exhibit individual differences in temperament. Such differences have been shown to be influenced by genetic variants that are similar functionally to those present in humans. These polymorphisms predict traits such as impulsivity, anxious responding, novelty seeking, social attachment, and alcohol consumption, often such that genetic effects are observed only in particular environmental contexts. Candidate gene–based studies performed in nonhuman primates appear to have translational value for investigating effects of genetic variation on traits that increase risk for psychopathology (Barr, Newman, Lindell, et al., 2004; Barr, Newman, Schwandt, et al., 2004; Barr et al., 2009, 2010; Lindell et al., 2010) and demonstrate how temperament traits that could have conferred selective advantage at some point in the evolutionary history of humans can also increase risk for stress-related, addictive, or other psychiatric disorders in modern society.

Further Reading

Darwin, C. (1896). *The expression of the emotions in man and animals*. New York: Appleton.

Diamond, S. (1957). *Personality and temperament*. New York: Harper & Brothers.

Panksepp, J. (1998). *Affective neuroscience: The foundations of human and animal emotions*. New York: Oxford University Press.

References

Albert, F. W., Carlborg, O., Plyusnina, I., Besnier, F., Hedwig, D., Lautenschläger, S., et al. (2009). Genetic architecture of tameness in a rat model of animal domestication. *Genetics*, 182(2), 541–554.

Bailey, J. N., Breidenthal, S. E., Jorgensen, M. J., McCracken, J. T., & Fairbanks, L. A. (2007). The association of DRD4 and novelty seeking is found in a nonhuman primate model. *Psychiatric Genetics*, 17(1), 23–27.

Barr, C. S., Chen, S. A., Schwandt, M. L., Lindell, S. G., Sun, H., Suomi, S. J., et al. (2010). Suppression of alcohol preference by naltrexone in the rhesus macaque: A critical role of genetic variation at the micro-opioid receptor gene locus. *Biological Psychiatry*, 67, 78–80.

Barr, C. S., Dvoskin, R. L., Gupte, M., Sommer, W., Sun, H., Schwandt, M. L., et al. (2009). Functional CRH promoter variation drives stress-induced alcohol consumption in primates. *Proceedings of the National Academy of Sciences*, 106, 14593–14598.

Barr, C. S., Dvoskin, R. L., Yuan, Q., Lipsky, R. H., Gupte, M., Hu, X., et al. (2008). *CRH* haplotype as a factor influencing cerebrospinal fluid levels of corticotropin-releasing hormone, hypothalamic–pituitary–adrenal axis activity, temperament, and alcohol consumption in rhesus macaques. *Archives of General Psychiatry*, 65(8), 934–944.

Barr, C. S., & Goldman, D. (2006). Nonhuman primate models of inheritance of vulnerability to alcohol abuse and addiction. *Addiction Biology*, 11, 374–385.

Barr, C. S., Newman, T. K., Becker, M. L., Parker, C. C., Champoux, M., Lesch, K. P., et al. (2003). The utility of the non-human primate model for studying gene by environment interactions in behavioral research. *Genes, Brain and Behavior*, 2, 336–340.

Barr, C. S., Newman, T. K., Lindell, S., Shannon, C., Champoux, M., Lesch, K. P., et al. (2004). Interaction between serotonin transporter gene variation and rearing condition in alcohol preference and consumption in female primates. *Archives of General Psychiatry*, 61, 1146–1152.

Barr, C. S., Newman, T. K., Schwandt, M., Shannon, C., Dvoskin, R. L., Lindell, S. G., et al. (2004). Sexual dichotomy of an interaction between early adversity and the serotonin transporter gene promoter variant in rhesus macaques. *Proceedings of the National Academy of Sciences*, 101, 12358–12363.

Barr, C. S., Newman, T. K., Shannon, C., Parker, C. C., Dvoskin, R. L., Becker, M. L., et al. (2004). Rearing condition and rh5-HTTLPR interact to influence limbic–hypothalamic–pituitary–adrenal axis response to stress in infant macaques. *Biological Psychiatry*, 55, 733–738.

Barr, C. S., Schwandt, M., Newman, T. K., & Higley, J. D. (2004). The use of adolescent nonhuman primates to model human alcohol intake: Neurobiological, genetic and environmental variables. *Annals of the New York Academy of Sciences*, *1021*, 221–233.

Barr, C. S., Schwandt, M. L., Lindell, S. G., Chen, S. A., Suomi, S. J., Goldman, D., et al. (2007). Mu opioid receptor gene variation is associated with alcohol response and consumption in rhesus monkeys. *Archives of General Psychiatry*, *64*, 369–376.

Barr, C. S., Schwandt, M. L., Lindell, S. G., Higley, J. D., Maestripieri, D., Goldman, D., et al. (2008). A functional *OPRM1* variant is associated with attachment behavior in infant rhesus macaques. *Proceedings of the National Academy of Sciences*, *105*, 5277–5281.

Benjamin, J., Li, L., Patterson, C., Greenberg, B. D., Murphy, D. L., & Hamer, D. H. (1996). Population and familial association between the D4 dopamine receptor gene and measures of novelty seeking. *Nature Genetics*, *12*, 81–84.

Bennett, A. J., Lesch, K.-P., Heils, A., Long, J. C., Lorenz, J. G., Shoaf, S. E., et al. (2002). Early experience and serotonin transporter gene variation interact to influence primate CNS function. *Molecular Psychiatry*, *7*, 118–122.

Bethea, C. L., Streicher, J. M., Mirkes, S. J., Sanchez, R. L., Reddy, A. P., & Cameron, J. L. (2005). Serotonin-related gene expression in female monkeys with individual sensitivity to stress. *Neuroscience*, *132*, 151–166.

Bevilacqua, L., Doly, S., Kaprio, J., Yuan, Q., Tikkanen, R., Paunio, T., et al. (2010). A population-specific HTR2B stop codon predisposes to severe impulsivity. *Nature*, *468*, 1061–1066.

Bond, C., LaForge, K. S., Tian, M. T., Melia, D., Zhang, S. W., Borg, L., et al. (1998). Single-nucleotide polymorphism in the human mu opioid receptor gene alters beta-endorphin binding and activity: Possible implications for opiate addiction. *Proceedings of the National Academy of Sciences*, *95*, 9608–9613.

Bowlby, J. (1969). *Attachment and loss: Vol. 1. Attachment.* New York: Basic Books.

Bowlby, J. (1973). *Attachment and loss: Vol. 2. Separation, anxiety and anger.* New York: Basic Books.

Bradwejn, J., Kosycki, D., Deutetre-Couteax, A., Bourin, M., Palmour, R. M., & Ervin, F. R. (1992). The cholecystokinin hypothesis of panic and anxiety disorders: A review. *Journal of Psychopharmacology*, *6*, 345–351.

Buckholtz, J. W., & Meyer-Lindenberg, A. (2008). MAOA and the neurogenetic architecture of human aggression. *Trends in Neuroscience*, *31*(3), 120–129.

Burkett, J. P., Spiegel, L. L., Inoue, K., Murphy, A. Z., & Young, L. J. (2011). Activation of the mu-opioid receptors in the dorsal striatum is necessary for adult social attachment in monogamous prarie voles. *Neuropsychopharmacology*, *36*(11), 2200–2210.

Buss, A. H., & Plomin, R. (1984). *Temperament: Early developing personality traits.* Hillsdale, NJ: Erlbaum.

Cabib, S., Puglisi-Allegra, S., & Ventura, R. (2002). The contribution of comparative studies in inbred strains of mice to the understanding of the hyperactive phenotype. *Behavioral Brain Research*, *10*(130), 103–109.

Capitanio, J. P., & Widaman, K. F. (2005). Confirmatory factor analysis of personality structure in adult male rhesus monkeys (*Macaca mulatta*). *American Journal of Primatology*, *65*, 289–294.

Caspi, A., Hariri, A. R., Holmes, A., Uher, R., & Moffitt, T. E. (2010). Genetic sensitivity to the environment: The case of the serotonin transporter gene and its implications for studying complex diseases and traits. *American Journal of Psychiatry*, *167*(5), 509–527.

Caspi, A., McClay, J., Moffitt, T. E., Mill, J., Martin, J., Craig, I. W., et al. (2002). Role of genotype in the cycle of violence in maltreated children. *Science*, *297*, 851–854.

Caspi, A., Sugden, K., Moffitt, T. E., Taylor, A., Craig, I. W., Harrington, H., et al. (2003). Influence of life stress on depression: Moderation by a polymorphism in the 5-HTT gene. *Science*, *301*, 386–389.

Chamove, A. S., Eysenck, H. J., & Harlow, H. F. (1972). Personality in monkeys: Factor analyses of rhesus social behaviour. *Quarterly Journal of Experimental Psychology*, *24*, 496–504.

Champoux, M., Bennett, A., Shannon, C., Higley, J. D., Lesch, K. P., & Suomi, S. J. (2002). Serotonin transporter gene polymorphism, differential early rearing, and behavior in rhesus monkey neonates. *Molecular Psychiatry*, *7*, 1058–1063.

Chong, R. Y., Oswald, L., Yang, X., Uhart, M., Lin, P. I., & Wand, G. S. (2006). The mu-opioid receptor polymorphism A118G predicts cortisol responses to naloxone and stress. *Neuropsychopharmacology*, *31*, 204–211.

Cloninger, C. R. (1987). A systematic method for clinical description and classification of personality variants. *Archives of General Psychiatry*, *44*, 573–588.

Copeland, W. E., Sun, H., Costello, E. J., Angold, A., Heilig, M. A., & Barr, C. S. (2011). Child μ-opioid receptor gene variant influences parent–child relations. *Neuropsychopharmacology*, *36*(6), 1165–1170.

Darwin, C. (1896). *The expression of the emotions in man and animals.* New York: Appleton.

Depue, R., & Collins, P. (1999). Neurobiology of the structure of personality: Dopamine, facilitation of incentive motivation and extraversion. *Behavioral and Brain Sciences*, *22*(3), 491–517.

Diamond, S. (1957). *Personality and temperament.* New York: Harper & Brothers.

Duberstein, K. J., & Gilkeson, J. A. (2010). Determination of sex differences in personality and trainability of yearling horses utilizing a handler questionnaire. *Applied Animal Behaviour Science, 128,* 57–63.

Dunn, A. J., & Berridge, C. W. (1990). Physiological and behavioral responses to corticotropin-releasing factor administration: Is CRF a mediator of anxiety or stress responses? *Brain Research Reviews, 15*(2), 71–100.

Ebstein, R. P., Novick, O., Umansky, R., Priel, B., Osher, Y., Blaine, D., et al. (1996). Dopamine D4 receptor (D4DR) exon III polymorphism associated with the human personality trait of novelty seeking. *Nature Genetics, 12,* 78–80.

Fairbanks, L. A., Melega, W. P., & Jorgensen, M. J. (2001). Social impulsivity inversely associated with CSF 5-HIAA and fluoxetine exposure in vervet monkeys. *Neuropsychopharmacology, 24,* 370–378.

Fairbanks, L. A., Newman, T. K., Bailey, J. N., Jorgensen, M. J., Breidenthal, S. E., Ophoff, R. A., et al. (2004). Genetic contributions to social impulsivity and aggressiveness in vervet monkeys. *Biological Psychiatry, 55,* 642–647.

Fan, X., Bruno, K. J., & Hess, E. J. (2012). Rodent models of ADHD. *Current Topics in Behavioral Neuroscience, 9,* 273–300.

Fiskerstrand, C. E., Lovejoy, E. A., & Quinn, J. P. (1999). An intronic polymorphic domain often associated with susceptibility to affective disorders has allele dependent differential enhancer activity in embryonic stem cells. *FEBS Letters, 458,* 171–174.

Freeman, H. D., & Gosling, S. D. (2010). Personality in nonhuman primates: A review and evaluation of past research. *American Journal of Primatology, 71,* 1–19.

Gold, P. W., & Chrousos, G. P. (2002). Organization of the stress system and its dysregulation in melancholic and atypical depression: High vs. low CRH/NE states. *Molecular Psychiatry, 7,* 254–275.

Goldman, D., & Barr, C. S. (2002). Restoring the addicted brain. *New England Journal of Medicine, 347,* 843–845.

Grandin, T. (2005). *Animals in translation: Using the mysteries of autism to decode animal behavior.* New York: Scribner.

Hausberger, M., Bruderer, C., Le Scolan, N., & Pierre, J. S. (2004). Interplay between environmental and genetic factors in temperament/personality traits in horses (*Equus caballus*). *Journal of Comparative Psychology, 118*(4), 434–446.

Hejjas, K., Kubinyi, E., Ronai, Z., Szekely, A., Vas, J., Miklósi, A., et al. (2009). Molecular and behavioral analysis of the intron 2 repeat polymorphism in the canine dopamine D4 receptor gene. *Genes, Brain and Behavior, 8*(3), 330–336.

Higham, J. P., Barr, C. S., Hoffman, C. L., Mandalaywala, T. M., Parker, K. J., & Maestripieri, D. (2011). Interaction between *OPRM1* genotype and reproductive status on CSF levels of oxytocin in free-ranging rhesus macaques. *Behavioral Neuroscience, 125*(2), 131–136.

Higley, J. D., & Suomi, S. J. (1989). Temperamental reactivity in non-human primates. In D. Kohnstamm, H. E. Bates, & M. K. Rothbart (Eds.), *Temperament in childhood.* Chichester, UK: Wiley.

Higley, J. D., Suomi, S. J., & Linnoila, M. (1996). A nonhuman primate model of type II excessive alcohol consumption?: Part 1. Low cerebrospinal fluid 5-hydroxyindoleacetic acid concentrations and diminished social competence correlate with excessive alcohol consumption. *Alcoholism: Clinical and Experimental Research, 20,* 629–642.

Homberg, J. R., & Lesch, K. P. (2011). Looking on the bright side of serotonin transporter gene variation. *Biological Psychiatry, 69*(16), 513–519.

Hu, X. Z., Lipsky, R. H., Zhu, G., Akhtar, L., Taubman, J., Greenberg, B. D., et al. (2006). Additional functional variation at the SLC6A4 gene. *American Journal of Human Genetics, 78,* 815–826.

Hundt, W., Zimmermann, U., Pottig, M., Spring, K., & Holsboer, F. (2001). The combined dexamethasone-suppression/CRH stimulation test in alcoholics during and after acute withdrawal. *Alcohol: Clinical and Experimental Research, 25,* 687–691.

Jaferi, A., & Bhatnagar, S. (2007). Corticotropin-releasing hormone receptors in the medial prefrontal cortex regulate HPA activity and anxiety-related behavior regardless of prior stress experience. *Brain Research, 1186,* 212–223.

Kagan, J. (1984a). The idea of emotion in human development. In C. E. Izard, J. Kagan, & R. B. Zajonic (Eds.), *Emotions, cognition and behavior.* Cambridge, UK: Cambridge University Press.

Kagan, J. (1984b). *The nature of the child.* Cambridge, MA: Harvard University Press.

Kagan, J., Resnick, J. S., & Snidman, N. (1988). Biological basis of childhood shyness. *Science, 240,* 167–171.

Kalin, N. H., & Shelton, S. E. (2003). Nonhuman primate models to study anxiety, emotion regulation and psychopathology. *Annals of the New York Academy of Sciences, 1008,* 189–200.

Kalin, N. H., Shelton, S. E., & Davidson, R. J. (2000). Cerebrospinal fluid corticotropin-releasing hormone levels are elevated in monkeys with patterns of brain activity associated with fearful temperament. *Biological Psychiatry, 47*(7), 579–585.

Kinnally, E. L., Capitanio, J. P., Leibel, R., Deng,

L., Leduc, C., Haghighi, F., et al. (2010). Epigenetic regulation of serotonin transporter expression and behavior in infant rhesus macaques. *Genes, Brain and Behavior, 9*(6), 575–582.

Koob, G. F., & Le Moal, M. (2001). Drug addiction, dysregulation of reward, and allostasis. *Neuropsychopharmacology, 24,* 97–129.

Korte, S. M., Koolhaas, J. M., Wingfield, J. C., & McEwen, B. S. (2005). The Darwinian concept of stress: Benefits of allostasis and costs of allostatic load and the tradeoffs in health and disease. *Neuroscience and Biobehavioral Reviews, 29,* 3–38.

Kraemer, G. W., Moore, C. F., Newman, T. K., Barr, C. S., & Schneider, M. L. (2008). Moderate levels of fetal alcohol exposure and serotonin transporter gene promoter polymorphism affect neonatal temperament and LHPA axis regulation in monkeys. *Biological Psychiatry, 63*(3), 317–324.

Krawczak, M., Trefilov, A., Berard, J., Bercovitch, F., Kessler, M., Sauermann, U., et al. (2005). Male reproductive timing in rhesus macaques is influenced by the HTTLPR promoter polymorphism of the serotonin transporter gene. *Biology of Reproduction, 72,* 1109–1113.

Lafenêtre, P., Chaouloff, F., & Marsicano, G. (2009). Bidirectional regulation of novelty-induced behavioral inhibition by the endocannabinoid system. *Neuropsychopharmacology, 57*(7–8), 715–721.

Lanfumey, L., Mannoury La Cour, C., Froger, N., & Hamon, M. (2000). 5-HT-HPA interactions in two models of transgenic mice relevant to major depression. *Neurochemical Research, 25,* 1199–1206.

Lansade, L., Bouissou, M.-F., & Erhard, H. W. (2008). Fearfulness in horses: A temperament trait stable across time and situations. *Applied Animal Behaviour Science, 115,* 182–200.

Lesch, K. P., Meyer, J., Glatz, K., Flügge, G., Hinney, A., Hebebrand, J., et al. (1997). The 5-HT transporter gene-linked polymorphic region (5-HTTLPR) in evolutionary perspective: Alternative biallelic variation in rhesus monkeys. *Journal of Neural Transmission, 104,* 1259–1266.

Lesimple, C., Fureix, C., LeScolan, N., Richard-Yris, M., & Hausberger, M. (2011). Housing conditions and breed are associated with emotionality and cognitive abilities in riding school horses. *Applied Animal Behaviour Science, 129,* 92–99.

Ley, J. M., McGreevy, P., & Bennett, P. C. (2009). Inter-rater and test–retest reliability of the Monash Canine Personality Questionnaire—Revised (MCPQ-R). *Applied Animal Behaviour Science, 119,* 85–90.

Li, Q., Wichems, C., Heils, A., Van de Dar, L. D., Lesch, K.-P., & Murphy, D. L. (1999). Reduction of 5-HT1A binding sites in 5-HT transporter knockout mice. *Journal of Pharmacology and Experimental Therapy, 291,* 999–1007.

Lindell, S. G., Schwandt, M. L., Sun, H., Sparenborg, J. D., Bjoerk, K., Kasckow, J. W., et al. (2010). Functional NPY variation as a factor in stress resilience in rhesus macaques. *Archives of General Psychiatry, 67*(4), 423–431.

Lloyd, A. S., Martin, J. E., Bornett-Gauci, H. L., & Wilkinson, R. G. (2008). Horse personality: Variation between breeds. *Applied Animal Behaviour Science, 112,* 369–383.

Lopez, J. F., & Higley, J. D. (2002). The effect of early experience on brain corticosteroid and serotonin receptors in rhesus monkeys. *Biological Psychiatry, 51,* 294.

Luo, X., Zuo, L., Kranzler, H., Zhang, H., Wang, S., & Gelernter, J. (2008). Multiple OPR genes influence personality traits in substance dependent and healthy subjects in two American populations. *American Journal of Medical Genetics B: Neuropsychiatric Genetics, 147,* 1028–1039.

MacDonald, K. B. (1988). *Social and personality development, an evolutionary synthesis.* New York: Springer.

Manuck, S. B., Kaplan, J. R., & Rymeski, B. A. (2003). Approach to a social stranger is associated with low central nervous system serotonergic responsivity in female cynomolgus monkeys (*Macaca fascicularis*). *American Journal of Primatology, 61,* 187–194.

Mazzanti, C. M., Lappalainen, J., Long, J. C., Bengel, D., Naukkarinen, H., Eggert, M., et al. (1998). Role of the serotonin transporter promoter polymorphism in anxiety-related traits. *Archives of General Psychiatry, 55,* 936–940.

McEwen, B. S. (2006). Protective and damaging effects of stress mediators: Central role of the brain. *Dialogues in Clinical Neuroscience, 8,* 367–381.

McGrogan, C., Hutchison, M. D., & King, J. E. (2008). Dimensions of horse personality based on owner and trainer supplied personality traits. *Applied Animal Behaviour Science, 113,* 206–214.

Mehlman, P. T., Higley, J. D., Faucher, I., Lilly, A. A., Taub, D. M., Vickers, J., et al. (1994). Low CSF 5-HIAA concentrations and severe aggression and impaired impulse control in nonhuman primates. *American Journal of Psychiatry, 151,* 1485–1491.

Mehlman, P. T., Higley, J. D., Faucher, I., Lilly, A. A., Taub, D. M., Vickers, J., et al. (1995). Correlation of CSF 5-HIAA concentration with sociality and the timing of emigration in free-ranging primates. *American Journal of Psychiatry, 152,* 907–913.

Meyer-Lindenberg, A., Buckholtz, J. W., Koachana, B., Hariri, A., Pezawas, L., Blasi, G., et al. (2006). Neural mechanisms of genetic risk for impulsivity and violence in humans. *Proceedings of the National Academy of Sciences, 103*(16), 6269–6274.

Miller, G. M., Bendor, J., Tiefenbacher, S., Yang,

H., Novak, M. A., & Madras, B. K. (2004). A mu-opioid receptor single nucleotide polymorphism in rhesus monkey: Association with stress response and aggression. *Molelcular Psychiatry, 9*(1), 99–108.

Moles, A., Kieffer, B. L., & D'Amato, F. R. (2004). Deficit in attachment behavior in mice lacking the mu-opioid receptor gene. *Science, 304,* 1983–1986.

Newman, T. K., Syagailo, Y. V., Barr, C. S., Wendland, J. R., Champoux, M., Graessle, M., et al. (2005). Monoamine oxidase A gene promoter variation and rearing experience influences aggressive behavior in rhesus monkeys. *Biological Psychiatry, 57,* 167–172.

Oki, H., Kusunose, R., Nakaoka, H., Nishiura, A., Miyake, T., & Sasaki, Y. (2007). Estimation of heritability and genetic correlation for behavioural responses by Gibbs sampling in the Thoroughbred racehorse. *Genetics, 124*(4), 185–191.

Olmstead, M. C., Ouagazzal, A. M., & Kieffer, B. L. (2009). Mu and delta opioid receptors oppositely regulate motor impulsivity in the signaled nose poke task. *PLoS ONE, 4*(2), 4410.

Overall, K. L. (1997). *Clinical behavioral medicine for small animals.* St. Louis, MO: Mosby.

Pang, G., Wang, J., Wang, Z., Goh, C., & Lee, C. (2009). The G allele of SNP E1/A118G at the μ-opioid receptor gene locus shows genomic evidence of recent positive selection. *Pharmacogenomics, 10,* 1101–1109.

Panksepp, J. B., & Lahvis, G. P. (2011). Rodent empathy and affective neuroscience. *Neuroscience and Biobehavioral Reviews, 35*(9), 1864–18675.

Ray, L. A., & Hutchison, K. E. (2004). A polymorphism of the mu-opioid receptor gene (*OPRM1*) and sensitivity to the effects of alcohol in humans. *Alcoholism: Clinical and Experimental Research, 28,* 1789–1795.

Reale, D., Reader, S. M., Sol, D., McDouball, P. T., & Dingermanse, N. J. (2007). Integrating animal temperament within ecology and evolution. *Biological Reviews of the Cambridge Philosophical Society, 82*(2), 291–318.

Reisner, I. R., Mann, J. J., Stanley, M., Huang, Y. Y., & Houpt, K. A. (1996). Comparison of CSF monoamine metabolite levels in dominantly aggressive and non-aggressive dogs. *Brain Research, 714*(1–2), 57–64.

Reist, C., Mazzanti, C., Vu, R., Fujimoto, K., & Goldman, D. (2004). Inter-relationships of intermediate phenotypes for serotonin function, impulsivity, and a 5-HT2A candidate allele: His452Tyr. *Molecular Psychiatry, 9*(9), 871–878.

Rothbart, M. K., & Derryberry, D. (1981). Development of individual differences in temperament. In M. E. Lamb & A. L. Brown (Eds.), *Advances in developmental psychology* (Vol. 1). Hillsdale, NJ: Erlbaum.

Russell, V. A. (2011). Overview of animal models of attention deficit hyperactivity disorder (ADHD). *Current Protocols in Neuroscience, 54,* 1–9.

Sabol, S. Z., Hu, S., & Hamer, D. (1998). A functional polymorphism in the monoamine oxidase A gene promoter. *Human Genetics, 103,* 273–279.

Saetre, P., Strandberg, E., Sundgren, P. E., Pettersson, U., Jazin, E., & Bergström, T. F. (2006). The genetic contribution to canine personality. *Genes, Brain and Behavior, 5*(3), 240–248.

Samochowiez, J., Lesch, K. P., Rottmann, M., Smolka, M., Syagailo, Y. V., Okladnova, O., et al. (1999). Association of a regulatory polymorphism in the promoter region of the monoamine oxidase A gene with antisocial alcoholism. *Psychiatry Research, 86,* 67–72.

Sanders, M. J., Kieffer, B. L., & Fanselow, M. S. (2005). Deletion of the mu opioid receptor results in impaired acquisition of Pavlovian context fear. *Neurobiology of Learning and Memory, 84*(1), 33–41.

Sapolsky, R. M. (2001). *A primate's memoir: A neuroscientist's unconventional life among the baboons.* New York: Scribner.

Schjerlderup-Ebbe, T. (1935). Social behavior of birds. In C. Murchison (Ed.), *Handbook of social psychology* (pp. 947–972). Worcester, MA: Clark University Press.

Schneider, M. L., Moore, C. F., Larson, J. A., Barr, C. S., Dejesus, O. T., & Roberts, A. D. (2010). Timing of moderate level prenatal alcohol exposure influences gene expression of sensory processing behavior in rhesus monkeys. *Frontiers in Integrative Neuroscience, 3,* 30–38.

Schwandt, M. L., Lindell, S. G., Higley, J. D., Suomi, S. J., Heilig, M., & Barr, C. S. (2011). OPRM1 gene variation influences HPA axis function in response to a variety of stressors in rhesus macaques. *Psychoneuroendocrinology, 36,* 1303–1311.

Schwandt, M. L., Lindell, S. G., Sjoberg, R. L., Chisholm, K. L., Higley, J. D., Suomi, S. J., et al. (2010). Gene–environment interactions and response to social intrusion in male and female rhesus macaques. *Biological Psychiatry, 67,* 323–330.

Shannon, C., Schwandt, M. L., Champoux, M., Shoaf, S. E., Suomi, S. J., Linnoila, M., et al. (2005). Maternal absence and stability of individual differences in CSF 5-HIAA concentrations in rhesus monkey infants. *American Journal of Psychiatry, 162,* 1658–1664.

Sjoberg, R. L., Ducci, F., Barr, C. S., Newman, T. K., Dell'Osso, L., Virkkunen, M., et al. (2008). A non-additive interaction of a functional MAOA VNTR and testosterone predicts antisocial behavior. *Neuropsychopharmacology, 33*(2), 425–430.

Smith, M. J. (1984). Paleontology at the high table. *Nature, 309,* 401–402.

Smoller, J. W., Rosenbaum, J. F., Biederman, J., Kennedy, J., Dai, D., Racette, S. R., et al. (2003). Association of a genetic marker at the corticotropin-releasing hormone locus with behavioral inhibition. *Biological Psychiatry*, 54(12), 1376–1381.

Soeby, K., Larsen, S. A., Olsen, L., Rasmussen, H. B., & Werge, T. (2005). Serotonin transporter: Evolution and impact of polymorphic transcriptional regulation. *American Journal of Human Genetics*, 136, 53–57.

Southwick, S. M., Vythilingam, M., & Charney, D. S. (2005). The psychobiology of depression and resilience to stress: Implications for prevention and treatment. *Annual Review of Clinical Psychology*, 1, 255–291.

Spinelli, S., Schwandt, M. L., Lindell, S. G., Newman, T. K., Heilig, M., Higley, J. D., et al. (2007). Association between the rh-*5HTTLPR* polymorphism and behavior in rhesus macaques during social separation stress. *Developmental Psychopathology*, 19(4), 977–987.

Strome, E. M., Wheler, G. H., Higley, J. D., Loriaux, D. L., Suomi, S. J., & Doudet, D. J. (2002). Intracerebroventricular corticotropin-releasing factor increases limbic glucose metabolism and has social context-dependent behavioral effects in nonhuman primates. *Proceedings of the National Academy of Sciences*, 99, 15749–15754.

Thomas, A., & Chess, S. (1977). *Temperament and development*. New York: Brunner/Mazel.

Thomas, A., & Chess, S. (1986). The New York Longitudinal Study: From infancy to early adolescence. In R. Plomin & J. Dunn (Eds.), *The study of temperament: Changes, continuities and challenges*. Hillsdale, NJ: Erlbaum.

Tikkanen, R., Sjoberg, R. L., Ducci, F., Goldman, D., Holi, M., Tiihonen, J., et al. (2009). Effects of MAOA-genotype, alcohol consumption and aging on violent behavior. *Alcohol: Clinical and Experimental Research*, 33, 428–443.

Trefilov, A., Berard, J., Krawczak, M., & Schmidtke, J. (2000). Natal dispersal in rhesus macaques is related to serotonin transporter gene promoter variation. *Behavior Genetics*, 30, 295–301.

Turcsán, B., Kubinyi, E., & Miklósi, A. (2011). Trainability and boldness traits differ between dog breed clusters based on conventional breed categories and genetic relatedness. *Applied Animal Behaviour Science*, 81(3), 392–401.

Vallender, E. J., Priddy, C. M., Haki, S., Yang, H., Chen, G. L., & Miller, G. M. (2008). Functional variation in the 3' UTR of the serotonin transporter in human rhesus macaque. *Genes, Brain Behavior*, 7, 690–697.

Van den Berg, S. M., Heuven, H. C. M., van den Berg, L., Duffy, D. L., & Serpell, J. A. (2010). Evaluation of the C-BARQ as a measure of stranger-directed aggression in three common dog breeds. *Applied Animal Behaviour Science*, 124, 136–141.

Veenema, A. H., & Neumann, I. D. (2007). Neurobiological mechanisms of aggression and stress coping: A comparative study in mouse and rat. *Brain, Behavior and Evolution*, 70, 274–285.

von Borstel, U. U. K., Duncan, I. J. H., Lundin, M. C., & Keeling, L. J. (2010). Fear reactions in trained and untrained horses from dressage and show-jumping breeding lines. *Applied Animal Behaviour Science*, 125, 124–131.

Way, B. M., Taylor, S. E., & Eisenberger, N. L. (2009). Variation in the µ-opioid receptor gene is associated with dispositional and neural sensitivity to social rejection. *Proceedings of the National Academy of Sciences*, 106, 15079–15084.

Wendland, J. R., Hampe, M., Newman, T. K., Syagailo, Y., Meyer, J., Schempp, W., et al. (2006). Structural variation of the monoamine oxidase A gene promoter repeat polymorphism in nonhuman primates. *Genes, Brain and Behavior*, 5, 40–45.

Wendland, J. R., Lesch, K. P., Newman, T. K., Timme, A., Gachot-Neveu, H., Thierry, B., et al. (2005). Differential functional variability of serotonin transporter and monoamine oxidase A genes in macaque species displaying contrasting levels of aggression-related behavior. *Behavior Genetics*, 30, 1–10.

Westergaard, G. C., Suomi, S. J., Chavanne, T. J., Houser, L., Hurley, A., Cleveland, A., et al. (2003). Physiological correlates of aggression and impulsivity in free-ranging female primates. *Neuropsychopharmacology*, 28, 1045–1055.

Williamson, D. E., Coleman, K., Bacanu, S., Devlin, B. J., Rogers, J., Ryan, N. D., et al. (2003). Heritability of fearful–anxious endophenotypes in infant rhesus macaques: A preliminary report. *Biological Psychiatry*, 53, 284–291.

Yeh, S. R., Fricke, R. A., & Edwards, D. H. (1996). The effect of social experience on serotonergic modulation of the escape circuit of crayfish. *Science*, 271, 366–369.

Yerkes, R. M., & Yerkes, A. W. (1917). Individuality, temperament, and genius in animals: Research that lets us appreciate human individuality. *Natural History*, p. 3.

Zentner, M., & Bates, J. E. (2008). Child temperament: An integrative review of concepts, research programs, and measures. *European Journal of Developmental Science*, 2, 7–37.

Zuckerman, M. (1983). A biological theory of sensation seeking. In M. Zuckerman (Ed.), *Biological bases of sensation seeking, impulsivity, and anxiety*. Hillsdale, NJ: Erlbaum.

Chapter 14

Temperament and Evolution

Kevin B. MacDonald

The promise and challenge of evolutionary psychology are to chart the set of human psychological adaptations—mechanisms designed by natural selection over the course of evolution that solve particular adaptive problems. These mechanisms are conceptualized as adaptive systems that served a variety of functions in the environment of evolutionary adaptedness (EEA)—the environment in which humans evolved and which presented the set of problems whose solutions are the set of human adaptations (also see Depue & Fu, Chapter 18, this volume). This perspective expects to find *homologous* (i.e., inherited from a common ancestor) systems in animals that serve similar adaptive functions, and it expects that these systems will be organized within the brain as discrete neurophysiological systems (see Buss, 2008, for a review focused on personality psychology). It expects that each system will be responsive to particular environmental contexts, and that different temperament and personality systems will be in competition with each other within individuals, leading at times to psychological ambivalence (MacDonald, 2005).

Here I review theory and data on temperament from an evolutionary perspective. Standard definitions of temperament acknowledge the centrality of biology. Rothbart's definition focuses on the two broad functional domains of temperament: constitutionally based individual differences in reactivity and in self-regulation (see Rothbart & Bates, 2006; also see Rothbart, Chapter 1, this volume). Rothbart and Bates (2006) distinguish temperament from personality by defining *temperament* as the affective, activational, and attentional core of personality—all of which are strongly biological, while *personality* is a larger category that includes also beliefs, social cognition, morals, skills, habits, and so forth, and is more characteristically human.

Evolution and Individual Differences

The term *trait* implies that individual differences are critical to temperament. In general, evolutionary psychologists regard adaptations as specieswide universals. However, genetic variation is ubiquitous, even for adaptations (e.g., West-Eberhard, 2003), leading to the evolution of appraisal mechanisms in which the value of different personality traits may be appraised differently depending on the perceived interests of evaluators—potential spouses, lovers, employees, employers, friends, leaders, and so forth (Lusk, MacDonald, & Newman, 1998). For example, finding mates is an evolutionarily ancient problem for both sexes, resulting in substantial cross-cultural commonality in how people evaluate variation in the personality trait of ambition–industriousness in potential spouses, with theoretically expected sex differences whereby females value this trait more highly in a potential spouse than males (Buss, 1989). In turn this suggests an evolutionary basis for valuations of personality, similar to Singh's (1993) findings for male appraisals of waist–hip ratio in females.

From an evolutionary perspective, individual differences within the normal range are seen as variation in evolved systems. The most accepted proposal for why genetic and phenotypic variation in adaptive systems remains in populations is environmental heterogeneity (MacDonald, 1995; Nettle, 2006; Penke, Denissen, & Miller, 2007). This is well established in animal research (Carere & Eens, 2005; Dingemanse, Both, Drent, & Tinbergen, 2004; Dingemanse & Réale, 2005; Van Oers, de Jong, van Noordwijk, Kempenaers, & Drent, 2005). For example, Dingemanse and colleagues (2004) found that exploratory males (but not females) had higher fitness in a year with high resource availability, but the reverse pattern occurred in resource-poor years. Thus, there are tradeoffs such that beneficial traits in some environments impose costs in others, depending on local environmental conditions—results compatible with models of fluctuating selection due to rapid changes in the physical and biotic environment (Bell, 2010). Dingemanse and Réale (2005) reviewed data indicating that the fitness of a personality trait may depend on sex, age, and the ecological quality of the environment. In most years, an intermediate phenotype had the highest fitness; interestingly, birds with extreme phenotypes mated disassortatively, thereby producing intermediate phenotypes in their offspring, suggesting that this is an adaptive strategy.

A Top-Down Perspective Aimed at Carving Nature at Its Joints

An evolutionary theory seeks to establish the set of adaptations that underlie temperament and personality. This is not the same as showing that a temperament trait has a biological basis, or that it is genetically influenced. An evolutionary theory seeks to "carve nature at its joints" on the basis of functional units—systems that have been the focus of natural selection. An illustrative example of a trait that shows genetic variation but is not an adaptation is proneness to divorce. McGue and Lykken (1992) found that proneness to divorce is heritable. However, proneness to divorce does not reflect variation in an adaptation. Different people are prone to divorce for different reasons (e.g., emotional instability [high neuroticism], selfishness, or proneness to philandering).

The standard psychometric approach is not ideal for discovering the adaptations underlying personality and temperament. For example, Freeman and Gosling's (2010) review of studies of primate personality found 14 categories: sociability, fearfulness, playfulness, confidence/aggression, activity, excitability, curiosity, dominance, agreeableness, irritability, intelligence, impulsiveness, anxiousness, and independence. Support for putative personality dimensions depends on interrater reliability, as well as convergent and discriminant validity, all of which are at least promising. From an evolutionary perspective, however, discerning reliable and valid traits is only an essential first step. In addition, an evolutionary analysis requires evidence that these traits are real foci of natural selection. Ideally, one would need to find independent evidence that the traits represent variation in adaptive systems designed to solve particular problems. Was variation in curiosity or playfulness a focus of natural selection or is it simply "noise"—nonadaptive genetic variation that is not undergoing natural selection and does not contribute to fitness, as Tooby and Cosmides (1990) proposed for personality variation in general? Are these traits like the divorce example—complexly influenced by a variety of evolved systems, in which different animals may be playful or curious for different reasons? Is the variation linked to differences in adaptive outcomes in the different environments that the animal's ancestors encountered over evolutionary time, or is it merely variation that human observers find interesting?

In general, evolutionary psychologists are

"splitters" in studying adaptations; that is, they study each putative adaptation separately. The emphasis is on universality rather than on correlations among individual differences among different adaptations. For example, evolutionary psychologists study anger as an adaptation (Sell, Tooby, & Cosmides, 2009), without considering how individual differences in anger are correlated with individual differences in other traits. Because of the centrality of individual differences, personality psychology has naturally been interested in the correlational patterns among traits, leading to an important role for higher-order factor analyses, such as the Five-Factor Model (FFM). This review proposes that several general adaptive spaces can be meaningfully related to the FFM, if not in a 1:1 manner. As Dingemanse and Réale (2005, p. 1180) point out, "Functional explanations for personality variation (i.e., *consistent* individual differences in suites of *correlated* behavioural traits) would require insight into conditions favouring phenotypic (or genetic) correlations among behavioral traits" (emphasis in original). The proposal in the following is that the concept of adaptive space provides a rationale for why there are correlations among particular suites of behavioral traits.

The concept of an adaptive space is an abstraction in the sense that it refers not to a particular adaptation but to a suite of adaptations with the following attributes:

- There are phenotypic correlations among individual differences in the traits detectable by factor analysis.
- There is shared genetic variation among the traits.
- There are broadly similar functions among this suite of adaptations.
- There are shared motivational, attentional, perceptual and, in addition for personality, cognitive mechanisms (there may also be motivational, attentional, perceptual, and cognitive mechanisms that are unique to a particular subsystem).
- This suite of adaptations results from an evolutionary history of elaboration and differentiation from systems that existed in common ancestors.

The adaptive space idea proposes that personality systems should be conceptualized hierarchically, from more specific to more general, within a generally defined adaptive space. For example, the behavioral approach adaptive space (BAAS) is at the highest level of evolutionary analysis—the highest level of meaningful adaptive space, with more specific systems arrayed beneath it. As described more fully below, the BAAS functions to motivate animals to interface actively with the environment. Research on animal personality supports correlations and genetic overlap among functionally distinct behavioral traits related to behavioral approach. For example, Dingamanse and Réale (2005) describe suites of "autocorrelated traits" based on the finding that animals that are relatively aggressive toward conspecifics are also bolder in exploring novel environments and predators; they are more prone to taking risks, more liable to scrounge during foraging, and are more responsive to stress. The correlations among these conceptually related traits are typically based on strong underlying genetic correlations (Dingamanse & Réale, 2005; Van Oers et al., 2005), for example, a genetic correlation of .84 between early exploratory behavior and risk taking in laboratory conditions in great tits (*Parus major*). Reported genetic correlations for boldness and aggression ranged from .37 in German shepherd dogs to .84 in three-spined stickleback fish (*Gasterosteus aculeatus*) (see Van Oers et al., 2004). Thus Barr (Chapter 13, this volume), discussing Korte, Koolhaas, Wingfield, and McEwen (2005), notes that traits of aggression and exploration likely did not evolve in isolation, but rather as a package of traits resulting from genetic linkage. Similarly, Hur and Bouchard (1997) found a genetic correlation of .55 between sensation seeking and impulsivity in a sample of identical twins reared apart, with the remaining genetic variance unique to impulsivity.

An evolutionary interpretation proposes that these different subsystems accrued over evolutionary time as primitive foraging and mate attraction systems became elaborated and somewhat differentiated in response to specialized features of the "approach" adaptive space, effectively resulting in subsystems or "facets" of temperament and personality. These subsystems share anatomical and neurological structures, as well as genetic and phenotypic variance, and may therefore be nested under one or more of the superfactors of higher-order models, prototypically the FFM. Thus, for example, testosterone influences aggression, dominance, sexual activity, mating effort, antisocial behavior, rough-and-tumble play, and personality traits (extraversion, sociability, disinhibition, sensation seeking, and instrumental effort) (Archer, 2006). Despite important differences among these behaviors and dispositions, as well as the mechanisms underlying them, they also share common mechanisms.

All of these characteristics of an adaptive space are falsifiable empirical propositions. Evidence against genetic correlations for traits that are phenotypically correlated would be evidence that two traits are not part of the same adaptive space. As discussed below, phenotypic overlap in the absence of genetic correlations could occur if people tended to group quite different types of negative affect together (e.g., fear and anger) even though fear and anger are quite different in terms of evolutionary function and in their neuropsychology.

Tools of an Evolutionary Theory: Evolution, Sex, Age, and Life History Theory

An important tool for carving nature at its joints is the evolutionary theory of sex (Trivers, 1972). The sex with the higher level of parental investment (typically the females, especially for mammals) is expected to be relatively more discriminating in choosing mates because the typically greater female investment implies that females will be a valued resource in the mating game. Mating is expected to be problematic for the low-investment sex, with the result that males must often compete with other males for access to females. This results in a large number of predictions related to personality: Males are expected to take a more proactive approach to the environment, whereas females benefit from a more conservative strategy. This is because males have more to gain by controlling the social and nonsocial environment than females. In all of the traditional societies of the world, males who have had relatively high levels of control of social and nonsocial resources have had higher reproductive success because they have had access to additional mates (polygyny, extramarital relationships) and to higher-quality mates (Betzig, 1986). Females, because they do not similarly benefit from additional matings, are predicted to adopt a more conservative strategy, primarily because, since mating is less problematic for females under conditions of sexual competition, there is less benefit of engaging in risky, dangerous strategies. Thus, by conquering most of Asia (a risky endeavor), Genghis Khan was able to have millions of descendants in the contemporary world because his conquests enabled intensive polygyny by himself and his male descendants (Zerjal et al., 2003). Because of inherent reproductive limitations, no female could have benefited to a similar extent by pursuing such a strategy.

The evolutionary theory of sex also has implications for age-related changes in at least some personality systems. The *young male syndrome* describes the pattern in which sensation seeking, impulsivity, and aggression (all associated with the BAAS described earlier) peak in young adulthood at the time when young males must compete for mates and establish themselves in the dominance hierarchy (Wilson & Daly, 1985). Similarly, sex differences related to intimacy peak during the reproductive years (Turner, 1981), that is, during the period when sex differences are maximally divergent, and when finding a spouse who is loving and empathic is a critical adaptive challenge, particularly for females.

Life history theory attempts to explain the evolution of *resource allocation strategies* that optimize the utilization of resources over the life course and across varying ecological conditions. Life history traits are characteristics that determine rates of reproduction and associated patterns of growth, aging, and parental investment, including current versus future reproduction, short versus long period of preadult dependency, and offspring quality versus quantity (Charnov, 1993; Roff, 1992; Stearns, 1992).

Animal research has shown that individual differences in the systems underlying a species' life history profile become intercorrelated because they constitute a coherent manner of responding to the exigencies of life—survival, development, and reproduction. For example, Mehlman and colleagues

(1997) found a variety of personality- and life history–related responses in rhesus macaques that varied depending on levels of serotonin. Males with low serotonin levels were more violently aggressive and dispersed at an earlier age. They were also more likely to engage in risky behavior and to suffer premature death, but less likely to be sexually involved with females. Thus, variation in serotonin levels is associated with a wide range of phenomena expressed in different ways at different ages throughout the lifespan.

Research on humans inspired by life history theory has focused on finding evidence for a general personality factor. Rushton and colleagues have provided evidence for a general factor of personality using FFM questionnaires (Rushton, Bons, & Hur, 2008; Rushton & Irwing, 2009). Figueredo and colleagues have linked this general personality factor to what is termed a *K-style reproductive strategy*, defined as relatively late reproduction, strong pair-bonds, and high parental investment (Figueredo, Vásquez, Brumbach, & Schneider, 2007; see also Figueredo et al., 2006; Figueredo, Vásquez, Brumbach, & Schneider, 2004). (The opposite of a K-style reproductive pattern is labeled an *r-style reproductive pattern*, characterized by relatively early reproduction, weak pair-bonds, and minimal parental investment.) A single factor emerged from 20 scales of personal, familial, and social functioning. Subjects with high factor scores reported higher quality of relationship with their parents, spouse, and children; they provided and received greater support from friends and relatives; and they scored higher on measures of long-term planning, impulse control, relationship stability, and degree of community organization or involvement. This K factor was correlated with a general personality factor characterized by relatively high scores on Extraversion, Agreeableness, Emotional Stability (the inverse of Neuroticism), Conscientiousness, and Openness to Experience.

The finding of a single personality factor implies that traits become intercorrelated because of the need to develop a coordinated life history response to the environment; that is, a mix of traits, some of which fit into a K-style life history pattern (e.g., long-term planning) and some of which fit into an r-style reproductive pattern (e.g., low impulse control), would be maladaptive. This coordinated response cuts across the adaptive space concept; that is, the emergence of a single personality factor implies intercorrelations among all the systems related to personality, including systems designed to solve very different adaptive problems. On the other hand, the adaptive space concept rests on the possibility of finding correlations based on a common evolutionary history of elaboration and differentiation of adaptations that existed in common ancestors. These are mutually compatible ways of conceptualizing personality from an evolutionary perspective.

Six Adaptive Spaces

The following sketches six adaptive spaces reflected in the temperament and personality literature. The procedure is to sketch out these adaptive spaces, then, by using the evolutionary tools mentioned earlier, discuss how the results of factor-analytic studies map onto these adaptive spaces.

The BAAS

Among even the most primitive mammals, there must be systems designed to approach the environment to obtain resources, prototypically foraging and mate attraction systems. As used here, a temperament/personality system includes a specific neuropsychological substrate influencing motivation, perception, and behavior. For example, Panksepp (1998) has argued that the mammalian brain contains a "foraging/exploration/investigation/curiosity/interest/expectancy/SEEKING" system (p. 145; see also Panksepp & Moskal, 2008). Thus, the SEEKING system includes neuropsychological substrates for motivational mechanisms that make curiosity and exploration psychologically rewarding, as well as perceptual biases toward attending to novel stimuli and specific exploratory behaviors, such as smelling novel aspects of the environment, seen in many mammals.

The behavioral approach system (BAS; Gray, 1987, 2000) evolved from systems designed to motivate approach toward sources of reward (e.g., sexual gratification, dominance, control of territory) that occurred as enduring and recurrent features of the environments in which animals or humans evolved. These systems overlap anatomically and neurophysiologically with aggression, perhaps because aggression is a prepotent way of dealing with the frustration of positive expectancies (Panksepp, 1998, p. 191). Several of the primate traits studied by Freeman and Gosling (2010; confidence/aggression, dominance, impulsiveness, activity, curiosity, and perhaps playfulness) have a surface plausibility as components of the BAAS for primates (see also Barr, Chapter 13, this volume, on confidence/aggression as a consensus temperament trait in rhesus). Furthermore, the autocorrelated traits of aggression, exploratory behavior, and risk taking revealed in animal research (see Dingamanse & Réale, 2005; Van Oers et al., 2005; see earlier discussion) all concern traits conceptually related to behavioral approach. Similarly, working with human data, De Pauw, Mervielde, and Van Leeuwen (2009) found that activity level loads on the same factor as impulsivity and high-intensity pleasure, and in Larsen and Diener's (1992) study, activity level appears in the same factor-analytic space as dominance and sensation seeking.

Important components of the BAAS are dopaminergic reward-seeking mechanisms (Gray, 1987, 2000; Panksepp, 1982, 1998; Panksepp & Moskal, 2008; Zuckerman, 1991; see also Putnam, Chapter 6, and Depue & Fu, Chapter 18, this volume). Evolution has resulted in affective motivational systems triggered by specific feeling states that motivate active interface with the environment (e.g., the taste of sweet foods, the pleasure of sexual intercourse, the joy of the infant in close intimate contact with its mother; E. O. Wilson, 1975). For example, in rats, these mechanisms underlie energetic searching, investigating, and sniffing objects in the environment as possible sources of reward (Panksepp, 1998).

There are species differences in behavioral approach related to the animal's ecology. For example, predatory aggression is a component of behavioral approach in cats, but not in rats (Panksepp, 1998, p. 194). Over evolutionary time, the BAAS has become elaborated and differentiated according to the unique adaptive demands of each species. As a result, carnivores seek different sorts of food than do herbivores, with the former requiring mechanisms involved in stalking and taking down prey, and the latter requiring mechanisms for locating edible plants. Dominance mechanisms are an important component of behavioral approach for many social species, but not for solitary species.

The behavioral approach system is related to Surgency/Extraversion in the FFM (see also Rothbart, Chapter 1, and Putnam, Chapter 6, this volume) and Dominance in the circumplex model of interpersonal descriptors (Trapnell & Wiggins, 1990; Wiggins, 1991; Wiggins & Trapnell, 1996). At the heart of behavioral approach is Dominance/Sensation Seeking, which consists of individual differences in social dominance, as well as several other highly sex-differentiated behaviors, including sensation seeking, impulsivity, and sensitivity to reward. Newman (1987; also see Derryberry, 1987) found that compared to introverts, extraverts have a stronger response to reward. Among human adults, behavioral approach is also associated with aggressiveness and higher levels of sexual experiences (Gray, 1987, 2000; Zuckerman, 1991) and positive emotionality (Gray, 1987, 2000; Heller, 1990), while impulsivity, "high-intensity pleasure," and aggressiveness are components of behavioral approach in young children (Rothbart, Ahadi, Hershey, & Fisher, 2001).

Sensitivity to reward emerges very early in life as a dimension of temperament (Bates, 1989; Rothbart, 1989b; Rothbart & Bates, 2006). In early infancy there are individual differences in the extent to which infants approach rewarding stimulation, as indicated by attraction to sweet food, grasping objects, or attending to novel visual patterns. This trait is sometimes labeled *exuberance*, defined as an "approach-oriented facet of positive emotionality" (Pfiefer, Goldsmith, Davidson, & Rickman, 2002, p. 1475; see also Fox, Henderson, Rubin, Calkins, & Schmidt, 2001). Children who score high on behavioral approach are prone to positive emotional responses, including smiling, joy, and laughter available in rewarding situations and in the pleasant social interaction sought by sociable children (see Putnam, Chapter 6, this volume).

Sensation seeking, including promiscuous sexual activity (which loads on the Disinhibition subscale of the Sensation Seeking Scale; Zuckerman, 1979), and aggression (Wilson & Daly, 1985) peak in late adolescence and young adulthood, followed by a gradual decline during adulthood. As noted earlier, this "young male syndrome" is highly compatible with evolutionary thinking: Sex-differentiated systems are expected to be strongest at the time of sexual maturation and maximum divergence of male and female reproductive strategies. Because mating is theorized to involve competition with other males, the male tendencies toward sensation seeking, risk taking, and aggression are expected to be at their peak during young adulthood, when males are attempting to establish themselves in the wider group and accumulate resources necessary for mating.

However, boys score higher on behavioral approach even during infancy in cross-cultural samples (reviewed in Rothbart, 1989b). Furthermore, sex differences in aggression (Eagly & Steffan, 1986), high-intensity pleasure (see Else-Quest, Chapter 23, this volume), externalizing psychiatric disorders (conduct disorder, oppositional defiant disorder), risk taking and aggression (Klein, 1995; LaFreniére et al., 2002), and rough-and-tumble play (which is often associated with aggression [Collaer & Hines, 1995; Hines, 2011; Humphreys & Smith, 1987; MacDonald & Parke, 1986]) can first be seen in early childhood. Beginning in infancy, boys engage in more large-motor, physically intense activity (Eaton & Yu, 1989; Else-Quest, Hyde, Goldsmith, & Van Hulle, 2006). Genetic females exposed to testosterone-like hormones prenatally are more aggressive (Matthews, Fane, Conway, Brook, & Hines, 2009; Pasterski et al., 2007) and more active than girls without such exposure (Ehrhardt, 1985). Moreover, the social interactions of boys are more characterized by dominance interactions and forceful, demanding interpersonal styles (LaFreniére & Charlesworth, 1983; LaFreniére et al., 2002). On the other hand, females are more prone to depression, which is associated with low levels of behavioral approach (Davidson, 1993; Fox, 1994). Indeed, *anhedonia* (lack of ability to experience pleasure) and negative mood are primary symptoms of depression within the *Diagnostic and Statistical Manual of Mental Disorders* (DSM-IV) classification (American Psychiatric Association, 2000).

In general, the results for behavioral approach fit well with the idea of an adaptive space of approach traits linked psychometrically and neurophysiologically, and showing evolutionarily expected sex differences and developmental trajectories (i.e., the young male syndrome).

The Behavioral Withdrawal Adaptive Space

While behavioral approach systems motivate active engagement with the environment, specialized systems are required to respond to environmental threats, prototypically by withdrawal or defensive aggression. The behavioral inhibition system (BIS) functions to monitor the environment for dangers and impending punishments (Gray, 1987, 2000; LeDoux, 1996). Recent conceptualizations distinguish between a fear system and an anxiety system, with different neuropsychologies and adaptive functions (see Depue & Fu, Chapter 18, this volume). The fear system is designed to respond to unconditioned (e.g., pain, snakes, spiders) or conditioned aversive stimuli, while anxiety is designed to respond to situations of uncertainty and unpredictability.

Individual differences in behavioral inhibition are observable beginning in the second half of the first year of life with the development of the emotion of fear and expressions of distress and hesitation in the presence of novelty (Rothbart, 1989a; Rothbart & Bates, 2006). Children who score high on behavioral inhibition respond negatively to new people and other types of novel stimulation (Fox et al., 2001; Kagan, Reznick, & Snidman, 1987; also see Kagan, Chapter 4, and White, Lamm, Helfinstein, & Fox, Chapter 17, this volume).

Fearfulness is a well-established temperament trait in children (see Kagan, Chapter 4, this volume) and in primates (Freeman & Gosling, 2010), and, indeed, in all animals studied (see Barr, Chapter 13, this volume). It is most closely related to Neuroticism in five-factor personality scales (see below). The evolutionary theory of sex predicts that females will be more sensitive than males to signals of personal threat. Females are more prone to most anxiety disorders, including agoraphobia and panic disorder (e.g., American Psychiatric Association, 2000; Weissman, 1985). Girls report being more fearful and timid than boys in uncertain situations and are more cautious and take fewer risks than boys (Christopherson, 1989; Ginsburg & Miller, 1982).

The Reactivity/Affect Intensity Adaptive Space

A third important adaptive space is reactivity (affect intensity). Arousal functions to energize the animal to meet environmental challenges or opportunities. In the absence of such a system, the animal would either be permanently overaroused, which would needlessly consume resources, or permanently underaroused and less able to meet environmental challenges. Indeed, Quinkert and colleagues (2011, p. 15617) identify generalized arousal mechanisms as "the most powerful and essential activity in any vertebrate nervous system."

Affect intensity functions to mobilize behavioral resources by increasing arousal in acutely demanding situations in the service of either approach or withdrawal. It is a behavioral scaling system that allows the organism to scale its responses to current environmental opportunities and threats. This system is well studied at the neurophysiological level; research implicates systems that energize both positive and negative emotion systems. Thus, Schiff and Pfaff (2009) and Quinkert and colleagues (2011) conceptualize arousal as a generalized, valence-free force that supplies the energy for emotionally charged responses, thereby regulating their intensity (also see Panksepp, 1998, pp. 109–110, 117). These generalized arousal mechanisms utilize a variety of neurotransmitters (Quinkert et al., 2011). Anatomically, the reticular formation is critical for regulating arousal levels of the central nervous system through its connections with the limbic system and thalamus (Posner, Russell, & Peterson, 2005; Posner et al., 2008; Quinkert et al., 2011). Freeman and Gosling's (2010) finding of an excitability dimension provides evidence for an individual-differences dimension of reactivity/affect intensity in primates. Garey and colleagues (2003) identified a generalized arousal component in the behavior of mice across experiments, investigators, and mouse populations.

Reactivity, along with self-regulation, is one of the two fundamental realms of temperament in Rothbart's scheme (see, e.g., Rothbart & Bates, 2006). Children who are highly reactive respond intensely to stimulation, reach peak arousal at lower stimulus intensity, and have a relatively low threshold for arousal (Rothbart, 1989a, 1989b; Strelau, 1989). Low-reactive children have a relatively high threshold of stimulation and do not become aroused by stimulation that would overwhelm a high-reactive individual. Emotionally intense individuals respond relatively strongly to emotional stimulation, independent of the emotion involved, including both positive and negative emotions (Aron & Aron, 1997; Benham, 2006; Larsen & Diener, 1992). Smolewska, Scott, McCabe, and Woody (2006) found that people who score high on the Highly Sensitive Person Scale (a measure of reactivity; Aron & Aron, 1997) also scored higher on measures of Neuroticism, Behavioral Inhibition (which measures proneness to fear), and Responsiveness to Reward (a component of the behavioral approach system). Highly reactive individuals thus react intensely both to situations perceived as threatening and potentially rewarding.

An independent arousal regulation system is also implied in two-dimensional models of mood that distinguish between activation (arousal) and valence (Russell, 2003; also see Posner et al., 2005). Nevertheless, it should be noted that acknowledging the independence of arousal and valence need not entail a rejection of discrete negatively valenced emotions energized by the generalized arousal system. Here evidence is provided that fear and anger are associated with different adaptive spaces (behavioral withdrawal and behavioral approach, respectively) and have different neuropsychologies (see below).

Larsen and Diener (1992) found that affect intensity is most closely associated with Neuroticism in the FFM; similarly, Smolewska et al. (2006) found that reactivity to stimulation as measured by the Highly Sensitive Person Scale was most strongly correlated with Neuroticism in the FFM. Similarly, Depue and Fu (Chapter 18, this volume) analyze neuroticism as reactivity to stressful situations and "labile, reactive moods." Watson and Clark (1992) show that Neuroticism is associated with all four of their dimensions of negative affect—guilt, hostility, fear, and sadness. However, these negative emotions also tend to be associated with the other systems associated with the FFM: hostility (negatively) with Nurturance/Love, sadness with Introversion, and guilt with Nurturance/Love and Conscientiousness. Neuroticism also appears to be related to a wide range of personality disorders that also load on other systems (Costa & McCrae, 1986; Widiger & Trull, 1992; see below). High affect intensity thus energizes negative emotional responding in general. However, affect intensity also provides a powerful engine for positive emotional responses that are central to other physiologically and psychometrically independent systems (Aron & Aron, 1997; Benham, 2006; Panksepp, 1998, p. 117; Smolewska et al., 2006; see below).

The Nurturance and Pair-Bonding Adaptive Space

Mammalian females give birth to and suckle their young. This has led to a host of adaptations for mothering, an outgrowth of which are pair-bonding mechanisms present also in males (MacDonald, 1992). For species that develop pair-bonds and other types of close relationships involving nurturance and empathy, one expects the evolution of a system designed to make such relationships psychologically rewarding. The adaptive space of nurturance/pair-bonding therefore becomes elaborated into a mechanism for cementing adult relationships of love and empathy, prototypically within the family.

Variation in Nurturance/Love, the second factor emerging from the circumplex model, is associated with intimacy and other long-term relationships, especially family relationships involving reciprocity and transfer of resources to others (e. g., investment in children; Kiesler, 1983; Trapnell & Wiggins, 1990; Wiggins & Trapnell, 1996; Wiggins, Trapnell, & Phillips, 1988). Recently, models of temperament have included a temperament dimension of Affiliativeness (Rothbart, 1994; see also Evans & Rothbart, 2007; Rothbart & Bates, 2006, also see Knafo & Israel, Chapter 9, this volume). Affiliativeness involves warmth, love, closeness, empathic concern, and a desire to nurture others. Individual differences in warmth and affection observable early in parent–child relationships, including secure attachments, are conceptually linked with Nurturance/Love later in life (MacDonald, 1992, 1999a). Secure attachments and warm, affectionate parent–child relationships have been found to be associated with a high-investment style of parenting characterized by later sexual maturation; stable pair-bonding; and warm, reciprocally rewarding, nonexploitative interpersonal relationships (Belsky, Steinberg, & Draper, 1991).

The physiological basis of pair-bonding involves specific brain regions (Bartels & Zeki, 2000; Burkett, Spiegel, Inoue, Murphy, & Young, 2011) and the hormones oxytocin and vasopressin, as well as opiates and dopamine (Atzil, Hendler, & Feldman, 2011; Burkett et al., 2011; Insel, Winslow, Wang, & Young, 1998; Panksepp, 1998; also see Barr, Chapter 13, and Depue & Fu, Chapter 18, this volume). In prairie voles (*Microtus ochrogaster*), a monogamous species with paternal involvement in provisioning the young, oxytocin receptors (Insel et al., 1998) and opioid receptors (Burkett et al., 2011) are found in brain regions associated with reward and with pair-bonding, supporting the proposal that pair-bonding is a reward-based system that functions to facilitate intimate family relationships and parental investment (MacDonald, 1992). The stimuli that activate this system act as natural clues (in the sense of Bowlby, 1969) for pleasurable affective response. Intimate relationships and nurturance of the objects of affection are pleasurable, and such relationships are sought out by those sensitive to the reward value of this stimulation.

If, indeed, the main evolutionary impetus for the development of the human affectional system is the need for high-investment parenting, females are expected to have a greater elaboration of mechanisms related to parental investment than males. The evolutionary theory of sex implies that females are expected to be highly discriminating maters compared to males and more committed to long-term relationships of nurturance and affection; cues of nurturance and love in males are expected to be highly valued by females seeking paternal investment.

There are robust sex differences (higher in females) on the Interpersonal Adjective Scale—Big Five version (IAS-R-B5) Love

(LOV) scale, which measures the Nurturance/Love dimension of the circumplex model (Trapnell & Wiggins, 1990). This dimension involving the tendency to provide aid for those needing help, including children and people who are ill (Wiggins & Broughton, 1985), would therefore be expected to be associated with high-investment childrearing. This dimension is strongly associated with measures of femininity, and with warm, empathic personal relationships and dependence (Wiggins & Broughton, 1985). Girls are more prone to engage in intimate, confiding relationships than boys throughout development (Berndt, 1986; Buhrmester & Furman, 1987; Douvan & Adelson, 1966). Females also tend to place generally greater emphasis than males on love and personal intimacy in sexual relationships (e.g., Buss & Schmitt, 1993; Douvan & Adelson, 1966). Females are more empathic and desire higher intimacy in relationships (Lang-Takoc & Osterweil, 1992), and both sexes perceive friendships with women as closer, richer, more intimate, more empathic, and more therapeutic (e.g., Wright & Scanlon, 1991). Females exposed prenatally to testosterone-like hormones show reduced emphaty (Mathews et al., 2009), and testosterone measured in amniotic fluid relates negatively to empathy in both boys and girls (Chapman et al., 2006). Developmentally, sex differences related to intimacy peak during the reproductive years (Turner, 1981), a finding that is compatible with the present perspective that sex differences in intimacy are related to reproductive behavior.

The Prefrontal Executive Control Adaptive Space

Top-down control enables coordination of specialized adaptations, including all of the mechanisms associated with the four general adaptive spaces discussed earlier (MacDonald, 2008). For many mammals, the prefrontal cortex or its analogues underlie executive control of behavior that takes into account not only subcortically generated affective cues routed though the orbitofrontal cortex (OFC) but also sensory input and other information (e.g., learned contingencies) available to working memory (Uylings, Groenewegen, & Kolb, 2003).

Humans have greatly elaborated this general adaptive space, resulting in top-down effortful mechanisms able to control not only a very wide array of mechanisms encompassed in the four general adaptive spaces mentioned earlier, but also capable of incorporating explicit construals of context in generating behavior, most notably linguistic and symbolic information (MacDonald, 2008). For example, affective states resulting from evolutionary regularities place people in a prepotently aggressive state energized by anger—an emotional state that is one of the subsystems of the BAAS discussed earlier. However, whether or not aggression actually occurs may also be influenced, at least for people with sufficient levels of effortful control, by explicit evaluation of the wider context, including explicit evaluation of the possible costs and benefits of the aggressive act (e.g., penalties at law, possible retaliation). These explicitly calculated costs and benefits are not recurrent over evolutionary time but are products of the analytic system evaluating current environments and producing mental models of possible consequences of behavior.

Rothbart has pioneered the idea that effortful control is a fundamental aspect of temperament related to self-regulation (e.g., Posner & Rothbart, 1998; also see Rueda, Chapter 8, this volume). In human children, there is increasing coherence between 22 and 33 months of age among a variety of tasks assessing the ability to suppress dominant socioaffective responses—for example, waiting for a signal before eating a snack, not peeking while a gift is wrapped, not touching a wrapped gift until the experimenter returns (Kochanska, Murray, & Harlan, 2000). In general, effortful control increases with age, with girls superior to boys (Kochanska & Knaack, 2003; Kochanska et al., 2000). The superior performance of girls on effortful control fits well with the evolutionary theory of sex discussed earlier. Males are expected to score higher on behavioral approach systems (sensation seeking, impulsivity, reward seeking, aggression) and therefore, on average, to be less prone to control prepotent approach responses.

The increasing efficiency of effortful control with advancing age parallels developmental changes in the prefrontal cortex

(PFC). In general there is linear development of PFC from childhood to adulthood; however, age changes in sensation-seeking and reward-oriented behavior are nonlinear because behavior is also influenced by the degree of maturation of limbic structures underlying the behavioral approach (Casey, Jones, & Hare, 2008) (see Figure 14.1). Adolescents are relatively uncontrolled when the development of subcortical structures underlying risk taking (a component of behavioral approach) outpaces the development of prefrontal control structures. This illustrates the complex, dynamically interactive nature of temperament systems, as well as normative changes over age in the relative strength of temperament systems.

Several authors have proposed that the personality system most closely associated with effortful control is Conscientiousness (Caspi, 1998; Kochanska & Knaack, 2003; Rothbart, Ahadi, & Evans, 2000). The only temperament factor of Rothbart's Adult Temperament Questionnaire that is correlated with Conscientiousness is the effortful control factor, which includes measures of attention shifting from reward and from punishment (MacDonald, Figueredo, Wenner, & Howrigan, 2007; Rothbart et al., 2000).

There are also strong conceptual links between Conscientiousness and the effortful control of prepotent socioaffective responses. Conscientiousness is a dimension in the FFM of personality (Costa & McCrae, 1992a; Digman, 1990, 1996; Goldberg, 1981; John, Caspi, Robins, Moffitt, & Stouthamer-Loeber, 1994) referring to *"socially prescribed impulse control* that facilitates task and goal-directed behavior" (John & Srivastava, 1999, p. 121; emphasis in original). Conscientiousness involves variation in the ability to defer gratification in the service of attaining long-term goals; to persevere in unpleasant tasks; to pay close attention to detail; and to behave in a responsible, dependable, cooperative manner (Digman & Inouye, 1986; Digman & Takemoto-Chock, 1981).

Conscientiousness is associated with academic success (Digman & Takemoto-Chock, 1981; Dollinger & Orf, 1991; John et al., 1994), an area in which there are sex differences favoring females throughout the school years, including college (King, 2006). Correlations between high school grades and assessments of Conscientiousness performed 6 years previously were in the .50 range. There are similar correlations between higher Conscientiousness and higher occupational status and income assessed when subjects were in their mid-20s.

The Orienting Sensitivity Adaptive Space

Evans and Rothbart (2007) propose that the temperamental basis for Openness is *Orienting Sensitivity*, a trait that taps perceptual sensitivity and is substantially correlated with standard personality measures of Openness. Markon, Krueger, and Watson (2005) show that Openness splits off from Positive Emotionality when moving from a four-factor to a five-factor solution. Moreover, Openness and Extraversion appear on the same factor in two-, three-, and four-factor models, but they split off in the five-factor solution (Caruso & Cliff, 1997; DeYoung, 2006; Digman, 1997; Rushton & Irwing, 2009).

This suggests that Openness is part of the BAAS, but that it became an adaptive space of its own as a result of differentiation and elaboration. This is intuitively plausible because people who score high in Orienting Sensitivity are intensely engaged with the

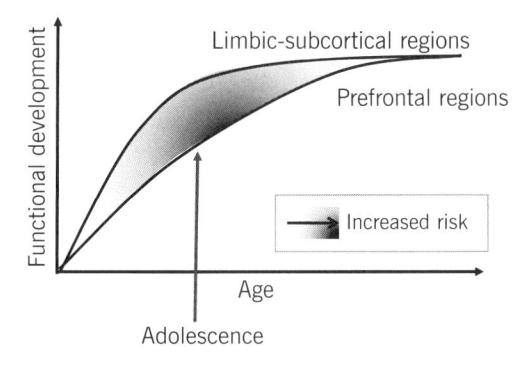

FIGURE 14.1. Illustration of different maturation patterns of prefrontal cortex and subcortical limbic regions (e.g., nucleus accumbens and amygdala) implicated in adolescent risk taking. From Casey, Jones, and Hare (2008). Copyright 2008 by the New York Academy of Sciences. Reprinted by permission.

environment in a positive manner. As with Behavioral Approach generally, people who score high on Orienting Sensitivity approach rewarding stimulation. In the case of Orienting Sensitivity this involves approaching novel aesthetic, perceptual, and intellectual experience characteristic of Openness.

Fitting the Adaptive Spaces to the Results of Factor-Analytic Studies

Animal Research

Individual differences in personality among chimpanzees can be understood within the FFM framework (Figueredo & King, 1996; King & Figueredo, 1994). Reviewing data for 12 quite different species, Gosling and John (1999) found evidence for Extraversion (E), Neuroticism (N), and Agreeableness (A) in most species: E was found in 10 species (but not rats and hyenas); N was found in nine species (but not in vervet monkeys, donkeys, and pigs); A was found in 10 species (but not in guppies and octopi); Conscientiousness (C) was found only in humans and chimpanzees (also see Barr, Chapter 13, this volume).

As noted earlier, Extraversion is associated with the BAAS. Gosling and John's (1999) results do not mean that rats and hyenas do not have behavioral approach systems designed to obtain resources or that vervet monkeys do not have fear systems (a system common to all animals studied; Barr, Chapter 13, this volume) or systems of arousal regulation (reactivity/affect intensity, a system common to all vertebrates; Quinkert et al., 2011). These findings may indicate that although these animals have these systems, individual differences are not conspicuous enough to be captured by the observer rating methodology.

On the other hand, it would not be surprising that guppies and octopi do not have mechanisms of pair-bonding and close relationships, since such relationships are not part of the ecology of these animals. Nor is it surprising that only humans and chimpanzees showed differences in Conscientiousness, since these species are involved in long-term projects requiring delay of gratification and close attention to detail; less cognitively advanced species (i.e., species that respond to environmental challenges mainly via preprogrammed responses) may fail to exhibit differences in focused effort. The point is that the systems perspective expects animal personality psychology to mirror the ecology of the animal.

Human Research

Rothbart and Bates (2006) review studies that yielded from two to eight factors, depending on the items in the item pool. They note support for strong conceptual similarities between three of the dimensions of the FFM: Negative Emotionality (Neuroticism), Positive Emotionality (Extraversion), and Effortful Control (Conscientiousness). Subsequently, Rothbart has added items intended to tap the other dimensions of the FFM, as reviewed earlier: Affiliation, tapping the Nurturance/Pair-Bonding Adaptive Space, and Orienting Sensitivity, intended to tap the temperamental basis for Openness on the FFM (see Evans & Rothbart, 2007).

These developments indicate a powerful convergence between research on temperament and personality centered around the FFM. In seeking to determine how this factor-analytic research fits with an adaptationist perspective, I consider an important paper by Markon and colleagues (2005), which may be considered paradigmatic of a factor-analytic approach that could potentially be incorporated into an evolutionary account. This is because it shows an orderly sequence in factor solutions, from two factors to five factors. The question is: Is it reasonable to view this result as mapping a 1:1 congruence between adaptive spaces and personality factors? In particular, could the branching pattern noted in Figure 14.2 reflect a real evolutionary sequence of elaboration and differentiation of primitive structures?

The Markon and colleagues (2005) α- and β-factors refer to withdrawal (Negative Emotionality) and approach (Positive Emotionality), respectively. The three-factor solution adds Disinhibition, and the four-factor solution distinguishes between Disagreeable Disinhibition and Unconscientious Disinhibition. As mentioned earlier, the fifth factor arises when Openness splits off from Extraversion. The differentiation of Negative Emotionality into Nega-

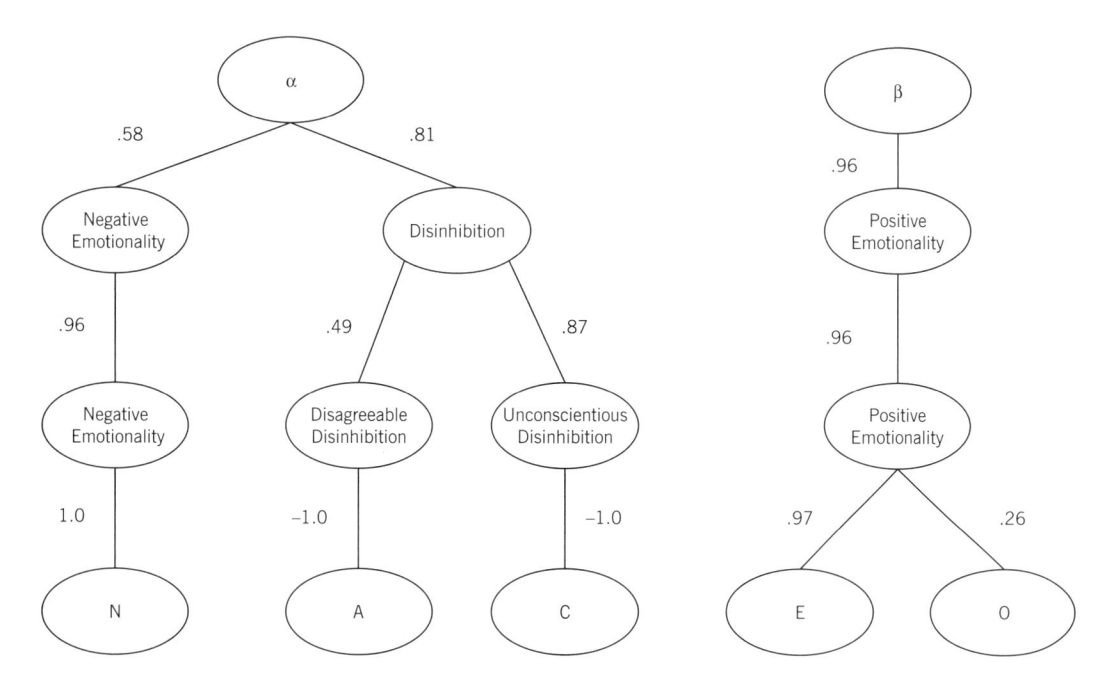

FIGURE 14.2. Correlations between subordinate and superordinate factors. From Markon, Krueger, and Watson (2005). Copyright 2005 by the American Psychological Association. Reprinted by permission. N, Neuroticism; A, Agreeableness; C, Conscientiousness; E, Extraversion; O, Openness.

tive Emotionality, Disagreeable Disinhibition, and Unconscientious Disinhibition reflects clinical categorizations rather than a reasonable interpretation of evolutionary adaptive spaces. Disagreeable Disinhibition is related to the reverse of the Nurturance/Pair-Bonding Adaptive Space, and Unconscientious Disinhibition is the reverse of Effortful Control/Conscientiousness within the prefrontal executive control adaptive space. Evolution has likely selected for these positive traits rather than their reverse. In the case of pair-bonding, there is a clear evolutionary rationale for the development of nurturance and pair-bonding mechanisms derived from parental investment theory, as noted earlier. In the case of effortful control, the prefrontal machinery of top-down control has clear adaptive benefits deriving from planning and impulse control.

One gap between an evolutionary perspective and factor analyses such as the one presented by Markon and colleagues (2005) is that an evolutionary perspective is more compatible with a factor rotation yielding factors of Dominance/Sensation Seeking and Nurturance/Love rather than Extraversion and Agreeableness (MacDonald, 1995, 1999a, 1999b). The Markon and colleagues five-factor solution is typical of many others emphasizing Extraversion-like traits as a basic factor. For example, Depue and Collins (1999) advocate Gregarious/Aloof and Arrogant/Unassuming as fundamental causal dimensions of personality covering the same factor space. Extraversion is also a factor in the NEO Personality Inventory (Costa & McCrae, 1992b) and the Schedule for Nonadaptive and Adaptive Personality (SNAP; Clark, 1993) utilized by Markon and colleagues.

As Trapnell and Wiggins (1990) note, the difference amounts to a rotational difference between two ways of conceptualizing the same interpersonal space. Nevertheless, an evolutionary perspective is better conceptualized with Dominance/Sensation Seeking and Nurturance/Love as the primary axes of interpersonal space, since this conceptualization maximizes theoretically important sex differences and is thus likely to have been the focus of natural selection. As noted earlier, evolutionary theory predicts that in species with sex-differentiated patterns of parental investment, the sex with the lower level of parental investment (typically males) is expected to pursue a more high-risk strategy compared to females, which includes being prone to risk taking and reward seeking, and less sensitive to cues of punishment. Depue and Collins (1999) claim that the traits associated with Behavioral Approach (i.e., dominance, aggression, sensation seeking, risk taking, boldness, sensitivity to reward, and impulsivity) are heterogeneous. But within the evolutionary theory of sex, they form a natural unit: They all involve risky behavior that would benefit males more than females. They are indeed heterogeneous at the level of mechanism, but they also have mechanisms in common, notably testosterone (Archer, 2006). As noted earlier, testosterone is implicated in sex differences both in Behavioral Approach (aggression, activity level) and in empathy, a central emotion of the nurturance/pair-bonding adaptive space. These mechanisms are thus much more likely to be the focus of natural selection than are Extraversion and Agreeableness. And, as noted earlier, there is a clear evolutionary logic in supposing mechanisms that promote parental investment are a critically important adaptive space, with clear implications for sex differences favoring females.

Whereas there are robust sex differences favoring males in Dominance and Sensation Seeking (Trapnell & Wiggins, 1990; Zuckerman, 1991), sex differences in Extraversion are relatively modest and actually favor females in some studies (McCrae et al., 2002; Srivastava, John, Gosling, & Potter, 2003). These results are compatible with Else-Quest's review of data indicating inconsistent and negligible sex differences in Extraversion and Surgency (Chapter 23, this volume).

This pattern of results occurs because Extraversion scales include items related to dominance and venturesomeness, which are higher among males, as well as items related to warmth and affiliation, which are higher among females (see discussion in Lucas, Deiner, Grob, Suh, & Shao, 2000). A good example of this is the Markon and colleagues (2005) study in which warmth loaded approximately equally on Extraversion and (negatively) on Disagreeable Disinhibition; similar results were obtained by Evans and Rothbart (2007). From the evolved systems perspective developed here, it is unlikely that combining warmth and affiliation with Dominance, Sensation Seeking, and Exploratory Behavior cuts nature at its joints.

Moreover, at the level of brain functioning, these systems are quite separate: There are unique neurochemical and neuroanatomical substrates for Nurturance/Love and Behavioral Approach, respectively (Archer, 2006; Bartels & Zeki, 2000; Depue & Morrone-Strupinsky, 2005; Panksepp, 1998; Depue & Fu, Chapter 18, this volume). The highly sex-differentiated traits of dominance, aggression, and sensation seeking on the one hand, and nurturance and love on the other, are thus compatible with neurological findings.

A related reason for focusing on these highly sex-differentiated traits is that they exhibit theoretically expected age changes, whereas there is little evidence for mean age changes in Extraversion (McCrae & Costa, 1990; McCrae et al., 2002). The "young male syndrome" describes the pattern in which sensation seeking, impulsivity, and aggression—all associated with the behavioral approach systems—peak in young adulthood exactly at the time when young males must compete for mates and establish themselves in the dominance hierarchy.

An important part of current-day personality psychology is based on ratings of people by themselves and others, so that the most socially salient features of people are emphasized. These may bear only indirectly on the underlying systems. For example, the factor of Neuroticism refers to a tendency toward negative emotionality, but at the systems level, the research discussed earlier reveals separate systems of reactivity/affect intensity (involving a general tendency toward both positive and negative emotionality) and the behavioral withdrawal adaptive space dominated by the emotions of fear and anxiety. Reactivity/Affect Intensity should be understood to be a separable component of temperament systems apart from motivation (MacDonald, 1988; Rothbart & Bates, 2006). At the motivational core of behavioral withdrawal are the emotions of fear and anxiety, whereas reactivity/affect intensity makes an independent contribution, heightening these emotions in people who score high on Reactivity/Affect Intensity.

This implies that the psychological salience of Neuroticism in everyday evaluations of self and others provides an imperfect guide to the underlying adaptations. Indeed, Vaish, Grossmann, and Woodward (2008) review data showing that, beginning early in life, people have a negativity bias whereby they attend to, learn from, and use negative emotional expressions more than positive emotional expressions in evaluating people. This is evolutionarily adaptive because cues to danger are often of immediate and irreversible relevance to survival, whereas missed opportunities are often reversible. This would result in emotional reactivity tending to be conflated with negative emotionality, so that positive emotional expressions by highly reactive, emotionally intense people are not given equal weight. The result is a temperament trait dominated by negative emotionality (Neuroticism), while positive emotionality is a much less dominant characteristic associated with Extraversion.

Moreover, the fact that the negative emotion of anger is associated with positive emotionality at the neurological level (Dawson, 1994; Fox, 1991; Fox et al., 2001; Harmon-Jones, Peterson, Gable, & Harmon-Jones, 2008; Harmon-Jones & Sigelman, 2001; see below) makes excellent sense within an evolved systems perspective where these emotions are linked to a variety of approach behaviors underlying reward (e.g., sexual gratification), aggression, social dominance, risk taking, and sensation seeking.

Similarly, the emergence of Extraversion in factor analysis may well reflect combinations of socially valued traits: Extraverts combine warmth and gregariousness with assertiveness and excitement seeking (see, e.g., the Markon et al. [2005] five-factor solution, Table 10, p. 151; Else-Quest, Chapter 23, this volume).

Moreover, in the model presented by Markon and colleagues (2005), the reactivity/affect intensity adaptive space is split into Positive Emotionality and Negative Emotionality. Negative Emotionality includes hostility and aggression, both loading on the Disagreeable Disinhibition (reverse of Agreeableness) factor in the five-factor solution.

However, this is unlikely to reflect neurological structure. Fox (1991; Fox et al., 2001; see also Dawson, 1994; Harmon-Jones & Sigelman, 2001; Harmon-Jones et al., 2008) has shown that in terms of brain organization, anger is associated with left cortical activation, along with positive emotions of joy and interest, and therefore is categorized as part of the behavioral approach adaptive space (discussed earlier). On the other hand, right cortical activation is associated with fear, disgust, and distress—key components of the behavioral withdrawal adaptive space (White et al., Chapter 17, and Depue & Fu, Chapter 18, this volume).

Furthermore, Evans and Rothbart (2007) found that aggressive and nonaggressive negative affect scales loaded on the same general Negative Affect factor, while Saucier's (2003) Multi-Language Seven Questionnaire separates Neuroticism into aggressive components ("angry" and "irritable" vs. "calm" and "patient") and nonaggressive components ("fearful" and "scared" vs. "tough"). The separation of aggressive and nonaggressive negative affect is consistent with an evolutionary perspective, since anger-type emotions (conceptually and neuropsychologically linked to the behavioral approach adaptive space) are vastly different functionally from fear-type emotions (conceptually and neurologically associated with the behavioral withdrawal adaptive space). However, the results from the Markon and colleagues (2005) study indicate that these traits load on the same factor in higher-order analyses all the way up to the two-factor solution, implying that anger never appears along with the positive emotionality cluster. This conflicts with the data on the neuropsychology of anger cited earlier (Dawson, 1994; Fox, 1991; Fox et al., 2001; Depue & Fu, Chapter 18, this volume), indicating that anger is associated with positive emotionality as an aspect of behavioral approach at the level of neuropsychology. It also conflicts with the data reviewed earlier indicating close ties between reward-seeking mechanisms and aggression at not only the level of neurobiology but also in terms of individual differences: People who are prone to aggression are also prone to strong attraction to reward. Again, the results of factor analyses of questionnaire-based data are poor guides to carving nature at its joints. These results suggest that people mistakenly tend to group all negative emotionality together. A more appropriate classification is based on individual differences in reactivity/affect intensity: People who score high on affect intensity tend toward intense emotions of all types, including anger, fear, and anxiety, therefore scoring high on measures of Neuroticism. It would be expected that some of these people would also score high on measures of Positive Emotionality, but, as noted earlier, this would be less salient as an aspect of personality because of the negativity bias.

As noted, at the level of neuropsychology, reactivity/affect intensity is a general behavioral energizer, with connections to both behavioral approach mechanisms and behavioral withdrawal mechanisms. This suggests that at the level of phenotypic temperament and personality descriptions, affect regulation will not appear as a separable component but will be intertwined with approach and withdrawal tendencies, respectively (see Figure 14.3). Individuals who score high in reactivity/affect intensity and behavioral approach also score high on measures of Positive Emotionality; individuals who score high in reactivity/affect intensity and behavioral withdrawal also score high on measures of negative emotionality (Neuroticism).

The intertwining of reactivity with approach and withdrawal mechanisms, respectively, is compatible with Larsen and Diener's (1992) findings that activated positive affect is associated with Extraversion, while activated negative affect is associated with Neuroticism. Furthermore, Heller (1990) notes that an activation system centered in the parietal region of the right hemisphere plays a role in both cortical and autonomic arousal. Emotional valence involves the balance between the frontal regions of the left and right hemispheres, with the former associated with positive emotions and the latter with negative emotions.

Again, it is important to distinguish the arousal component of temperament systems as separate from motivational components (MacDonald, 1988, 1995; Rothbart & Bates, 2006). For example, motivation for behavioral approach includes mechanisms such as sensitivity to reward, discussed earlier. As a result, people can score high on behavioral approach without being intensely emotional. This perspective is congruent with two-dimensional perspectives on affect that distinguish arousal components from valence components (Posner et al., 2005, 2008; Russell, 2003). Thus, as noted earlier in the discussion of the reactivity/affect intensity adaptive space, whereas the reticular formation is central to arousal, Posner and colleagues (2005, 2008) show that valence is linked to the mesolimbic dopamine reward system activated with pleasurable stimulation and the mesolimbic ventral striatum activated with aversive stimulation.

Indeed, a very large literature shows that many people who are highly aggressive and prone to sensation seeking are emotionally hyporeactive. For example, Adrian Raine and colleagues (e.g., Ortiz & Raine, 2004; Raine, 2002) have provided evidence that reduced adrenergic function, as indicated by low resting heart rate, is the best biological correlate of aggression, antisocial behavior, and sensation seeking. As noted earlier, the biological substrate of reactivity/affect intensity is the adrenergic arousal system, indicating that these children score low on Reactivity/Affect Intensity, while nevertheless scoring high on Behavioral Approach. Deficits in prefrontal structures associated with Effortful Control/Conscientiousness are also implicated. Low resting heart rate at age 3 predicts aggressive behavior at age 11 and is heritable. Furthermore, sex differences are in the expected direction: Males are more likely than females to have low resting heart rate.

Such results are compatible with proposals that people who score low on autonomic arousal use aggression and sensation seeking to attain an optimal level of arousal (Eysenck, 1997; Quay, 1965; Raine, 1997). These results are also compatible with the idea that people high in Reactivity/Affect Intensity would avoid sensation seeking and aggression because these activities would be emotionally overwhelming (MacDonald, 1995); that is, highly reactive people—people with weak nervous systems (Strelau, 1989)—withdraw in the presence of even moderate levels of stimulation. These findings fit well with the common distinction between aggression accompanied by anger ("hostile or reactive aggression") and unemotional aggression (proactive aggression). For example, Frick and Ellis (1999) show that children with reactive aggression are prone to anger and emotional dysregulation, but this is not the case for children diagnosed with proactive aggression. Children labeled as callous/unemotional were found to have the most severe type of conduct disorder. Such children score low on not only empathy, guilt, and concern for others (associated with low levels of Nurturance/Love), but also generally low on emotional expressiveness ("does not show emotion"), including fearfulness and anxiety. Similarly, psychopathic adults show a pattern of "lower anxiety, less fearfulness, and other evidence for deficits in their processing of emotional stimuli" (Frick & Ellis, p. 160). This low-emotional subtype is also prone to sensation seeking and reward seeking, indicating that such people score high on behavioral approach.

Bushman and Anderson (1999; see also Anderson & Bushman, 2002) note that emotionally charged, angry aggression and aggression unaccompanied by anger may have similar motives (e.g., harming another, reclaiming self-esteem). In terms of the present framework, people who combine high levels of behavioral approach with high reactivity/affect intensity are prone to emotionally charged, angry, hostile aggression; they are also prone to reward seeking accompanied by positive emotionality. On the other hand, the combination of high behavioral approach with low reactivity/affect intensity is associated with aggression unaccompanied by anger (instrumental, proactive aggression) and reward seeking unaccompanied by strong positive emotionality.

An Evolutionary Proposal

Ideally, one would be able to trace the evolution of these systems over time and chart their differentiation in different lineages, for example, as approach systems originally designed for foraging and mating become linked with social dominance and intraspecific aggression in social species, and with systems assessing risk (impulsivity, sensation seeking, etc.), self-confidence, and sociability. Figure 14.3 provides an illustration of the proposed evolutionary lineages of the six adaptive spaces discussed here, based partly on MacLean's (1990, 1993) work on the triune brain. MacLean shows that the reptilian brain included mechanisms of behavioral approach, while the distinguishing feature of the paleomammalian brain was adaptations for nurturance; these later evolved into pair-bonding mechanisms in some lineages, including humans (MacDonald, 1992). The neomammalian brain is dominated by the cortex, with top-down processing utilizing prefrontal control mechanisms exerting inhibitory control over the more evolutionarily ancient subcortical areas. In humans these are elaborated in the prefrontal executive control adaptive space. The figure suggests that prefrontal executive control shares some mechanisms with Nurturance/Pair-Bonding. This fits with the Markon and colleagues (2005) findings that Disinhibition (Eysenck's Psychoticism) breaks down into Disagreeable and Unconscientious Disinhibition in the four-factor solution. Watson and Clark (1992) found that guilt was an emotion common to the two systems. Figure 14.3 also illustrates the orienting sensitivity adaptive space branching off from the behavioral approach adaptive space, as discussed earlier.

Figure 14.3 also illustrates the proposed linkages between the six adaptive spaces to personality factors as delineated in the FFM, a six-factor model based on Saucier (2003), in which Neuroticism is broken down into Nonaggressive Negative Emotionality (i.e., Saucier's Self-Assured reversed: e.g., fearful, scared, cowardly) and Aggressive Negative Emotionality (i.e., Saucier's Temperamental: e.g., hot-tempered, short-tempered, impatient; Freeman & Gosling's [2010] trait of irritability would seem to tap this aggressive negative emotionality in primates generally). Figure 14.3 also illustrates the linkages between evolved systems and an evolutionarily informed factor analysis with Dominance/Sensation Seeking, Nurturance/Love and Behavioral Withdrawal as primary factors, as discussed earlier.

Conclusion

The fundamental goal of an evolutionary approach is to cut nature at its joints. The foregoing shows that doing so requires an integration at several levels—the neuropsychological (e.g., how behavioral approach

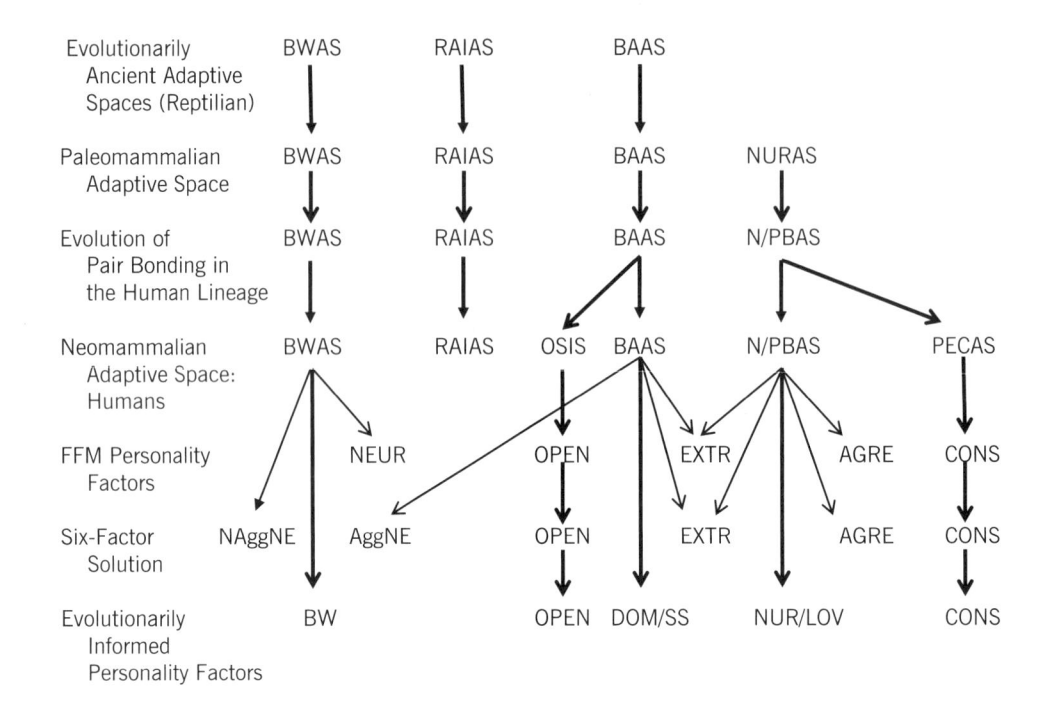

FIGURE 14.3. Illustration of the proposed evolutionary history of the adaptive spaces and their relation to personality factors. The thick arrows indicate evolutionary relationships of homology (identity by common descent). The thin arrows indicate influences of neomammallian adaptive systems on personality. Individual differences in reactivity/affect intensity influence all personality factors; the lines connecting the reactivity/affect intensity adaptive space (RAIAS) and the personality factors are not drawn for reasons of clarity. BWAS, behavioral withdrawal adaptive space; BAAS, behavioral approach adaptive space; NURAS, nurturance adaptive space; N/PBAS, nurturance/pair bonding adaptive space; OSAS, orienting sensitivity adaptive space; PECAS, prefrontal executive control adaptive space; NEUR, Neuroticism; EXTR, Extraversion; OPEN, Openness; AGRE, Agreeableness; CONS, Conscientiousness; AggNE, Aggressive Negative Emotionality; NaggNE, Nonaggressive Negative Emotionality; BW, Behavioral Withdrawal; DOM/SS, Dominance/Sensation Seeking; NUR/LOVE, Nurturance/Love.

and emotionality are organized in the brain), the comparative (species differences in adaptations related to temperament and personality), the theoretical (e.g., the evolutionary theory of sex, life history theory), and the results of factor analysis of temperament and personality questionnaires. While much remains to be learned in all these areas, it is clear at this point that an evolutionary perspective provides novel insights into the structure of personality.

Further Reading

Dingemanse, N. J., & Réale, D. (2005). Natural selection and animal personality. *Behaviour*, 142, 1165–1190.
Freeman, H. D., & Gosling, S. D. (2010). Personality in nonhuman primates: A review and evaluation of past research. *American Journal of Primatology*, 72, 653–671.
MacDonald, K. B. (2008). Effortful control, explicit processing and the regulation of human evolved predispositions. *Psychological Review*, 115(4), 1012–1031.
Rothbart, M. K. (2007). Temperament, development, and personality. *Current Directions in Psychology*, 16, 207–212.
Rothbart, M. K., & Bates, J. E. (2006). Temperament. In W. Damon, R. Lerner, & N. Eisenberg (Eds.), *Handbook of child psychology: Vol. 3. Social, emotional, and personality development* (6th ed., pp. 99–166). New York: Wiley.

References

American Psychiatric Association. (2000). *Diagnostic and statistical manual of mental disorders* (4th ed., text rev.). Washington, DC: Author.

Anderson, C. A., & Bushman, B. J. (2002). Human aggression. *Annual Review of Psychology, 53,* 27–51.

Archer, J. (2006). Testosterone and human aggression: An evaluation of the challenge hypothesis. *Neuroscience Biobehavioral Reviews, 30,* 319–345.

Aron, E. N., & Aron, A. (1997). Sensory-processing sensitivity and its relation to introversion and emotionality. *Journal of Personality and Social Psychology, 73,* 345–368.

Atzil, S., Hendler, T., & Feldman, R. (2011). Specifying the neurobiological basis of human attachment: Brain, hormones, and behavior in synchronous and intrusive mothers. *Neuropsychopharmacology, 36,* 2603–2615.

Bartels, A., & Zeki, S. (2000). The neural basis of romantic love. *NeuroReport, 11*(17), 3829–3834.

Bell, G. (2010). Fluctuating selection: The perpetual renewal of adaptation in variable environments. *Philosophical Transactions of the Royal Society B: Biological Sciences, 365,* 87–97.

Belsky, J., Steinberg, L., & Draper, P. (1991) Childhood experience, interpersonal development, and reproductive strategy: An evolutionary theory of socialization. *Child Development, 62,* 647–670.

Benham, G. (2006). The highly sensitive person: Stress and physical symptom reports. *Personality and Individual Differences, 40,* 1433–1440.

Berndt, T. J. (1986). Children's comments about their friendships. In M. Perlmutter (Ed.), *Minnesota Symposia in Child Development: Vol. 18. Cognitive perspectives on children's social and behavioral development* (pp. 189–212). Hillsdale, NJ: Erlbaum.

Betzig, L. (1986). *Despotism and differential reproduction.* Hawthorne, NY: Aldine.

Bowlby, J. (1969). *Attachment and loss: Vol. I. Attachment.* London: Hogarth Press/Institute of Psychoanalysis.

Buhrmester, D., & Furman, W. (1987). The development of companionship and intimacy. *Child Development, 58,* 1101–1113.

Burkett, J. P., Spiegel, L. L., Inoue, K., Murphy, A. Z., & Young, L. J. (2011). Activation of μ-opioid receptors in the dorsal striatum is necessary for adult social attachment in monogamous prairie voles. *Neuropsychopharmacology, 36,* 2200–2210.

Bushman, B. J., & Anderson, C. A. (2001). Is it time to pull the plug on the hostile versus instrumental aggression dichotomy? *Psychological Review, 108,* 273–279.

Buss, D. M. (1989). Sex differences in human mate preferences: Evolutionary hypotheses tested in 37 cultures. *Behavioral and Brain Sciences, 12,* 1–49.

Buss, D. M. (2008). Human nature and individual differences: Evolution of human personality. In O. P. John, R. W. Robins, & L. A. Pervin (Eds.), *Handbook of personality: Theory and research* (3rd ed., pp. 29–61). New York: Guilford Press.

Buss, D. M., & Schmitt, D. P. (1993). Sexual strategies theory: An evolutionary perspective on human mating. *Psychological Review, 100,* 204–232.

Carere, C., & Eens, M. (2005). Unravelling animal personalities: How and why individuals consistently differ. *Behaviour, 142,* 1155–1163.

Caruso, J. C., & Cliff, N. (1997). An examination of the five-factor model of normal personality variation with reliable component analysis. *Personality and Individual Differences, 23*(2), 317–325.

Casey, B. J., Jones, R. M., & Hare, T. A. (2008). The adolescent brain. *Annals of the New York Academy of Sciences, 1124,* 111–126.

Caspi, A. (1998). Personality development across the lifespan. In N. Eisenberg (Ed.), *Handbook of child psychology* (Vol. 3, pp. 105–176). New York: Wiley.

Chapman, E., Baron-Cohen, S., Auyeung, B., Knickmeyer, R., Taylor, K., & Hackett, G. (2006). Fetal testosterone and empathy: evidence from the Empathy Quotient (EQ) and the "reading the mind in the eyes" test. *Social Neuroscience, 1,* 135–148.

Charnov, E. L. (1993). *Life history invariants.* Oxford, UK: Oxford University Press.

Christopherson, E. R. (1989). Injury control. *American Psychologist, 44,* 237–241.

Clark, L. A. (1993). *Manual for the Schedule for Nonadaptive and Adaptive Personality.* Minneapolis: University of Minnesota Press.

Collaer, M. L., & Hines, M. (1995). Human behavioral sex differences: A role for gonadal hormones during early development? *Psychological Bulletin, 118,* 55–107.

Costa, P. T., & McCrae, R. R. (1986). Personality stability and its implications for clinical psychology. *Clinical Psychology Review, 6,* 407–423.

Costa, P. T., Jr., & McCrae, R. R. (1992a). Normal personality assessment in clinical practice: The NEO Personality Inventory. *Psychological Assessment, 4,* 5–13.

Costa, P. T., & McCrae, R. R. (1992b). *Revised NEO Personality Inventory (NEO-PI-R) and NEO Five-Factor Inventory (NEO-FFI) professional manual.* Odessa, FL: Psychological Assessment Resources.

Davidson, R. J. (1993). The neuropsychology of emotion and affective style. In M. Lewis & J. M. Haviland (Eds.), *Handbook of emotions* (pp. 143–154). New York: Guilford Press.

Dawson, G. (1994). Development of emotional expression and emotion regulation in infancy: Contributions of the frontal lobe. In G. Dawson & K. W. Fischer (Eds.), *Human behavior and the developing brain* (pp. 346–379). New York: Guilford Press.

De Pauw, S. S. W., Mervielde, I., & Van Leeuwen, K. G. (2009). How are traits related to problem behavior in preschoolers?: Similarities and contrasts between temperament and personality. *Journal of Abnormal Child Psychology, 37,* 309–325

Depue, R. A., & Collins, P. F. (1999). Neurobiology of the structure of personality: Dopamine facilitation of incentive motivation and extraversion. *Brain and Behavioral Sciences, 22,* 491–569.

Depue, R. A., & Morrone-Strupinsky, J. V. (2005). A neurobehavioral model of behavioral bonding: Implications for conceptualizing a human trait of affiliation. *Behavioral and Brain Sciences, 28*(3), 313–378.

Derryberry, D. (1987). Incentive and feedback effects on target detection: A chronometric analysis of Gray's theory of temperament. *Personality and Individual Differences, 8,* 855–865.

DeYoung, C. G. (2006). Higher-order factors of the Big Five in a multi-informant sample. *Journal of Personality and Social Psychology, 91,* 1138–1151.

Digman, J. M. (1990). Personality structure: Emergence of the five-factor model. *Annual Review of Psychology, 41,* 417–440.

Digman, J. M. (1996). The curious history of the five-factor model. In J. S. Wiggins (Ed.), *The five-factor model of personality: Theoretical perspectives* (pp. 1–20). New York: Guilford Press.

Digman, J. M. (1997). Higher-order factors of the Big Five. *Journal of Personality and Social Psychology, 73,* 1246–1256.

Digman, J. M., & Inouye, J. (1986). Further specification of the five robust factors of personality. *Journal of Personality and Social Psychology, 50,* 116–123.

Digman, J. M., & Takemoto-Chock, N. K. (1981). Factors in the natural language of personality: Re-analysis, comparison, and interpretation of six major studies. *Multivariate Behavioral Research, 16,* 149–170.

Dingemanse, N. J., Both, C., Drent, P. J., & Tinbergen, J. M. (2004). Fitness consequences of avian personalities in a fluctuating environment. *Proceedings of the Royal Society of London B: Biological Sciences, 271,* 847–852.

Dingemanse, N. J., & Réale, D. (2005). Natural selection and animal personality. *Behaviour, 142,* 1165–1190.

Dollinger, S. J., & Orf, L. A. (1991). Personality and performance in "personality": Conscientiousness and openness. *Journal of Research in Personality, 25,* 276–284.

Douvan, E. A., & Adelson, J. (1966). *The adolescent experience.* New York: Wiley.

Eagly, A. H., & Steffan, V. J. (1986). Gender and aggressive behavior: A meta-analytic review of the social psychological literature. *Psychological Bulletin, 100,* 283–308.

Eaton, W. O., & Yu, A. P. (1989). Are sex differences in child motor activity level a function of sex differences in maturational status? *Child Development, 60,* 1005–1011.

Ehrhardt, A. A. (1985). The psychobiology of gender. In A. S. Rossi (Ed.), *Gender and the life course* (pp. 81–96). New York: Aldine.

Else-Quest, N. M., Hyde, J. S., Goldsmith, H. H., & Van Hulle, C. (2006). Gender differences in temperament: A meta-analysis. *Psychological Bulletin, 132,* 33–72.

Evans, D. E., & Rothbart, M. K. (2007). Developing a model for adult temperament. *Journal of Research in Personality, 41,* 868–888.

Eysenck, H. J. (1997). Personality and the biosocial model of antisocial and criminal behavior. In A. Raine, P. Brennan, D. P. Farrington, & S. A. Mednick (Eds.), *Biosocial bases of violence* (pp. 21–38). New York: Plenum Press.

Figueredo, A. J., & King, J. E. (1996). The evolution of individual differences in behavior. *Western Comparative Psychological Association Observer, 2*(2), 1–4.

Figueredo, A. J., Vásquez, G., Brumbach, B. H., & Schneider, S. M. R. (2004). The heritability of life history strategy: The K-factor, covitality, and personality. *Social Biology, 51,* 121–143.

Figueredo, A. J., Vásquez, G., Brumbach, B. H., & Schneider, S. M. R. (2007). The K-factor, covitality, and personality: A psychometric test of life history theory. *Human Nature, 18,* 47–73.

Figueredo, A. J., Vásquez, G., Brumbach, B. H., Schneider, S. M. R., Sefcek, J. A., Tal, I. R., et al. (2006). Consilience and life history theory: From genes to brain to reproductive strategy. *Developmental Review, 26,* 243–275.

Fox, N. A. (1991). If it's not left, it's right: Electroencephalograph asymmetry and the development of emotion. *American Psychologist, 46,* 863–872.

Fox, N. A. (1994). Dynamic cerebral processes underlying emotion regulation. *Monographs of the Society for Research in Child Development, 59*(2/3, Serial No. 240), 152–166.

Fox, N. A., Henderson, H. A., Rubin, K. H., Calkins, S. D., & Schmidt, L. A. (2001). Continuity and discontinuity of behavioral inhibition and exuberance: Psychophysiological and behavioral influences across the first four years of life. *Child Development, 72,* 1–21.

Freeman, H. D., & Gosling, S. D. (2010). Personality in nonhuman primates: A review and evaluation of past research. *American Journal of Primatology, 72,* 653–671.

Frick, P. J., & Ellis, M. (1999). Callous–unemotional traits and sub-types of conduct disorder. *Clini-*

cal *Child and Family Psychology Review, 2,* 149–168.
Garey, J., Goodwillie, A., Frohlich, J., Morgan, M., Gustafsson, J.-A., Smithies, O., et al. (2003). Genetic contributions of generalized arousal of brain and behavior. *Proceedings of the National Academy of Science USA, 100,* 11019–11022.
Ginsburg, H. J., & Miller, S. M. (1982). Sex differences in children's risk-taking behavior. *Child Development, 53,* 426–428.
Goldberg, L. R. (1981). Language and individual differences: The search for universals in personality lexicons. In L. Wheeler (Ed.), *Review of personality and social psychology* (Vol. 2, pp. 141–165). Beverly Hills, CA: Sage.
Gosling, S. D., & John, O. P. (1999). Personality dimensions in nonhuman animals: A cross-species review. *Current Directions in Psychological Science, 8*(3), 69–75.
Gray, J. A. (1987). *The psychology of fear and stress* (2nd ed.). Cambridge, UK: Cambridge University Press.
Gray, J. A. (2000). *The neuropsychology of anxiety: An enquiry into the functions of the septo-hippocampal system* (2nd ed.). Oxford, UK: Oxford University Press.
Harmon-Jones, E., Peterson, C., Gable, P. A., & Harmon-Jones, C. (2008). Anger and approach-avoidance motivation. In A. J. Elliot (Ed.), *Handbook of approach and avoidance motivation* (pp., 399–413). New York: Psychology Press.
Harmon-Jones, E., & Sigelman, J. (2001). State anger and prefrontal brain activity: Evidence that insult-related relative left-prefrontal activation is associated with experienced anger and aggression. *Journal of Personality and Social Psychology, 80,* 797–803.
Heller, W. (1990). The neuropsychology of emotion: Developmental patterns and implications for psychopathology. In N. L. Stein, B. Leventhal, & T. Trabasso (Eds.), *Psychological and biological approaches to emotion* (pp. 167–211). Hillsdale, NJ: Erlbaum.
Hines, M. (2011). Gender development in the human brain. *Annual Review of Neuroscience, 34,* 69–88.
Humphreys, A. P., & Smith, P. K. (1987). Rough and tumble, friendship, and dominance in school children: Evidence for continuity and change with age. *Child Development, 58,* 201–212.
Hur, Y., & Bouchard, T. J. (1997). The genetic correlation between impulsivity and sensation seeking traits. *Behavior Genetics, 27,* 455–463.
Insel, T. R., Winslow, J. T., Wang, Z., & Young, L. J. (1998). Oxytocin, vasopressin, and the neuroendocrine basis of pair bond formation. *Advances in Experimental Medicine and Biology, 449,* 215–224.
John, O., Caspi, A., Robins, R. W., Moffitt, T. E., & Stouthamer-Loeber, M. (1994). The "little five": Exploring the nomological network of the five-factor model of personality in adolescent boys. *Child Development, 65,* 160–178.
John, O. P., & Srivastava, S. (1999). The Big Five trait taxonomy: History, measurement, and theoretical perspectives. In L. A. Pervin & O. P. John (Eds.), *Handbook of personality: Theory and research* (2nd ed., pp. 102–138). New York: Guilford Press.
Kagan, J., Reznick, J. S., & Snidman, N. (1987). The physiology and psychology of behavioral inhibition. *Child Development, 58,* 1459–1473.
Kiesler, D. J. (1983). The 1982 interpersonal circle: A taxonomy for complementarity in human transactions. *Psychological Review, 90,* 185–214.
King, J. (2006). *Gender equity in education: 2006.* Washington, DC: American Council on Education.
King, J. E., & Figueredo, A. J. (1994, April). *Human personality factors in zoo chimpanzees?* Paper presented at the Western Psychological Association Convention, Kona, Hawaii.
Klein, Z. (1995). Safety-seeking and risk-taking behavioral patterns in *Homo sapiens. Ethology and Sociobiology.*
Kochanska, G., Murray, K. T., & Harlan, E. T. (2000). Effortful control in early childhood: Continuity and change, antecedents, and implications for social development. *Developmental Psychology, 36,* 220–232.
Kochanska, G., & Knaack, A. (2003). Effortful control as a personality characteristic of young children: Antecedents, correlates, and consequences. *Journal of Personality, 71,* 1087–1112.
Korte, S. M., Koolhaas, J. M., Wingfield, J. C., & McEwen, B. S. (2005). The Darwinian concept of stress: Benefits of allostasis and costs of allostatic load and the trade offs in health and disease. *Neuroscience and Biobehavioral Reviews, 29,* 3–38.
LaFreniére, P. J., & Charlesworth, W. R. (1983). Dominance, affiliation and attention in a preschool group: A nine-month longitudinal study. *Ethology and Sociobiology, 4,* 55–67.
LaFreniére, P. J., Masataka, N., Butovskaya, M., Chen, Q., Dessen, M. A., Atwanger, K., et al. (2002). Cross-cultural analysis of social competence and behavior problems in preschoolers. *Early Education and Development, 13,* 201–220.
Lang-Takoc, E., & Osterweil, Z. (1992). Separateness and connectedness: Differences between the genders. *Sex Roles, 27,* 277–289.
Larsen, R. J., & Diener, E. (1992). Problems and promises with the circumplex model of emotion. *Review of Personality and Social Psychology, 13,* 25–59.
LeDoux, J. (1996). *The emotional brain: The mys-

terious underpinnings of emotional life. New York: Simon & Schuster.

Lucas, R. E., Deiner, E., Grob, A., Suh, E. M., & Shao, L. (2000). Cross-cultural evidence for the fundamental features of extraversion. *Journal of Personality and Social Psychology, 79,* 452–468.

Lusk, J., MacDonald, K., & Newman, J. R. (1998). Resource appraisals among self, friend and leader: Implications for an evolutionary perspective on individual differences and a resource/reciprocity perspective on friendship. *Personality and Individual Differences, 24,* 685–700.

MacDonald, K. B. (1988). *Social and personality development: An evolutionary synthesis.* New York: Plenum Press.

MacDonald, K. B. (1992). Warmth as a developmental construct: An evolutionary analysis. *Child Development, 63,* 753–773.

MacDonald, K. B. (1995). Evolution, the five-factor model, and levels of personality. *Journal of Personality, 63,* 525–567.

MacDonald, K. B. (1999a). Love and security of attachment as two independent systems underlying intimate relationships. *Journal of Family Psychology, 13*(4), 492–495.

MacDonald, K. B. (1999b). What about sex differences?: An adaptationist perspective on "the lines of causal influence" of personality systems: Commentary on "Neurobiology of the Structure of Personality: Dopamine Facilitation of Incentive Motivation and Extraversion," by R. A. Depue & P. F. Collins. *Behavioral and Brain Sciences, 22*(3), 530–531.

MacDonald, K. B. (2005). Personality, development, and evolution. In R. Burgess & K. MacDonald (Eds.), *Evolutionary perspectives on human development* (2nd ed., pp. 207–242). Thousand Oaks, CA: Sage.

MacDonald, K. B. (2008). Effortful control, explicit processing and the regulation of human evolved predispositions. *Psychological Review, 115*(4), 1012–1031.

MacDonald, K. B., Figueredo, A. J., Wenner, C. J., & Howrigan, D. (2007, June). *Life history strategy, executive functions, and personality.* Paper presented at the meeting of the Human Behavior and Evolution Society, William and Mary College, Williamsburg, VA.

MacDonald, K. B., & Parke, R. D. (1986). Parent–child physical play: The effects of sex and age of children and parents. *Sex Roles, 15,* 367–378.

MacLean, P. D. (1990). *The triune brain in evolution: Role in paleocerebral functions.* New York: Plenum Press.

MacLean, P. D. (1993). Cerebral evolution of emotion. In M. Lewis & J. M. Haviland (Eds.), *Handbook of emotions* (pp. 67–86). New York: Guilford Press.

Markon, K. E., Krueger, R. F., & Watson, D. (2005). Delineating the structure of normal and abnormal personality: An integrative hierarchical approach. *Journal of Personality and Social Psychology, 88*(1), 139–157.

Mathews, G. A., Fane, B. A., Conway, G. S., Brook, C., & Hines, M. (2009). Personality and congenital adrenal hyperplasia: Possible effects of prenatal androgen exposure. *Hormones and Behavior, 55,* 285–291.

McCrae, R. R., & Costa, P. T. (1990). *Personality in adulthood.* New York: Guilford Press.

McCrae, R. R., Costa, P. T., Terracciano, A., Parker, W. D., Mills, C. J., De Fruyt, F., et al. (2002). Personality trait development from age 12 to age 18: Longitudinal, cross-sectional, and cross-cultural analysis. *Journal of Personality and Social Psychology, 83,* 1456–1468.

McGue, M., & Lykken, D. T. (1992). Genetic influence on risk of divorce. *Psychological Science, 3,* 368–373.

Mehlman, P. T., Higley, J. D., Fernald, B. J., Sallee, F. R., Suomi, S. J., & Linnoila, M. (1997). CSF 5-HIAA, testosterone, and sociosexual behaviors in free-ranging male rhesus macaques in the mating season. *Psychiatric Research, 72,* 89–102.

Nettle, D. (2006). The evolution of personality variation in humans and other animals. *American Psychologist, 61,* 622–631.

Newman, J. P. (1987). Reaction to punishment in extraverts and psychopaths: Implications for the impulsive behavior of disinhibited individuals. *Journal of Personality Research, 21,* 464–480.

Ortiz, J., & Raine, A. (2004). Heart-rate level and antisocial behavior in children: A meta-analysis. *Journal of the American Academy of Child and Adolescent Psychiatry, 43*(2), 154–162.

Panksepp, J. (1982). Toward a general psychobiological theory of emotions. *Behavioral and Brain Sciences, 5,* 407–422.

Panksepp, J. (1998). *Affective neuroscience: The foundations of human and animal emotions.* New York: Oxford University Press.

Panksepp, J., & Moskal, J. (2008). Dopamine and SEEKING: Sub-cortical "reward" systems and appetitive urges. In A. J. Elliot (Ed.), *Handbook of approach and avoidance motivation* (pp. 67–88). New York: Psychology Press.

Pasterski, V. L., Hindmarsh, P., Geffner, M., Brook, C., Brain, C., & Hines, M. (2007). Increased aggression and activity level in 3- to 11-year-old girls with congenital adrenal hyperplasia (CAH). *Hormones and Behavior, 52,* 368–374.

Penke, L., Denissen, J. J. A., & Miller, G. (2007). The evolutionary genetics of personality. *European Journal of Personality, 21,* 549–587.

Pfiefer, M., Goldsmith, H. H., Davidson, R. J., & Rickman, M. (2002). Continuity and change in inhibited and uninhibited children. *Child Development, 73,* 1474–1485.

Posner, J., Russell, J. A., Gerber, A., Tiziano, C.,

Shan, Y., Wang, Z., et al. (2008). The neurophysiological bases of emotion: An fMRI study of the affective circumplex using emotion-denoting words. *Human Brain Mapping, 30,* 883–895.

Posner, J., Russell, J. A., & Peterson, B. S. (2005). The circumplex model of affect: An integrative approach to affective neuroscience, cognitive development, and psychopathology. *Development and Psychopathology, 17,* 715–734.

Posner, M. I., & Rothbart, M. K. (1998). Attention, self-regulation, and consciousness. *Philosophical Transactions of the Royal Society of London B, 353,* 1915–1927.

Quay, H. C. (1965). Psychopathic personality as pathological stimulation-seeking. *American Journal of Psychiatry, 122,* 180–183.

Quinkert, A. W., Vimala, V., Weila, Z. M., Reekeb, G. N., Schiff, N. D., Banavard, J. R., et al. (2011). Quantitative descriptions of generalized arousal, an elementary function of the vertebrate brain. *Proceedings of the National Academy of Sciences USA, 108*(Suppl. 3), 15617–15623.

Raine, A. (1997). Psychophysiology and antisocial behavior: A biosocial perspective and a prefrontal dysfunction hypothesis. In D. Stoff, J. Breiling, & J. D. Maser (Eds.), *Handbook of antisocial behavior* (pp. 289–304). New York: Wiley.

Raine, A. (2002). Annotation: The role of prefrontal deficits, low autonomic arousal, and early health factors in the development of antisocial and aggressive behavior in children. *Journal of Child Psychology and Psychiatry, 43*(4), 417–434.

Roff, D. (1992). *The evolution of life histories: Theory and analysis.* New York: Chapman & Hall.

Rothbart, M. K. (1989a). Biological processes in temperament. In G. A. Kohnstamm, J. Bates, & M. K. Rothbart (Eds.), *Temperament in childhood* (pp. 77–110). Chichester, UK: Wiley.

Rothbart, M. K. (1989b). Temperament in childhood: A framework. In G. A. Kohnstamm, J. Bates, & M. K. Rothbart (Eds.), *Temperament in childhood* (pp. 59–73). Chichester, UK: Wiley.

Rothbart, M. K. (1994). Broad dimensions of temperament and personality. In P. Ekman & R. J. Davidson (Eds.), *The nature of emotion* (pp. 337–341). New York: Oxford University Press.

Rothbart, M. K., Ahadi, S. A., & Evans, D. (2000). Temperament and personality: Origins and outcomes. *Journal of Personality and Social Psychology, 78,* 122–135.

Rothbart, M. K., Ahadi, S. A., Hershey, K. L., & Fisher, P. (2001). Investigations of temperament at three to seven years: The Children's Behavior Questionnaire. *Child Development, 72,* 1394–1408.

Rothbart, M. K., & Bates, J. E. (2006). Temperament. In W. Damon, R. Lerner, & N. Eisenberg (Eds.), *Handbook of child psychology: Vol. 3. Social, emotional, and personality development* (6th ed., pp. 99–166). New York: Wiley.

Rushton, J. P., Bons, T. A., & Hur, Y.-M. (2008). The genetics and evolution of a general factor of personality. *Journal of Research in Personality, 42,* 1136–1149.

Rushton, J. P., & Irwing, P. (2009). A general factor of personality in 16 sets of the Big Five, the Guilford–Zimmerman Temperament Survey, the California Psychological Inventory, and the Temperament and Character Inventory. *Personality and Individual Differences, 47,* 558–564.

Russell, J. A. (2003). Core affect and the psychological construction of emotion. *Psychological Review, 110*(1), 145–172.

Saucier, G. (2003). An alternative multiple-language structure of personality attributes. *European Journal of Personality, 17,* 179–205.

Schiff, N. D., & Pfaff, D. W. (2009). Neural perspectives on activation and arousal. In G. G. Berntson & J. T. Cacioppo (Eds.), *Handbook of neuroscience for the behavioral sciences* (pp. 454–460). New York: Wiley.

Sell, A., Tooby, J., & Cosmides, L. (2009). Formidability and the logic of human anger. *Proceedings of the National Academy of Sciences, 106,* 15073–15078.

Singh, D. (1993). Body shape and women's attractiveness: The critical role of waist-to-hip ratio. *Human Nature, 4,* 297–321.

Smolewska, K. A., Scott, B., McCabe, S. B., & Woody, E. Z. (2006). A psychometric evaluation of the Highly Sensitive Person Scale: The components of sensory–processing sensitivity and their relation to the BIS/BAS and "Big Five." *Personality and Individual Differences, 40,* 1269–1279.

Srivastava, S., John, O. P., Gosling, S. D., & Potter, J. (2003). Development of personality in early and middle adulthood: Set like plaster or persistent change? *Journal of Personality and Social Psychology, 84,* 1041–1053.

Stearns, S. (1992). *The evolution of life histories.* Oxford, UK: Oxford University Press.

Strelau, J. (1989). The regulative theory of temperament as a result of East–West influences. In G. A. Kohnstamm, J. Bates, & M. K. Rothbart (Eds.), *Temperament in childhood* (pp. 35–48). Chichester, UK: Wiley.

Tooby, J., & Cosmides, L. (1990). On the universality of human nature and the uniqueness of the individual: The role of genetics and adaptation. *Journal of Personality, 58,* 17–68.

Trapnell, P. D., & Wiggins, J. S. (1990). Extension of the Interpersonal Adjective Scales to include the Big Five dimensions of personality. *Journal of Personality and Social Psychology, 59,* 781–790.

Trivers, R. L. (1972). Parental investment and sexual selection. In B. Campbell (Ed.), *Sexual selection and the descent of man, 1871–1971* (pp. 136–179). Chicago: Aldine.

Turner, B. (1981). Sex-related differences in aging. In B. B. Wolman & G. Stricker (Eds.), *Handbook of developmental psychology* (pp. 493–512). Englewood Cliffs, NJ: Prentice-Hall.

Uylings, H. B. M., Groenewegen, H. J., & Kolb, B. (2003). Do rats have a prefrontal cortex? *Behavioural Brain Research, 146,* 3–17.

Vaish, A., Grossmann, T., Woodward, A. (2008). Not all emotions are created equal: The negativity bias in social–emotional development. *Psychological Bulletin, 134,* 383–403.

Van Oers, K., de Jong, G., van Noordwijk, A. J., Kempenaers, B., & Drent, P. A. (2005). Contribution of genetics to the study of animal personalities: A review of case studies. *Behaviour, 142,* 1191–1212.

Watson, D., & Clark, L. A. (1992). On traits and temperament: General and specific factors of emotional experience and their relation to the five-factor model. *Journal of Personality, 60,* 441–476.

Weissman, M. M. (1985). The epidemiology of anxiety disorders: Rates, risks, and familial patterns. In A. H. Tuma & J. Maser (Eds.), *Anxiety and the anxiety disorders* (pp. 275–296). Hillsdale, NJ: Erlbaum.

West-Eberhard, M. J. (2003). *Developmental plasticity and evolution*. New York: Oxford University Press.

Widiger, T. A., & Trull, T. J. (1992). Personality and psychopathology: An application of the five-factor model. *Journal of Personality, 60,* 363–393.

Wiggins, J. S. (1991). Agency and communion as conceptual coordinates for the understanding and measurement of interpersonal behavior. In W. M. Grove & D. Cicchetti (Eds.), *Thinking clearly about psychology: Vol. 2. Personality and psychopathology* (pp. 89–113). Minneapolis: University of Minnesota Press.

Wiggins, J. S., & Broughton, R. (1985). The interpersonal circle: A structural model for the integration of personality research. *Perspectives in Personality, 1,* 1–47.

Wiggins, J. S., Trapnell, P., & Phillips, N. (1988). Psychometric and geometric characteristics of the Revised Interpersonal Adjective Scales (IAS-R). *Multivariate Behavioral Research, 23,* 517–530.

Wiggins, J. S., & Trapnell, P. D. (1996). A dyadic interactional perspective on the five-factor model. In J. S. Wiggins (Ed.), *The five-factor model of personality: Theoretical perspectives* (pp. 88–162). New York: Guilford Press.

Wilson, E. O. (1975). *Sociobiology: The new synthesis*. Cambridge, MA: Harvard University Press.

Wilson, M. A., & Daly, M. (1985). Competitiveness, risk taking, and violence: The young male syndrome. *Ethology and Sociobiology, 6,* 59–73.

Wright, P. H., & Scanlon, M. B. (1991). Gender role orientation and friendship: Some attenuation, but gender differences abound. *Sex Roles, 24,* 551–566.

Zerjal, T., Xue, Y., Bertorelle, G., Wells, R. S., Bao, W., Zhu, S., et al. (2003). The genetic legacy of the Mongols. *American Journal of Human Genetics, 72,* 717–721.

Zuckerman, M. (1979). *Sensation seeking: Beyond the optimal level of arousal*. Hillsdale, NJ: Erlbaum.

Zuckerman, M. (1991). *Psychobiology of personality*. Cambridge, UK: Cambridge University Press.

CHAPTER 15

Prenatal Factors in Temperament
The Role of Prenatal Stress and Substance Use Exposure

Anja C. Huizink

The prenatal period has been regarded as an important phase in human development since ancient times, when people already believed that the emotional state of a pregnant woman could affect the unborn child (for a review, see Ferreira, 1965). However, most theories and models of child development until the mid-20th century more or less ignored the prenatal origins of health and development, and focused on various aspects of child development from birth onwards. Similarly, gynaecologists, who were aware of the importance of the prenatal period for birth outcomes, were mainly interested in short-term outcomes of prenatal influences on neonatal health, but to a lesser extent in longer-term developmental and behavioral outcomes, such as temperament. Only since the last decade have the prenatal, neonatal, and child phases been linked through several longitudinal studies. Indeed, in the last few years, a wealth of new studies has emerged, focusing on fetal exposure *in utero* to maternal anxiety and stress, and related levels of stress hormones, and the offspring's developmental and behavioral outcomes, including temperament. The same is true for studies linking maternal use of substances, such as tobacco, alcohol, and cannabis, to these offspring outcomes. These recent studies are often grounded in the theory that during fetal development, disturbances caused by exposure to stress hormones or substances may yield so-called "prenatal programming" effects, resulting in long-term effects on a wide range of outcomes in the offspring.

Prenatal Programming and Behavioral Teratology

An abundant number of studies published in the last couple of years suggests that prenatal influences exist on fetal brain development in humans, which may result in alterations of offspring behavior, including temperament. This concept of early life physiological "programming" has been proposed to explain the associations between prenatal environmental events, birth outcome, and postnatal development and behavior (Barker, 1998; Huizink, Mulder, & Buitelaar, 2004).

Barker and colleagues (1993) first formulated the idea of fetal origins of adult disease, which is now often referred to as the "Barker hypothesis." This hypothesis suggested that several adult diseases, including Type 2 diabetes, coronary heart disease, stroke, and hypertension, originated in the fetal period, through developmental plasticity as a result of fetal malnutrition (Barker et al., 1993). In short, because fetuses were undernourished in harsh times, their physiological systems were programmed to function as efficiently as possible with little energy. When these fetuses were born and raised in an environment that by then provided them with plenty of nutrition, their very efficient physiological system yielded leftover energy of their food intake. This energy was subsequently stored in their bodies for times of low nutrition, leading to more obesity and other risk factors associated with adult cardiovascular diseases. Thus, the Barker hypothesis suggested that the fetal physiology can adapt to its intrauterine environment, a process of so-called "prenatal programming."

Several decades before the Barker hypothesis was postulated and applied to a much wider array of prenatal exposures and offspring outcomes, the identification of fetal alcohol syndrome (FAS) led to first attempts of studying how prenatal exposure to substances, like alcohol, could affect the developing fetus. These studies were framed within a behavioral teratology approach. In this approach, agents, relatively harmless to the expectant mother, are considered to be potentially harmful to the fetus. Two principles of this field of research, postulated by Vorhees (1989), have guided this approach (see Fried, 1998): (1) Vulnerability of the central nervous system (CNS) to injury extends beyond the fetal, neonatal, and infancy stage; and (2) the most frequent manifestation of injury to the developing CNS results not in nervous system malformation but in functional abnormalities that may not be detectable at birth.

Given these developments in behavioral teratology, and with increasing interest in studies within the Barker hypothesis framework, it is not surprising that so many researchers have published on prenatal exposure to, for instance, maternal stress and anxiety or substance use, and its relation to a variety of behavioral outcomes in infancy and childhood, including temperamental aspects and (first expressions of) psychopathology. There is accumulating evidence that maternal stress or substance use during pregnancy, probably in interaction with genetic factors, may have long-lasting adverse consequences on the brain and behavior of the offspring. This result is consistent with the original ideas of Thomas and Chess (1977) on the etiology of temperament, which included mention of prenatal factors. This chapter gives an overview of findings derived from animal and human studies that have focused on the relation between prenatal exposure to stress and substances on the one hand, and offspring temperament and other behavioral outcomes on the other, and introduces the methodological challenges and innovations associated with this field of research.

Animal Studies on Prenatal Stress

Summary of Results

A clear advantage of animal studies on prenatal stress effects on offspring behavior is that they commonly use a circumscribed and well-defined form of stress (e.g., restraint, noise, or tail shocks) in pregnant dams. Indeed, animal models of prenatal stress can provide insight into which mechanisms underlie the association between exposure to stress or substances *in utero* and offspring outcome (Huizink et al., 2004).

In these animal models, pregnant females were subjected to an experimentally controlled stressful situation leading to changes in the maternal physiology. Stressors included several forms, such as suspension (Alonso, Arevalo, Afonso, & Rodriguez, 1991), crowding (Dahlof, Hard, & Larsson, 1978), rehousing with unfamiliar confederates (Schneider & Coe, 1993), social isolation, repeated electric tail shocks (Takahashi, Haglin, & Kalin, 1992), noise (Clarke, Wittwer, Abbott, & Schneider, 1994), saline injections (Cratty, Ward, Johnson, Azzaro, & Birkle, 1995; Peters, 1982), immobilization (Ward & Weisz, 1984), and restraint (Deminiere et al., 1992). Some nonhuman primate studies that have also applied a social stress paradigm have more ecological relevance for human studies of prenatal stress exposure. For instance, Schneider and Coe (1993) exposed pregnant animals to unfamiliar confederates after changing their housing conditions. Of particular interest also are studies by Sachser and colleagues in guinea pigs (e.g., Sachser & Kaiser, 1997) and by Nemeroff and colleagues in monkeys (reviewed in Gutman & Nemeroff, 2002) that emphasized the impact of social support and daily hassles, respectively, in animal models.

Aspects of offspring behavior that have been studied after *in utero* exposure to stress include exploration in a novel environment, such as an open field or a plus-maze, disturbance behavior under stressful conditions (e.g., social isolation, forced swimming), and social behaviors (Alonso et al., 1991; Grimm & Frieder, 1987; Takahashi et al., 1992; Wakshlak & Weinstock, 1990; Weinstock, Matlina, Maor, Rosen, & McEwen, 1992). Another outcome measure of interest was reduced vocalization, which can be regarded as an index of behavioral inhibition that generally occurs in response to threatening situations, such as social isolation (Takahashi, 1994).

Findings of research in rodents show fairly consistent evidence that exposure to prenatal stress is associated with increased emotionality, decreased exploratory behavior, and reduced attention in offspring (Grimm & Frieder, 1987; Schneider & Coe, 1993; Wakshlak & Weinstock, 1990; Weinstock et al., 1992). In addition, adaptation to stressful conditions seemed hampered in prenatally stressed 14-day-old rat pups because they produced fewer ultrasonic vocalizations in social isolation (Takahashi et al., 1992).

Schneider (1992) looked at prenatal stress effects in nonhuman primate offspring. In their model of stress, they used mild stressors, such as applying loud noise five times per week to pregnant monkeys. Offspring of these monkeys at 6 months of age showed significantly more disturbance behaviors and fewer exploratory behaviors in a novel environment compared to controls (Schneider, 1992). A similar study by Worlein and Sackett (1995) found more fearful behavior in a novel environment of prenatally stressed monkeys. Furthermore, during the first 8 months postpartum, the stressed infants appeared to be less social in interaction with other animals; they initiated fewer social interactions and withdrew from social interactions more often.

Possible Mechanisms

Besides the effects of prenatal stress exposure on observed offspring behavior, animal studies have shown that prenatal maternal stress leads to enhanced activity of the hypothalamic–pituitary–adrenal (HPA) axis (for a review, see Huizink et al., 2004), resulting in release of stress hormones, such as the glucocorticoid corticosterone in animals, which is similar to cortisol in humans. This stress hormone can enter the fetal circulation and is able to affect fetal HPA axis regulation in rodents and nonhuman primates (Huizink et al., 2004; McEwen, 1991; Sapolsky, Uno, Rebert, & Finch, 1990) and may also be involved in humans. Maternal stress hormones, such as glucocorticoids resulting from HPA axis activity, can be transferred to the fetus either by transplacental transport or by maternal stress-induced release of placental hormones, which in turn enter the fetal circulation.

In contrast to several rodent species, human and nonhuman primate fetuses are relatively protected from the two to 10 times higher maternal levels of cortisol by the placental enzyme 11ß-hydroxysteroid dehydrogenase (11ß-HSD). This enzyme converts cortisol into the bioinactive cortisone (Benediktsson, Calder, Edwards, & Seckl, 1997). Despite the placental 11ß-HSD barrier, maternal cortisol still passes through the placenta. A contribution of 10–20% from the mother could still double fetal concentrations (Gitau, Cameron, Fisk, & Glover, 1998). Increases in maternal cortisol have consequences for fetal development (Weinstock, 2005).

In addition to the transport of maternal glucocorticoids into the fetal circulation, the placenta is another source of HPA axis hormones, such as corticotropin-releasing hormone (CRH; Petraglia, Florio, Nappi, & Genazzani, 1996). Placental CRH, entering the fetal circulation through the umbilical vein, stimulates the fetal HPA axis, which, by means of a positive feedback loop, stimulates further placental CRH secretion (Majzoub & Karalis, 1999). Finally, maternal stress may reduce uteroplacental blood flow (Teixeira, Fisk, & Glover, 1999), which may hamper transplacental transport of oxygen and nutrients to the fetus. Through these mechanisms fetal (brain) development may be affected, resulting in altered HPA axis regulation, alterations in neurotransmitter systems, such as the serotonergic, noradrenergic, dopaminergic, and cholinergic systems (for details, see Huizink et al., 2004). Several of these mechanisms may underlie the changes found in behavior of prenatally stressed offspring.

Human Studies on Prenatal Stress: Summary of Findings

What can be learned from the abundant animal literature on prenatal stress is that various aspects of offspring behavior may be affected after exposure to prenatal stress. More specifically, exposure to prenatal stress may be associated with increased behavioral inhibition, anxious or depressive behavior, reduced attention, and less social interaction.

Temperament

Human studies on prenatal stress exposure reveal a similar pattern of altered behavior. It is important to note that temperament was specifically measured only in a relatively small number of these studies. More typically, the assessed behaviors seem to share features with temperamental traits. In what follows, I therefore use the term *temperament* if actual temperament measures were used, and *temperament-like* behaviors when this was not the case but the behaviors resemble common early childhood temperament traits (Zentner & Bates, 2008, also see Mervielde & De Pauw, Chapter 2, this volume).

Overall, the findings of several older studies suggest that infants of emotionally disturbed or high-anxious pregnant women more often exhibited temperament-like behaviors, such as restlessness, irritability, overactivity, poor sleep, and less alertness and responsiveness compared to infants of undisturbed or low-anxious women (Farber, Vaughn, & Egeland, 1981; Ferreira, 1960; Ottinger & Simmons, 1964; Turner, 1956). Some caution must be taken with regard to the validity of these findings, however, due to limitations of the retrospective designs, small sample sizes, and/or nonstandardized measurements (for a more detailed review of methodological issues involved in these studies, see Huizink et al., 2004). Of course, other pregnancy-related factors, such as growth restriction or premature birthweight, may also be related to both prenatal stress exposure and infant temperament and behavior (see Lengua & Wachs, Chapter 25, this volume). Two older studies also examined the association between maternal anxiety during pregnancy, assessed prospectively during pregnancy by means of a self-report anxiety scale, and difficult temperament of the baby 4 months after birth, assessed with the Carey Infant Temperament Questionnaire (Vaughn, Bradley, Joffe, Seifer, & Barglow, 1987), or at 7 months of age, using the Infant Characteristics Questionnaire (Van den Bergh, 1990). Since temperamental ratings were also obtained from the mothers, the association between pregnancy anxiety and later temperament may well be due to report bias (i.e., personality factors of the mother).

A study examined how infant temperament (assessed with the Infant Behavior Questionnaire) within the first year of life was affected by a "naturally occurring stressor" during pregnancy that might be more comparable to animal models of "sudden stressors," namely, the 9/11 World Trade Center terrorist attacks. Findings showed that women who developed posttraumatic stress disorder (PTSD) after being exposed to this attack while pregnant rated their infants as showing more distress in response to novelty at 9 months compared to women who did not develop PTSD after the attack (Brand, Engel, Canfield, & Yehuda, 2006).

Another study that investigated the effect of a naturally occurring stressor, namely, exposure to Hurricane Katrina and its aftermath, on infant temperament found similar results (Tees et al., 2010). In that study, infant temperament characteristics were reported by the mother 2 and 12 months postpartum, and rated on the Early Infant and Toddler Temperament Questionnaires. Women who experienced serious stress due to Hurricane Katrina while pregnant did not have an increased risk of having a child with a difficult temperament. However, if these women suffered from PTSD, then they were more likely to report having an infant with a difficult temperament at the age of 12 months. Thus, these two studies seem to suggest that the mother's mental health in the postpartum period may explain some of the effects of prenatal stress exposure on infant temperament, although both studies relied on maternal ratings only, and their reports may be biased. The mechanisms relating

PTSD and difficult temperament were not addressed in these studies. However, there is reason to believe that the HPA axis plays an important role, and direct exposure to cortisol *in utero* may be related to behavioral outcomes.

Only very few studies have related HPA axis measures during pregnancy to infant temperament. In a small sample ($N = 17$), de Weerth, van Hees, and Buitelaar (2003) examined the association between maternal saliva cortisol levels in pregnancy on the one hand, and maternal reports of infant temperament and observed behavior at several occasions during the first 5 months of life on the other. Higher levels of maternal cortisol, an end product of the HPA axis, were related to more observed temperament-like behaviors, such as crying, fussing, and negative facial expressions of the infants. The same infants were also rated as more difficult on the Infant Characteristics Questionnaire. Davis and colleagues (2007) collected CRH levels from blood samples in a much larger sample of pregnant women ($N = 248$) and found that low levels of CRH in midpregnancy was related to low maternal-reported fear and distress scores at 2 months on the Infant Temperament Questionnaire.

Finally, one recent study examined whether *in utero* exposure to cortisol was related to fear reactivity in infancy, assessed by administering the Laboratory Temperament Assessment Battery to 108 infants between 14 and 19 months of age (Bergman, Glover, Sarkar, Abbott, & O'Connor, 2010). Researchers were able to measure the amount of cortisol *in utero* because the participants in their study were undergoing clinically indicated amniocentesis, which is a procedure used to diagnose fetal defects in the early second trimester by testing a sample of amniotic fluid. Within this sample, the level of cortisol could be determined. Bergman and colleagues (2010) found no significant association between fetal cortisol exposure and fear reactivity. Thus, some evidence is found for an association between exposure to HPA hormones and infant temperament, although the study of Bergman and colleagues does not support this link. The authors suggest that their results may reflect either a false-negative finding or the HPA-mediated link between prenatal stress on the one hand, and infant temperament on the other, may be weaker or more complicated than assumed.

Other Behavioral Outcomes

Several prospective studies related prenatal maternal stress or anxiety to hyperactivity, emotional, and inattention problems in infants and children (Gutteling et al., 2005; Huizink, de Medina, Mulder, Visser, & Buitelaar, 2002; O'Connor, Heron, Golding, Beveridge, & Glover, 2002; O'Connor, Heron, Golding, & Glover, 2003; Van den Bergh & Marcoen, 2004). These human studies were mainly based on maternal report of exposure to prenatal stressors in contrast to the inflicted stressors in animal studies. An overview of associations of prenatal maternal stress exposure and infant or child temperamental and behavioral characteristics is presented in Table 15.1.

Animal Studies on Prenatal Substance Use

Summary of Results

Much of the evidence of prenatal exposure to substances on offspring outcomes originates from animal models, which have been employed extensively. In human pregnancy, the most common substances being used are nicotine, alcohol, and cannabis. Therefore, a brief summary of animal studies with regard to exposure *in utero* to these substances is provided below. As with animal models of prenatal stress, the obvious advantage of these studies is that an adequate control of both dose and timing of substance exposure *in utero* is theoretically possible. Nonetheless, in most animal models of prenatal maternal smoking, pregnant animals received nicotine throughout their pregnancy, excluding the possibility to identify specific periods of increased fetal vulnerability to nicotine effects.

When the results of animal models of prenatal maternal smoking and its effect on offspring behavior are summarized, attentional dysfunction (Ernst, Moolchan & Robinson, 2001; Knopik, 2009), increased locomotor activity or hyperactivity (Pauly, Sparks, Hauser, & Pauly, 2004; Vaglenova, Birru, Pandiella, & Breese, 2004), and increased

TABLE 15.1. Overview of Prenatal Stress Associations with Temperament in Human Offspring

Prenatal anxiety/stress measure or exposure	Design	Temperament/behavior	Relevant studies
Personality Testing and Assessment Anxiety scale	Prospective, self-reported measure	Difficulty, maternal rating on the ITQ	Vaughn et al. (1987)
State–Trait Anxiety Inventory	Prospective, self-reported measure	Difficulty, maternal rating on ICQ	Van den Bergh (1990)
		ADHD, maternal and teacher rating on CBCL and TRF	Van den Bergh & Marcoen (2004)
		Externalizing behavior, maternal and teacher rating on CBCL and TRF	
		Anxiety, child rating on STAIC	
Perceived stress, pregnancy-related anxiety	Prospective, self-reported measures	Adaptability to novelty, attention regulation; observed behavior during test	Huizink et al. (2002); Gutteling et al. (2005)
		Disruptive behavior, maternal rating on ICQ	Gutteling et al. (2005)
Crown–Crisp Index, Anxiety scale	Prospective, self-reported measures	Inattention/hyperactivity, emotional problems, conduct problems; maternal rating on CDQ	O'Connor et al. (2002, 2003)
9/11 World Trade Center terrorist attack	Short-term retrospective design, disaster exposure	Adaptability to novel situations, maternal rating on IBQ	Brand et al. (2006)
Hurricane Katrina	Short-term retrospective design, disaster exposure	Difficulty, maternal rating on EITQ	Tees et al. (2010)
Cortisol	Prospective design–HPA axis measures	Crying/fussing, negative facial expressions, observed behavior	de Weerth et al. (2003)
		Difficulty, maternal rating on ICQ	
Cortisol	Prospective design–HPA axis measures	Fear/distress, observed behavior	Davis et al. (2007)
Corticotropin-releasing hormone (CRH)	Prospective design–HPA axis measures	Fear reactivity, observed with Lab-TAB: n.s.	Bergman et al. (2010)

Note. n.s., not significant; CBCL, Child Behavior Checklist; EITQ, Early Infant Temperament Questionnaire; HPA, hypothalamic–pituitary–adrenal; ICQ, Infant Characteristics Questionnaire; ITQ, Infant Temperament Questionnaire; Lab-TAB, Laboratory Temperament Assessment Battery; SDQ, Strengths and Difficulties Questionnaire; STAIC, State–Trait Anxiety Inventory for Children; TRF, Teacher Rating Form.

anxiety (Huang, Liu, Griffith, & Winzer-Serhan, 2007; Vaglenova et al., 2004) in offspring have been found. Notably, most of these animal studies are limited to nicotine exposure, which is just one toxic component of cigarettes used by humans.

Most animal studies concerning alcohol exposure *in utero* used heavy levels of alcohol (ethanol) exposure. A few studies have described effects of more moderate alcohol exposure *in utero* as well, showing an association with disinhibition and attention problems in rodents and nonhuman primates (Driscoll, Streissguth, & Riley, 1990). The magnitude of these effects was often dose-related. A voluntary drinking paradigm, applied in a mouse model of prenatal alcohol exposure, also showed increased exploratory behavior in the offspring (Allen, Chynoweth, Tyler, & Caldewell, 2003). In this model, the effects of moderate prenatal exposure to ethanol can be examined without imposing additional stress on the pregnant animals caused by intubation or injection because the ethanol was consumed voluntarily. This method more closely resembles the human situation.

In that respect, an interesting new model of nicotine exposure *in utero* for animal studies was developed recently by Schneider, Bizarro, Asherson, and Stolerman (2010). In order to model more closely the chronic exposure to nicotine of human regular smokers, nicotine in drinking water was administered to pregnant rats. This method has the advantage that it is relatively stress free and results in episodic exposure rather than the chronic high level of nicotine seen previously with the often used osmotic minipump method. Schneider and colleagues only examined maturational and developmental outcomes, but their method can be applied in future studies on behavioral outcomes as well, which may be of interest for temperament researchers.

Finally, effects of cannabis exposure *in utero* in animal studies have been reviewed by Navarro, Rubio, and de Fonseca (1995). Findings showed reduced exploratory behavior; persistent alterations in the behavioral response to novelty and social interactions; diminished habituation; reactivity to a variety of stimuli (Navarro et al., 1995); and hyperactivity (Mereu et al., 2003) in rodents exposed to cannabis *in utero*.

Possible Mechanisms

With regard to *in utero* exposure to substances and offspring behavioral outcomes, animal studies also have examined possible underlying mechanisms. One of the most common substances used during human pregnancy is cigarette smoking (Coleman, 2004; DiFranza & Lew, 1995). It is therefore not surprising that many animal studies have examined potential harmful effects of nicotine exposure during pregnancy on offspring outcomes. Nicotine acts as a neuroteratogen that interacts with the nicotinic acetylcholine receptors (nAChRs). These receptors are present already in the developing fetal brains of both rodents and humans (Hellstrom-Lindahl, Gorbounova, Seiger, Mousavi, & Nordberg, 1998; Levin & Slotkin, 1998; Slikker, Xu, Levin, & Slotkin, 2005; Sugiyama, Hagino, Moore, & Lee, 1985). The nAChR promotes cell division and the subsequent switch from cell replication to cell differentiation in terminal neuronal differentiation during fetal brain development (Shea & Steiner, 2008). Fetal nAChR may show increased receptor density, and thus an up-regulation, as a result of binding of nicotine to these receptors (Slotkin, 1998). This in turn could result in a premature switch from cell replication to differentiation (Ernst et al., 2001), which could lead to brain cell death, structural changes in regional brain areas, and altered neurotransmitter systems (Knopik, 2009; Shea & Steiner, 2008; Slikker et al., 2005). Some evidence for this process has indeed been found in animal models, showing that persistent cholinergic, noradrenergic, and dopaminergic hypoactivity in offspring was found after prenatal exposure to nicotine (Abreu-Villaca, Seidler, Tate, Cousins, & Slotkin, 2004; Slotkin, 1998). A variety of behavioral outcomes found after prenatal nicotine exposure may be due to these alternations on neurotransmitter level. In addition, nicotine is a vasoconstrictor, reducing the flow of oxygen and nutrients to the developing fetus, and can have an impact on several aspects of fetal development.

Likewise, prenatal alcohol exposure in animals has been shown to affect brain development. For instance, prenatal alcohol exposure was associated with neuronal loss, and altered neuronal circuitry (Ikonomidou et al., 2000; Miller & Potempa, 1990; West & Hamre, 1985) of the corpus callosum (Qiang, Wang, & Elberger, 2002) and glutamatergic neurotransmitter function in the hippocampus (Savage, Becher, de la Torre, & Sutherland, 2002).

Finally, animal studies have shown that delta-9-tetrahydrocannabinol (THC), the active compound of cannabis, and its metabolites, just like alcohol, freely pass the placental barrier (Little & Van Beveren, 1996; Vardaris, Weisz, Fazel, & Rawitch, 1976), and by entering the fetal circulation, may affect the developing fetus. More specifically, THC influences gene expression of a key protein for brain development, the neural adhesion molecule L1, which plays an important role in processes of cell proliferation and migration, and in synaptogenesis (Gomez et al., 2003). These mechanisms in animal models could possibly underlie the associations between prenatal substance exposure and behavioral outcomes found in human offspring as well.

Human Studies on Prenatal Substance Use: Summary of Findings

Animal studies show increased anxiety, attentional problems, and hyperactive behavior after exposure to substances *in utero*. In line with these studies, prenatal exposure to substances that are most commonly used by humans, such as alcohol, nicotine, or cannabis, has been associated with similar behavioral outcomes in humans, including temperament (for reviews, see Ernst et al., 2001; Fried, 2002; Huizink & Mulder, 2006; Linnet et al., 2003).

Temperament

Even though the mechanisms related to maternal substance use and offspring outcomes are to some extent specific for each substance and may differ from mechanisms relating prenatal stress exposure to offspring outcome, this field of research shows that perturbation during fetal development may have (enduring) effects on offspring behavior. For instance, on a standard neurobehavioral assessment to determine temperament-like behaviors, nicotine-exposed newborns were more excitable and hypertonic, and showed more stress/abstinence signs than newborns not exposed to nicotine (Law et al., 2003). In line with this study, nicotine-exposed infants also had higher scores on negativity, assessed by a composite of three subscales of toddler's troublesome behaviors, namely, Impulsivity, Risk Taking, and Rebelliousness (Brook, Brook, & Whiteman, 2000).

A recent, interesting study investigated the impact of prenatal maternal smoking on the early development of regulatory processes across the neonatal period in a prospective design, using both self-reported measures of smoking and bioassay indices of exposure collected at several times throughout pregnancy (N = 304). At 2 days, 2 weeks, and 4 weeks postpartum, the Neonatal Temperament Assessment (NTA) was administered to measure regulatory skills of the neonate. It was found that infants exposed to maternal smoking during pregnancy had poorer attentional skills after birth, and this effect attenuated in the first 4 weeks of life. In contrast, irritability of the infant after prenatal exposure to smoking became apparent (marginally) only after 4 weeks of life (Espy, Fang, Johnson, Stopp, & Wiebe, 2011). This study shows the importance of studying the developmental pattern of temperamental outcomes from early life onward in relation to prenatal substance use exposure.

Other Behavioral Outcomes

More studies were concerned with whether specific forms of externalizing behavior, such as (symptoms of) attention-deficit/hyperactivity disorder (ADHD) or conduct disorder, were more commonly found in offspring of mothers who smoked during pregnancy. Several review articles summarize findings of these studies. Ernst and colleagues (2001) concluded, after a thorough review of empirical studies, that the effects of maternal smoking during pregnancy on neurobehavioral outcomes in infants were inconsistent, while studies reviewed by Linnet and colleagues (2003) revealed some effects on a variety of symptoms related to ADHD in children. Furthermore, Knopik (2009) published a review that describes genetically sensitive designs, in which genetic influences on the child behavioral outcomes are included, and genetic and environmental factors can be disentangled. Examples of these studies include adoptive samples, studies that compare offspring of female twins, and studies that include DNA material of mothers. These reviews focus mainly on maternal smoking during pregnancy and child outcomes. Huizink and Mulder (2006) also include studies on maternal alcohol or cannabis use during pregnancy. In their review, the authors suggest that some evidence may be found for mostly subtle increased levels of ADHD and externalizing behavior, and increased tendencies to use substances in adolescence or adulthood in offspring of mothers who moderately used alcohol or tobacco, or heavily used cannabis, while pregnant (Huizink & Mulder, 2006).

New Directions for Human Studies

Given the summarized findings in human studies, one could conclude that prenatal exposure to stress or substances is indeed of importance in predicting infant or child temperament and other behavioral outcomes. However, the aforementioned statistical associations between prenatal influences and offspring outcomes may not reflect causation. It is important for public health policy to be able to separate causal associations from noncausal or perhaps even spurious associations (Knopik, 2009). This is of particular concern when prenatal influences on offspring outcomes are the focus of study (Huizink, 2009). Causal factors provide the possibility of intervention, and especially prenatal substance use seems to be a preventable "cause." Most results of animal studies point in the direction of neuroteratological effects of both substance use exposure *in utero* on fetal brain development and stress effects in the developing fetus, and thus on offspring behavior. Nonetheless, the human situation is much more complex. Several sophisticated new approaches have been applied recently in human studies in further efforts to delineate actual *in utero* exposure effects from associated confounding effects. Most of these approaches have been applied for prenatal substance use exposure studies, and only very few for prenatal stress exposure effects. Below, these approaches are outlined, along with findings of several recent studies (see also Huizink, 2009).

Application of Novel Approaches to Disentangle Causal and Noncausal Factors

Measuring of Maternal and Paternal Exposure Associations with Offspring Outcomes

One way of testing direct biological effects of exposure to stress or substances *in utero* may be to compare the strength of associations between maternal exposure *in utero* and offspring outcomes with the strength of associations between paternal exposure to the same stress or substance and offspring outcomes (Alati et al., 2008; Smith, 2008). Thus, if the link of maternal exposure with offspring outcomes is significantly stronger than that of paternal exposure, one can assume that *in utero* exposure probably plays a more important role in the effect on offspring outcome. This approach has been used by several studies focusing on several kinds of prenatal substance use, although most studies did not focus on behavioral outcomes. An example comes from our own recent work within the Generation R Study, which is a large-scale multiethnic, population-based, prospective cohort study from fetal life until young adulthood in the city of Rotterdam, the Netherlands. We compared maternal and paternal cannabis use effects on fetal growth. Fetal growth was determined using ultrasound measures in early, mid-, and late pregnancy, and birthweight. Our findings suggested that maternal cannabis use during mid- and late pregnancy was associated with growth restriction and lower birthweight, while no such association was found for paternal cannabis use in the same period (El Marroun et al., 2009). Similarly, maternal cannabis use during pregnancy was associated with increased levels of Aggression and Inattention scores on the Child Behavior Checklist among girls but not among boys at age 18 months, whereas no such association was found for paternal cannabis use (El Marroun et al., 2011). These results indicate a direct biological effect of *in utero* exposure to cannabis on fetal growth and on behavior of infant girls. No studies on prenatal stress exposure have used this approach as yet.

Adoption Studies

Adoption studies examine infants who are prenatally exposed to stress or substance use of their biological mother, but subsequently are raised by others (also see Saudino & Wang, Chapter 16, this volume). In these studies, genetic and environmental sources of variation can be differentiated by comparing the resemblance between children who share their family environment in their (adoptive) home but are not genetically related, with similarity among those who share their genetic background but are adopted into different families. It is important, however, to realize that highly selective placement in most adoptive cases, for instance, very little environmental risk in the adoptive families, hampers the variation in environmental factors in such designs (Knopik, 2009). A similar strategy could be used to unravel the effects of prenatal stress exposure, distinguishing it from postnatal stress exposure, but until now, such studies have not been conducted.

A few of years ago, Crea, Barth, Guo, and Brooks (2008) published a study focusing on behaviors of children 14 years after their adoption who were prenatally exposed to substance (crack cocaine, cannabis, or heroin), using a shortened form of the Behavior Problems Index. Significantly more behavioral problems were found in adoptees after prenatal exposure, but with increasing age, the differences became small when compared to their nonexposed adoptive counterparts. The authors therefore concluded that prenatal substance use exposure alone was not responsible for adverse long-term behavioral outcomes, and positive postnatal rearing environments may buffer the impact of this exposure.

Children-of-Twins Design

Another interesting new approach to study of prenatal influences on offspring behavior is the children-of-twins (CoT) design, which is able to delineate between environmental exposure (i.e., prenatal stress or substance use) shared by siblings and genetic transmission from parents to their offspring (Silberg & Eaves, 2004). Furthermore, it can include environmental confounds that vary between families (for reviews, see D'Onofrio et al., 2003, 2005). General information on twin designs can be found in Saudino and Wang (Chapter 16, this volume). In this particular CoT design, children of discordant identical (monozygotic, MZ) or fraternal (dizygotic, DZ) female twins were compared. Children of MZ twins share half of their genes with both their own parent and their parent's co-twin (the child's aunt in this case), while children of DZ twins also share half of their genes with their mother, but only about 25% with their aunt. Those twin-mothers could be discordant for the exposure measure (e.g., one of them smoked during pregnancy and the other did not), or for any behavioral or environmental measure that could confound offspring behavioral outcomes. This design is applied to offspring of both discordant MZ and DZ twins, by comparing the rates of similarity in offspring behaviors.

Several researchers have applied this design to study the effect of prenatal maternal smoking and offspring outcomes, such as birthweight (D'Onofrio et al., 2003) or ADHD symptoms (Knopik, Jacob, Haber, Swenson, & Howell, 2009). The latter study also included parental alcoholism as an important factor. Their findings suggested that the association between parental alcohol dependence and offspring ADHD is genetically mediated. This genetic risk, transmitted from parents to their offspring, accounts for an important part of the association between prenatal maternal smoking and offspring ADHD. Knopik and colleagues (2006) similarly tested whether maternal smoking during pregnancy and maternal alcohol use disorders predicted ADHD risk in the CoT offspring. The pattern of findings clearly indicated that the association between maternal alcohol use disorder and ADHD in offspring was due mostly to genetic factors. However, a small independent effect of prenatal smoking on ADHD was also found. Again, no studies have used this approach to examine prenatal stress effects on infant behavioral outcomes.

Case-Crossover or Quasi-Experimental Design

Another interesting and novel approach is offered by the so-called case-crossover or quasi-experimental design, or within-mother between-pregnancy design. In this design, children born after subsequent pregnancies of the same mother, and with varying exposure to factors such as stress or maternal substance use during each pregnancy, are compared with each other (Knopik, 2009). This design offers the opportunity to control for various confounding factors related to behavior of the mother, including her heritable traits, and environmental circumstances of the family, such as socioeconomic status, marital status, nutrition, and adverse home environment in which the children grow up.

Nevertheless, there are also some limitations to consider that may affect the generalizability of the results. For instance, women who are able to quit using substances, such as nicotine or alcohol, during at least one of their pregnancies are less addicted to that substance, or use it less, on average, than women who continue to use substances during all of their pregnancies. Moreover, these women will probably have other personality characteristics and other related risk factors that should be accounted for in the analysis. Furthermore, an underlying assumption to take into account is that parenting factors and environmental factors are similar for each child. Nonetheless, given a large enough sample size for complex analyses, this design is an innovative extension of previous retrospective case–control designs. In those previous studies, cases (i.e., "exposed infants") were compared with controls (i.e., "unexposed infants") from different families. Although this design cannot prove a causal effect of maternal substance use on offspring outcome, the absence of significant associations in such a study would raise some doubts regarding causality.

Some results of this approach have been published. For instance, Gilman, Gardener, and Buka (2008) reported on smoking during pregnancy and children's development, by including in their analyses over 2,000 sibling sets in which there was variability in exposure to maternal smoking during pregnancy. While a significant association between maternal smoking during pregnancy and lower birthweight was found, no significant effect on children's cognitive outcomes at age 4 and 7, or conduct problems at age 7, could be found. Using the same approach, D'Onofrio and colleagues (2007, 2008) found no indication for a biological effect of *in utero* exposure to either maternal smoking (2008) or maternal alcohol use (2007) on externalizing behavior, including conduct disorder, oppositional disorder, and ADHD in 4- to 10-year-olds.

Prenatal Cross-Fostering Design as a Result of In Vitro *Fertilization*

An unusual design using women who became pregnant through *in vitro* fertilization (IVF) is described in one study of Rice and colleagues (2009). They formed two groups of women: one in which women became pregnant using a donor egg or donor embryo, and thus were not biologically related to the children they were carrying; and another comprising women who were biologically related to their child. Offspring of these women were compared with regard to birthweight and behavioral outcomes after prenatal exposure to nicotine use. This represents an example of a human prenatal cross-fostering design, an experimental method that had been applied in animal studies only. A clear advantage of this design is that prenatal exposure effects, as such, can be differentiated from genetic effects, or gene–exposure interaction effects. The findings of Rice and colleagues suggested that prenatal smoking was related to lower birthweight. In contrast, the relationship with more antisocial behavior in prenatally nicotine-exposed offspring was entirely explained by inherited pathways. Thus, no differences based on prenatal exposure to nicotine were found in offspring of mothers who were biologically unrelated to the children they were carrying. Although this is an interesting and novel design to study prenatal substance use exposure effects on offspring outcome, the very low prevalence of substance use in this group of women limits the feasibility and power of this approach for future studies. The same design was used to test the links between maternally reported prenatal stress with offspring birthweight, gestational age, anxiety symptoms, antisocial behavior, and ADHD (Rice et al., 2010). For all outcomes except ADHD, in both unrelated and related mother–child dyads, a relationship was found with prenatal stress levels. This suggests that prenatal stress may indeed affect birth outcomes and result in more anxiety and antisocial behavior. These outcomes could not be attributed to genetic factors.

Genotype–Exposure Interactions

Until now, very few human studies have focused on individual vulnerability to prenatal exposure, suggestive of gene–exposure interaction effects. For prenatal maternal smoking, such vulnerability may be reflected in polymorphisms in one or more genes related to nicotine acetylcholine receptors and nicotine metabolism, and genes that mediate effects of nicotine via modulation of brain cholinergic neurotransmission. Recently, several reports have described the function of a gene that regulates nicotine inactivation (*CYP2A6*), through which it controls nicotine metabolism (Malaiyandi, Sellers, & Tyndale, 2005). If the fetus has a *CYP2A6* genetic variant that is associated with slow inactivation of nicotine, it will be exposed to nicotine for a prolonged period compared to fetuses with a normal inactivation rate of nicotine, even if the amount of cigarettes smoked by their mothers is equal. Other genotypes may also modify the effect of prenatal maternal smoking on offspring behavior. For instance, a common dopamine transporter polymorphism (*DAT1*) has been related to an increased risk of ADHD in children. Becker, El-Faddagh, Schmidt, Esser, and Laucht (2008) found that boys who were homozygous for *DAT1* were more vulnerable to prenatal exposure to maternal smoking. No such effect was found for females. This study thus supports the idea that some prenatal substance use effects may be operating through gene–environment interactions (Becker et al., 2008).

A summary of findings of these studies that used novel approaches in order to delineate prenatal influences from associated or inherited factors is presented in Table 15.2.

Conclusion and Implications

Interest in fetal origins of later behavior originated in ancient times but has grown extensively in the last decade. We now know that the fetal physiology can indeed adapt to its intrauterine environment and may produce programming effects on later development, including behavior. The human situation is, however, rather complex because of several factors correlated with exposure to either stress or substances *in utero*. Therefore, it is essential to set a higher bar for implicative evidence of fetal exposure effects, as was noted roughly 18 years ago by Paneth (1994) and reiterated more recently by Breslau (2007). It remains a challenge to tease apart true biological (thus causal) effects on fetal development and later offspring behavior, and confounding effects in human studies.

TABLE 15.2. Examples of Studies That Used Novel Approaches to Examine Prenatal Influences on Infant–Child Behavior and Their Findings

Design	Type of prenatal influence	Behavior	Evidence for prenatal influences	Authors
Maternal versus paternal substance use	Cannabis use	Aggression Inattention (girls)	Yes	El Marroun et al. (2011)
Adoption	(Crack) cocaine, cannabis, heroin	Behavioral problems	Maybe (but small)	Crea et al. (2008)
Children of twins	Smoking	ADHD	Maybe (but small)	Knopik et al. (2006, 2009)
Case-crossover	Smoking	Conduct problems	No	Gilman et al. (2008)
	Smoking	Externalizing behavior	No	D'Onofrio et al. (2008)
	Alcohol	Externalizing behavior	No	D'Onofrio et al. (2007)
Prenatal cross-fostering	Smoking	Antisocial behavior	No	Rice et al. (2009)
	Stress	Anxiety	Yes	Rice et al. (2010)
	Stress	Antisocial behavior	Yes	Rice et al. (2010)
	Stress	ADHD	No	Rice et al. (2010)
Gene–exposure interaction	Smoking	ADHD (boys)	Yes	Becker et al. (2008)

The best strategy may be to combine several new methods of study, which can be used to tackle the various methodological pitfalls. We must realize that it is unlikely for a single study using a particular design to provide enough evidence for the complicated question of how prenatal exposure to either stress or substance use may affect the developing fetus, yielding changes in temperament.

In this chapter, several new approaches that have been highlighted may elucidate how several aspects, mostly related to maternal substance use during pregnancy and some to maternal stress during pregnancy, may be associated with infant behavioral outcomes. It seems that individual vulnerability to exposures may be a key factor in explaining the (lack of) harmful effects. It is also important to note, however, that most of these new approaches have been applied neither to prenatal stress effects nor to temperamental outcomes. In this regard, much can be learned from innovations in the field of prenatal substance use exposure. For smoking during pregnancy, some studies have focused on the biological metabolism of nicotine in trying to explain the behavioral outcome of the child. Other studies have focused on the potential buffering effect of the postnatal environment. Behavioral genetic studies, including adoption studies, CoT studies, case-crossover designs, and prenatal cross-fostering designs, are especially well equipped to elucidate how genetic confounds may affect the association under study. All these approaches assist in delineating whether a real or a spurious effect of prenatal stress or substance use on offspring behavior is found (Knopik, 2009).

When the pattern of results of these new approaches is considered, it appears that inconsistencies in the findings oppose the claim of strong causal risk effects of prenatal substance use on adverse behavioral outcomes in the offspring. With regard to prenatal stress effects on behavioral outcomes, too few studies have used these approaches to draw strong conclusions. Some small and sometimes independent effects were found in several differently designed studies, particularly of prenatal nicotine exposure on birthweight (D'Onofrio et al., 2003; Gilman et al., 2008; Rice et al., 2009), and ADHD phenotypes (e.g., Button, Thapar, & McGuffin, 2005; Knopik et al., 2005; Thapar et al., 2003). However, in most studies, exposure to prenatal substance use alone was unlikely to be responsible for adverse long-term behavioral outcomes. It can therefore be questioned whether these recent findings actually offer enough scientific evidence for a vigorous public health policy to reduce maternal stress or maternal substance use during pregnancy. Furthermore, some researchers suggest that positive postnatal rearing environments may buffer the impact of this exposure. Therefore, the focus of concern could be directed to the correlated factors that often accompany prenatal risk factors, as described in this chapter, such as other adverse health behaviors, detrimental family environment, and psychopathology.

Although the postnatal environment holds a risk for child development, enrichment of the rearing environment can also compensate for part of the gestational stress effect. Some animal studies have shown that after prenatal exposure to stress, environmental enrichment in the postnatal period resulted in normalized behavioral responses to stress (Francis, Diorio, Plotsky, & Meaney, 2002) and social play (Morley-Fletcher, Rea, Maccari, & Laviola, 2003). Also, Meaney's research group focused on long-term effects of different patterns of early maternal caregiving behavior in rodents. Their findings indicated that mothers showing more nursing and licking (grooming) behavior had offspring that exhibited less anxious behavior as adults (Zhang, Parent, Weaver, & Meaney, 2004). These animal findings are in line with results from human studies showing that maternal sensitivity in mother–child interactions influences infant responsiveness to stress (Kaplan, Evans, & Monk, 2008). A recent human study showed that prenatal cortisol exposure negatively predicted cognitive scores on the Bayley Scales of Infant Development, but only in children with an insecure attachment to their mothers. In children with a secure attachment, according to Ainsworth's Strange Situation, no such negative effect of prenatal cortisol exposure was found (Bergman, Sarkar, Glover, & O'Connor, 2010). Thus, potentially harmful prenatal effects may be attenuated if a child grows up in a caring and secure family.

In conclusion, future studies could take advantage of novel approaches in tackling the question of whether prenatal stress or prenatal substance use is causing altered behavior in the child. Finally, for clinicians, it is important to note that early caregiving experiences may moderate prenatal influences on child development and on infant temperament, and therefore hold potential for effective interventions.

Further Reading

Huizink, A. C., & Mulder, E. J. (2006). Maternal smoking, drinking or cannabis use during pregnancy and neurobehavioral and cognitive functioning in human offspring. *Neuroscience and Biobehavioral Reviews*, 30, 24–41.

Huizink, A. C., Mulder, E. J., & Buitelaar, J. K. (2004). Prenatal stress and risk for psychopathology: specific effects or induction of general susceptibility? *Psychological Bulletin*, 130, 115–142.

Rice, F., Jones, I., & Thapar, A. (2007). The impact of gestational stress and prenatal growth on emotional problems in offspring: A review. *Acta Psychiatrica Scandinavica*, 115, 171–183.

References

Abreu-Villaca, Y., Seidler, F. J., Tate, C. A., Cousins, M. M., & Slotkin, T. A. (2004). Prenatal nicotine exposure alters the response to nicotine administration in adolescence: Effects on cholinergic systems during exposure and withdrawal. *Neuropsychopharmacology*, 29, 879–890.

Alati, R., Macleod, J., Hickman, M., Sayal, K., May, M., Smith, G. D., et al. (2008). Intrauterine exposure to alcohol and tobacco use and childhood IQ: Findings from a parental–offspring comparison within the Avon Longitudinal Study of Parents and Children. *Pediatrics Research*, 64, 659–66.

Allen, A. M., Chynoweth, J., Tyler, L. A., & Caldewell, K. K. A. (2003). A mouse model of prenatal ethanol exposure using a voluntary drinking paradigm. *Alcoholism: Clinical and Experimental Research*, 27, 2009–2016.

Alonso, S. J., Arevalo, R., Afonso, D., & Rodriguez, M. (1991). Effects of maternal stress during pregnancy on forced swimming test behavior of the offspring. *Physiology and Behavior*, 50, 511–517.

Barker, D. J. (1998). *In utero* programming of chronic disease. *Clinical Science (London)*, 95, 115–128.

Barker, D. J., Gluckman, P. D., Godfrey, K. M., Harding, J. E., Owens, J. A., & Robinson, J. S. (1993). Fetal nutrition and cardiovascular disease in adult life. *Lancet*, 341, 938–941.

Becker, K., El-Faddagh, M., Schmidt, M. H., Esser, G., & Laucht, M. (2008). Interaction of dopamine transporter genotype with prenatal smoke exposure on ADHD symptoms. *Journal of Pediatrics*, 152, 263–269.

Benediktsson, R., Calder, A. A., Edwards, C. R., & Seckl, J. R. (1997). Placental 11 beta-hydroxysteroid dehydrogenase: A key regulator of fetal glucocorticoid exposure. *Clinical Endocrinology (Oxford)*, 46, 161–166.

Bergman, K., Glover, V., Sarkar, P., Abbott, D. H., & O'Connor, T. G. (2010). In utero cortisol and testosterone exposure and fear reactivity in infancy. *Hormones and Behavior*, 57, 306–312.

Bergman, K., Sarkar, P., Glover, V., & O'Connor, T. G. (2010). Maternal prenatal cortisol and infant cognitive development: Moderation by infant–mother attachment. *Biological Psychiatry*, 67, 1026–1032.

Brand, S. R., Engel, S. M., Canfield, R. L., & Yehuda, R. (2006). The effect of maternal PTSD following *in utero* trauma exposure on behavior and temperament in the 9-month-old infant. *Annals of the New York Academy of Sciences USA*, 1071, 454–458.

Breslau, N. (2007). Commentary: Maternal smoking during pregnancy: Hazard for what? *International Journal of Epidemiology*, 36, 832–833.

Brook, J. S., Brook, D. W., & Whiteman, M. (2000). The influence of maternal smoking during pregnancy on the toddler's negativity. *Archives of Pediatrics and Adolescent Medicine*, 154, 381–385.

Button, T. M., Thapar, A., & McGuffin, P. (2005). Relationship between antisocial behaviour, attention-deficit hyperactivity disorder and maternal prenatal smoking. *British Journal of Psychiatry*, 187, 155–160.

Clarke, A. S., Wittwer, D. J., Abbott, D. H., & Schneider, M. L. (1994). Long-term effects of prenatal stress on HPA axis activity in juvenile rhesus monkeys. *Developmental Psychobiology*, 27, 257–269.

Coleman, T. (2004). ABC of smoking cessation: Special groups of smokers. *British Medical Journal*, 328, 575–577.

Cratty, M. S., Ward, H. E., Johnson, E. A., Azzaro, A. J., & Birkle, D. L. (1995). Prenatal stress increases corticotropin-releasing factor (CRF) content and release in rat amygdala minces. *Brain Research*, 675, 297–302.

Crea, T. M., Barth, R. P., Guo, S., & Brooks, D. (2008). Behavioral outcomes for substance exposed adopted children: Fourteen years postadoption. *American Journal of Orthopsychiatry*, 78, 11–19.

Dahlof, L. G., Hard, E., & Larsson, K. (1978). Influence of maternal stress on the development of the fetal genital system. *Physiology and Behavior*, 20, 193–195.

Davis, E. P., Glynn, L. M., Schetter, C. D., Hobel,

C., Chicz-Demet, A., & Sandman, C. A. (2007). Prenatal exposure to maternal depression and cortisol influences infant temperament. *Journal of the American Academy of Child and Adolescent Psychiatry, 46*, 737–746.

Deminiere, J. M., Piazza, P. V., Guegan, G., Abrous, N., Maccari, S., Le Moal, M., et al. (1992). Increased locomotor response to novelty and propensity to intravenous amphetamine self-administration in adult offspring of stressed mothers. *Brain Research, 586*, 135–139.

de Weerth, C., van Hees, Y., & Buitelaar, J. K. (2003). Prenatal maternal cortisol levels and infant behavior during the first 5 months. *Early Human Development, 74*, 139–151.

DiFranza, J. R., & Lew, R. A. (1995). Effect of maternal cigarette smoking on pregnancy complications and sudden infant death syndrome. *Journal of Family Practice, 40*, 385–394.

D'Onofrio, B. M., Turkheimer, E. N., Eaves, L. J., Corey, L. A., Berg, K., & Solaas, M. H. (2003). The role of the children of twins design in elucidating causal relations between parent characteristics and child outcomes. *Journal of Child Psychology and Psychiatry, 44*, 1130–1144.

D'Onofrio, B. M., Turkheimer, E. N., Emery, R. E., Slutske, W., Heath, A., Madden, P. A. F., et al. (2005). A genetically informed study of marital instability and its association with offspring psychopathology. *Journal of Abnormal Psychology, 114*, 570–586.

D'Onofrio, B. M., Van Hulle, C. A., Waldman, I. D., Rodgers, J. L., Harden, K. P., Rathouz, P. J., et al. (2008). Smoking during pregnancy and offspring externalizing problems: An exploration of genetic and environmental confounds. *Development and Psychopathology, 20*, 139–164.

D'Onofrio, B. M., Van Hulle, C. A., Waldman, I. D., Rodgers, J. L., Rathouz, P. J., & Lahey, B. B. (2007). Causal inferences regarding prenatal alcohol exposure and childhood externalizing problems. *Archives of General Psychiatry, 64*, 1296–1304.

Driscoll, C. D., Streissguth, A. P., & Riley, E. P. (1990). Prenatal alcohol exposure: Comparability of effects in humans and animal models. *Neurotoxicology and Teratology, 12*, 231–237.

El Marroun, H. E., Hudziak, J. J., Tiemeier, H., Creemers, H., Steegers, E. A., Jaddoe, V. W., et al. (2011). Intrauterine cannabis exposure leads to more aggressive behavior and attention problems in 18-month-old girls. *Drug and Alcohol Dependence, 118*, 470–474.

El Marroun, H., Tiemeier, H., Steegers, E. A., Jaddoe, V. W., Hofman, A., Verhulst, F. C., et al. (2009). Intrauterine cannabis exposure affects fetal growth trajectories: The Generation R Study. *Journal of the American Academy of Child and Adolescent Psychiatry, 48*, 1173–1181.

Ernst, M., Moolchan, E. T., & Robinson, M. L. (2001). Behavioral and neural consequences of prenatal exposure to nicotine. *Journal of the American Academy of Child and Adolescent Psychiatry, 40*, 630–641.

Espy, K. A., Fang, H., Johnson, C., Stopp, C., & Wiebe, S. A. (2011). Prenatal tobacco exposure: Developmental outcomes in the neonatal period. *Developmental Psychology, 47*, 153–156.

Farber, E. A., Vaughn, B., & Egeland, B. (1981). The relationship of prenatal maternal anxiety to infant behavior and mother–child interactions during the first six months of life. *Early Human Development, 5*, 267–277.

Ferreira, A. J. (1960). The pregnant woman's emotional attitude and its reflection of the newborn. *American Journal of Orthopsychiatry, 30*, 553–561.

Ferreira, A. J. (1965). Emotional factors in prenatal environment. A review. *Journal of Nervous and Mental Disease, 141*, 108–118.

Francis, D. D., Diorio, J., Plotsky, P. M., & Meaney, M. J. (2002). Environmental enrichment reverses the effects of maternal separation on stress reactivity. *Journal of Neuroscience, 22*, 7840–7843.

Fried, P. A. (1998). Behavioral evaluation of the older infant and child. In W. Sliker, Jr., & L. W. Chang (Eds.), *Handbook of developmental neurotoxicology* (pp. 469–486). San Diego, CA: Academic Press.

Fried, P. A. (2002). Conceptual issues in behavioral teratology and their application in determining long-term sequelae of prenatal marihuana exposure. *Journal of Child and Adolescent Psychiatry, 42*, 81–102.

Gilman, S. E., Gardener, H., & Buka, S. L. (2008). Maternal smoking during pregnancy and children's cognitive and physical development: A causal risk factor? *American Journal of Epidemiology, 168*, 522–531.

Gitau, R., Cameron, A., Fisk, N. M., & Glover, V. (1998). Fetal exposure to maternal cortisol. *Lancet, 352*, 707–708.

Gomez, M., Hernandez, M., Johansson, B., de Miguel, R., Ramos, J. A., & Fernández-Ruiz, J. (2003). Prenatal cannabinoid and gene expression for neural adhesion molecule L1 in the fetal rat brain. *Brain Research: Developmental Brain Research, 147*, 201–207.

Grimm, V. E., & Frieder, B. (1987). The effects of mild maternal stress during pregnancy on the behavior of rat pups. *International Journal of Neuroscience, 35*, 65–72.

Gutman, D. A., & Nemeroff, C. B. (2002). Neurobiology of early life stress: Rodent studies. *Seminars in Clinical Neuropsychiatry, 7*, 89–95.

Gutteling, B. M., de Weerth, C., Willemsen-Swinkels, S. H., Huizink, A. C., Mulder, E. J., Visser, G. H., et al. (2005). The effects of prenatal stress on temperament and problem behavior of 27-month-old toddlers. *European Child and Adolescent Psychiatry, 14*, 41–51.

Hellstrom-Lindahl, E., Gorbounova, O., Seiger, A., Mousavi, M., & Nordberg, A. (1998). Regional distribution of nicotinic receptors during prenatal development of human brain and spinal cord. *Brain Research: Developmental Brain Research, 108*, 147–160.

Huang, L. Z., Liu, X., Griffith, W. H., & Winzer-Serhan, U. H. (2007). Chronic neonatal nicotine increases anxiety but does not impair cognition in adult rats. *Behavioral Neuroscience, 121*, 1342–1352.

Huizink, A. C. (2009). Moderate use of alcohol, tobacco and cannabis during pregnancy: New approaches and update on research findings. *Reproductive Toxicology, 28*, 143–151.

Huizink, A. C., de Medina, P. G., Mulder, E. J., Visser, G. H., & Buitelaar, J. K. (2002). Psychological measures of prenatal stress as predictors of infant temperament. *Journal of the American Academy of Child and Adolescent Psychiatry, 41*, 1078–1085.

Huizink, A. C., & Mulder, E. J. (2006). Maternal smoking, drinking or cannabis use during pregnancy and neurobehavioral and cognitive functioning in human offspring. *Neuroscience and Biobehavioral Reviews, 30*, 24–41.

Huizink, A. C., Mulder, E. J., & Buitelaar, J. K. (2004). Prenatal stress and risk for psychopathology: Specific effects or induction of general susceptibility? *Psychological Bulletin, 130*, 115–142.

Ikonomidou, C., Bittigau, P., Ishimaru, M. J., Wozniak, D. F., Koch, C., Genz, K., et al. (2000). Ethanol-induced apoptotic neurodegeneration and fetal alcohol syndrome. *Science, 287*, 1056–1060.

Kaplan, L. A., Evans, L., & Monk, C. (2008). Effects of mothers' prenatal psychiatric status and postnatal caregiving on infant biobehavioral regulation: Can prenatal programming be modified? *Early Human Development, 84*, 249–256.

Knopik, V. S. (2009). Maternal smoking during pregnancy and child outcomes: Real or spurious effect? *Developmental Neuropsychology, 34*, 1–36.

Knopik, V. S., Heath, A. C., Jacob, T., Slutske, W. S., Bucholz, K. K., Madden, P. A., et al. (2006). Maternal alcohol use disorder and offspring ADHD: Disentangling genetic and environmental effects using a children-of-twins design. *Psychological Medicine, 36*, 1461–1471.

Knopik, V. S., Jacob, T., Haber, J. R., Swenson, L. P., & Howell, D. N. (2009). Paternal alcoholism and offspring ADHD problems: A children of twins design. *Twin Research and Human Genetics, 12*, 53–62.

Knopik, V. S., Sparrow, E. P., Madden, P. A., Bucholz, K. K., Hudziak, J. J., Reich, W., et al. (2005). Contributions of parental alcoholism, prenatal substance exposure, and genetic transmission to child ADHD risk: A female twin study. *Psychological Medicine, 35*, 625–635.

Law, K. L., Stroud, L. R., LaGasse, L. L., Niaura, R., Liu, J., & Lester, B. M. (2003). Smoking during pregnancy and newborn neurobehavior. *Pediatrics, 111*, 1318–1323.

Levin, E. D., & Slotkin, T. A. (1998). Developmental neurotoxicity of nicotine. In W. Slikker & L. W. Chang (Eds.), *Handbook of developmental neurotoxicity* (pp. 587–615). New York: Academic Press.

Linnet, K. M., Dalsgaard, S., Obel, C., Wisborg, K., Henriksen, T. B., Rodriguez, A., et al. (2003). Maternal lifestyle factors in pregnancy risk of attention deficit hyperactivity disorder and associated behaviors: Review of the current evidence. *American Journal of Psychiatry, 160*, 1028–1040.

Little, B. B., & Van Beveren, T. T. (1996). Placental transfer of selected substances of abuse. *Seminars in Perinatology, 20*, 147–153.

Majzoub, J. A., & Karalis, K. P. (1999). Placental corticotropin-releasing hormone: Function and regulation. *American Journal of Obstetrics and Gynecology, 180*, S242–S246.

Malaiyandi, V., Sellers, E. M., & Tyndale, R. F. (2005). Implications of CYP2A6 genetic variation for smoking behaviors and nicotine dependence. *Clinical Pharmacology and Therapy, 77*, 145–158.

McEwen, B. S. (1991). Non-genomic and genomic effects of steroids on neural activity. *Trends in Pharmacological Science, 12*, 141–147.

Mereu, G., Fa, M., Ferraro, L., Cagiano, R., Antonelli, T., Tattoli, M., et al. (2003). Prenatal exposure to a cannabinoid agonist produces memory deficits linked to dysfunction in hippocampal long-term potentiation and glutamate release. *Proceedings of the National Academy of Sciences USA, 100*, 4915–4920.

Miller, M. W., & Potempa, G. (1990). Numbers of neurons and glia in mature rat somatosensory cortex: Effects of prenatal exposure to ethanol. *Journal of Comparative Neurology, 293*, 92–102.

Morley-Fletcher, S., Rea, M., Maccari, S., & Laviola, G. (2003). Environmental enrichment during adolescence reverses the effects of prenatal stress on play behaviour and HPA axis reactivity in rats. *European Journal of Neuroscience, 18*, 3367–3374.

Navarro, M., Rubio, P., & de Fonseca, F. R. (1995). Behavioural consequences of maternal exposure to natural cannabinoids in rats. *Psychopharmacology (Berlin), 122*, 1–14.

O'Connor, T. G., Heron, J., Golding, J., Beveridge, M., & Glover, V. (2002). Maternal antenatal anxiety and children's behavioural/emotional problems at 4 years: Report from the Avon Longitudinal Study of Parents and Children. *British Journal of Psychiatry, 180,* 502–508.

O'Connor, T. G., Heron, J., Golding, J., & Glover, V. (2003). Maternal antenatal anxiety and behavioural/emotional problems in children: A test of a programming hypothesis. *Journal of Child Psychology and Psychiatry, 44,* 1025–1036.

Ottinger, D. R., & Simmons, J. E. (1964). Behavior of human neonates and prenatal maternal anxiety. *Psychological Reports, 14,* 391–394.

Paneth, N. (1994). The impressionable fetus?: Fetal life and adult health. *American Journal of Public Health, 84,* 1372–1374.

Pauly, J. R., Sparks, J. A., Hauser, K. F., & Pauly, T. H. (2004). In utero nicotine exposure causes persistent, gender-dependant changes in locomotor activity and sensitivity to nicotine in C57Bl/6 mice. *International Journal of Developmental Neuroscience, 22,* 329–337.

Peters, D. A. (1982). Prenatal stress: Effects on brain biogenic amine and plasma corticosterone levels. *Pharmacology, Biochemistry and Behavior, 17,* 721–725.

Petraglia, F., Florio, P., Nappi, C., & Genazzani, A. R. (1996). Peptide signaling in human placenta and membranes: Autocrine, paracrine, and endocrine mechanisms. *Endocrine Reviews, 17,* 156–186.

Qiang, M., Wang, M. W., & Elberger, A. J. (2002). Second trimester prenatal alcohol exposure alters development of rat corpus callosum. *Neurotoxicology and Teratology, 24,* 719–732.

Rice, F., Harold, G. T., Boivin, J., Hay, D. F., van den Bree, M., & Thapar, A. (2009). Disentangling prenatal and inherited influences in humans with an experimental design. *Proceedings of the National Academy of Sciences USA, 17*(106), 2464–2467.

Rice, F., Harold, G. T., Boivin, J., van den Bree, M., Hay, D. F., & Thapar, A. (2010). The links between prenatal stress and offspring development and psychopathology: Disentangling environmental and inherited influences. *Psychological Medicine, 40,* 335–345.

Sachser, N., & Kaiser, S. (1997). The social environment, behaviour and stress—a case study in guinea pigs. *Acta Physiolica Scandinavica Supplement, 640,* 83–87.

Sapolsky, R. M., Uno, H., Rebert, C. S., & Finch, C. E. (1990). Hippocampal damage associated with prolonged glucocorticoid exposure in primates. *Journal of Neuroscience, 10,* 2897–2902.

Savage, D. D., Becher, M., de la Torre, A. J., & Sutherland, R. J. (2002). Dose-dependent effects of prenatal ethanol exposure on synaptic plasticity and learning in mature offspring. *Alcoholism: Clinical and Experimental Research, 26,* 1752–1758.

Schneider, M. L. (1992). Prenatal stress exposure alters postnatal behavioral expression under conditions of novelty challenge in rhesus monkey infants. *Developmental Psychobiology, 25*(7), 529–540.

Schneider, M. L., & Coe, C. L. (1993). Repeated social stress during pregnancy impairs neuromotor development of the primate infant. *Journal of Development and Behavioral Pediatrics, 14,* 81–87.

Schneider, T., Bizarro, L., Asherson, P. J., & Stolerman, I. P. (2010).Gestational exposure to nicotine in drinking water: Teratogenic effects and methodological issues. *Behavioral Pharmacology, 21,* 206–216.

Shea, A. K., & Steiner, M. (2008). Cigarette smoking during pregnancy. *Nicotine and Tobacco Research, 10,* 267–278.

Silberg, J. L., & Eaves, L. J. (2004). Analysing the contributions of genes and parent–child interaction to childhood behavioural and emotional problems: A model for the children of twins. *Psychological Medicine, 34,* 347–356.

Slikker, W., Jr., Xu, Z. A., Levin, E. D., & Slotkin, T. A. (2005). Mode of action: Disruption of brain cell replication, second messenger, and neurotransmitter systems during development leading to cognitive dysfunction—developmental neurotoxicity of nicotine. *Critical Reviews in Toxicology, 35,* 703–711.

Slotkin, T. A. (1998). Fetal nicotine or cocaine exposure: Which one is worse? *Journal of Pharmacology and Experimental Therapy, 285,* 931–945.

Smith, G. D. (2008). Assessing intrauterine influences on offspring health outcomes: Can epidemiological studies yield robust findings? *Basic Clinical Pharmacological Toxicology, 102,* 245–256.

Sugiyama, H., Hagino, N., Moore, G., & Lee, J. W. (1985). [^{3}H]Nicotine binding sites in developing fetal brains in rats. *Neuroscience Research, 2,* 387–392.

Takahashi, L. K., Haglin, C., & Kalin, N. H. (1992). Prenatal stress potentiates stress-induced behavior and reduces the propensity to play in juvenile rats. *Physiology and Behavior, 51,* 319–323.

Tees, M. T., Harville, E. W., Xiong, X., Buekens, P., Pridjian, G., & Elkind-Hirsch, K. (2010). Hurricane Katrina–related maternal stress, maternal mental health, and early infant temperament. *Maternal and Child Health Journal, 14,* 511–518.

Teixeira, J. M., Fisk, N. M., & Glover, V. (1999). Association between maternal anxiety in pregnancy and increased uterine artery resistance index: Cohort based study. *British Medical Journal, 318,* 153–157.

Thapar, A., Fowler, T., Rice, F., Scourfield, J., van den Bree, M., Thomas, H., et al. (2003). Maternal smoking during pregnancy and attention deficit hyperactivity disorder symptoms in offspring. *American Journal of Psychiatry, 160,* 1985–1989.

Thomas, A., & Chess, S. (1977). *Temperament and development*. New York: Brunner/Mazel.

Turner, E. K. (1956). The syndrome in the infant resulting from maternal emotional tension during pregnancy. *Medical Journal of Australia, 4*, 221–222.

Vaglenova, J., Birru, S., Pandiella, N. M., & Breese, C. R. (2004). An assessment of the long-term developmental and behavioral teratogenicity of prenatal nicotine exposure. *Behavioral Brain Research, 150*, 159–170.

Van den Bergh, B. (1990). The influence of maternal emotions during pregnancy on fetal and neonatal behavior. *Pre- and Perinatal Psychology, 5*, 119–130.

Van den Bergh, B. R., & Marcoen, A. (2004). High antenatal maternal anxiety is related to ADHD symptoms, externalizing problems, and anxiety in 8- and 9-year-olds. *Child Development, 75*, 1085–1097.

Vardaris, R. M., Weisz, D. J., Fazel, A., & Rawitch, A. B. (1976). Chronic administration of delta-9-tetrahydrocannabinol to pregnant rats: Studies of pup behavior and placental transfer. *Pharmacology, Biochemistry and Behavior, 4*, 249–254.

Vaughn, B. E., Bradley, C. F., Joffe, L. S., Seifer, R., & Barglow, P. (1987). Maternal characteristics measured prenatally are predictive of ratings of temperamental "difficulty" on the Carey Infant Temperament Questionnaire. *Developmental Psychology, 23*, 152–161.

Vorhees, C. V. (1989). Concepts in teratology and developmental toxicology derived from animal research. *Annals of the New York Academy of Sciences, 562*, 31–41.

Wakshlak, A., & Weinstock, M. (1990). Neonatal handling reverses behavioral abnormalities induced in rats by prenatal stress. *Physiology and Behavior, 48*, 289–292.

Ward, I. L., & Weisz, J. (1984). Differential effects of maternal stress on circulating levels of corticosterone, progesterone, and testosterone in male and female rat fetuses and their mothers. *Endocrinology, 114*, 1635–1644.

Weinstock, M. (2005). The potential influence of maternal stress hormones on development and mental health of the offspring. *Brain, Behavior and Immunity, 19*, 296–308.

Weinstock, M., Matlina, E., Maor, G. I., Rosen, H., & McEwen, B. S. (1992). Prenatal stress selectively alters the reactivity of the hypothalamic–pituitary–adrenal system in the female rat. *Brain Research, 595*, 195–200.

West, J. R., & Hamre, K. M. (1985). Effects of alcohol exposure during different periods of development: Changes in hippocampal mossy fibers. *Brain Research, 349*, 280–284.

Worlein, J. M., & Sackett, G. P. (1995). Maternal exposure to stress during pregnancy: Its significance for infant behavior in pigtail macaques (*Macaca nemestrina*). In C. R. Pryce, R. D. Martin, & D. Skuse (Eds.), *Motherhood in human and nonhuman primates* (pp. 142–151). Basel: Karger.

Zentner, M., & Bates, J. E. (2008). Child temperament: An integrative review of concepts, research programs, and measures. *European Journal of Developmental Science, 2*, 7–37.

Zhang, T. Y., Parent, C., Weaver, I., & Meaney, M. J. (2004). Maternal programming of individual differences in defensive responses in the rat. *Annals of the New York Academy of Science, 1032*, 85–103.

# CHAPTER 16

Quantitative and Molecular Genetic Studies of Temperament

Kimberly J. Saudino
Manjie Wang

As can be seen from the other chapters in this handbook, temperament research has found that individual differences in temperament dimensions are substantial, and that these differences are of considerable developmental significance. People differ from each other in those behaviors thought to be temperamental, and this temperamental variation is meaningful, as it predicts a wide variety of developmental outcomes. The goal of behavioral genetic approaches to the study of temperament is to understand *why* people differ in their temperaments. What are the factors that explain the variation in temperaments that we see in the population? At the broadest level of explanation, behavioral variation, or individual differences, can be due to two factors: genes and the environment. *Quantitative genetics* research can inform about the relative influence of both genes and environments on individual differences in temperament. *Molecular genetics* research seeks to identify specific genes associated with behavioral variations in temperament. Both approaches, however, have more to offer than simply indicating whether or not temperament is genetically influenced. In addition to describing the basic methodologies and presenting quantitative and molecular genetics findings regarding the factors that influence individual differences in temperament, this chapter reviews research that examines genetic and environmental influences on developmental stability and change; genetic and environmental links between temperament and outcome; and genotype–environment correlations and interactions between genetic effects on temperament and specific environments. The study of genetic influences on behavior has moved beyond the simple heritability question and, in doing so, continues to make significant contributions to our understanding of temperament.

Genetic Influences on Temperament

Quantitative Genetics Research

Methods

Quantitative genetic methods decompose the observed (i.e., phenotypic) variance of a trait into genetic and environmental variance components. *Heritability*, the genetic effect size, is the proportion of phenotypic variance that can be attributed to genetic factors. The remaining variance is attributed to environmental factors that comprise all nonheritable influences, including prenatal factors. Envi-

315

ronmental variance can be further decomposed into "shared" and "nonshared" environmental influences. *Shared environmental variance* is familial resemblance that is not explained by genetic effects. This includes environmental influences that are shared by family members, such as family demographics, rearing neighborhood, family climate, and even the number of TVs or books in the house. If shared environments are important to individual differences in temperament, then they should act to make family members *similar* in temperament irrespective of their genetic similarity. *Nonshared environmental variance* is a residual variance that includes environmental influences that are unique to each individual. These unique environmental influences operate to make members of the same family *different* from one another. Possible sources of nonshared environmental variance include differential parental treatment; extrafamilial relationships with friends, peers, and teachers; nonsystematic factors, such as accidents or illness; and measurement error.

Genetic, shared, and nonshared environmental contributions to individual differences in temperament or other behaviors of interest can be estimated by examining pairs of individuals who vary systematically in their genetic and/or environmental similarity. If genetic influences are important to a trait or behavior, then behavioral similarity should covary with genetic relatedness (i.e., individuals who are more genetically similar should be more behaviorally similar). In other words, traits that are genetically influenced should "run in families." Relatives should be more similar for the behavior than unrelated individuals, and the more closely related the family members, the more similar they should be for the behavior. However, it is a bit more complicated than simply studying the resemblances of family members because relatives share environments as well as genes, and the more genetically related relatives are, the more similar their environments (Plomin, 1990). Therefore, family members may resemble each other for environmental as well as genetic reasons, and simple family studies cannot separate the two.

The two designs most frequently used to disentangle genetic and environmental sources of variance in temperament are the twin design and the adoptive/nonadoptive sibling design. The *twin method* involves comparing genetically identical monozygotic (MZ) twins with fraternal dizygotic (DZ) twins who share approximately 50% of their segregating genes. Segregating genes refer to genes that *differ* in the population. Over 99% of the human genome is similar between all individuals (Venter, 2007), but these genetic effects are of little interest to behavioral geneticists because they cannot explain variation in the population. Only genes that differ among individuals can contribute to individual differences. If a trait is genetically influenced, the twofold greater genetic similarity of MZ twins is expected to make them more similar than DZ twins. Intraclass correlations typically serve as indices of co-twin similarity. An MZ correlation that is greater than the DZ correlation suggests genetic influence. A DZ correlation that exceeds one-half the MZ correlation indicates familial resemblance that is not explained by genetic factors and suggests the presence of shared environmental influences. Because MZ twins share all of their genes, differences within pairs of identical twins can only be due to environmental influences that are unique to each individual; thus MZ correlations that are less than 1 indicate nonshared environmental influences. The *adoptive/nonadoptive sibling design* shares a similar logic but compares the similarity of adoptive and nonadoptive sibling pairs. Genetic influences are implied when nonadoptive siblings (i.e., first-degree siblings) who share approximately 50% of their segregating genes are more similar than adoptive siblings who are not genetically related. Shared environmental influences are suggested when genetically unrelated adoptive siblings resemble each other. Under this design, nonshared environmental variance is the remaining variance not accounted for by genetic or shared environmental influences.

Most of the quantitative research reviewed in this chapter is based on the twin and adoptive–nonadoptive sibling designs; however, a handful of studies employ designs that are a combination of twin, sibling, and/or adoption designs. For example, the Nonshared Environment Adolescent Development (NEAD) project sample comprises MZ and DZ twin pairs; full siblings in nondivorced families; and full, half, and unrelated siblings in step families. Although not as powerful as the twin or adoption design, the twin–sibling design of NEAD does permit tests of whether nondivorced and stepfamilies differ with regard to genetic and environmental influences on the behavior of interest (Plomin, DeFries, McClearn, & McGuffin, 2008). A discussion of the full range of behavioral genetic designs is beyond the scope of this chapter, but the interested reader is encouraged to consult Plomin and colleagues (2008) for more detailed information about behavioral genetics methods.

Findings

GENETIC INFLUENCES

Temperament theories suggest that individual differences in temperament have a biological or constitutional foundation, but the environment is also important (Goldsmith et al., 1987). The results from quantitative behavior genetic studies provide strong support for this premise. Studies of both reactive temperaments (e.g., emotionality, activity, shyness, sociability, adaptability, and positive affect) and regulatory temperaments (e.g., effortful control, inhibitory control, behavioral inhibition, and attentional focusing) consistently find significant genetic effects in infancy (Braungart, Plomin, DeFries, & Fulker, 1992; Roisman & Fraley, 2006; Saudino & Eaton, 1991; Silberg et al., 2005), early childhood (Gagne & Saudino, 2010; Goldsmith, Buss, & Lemery, 1997; Saudino, Plomin, & DeFries, 1996), middle childhood (Lemery-Chalfant, Doelger, & Goldsmith, 2008; Mullineaux, Deater-Deckard, Petrill, Thompson, & DeThorne, 2009; Schmitz, Saudino, Plomin, & Fulkner, 1996; Wood, Saudino, Rogers, Asherson, & Kuntsi, 2007), and adolescence (Ganiban, Saudino, Ulbricht, Neiderhiser, & Reiss, 2008; Saudino, McGuire, Reiss, Hetherington, & Plomin, 1995; Yamagata et al., 2005). Similarly, although most frequently studied in adulthood, the related temperament dimensions of novelty seeking, harm avoidance, and reward dependence also appear to be genetically influenced (Ando et al., 2004; Heiman, Stallings, Hofer, & Hewitt, 2003; Heiman, Stallings, Young, & Hewitt, 2004; Isen, Baker, Raine, & Bezdjian, 2009; Keller, Coventry, Heath, & Martin, 2005). Thus, the reason why people differ from one another in their temperaments is in part due to the fact that they differ genetically.

Genetic Effect Sizes. Estimates of heritability vary across studies; however, they generally fall within the range of .20 to .60, suggesting that genetic differences among individuals account for approximately 20 to 60% of the variability of temperament within a population. With few exceptions, for example, soothability and rhythmicity, which show little genetic influence (Goldsmith et al., 1997), there is no consistent pattern of differential heritability across dimensions. In other words, across most research, there is little evidence to suggest that some temperament dimensions are more heritable than others. There is also little evidence to suggest that cultural differences substantially influence the etiology of individual differences in temperament. For example, twin studies with Korean and Japanese samples yield estimates of heritability for temperament dimensions that are remarkably similar to those for Western samples (Ando et al., 2004; Hur, 2009; Yamagata et al., 2005), but more research is needed—particularly with more diverse cultures (e.g., nonindustrialized countries).

The broad range of heritability estimates for temperament dimensions across studies may be due to a number of factors. First, it may reflect sample characteristics. For example, sample sizes vary across studies and, as with all statistics, larger samples allow more precise estimates. Similarly, age differences between samples might account for differences in heritability estimates (see "Genetic Influences on Change in Temperament" section). Second, differences in the genetic effect sizes across studies may reflect methodological differences in the assessment of temperament, which we explain below.

Measure-Specific Effects. An important, but often overlooked, consideration when examining genetic influences on temperament is possible measure-specific effects. There are many different methods for assessing temperament. The most frequently employed method is the parent-rating questionnaire, which asks parents to rate their child's typical behaviors on a series of questions designed to tap various temperament dimensions. Observational measures, such as tester ratings or observed behavioral coding (e.g., the Laboratory Temperament Assessment Battery [Lab-TAB]; Goldsmith, Reilly, Lemery, Longley, & Prescott, 1994), are sometimes used to provide a measure of temperament, typically within the laboratory situation. In addition, some dimensions of temperament are amenable to methods of assessment that do not require human inferences about child behavior, for example, computer-based measures of attention and mechanical measures of activity level. It is generally assumed that these different methods of assessment are tapping the same underlying constructs, but this is an empirical question. Multivariate quantitative genetics research can test this assumption by exploring the extent to which different methods of assessing temperament are influenced by the same genetic and environmental factors.

One potential problem when exploring possible method-specific effects is that different methods are often used in different situations (e.g., parent ratings in the home, teacher ratings in the school, and tester ratings in the laboratory), thus confounding methods with situations (cf. Philips & Matheny, 1997; Wood, Rijsdijk, Saudino, Asherson, & Kuntsi, 2008). In order to tease apart method and situation effects it is necessary to use *different* methods of assessing temperament within the *same* situation. Few studies meet this criteria, but a recent study of activity level in early childhood (Saudino, 2009b) found that there was only modest overlap between the genetic factors that influenced *actigraph* (mechanical devices that record the frequency and amplitude of acceleration associated with human movement) and parent rating measures of activity in the home. The genetic correlation (r_G) indexing the extent to which the same genetic effects operate across the two methods was .38. In other words, although both measures were genetically influenced, the genetic effects on each measure were largely independent of each other. There was no overlap in environmental factors that influenced each measure, suggesting that despite the fact that the genetic overlap between the two methods was modest, it was these overlapping genetic effects that fully accounted for the phenotypic correlation ($r = .25$) between the two measures of activity level.

The fact that different measures of the same temperament domain within the same situation can have different etiologies means that researchers should not assume that all measures of temperament are interchangeable. Findings with one method may not generalize to another, not because of contextual factors, but because different methods engage different processes.

Context-Specific Effects. The etiology of individual differences in temperaments may also differ across situations. Quantitative genetic studies using the *same method* of assessing temperament across *different situations* suggest that there may be contextual or situation-specific genetic effects. To our knowledge, only two studies have taken this stringent approach to explore cross-situational and situationally specific genetic influences on temperament. A study of observer-assessed shyness in infancy found that although there was substantial genetic overlap between shyness assessed in the laboratory and home ($r_G = .81$), there were also some modest, but significant, genetic effects that were specific to the home situation (Cherny, Fulker, Corley, Plomin, & DeFries, 1994; Cherny et al., 2001). Similarly, the activity level of toddler twins assessed by actigraphs in the home, laboratory test, and laboratory play situations also showed a pattern of cross-situational genetic effects (i.e., genetic overlap across situations, with r_G ranging from .68 to 1.0) and genetic variance that was specific to the home environment (Saudino & Zapfe, 2008). In fact, approximately 50% of the genetic variance on activity in the home was situation-specific (i.e., half of the genetic effects that influence activity in the home are independent of the genetic effects that influenced activity in the laboratory).

We tend to think that behavioral change across situations as being due to environmental factors, but findings from these three studies suggest that this need not be the case. Different situations place different demands on the individual and elicit different behaviors, and it is possible that genetic influences contribute to behavioral change as the individual goes from situation to situation; that is, individual differences in temperamental responding to specific situations might be influenced by genetic effects

(Philips & Matheny, 1997). Therefore, it is important to consider the context in which temperament is assessed when exploring the etiology of temperament and, more generally, the links between temperament and developmental outcomes.

ENVIRONMENTAL INFLUENCES

Thus far, we have focused on genetic influences on individual differences in temperament, but it is important to note that quantitative genetic research also has a great deal to say about environmental influences on behaviors. As indicated earlier, genetic influences account for approximately 20 to 60% of the observed variance in temperament; hence, the remaining variance must be due to environmental influences (i.e., the environment accounts for between 40 and 80% of the variance). Clearly, the environment plays an important role in the development of temperament. What is interesting, however, is that quantitative genetics research suggests that the types of environments traditionally assumed to influence child behavior may not operate the way we think they do.

Shared Environmental Influences. The environments that are most frequently studied in developmental research on temperament are those thought to operate on a familywide basis (e.g., parenting style, family functioning, or socioeconomic status). Such environments would be classified as *shared environments* in quantitative genetics research because they are environments that are common among family members. If shared environmental influences are important to temperament, then they should contribute to familial resemblance in temperament, but quantitative genetics research consistently suggests that, for most dimensions, family members are similar in temperaments primarily because of shared genes, not shared environments (e.g., Braungart et al., 1992; Cyphers, Phillips, Fulker, & Mrazek, 1990; Gagne, Saudino, & Cherny, 2003; Lemery-Chalfant et al., 2008; Mullineaux, Deater-Deckard, Petrill, Thompson, et al., 2009; Robinson, Kagan, Reznick, & Corley, 1992; Saudino & Cherny, 2001a, 2001b). For example, in the Colorado Adoption Project, correlations for tester-rated temperament in infancy were approximately .00 for genetically unrelated adoptive siblings and .20 for genetically related nonadoptive siblings (Braungart et al., 1992). The zero correlation for adoptive siblings raised together indicates that being raised in the same family did not make adoptive siblings resemble each other in temperaments. Only those siblings who shared genes were similar in temperament.

There are some exceptions to the general finding of no shared environmental influences on temperament. Positive affect and related behaviors (e.g., smiling, interest in others) display moderate shared environmental influences during infancy and early childhood (Cohen, Dibble, & Grawe, 1977; Goldsmith et al., 1997; Goldsmith & Campos, 1986; Goldsmith & Gottesman, 1981; Goldsmith, Lemery, Buss, & Campos, 1999; Lytton, 1980), perhaps reflecting the influence of maternal personality and attachment security on this temperament dimension (Goldsmith et al., 1999). Similarly, shared environmental influences are substantial for actigraph-assessed activity level within the home, but not within laboratory play or test situations (Saudino & Zapfe, 2008). Family practices and schedules (e.g., mealtimes, bedtimes, family outings, and caretakers' tolerances for their children's activity levels) are a likely source of common variance between siblings, but these familywide factors do not appear to influence activity beyond the home situation. Despite these exceptions, the overall evidence suggests that growing up in the same family does not make family members resemble each other in temperaments.

Nonshared Environmental Influences. The environments that influence temperament are those that are unique to individuals within a family and make family members different (i.e., nonshared environments). These effects are substantial, typically exceeding estimates of measure unreliability, thus indicating that nonshared environmental influences on temperament are more than simply measurement error. This provides an important focus for researchers interested in environmental effects on temperament. Instead of examining environmental factors that differ *across* families (e.g., studies of general parenting style), it will be more profitable to focus on environmental factors that differ *within* families (e.g., differential parenting). That is, research should explore why individuals within the same family differ so much with regard to temperament. This requires studying more than one individual per family and relating experiential differences within a family to sibling differences in temperament. Research of this sort is rare, due in part to the dearth of environmental measures that are specific to the individual; however, a handful of studies have begun to identify possible nonshared environmental influences on temperament. For example, a study of adolescent and young adult siblings found that sibling differences in temperament were related to differences within the sibling relationship (Daniels, 1986). Differences in shyness and sociability were related to differential sibling closeness, and differences in emotionality were related to differential sibling jealousy and antagonism; that is, within sibling pairs, the sibling who was more shy or less sociable experienced less closeness, and the sibling who displayed more anger and distress experienced more antagonism and jealousy within the sibling relationship. Similarly, in middle childhood, sibling differences in shyness and activity level have been associated with differential parental treatment, such that the sibling who was rated by the mother as being more shy received more sensitive maternal treatment, and the sibling who had higher actigraph activity scores experienced more maternal control (Saudino, Wertz, Gagne, & Chawla, 2004).

These sibling studies provide a good start at identifying potential nonshared environments that may influence temperament, but they are limited by the fact that siblings differ in genetic makeup, as well as nonshared environments. Associations between temperamental differences and experiential differences for MZ twins provide a more powerful test of nonshared environmental influences because differences between MZ twins can *only* be due to nonshared environmental influences (i.e., are not contaminated with genetic effects). This method has largely been used to examine possible sources of nonshared environmental influences on behavior problems (e.g., Asbury, Dunn, Pike, & Plomin, 2003; Asbury, Dunn, & Plomin, 2006; Mullineaux, Deater-Deckard, Petrill, & Thompson, 2009), but one study found that MZ within-pair differences in temperament were correlated with experiential differences (Deater-Deckard, Petrill, & Thompson, 2007b). Within pairs, the twin who was rated lower on the dimensions of surgency and negative affect, and higher on the dimension of effortful control was heavier at birth, experienced less maternal negativity and more maternal positivity. Thus, differences in birthweight and parenting may be important sources of nonshared environmental influences accounting for temperamental differences between MZ twins. A caveat is that it is difficult to know the direction of effects given that parenting and temperament were assessed contemporaneously. Differences in parenting could result in differences in temperament, but it is also possible that differences in temperament could result in differential parental treatment. Longitudinal studies that explore the association of experiential differences within a family with differences in temperament are needed to identify specific nonshared environments that impact the development of temperament. Again, a limiting factor for research of this type is the lack of environmental measures that are specific to the individual. Thus, the development of such measures will play an important role in advancing our understanding of individual differences in temperament. This is especially important given that nonshared environmental influences account for a substantial proportion of the variance in temperament.

Molecular Genetics Research

Quantitative genetic research clearly indicates that genes influence individual differences in temperament; however, the genetic effects in these analyses are anonymous. That is, twin and adoption studies indicate the magnitude of genetic influence but do not identify specific genes responsible for variation in temperament. One of the most exciting new directions for research on temperament comes from recent advances in molecular genetic techniques that now make it possible to identify genes associated with complex phenotypes. The identification of specific genes for temperament dimensions will provide an important first step in understanding *how* genes influence temperament.

Complex behavioral dimensions such as temperament are typically distributed continuously; show substantial environmental influence, as well as genetic influence; and are likely to be influenced by many genes, each of varying effect (Plomin & Saudino, 1994). Genes of small and varying effect sizes, which contribute to quantitative traits, are referred to as *quantitative trait loci* (QTLs). The challenge for contemporary molecular geneticists is to use the power of modern molecular techniques to identify QTLs for complex traits, such as temperament dimensions, that involve multiple genetic and nongenetic factors. The goal of applying molecular genetic techniques to the study of behavior is not to identify *the* gene for a particular behavioral dimension—it is unlikely that a single major gene explains variation in complex behavioral dimensions (Plomin, Owen, & McGuffin, 1994)—but rather to identify some of the many genes that each make a small contribution to variability in a particular trait.

Methods

Allelic association is the research strategy that has been most frequently used to identify QTLs that affect temperament. An *allele* refers to different forms of a gene at a specific locus. When there are two or more alleles for a gene occurring in at least 1% of the population, the gene is said to be *polymorphic*, and the genetic variations are referred to as *polymorphisms* (Attia et al., 2009). Some polymorphisms reflect a difference in a single base pair in the DNA sequence (i.e., single-nucleotide polymorphisms [SNPs]); others include repeating units of one to a few hundred base pairs in which the number of repeats vary among individuals (i.e., variable number tandem repeat [VNTR] polymorphism) or larger-scale copy number variations in which duplications of long stretches of DNA differ among individuals (i.e., copy number polymorphisms [CNPs]). Allelic association explores whether variations in DNA (i.e., alleles or polymorphisms) are associated with behavioral variations (e.g., individual differences in a specific temperament trait). A particular allele is considered to be associated with a trait if it occurs at a different frequency across different levels of a trait, or in groups of individuals who score high versus low on some measure of the trait in question (Plomin et al., 2008). For example, say a gene "A" has two variants (i.e., alleles) A1 and A2, and we find that the A2 allele occurs at a higher frequency in a high shy group as compared to a low shy group, we would say that the A2 allele is associated with high shyness. Allelic association occurs when a DNA marker is so close to a trait-relevant gene (or is part of the gene) that its alleles are correlated with the trait in unrelated individuals in the population (Edwards, 1991). (We again refer the interested reader to Plomin et al. [2008] for a good overview of molecular genetics concepts and methods.)

Findings

Typically, association studies of temperament have employed a *candidate gene* approach; that is, specific genes are selected a priori as possible candidates explaining some of the genetic variation in temperament on the basis of their known function and hypotheses about neurological relevance. Genes that regulate dopaminergic or serotonergic functions are among the most frequently studied candidate genes for temperament. The neurotransmitter dopamine has been implicated in the activation and intensity of behavioral responses in reward situations and is thought to be linked with approach to novel stimuli (Auerbach, Benjamin, Faroy, Geller, & Ebstein, 2001; Cloninger, 1987). Neurological and pharmacological studies suggest that dopamine plays a role in emotional response; the regulation of movement; motivated behavior; the control of cognition, including learning, memory and attention (Glickstein & Schmauss, 2001; Jaber, Robinson, Missale, & Caron, 1996); and impulsivity (Buckholtz et al., 2010). Serotonin influences the regulation of mood and emotional states, and drugs that modulate serotonin reuptake are often used in the treatment of mood disorders such as anxiety and depression (Westernberg, Murphy, & Den Boer, 1996). Moreover, serotonin has been linked to impulsivity (Carver & Miller, 2006) and behavioral inhibition/harm avoidance (Peirson et al., 1999; Sourbrie, 1986). Given the links between these neurotransmitters and temperamentally related behaviors, it seems reasonable that genes that either directly or indirectly play a role in the functioning of dopamine or serotonin are the most commonly considered candidate genes for temperament. However, a small number of molecular genetic studies look at genes in noradrenergic (i.e., norepinephrine transporter [*NET*] and phenylethanolamine-N-methyltransferase [*PNMT*] genes) and glutamatergic (i.e., glutamate receptor kainite 3 [*GRIK3*] and excitatory amino acid transporter [*EAAT2*] genes) systems.

Table 16.1 lists genes that have been associated with specific temperament dimensions in nonclinical samples. These early temperament results should be viewed with caution until they have been consistently replicated in a variety of samples. Nonetheless, they hint at the potential for the application of molecular genetic approaches to the study of temperament. Overall, the results are mixed and there are many failures to replicate, but the general pattern of findings suggests that genes linked to dopaminergic functions are more often associated with attention and regulatory temperaments, whereas genes with serotonergic functions are more frequently associated with socio-affective temperaments. In this section we focus on two genes, the dopamine receptor D4 gene (*DRD4*) and the serotonin transporter gene (*5-HTT*). These genes show the strongest evidence for being temperament-relevant. We refer the interested reader to White, Lamm, Helfinstein, and Fox (Chapter 17) and Depue and Fu (Chapter 18) in this volume for a discussion of *DRD4* and *5-HTT* in the context of the neurobiological and neurochemical bases of temperament in children and adults.

DRD4 is a dopamine receptor gene that has several functional polymorphisms. The most frequently studied *DRD4* polymorphism with respect to temperament is the 48-base pair repeat in *exon 3 VNTR* polymorphism. Genotypes for the *DRD4 VNTR* polymorphism are typically classified in terms of the number of repeats (>6 repeats = long vs. 2–5 repeats = short). The *DRD4 VNTR* polymorphism has been associated with activity level, impulsivity/novelty seeking, negative emotionality, shyness/withdrawal, attention/persistence, effortful control, harm avoidance, and adaptability (see Table 16.1). Note, however, the high number of failures to replicate—even within the same sample. For example, De Luca and colleagues (2001) found that *DRD4* was associated with infant adaptability at 1 month but not at 5 months of age. Moreover, in some instances, within those studies that find a significant association between *DRD4* and a particular dimension, the direction of effects varies. That is, the long allele of *DRD4* has been associated with both higher and lower scores on attention/persistence (Auerbach, Faroy, Ebstein, Kahana, & Levine, 2001; Ebstein et al., 1998; Strobel, Wehr, Michel, & Brocke, 1999; Szekely et al., 2004); and reactivity (De Luca et al., 2003; Ebstein et al., 1998).

The *5-HTT* gene, which codes for a serotonin transporter promoter, also has several functional polymorphisms. A polymorphism in the regulatory region of the *5-HTT* gene (*5-HTTLPR*) has been found to be associated with several temperament dimensions, including activity level, negative emotionality, positive emotionality, shyness/withdrawal, attention/persistence, harm avoidance, and reward dependence (see Table 16.1). There is also evidence of possible interactions between *5-HTTLPR* and *DRD4* for shyness/approach (Lakatos et al., 2003), negative emotionality (Auerbach et al., 1999) and orientation (Ebstein et al., 1998). Again, there are many replication failures and conflicting results. The short allele for *5-HTTLPR* has been associated with both high and low levels of emotionality (Auerbach, Faroy, et al., 2001; Auerbach et al., 1999; Hayden et al., 2007) and shyness (Arbelle et al., 2003; Battaglia et al., 2005; Hayden et al., 2007; Jorm et al., 2000; Lakatos et al., 2003).

The large number of failures to replicate and inconsistencies in the direction of effects across studies are not unique to molecular genetic studies of temperament—this pattern also emerges for molecular genetic research examining genes associated with other complex phenotypes. A possible reason for this may lie in the small effect sizes that are typical of molecular genetic studies of complex phenotypes. For the studies of temperament discussed earlier, the genetic polymorphisms accounted for approximately 5% of the total variance. Consequently, very large samples

(text resumes on page 329)

TABLE 16.1. Summary of Molecular Genetic Studies of Temperament

Dimension	Significant findings	Null findings
DRD4 gene		
Activity level	Auerbach, Faroy, et al. (2001) (I, Obs) Ebstein et al. (1998) (I, Obs)	Auerbach, Geller, Lezer, et al. (1999) (I, PR) De Luca et al. (2003) (C, PR) Ilott et al. (2010) (I, Act) Ivorra et al. (2011) (I, Obs)
Impulsivity/ sensation seeking/ novelty seeking	Becker et al. (2005) (A, SR) Ekelund et al. (1999) (Ad, SR) Keltikangas-Järvinen et al. (2003) (Ad, SR) Lee et al. (2003) (A, SR) Mitsuyasu et al. (2001) (Ad, SR) Noble et al. (1998) (A, SR) Reiner & Spangler (2011) (Ad, SR) Ronai et al. (2004) (Ad, SR) Strobel et al. (1999) (Ad, SR) Tsuchimine et al. (2009) (Ad, SR)	Gebhardt et al. (2000) (Ad, SR) Herbst et al. (2000) (Ad, SR) Kim, Kim, Kim, & Lee (2006) (Ad, SR) Noble et al. (1998) (A, SR) Nyman et al. (2009) (Ad, SR) Okuyama et al. (2000) (Ad, SR) Ono et al. (1997) (Ad, SR) Szekely et al. (2004) (Ad, SR) Van Gestel et al. (2002) (Ad, SR)
Negative emotionality	Auerbach et al. (1999) (I, PR) Holmboe et al. (2011) (I, PR) Oniszczenko & Dragan (2005) (Ad, SR)	Lakatos et al. (2003) (I, PR/Obs) Sheese et al. (2009) (I, PR)
Shyness/approach– withdrawal	De Luca et al. (2003) (C, PR) Noble et al. (1998) (A, SR)	
Attention/ persistence orientation	Auerbach, Faroy, et al. (2001) (I, Obs) Ebstein et al. (1998) (I, Obs) Ivorra et al. (2011) (I, Obs) Strobel et al. (1999) (Ad, SR) Szekely et al. (2004) (Ad, SR) Tsuchimine et al. (2009) (Ad, SR)	De Luca et al. (2003) (C, PR) Gebhardt et al. (2000) (Ad, SR) Kim, Kim, Kim, & Lee (2006) (Ad, SR) Mitsuyasu et al. (2001) (Ad, SR) Nyman et al. (2009) (Ad, SR) Okuyama et al. (2000) (Ad, SR) Ronai et al. (2004) (Ad, SR)
Effortful control	Ebstein et al. (1998) (I, Obs)	Holmboe et al. (2011) (I, PR) Ivorra et al. (2011) (I, Obs) Sheese et al. (2007, 2009) (I, PR)
Harm avoidance	Szekely et al. (2004) (Ad, SR)[a] Van Gestel et al. (2002) (Ad, SR)	Gebhardt et al. (2000) (Ad, SR) Kim, Kim, Kim, & Lee (2006) (Ad, SR) Mitsuyasu et al. (2001) (Ad, SR) Nyman et al. (2009) (Ad, SR) Okuyama et al. (2000) (Ad, SR) Ronai et al. (2004) (Ad, SR) Strobel et al. (1999) (Ad, SR) Tsuchimine et al. (2009) (Ad, SR)
Reward dependence	Mitsuyasu et al. (2001) (Ad, SR)	Gebhardt et al. (2000) (Ad, SR) Kim, Kim, Lee, Kim, & Kim (2006) (Ad, SR) Nyman et al. (2009) (Ad, SR) Okuyama et al. (2000) (Ad, SR) Ronai et al. (2004) (Ad, SR) Strobel et al. (1999) (Ad, SR) Szekely et al. (2004) (Ad, SR) Tsuchimine et al. (2009) (Ad, SR)

(cont.)

TABLE 16.1. *(cont.)*

Dimension	Significant findings	Null findings
Adaptability	De Luca et al. (2001) (I, PR)	De Luca et al. (2001) (I, PR) De Luca et al. (2003) (C, PR)
Reactivity	De Luca et al. (2003) (C, PR) Ebstein et al. (1998) (I, Obs)	Ivorra et al. (2011) (I, Obs)
5-HTT gene		
Activity level	Dragan & Oniszczenko (2005, 2006) (Ad, SR)	
Impulsivity/ sensation seeking/ novelty seeking	Saiz et al. (2010) (Ad, SR)[b] Suzuki et al. (2008) (Ad, SR)[c]	Aoki et al. (2010) (Ad, SR) Ebstein et al. (1997) (Ad, SR) Gonda et al. (2009) (Ad, SR) Ham et al. (2004) (Ad, SR) Joo et al. (2007) (Ad, SR) Kazantseva et al. (2008) (Ad, SR) Kim et al. (2005) (Ad, SR) Kim, Kim, Lee, Kim, & Kim (2006) (Ad, SR) Kumakiri et al. (1999) (Ad, SR) Samochowiec et al. (2001) (Ad, SR) Samochowiec et al. (2004) (Ad, SR) Szekely et al. (2004) (Ad, SR) Van Gestel et al. (2002) (Ad, SR)
Negative emotionality	Auerbach, Faroy, et al. (2001) (I, Obs) Auerbach et al. (1999) (I, PR) Hayden et al. (2007) (C, Obs) Holmboe et al. (2011) (I, PR)[e]	Dragan & Oniszczenko (2005) (Ad, SR) Dragan & Oniszczenko (2006) (Ad, SR) Hayden et al. (2007) (C, PR) Hayden et al. (2011) (C, Obs) Lakatos et al. (2003) (I, PR) Pluess et al. (2011) (I, PR) Sheese et al. (2009) (I, PR)
Positive emotionality	Auerbach, Faroy, et al. (2001) (I, Obs)	Auerbach et al. (1999) (I, PR) Hayden et al. (2011) (C, Obs) Sheese et al. (2009) (I, PR)
Shyness/approach–withdrawal	Arbelle et al. (2003) (C, SR/PR/TR) Battaglia et al. (2005) (C, TR/Obs) Hayden et al. (2007) (C, PR) Jorm et al. (2000) (A, PR) Lakatos et al. (2003) (I, Obs)	Schmidt et al. (2002) (C, Obs) Jorm et al. (2000) (I, C, PR)
Attention/ persistence orientation	Kazantseva et al. (2008) (Ad, SR) Kim et al. (2005) (Ad, SR) Dragan & Oniszczenko (2006) (Ad, SR)	Aoki et al. (2010) (Ad, SR) Ebstein et al. (1997) (Ad, SR) Gonda et al. (2009) (Ad, SR) Ham et al. (2004) (Ad, SR) Joo et al. (2007) (Ad, SR) Kim, Kim, Lee, Kim, & Kim (2006) (Ad, SR) Kumakiri et al. (1999) (Ad, SR) Saiz et al. (2010) (Ad, SR) Samochowiec et al. (2001) (Ad, SR) Samochowiec et al. (2004) (Ad, SR) Szekely et al. (2004) (Ad, SR)

(cont.)

TABLE 16.1. *(cont.)*

Dimension	Significant findings	Null findings
Harm avoidance	Kazantseva et al. (2008) (Ad, SR) Kim, Kim, Lee, Kim, & Kim (2006) (Ad, SR)[d] Saiz et al. (2010) (Ad, SR) Suzuki et al. (2008) (Ad, SR)[c] Van Gestel et al. (2002) (Ad, SR)	Aoki et al. (2010) (Ad, SR) Ebstein et al. (1997) (Ad, SR) Gonda et al. (2009) (Ad, SR) Ham et al. (2004) (Ad, SR) Hamer et al. (1999) (Ad, SR) Herbst et al. (2000) (Ad, SR) Joo et al. (2007) (Ad, SR) Kim et al. (2005) (Ad, SR) Kumakiri et al. (1999) (Ad, SR) Samochowiec et al. (2001) (Ad, SR) Samochowiec et al. (2004) (Ad, SR) Szekely et al. (2004) (Ad, SR)
Reward dependence	Samochowiec et al. (2004) (Ad, SR) Kim, Kim, Lee, Kim, & Kim (2006) (Ad, SR)[d]	Aoki et al. (2010) (Ad, SR) Ebstein et al. (1997) (Ad, SR) Gonda et al. (2009) (Ad, SR) Ham et al. (2004) (Ad, SR) Hamer et al. (1999) (Ad, SR) Joo et al. (2007) (Ad, SR) Kazantseva et al. (2008) (Ad, SR) Kim et al. (2005) (Ad, SR) Kumakiri et al. (1999) (Ad, SR) Saiz et al. (2010) (Ad, SR) Samochowiec et al. (2001) (Ad, SR) Suzuki et al. (2008) (Ad, SR) Szekely et al. (2004) (Ad, SR)
Reactivity	Ivorra et al. (2011) (I, Obs)	
DRD2 gene		
Impulsivity/ sensation seeking/ novelty seeking	Kazantseva et al. (2011) (Ad, SR) Noble et al. (1998) (A, SR) Nyman et al. (2009) (Ad, SR)	Gebhardt et al. (2000) (Ad, SR) Lee et al. (2008) (Ad, SR) Lee et al. (2003) (A, SR) Noble et al. (1998) (A, SR)
Shyness/approach–withdrawal	Noble et al. (1998) (A, SR)	
Attention/ persistence orientation	Noble et al. (1998) (A, SR) Nyman et al. (2009) (Ad, SR)	Gebhardt et al. (2000) (Ad, SR) Lee et al. (2007) (Ad, SR) Lee et al. (2003) (A, SR)
Harm avoidance	Nyman et al. (2009) (Ad, SR)	Gebhardt et al. (2000) (Ad, SR) Lee et al. (2007) (Ad, SR)
Reward dependence	Kazantseva et al. (2011) (Ad, SR) Noble et al. (1998) (A, SR)	Gebhardt et al. (2000) (Ad, SR) Lee et al. (2007) (Ad, SR) Lee et al. (2003) (A, SR)
DAT1 gene		
Effortful control	Rueda et al. (2005) (C, PR)	Sheese et al. (2009) (I, PR)
Surgency	Rueda et al. (2005) (C, PR)	
Impulsivity/ sensation seeking/ novelty seeking	Van Gestel et al. (2002) (Ad, SR)	Kim, Kim, Kim, & Lee (2006); Kim, Kim, Lee, Kim, & Kim (2006) (Ad, SR) Samochowiec et al. (2001) (Ad, SR) Schosser et al. (2010) (Ad, SR)

(cont.)

TABLE 16.1. *(cont.)*

Dimension	Significant findings	Null findings
Attention/persistence orientation	Kazantseva et al. (2011) (Ad, SR)	
EGF gene		
Impulsivity/sensation seeking/novelty seeking	Keltikangas-Järvinen et al. (2006) (Ad, SR)	
Reward dependence	Keltikangas-Järvinen et al. (2006) (Ad, SR)	
MAOA gene		
Impulsivity/sensation seeking/novelty seeking	Lee et al. (2008) (Ad, SR)[c] Shiraishi et al. (2006) (Ad, SR)	Garpenstrand et al. (2002) (Ad, SR) Hakamata et al. (2005) (Ad, SR) Kim, Kim, Kim, & Lee (2006) (Ad, SR) Samochowiec et al. (2004) (Ad, SR) Tsuchimine et al. (2008) (Ad, SR)
Attention/persistence orientation	Tsuchimine et al. (2008) (Ad, SR)	Garpenstrand et al. (2002) (Ad, SR) Hakamata, Takahashi et al. (2005) (Ad, SR) Kim, Kim, Kim, Lee, & Kim (2006) (Ad, SR) Lee et al. (2008) (Ad, SR) Samochowiec et al. (2004) (Ad, SR) Shiraishi et al. (2006) (Ad, SR)
APOE gene		
Activity level	Keltikangas-Järvinen et al. (1993) (C, PR)	Keltikangas-Järvinen et al. (1993) (A/Ad, PR/SR) Jorm et al. (2003 (I/C/A, PR)
Positive emotionality	Keltikangas-Järvinen et al. (1993) (A/Ad, PR/SR)	Keltikangas-Järvinen et al. (1993) (C/A, PR) Sheese et al. (2009) (I, PR)
Sociability	Keltikangas-Järvinen et al. (1993) (A/Ad, PR)	Keltikangas-Järvinen et al. (1993) (C/A, PR)
COMT gene		
Positive emotionality	Sheese et al. (2009) (I, PR)	Sheese et al. (2009) (I, PR)
Harm avoidance	Hashimoto et al. (2007) (Ad, SR) Kim, Kim, Kim, Lee, & Kim (2006) (Ad, SR)	Drabant et al. (2006) (Ad, SR)
Impulsivity/sensation seeking/novelty seeking	Salo et al. (2010) (Ad, SR)[c]	

(cont.)

TABLE 16.1. *(cont.)*

Dimension	Significant findings	Null findings
CYP2C19 gene		
Harm avoidance	Yasui-Furukori et al. (2007) (Ad, SR)	Ishii et al. (2007) (Ad, SR)
Shyness/approach–withdrawal	Yasui-Furukori et al. (2007) (Ad, SR)	
Reward dependence	Ishii et al. (2007) (Ad, SR)	Yasui-Furukori et al. (2007) (Ad, SR)
5-HTR2A gene		
Impulsivity/sensation seeking/novelty seeking	Nakamura et al. (2011) (Ad, SR)	Ham et al. (2004) (Ad, SR) Kusumi et al. (2002) (Ad, SR) Saiz et al. (2010) (Ad, SR) Schosser et al. (2010) (Ad, SR)
5-HTR2C gene		
Reward dependence	Ebstein et al. (1997) (Ad, SR)	Kühn et al. (2002) (Ad, SR)
Attention/persistence orientation	Ebstein et al. (1997) (Ad, SR)	Kühn et al. (2002) (Ad, SR)
5-HTR3A		
Harm avoidance	Melke et al. (2003) (Ad, SR)	
Shyness/approach–withdrawal	Melke et al. (2003) (Ad, SR)	
BDNF gene		
Harm avoidance	Montag et al. (2010) (Ad, SR)	Itoh et al. (2004) (Ad, SR) Minelli et al. (2011) (Ad, SR)
Reward dependence	Itoh et al. (2004) (Ad, SR)	Minelli et al. (2011) (Ad, SR)
ESR1 gene		
Harm avoidance	Gade-Andavolu et al. (2009) (Ad, SR)	
Shyness/approach–withdrawal	Gade-Andavolu et al. (2009) (Ad, SR)	
GRIK3 gene		
Harm avoidance	Minelli et al. (2009) (Ad, SR)	
Shyness/approach–withdrawal	Minelli et al. (2009) (Ad, SR)	
Reactivity	Jorm et al. (2002) (C, PR)	
TPH2 gene		
Harm avoidance	Reuter et al. (2007) (Ad, SR)	Inoue et al. (2010) (Ad, SR)
Reward dependence	Inoue, Yamasue et al. (2010) (Ad, SR)	Reuter et al. (2007) (Ad, SR)

(cont.)

TABLE 16.1. *(cont.)*

Dimension	Significant findings	Null findings
NET gene		
Reward dependence	Ham, Choi et al. (2005) (Ad, SR)	Lee et al. (2008) (Ad, SR) Samochowiec et al. (2001) (Ad, SR) Suzuki et al. (2007) (Ad, SR) Suzuki et al. (2008) (Ad, SR)
ACE gene		
Impulsivity/sensation seeking/novelty seeking	Shimizu et al. (2006) (Ad, SR)	
CHRNA4 gene		
Effortful control	Sheese et al. (2009) (I, PR)	Sheese et al. (2009) (I, PR)
CRH gene		
Behavioral inhibition	Smoller et al. (2005 (I/C, Obs)	
CYP17 gene		
Impulsivity/sensation seeking/novelty seeking	Matsumoto et al. (2008) (Ad, SR)	
CYP19 gene		
Harm avoidance	Matsumoto et al. (2009) (Ad, SR)	
DBH gene		
Harm avoidance	Kamata et al. (2009) (Ad, SR)	
EAAT2 gene		
Reward dependence	Matsumoto et al. (2007) (Ad, SR)	
PNMT gene		
Reward dependence	Yamano et al. (2008) (Ad, SR)	
RGS2 gene		
Behavioral inhibition	Smoller et al. (2008 (I/C, Obs)	
SNAP25 gene		
Negative emotionality	Sheese et al. (2009) (I, PR)	

(cont.)

TABLE 16.1. *(cont.)*

Dimension	Significant findings	Null findings
TH gene		
Impulsivity/ sensation seeking/ novelty seeking	Sadahiro et al. (2010) (Ad, SR)	
GABRA6 gene		
Harm avoidance	Arias et al. (2012) (Ad, SR)	
GCH1 gene		
Impulsivity/ sensation seeking/ novelty seeking	Sadahiro et al. (2011) (Ad, SR)	
TFAP2B gene		
Reactivity	Ivorra et al. (2011) (I, Obs)	
FKBP5 gene		
Harm avoidance	Shibuya et al. (2011) (Ad, SR)	
OXTR gene		
Reward dependence	Tost et al. (2010) (Ad, SR)	

Note. I, infancy; C, childhood; A, adolescence; Ad, adulthood; Act, actigraph; Obs, observational measure; PR, parent report; TR, teacher report; SR, self-report.
[a]No main effect, interaction with *5-HTT*. [b]No main effect, interaction with *5-HTR2A*. [c]No main effect, interaction with *NET*. [d]No main effect, interaction with *DAT1*. [e]No main effect, interaction with *DRD4*.

are needed to detect such small effects. In addition, failures to replicate may reflect differences in the ages of the populations studied, the measurement of temperament, and/or conceptual definitions of the temperament dimensions studied. As indicated earlier, quantitative genetic analyses have found measure-specific and situation-specific genetic effects that might explain the many failures to replicate. A critical issue for molecular genetics studies of temperament (and other complex phenotypes) is the definition and measurement of the phenotype.

Genetic Influences on Change in Temperament

Quantitative behavior genetic research has approached the issue of developmental change in temperament in two general ways. First, by exploring whether the relative importance of genetic and environmental influences on temperament changes with age; that is, do estimates of heritability and environmentality differ across age? Second, by exploring genetic influences on age-to-age change or continuity of individual differences in temperament during development (i.e., to what extent is behavioral change or continuity in temperament due to genetic influences?). The first question can be answered with cross-sectional research; the second requires longitudinal studies of temperament within a genetically sensitive design.

Genes switch on and off throughout development, and there may be changes in the quantity and quality of genetic effects across age (Plomin & Nesselroade, 1990). Similarly, the environments that we experience differ across age, and the role of the environment on individual differences in temperament may change as environments change. This dynamic nature of genes and environments means that there may be developmental differences in the relative importance of genetic and environmental influences on temperament, and that one should not assume that behavioral genetics findings about the etiology of temperament at one age apply to another.

Differential Heritability across Age

It is possible that temperament may be differentially heritable across age. On an intuitive level, most people might predict that as children develop, they are exposed to more diverse environments that may influence temperament; therefore, the importance of genetic factors on temperament might wane. However, the findings from quantitative genetics research do not support this intuition. Many studies find no evidence of differential heritability across age (e.g., Cyphers et al., 1990; Gagne et al., 2003; McCartney, Harris, & Bernieri, 1990; Plomin et al., 1993; Saudino, 2012; Saudino & Cherny, 2001b). Moreover, developmental differences in genetic influences on temperament that are found tend to be in the direction of *increased* genetic variance (e.g., Braungart et al., 1992; Buss, Plomin, & Willerman, 1973; Ganiban et al., 2008; Stevenson & Fielding, 1985). For example, in the Louisville Twin Study, observer-rated temperament was not genetically influenced during the neonatal period (Riese, 1990), but it was moderately heritable in later infancy and early childhood (Matheny, 1983, 1989).

A number of explanations for increases in heritability across age have been put forth. First, genetic influences on temperament in early infancy might be masked because of perinatal environmental influences (Torgersen, 1985). Second, genetic effects that create small individual differences in infancy become amplified with age (Plomin & DeFries, 1985). Third, with age there is a shift from passive to reactive and active genotype–environment correlations (Scarr & McCartney, 1983). That is, with development, individuals elicit and select environments that reflect their unique genotypes; hence, DZ twins become less similar relative to MZ twins, and estimates of heritability increase. Finally, it is also possible that apparent increases in the heritability of temperament reflect differential measure reliability and validity across age (see Saudino, 2009a, for a detailed discussion of these explanations).

Sources of Continuity and Change in Temperament

Although the evidence for age-dependent differential heritability of temperament is mixed, it is clear that temperament in infancy, early childhood, middle childhood, adolescence, and adulthood is genetically influenced. This does not mean, however, that the same genetic influences operate across age; that is, the genes that influence temperament in infancy may differ from those that influence temperament in later developmental periods. This is true even if estimates of heritability are the same across age. Similarly, age differences in estimates of heritability do not mean that the genes operating on temperament differ from one age to the next—only that there is a difference in the extent to which genetic factors contribute to behavioral variability in temperament. Thus, comparing heritability estimates across age cannot inform about sources of continuity and change and does not address developmental processes.

Genetic and environmental influences on developmental change can be addressed by assessing genetic contributions to phenotypic continuity and change across age (i.e., age-to-age stability and instability). Analyses of genetic contributions to phenotypic continuity permit the estimation of the extent to which genetic effects on a trait at one age overlap with genetic effects on the same trait at another age (i.e., the genetic correlation) and, furthermore, whether new genetic influences on the trait emerge across time. Such analyses inform about environmental sources of continuity and change, and can therefore provide important information about developmental processes.

In the MacArthur Longitudinal Twin Study, observer-rated Activity, Affect/Extraversion, Task Orientation, and Behavioral Inhibition displayed moderate stability across 14, 20, 24, and 36 months of age (i.e., the average age-to-age correlation was .24). Genetic analyses of continuity and change found that the age-to-age stability of Activity, Affect/Extraversion, Task Orientation, and Behavioral Inhibition was entirely due to genetic factors (Saudino & Cherny, 2001b; Saudino et al., 1996). Shyness was an exception in that both genetic and shared environmental influences contributed to developmental continuity. If genetic factors explain continuity for most temperament dimensions, what explains developmental change in temperament across toddlerhood? The answer to some extent varies across temperament dimensions, but for all dimensions, new nonshared environmental influences emerged at each age. In other words, individual differences in the development of early temperament are due, in part, to differences within the family environment, such as differential treatment, experiences, or accidents. With the exception of Shyness, genetic factors also contributed to developmental change. New genetic effects emerged at 20, 24, and 36 months of age for Behavioral Inhibition; at 20 months for Affect/Extraversion; and at 36 months for both Activity and Task Orientation. Thus, for these temperament dimensions, genetic factors influence both continuity and change in temperament across age.

The new genetic effects on Affect/Extraversion at 20 months of age are intriguing because this is the age when children's sociocognitive competencies (e.g., self-awareness and other-awareness) dramatically increase (Asendorpf & Baudonnière, 1993; Asendorpf, Warkentin, & Baudonnière, 1996). Consequently, the novel genetic effects for Affect/Extraversion observed within the laboratory situation at 20 months might be a result of these new processes coming online. The issue of possible sources of genetic change is murkier, however, for Behavioral Inhibition, Activity, and Task Orientation because genetic change coincided with subtle changes in the measures used to assess these dimensions. As indicated earlier, different methods of assessing temperament can tap different genetic effects, which raises the possibility that, for these dimensions, the emergence of new genetic effects from one age period to the next could be due to differences in measures, not development.

More recent research in which the same temperament measures were used across age provides stronger evidence for genetic change in temperament. A study of actigraph-assessed activity level in toddlers found that for activity in the laboratory at ages 2 and 3 years, age-to-age stability ($r = .46$) was entirely due to genetic factors, however, there were significant new genetic effects on activity level at age 3 (Saudino, 2012). Thus, genes contributed to both continuity and change for activity in the laboratory. Interestingly, there was no evidence of genetic contributions to change for actigraph activity within the home situation. The genetic effects that influenced activity in the home at age 2 were entirely overlapping with those at age 3 (i.e., $r_G = 1.0$). These results indicated that the processes influencing developmental change in activity level in toddlerhood may differ across contexts. The laboratory findings mirror those from the MacArthur Longitudinal Twin Study, which also found novel genetic variance on observed activity within the laboratory at age 3; however, the use of actigraphs to assess activity level across age eliminates measure differences as a possible source of change and allows for more interesting hypotheses regarding the new genetic variance. For example, it is possible that the new genetic effects in the laboratory at age 3 may reflect children's increased self-control/self-regulation or adaptability to novel social situations.

There is also evidence of genetic contributions to temperamental change in adolescence. Parents in the NEAD project rated the temperaments of their adolescent children at two time points, approximately 3 years apart (Ganiban et al., 2008). Cross-age stability correlations ranged from .32 to .56 for mothers' ratings, and from .42 to .53 for fathers' ratings. As was found for toddlers, stability in temperament across mid- to late adolescence was largely due to genetic effects, and change was due to both genetic and nonshared environmental influences; that is, for both mothers' and fathers' ratings of their adolescent children's temperaments, there was substantial new genetic variance in the Time 2 ratings that was independent of the genetic effects on Time 1 ratings. It is possible that the genetic factors contributing to changes in temperament in adolescence reflect the activation of new genes during puberty (Ganiban et al., 2008).

The finding that genetic influences largely explain the behavioral consistency of temperament across age probably comes as no surprise, as it fits with the commonly held static view of genetic effects. Genetic contributions to behavioral consistency are, however, only part of the story. In accordance with a more dynamic view of genetic effects, longitudinal quantitative analyses provide evidence that genes also contribute to developmental change in temperament. This has important implications for developmental researchers interested in temperament. Specifically, findings based on an assessment of temperament at one age may not generalize to another age, and the factors that influence developmental processes in temperament may differ across contexts. This is particularly relevant to molecular genetics research because it means that the specific genes that are associated with temperament will, to some extent, differ across age. Indeed, in a longitudinal study of temperament from infancy to midadolescence, the *5-HTTLPR* polymorphism was associated with shyness/approach–withdrawal only in adolescence (Jorm et al., 2000)—a finding that would be consistent with the quantitative results from the NEAD project suggesting the emergence of new genetic effects in adolescence (Ganiban et al., 2008).

Other longitudinal molecular genetics studies of temperament also hint at developmental changes in specific genes that influence temperament. For example, the catechol-O-methyltransferase gene (*COMT*) has been associated with positive emotionality in early, but not late, infancy; and the nicotinic acetylcholine receptor alpha-4 subunit gene (*CHRNA4*) has been associated with effortful control in late, but not early, infancy (Sheese, Voelker, Posner, & Rothbart, 2009). Similarly, De Luca and colleagues (2001) found that *DRD4* was associated with infant adaptability at 1 month, but not at 5 months, of age. Although intriguing, these findings must be considered cautiously, as the sample sizes are small, which limits the power to detect significant effects, and the measures used to assess temperament differed across age. Thus, these methodological issues could account for what appears to be genetic change. Replication with larger samples, using the same measures at each age, is needed to resolve the question of developmental changes in specific genes that influence behavior.

Genetic Links between Temperament and Developmental Outcomes

As indicated by Shiner and Caspi (Chapter 24), Lengua and Wachs (Chapter 25), Klein, Dyson, Kujawa, and Kotov (Chapter 26), Tackett, Martel, and Kushner (Chapter 27), and Hampson and Vollrath (Chapter 28) in this volume, temperament has been associated with a variety of developmental outcomes. This raises the question of what factors explain these associations; that is, what are the mechanisms that link temperament and outcome? Quantitative genetics research can address this question by examining the extent to which the association between temperament and outcome is due to common genetic and/or environmental factors. Surprisingly, although there is an abundance of phenotypic research linking temperament to developmental outcome, there is relatively little behavioral genetic research exploring the etiology of these associations.

Most of the behavioral genetics research exploring temperament and developmental outcome has focused on links between temperament and behavior problems. Like temperament, individual differences in behavior problems are, in part, influenced by genetic factors (Rhee & Waldman, 2002; Rietveld, Hudziak, Bartels, van Beijsterveldt, & Boomsma, 2004; Saudino, Carter, Purper-Ouakil, & Gorwood, 2008). Thus, it is reasonable to ask if the association between temperament and behavior problems arises because of common genetic effects. With a few exceptions, this would appear to be the case. For example, multivariate genetic analyses show that the genetic factors influencing the temperament dimensions of emotionality and effortful control overlap significantly with those that influence internalizing and externalizing behavior problems in early and middle childhood (Lemery-Chalfant et al., 2008; Schmitz et al., 1999; Schmitz & Saudino, 2003). Similarly, both parent-rated and observed inhibitory control are genetically linked to externalizing and hyperactivity problems in toddlers (Gagne, Saudino, & Asherson, 2011) and observed attention/persistence and anger/frustration show substantial genetic covariance with conduct problems in middle childhood (Deater-Deckard, Petrill, & Thompson, 2007a). In all of these analyses, the phenotypic correlations between temperament and behavior problems are primarily a result of common genetic influences.

Findings in regard to links between shyness and internalizing problems are less clear. Although genetic factors explain the association between shyness and internalizing problems in early childhood (Schmitz et al., 1999), shared environmental influences appear to mediate the longitudinal association between shyness in early childhood and internalizing problems in middle childhood (Rhee et al., 2007). Given that this latter study collapsed across multiple measures of both parent-rated temperament and behavior problems, it is possible that the findings of shared environmental covariance may reflect method covariance; however, it is also possible that sources of covariance between shyness and internalizing change across age. The use of multiple assessment methods would help to clarify these findings.

Other research has looked at more specific problem behaviors, but a similar pattern emerges. In a sample of middle childhood and adolescent twins, emotionality significantly predicted anxious/depressed, attention, delinquent, and aggressive behavior problems assessed 2 years later (Gjone & Stevenson, 1997). The phenotypic correlations between emotionality and aggression and attention problems were due only to common genetic factors. Similarly, genetic effects accounted for the majority of the covariation between negative emotionality, self-esteem, and depression in a study of temperament and outcome in adolescent females, although there was also some modest nonshared environmental covariation among the three constructs (Neiss, Stevenson, Legrand, Iacono, & Sedikides, 2009). Finally, a study of fear and anxiety symptoms in early childhood suggests that the associations between fear and general anxiety, and between fear and separation anxiety, arise for different reasons (Goldsmith & Lemery, 2000). Despite only modest overlap in the genetic influences on fear and general anxiety, it was these modest overlapping genetic influences that almost entirely accounted for the phenotypic correlation between the two domains. In contrast, fear and separation anxiety were genetically distinct and were associated because of common shared and nonshared environmental influences.

Quantitative genetic research examining genetic and environmental links between temperament and behavior problems has significance for molecular genetic research. A finding of substantial overlap in genetic influences on the two domains provides support for the hypothesis that certain behavior problems may be the extreme manifestation of specific temperament dimensions. This hypothesis is further supported by the finding of specific genes that operate for both temperament and behavior problems. For example, *DRD4*, the dopamine transporter gene (*DAT1*), and *5-HTTLPR* have been associated with attention-deficit/hyperactivity disorder (ADHD) in a number of studies (see Banaschewski, Becker, Scherag, Franke, & Coghill, 2010, for a review). As indicated in Table 16.1, these genes are also associated with the temperament dimensions of Activity Level, Impulsivity/Novelty Seeking, Attention/Persistence, and Effortful Control, suggesting that ADHD symptoms may indeed reflect the extremes of these temperament dimensions.

Alternatively, it has been proposed that temperament dimensions may be endophenotypes for clinical disorders; for example, Activity Level has been viewed as a possible endophenotype for ADHD (Wood & Neale, 2010). *Endophenotypes* are heritable characteristics that are less complex than the disorder and more proximal to the genetic etiology of a disorder than the diagnosis (i.e., intermediate phenotypes between the gene and the disorder). Because endophenotypes are simpler and closer to the genetic etiology, it should be easier to discover genes for endophenotypes than for complex disorders (Gottesman & Gould, 2003). Hence, temperament, as a putative endophenotype, has the potential to contribute to our understanding of the specific genetic mechanisms that influence psychopathology.

Temperament and the Interface between Nature and Nurture

As discussed earlier, quantitative behavior genetics research has clearly indicated that the environment contributes to both individual differences in temperament and to developmental change in temperament. Behavior genetics research is also able to elucidate environmental mechanisms relevant to temperament via the study of genotype–environment correlations and interactions.

Genotype–Environment Correlations

Genotype–environment correlations (GEr) occur when the environment covaries with genetically influenced characteristics of the individual (Plomin, DeFries, & Loehlin, 1977); that is, individuals are differentially exposed to environments as a function of their genetically influenced characteristics. There are three types of GEr. *Passive* GE correlations occur when the environment reflects parental traits that are related genetically to infant characteristics. Thus, children can passively "inherit" environments that are correlated with their genetic propensities as a result of sharing heredity and family environment with their parents. *Reactive/evocative* GE correlations refer to experiences that occur as a consequence of other people's reactions to genetically influenced characteristics of the individual. *Active* GE correlations occur when individuals actively select or create environments correlated with their genetically influenced characteristics. In other words, people seek out environments or experiences that are compatible with their temperaments. These temperament × environment transactions are described in more detail later in this volume (see Shiner & Caspi, Chapter 24).

One of the most provocative findings to emerge from behavioral genetic research is that genetic factors contribute substantially to many measures that assess the environments of individuals. For example, genetic analyses of family environment, peer groups, social support, life events, and divorce often yield moderate heritability estimates (Plomin, 1994). Environments have no DNA; thus, genetic influences on environmental measures suggest the presence of GE correlations (i.e., the environment reflects genetically influenced characteristics of individuals). The question, then, is to what extent do one's environments reflect genetically influenced temperament characteristics? This can be explored by using multivariate quantitative genetic models that examine genetic and environmental contributions to the covariance between measures of the environment and temperament. These models can test whether genetic influences on temperament mediate the genetic influences on measures of the environment.

Parenting behaviors, such as negativity and warmth, are an important facet of the child's environment, and it is likely that parents' behaviors toward their children are, in part, in response to their children's temperaments. Numerous studies have found genetic effects on parenting (e.g., Deater-Deckard, 2000; Forget-Dubois et al., 2007; Neiderhiser et al., 2004; Ulbricht & Neiderhiser, 2009). These genetic effects are *child effects*, in that they represent the genetic contributions of children to their parents' behavior, and suggest that parents are responding to genetically influenced characteristics of their children (i.e., genotype–environment correlation). Although studies of child-based genetic effects on parenting are plentiful, only a handful of studies have explored whether child temperament mediates these genetic effects. Nonetheless, it appears that genetic influences on negative (i.e., hostile or harsh) parenting are mediated, in part, by genetic influences on negative emotionality/difficult temperament. For example, negative emotionality/difficult temperament explained approximately 50% of the genetic effects on maternal negative parenting in 5-month-olds (Boivin et al., 2005) and 2-year-olds (Ganiban & Saudino, 2009). Similar results have emerged for adolescents, although perhaps not as strongly. In the NEAD project, adolescent negative emotionality accounted for 22 and 39%, respectively, of the genetic effects on maternal and paternal negativity (Ganiban et al., 2011). Taken together, these results demonstrate that negative emotionality/difficult temperament is an important avenue through which the child's genotype influences parent behaviors.

Child temperament may also influence how parents structure the physical environments of their children. Genetic effects on an observational/interview measure of the home environment of infants at age 2 were mediated predominantly by genetic effects on tester ratings of Task Orientation, a temperament dimension reflecting attention span, persistence, and goal directedness (Saudino & Plomin, 1997). This suggests that, to some extent, infants' environments reflect their genetically influenced attentional characteristics. However, genetic influences on parent-report measures of the family environment in middle childhood were largely independent of genetic influences on observed temperament in infancy and early childhood (Braungart, 1994). Thus, although more research is needed, it appears that genetic effects on the environment reflects genetic influences on one's current, not past, temperaments.

Genotype–Environment Interactions (G × E)

Although it is tempting to interpret genotype–environment interactions (G × E) as meaning that a phenotype, such as temperament, is the product of both genes and environments, this would be wrong. G × E interactions refer to genetic sensitivity to the environment (Plomin et al., 2008). That is, the effect of the environment on specific phenotypes may differ across genotypes (i.e., different genotypes may be differentially susceptible to the environment; see van IJzendoorn & Bakermans-Kranenburg, Chapter 19, this volume, for extensive coverage of the differential susceptibility hypothesis), or the effect of the genotype on the phenotype may differ across environments (i.e., the same genotype may be associated with different phenotypic outcomes depending on the environment). In this way, G × E interactions inform about genetic and environmental risk mechanisms.

Quantitative genetic studies of G × E interactions typically focus on differences in heritability as a function of the environment. The two studies that have examined the heritability of temperament as a function of the environment have explored parenting as the potential moderating variable (i.e., the environment in G × E interaction analyses). A twin study of toddlers found that genetic contributions to negative emotionality were strongest when maternal negativity was extremely high or low (Ganiban & Saudino, 2009), indicating that parenting moderates the expression of children's genetically influenced characteristics. Maternal negativity also moderated environmental influences on emotionality. At higher levels of maternal negativity, co-twins demonstrated greater differences in emotionality as a result of their unique, nonshared experiences. When maternal negativity was low, however, familywide shared environmental influences contributed more to emotionality. Similar, though not identical, results have emerged from a study of perceived parenting in adolescents. Genetic effects on both positive and negative emotionality were greater when adolescents perceived that parents displayed higher levels of regard/warmth (Krueger, South, Johnson, & Iacono, 2008). At lower levels of parental regard/warmth, genetic influences diminished and the relative influence of the environment increased. Adolescents' perceptions of conflict within the parent–child relationship also moderated genetic influences on negative and positive emotionality, such that the relative impact of genetic influences decreased and the importance of the shared environment increased as conflict increased.

More research is needed, but these G × E findings suggest a dynamic interplay between parenting and temperament that might be more satisfying to developmentalists, who are often surprised by the lack of shared genetic influences on temperament. The basic twin design presents the average effects in the population (i.e., collapsing across all levels of parenting). Results from the basic design are accurate but general (Krueger et al., 2008). G × E analyses permit a more nuanced understanding of the etiology of temperament and suggest that familywide environments may influence individual differences in temperament under certain conditions (e.g., when the child experiences poorer parenting). This theme is elaborated on later in the volume, notably in Chapters 19, 20, and 25.

Other quantitative G × E research has viewed temperament as a context for parenting and examined the extent to which child temperament moderates child-based genetic and environmental influences on parenting behaviors. That is, does the relative influence of genes and environments on parenting behavior vary across levels of child temperament? Although studies that have explored this question do find evidence of G × E interaction in adolescence, the findings are inconsistent. In one study, genetic contributions to adolescents' perceptions of parental regard/warmth were highest when the children had less problematic temperaments (i.e., higher levels of positive emotionality or lower levels of negative emotionality). When adolescents had more difficult temperaments, variance in perceived regard/warmth in the parent–child relationship was largely due to shared environmental influences (South, Krueger, Johnson, & Iacono, 2008). However, in the NEAD project, shared environmental influences on mothers' and fathers' negativity toward their children were lowest when adolescents demonstrated more challenging temperaments (Ganiban et al., 2011). Genetic contributions to parental negativity increased as a function of child negative emotionality and sociability, and for fathers, decreased as a function of child shyness. For parental warmth, only fathers' warmth was moderated by child temperament. Genetic contributions to fathers' warmth decreased and nonshared environmental contributions increased when children demonstrated high activity levels. Nonshared environmental contributions to father warmth increased when children demonstrated higher levels of sociability and lower levels of shyness. Methodological differences between the two studies may, in part, account for differences in findings. South and colleagues (2008) relied on adolescent perceptions of parenting behaviors, whereas in the NEAD study, parenting was based on a composite of mother, child, and adolescent ratings. Nonetheless, these studies are consistent in indicating that adolescents' temperament characteristics provide an important context for parenting behavior, in that the etiology of parenting varies as a function of child temperament.

Molecular genetic studies of G × E interactions have identified specific genes that may moderate the effect of the environment on temperament. In particular, the short allele of the *5-HTTLPR* polymorphism appears to confer genetic risk to environmental influences in childhood. For example, in children with the short *5-HTTLPR* allele, maternal prenatal and postnatal anxiety predicts infant negative emotionality/irritability (Ivorra et al., 2010; Pluess et al., 2011); family social support predicts behavioral inhibition and shyness (Fox et al., 2005); and insecure parent–child attachment predicts poor self-regulation (Kochanska, Philibert, & Barry, 2009), stranger approach, and negative emotionality (Pauli-Pott, Friedel, Hinney, & Hebebrand, 2009). In contrast, temperament was not related to these environmental variations for children with two long *5-HTTLPR* alleles. Other research found an interaction between *DRD4 VNTR* polymorphism and parenting on early childhood temperament, in which sensation seeking was negatively associated with parenting quality only for children who had the 7-repeat allele (Sheese, Voelker, Rothbart, & Posner, 2007). Similarly, the effect of childhood environment (e.g., parental socioeconomic status and parenting) on harm avoidance in adulthood has been shown to be moderated by the tryptophan hydroxylase 1 (*THP1*) gene (Keltikangas-Järvinen et al., 2007) and the serotonin receptor 2A (*HTR2A*) gene (Jokela, Lehtimaki, & Keltikangas-Järvinen, 2007). Again, these results should be viewed cautiously, as replication is needed; however, they highlight the potential of G × E research in identifying individuals at genetic and environmental risk for developing less adaptive temperaments and could inform strategies for prevention and intervention.

Conclusion

In the past 20 years, an abundance of behavioral genetics research has indicated that genetic factors play a role in individual differences in temperament. This, however, is just the beginning of the story. Current behavioral genetic studies rarely focus on simple heritability estimates because whether or not a given temperament is heritable is no longer the interesting question. Most temperament dimensions are heritable, but recent research suggests that the issue of genetic influences on temperament is much more complex, and the story of genetic influences on temperament is much more interesting. The genetic factors that influence temperament may differ across age, measures, and situations. Moreover, environmental experiences may moderate genetic influences on temperament, and genes may moderate the impact of environments on temperament. As illustrated in the next four chapters, these complexities have implications for research exploring links between temperament and developmental outcomes and for research that seeks to identify specific genes that influence temperament. As molecular genetics studies of temperament become more common, the relevance of quantitative genetic studies is often questioned. However, as the research reviewed here indicates, quantitative genetics research plays an important role in informing molecular genetics studies of temperament. A key issue in both quantitative and molecular genetics research is the precise definition and measurement of temperament.

Further Reading

Eley, T. C., & Craig, I. W. (2005). Introductory guide to the language of molecular genetics. *Journal of Child Psychology and Psychiatry*, 46(10), 1039–1041.

Eley, T. C., & Rijsdijk, F. H. (2005). Introductory guide to the statistics of molecular genetics. *Journal of Child Psychology and Psychiatry*, 46(10), 1042–1044.

Goldsmith, H. H., Lemery, K. S., Essex, M. J., & DiLalla, L. F. (2004). Temperament as a liability factor for childhood behavioral disorders: The concept of liability. In L. F. DiLalla (Ed.), *Behavior genetics principles: Perspectives in development, personality, and psychopathology* (pp. 19–39). Washington, DC: American Psychological Association.

Plomin, R., DeFries, J. C., McClearn, G. E., & McGuffin, P. (2008). *Behavioral genetics* (5th ed.). New York: Worth.

Saudino, K. J. (2003). Parent ratings of infant temperament lessons from twin studies. *Infant Behavior and Development*, 26, 100–107.

References

Ando, J., Suzuki, A., Yamagata, S., Kijima, N., Maekawa, H., Ono, Y., et al. (2004). Genetic and environmental structure of Cloninger's temperament and character dimensions. *Journal of Personality Disorders*, 18(4), 379–393.

Aoki, J., Ikeda, K., Murayama, O., Yoshihara, E., Ogai, Y., & Iwahashi, K. (2010). The association between personality, pain threshold and a single nucleotide polymorphism (rs3813034) in the 3′-untranslated region of the serotonin transporter gene (SLC6A4). *Journal of Clinical Neuroscience*, 17(5), 574–578.

Arbelle, S., Benjamin, J., Golin, M., Kremer, I., Belmaker, R. H., & Ebstein, R. P. (2003). Relation of shyness in grade school children to the genotype for the long form of the serotonin promoter region polymorphism. *American Journal of Psychiatry*, 160(4), 671–676.

Arias, B., Aguilera, M., Moya, J., Saiz, P. A., Villa, H., Ibanez, M. I., et al. (2012). The role of genetic variability in the SLC6A4, BDNF and GABRA6 genes in anxiety-related traits. *Acta Psychiatrica Scandinavica*, 125, 194–202.

Asbury, K., Dunn, J., Pike, A., & Plomin, R. (2003). Nonshared environmental influences on individual differences in early behavioral development: A monozygotic twin differences study. *Child Development*, 74(3), 933–943.

Asbury, K., Dunn, J., & Plomin, R. (2006). Birthweight-discordance and differences in early parenting relate to monozygotic twin differences in behaviour problems and academic achievement at age 7. *Developmental Science*, 9(2), F22–F31.

Asendorpf, J. B., & Baudonnière, P.-M. (1993). Self-awareness and other-awareness: Mirror self-recognition and synchronic imitation among unfamiliar peers. *Developmental Psychology*, 29(1), 88–95.

Asendorpf, J. B., Warkentin, V., & Baudonnière, P.-M. (1996). Self-awareness and other-awareness: II. Mirror self-recognition, social contingency awareness, and synchronic imitation. *Developmental Psychology*, 32(2), 313–321.

Attia, J., Ioannidis, J. P. A., Thakkinstian, A., McEvoy, M., Scott, R. J., Minelli, C., et al. (2009). How to use an article about genetic association: A: Background concepts. *Journal of the American Medical Association*, 301(1), 74–81.

Auerbach, J. G., Benjamin, J., Faroy, M., Geller, V., & Ebstein, R. (2001). DRD4 related to infant attention and information processing: A developmental link to ADHD? *Psychiatric Genetics*, 11, 31–35.

Auerbach, J. G., Faroy, M., Ebstein, R., Kahana, M., & Levine, J. (2001). The association of the dopamine D4 receptor gene (DRD4) and the serotonin transporter promoter gene (5-HTTLPR) with temperament in 12-month-old infants. *Journal of Child Psychology and Psychiatry*, 42, 777–783.

Auerbach, J. G., Geller, V., Lezer, S., Shinwell, E., Belmaker, R. H., Levine, J., et al. (1999). Dopamine D4 receptor (D4DR) and serotonin transporter promoter (5-HTTLPR) polymorphisms in the determination of temperament in 2-month-old infants. *Molecular Psychiatry*, 4, 369–373.

Banaschewski, T., Becker, K., Scherag, S., Franke, B., & Coghill, D. (2010). Molecular genetics of attention-deficit/hyperactivity disorder: An overview. *European Child and Adolescent Psychiatry*, 19(3), 237–257.

Battaglia, M., Ogliari, A., Zanoni, A., Citterio, A., Pozzoli, U., Giorda, R., et al. (2005). Influence of the serotonin transporter promoter gene and shyness on children's cerebral responses to facial expressions. *Archives of General Psychiatry*, 62(1), 85–94.

Becker, K., Laucht, M., El-Faddagh, M., & Schmidt, M. H. (2005). The dopamine D4 receptor gene exon III polymorphism is associated with novelty seeking in 15-year-old males from a high-risk community sample. *Journal of Neural Transmission, 112*(6), 847–858.

Boivin, M., Pérusse, D., Dionne, G., Saysset, V., Zoccolillo, M., Tarabulsy, G. M., et al. (2005). The genetic–environmental etiology of parents' perceptions and self-assessed behaviours toward their 5-month-old infants in a large twin and singleton sample. *Journal of Child Psychology and Psychiatry, 46*(6), 612–630.

Braungart, J. M. (1994). Genetic influences on "environmental" measures. In J. C. DeFries, R. Plomin, & D. W. Fulker (Eds.), *Nature and nurture during middle childhood* (pp. 233–248). Cambridge, MA: Blackwell.

Braungart, J. M., Plomin, R., DeFries, J. C., & Fulker, D. (1992). Genetic influences on tester-rated infant temperament as assessed by Bayley's Infant Behavior Record: Nonadoptive and adoptive siblings and twins. *Developmental Psychology, 28*, 40–47.

Buckholtz, J. W., Treadway, M. T., Cowan, R. L., Woodward, N. D., Li, R., Ansari, M. S., et al. (2010). Dopaminergic network differences in human impulsivity. *Science, 329*, 532.

Buss, A. H., Plomin, R., & Willerman, L. (1973). The inheritance of temperaments. *Journal of Personality, 41*, 513–524.

Carver, C. S., & Miller, C. J. (2006). Relations of serotonin function to personality: Current views and a key methodological issue. *Psychiatry Research, 144*(1), 1–15.

Cherny, S. S., Fulker, D. W., Corley, R. P., Plomin, R., & DeFries, J. C. (1994). Continuity and change in infant shyness from 14 to 20 months. *Behavior Genetics, 24*, 365–379.

Cherny, S. S., Saudino, K. J., Fulker, D. W., Plomin, R., Corley, R. P., & DeFries, J. C. (2001). The development of observed shyness from 14 to 20 months: Shyness in context. In R. N. Emde & J. K. Hewitt (Eds.), *Infancy to early childhood: Genetic and environmental influences on developmental change* (pp. 269–282). New York: Oxford University Press.

Cloninger, C. R. (1987). A systematic method of clinical description and classification of personality variants. *Archives of General Psychiatry, 44*, 573–588.

Cohen, D. J., Dibble, E., & Grawe, J. M. (1977). Fathers' and mothers' perceptions of children's personality. *Archives of General Psychiatry, 34*, 480–487.

Cyphers, L. H., Phillips, K., Fulker, D. W., & Mrazek, D. A. (1990). Twin temperament during the transition from infancy to early childhood. *Journal of the American Academy of Child and Adolescent Psychiatry, 29*, 392–397.

Daniels, D. (1986). Differential experiences of siblings in the same family as predictors of adolescent sibling personality differences. *Journal of Personality and Social Psychology, 51*, 339–346.

Deater-Deckard, K. (2000). Parenting and child behavioral adjustment in early childhood: A quantitative genetic approach to studying family processes. *Child Development, 71*(2), 468–484.

Deater-Deckard, K., Petrill, S. A., & Thompson, L. A. (2007a). Anger/frustration, task persistence, and conduct problems in childhood: A behavioral genetic analysis. *Journal of Child Psychology and Psychiatry, 48*(1), 80–87.

Deater-Deckard, K., Petrill, S. A., & Thompson, L. A. (2007b, April). *Nonshared environmental influences on temperament in middle childhood.* Paper presented at the annual meeting of the Society for Research in Child Development, Boston.

De Luca, A., Rizzardi, M., Buccino, A., Alessandroni, R., Salvioli, G., Filograsso, N., et al. (2003). Association of dopamine D4 receptor (DRD4) exon III repeat polymorphism with temperament in 3-year-old infants. *Neurogenetics, 4*(4), 207–212.

De Luca, A., Rizzardi, M., Torrente, T., Alessandroni, R., Salvioli, G. P., & Filograsso, N. (2001). Dopamine D4 receptor (DRD4) polymorphism and adaptability trait during infancy: A longitudinal study in 1- to 5-month-old neonates. *Neurogenetics, 3*, 79–82.

Drabant, E. M., Hariri, A. R., Meyer-Lindenberg, A., Munoz, K. E., Mattay, V. S., Kolachana, B. S., et al. (2006). Catechol-O-methyltransferase val-158met genotype and neural mechanisms related to affective arousal and regulation. *Archives of General Psychiatry, 63*(12), 1396–1406.

Dragan, W. L., & Oniszczenko, W. (2005). Polymorphisms in the serotonin transporter gene and their relationship to two temperamental traits measured by the Formal Characteristics of Behavior–Temperament Inventory: Activity and emotional reactivity. *Neuropsychobiology, 51*(4), 269–274.

Dragan, W. L., & Oniszczenko, W. (2006). Association of a functional polymorphism in the serotonin transporter gene with personality traits in females in a Polish population. *Neuropsychobiology, 54*(1), 45–50.

Ebstein, R. P., Levine, J., Geller, V., Auerbach, J. G., Gritsenko, I., & Belmaker, R. H. (1998). Dopamine D4 receptor and serotonin transporter promoter in the determination of neonatal temperament. *Molecular Psychiatry, 3*, 238–246.

Ebstein, R. P., Segman, R., Benjamin, J., Osher, Y., Nemanov, L., & Belmaker, R. H. (1997). 5-HT2C (HTR2C) serotonin receptor gene polymorphism associated with the human personality trait of reward dependence: interaction with dopamine D4 receptor (D4DR) and dopamine D3 receptor (D3DR) polymorphisms. *American Journal of Medical Genetics, 74*(1), 65–72.

Edwards, J. H. (1991). The formal problems of linkage. In P. McGuffin & M. Murray (Eds.), *The new genetics of mental illness* (pp. 58–70). London: Butterworth-Heinemann.

Ekelund, J., Lichtermann, D., Jarvelin, M. R., & Peltonen, L. (1999). Association between novelty seeking and the type 4 dopamine receptor gene in a large Finnish cohort sample. *American Journal of Psychiatry, 156*(9), 1453–1455.

Forget-Dubois, N., Boivin, M., Dionne, G., Pierce, T., Tremblay, R. E., & Pérusse, D. (2007). A longitudinal twin study of the genetic and environmental etiology of maternal hostile-reactive behavior during infancy and toddlerhood. *Infant Behavior and Development, 30*(3), 453–465.

Fox, N. A., Nichols, K. E., Henderson, H. A., Rubin, K., Schmidt, L., Hamer, D., et al. (2005). Evidence for a gene–environment interaction in predicting behavioral inhibition in middle childhood. *Psychological Science, 16*(12), 921–926.

Gade-Andavolu, R., Macmurray, J., Comings, D. E., Calati, R., Chiesa, A., & Serretti, A. (2009). Association between the estrogen receptor TA polymorphism and harm avoidance. *Neuroscience Letters, 467*(2), 155–158.

Gagne, J. R., & Saudino, K. J. (2010). Wait for it!: A twin study of inhibitory control in early childhood. *Behavior Genetics, 40*, 327–337.

Gagne, J. R., Saudino, K. J., & Asherson, P. (2011). The genetic etiology of inhibitory control and behavior problems at 24 months of age. *Journal of Child Psychology and Psychiatry, 52*, 1155–1163.

Gagne, J. R., Saudino, K. J., & Cherny, S. S. (2003). Genetic influences on temperament in early adolescence: A multimethod perspective. In S. A. Petrill, R. Plomin, J. C. DeFries, & J. K. Hewitt (Eds.), *Nature nurture, and the transition to early adolescence* (pp. 166–184). Oxford, UK: Oxford University Press.

Ganiban, J. M., & Saudino, K. J. (2009, April). *Interplay between negative emotionality and parenting during early childhood: reciprocal influences and effects.* Paper presented at the annual meeting of the Society for Research in Child Development, Denver, CO.

Ganiban, J. M., Saudino, K. J., Ulbricht, J., Neiderhiser, J. M., & Reiss, D. (2008). Continuity and change in temperament during adolescence. *Journal of Personality and Social Psychology, 95*, 222–236.

Ganiban, J. M., Ulbricht, J., Saudino, K. J., Neiderhiser, J., Hauptman, D., & Reiss, D. (2011). Understanding child-based effects on parenting: Temperament as a moderator of genetic and environmental contributions to parenting. *Developmental Psychology, 47*, 676–692.

Garpenstrand, H., Norton, N., Damberg, M., Rylander, G., Forslund, K., Mattila-Evenden, M., et al. (2002). A regulatory monoamine oxidase a promoter polymorphism and personality traits. *Neuropsychobiology, 46*(4), 190–193.

Gebhardt, C., Leisch, F., Schussler, P., Fuchs, K., Stompe, T., Sieghart, W., et al. (2000). Non-association of dopamine D4 and D2 receptor genes with personality in healthy individuals. *Psychiatric Genetics, 10*(3), 131–137.

Gjone, H., & Stevenson, J. (1997). A longitudinal twin study of temperament and behaviour problems: Common genetic or environmental influences? *Journal of the American Academy of Child and Adolescent Psychiatry, 36*, 1448–1456.

Glickstein, S. B., & Schmauss, C. (2001). Dopamine receptor functions: Lessons from knockout mice. *Pharmacological Therapy, 91*(1), 63–83.

Goldsmith, H. H., Buss, K. A., & Lemery, K. S. (1997). Toddler and childhood temperament: Expended content, stronger genetic evidence, new evidence for the importance of environment. *Developmental Psychology, 33*, 891–905.

Goldsmith, H. H., Buss, K. A., Plomin, R., Rothbart, M. K., Thomas, A., Chess, S., et al. (1987). Roundtable: What is temperament? Four approaches. *Child Development, 58*, 505–529.

Goldsmith, H. H., & Campos, J. J. (1986). Fundamental issues in the study of early temperament: The Denver Twin Temperament Study. In M. E. Lamb, A. L. Brown, & B. Rogoff (Eds.), *Advances in developmental psychology* (Vol. 4, pp. 231–283). Hillsdale, NJ: Erlbaum.

Goldsmith, H. H., & Gottesman, I. I. (1981). Origins of variation in behavioral style: A longitudinal study of temperament in young twins. *Child Development, 52*, 91–103.

Goldsmith, H. H., & Lemery, K. S. (2000). Linking temperamental fearfulness and anxiety symptoms: A behavior-genetic perspective. *Biological Psychiatry, 48*, 1199–1209.

Goldsmith, H. H., Lemery, K. S., Buss, K. A., & Campos, J. J. (1999). Genetic analyses of focal aspects of infant temperament. *Developmental Psychology, 35*, 972–985.

Goldsmith, H. H., Reilly, H. H., Lemery, K. S., Longley, S., & Prescott, A. (1994). *Manual for the Preschool Laboratory Temperament Assessment Battery.* Unpublished manual.

Gonda, X., Fountoulakis, K. N., Juhasz, G., Rihmer, Z., Lazary, J., Laszik, A., et al. (2009). Association of the s allele of the 5-HTTLPR with neuroticism-related traits and temperaments in a psychiatrically healthy population. *European Archives of Psychiatry and Clinical Neuroscience, 259*(2), 106–113.

Gottesman, I. I., & Gould, T. D. (2003). The endophenotype concept in psychiatry: Etymology and strategic intentions. *American Journal of Psychiatry, 160*(4), 636–645.

Hakamata, Y., Takahashi, N., Ishihara, R., Saito, S., Ozaki, N., Honjo, S., et al. (2005). No association between monoamine oxidase A promoter polymorphism and personality traits in Japanese females. *Neuroscience Letters*, *389*(3), 121–123.

Ham, B. J., Choi, M. J., Lee, H. J., Kang, R. H., & Lee, M. S. (2005). Reward dependence is related to norepinephrine transporter T-182C gene polymorphism in a Korean population. *Psychiatric Genetics*, *15*(2), 145–147.

Ham, B. J., Kim, Y. H., Choi, M. J., Cha, J. H., Choi, Y. K., & Lee, M. S. (2004). Serotonergic genes and personality traits in the Korean population. *Neuroscience Letters*, *354*(1), 2–5.

Hamer, D. H., Greenberg, B. D., Sabol, S. Z., & Murphy, D. L. (1999). Role of the serotonin transporter gene in temperament and character. *Journal of Personality Disorders*, *13*(4), 312–327.

Hashimoto, R., Noguchi, H., Hori, H., Ohi, K., Yasuda, Y., Takeda, M., et al. (2007). A possible association between the Val158Met polymorphism of the catechol-O-methyl transferase gene and the personality trait of harm avoidance in Japanese healthy subjects. *Neuroscience Letters*, *428*(1), 17–20.

Hayden, E. P., Dougherty, L. R., Maloney, B., Durbin, C. E., Olino, T. M., Nurnberger, J. I., Jr., et al. (2007). Temperamental fearfulness in childhood and the serotonin transporter promoter region polymorphism: A multimethod association study. *Psychiatric Genetics*, *17*(3), 135–142.

Hayden, E. P., Klein, D. N., Sheikh, H. I., Olino, T. M., Dougherty, L. R., Dyson, M. W., et al. (2011). The serotonin transporter promoter polymorphism and childhood positive and negative emotionality. *Emotion*, *10*(5), 696–702.

Heiman, N., Stallings, M. C., Hofer, S. M., & Hewitt, J. K. (2003). Investigating age differences in the genetic and environmental structure of the tridimensional personality questionnaire in later adulthood. *Behavior Genetics*, *33*(2), 171–180.

Heiman, N., Stallings, M. C., Young, S. E., & Hewitt, J. K. (2004). Investigating the genetic and environmental structure of Cloninger's personality dimensions in adolescence. *Twin Research*, *7*(5), 462–470.

Herbst, J. H., Zonderman, A. B., McCrae, R. R., & Costa, P. T., Jr. (2000). Do the dimensions of the temperament and character inventory map a simple genetic architecture?: Evidence from molecular genetics and factor analysis. *American Journal of Psychiatry*, *157*(8), 1285–1290.

Holmboe, K., Nemoda, Z., Fearon, R. M., Sasvari-Szekely, M., & Johnson, M. H. (2011). Dopamine D4 receptor and serotonin transporter gene effects on the longitudinal development of infant temperament. *Genes, Brain and Behavior*, *10*(5), 513–522.

Hur, Y.-M. (2009). Genetic and environmental contributions to childhood temperament in South Korean twins. *Twin Research and Human Genetics*, *12*(6), 549–551.

Ilott, N., Saudino, K. J., Wood, A., & Asherson, P. (2010). A genetic study of ADHD and activity level in infancy. *Genes, Brain and Behavior*, *9*, 296–304.

Inoue, H., Yamasue, H., Tochigi, M., Takei, K., Suga, M., Abe, O., et al. (2010). Effect of tryptophan hydroxylase-2 gene variants on amygdalar and hippocampal volumes. *Brain Research*, *1331*, 51–57.

Isen, J. D., Baker, L. A., Raine, A., & Bezdjian, S. (2009). Genetic and environmental influences on the Junior Temperament and Character Inventory in a preadolescent twin sample. *Behavior Genetics*, *39*(1), 36–47.

Ishii, G., Suzuki, A., Oshino, S., Shiraishi, H., & Otani, K. (2007). CYP2C19 polymorphism affects personality traits of Japanese females. *Neuroscience Letters*, *411*(1), 77–80.

Itoh, K., Hashimoto, K., Kumakiri, C., Shimizu, E., & Iyo, M. (2004). Association between brain-derived neurotrophic factor 196 G/A polymorphism and personality traits in healthy subjects. *American Journal of Medical Genetics B: Neuropsychiatric Genetics*, *124*(1), 61–63.

Ivorra, J. L., D'Souza, U. M., Jover, M., Arranz, M. J., Williams, B. P., Henry, S. E., et al. (2011). Association between neonatal temperament, SLC6A4, DRD4 and a functional polymorphism located in TFAP2B. *Genes, Brain and Behavior*, *10*(5), 570–578.

Ivorra, J. L., Sanjuan, J., Jover, M., Carot, J. M., Frutos, R., & Molto, M. D. (2010). Gene–environment interaction of child temperament. *Journal of Developmental and Behavioral Pediatrics*, *31*(7), 545–554.

Jaber, M., Robinson, S. W., Missale, C., & Caron, M. G. (1996). Dopamine receptors and brain function. *Neuropharmacology*, *35*(11), 1503–1520.

Jokela, M., Lehtimaki, T., & Keltikangas-Järvinen, L. (2007). The serotonin receptor 2A gene moderates the influence of parental socioeconomic status on adulthood harm avoidance. *Behavior Genetics*, *37*(4), 567–574.

Joo, Y. H., Oh, H. B., Kim, B., Jung, S. H., Chung, J. K., Hong, J. P., et al. (2007). No association between 5-HTTLPR and harm avoidance in Korean college students. *Journal of Korean Medical Science*, *22*(1), 138–141.

Jorm, A. F., Prior, M., Sanson, A., Smart, D., Zhang, Y., & Easteal, S. (2000). Association of a functional polymorphism of the serotonin transporter gene with anxiety-related temperament and behavior problems in children: A longitudinal study from infancy to the mid-teens. *Molecular Psychiatry*, *5*, 542–547.

Jorm, A. F., Prior, M., Sanson, A., Smart, D., Zhang, Y., & Easteal, S. (2003). Apolipoprotein

E genotype and temperament: A longitudinal study from infancy to the late teens. *Psychosomatic Medicine, 65*(4), 662–664.

Jorm, A. F., Prior, M., Sanson, A., Smart, D., Zhang, Y., Tan, S., et al. (2002). Lack of association of a single-nucleotide polymorphism of the mu-opioid receptor gene with anxiety-related traits: Results from a cross-sectional study of adults and a longitudinal study of children. *American Journal of Medical Genetics, 114*(6), 659–664.

Kamata, M., Suzuki, A., Matsumoto, Y., Shibuya, N., Togashi, H., Goto, K., et al. (2009). Association study between the -1021C/T polymorphism of the dopamine-beta-hydroxylase gene promoter and personality traits in healthy subjects. *Neuroscience Letters, 462*(1), 54–57.

Kazantseva, A., Gaysina, D., Malykh, S., & Khusnutdinova, E. (2011). The role of dopamine transporter (SLC6A3) and dopamine D2 receptor/ankyrin repeat and kinase domain containing 1 (DRD2/ANKK1) gene polymorphisms in personality traits. *Progress in Neuropsychopharmacology and Biological Psychiatry, 35*(4), 1033–1040.

Kazantseva, A. V., Gaysina, D. A., Faskhutdinova, G. G., Noskova, T., Malykh, S. B., & Khusnutdinova, E. K. (2008). Polymorphisms of the serotonin transporter gene (5-HTTLPR, A/G SNP in 5-HTTLPR, and STin2 VNTR) and their relation to personality traits in healthy individuals from Russia. *Psychiatric Genetics, 18*(4), 167–176.

Keller, M. C., Coventry, W. L., Heath, A. C., & Martin, N. G. (2005). Widespread evidence for non-additive genetic variation in Cloninger's and Eysenck's personality dimensions using a twin plus sibling design. *Behavior Genetics, 35*(6), 707–721.

Keltikangas-Järvinen, L., Elovainio, M., Kivimäki, M., Lichtermann, D., Ekelund, J., & Peltonen, L. (2003). Association between the type 4 dopamine receptor gene polymorphism and novelty seeking. *Psychosomatic Medicine, 65*(3), 471–476.

Keltikangas-Järvinen, L., Puttonen, S., Kivimäki, M., Elovainio, M., Rontu, R., & Lehtimäki, T. (2007). Tryptophan hydroxylase 1 gene haplotypes modify the effect of a hostile childhood environment on adulthood harm avoidance. *Genes, Brain and Behavior, 6*(4), 305–313.

Keltikangas-Järvinen, L., Puttonen, S., Kivimäki, M., Rontu, R., & Lehtimäki, T. (2006). Cloninger's temperament dimensions and epidermal growth factor A61G polymorphism in Finnish adults. *Genes, Brain, and Behavior, 5*(1), 11–18.

Keltikangas-Järvinen, L., Räikkönen, K., & Lehtimäki, T. (1993). Dependence between apolipoprotein E phenotypes and temperament in children, adolescents, and young adults. *Psychosomatic Medicine, 55*, 155–163.

Kim, S. J., Kim, Y. S., Choi, N. K., Hong, H. J., Lee, H. S., & Kim, C. H. (2005). Serotonin transporter gene polymorphism and personality traits in a Korean population. *Neuropsychobiology, 51*(4), 243–247.

Kim, S. J., Kim, Y. S., Kim, C. H., & Lee, H. S. (2006). Lack of association between polymorphisms of the dopamine receptor D4 and dopamine transporter genes and personality traits in a Korean population. *Yonsei Medical Journal, 47*(6), 787–792.

Kim, S. J., Kim, Y. S., Kim, S. Y., Lee, H. S., & Kim, C. H. (2006). An association study of catechol-O-methyltransferase and monoamine oxidase A polymorphisms and personality traits in Koreans. *Neuroscience Letters, 401*(1–2), 154–158.

Kim, S. J., Kim, Y. S., Lee, H. S., Kim, S. Y., & Kim, C. H. (2006). An interaction between the serotonin transporter promoter region and dopamine transporter polymorphisms contributes to harm avoidance and reward dependence traits in normal healthy subjects. *Journal of Neural Transmission, 113*(7), 877–886.

Kochanska, G., Philibert, R. A., & Barry, R. A. (2009). Interplay of genes and early mother–child relationship in the development of self-regulation from toddler to preschool age. *Journal of Child Psychology and Psychiatry, 50*(11), 1331–1338.

Krueger, R. F., South, S., Johnson, W., & Iacono, W. (2008). The heritability of personality is not always 50%: Gene–environment interactions and correlations between personality and parenting. *Journal of Personality, 76*(6), 1485–1522.

Kühn, K. U., Quednow, B. B., Bagli, M., Meyer, K., Feuchtl, A., Westheide, J., et al. (2002). Allelic variants of the serotonin(2C) receptor and neuroendocrinological responses to the serotonin(2C) receptor agonist m-chlorophenylpiperazine in healthy male volunteers. *Pharmacopsychiatry, 35*(6), 226–230.

Kumakiri, C., Kodama, K., Shimizu, E., Yamanouchi, N., Okada, S., Noda, S., et al. (1999). Study of the association between the serotonin transporter gene regulatory region polymorphism and personality traits in a Japanese population. *Neuroscience Letters, 263*(2–3), 205–207.

Kusumi, I., Suzuki, K., Sasaki, Y., Kameda, K., Sasaki, T., & Koyama, T. (2002). Serotonin 5-HT(2A) receptor gene polymorphism, 5-HT(2A) receptor function and personality traits in healthy subjects: A negative study. *Journal of Affective Disorders, 68*, 235–241.

Lakatos, K., Nemoda, Z., Birkas, E., Ronai, Z., Kovacs, E., Ney, K., et al. (2003). Association of D4 dopamine receptor gene and serotonin transporter promoter polymorphisms with infants' response to novelty. *Molecular Psychiatry, 8*, 90–97.

Lee, B. C., Yang, J. W., Lee, S. H., Kim, S. H., Joe, S. H., Jung, I. K., et al. (2008). An interaction between the norepinephrine transporter and monoamine oxidase A polymorphisms, and novelty-seeking personality traits in Korean females. *Progress in Neuropsychopharmacology and Biological Psychiatry, 32*(1), 238–242.

Lee, H. J., Lee, H. S., Kim, Y. K., Kim, S. H., Kim, L., Lee, M. S., et al. (2003). Allelic variants interaction of dopamine receptor D4 polymorphism correlate with personality traits in young Korean female population. *American Journal of Medical Genetics B: Neuropsychiatric Genetics, 118*(1), 76–80.

Lemery-Chalfant, K., Doelger, L., & Goldsmith, H. H. (2008). Genetic relations between effortful and attentional control and symptoms of psychopathology in middle childhood. *Infant and Child Development, 17*(4), 365–385.

Lytton, H. (1980). *Parent–child interaction: The socialization processes observed in twin and singleton families*. New York: Plenum Press.

Matheny, A. P. (1983). A longitudinal twin study of stability of components from Bayley's Infant Behavior Record. *Child Development, 54*, 356–360.

Matheny, A. P. (1989). Children's behavioral inhibition over age and across situations: Genetic similarity for a trait during change. *Journal of Personality, 57*, 215–235.

Matsumoto, Y., Suzuki, A., Ishii, G., Oshino, S., Otani, K., & Goto, K. (2007). The -181 A/C polymorphism in the excitatory amino acid transporter-2 gene promoter affects the personality trait of reward dependence in healthy subjects. *Neuroscience Letters, 427*(2), 99–102.

Matsumoto, Y., Suzuki, A., Shibuya, N., Oshino, S., Kamata, M., Goto, K., et al. (2008). Association study of the cytochrome P450 17 gene polymorphism with personality traits in healthy subjects. *Behavioural Brain Research, 194*(1), 21–24.

Matsumoto, Y., Suzuki, A., Shibuya, N., Sadahiro, R., Kamata, M., Goto, K., et al. (2009). Effect of the cytochrome P450 19 (aromatase) gene polymorphism on personality traits in healthy subjects. *Behavioural Brain Research, 205*(1), 234–237.

McCartney, K., Harris, M. J., & Bernieri, F. (1990). Growing up and growing apart: A developmental meta-analysis of twin studies. *Psychological Bulletin, 107*, 226–237.

Melke, J., Westberg, L., Nilsson, S., Landen, M., Soderstrom, H., Baghaei, F., et al. (2003). A polymorphism in the serotonin receptor 3A (HTR3A) gene and its association with harm avoidance in women. *Archives of General Psychiatry, 60*(10), 1017–1023.

Minelli, A., Scassellati, C., Bonvicini, C., Perez, J., & Gennarelli, M. (2009). An association of GRIK3 Ser310Ala functional polymorphism with personality traits. *Neuropsychobiology, 59*(1), 28–33.

Minelli, A., Zanardini, R., Bonvicini, C., Sartori, R., Pedrini, L., Gennarelli, M., et al. (2011). BDNF serum levels, but not BDNF Val66Met genotype, are correlated with personality traits in healthy subjects. *European Archives of Psychiatry and Clinical Neuroscience, 261*(5), 323–329.

Mitsuyasu, H., Hirata, N., Sakai, Y., Shibata, H., Takeda, Y., Ninomiya, H., et al. (2001). Association analysis of polymorphisms in the upstream region of the human dopamine D4 receptor gene (DRD4) with schizophrenia and personality traits. *Journal of Human Genetics, 46*(1), 26–31.

Montag, C., Basten, U., Stelzel, C., Fiebach, C. J., & Reuter, M. (2010). The BDNF Val66Met polymorphism and anxiety: Support for animal knock-in-studies from a genetic association study in humans. *Psychiatry Research, 179*, 86–90.

Mullineaux, P. Y., Deater-Deckard, K., Petrill, S. A., & Thompson, L. A. (2009). Parenting and child behaviour problems: A longitudinal analysis of non-shared environment. *Infant and Child Development, 18*, 133–148.

Mullineaux, P. Y., Deater-Deckard, K., Petrill, S. A., Thompson, L. A., & DeThorne, L. S. (2009). Temperament in middle childhood: A behavioral genetic analysis of fathers' and mothers' reports. *Journal of Research in Personality, 43*(5), 737–746.

Nakamura, Y., Ito, Y., Aleksic, B., Kushima, I., Yasui-Furukori, N., Inada, T., et al. (2011). Influence of HTR2A polymorphisms and parental rearing on personality traits in healthy Japanese subjects. *Journal of Human Genetics, 55*(12), 838–841.

Neiderhiser, J. M., Reiss, D., Pedersen, N. L., Lichtenstein, P., Spotts, E. L., & Hansson, K. (2004). Genetic and environmental influences on mothering of adolescents: A comparison of two samples. *Developmental Psychology, 40*, 335–351.

Neiss, M. B., Stevenson, J., Legrand, L. N., Iacono, W. G., & Sedikides, C. (2009). Self-esteem, negative emotionality, and depression as a common temperamental core: A study of mid-adolescent twin girls. *Journal of Personality, 77*, 327–346.

Noble, E. P., Ozkaragoz, T. Z., Ritchie, T. L., Zhang, X., Belin, T. R., & Sparkes, R. S. (1998). D2 and D4 dopamine receptor polymorphisms and personality. *American Journal of Medical Genetics, 81*(3), 257–267.

Nyman, E. S., Loukola, A., Varilo, T., Ekelund, J., Veijola, J., Joukamaa, M., et al. (2009). Impact of the dopamine receptor gene family on temperament traits in a population-based birth cohort. *American Journal of Medical Genetics B: Neuropsychiatric Genetics, 150*(6), 854–865.

Okuyama, Y., Ishiguro, H., Nankai, M., Shibuya, H., Watanabe, A., & Arinami, T. (2000). Identification of a polymorphism in the promoter region of DRD4 associated with the human novelty seeking personality trait. *Molecular Psychiatry, 5*(1), 64–69.

Oniszczenko, W., & Dragan, W. L. (2005). Association between dopamine D4 receptor exon III polymorphism and emotional reactivity as a temperamental trait. *Twin Research and Human Genetics, 8*(6), 633–637.

Ono, Y., Manki, H., Yoshimura, K., Muramatsu, T., Mizushima, H., Higuchi, S., et al. (1997). Association between dopamine D4 receptor (D4DR) exon III polymorphism and novelty seeking in Japanese subjects. *American Journal of Medical Genetics, 74*(5), 501–503.

Pauli-Pott, U., Friedel, S., Hinney, A., & Hebebrand, J. (2009). Serotonin transporter gene polymorphism (5-HTTLPR), environmental conditions, and developing negative emotionality and fear in early childhood. *Journal of Neural Transmission, 116*(4), 503–512.

Peirson, A. R., Heuchert, J. W., Thomala, L., Berk, M., Plein, H., & Cloninger, C. R. (1999). Relationship between serotonin and the Temperament and Character Inventory. *Psychiatry Research, 89*(1), 29–37.

Philips, K., & Matheny, A. P. (1997). Evidence for genetic influence on both cross-situation and situation-specific components of behavior. *Journal of Personality and Social Psychology, 73,* 129–138.

Plomin, R. (1990). *Nature and nurture: An introduction to human behavioral genetics.* Belmont, CA: Brooks/Cole.

Plomin, R. (1994). *Genetics and experience: The developmental interplay between nature and nurture.* Thousand Oaks, CA: Sage.

Plomin, R., Chipuer, H. M., & Neiderhiser, J. M. (1994). Behavioral genetic evidence for the importance of nonshared environment. In E. M. Hetherington, D. Reiss, & R. Plomin (Eds.), *Separate social worlds of siblings: Importance of nonshared environment on development* (pp. 1–31). Hillsdale, NJ: Erlbaum.

Plomin, R., & DeFries, J. C. (1985). *Origins of individual differences in infancy: The Colorado Adoption Project.* Toronto: Academic Press.

Plomin, R., DeFries, J. C., & Loehlin, J. C. (1977). Genotype–environment interaction and correlation in the analysis of human behavior. *Psychological Bulletin, 84,* 309–322.

Plomin, R., DeFries, J. C., McClearn, G. E., & McGuffin, P. (2008). *Behavioral genetics* (5th ed.). New York: Worth.

Plomin, R., Emde, R. N., Braungart, J. M., Campos, J., Corley, R., & Fulker, D. W. (1993). Genetic change and continuity from 14 to 20 months: The MacArthur Longitudinal Twin Study. *Child Development, 64,* 1354–1376.

Plomin, R., & Nesselroade, J. R. (1990). Behavioural genetics and personality changes. *Journal of Personality, 58,* 191–220.

Plomin, R., Owen, M. J., & McGuffin, P. (1994). The genetic basis of complex human behaviors. *Science, 264,* 1733–1739.

Plomin, R., & Saudino, K. J. (1994). Quantitative genetics and molecular genetics. In J. E. Bates & T. D. Wachs (Eds.), *Temperament: Individual differences at the interface of biology and behavior* (pp. 143–171). Washington, DC: American Psychological Association.

Pluess, M., Velders, F. P., Belsky, J., van IJzendoorn, M. H., Bakermans-Kranenburg, M. J., Jaddoe, V. W. V., et al. (2011). Serotonin transporter polymorphism moderates effects of prenatal maternal anxiety on infant negative emotionality. *Biological Psychiatry, 69*(6), 520–525.

Reiner, I., & Spangler, G. (2011). Dopamine D4 receptor exon III polymorphism, adverse life events and personality traits in a nonclinical German adult sample. *Neuropsychobiology, 63*(1), 52–58.

Reuter, M., Kuepper, Y., & Hennig, J. (2007). Association between a polymorphism in the promoter region of the TPH2 gene and the personality trait of harm avoidance. *International Journal of Neuropsychopharmacology, 10*(3), 401–404.

Rhee, S. H., Cosgrove, V. E., Schmitz, S., Haberstick, B. C., Corley, R., & Hewitt, J. K. (2007). Early childhood temperament and the covariation between internalizing and externalizing behavior in school-aged children. *Twin Research and Human Genetics, 10,* 33–44.

Rhee, S. H., & Waldman, I. D. (2002). Genetic and environmental influences on antisocial behavior: A meta-analysis of twin and adoption studies. *Psychological Bulletin, 128,* 490–529.

Riese, M. L. (1990). Neonatal temperament in monozygotic and dizygotic twin pairs. *Child Development, 61,* 1230–1237.

Rietveld, M. J. H., Hudziak, J. J., Bartels, M., van Beijsterveldt, C. E. M., & Boomsma, D. I. (2004). Heritability of attention problems in children: Longitudinal results from a study of twins, age 3 to 12. *Journal of Child Psychology and Psychiatry, 45*(3), 577–588.

Robinson, J. L., Kagan, J., Reznick, J. S., & Corley, R. (1992). The heritability of inhibited and unihibited behavior: A twin study. *Developmental Psychology, 28,* 1030–1037.

Roisman, G. I., & Fraley, R. C. (2006). The limits of genetic influence: A behavior–genetic analysis of infant–caregiver relationship quality and temperament. *Child Development, 77*(6), 1656–1667.

Ronai, Z., Szantai, E., Szmola, R., Nemoda, Z., Szekely, A., Gervai, J., et al. (2004). A novel A/G SNP in the -615th position of the dopamine D4 receptor promoter region as a source of misgenotyping of the -616 C/G SNP. *American Journal of Medical Genetics B: Neuropsychiatric Genetics, 126*(1), 74–78.

Rueda, M. R., Rothbart, M. K., McCandliss, B. D., Saccomanno, L., & Posner, M. I. (2005). Training, maturation, and genetic influences on the development of executive attention. *Proceedings of the National Academy of Sciences, 102*(41), 14931–14936.

Sadahiro, R., Suzuki, A., Matsumoto, Y., Shibuya, N., Enokido, M., Kamata, M., et al. (2011). Functional polymorphism of the GTP cyclohydrolase 1 gene affects the personality trait of novelty seeking in healthy subjects. *Neuroscience Letters, 503*(3), 220–223.

Sadahiro, R., Suzuki, A., Shibuya, N., Kamata, M., Matsumoto, Y., Goto, K., et al. (2010). Association study between a functional polymorphism of tyrosine hydroxylase gene promoter and personality traits in healthy subjects. *Behavioural Brain Research, 208*(1), 209–212.

Saiz, P. A., Garcia-Portilla, M. P., Herrero, R., Arango, C., Corcoran, P., Morales, B., et al. (2010). Interactions between functional serotonergic polymorphisms and demographic factors influence personality traits in healthy Spanish Caucasians. *Psychiatric Genetics, 20*(4), 171–178.

Salo, J., Pulkki-Raback, L., Hintsanen, M., Lehtimaki, T., & Keltikangas-Järvinen, L. (2010). The interaction between serotonin receptor 2A and catechol-O-methyltransferase gene polymorphisms is associated with the novelty-seeking subscale impulsiveness. *Psychiatric Genetics, 20*(6), 273–281.

Samochowiec, J., Rybakowski, F., Czerski, P., Zakrzewska, M., Stepien, G., Pelka-Wysiecka, J., et al. (2001). Polymorphisms in the dopamine, serotonin, and norepinephrine transporter genes and their relationship to temperamental dimensions measured by the Temperament and Character Inventory in healthy volunteers. *Neuropsychobiology, 43*(4), 248–253.

Samochowiec, J., Syrek, S., Michal, P., Ryzewska-Wodecka, A., Samochowiec, A., Horodnicki, J., et al. (2004). Polymorphisms in the serotonin transporter and monoamine oxidase A genes and their relationship to personality traits measured by the Temperament and Character Inventory and NEO Five-Factor Inventory in healthy volunteers. *Neuropsychobiology, 50*(2), 174–181.

Saudino, K. J. (2009a). The development of temperament from a behavioral genetics perspective. In P. Bauer (Ed.), *Advances in child development and behavior* (Vol. 37, pp. 203–233). Cambridge, UK: Elsevier.

Saudino, K. J. (2009b). Do different measures tap the same genetic influences?: A multi-method study of activity level in young twins. *Developmental Science, 12*, 626–633.

Saudino, K. J. (2012). Sources of continuity and change in activity level in early childhood. *Child Development, 83*, 266–281.

Saudino, K. J., Carter, A. S., Purper-Ouakil, D., & Gorwood, P. (2008). The etiology of behavioral problems and competences in very young twins. *Journal of Abnormal Psychology, 117*, 48–62.

Saudino, K. J., & Cherny, S. S. (2001a). Parent ratings of temperament in twins. In R. N. Emde & J. K. Hewitt (Eds.), *The transition from infancy to early childhood: Genetic and environmental influences in the MacArthur Longitudinal Twin Study* (pp. 73–88). New York: Oxford University Press.

Saudino, K. J., & Cherny, S. S. (2001b). Sources of continuity and change in observed temperament. In R. N. Emde & J. K. Hewitt (Eds.), *The transition from infancy to early childhood: Genetic and environmental influences in the MacArthur Longitudinal Twin Study* (pp. 89–110). New York: Oxford University Press.

Saudino, K. J., & Eaton, W. O. (1991). Infant temperament and genetics: An objective twin study of motor activity level. *Child Development, 62*, 1167–1174.

Saudino, K. J., McGuire, S., Reiss, D., Hetherington, E. M., & Plomin, R. (1995). Parent ratings of EAS temperaments in twins, full siblings, half siblings, and step siblings. *Journal of Personality and Social Psychology, 68*, 723–733.

Saudino, K. J., & Plomin, R. (1997). Cognitive and temperamental mediators of genetic contributions to the home environment during infancy. *Merrill–Palmer Quarterly, 43*, 1–23.

Saudino, K. J., Plomin, R., & DeFries, J. C. (1996). Tester-related temperament at 14, 20, and 24 months: Environmental change and genetic continuity. *British Journal of Developmental Psychology, 14*, 129–144.

Saudino, K. J., Wertz, A. E., Gagne, J. R., & Chawla, S. (2004). Night and day: Are siblings as different in temperament as parents say they are? *Journal of Personality and Social Psychology, 87*, 698–706.

Saudino, K. J., & Zapfe, J. A. (2008). Genetic influences on activity level in early childhood: Do situations matter? *Child Development, 79*, 930–943.

Scarr, S., & McCartney, K. (1983). How people make their own environments: A theory of genotype–environment effects. *Child Development, 54*, 424–435.

Schmidt, L. A., Fox, N. A., Rubin, K. H., Hu, S., & Hammer, D. H. (2002). Molecular genetics of shyness and aggression in preschoolers. *Personality and Individual Differences, 33*, 227–238.

Schmitz, S., Fulker, D. W., Plomin, R., Zahn-Waxler, C., Emde, R. N., & DeFries, J. C. (1999). Temperament and problem behavior during early childhood. *International Journal of Behavioral Development, 23*, 333–355.

Schmitz, S., & Saudino, K. J. (2003). Links between temperament and behavior problems in children. In S. Petrill, R. Plomin, J. C. DeFries, & J. K.

Hewitt (Eds.), *The transition to early adolescence: Nature and nurture* (pp. 185–198). New York: Oxford University Press.

Schmitz, S., Saudino, K. J., Plomin, R., & Fulkner, D. W. (1996). Genetic and environmental influences on temperament in middle childhood: Analyses of teacher and tester ratings. *Child Development, 67,* 409–422.

Schosser, A., Fuchs, K., Scharl, T., Schloegelhofer, M., Kindler, J., Mossaheb, N., et al. (2010). Interaction between serotonin 5-HT2A receptor gene and dopamine transporter (DAT1) gene polymorphisms influences personality trait of persistence in Austrian Caucasians. *World Journal of Biological Psychiatry, 11,* 417–424.

Sheese, B. E., Voelker, P. M., Posner, M. I., & Rothbart, M. K. (2009). Genetic variation influences on the early development of reactive emotions and their regulation by attention. *Cognitive Neuropsychiatry, 14*(4–5), 332–355.

Sheese, B. E., Voelker, P. M., Rothbart, M. K., & Posner, M. I. (2007). Parenting quality interacts with genetic variation in dopamine receptor D4 to influence temperament in early childhood. *Development and Psychopathology, 19*(4), 1039–1046.

Shibuya, N., Suzuki, A., Sadahiro, R., Kamata, M., Matsumoto, Y., Goto, K., et al. (2011). Association study between a functional polymorphism of FK506-binding protein 51 (FKBP5) gene and personality traits in healthy subjects. *Neuroscience Letters, 485*(3), 194–197.

Shimizu, E., Hashimoto, K., Ohgake, S., Koizumi, H., Okamura, N., Koike, K., et al. (2006). Association between angiotensin I-converting enzyme insertion/deletion gene functional polymorphism and novelty seeking personality in healthy females. *Progress in Neuropsychopharmacology and Biological Psychiatry, 30*(1), 99–103.

Shiraishi, H., Suzuki, A., Fukasawa, T., Aoshima, T., Ujiie, Y., Ishii, G., et al. (2006). Monoamine oxidase A gene promoter polymorphism affects novelty seeking and reward dependence in healthy study participants. *Psychiatric Genetics, 16*(2), 55–58.

Silberg, J. L., San Miguel, V. F., Murrelle, E. L., Prom, E., Bates, J. E., Canino, G., et al. (2005). Genetic and environmental influences on temperament in the first year of life: The Puerto Rico Infant Twin Study (PRINTS). *Twin Research and Human Genetics, 8*(4), 328–336.

Smoller, J. W., Paulus, M. P., Fagerness, J. A., Purcell, S., Yamaki, L. H., Hirshfeld-Becker, D., et al. (2008). Influence of RGS2 on anxiety-related temperament, personality, and brain function. *Archives of General Psychiatry, 65*(3), 298–308.

Smoller, J. W., Yamaki, L. H., Fagerness, J. A., Biederman, J., Racette, S., Laird, N. M., et al. (2005). The corticotropin-releasing hormone gene and behavioral inhibition in children at risk for panic disorder. *Biological Psychiatry, 57*(12), 1485–1492.

Sourbrie, P. (1986). Reconciling the role of central serotonin neurons in human and animal behavior. *Behavioral and Brain Sciences, 9,* 319–364.

South, S. C., Krueger, R. F., Johnson, W., & Iacono, W. G. (2008). Adolescent personality moderates genetic and environmental influences on relationships with parents. *Journal of Personality and Social Psychology, 94*(5), 899–912.

Stevenson, J., & Fielding, J. (1985). Ratings of temperament in families of young twins. *British Journal of Developmental Psychology, 3,* 143–152.

Strobel, A., Wehr, A., Michel, A., & Brocke, B. (1999). Association between the dopamine D4 receptor (DRD4) exon III polymorphism and measures of novelty seeking in a German population. *Molecular Psychiatry, 4*(4), 378–384.

Suzuki, A., Matsumoto, Y., Ishii, G., Oshino, S., Goto, K., & Otani, K. (2007). No association between the -3081A/T polymorphism in the norepinephrine transporter gene promoter and personality traits in healthy subjects. *Neuroscience Letters, 425*(3), 192–194.

Suzuki, A., Matsumoto, Y., Oshino, S., Kamata, M., Goto, K., & Otani, K. (2008). Combination of the serotonin transporter and norepinephrine transporter gene promoter polymorphisms might influence harm avoidance and novelty seeking in healthy females. *Neuroscience Letters, 439*(1), 52–55.

Szekely, A., Ronai, Z., Nemoda, Z., Kolmann, G., Gervai, J., & Sasvari-Szekely, M. (2004). Human personality dimensions of persistence and harm avoidance associated with DRD4 and 5-HTTLPR polymorphisms. *American Journal of Medical Genetics B: Neuropsychiatric Genetics, 126*(1), 106–110.

Torgersen, A. M. (1985). Temperamental differences in infants and 6-year-old children: A follow-up study of twins. In J. Strelau, F. H. Farley, & A. Gale (Eds.), *The biological basis of personality and behavior: Theories, measurement techniques, and development* (Vol. 1, pp. 227–239). Washington, DC: Hemisphere.

Tost, H., Kolachana, B., Hakimi, S., Lemaitre, H., Verchinski, B. A., Mattay, V. S., et al. (2010). A common allele in the oxytocin receptor gene (OXTR) impacts prosocial temperament and human hypothalamic–limbic structure and function. *Proceedings of the National Academy of Sciences, 107*(31), 13936–13941.

Tsuchimine, S., Yasui-Furukori, N., Kaneda, A., Saito, M., Nakagami, T., Sato, K., et al. (2008). Association between monoamine oxidase A (MAOA) and personality traits in Japanese individuals. *Progress in Neuropsychopharmacology and Biological Psychiatry, 32*(8), 1932–1935.

Tsuchimine, S., Yasui-Furukori, N., Kaneda, A., Saito, M., Sugawara, N., & Kaneko, S. (2009). Minor genetic variants of the dopamine D4 receptor (DRD4) polymorphism are associated with novelty seeking in healthy Japanese subjects. *Progress in Neuropsychopharmacology and Biological Psychiatry, 33*(7), 1232–1235.

Ulbricht, J. A., & Neiderhiser, J. M. (2009). Genotype–environment correlation and family relationships. In Y.-K. Kim (Ed.), *Handbook of behavior genetics* (pp. 209–221). New York: Springer Science + Business Media.

Van Gestel, S., Forsgren, T., Claes, S., Del-Favero, J., Van Duijn, C. M., Sluijs, S., et al. (2002). Epistatic effect of genes from the dopamine and serotonin systems on the temperament traits of novelty seeking and harm avoidance. *Molecular Psychiatry, 7*(5), 448–450.

Venter, J. C. (2007, September 4). First diploid human genome sequence shows we're surprisingly different. *Science Daily.* Retrieved from *www.sciencedaily.com/releases/2007/09/070904072204.htm.*

Westernberg, H. G., Murphy, D. L., & Den Boer, J. A. (1996). *Advances in the neurobiology of anxiety disorders.* New York: Wiley.

Wood, A. C., & Neale, M. C. (2010). Twin studies and their implications for molecular genetic studies: Endophenotypes integrate quantitative and molecular genetics in ADHD research. *Journal of the American Academy of Child and Adolescent Psychiatry, 49*(9), 874–883.

Wood, A. C., Rijsdijk, F., Saudino, K. J., Asherson, P., & Kuntsi, J. (2008). High heritability for a composite index of children's activity level measures. *Behavior Genetics, 38*(3), 266–276.

Wood, A. C., Saudino, K. J., Rogers, H., Asherson, P., & Kuntsi, J. (2007). Genetic influences on mechanically-assessed activity level in children. *Journal of Child Psychology and Psychiatry, 48,* 695–702.

Yamagata, S., Takahashi, Y., Kijima, N., Maekawa, H., Ono, Y., & Ando, J. (2005). Genetic and environmental etiology of effortful control. *Twin Research and Human Genetics, 8*(4), 300–306.

Yamano, E., Isowa, T., Nakano, Y., Matsuda, F., Hashimoto-Tamaoki, T., Ohira, H., et al. (2008). Association study between reward dependence temperament and a polymorphism in the phenylethanolamine N-methyltransferase gene in a Japanese female population. *Comprehensive Psychiatry, 49*(5), 503–507.

Yasui-Furukori, N., Kaneda, A., Iwashima, K., Saito, M., Nakagami, T., Tsuchimine, S., et al. (2007). Association between cytochrome P450 (CYP) 2C19 polymorphisms and harm avoidance in Japanese. *American Journal of Medical Genetics B: Neuropsychiatric Genetics, 144*(6), 724–727.

CHAPTER 17

Neurobiology and Neurochemistry of Temperament in Children

Lauren K. White
Connie Lamm
Sarah M. Helfinstein
Nathan A. Fox

For centuries, humans have noted individual differences in the way infants and children react and adapt to everyday situations. As such, the study of temperament involves a rich history of theories and research spanning many disciplines, all aimed at understanding the differences in how individuals react to their environment. Two investigators have profoundly influenced the contemporary study of individual differences in human temperament: Mary Rothbart and Jerome Kagan. Working from a model first articulated by European personality psychologists such as Jan Strelau (1987), Rothbart stressed the dual dimensions of reactivity and regulation, in which a child's temperament is a reflection of differences in the degree of reactivity and the manner in which the child can successfully engage regulative processes to regulate said reactivity. According to this framework, temperaments vary as a function of children's behavioral, emotional, attentional, and physiological reactions, as well as the manner in which they adapt or regulate their reactivity (Rothbart & Derryberry, 1981). Rothbart does not view temperament, particularly the regulatory side of temperament, as static, but rather as elements of individual differences that emerge over childhood and, coupled with environment and experience, form the basis of personality. Her collaborative writings with Michael Posner elaborate on the processes and brain networks that underlie the development of temperament, particularly the dimension of regulation.

Since his time at the Fels Institute, Jerome Kagan was interested in individual differences in temperament and personality, particularly in understanding these differences within the context of response to novelty and unfamiliarity (Kagan, 1962). He and his colleagues first described young children, who, in the face of unfamiliar people or objects, ceased their activity and assumed a heightened vigilant, attentive state, a temperament construct referred to as *behavioral inhibition* (BI; see Kagan, Chapter 4, this volume). Recent research has begun to explore those children who, in the face of unfamiliar people and objects, show high levels of approach behaviors and positive affect, and often are referred to as *exuberant children* (e.g., Degnan et al., 2011). During the time that Kagan first published on behaviorally inhibited children, he made the connection between his work examining BI and the work of neuroscientists, such as Joseph LeDoux and Michael Davis, examining the role of the amygdala in fear, fear conditioning, and anxiety. As a result, Kagan focused his subsequent studies on linking the neuroscience work on the amygdala and fear conditioning to an understanding of the biology of BI, thereby exemplifying a strong link between biology and child temperament.

For the past 20 years, we have attempted to merge both the Rothbart and the Kagan approaches to studying infant temperament and its influence on children's social and emotional development. We have utilized Kagan's approach of selecting infants who in the early months of life display heightened reactivity to unfamiliar visual and auditory stimuli, and examine the temperamental reactive characteristics, both at behavioral and psychophysiological levels of analyses, of these children across childhood. At the same time, we have been interested in understanding the discontinuities in overt expression of temperament over time, particularly in regard to BI, and the role that regulative cognitive processes (i.e., effortful control; see Rueda, Chapter 8, this volume) play in the modulation of temperamental reactivity across development. Thus, we have adopted Rothbart's approach to examining the role of cognitive regulatory processes as moderators of reactivity.

In the following review, we first provide a discussion of the underlying neural circuitry believed to be involved in temperamental reactivity. Our focus is on the limbic region, specifically on the role of the amygdala and the striatum in a child's temperamental reactivity. We then discuss the development of the neural underpinnings of temperamental regulation. Subsequently, we examine the manner in which the neural circuitry underlying children's reactive and regulative tendencies interact to influence the expression of temperament, exploring how the cognitive processes associated with regulation either exacerbate or moderate the continuity of temperamental reactivity in children. We end with new directions in our own research on how neural circuitry underlying reward processing may influence the behavior of temperamentally fearful children.

Temperamental Reactivity

Reactivity reflects the tendency and predisposition of one's emotional, psychological, physiological, and behavioral responses to stimuli in the environment (Rothbart, 1988). Some infants show high levels of negative reactivity to unknown objects, people, or locations, a pattern of reactivity that is associated with BI in later childhood. This fearful behavior tends to develop in the middle of the first year of life (Bronson, 1968) and is behaviorally expressed by an increase in motor activity and negative affect (including increases in crying) in the presence of novelty (Kagan & Snidman, 1991). The developmental trajectory of these fearful behaviors tends to be relatively stable (e.g., Bronson, 1970; Kagan & Snidman, 1991; Schmidt & Fox, 1998) and is associated with an increased risk of anxiety disorders later in life (e.g., Chronis-Tuscano et al., 2009). Hence, many infants and young children who are high in negative reactivity (e.g., fearful of novel situations) continue to display fearful, inhibited, and anxious behaviors throughout development.

Conversely, infants who show high positive reactivity to unknown objects, people, or locations tend to show high levels of approach behaviors, sociability, and positive affect across childhood (Degnan et al., 2011; Fox, Henderson, Rubin, Calkins, & Schmidt, 2001). This type of approach-oriented temperamental reactivity is often referred to as *exuberance*. Although less is known about this temperamental characteristic compared to BI, we have recently shown in our laboratory that exuberance is a stable temperamental trait in children. Stability in this type of reactivity across childhood is associated with both maladaptive (e.g., high externalizing) and adaptive (e.g., social competence) outcomes (Degnan et al., 2011).

Neurobiological Basis of Reactivity

Negative reactivity is in part due to a biological predisposition for a low threshold of arousal in forebrain limbic structures (Kagan, Reznick, & Snidman, 1987; Kagan & Snidman, 1991; also see Kagan, Chapter 4, this volume). For example, research has shown that BI and negative reactivity are associated with high levels of cardiac acceleration to stressful events (Kagan, Reznick, Snidman, Gibbons, & Johnson, 1988); high and stable heart rates; tonically dilated pupils; and high levels of cortisol and norepinephrine—all markers of sympathetic arousal (Kagan et al., 1987). Since amygdala activation is part of our threat response system and thus contributes to sympathetic arousal (LeDoux, Iwata, Cicchetti, & Reis, 1988), it is thought that the sensitivity of the sympathetic nervous system associated with BI largely results from a hyperresponsive amygdala (Kagan et al., 1987).

The amygdala is associated with fearful states (LeDoux, 1996) and hypersensitive amygdala activation has been implicated in individual differences in state and trait anxiety (e.g., Bishop, Duncan, Brett, & Lawrence, 2004; Etkin et al., 2004; Somerville, Kim, Johnstone, Alexander, & Whalen, 2004). Research has shown that amygdala activation increases as a function of perceived threat (Aggleton, 2000) and subjective experience of fear (Monk et al., 2003). For example, Bishop and colleagues (2004) instructed participants to direct their attention either toward or away from fearful facial expressions, and found that participants low in state anxiety only revealed elevated amygdala activation when attending to fearful faces, whereas participants high in state anxiety revealed indiscriminately high amygdala activation, regardless of whether they attended to fearful faces or not. Individuals high in state anxiety also show increased amygdala activity when viewing neutral or ambiguous information (Somerville et al., 2004), suggestive of threat-related evaluations of neutral information during anxious states. Additionally, Etkin and colleagues (2004) used a backward-masked fearful face task and found that individual differences in trait anxiety predicted amygdala activation in response to the unconscious viewing of fearful faces, but not for conscious viewing.

Neuroimaging research has also begun to establish a hyperresponsive amygdala in BI populations. In a series of studies, Schwartz and colleagues (in press; Schwartz, Wright, Shin, Kagan, & Rauch, 2003) have demonstrated that compared individuals with no history of BI, adults identified as highly reactive in infancy or behaviorally inhibited in childhood show greater amygdala activation when viewing novel faces, compared to familiar faces. Pérez-Edgar and colleagues (2007) found that when adolescents were asked to provide subjective ratings of their fear response when viewing emotionally evocative faces, relative to adolescents with no history of BI, adolescents characterized as behaviorally inhibited in childhood revealed greater amygdala activation. This study also showed heighted amygdala response in adolescents with BI during situations involving novelty and uncertainty. Furthermore, Monk and colleagues (2008), using an attention-orienting task, found a positive correlation between amygdala activation while viewing angry faces and anxiety severity in a sample of anxious youth (mean age 13.73 years). Taken together, the current results suggest that children high in fear and anxiety-related temperamental traits have a hyperresponsive amygdala, indicative of a lower threshold for arousal. The frequent activation of this neural structure likely leads to increases in the experience of fear and anxiety for these children.

Furthermore, electroencephalogram (EEG) and event-related potential (ERP) research have shown particular patterns of neural activity that are associated with BI and other fear-related temperamental traits. For example, negative reactivity and BI in childhood is associated with right frontal EEG asymmetry (Davidson & Fox, 1989; Fox, Bell, & Jones, 1992). For example, Calkins, Fox, and Marshall (1996) found that children selected early in the first year of life for high frequencies of motor activity and negative affect in response to novelty also exhibited greater relative right frontal EEG activation at 9 months of age. Furthermore, Hane, Fox, Henderson, and Marshal (2008) found that negatively reactive infants showed high levels of avoidance and displayed a pattern of right frontal EEG asymmetry. EEG cannot capture amygdala activation; however, reciprocal innervations between the amygdala and prefrontal regions are well documented (e.g., LeDoux, 2000). Thus, as hypothesized by Calkins and colleagues (1996), this pattern of prefrontal EEG may reflect, in part, limbic arousal.

Differences in novelty sensitivity between fearful and nonfearful children have also been illustrated using ERP methodology. Marshall, Reeb, and Fox (2009) found differences in ERP (averaged EEG) activation in response to deviant stimuli in 9-month-old infants. Specifically, the study found that compared to nonreactive and positively reactive infants, negatively reactive infants (i.e., temperamentally inhibited infants) displayed greater positive frontal activation in the ERP response to deviant tones relative to standard tones. These ERP results further suggest increased sensory or attention reactivity—potentially due to amygdala arousal—to a novel stimulus for temperamentally fearful infants. This interpretation is supported by a study by Reeb-Sutherland and colleagues (2009), who found that elevated P3 amplitudes, an ERP component associated with an orienting response, in adolescents moderated the association between early identified BI and adolescent anxiety problems. Specifically, adolescents with a history of BI who concurrently displayed heightened attention reactivity to novelty, as indexed by increased P3 amplitudes, were more likely to have a history of anxiety disorders compared to BI adolescents who displayed small P3 amplitudes. Taken together, negative temperamental reactivity and fearfulness is associated with heightened psychophysiological reactivity, with a particular sensitivity to novelty, and this hypersensitivity may be a risk factor for poor socioemotional functioning.

Fearful and anxious individuals tend preferentially to allocate their attention toward threatening information in the environment (i.e., an attention bias toward threat), and such bias has been implicated in the development and maintenance of anxiety in children (Eldar, Ricon, & Bar-Haim, 2008) and adults (MacLeod, Rutherford, Campbell, Ebsworthy, & Holker, 2002). Similar to the sensitivity toward novelty, this increased sensitivity to threatening or potentially threatening stimuli is thought to result largely from a hyperresponsive amygdala (e.g., Bishop et al., 2004; Monk et al., 2008). A growing body of research has established a link between children with fearful and anxious temperaments and an attention bias toward threat (Lonigan & Vasey, 2009; Pérez-Edgar, Bar-Haim, McDermott, Chronis-Tuscano, et al., 2010; Waters, Wharton, Zimmer-Gembeck, & Craske, 2008), further supporting the notion of a hypersensitive amygdala in these children across development. Adolescents identified as temperamentally fearful in childhood show an increased allocation of attention to threat faces compared to their noninhibited peers (Pérez-Edgar, Bar-Haim, McDermott, Chronis-Tuscano, et al., 2010). Moreover, a series of longitudinal studies have found that the presence of an attention bias to threat moderates the link between early BI and negative developmental outcomes; BI is only associated with social withdrawal for youth showing an attention bias toward threat (Pérez-Edgar, Bar-Haim, McDermott, Chronis-Tuscano, et al., 2010; Pérez-Edgar et al., 2011). Thus, given the association between amygdala sensitivity and attention bias to threat, these longitudinal findings suggest that fearful children in certain contexts may activate limbic circuitry, and this reactivity may make them more vulnerable to the development of anxious behaviors.

In addition to their role in reactivity to novelty and threat, areas of the limbic region are associated with temperamental traits linked to reward sensitivity and approach behaviors. Specifically, the striatum is an area in the brain thought to play a particularly important role in reward behavior. The striatum is composed of three subregions—the nucleus accumbens, the caudate, and the putamen. Along with the ventral tegmental area (VTA; a small nucleus that sends dense dopaminergic projects to the striatum), the striatum is thought to play a critical role in processing information about salient stimuli in the environment and initiating appropriate actions (see Depue & Fu, Chapter 18, this volume).

The striatum is known to play an important role in initiating stimulus-driven, or habitual, behavior (Yin & Knowlton, 2006), particularly approach and avoidance behavior (Reynolds & Berridge, 2002). Thus, while the amygdala may be most directly linked to physiological processes that are associated with fearful reactivity, such as potentiated startle or reactivity to threat, functional differences in the striatum are likely to underlie most directly some of the basic differences in approach–withdrawal behavior seen across different temperament groups. Neuroimaging work indicates that differences in striatal function are related to stable individual differences in temperament and personality, and shifts in striatal activity are thought to be directly related to the shifts in risk taking and approach behavior seen across development (e.g., Abler, Walter, Erk, Kammerer, & Spitzer, 2006; Wittmann, Daw, Seymour, & Dolan, 2008).

Functional magnetic resonance imaging (fMRI) studies indicate that the striatum is important for processing salient information. Classic fMRI studies indicate that the striatum responds to rewarding cues (Delgado, Nystrom, Fissell, Noll, & Fiez, 2000; Knutson, Adams, Fong, & Hommer, 2001); however, there is an abundance of evidence that the striatum responds robustly to a wide range of different types of rewarding stimuli, including money (Knutson, Westdorp, Kaiser, & Hommer, 2000), pleasant sounds (Levita et al., 2009), pleasant tastes (Pagnoni, Zink, Montague, & Berns, 2002), images of loved ones (Aron et al., 2005), pornography (Walter et al., 2008), and pictures of "cute" babies (Glocker et al., 2009). While this has led to a representation of the striatal circuitry as "reward circuitry" (e.g., Knutson & Cooper, 2005), there is also a great deal of evidence suggesting that the striatum responds robustly to all salient stimuli, including punishing stimuli, such as loss of money (Seymour, Daw, Dayan, Singer, & Dolan, 2007), shocks (Seymour et al., 2004), thermal pain (Becerra, Breiter, Wise, Gonzalez, & Borsook, 2001) and aversive sounds (Levita et al., 2009). The striatum also responds to neutrally valenced stimuli that are novel (Wittmann et al., 2008). Functional striatal responses to rewarding (Cohen et al., 2010; Pagnoni et al., 2002), punishing (Seymour et al., 2004, 2007), and novel (Wittmann et al., 2008) stimuli have all been shown to follow the same "prediction error" pattern that is seen in the firing of VTA neurons (Schultz, Dayan, & Montague, 1997), indicating that the functional striatal responses are related to dopaminergic signaling from the VTA, which has long been linked with individual differences in personality (see Depue & Fu, Chapter 18, this volume).

Several recent neuroimaging studies indicate that individual differences in striatal and VTA response to salient stimuli are related to personality in the adult. Abler and colleagues (2006) showed that self-report measures of approach-oriented traits (i.e., exploratory excitability and thrill- and adventure-seeking) related to striatal activity in response to cues indicating that the participant would receive a reward. Wittmann and colleagues (2008) showed that striatal responses to novel stimuli, independent of their reward value, correlated with self-reported novelty seeking. Krebs, Schott, and Duzel (2009) found a similar dissociation in activation in the VTA and the substantia nigra: Response to novel stimuli that did not predict reward correlated with the trait of novelty seeking, whereas response to novel stimuli that did predict reward correlated with the trait of reward dependence. Taken together, this neuroimaging work suggests that the striatum, VTA, and related neural circuitry underlie aspects of personality and temperament, particularly traits related to reward sensitivity and approach behaviors.

Neurobiological Basis of Reactivity across Development

In addition to the evidence indicating that differences in the limbic region of the brain are related to interindividual differences in temperament and personality, functional changes also appear to be linked to changes in temperament and personality across the lifespan. For example, developmental changes in the striatum are thought to underlie the peak in risk-taking and reward-seeking behavior seen in adolescence. Numerous studies have shown a systematic shift in sensation-seeking and risk-taking behaviors during the period of adolescence relative to childhood or adulthood (Furby & Beythmarom, 1992; Steinberg, 2004). Adolescents engage in more risky behaviors than do children and adults (Somerville, Jones, & Casey, 2010) and they are better at learning to approach a reward (Cauffman et al., 2010), particularly in "hot" contexts (Figner, Mackinlay, Wilkening, & Weber, 2009). These developmental patterns do not seem to be species-specific, since adolescent rats also show an increase in novelty seeking, impulsivity, and restlessness (Laviola, Macri, Morley-Fletcher, & Adriani, 2003).

Evidence suggests that these developmental shifts may be related to shifts in striatal functioning. Multiple studies have shown that adolescents show greater striatal activation in response to reward feedback than do children or adults (Ernst et al., 2005; Galvan et al., 2006). This increased neural sensitivity to reward detected in adolescents has been demonstrated in the context of rewards after high-risk gambles (Van Leijenhorst et al., 2010) and through an increased dopaminergic prediction error response (Cohen et al., 2010), although, interestingly, this increased responsivity is not seen in response to cues that indicate the possibility of reward (Bjork et al., 2004). This activation also appears to be directly related to risk-seeking behavior: In a study by Galvan, Hare, Voss, Glover, and Casey (2007), participants' accumbens activation in response to reward feedback was related to their risk seeking.

Neurochemical Basis of Reactivity

Similar to the neurobiological basis associated with temperamental reactivity highlighted earlier, research suggests a neurochemical basis underlying temperamental reactivity (see Saudino & Wang, Chapter 16, and Depue & Fu, Chapter 18, this volume). One candidate gene thought to be associated with BI is the *5-HTT* serotonin transporter (see Depue & Fu, Chapter 18, this volume). Variations in this allele have been associated with negative affect, including anxiety, depression, and negative emotionality (e.g., Gonda et al., 2009; Munafo et al., 2003). The short allele of the *5-HTT* has also been related to amygdala reactivity (Hariri et al., 2002). Recently, Pérez-Edgar and colleagues (2010) showed that the availability of an adolescent's serotonin, indexed by allelic variations, was systematically related to how the adolescent attended to threat; that is, adolescents with the lowest amount of serotonin availability showed the greatest attention bias toward threat compared to adolescents with intermediate and high levels of serotonin availability. However, it should be noted that findings regarding *5-HTT* allelic differences between behaviorally inhibited and noninhibited children have been mixed (Battaglia et al., 2005), suggesting that rather than examining these genetic variations in isolation, the contribution of the neuromodulator to temperament traits should be examined in the context of a child's environment (see Saudino & Wang, Chapter 16, this volume).

There has also been a line of genetic work linking aspects of positive reactivity to the dopaminergic system (see Schinka, Letsch, & Crawford, 2002; Depue & Fu, Chapter 18, this volume). However, similar to the *5-HTT* findings, studies linking *DRD4* to approach-related behaviors have yielded inconsistent results (e.g., Malhotra et al., 1996), further suggesting an intricate relation among genes, environment, and temperamental reactivity. For example, Sheese and colleagues (Sheese, Voelker, Rothbart, & Posner, 2007; Voelker, Sheese, Rothbart, & Posner, 2009) found that parenting behaviors differentially influenced a child's level of sensation seeking depending on the child's allelic variation of the *DRD4* gene. Specifically, in children with the 7-repeat allele, parenting behaviors significantly influenced a child's level of sensation seeking, such that lower parenting quality predicted higher sensation seeking. No link between parenting behaviors and sensation seeking was found in children without the 7-repeat allele. Taken together, the contribution of children's genetic predisposition to the development of their temperamental reactivity is significantly influenced by their experiences and environment. Therefore, individual differences in serotonergic and dopamanergic systems, coupled with environmental factors, strongly influence the developmental trajectories of a child's temperamental reactivity.

Temperamental Regulation

Temperamental regulation, often referred to as effortful control or self-regulation, reflects the ability to activate or inhibit responses and voluntarily control attention in order to alter actions, thoughts, and emotions. Successful regulation is achieved through efficient and flexible recruitment of higher-order executive processes such as attention flexibility, attention focusing, and inhibitory control (Kopp, 1982; Rothbart & Rueda, 2005). Efficient regulation in childhood is associated with positive development outcomes (Moffitt et al., 2011). Whereas the reactive tendencies previously described in this chapter (i.e., amygdala hyperresponsivity) typically reflect more automatic or involuntary biological responses, the cognitive processes underlying temperamental regulation are typically considered more effortful or voluntary processes (Rothbart, Sheese, & Posner, 2007), recruited to modulate automatic reactive tendencies (Rothbart & Derryberry, 1981).

The ability to recruit regulatory mechanisms successfully to modulate emotions and behaviors shows remarkable improvement across childhood. While infants' regulatory abilities are limited and rely heavily on external means (e.g., soothing from the caregiver), infants do show rudimentary abilities to regulate their distress states and control attention (Buss & Goldsmith, 1998; Calkins & Fox, 2002; Kopp, 1982; Sheese, Rothbart, Posner, White, & Fraundorf, 2008). During toddlerhood, remarkable improvements in children's ability to recruit and efficiently employ cognitive regulatory abilities are detected (Gerardi-Caulton, 2000), with vast improvements occurring during the preschool years (e.g., Gerstadt, Hong, & Diamond, 1994; Rueda et al., 2004; Zelazo, 2006). Notable improvements in regulatory abilities continue to be detected well into middle childhood (e.g., Simonds, Kieras, Rueda, & Rothbart, 2007) and occasionally adolescence (e.g., Anderson, 2002; Huizinga, Dolan, & van der Molen, 2006). Developmental work illustrates a robust positive correlation between age and cognitive regulatory abilities (e.g., Luna & Sweeney, 2004; Rubia, Smith, Taylor, & Brammer, 2007), and these improvements engender the parallel improvements detected in individuals' ability to regulate their emotions (Calkins, 1994; Derryberry & Rothbart, 1997).

Neurobiological Basis of Temperamental Regulation

Temperamental regulation is thought to have a strong neural basis involving the anterior cingulate cortex (ACC) and the lateral prefrontal cortex (PFC; Luna, Padmanabhan, & O'Hearn, 2010; Posner & Fan, 2004; Posner & Rothbart, 2009). A large body of neurophysiological work provides evidence that during the recruitment of regulative processes (i.e., conflict and error detection, error correction, attention shifting, attention focusing, and inhibitory control) areas of the ACC and PFC are consistently activated (Botvinick, 2007; Botvinick, Braver, Barch, Carter, & Cohen, 2001; McDermott & Fox, 2010; Ochsner, Bunge, Gross, & Gabrieli, 2002; Raz & Buhle, 2006). These regions are involved in both the up- and down-regulation of other neural networks to modulate an individual's emotion and behavior (Beauregard, Levesque, & Bourgouin, 2001; Miller & Cohen, 2001; Ochsner et al., 2002; Posner & Rothbart, 2009).

The ACC serves to integrate and modulate visceral, motor, attention, and emotion processes and allows for the flexible recruitment of higher-order regulatory processes (Bush, Luu, & Posner, 2000; Dennis, 2010; Devinsky, Morrell, & Vogt, 1995; Fox, Henderson, Pérez-Edgar, & White, 2008; Kerns et al., 2004; Posner, Rothbart, Sheese, & Tang, 2007). Although the ACC and PFC are often coactivated when individuals perform tasks that tap regulatory processes (e.g., Stroop, flanker, and go/no-go tasks), the ACC shows a separable pattern of activation associated with the detection and monitoring of conflict, both in the external environment and in the individual's own behavior (e.g., Carter & van Veen, 2007; Casey, Trainor, Giedd, et al., 1997; Fan, Flombaum, McCandliss, Thomas, & Posner, 2003; Posner & Fan, 2004). Once conflict has been detected, the ACC signals for the recruitment of higher-order cognitive processes, located in the PFC, in order to resolve said conflict (Kerns et al., 2004)—regulating thoughts, actions, and emotions. Although the majority of neuroimaging work demonstrating the role of ACC in conflict monitoring has been conducted in adult populations, research implicates that this structure also underlies conflict monitoring in children and adolescents (Rubia et al., 2007).

A particularly relevant function of the ACC to the study of temperament is the role it plays in the regulation of emotions (Beauregard et al., 2001; Ochsner et al., 2006). During emotion regulation, the ACC is associated with the monitoring of an individual's emotional response and evaluation (Ochsner et al., 2006). When viewing emotional stimuli, ACC activation increases as a function of increasing emotional intensity (Blair, Morris, Frith, Perrett, & Dolan, 1999; Morris et al., 1998), and is thought to reflect increases in emotional conflict produced by the stimuli. Moreover, the detection of emotional conflict (i.e., level of ACC activation) is thought to be related to the level of control processes that are recruited in a given situation. Using ERP methodology, Lewis and colleagues (Lamm & Lewis, 2010; Lewis, Lamm, Segalowitz, Stieben, & Zelazo, 2006; Lewis, Todd, & Honsberger, 2007) have investigated emotion regulation in children by examining the N2, an ERP component often associated with temperamental regulation (Rueda, Posner, & Rothbart, 2005). The N2 is a medial-frontal component occurring between 200–500 ms after stimulus onset and is thought to, in part, reflect activation of the ACC (Van Veen & Carter, 2002b): Greater N2 amplitude is associated with increased conflict monitoring and greater recruitment of control processes

(Lamm, Zelazo, & Lewis, 2006; Lewis et al., 2006; van Veen & Carter, 2002a). On a go/no-go task with emotional images, children ages 4–6 showed greater N2 amplitude and shorter N2 latencies when viewing angry faces than when viewing happy faces (Lewis et al., 2007). The authors interpreted these findings to suggest that when faced with threatening information, children recruit more regulative processes and do so in a more pressing manner. In support of this interpretation, children had the slowest reaction times on angry go-trials. Additionally, during a modified go/no-go task, older children and adolescents also showed an increase in N2 amplitude after an emotion induction procedure, likely reflecting the greater recruitment of regulative processes (Lamm et al., 2006; Luna & Sweeney, 2004).

Whereas the ACC is thought to play a crucial role in monitoring conflict and signaling the amount of control needed in a given situation, it is not necessarily thought to regulate reactivity itself. The ACC recruits higher-order regulatory processes subserved by the lateral PFC to modulate responses and emotions (see Carter & van Veen, 2007, for a review; also see MacDonald, Cohen, Stenger, & Carter, 2000; Miller & Cohen, 2001). Areas of the lateral PFC are associated with the processes recruited to modulate an individual's neural, behavioral, and emotional reactivity. Regulatory processes subserved by this area include attentional focusing, attention shifting, inhibitory control, and the ability to represent internal goals (Bunge, Dudukovic, Thomason, Vaidya, & Gabrieli, 2002; Casey, Trainor, Orendi, et al., 1997; Luna et al., 2010; MacDonald et al., 2000; Miller, 2000). Developmental neuroimaging studies have shown that while employing regulative processes, children and adolescents recruit similar regions of the PFC as adults (Casey, Trainor, Orendi, et al., 1997). However, Bunge and colleagues (2002) found that although 8- to 12-year-old children showed activation similar to that of adults in several PFC regions (i.e., left ventrolateral PFC), during two cognitive control tasks, they failed to recruit their right ventrolateral PFC, the region that showed the strongest, most consistent activation in the adult group across the two tasks. This suggests that, while employing certain cognitive regulatory processes, children recruit both similar and alternative PFC circuitry to that of adults.

Similar to the ACC, the lateral PFC plays a critical role in emotion regulation (see Ochsner & Gross, 2005). Hariri, Mattay, Tessitore, Fera, and Weinberger (2003) detected increased amygdala activation when participants were passively viewing threatening pictures; however, when participants were asked to categorize the pictures as either "natural" or "artificial," their amygdala activation decreased and right ventrolateral PFC activation increased during the presentation of threatening pictures. This suggests that by shifting attention away from the emotional salience of a stimulus, increasing activation in the circuitry associated with cognitive regulatory processes, areas associated with emotional reactivity are modulated. A large body of neuroimaging work also has shown that the effortful regulation of emotions is associated with PFC–amygdala coupling; that is, when individuals are instructed to down-regulate their negative emotions voluntarily, areas of the PFC are activated; this activation is linked to the modulation of brain areas (e.g., the amygdala) associated with emotional reactivity (Kim & Hamann, 2007; Levesque et al., 2003; Ochsner et al., 2002, 2004). Similar patterns of activation have been observed when individuals are asked to up-regulate positive emotions (Kim & Hamann, 2007). Thus, the connections between the PFC and subcortical neural structures underlying emotional reactivity are critical for the modulation of emotional responses.

Although the ACC and PFC subserve the multiple cognitive regulatory processes associated with temperamental regulation (e.g., inhibitory control, attention focusing, attention shifting), neuroimaging work has identified separable patterns of activation associated with the different regulatory processes (for a review, see Aron, 2008; Ochsner & Gross, 2005). For example, Ochsner and colleagues (2002) showed that although similar brain regions were activated across the employment of multiple emotional regulatory strategies, the patterns of neural activation associated with each strategy were different. Thus, while ACC and PFC are the neurological basis of temperamental regulation, the specific pattern of neural circuitry activated during regulation is influenced by a child's regulation goals (e.g., decrease anxious state vs. increase positive affect), the strategy employed (e.g., distraction vs. reappraisal), and the child's underlying capacity in his or her regulatory processes (e.g., high vs. low attention-shifting abilities). Moreover, as indicated below, the circuitry associated with each regulatory process may have a different developmental trajectory.

Neurobiological Basis of Temperamental Regulation across Development

The same neural circuitry underlying cognitive regulatory processes in healthy adults appear to be online, for the most part, in children and adolescents. However, drastic maturation of this network occurs over the course of development (see Luna et al., 2010), differentially influencing regulatory abilities in children and adolescents. In fact, the remarkable behavioral improvements in a child's ability to efficiently recruit and employ self-regulatory processes that occur across development are thought to result, in large part, from the protracted development of the ACC and PFC. Neurophysiological studies demonstrate considerable changes in the structural, functional, and connective properties of the ACC, PFC, and associated brain networks across development (e.g., Bunge et al., 2002; Casey, Trainor, Orendi, et al., 1997; Davies, Segalowitz, & Gavin, 2004a, 2004b; Ladouceur, Dahl, & Carter, 2004, 2007; Lamm & Lewis, 2010; Marsh et al., 2006; Rubia et al., 2007). Neuroimaging work has shown that although children and adults typically display activation in similar brain regions when performing tasks that tap regulatory processes, the pattern and extent of this activation differs. For example, decreased and more localized activation of specific brain regions underlying temperamental regulation is often positively associated with age, likely reflecting increased maturation and neural efficiency (e.g., Bunge et al., 2002; Casey, Trainor, Orendi, et al., 1997). Some studies, however, report a positive association between age and increased prefrontal activation (e.g., Konrad et al., 2005; Marsh et al., 2006). The discrepant age-related activation patterns detected across studies are likely a function of the task used, the regulatory processes assessed, and the specific brain regions examined. Nevertheless, this developmental change in activation, be it an increase or decrease, is thought to represent more efficient recruitment and implementation of regulatory abilities. To support this notion, many neuroimaging studies have found that the age-related changes detected in ACC and PFC activation are also associated with improved behavioral performance on the tasks designed to assess cognitive regulative abilities (Casey, Trainor, Orendi, et al., 1997; Konrad et al., 2005; Stevens, Kiehl, Pearlson, & Calhoun, 2007).

The dynamic functional and anatomical connectivity between brain regions such as the PFC and ACC show dramatic maturation across development (Stevens et al., 2007). The circuitry associated with regulation and social and emotional functions appears to undergo the most dramatic changes across development (Kelly et al., 2009). Functional connectivity analyses illustrate that, over the course of development, the connections of brain regions subserving regulative processes become more specialized and segregated, indexed by a decrease in short-range synaptic connections, and become more integrated into functional networks, indexed by an increase in long-range connections (Fair et al., 2007, 2009). That is, over the course of development, brain connectivity becomes less localized and more distributed, forming mature, functional neural networks. These changes in connectivity and the patterns of neural activation are related to better behavioral performance on cognitive regulation tasks (Liston et al., 2006; Rubia et al., 2007; Stevens et al., 2007). Taken together, the body of developmental neuroimaging work examining cognitive regulatory processes shows robust structural and functional changes across development in the ACC and PFC, and these changes appear to be directly related to a child's increased ability to regulate his or her thoughts, actions, and emotions.

ERP methodology has proven to be a useful tool in the examination of developmental changes in the neurophysiological underpinnings of temperamental regulation in children and adolescents. Compared to adults, young children show longer latencies and larger amplitudes of the N2 (Rueda et al., 2005), suggesting less proficient regulation. However, in samples of children between the ages of 5 and 16, Lewis and colleagues (2006) demonstrated a steady decrease in N2 amplitude across development. Moreover, this developmental reduction in N2 activation appears to be closely linked to behavioral improvements in children's cognitive regulatory processes (Lamm et al., 2006). The reduction in N2 amplitude found across development dovetails nicely with the developmental neuroimaging findings, further signifying a developmental increase in efficiency of the neural circuitry underlying self-regulation.

Another ERP component closely associated with temperamental regulation that shows a protracted developmental pattern is error-related negativity (ERN; McDermott & Fox, 2010). ERN is a fronto-central component, time-locked to the execution of a response, usually appearing 150 ms after the commission of an error. ERN is thought to reflect the monitoring of an individual's current behavior and how the behavior relates to his or her goals and/or anticipated behavior. ERN is also thought largely to reflect activity of the ACC (van Veen & Carter, 2002b). Developmental research suggests that ERN becomes more prominent across development (Davies et al., 2004b; Ladouceur et al., 2007; Santesso, Segalowitz, & Schmidt, 2006), indicating maturation of response monitoring. For example, compared to adults, children (Santesso et al., 2006) and adolescents (Ladouceur et al., 2007; Santesso & Segalowitz, 2008) showed decreased ERNs. Moreover, in a sample of 7- to 25-year-olds, Davies and colleagues (2004b) showed that ERNs became more robust across development, continuing to develop into adulthood. The developmental change in the ERN is thought to reflect protracted development of an individual's ability to monitor his or her performance, engendered by the extended maturation of the ACC and associated circuitry.

Taken together, a rich body of neuroimaging research indicates that there is a strong neural architecture, including the ACC and PFC, associated with temperamental regulation. Dramatic increases in this neural circuitry occur across development, often still maturing well into adulthood (Casey, Tottenham, Liston, & Durston, 2005). These changes are related to the dramatic progress in children's ability to regulate their thoughts, actions, and emotions, detected across development.

Neurochemical Basis of Temperamental Regulation

Given the strong neural correlates of temperamental regulation, research has also pinpointed a neurochemical basis of temperamental regulation, focusing on the chemical modulators underlying the ACC, PFC, and associated circuitry. Dopamine neurons permeate the neural circuitry underlying temperamental regulation, and accordingly, dopaminergic genes (e.g., *DRD4*, catechol-O-methyltransferase [*COMT*]) have been the focus of much research to identify genetic markers of cognitive regulatory processes. In support of this notion, genetic differences in the dopamine system have been shown to predict performance on cognitive regulatory tasks (Blasi et al., 2005; Fan, Fossella, Sommer, Wu, & Posner, 2003; Wahlstrom et al., 2007). For example, in a group of 200 adults, the level of interference caused by conflict on a flanker task was related to variations in two dopamine genes, *DRD4* and monoamine oxidase (*MAOA*) (Fossella et al., 2002). A similar pattern has also been detected in toddlers (Sheese, Voelker, Posner, & Rothbart, 2009; Voelker et al., 2009). Genes related to serotonin are also thought to play a role in regulatory processes (Canli et al., 2005; Reuter, Ott, Vaitl, & Hennig, 2007), and may have a particularly important role in emotion regulation (Hariri & Holmes, 2006).

Akin to the protracted development of the ACC and PFC, animal studies have shown that the dopaminergic system does not reach adult levels until late adolescence (Rosenberg & Lewis, 1995; Tarazi, Tomasini, & Baldessarini, 1998). In addition, the functional changes seen in the ACC and PFC across development (and the associated increases in regulatory abilities) likely reflect the maturation of the dopaminergic system.

Interactions between Temperamental Reactivity and Regulation

The fundamental function of temperamental regulation is to modulate a child's reactivity and automatic response tendencies. This ability relies heavily on the interconnections between the neural regions that subserve temperamental reactivity and regulation

(Dennis, 2010; Henderson & Wachs, 2007), and it is through these vast connections with the limbic system, motor areas, and nearly all sensory systems that the modulatory functions of ACC and PFC are afforded (see Miller & Cohen, 2001). The ongoing interactions between these systems (i.e., a child's reactivity and regulation) largely determine the expression of a child's temperament (see Figure 17.1 for an illustration of these interactions) and the associated social, emotional, and behavioral outcomes (Dennis, 2010; Derryberry & Rothbart, 1997; Henderson & Wachs, 2007; White, Helfinstein, & Fox, 2010; White, Helfinstein, Reeb-Sutherland, Degnan, & Fox, 2009). Neuroimaging research has underscored this notion, demonstrating that individual differences in coupling between the neural circuits subserving reactivity and regulation significantly affect an individual's ability to effectively regulate their reactivity (Davidson, 2000; Hariri et al., 2003; Ochsner & Gross, 2005). Moreover, a strong body of neurophysiological research with children, adolescents, and adults suggests that high levels of anxiety and fear-related temperamental traits (Bishop et al., 2004; Hajcak, McDonald, & Simons, 2004; Ladouceur, Conway, & Dahl, 2010; Lamm & Lewis, 2010; Pérez-Edgar, Bar-Haim, McDermott, Chronis-Tuscano, et al., 2010) and high reward-seeking tendencies (Casey, Jones, & Hare, 2008; Ernst, Pine, & Hardin, 2006) are associated with perturbations in the recruitment of regulatory processes.

A substantial body of neuoimaging work underscores perturbations in the functional connectivity between brain regions subserving regulation and reactivity processes in temperamentally fearful individuals. When viewing fearful stimuli, individuals with the short allele for *5-HTT*, a genetic predisposition for fearful temperamental traits, showed a lower correlation between ACC and amygdala activation compared to individuals without the short allele (Pezawas et al., 2005). Moreover, Pezawas and colleagues (2005) found that the level of coupling between ACC and amygdala activation

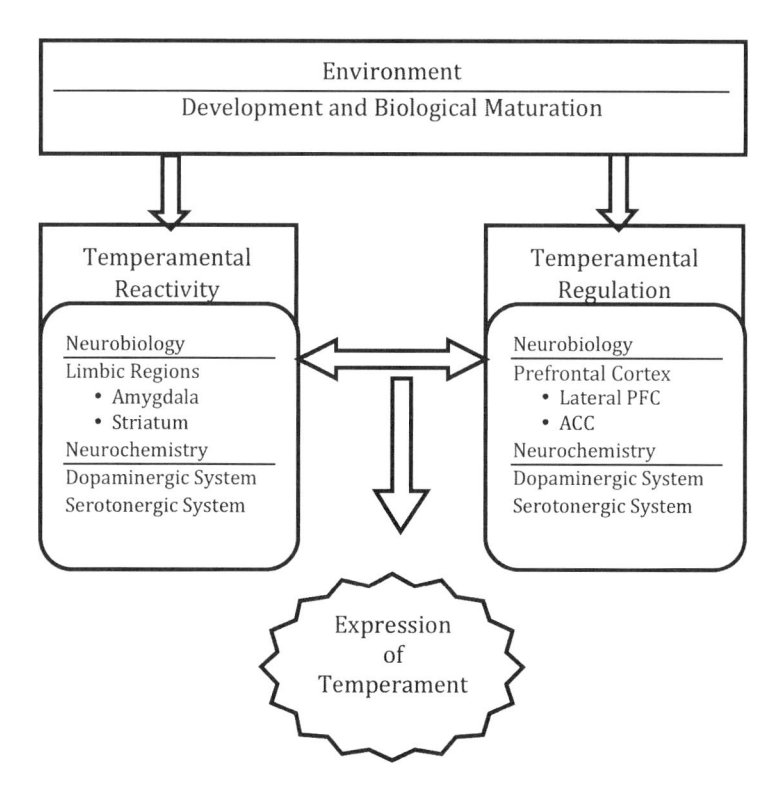

FIGURE 17.1. An illustration of the factors that contribute to the expression of a child's temperament.

explained 30% of the variance in anxiety-related temperament traits. This suggests that the circuitry between the limbic and prefrontal regions may not be functioning effectively in individuals with fearful temperamental traits. In support of this notion, Cremers and colleagues (2010) found that the amount of left amygdala–ACC connectivity detected while participants viewed negative facial expressions was negatively correlated to a participants' level of neuroticism. Using a probe detection task, Monk and colleagues (2008) reported reduced coupling between the PFC and amygdala in children and adolescents with an anxiety diagnosis compared to healthy controls. These results suggest that during times of emotional reactivity, children with fearful and anxiety-related temperamental traits have perturbations in the neural coupling between regions associated with reactivity and those associated with regulation, likely leaving the child vulnerable to tonic levels of negative reactivity and information-processing biases.

Differences in the ability of temperamentally fearful or anxious children efficiently to recruit the circuitry needed to regulate their reactivity effectively may also be influenced by the type of cognitive regulatory processes employed. In a recent behavioral study examining how interactions between temperamental reactivity and regulation influence emotional development, White, McDermott, Degnan, Henderson, and Fox (2011) found that the association between high BI in toddlerhood and high anxiety problems during the preschool years was moderated differentially by two regulatory processes: attention shifting and inhibitory control. Children who were high in BI in toddlerhood and displayed poor levels of attention shifting showed increased anxiety problems during the preschool years, a link that was not present for BI children with high levels of attention shifting. Interestingly, those children with a history of high BI and high levels of inhibitory control had more anxiety problems during the preschool years; BI was not related to anxiety problems in children showing medium to low levels of inhibitory control.

Recent psychophysiological work also supports this finding: Henderson (2010) showed that children rated high in shyness who were also sensitive to conflict, as indexed by greater N2 amplitudes during a flanker task, had worse socioemotional functioning compared to children with lower N2 amplitudes. McDermott and colleagues (2009) found a similar pattern when examining ERNs in behaviorally inhibited youth: In a group of adolescents who had a history of BI, those with higher ERNs, an index of behavioral monitoring, were more at risk for anxiety problems. Thus, certain aspects underlying temperamental regulation (i.e., attention shifting) may better modulate fear-related reactivity, contributing to reduction of fearful temperamental traits over time, decreasing a child's risk for negative outcomes. Conversely, other aspects of temperamental regulation (i.e., heightened inhibitory control, sensitivity to conflict and error) may contribute to the stability of fear-related temperamental traits across childhood.

Interactions between the Neurobiological Bases of Reactivity and Regulation across Development

Adding to the complexity of how the neural systems that underlie reactivity and regulation interact to influence the expression of temperament, developmental research has shown that these interactions and connections between the neural correlates of reactivity and regulation change across development. That is, children, adolescents, and adults differ in the connectivity between brain regions subserving regulation and regions associated with reactivity (Casey et al., 2008; Hare et al., 2008; Hariri et al., 2003; Monk et al., 2008). The circuitry underlying both temperamental reactivity and regulation has different developmental trajectories, and as a result, the coupling between the two networks changes with age.

Adolescence appears to be a period in which differences in the maturity between these two neural systems is abnormally large, resulting in an imbalance in coupling between the systems. This imbalance in maturation levels between the circuits associated with reactivity and regulation is thought to underlie many of the behavioral and emotional problems, such as anxiety, depression, and high reward seeking, often seen in adolescence (for a review, see Casey et al., 2008). Recent neuroimaging work in adolescents provides evidence of an imbalance in the maturational trajectories of the two systems. During an emotion go/no-go task, a group of healthy adolescents showed exaggerated amygdala activity compared to children and adults (Hare et al., 2008), suggesting a need for increased regulatory processes during this stage of development. However, given the protracted development of the neural circuitry underlying regulation, adolescents, particularly those with hypersensitive amygdala (e.g., temperamentally fearful adolescents), may not have adequate neural architecture in place to regulate their emotional reactivity properly.

Supporting this assertion, when performing a dot-probe task, youth with generalized anxiety disorder show increased amygdala hypersensitivity and perturbations in the recruitment of lateral PFC (Monk et al., 2008). In a subsequent study, Casey and colleagues (Galvan et al., 2006) showed that, compared to children and adults, adolescents showed increased accumbens activity when anticipating a reward. However, recruitment of prefrontal regions in adolescents was more similar to PFC activation found in children than that found in adults. Thus, both high negative- and high positive-reactive adolescents may be particularly vulnerable to outcomes related to anxiety/depression or risky behaviors because they are not able to control or inhibit the increased responsiveness of their limbic system properly. Given the importance of the interactions between reactivity and regulation, the imbalance in the coupling between the networks underlying regulation and those underlying reactivity detected across development has important consequences for the expression of temperament in children and adolescents.

Interactions between the Neurochemical Bases of Reactivity and Regulation

Interactions between genetic polymorphisms relating to an individual's temperamental regulation and reactivity are also thought to play a significant role in the expression of temperament (Auerbach, Faroy, Ebstein, Kahana, & Levine, 2001; Posner, Rothbart, & Sheese, 2007) and developmental outcomes (Auerbach, Benjamin, Faroy, Geller, & Ebstein, 2001; Chappie et al., 2007). For example, a child with a polymorphism in *5-HTT*, a gene associated with increased negative affect and anxiety vulnerability (Lesch et al., 1996; Pérez-Edgar, Bar-Haim, McDermott, Gorodetsky, et al., 2010), who also has a specific polymorphism in dopamine genes related to poor attention control may be at risk for negative outcomes resulting from an inability to regulate reactivity associated with the serotonin system. On the other hand, a child with the same *5-HTT* polymorphism may be protected against the negative outcomes associated with the polymorphism if he or she also has dopaminergic genetic allelic variations that support efficient attentional control.

New Directions: The Role of the Striatum in the Development of Fearful Temperament

Recent work from our laboratory has suggested that the striatum, an area in the brain once thought to be involved solely in reward behavior, may in fact play an important role in the development of social behavior in behaviorally inhibited children. Fox and colleagues (Bar-Haim et al., 2009; Guyer et al., 2006; Helfinstein et al., 2011) investigated whether striatal response to salient stimuli differs between adolescents who have a stable pattern of BI across childhood and those who do not. Guyer and colleagues (2006) examined striatal responses to cues that indicated the amount of reward or punishment at stake on a timed responding task. They reported that adolescents characterized as behaviorally inhibited in childhood showed greater activation to these cues in both the striatum and the amygdala, and the larger the amount of money at stake, the greater the increase in activation for these inhibited adolescents. In a second study, a different group of adolescents also characterized with BI in childhood (Bar-Haim et al., 2009) saw two different types of cues: noncontingent cues, which contained either the number 1 or 2, in which participants simply had to press the indicated number to receive a reward; and contingent cues, which contained a question mark, in which participants had to guess correctly whether 1 or 2 was the correct number to receive a reward. Bar-Haim and colleagues (2009) reported that there were no differences between inhibited and noninhibited adolescents in their response to the noncontingent cues, for which a reward was guaranteed, but the behaviorally inhibited adolescents showed greater activation in response to the contingent cues that indicated the participant had to guess correctly to receive a reward.

These data revealed clear functional differences between behaviorally inhibited and noninhibited adolescents in their striatal response to salient information, but it was unclear from these reports whether this response had any valence specificity. To explore this question, Helfinstein and colleagues (2011) examined striatal response to the feedback received on contingent trials, which was unpredictable, and indicated a gain half the time, and a failure to gain half the time. Results revealed a group by valence interaction in the caudate: Behaviorally inhibited adolescents showed greater striatal activation to the salient aversive information (i.e., the failure to receive a reward), while noninhibited adolescents showed greater activation to the salient rewarding information (i.e., the feedback indicating that they had performed correctly and would receive a reward).

These data raise the interesting possibility that behaviorally inhibited adolescents show enhanced striatal responses specifically to salient negative information. This would be consistent with the large corpus of research indicating that behaviorally inhibited individuals tend to focus on the aversive or threatening, rather than positive, stimuli in their environment (e.g., Pérez-Edgar, Bar-Haim, McDermott, Chronis-Tuscano, et al., 2010; Pérez-Edgar et al., 2011). This is also consistent with the heightened avoidance and withdrawal behavior that characterizes behaviorally inhibited individuals. Studies in rats (Reynolds & Berridge, 2002) have shown that stimulation of the rostral part of the nucleus accumbens shell elicits approach and feeding behavior, while stimulation of the caudal part elicits defensive treading and feeding behavior. Moreover, this gradient is malleable: When rats are placed in a dark, quiet, comfortable environment, stimulation of most of the shell produces approach behavior, and only the most caudal tip elicits avoidance behavior; when rats are placed in a loud, bright, threatening environment instead, avoidance behavior is elicited by all but the most rostral tip of the shell (Reynolds & Berridge, 2008). Thus, if behaviorally inhibited individuals are showing a more robust striatal response to salient aversive events, this could be directly linked to their greater tendency toward avoidance behavior.

Conclusion

In this chapter we have attempted to provide a synthesis of research that examines the underlying neural structures and mechanisms involved in temperamental reactivity and regulation. We have described research from our own and other laboratories that integrates two important programs of research in temperament within developmental psychology: those of Jerome Kagan and Mary Rothbart. Our work provides a framework for describing the link between biology and temperament in children and adolescents, highlighting the neurophysiological correlates of both temperamental reactivity and regulation. We have highlighted the developmental importance of these biological correlates, as well as the significant interactions between the neural circuitry associated with reactivity and regulation, as it relates to the expression of temperament in children. Finally, we have described a new program of research connecting a network of structures in the brain, often associated with positive reactivity and approach, to fearful temperaments. It appears that individual differences in striatal activation play a crucial role in the development of reticent and fearful behavior in temperamentally behaviorally inhibited children. The interconnections between this brain network and others that have been more traditionally associated with anxiety and fear comprise a research agenda for the future.

Acknowledgments

Manuscript preparation was supported in part by National Research Service Award No. 1F31MH085424 to Lauren K. White and Grant No. R37HD17899 to Nathan A. Fox from the National Institutes of Health.

Further Reading

Fox, N. A., Henderson, H. A., Pérez-Edgar, K., & White, L. K. (2008). The biology of temperament:

An intergrative approach. In C. A. Nelson & M. L. Collins (Eds.), *Handbook of developmental cognitive neuroscience* (2nd ed., pp. 839–854). Cambridge, MA: MIT Press.

Helfinstein, S. M., Fox, N. A., & Pine, D. S. (2012). Approach–withdrawal and the role of the striatum in the temperament of behavioral inhibition. *Developmental Psychology, 48,* 815–826.

Kagan, J., & Snidman, N. (1991). Temperamental factors in human development. *American Psychologist, 46,* 856–862.

White, L. K., Helfinstein, S. M., Reeb-Sutherland, B. C., Degnan, K. A., & Fox, N. A. (2009). Role of attention in the regulation of fear and anxiety. *Developmental Neuroscience, 31*(4), 309–317.

References

Abler, B., Walter, H., Erk, S., Kammerer, H., & Spitzer, M. (2006). Prediction error as a linear function of reward probability is coded in human nucleus accumbens. *NeuroImage, 31,* 790–795.

Aggleton, J. P. (2000). *The amygdala: A functional analysis.* Oxford, UK: Oxford University Press.

Anderson, P. (2002). Assessment and development of executive function (EF) during childhood. *Child Neuropsychology, 8*(2), 71–82.

Aron, A. (2008). Progress in executive-function research: From tasks to functions to regions to network. *Current Directions in Psychological Science, 17,* 124–129.

Aron, A., Fisher, H., Mashek, D. J., Strong, G., Li, H., & Brown, L. L. (2005). Reward, motivation, and emotion systems associated with early-stage intense romantic love. *Journal of Neurophysiology, 94*(1), 327–337.

Auerbach, J. G., Benjamin, J., Faroy, M., Geller, V., & Ebstein, R. (2001). DRD4 related to infant attention and information processing: A developmental link to ADHD? *Psychiatric Genetics, 11*(1), 31–35.

Auerbach, J. G., Faroy, M., Ebstein, R., Kahana, M., & Levine, J. (2001). The association of the dopamine D4 receptor gene (DRD4) and the serotonin transporter promoter gene (5-HTTLPR) with temperament in 12-month-old infants. *Journal of Child Psychology and Psychiatry, 42*(6), 777–783.

Bar-Haim, Y., Fox, N. A., Benson, B., Guyer, A. E., Williams, A., Nelson, E. E., et al. (2009). Neural correlates of reward processing in adolescents with a history of inhibited temperament. *Psychological Science, 20*(8), 1009–1018.

Battaglia, M., Ogliari, A., Zanoni, A., Citterio, A., Pozzoli, U., Giorda, R., et al. (2005). Influence of the serotonin transporter promoter gene and shyness on children's cerebral responses to facial expressions. *Archives of General Psychiatry, 62,* 85–94.

Beauregard, M., Levesque, J., & Bourgouin, P. (2001). Neural correlates of conscious self-regulation of emotion. *Journal of Neuroscience, 21,* Rc165(1–6)

Becerra, L., Breiter, H. C., Wise, R., Gonzalez, R. G., & Borsook, D. (2001). Reward circuitry activation by noxious thermal stimuli. *Neuron, 32*(5), 927–946.

Bishop, S., Duncan, J., Brett, M., & Lawrence, A. D. (2004). Prefrontal cortical function and anxiety: Controlling attention to threat-related stimuli. *Nature Neuroscience, 7*(2), 184–188.

Bjork, J. M., Knutson, B., Fong, G. W., Caggiano, D. M., Bennett, S. M., & Hommer, D. W. (2004). Incentive-elicited brain activation in adolescents: Similarities and differences from young adults. *Journal of Neuroscience, 24*(8), 1793–1802.

Blair, R. J., Morris, J. S., Frith, C. D., Perrett, D. I., & Dolan, R. J. (1999). Dissociable neural responses to facial expressions of sadness and anger. *Brain, 122*(5), 883–893.

Blasi, G., Mattay, V. S., Bertolino, A., Elvevag, B., Callicott, J. H., Das, S., et al. (2005). Effect of catechol-O-methyltransferase val158met genotype on attentional control. *Journal of Neuroscience, 25*(20), 5038–5045.

Botvinick, M. M. (2007). Conflict monitoring and decision making: Reconciling two perspectives on anterior cingulate function. *Cognitive, Affective, and Behavioral Neuroscience, 7*(4), 356–366.

Botvinick, M. M., Braver, T. S., Barch, D. M., Carter, C. S., & Cohen, J. D. (2001). Conflict monitoring and cognitive control. *Psychological Review, 108*(3), 624–652.

Bronson, G. W. (1968). The fear of novelty. *Psychological Bulletin, 69,* 350–358.

Bronson, G. W. (1970). Fear of visual novelty: Developmental patterns in males and females. *Developmental Psychology, 2,* 33–40.

Bunge, S. A., Dudukovic, N. M., Thomason, M. E., Vaidya, C. J., & Gabrieli, J. D. (2002). Immature frontal lobe contributions to cognitive control in children: Evidence from fMRI. *Neuron, 33*(2), 301–311.

Bush, G., Luu, P., & Posner, M. I. (2000). Cognitive and emotional influences in anterior cingulate cortex. *Trends in Cognitive Sciences, 4*(6), 215–222.

Buss, K. A., & Goldsmith, H. H. (1998). Fear and anger regulation in infancy: Effects on the temporal dynamics of affective expression. *Child Development, 69*(2), 359–374.

Calkins, S. D. (1994). Origins and outcomes of individual differences in emotion regulation. *Monographs of the Society for Research in Child Development, 59*(2–3), 53–72.

Calkins, S. D., & Fox, N. A. (2002). Self-regulatory processes in early personality development: A multilevel approach to the study of childhood social withdrawal and aggression. *Development and Psychopathology, 14*(3), 477–498.

Calkins, S. D., Fox, N. A., & Marshall, T. R.

(1996). Behavior and psychological antecedents of Inhibited and uninhibited behavior. *Child Development, 67,* 523–540.

Canli, T., Omura, K., Haas, B. W., Fallgatter, A., Constable, R. T., & Lesch, K. P. (2005). Beyond affect: A role for genetic variation of the serotonin transporter in neural activation during a cognitive attention task. *Proceedings of the National Academy of Sciences, 102*(34), 12224–12229.

Carter, C. S., & van Veen, V. (2007). Anterior cingulate cortex and conflict detection: An update of theory and data. *Cognitive, Affective, and Behavioral Neuroscience, 7*(4), 367–379.

Casey, B. J., Jones, R. M., & Hare, T. A. (2008). The adolescent brain. *Annals of the New York Academy of Sciences, 1124,* 111–126.

Casey, B. J., Tottenham, N., Liston, C., & Durston, S. (2005). Imaging the developing brain: What have we learned about cognitive development? *Trends in Cognitive Sciences, 9*(3), 104–110.

Casey, B. J., Trainor, R., Giedd, J., Vauss, Y., Vaituzis, C. K., Hamburger, S., et al. (1997). The role of the anterior cingulate in automatic and controlled processes: A developmental neuroanatomical study. *Developmental Psychobiology, 30*(1), 61–69.

Casey, B. J., Trainor, R. J., Orendi, J. L., Schubert, A. B., Nystrom, L. E., Giedd, J. N., et al. (1997). A developmental functional MRI study of prefrontal activation during performance of a Go–No-Go task. *Journal of Cognitive Neuroscience, 9*(6), 835–847.

Cauffman, E., Shulman, E. P., Steinberg, L., Claus, E., Banich, M. T., Graham, S., et al. (2010). Age differences in affective decision making as indexed by performance on the Iowa Gambling Task. *Developmental Psychology, 46*(1), 193–207.

Chappie, T. A., Humphrey, J. M., Allen, M. P., Estep, K. G., Fox, C. B., Lebel, L. A., et al. (2007). Discovery of a series of 6,7-dimethoxy-4-pyrrolidylquinazoline PDE10A inhibitors. *Journal of Medicinal Chemistry, 50*(2), 182–185.

Chronis-Tuscano, A., Degnan, K. A., Pine, D. S., Pérez-Edgar, K., Henderson, H. A., Diaz, Y., et al. (2009). Stable, early behavioral inhibition predicts the development of social anxiety disorder in adolescence. *Journal of the American Academy of Child and Adolescent Psychiatry, 49,* 928–935.

Cohen, J. R., Asarnow, R. F., Sabb, F. W., Bilder, R. M., Bookheimer, S. Y., Knowlton, B. J., et al. (2010). A unique adolescent response to reward prediction errors. *Nature Neuroscience, 13*(6), 669–671.

Cremers, H. R., Demenescu, L. R., Aleman, A., Renken, R., van Tol, M. J., van der Wee, N. J., et al. (2010). Neuroticism modulates amygdala–prefrontal connectivity in response to negative emotional facial expressions. *NeuroImage, 49*(1), 963–970.

Davidson, R. J. (2000). Affective style, psychopathology, and resilience: Brain mechanisms and plasticity. *American Psychologist, 55*(11), 1196–1214.

Davidson, R. J., & Fox, N. A. (1989). Frontal brain asymmetry predicts infants' response to maternal separation. *Journal of Abnormal Psychology, 98,* 127–131.

Davies, P. L., Segalowitz, S. J., & Gavin, W. J. (2004a). Development of error-monitoring event-related potentials in adolescents. *Annals of the New York Academy of Sciences, 1021,* 324–328.

Davies, P. L., Segalowitz, S. J., & Gavin, W. J. (2004b). Development of response-monitoring ERPs in 7- to 25-year-olds. *Developmental Neuropsychology, 25*(3), 355–376.

Degnan, K. A., Hane, A. A., Henderson, H. A., Moas, O. L., Reeb-Sutherland, B. C., & Fox, N. A. (2011). Longitudinal stability of temperamental exuberance and social–emotional outcomes in early childhood. *Developmental Psychology, 47*(3), 765–780.

Delgado, M. R., Nystrom, L. E., Fissell, C., Noll, D. C., & Fiez, J. A. (2000). Tracking the hemodynamic responses to reward and punishment in the striatum. *Journal of Neurophysiology, 84*(6), 3072–3077.

Dennis, T. A. (2010). Neurophysiological markers for child emotion regulation from the perspective of emotion–cognition integration: Current directions and future challenges. *Developmental Neuropsychology, 35*(2), 212–230.

Derryberry, D., & Rothbart, M. K. (1997). Reactive and effortful processes in the organization of temperament. *Developmental Psychopathology, 9*(4), 633–652.

Devinsky, O., Morrell, M. J., & Vogt, B. A. (1995). Contributions of anterior cingulate cortex to behaviour. *Brain, 118*(1), 279–306.

Eldar, S., Ricon, T., & Bar-Haim, Y. (2008). Plasticity in attention: Implications for stress response in children. *Behaviour Research and Therapy, 46,* 450–461.

Ernst, M., Nelson, E. E., Jazbec, S., McClure, E. B., Monk, C. S., Leibenluft, E., et al. (2005). Amygdala and nucleus accumbens in responses to receipt and omission of gains in adults and adolescents. *NeuroImage, 25*(4), 1279–1291.

Ernst, M., Pine, D. S., & Hardin, M. (2006). Triadic model of the neurobiology of motivated behavior in adolescence. *Psychological Medicine, 36*(3), 299–312.

Etkin, A., Klemenhagen, K. C., Dudman, J. T., Rogan, M. T., Hen, R., Kandel, E. R., et al. (2004). Individual differences in trait anxiety predict the response of the basolateral amygdala to unconsciously processed fearful faces. *Neuron, 44,* 1043–1055.

Fair, D. A., Cohen, A. L., Power, J. D., Dosenbach, N. U., Church, J. A., Miezin, F. M., et al. (2009).

Functional brain networks develop from a "local to distributed" organization. *PLoS Computational Biology, 5*(5), e1000381.

Fair, D. A., Dosenbach, N. U., Church, J. A., Cohen, A. L., Brahmbhatt, S., Miezin, F. M., et al. (2007). Development of distinct control networks through segregation and integration. *Proceedings of the National Academy of Sciences, 104*(33), 13507–13512.

Fan, J., Flombaum, J. I., McCandliss, B. D., Thomas, K. M., & Posner, M. I. (2003). Cognitive and brain consequences of conflict. *NeuroImage, 18*(1), 42–57.

Fan, J., Fossella, J., Sommer, T., Wu, Y., & Posner, M. I. (2003). Mapping the genetic variation of executive attention onto brain activity. *Proceedings of the National Academy of Sciences, 100*(12), 7406–7411.

Figner, B., Mackinlay, R. J., Wilkening, F., & Weber, E. U. (2009). Affective and deliberative processes in risky choice: Age differences in risk taking in the Columbia Card Task. *Journal of Experimental Psychology: Learning, Memory, and Cognition, 35*(3), 709–730.

Fossella, J., Sommer, T., Fan, J., Wu, Y., Swansom, J. M., Pfaff, D. W., et al. (2002). Assessing the molecular genetics of attention networks. *BMC Neuroscience, 3*, 14.

Fox, N. A., Bell, M. A., & Jones, N. A. (1992). Individual differences in response to stress and cerebral asymmetry. *Developmental Neuropsychology, 8*, 161–184.

Fox, N. A., Henderson, H. A., Pérez-Edgar, K., & White, L. K. (2008). The biology of temperament: An intergrative approach. In C. A. Nelson & M. L. Collins (Eds.), *Handbook of developmental cognitive neuroscience* (2nd ed., pp. 839–854). Cambridge, MA: MIT Press.

Fox, N. A., Henderson, H. A., Rubin, K. H., Calkins, S. D., & Schmidt, L. A. (2001). Continuity and discontinuity of behavioral inhibition and exuberance: Psychophysiological and behavioral influences across the first four years of life. *Child Development, 72*, 1–21.

Furby, L., & Beythmarom, R. (1992). Risk-taking in adolescence—a decision-making perspective. *Developmental Review, 12*(1), 1–44.

Galvan, A., Hare, T., Voss, H., Glover, G., & Casey, B. J. (2007). Risk-taking and the adolescent brain: Who is at risk? *Developmental Science, 10*(2), F8–F14.

Galvan, A., Hare, T. A., Parra, C. E., Penn, J., Voss, H., Glover, G., et al. (2006). Earlier development of the accumbens relative to orbitofrontal cortex might underlie risk-taking behavior in adolescents. *Journal of Neuroscience, 26*(25), 6885–6892.

Gerardi-Caulton, G. (2000). Sensitivity to spatial conflict and the development of self-regulation in children 24–26 months of age. *Developmental Science, 3*(4), 397–404.

Gerstadt, C. L., Hong, Y. J., & Diamond, A. (1994). The relationship between cognition and action: performance of children 3½–7 years old on a Stroop-like day–night test. *Cognition, 53*, 129–153.

Glocker, M. L., Langleben, D. D., Ruparel, K., Loughead, J. W., Valdez, J. N., Griffin, M. D., et al. (2009). Baby schema modulates the brain reward system in nulliparous women. *Proceedings of the National Academy of Sciences, 106*(22), 9115–9119.

Gonda, X., Fountoulakis, K. N., Juhasz, G., Rihmer, Z., Lazary, J., Laszik, A., et al. (2009). Association of the s allele of the 5-HTTLPR with neuroticism-related traits and temperaments in a psychiatrically healthy population. *European Archives of Psychiatry and Clinical Neuroscience, 259*(2), 106–113.

Guyer, A. E., Kaufman, J., Hodgdon, H. B., Masten, C. L., Jazbec, S., Pine, D. S., et al. (2006). Behavioral alterations in reward system function: The role of childhood maltreatment and psychopathology. *Journal of the American Academy of Child and Adolescent Psychiatry, 45*(9), 1059–1067.

Hajcak, G., McDonald, N., & Simons, R. F. (2004). Error-related psychophysiology and negative affect. *Brain and Cognition, 56*(2), 189–197.

Hane, N. A., Fox, N. A., Henderson, H. A., & Marshal, P. J. (2008). Behavioral reactivity and approach–withdrawal bias in infancy. *Child Development, 44*, 1491–1496.

Hare, T. A., Tottenham, N., Galvan, A., Voss, H. U., Glover, G. H., & Casey, B. J. (2008). Biological substrates of emotional reactivity and regulation in adolescence during an emotional go–no go task. *Biological Psychiatry, 63*(10), 927–934.

Hariri, A. R., & Holmes, A. (2006). Genetics of emotional regulation: The role of the serotonin transporter in neural function. *Trends in Cognitive Sciences, 10*(4), 182–191.

Hariri, A. R., Mattay, V. S., Tessitore, A., Fera, F., & Weinberger, D. R. (2003). Neocortical modulation of the amygdala response to fearful stimuli. *Biological Psychiatry, 53*, 494–501.

Hariri, A. R., Mattay, V. S., Tessitore, A., Kolachana, B., Fera, F., Goldman, D., et al. (2002). Serotonin transporter genetic variation and the response of the human amygdala. *Science, 297*, 400–403.

Helfinstein, S. M., Benson, B., Pérez-Edgar, K., Bar-Haim, Y., Detloff, A., Pine, D. S., et al. (2011). Striatal responses to negative monetary outcomes differ between temperamentally inhibited and non-inhibited adolescents. *Neuropsychologia, 49*(3), 479–485.

Henderson, H. A. (2010). Electrophysiological correlates of cognitive control and the regulation of shyness in children. *Developmental Neuropsychology, 35*(2), 177–193.

Henderson, H. A., & Wachs, T. D. (2007). Temperament theory and the study of cognition–emotion interactions across development. *Developmental Review*, 27, 396–427.

Huizinga, M., Dolan, C. V., & van der Molen, M. W. (2006). Age-related change in executive function: Developmental trends and a latent variable analysis. *Neuropsychologia*, 44(11), 2017–2036.

Kagan, J. (1962). *Birth to maturity*. New York: Wiley.

Kagan, J., Reznick, J. S., & Snidman, N. (1987). The physiology and psychology of behavioral inhibition in children. *Child Development*, 58, 1459–1473.

Kagan, J., Reznick, J. S., Snidman, N., Gibbons, J., & Johnson, M. O. (1988). Childhood derivatives of inhibition and lack of inhibition to the unfamiliar. *Child Development*, 59, 1580–1589.

Kagan, J., & Snidman, N. (1991). Temperamental factors in human development. *American Psychologist*, 46, 856–862.

Kelly, A. M., Di Martino, A., Uddin, L. Q., Shehzad, Z., Gee, D. G., Reiss, P. T., et al. (2009). Development of anterior cingulate functional connectivity from late childhood to early adulthood. *Cerebral Cortex*, 19(3), 640–657.

Kerns, J. G., Cohen, J. D., MacDonald, A. W., III, Cho, R. Y., Stenger, V. A., & Carter, C. S. (2004). Anterior cingulate conflict monitoring and adjustments in control. *Science*, 303, 1023–1026.

Kim, S. H., & Hamann, S. (2007). Neural correlates of positive and negative emotion regulation. *Journal of Cognitive Neuroscience*, 19(5), 776–798.

Knutson, B., Adams, C. M., Fong, G. W., & Hommer, D. (2001). Anticipation of increasing monetary reward selectively recruits nucleus accumbens. *Journal of Neuroscience*, 21(16), RC159.

Knutson, B., & Cooper, J. C. (2005). Functional magnetic resonance imaging of reward prediction. *Current Opinion in Neurology*, 18(4), 411–417.

Knutson, B., Westdorp, A., Kaiser, E., & Hommer, D. (2000). FMRI visualization of brain activity during a monetary incentive delay task. *NeuroImage*, 12(1), 20–27.

Konrad, K., Neufang, S., Thiel, C. M., Specht, K., Hanisch, C., Fan, J., et al. (2005). Development of attentional networks: An fMRI study with children and adults. *NeuroImage*, 28(2), 429–439.

Kopp, C. (1982). Antecedents of self-regulation: A developmental perspective. *Developmental Psychology*, 18, 199–214.

Krebs, R. M., Schott, B. H., & Duzel, E. (2009). Personality traits are differentially associated with patterns of reward and novelty processing in the human substantia nigra/ventral tegmental area. *Biological Psychiatry*, 65(2), 103–110.

Ladouceur, C. D., Conway, A., & Dahl, R. E. (2010). Attentional control moderates relations between negative affect and neural correlates of action monitoring in adolescence. *Developmental Neuropsychology*, 35(2), 194–211.

Ladouceur, C. D., Dahl, R. E., & Carter, C. S. (2004). ERP correlates of action monitoring in adolescence. *Annals of the New York Academy of Sciences*, 1021, 329–336.

Ladouceur, C. D., Dahl, R. E., & Carter, C. S. (2007). Development of action monitoring through adolescence into adulthood: ERP and source localization. *Developmental Science*, 10(6), 874–891.

Lamm, C., & Lewis, M. D. (2010). Developmental change in the neurophysiological correlates of self-regulation in high- and low-emotion conditions. *Developmental Neuropsychology*, 35(2), 156–176.

Lamm, C., Zelazo, P. D., & Lewis, M. D. (2006). Neural correlates of cognitive control in childhood and adolescence: Disentangling the contributions of age and executive function. *Neuropsychologia*, 44, 2139–2148.

Laviola, G., Macri, S., Morley-Fletcher, S., & Adriani, W. (2003). Risk-taking behavior in adolescent mice: Psychobiological determinants and early epigenetic influence. *Neuroscience and Biobehavioral Reviews*, 27(1–2), 19–31.

LeDoux, J. E. (1996). Emotional networks and motor control: A fearful view. *Progress in Brain Research*, 107, 437–446.

LeDoux, J. E. (2000). Emotion circuits of the Brain. *Annual Review of Neuroscience*, 23, 155–184.

LeDoux, J. E., Iwata, J., Cicchetti, P., & Reis, D. J. (1988). Different projections of the central amygdaloid nucleus mediate autonomic and behavioral correlates of conditioned fear. *Journal of Neuroscience*, 8(7), 2517–2529.

Lesch, K. P., Bengel, D., Heils, A., Sabol, S. Z., Greenberg, B. D., Petri, S., et al. (1996). Association of anxiety-related traits with a polymorphism in the serotonin transporter gene regulatory region. *Science*, 274, 1527–1531.

Levesque, J., Eugene, F., Joanette, Y., Paquette, V., Mensour, B., Beaudoin, G., et al. (2003). Neural circuitry underlying voluntary suppression of sadness. *Biological Psychiatry*, 53(6), 502–510.

Levita, L., Hare, T. A., Voss, H. U., Glover, G., Ballon, D. J., & Casey, B. J. (2009). The bivalent side of the nucleus accumbens. *NeuroImage*, 44(3), 1178–1187.

Lewis, M. D., Lamm, C., Segalowitz, S. J., Stieben, J., & Zelazo, P. D. (2006). Neurophysiological correlates of emotion regulation in children and adolescents. *Journal of Cognitive Neuroscience*, 18(3), 430–443.

Lewis, M. D., Todd, R. M., & Honsberger, M. J. (2007). Event-related potential measures of emotion regulation in early childhood. *NeuroReport*, 18, 61–65.

Liston, C., Watts, R., Tottenham, N., Davidson, M. C., Niogi, S., Ulug, A. M., et al. (2006). Frontostriatal microstructure modulates efficient recruitment of cognitive control. *Cerebral Cortex, 16*(4), 553–560.

Lonigan, C. J., & Vasey, M. W. (2009). Negative affectivity, effortful control, and attention to threat-relevant stimuli. *Journal of Abnormal Child Psychology, 37*(3), 387–399.

Luna, B., Padmanabhan, A., & O'Hearn, K. (2010). What has fMRI told us about the development of cognitive control through adolescence? *Brain and Cognition, 72*(1), 101–113.

Luna, B., & Sweeney, J. A. (2004). The emergence of collaborative brain function: FMRI studies of the development of response inhibition. *Annals of the New York Academy of Sciences, 1021*, 296–309.

MacDonald, A. W., III, Cohen, J. D., Stenger, V. A., & Carter, C. S. (2000). Dissociating the role of the dorsolateral prefrontal and anterior cingulate cortex in cognitive control. *Science, 288*, 1835–1838.

MacLeod, C., Rutherford, E., Campbell, L., Ebsworthy, G., & Holker, L. (2002). Selective attention and emotional vulnerability: Assessing the causal basis of their association through the experimental manipulation of attentional bias. *Journal of Abnormal Psychology, 111*(1), 107–123.

Malhotra, A. K., Virkkunen, M., Rooney, W., Eggert, M., Linnoila, M., & Goldman, D. (1996). The association between the dopamine D4 receptor (D4DR) 16 amino acid repeat polymorphism and novelty seeking. *Molecular Psychiatry, 1*(5), 388–391.

Marsh, R., Zhu, H., Schultz, R. T., Quackenbush, G., Royal, J., Skudlarski, P., et al. (2006). A developmental fMRI study of self-regulatory control. *Human Brain Mapping, 27*(11), 848–863.

Marshall, P. J., Reeb, B. C., & Fox, N. A. (2009). Electrophysiological responses to auditory novelty in temperamentally different 9-month-old Infants. *Developmental Science, 12*, 568–582.

McDermott, J. M., & Fox, N. A. (2010). Exploring response-monitoring: Developmental differences and contributions to self-regulation. In R. H. Hoyle (Ed.), *Handbook of self-regulation and personality* (pp. 91–113). Oxford, UK: Wiley/Blackwell.

McDermott, J. M., Pérez-Edgar, K., Henderson, H. A., Chronis-Tuscano, A., Pine, D. S., & Fox, N. A. (2009). A history of childhood behavioral inhibition and enhanced response monitoring in adolescence are linked to clinical anxiety. *Biological Psychiatry, 65*, 445–448.

Miller, E. K. (2000). The prefrontal cortex and cognitive control. *Nature Reviews Neuroscience, 1*(1), 59–65.

Miller, E. K., & Cohen, J. D. (2001). An integrative theory of prefrontal cortex function. *Annual Review of Neuroscience, 24*, 167–202.

Moffitt, T. E., Arseneault, L., Belsky, D., Dickson, N., Hancox, R. J., Harrington, H., et al. (2011). A gradient of childhood self-control predicts health, wealth, and public safety. *Proceedings of the National Academy of Sciences, 108*(7), 2693–2698.

Monk, C. S., Grillon, C., Baas, J. M., McClure, E. B., Nelson, E. E., Zarahn, E., et al. (2003). A neuroimaging method for the study of threat in adolescents. *Developmental Psychobiology, 43*(4), 359–366.

Monk, C. S., Telzer, E. H., Mogg, K., Bradley, B. P., Mai, X., Louro, H. M., et al. (2008). Amygdala and ventrolateral prefrontal cortex activation to masked angry faces in children and adolescents with generalized anxiety disorders. *Archives of General Psychiatry, 65*, 568–576.

Morris, J. S., Friston, K. J., Buchel, C., Frith, C. D., Young, A. W., Calder, A. J., et al. (1998). A neuromodulatory role for the human amygdala in processing emotional facial expressions. *Brain, 121*(1), 47–57.

Munafo, M. R., Clark, T. G., Moore, L. R., Payne, E., Walton, R., & Flint, J. (2003). Genetic polymorphisms and personality in healthy adults: A systematic review and meta-analysis. *Molecular Psychiatry, 8*(5), 471–484.

Ochsner, K. N., Bunge, S. A., Gross, J. J., & Gabrieli, J. D. E. (2002). Rethinking feelings: An fMRI study of the cognitive regulation of emotion. *Journal of Cognitive Neuroscience, 14*(8), 1215–1229.

Ochsner, K. N., & Gross, J. J. (2005). The cognitive control of emotion. *Trends in Cognitive Sciences, 9*, 242–249.

Ochsner, K. N., Ludlow, D. H., Knierim, K., Hanelin, J., Ramachandran, T., Glover, G. C., et al. (2006). Neural correlates of individual differences in pain-related fear and anxiety. *Pain, 120*(1–2), 69–77.

Ochsner, K. N., Ray, R. D., Cooper, J. C., Robertson, E. R., Chopra, S., Gabrieli, J. D., et al. (2004). For better or for worse: Neural systems supporting the cognitive down- and up-regulation of negative emotion. *NeuroImage, 23*, 483–499.

Pagnoni, G., Zink, C. F., Montague, P. R., & Berns, G. S. (2002). Activity in human ventral striatum locked to errors of reward prediction. *Nature Neuroscience, 5*(2), 97–98.

Pérez-Edgar, K., Bar-Haim, Y., McDermott, J. M., Chronis-Tuscano, A., Pine, D. S., & Fox, N. A. (2010). Attention biases to threat and behavioral inhibition in early childhood shape adolescent social withdrawal. *Emotion, 10*(3), 349–357.

Pérez-Edgar, K., Bar-Haim, Y., McDermott, J. M., Gorodetsky, E., Hodgkinson, C. A., Goldman, D., et al. (2010). Variations in the serotonin-transporter gene are associated with attention bias patterns to positive and negative emotion faces. *Biological Psychology, 83*(3), 269–271.

Pérez-Edgar, K., Reeb-Sutherland, B. C., McDermott, J. M., White, L. K., Henderson, H. A., Degnan, K. A., et al. (2011). Attention biases to threat link behavioral inhibition to social withdrawal over time in very young children. *Journal of Abnormal Child Psychology, 39*(6), 885–895.

Pérez-Edgar, K., Roberson-Nay, R., Hardin, M. G., Poeth, K., Guyer, A. E., Nelson, E. E., et al. (2007). Attention alters neural responses to evocative faces in behaviorally inhibited adolescents. *NeuroImage, 35*(4), 1538–1546.

Pezawas, L., Meyer-Lindenberg, A., Drabant, E. M., Verchinski, B. A., Munoz, K. E., Kolachana, B. S., et al. (2005). 5-HTTLPR polymorphism impacts human cingulate-amygdala interactions: A genetic susceptibility mechanism for depression. *Nature Neuroscience, 8*(6), 828–834.

Posner, M. I., & Fan, J. (2004). *Attention as an organ system*. Cambridge, UK: Cambridge University Press.

Posner, M. I., & Rothbart, M. K. (2009). Toward a physical basis of attention and self regulation. *Physics of Life Reviews, 6*(2), 103–120.

Posner, M. I., Rothbart, M. K., & Sheese, B. E. (2007). Attention genes. *Developmental Science, 10*(1), 24–29.

Posner, M. I., Rothbart, M. K., Sheese, B. E., & Tang, Y. (2007). The anterior cingulate gyrus and the mechanism of self-regulation. *Cognitive, Affective, and Behavioral Neuroscience, 7*(4), 391–395.

Raz, A., & Buhle, J. (2006). Typologies of attentional networks. *Nature Reviews Neuroscience, 7*, 367–379.

Reeb-Sutherland, B. C., Vanderwert, R. E., Degnan, K. A., Marshall, P. J., Pérez-Edgar, K., Chronis-Tuscano, A., et al. (2009). Attention to novelty in behaviorally inhibited adolescents moderates risk for anxiety. *Journal of Child Psychology and Psychiatry, 50*, 1365–1372.

Reuter, M., Ott, U., Vaitl, D., & Hennig, J. (2007). Impaired executive control is associated with a variation in the promoter region of the tryptophan hydroxylase 2 gene. *Journal of Cognitive Neuroscience, 19*(3), 401–408.

Reynolds, S. M., & Berridge, K. C. (2002). Positive and negative motivation in nucleus accumbens shell: Bivalent rostrocaudal gradients for GABA-elicited eating, taste "liking"/"disliking" reactions, place preference/avoidance, and fear. *Journal of Neuroscience, 22*(16), 7308–7320.

Rosenberg, D. R., & Lewis, D. A. (1995). Postnatal maturation of the dopaminergic innervation of monkey prefrontal and motor cortices: A tyrosine hydroxylase immunohistochemical analysis. *Journal of Comparative Neurology, 358*(3), 383–400.

Rothbart, M. K. (1988). Temperament and the development of inhibited approach. *Child Development, 59*, 1241–1250.

Rothbart, M. K., & Derryberry, D. (1981). Development of individual differences in temperament. In M. E. Lamb & A. L. Brown (Eds.), *Advances in developmental psychology* (Vol. 1, pp. 37–86). Hillsdale, NJ: Erlbaum.

Rothbart, M. K., & Rueda, M. R. (2005). The development of effortful control. In U. Mayr, E. Awh, & S. Keele (Eds.), *Developing individuality in the human brain: A tribute to Michael I. Posner* (pp. 167–188). Washington, DC: American Psychological Association.

Rothbart, M. K., Sheese, B. E., & Posner, M. I. (2007). Executive attention and effortful control: Linking temperament, brain networks, and genes. *Child Development Perspectives, 1*, 2–7.

Rubia, K., Smith, A. B., Taylor, E., & Brammer, M. (2007). Linear age-correlated functional development of right inferior fronto-striato-cerebellar networks during response inhibition and anterior cingulate during error-related processes. *Human Brain Mapping, 28*(11), 1163–1177.

Rueda, M. R., Fan, J., McCandliss, B. D., Halparin, J. D., Gruber, D. B., Lercari, L. P., et al. (2004). Development of attentional networks in childhood. *Neuropsychologia, 42*(8), 1029–1040.

Rueda, M. R., Posner, M. I., & Rothbart, M. K. (2005). The development of executive attention: Contributions to the emergence of self-regulation. *Developmental Neuropsychology, 28*(2), 573–594.

Santesso, D. L., & Segalowitz, S. J. (2008). Developmental differences in error-related ERPs in middle- to late-adolescent males. *Developmental Psychology, 44*(1), 205–217.

Santesso, D. L., Segalowitz, S. J., & Schmidt, L. A. (2006). Error-related electrocortical responses in 10-year-old children and young adults. *Developmental Science, 9*(5), 473–481.

Schinka, J. A., Letsch, E. A., & Crawford, F. C. (2002). DRD4 and novelty seeking: Results of meta-analyses. *American Journal of Medical Genetics, 114*(6), 643–648.

Schmidt, L. A., & Fox, N. A. (1998). Fear-potentiated startle responses in temperamentally different human infants. *Developmental Psychobiology, 32*(2), 113–120.

Schultz, W., Dayan, P., & Montague, P. R. (1997). A neural substrate of prediction and reward. *Science, 275*, 1593–1599.

Schwartz, C. E., Kunwar, P. S., Greve, D. N., Kagan, J., Snidman, N. C., & Bloch, R. B. (in press). A phenotype of early infancy predicts reactivity of the amygdala in male adults. *Molecular Psychiatry*.

Schwartz, C. E., Wright, C. I., Shin, L. M., Kagan, J., & Rauch, S. L. (2003). Inhibited and uninhibited infants "grown up": Adult amygdalar response to novelty. *Science, 300*, 1952–1953.

Seymour, B., Daw, N., Dayan, P., Singer, T., &

Dolan, R. (2007). Differential encoding of losses and gains in the human striatum. *Journal of Neuroscience, 27*(18), 4826–4831.

Seymour, B., O'Doherty, J. P., Dayan, P., Koltzenburg, M., Jones, A. K., Dolan, R. J., et al. (2004). Temporal difference models describe higher-order learning in humans. *Nature, 429,* 664–667.

Sheese, B. E., Rothbart, M. K., Posner, M. I., White, L. K., & Fraundorf, S. H. (2008). Executive attention and self-regulation in infancy. *Infant Behavior and Development, 31*(3), 501–510.

Sheese, B. E., Voelker, P., Posner, M. I., & Rothbart, M. K. (2009). Genetic variation influences on the early development of reactive emotions and their regulation by attention. *Cognitive Neuropsychiatry, 14*(4–5), 332–355.

Sheese, B. E., Voelker, P. M., Rothbart, M. K., & Posner, M. I. (2007). Parenting quality interacts with genetic variation in dopamine receptor D4 to influence temperament in early childhood. *Development and Psychopathology, 19*(4), 1039–1046.

Simonds, J., Kieras, J. E., Rueda, M. R., & Rothbart, M. K. (2007). Effortful control, executive attention, and emotional regulation in 7–10-year-old children. *Cognitive Development, 22,* 474–488.

Somerville, L. H., Jones, R. M., & Casey, B. J. (2010). A time of change: Behavioral and neural correlates of adolescent sensitivity to appetitive and aversive environmental cues. *Brain and Cognition, 72*(1), 124–133.

Somerville, L. H., Kim, H., Johnstone, T., Alexander, A. L., & Whalen, P. J. (2004). Human amygdala responses during presentation of happy and neutral faces: Correlations with state anxiety. *Biological Psychiatry, 55*(9), 897–903.

Steinberg, L. (2004). Risk taking in adolescence: What changes, and why? *Annals of the New York Academy of Sciences, 1021,* 51–58.

Stevens, M. C., Kiehl, K. A., Pearlson, G. D., & Calhoun, V. D. (2007). Functional neural networks underlying response inhibition in adolescents and adults. *Behavioural Brain Research, 181*(1), 12–22.

Strelau, J. (1987). The concept of temperament in personality research. *European Journal of Personality, 1,* 107–117.

Tarazi, F. I., Tomasini, E. C., & Baldessarini, R. J. (1998). Postnatal development of dopamine and serotonin transporters in rat caudate-putamen and nucleus accumbens septi. *Neuroscience Letters, 254*(1), 21–24.

Van Leijenhorst, L., Moor, B. G., Op de Macks, Z. A., Rombouts, S. A. R. B., Westenberg, P. M., & Crone, E. A. (2010). Adolescent risky decision-making: Neurocognitive development of reward and control regions. *NeuroImage, 51,* 345–355.

Van Veen, V., & Carter, C. S. (2002a). The anterior cingulate as a conflict monitor: fMRI and ERP studies. *Physiology and Behavior, 77*(4–5), 477–482.

Van Veen, V., & Carter, C. S. (2002b). The timing of action-monitoring processes in the anterior cingulate cortex. *Journal of Cognitive Neuroscience, 14*(4), 593–602.

Voelker, P., Sheese, B. E., Rothbart, M. K., & Posner, M. I. (2009). Variations in catechol-O-methyltransferase gene interact with parenting to influence attention in early development. *Neuroscience, 164*(1), 121–130.

Wahlstrom, D., White, T., Hooper, C. J., Vrshek-Schallhorn, S., Oetting, W. S., Brott, M. J., et al. (2007). Variations in the catechol O-methyltransferase polymorphism and prefrontally guided behaviors in adolescents. *Biological Psychiatry, 61*(5), 626–632.

Walter, M., Bermpohl, F., Mouras, H., Schiltz, K., Tempelmann, C., Rotte, M., et al. (2008). Distinguishing specific sexual and general emotional effects in fMRI-subcortical and cortical arousal during erotic picture viewing. *NeuroImage, 40*(4), 1482–1494.

Waters, A. M., Wharton, T. A., Zimmer-Gembeck, M. J., & Craske, M. G. (2008). Threat-based cognitive biases in anxious children: Comparison with non-anxious children before and after cognitive behavioural treatment. *Behaviour Research Therapy, 46*(3), 358–374.

White, L. K., Helfinstein, S. M., & Fox, N. A. (2010). Temperamental factors associated with the acquisition of information processing biases and anxiety. In J. A. Hadwin & A. P. Field (Eds.), *Information processing biases and anxiety: A developmental perspective* (pp. 233–252). West Sussex, UK: Wiley-Blackwell.

White, L. K., Helfinstein, S. M., Reeb-Sutherland, B. C., Degnan, K. A., & Fox, N. A. (2009). Role of attention in the regulation of fear and anxiety. *Developmental Neuroscience, 31*(4), 309–317.

White, L. K., McDermott, J. M., Degnan, K. A., Henderson, H. A., & Fox, N. A. (2011). Behavioral inhibition and anxiety: The moderating roles of inhibitory control and attention shifting. *Journal of Abnormal Child Psychology, 39*(5), 735–747.

Wittmann, B., Daw, N., Seymour, B., & Dolan, R. (2008). Striatal activity underlies novelty-based choice in humans. *Neuron, 58,* 967–973.

Yin, H. H., & Knowlton, B. J. (2006). The role of the basal ganglia in habit formation. *Nature Reviews Neuroscience, 7*(6), 464–476.

Zelazo, P. D. (2006). The dimensional change card sort (DCCS): A method of assessing executive function in children. *Nature Protocols, 1,* 297–301.

CHAPTER 18

Neurobiology and Neurochemistry of Temperament in Adults

Richard A. Depue
Yu Fu

The Construct of Temperament

Forty years ago, Gray (1973) revolutionized thinking about the nature and structure of human behavior. He argued that behavior reflects the activity of emotional–motivational systems that evolved to increase adaptation to broad classes of stimuli associated with positive and negative outcomes, such as incentive and aversive stimuli. Individual differences in these systems reflect variation in the sensitivity to such stimuli, where *sensitivity* ultimately refers to the threshold of stimulus-elicited reactivity of the neurobiology associated with an emotional/motivational system.

Gray and others (Cloninger, 1986; Depue & Collins, 1999; Depue & Morrone-Strupinsky, 2005) extended this framework by suggesting that the higher-order traits of personality reflect the structure of these emotional/motivational systems. This implies that individual differences in personality reflect variation in the neurobiological underpinnings of emotional/motivational systems. These individual differences arise from variation in the regulation of gene expression and in environmental influences affecting gene regulation, a process known as *epigenetics*. In our view, the basic nature and structure of temperament is the same as that described earlier for personality: *Temperament* is the early expression of individual differences in reactivity of emotional–motivational systems to broad classes of critical stimuli. In this way, temperament may be thought of as the reflection of the genetic foundation of these systems prior to significant postnatal, but not prenatal (Davis & Sandman, 2010; Eysenck, 1981), environmental influence.

As we hope to demonstrate in this chapter, the significance of the construct of temperament is that it defines the neurogenetic foundation upon which epigenetic influences operate during the early postnatal period. It is in this early postnatal period that an extended period of synapse formation and adjustment takes place in the forebrain, enhancing neural circuitries and networks (Fox, Levitt, & Nelson, 2010). Particularly during this period, and perhaps in other experience-expectant periods as well (e.g., adolescence, Paus, Keshavan, & Giedd, 2008), the development of neural circuitries is highly sensitive to experience. This is because experience-dependent activity modulates the expression of transcription factors that affect gene expression of structural proteins, receptors, and signaling molecules (Gaspar, Cases, & Maroteaux, 2003; Meaney, 2001). Thus, in this period, genetic variation interacts with experience to establish an enduring basic neural foundation underlying emotional behavior. Indeed, as we discuss below, similar experiences occurring after the early postnatal period may have no discernible effects on neural or behavioral functioning. Perhaps this is one major reason that temperament/personality is unstable before age 3 but relatively stable thereafter into adulthood (Caspi, Roberts, & Shiner, 2005).

Overall, then, it is in this early postnatal period of forebrain neural development that the construct of temperament is most important. The individual differences in neurogenetic processes underlying variation in the emotional/motivational systems of temperament condition or modulate the *extent* of the influence of experience on neurobiology. That is what the concept of gene–environment interaction implies (Meaney, 2001). Thus, the degree to which different types of experience affect gene regulation will depend in large part upon an individual's neurogenetic characteristics (temperament) during the early postnatal period (see also van IJzendoorn & Bakermans-Kranenburg, Chapter 19, this volume).

Neurogenetic and Experiential Processes in the Development of Individual Differences in Higher-Order Temperament/Personality Traits

Here we use the common names of higher-order personality traits, since they are well established and have a relatively common understanding. We understand, however, that the earliest expression of these traits represents temperament traits, which more closely reflect the activity of emotional/motivational systems. In a revised concept of temperament that follows our line of thinking, it would probably be best to refer to temperament traits directly by the name of the emotional/motivational systems underlying personality traits. Since these systems are not as commonly known or understood, however, we begin our effort to define temperament by using the names of personality traits.

If higher-order temperament/personality traits reflect the activity of affective neurobehavioral systems, the manner in which individual differences develop within these systems comprises the essence of personality research. In this section we focus particularly on the higher-order traits of Neuroticism, Extraversion, Social Closeness/Agreeableness, and Constraint/Conscientiousness, plus a social trait unduly overlooked—Social Rejection Sensitivity—because their phenotypes correspond most closely and most comprehensively to the characterizations of the major temperament traits (Caspi et al., 2005; Eysenck, 1981). These five traits are discussed in terms of their (1) phenotype and affective system, and (2) neurogenetic and experiential processes that interact over time to create individual variation. Some traits, or the affective systems they reflect, have been associated with several neurobiological factors, and we attempt to organize their relation to each other through final common pathways. In our discussion, we have also relied on animal research on neurobehavioral variables that are analogous to the central behavioral and affective features that characterize higher-order traits, even if such variables have not been directly related to the personality trait thus far. Where data are available, we also address the importance of early postnatal experience in the development of individual differences. Thus, our goal is to provide a neurobehavioral framework of higher-order traits that can be used as a guide for further research on temperament at the human trait level.

Neuroticism

Phenotype and Affective System

Anxiety and stress reactivity are among the best-studied traits with neurobiological foundations. To do justice to the extensive literature this section on Neuroticism will be somewhat more extensive relative to the section on the other traits.

The content of Neuroticism scales reflects in large part a state of heightened reactivity to stress, with groups of items describing (1) negative affect of various types (anxious, distressed, nervous, irritable, touchy, depressed, worried, hostile, jittery); (2) labile, reactive moods; and (3) negative valuation of self and others. Accordingly, the trait has also been termed *Negative Emotionality* (Markon, Krueger, & Watson, 2005; Tellegen & Waller, 2008); in Tellegen's scheme, the strongest primary trait marker is Stress Reactivity. External validity of this view of the content of Neuroticism is shown by the strong association of Neuroticism with longitudinally assessed negative affect (Tellegen & Waller, 2008), and with responsiveness to negative mood induction (Canli, 2008).

We conceive of the core aspects of Neuroticism as reflecting the affective system of anxiety. Therefore, we review below research areas that are relevant to the anxiety system, which is associated with heightened stress reactivity. Although many researchers combine anxiety and fear as if they are similar emotions, they are, in fact, independent as affective systems and as personality traits (White & Depue, 1999). That is, they are elicited by different stimulus properties that travel different neural routes, they involve different main neural endpoints and neuromodulators, and as traits they correlate near zero and load on different factors (Cooper, Perkins, & Corr, 2007; Davis, 2006; Depue, 2009; Tellegen & Waller, 2008). Fear evolved as a means of escaping unconditioned aversive stimuli that are inherently dangerous to survival, such as tactile pain, injury contexts, snakes, spiders, heights, predators, and sudden sounds. These stimuli are specific, discrete, and explicit, and in turn elicit specific, short-latency, high-magnitude phasic responses of autonomic arousal, subjective feelings of panic, and behavioral escape via brainstem circuitries in the periacqueductal gray when escape is possible (Davis, 2006; Somerville, Whalen, & Kelley, 2010). Specific, discrete, neutral contextual stimuli associated with these unconditioned events elicit conditioned fear, which at the trait level is not anxiety but rather is fearfulness, harm avoidance, and timidity.

There are, however, many aversive contexts that include nondiscrete contextual stimuli associated with an elevated *potential* risk of danger or aversive consequences. Such stimuli can be unconditioned (USs; e.g., darkness, open spaces, unfamiliarity, approaching strangers, predator odors) or conditioned contextual cues (CSs; e.g., general textures, colors, relative spatial locations, sounds) (Davis, 2006; Fendt, Endres, & Apfelbach, 2003). Conceptually, these stimuli are commonly characterized by unpredictability and uncontrollability—or, more simply, uncertainty.

In order to reduce the risk of danger in circumstances of uncertainty, a second behavioral system evolved—anxiety. *Anxiety* is characterized by negative affect that serves the purpose of informing the individual that, although no explicit, specific aversive stimuli may be present, conditions are potentially threatening (e.g., consider a deer entering an open meadow; Davis, 2006; White & Depue, 1999). This affective state, and the physiological arousal that accompanies it, continues or reverberates until the uncertainty is resolved (Gray & McNaughton, 2000; Somerville et al., 2010). Associated responses that may functionally help to resolve the uncertainty are heightened attentional scanning of the uncertain environment, and cognitive worrying and rumination over possible negative response outcome scenarios. These stimulus conditions indicate why the trait of Neuroticism is characterized by *both* anxiety and stress reactivity, among other emotional and cognitive components. Contexts that are anxiety-inducing are essentially stressors. In other words, aversive situations that are characterized by uncontrollability, unpredictability, unfamiliarity, unavoidability, and uncertainty are considered stressful and elicit anxiety. Put differently, anxiety is essentially an affective response to the uncertainty that characterizes stressful events.

Thus, several researchers (Barlow, 2002; Cooper et al., 2007; Davis, 2006; White & Depue, 1999) have suggested that the stimulus conditions and behavioral characteristics of fear and anxiety are different, and are independent traits psychometrically, although a similar state of intense autonomic arousal is associated with both emotional states, rendering their overlap at the subjective level. It is important to emphasize, however, that the *prolonged* negative subjective state of anxiety distinguishes it from the rapid, brief state of panic elicited by the presence of a specific fear stimulus.

Neurobiological, Genetic, and Experiential Factors

Neuroanatomical research with animals demonstrates that fear and anxiety reflect different affective systems. It is now well established that cortical uni- and polymodal sensory efferents convey discrete, explicit stimuli to the basolateral complex of the amygdala (BLA), where they are affectively encoded (Davis, 2006; Kalin, Shelton, & Davidson, 2004; LeDoux, 1998). In the case of discrete aversive USs (e.g., a shock) and CSs (e.g., a tone), fear is expressed as a diverse pattern of behavioral, neuropeptide, and autonomic responses via output from the BLA to the central amygdala (Ce), which in turn sends functionally separable efferents to many hypothalamic and brainstem targets (Davis, 2006; LeDoux, 1998; Somerville et al., 2010).

In contrast, nondiscrete, contextually related rewarding or aversive stimuli (e.g., an open space or darkness) are affectively encoded by a group of structures collectively referred to as the *extended amygdala*. The extended amygdala receives massive projections from BLA, and olfactory amygdala complexes and the hippocampus, and represents a macrostructure characterized by two divisions, central and medial (Heimer, 2003; Kalin, Shelton, Davidson, & Kelley, 2001). The central division consists of distributed cell groups that include the bed nucleus of the stria terminalis (BNST). The BNST appears to associate *general contextual features and nonexplicit, nondiscrete* CSs and USs with reward or punishment (e.g., spatial layout and relations; color and brightness of light; physical features such as texture; availability of hiding places) (Davis, 2006; McDonald, Shammah-Lagnado, Shi, & Davis, 1999). Similar to the outputs from the Ce, the BNST can transmit this motivationally relevant information to some or all hypothalamic and brainstem structures related to emotional expression (Heimer, 2003). Significantly, there is a double dissociation of fear and anxiety as mediated by the Ce and lateral BNST, respectively (Davis, 2006). As discussed further below, the lateral BNST is particularly critical in mediating the prolonged-duration, variable-magnitude negative affective states characterizing anxiety as opposed to fear (Somerville et al., 2010).

Animal and human research have identified four major neurobiological factors that are associated with anxiety and stress reactivity: (1) the central corticotropin-releasing hormone (CRH) system, (2) a genetic polymorphism in the gene that codes for the serotonin transporter, (3) variation in the gene that codes for the serotonin 1A receptor, and (4) the peripheral glucocorticoid system. Norepinephrine does not appear to have a primary role in anxiety, but it may have a strong modulatory effect (Aston-Jones & Cohen, 2005). Importantly, most of these neurobiological factors are subject to modification by adverse events, particularly in early postnatal development, raising the possibility of gene–environment interactions in the expression of anxiety and stress reactivity. By necessity, we review these areas of research briefly, but in a final subsection, we provide an integrated final common pathway model of how these various factors may jointly influence individual variation in the trait of Neuroticism.

Central CRH System: Integration of an Anxiety/Stress Response Network

Stressful contexts are complex sensory events that can include both aversive explicit, discrete stimuli and nonexplicit stimuli associated with uncertainty, eliciting a mélange of negative affective feelings. (Imagine a deer entering an open meadow, which is characterized by uncertainty, and subsequently a wolf entering the same meadow—an explicit aversive stimulus. This complex context then contains both fear- and anxiety-inducing cues.) Both the BLA and the lateral BNST are involved in responding to such complex contexts. Indeed, the amygdala has often been viewed as a threat detector that rapidly activates other neural structures in the presence of discrete danger cues, including the BNST, to set in motion an array of adaptive responses at times of stress. The BNST has also been implicated in threat detection but activates *sustained* vigilance in ambiguous, uncertain contexts (Somerville et al., 2010).

The BLA and BNST sit at the head of a network of structures that integrate behavioral, neuroendocrine, and autonomic responses to stressful circumstances (Leri, Flores, Rodaros, & Stewart, 2002). This integration is accomplished by the activity of both the peripheral and central CRH systems. The *peripheral* system involves CRH neurons located in the paraventricular nucleus of the hypothalamus (PVN), which, when activated, initiates the series of events that ends in the release of cortisol from the adrenal cortex (Kim & Diamond, 2002). In contrast, the *central* CRH system is composed of CRH neurons located in many different brain regions. A set of the CRH-containing regions that are important in mediating stress effects is illustrated in Figure 18.1. In particular, the BLA rapidly detects specific threatening aversive stimuli associated with stressful circumstances and activates the extensive array of CRH neurons located in the Ce (approximately 1,750 neurons per hemisphere) (Merali, Michaud, McIntosh, Kent, & Anisman, 2003; Somerville et al., 2010). These CRH neurons project to many brain regions that modulate emotion, memory, and arousal, including the BNST and the peripheral CRH neurons in the PVN. Stress

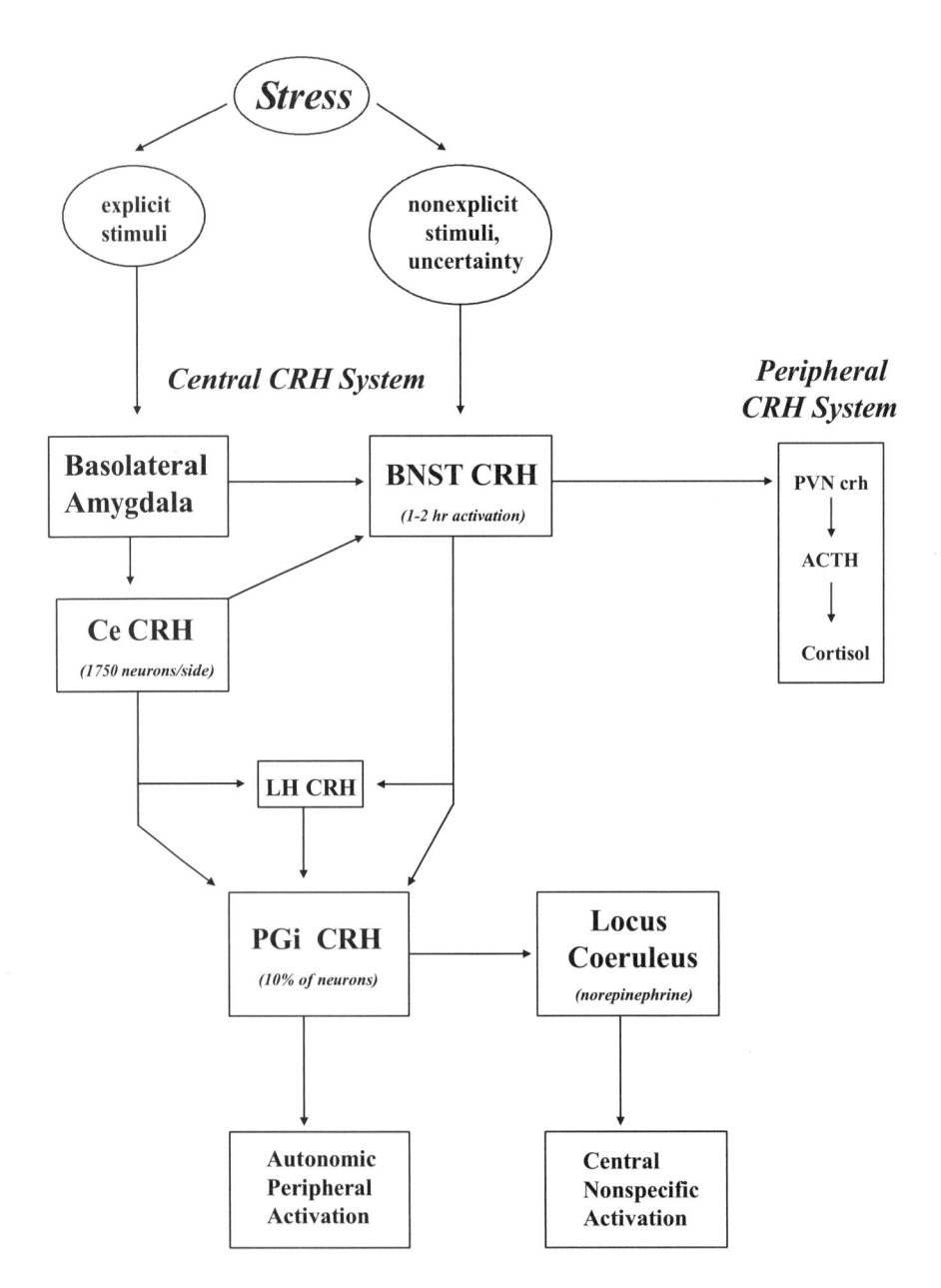

FIGURE 18.1. Components of the central and peripheral corticotropin-releasing hormone (CRH) systems. ACTH, adrenocorticotropic hormone from the anterior pituitary; BNST, bed nucleus of the stria terminalis; Ce, central amygdala nucleus; LH, lateral hypothalamus; Pgi, paragiganticocellularis; PVN, paraventricular nucleus of the hypothalamus.

variables associated with context and uncertainty activate CRH neurons in the BNST, which have similar projection targets as the Ce (Macey, Smith, Nader, & Porrino, 2003). Both the Ce and BNST can activate CRH neurons in the lateral hypothalamus (LH), a region that integrates central nervous system (CNS) arousal and, in turn, modulates autonomic nervous system (ANS) activity.

Importantly, as illustrated in Figure 18.1, all three sources of CRH projections—the Ce, BNST, and LH—innervate CRH neurons in the paragigantocellularis (Pgi) (Aston-Jones & Cohen, 2005; Aston-Jones, Rajkowski, Kubiak, Valentino, & Shiptley, 1996), which is located in the rostral ventrolateral area of the medulla. The PGi is a massive nucleus that provides major integration of central and autonomic arousal and, in turn, coordinates and triggers arousal responses to urgent stimuli via two main pathways emanating from its own population of CRH neurons, which make up 10% of PGi neurons (Aston-Jones et al., 1996). One CRH pathway modulates the ANS via projections to the intermediolateral cell column of the spinal cord, activating sympathetic preganglionic autonomic neurons. The other CRH pathway modulates central arousal via activation of the locus coeruleus (LC), where PGi CRH innervation of the LC in humans and monkeys is dense (Aston-Jones et al., 1996). The LC, whose neurons provide the major source of norepinephrine (NE) in the brain, innervates the entire brain. LC neurons that release NE onto beta-adrenergic receptors are responsible for producing a nonspecific emotional activation pattern that comprises a global urgent response system. And this central arousal can be enduring: PGi CRH activation of LC neurons peaks 40 minutes after stimulation of the PGi (Aston-Jones et al., 1996). Thus, taken together, the central CRH neuron system is capable of activating a vast array of behaviorally relevant neural and hormonal processes during stressful conditions, including activation of the peripheral CRH system.

Early research demonstrated that CRH injected into the BNST, as opposed to the Ce, activates an anxious behavioral profile and, importantly, that the effect is temporally prolonged (for up to 2 hours), a phenotypic characteristic of anxiety but not Ce-mediated fear. Subsequent work has confirmed a specific role for CRH in the BNST in the mediation of anxiogenic effects. For instance, marked anxiety lasting longer than 24 hours is produced after administration of three doses of CRH over 1.5 hours, despite the lack of a lasting effect on peripheral release of corticosterone (Servatius et al., 2005). The source of naturally occurring CRH in the BNST is the Ce's population of CRH neurons: CRH release from the Ce after a psychogenic stressor causes long-term (up to 7 days) anxiety effects in rats, which correlates with cerebrospinal fluid (CSF) CRH concentrations (Merali et al., 2003).

The anxiogenic effects of CRH are specific to the lateral region of the BNST. Intralateral BNST (but not intra-Ce) administration of CRH in rats elicits dose-dependent anxiogenic effects (Nie et al., 2004), as well as aversion to an environment paired with CRH injections (Sahuque et al., 2006). Moreover, forebrain *CRH-R1* receptors mediate these anxiogenic effects. Transgenic mice with elevated *CRH-R1* (but not with elevated R2) receptors in the central forebrain (but with no elevation peripherally in the hypothalamus or pituitary) show extreme indications of anxiety. In contrast, mice with knockout of the *CRH-R1* (but not R2) receptor gene in the central (but not peripheral) forebrain show little anxiety in the elevated-T maze or in the light–dark test (both being aversive USs; Deussing & Wurst, 2005).

Individual differences in anxious temperament are associated with individual variation in BNST metabolism at rest in primates (Fox, Shelton, Oakes, Davidson, & Kalin, 2008; Oler et al., 2009) and with exaggerated tracking of threat proximity in humans (Somerville et al., 2010). In contrast, BNST lesions eliminate individual variability in anxiety behaviors in rodents (Durvarci, Bauer, & Pare, 2009). Moreover, several *CRH-R1* gene variants taken together as the TAT haplotype appear to reduce cortisol response to stress and decrease the risk of anxiety and depression in humans who experienced early life adversity (Binder & Nemeroff, 2010). Concordant with these findings, one study demonstrated that extreme trait levels of anxiety may be ameliorated in male monkeys via a *CRH-R1* antagonist (Habib et al., 2000).

Neural factors that contribute to the trait of Neuroticism may be influenced by experience earlier in life. Early postnatal adversity, including separations from mother rats, caused in pups later in life to experience enhanced reactivity to brief stressors in the form of (1) anxiety behaviors, (2) corticosterone secretion, (3) CRH messenger RNA (mRNA) expression in the Ce, and (4) increased hypothalamic–pituitary–adrenal (HPA) axis responsiveness (Gillespie & Nemeroff, 2007; Ladd et al., 2000; Plotsky & Meaney, 1993; Plotsky et al., 2005). Similarly, monkeys reared under stressful conditions show increased CSF CRH relative to monkeys reared under nonstressful conditions (Coplan et al., 1996; Sanchez et al., 2005). In humans, early life trauma is a robust predictor of CSF CRH concentrations in adulthood (Carpenter et al., 2004; Lee, Geracioti, Kasckow, & Coccaro, 2005; Lee, Gollan, Kasckow, Geracioti, & Coccaro, 2006). This set of findings raises the possibility that early adverse experience affectively encoded in BLA may result in a persistent Ce-induced *CRH-R1* activation in the lateral BNST. Importantly, one study indicates that such repeated activation can sensitize CRH receptors in the BNST, leading to prolonged anxiety effects (Lee, Fitz, Johnson, & Shekhar, 2008).

Taken together, the CRH findings strongly suggest that anxiety is essentially a stress response system that relies on a central network of CRH neuron populations acting via *CRH-R1* receptors that provide integrated responses (hormonal, behavioral, autonomic, and central arousal) to the stressor (see Figure 18.1). CRH, especially in the lateral BNST, mediates what is a defining characteristic of anxiety as opposed to fear: *prolonged* anxiogenic effects that last as long as uncertainty is unresolved, and aversive *contextual* conditioning (Davis, 2006; Somerville et al., 2010; White & Depue, 1999). These CRH-induced psychological effects appear to strongly match the content of trait Neuroticism measures.

Polymorphism of the Serotonin Transporter Gene

Serotonin (5-HT) is mainly inactivated by an uptake process that requires active transport across the presynaptic membrane by the 5-HT transporter (*5-HTT*). Although there are a number of polymorphisms in the gene (*SLC6A4*) that code for *5-HTT*, most work has focused on a polymorphism in the promotor region of the gene. This polymorphism results in two common alleles, referred to as long (l) and short (s) alleles, since their respective promotor regions differ in nucleotide number (Lesch & Canli, 2006). The l-allele codes for enhanced mRNA production and, due to the facilitatory effects of the promotor region on gene transcription, therefore produces more transporter protein than the s-allele. The s-allele is characterized by reduced *5-HTT* promotor activity and *5-HTT* expression, although the functional effects of these differences remain uncertain (Lesch & Canli, 2006).

This l/s polymorphism is associated with effects at both behavioral and neural levels. At the behavioral level, two meta-analyses and reanalysis of a third meta-analysis found that individuals who carry one or two copies of the s-allele have higher Neuroticism scores than individuals who carry two l-alleles (Canli, 2008). The association is characterized by a small effect size, accounting for only 3–4% of the total observed variance, indicating that many genes may be associated with variation in the broad phenotype of Neuroticism. Furthermore, this indicates that there is a long distance between the gene's molecular coding and the measured phenotype (referred to as the *exo*phenotype of the trait; Meyer-Lindenberg & Weinberger, 2006). With reference to the last point, as we discuss below, *endo*phenotypes of Neuroticism, that is, phenotypes closer to the level of gene activity (e.g., neural functioning), do have a stronger association with Neuroticism scores. Nevertheless, the *5-HTT* association is striking because no other gene variants have shown a consistent association with Neuroticism (Canli, 2008). Moreover, animal and human behavioral work is consistent with the genotype-trait findings. Thus, *5-HTT* knockout mice exhibit increased anxiety and reduced exploration, and primates who carry the homologue of the s-allele express increased behavioral anxiety and reduced social interaction (Hariri, 2006). In addition, human carriers of the s-allele show a stronger attentional bias for anxiety-related words than carriers of only the l-allele (Canli, 2008).

On the neural level, the s-allele has been associated with both neural function and structure. A meta-analysis demonstrated that the s-allele has been consistently associated in both human males and females with enhanced amygdala reactivity to many forms of negative emotional stimuli relative to neutral cues, including fear and angry faces, and negative scenes and words (Canli & Lesch, 2007; Hariri, 2006). The effect size of this association is about six times greater than that found for self-report measures (also see Kagan, Chapter 4, this volume). Importantly, social threat appears to be a potent elicitor of activation in s-allele carriers. Thus, increased activation was found in the BNST, as well as the amygdala, specifically in uncertain social threat conditions in rhesus monkeys carrying the homologue of the human s-allele (Kalin et al., 2008). Moreover, human s-allele carriers had increased anterior cingulate activity that was associated with a profound effect on cortisol secretion—especially in response to social threat (Jahn et al., 2010; Way & Taylor, 2010). Finally, the s-allele is also associated with reduced gray matter volume in the human amygdala, which may reflect reduced dendritic branching and axonal arborization (Hariri, 2006; Pezawas et al., 2005). Overall, then, there is a link between gene variation and basic brain mechanisms involved in processing negative emotion.

The reduced gray matter volume and increased reactivity of the amygdala in s-allele carriers (both s/s and l/s) raises the possibility that the amygdala's neural circuitry interactions (i.e., its projections to and efferents from other brain regions) may be influenced. Reviews have shown that increased amygdala responsivity is associated with reduced connectivity between the amygdala and other brain regions that regulate cognitive and emotional processes. Indeed, recent research on s-allele neural correlates shows that the anterior cingulate cortex (ACC)–amygdala circuitry confirms this possibility. Specifically, the perigenual portion of the ACC (pACC), which surrounds the genua of the corpus collosum, is composed of the subgenual, rostral (rACC) and the supragenual, caudal (cACC) regions. As illustrated in Figure 18.2, animal research indicates that the rACC receives the most dense projections from the amygdala and conveys that information to the cACC, which in turn sends inhibitory efferents back to the amygdala (Pezawas et al., 2005). This circuitry is critical in modulating amygdala reactivity via inhibitory feedback from cACC to the amygdala during times of emotional stress, and thus serves as an important emotion regulation circuit.

Pezawas and colleagues (2005) found nonclinical human s-allele carriers to have reduced gray matter volume of both the pACC and the amygdala, with the most pronounced reduction in the rACC region, and a reduced covariance of pACC (especially rACC)–amygdala volumes. Furthermore, during the processing of fearfuls and angry faces, there was greatly reduced positive cova-

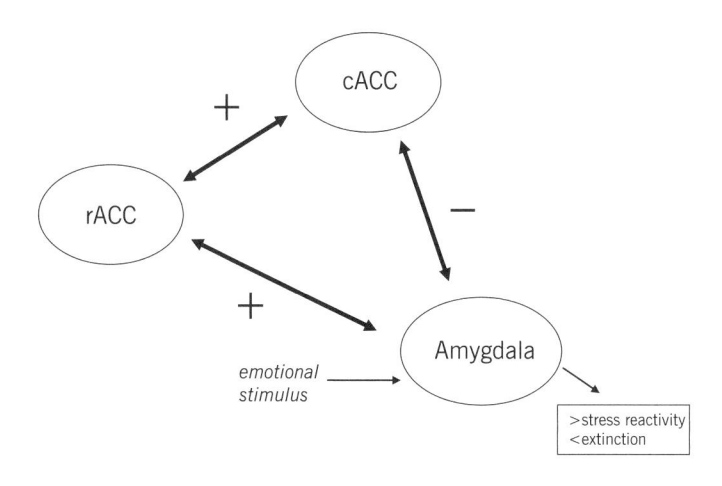

FIGURE 18.2. Anterior cingulate–amygdala circuitry that provides negative feedback to modulate activity of the amygdala. See text for details. rACC, subgenual rostral anterior cingulate cortex; cACC, supragenual caudal cingulate cortex.

riance between rACC–amygdala activation, and reduced negative covariance between cACC–amygdala activation, suggesting a reduced negative feedback of the cACC on amygdala reactivity to stressful stimuli. Covariance between rACC–amygdala activation accounted for approximately 30% of the variance in Neuroticism scores in the entire sample, whereas no single region was significantly related to Neuroticism. Thus, it is possibly the reduced coherence of activity across brain regions associated with the s-allele that most markedly affects enhanced reactivity to stress.

Interactions (epistasis) with other genetic polymorphisms modify the effects of the *5-HTT* genotype on brain circuitry and behavior. Serotonergic postsynaptic action increases the secretion of brain-derived neurotrophic factor (BDNF), which in turn sculpts glutamate (the major excitatory neurotransmitter in the CNS) innervation patterns of dendrites and axons, thereby increasing synaptic efficacy of glutamate. A common single-nucleotide polymorphism (SNP) in the BDNF gene, a methionine (Met) substitution for valine (Val) at codon 66 (*Val66Met*), is associated with a reduced BDNF responsiveness to 5-HT. The Met-allele protected against the effects of the *5-HTT* genotype (s-allele carriers) on pACC–amygdala circuitry (Pezawas et al., 2008). Similarly, two Met-alleles of the gene that codes for catechol-O-methyltransferase (COMT: *Val158Met*), which shows reduced enzyme activity in degrading 5-HT at the postsynaptic receptor and hence enhanced 5-HT postsynaptic effects, interact with two s-alleles to cause a twofold reduction in persistence of anxiety across adolescence (Olsson et al., 2007).

The altered coherence in gray matter volume and functional activity, as well as the reduced threshold for stimulus-induced arousal, in pACC–amygdala and perhaps BNST circuitries associated with the s-allele, implies (1) reduced dendritic branching and axonal arborization, and thus (2) modified connections between brain regions (Pezawas et al., 2005). Indeed, these findings are not limited to the ACC, amygdala, and BNST. The s- (and lg-, which has similar associations as s-) allele is also associated with reduced human gray matter volume in many lateral and medial cortical regions, including prefrontal cortex (PFC) and ventrolateral temporal, inferior parietal, and hippocampus regions (Frodl et al., 2008). This raises the possibility that the s-allele affects the development of basic neurocircuitry in general. Significantly, 5-HT plays a critical role in the development and plasticity of the brain (Gaspar et al., 2003), with especially strong effects during early development as opposed to later in life (Ansorge, Zhou, Lira, Hen, & Gingrich, 2004; Fox et al., 2010; Gaspar et al., 2003; Gross & Hen, 2004; Leonardo & Hen, 2006; Meaney, 2001): In rodents during the first 3 weeks postnatally, in nonhuman primates during approximately the first 6 postnatal months, and in humans during approximately the first 3 years (Fox et al., 2010). This represents, then, one of the means by which l- and s-allele variations could influence experience-dependent 5-HT activity and, hence, interconnections between brain regions.

The importance of early postnatal effects of 5-HT on neural development may be one of the reasons that early adverse environments appear to interact with the *5-HTT* polymorphism in determining affective and social behavioral patterns. Thus, deprivation of early maternal care (which in nonhuman primates causes reduced 5-HT levels and later increased aggression-, anxiety-, and depression-related behavior) interacts with the *5-HTT* polymorphism in that peer-reared or early stressed monkeys carrying a homologue of the human s-allele show greater reduction in 5-HT functioning, increased behavioral signs of anxiety and depression, reduced engagement in play and greater aggression, and a higher preference for alcohol in females (Champoux et al., 2002; Meaney, 2010; Nelson et al., 2009). In all cases, mother- rearing eliminated differences between carriers and noncarriers. A similar interaction between an adverse rearing environment and the *5-HTT* polymorphism was found in recent studies in humans, in which the effects of the s-allele on anxiety, depression, and cortisol secretion were enhanced by such adversity (Caspi, Sugden, Moffitt, Taylor, & Craig, 2003; Stein, Schork, & Glertner, 2008; Taylor et al., 2006) or negative life experiences (Caspi et al., 2003; Gunthert et al., 2007; Wilhelm et al., 2006), and was associated with a negative emotionality temperament in infants who experienced poor rearing conditions (Auerbach, Farou, Ebstein, Kahana, & Levine, 2001). Furthermore, in young adults, an interaction between life stress and the *5-HTT* polymorphism was demonstrated: Carriers of the s-allele with increased levels of stress had the greatest resting and emotionally induced activation in the amygdala and hippocampus, and increased rumination relative to noncarriers (Canli & Lesch, 2007). Similarly, early maternal separation, or early developmental exposure to selective serotonin reuptake inhibitors (SSRIs), caused transgenic mice with reduced *5-HTT* expression to show intensified anxiety and depression-like behaviors, and reduced dendritic morphology and spine density in the orbital cortex and BLA (Ansorge et al., 2004; Murphy & Lesch, 2008). And, finally, a genetic protection from anxiety in adolescents found for the Met/Met *COMT* + s/s *5-HTT* interaction was especially effective under conditions of high early-life stress (Olsson et al., 2007).

In summary, then, it is hypothesized that the *5-HTT* polymorphism affects 5-HT–modulated development of dendritic and axonal development and fine-tuning of connectivity patterns in the forebrain. Variation in the connectivity of the pACC–amygdala and perhaps BNST circuits would manifest neurally as amygdala–BNST hyperreactivity to stress. The implications of this overreactivity are consistent with the phenotypic features of Neuroticism. One can expect the persistent increased arousal being conveyed by amygdala and BNST efferents to other brain regions to be associated with anxiety and feelings of distress, persistent enhancement of vigilance for threat, increased rumination of negative thoughts (especially under stress), increased acquisition of negative emotional memories, and decreased extinction of anxiety elicited by environmental contexts.

It is worth noting, however, that the *5-HTT* polymorphism may not be related in any exclusive way to anxiety and depression because it has shown broad pleiotropic effects on more than 50 phenotypic changes. The s-allele has been associated with bipolar and unipolar affective disorder, obsessive–compulsive disorder, suicide, eating disorders, attention-deficit/hyperactivity disorder (ADHD), and neurodegenerative disorders (Murphy & Lesch, 2008). Furthermore, it may be that this polymorphism affects neural reactivity in general, irrespective of negative environmental effects, where reactivity would increase across l/l, l/s, to s/s genotypes. Thus, human and monkey s-allele carriers are also more responsive at *rest* in many cortical sites (Canli, 2008), and more responsive to reward, positive emotional stimuli, and the absence of negative environments (Belsky et al., 2009). Moreover, when childhood adversity is present, the s-allele has been found to predict generalized *impulsivity* across many different emotionally evocative situations, not just those that are anxiety-inducing (Carver, Johnson, Joormann, & Nam, 2010).

5-HT1A Receptor

5-HT1A receptors serve as autoreceptors when localized to the soma and dendrites of 5-HT synthesizing raphe neurons in the brainstem. Autoreceptors control the functioning of raphe neurons: They are activated by 5-HT released from the soma of raphe neurons, and regulate via negative feedback 5-HT synthesis and the rate of phasic firing of raphe neurons. *5-HT1A* receptors also serve as postsynaptic receptors, which are broadly expressed in forebrain cortical areas (e.g., hippocampus, amygdala, orbital cortex, ACC). Their activation by 5-HT induces marked inhibition of and reduced neuronal excitability in postsynaptic neurons (Gaspar et al., 2003; Murphy & Lesch, 2008). *5-HT1A* knockout mice manifest increased anxiety behavior and autonomic indicators of anxiety, overreact to ambiguous predictors of aversive stimuli, and more rapidly condition ambiguous cues to aversive stimuli (Akimova, Lanzenberger, & Kasper, 2009; Tsetsenis, Ma, Iacono, Beck, & Gross, 2007). If *5-HT1A* receptors in rats are pharmacologically blocked in the first 4 weeks of the early postnatal period, there is a strong enhancement of adult anxiety, which first appears in Week 3—but no anxiety enhancement occurs when the receptor is blocked in adulthood (Akimova et al., 2009; Lesch & Canli, 2006; Tsetsenis et al., 2007).

Research on the association of *5-HT1A* receptor variations in social anxiety disorder (SAD), a human model of extreme anxiety, has shown reduced *5-HT1A* receptor density in both brainstem and cortical regions in patients with SAD and in high-trait-anxious healthy controls, including in amygdala (<21%), ACC (<24%), medial orbital (<19%), insula (<28%), and raphe (<36%) (Akimova et al., 2009; Fisher et al., 2006; Lanzenberger et al., 2007). These brain regions also show increased neural reactivity to anticipatory anxiety conditions that is inversely correlated with 5-HT1A receptor density.

Carriers of the 5-HTT s-allele have also shown reduced density of 5-HT1A autoreceptors, so that the two factors may interact to produce anxiety (Lanzenberger et al., 2007). Interestingly, Gross and Hen (2004), in a transgenic mouse model using time-dependent and tissue-specific regulation of 5-HT1A receptor expression, showed that the early postnatal period is critical for the establishment of adult anxiety behavior. Thus, both 5-HT1A receptors and 5-HTT may influence neural circuitry development. The 5-HT1A receptor appears in Week 2 postnatally in hippocampus, amygdala, and ACC. 5-HT1A *autoreceptors* enhance dendritic maturation; thus, their blockade could affect neural circuitry, whereas 5-HT1A *postsynaptic* receptors induce marked inhibition of and reduce neuronal excitability in postsynaptic neurons—thus increasing the threshold for firing the postsynaptic neuron (Gaspar et al., 2003). Reduction of this latter effect could contribute to overreactivity in postsynaptic neurons in the amygdala.

These findings raise the possibility that high levels of trait anxiety and SAD are characterized by reduced 5-HT1A autoreceptor and postsynaptic receptor density. The reduced autoreceptor density would permit enhanced phasic firing of raphe neurons and subsequent increased release of 5-HT into the synaptic cleft. Research has shown that the latter effect induces down-regulation of 5-HT1A postsynaptic receptors, which appear to be already in low density, thereby reducing 5-HT-induced postsynaptic inhibition (Gaspar et al., 2003). This state of affairs could produce amygdala overreactivity to emotionally evocative stimulation. Importantly, stress-induced increases in cortisol have been shown to repress transcription factors that activate the 5-HT1A receptor gene promotor (Meaney, 2001). Thus, a gene (5-HT1A density) × environment (stress-induced cortisol inhibition of the 5-HT1A receptor gene) interaction may enhance the development of anxiety, perhaps particularly if the environmental stress occurs in the early postnatal period (Gross & Hen, 2004).

Peripheral Glucocorticoid System

Under conditions of stress, CRH is released from PVN CRH neurons, eventually activating the adrenal cortex, which secretes cortisol. Cortisol travels through the bloodstream and has a diverse set of effects on energy metabolism and neural functioning. In humans and rodents, there are two types of stress-induced cortisol receptors. Type I, or mineralocorticoid receptors (MRs), have a high affinity for cortisol and thereby mediate the acute stress-induced effects of cortisol on bodily responses. Type II, or glucocorticoid receptors (GRs), have a low affinity for cortisol, and thereby become bound to cortisol only at high levels of cortisol concentration. Such high levels of cortisol in the hippocampus, acting via GRs, activate inhibitory output from the hippocampus to the Ce CRH and PVN CRH neurons, thereby reducing the activity of the CRH–cortisol stress response system. This pathway represents the major negative feedback system for controlling stress-induced CRH–cortisol responses.

The relations between early adversity and environmental poverty on the one hand, and adulthood health on the other, appear to be mediated by parental influences. Therefore, researchers, using mainly rats and monkeys as subjects, have begun to explore whether these parental influences operate via effects on the development of neural systems that underlie the expression of behavioral and endocrine responses to stress (Gross & Hen, 2004; Meaney, 2010; Sapolsky, 2004; also see van IJzendoorn & Bakermans-Kranenburg, Chapter 19; Bates, Schermerhorn, & Petersen, Chapter 20; and Lengua & Wachs, Chapter 25, this volume). Postnatal handling studies in rats provided early support for this notion, since handling resulted in reduced stress reactivity and anxiety effects only if handling was within the first 3 weeks of the rat's life (Meaney, 2001). In contrast, separation of rat pups from their mothers had the opposite effects of postnatal handling, yielding increases in CRH mRNA expression in the Ce and PVN; reduced *5-HT1A* responses in the hippocampus; and decreased *GR* mRNA and reduced *GR* binding in the hippocampus, hypothalamus, and frontal cortex, all of which blunt the CRH negative feedback system. Importantly, these pups also manifested a lifetime hyperresponsivity to unfamiliar stressors.

A series of studies of individual differences in rat maternal behavior toward pups has also supported these findings (Champagne et al., 2008; Leonardo & Hen, 2006; Meaney, 2010; Weaver et al., 2004). Pups of rat mothers with high levels of licking/grooming and arched-back nursing (LG-ABN, which is less stressful for pups than being compressed by the mother's body during nursing) experienced reduced startle responses, increased open-field exploration, and reduced latencies to eat food in a novel environment. Neurobiologically, these pups exhibited reduced corticosterone responses to acute stress; increased hippocampal *GR* mRNA expression and hence increased glucocorticoid negative feedback sensitivity; decreased CRH mRNA levels in PVN; and increased 5-HT release in the hippocampus.

Thus, the behavior of the mother toward offspring can apparently "program" behavioral and endocrine responses to stress that endure the entire lifespan. Moreover, individual differences in stress reactivity mediated by maternal care are transmitted across generations (Gross & Hen, 2004). When offspring of low LG mothers are raised from birth by high LG mothers (i.e., cross-fostering), these offspring manifest low stress reactivity and anxiety as pups and adults. Raising offspring of high LG mothers with low LG mothers, however, has not consistently produced stress-reactive offspring, indicating that perhaps genetic factors that contribute to high LG behavior and low anxiety are not reversible by poor early maternal care alone (Gross & Hen, 2004). Nevertheless, the results as a whole indicate that variation in rat maternal care can affect development of neural systems that mediate anxiety and stress reactivity (Meaney, 2001).

The critical question concerning the findings on early handling, separation, and maternal care is how these influences on stress reactivity and anxiety become long-lasting. Rat research thus far has supported the role of two epigenetic mechanisms (chromatin structure and DNA methylation), both of which involve an environmentally induced functional modification of DNA (particularly, gene expression) that does not alter nucleotide sequence (Meaney, 2001; Tsankova, Renthal, Kumar, & Nestler, 2007). Importantly, experience, mediated via neurotransmitter (e.g., 5-HT) and hormone (e.g., cortisol) postsynaptic effects, can alter regulators of gene transcription, and hence behavior, in an enduring manner. Furthermore, genes can be stably silenced for substantial periods of time when a methyl group is attached to nucleotides in a gene's promotor or exon regions, in which the methyl group tightly binds a repressor protein, which inhibits access to genes. In contrast, demethylation of a gene leads to enhanced expression of its protein product.

In the case of maternally induced epigenetic effects, the focus has been on modification of the expression of the *GR* gene in the hippocampus, since *GR*s serve as the foundation of feedback inhibition over Ce CRH and PVN CRH production in the stress response. Changes in both chromatin structure and DNA methylation state are implicated strongly in the effects of handling and maternal style. In the latter case, a hypothesized chain of events (Champagne et al., 2008; Sapolsky, 2004; Tsankova et al., 2007) is that high LG rearing results in increased 5-HT neurotransmission in the hippocampus of pups, which leads to strong activation of a biochemical cascade within the postsynaptic neuron that increases (1) openness of chromatin, (2) expression of transcription factors, and (3) transcription factor binding to the *GR* gene. Such binding enhances the expression of *GR*s in the hippocampus, providing enhanced negative feedback effects on Ce CRH and PVN CRH release. In terms of DNA methylation, it has been found that the methylation state of the transcription binding site on the first exon of the *GR* gene is plastic around the time of birth. The site is then methylated the first day after birth, decreasing transcription of the hippocampal *GR* gene. Over the next week, exposure to high LG mothering (by biological or cross-fostering females) caused the binding site of pups to be demethylated, increasing transcription of the *GR* gene and hence hippocampal *GR*s.

Significantly, handling, maternal style, and methylation status all must be present in the first week of life to have an effect in rodents (Champagne et al., 2008; Gross & Hen, 2004; Leonardo & Hen, 2006; Meaney, 2001). This is consistent with the findings discussed earlier, since the first 3 weeks in rodents were critical in the developmental effects of 5-HT, the effects of knocking out *5-HT1A* receptors, and in CRH reactivity. Similarly, SSRIs (which result in enhanced 5-HT availability) administered during Weeks 1–3 (but not during Weeks 6–8) normalize the glucocorticoid response in parentally stressed mice, indicating that this critical developmental period may have a relatively narrow window. Thus, experience during early postnatal weeks in rodents, and perhaps early months in primates, appear to interact with functional effects of genetic polymorphisms in 5-HT (and likely other variables), creating a critical period for establishing effective synaptic development in the forebrain structures that mediate anxiety in response to experience-dependent signals.

Integration of Neurogenetic and Environmental Variables

The previous discussion suggests that individual differences in anxiety and stress reactivity, and hypothetically the trait of Neuroticism, are influenced by four major systems: (1) central CRH sensitivity, (2) *5-HTT* genotype, and (3) *5-HT1A* receptor density (and the possible influence of (2) and (3) on development of neural connectivity), and (4) the epigenetic effects of early maternal care and perhaps other aspects of the childhood environment. It is quite possible that additional contributors will be discovered. It may be, however, that although genetically independent, these disparate systems can be integrated in their functional influence on the phenotype of anxiety and stress reactivity. As illustrated in Figure 18.3, the effects of stressful contexts on anxiety and stress reactivity are mediated through the activation of a central CRH system final common pathway (see Figure 18.1). This pathway comprises a rapid elicitation by the threat-detecting BLA and behavioral activation by the Ce, as well as an enduring activation by the lateral BNST. Both types of activation, taken together, provides an integrated behavioral, hormonal, autonomic, and neural responses to the stress. Key to this activation of the central CRH system is (1) the sensitivity of the *central* CRH system itself; (2) the sensitivity of the amygdala to activation by stressful stimuli, hence the amygdala's initiation of the central CRH system; and (3) sensitivity of the BNST to CRH activation (i.e., sensitivity of *CRH-R1* receptors). Any factor that decreases the threshold of arousability, or increases tonic arousal, of the amygdala and BNST would be seen as also enhancing stress-induced activation of the central CRH system. The left side of Figure 18.3 illustrates previously discussed factors associated with increased amygdala reactivity, including the *5-HTT* genotype, *5-HT1A* receptors, and the epigenetic effects of early maternal care on *GR* gene expression. Also shown in Figure 18.3 are two other genetic polymorphisms that reduce 5-HT functioning and have been associated with amygdala arousal; therefore, they could be relevant contributors to individual differences in anxiety and stress reactivity (Depue, 2009). Thus, the finding outlined earlier, that poor maternal care in rats results in reduced 5-HT tone that can subsequently affect *GR* number, is also of interest. Because reduced 5-HT release from raphe projections in the amygdala can decrease the threshold of amygdala response to provoking stimuli (Depue & Spoont, 1986; Spoont, 1992), perhaps many of the variables discussed earlier commonly affect amygdala arousal via a 5-HT component.

Extraversion

Phenotype and Affective System

Through empirical studies and integrative reviews, we have provided evidence that Extraversion to a large extent reflects the activity of a mammalian behavioral approach system based on positive incentive motivation (Depue, 2006; Depue & Collins, 1999; Depue & Morrone-Strupinsky, 2005). This system is activated by, and serves to bring an animal in contact with, unconditioned and conditioned rewarding incentive

Stressful Context
↓
Amygdala/BNST Arousal

Modulators of Amygdala/BNST Arousal →

- valCOMTmet: 5-HT at receptor sites
- gTPH2t, 5-HT1A receptor: 5-HT postsynaptic inhibition
- 5-HTT & Early Postnatal Neural Development
  - neural connectivity in emotion regulation circuitries
  - amygdala
  - caudal ACC ← subgenual ACC

- Early Childhood Environment
  - maternal behavioral style, maltreatment, separations, neglect
  - ↓
  - 5-HT
  - ↓
  - NGFI-A
  - ↓
  - hippocampal GRs → negative feedback
  - ↓
  - peripheral cortisol

Basolateral Amygdala/ Lateral BNST (CRH-R1 functioning)
- strength of negative affective encoding
- ↓
- strength & breadth of negative associative conditioning

Central Amygdala CRH Neurons
↓
BNST
↓
Central CRH Stress Network

Peripheral CRH network

FINAL COMMON PATHWAY

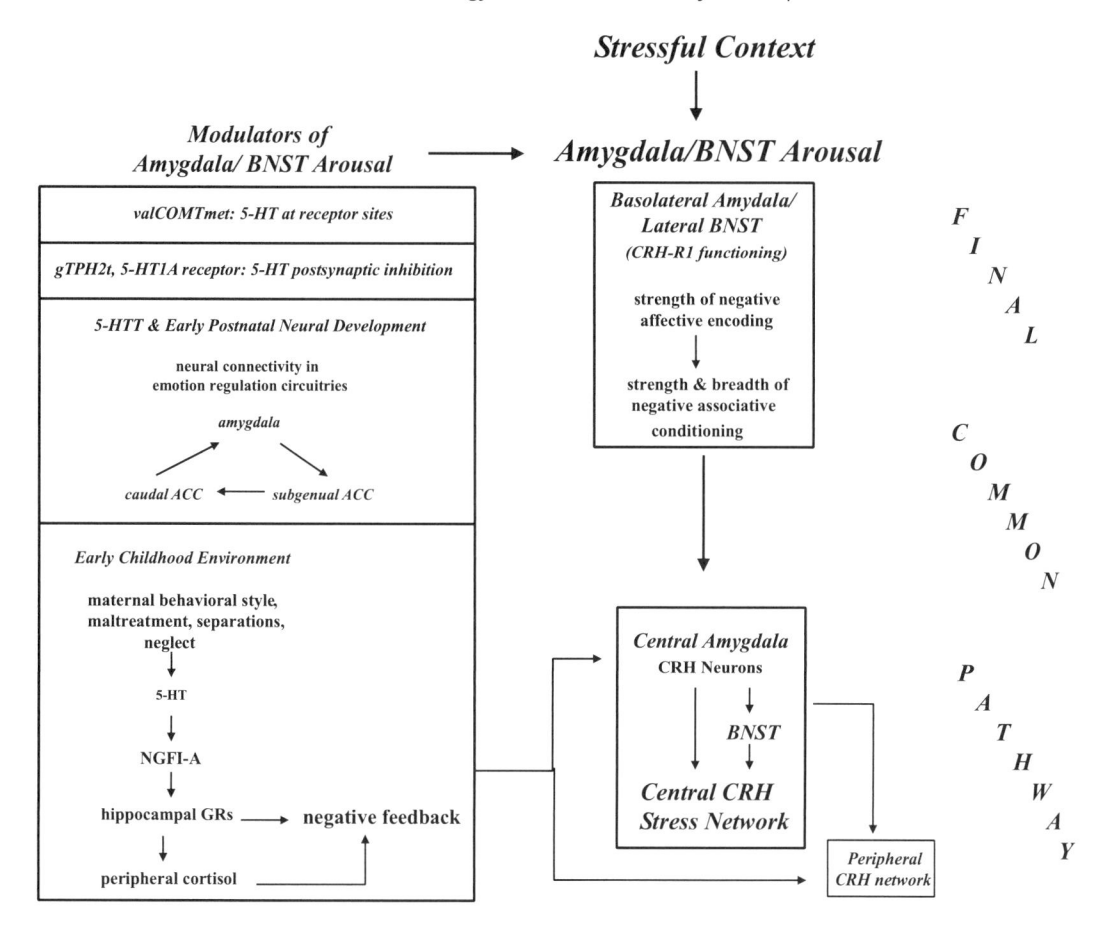

FIGURE 18.3. An illustration of how many disparate variables (left side) may modulate amygdala arousal to stressful stimuli, which subsequently provides activation of the final common pathway of the central CRH system that integrates behavioral, hormonal, autonomic, and neural responses to the stressor. ACC, anterior cingulate cortex; BNST, bed nucleus of the stria terminalis; COMT, catechol-O-methyltransferase; CRH, corticotropin-releasing hormone; 5-HT, serotonin; 5-HTT, serotonin transporter; NGFI-A, nerve growth factor-inducible protein A; TPH2, tyrosine hydroxylase.

stimuli. Incentives are inherently evaluated as positive in valence, and activate incentive motivation, increased energy through sympathetic nervous system and endocrine activity, and forward locomotion as a means of bringing individuals into close proximity to rewards. The incentive state is clearly evident in the phenotypic features of Extraversion: social dominance, persistence and striving, achievement ambition, positive affect, and assertiveness, as well as subjective feelings of desire, wanting, excitement, elation, enthusiasm, potency, and self-efficacy that are distinct from, but typically co-occur with, feelings of pleasure and liking. It is important to distinguish this emotional/motivational system from the consummatory reward state of quiescence, gratification, and liking that brings goal-directed behavior to a gratifying conclusion (see the trait "Social Closeness/ Agreeableness" below; Depue, 2006; Depue & Morrone-Strupinsky, 2005). The phenotype of Extraversion is also characterized by (1) active seeking of novelty, since novelty serves as a reward and is an elicitor of incentive motivation, and (2) an impulsivity in attempts to obtain immediate reward (this complex topic is beyond our current focus; therefore, the reader is directed to Depue & Collins, 1999).

Neurobiological, Genetic, and Experiential Factors

Dopamine and Incentive-Induced Reward

Animal research demonstrates that the positive incentive motivation and experience of reward that underlies a behavioral system of approach is dependent on the functional properties of the midbrain ventral tegmental area (VTA) dopamine (DA) projection system. DA agonists or antagonists in the VTA or nucleus accumbens (NAcc), which is a major ventral striatal terminal site of VTA DA projections facilitate or markedly impair, in rats and monkeys, respectively, a broad array of incentive motivated behaviors, including novelty- and food-induced exploration, affective aggression, and social and sexual approach. Furthermore, dose-dependent DA receptor activation in the VTA–NAcc pathway facilitates the acute rewarding effects of stimulants (Belin, Mar, Dalley, Robbins, & Everitt, 2008), and the NAcc is a particularly strong site for intracranial self-administration of DA agonists. DA agonists injected in the NAcc also modulate behavioral responses to *conditioned* incentive stimuli in a dose-dependent fashion. In single-unit recording studies, VTA DA neurons are activated preferentially by appetitive incentive stimuli, and DA cells, most numerous in the VTA, respond vigorously to and in proportion to the magnitude of both conditioned and unconditioned incentive stimuli and in anticipation of reward (Schultz, 2007). Similarly, in human neuroimaging studies, increased activation in the VTA and NAcc regions correlates with the occurrence of unanticipated reward, the positive prediction of reward, amount of reward anticipated, and ratings of excitement preceding the reward (D'Ardenne, McClure, Nystrom, & Cohen, 2008; Knutson & Bhanji, 2006). Moreover, during acute administration the intensity of a participant's subjective euphoria increased in a dose-dependent manner in proportion to cocaine binding to the DA uptake transporter (and hence to DA levels) in the striatum (Drevets et al., 2001; Volkow et al., 1997). Hence, taken together, the animal and human evidence demonstrates that the VTA DA–NAcc pathway is a primary neural circuit for incentive motivation and its accompanying subjective state of reward and positive affect.

Individual Differences in Dopamine Functioning and Extraversion-Like Traits

Individual differences in DA functioning assessed in various ways have consistently been related to variation in Extraversion-like behaviors or traits. In rats and mice, DA neuron number in the VTA is strongly positively related to incentive-induced behaviors, such as novelty- and food-induced exploration, affective aggression, and social and sexual approach (Depue & Collins, 1999). In addition, the level of responsiveness to novelty in rats is correlated with higher basal and stimulated extracellular DA levels in the NAcc (Depue & Collins, 1999). In humans, DA-facilitated hormonal release and eyeblink rates have been associated specifically and highly (.67 to .75) with the trait of Extraversion (Depue, Luciana, Arbisi, Collins, & Leon, 1994). Also, the preference for immediate over delayed rewards is associated with the magnitude of activity in the NAcc region (Hariri et al., 2006). Furthermore, two recent studies have demonstrated an association between the density of *DA D2* receptors and Extraversion-like traits (novelty-seeking, impulsivity; Buckholtz et al., 2010; Zald et al., 2008). Within VTA DA neurons, somatodendritic D2-like autoreceptors provide inhibitory regulation of frequency and duration of VTA DA neuron firing, and influence DA release in the NAcc and other projection sites (Marinelli & White, 2000; Zald et al., 2008). Variation in D2 density in the VTA is reflected in individual differences in incentive-motivated behaviors in rats, such as the degree of responsivity to novel stimuli (Marinelli & White, 2000). As illustrated in Figure 18.4, Zald and colleagues (2008) found in humans that D2-like (a combination of D2 and D3 receptors) density was correlated inversely (approximately –.70) with novelty-seeking traits. This might explain the positive association in fMRI studies between (1) neural activation in the VTA region and anticipation or viewing of novel pictures or positive predictions of reward (Abler, Walter, Erk, Kammerer, & Spitzer, 2006; Bunzeck & Duzel, 2006; Schott et al., 2004; Wittmann, Bunzeck, Dolan, & Duzel, 2007), (2) novelty-seeking and DA release in the NAcc region (Leyton et al., 2002), and (3) degree of sensitization to repeated amphetamine

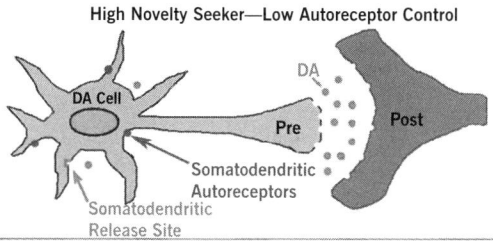

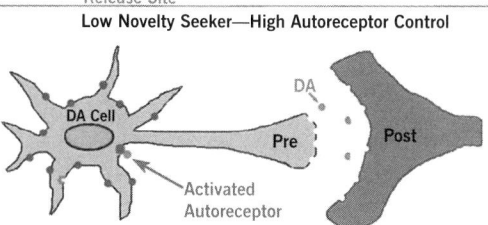

FIGURE 18.4. Model of autoreceptor control and individual differences in novelty seeking. DA, dopamine. From Zald et al. (2008). Copyright 2008 by the Society for Neuroscience. Reprinted by permission.

doses (Boileau et al., 2006). Buckholtz and colleagues (2010) extended the study of Zald and colleagues (2008) by demonstrating that D2-like density in the VTA region is inversely related not only to novelty-seeking/impulsivity traits (−.73) but also to amphetamine-induced release of DA in the NAcc region, which in turn was also correlated positively with Extraversion-like traits (.65) and with the subjective rating of wanting or desire for more amphetamine (.48). In contrast, D2 agonists block responsiveness to primary reward in animals (Liu, Shin, & Ikemoto, 2008).

Dopamine Genetic Polymorphisms and Extraversion-Like Traits

Consistent with the previous findings are studies on genetic polymorphisms associated with different variables that affect DA functioning (Munafo et al., 2003). The D4 receptor is part of the D2 family of DA receptors, which are generally inhibitory in nature. The D4 gene polymorphism is characterized by variation in the number of repeats of a 48-base-pair unit in exon 3. The most common repeats in the population are 4 and 7 repeats, where the 7-repeat allele is characterized by a twofold reduction in inhibitory effects on postsynaptic neurons relative to the 4-repeat allele. Several small studies have found the 7-repeat allele to be associated with increased Extraversion levels relative to the 4-repeat allele, and this was also found in studies using behavioral features of positive emotion (e.g., frequency of smiling) in a study of 8- to 12-month-old infants (Lakatos, Johnson, & Young, 2003). One meta-analysis, however, found this polymorphism to be related more to novelty seeking and impulsivity than to Extraversion per se (Munafo, Yalcin, Willis-Owen, & Flint, 2008). When this polymorphism was taken in interaction with a polymorphism of the DA transporter gene (*DAT1*; an allele associated with reduced DA uptake; hence, increased time of DA in the synapse to activate postsynaptic receptors), impulsivity was significantly increased in terms of number of commission errors in a go/no-go task (Congdon, Lesch, & Canli, 2008). Furthermore, in an fMRI study of neural reactivity to monetary reward, NAcc activation, as well as impulsivity scores, were increased with genetic variants associated with relatively increased DA release (*D2-141C* deletion) and availability (*DAT1* 9-repeat allele), as well as diminished inhibitory postsynaptic DA effects (*D2-141C* deletion, D4 7-repeat allele) (Forbes et al., 2009).

Individual Differences in Dopamine Functioning and Associative Conditioning to Reward

One of the functions of DA release in the NAcc is to signal the occurrence of an unpredicted (change in) reward and to encode that reward for the magnitude of its incentive salience (Abler et al., 2006; Berridge, 2007; Liu et al., 2008; O'Doherty, Kringelbach, Rolls, Hornack, & Andrews, 2001). Corticolimbic regions processing rewards and their stimulus contexts activate the VTA DA neurons in proportion to the magnitude of reward, and DA is subsequently released into the NAcc (Depue & Morrone-Strupinsky, 2005). As contextual cues are progressively associated with reward in corticolimbic regions, VTA DA neurons are activated by such cues, so that DA release in the NAcc follows those associations, ratcheting backwards in time to earlier and earlier predictive cues that become associated with an anticipated reward (Knutson & Wimmer,

2007; Stuber et al., 2008). Thus, DA release in the NAcc provides a reward signal that is dynamically modified by associative learning (Costa, 2007; Day, Roitman, Wightman, & Carelli, 2007). Since in animals variation in DA functioning is positively related to the degree of conditioning of contextual cues to reward (Depue & Collins, 1999), we hypothesized that a similar association would be found in relation to the trait of Extraversion (Depue, 2006). In support of this hypothesis, we found that when exposed to DA-agonist–induced subjective reward for 4 consecutive days compared to placebo, high extraverts more readily associated specific and general contextual cues to reward, as indicated by strong cue-induced activation of a range of DA-activated motor, affective, and cognitive processes. In contrast, low extraverts showed no associative conditioning at the dose level of DA agonist used in the studies. This suggests that higher extraverts will develop over time stronger and broader contextual networks that activate incentive-motivated behavior and positive affect. If these differences in DA and associative conditioning exist early in life as a temperamental foundation, then quite divergent trajectories in traitwise incentive behavior and positive affect (Extraversion) may develop across the lifespan.

Early Adversity and Dopamine Functioning

Early adverse experience in animals has a marked effect on DA functioning, as summarized in Figure 18.5. Single, intense stressors or repeated, prolonged stressors, including maternal separations in neonatal rats and monkeys, lead to a sensitization of NAcc DA release to repetition of the same stressor or to novel stressors and DA agonists later in life (Point 6 in Figure 18.5; Depue & Collins, 1999; Meaney, Brake, & Cratton, 2002). There is also an increase in the acquisition of self-administration and a reduced threshold in terms of effective dosage of psychostimulants, alcohol, and opiates, and an increased intensity of effort (incentive craving?) to obtain these drugs (Meaney et al., 2002). Furthermore, rat pups exposed to maternal separations have a 250% reduction in DA transporters in the NAcc as adults, which increases time of DA availability at postsynaptic receptors, whereas rats with a history of handling show reduced DA release in the NAcc to stress and DA-agonist drugs (Point 5 in Figure 18.5; Meaney et al., 2002). These results are supported by the fact that 18- to 24-month-old toddlers who carry the D4 7-repeat allele and also have poor-quality parenting show increased sensation seeking, suggesting that the weaker inhibition associated with the 7-repeat allele permits stress-related poor parenting to overactivate DA activity (Paterson, Sunohara, & Kennedy, 1999).

These effects appear to be enhanced by an interaction of glucocorticoid activation of *GR*s with DA. Amphetamine and stress both increase corticosterone (cortisol) secretion and NAcc DA release, which together correlate with positive subjective responses in humans (McArthur, Dalley, Buckingham, & Gillies, 2005). Administration of dexamethasone (synthetic cortisol) prenatally and during the first 7 postnatal days in rats results in a 50% increase in VTA DA neurons (Point 4 in Figure 18.5), and increased corticosterone and NAcc DA release to stress and DA-agonists in adulthood (McArthur et al., 2005). Even adult humans who report having had poor maternal care as children have stress-induced increased cortisol levels that correlate positively ($r = .78$) with increased NAcc DA release (Pruessner, Champagne, Meaney, & Dagher, 2004). This effect is enhanced by stressor-induced prolonged oversecretion of cortisol (Point 1 in Figure 18.5) that activates *GR*s located on VTA DA neurons (Oswald et al., 2005). Such activation has the effect of increasing DA cell responses to input from corticolimbic regions (Point 2 in Figure 18.5), possibly from an enhancement of glutamate release mediated by *GR*s on glutamate terminals that synapse on VTA DA neurons. In addition, cortisol activation of *GR*s on VTA DA neurons enhances the frequency of DA cell firing (Point 3 in Figure 18.5). Taken together, these results suggest that prolonged stressors, such as poor, conflictual, violent, or inconsistent familial environments, or physical and/or sexual abuse early in life, can sensitize the VTA–NAcc DA system in an enduring manner. It is equally possible that frequent rewarding childhood contexts could enhance DA functioning, as is found with early treatment with psychostimulants (Depue & Collins, 1999).

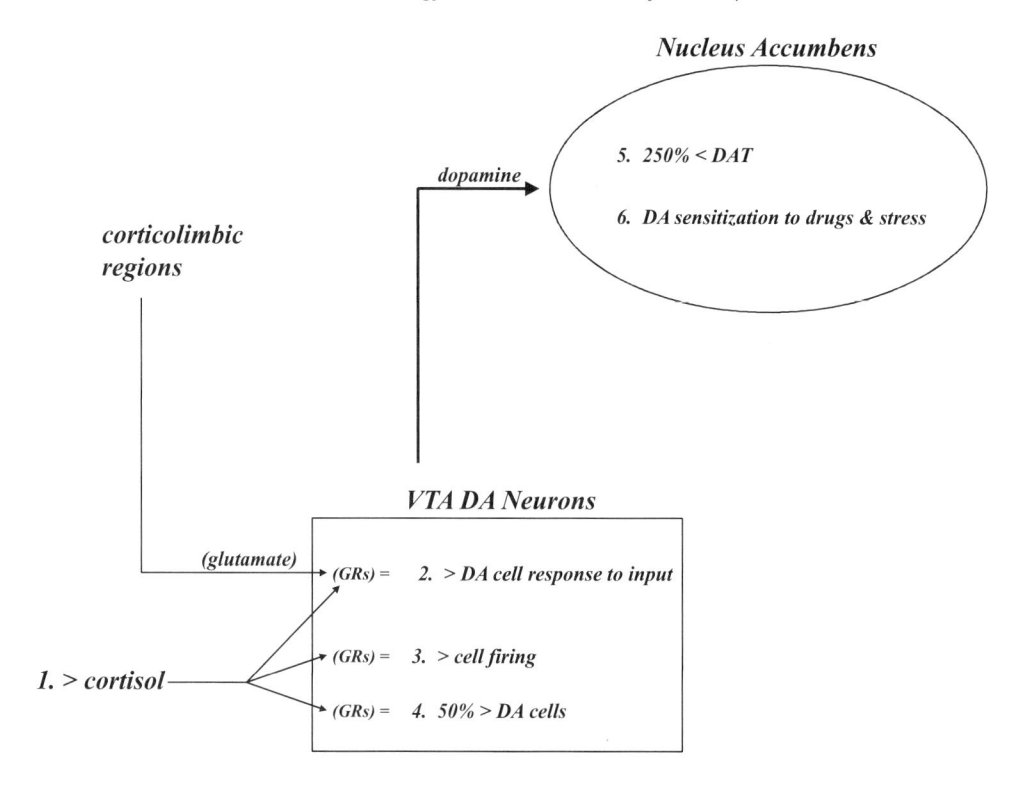

FIGURE 18.5. Summary of effects of early adversity on DA functioning. See text for details. DA, dopamine; DAT, dopamine transporter; GR, glucocorticoid receptor; VTA, ventral tegmental area.

Integration of Neurogenetic and Environmental Variables

Consistent with our initial hypothesis (Depue & Collins, 1999), there is now broad support from neuroendocrine, neuroimaging, and neurogenetic work for the association of the VTA–NAcc DA projection system with Extraversion and its related traits of novelty-seeking and impulsivity to reward. DA encodes the incentive salience of rewarding events, and is involved in associative learning processes, in which DA encodes neutral events that predict reward with incentive salience. Individual differences in Extraversion contribute to variation in such associative learning of predictive contexts; higher levels of Extraversion are likely associated with broader, stronger-conditioned networks that create variation in context-facilitated incentive-motivated behavior, positive affect, social dominance, and persistence in goal-directed behavior. On the basis of early adversity studies showing a strong environmental effect on DA functioning, one might predict that variations in temperamental trait levels of DA functioning will influence the magnitude of effects of *both* rewarding and stressful environments, and that higher trait levels will be more susceptible to environmental impact. One can imagine dramatic differences in developmental trajectories in Extraversion associated with such gene–environment interactions.

Social Closeness/Agreeableness

Phenotype and Affective System

In contrast to the highly motivating incentive state associated with Extraversion, the core content of Social Closeness and Agreeableness scales reflects the operation of neural processes that create a warm, affectionate, gratifying subjective emotional state elicited by affiliative stimuli, such as soft touch (kissing, caressing, stroking, play); sexual touch; hair grooming; psychological and physical warmth; a caring, smiling, friendly face;

soft, caring vocalizations; and shared intimacy (symbolic touching). Our hypothesis is that the subjective emotional experience of warmth and affection reflects the *capacity to experience consummatory reward that is elicited by a broad array of affiliative stimuli* (Depue & Morrone-Strupinsky, 2005). Such consummatory reward is likely to be the same system that is elicited by nonsocial stimuli (good food/drink, sexual intercourse, a warm bath, the sun on the beach, etc.). This reward capacity is viewed as providing the key element utilized in associative conditioning processes that permit the development and maintenance of longer-term affective bonds characteristic of social organization in human and other primate societies.

Neurobiological, Genetic, and Experiential Factors

Four neurobiological variables have been associated with social bonding: oxytocin, vasopressin, opiates, and dopamine. The role of oxytocin and vasopressin in rodents (Donaldson & Young, 2008; Insel, 2010; Lim & Young, 2006; Young & Wang, 2004) and humans (Heinrichs & Domes, 2008) has been reviewed previously, so we focus on opiates here. A broad range of evidence suggests a role for an endogenous opiate neuropeptide in reward that is exerted by opiate neurons in the hypothalamic arcuate nucleus that project to many brain regions. Most relevant to affiliative reward is the mu-opiate receptor (OR) family, which is the main site of exogenously administered opiate drugs (e.g., morphine) and of endogenous neuropeptide endorphins (particularly, beta-endorphin; Depue & Morrone-Strupinsky, 2005). Rewarding properties of mu-OR agonists are directly indicated by the fact that animals will work for the prototypical mu-agonists morphine and heroin, and that they are dose-dependently self-administered in animals and humans. We are not aware of such support for oxytocin and vasopressin in reward. Beta-endorphin release on mu-OR receptors is increased in rats, monkeys, and humans by lactation and nursing, sexual activity, vaginocervical stimulation, maternal social interaction, brief social isolation, and grooming and other nonsexual tactile stimulation (Depue & Morrone-Strupinsky, 2005).

The rewarding effect of opiates may be especially mediated by mu-ORs located in the NAcc and VTA, both of which support self-administration of mu-OR agonists that is attenuated by intracranially administered mu-OR antagonists. Destruction of DA terminals in the NAcc also showed that opiate self-administration is independent of DA function, at least at the level of the NAcc (Laviolette, Gallegos, Henriksen, & van der Kooy, 2004). Furthermore, rewarding effects of opiates are directly indicated by the fact that a range of mu-OR agonists, when injected intracerebroventricularly or directly into the NAcc, serve as unconditioned rewarding stimuli in a dose-dependent manner in producing a conditioned place preference, a behavioral measure of reward. VTA-localized mu-Ors, particularly in the rostral zone of the VTA mediate (1) rewarding effects, such as self-administration behavior and conditioned place preference; (2) increased sexual activity and maternal behaviors; and (3) the persistently increased play behavior, social grooming, and social approach of rats subjected to morphine *in utero*. Transgenic mice lacking the mu-OR gene show neither morphine-induced place preferences nor physical dependence when consuming morphine.

Soft tactile stimulation between mother and infant or mates appears to be the most effective source of bonding. Indeed, in monkeys and rodents, social bonding is not possible without soft tactile stimulation from the mother (Fleming, Korsmit, & Deller, 1994; Fleming, O'Day, & Kraemer, 1999). Importantly, such stimulation serves as reward in associative conditioning to odor in rats, which was eliminated by blocking mu-ORs (Roth & Sullivan, 2005), and soft-touch reward was associated to odor in human neonates (Sullivan, 1991). Mammals, and especially primates, have evolved particular receptors on hairy skin and a sensory pathway for soft touch (Liu et al., 2007; Olausson et al., 2002) that projects to the anterior insular cortex, a structure that mediates awareness of the subjective experience of emotions (Craig, 2009). In turn, the anterior insula can activate in the arcuate nucleus beta-endorphin neurons, which activate reward and physiological quiescence via projections to VTA–NAcc and brainstem regions.

Individual differences in the trait of social closeness are subject to strong genetic influence (Tellegen et al., 1988), but it is unknown whether variation in mu-ORs underlies trait variation. Individual differences in humans and rodents have been demonstrated in levels of mu-OR expression and binding that are associated with a preference for mu-OR-agonists, such as morphine (Uhl, Sora, & Wang, 1999; Zubieta et al., 2001). In humans, individual differences in CNS mu-OR densities show a range of up to 75% between lower and upper thirds of the distribution (Uhl et al., 1999), differences that appear to be related to variation in the rewarding effects of alcohol in humans and rodents.

One source of this individual variation is different SNPs in the mu-OR gene *OPRM1* (Bond et al., 1998; Gelernter, Kranzler, & Cubells, 1999). The most prevalent of these is *A118G*, with an allelic frequency of approximately 10%. Importantly, this genetic variation in mu-OR properties is related to response to rewarding drugs and to opiate self-administration behavior in animals (Zhang et al., 2007). Taken together, these studies suggest that genetic variation in mu-OR properties in humans and rodents is (1) substantial, (2) an essential element in variation in the rewarding value of opiate agonists, and (3) critical in accounting for variation in the Pavlovian learning that underlies the association between contextual cues and reward, as occurs in partner and place preferences (Van den Oever et al., 2008).

Two studies have found that variation in mu-ORs is associated with the strength of attachment behaviors in animals. Transgenic mice lacking the mu-OR gene showed markedly *reduced* (1) opiate self-administration reward, (2) acquisition of place and mate/pup preferences, (3) maternal behaviors (pup tactile stimulation, pup retrieval, nursing), (4) play and social grooming, and (5) NAcc DA release to ethanol and amphetamine (Moles, Kieffer, & D'Amato, 2004). Also, juvenile monkeys having the homologue of the mu-OR gene polymorphism that is characterized by enhanced beta-endorphin functioning showed greatly enhanced distress and reduced attachment behavior as a function of a series of maternal separations (Barr et al., 2008). And, finally, we have shown that a mu-OR antagonist in participants with high trait levels of social closeness *reversed* their heightened ratings of affection in response to film scenes and their greater tolerance to heat (mediated by mu-ORs), such that they now expressed levels not statistically different from participants with low trait social closeness (Depue, 2006).

In terms of effects of experience on social closeness, it is the only higher-order trait that shows significant within-family experience effects (Tellegen et al., 1988), indicating that both familial and nonfamilial relationships have a marked effect on trait levels. Of course, an immense animal and human literature demonstrates that level of attachment is affected by interpersonal experience starting in the postnatal period (Fleming et al., 1999, also see van IJzendoorn & Bakermans-Kranenburg, Chapter 19, this volume). Unfortunately, no studies of experience-dependent modulations of the mu-OR system have been reported, so it is unclear whether experience operates on social bonding via this system. There is emerging evidence, however, that social interactions during the neonatal period organize the subsequent expression of affiliative behavior by altering sensitivity to neuropeptides (Cushing & Kramer, 2005).

Social Rejection Sensitivity

Items covering the nature of social rejection sensitivity (SRS) have not been included in personality questionnaires. We view this as a serious oversight, since close interpersonal relationships are modulated by at least two very strong emotional systems: social bonding (drawing people together) and SRS (which can substantially inhibit social interactions). SRS is elicited by social separation due to group exclusion and whenever social relationships are threatened, damaged, or lost. It is also elicited by more symbolic forms of withdrawal of love or acceptance, including negative feedback about the self; verbal devaluation; disapproving, frowning faces; averted gazes; and expressions of the social emotions of contempt, indignation, and disgust by others. In response, people experience hurt, pain, anxiety and agitation, sadness, and the social emotions of guilt, shame, and embarrassment. Such a neurobehavioral system allows others to control social transgressions, and the rejected person avoids social ostracization that would follow if no anxiety or guilt were experienced—which in monkeys in natural settings leads to death within weeks. From an evolutionary standpoint, SRS may have developed to maintain closeness of long-developing toddlers to nourishment- and safety-providing caregivers (Eisenberger & Lieberman, 2004).

Thus, SRS may be based on *social pain*—the distressing experience arising from the perception of or potential psychological distance from close others or a social group (Eisenberger & Lieberman, 2004). The description of the distress associated with social rejection is dominated by the terms *pain* and *hurt*, terms that are not ordinarily associated with other negative emotions. Pain has two components: physical sensory experience, and affective experience of unpleasantness and psychological pain and hurt. The latter component is associated with activation in the dorsal region of the ACC (dACC). This region is also the location of neurons that provide an aversive, punishment signal to the basolateral amygdala, where that aversive signal is paired with neutral cues in emotional associative learning (Johansen & Fields, 2004). Thus, the dACC may provide the foundation for affectively aversive signals during the experience of harm—either physical harm or social harm. Indeed, recent studies have revealed that during the experience of social rejection, humans show intense activation of the dACC, which presumably activates the amygdala to generate the bodily responses that create the unpleasant emotional experience (Eisenberger & Lieberman, 2004; Somerville, Heatherton, & Kelley, 2006). Interestingly, there may be a link between social bonding and SRS in humans. While the *A118G* polymorphism of the mu-OR gene is associated with increased attachment behavior, it is also associated with increased sensitivity to the pain of social rejection (Way, Taylor, & Eisenberger, 2009). Our view is that social bonding and SRS represent different neurobehavioral systems, the former being associated with reward that binds people together, the latter with intense anxiety in being ostracized from the social group. It may be that opiates modify both systems in that individuals with high mu-opiate functioning derive greater reward from interpersonal contact and therefore experience enhanced rejection anxiety when those contacts are threatened.

Though we are not aware of any research on the effects of experience on SRS levels or dACC activation levels, it is clear that familial and nonfamilial experiences of social rejection affect trust and security of attachments. The entire area of SRS is understudied in psychology and neuroscience.

Constraint/Conscientiousness

The Nature of Constraint

Constraint (which may have some relation to effortful control as described in this volume [Rothbart, Chapter 1, and Rueda, Chapter 8] and conscientiousness in the Five-Factor Model) represents a broad trait of impulsivity that modulates the expression of many domains of behavior, including emotional, motor, cognitive, and sensory reactivity (Carver & Miller, 2006; Depue & Collins, 1999; Depue & Lenzenweger, 2005; Depue & Spoont, 1986; Spoont, 1992; Zald & Depue, 2001). Whereas the three higher-order traits described earlier (Neuroticism, Extraversion, Social Closeness) reflect the activity of neurobehavioral systems, constraint lacks ties to any specific emotional/motivational system (Carver & Miller, 2006; Depue & Collins, 1999; Spoont, 1992). Based on a vast body of animal and human literature, we and others have proposed that constraint reflects a robust, generalized influence on the threshold of elicitation of behavior, where the threshold represents a weighting of external and internal CNS factors that contribute to the probability of response expression (Carver & Miller, 2006; Coccaro & Siever, 1991; Cools, Roberts, & Robbins, 2007; Depue, 1995; Depue & Spoont, 1986; Lesch & Canli, 2006; Panksepp, 1998; Spoont, 1992; Zald & Depue, 2001; Zuckerman, 1994). In this model, constraint would reflect a broadly distributed CNS variable (e.g., a neurotransmitter of broad distribution) that modulates the threshold of stimulus elicitation of neural circuitries associated with a range of psychological processes, including motor behavior, emotions, memory, attention, and cognition. In this view, emotional higher-order personality traits, such as Neuroticism and Extraversion, reflect the influence of neurobiological variables that strongly contribute to the threshold of elicitation of specific emotional responses, such as DA in the facilitation of incentive motivated behavior and positive affect, CRH in the potentiation of anxiety, and mu-ORs in the mediation of affiliative reward. Constraint would be viewed as modulating the probability of elicitation of all of those variables; hence, it exerts a general inhibitory influence over the elicitation of any affective behavior.

As shown in Figure 18.6, constraint in its modulatory interaction with an emotional personality trait creates a diagonal of stability of emotional behavior. This diagonal extends from *lability*, where the emotional trait's level is high and constraint is low (i.e., increasingly easy stimulus elicitation of affective responses) to *rigidity*, where the emotional trait's level is low and constraint is high (i.e., increasingly difficult stimulus elicitation of affective responses). Therefore, lability will increase as a joint function of decreasing constraint plus increasing stimulus influences on response elicitation of other affective systems (Depue & Spoont, 1986; Spoont, 1992). For instance, low constraint would increase the probability that an individual high in Extraversion would impulsively (without planning or thinking of the negative consequences) seek immediate rewards and express positive affect. Thus, the *qualitative content* of emotional behavior will depend on which *affective* personality trait is being elicited at any point in time, whereas the magnitude and latency of affective responses will depend on trait levels of constraint (Zald & Depue, 2001; although differential strength of various personality traits will obviously produce relative predominance of particular affective behaviors within individuals).

Constraint and Serotonin Functioning

Functional levels of neurotransmitters that provide a strong, relatively generalized *tonic inhibitory* influence on behavioral responding would be good candidates as significant modulators of response elicitation thresholds; hence, they would hypothetically account for a large proportion of the variance in the trait of constraint. We and others (Carver & Miller, 2006; Coccaro & Siever, 1991; Cools et al., 2007; Depue, 1995; Depue & Spoont, 1986; Lesch & Canli, 2006; Panksepp, 1998; Spoont, 1992; Zald & Depue, 2001; Zuckerman, 1994) have suggested that 5-HT, acting at multiple receptor sites in most brain regions, is such a modulator. 5-HT modulates a diverse set of functions—including emotion, motivation, motor, affiliation, cognition, food intake, sleep, sexual activity, and sensory reactivity—indicating broad effects across the brain (Carver & Miller, 2006; Cools et al., 2007; Depue & Spoont, 1986; Lesch & Canli, 2006; Spoont, 1992).

Importantly, *reduced* 5-HT functioning in animals (Depue & Spoont, 1986; Spoont, 1992) and humans (Coccaro & Siever, 1991; Cools et al., 2007) is associated with many labile emotional impulsive conditions, including human impulsive suicide across several types of disorder, obsessive–compulsive disorder, disorders of impulse control, aggression and irritability, depression, anxiety and enhanced stress reactivity, arson, unconstrained sexual behavior, and substance abuse, suggesting marked disinhibition of many brain processes (Carver & Miller, 2006; Coccaro & Siever, 1991; Depue & Spoont, 1986; Winstanley, Theobald, Dalley, & Robbins, 2005). Research on several polymorphisms of the gene for tryptophan hydroxylase (*TPH2*, which is localized in brain rather than the periphery), the rate-limiting enzyme in the synthesis of 5-HT, supports these findings. In particular, T-carriers of the *T-703G* SNP in the upstream promotor region, which is associated with

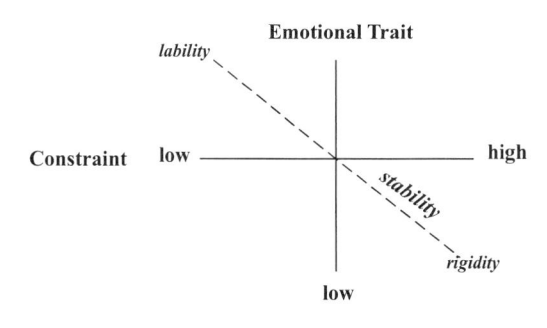

FIGURE 18.6. The interaction of an emotional trait with the higher-order trait of constraint, forming a diagonal of behavioral stability extending from labile to rigid.

50% reduction in brain 5-HT levels, manifest marked impulsivity, affective aggression, and suicidality, and increased occipital cortex and amygdala reactivity at rest and in response to happy, fearful, and sad facial expressions. These findings were exaggerated in T-carriers who also had one or two copies of the s-allele (Hennig, Reuter, Netter, & Burk, 2005; Manuck et al., 1999; Rujescu et al., 2002).

One distinction worth considering is the different roles that 5-HT may play in Neuroticism and Constraint. Whereas genetic variation in transmission properties of 5-HT (e.g., *5-HTT, 5-HT1A* receptors) may influence the postnatal development of neural processes and hence the connectivity within neural circuitries in Neuroticism, Constraint may be more related to the level of neurotransmitter availability across the brain. In this latter case, perhaps the main effect of 5-HT level is less on neural development than primarily on magnitude of functional influence on resting response thresholds of other neurons it innervates. This is a critical issue for future research.

Thus, variation in 5-HT level plays a substantial modulatory role in general neurobiological reactivity to exogenous stimuli that affects the expression of many forms of emotional/motivated behavior. As illustrated in Figure 18.7, this relationship may be modeled using the response threshold construct discussed earlier. In this sense, constraint might be viewed as reflecting the influence of the CNS variable of 5-HT. In support of this notion, we found that 5-HT agonist-induced increases in serum prolactin secretion correlated significantly only with the Impulsivity scale from Tellegen's measure of Constraint (Depue, 1995).

An example of the interaction of neurobiological variables associated with Constraint (5-HT) and Extraversion (DA) helps to illustrate the model in Figure 18.7. 5-HT is an inhibitory modulator of a host of DA-facilitated behaviors, including the rewarding properties of psychostimulants, novelty-induced locomotor activity, the acquisition of self-administration of cocaine, and DA utilization in the NAcc (Depue & Collins, 1999; Depue & Spoont, 1986; Spoont, 1992). This

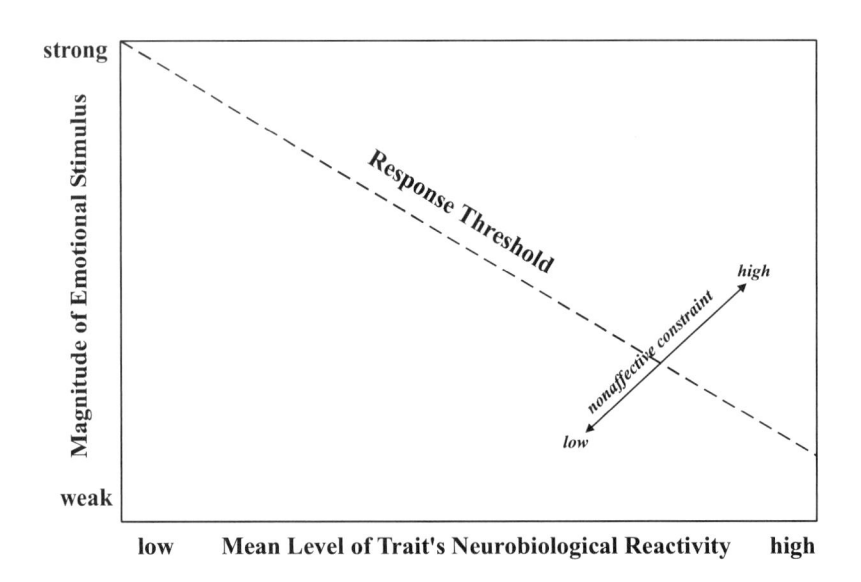

FIGURE 18.7. A minimum threshold of emotional elicitation model illustrated as a tradeoff function between the influence of (1) trait level of a neurobiological variable associated with the emotional trait (e.g., DA in Extraversion, CRH in Neuroticism, opiates in Social Closeness) (horizontal axis); (2) magnitude of a stimulus relevant to the emotional system in question (e.g., incentive for Extraversion, uncertainty for Neuroticism, soft touch for Social Closeness) (left vertical axis); and (3) the inhibitory modulation of the response threshold by the trait of constraint (perpendicular to the response threshold diagonal), which reflects the influence of 5-HT functional activity on the emotional trait's neurobiology (e.g., DA × 5-HT in Extraversion).

modulatory influence arises in large part from the dense dorsal raphe 5-HT efferents to the VTA and NAcc, connections that are known to modulate DA activity (Spoont, 1992). A reduction in 5-HT inhibitory modulation of the threshold of DA facilitation of behavior results in an exaggerated response to incentive stimuli, which is most apparent in reward–punishment conflict situations. In such situations, exaggerated responding to incentives results in (1) a greater weighting of immediate versus delayed future rewards, (2) increased reactivity to the reward of safety or relief associated with active avoidance (e.g., suicidal behavior), (3) impulsive behavior (i.e., a propensity to respond to reward even though withholding or delaying a response may produce a more favorable long-term outcome), and (4) various attempts to experience the increased magnitude and frequency of incentive reward, such as self-administration of DA-active substances (Coccaro & Siever, 1991; Depue & Collins, 1999; Lesch & Canli, 2006; Winstanley et al., 2005). These findings illustrate that the impact of environmental stimulation on neurobiological variables underlying emotional traits (e.g., DA and Extraversion) is modulated by 5-HT functioning.

Finally, stress in the form of early adversity may also influence the elicitation threshold of emotional traits in an enduring manner: Animal research has shown that stressors of many types, but especially perceived or actual social aggression and social isolation, elicit prolonged decreases in 5-HT functioning (Spoont, 1992).

A General Model of Emotional Traits

Of the five traits we have discussed, four reflect the activity of emotional/motivational systems: Neuroticism (anxiety), Extraversion (incentive motivation, positive affect), Social Closeness (consummatory affiliative reward), and SRS (social anxiety and guilt). As illustrated in Figures 18.6 and 18.7, the expression of all of these traits would be modified by the trait of constraint. This view seems relatively consistent with the view that temperament consists of two components, one relating to emotional reactivity and the other to self-regulatory processes (see Rothbart, Chapter 1, and Rueda, Chapter 8, this volume). Based on the previous discussion of the traits, the critical components in the development of individual differences in emotional traits relevant to temperament might profitably be modeled as in Figure 18.8. In this model, each trait would be sensitive to specific classes of stimuli that interact with variation in genetic factors associated with specific, broadly distributed neuromodulators that underlie the trait, such as DA, CRH, mu-opiates, and 5-HT. These genetic polymorphisms would condition the effects of critical stimuli, thereby modifying the epigenetic influences on the trait's neurobiology, as in the case of the s- and l-allele interactions with early experience. The neurobiological outcome of this interaction (e.g., the functional properties of DA) will in turn influence the core processes of an emotional trait. These core processes consist of the magnitude of affective encoding of the critical stimuli (e.g., efficacy of DA activation in the NAcc, which encodes incentive salience of environmental stimuli), and hence the breadth and strength of the associative conditioning of neutral cues to the affective code (e.g., the breadth of contextual conditioning to DA-induced reward; Depue, 2006). Variation in these core trait processes will have a *biasing* effect on many cognitive, memory, and social processes that are dependent on the magnitude of affective encoding (correlated trait processes). For instance, the magnitude of incentive encoding (core trait process), which is attached to estimates of outcome expectations formulated in the orbital cortex, will influence decisional processes and consolidation of memories of the evolving context (Depue & Collins, 1999; Depue & Morrone-Strupinsky, 2005). The correlated trait processes will thus be influenced by the core trait processes, and thereby come to define (as primary traits) the nature of the higher-order trait. The higher-order trait can be indexed by exophenotypic (behavioral, psychometric) or endophenotypic (genetic, neural, and cognitive) methods.

The biasing influence of core trait processes on correlated trait processes has a neural foundation. Affective encoding in the BLA (and perhaps the BNST) can occur within approximately 20 milliseconds via a subcortical visual pathway from the superior colliculus through the medial puvinar to the

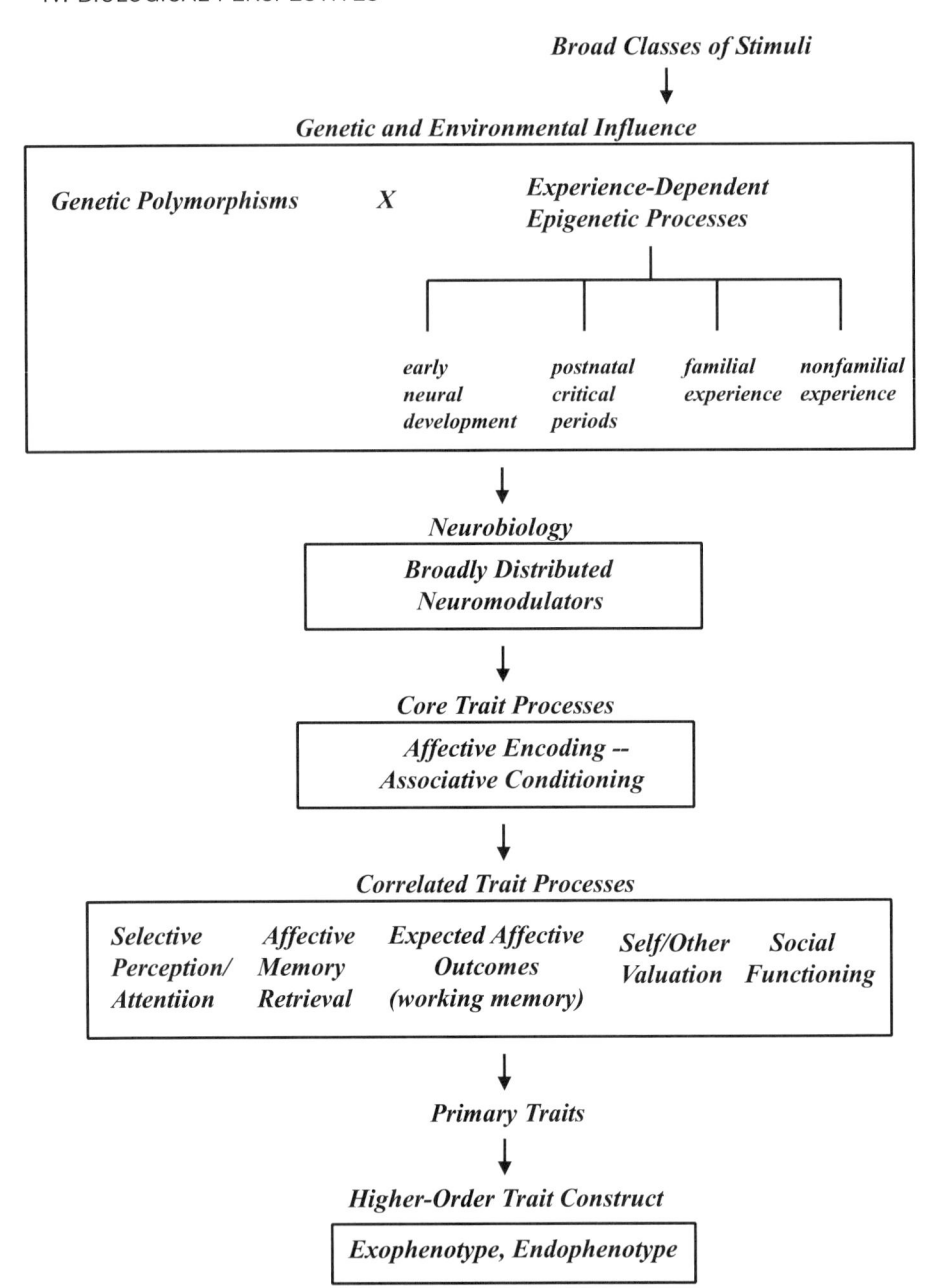

FIGURE 18.8. The critical components in the development of individual differences in emotional traits relevant to temperament and personality.

BLA (Tamietto & de Gelder, 2010). Only crude visual representations (e.g., amount of white of the eyes) are achieved in this way, outside of sensory awareness, but they do activate (1) BLA output to the Ce in order to initiate emotional responses, and (2) backprojections from the BLA to many cortical and subcortical regions to bias processing in sensory pathways, attentional networks, arousal-inducing acetylcholine projections from the basal nucleus to the cortex, outcome expectations in the orbital cortex, and affective memory consolidation and retrieval in the hippocampus. Therefore, the magnitude of BLA backprojection activity, based on magnitude of affective encoding in the BLA (in turn reflecting trait differences in reactivity to the relevant eliciting class of stimuli), can facilitate rapid processing of similar affective cues in the environment. This process may be one contribution to the biased perception, attention, and memory performance with respect to negative stimuli found in studies of Neuroticism and with respect to positive stimuli in Extraversion (Canli, 2008; Knutson & Bhanji, 2006).

In conclusion, a growing literature indicates that positive and negative environmental experiences have a robust effect through epigenetic processes on the functioning of neurobiological variables underlying temperament and personality traits. These experiences may derive from environmental conditions that are external (e.g., poverty, dangerous neighborhoods, enriching educational environment), within the family (e.g., conflict, violence, sexual abuse, caregiver separation or neglect, exuberant reward), or within the caregiver (e.g., negative vs. affectionate maternal styles). The exciting aspect of this area of research is that we are beginning to understand how these environmental influences affect neurobiological functioning and hence behavioral variation in enduring ways. The important role of temperament in these processes derives from the fact that both genetic and environmental variables that modulate brain functioning underlying emotional behavior appear to have their most profound and enduring effects during early periods of brain development. Of course, other periods of experience-expectant brain growth in childhood and in the robust growth in corticocortical connections between prefrontal and posterior brain regions in adolescence may also be critical periods for gene–environment interactions (Paus et al., 2008). Thus, temperament may represent the neural foundation against which these genetic and environmental interactions unfold.

Acknowledgment

This work was supported by Research Grant No. MH55347 awarded to Richard A. Depue.

Further Reading

Depue, R. A., & Collins, P. F. (1999). Neurobiology of the structure of personality: Dopamine, facilitation of incentive motivation, and extraversion. *Behavioral and Brain Sciences*, 22, 491–569.

Depue, R. A., & Morrone-Strupinsky, J. (2005). A neurobehavioral model of affiliative bonding: Implications for conceptualizing a human trait of affiliation. *Behavioral and Brain Sciences*, 28, 313–395.

Eisenberger, N., & Lieberman, M. (2004). Why rejection hurts: A common neural alarm system for physical and social pain. *Trends in Cognitive Sciences*, 8, 294–300.

Meaney, M. (2001). Epigenetics and the biological definition of gene × environment interactions. *Child Development*, 81, 41–79.

References

Abler, B., Walter, H., Erk, S., Kammerer, H., & Spitzer, M. (2006). Prediction error as a linear function of reward probability is coded in human nucleus accumbens. *NeuroImage*, 31, 790–795.

Akimova, E., Lanzenberger, R., & Kasper, S. (2009). The serotonin-1A receptor in anxiety disorders. *Biological Psychiatry*, 66, 627–635.

Ansorge, M., Zhou, M., Lira, A., Hen, R., & Gingrich, J. (2004). Early-life blockade of the 5-HT transporter alters emotional behavior in adult mice. *Science*, 306, 879–881.

Aston-Jones, G., & Cohen, J. D. (2005). The norepinephrine system. *Annual Review of Neuroscience*, 28, 403–435.

Aston-Jones, G., Rajkowski, J., Kubiak, P., Valentino, R., & Shiptley, M. (1996). Role of the locus coeruleus in emotional activation. In G. Holstege, R. Bandler, & C. Saper (Eds.), *The emotional motor system* (pp. 254–279). New York: Elsevier.

Auerbach, J. G., Farou, M., Ebstein, R., Kahana, M., & Levine, J. (2001). The association of the dopamine D4 receptor gene (DRD4) and the serotonin transporter promoter gene (5-HTTLPR) with temperament in 12-month-old infants. *Journal of Child Psychology and Psychiatry, 42,* 777–783.

Barlow, D. H. (2002). *Anxiety and its disorders: The nature and treatment of anxiety and panic* (2nd ed.). New York: Guilford Press.

Barr, C., Schwandt, M., Lindell, S., Higley, J., Maestripieri, D., Goldman, D., et al. (2008). Variation at the mu-opioid receptor gene (OPRM1) influences attachment behavior in infant primates. *Proceedings of the National Academy of Sciences, 105,* 5277–5281.

Belin, D., Mar, A. C., Dalley, J. W., Robbins, T. W., & Everitt, B. J. (2008). High impulsivity predicts the switch to compulsive cocaine-taking. *Science, 320,* 1352–1355.

Belsky, J., Jonassaint, C., Pleuss, M., Stanton, M., Brummett, B., & Williams, R. (2009). Vulnerability genes or plasticity genes? *Molecular Psychiatry, 14,* 746–754.

Berridge, K. C. (2007). The debate over dopamine's role in reward: The case for incentive salience. *Psychopharmacology (Berlin), 191,* 391–431.

Binder, E. B., & Nemeroff, C. B. (2010). The CRF system, stress, depression and anxiety—insights from human genetic studies. *Molecular Psychiatry, 15,* 574–588.

Boileau, I., Dagher, A., Leyton, M., Gunn, R. N., Baker, G. B., Diksic, M., et al. (2006). Modeling sensitization to stimulants in humans: An [11C] raclopride/positron emission tomography study in healthy men. *Archives of General Psychiatry, 63,* 1386–1395.

Bond, C., LaForge, K. S., Tian, M., Melia, D., Zhang, S., Borg, L., et al. (1998). Single-nucleotide polymorphism in the human mu opioid receptor gene alters β-endorphin binding and activity: Possible implications for opiate addiction. *Proceedings of the National Academy of Sciences, 95,* 9608–9613.

Buckholtz, J. W., Treadway, M. T., Cowan, R. L., Woodward, N. D., Li, R., Ansari, M., et al. (2010). Dopaminergic network differences in human impulsivity. *Science, 329,* 532.

Bunzeck, N., & Duzel, E. (2006). Absolute coding of stimulus novelty in the human substantia nigra/VTA. *Neuron, 51,* 369–379.

Canli, T. (2008). Toward a neurogenetic theory of neuroticism. *Annals of the New York Academy of Sciences, 1129,* 153–174.

Canli, T., & Lesch, K.-P. (2007). Long story short: The serotonin transporter in emotion regulation and social cognition. *Nature Neuroscience, 10,* 1103–1109.

Carpenter, L. L., Tyrka, A. R., McDougle, C. J., Malison, R. T., Owens, M. G., & Nemeroff, C. B. (2004). Cerebrospinal fluid corticotropin-releasing factor and perceived early-life stress in depressed patients and healthy control subjects. *Neuropsychopharmacology, 29,* 777–784.

Carver, C. S., Johnson, S. L., Joormann, J., & Nam, J. Y. (2010). Serotonin transporter polymorphism interacts with childhood adversity to predict aspects of impulsivity. *Psychological Science, 15,* 25–41.

Carver, C. S., & Miller, C. J. (2006). Relations of serotonin function to personality: Current views and a key methodological issue. *Psychiatry Research, 144,* 1–15.

Caspi, A., Roberts, B. W., & Shiner, R. L. (2005). Personality development: Stability and change. *Annual Review of Psychology, 56,* 453–484.

Caspi, A., Sugden, K., Moffitt, T., Taylor, A., & Craig, I. (2003). Influence of life stress on depression: Moderation by a polymorphism in the 5-HTT gene. *Science, 301,* 386–389.

Champagne, D., Bagot, R., Hasselt, F., Ramakers, G., Meaney, M., de Kloet, E., et al. (2008). Maternal care and hipocampal plasticity: Evidence for experience-dependent structural plasticity, altered synaptic functioning, and differential responsiveness to glucocorticoids and stress. *Journal of Neuroscience, 28,* 6037–6045.

Champoux, M., Bennett, A., Shannon, C., Higley, J., Lesch, K., & Suomi, S. (2002). Serotonin transporter gene polymorphism, differential early rearing, and behavior in rhesus monkey neonates. *Molecular Psychiatry, 7,* 1058–1063.

Cloninger, C. R. (1986). A unified biosocial theory of personality and its role in the development of anxiety states. *Psychiatric Developments, 3,* 167–226.

Coccaro, E., & Siever, L. (1991). *Serotonin and psychiatric disorders.* Washington, DC: American Psychiatric Association Press.

Congdon, E., Lesch, K.-P., & Canli, T. (2008). Analysis of DRD4 and DAT plymorphisms and behavioral inhibition in healthy adults. *American Journal of medical Genetics B: Neuropsychiatric Genetics, 147,* 27–32.

Cools, R., Roberts, A. C., & Robbins, T. W. (2007). Serotoninergic regulation of emotional and behavioural control processes. *Trends in Cognitive Sciences, 12,* 31–40.

Cooper, A. J., Perkins, A. M., & Corr, P. J. (2007). A confirmatory factor analytic study of anxiety, fear, and behavioral inhibition system measures. *Journal of Individual Differences, 28,* 179–187.

Coplan, J. D., Andrews, M. W., Rosenblum, L. A., Owens, M. J., Friedman, S., & Gorman, J. M. (1996). Persistent elevations of cerebrospinal fluid concentrations of corticotropin-releasing factor in adult nonhuman primates exposed to early-life stressors: Implications for the pathophysiology of mood and anxiety disorders. *Proceedings of the National Academy of Sciences, 93,* 1619–1623.

Costa, R. M. (2007). Plastic corticostriatal circuits for action learning. *Annals of the New York Academy of Science, 1104,* 172–191.

Craig, A. (2009). How do you feel—now?: The anterior insula and human awareness. *Nature Neuroscience, 10,* 59–70.

Cushing, B., & Kramer, K. (2005). Mechanisms underlying epigenetic effects of early social experience: The role of neuropeptides and steroids. *Neuroscience and Biobehavioral Reviews, 29,* 1089–1105.

D'Ardenne, K., McClure, S. M., Nystrom, L. E., & Cohen, J. D. (2008). BOLD responses reflecting dopmainergic signals in the human ventral tegmental area. *Science, 319,* 1264–1267.

Davis, E. P., & Sandman, C. A. (2010). The timing of prenatal exposure to maternal cortisol and psychosocial stress is associated with human infant cognitive development. *Child Development, 81,* 131–148.

Davis, M. (2006). Neural systems involved in fear and anxiety measured with fear-potentiated startle. *American Psychologist, 61,* 741–756.

Day, J. J., Roitman, M. F., Wightman, R. M., & Carelli, R. M. (2007). Associative learning mediates dynamic shifts in dopamine signaling in the nucleus accumbens. *Nature Neuroscience, 10,* 1020–1028.

Depue, R. A. (1995). Neurobiological factors in personality and depression. *European Journal of Personality, 9,* 413–439.

Depue, R. A. (2006). Interpersonal behavior and the structure of personality: Neurobehavioral foundation of agentic extraversion and affiliation. In T. Canli (Ed.), *Biology of personality and individual differences* (pp. 60–92). New York: Guilford Press.

Depue, R. A. (2009). Genetic, environmental, and epigenetic factors in the development of personality disturbance [*Special issue*]. *Developmental Psychopathology, 21*(4), 1031–1063.

Depue, R. A., & Collins, P. F. (1999). Neurobiology of the structure of personality: Dopamine, facilitation of incentive motivation, and extraversion. *Behavioral and Brain Sciences, 22,* 491–569.

Depue, R. A., & Lenzenweger, M. F. (2005). A neurobehavioral dimensional model of personality disturbance. In M. F. Lenzenweger & J. F. Clarkin (Eds.), *Major theories of personality disorders* (2nd ed., pp. 391–454). New York: Guilford Press.

Depue, R., Luciana, M., Arbisi, P., Collins, P., & Leon, A. (1994). Dopamine and the structure of personality: Relation of agonist-induced dopamine D2 activity to positive emotionality. *Journal of Personality and Social Psychology, 67,* 485–498.

Depue, R. A., & Morrone-Strupinsky, J. (2005). A neurobehavioral model of affiliative bonding: Implications for coneptualizing a human trait of affiliation. *Behavioral and Brain Sciences, 28,* 313–395.

Depue, R., & Spoont, M. (1986). Conceptualizing a serotonin trait: A behavioral dimension of constraint. *Annals of the New York Academy of Sciences, 487,* 47–62.

Deussing, J., & Wurst, W. (2005). Dissecting the genetic effect of the CRH system on anxiety and stress-related behaviour. *Comptes Rendus Biologies, 328,* 199–212.

Donaldson, Z. R., & Young, L. J. (2008). Oxytocin, vasopressin, and the neurogenetics of sociality. *Science, 322,* 900–904.

Drevets, W. C., Gautier, C., Price, J. C., Kupfer, D. J., Kinahan, P. E., Grace, A. A., et al. (2001). Amphetamine-induced dopamine release in human ventral striatum correlates with euphoria. *Biological Psychiatry, 49,* 81–96.

Durvarci, S., Bauer, E. P., & Pare, D. (2009). The bed nucleus of the stria terminalis mediates interindividual variations in anxiety and fear. *Journal of Neuroscience, 29,* 10357–10361.

Eisenberger, N., & Lieberman, M. (2004). Why rejection hurts: A common neural alarm system for physical and social pain. *Trends in Cognitive Sciences, 8,* 294–300.

Eysenck, H. J. (1981). *A model for personality.* New York: Springer-Verlag.

Fendt, M., Endres, T., & Apfelbach, R. (2003). Temporary inactivation of the bed nucleus of the stria terminalis but not of the amygdala blocks freezing induced by trimethylthiazoline, a component of fox feces. *Journal of Neuroscience, 23,* 23–28.

Fisher, P. M., Meltzer, C. C., Ziolko, S. K., Price, J. C., Moses-Kolko, E. L., Berga, S. L., et al. (2006). Capacity for 5-HT1A-mediated autoregulation predicts amygdala reactivity. *Nature Neuroscience, 9,* 1362–1363.

Fleming, A. S., Korsmit, M., & Deller, M. (1994). Rat pups are potent reinforcers to the maternal animal: Effects of experience, parity, hormones, and dopamine function. *Psychobiology, 22,* 44–53.

Fleming, A. S., O'Day, D. H., & Kraemer, G. W. (1999). Neurobiology of mother–infant interactions: Experience and central nervous system plasticity across development and generations. *Neuroscience and Biobehavioral Reviews, 23,* 673–685.

Forbes, E. E., Brown, S. M., Kimak, M., Ferrell, R. E., Manuck, S. B., & Hariri, A. R. (2009). Genetic variation in components of dopamine neurotransmission impacts ventral striatal reactivity associated with impulsivity. *Molecular Psychiatry, 14,* 60–70.

Fox, A., Shelton, S. E., Oakes, T. R., Davidson, R. J., & Kalin, N. H. (2008). Trait-like brain activity during adolescence predicts anxious temperament in primates. *PLoS ONE, 3,* e2570.

Fox, S., Levitt, P., & Nelson, C. A. (2010). How the timing and quality of early experiences influence the development of brain architecture. *Child Development, 81,* 28–40.

Frodl, T., Outsouleris, N., Bottlender, R., Bom, C., Er, A., Enthaler, O. R., et al. (2008). Reduced gray matter brain volumes are associated with variants of the serotonin transporter gene in

major depression. *Molecular Psychiatry, 13,* 1093–1101.
Gaspar, P., Cases, O., & Maroteaux, L. (2003). The developmental role of serotonin: News from mouse molecular genetics. *Nature Reviews Neuroscience, 4,* 1002–1012.
Gelernter, J., Kranzler, H., & Cubells, J. (1999). Genetics of two μ opioid receptor gene (OPRM1) exon I polymorphisms: Population studies, and allele frequencies in alcohol- and drug-dependent subjects. *Molecular Psychiatry, 4,* 476–483.
Gillespie, S., & Nemeroff, S. (2007). Corticotropin-releasing factor and the psychobiology of early-life stress. *Current Directions in Psychological Science, 16,* 85–89.
Gray, J. A. (1973). Causal theories of personality and how to test them. In J. R. Royce (Ed.), *Multivariate analysis and psychological theory* (pp. 75–102). New York: Academic Press.
Gray, J. A., & McNaughton, N. (2000). *The neuropsychology of anxiety: An enquiry into the functions of the septo-hippocampal system* (2nd ed.). Oxford, UK: Oxford University Press.
Gross, E., & Hen, R. (2004). Developmental origins of anxiety. *Nature Reviews Neuroscience, 5,* 545–552.
Gunthert, K. C., Conner, T. S., Armeli, S., Tennen, H., Covault, J., & Kranzler, H. R. (2007). Serotonin transporter gene polymorphism (5-HTTLPR) and anxiety reactivity in daily life: A daily process approach to gene–environment interaction. *Psychosomatic Medicine, 69,* 762–768.
Habib, K., Weld, K., Rice, K., Pushkas, J., Champoux, M., Listwak, S., et al. (2000). Oral administration of a corticotropin-releasing hormone receptor antagonist significantly attenuates behavioral, neuroendocrine, and autonomic response to stress in primates. *Proceedings of the National Academy of Sciences, 97,* 6079–6084.
Hariri, A. R. (2006). Genetically driven variation in serotonin function: Impact on amygdala reactivity and individual differences in fearful and anxious personality. In T. Canli (Ed.), *Biology of personality and individual differences* (pp. 295–316). New York: Guilford Press.
Hariri, A. R., Brown, S. M., Williamson, D. E., Flory, J. D., de Wit, H., & Manuck, S. B. (2006). Preference for immediate over delayed rewards is associated with magnitude of ventral striatal activity. *Journal of Neuroscience, 26,* 13213–13217.
Heimer, L. (2003). A new anatomical framework for neuropsychiatric disorders and drug abuse. *American Journal of Psychiatry, 160,* 1726–1739.
Heinrichs, M., & Domes, G. (2008). Neuropeptides and social behaviour: Effects of oxytocin and vasopressin in humans. *Progress in Brain Research, 170,* 337–350.
Hennig, J., Reuter, M., Netter, P., & Burk, C. (2005). Two types of aggression are differentially related to serotonergic activity and the A779C TPH polymorphism. *Behavioral Neuroscience, 119,* 16–25.
Insel, T. R. (2010). The challenge of translation in social neuroscience: A review of oxytocin, vasopressin, and affiliative behavior. *Neuron, 65,* 768–779.
Jahn, A. L., Fox, A. S., Abercrombie, H. C., Shelton, S. E., Oakes, T. R., Davidson, R. J., et al. (2010). Subgenual prefrontal cortex activity predicts individual differences in hypothalamic–pituitary–adrenal activity across different contexts. *Biological Psychiatry, 67,* 175–181.
Johansen, J., & Fields, H. (2004). Glutamatergic activation of anterior cigulate cortex produces an aversive teaching signal. *Nature Neuroscience, 7,* 398–403.
Kalin, N., Shelton, S., & Davidson, R. (2004). The role of the central nucleus of the amygdala in mediating fear and anxiety in the primate. *Journal of Neuroscience, 24,* 5506–5515.
Kalin, N., Shelton, S., Davidson, R., & Kelley, A. (2001). The primate amygdala mediates acute fear but not the behavioral and physiological components of anxious temperament. *Journal of Neuroscience, 21,* 2067–2074.
Kalin, N., Shelton, S., Fox, A. S., Rogers, J., Oakes, T. R., & Davidson, R. J. (2008). The serotonin transporter genotype is associated with intermediate brain phenotypes that depend on the context of eliciting stressor. *Molecular Psychiatry, 13,* 1021–1027.
Kim, J., & Diamond, D. (2002). The stressed hippocampus, synaptic plasticity and lost memories. *Nature Reviews Neuroscience, 3,* 453–462.
Knutson, B., & Bhanji, J. (2006). Neural substrates for emotional traits?: The case of extraversion. In T. Canli (Ed.), *Biology of personality and individual differences* (pp. 116–132). New York: Guilford Press.
Knutson, B., & Wimmer, G. E. (2007). Splitting the difference: How does the brain code reward episodes? *Annals of the New York Academy of Sciences, 1104,* 54–69.
Ladd, C. O., Huot, R. L., Thrivikraman, K. V., Nemeroff, C. B., Meaney, M. J., & Plotsky, P. M. (2000). Long-term behavioral and neuroendocrine adaptations to adverse early experience. *Progress in Brain Research, 122,* 81–103.
Lakatos, M., Johnson, C., & Young, G. (2003). Association of D4 dopamine receptor gene and serotonin transporter promotor polymorphisms with infants response to novelty. *Molecular Psychiatry, 8,* 90–97.
Lanzenberger, R. R., Mitterhauser, M., Spindelegger, C., Wadsak, W., Klein, N., Mien, L., et al. (2007). Reduced serotonin-1A receptor binding in social anxiety disorder. *Biological Psychiatry, 61,* 1081–1089.
Laviolette, S. R., Gallegos, R. A., Henriksen, S. J., & van der Kooy, D. (2004). Opiate state controls

bi-directional reward signaling via GABA-A receptors in the ventral tegmental area. *Nature Neuroscience, 10,* 160–169.

LeDoux, J. (1998). *The emotional brain.* New York: Simon & Schuster.

Lee, R., Geracioti, T. D., Kasckow, J. W., & Coccaro, E. F. (2005). Childhood trauma and personality disorder: Positive correlation with adult CSF corticotropin-releasing factor concentrations. *American Journal of Psychiatry, 162,* 995–997.

Lee, R., Gollan, J., Kasckow, J., Geracioti, T., & Coccaro, E. F. (2006). CSF corticotropin-releasing factor in personality disorder: Relationship with self-reported parental care. *Neuropsychopharmacology, 31,* 2289–2295.

Lee, Y., Fitz, S., Johnson, P., & Shekhar, A. (2008). Repeated stimulation of CRF receptors in the BNST of rats selectively induces social but not panic-like anxiety. *Neuropsychopharmacology, 33,* 2586–2594.

Leonardo, A., & Hen, R. (2006). Genetics of affective and anxiety disorders. *Annual Review of Psychology, 57,* 117–137.

Leri, F., Flores, J., Rodaros, D., & Stewart, J. (2002). Blockade of stress-induced but not cocaine-induced reinstatement by infusion of noradrenergic antagonists into the bed nucleus of the stria terminalis or the central nucleus of the amygdala. *Journal of Neuroscience, 22,* 5713–5718.

Lesch, K.-P., & Canli, T. (2006). 5-HT1A receptor and anxiety-related traits: Pharmacology, genetics, and imaging. In T. Canli (Ed.), *Biology of personality and individual differences* (pp. 273–294). New York: Guilford Press.

Leyton, M., Boileau, I., Benkelfat, C., Diksic, M., Baker, H. F., & Dagher, A. (2002). Extracellular dopamine, drug wanting, and novelty seeking: A PET/[11C]raclopride study in healthy men. *Neuropharmacology, 6,* 145–163.

Lim, M. M., & Young, L. J. (2006). Neuropeptidergic regulation of affiliative behavior and social bonding in animals. *Hormones and Behavior, 50,* 506–517.

Liu, Q., Vrontou, S., Rice, F., Zylka, M., Dong, X., & Anderson, D. (2007). Molecular genetic visualization of a rare subset of unmyelinated sensory neurons that may detect gentle touch. *Nature Neuroscience, 10,* 946–948.

Liu, Z.-H., Shin, R., & Ikemoto, S. (2008). Dual role of medial A10 dopamine neurons in affective encoding. *Neuropsychopharmacology, 33,* 3010–3020.

Macey, D., Smith, H., Nader, M., & Porrino, L. (2003). Chronic cocaine self-administration upregulates the norepinephrine transporter and alters functional activity in the bed nucleus of the stria terminalis of the rhesus monkey. *Journal of Neuroscience, 23,* 12–16.

Manuck, S., Flory, J., Ferrell, R., Dent, K., Mann, J., & Muldoon, M. (1999). Aggression and anger-related traits associated with a polymorphism of the tryptophan hydroxylase gene. *Biological Psychiatry, 45,* 603–614.

Marinelli, M., & White, F. (2000). Enhanced vulnerability to cocaine self-administration is associated with elevated impulse activity of midbrain dopamine neurons. *Journal of Neuroscience, 20,* 8876–8885.

Markon, K., Krueger, R., & Watson, D. (2005). Delineating the structure of normal and abnormal personality: An integrative hierarchical approach. *Journal of Personality and Social Psychology, 88,* 139–157.

McArthur, S., Dalley, J., Buckingham, J., & Gillies, G. (2005). Altered mesencephalic dopaminergic populations in adulthood as a consequence of brief perinatal glucocorticoid exposure. *Journal of Neuroendocrinology, 17,* 475–482.

McDonald, A., Shammah-Lagnado, S., Shi, C., & Davis, M. (1999). Cortical afferents to the extended amygdala. *Annals of New York Academy of Sciences, 877,* 309–338.

Meaney, M. (2001). Epigenetics and the biological definition of gene × environment interactions. *Child Development, 81,* 41–79.

Meaney, M. (2010). Maternal care, gene expression, and the transmission of individual differences in stress reactivity across generations. *Annual Review of Neuroscience, 24,* 1161–1192.

Meaney, M., Brake, W., & Cratton, A. (2002). Environmental regulation of the development of mesolimbic dopamine systems: A neurobiological mechanism for vulnerability to drug abuse? *Psychoneuroendocrinology, 27,* 127–138.

Merali, Z., Michaud, D., McIntosh, J., Kent, P., & Anisman, H. (2003). Differential involvement of amygdaloid CRH system(s) in the salience and valence of the stimuli. *Progress in Neuro-Psychopharmacology and Biological Psychiatry, 27,* 1201–1212.

Meyer-Lindenberg, A., & Weinberger, D. (2006). Intermediate phenotypes and genetic mechanisms of psychiatric disorders. *Nature Reviews Neuroscience, 7,* 818–827.

Moles, A., Kieffer, B., & D'Amato, F. (2004). Deficit in attachment behavior in mice lacking the *u*-opioid receptor gene. *Science, 304,* 1983–1986.

Munafo, M., Clark, T., Moore, L., Payne, E., Walton, R., & Flint, J. (2003). Genetic polymorphisms and personality in healthy adults: A systematic review and meta-analysis. *Molecular Psychiatry, 8,* 471–484.

Munafo, M., Yalcin, B., Willis-Owen, S. A., & Flint, J. (2008). Association of the dopamine D4 receptor (*DRD4*) gene and approach-related personality traits: Meta-analysis and new data. *Biological Psychiatry, 63,* 197–206.

Murphy, D. L., & Lesch, K.-P. (2008). Targeting the murine serotonin transporter: Insights into human neurobiology. *Nature Reviews Neuroscience, 9,* 45–61.

Nelson, E. E., Hermann, K. N., Barrett, C., Noble,

P. L., Wojteczko, K., Chisholm, K., et al. (2009). Adverse rearing experiences enhance responding to both aversive and rewarding stimuli in juvenile Rhesus monkeys. *Biological Psychiatry*, 66, 702–704.

Nie, Z., Schweitzer, P., Roberts, A., Madamba, S., Moore, S., & Siggins, G. (2004). Ethanol augments GABAergic transmission in the central amygdala via CRF1 receptors. *Science*, 303, 1512–1514

O'Doherty, J., Kringelbach, M., Rolls, E., Hornack, J., & Andrews, C. (2001). Abstract reward and punishment representations in the human orbitofrontal cortex. *Nature Neuroscience*, 4, 95–102.

Olausson, H., Lamarre, Y., Backlund, H., Morin, C., Wallin, B. G., Starck, G., et al. (2002). Unmyelinated tactile afferents signal touch and project to insular cortex. *Nature Neuroscience*, 5, 900–904.

Oler, J., Fox, A., Shelton, S. E., Christian, B. T., Murali, D., & Oakes, T. R. (2009). Serotonin transporter availability in the amygdala and bed nucleus of the stria terminalis predicts anxious temperament and brain glucose metabolic activity. *Journal of Neuroscience*, 29, 9961–9966.

Olsson, C. A., Byrnes, G. B., Anney, R. J., Collins, V., Hemphill, S. A., Williamson, R., et al. (2007). COMT val158MET and 5HTTLPR functional loci interact to predict persistence of anxiety across adolescence: Results from the Victorian Adolescent Health Cohort Study. *Genes, Brain and Behavior*, 6, 647–652.

Oswald, L., Wong, D., McCaul, M., Zhou, Y., Kuwabara, H., Choi, L., et al. (2005). Relationships among ventral striatal dopamine release, cortisol secretion, and subjective responses to amphetamine. *Neuropsychopharmacology*, 30, 821–832.

Panksepp, J. (1998). *Affective neuroscience: The foundations of human and animal emotions.* New York: Oxford University Press.

Paterson, A. D., Sunohara, G. A., & Kennedy, J. L. (1999). Dopamine D4 receptor gene: Novelty or nonsense. *Neuropsychopharmacology*, 21, 3–16.

Paus, T., Keshavan, M., & Giedd, J. N. (2008). Why do many psychiatric disorders emerge during adolescence? *Nature Reviews Neuroscience*, 9, 947–957.

Pezawas, L., Meyer-Lindenberg, A., Drabant, E., Verchinski, B., Munoz, K., Kolachana, B., et al. (2005). 5-HTTLPR polymorphism impacts human cingulate amygdala interactions. *Nature Neuroscience*, 8, 828–834.

Pezawas, L., Meyer-Lindenberg, A., Goldman, A. L., Verchinski, B. A., Chen, G., Kolachana, B. S., et al. (2008). Evidence of biologic epistasis between BDNF and SLC6A4 and implications for depression. *Molecular Psychiatry*, 13, 709–716.

Plotsky, P. M., & Meaney, M. J. (1993). Early postnatal experience alters hypothalamic corticotropin-releasing factor (CRF) mRNA, median eminence CRF content and stress-induced release in adult rats. *Molecular Brain Research*, 18, 195–200.

Plotsky, P. M., Thrivikraman, K. V., Nemeroff, C. B., Caldji, C., Sharma, S., & Meaney, M. J. (2005). Long-term consequences of neonatal rearing on central corticotropin-releasing factor systems in adult male rat offspring. *Neuropsychopharmacology*, 30, 2192–2204.

Pruessner, J., Champagne, F., Meaney, M., & Dagher, A. (2004). Dopamine release in response to a psychological stress in humans and its relationship to early life maternal care: A positron emission tomography study using [11C]raclopride. *Journal of Neuroscience*, 24, 2825–2831.

Rujescu, D., Giegling, I., Bondy, B., Gietl, A., Zill, P., & Moller, H.-J. (2002). Association of anger-related traits with SNPs in the TPH gene. *Molecular Psychiatry*, 7, 1023–1029.

Roth, T., & Sullivan, R. (2005). Examining the role of endogenous opioids in learned odor-stroke associations in infant rats. *Journal of Neuroscience*, 54, 71–78.

Sahuque, L., Kullberg, E., McGeehan, A., Kinder, J., Hicks, M., Blanton, M., et al. (2006). Anxiogenic and aversive effects of corticotropin releasing factor (CRF) in the bed nucleus of the stria terminalis in the rat: Role of CRF receptor subtypes. *Psychopharmacology*, 186, 122–132.

Sanchez, M. M., Noble, P. M., Lyon, C. K., Plotsky, P. M., Davis, M., & Nemeroff, C. B. (2005). Alterations in diurnal cortisol rhythm and acoustic startle response in nonhuman primates with adverse rearing. *Biological Psychiatry*, 57, 373–381.

Sapolsky, R. (2004). Mothering style and methylation. *Nature Neuroscience*, 7, 791–792.

Schott, B. H., Sellner, D. B., Lauer, C. J., Habib, R., Frey, J. U., Guderian, S., et al. (2004). Activation of midbrain structures by associative novelty and the formation of explicit memory in humans. *Learning and Memory*, 11, 383–387.

Schultz, W. (2007). Multiple dopamine functions at different time courses. *Annual Review of Neuroscience*, 30, 259–288.

Servatius, R., Beck, K., Moldow, R., Salameh, G., Tumminello, T., & Short, K. (2005). A stress-induced anxious state in male rats: Corticotropin-releasing hormone induces persistent changes in associative learning and startle reactivity. *Biological Psychiatry*, 57, 865–872.

Somerville, L., Heatherton, T., & Kelley, W. (2006). Anterior cingulate cortex responds differentially to expectancy violation and social rejection. *Nature Neuroscience*, 9, 1007–1008.

Somerville, L., Whalen, P., & Kelley, W. (2010). Human bed nucleus of the stria terminalis indexes hypervigilant threat monitoring. *Biological Psychiatry*, 68, 416–424.

Spoont, M. (1992). Modulatory role of serotonin in neural information processing: Implications for human psychopathology. *Psychological Bulletin, 112*, 330–350.

Stein, M. B., Schork, N. J., & Glernter, J. (2008). Gene-by-environment (serotonin transporter and childhood maltreatment) interaction for anxiety sensitivity, an intermediate phenotype for anxiety disorders. *Neuropsychopharmacology, 33*, 312–319.

Stuber, G. D., Klanker, M., de Ridder, B., Bowers, M. S., Joosten, R. N., Feenstra, M. G., et al. (2008). Reward-predictive cues enhance excitatory synaptic strength onto midbrain dopamine neurons. *Science, 321*, 1690–1692.

Sullivan, R. (1991). Olfactory classical conditioning in neonates. *Pediatrics, 87*, 511–518.

Tamietto, M., & de Gelder, B. (2010). Neural bases of the non-conscious perception of emotional signals. *Nature Reviews Neuroscience, 11*, 697–709.

Taylor, S., Way, B., Walch, W., Hilmert, C., Lehman, B., & Eisenberger, N. (2006). Early family environment, current adversity, the serotonin transporter promotor polymorphism, and depressive symptomatology. *Biological Psychiatry, 60*, 671–676.

Tellegen, A., Lykken, D. T., Bouchard, T. J., Wilcox, K. J., Segal, N. L., & Rich, S. (1988). Personality similarity in twins reared apart and together. *Journal of Personality and Social Psychology, 54*, 1031–1039.

Tellegen, A., & Waller, N. G. (2008). Exploring personality through test construction: Development of the Multidimensional Personality Questionnaire. In G. J. Boyle, G. Mathews, & D. H. Saklofske (Eds.), *The Sage handbook of personality theory and assessment: Vol. 2. Personality measurement and testing* (pp. 189–213). New York: Sage.

Tsankova, S., Renthal, D., Kumar, A., & Nestler, E. (2007). Epigenetic regulation in psychiatric disorders. *Nature Reviews Neuroscience, 8*, 355–367.

Tsetsenis, T., Ma, X.-H., Iacono, L., Beck, S., & Gross, C. (2007). Suppression of conditioning to ambiguous cues by pharmacogenetic inhibition of the dentate gyrus. *Nature Neuroscience, 10*, 896–902.

Uhl, G. R., Sora, I., & Wang, Z. (1999). The μ opiate receptor as a candidate gene for pain: Polymorphisms, variations in expression, nociception, and opiate responses. *Proceedings of the National Academy of Sciences, 96*, 7752–7755.

Van den Oever, M., Goriounova, N., Li, K., Van der Schors, R., Binnekade, R., Schoffelmeer, A., et al. (2008). Prefrontal cortex AMPA receptor plasticity is crucial for cue-induced relapse to heroin-seeking. *Nature Neuroscience, 11*, 1053–1058.

Volkow, N., Wang, G., Fischman, M., Foltin, R., Fowler, J., Abumrad, N., et al. (1997). Relationship between subjective effects of cocaine and dopamine transporter occupancy. *Nature, 386*, 827–829.

Way, B. M., & Taylor, S. E. (2010). The serotonin transporter promoter polymorphism is associated with cortisol responses to psychosocial stress. *Biological Psychiatry, 67*, 487–492.

Way, B. M., Taylor, S. E., & Eisenberger, N. I. (2009). Variation in the μ-opioid receptor gene (OPRM1) is associated with dispositional and neural sensitivity to social rejection. *Proceedings of the National Academy of Sciences, 106*, 15079–15084.

Weaver, I., Cervoni, N., Champagne, F., D'Alessio, A., Sharma, S., Seckl, J., et al. (2004). Epigenetic programming by maternal behavior. *Nature Neuroscience, 7*, 847–853.

White, T. L., & Depue, R. A. (1999). Differential association of traits of fear and anxiety with norepinephrine- and dark-induced pupil reactivity. *Journal of Personality and Social Psychology, 77*, 863–877.

Wilhelm, K., Mitchell, P. B., Niven, H., Finch, A., Wedgwood, L,, & Scimone, A. (2006). Life events, first depression onset and the serotonin transporter gene. *British Journal of Psychiatry, 188*, 210–215.

Winstanley, C., Theobald, D., Dalley, J., & Robbins, T. (2005). Interactions between serotonin and dopamine in the control of impulsive choice in rats: Therapeutic implications for impulse control disorders. *Neuropsychopharacology, 5*, 1–14.

Wittmann, B. C., Bunzeck, N., Dolan, R. J., & Duzel, E. (2007). Anticipation of novelty recruits reward system and hippocampus while promoting recollection. *NeuroImage, 38*, 194–202.

Young, L. J., & Wang, D. A. (2004). The neurobiology of pair bonding. *Nature Neuroscience, 7*, 1048–1054.

Zald, D., Cowan, R. L., Riccardi, P., Baldwin, R. M., Ansari, M., Li, R., et al. (2008). Midbrain dopamine receptor availability is inversely associated with novelty-seeking traits in humans. *Journal of Neuroscience, 28*, 14372–14378.

Zald, D., & Depue, R. (2001). Serotonergic modulation of positive and negative affect in psychiatrically healthy males. *Personality and Individual Differences, 30*, 71–86.

Zhang, D., Shao, C., Shao, M., Yan, P., Wang, Y., Liu, Y., et al. (2007). Effect of μ-opioid receptor gene polymorphisms on heroin-induced subjective responses in a Chinese population. *Biological Psychiatry, 61*, 1244–1251.

Zubieta, J.-K., Smith, Y., Bueller, J., Xu, Y., Kilbourn, M., Jewett, D., et al. (2001). Regional mu opioid receptor regulation of sensory and affective dimensions of pain. *Science, 293*, 311–315.

Zuckerman, M. (1994). An alternative five-factor model for personality. In C. Halverson, G. Kohnstamm, & R. Marten (Eds.), *The developing structure of temperament and personality from infancy to adulthood* (pp. 34–57). Hillsdale, NJ: Erlbaum.

PART V

TEMPERAMENT IN CONTEXT

CHAPTER 19

Integrating Temperament and Attachment
The Differential Susceptibility Paradigm

Marinus H. van IJzendoorn
Marian J. Bakermans-Kranenburg

For years on end, attachment and temperament seemed natural enemies in a deadly war over dominance and territory. At one side of the border, followers of temperament theory basically reduced attachment to temperamental inhibition in the Strange Situation (Kagan, 1995). At the other side, adherents of attachment theory declared temperament obsolete because of its outmoded emphasis on inherited or constitutional individual differences (Sroufe, 1985). Recent research in the fields of both attachment and temperament, however, has shown convincingly that caregiving environments fostering the formation of secure attachment not only shape neurophysiological substrates of temperamental inhibition but also help to regulate infant emotional reactivity (Hane & Fox, 2006). Inspired by the seminal work of Meaney (2010) and his group on the crucial role of caregiving in determining stress reactivity in rodents, the domains of temperament and attachment have come closer to each other in the converging identification of the significance of the caregiving environment. At the same time the idea that the effect of parenting on the child also depends on the child's temperament has almost become a truism.

In recent years temperament and attachment have thus become intertwined more intimately. Although much work still focuses on parenting effects, with the assumption that they apply equally to all children, recent studies have tested the moderating effect of the child's temperament, following Belsky's (1997b) ideas about temperamental differential susceptibility. For example, Klein Velderman, Bakermans-Kranenburg, Juffer, and van IJzendoorn (2006) found that experimentally induced changes in maternal sensitivity exerted greater impact on the attachment security of highly reactive infants than it did on other infants. The very temperamental characteristics of individuals that make them disproportionately vulnerable to adversity may also make them disproportionately likely to benefit from contextual support, which is the core hypothesis of the differential susceptibility paradigm (Ellis, Boyce, Belsky, Bakermans-Kranenburg, & van IJzendoorn, 2011).

In this chapter we describe the various interpretations of the complicated relation between attachment and temperament, and we show how their borders have become permeable. In fact, the differential susceptibility paradigm integrates temperament and attachment in a constructive, complementary, and productive way. Although some decades ago it seemed "never the twain shall meet," a reconciliation is now emerging, and bridges are being built between two major theoretical strands in developmental science. In this chapter we highlight some milestones in this rapprochement, with an emphasis on recent, exciting developments based on the differential susceptibility paradigm as the integrative template of temperament and attachment theory and research.

The Nature and Nurture of Attachment and Temperament

Attachment

Attachment has been briefly defined as children's "strong disposition to seek proximity to and contact with a specific figure and to do so in certain situations, notably when they are frightened, tired or ill" (Bowlby, 1969, p. 371). Inspired by Darwinian evolutionary theory and Harlow's (1958) experimental work with rhesus monkeys, Bowlby (1969) was the first to propose that human genetic selection had favored attachment behaviors, since they increased infant–parent proximity, which in turn enhanced the chances for infant survival. Although Bowlby did not use the concept of "inclusive fitness" to hint at the transmission of parental genes into the next generations, he can certainly be considered the first evolutionary psychologist after Darwin (see Simpson & Belsky, 2008, for a more sophisticated treatment of the evolutionary background of attachment). Attachment is considered to be an inborn capacity of every exemplar of the human species. Individual differences in the quality of attachment emerge in the first years of life, and central to attachment theory is the idea that parenting, more specifically, parental sensitive responsiveness to the infant's distress signals, determines whether children develop a secure or an insecure attachment relationship with their primary caregiver (Ainsworth, 1967; Ainsworth, Blehar, Waters, & Wall, 1978).

Individual differences in infant attachment security are typically observed in the Strange Situation, a mildly stressful procedure with two separations from the caregiver in an unfamiliar room, with and without a "stranger" present (Ainsworth et al., 1978). The procedure is supposed to activate the infant's attachment system, and the pattern of behavior observed during the procedure, in particular, upon reunion with the caregiver, is indicative of the quality of the infant–caregiver attachment relationship. When distressed, secure children direct attachment behaviors to their caregivers and take comfort in the reassurance offered by them. Experience has taught securely attached children that they can rely on their caregivers to be there and alleviate their stress. Infants with insecure attachments have not experienced sensitive caregiving and are anxious about the availability of their caregivers. They either avoid showing attachment behavior upon reunion with the caregiver in the Strange Situation procedure because of fear of triggering a negative parental response, or they display anger toward their caregivers, showing ambivalence in the reunion episodes: In the latter case, children seek contact, then resist contact angrily when it is achieved, as if to punish the caregiver for his or her unwanted absence (Sroufe, Egeland, Carlson, & Collins, 2005).

Temperament

The number of definitions and measures of attachment is limited, and, in fact, the dependence of attachment theory on one or a few "gold standard" assessments has been deplored as too restrictive (Kagan, 1995, 2009). In contrast, the origins of temperament theory are manifold, as are the definitions, interpretations, dimensions, and measures of temperament. Of course, Thomas and Chess (1977), who started their seminal New York Longitudinal Study in 1956, were the singular crucial source of inspiration for many temperament researchers in the 1970s and 1980s of the previous century. Thomas and Chess searched for child characteristics that would influence the course of child development relatively independent of, or in addition to, parenting and other environmental pressures, as they had noted that parenting had only limited success in shaping the development of many children in their clinical practice, as well as in their longitudinal study. They differentiated various temperamental dimensions, including, among others, activity level, rhythmicity, adaptability, sensory threshold, intensity of reaction, mood, and distractibility. Their typology of child temperaments presented the "difficult," the "slow-to-warm," and the "easy" child. In their "goodness-of-fit" concept they pointed at the critical role of the environment in adapting to temperamental features of the individual child, thus preparing the field for a transactional perspective on development emphasizing the combined and evolving interplay of children's constitutional characteristics and the caregiving environment (Sameroff, 1975).

After decades of temperament research, the field has become replete with diverging models and measures, but all temperament researchers seem to agree that temperamental characteristics should appear early in development, show moderate stability, and have distinctive neurobiological indices (Rothbart & Bates, 2006; Zentner & Bates, 2008). Heritability of temperament is widely considered to be present, albeit in varying degrees depending on the specific temperamental dimension. A large number of temperament dimensions are recognized by temperament researchers (Caspi & Shiner, 2006), but two important dimensions emerging from various temperament models are "behavioral inhibition" (see Kagan, Chapter 4, this volume) and "irritability" or "difficultness" (see Bates, Freeland, & Lounsbury, 1979; Deater-Deckard & Wang, Chapter 7, this volume). *Inhibition* points at behavior in response to novelty, unfamiliar people, and strange situations, and it is related to harm avoidance and shyness. *Irritability* is aggressive or irritated behavior in response to painful and/or frustrating input, and it is related to difficultness, distress to limitations, and anger proneness. Inhibition is thought to be a rather stable, inherited characteristic influencing the individual's interaction with the environment (without denying a reversed influence), whereas irritability is considered to be the outcome of constitutional and parenting influences, thus leaving considerable room for environmental input (Bates et al., 1979). It seems compatible with the old idea of goodness of fit (Thomas & Chess, 1977). It should be noted that various other temperamental traits have been identified (see Mervielde & De Pauw, Chapter 2, this volume), but inhibition and irritability (both lower-order aspects of a broader negative emotionality trait) have received the most attention in research on differential susceptibility.

Similar to evolutionary explanations of attachment, evolutionary pressures have been speculated to be at the root of temperament. Whereas attachment theory assumes that evolution created in all newborns an inborn bias to become attached, temperament theory seems to prefer an evolutionary explanation of temperamental diversity. As Zentner and Bates (2008) argued, temperamental diversity probably evolved as a result of "fluctuating selection." Survival in a variety of ecological niches would require the presence of diversity of temperamental traits suited to each of those niches. Thus, there appears to be no "ideal" temperament independent of context or circumstances. Of course, this view on temperamental diversity does not preclude the idea that temperament traits are related to biological systems that were essential for survival, existing across all humans (e.g., the fight-or-flight system). Individuals, however, may differ in the strengths of these systems, probably due in part to the different contexts they experience (for further elaboration of these ideas see MacDonald, Chapter 14, this volume).

One of the earliest pieces of evidence that the benefits of temperament traits depend on context comes from DeVries's (1984, 1987) study of temperament among Masai pastoralists in Kenya. DeVries arrived in Kenya at the height of a 10-year drought, when children and infants were the first in a population to starve. During this particular famine, infant mortality rose to 50%. Of 15 newborn infants observed in the initial study population, he could locate only six by the end of his study; all others had died. Only one of the six infants with difficult, "fussy" temperaments had died, whereas five of the seven with "easy" temperaments had done so. In this case temperamental difficultness appeared to be of vital importance, presumably to attract the mother's attention and elicit her reaction to the infant's hunger signals. The infant's temperament may be an important factor for the child's survival, but, as mentioned before, there appears to be no ideal temperament independent of context. In some circumstances, "easy" children may elicit their parent's sensitive responsiveness, whereas in others a baby's frequent crying may enhance the chance of a parent's adequate response (van IJzendoorn & Bakermans-Kranenburg, 2004).

Is Attachment Temperament?

According to Kagan (1995), children's behavior in the Strange Situation is largely determined by temperament. He challenges attachment researchers to disentangle attachment from temperamental features, such as inhibition, and assumes that not much would remain after taking temperament into account. His reasoning is simple and at first sight convincing. The majority of children are not inhibited and do not show excessive distress in strange environments or when confronted with strangers, and if distressed they are soothed rather easily. Kagan describes these children as follows: "These children, who are likely to be classified as securely attached, are temperamentally uninhibited infants who inherited a physiology that mutes a fearful reaction in unfamiliar places" (p. 105). A minority of children with temperamental inhibition responds in a fearful manner to unfamiliar settings, and they start to cry when confronted with a stranger. These children, who can only be comforted by their parent after much effort, are classified as insecurely attached and considered to be at risk for behavior problems in later childhood. Thus, according to this point of view, the patterns of attachment behaviors in the Strange Situation are isomorphic with, or at least largely determined by, temperamental inhibition.

Is insecure attachment essentially temperamental inhibition and, in fact, can attachment not be differentiated from temperament? A first observation would be that secure and insecure children display both high and low levels of distress in the Strange Situation depending on their subclassification, and children acting aloof in the Strange Situation (categorized as avoidantly attached), might show highly irritable behavior at home (see Ainsworth et al., 1978; van den Boom, 1994). We would like to offer two additional strands of argument that run counter the temperamental redefinition of attachment. The first strand is meta-analytic, and the second strand concerns behavioral and molecular genetics. First, if attachment were simply temperament, and if temperament were based on "inherited physiology," then infants' attachments to their two parents should be largely similar. However, in a meta-analysis of 14 pertinent studies on more than 900 families, we found a modest correlation of $r = .17$ between infant–mother and infant–father attachment, indicating less than 3% overlap in variance (van IJzendoorn & DeWolff, 1997). More important, some overlap between infant–mother and infant–father attachment security might be expected because mothers and fathers tend to interact in similar ways with their children. In terms of attachment representations, we found significant similarity between husbands and wives within the same family in a set of five studies (van IJzendoorn & Bakermans-Kranenburg, 1996). Birds of a feather indeed seem to flock together. Therefore, not only infant temperament but also assortative mating or more direct influences of the partner may cause similarity in attachment and in parenting style of a father and a mother within the same family, resulting in a modest association between infant–mother and infant–father attachment security (van IJzendoorn & DeWolff, 1997).

Second, behavioral and molecular genetics illustrate the divergent roots of individual differences in attachment and temperament. In a twin study we found that about half of the variance in attachment security as observed in the Strange Situation was explained by shared environment, and the other half by unique environmental factors and measurement error (Bokhorst et al., 2003). The role of genetic factors was negligible. In the same study on the same sample, genetic factors explained almost 80% of the variance in temperamental reactivity (and nonshared environmental factors and measurement error more than 20%). Differences in temperamental reactivity were not associated with attachment concordance within twins. Similar results were shown for infant–father attachment and temperamental dependency (Bakermans-Kranenburg, van IJzendoorn, Bokhorst, & Schuengel, 2004), both assessed with the Attachment Q-Sort that also contains temperamental items (Vaughn & Waters, 1990). Attachment security was largely explained by shared environmental (59%) and nonshared environmental (41%)

factors, whereas genetic factors explained 66% of the variance in temperamental dependency, with nonshared environmental factors, including measurement error, explaining the remaining 34% of the variance. These results have been found in several other studies (O'Connor & Croft, 2001; Ricciuti, 1992; Roisman & Fraley, 2008).

Molecular genetic analyses also fail to support the temperamental redefinition of attachment. In a genomewide association (GWAS) and pathway analysis on attachment security and temperamental fearfulness in a Dutch sample of about 700 infants, we did not find the same genetic roots for the two phenotypes (Székely et al., 2011). The children of the Generation R Study (Jaddoe et al., 2007) were observed in the Strange Situation at 14 months of age, and at 36 months of age with the Laboratory Temperament Assessment Battery—Preschool Version (Lab-TAB; Goldsmith, Reilly, Lemery, Longley, & Prescott, 1999). Fearful temperament was measured with the Stranger Approach Episode, which indicates social fear when a novel, slightly threatening stranger approaches—quite similar to the first stranger episode of the Strange Situation. As expected, no significant GWAS results for attachment security were found; that is, no pathway was associated with increased chances of secure attachment. For temperamental fearfulness, a significant asparagine and aspartate biosynthesis pathway was found. Aspartate has been proposed to be a glutamate-like neurotransmitter in the central nervous system, as both glutamate and aspartate use the same reuptake mechanisms and have similar postsynaptic effects. It should be noted that in this large sample, attachment security and temperamental fearfulness were again not associated (Székely et al., 2011). Moreover, using a more powerful candidate genes approach in two birth cohort studies including more than 1,000 infants in total, we failed to show associations of attachment security with the genetic "usual suspects" related to the dopamine, serotonin, and oxytocin systems (*DRD4, DRD2, COMT, 5-HTT, OXTR*), with the exception of a co-dominant risk model for *COMT* Val158Met, as children with the Val/Met combination seemed most disorganized. However, this unexpected single finding is difficult to interpret and badly in need of replication (Luijk et al., 2011).

We conclude that attachment cannot be reduced to temperament, most importantly because they are phenotypically different, and show different genetic roots. Whereas there is some evidence for a genetic basis of temperamental differences (see Saudino & Wang, Chapter 16, this volume), individual differences in attachment security cannot be ascribed to genetic determinants.

Three Traditional Views on Temperament and Attachment: Orthogonal, Oblique, and Reciprocal

Besides the reductionist view articulated in the previous section (attachment can be reduced to temperament) three other views on the relation between attachment and temperament can be differentiated. The first view considers attachment and temperament as two orthogonal constructs, and the "never the twain shall meet." From an early stage, however, this view was contested by Crockenberg (1981), who sought to study attachment from an interactive perspective, investigating both the simple and interactive effects of early irritability and parental sensitivity on attachment security. This opened ways to consider the relation between attachment and temperament as partially overlapping (oblique) or as reciprocally influencing each other through moderation (reciprocal).

Temperament and Attachment as Orthogonal Constructs

Reacting to the claim that attachment would merely or essentially be a reflection of temperamental differences, Sroufe (1985) vehemently argued that attachment and temperament constitute *orthogonal* categories, situated at different levels of analysis. In his view, attachment is a relationship construct, characterized by a dyadic origin and nature, whereas temperament is an individual category, characterized by an organismic origin and nature. To try to reduce attachment to temperament (or the other way around) would be a logical category mistake. Sroufe stressed that within a relationship perspective, temperamental differences may influence various aspects of behavior in strange environments and toward a stranger and attachment figures. It does not, however, affect the (dyadic) organization of attachment behavior that is the essence of an attachment classification. The relationship history would override constitutional temperamental differences, and the contribution of temperamental features to Strange Situation behavior or attachment more generally would be negligible (Sroufe, 1985).

The idea that the environment plays a major part in explaining individual differences in quality of the infant–parent attachment relationship is indeed central to attachment theory. Inspired by Ainsworth's seminal work on attachment and childrearing in her Uganda and Baltimore samples (Ainsworth, 1967; Ainsworth et al., 1978), attachment researchers have considered parental sensitivity to be the single most important determinant of infant attachment security, particularly for the three organized attachment strategies: secure, insecure–avoidant, and insecure–ambivalent attachment (Cassidy & Shaver, 2008). Observational and experimental studies of attachment have generally confirmed this core hypothesis, although the combined effect size across numerous correlational studies for the association between parental sensitivity and attachment security is relatively modest. In De Wolff and van IJzendoorn's (1997) meta-analysis, the combined effect amounted to a correlation of $r = .24$. In addition, a large number of experimental studies with attachment-based interventions have documented the causal nature of the relation between parental sensitivity and infant attachment, showing that interventions that more effectively enhanced parental sensitivity also more effectively changed the quality of the attachment relationship (see Bakermans-Kranenburg, van IJzendoorn, & Juffer, 2003, for a meta-analysis on the experimental evidence). Thus, parenting has been proven partly to determine differences in attachment security between children, as elevated levels of parental sensitivity enhance the chance for the child to become secure, whereas lower levels of parental sensitivity lead to a higher risk for insecure attachment. However, these findings certainly leave room for other influences, including those of a more constitutional nature.

Temperament and Attachment Related in an Oblique Way

The oblique point of view acknowledges the environmental influences on attachment security and at the same time stresses the possibility of other determinants, such as temperament, to impact on the child's development of attachment. Several studies have demonstrated that parents' sensitivity to their infants' attachment signals is strongly determined by parents' own secure or insecure mental representation of childhood attachment experiences (Hesse, 2008; Main, Kaplan, & Cassidy, 1985). But parental sensitivity accounts for only one-third of the association between parental attachment representation and infant attachment, leaving a *transmission gap* of unexplained variance in infant attachment security (van IJzendoorn, 1995a, 1995b). Most importantly, although attachment is a relationship construct, at least in the first few years of life, the meta-analyses of correlational and experimental studies on attachment and sensitivity show that attachment is only partly reflected in the interactive history of the parent–infant dyad.

This leaves room for the idea that temperament and attachment are related in an *oblique* way (Belsky & Rovine, 1987; Kochanska, 1998; Marshall & Fox, 2005; Thompson & Lamb, 1984; Vaughn & Bost, 1999). For example, temperamentally inhibited infants may develop an insecure–resistant attachment to their insensitive caregiver, whereas more robust, uninhibited infants may become insecure–avoidant in their attachment to an insensitive parent (Vaughn, Bost, & van IJzendoorn, 2008). Belsky (personal communication, February 10, 2011) even suggests that some temperamentally sturdy and adaptable infants may become securely attached to an insensitive caregiver, explaining the incomplete determination of attachment security by parenting. The sturdiness of temperamentally adaptive children may also explain the remarkable resilience of some orphans growing up in the institutional environment of structural neglect but, against all odds, nevertheless developing secure attachments (van IJzendoorn et al., 2011). Thus, temperament influences the type of insecurity that children develop, and in some cases might even make children less receptive for environmental input.

Reciprocal: Moderating Models

Attachment might be a moderator of the influence of earlier temperament on later emotional reactivity to strange environments or persons. Calkins and Fox (1992), for example, found an interaction effect between infants' reactivity to frustration at 5 months and attachment classification at 14 months, predicting inhibition at 24 months. Because inhibition was measured at a later point in time (24 months) than attachment classification (14 months), one may argue that the interaction effect shows the influence of attachment security on inhibition, or is at least not incompatible with this reversed interpretation (van IJzendoorn & Bakermans-Kranenburg, 2004). In the same vein, Nachmias, Gunnar, Mangelsdorf, Parritz, and Buss (1996) examined the moderating role of attachment security in buffering the effects of temperamental inhibition on stress reactivity as assessed by cortisol levels. They assessed cortisol levels before and after a stressful session confronting the child with novel, arousing stimuli, as well as after the Strange Situation. They found no association between behavioral inhibition and security of attachment; they did find that children with higher behavioral inhibition had higher poststress cortisol levels if they were also insecure, but not when they were securely attached to their mother. In a study on behavioral inhibition and heart rate after stressful episodes, Stevenson-Hinde and Marshall (1999) found that low inhibition was associated with high heart rate periods, but only in secure children. Security of attachment can thus be viewed as a buffer against stress or as a moderator of the initial physiological disposition (van IJzendoorn & Bakermans-Kranenburg, 2004).

In the early 1990s Belsky, Fish, and Isabella (1991) showed that infants' change in temperament from 3 to 9 months was predictable from the quality of the rearing environment, and that resultant change in temperament was predictive of attachment security, consistent with the view that attachment reflects, in part, the regulation of temperament. Research examining associations between parenting and temperament has suggested that the caregiving environment supporting the formation of attachment relationships (i.e., parental sensitivity) may also serve to influence and regulate infant reactivity (see Sheese, Voelker, Rothbart, & Posner, 2007, for an example). A paramount example of this line of research is a study by Hane and Fox (2006), who broke through the barrier between attachment and temperament theory by focusing on important indices of fearful temperament (electroencephalographic [EEG] asymmetries in the frontal cortex and fearful reactivity to stimuli in the Lab-TAB assessment) in relation to maternal sensitivity to infants at 9 months of age. The mothers' behavior during a home visit was video-recorded and subsequently rated for degree of sensitivity using the classic Ainsworth sensitivity rating scales central to most of the work on antecedents of attachment (Ainsworth et al., 1978). Relative to infants who experienced highly sensitive maternal care, infants who experienced low sensitive care displayed more temperamental fearfulness and more right frontal asymmetry, an important marker of an infant's disposition toward withdrawal behaviors. Temperament assessed at 4 month of age did not predict these outcomes (Hane & Fox, 2006). This correlational study cannot determine the causal direction of the associations between sensitive parenting and temperamental fearfulness, but the finding that earlier temperament did not predict later fearfulness, whereas maternal sensitivity did, is certainly convergent with a transactional model (Sameroff, 1983) that places sensitive, responsive care in the center of early temperament, as well as attachment, development. Most important, in support of Meaney's (2010) theory of early development based on his extensive studies of rodents, early maternal sensitive care seemed able to change even basic parameters of brain functioning, in the case of Hane and Fox's (2006) study of human infants' patterns of right versus left frontal EEG asymmetry.

In summary, the relations between parenting, attachment, and temperament seem much more complicated and multidirectional than originally conceptualized by Kagan (1995) and Sroufe (1985). A few decades after their debate about the direction of the influences between temperament and attachment, the general consensus seems to be that

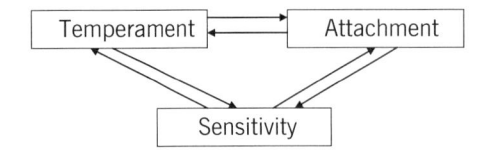

FIGURE 19.1. Various causal pathways between temperament, attachment, and parental sensitivity.

both temperament and attachment are influencing each other in a transactional way, and both are more or less open to environmental input such as parenting (see Figure 19.1). Despite different origins and a somewhat agonistic tradition, temperament and attachment theory now seem ready for further exploration of mutual fertilization. The differential susceptibility paradigm offers such a new perspective.

Reconciliation and Integration: Diathesis–Stress and Differential Susceptibility

Diathesis–Stress

Not only has research shown that the caregiving environment may influence and regulate infant reactivity, as we noted earlier, but there is also growing evidence that not all children are equally affected by their caregiving environment. Research on temperament × parenting interactions, or broader temperament × environment interactions, is based on the premise that negative effects of the environment (e.g., inadequate parenting or low-quality day care) are observed in some children but are virtually absent in others. Some children appear to be especially reactive to adversity, whereas other children—lacking such vulnerabilities—do not succumb to a specific adversity and are considered resilient (e.g., Cicchetti, 1993; Masten & Obradović, 2006; also see Lengua & Wachs, Chapter 25, this volume), often as a result of personal protective factors such as easygoing temperament, low stress reactivity, or a specific genetic makeup. Implicit in this diathesis–stress framework is the view that children who are vulnerable or resilient due to their personal characteristics thrive similarly in nonadverse and supportive environments. One of the consequences of this focus on developmental psychopathology is that many studies do not measure the full range of either environments or outcomes, but are restricted to just adversity and its absence (e.g., maltreatment vs. no maltreatment) or just dysfunction and its absence (e.g., externalizing behavior problems). However, the temperamental characteristics of individuals that make them disproportionately vulnerable to adversity may also make them benefit more from contextual support. This idea is central to the model of differential susceptibility.

Differential Susceptibility: For Better and for Worse

According to the differential susceptibility model, individuals characterized by heightened susceptibility are more sensitive to *both* negative and positive environments (i.e., to both risk-promoting and development-enhancing environmental conditions), for better *and* for worse. Several introductions and reviews have been devoted to defining differential susceptibility in contrast to diathesis–stress and cumulative risk (e.g., Bakermans-Kranenburg & van IJzendoorn, 2007; Belsky, 1997a, 1997b, 2005; Belsky, Bakermans-Kranenburg, & van IJzendoorn, 2007; Boyce & Ellis, 2005; Ellis et al., 2011). Temperamental reactivity was one of the differential susceptibility factors taken into account in the first wave of studies pioneered by Belsky, Hsieh, and Crnic (1998), and most of the remainder of this chapter is devoted to a discussion of this temperamental marker of differential susceptibility, though other markers of negative emotionality (including inhibition, irritability, and fearfulness) also appear in this review.

Genetic differential susceptibility was introduced by the Leiden group, with special emphasis on dopamine system–related genes such as *DRD4* (Bakermans-Kranenburg & van IJzendoorn, 2006), whereas physiological factors (i.e., biological reactivity defined by children's autonomic, adrenocortical, or immune reactivity to psychosocial stressors) were introduced by Boyce and his team (1995). Boyce and Ellis (2005) coined the expressive epithets *orchid* and *dandelion* to describe two types of children. More physiologically reactive children displaying heightened sensitivity to both positive and negative environmental influences were given the shorthand designation of *orchid* children, signifying their special susceptibility to both highly stressful and highly nurturing environments. Children low in reactivity, on the other hand, were designated as *dandelion* children, reflecting their relative ability to function adequately in species-typical circumstances of all varieties. Such typologies, though persuasive, should not inadvertently give rise to a misunderstanding; susceptibility is generally considered to be continuously distributed and not as a category that is absent or present (Ellis et al., 2011).

Defining Steps in the Test for Differential Susceptibility

Not all temperament × parenting interactions provide evidence for differential susceptibility. Differential susceptibility needs to be distinguished from other interaction effects, including that of *dual risk*, which arises when the most vulnerable individuals are disproportionately affected in an adverse manner by a negative environment but do not also benefit disproportionately from positive environmental conditions.

The formal test of differential susceptibility consists of five steps (see Figure 19.2; Belsky et al., 2007). Step 1 concerns the application of conventional statistical criteria for evaluating genuine moderation (Dearing & Hamilton, 2006), with some emphasis on excluding interactions with regression lines that do not cross (sometimes referred to as *removable* interactions). The next steps distinguish differential susceptibility from temperament–environment correlations that may reflect rearing experiences evoked by specific child characteristics and from dual-risk models. It is important to ascertain that there is no association between the moderator (i.e., the susceptibility factor) and the environment (Step 2). Belsky and colleagues (1998), examining the effects of infant negative emotionality and parenting on 3-year-old boys' externalizing problems and inhibition, explicitly tested the independence of negative emotionality and parenting as a step in their investigation of differential suscep-

---

1. Is the interaction between the moderator (e.g., temperament) and the environment statistically significant? Do the regression lines cross?
2. Are the moderator and the environment independent?
3. Is the moderator related to the outcome? If the association between the moderator and the outcome is significant, there is no support for differential susceptibility
4. What does the regression plot look like? The prototypical graphical display of the differential susceptibility model is shown in Figure 19.3a. Figure 19.3b shows a main effect of the supposed moderator, independent of the environment. Figures 19.3c and 19.3d represent dual risk or dual gain; the effect of the environment is unidirectional. At one of the extremes of the environmental range there is no difference between the two groups that are distinguished on the basis of the moderator. Figure 19.3e shows contrastive effects; both groups are equally susceptible to environmental influences, though in divergent directions.
5. Is the effect specific to this moderator?

FIGURE 19.2. Steps in testing for differential susceptibility. From Belsky, Bakermans-Kranenburg, and van IJzendoorn (2007). Copyright 2007 by the Association for Psychological Science. Adapted by permission.

---

tibility. Had these factors been correlated, the evidence would not have shown that the predictive power of parenting was greater for highly negative infants; it would instead have indicated that either highly negative infants elicit negative parenting or that negative parenting fosters infant negativity. If the susceptibility factor and the outcome are related (Step 3), dual risk—or dual gain, when positive factors are involved—is suggested. For example, early negativity would itself lead to externalizing behavior, but even more so when combined with negative parenting.

Differential susceptibility is demonstrated (Step 4) when the moderation reflects a crossover interaction that covers both the positive and the negative aspects of the environment; see Figure 19.3a. The slope for the susceptible subgroup should be significantly different from zero and at the same time significantly steeper than the slope for the nonsusceptible subgroup. The two groups may also show

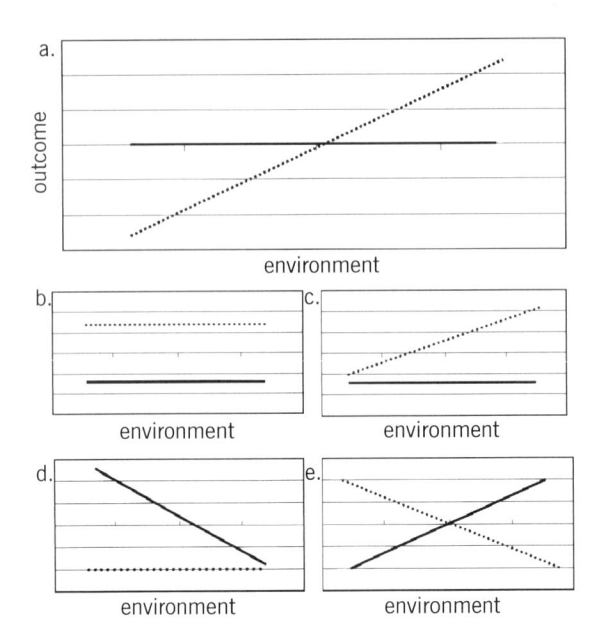

FIGURE 19.3. Graphical display of differential susceptibility in comparison with other interaction effects. From Bakermans-Kranenburg and van IJzendoorn (2007). Copyright 2007 by the Association for Psychological Science. Adapted by permission.

different outcomes independent of the environment. Figure 19.3b displays the results of this scenario; it shows a main effect of the supposed moderator, which in this case is in fact not a moderator. Figure 19.3c and 19.3d represent dual risk or dual gain; the effect of the environment is unidirectional. At one end of the environmental range there is no difference between the two groups (groups distinguished on the basis of the moderator). Figure 19.3e shows contrastive effects; both groups are susceptible to environmental influences, though in divergent directions. As a consequence both slopes are significantly different from zero but in opposite directions, as in the case of positive and negative effects of harsh discipline on, respectively, African American and European American children (Deater-Deckard, Bates, Dodge, & Pettit, 1996). Although clearly different, this is not what is meant in the differential susceptibility model. The specificity of the effect (Step 5 in Figure 19.2) is shown if the model is not replicated when other susceptibility factors are used as moderators (e.g., Bakermans-Kranenburg, van IJzendoorn, Caspers, & Philibert, 2011; Caspi & Moffitt, 2006).

The Moderating Role of Temperament

When temperament moderates the association between some environmental factor and developmental outcome, it may do so in several ways, as outlined earlier. In the following sections we highlight and illustrate the distinct patterns of interaction. First we review studies with temperamental reactivity or irritability as a *vulnerability* factor, adding to the negative effects of an unsupportive environment. Second, we shift the focus to the bright side of life, where temperament as a *susceptibility* factor enhances the openness to positive influences of a specific subgroup of individuals. Third, we present studies substantiating the bidirectional *for-better-and-for-worse* predictions of the differential susceptibility hypothesis in a single sample. Last, at the end of the chapter, we present the first meta-analytic evidence for differential susceptibility. It should be noted that the discussion of the moderating role of temperament covers a much broader set of concepts and environments than that included in the attachment paradigm.

Temperament as Vulnerability Factor

Difficult temperament has more than once been found to increase the vulnerability to negative environmental influences. Here we briefly present some key findings as a background for our treatment of the differential susceptibility model (see Lengua & Wachs, Chapter 25, this volume, for an extensive discussion of temperament as a vulnerability factor). For example, in Morrell and Murray's (2003) study, only the highly distressed and irritable 4-month-old boys who experienced coercive and rejecting mothering at this age continued to show evidence, 5 months later, of emotional and behavioral dysregulation. These results reflect a double risk model (Figure 19.3c), where the negative effect of the environment (i.e. coercive, rejecting parenting) is strongest or only apparent in the group of children with a difficult temperament. Other studies have reported similar effects. Belsky and colleagues (1998) observed that infants who scored high in negative emotionality at 12 months of age, and who experienced the least supportive mothering and fathering across their second and third years of life, scored highest on externalizing problems at 36 months of age. Deater-Deckard and Dodge (1997) reported that children rated highest on externalizing behavior problems by teachers across the primary school years were those who experienced the most harsh discipline prior to kindergarten entry and were characterized by mothers at age 5 as being negatively reactive infants. Similarly, in a study on the effects of day care, instability of child care arrangements, as indicated by the number of different care arrangements in the course of a single day or week, was found to be associated with internalizing behavior problems among children with a difficult temperament. In the group of less difficult children, the association between multiple care arrangements and internalizing problems was absent (De Schipper, Tavecchio, van IJzendoorn, & van Zeijl, 2004). These studies illustrate how difficult temperament, in combination with low parental or caregiver support, leads to elevated levels of child problem behaviors.

The generalizability of this dual-risk model of parenting and temperament to non-Western immigrant families with young children was recently supported in a longitudinal study in The Netherlands. We investigated the influence of parenting practices in the prediction of child physical aggression in 94 second-generation Turkish immigrant families with 2-year-old toddlers, and the moderating role of child temperament (Yaman, Mesman, van IJzendoorn, & Bakermans-Kranenburg, 2010). Observational data were obtained for mothers' parenting quality and authoritarian discipline, and maternal reports for child temperament and physical aggression. All measures were repeated 1 year later. Child temperament at age 2 years was a significant predictor of child aggression 1 year later; moreover, toddlers with difficult temperaments were more adversely affected by a lack of positive parenting than were other children.

As in the Yaman and colleagues (2010) study, sometimes a main effect for difficult temperament in the prediction of behavior problems also emerges (which may partly be explained by overlapping items in the measures of the constructs), pointing to the double-risk nature of the pattern of results: Effects are worst for those children who share both temperamental and environmental disadvantages. Essential for a dual-risk model is that children with difficult temperaments are more adversely affected by negative environmental factors (including the lack of positive support), but they do not benefit more from positive environments than do children with more easy temperaments.

Temperament as Susceptibility Factor: The Bright Side

We already noted the preference to focus on adversity and dysfunction in empirical studies. Fortunately, in recent years, a considerable number of studies have included environmental factors or developmental outcomes that reflect what we consider the bright side of life: warm, supportive parenting, attachment security, and prosocial behavior. Where *vulnerability* refers to a unidirectional negative effect of the environment for a subgroup of children (e.g., temperamentally difficult children), *susceptibility* may be used to describe the openness to positive influences of a specific subgroup of individuals.

One of the correlational studies addressing the bright side is that of Denham and colleagues (2000). They reported that the beneficial effects of proactive parenting (i.e., supportive presence, clear limit setting) at age 7 and/or age 9 were most pronounced in the case of children with high levels of disobedient, aggressive, or angry behavior at an earlier time of measurement, even after controlling for problem behavior at the initial measurement occasion. Belsky (1997a, 1997b, 2005) observed that children high in negative emotion, particularly in the early years, appeared to benefit disproportionately from supportive rearing environments. Crockenberg (1981) showed that social support predicted infant attachment security, but only in the case of highly irritable infants. Kochanska (1995) showed the larger effect of gentle parental discipline, deemphasizing power on compliance, in more fearful children compared to less fearful children.

Experimental studies are even more suggestive than the longitudinal correlational evidence. In such experiments, the environment is changed for the better, and susceptible children may profit most from this change. At the same time, this might explain why most interventions are only moderately effective; the average intervention effect may hide a large effect for a subgroup of susceptible children because their larger outcomes are averaged together with the smaller effects for the less-susceptible children. One of the first studies pointing to temperamentally difficult children as being highly susceptible to intervention efforts was van den Boom (1994), who demonstrated the extraordinary effectiveness of an attachment-based intervention on irritable infants and their low-socioeconomic-status (SES) mothers. The intervention helped to elevate the level of maternal sensitivity, which in turn enhanced the children's attachment security. LaFreniere and Capuano (1997) reported intervention effects on anxiously withdrawn children. Mothers in the treatment group started to behave less intrusively, while their children showed an increase in cooperation and enthusiasm during a problem-solving task with the mother, and elevated teacher-rated social competence. Drawing on data from the Infant Health and Development Program, in which premature, low birthweight infants from economically disadvantaged homes were randomly assigned to experimental and control treatment conditions, Blair (2002) examined differential outcomes for infants who varied in negative emotionality. He found that infants who were highly negatively emotional and assigned to the early intervention treatment group scored substantially lower on externalizing problems and higher on cognitive functioning at 3 years of age than did similarly tempered control infants, with no such treatment effect detectable in the case of other infants with less negative emotionality.

Klein Velderman and colleagues (2006) found that experimentally induced changes in maternal sensitivity exerted greater impact on the attachment security of highly negatively reactive infants than it did on other infants. Their Video-Feedback Intervention to Promote Positive Parenting (VIPP; Juffer, Bakermans-Kranenburg, & van IJzendoorn, 2008) effectively enhanced maternal sensitivity. In the group of highly reactive infants, change in pre- to posttest maternal sensitivity and attachment security were significantly correlated, $r = .57$. In the less reactive group, the correlation was $r = .08$. Thus, the experimentally induced change in maternal sensitivity appeared to have a stronger impact on attachment security in the highly reactive infant group; that is, for highly reactive infants, attachment security was significantly associated with their mothers' gains in sensitivity between pre- and posttest. This was not true for less reactive infants; their attachment security was not related to improvements in sensitivity of their mothers. Highly reactive children were more susceptible to experimentally induced environmental change than were less reactive infants. In a similar vein, Cassidy, Woodhouse, Sherman, Stupica, and Lejuez (2011) found that only temperamentally irritable infants profited from a home visit intervention aimed at enhancing attachment security.

It should be noted that in each of the aforementioned experiments, random assignment to intervention and control conditions was done according to the experimental manipulation of the environment, not according to temperamental factors in the child. Importantly, the model of differential susceptibility has not yet been tested experimentally in a *randomized controlled trial*, with intervention and control groups stratified according to (temperamental) susceptibility factors.

Temperament as a Factor in Bidirectional Differential Susceptibility

So far we have reviewed studies highlighting the heightened susceptibility of temperamentally difficult children to either positive or negative rearing influences (Figures 19.3c and 19.3d). Even more compelling are data on a single sample substantiating the for-better-*and*-for-worse predictions of the differential susceptibility hypothesis. Feldman, Greenbaum, and Yirmiya (1999) found that 9-month-olds scoring high on negativity who experienced low levels of synchrony in mother–infant interaction manifested more noncompliance during cleanup at age 2 than other children did. When such infants experienced mutually synchronous mother–infant interaction, however, they displayed greater self-control than did children manifesting much less negativity as infants. Kochanska, Aksan, and Joy (2007) observed that highly fearful 15-month-olds experiencing high levels of power-assertive paternal discipline were most likely to cheat in a game at 38 months, yet when cared for in a supportive manner, such negatively emotional, fearful toddlers manifested the most rule-compatible conduct.

In a study of temperament and maternal discipline in relation to externalizing problems in early childhood, van Zeijl and colleagues (2006, 2007) found that children with difficult temperaments were more susceptible to both negative and positive discipline than were children of relatively easy temperament. Bohlin, Hagekull, and Andersson (2005) found that inhibition moderated the effect of attachment security on social competence at 8 years. For preschool-age children who showed low levels of behavioral inhibition, attachment security did not make much of a difference for their social competence some years later. In contrast, inhibited children who were insecurely attached showed the lowest levels of social competence, and securely attached inhibited children showed the highest levels of social competence at 8 years. Gilissen, Bakermans-Kranenburg, van IJzendoorn, and van der Veer (2008) showed that temperamentally fearful children were more susceptible to both secure and insecure attachment relationships in their physiological reactivity when looking at fear-inducing film clips. Temperamentally fearful children with less secure relationships showed the highest skin conductance reactivity to the film clip, whereas comparable children with more secure relationships showed the lowest skin conductance activity.

The studies on bidirectional differential susceptibility reviewed thus far all addressed parental care as context or environmental dimension. Evidence for differential susceptibility, for-better-and-for-worse, however, has not been limited to the effects of parental care but includes nonparental care as well. Children in the National Institute of Child Health and Human Development (NICHD) study of early child care who had been temperamentally difficult infants showed the worst outcomes when they experienced inadequate parenting and the best outcomes when they experienced excellent parenting (Bradley & Corwyn, 2008; Stright, Kelley, & Gallagher, 2008). For children who attended child care, the professional caregiver's sensitivity interacted with child temperament in the prediction of children's social competence and behavior problems as assessed with the Child Behavior Checklist (CBCL). Children who had been temperamentally difficult as infants scored low on social competence and high on teacher-reported externalizing behavior problems at 54 months when their caregivers were insensitive, but they scored high on social competence and low on behavior problems when their caregivers were sensitive. For those children who were not difficult in infancy, caregiver sensitivity was not related to social competence and behavior problems at 54 months (Pluess & Belsky, 2009). A much smaller study in The Netherlands showed that fearful children with more stressed professional caregivers (as indicated by an increase in cortisol during the day) showed the lowest levels of well-being in day care, but those with unstressed caregivers (whose cortisol levels decreased over the day) scored higher on caregiver-reported well-being in the child care setting than their less fearful peers (Groeneveld, Vermeer, van IJzendoorn, & Linting, 2012). Thus, fearful infants appear to be more affected by the quality of day care they experience—both negatively and positively—than less fearful children.

Extending the issue of nonparental care beyond kindergarten age, Essex, Armstrong, Burk, Goldsmith, and Boyce (2011) examined the effect of grade 1 teacher–child relationships on mental health symptoms at grade 7. Distinguishing between teacher–child closeness and teacher–child conflict as two only partly overlapping dimensions of the relationship at grade 1, they found that behaviorally inhibited children developed the most severe mental health symptoms by grade 7 under conditions of high grade 1 teacher conflict, but the lowest levels of symptoms under conditions of low teacher conflict. The inhibited children were thus more susceptible to teacher conflict than children with lower levels of inhibition. At the same time, highly *disinhibited* children were more susceptible to teacher–child closeness; they developed the most severe mental health symptoms when they experienced low levels of teacher closeness, and fewest symptoms under conditions of high teacher closeness. The study may point to temperamental inhibition and disinhibition as markers of differential susceptibility dependent on the environmental dimension that is examined. In an environment with conflict, inhibition seems to increase differential susceptibility, whereas in an environment with close contact, disinhibition might operate as a differential susceptibility marker.

Adult Differential Susceptibility

Not only children but also *parents* may be differentially susceptible to stressors and supportive experiences. Both positive and negative environmental factors may have more impact on parents who for temperamental or genetic reasons are more susceptible to such influences—with traceable effects on their parenting behavior. We found that parents with a specific genetic makeup (carrying a *DRD4* 7-repeat allele, as well as a *COMT* Val allele) showed increased susceptibility to daily stresses (van IJzendoorn, Bakermans-Kranenburg, & Mesman, 2008). Parents with these gene combinations were less sensitive to their children's needs when they had to deal with many daily hassles, but they showed higher levels of sensitive parenting compared with other parents in the case of few daily hassles. In replicating this study with parents of twins, Fortuna et al. (2011) found that when parents of twins with various birth risks (low gestational age, low birthweight, long stay in neonatal intensive care) were least sensitive to their twins about 3 years later when they were carriers of the *DRD4* 7-repeat allele. Without these child birth risks, parents with the 7-repeat alleles were the most sensitive to their children.

Two other studies involving adults, but not in their parental role, should be mentioned briefly. First, in a study on adults adopted as children, we found that *DRD4* moderated the association of parental problems during the participants' childhood (e.g., parental depression, marital discord) with unresolved loss or trauma (that is associated with posttraumatic stress and dissociative symptoms). Participants with the *DRD4* 7-repeat allele who experienced parental problems had the highest scores for unresolved loss or trauma, whereas participants with the *DRD4* 7-repeat allele who did *not* experience parental problems showed the lowest posttraumatic stress symptoms. Among participants without the *DRD4* 7-repeat allele, the parental problems during childhood did not make much of a difference. Second, in a study on political preferences, more than 2,000 young adults listed up to 10 best friends, and answered one question about political preference: whether they considered themselves to be more conservative, middle-of-the road, or liberal (Settle, Dawes, Christakis, & Fowler, 2010). The authors argued that having more friends would mean more exposure to divergent ideas and worldviews, and thus a more liberal perspective. Without referring to differential susceptibility the authors nevertheless found clear support for the differential susceptibility model: only in carriers of the 7-repeat alleles was having more friends related to more liberal views, and fewer friends, to more conservative attitudes.

The application of the differential susceptibility hypothesis to adults in general and parents in particular is virtually uncharted territory: To our knowledge there is no other published study with temperamental or genetic factors as moderators of environmental effects on parenting. In the Klein Velderman and colleagues' (2006) intervention study, mothers of highly reactive infants profited more from the intervention. They might have been more readily reinforced by their infants' positive behavioral changes in the dyadic context, but an alternative interpretation would be that it was the temperamentally reactive mothers who profited most from intervention efforts. Given that emotional reactivity has been found to be substantially genetically determined (Bokhorst et al., 2003; Goldsmith, Lemery, Buss, & Campos, 1999), the mothers of highly reactive children may have been as temperamentally reactive as their children. Similar to the children's case, differential susceptibility of parents should be tested in an experimental design, with random assignment of parents to the experimental and control conditions based on their supposed (temperamental or genetic) susceptibility.

We therefore advance the exciting hypothesis that adult personality may also be considered a marker of differential susceptibility, and in terms of the Big Five, adults with high levels of Openness to Experience may indeed be highly sensitive personalities (E. Aron, Aron, & Davies, 2005; also see Aron, Chapter 31, this volume) across a variety of domains, from parenting to political ideologies, for-better-*and*-for-worse.

It would, of course, be most compelling to test the model of bidirectional differential susceptibility in an experimental design, in order to examine whether the same individuals who profit most from a positive change in the environment would also suffer the most from an experimentally induced deterioration of their environment. A limitation inherent to experiments with human beings is that this is unethical and thus impossible. In limited probabilistic learning tasks (e.g., Klein et al., 2007) or stress paradigms, the use of positive or negative feedback in case of "errors" can experimentally induce changes in the microenvironment of the same subjects, which can then be examined in terms of their impact on immediate outcomes. But this is different than testing the differential susceptibility hypothesis, which involves sustained and at least somewhat enduring change in response to environmental exposures (Ellis et al., 2011). It would simply not be justifiable experimentally to induce negative changes in the caregiving environment. In his seminal work with inhibited rhesus monkeys, Suomi (1997) illustrated the vast potential of studies on nonhuman primates for gaining insight into human development. Perhaps experimental animal models might be used to mimic the basic temperament × environment interactions illustrating the moderating role of temperament in human development for-better-*and*-for-worse.

Meta-Analytic Evidence for Differential Susceptibility: Dopamine-Related Genes as Susceptibility Factors

The idea that dopamine-related genetic polymorphisms may play a role in differential susceptibility to the rearing environment is not far-fetched. Low dopaminergic efficiency is associated with decreased attentional and reward mechanisms (Robbins & Everitt, 1999), which may be advantageous or disadvantageous depending on specific environmental characteristics (Suomi, 1997). The role of dopamine in feedback-based learning was tested in a neuroimaging study (Klein et al., 2007). Subjects were grouped according to their *DRD2* genotype. Carriers of the A1-allele had significantly more difficulties learning from negative feedback. Moreover, their posterior medial frontal cortex, involved in feedback monitoring, responded less to negative feedback than did that of their comparison subjects. However, they did not perform worse than comparisons when provided with positive feedback. The study might explain why experimental interventions emphasizing prompt positive feedback trigger the high potentials of children who otherwise show most behavior problems (Bakermans-Kranenburg, van IJzendoorn, Mesman, et al., 2008; Bakermans-Kranenburg, van IJzendoorn, Pijlman, et al., 2008) or display the lowest level of prereading abilities (Kegel, Bus, & van IJzendoorn, 2011).

We conducted a meta-analysis on the role of dopamine-related genes in making children more or less susceptible to rearing influences, for-better-and-for-worse (see Bakermans-Kranenburg & van IJzendoorn, 2011, for details on the studies included in the meta-analysis). Because the number of gene × environment (G × E) interaction studies including dopamine-related gene polymorphisms has steeply increased in recent years, sufficient empirical studies were available to conduct a meta-analysis to explore the effects of G × E interactions on development and to compare the combined effect sizes for both negative and positive effects. The studies included in the meta-analysis examined the moderating role of three dopamine-related genes, *DRD2*, *DAT*, and *DRD4*, in children up to age 10 years, although most studies did not look explicitly for both the dark and the bright side of differential susceptibility.

We identified 15 pertinent effect sizes on 1,232 subjects, providing data for two meta-analyses of the moderating role of dopamine-related genes on the impact of rearing environment on development (for details, see Bakermans-Kranenburg & van IJzendoorn, 2011). Nine effect sizes concerned vulnerability, that is, susceptibility to *negative* environmental factors. These studies examined the effect of dopamine-related "risk alleles" (*DRD2*-A1, *DAT* 10-repeat, *DRD4* 7-repeat) on the association between adverse rearing environment and behavioral disturbance, such as externalizing behavior, sensation seeking, and attention-deficit/hyperactivity disorder (ADHD). Six effect sizes—enabling a focus on the "bright side"—pertained to moderation of the relation between supportive contexts (e.g., warm, responsive parenting) and positive behavioral outcomes (e.g., effortful control or prosocial behavior), or the absence or reduction of negative behaviors (e.g., decrease in externalizing behavior after intervention). The meta-analyses thus took into account both sides of the differential susceptibility hypothesis but could not directly examine whether the same children who do worse than comparisons in adverse environments also do better in supportive environments—this has simply not yet been tested in empirical studies.

The combined effect size for behavioral disturbance in the presence of adverse rearing influences amounted to $r = .37$ for carriers of the "risk alleles," and $r = .10$ for the comparisons without the risk alleles. The difference was significant ($p = .02$), supporting the idea that carriers of the risk alleles were more vulnerable to environmental adversity. Turning to the bright side, that is, the association between parental support and better adaptation, we found a combined effect size of $r = .31$ for carriers of the putative risk alleles, whereas the combined effect size for children without the risk alleles was $r = -.03$. Again, the difference was significant ($p < .01$). Children with alleles that put them at risk for behavioral disturbances in adverse contexts benefited significantly more from parental support than did their counterparts.

The combined effect size for children carrying the risk alleles pertaining to vulnerability was not larger than the combined effect size derived from the positive outcomes. In other words, children with the putative risk alleles were equally susceptible to negative and supportive influences. In fact, the difference between the combined effect sizes of the genetically "at-risk" children and their genetically "low-risk" counterparts were .29 (Fisher's Z) for the vulnerability studies and .35 (Fisher's Z) for studies focusing on the bright side (Bakermans-Kranenburg & van IJzendoorn, 2011). The difference between the combined effect sizes in the second set of studies was thus comparable to and even somewhat larger than the difference in the first set of studies, suggesting that the promotive susceptibility effect is certainly not weaker than the vulnerability effect. In other words, these meta-analytic results provide support for the hypothesis that genetically "vulnerable" individuals are actually more susceptible to the environment, for-better-*and*-for-worse.

Directions for Future Research

Three critical issues should be high on the agenda for future research. First, the diversity of temperamental characteristics found to play a role in differential susceptibility models points to the question of whether different temperamental features may be identified as susceptibility factors dependent on the specific environmental influence and the specific developmental outcome. Irritable or difficult and inhibited or fearful temperaments have appeared on the stage as susceptibility factors with varying success. The fact that some studies use inhibition or fearfulness, whereas others use irritability or reactivity to distinguish more susceptible individuals from less susceptible individuals, has mostly been passed over in order to stress the converging support for the differential susceptibility model. Future studies should explicitly aim at distinguishing among temperament dimensions such as inhibition, irritability (Zentner & Bates, 2008), and sensory sensitivity (Aron et al., 2005; see also Aron, Chapter 31, this volume), and test to what extent these dimensions function as susceptibility factors depending on the specific environmental influences and developmental outcomes. Other (adult) personality traits also deserve more attention as potential markers of differential susceptibility, and Openness to Experience might be a good candidate because it has been found to be associated with dopamine system–related genes.

Temperament has only been one of the differential susceptibility factors taken into account in the first wave of studies pioneered by Belsky and colleagues (1998). Physiological factors (i.e., biological reactivity) were introduced by Boyce and colleagues (1995), whereas genetic differential susceptibility was introduced by the Leiden group (Bakermans-Kranenburg & van IJzendoorn, 2006). The second critical issue concerns the associations between these susceptibility candidates. Their interrelations should be explored because it seems theoretically evident that genetic, endophenotypical, physiological, and phenotypical susceptibility factors would be associated to a larger or smaller degree. For example, it would be critical to know whether dopamine system–related genes are involved in specific temperamental features, and whether the accumulating evidence on the susceptibility role of these genes in fact translates to one of the temperamental dimensions, or whether they operate in an additive (or even interactive) way. There is evidence linking susceptibility factors, but we do not know whether the moderating effect of one susceptibility factor overlaps with the moderating effect of another such factor. Carriers of the *DRD4* 7-repeat alleles might be more temperamentally reactive, but whether these two markers of differential susceptibility have similar roles in similar domains of functioning and in similar contexts remains to be seen. On another score, it has been demonstrated that the carriers of the short variant of the serotonin transporter gene (*5-HTTLPR*) are prone to negative emotionality, and both variants have been found to be markers of differential susceptibility in some studies (see Belsky & Pluess, 2009, for a review). Including various susceptibility factors in the same study (e.g., Essex et al., 2011) creates the opportunity to test interrelations and to examine the varying predictive power of the moderators.

Careful measurement of the environment, the outcome, and the temperamental moderator is a prerequisite for valid tests of the differential susceptibility paradigm. The importance of this third critical issue cannot be overestimated. Kagan (2007, 2009) eloquently argued that temperament should be measured in observational settings, as the concept of temperament refers to a behavioral style, and not to parental or self-perceptions (but see Crockenberg & Leerkes, 2006, who make a case for temperament questionnaires controlling for response biases). Similarly, parenting and other environmental influences should be assessed with greater precision and validity than has been done in several large-scale temperament × parenting or G × E studies, with sometimes disappointing results. As an illustration, two meta-analyses (Munafo, Durrant, Lewis, & Flint, 2009; Risch et al., 2009) failed to find support for the much cited interaction between negative life events and the serotonin transporter gene (*5-HTTLPR*) in depression (Caspi et al., 2003). However, Uher and McGuffin (2010) showed that the method of assessment of environmental adversity was an important determinant of the outcome of the study. Detailed interview-based approaches were associated with significant G × E findings, whereas all nonreplications used self-report questionnaires.

The differential susceptibility paradigm has created myriad opportunities for temperament and attachment researchers to join forces and exploit the best of both theoretical perspectives to gain more insight into human development. It is time to recognize that the battle between two highly influential schools of thought is over, and that "everybody has won, and all must have prizes," to quote Lewis Carroll's *Alice in Wonderland*.

Acknowledgments

This work was supported by awards from the Netherlands Organization for Scientific Research (VIDI Grant No. 452-04-306 and VICI Grant No. 453-09-003 to Marian J. Bakermans-Kranenburg and the Spinoza Prize to Marinus H. van IJzendoorn).

Further Reading

Bakermans-Kranenburg, M. J., & van IJzendoorn, M. H. (2007). Genetic vulnerability or differential susceptibility in child development: The case of attachment. *Journal of Child Psychology and Psychiatry, 48*(12), 1160–1173.

Ellis, B. J., Boyce, W. T., Belsky, J., Bakermans-Kranenburg, M. J., & van IJzendoorn, M. H. (2011). Differential susceptibility to the environment: A neurodevelopmental theory. *Development and Psychopathology, 23,* 7–28.

Vaughn, B. E., Bost, K. K., & van IJzendoorn, M. H. (2008). Attachment and temperament: Additive and interactive influences on behavior, affect, and cognition during infancy and childhood. In J. Cassidy & P. R. Shaver (Eds.), *Handbook of attachment: Theory, research, and clinical applications* (2nd ed., pp. 192–216). New York: Guilford Press.

References

Ainsworth, M. D. (1967). *Infancy in Uganda: Infant care and the growth of love.* Baltimore: Johns Hopkins University Press.

Ainsworth, M. D., Blehar, M. C., Waters, E., & Wall, S. (1978). *Patterns of attachment: A psychological study of the Strange Situation.* Hillsdale, NJ: Erlbaum.

Aron, E., Aron, A., & Davies, K. M. (2005). Adult shyness: The interaction of temperamental sensitivity and an adverse childhood environment. *Personality and Social Psychology Bulletin, 31,* 181–197.

Bakermans-Kranenburg, M. J., & van IJzendoorn, M. H. (2006). Gene–environment interaction of the dopamine D4 receptor (DRD4) and observed maternal insensitivity predicting externalizing behavior in preschoolers. *Developmental Psychobiology, 48,* 406–409.

Bakermans-Kranenburg, M. J., & van IJzendoorn, M. H. (2007). Genetic vulnerability or differential susceptibility in child development: The case of attachment. *Journal of Child Psychology and Psychiatry, 48*(12), 1160–1173.

Bakermans-Kranenburg, M. J., & van IJzendoorn, M. H. (2011). Differential susceptibility to rearing environment depending on dopamine-related genes: New evidence and a meta-analysis. *Development and Psychopathology, 23,* 39–52.

Bakermans-Kranenburg, M. J., van IJzendoorn, M. H., Bokhorst, C. L., & Schuengel, C. (2004). The importance of shared environment in infant–father attachment: A behavioral genetic study of the Attachment Q-Sort. *Journal of Family Psychology, 18,* 545–549.

Bakermans-Kranenburg, M. J., van IJzendoorn, M. H., Caspers, K., & Philibert, R. (2011). DRD4 genotype moderates the impact of parental problems on unresolved loss or trauma. *Attachment and Human Development, 13*(3), 253–269.

Bakermans-Kranenburg, M. J., van IJzendoorn, M. H., & Juffer, F. (2003). Less is more: Meta-analyses of sensitivity and attachment interventions in early childhood. *Psychological Bulletin, 129,* 195–215.

Bakermans-Kranenburg, M. J., van IJzendoorn, M. H., Mesman, J., Alink, L. R., & Juffer, F. (2008). Effects of an attachment-based intervention on daily cortisol moderated by dopamine receptor D4: R randomized control trial on 1- to 3-year-olds screened for externalizing behavior. *Developmental and Psychopathology, 20,* 805–820.

Bakermans-Kranenburg, M. J., van IJzendoorn, M. H., Pijlman, F. T. A., Mesman, J., & Juffer, F. (2008). Experimental evidence for differential susceptibility: Dopamine D4 receptor polymorphism (DRD4 VNTR) moderates intervention effects on toddlers' externalizing behavior in a randomized trial. *Developmental Psychology, 44,* 293–300.

Bates, J. E., Freeland, C. A. B., & Lounsbury, M. L. (1979). Measurement of infant difficultness. *Child Development, 50,* 794–803.

Belsky, J. (1997a). Theory testing, effect-size evaluation, and differential susceptibility to rearing influence: The case of mothering and attachment. *Child Development, 68,* 598–600.

Belsky, J. (1997b). Variation in susceptibility to rearing influences: An evolutionary argument. *Psychological Inquiry, 8,* 182–186.

Belsky, J. (2005). Differential susceptibility to rearing influence: An evolutionary hypothesis and some evidence. In B. J. Ellis & D. F. Bjorklund (Eds.), *Origins of the social mind: Evolutionary psychology and child development* (pp. 139–163). New York: Guilford Press.

Belsky, J., Bakermans-Kranenburg, M. J., & van IJzendoorn, M. H. (2007). For better and for worse: Differential susceptibility to environmental influences. *Current Directions in Psychological Science, 16*(6), 300–304

Belsky, J., Fish, M., & Isabella, R. (1991). Continuity and discontinuity in infant negative and positive emotionality: Family antecedents and attachment consequences. *Developmental Psychology, 27,* 421–431.

Belsky, J., Hsieh, K., & Crnic, K. (1998). Mothering, fathering, and infant negativity as antecedents of boys' externalizing problems and inhibition at age 3: Differential susceptibility to rearing influence? *Development and Psychopathology, 10,* 301–319.

Belsky, J., & Pluess, M. (2009). Beyond diathesis–stress. *Psychological Bulletin, 135,* 885–908.

Belsky, J., & Rovine, M. (1987). Temperament and attachment security in the Strange Situation: An empirical rapprochement. *Child Development, 58,* 787–795.

Blair, C. (2002). Early intervention for low birth weight preterm infants: The role of negative emotionality in the specification of effects. *Development and Psychopathology, 14,* 311–332.

Bohlin, G., Hagekull, B., & Andersson, A. (2005). Behavioral inhibition as a precursor of peer social competence in early school age: The interplay with attachment and non-parental care. *Merrill–Palmer Quarterly, 51,* 1–19.

Bokhorst, C. L., Bakermans-Kranenburg, M. J., Fearon, P., van IJzendoorn, M. H., Fonagy, P., & Schuengel, C. (2003). The importance of shared environment in mother–infant attachment security: A behavioral genetic study. *Child Development, 74,* 1769–1782.

Bowlby, J. (1969). *Attachment and loss: Vol. 1. Attachment.* London: Penguin.

Boyce, W. T., Chesney, M., Alkon, A., Tschann, J. M., Adams, S., Chesterman, B., et al. (1995). Psychobiologic reactivity to stress and childhood respiratory illnesses: Results of two prospective studies. *Psychosomatic Medicine, 57*(5), 411–422.

Boyce, W. T., & Ellis, B. J. (2005). Biological sensitivity to context: I. An evolutionary–developmental theory of the origins and functions of stress reactivity. *Development and Psychopathology, 17,* 271–301.

Bradley, R. H., & Corwyn, R. F. (2008). Infant temperament, parenting, and externalizing behavior in first grade: A test of the differential susceptibility hypothesis. *Journal of Child Psychology and Psychiatry and Allied Disciplines, 49,* 124–131.

Calkins, S. D., & Fox, N. A. (1992). The relations among infant temperament, security of attachment, and behavioral inhibition at twenty-four months. *Child Development, 3,* 1456–1472.

Caspi, A., & Moffitt, T. E. (2006). Gene–environment interactions in psychiatry: Joining forces with neuroscience. *Nature Reviews Neuroscience, 7,* 583–590.

Caspi, A., & Shiner, R. L. (2006). Personality development. In W. Damon & R. Lerner (Eds.), *Child development: An advanced course* (pp. 181–214). New York: Wiley.

Caspi, A., Sugden, K., Moffitt, T. E., Taylor, A., Craig, I. W., Harrington, H., et al. (2003). Influence of life stress on depression: Moderation by a polymorphism in the 5 HTT gene. *Science, 301,* 386–389.

Cassidy, J., & Shaver, P. R. (Eds.). (2008). *Handbook of attachment: Theory, research, and clinical applications* (2nd ed.). New York: Guilford Press.

Cassidy, J., Woodhouse, S. S., Sherman, L. J., Stupica, B., & Lejuez, C. W. (2011). Enhancing infant attachment security: An examination of treatment efficacy and differential susceptibility. *Development and Psychopathology, 23,* 131–148.

Cicchetti, D. (1993). Developmental psychopathology—reactions, reflections, projections. *Developmental Review, 13,* 471–502.

Crockenberg, S. B. (1981). Infant irritability, mother responsiveness, and social support influences on the security of infant–mother attachment. *Child Development, 52,* 857–865.

Crockenberg, S. C., & Leerkes, E. M. (2006). Infant and maternal behavior moderate reactivity to novelty to predict anxious behavior at 2.5 years. *Development and Psychopathology, 18,* 17–34.

Dearing, E., & Hamilton, L. C. (2006). Contemporary advances and classic advice for analyzing mediating and moderating variables. *Monographs of the Society for Research in Child Development, 71,* 88–104.

Deater-Deckard, K., Bates, J. E., Dodge, K. A., & Pettit, G. S. (1996). Physical discipline among African American and European American mothers: Links to children's externalizing behaviors. *Developmental Psychology, 32,* 1065–1072.

Deater-Deckard, K., & Dodge, K. A. (1997). Externalizing behavior problems and discipline revisited: Nonlinear effects and variation by culture, context, and gender. *Psychological Inquiry, 8*(3), 161–175.

Denham, S. A., Workman, E., Cole, P. M., Weissbrod, C., Kendziora, K. T., & Zahn-Waxler, C. (2000). Prediction of externalizing behavior problems from early to middle childhood: The role of parental socialization and emotion expression. *Development and Psychopathology, 12*(1), 23–45.

De Schipper, J. C., Tavecchio, L. W. C., van IJzendoorn, M. H., & van Zeijl, J. (2004). Goodness-of-fit in center day care: Relations of temperament, stability, and quality of care with the child's adjustment. *Early Childhood Research Quarterly, 19,* 257–272.

DeVries, M. W. (1984). Temperament and infant mortality among the Masai of East Africa. *American Journal of Psychiatry, 141,* 1189–1194.

DeVries, M. W. (1987). Cry babies, culture and catastrophe. Infant temperament among the Masai. In N. Scheper-Hughes (Ed.), *Anthropological approaches to the treatment and maltreatment of children* (pp. 165–186). Dordrecht, The Netherlands: Reidel.

De Wolff, M., & van IJzendoorn, M. H. (1997). Sensivity and attachment. A meta-analysis on parental antecedents of infant attachment. *Child Development, 68,* 571–591.

Ellis, B. J., Boyce, W. T., Belsky, J., Bakermans-Kranenburg, M. J., & van IJzendoorn, M. H. (2011). Differential susceptibility to the environment: An evolutionary–neurodevelopmental theory. *Development and Psychopathology, 23*(1), 7–28.

Essex, M. J., Armstrong, J. M., Burk, L. R., Goldsmith, H. H., & Boyce, W. T. (2011). Biological sensitivity to context moderates the effects of the early teacher–child relationship on the development of mental health by adolescence. *Development and Psychopathology, 23*, 149–161.

Feldman, R., Greenbaum, C. W., & Yirmiya, N. (1999). Mother–infant affect synchrony as an antecedent of the emergence of self-control. *Developmental Psychology, 35*, 223–231.

Fortuna, K., van IJzendoorn, M. H., Mankuta, D., Kaitz, M., Avinun, R., Ebstein, R. P., et al. (2011). Differential genetic susceptibility to child risk at birth in predicting observed maternal behavior. *PLoS ONE, 6*(5), e19765.

Gilissen, R., Bakermans-Kranenburg, M. J., van IJzendoorn, H. W., & van der Veer, R. (2008). Parent–child relationship, temperament, and physiological reactions to fear-inducing film clips: Further evidence for differential susceptibility. *Journal of Experimental Child Psychology, 99*(3), 182–195.

Goldsmith, H. H., Lemery, K. S., Buss, K. A., & Campos, J. J. (1999). Genetic analyses of focal aspects of infant temperament. *Developmental Psychology, 35*(4), 972–985.

Goldsmith, H. H., Reilly, J., Lemery, K. S., Longley, S., & Prescott, A. (1999). *The Laboratory Temperament Assessment Battery: Preschool Version.* Unpublished manuscript.

Groeneveld, M. G., Vermeer, H. J., van IJzendoorn, M. H., & Linting, M. (2012). Stress, cortisol, and well-being of caregivers and children in home-based childcare: A case for differential susceptibility. *Child: Care, Health and Development, 38*(2), 251–260.

Hane, A. A., & Fox, N. A. (2006). Ordinary variations in maternal caregiving influence human infants' stress reactivity. *Psychological Science, 17*, 550–556.

Harlow, H. F. (1958). The nature of love. *American Psychologist, 13*, 673–685.

Hesse, E. (2008). The Adult Attachment Interview: Protocol, method of analysis, and empirical studies. In J. Cassidy & P. R. Shaver (Eds.), *Handbook of attachment* (pp. 552–598). New York: Guilford Press.

Jaddoe, V. W., Bakker, R., van Duijn, C. M., van der Heijden, A. J., Lindemans, J., Mackenbach, J. P., et al. (2007). The Generation R Study Biobank: A resource for epidemiological studies in children and their parents. *European Journal of Epidemiology, 22*(12), 917–923.

Juffer, F., Bakermans-Kranenburg, M. J., & van IJzendoorn, M. H. (Eds.). (2008). *Promoting positive parenting.* New York: Taylor & Francis.

Kagan, J. (1995). On attachment. *Harvard Review of Psychiatry, 3*, 104–106.

Kagan, J. (2007). A trio of concerns. *Perspectives on Psychological Science, 2*, 361–376.

Kagan, J. (2009). Two is better than one. *Perspectives on Psychological Science, 4*, 22–23.

Kegel, C. A. T., Bus, A. G., & van IJzendoorn, M. H. (2011). Differential susceptibility in early literacy instruction through computer games: The role of the dopamine D4 receptor gene (DRD4). *Mind, Brain and Education, 5*, 71–79.

Klein, T. A., Neumann, J., Reuter, M., Hennig, J., Von Cramon, D. Y., & Ullsperger, M. (2007). Genetically determined learning from errors. *Science, 318*, 1642–1645.

Klein Velderman, M., Bakermans-Kranenburg, M. J., Juffer, F., & van IJzendoorn, M. H. (2006). Effects of attachment-based interventions on maternal sensitivity and infant attachment: Differential susceptibility of highly reactive infants. *Journal of Family Psychology, 20*, 266–274.

Kochanska, G. (1995). Children's temperament, mothers discipline, and security of attachment: Multiple pathways to emerging internalization. *Child Development, 66*(3), 597–615.

Kochanska, G. (1998). Mother–child relationship, child fearfulness, and emerging attachment: A short-term longitudinal study. *Developmental Psychology, 34*, 480–490.

Kochanska, G., Aksan, N., & Joy, M. E. (2007). Children's fearfulness as a moderator of parenting in early socialization. *Developmental Psychology, 43*, 222–237.

LaFreniere, P. J., & Capuano, F. (1997). Preventive intervention as means of clarifying direction of effects in socialization: Anxious–withdrawn preschoolers case. *Development and Psychopathology, 9*, 551–564.

Luijk, M. P. C. M., Roisman, G. I., Haltigan, J. D., Tiemeier, H., Booth-LaForce, C., van IJzendoorn, M. H., et al. (2011). Dopaminergic, serotonergic, and oxytonergic candidate genes associated with infant attachment security and disorganization?: In search of main effects and G × E interactions. *Journal of Child Psychology and Psychiatry, 52*(12), 1295–1307.

Main, M., Kaplan, N., & Cassidy, J. (1985). Security in infancy, childhood, and adulthood: A move to the level of representation. *Monographs of the Society for Research in Child Development, 50*, 66–106.

Marshall, P. J., & Fox, N. A. (2005). Relations between behavioral reactivity at 4 months and attachment classification at 14 months in a selected sample. *Infant Behavior and Development, 28*, 492–502.

Masten, A. S., & Obradović, J. (2006). Competence and resilience in development. *Annals of the New York Academy of Sciences, 1094*, 13–27.

Meaney, M. J. (2010). Epigenetics and the biological definition of gene × environment interactions. *Child Development, 81*, 41–79.

Morrell, J., & Murray, L. (2003). Parenting and the development of conduct disorder and hyperactive symptoms in childhood: A prospective longitudinal study from 2 months to 8 years. *Journal of Child Psychology and Psychiatry, 44,* 489–508.

Munafo, M. R., Durrant, C., Lewis, G., & Flint, J. (2009). Gene × environment interactions at the serotonin transporter locus. *Biological Psychiatry, 65,* 211–219.

Nachmias, M., Gunnar, M., Mangelsdorf, S., Parritz, R., & Buss, K. (1996). Behavioral inhibition and stress reactivity: The moderating role of attachment security. *Child Development, 67,* 508–522.

O'Connor, T. G., & Croft, C. M. (2001). A twin study of attachment in preschool children. *Child Development, 72,* 1501–1511.

Pluess, M., & Belsky, J. (2009). Differential susceptibility to rearing experience: The case of childcare. *Journal of Child Psychology and Psychiatry Allied Disciplines, 50,* 396–404.

Ricciuti, A. E. (1992). Child–mother attachment: A twin study. *Dissertation Abstracts International, 54,* 3364–3364. (University Microfilms No. 9324873)

Risch, N., Herrell, R., Lehner, T., Liang, K., Eaves, L., Hoh, J., et al. (2009). Interaction between the serotonin transporter gene (5-HTTLPR), stressful life events, and risk of depression. *Journal of the American Medical Association, 301*(23), 2462–2471.

Robbins, T. W., & Everitt, B. J. (1999). Motivation and reward. In M. J. Zigmond, F. E. Bloom, S. C. Landis, J. L. Roberts, & L. R. Squire (Eds.), *Fundamental neuroscience* (pp. 1246–1260). San Diego, CA: Academic Press.

Roisman, G. I., & Fraley, R. C. (2008). A behavior-genetic study of parenting quality, infant attachment security, and their covariation in a nationally representative sample. *Developmental Psychology, 44*(3), 831–839.

Rothbart, M. K., & Bates, J. E. (2006). Temperament. In N. Eisenberg, W. Damon, & R. M. Lerner (Eds.), *Handbook of child psychology: Vol. 3. Social, emotional, and personality development* (6th ed., pp. 99–166). Hoboken, NJ: Wiley.

Sameroff, A. (1975). Transactional models in early social-relations. *Human Development, 18,* 65–79.

Sameroff, A. J. (1983). Developmental systems: Contexts and evolution. In P. Mussen (Ed.), *Handbook of child psychology* (Vol. 1, pp. 237–294). New York: Wiley.

Settle, J. E., Dawes, C. T., Christakis, N. A., & Fowler, J. H. (2010). Friendships moderate an association between a dopamine gene variant and political ideology. *Journal of Politics, 72,* 1189-1198.

Sheese, B. E., Voelker, P. M., Rothbart, M. K., & Posner, M. I. (2007). Parenting quality interacts with genetic variation in dopamine receptor D4 to influence temperament in early childhood. *Development and Psychopathology, 19,* 1039–1046.

Simpson, J. A., & Belsky, J. (2008). Attachment theory within a modern evolutionary framework. In P. R. Shaver & J. Cassidy (Eds.), *Handbook of attachment: Theory, research, and clinical applications* (2nd ed., pp. 131–157). New York: Guilford Press.

Sroufe, L. A. (1985). Attachment classification from the perspective of infant–caregiver relationships and infant temperament. *Child Development, 56,* 1–14.

Sroufe, L. A., Egeland, B., Carlson, E., & Collins, W. A. (2005). *The development of the person: The Minnesota Study of Risk and Adaptation from Birth to Adulthood.* New York: Guilford Press.

Stevenson-Hinde, J., & Marshall, P. J. (1999). Behavioral inhibition, heart period, and respiratory sinus arrhythmia: An attachment perspective. *Child Development, 70,* 805–816.

Stright, A. D., Kelley, K., & Gallagher, K. C. (2008). Infant temperament moderates relations between maternal parenting in early childhood and children's adjustment in first grade. *Child Development, 79,* 186–200.

Suomi, S. (1997). Early determinants of behaviour. *British Medical Bulletin, 53,* 170–184.

Székely, E., van IJzendoorn, M. H., Bakermans-Kranenburg, M. J., Kok, R., Luijk, M., Tharner, A. et al. (2011). *Beyond the usual suspects: In search of the genetic basis of attachment and temperamental fearfulness with pathway analysis based on genome wide associations.* Manuscript in preparation.

Thomas, A., & Chess, S. (1977). *Temperament and development.* New York: Brunner/Mazel.

Thompson, R. A., & Lamb, M. E. (1984). Assessing qualitative dimensions of emotional responsiveness in infants: Separation reactions in the strange situation. *Infant Behavior and Development, 7,* 423–445.

Uher, R., & McGuffin, P. (2008). The moderation by the serotonin transporter gene of environmental adversity in the etiology of mental illness: Review and methodological analysis. *Molecular Psychiatry, 13,* 131–146.

Uher, R., & McGuffin, P. (2010). The moderation by the serotonin transporter gene of environmental adversity in the etiology of depression: 2009 update. *Molecular Psychiatry, 15,* 18–22.

van den Boom, D. C. (1994). The influence of temperament and mothering on attachment and exploration: An experimental manipulation of sensitive responsiveness among lower-class mothers with irritable infants. *Child Development, 65,* 1457–1477.

van IJzendoorn, M. H. (1995a). Adult attachment

representations, parental responsiveness, and infant attachment: A meta-analysis on the predictive validity of the Adult Attachment Interview. *Psychological Bulletin, 117,* 387–403.

van IJzendoorn, M. H. (1995b). Of the way we are: On temperament, attachment and the transmission gap: A rejoinder to Fox. *Psychological Bulletin, 117,* 411–415.

van IJzendoorn, M. H., & Bakermans-Kranenburg, M. J. (1996). Attachment representations in mothers, fathers, adolescents, and clinical groups: A meta-analytic search for normative data. *Journal of Consulting and Clinical Psychology, 64,* 8–21.

van IJzendoorn, M. H., & Bakermans-Kranenburg, M. J. (2004). Maternal sensitivity and infant temperament in the formation of attachment. In G. Bremner & A. Slater (Eds.), *Theories of infant development* (pp. 233–258). London: Blackwell.

van IJzendoorn, M. H., Bakermans-Kranenburg, M. J., & Mesman, J. (2008). Dopamine system genes associated with parenting in the context of daily hassles. *Genes, Brain and Behavior, 7,* 403–410.

van IJzendoorn, M. H., & DeWolff, M. W. E. (1997). In search of the absent father: Meta-analyses of infant–father attachment: A rejoinder to our discussants. *Child Development, 68,* 604–609.

van IJzendoorn, M. H., Palacios, J., Sonuga-Barke, E. J. S., Gunnar, M. R., Vorria, P., McCall, R. B., et al. (2011). Children in institutional care: Delayed development and resilience. *Monographs of the Society for Research of Child Development, 76*(4), 8–30.

van Zeijl, J., Mesman, J., Stolk, M. N., Alink, L. R. A., van IJzendoorn, M. H., Bakermans-Kranenburg, M. J., et al. (2007). Differential susceptibility to discipline: The moderating effect of child temperament on the association between maternal discipline and early childhood externalizing problems. *Journal of Family Psychology, 21,* 626–636.

van Zeijl, J., Mesman, J., van IJzendoorn, M. H., Bakermans-Kranenburg, M. J., Juffer, F., Stolk, M. N., et al. (2006). Attachment-based intervention for enhancing sensitive discipline in mothers of 1- to 3-year-old children at risk for externalizing behavior problems: A randomized controlled trial. *Journal of Consulting and Clinical Psychology, 47,* 801–810.

Vaughn, B. E., & Bost, K. K. (1999). Attachment and temperament: Redundant, independent, or interacting influences on interpersonal adaptation and personality development. In J. Cassidy & P. R. Shaver (Eds.), *Handbook of attachment: Theory, research, and clinical applications* (pp. 198–225). New York: Guilford Press.

Vaughn, B. E., Bost, K. K., & van IJzendoorn, M. H. (2008). Attachment and temperament: Additive and interactive influences on behavior, affect, and cognition during infancy and childhood. In J. Cassidy & P. R. Shaver (Eds.), *Handbook of attachment* (pp. 192–216). New York: Guilford Press.

Vaughn, B. E., & Waters, E. (1990). Attachment behavior at home and in the laboratory: Q-sort observations and Strange Situation classifications of one-year-olds. *Child Development, 61,* 1965–1973.

Yaman, A., Mesman, J., van IJzendoorn, M. H., & Bakermans-Kranenburg, M. J. (2010). Parenting and toddler aggression in second-generation immigrant families: The moderating role of child temperament. *Journal of Family Psychology, 24,* 208–211.

Zentner, M., & Bates, J. E. (2008). Child temperament: An integrative review of concepts, research programs, and measures. *European Journal of Developmental Science, 1/2,* 7–37.

CHAPTER 20

Temperament and Parenting in Developmental Perspective

John E. Bates
Alice C. Schermerhorn
Isaac T. Petersen

In this chapter we consider how child temperament and parenting differences might influence one another and interact in shaping child adjustment. By temperament we mean concepts of individual differences in both reactivity and regulation (Rothbart & Bates, 2006). The frequently used three-factor model of temperament includes positive emotional reactivity, negative emotional reactivity, and self-regulation. Parenting differences are important because they occur in the primary context for socializing children (Maccoby & Martin, 1983). Parenting dimensions are not as well established as temperament dimensions, but research has shown dimensions of warmth—including supportiveness, positive involvement, responsiveness, affection, and nurturance—and control, which is often described in terms of harsh versus gentle and autonomy encouraging versus suppressing styles of control (Maccoby & Martin, 1983). Parental control probably includes more than one subdimension (Barber, Stolz, & Olsen, 2005; Bugental & Grusec, 2006), so in this chapter, we specify types of control when citing particular studies. One could treat temperament and parenting as independent, separate factors in accounting for adjustment outcomes, but studies suggest that they are related.

Temperament traits involve social behaviors and, as such, child temperament traits could elicit parenting behaviors. At the same time, parenting behaviors could shape the social behaviors that constitute the phenotype of temperament. For example, a child who laughs and smiles often would seem likely to elicit similar positive behavior from parents, compared with a child who is predominantly sober. And the positive emotionality of the child could, at least partly, reflect the normal environmental press of a happy, interested, affectionate, responsive parent (Rothbart & Bates, 2006). This view of child temperament and parenting influencing each other and interacting to shape adjustment is based in developmental theory.

It is generally agreed that parents' cognitive and social skills enable them to choose how they will respond to the behavioral cues of their children, and that parents are capable of shaping at least some child behavior (Collins, Maccoby, Steinberg, Hetherington, & Bornstein, 2000), but modern theory (e.g., Sameroff, 2009) recognizes that children can influence the behavior of parents. Empirical work provides evidence of children's influence (Schermerhorn & Cummings, 2008). For example, findings of evocative effects of genetically influenced behavior (Ge et al.,

1996), and findings of parental differential treatment of children (Suitor, Sechrist, Plikuhn, Pardo, & Pillemer, 2008) suggest that children's social behavior influences the caregiving environment. Child temperament traits such as negative emotional reactivity could elicit either directly reciprocal (distress, fear, or anger) or compensatory patterns of parent behavior (soothing or protecting). In fact, as we describe, research has considered the possible influence of temperament upon parenting.

Similarly, although temperament is generally considered a largely constitutional trait, the phenotypes that reflect temperament continue to develop after birth and are shaped by contextual factors, including parenting and family processes (Rothbart & Bates, 2006). Despite being fairly stable over the lifespan, temperament shows mean-level (i.e., group-level) and rank-order (i.e., between-person) change (Neyer & Lehnart, 2007). Twin studies affirm the importance of the environment in the development of temperament (Ganiban, Saudino, Ulbricht, Neiderhiser, & Reiss, 2008; Goldsmith, Buss, & Lemery, 1997; Goldsmith, Lemery, Buss, & Campos, 1999; Saudino, 2005; also see Saudino & Wang, Chapter 16, this volume). Parenting could influence the development of temperament through several possible mechanisms. It is known that caregiving and other environmental factors can influence children's biological development, including physiological responses (Gunnar & Donzella, 2002; Propper & Moore, 2006) and brain development (Glaser, 2000; Schore, 1996). Children gradually internalize their parents' modeling of impulse control (Kopp, 1982), styles of emotional responding (Fox, 2006), and behavioral compliance (Kopp, 1982), perhaps because of parental modeling of appropriately warm and well-regulated social behavior and the encouragement of a secure attachment. In short, despite the field's tendency to define temperament as reflections of the child's constitution, there are also good reasons to think that parenting qualities could affect temperament, especially children's complexly determined behavioral phenotypes.

This chapter considers studies in which temperament differences are conceptualized as predictors of parenting differences, as well as those in which parenting is conceptualized as a factor contributing to temperament and changes in temperament. And, finally, it considers how temperament and parenting might combine, especially in the form of interaction effects, in predicting social-developmental outcomes in children. It is becoming increasingly clear (Bates & Pettit, 2007; Bates, Schermerhorn, & Goodnight, 2010; Degnan & Fox, 2007; Henderson & Wachs, 2007; Rothbart & Bates, 2006) that child temperament differences help explain how a given style of parenting is related to child adjustment and, alternatively, that a given temperament predicts child adjustment as a function of parenting qualities. In what follows, we describe studies on how temperament and parenting relate, organized according to the design of the study. Design affects inferences regarding developmental processes involving temperament and parenting. Within major methodological categories, we organize, as far as possible, by the child temperament domain and by the domain of parenting, emphasizing warmth and control. Temperament and parenting constructs are operationally measured in multiple ways. Commonly, different studies we cite in a given section have different, specific measures of the broad categories in which we place them. There is some convergence between different measures, especially questionnaire measures (for temperament: Bates & Bayles, 1984; Goldsmith et al., 1997; Rothbart & Bates, 2006; for parenting: Hawes & Dadds, 2006). This is not the occasion for a methodologically rigorous comparison of studies, but we occasionally mention a few key method details.

Nondirectional Association Studies

In this section we describe studies of associations between child temperament and parenting that used cross-sectional, correlational data. Many of the findings were interpreted by their authors as reflecting the influence of temperament on parenting or, in other cases, as the influence of parenting on temperament. However, because of the cross-sectional design, we interpret the studies merely as showing an association. The authors' original causal interpretations may turn out to be correct, and with a transactional model (Sameroff, 2009) both child and parent effects can operate. For now, it is useful just to know the basic correlations, which may suggest areas for fruitful longitudinal and experimental studies.

Child Positive Reactivity and Parenting

A few cross-sectional studies have shown associations between child positive reactivity and parental warmth, as measured in children by observation (Kochanska, Friesenborg, Lange, & Martel, 2004), and in adolescence by questionnaire (Latzman, Elkovitch, & Clark, 2009). Such association could reflect simple social reciprocity, shaping, or genetic similarity between parent and child in temperament.

A few cross-sectional studies have also examined associations between child positive reactivity and parental control. Among the findings, mothers of joyful infants tracked their infants' location more closely than did mothers of less joyful infants (Kochanska et al., 2004). Tracking might be interpreted as reflecting proactive control. In contrast, Latzman and colleagues (2009) found no associations between positivity and maternal monitoring, inconsistent discipline, or corporal punishment. Thus, we know little about concurrent associations between positive reactivity and parental control.

Child Negative Reactivity and Parenting

Many studies have measured a general negative reactivity, sometimes called *difficult temperament*, marked by frequent expressions of distress. Difficult temperament, referring to a general tendency to express negative emotions, is more general than the related constructs of fearful and angry negative reactivity (Rothbart & Bates, 2006). The different qualities of negative emotion could elicit or stem from different kinds of parenting. Depending on parents' adaptive capacities, negative emotionality could produce nurturance, neglect, or even reciprocal negativity. Likewise, parent habits of warmth could elicit child habits of equanimity or reinforce negative reactivity.

Negative Reactivity/Difficultness

Findings on associations between general negative reactivity and parental warmth have been fairly numerous but mixed (Paulussen-Hoogeboom, Stams, Hermanns, & Peetsma, 2007). One study found negative associations between toddlers' difficultness and maternal responsiveness concurrently but not longitudinally (Owens, Shaw, & Vondra, 1998). Another study found concurrent positive associations of infant difficultness, with only two of seven aspects of observed maternal warmth and responsiveness: higher levels of affection and stimulating the infant with an object (Bates, Olson, Pettit, & Bayles, 1982). This study included a substantial number of middle-class families. The Paulussen-Hoogeboom and colleagues (2007) meta-analysis suggests that child negative reactivity overall may be correlated with less parental warmth, but this is more so for lower-socioeconomic-status (SES) than upper-SES samples. As in the Bates and colleagues (1982) study (and see Crockenberg, 1986), some mothers, especially those with educational and economic resources, may respond in supportive ways to a fussy child, especially an infant, whereas others, especially those with fewer such resources, respond with less support for a child who is high in negativity than for one who is low in negativity.

Previous findings of child negative emotionality relating to parental control are less extensive than those relating to parental warmth. Nonetheless, Paulussen-Hoogeboom and colleagues (2007) did find a general tendency for parents of more negative children to exercise more restrictive control. Much of this effect may concern child anger, but some of it appears to involve difficultness or irritability, too. To consider one study, Coplan, Reichel, and Rowan (2009) found associations between child negative reactivity and lower levels of parent authoritative control, but not overprotective or coercive parenting. Thus, in overview, plausible associations have been found between child general negative reactivity and parental warmth and, to a lesser extent, parental control.

Fear and Inhibition

The Paulussen-Hoogeboom and colleagues (2007) meta-analysis tables do not suggest that child fearful reactivity is associated with either less or more parental support. The same is true for parents' restrictive control. Considering a few specific studies, two studies found concurrent associations in infancy and early childhood between fear/inhibition and more observed parental warmth (Kertes et al., 2009; Kochanska et al., 2004), but longitudinal tests were nonsignificant, even without autoregressive controls (Kochanska et al., 2004). In contrast, another study with 2-year-olds showed an association between child fearfulness and low levels of sensitivity/responsiveness (Rubin, Hastings, Stewart, Henderson, & Chen, 1997). In addition to these findings on parental warmth, one study found concurrent positive associations between child shyness and overprotective maternal parenting (Coplan et al., 2009). Thus, there is little consistent evidence of concurrent associations between children's fearful traits and parenting.

Frustration and Anger

A child's disposition to become frustrated and angry may be hard to distinguish from other forms of negative affect in early infancy, but it soon becomes more distinct from other forms of negative affect (Rothbart & Bates, 2006). Frustration and anger have greater likelihood of a negative association with supportive parenting than does fearful reactivity, and possibly with greater likelihood of a positive association with restrictive control, too (Paulussen-Hoogeboom et al., 2007). For example, infant anger has been concurrently associated with less parental warmth (Kochanska et al., 2004) and more harsh parenting (Rhoades et al., 2011).

Child Self-Regulation and Parenting

Self-regulation traits have been described in terms of a wide array of mechanisms, including behavioral, emotional, and physiological regulation. These traits are most often described as effortful control and executive functions. *Effortful control* is the ability to inhibit a dominant response in favor of a subdominant one. *Executive function* has been defined as "the set of higher order cognitive processes that underlie flexible goal-directed behaviors, such as inhibitory control, working memory, planning, and set shifting" (Bernier, Carlson, & Whipple, 2010, p. 326). Both can be considered related ways of talking about self-regulation (Zhou, Chen, & Main, 2012). The natural complement of child self-regulatory traits would be parental autonomy support and lower levels of control in general. Self-regulatory traits could also stem from and elicit parental warmth and low levels of hostility.

Tests of concurrent links between child self-regulation and parental warmth have been mixed, at least in early childhood. In a meta-analysis on concurrent associations between parenting and child self-regulation at ages 2 to 5, Karreman, van Tuijl, van Aken, and Dekovic (2006) found no associations between parental responsiveness and child self-regulation. In contrast, two studies that were not part of Karreman and colleagues' meta-analysis did find concurrent associations between parental warmth or responsiveness and child compliance (Dennis, 2006) and toddler self-regulation (Popp, Spinrad, & Smith, 2008).

Karreman and colleagues' (2006) meta-analysis found concurrent associations between children's self-regulation, measured by observation and questionnaire, and more positive, less negative parental control, measured by observation and questionnaire. Similar patterns have been reported in several more recent studies using observational and questionnaire measures of self-regulation (Karreman, van Tuijl, van Aken, & Dekovic, 2008; Latzman et al., 2009; Popp et al., 2008). In Karreman and colleagues' meta-analysis, when self-regulation was disaggregated into subcategories of compliance, inhibition, and emotion regulation, only compliance was correlated with parental control. Karreman and colleagues distinguished between positive control, referring to encouraging, guiding, and directive parenting, and negative control, or power-assertive, harsh, and possibly physical control. Compliance was positively related to positive control and negatively related to negative control.

In summary, children with better self-regulation tend to have parents who score high on warmth and low on negative kinds of control, similar to the associations between temperamental negative reactivity and parenting. The findings do not show, however, how the child and parent traits come to be associated. Next, we consider studies with design features that shed more light on the development of temperament–parenting links.

Directional Studies

In this section, we discuss longitudinal studies testing how children's temperament and parenting might influence one another.

Child Positive Reactivity and Parenting

Child Positive Reactivity Predicting Parenting

Very few longitudinal studies have tested whether child positivity elicits parental warmth, and their results are mixed. In one study, infants' joyfulness predicted neither subsequent parent–child shared positive affect nor maternal responsiveness (Kochanska et al., 2004). In contrast, Lengua and Kovacs (2005) found that during middle childhood, positive emotionality predicted more subsequent maternal acceptance, controlling for earlier acceptance. Thus, although both the assumption of reciprocity and child effects research (Bates, 1976) suggest that child positivity could elicit parental warmth, there is very little evidence on this issue. We have not seen any longitudinal studies examining the influence of child positivity on parental control.

Parenting Predicting Child Positive Reactivity

Two longitudinal studies show links between parental warmth and positive temperamental reactivity. Belsky, Fish, and Isabella (1991) found that greater parental involvement predicted increases in infants' positive reactivity, controlling for prior levels of positive reactivity. Halverson and Deal (2001) found that positive parenting predicted children's temperamental persistence, even after autoregressive controls. We place this study here, even though Halverson and Deal's persistence measure may involve self-regulation, because most of their persistence items refer to approach-type, assertive behaviors, such as mastering a physical skill, which relates to positive reactivity. These findings may suggest part of the mechanism that accounts for twin studies' findings of relatively strong shared environmental components in children's positive affectivity (Goldsmith et al., 1997). Shared environmental factors are those that make siblings more similar to one another. Thus, it may be that children of parents who have high levels of positive parenting are more similar to one another in (high levels of) positive affect. On the other hand, we did not find studies examining parental control as a predictor of positive temperamental reactivity.

Child Negative Reactivity and Parenting

Child Negative Reactivity Predicting Parenting

NEGATIVE REACTIVITY/DIFFICULTNESS

Several longitudinal studies have examined the association between children's general negative reactivity and parental warmth. For example, as noted earlier, Owens and colleagues (1998) did not find longitudinal associations between toddlers' difficultness and maternal responsiveness, although they did find a concurrent association. Gauvain and Fagot (1995) found that toddlers' difficultness was associated with not only more subsequent maternal problem-solving assistance but also less subsequent maternal encouragement and approval, and more disapproval; however, autoregressive controls were not used. Similarly, Boivin and colleagues (2005) found that maternal hostile-reactive parenting was partly due to infants' genetically influenced difficultness. In a further complexity, Frankel and Bates (1990) found that male infants' difficultness was associated with less discordant subsequent mother–child interactions, but female infants' difficultness was associated with more discordant subsequent interactions. Negative emotionality was also linked with more subsequent maternal sensitive responsiveness in a study by Paulussen-Hoogeboom, Stams, Hermanns, and Peetsma (2008). However, neither Frankel and Bates (1990) nor Paulussen-Hoogeboom and colleagues used autoregressive controls for earlier parenting. At this point, we would characterize the evidence for child negative reactivity upon parental warmth as quite mixed. Although negative reactivity appears to predict subsequent parental warmth, the valence of that relationship is consistent across neither studies nor child gender.

There also is some evidence that negative reactivity might elicit more parental control.

A longitudinal study found that difficultness during the first 2 years of life was associated with more maternal reactive control and mother–child conflict at age 2 (Lee & Bates, 1985). In Gauvain and Fagot's (1995) study, mentioned earlier, difficult temperament in toddlerhood was subsequently associated with more maternal directives. Neither of these studies used autoregressive controls for earlier parenting. However, two studies of middle childhood, which did control for earlier discipline, found that temperamental irritability predicted increases in inconsistent discipline (Lengua, 2006; Lengua & Kovacs, 2005). As with evidence of negative reactivity predicting parental warmth, negative reactivity may predict parental control, but the evidence is thin so far.

FEAR AND INHIBITION

Several longitudinal studies have examined associations between children's fear/inhibition and parental warmth. As noted earlier, although Kochanska and colleagues (2004) found concurrent associations in infancy and early childhood between fear/inhibition and more parental warmth, they did not find longitudinal associations, even without controls for earlier warmth. Interestingly, as with difficultness, male infants' inhibition has been linked with less discordant subsequent mother–child interactions, but female infants' inhibition has been linked with more discordant subsequent interactions (Frankel & Bates, 1990); however, autoregressive controls were not used. Fearfulness in middle childhood in one study predicted more subsequent maternal acceptance (Lengua & Kovacs, 2005), and in another also predicted decreases in maternal rejection, the inverse of warmth (Lengua, 2006), with both studies controlling for earlier parenting. Thus, several studies suggest that children's fearful traits function to increase maternal warmth.

In addition, one study examined the longitudinal association between child fearfulness and parental control. Fearfulness in middle childhood predicted decreases in inconsistent discipline, even after statistical controls for earlier discipline (Lengua, 2006). It is interesting that fearfulness, a child trait that could be a negative indicator, actually has predicted increased parental warmth and decreased inconsistency in control. This may be related to a tendency of fearful children to show less growth in externalizing problems (Keiley, Lofthouse, Bates, Dodge, & Pettit, 2003), but more replications are needed before detailed interpretation is indicated.

FRUSTRATION AND ANGER

Although Kochanska and colleagues (2004) found that infant anger predicted less parental warmth concurrently, as described earlier, their longitudinal tests were nonsignificant. Thus, there is little to suggest that children's anger elicits less warm parenting. We know of no longitudinal studies of associations between frustration or anger and parental control.

Parenting Predicting Child Negative Reactivity

NEGATIVE REACTIVITY/DIFFICULTNESS

A number of studies show longitudinal links between parenting and child negative reactivity. One of the stronger findings is that caregivers who score high in sensitivity/responsivity have children who end up scoring lower in negative reactivity, even with controls for initial levels of temperament (Belsky et al., 1991; Braungart-Rieker, Hill-Soderlund, & Karrass, 2010; Engfer, 1986; Pauli-Pott, Mertesacker, & Beckmann, 2004).

In addition to these findings for parental warmth, one study examined a measure of parental control as a predictor of child negative emotionality. In that study, parental punitive reactions, a form of harsh control, predicted higher levels of negative emotionality, even with controls for earlier negative emotionality (Eisenberg et al., 1999).

FEAR AND INHIBITION

Low levels of parental sensitivity/responsivity predict child fearfulness, with controls for prior levels of fearfulness (Braungart-Rieker et al., 2010; Pauli-Pott et al., 2004). This may be due to insecure attachment because parental sensitivity has also been associated with infant attachment security (De Wolff & van IJzendoorn, 1997).

FRUSTRATION AND ANGER

We failed to identify studies examining the longitudinal effects of parenting on child frustration or anger. We would expect future research to show that parental warmth or control influences children's frustration and anger.

Comparison of Parenting's Influence on Positive and Negative Reactivity

Studies that control for genetic similarities between parents and children tend to show stronger shared environmental influences on child positive reactivity than on negative reactivity (Goldsmith et al., 1997, 1999; Plomin et al., 1993). Studies that do not control for genetic effects, however, tend to show more evidence of associations between parenting and child negative reactivity than between parenting and positive reactivity. For example, Belsky and colleagues (1991) found that several aspects of parenting predicted increases in child positive reactivity over time when controlling for prior levels of positive reactivity, but they also noted that parenting factors were much more predictive of the development of negative, rather than positive, reactivity. Other studies including autoregressive controls have found that parenting predicts the development of child negative, but not positive, reactivity (Lengua & Kovacs, 2005; Pauli-Pott et al., 2004). Although the behavioral genetic studies' finding that positive reactivity has more shared environmental contributions than negative reactivity may seem to contradict behavioral studies' finding that negative reactivity may be more influenced by parenting than positive reactivity, they are not necessarily inconsistent. Behavior genetic studies do show that *nonshared environment*, which refers to factors that make siblings different from one another, accounts for some variance in negative emotionality. Nonshared environment could include how one sibling is parented differently than the other. In addition, nonshared environment also explains some of the change in both negative and positive reactivity traits across development (Ganiban et al., 2008; Saudino, 2005; Takahashi et al., 2007). Although it is notable that parenting can influence change in negative reactivity, and that shared family factors can make siblings similar in positive reactivity, further research is needed to chart the more fine-grained developmental processes underlying these findings.

Child Self-Regulation and Parenting

Child Self-Regulation Predicting Parenting

The standard view is that warm and supportive, but firm, parenting produces a self-regulated child (Baumrind, 1991). Even so, as suggested by Bell (1968), children's self-regulation could also influence parenting. Among the few studies that have examined infants' or young children's self-regulation as a predictor of parenting warmth, Popp and colleagues (2008) found that toddlers' self-regulation was linked with more subsequent maternal responsiveness, but not when controls for initial maternal responsiveness were added. In addition, in another study in early childhood, researchers found that higher child vagal tone, indexing higher regulation by the parasympathetic system, predicted more subsequent maternal supportive parenting, controlling for earlier supportive parenting (Kennedy, Rubin, Hastings, & Maisel, 2004). This suggests that better self-regulation elicits more supportive parenting.

In studies of older children, two studies examined associations between early adolescents' attention problems, which are likely related to deficiencies in self-regulation traits, and subsequent parenting. Even with statistical controls for initial parenting, attention problems predicted more subsequent mother–child (but not father–child) rejection (Lifford, Harold, & Thapar, 2008), and boys' (but not girls') attention problems predicted more subsequent mother–son (but not father–son) hostility (Lifford, Harold, & Thapar, 2009). Similarly, effortful control in late childhood and early adolescence predicted decreases in maternal rejection (Lengua, 2006), and adolescents' conscientiousness—a core personality trait linked to temperamental effortful control—predicted increases in paternal support (Asendorpf & van Aken, 2003). All four of these studies included controls for earlier parenting. Thus, the overall pattern of findings from these studies provides converging evidence that children's self-regulatory deficits produce less warm, supportive, and accepting parenting.

Several studies have found associations between self-regulatory difficulties and higher levels of parental control. For example, one study found longitudinal associations between children's self-regulation and less negative parental control (less over-reactivity, laxness, and verbosity), but the study did not include controls for earlier parenting (Bridgett et al., 2009). However, Kennedy and colleagues (2004) found that lower vagal tone, a marker of less effective self-regulation, in early childhood predicted more maternal restrictive parenting, controlling for earlier parenting. Further, restrictive parenting was stable over the observation period only for mothers of children with lower vagal tone. Studies using a variety of methods and examining a variety of child ages consistently suggest that child self-regulatory deficits elicit more negative parental control, especially in parents most at risk for such parenting.

Evidence for Parenting Predicting Child Self-Regulation

Research suggests that parenting can influence children's self-regulation. Parental warmth has been implicated in various outcomes involving behavioral regulation. For example, in a study that included autoregressive controls, maternal responsiveness predicted more child effortful control (Kochanska, Murray, & Harlan, 2000). Bernier and colleagues (2010) found that maternal sensitivity and autonomy support predicted children's later executive functioning, but they did not include autoregressive controls.

Ineffectual parental control has also been associated with child deficits in behavioral regulation. In the most relevant example, Eisenberg and colleagues (1999) found that parents' punitive reactions predicted poorer behavioral regulation, controlling for prior regulation.

Summary

Temperament Influences on Parenting

A few studies provide evidence that child positive reactivity might predict more parental warmth. Fewer studies have tested associations between positive reactivity and parental control, and these cross-sectional studies offer little evidence that child positive reactivity is directly linked with parental control. Findings on associations between child general negative reactivity and parenting warmth are complex and somewhat inconsistent. This could reflect developmental stages of sampled children (Crockenberg, 1986). It could also reflect differences between studies in how general negative emotionality or difficultness was measured (Bates, 1989). In contrast, there is more consistent evidence that fearfulness elicits more warmth. A few studies also suggest that negative reactivity may be linked with higher levels of parental control, whereas fearfulness is linked with less inconsistent parenting. We note that few studies have tested associations between negative reactivity and parenting during adolescence. Studies more consistently suggest that child self-regulation predicts parental warmth and positive forms of control. Longitudinal studies represent considerable progress in description of developmental processes involving temperament.

Parenting Influences on Temperament

Findings on parental influences on children's reactivity and regulation support the model that temperament, despite being biologically based and relatively stable, is shaped by environmental factors, including parenting. Specifically, parental warmth and positive control tend to be associated with children's more positive emotionality, less negative emotionality, and better self-regulation. In addition, parental warmth predicts less child fearfulness. These interpretations are tentative, however, because most relevant studies fail to control for prior levels and to test whether associations owe to parent or child effects. More studies with cross-lag, longitudinal designs would advance understanding of the unfolding development of temperament. In addition, more studies on intermediary processes will aid understanding of the mechanisms by which temperament affects parenting and parenting affects temperament.

Temperament × Parenting Interactions in Development

In the first two sections of this chapter we have described findings of linear relationships between temperament and parenting. Here we consider evidence that they interactively combine with one another in shaping social development. It is increasingly well established that temperament variables predict social functioning in developmentally important settings, even longitudinally (Bates, 1989; Kagan & Fox, 2006; Rothbart & Bates, 1998, 2006). Findings tend to converge in showing a differential linkage pattern (Bates, 1989), with general negative emotionality predicting both externalizing and internalizing behavior problems, fearful temperament predicting internalizing problems more than externalizing, and temperamental self-regulation deficits predicting externalizing more than internalizing problems (Janson & Mathiesen, 2008; Rothbart & Bates, 2006; Saudino, 2005; Zhou et al., 2009). These findings tend to converge across studies covering various age spans, using various parent- and teacher-report measures, and even observational measures of temperament. Such linkages partially reflect common genetic bases for both temperament and adjustment (Saudino, 2005). And, of course, it is well known that parenting helps explain development of child social outcomes (Rothbaum & Weisz, 1994).

Nevertheless, temperament and parenting account for only moderate portions of the variance in children's adjustment outcomes, even when they are additively combined (Deater-Deckard, Dodge, Bates, & Pettit, 1998). A particularly interesting type of additive model would be would be of temperament effects on adjustment outcomes as mediated by parenting or the reverse. Such models would show, for example, that some of temperament's effects on adjustment are explained by temperament's effects on parenting, which in turn explain adjustment. However, there have been too few reports of such mediation models to require a review at this point. Another kind of model involves nonlinear interactions between temperament and parenting in predicting child adjustment. Numbers of studies reporting temperament × parenting interactions as predictors of child adjustment have grown increasingly in recent years. Here we summarize recent reviews of the temperament × parenting literature and mention newer studies. We consider the same dimensions of temperament and parenting as in the previous sections. Some studies choose to describe interaction effects in terms of the moderating effects of parenting, and others in terms of the moderating effects of child temperament. Although these different descriptive approaches can provide different answers, in general, they should be highly complementary, so we intermix findings from the different perspectives.

Positive Reactivity × Parenting → Adjustment

We have seen few reports of child positive reactivity interacting with parenting. In one study, children who scored lower on positive emotionality were more likely to show both depression and conduct problems in conjunction with maternal rejection, but more positive children were buffered against the effects of maternal rejection (Lengua, Wolchik, Sandler, & West, 2000). A more recent study supports this pattern. Lahey and colleagues (2008) found that the prediction from spanking and restriction in infancy to childhood conduct problems was weak among infants scoring high in positive affect compared to low positive affect infants.

Negative Reactivity × Parenting → Adjustment

Many studies report child negative reactivity interactions with parenting. We have subdivided this section into studies concerning fearful, frustrated, and general negative emotionality variables.

General Negative Emotional Reactivity

As noted earlier, studies often use an overall adverse or "difficult" temperament measure that typically combines several theoretically separable dimensions, including fearful and frustrated reactivity, as well as general irritability and emotional dysregulation. This is especially so when the temperament is assessed in infancy and via parental report. All studies in this section used parent reports of temperament, but one (Belsky, Hsieh, & Crnic, 1998) defined negative reactivity with both parent report and behavior observed in the laboratory. Bates and Pettit (2007) concluded in their review that child negative emotionality has tended to amplify the harmful effects of negative parenting upon child adjustment outcomes, or conversely, negative parenting has amplified the effects of negative child temperament. A key early example is the finding by Belsky and colleagues (1998) that parents' intrusive control with toddlers predicted child externalizing behavior at age 3, but more for toddlers who scored high in negative reactivity than for those who scored low. Three recent papers report temperament × parenting interactions found in the National Institute of Child Health and Human Development (NICHD) child care study: Stright, Gallagher, and Kelley (2008) found that children's positive school adjustment in the first grade was predicted by mothers' sensitive, warm, and autonomy-supportive parenting, especially for children scoring high on adverse temperament at age 6 months. Bradley and Corwyn (2008) found a similar pattern with externalizing in first grade, using a difficultness composite from 1 and 6 months. They also found that harsh parenting predicted externalizing problems at school only for children scoring high on difficultness, and that mother productive activity (educational stimulation) predicted lower levels of externalizing for more difficult children. Pluess and Belsky (2010) found that lower levels of parenting quality were associated with lower academic and social adjustment across preschool to sixth grade but to a greater degree for children scoring high on temperamental negativity. For the academic skills measures, at high levels of parenting quality, temperament made no difference. However, for social skills, difficult children with high-quality parenting actually scored slightly higher than easygoing children, and those with low-quality parenting scored lower. Two additional studies provide similar findings. Mesman and colleagues (2009) found that maternal sensitivity predicted less growth of mother-reported externalizing problems from Time 1 (2–3 years of age) to Time 2 (3–4 years) only for children who scored high in adverse temperament. van Aken, Junger, Verhoeven, van Aken, and Deković (2007) similarly found that low levels of maternal warm, sensitive control, and high levels of hostile, intrusive control predicted increases in mother-reported externalizing behavior from 17 to 23 months only for difficult/dysregulated boys. One study found an effect opposite to the dominant pattern: Lahey and colleagues (2008) found that maternal spanking and restrictiveness, assessed in infancy, predicted conduct problems at ages 4–13 years more weakly for infants rated by their mothers as high in negative emotionality than for those low in negative emotionality. Perhaps this anomalous finding pertains to the relatively young age at which parenting was measured.

Fearful Reactivity

The Bates and Pettit (2007) review mentioned about 10 studies suggesting that the implications of fearful versus fearless traits depend on qualities of parenting, with a few patterns converging across studies. The most important of the patterns concerns high-fear toddlers developing signs of conscience better when their mothers are gentle than when their mothers are harsh in their control, and low-fear toddlers developing signs of conscience better when they have an emotionally positive relationship with their mothers than when they do not have such a relationship. The key early study showing this pattern was that by Kochanska (1995). This pattern was essentially replicated in two studies of toddlers by Kochanska, Aksan, and Joy (2007). In addition, Lahey and colleagues (2008) found that infants seen by their mothers as low in fear showed fewer conduct problems (mother-report) at ages 4–13 years if as infants they had mothers who were high in responsiveness. Furthermore, Lengua (2008) found that boys who were highly anxious in a laboratory game reported increased externalizing problems when they described their mothers as high in physical punishment. A second, highly intriguing pattern concerns high-fear children developing lower levels of internalizing behavior when their parents allow them to experience more rather than less frustration. Arcus (2001) found that infants who were negatively reactive in a laboratory situation, attributable to an early form of fearfulness, were less likely to show behavioral inhibition at age 14 months if their mothers were observed to be high in limit setting. Two studies provide additional support for this pattern. Lengua found that anxious 8- to 12-year-old boys who reported inconsistent parental discipline showed a decrease in self-reported internalizing problems over the next year. This can be construed as supporting the pattern because inconsistent parenting would produce frustration. Williams and colleagues (2009) found that for toddlers who were behaviorally inhibited, permissive parenting (inconsistent and ineffectual) predicted a high level of internalizing at age 4, whereas the parenting did not matter much for the low-inhibited children. Finally, we mention an interesting, qualitatively different moderator effect: Cornell and Frick (2007) found that relatively fearless preschoolers showed more advanced levels of guilt and empathy when they received more authoritarian and more consistent discipline, whereas parenting made little difference for the ratings of guilt of highly inhibited children. Low inhibition in this study may partly index a lack of self-regulation, in which case the finding would resemble a pattern we describe in the subsequent section on interactive effects of self-regulation.

Frustrated Reactivity

Theoretically, frustrated reactivity is quite different from fearful reactivity. It is often embedded in measures of general negative reactivity, but few studies have evaluated its effects separately. Two studies represent a promising interaction pattern. Degnan, Calkins, Keane, and Hill-Soderlund (2008) found that high-frustration toddlers whose mothers displayed overcontrol tended to show a high trajectory of mother-reported aggression across ages 2 to 5. Lengua (2008) found that parenting differences mattered more for children's adjustment when the children scored high in frustration. When mothers were seen by their children as inconsistent in discipline, low-frustration children showed decreased internalizing problems over a 1-year period, but high-frustration children showed increased internalizing problems. When mothers were seen as rejecting, high-frustration children increased in externalizing problems, but low-frustration children did not. In contrast, when mothers were seen as high in physical punishment, low-frustration boys showed increased externalizing problems, but high-frustration boys showed decreased externalizing problems.

Self-Regulation × Parenting → Adjustment

Our previous review (Bates & Pettit, 2007) highlighted a pattern in which high levels of negative parenting (e.g., harsh discipline) or low levels of positive parenting (e.g., warmth or effective control) were associated with adjustment problems, especially for children who scored low in temperamental manageability or self-regulation. This pattern was supported to a comparatively substantial degree. A key example is the study by Rubin, Burgess, Dwyer, and Hastings (2003), following children from ages 2–4. Subsequent studies have continued to support this pattern. King and Chassin (2004) found that teens' self-reported impulsivity at age 15 predicted more self-reported drug problems at age 20, especially for teens who described their parents as unsupportive. Interestingly, the King and Chassin study found that the moderator effect did not apply at extremely high levels of impulsivity. Lengua (2008) found that child-rated inconsistent parental discipline predicted increased externalizing behavior 1 year later for children scoring low in executive functioning.

The pattern in which parenting matters more for poorly regulated children than it does for well-regulated children does not preclude other patterns. Lengua (2008), for example, also found that child perceptions of parental physical punishment predicted no decrease in child externalizing behavior for children low in effortful control, but it did predict a decrease in the externalizing behavior of children high in effortful control. Thus, children with better effortful control showed bigger reductions in their externalizing behavior over 1 year in response to perceived punishment. This finding comes from a sample that represents an urban community in the United States, with a broad range of incomes and ethnic/racial minorities. A rather different interaction effect is reported by de Haan, Prinzie, and Dekovic (2010) in a broadly representative sample of families followed in Flanders, involving child conscientiousness as a marker of effortful control. Here, mothers who described themselves as unlikely to criticize and yell saw greater decreases in child aggression than mothers who described themselves as likely to criticize and yell, but only if the child scored high on the trait of conscientiousness. In a perhaps related vein, Degnan and colleagues (2008) used a physiological index of self-regulation—vagal suppression in response to a frustrating situation at age 2, that is, a measure of decreased vagal influence in response to challenge. Mothers who showed less harsh and more child-focused parenting less often saw their children on a subsequently high trajectory of disruptive behavior, if their children were high in vagal suppression. This parenting variable did not matter much for children with low vagal suppression. Similarly, Obradovic, Bush, Stamperdahl, Adler, and Boyce (2010) found that the behavioral and academic development of children with low vagal responsiveness was less sensitive to levels of parent-reported family adversity (which includes harsh and restrictive parenting) than that of children high in vagal suppression. Those with high vagal suppression in response to a laboratory challenge and low family adversity showed better baseline adjustment on parent-, teacher-, and child-report measures in the Fall of kindergarten, and increased growth in academic competence across the kindergarten year compared to children with high family adversity.

Across studies, findings suggest that there may be a pattern in which the social development of children with traits of lower behavioral self-regulation proceeds notably better in families with parental warmth and effective control than in families with low levels of warmth and effective control, and that for such children, parenting matters more than it does for children with higher self-regulation. This is still not sufficiently established, but it has become a solid hypothesis. There is also a trend for a similar effect for parenting to matter more for children high in vagal suppression in response to challenge.

Summary of Temperament × Parenting → Adjustment

The emerging literature on temperament × parenting interactions continues the trend of accelerating numbers of relevant findings. The pattern of more fearful children showing fewer externalizing behaviors when they receive gentle discipline, and for relatively fearless children to do this when they have a responsive, enjoyable relationship with their parent, continues to receive support. This fits the theoretical notion of two pathways to socialization, one based on optimal and not excessive amounts of fear of negative consequences for misbehavior, and the other based on desire to maintain a positive relationship (Kochanska, 1997). The pattern of fearful children developing fewer internalizing behaviors when they receive more demanding parenting has received only a bit of further support, and some challenges. Some recent studies suggest that easily frustrated children may be more sensitive to negative parenting in terms of developing behavior problems than less easily frustrated children. A few recent studies also suggest that children who score high on general negative emotionality develop higher levels of behavior problems in response to negative parenting, more so than children who score low on negative emotionality. At the same time, studies suggest that children who score high on negative emotionality might be likely to develop positive adjustment in response to positive parenting, more so than less negatively emotional children. We reiterate a previously noted pattern (Bates, Pettit, Dodge, & Ridge, 1998) in which children with lower levels of self-regulation develop better adjustment if they receive positive or effective parenting, whereas the absence of such parenting does not matter as much for children with higher self-regulation. And finally, another pattern may also be emerging, in which children with higher self-regulation may actually develop better adjustment in response to higher levels of negative parenting, whereas this matters less for poorly self-regulated children.

Conclusion

This chapter has considered how children's temperament relates to their experiences with parenting. Temperament characteristics are biologically rooted and relatively stable, so one might think of temperament as fundamentally independent of environmental pressures. Nevertheless, temperament, at least as it is measured, could actually be part of a transactional, developmental process with the environment, especially the parenting environment. Our review provides numerous examples that support this possibility, at least in a loose way. Studies show that child temperament predicts parental warmth and control. These studies have used a variety of operational definitions of temperament and parenting, including both self- or parent-report and observational measures, which increase our confidence that child temperament does have effects upon parenting. However, only a few of these studies show temperament predicting parenting at a later time even after statistically controlling for parenting at the initial time. Thus, we need more longitudinal data, modeled in ways that allow inferences about direction of effects. Controls for initial levels of parenting may be difficult in eras of development in which children's needs from parents change rapidly (e.g., infancy to toddlerhood or toddlerhood to the preschool era). However, it is probably possible to develop some additional parenting measures with cross-age validity. We also found studies showing that parenting variables predict child temperament variables. As with the studies of temperament influences upon parenting, parenting → temperament studies used various measures of parenting and temperament, but again, only some of them used longitudinal models controlling for initial levels of temperament. More such evidence is needed for confident conclusions. Also on our wish list for future research is more systematic coverage of the developmental spectrum. Adolescence has been least well considered, and we are not aware of any studies comparing the effects of temperament or parenting at multiple stages of development. In addition, if longitudinal, replicated transactional effects are found, it will be important to measure the more basic processes that mediate the correlations, such as genes, child or parent learning, active parental campaigns (Goodnight, Bates, Pettit, & Dodge, 2008), and dynamic cascades (Dodge et al., 2009). It will also be valuable to have a taxonomy of parenting dimensions that allows confident comparisons of the many different ways we measure temperament.

Finally, we also have considered recent studies that show how child temperament and parenting interact in predicting child social adjustment. Ultimately, replicated patterns of temperament × parenting interaction could specify how children with a given temperament may profit from different types of parenting, and conversely, how a given kind of parenting may have different implications for temperamentally different children. Such patterns are beginning to emerge. However, many gaps remain in the literature. In addition to the general need for further and more explicit replications of longitudinal studies, another need, as with the main effects of temperament or parenting, is for more evaluation of the influence of developmental stage. In a useful example of the work that is needed, Kochanska and colleagues (2007) suggested that interactions involving parental gentle control and child fearfulness may affect social development only when they occur in the first few years of life. Ultimately it is important to understand the developmental processes through which the temperament × parenting interactions influence child adjustment. We think it most likely that temperament could affect social learning processes (Patterson, Reid, & Dishion, 1992), perhaps through how the child perceives parent behaviors (e.g., whether parent social punishments or rewards are more salient; Goodnight et al., 2008) and the extent to which they motivate the child's social learning. Other processes, however, are also possible. We are eager to see future findings and theoretical developments on temperament–parenting transactions and interactions in shaping social development.

Further Reading

Caspi, A., & Shiner, R. L. (2006). Personality development. In W. Damon & R. Lerner (Series Eds.) & N. Eisenberg (Vol. Ed.), *Handbook of child psychology: Vol. 3. Social, emotional, and personality development* (6th ed., pp. 300–365). New York: Wiley.

Propper, C., & Moore, G. A. (2006). The influence of parenting on infant emotionality: A multilevel psychobiological perspective. *Developmental Review, 26,* 427–460.

Rothbart, M. K. (2011). *Becoming who we are: Temperament and personality in development.* New York: Guilford Press.

References

Arcus, D. (2001). Inhibited and uninhibited children: Biology in the social context. In T. D. Wachs & G. A. Kohnstamm (Eds.), *Temperament in context* (pp. 2043–2060). Mahwah, NJ: Erlbaum.

Asendorpf, J. B., & van Aken, M. A. G. (2003).

Personality–relationship transaction in adolescence: Core versus surface personality characteristics. *Journal of Personality, 71,* 629–666.
Barber, B. K., Stolz, H. E., & Olsen, J. A. (2005). Parental support, psychological control, and behavioral control: Assessing relevance across time, culture, and method. *Monographs of the Society for Research in Child Development, 70,* 1–147.
Bates, J. E. (1976). Effects of children's nonverbal behavior upon adults. *Child Development, 47,* 1079–1088.
Bates, J. E. (1989). Applications of temperament concepts. In G. A. Kohnstamm, J. E. Bates, & M. K. Rothbart (Eds.), *Temperament in childhood* (pp. 322–355). Chichester, UK: Wiley.
Bates, J. E., & Bayles, K. (1984). Objective and subjective components in mothers' perceptions of their children from age 6 months to 3 years. *Merrill–Palmer Quarterly, 30,* 111–130.
Bates, J. E., Olson, S. L., Pettit, G. S., & Bayles, K. (1982). Dimensions of individuality in the mother–infant relationship at six months of age. *Child Development, 53,* 446–461.
Bates, J. E., & Pettit, G. S. (2007). Temperament, parenting, and socialization. In J. E. Grusec & P. D. Hastings (Eds.), *Handbook of socialization: Theory and research* (pp. 153–177). New York: Guilford Press.
Bates, J. E., Pettit, G. S., Dodge, K. A., & Ridge, B. (1998). Interaction of temperamental resistance to control and restrictive parenting in the development of externalizing behavior. *Developmental Psychology, 34,* 982–995.
Bates, J. E., Schermerhorn, A. C., & Goodnight, J. A. (2010). Temperament and personality through the lifespan. In M. E. Lamb & A. Freund (Eds.), *Handbook of lifespan development* (pp. 208–253). Hoboken, NJ: Wiley.
Baumrind, D. (1991). The influence of parenting styles on adolescent competence and substance use. *Journal of Early Adolescence, 11,* 56–95.
Bell, R. Q. (1968). A reinterpretation of the direction of effects in studies of socialization. *Psychological Review, 75,* 81–95.
Belsky, J., Fish, M., & Isabella, R. A. (1991). Continuity and discontinuity in infant negative and positive emotionality: Family antecedents and attachment consequences. *Developmental Psychology, 27,* 421–431.
Belsky, J., Hsieh, K.-H., & Crnic, K. (1998). Mothering, fathering, and infant negativity as antecedents of boys' externalizing problems and inhibition at age 3 years: Differential susceptibility to rearing experience? *Development and Psychopathology, 10,* 301–319.
Bernier, A., Carlson, S. M., & Whipple, N. (2010). From external regulation to self-regulation: Early parenting precursors of young children's executive functioning. *Child Development, 81,* 326–339.

Boivin, M., Perusse, D., Dionne, G., Saysset, V., Zoccolillo, M., Tarabulsy, G. M., et al. (2005). The genetic–environmental etiology of parents' perceptions and self-assessed behaviours toward their 5-month-old infants in a large twin and singleton sample. *Journal of Child Psychology and Psychiatry, 46,* 612–630.
Bradley, R. H., & Corwyn, R. F. (2008). Infant temperament, parenting, and externalizing behavior in first grade: A test of the differential susceptibility hypothesis. *Journal of Child Psychology and Psychiatry, 49,* 124–131.
Braungart-Rieker, J. M., Hill-Soderlund, A. L., & Karrass, J. (2010). Fear and anger reactivity trajectories from 4 to 16 months: The roles of temperament, regulation, and maternal sensitivity. *Developmental Psychology, 46,* 791–804.
Bridgett, D. J., Gartstein, M. A., Putnam, S. P., McKay, T., Iddins, E., Robertson, C., et al. (2009). Maternal and contextual influences and the effect of temperament development during infancy on parenting in toddlerhood. *Infant Behavior and Development, 32,* 103–116.
Bugental, D. B., & Grusec, J. E. (2006). Socialization processes. In N. Eisenberg, W. Damon, & R. M. Lerner (Eds.), *Handbook of child psychology: Vol. 3, Social, emotional, and personality development* (6th ed., pp. 366–428). Hoboken, NJ: Wiley.
Collins, W. A., Maccoby, E. E., Steinberg, L., Hetherington, E. M., & Bornstein, M. H. (2000). Contemporary research on parenting: The case for nature and nurture. *American Psychologist, 55,* 218–232.
Coplan, R. J., Reichel, M., & Rowan, K. (2009). Exploring the associations between maternal personality, child temperament, and parenting: A focus on emotions. *Personality and Individual Differences, 46,* 241–246.
Cornell, A. H., & Frick, P. J. (2007). The moderating effects of parenting styles in the association between behavioral inhibition and parent-reported guilt and empathy in preschool children. *Journal of Clinical Child and Adolescent Psychology, 36,* 305–318.
Crockenberg, S. (1986). Are temperamental differences in babies associated with predictable differences in care giving? *New Directions for Child Development, 31,* 53–73.
Deater-Deckard, K., Dodge, K. A., Bates, J. E., & Pettit, G. S. (1998). Multiple risk factors in the development of externalizing behavior problems: Group and individual differences. *Development and Psychopathology, 10,* 469–493.
Degnan, K. A., Calkins, S. D., Keane, S. P., & Hill-Soderlund, A. L. (2008). Profiles of disruptive behavior across early childhood: Contributions of frustration reactivity, physiological regulation, and maternal behavior. *Child Development, 79,* 1357–1376.
Degnan, K. A., & Fox, N. A. (2007). Behavioral

inhibition and anxiety disorders: Multiple levels of a resilience process. *Development and Psychopathology, 19,* 729–746.

de Haan, A. D., Prinzie, P., & Dekovic, M. (2010). How and why children change in aggression and delinquency from childhood to adolescence: Moderation of overreactive parenting by child personality. *Journal of Child Psychology and Psychiatry, 51,* 725–733.

Dennis, T. (2006). Emotional self-regulation in preschoolers: The interplay of child approach reactivity, parenting, and control capacities. *Developmental Psychology, 42,* 84–97.

De Wolff, M. S., & van IJzendoorn, M. H. (1997). Sensitivity and attachment: A meta-analysis on parental antecedents of infant attachment. *Child Development, 68*(4), 571–591.

Dodge, K. A., Malone, P. S., Lansford, J. E., Miller, S., Pettit, G. S., & Bates, J. E. (2009). A dynamic cascade model of the development of substance-use onset. *Monographs of the Society for Research in Child Development, 74,* 1–134.

Eisenberg, N., Fabes, R. A., Shepard, S. A., Guthrie, I. K., Murphy, B. C., & Reiser, M. (1999). Parental reactions to children's negative emotions: Longitudinal relations to quality of children's social functioning. *Child Development, 70,* 513–534.

Engfer, A. (1986). Antecedents of perceived behaviour problems in infancy. In G. A. Kohnstamm (Ed.), *Temperament discussed: Temperament and development in infancy and childhood* (pp. 165–180). Lisse: Swets & Zeitlinger.

Fox, G. (2006). Development in family contexts. In L. Combrinck-Graham (Ed.), *Children in family contexts: Perspectives on treatment* (pp. 26–50). New York: Guilford Press.

Frankel, K. A., & Bates, J. E. (1990). Mother–toddler problem solving: Antecedents in attachment, home behavior, and temperament. *Child Development, 61,* 810–819.

Ganiban, J. M., Saudino, K. J., Ulbricht, J., Neiderhiser, J. M., & Reiss, D. (2008). Stability and change in temperament during adolescence. *Journal of Personality and Social Psychology, 95,* 222–236.

Gauvain, M., & Fagot, B. (1995). Child temperament as a mediator of mother–toddler problem solving. *Social Development, 4,* 257–276.

Ge, X., Conger, R. D., Cadoret, R. J., Neiderhiser, J. M., Yates, W., Troughton, E., et al. (1996). The developmental interface between nature and nurture: A mutual influence model of child antisocial behavior and parent behaviors. *Developmental Psychology, 32,* 574–589.

Glaser, D. (2000). Child abuse and neglect and the brain—a review. *Journal of Child Psychology and Psychiatry, 41,* 97–116.

Goldsmith, H. H., Buss, K. A., & Lemery, K. S. (1997). Toddler and childhood temperament: Expanded content, stronger genetic evidence, new evidence for the importance of environment. *Developmental Psychology, 33,* 891–905.

Goldsmith, H. H., Lemery, K. S., Buss, K. A., & Campos, J. J. (1999). Genetic analyses of focal aspects of infant temperament. *Developmental Psychology, 35,* 972–985.

Goodnight, J. A., Bates, J. E., Pettit, G. S., & Dodge, K. A. (2008). Parents' campaigns to reduce their children's conduct problems: Interactions with temperamental resistance to control. *European Journal of Developmental Science, 2,* 100–119.

Grusec, J. E., & Hastings, P. D. (Eds.). (2007). *Handbook of socialization: Theory and research.* New York: Guilford Press.

Gunnar, M. R., & Donzella, B. (2002). Social regulation of the cortisol levels in early human development [Special issue]. *Psychoneuroendocrinology, 27,* 199–220.

Halverson, C. F., & Deal, J. E. (2001). Temperamental change, parenting, and the family context. In T. D. Wachs & G. A. Kohnstamm (Eds.), *Temperament in context* (pp. 61–79). Mahwah, NJ: Erlbaum.

Hawes, D. J., & Dadds, M. R. (2006). Assessing parenting practices through parent-report and direct observation during parent-training. *Journal of Child and Family Studies, 15,* 555–568.

Henderson, H. A., & Wachs, T. D. (2007). Temperament theory and the study of cognition–emotion interactions across development. *Developmental Review, 27,* 396–427.

Janson, H., & Mathiesen, K. S. (2008). Temperament profiles from infancy to middle childhood: Development and associations with behavior problems. *Developmental Psychology, 44*(5), 1314–1328.

Kagan, J., & Fox, N. A. (2006). Biology, culture, and temperamental biases. In N. Eisenberg, W. Damon, & R. M. Lerner (Eds.), *Handbook of child psychology: Vol. 3. Social, emotional, and personality development* (6th ed., pp. 167–225). Hoboken, NJ: Wiley.

Karreman, A., van Tuijl, C., van Aken, M. A. G., & Dekovic, M. (2006). Parenting and self-regulation in preschoolers: A meta-analysis. *Infant and Child Development, 15,* 561–579.

Karreman, A., van Tuijl, C., van Aken, M. A. G., & Dekovic, M. (2008). The relation between parental personality and observed parenting: The moderating role of preschoolers' effortful control. *Personality and Individual Differences, 44,* 723–734.

Keiley, M. K., Lofthouse, N., Bates, J. E., Dodge, K. A., & Pettit, G. S. (2003). Differential risks of covarying and pure components in mother and teacher reports of externalizing and internalizing behavior across ages 5 to 14. *Journal of Abnormal Child Psychology, 31,* 267–283.

Kennedy, A. E., Rubin, K. H., Hastings, P. D., & Maisel, B. (2004). Longitudinal relations between child vagal tone and parenting behavior: 2 to 4 years. *Developmental Psychobiology, 45,* 10–21.

Kertes, D. A., Donzella, B., Talge, N. M., Garvin, M. C., Van Ryzin, M. J., & Gunnar, M. R. (2009). Inhibited temperament and parent emotional availability differentially predict young children's cortisol responses to novel social and nonsocial events. *Developmental Psychobiology, 51,* 521–532.

King, K. M., & Chassin, L. (2004). Mediating and moderated effects of adolescent behavioral undercontrol and parenting in the prediction of drug use disorders in emerging adulthood. *Psychology of Addictive Behaviors, 18,* 239–249.

Kochanska, G. (1995). Children's temperament, mother's discipline, and security of attachment: Multiple pathways to emerging internalization. *Child Development, 66,* 597–615.

Kochanska, G. (1997). Multiple pathways to conscience for children with different temperaments: From toddlerhood to age 5. *Developmental Psychology, 33,* 228–240.

Kochanska, G., Aksan, N., & Joy, M. E. (2007). Children's fearfulness as a moderator of parenting in early socialization: Two longitudinal studies. *Developmental Psychology, 43,* 222–237.

Kochanska, G., Friesenborg, A. E., Lange, L. A., & Martel, M. M. (2004). Parents' personality and infants' temperament as contributors to their emerging relationship. *Journal of Personality and Social Psychology, 86,* 744–759.

Kochanska, G., Murray, K. T., & Harlan, E. T. (2000). Effortful control in early childhood: Continuity and change, antecedents, and implications for social development. *Developmental Psychology, 36,* 220–232.

Kopp, C. B. (1982). Antecedents of self-regulation: A developmental perspective. *Developmental Psychology, 18,* 199–214.

Lahey, B. B., Van Hulle, C. A., Keenan, K., Rathouz, P. J., D'Onofrio, B. M., Rodgers, J. L., et al. (2008). Temperament and parenting during the first year of life predict future child conduct problems. *Journal of Abnormal Child Psychology, 36,* 1139–1158.

Latzman, R. D., Elkovitch, N., & Clark, L. A. (2009). Predicting parenting practices from maternal and adolescent sons' personality. *Journal of Research in Personality, 43,* 847–855.

Lee, C. L., & Bates, J. E. (1985). Mother–child interaction at age two years and perceived difficult temperament. *Child Development, 56,* 1314–1325.

Lengua, L. J. (2006). Growth in temperament and parenting as predictors of adjustment during children's transition to adolescence. *Developmental Psychology, 42,* 819–832.

Lengua, L. J. (2008). Anxiousness, frustration, and effortful control as moderators of the relation between parenting and adjustment in middle-childhood. *Social Development, 17,* 554–577.

Lengua, L. J., & Kovacs, E. A. (2005). Bidirectional associations between temperament and parenting and the prediction of adjustment problems in middle childhood. *Journal of Applied Developmental Psychology, 26,* 21–38.

Lengua, L. J., Wolchik, S. A., Sandler, I. N., & West, S. G. (2000). The additive and interactive effects of parenting and temperament in predicting problems of children of divorce. *Journal of Clinical Child Psychology, 29,* 232–244.

Lifford, K. J., Harold, G. T., & Thapar, A. (2008). Parent–child relationships and ADHD symptoms: A longitudinal analysis. *Journal of Abnormal Child Psychology, 36,* 285–296.

Lifford, K. J., Harold, G. T., & Thapar, A. (2009). Parent–child hostility and child ADHD symptoms: A genetically sensitive and longitudinal analysis. *Journal of Child Psychology and Psychiatry, 50,* 1468–1476.

Maccoby, E. E., & Martin, J. A. (1983). Socialization in the context of the family: Parent–child interaction. In P. H. Mussen & E. M. Hetherington (Eds.), *Handbook of child psychology: Vol. 4. Socialization, personality, and social development* (4th ed., pp. 1–101). New York: Wiley.

Mesman, J., Stoel, R., Bakermans-Kranenburg, M. J., van IJzendoorn, M. H., Juffer, F., Koot, H. M., et al. (2009). Predicting growth curves of early childhood externalizing problems: Differential susceptibility of children with difficult temperament. *Journal of Abnormal Child Psychology, 37,* 625–636.

Neyer, F. J., & Lehnart, J. (2007). Relationships matter in personality development: Evidence from an 8-year longitudinal study across young adulthood. *Journal of Personality, 75,* 535–568.

Obradovic, J., Bush, N. R., Stamperdahl, J., Adler, N. E., & Boyce, W. T. (2010). Biological sensitivity to context: The interactive effects of stress reactivity and family adversity on socioemotional behavior and school readiness. *Child Development, 81,* 270–289.

Owens, E. B., Shaw, D. S., & Vondra, J. I. (1998). Relations between infant irritability and maternal responsiveness in low-income families. *Infant Behavior and Development, 21,* 761–777.

Patterson, G. R., Reid, J. B., & Dishion, T. J. (1992). *Antisocial boys*. Eugene, OR: Castalia.

Pauli-Pott, U., Mertesacker, B., & Beckmann, D. (2004). Predicting the development of infant emotionality from maternal characteristics. *Development and Psychopathology, 16,* 19–42.

Paulussen-Hoogeboom, M. C., Stams, G. J. J. M., Hermanns, J. M. A., & Peetsma, T. T. D. (2007). Child negative emotionality and parenting from infancy to preschool: A meta-analytic review. *Developmental Psychology, 43,* 438–453.

Paulussen-Hoogeboom, M. C., Stams, G. J. J. M.,

Hermanns, J. M. A., & Peetsma, T. T. D. (2008). Relations among child negative emotionality, parenting stress, and maternal sensitive responsiveness in early childhood. *Parenting: Science and Practice*, 8, 1–16.

Plomin, R., Emde, R. N., Braungart, J. M., Campos, J., Corley, R., Fulker, D. W., et al. (1993). Genetic change and continuity from fourteen to twenty months: The MacArthur Longitudinal Twin Study. *Child Development*, 64, 1354–1376.

Pluess, M., & Belsky, J. (2010). Differential susceptibility to parenting and quality child care. *Developmental Psychology*, 46, 379–390.

Popp, T. K., Spinrad, T. L., & Smith, C. L. (2008). The relation of cumulative demographic risk to mothers' responsivity and control: Examining the role of toddler temperament. *Infancy*, 13, 496–518.

Propper, C., & Moore, G. A. (2006). The influence of parenting on infant emotionality: A multilevel psychobiological perspective. *Developmental Review*, 26, 427–460.

Rhoades, K. A., Leve, L. D., Harold, G. T., Neiderhiser, J. M., Shaw, D. S., & Reiss, D. (2011). Longitudinal pathways from marital hostility to child anger during toddlerhood: Genetic susceptibility and indirect effects via harsh parenting. *Journal of Family Psychology*, 25, 282–291.

Rothbart, M. K., & Bates, J. E. (1998). Temperament. In W. Damon & N. Eisenberg (Eds.), *Handbook of child psychology: Vol. 3. Social, emotional, and personality development* (5th ed., pp. 105–176). New York: Wiley.

Rothbart, M. K., & Bates, J. E. (2006). Temperament. In N. Eisenberg, W. Damon, & R. M. Lerner (Eds.), *Handbook of child psychology: Vol. 3. Social, emotional, and personality development* (6th ed., pp. 99–166). Hoboken, NJ: Wiley.

Rothbaum, F., & Weisz, J. R. (1994). Parental caregiving and child externalizing behavior in nonclinical samples: A meta-analysis. *Psychological Bulletin*, 116, 55–74.

Rubin, K. H., Burgess, K. B., Dwyer, K. M., & Hastings, P. D. (2003). Predicting preschoolers' externalizing behaviors from toddler temperament, conflict, and maternal negativity. *Developmental Psychology*, 39, 164–176.

Rubin, K. H., Hastings, P. D., Stewart, S. L., Henderson, H. A., & Chen, X. (1997). The consistency and concomitants of inhibition: Some of the children, all of the time. *Child Development*, 68, 467–483.

Sameroff, A. J. (2009). Conceptual issues in studying the development of self-regulation. In S. L. Olson & A. J. Sameroff (Eds.), *Biopsychosocial regulatory processes in the development of childhood behavioral problems* (pp. 1–18). New York: Cambridge University Press.

Saudino, K. J. (2005). Behavioral genetics and child temperament. *Developmental and Behavioral Pediatrics*, 26, 214–223.

Schermerhorn, A. C., & Cummings, E. M. (2008). Transactional family dynamics: A new framework for conceptualizing family influence processes. In R. V. Kail (Ed.), *Advances in child development and behavior* (Vol. 36, pp. 187–250). San Diego, CA: Elsevier.

Schore, A. N. (1996). The experience-dependent maturation of a regulatory system in the orbital prefrontal cortex and the origin of developmental psychopathology. *Development and Psychopathology*, 8, 59–87.

Stright, A. D., Gallagher, K. C., & Kelley, K. (2008). Infant temperament moderates relations between maternal parenting in early childhood and children's adjustment in first grade. *Child Development*, 79, 186–200.

Suitor, J. J., Sechrist, J., Plikuhn, M., Pardo, S. T., & Pillemer, K. (2008). Within-family differences in parent–child relations across the life course. *Current Directions in Psychological Science*, 17, 334–338.

Takahashi, Y., Yamagata, S., Kijima, N., Shigemasu, K., Ono, Y., & Ando, J. (2007). Continuity and change in behavioral inhibition and activation systems: A longitudinal behavioral genetic study. *Personality and Individual Differences*, 43, 1616–1625.

van Aken, C., Junger, M., Verhoeven, M., van Aken, M. A. G., & Deković, M. (2007). The interactive effects of temperament and maternal parenting on toddlers' externalizing behaviours. *Infant and Child Development*, 16, 553–572.

Williams, L. R., Degnan, K. A., Pérez-Edgar, K. E., Henderson, H. A., Rubin, K. H., Pine, D. S., et al. (2009). Impact of behavioral inhibition and parenting style on internalizing and externalizing problems from early childhood through adolescence. *Journal of Abnormal Child Psychology*, 37, 1063–1075.

Zhou, Q., Chen, S. H., & Main, A. (2012). Commonalities and differences in the research on children's effortful control and executive function: A call for an integrated model of self-regulation. *Child Development Perspectives*, 6, 112–121.

Zhou, Q., Lengua, L. J., & Wang, Y. (2009). The relations of temperament reactivity and effortful control to children's adjustment problems in China and the United States. *Developmental Psychology*, 45(3), 724–739.

Chapter 21

Temperament and Peer Relationships

Robert J. Coplan
Amanda Bullock

Child temperament has been defined as characteristic styles of behavioral responses (Thomas & Chess, 1977), inherited personality traits that appear early in life (Buss & Plomin, 1984), and relatively stable, primarily biologically based individual differences in reactivity and self-regulation (Rothbart & Bates, 2006). Notwithstanding variability in definitions, taxonomies, and conceptual approaches, most temperament researchers would agree that individual differences in child temperament impact children's behaviors across a wide range of contexts (Wachs & Kohnstamm, 2001).

From early childhood through adolescence, most children spend the majority of their waking hours in the company of peers (Ladd & Golter, 1988; Larson & Richards, 1991). Moreover, the peer group represents an important and unique context for children's social, emotional, social-cognitive, cognitive, linguistic, and moral development (Rubin, Bukowski, & Laursen, 2009). In this chapter, we consider links between child temperament and children's peer relationships. We begin with an overview of the nature and significance of children's relations with peers and the conceptual mechanisms that may underlie associations between temperament and peer interactions, relationships, and groups. The body of the chapter is then devoted to a review of the relevant literature exploring links between specific temperamental characteristics (e.g., behavioral inhibition, negative emotionality, positive affect, attentional control) and peer relation variables. Finally, we consider some unanswered questions and posit directions for future research.

Theoretical Overview of Children's Peer Relationships

The study of children's peer relationships has a long and rich history (for more extensive historical reviews, see Ladd, 2006; Renshaw, 1981; Rubin, Bukowski, & Parker, 2006). Over a hundred years ago, Cooley (1902) was among the first to suggest that children's peers (or *primary group*) made significant contributions to child socialization, particularly with regard to the development of the self-system. Building on these notions, Mead (1934) suggested that the distinct nature of peer interactions fostered young children's understanding of the self as both subject and object, promoted the emergence of self-reflection, and was integral in the early development of the self-system.

Piaget (1932) further emphasized the unique characteristics of peer relationships that serve to distinguish them from adult–child relationships. For example, whereas adult–child relationships were construed as being more *vertical* in nature (asymmetrical in terms of dominance, power assertion, abilities, etc.), relations between peers were portrayed comparatively as being *horizontal* (i.e., more balanced, egalitarian). Accordingly, these distinctive qualities of the peer context were seen as providing children with unparalleled opportunities to experience directly multiple and conflicting perspectives. In turn, these occurrences promoted the use of negotiation, compromise, and other conflict-resolution skills, and also served to develop perspective-taking skills and aid in reducing the *egocentrism* (i.e., the inability to consider others' points of view) that often characterizes young children's thinking.

Sullivan (1953) specifically emphasized the importance of best-friendships (which he labeled *chumships*) in children's development of concepts such as mutual respect, reciprocity, cooperation, and competition. In particular, Sullivan postulated that peers had a unique influence on children's developing personality. This notion was a core component of later social learning theories (Bandura & Walters, 1963), which highlighted the "powers" of the peer group to shape children's social behaviors and social norms directly through the mechanisms of peer tutelage, reinforcement, and punishment, and indirectly via the casual observation of peer behaviors.

Hinde (1987) proposed that children's peer relations should be considered using multiple and nested levels of social complexity, ranging from the individual to interactions, to relationships, and finally to groups. Peer relations research can be broadly construed within this structural paradigm (Rubin et al., 2009), which we employ herein as an organizing configuration and to set the scope of our review of the extant empirical literature. Child temperamental characteristics constitute an individual-level variable but will be explored in terms of how they impact upon peer relations constructs situated at each subsequent level.

For our purposes, the level of *interactions* comprises variables related to children's social behaviors (e.g., prosocial, empathetic, initiating peer contact, leadership, and other indices of social competence), asocial behaviors (e.g., social withdrawal, solitary play, submissiveness, social wariness), and antisocial behaviors (e.g., aggression, impulsivity, socially immature behaviors) that may be displayed within the context of peer exchanges. The level of *relationships* focuses primarily on friendships in terms of both the quantity and the quality (e.g., intimacy, conflict, support) of these dyadic, mutual, and reciprocal relationships. Finally, *group* level variables include assessments of social standing and reputation within the peer group (e.g., popularity, rejection), victimization by peers, and membership in broader social networks.

Conceptual Links between Temperament and Peer Relations

The importance of the peer group as a context for children's development has led to the extensive empirical study of a wide range of peer relationship variables situated at all levels of this conceptual model. Overall, it is now well documented and widely accepted that children who experience a poor quantity and quality of peer relations are at increased risk for a plethora of concurrent and later negative adjustment outcomes, including difficulties at school (e.g., poor academic achievement, absenteeism, school dropout), internalizing problems (e.g., anxiety, depression, low self-esteem), and externalizing problems (e.g., aggression, juvenile delinquency, substance abuse) (see Rubin, Bukowski, et al., 2006, for an extensive review).

Most conceptualizations of the underlying links between child temperament and peer relations have described sets of linear associations among constructs (e.g., Eisenberg, Vaughan, & Hofer, 2009; Hay, Payne, & Chadwick, 2004; Rubin, Bukowski, et al., 2006; Sanson, Hemphill, & Smart, 2004). For example, Eisenberg and colleagues (2009) outlined a theoretical model in which child temperamental characteristics influence the quality of children's behaviors with peers and friends, friendships, and status with peers, which in turn impacts children's psychosocial functioning. Similarly, Sterry and colleagues (2010) recently reported that the links between child temperamental traits (i.e., activity, attention focus, adaptability) and peer acceptance are mediated by children's social behaviors. From this perspective, the primary focus has been on how different child temperamental traits might predict children's *behaviors* in the peer context (which in turn predict aspects of children's socioemotional functioning). As we illustrate, the majority of empirical studies in this area have focused on the linear associations between temperament and aspects of peer relations.

Researchers and theorists have also formulated more complex *interactional* models that postulate differential outcomes based on child temperament × environment interactions (Rothbart & Bates, 2006). For example, Thomas and Chess (1977) coined the term *goodness of fit* to describe the match (or lack thereof) between children's temperamental characteristics and the demands, expectations, and opportunities of the environment. In this regard, children's peer relations can be considered a substantive context that serves to *moderate* the associations between child temperament and adjustment outcomes. Accordingly, specific experiences within the peer group context (e.g., exclusion) may have differential consequences for children with different temperamental characteristics (Gazelle & Ladd, 2003).

Specific temperamental traits may also interact in the prediction of peer relations outcomes (Eisenberg, Fabes, Bernzweig, Karbon, Poulin, & Hanish, 1993; Pérez-Edgar et al., 2010). For example, children who are highly reactive and easily upset may have a particularly difficult time in the peer group if they also possess poor regulatory abilities. However, considerably less empirical attention has been paid to these interactive effects in the temperament and peer relations literature. In Figure 21.1 we have synthesized these linear and interactive theoretical models and adapted them within Hinde's (1987) organizational framework.

Aside from a direct link to children's behaviors with peers, child temperament is also likely to be expressed in terms of a wider range of processes relevant to the peer

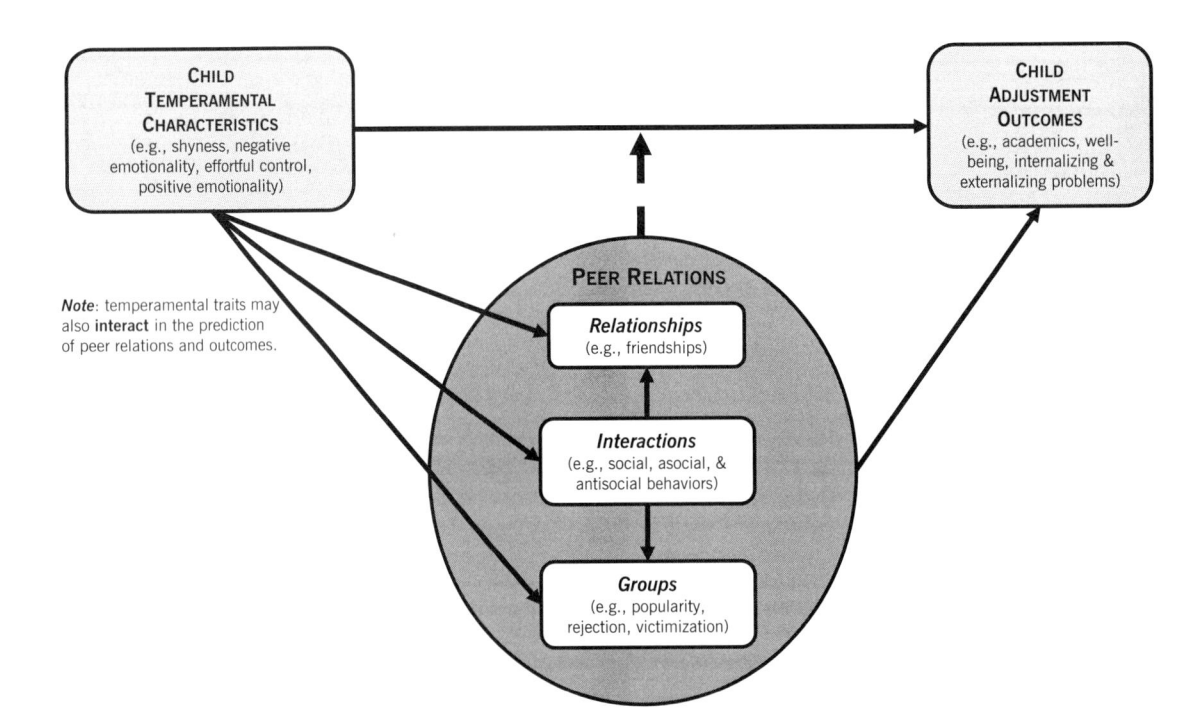

FIGURE 21.1. Conceptual model of the linear and interactive associations among temperament, peer relations, and adjustment outcomes.

group context, including social motivations (desires to approach and avoid peers), emotions (e.g., anger, fear), and social cognitions (e.g., attribution biases, threat perception, rejection sensitivity, perceived competence) (Rothbart & Bates, 2006). Moreover, the associations between these variables likely involve *bidirectional* and *transactional* processes that change over time (e.g., Cicchetti & Cohen, 1995). For example, Rubin, LeMare, and Lollis (1990) described the interplay between child characteristics and the peer group context over time. Children's temperamentally driven behaviors with peers (e.g., social withdrawal, aggression) evoke various peer responses (e.g., rejection, victimization), which helps to shape child emotions and social cognitions (e.g., perceived competence, felt-security), which in turn further impacts children's subsequent behaviors with peers.

Expanding this model, temperamental characteristics might be expected to affect not only children's initial social, asocial, and antisocial behaviors with peers, but also their social motivations, emotions, and social cognitions in the peer context. Children's behaviors in the peer group shape peers' reactions, evoke differential peer responses, and influence the quality of friendship relationships. In turn, these experiences provide salient feedback that serves to modulate children's motivations for peer interaction, emotional reactivity, and social cognitions, which, in concert with children's temperament, serve to impact children's subsequent behaviors with peers in a continuing transactional process over time. This type of conceptual model is illustrated in Figure 21.2.

The conceptual models presented in Figures 21.1 and 21.2 are meant to illustrate the rich theoretical framework that underlies links between child temperament and peer relations. In the following sections we provide an overview of the empirical literature in this area. In particular, we summarize findings that link to basic temperament characteristics with different aspects of children's peer relations (e.g., interactions, relationships, groups).

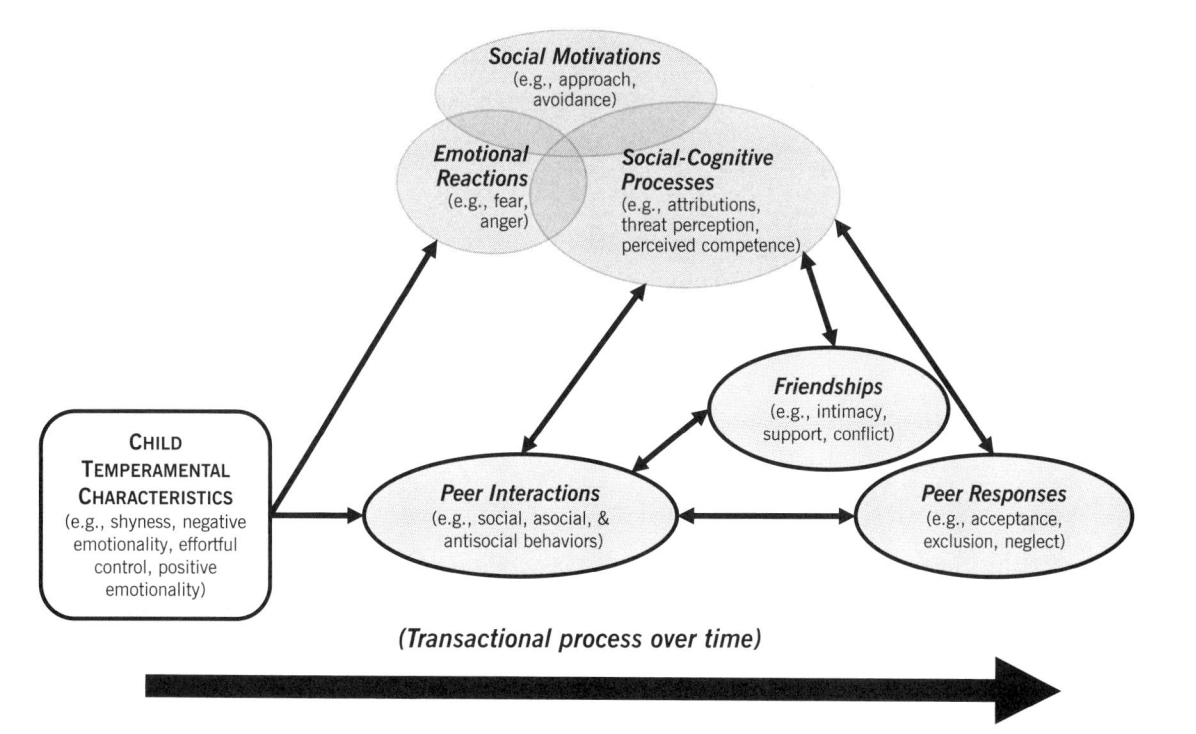

FIGURE 21.2. Conceptual model illustrating transactional associations between temperament and peer relations over time.

Empirical Links between Temperament and Peer Relations

Although subtle distinctions can be made within groups of conceptually related temperamental traits (e.g., behavioral inhibition vs. shyness; see Coplan & Rubin, 2010), such discriminations are beyond the scope of this chapter. Instead, our goal herein is to focus on four broad clusters of temperamental characteristics that are the most theoretically and empirically relevant with regard to their links with aspects of children's peer relations. These include (1) behavioral inhibition, shyness, and social fear; (2) negative emotionality (with a focus on irritability, anger, frustration); (3) positive emotionality, exuberance, and surgency; and (4) effortful control, attention, and self-regulation.

Behavioral Inhibition, Shyness, and Social Fear

One temperamental cluster that has received a lot of attention with regard to its contribution toward children's peer relations pertains to children's reactive and wary responses to social and (particularly novel social) situations. *Behavioral inhibition* (BI) describes a biologically based low threshold for arousal in response to novelty that is characterized by wariness during exposure to new people, things, and places (see Kagan, Chapter 4, this volume). Similarly, *shyness* has been conceptualized as temperamental wariness in the face of social novelty and/or self-conscious behavior in situations of perceived social evaluation (Schmidt & Buss, 2010). Other conceptually related terms include *social fear, (low) approach*, and *slow to warm up* (Coplan & Rubin, 2010).

The peer group appears to be a particularly salient and relevant context for the behavioral expression of the temperamental trait of inhibition/shyness (Rubin, Bowker, & Gazelle, 2010). From a motivation perspective, shyness is thought to be characterized by an underlying social approach–avoidance conflict (Coplan, Prakash, O'Neil, & Armer, 2004). That is, shy children are thought to desire social contact (i.e., high social approach motivation) but at the same time are fearful and wary of peer interaction (i.e., high social avoidance motivation). Moreover, the presence of peers is purported to evoke emotional responses in shy children, including fear/anxiety and embarrassment/self-consciousness (Schmidt & Buss, 2010). As well, peers are also thought to trigger negative and self-defeating social-cognitive processes in shy children (Boivin, Hymel, & Bukowski, 1995; Wichmann, Coplan, & Daniels, 2004).

Given their strong conceptual links, it should perhaps not be surprising that there is a substantial empirical literature demonstrating associations between shyness and various aspects of children's peer relations. To begin with, in terms of peer *interactions*, temperamentally shy/inhibited children tend to engage in a lower quantity of peer contact across a number of different peer contexts (Rubin et al., 2009). For example, the tendency to withdraw from and avoid social interactions in novel social settings has been used as a defining characteristic of behavioral inhibition (Kagan, Reznick, Clarke, Snidman, & Garcia-Coll, 1984). Indeed, results from several studies have indicated that extremely shy/inhibited children tend to "play less" with peers and spend more time engaged in onlooking behaviors (i.e., watching others but not joining in) and remaining unoccupied (i.e., staring off into space, wandering around aimlessly) when among peers (Coplan, 2011).

These findings have been reported across numerous social contexts, including the presence of unfamiliar peers in the laboratory playroom (e.g., Coplan, Rubin, Fox, Calkins, & Stewart, 1994; Rubin, Coplan, Fox, & Calkins, 1995; Rubin, Hastings, Stewart, Henderson, & Chen, 1997) and the first day of school (Coplan, 2000), as well as the presence of familiar peers several months into the school year (Coplan, Arbeau, & Armer, 2008; Coplan et al., 2004; Rimm-Kaufman & Kagan, 2005). Even outside the school context, there appears to be some consistency to this pattern of withdrawn behaviors (Schneider, Richard, Younger, & Freeman, 2000). For example, Coplan, DeBow, Schneider, and Graham (2009) had parents of extremely inhibited and uninhibited young children keep a diary of their children's social contacts outside of school. Among their results, extremely inhibited children were found to engage in significantly fewer peer activities outside of preschool compared to their more uninhibited counterparts. As a result, concerns have been raised because shy children may be *missing out* on the previously mentioned important and unique contributions of the peer group context toward children's development (Rubin, Wojslawowicz, et al., 2006).

Moreover, even when they do engage socially in the peer group, shy children tend to display a lack of social competence (Bohlin, Hagekull, & Anderson, 2005; Chen, DeSouza, Chen, & Wang, 2006) and a pattern of asocial and socially reticent behaviors (Coplan et al., 2008). Compared to their more uninhibited counterparts, shy children have a longer latency to initiate speech, make fewer verbal requests, and talk less overall to peers and teachers (Bishop, Spence, & McDonald, 2003; Coplan et al., 2004; Rimm-Kaufman & Kagan, 2005). For example, Asendorpf and Meier (1993) reported that parent-identified shy children spoke less upon arrival at school, in discussions, at break, and upon leaving for home. Moreover, shy children also tend to instigate fewer social initiations, and their requests to peers tend to be more passive and are more often refused and ignored (Chen et al., 2006; Rubin, Daniels-Beirness, & Bream, 1984).

Although there has been less research into the specific peer *relationships* of shy children, their pattern of asocial and submissive behaviors appears to have implications in this context as well. Interestingly, whereas shy children do not differ from their nonshy peers in terms of their likelihood to report a reciprocal best friendship (e.g., Ladd & Burgess, 1999; Rubin, Wojslawowicz, Rose-Krasnor, Booth-LaForce, & Burgess, 2006), there is some evidence to suggest that shy children tend to form fewer friendships overall than their nonshy peers (Gazelle, 2008; Pedersen, Vitaro, Barker, & Borge, 2007). As well, shy children do not seem to be viewed as particularly attractive potential friends (Coplan, Girardi, Findlay, & Frohlick, 2007). Moreover, the friendship relationships that shy children do establish are characterized as poorer in quality along a number of dimensions, including communication, intimate disclosure, helpfulness, guidance, and enjoyment (Fordham & Stevenson-Hinde, 1999; Rubin, Wojslawowicz, et al., 2006; Schneider, 1999, 2009).

Finally, in terms of status within the peer *group*, it appears that temperamentally shy children's behaviors do not generally tend to evoke positive responses from peers. Indeed, even in early childhood, shy children are more likely than other children to be disliked, excluded, and rejected by the peer group (e.g., Chen et al., 2006; Coplan et al., 2008; Gazelle & Ladd, 2003). Moreover, shy children's timidity, anxiety, and lack of assertiveness in the peer group may mark them as easy targets for victimization (Olweus, 1978; Perren & Alsaker, 2006; Perry, Kusel, & Perry, 1988; Rubin, Wojslawowicz, et al., 2006). Shy children's negative peer group experiences appear to increase with age (Ladd, 2006; Oh et al., 2008), perhaps because their asocial and reticent behaviors among peers become more negatively salient and are viewed as increasingly atypical and socially deviant (Boivin et al., 1995; Rubin et al., 1990; Younger, Gentile, & Burgess, 1993).

Indeed, results from longer-term longitudinal studies suggest that shyness and related temperamental constructs in childhood are predictive of poorer peer and romantic relationships in adulthood (Asendorpf, 2010; Caspi, Elder, & Bem, 1988; Rubin, Chen, McDougall, Bowker, & McKinnon, 1995). For example, in an almost 20-year longitudinal study, Asendorpf, Denissen, and van Aken (2008) found that as adults, inhibited children entered romantic relationships later than comparison peers.

Overall, there is growing evidence to suggest that temperamentally shy and inhibited children are more likely than their more outgoing counterparts to experience both reduced quantity and lower quality of peer relations. In and of itself, this is cause for some potential concern given the increased risk for a wide range of previously described negative outcomes associated with peer relationship difficulties in childhood (Rubin, Bukowski, et al., 2006). Unfortunately, temperamentally shy children also appear to be particularly vulnerable to the negative consequences of poor peer relations (Oh et al., 2008). Indeed, although friendships are generally presumed to have a positive influence on children's socioemotional development (Bernt, 2004), shy children may not always *benefit* from these close relationships with peers. For example, as compared to friends of other children, best friends of shy children tend to be more shy and socially withdrawn themselves, and are more likely to be victimized and excluded by their peers (Rubin, Wojslawowicz, et al., 2006). As well, peer exclusion and rejection appear to exacerbate the associations between shyness and internalizing problems, particularly with regards to depression (Gazelle & Ladd, 2003; Gazelle & Rudolph, 2004).

As such, extreme shyness/inhibition in early childhood has been used as a targeting criterion to indentify children who may benefit from ameliorative intervention (e.g., Rapee, Kennedy, Ingram, Edwards, & Sweeney, 2005). Moreover, there is at least some preliminary evidence to suggest that involving peers in such intervention efforts may serve to improve both the quantity and quality of shy children's peer experiences (e.g., Christopher, Hansen, & MacMillan, 1991; Coplan, Schneider, Matheson, & Graham, 2010).

Negative Emotionality: Irritability, Anger, and Frustration

Another temperamental cluster that has been often studied in terms of its contribution to children's peer relations encompasses children's threshold, intensity, and control of negative affect. *Negative emotionality* refers to children's expression and regulation of anger and frustration (Eisenberg et al., 2009; Rothbart, Ahadi, Hershey, & Fisher, 2001). Other conceptually related terms include *irritability*, *hostility*, and *hard to soothe* (Paulussen-Hoogeboom, Stams, Hermanns, & Peetsma, 2007, see Deater-Deckard & Wang, Chapter 7, this volume). Negative emotionality and irritability are also considered fundamental components of the temperamental composite of *difficultness* (Thomas & Chess, 1977). Although the term *negative emotionality* has also been used to describe other emotional responses (e.g., fear, which was touched upon in the previous section), the focus in this section pertains more specifically to anger and frustration.

Children who are emotionally *dysregulated* lack the ability adequately to modulate negative emotions (Cole, Michel, & Teti, 1994; Rubin et al., 1995). Although children may display negative emotions in both nonsocial and social settings, the peer group appears to be a conceptually salient context for this temperamental trait. For example, peers are evocative stimuli, directly provoking and threatening children, or making social demands (e.g., asking to share) that may *evoke* negative emotional responses (Calkins, Gill, Johnson, & Smith, 1999). Moreover, strong negative emotions such as anger and frustration may interfere with children's abilities to manage conflicts (Eisenberg et al., 2009). As well, children high in negative emotionality also tend to *elicit* antagonism and rejection from peers (Rubin, Bukowski, et al., 2006). Thus, the management of emotional arousal is necessary to secure effective social functioning (e.g., Calkins, 1994; Dodge & Garber, 1991), and temperamental negative emotionality is considered to be a significant theoretical contributor to multiple aspects of children's peer relations (Eisenberg & Fabes, 2006; Lemerise & Arsenio, 2000).

Like their previously described shy/inhibited counterparts, children prone to anger and frustration also tend to display maladaptive patterns of social behaviors with peers. Results from a number of studies have indicated inverse associations between temperamental negative emotionality and children's social skills, social competence, and prosocial behaviors with peers throughout childhood (Eisenberg et al., 1993; Eisenberg, Fabes, et al., 1997; Rydell, Thorell, & Bohlin, 2007; Zhou, Eisenberg, Wang, & Reiser, 2004). For example, Calkins and colleagues (1999) found that toddlers who were more easily frustrated experienced more conflicts and were less cooperative with peers. Fabes and colleagues (1999) reported that children higher in teacher-rated negative emotionality were observed to be less helpful and friendly with peers at school. In a recent study of early adolescents, Laible, Panfile, Eye, Carlo, and Parker (2010) found that self-reported negative emotionality was inversely associated with self-reported altruism and positively related to negative-dominant expressiveness.

It has also been postulated that negative emotionality also represents a predisposition for aggressive behavior with peers (Cairns & Cairns, 1991; Ledingham, 1991; Sanson, Smart, Prior, Oberklaid, & Pedlow, 1994). Indeed, extensive empirical evidence indicates that negative emotional, difficult, and anger/frustration-prone children are more likely to display aggressive, disruptive, and oppositional behaviors with peers (e.g., Diener & Kim, 2004; Eisenberg, Fabes, Guthrie, & Reiser, 2000; Hill, Degnan, Calkins, & Keane, 2006; Rydell et al., 2007).

Degnan, Calkins, Keane, and Hill-Soderlund (2008) examined temperamental contributions to the development of disruptive behaviors in a longitudinal study of children ages 2–5 years. Membership in the "high disruptive" profile was predicted by children's frustration reactivity. However, it is also worth noting that the effect of frustration reactivity was stronger at higher levels of maternal control. Indeed, there is growing evidence to suggest that maternal behaviors (i.e., control, positivity) moderate the associations between negative emotionality and children's problem behaviors in the peer group (e.g., Paterson & Sanson, 1999; see Paulussen-Hoogeboom et al., 2007, for an extensive review).

Only a handful of studies have specifically explored associations between negative emotionality and children's *friendships*. It has been suggested that particularly in early childhood, when emotion regulation is still a developing skill, having a friend who is prone to negative emotionality might be particularly problematic (Walden, Lemerise, & Smith, 1999). There is at least some evidence to support this notion. Parent and teacher ratings of negative emotionality have been related to observational assessments of poorer friendship quality (Dunn & Cutting, 1999) and greater conflict among friends (Pellegrini, Galda, Flor, Bartini, & Charak, 1997; Pike & Atzaba-Poria 2003). Gleason, Gower, Hohmann, and Gleason (2005) found that children rated by teachers as temperamentally "easy" (i.e., high in soothability) were more likely to be nominated as a preferred friend by peers. Interestingly, these authors also reported that similarity in temperament between children was *not* a significant predictive factor in reciprocal friendship selections.

Researchers have extensively explored the implications of negative emotionality at the level of the peer *group*. Overall, there is considerable research demonstrating that negative emotionality, anger, frustration reactivity, and hostility are associated with peer rejection and exclusion from early childhood through adolescence (Eisenberg et al., 1993, 2000; Fabes & Eisenberg, 1992; Kim & Cicchetti, 2010; Szewczyk-Sokolowski, Bost, & Wainwright, 2005; Trentacosta & Shaw, 2009). These findings are likely accounted for by the previously described links between negative emotionality and maladaptive behaviors with peers, including a lack of social competence and aggression. In particular, aggression is one of the strongest and most consistent behavioral predictors of peer rejection in childhood (Rubin, Bukowksi, et al., 2006).

It has been suggested that such negatively salient and provocative behaviors may also put children at increased risk for victimization by peers (Olweus, 1978). Indeed, growing empirical evidence indicates that negative emotionality (particularly with regard to the display of anger) is associated with peer victimization (Hanish, Kochenderfer-Ladd, Fabes, Martin, & Denning, 2004; Jensen-Campbell & Malcolm, 2007; Spence, De Young, Toon, & Bond, 2009). Hanish and colleagues (2004) reported that anger prone children are more likely to be victimized by peers than their more well-regulated counterparts. For boys, this association between anger and victimization appears to be mediated by the display of aggressive behaviors—particularly early in the school year.

Overall, these findings do not bode particularly well for children who are prone to anger, frustration, and negative emotions. As previously described, there are potentially negative long term implications associated with poor peer relations (Rubin, Bukowski, et al., 2006). Moreover, in and of themselves, the types of negative peer behaviors and experiences (i.e., aggression, victimization) incurred by children high in negative emotionality also carry with them significant risk for later, more serious adjustment difficulties, including both internalizing and externalizing problems (Dodge, Coie, & Lynam, 2006).

Positive Affect, Exuberance, and Surgency

A third cluster of temperamental traits encompasses the frequency and intensity of positive emotions. *Positive affect* involves the display of pleasure and excitement, and the tendency to seek out and approach reward-fulfilling stimulation (Bates, Wachs,

& Emde, 1994; Gray, 1991; Rothbart, 1989; Rothbart & Derryberry, 2002, see Putnam, Chapter 6, this volume). Similarly, *exuberance* is characterized by high levels of positive affect and sociability, a strong tendency to engage in approach behaviors, and little to no fear and inhibition in response to novel objects and people (Fox, Henderson, Rubin, Calkins, & Schmidt, 2001). Other related terms that can be included in this category include *surgency, extraversion, approach,* and *novelty seeking* (Zentner & Bates, 2008).

Positive affect has also been posited as an integral contributor to successful social interactions in the peer group context (Izard, 2009). For example, Fox and Henderson (1999) suggested that children who demonstrate happiness and pleasure in response to social stimulation create a unique and positive social environment. Accordingly, children who are prone to positive affect are better able to initiate and maintain social interactions in the peer group environment. Moreover, exuberant children's propensity to approach novel objects and unfamiliar people (Stifter, Putnam, & Jahromi, 2008) may help to facilitate social exchanges with peers.

Notwithstanding the conceptual links between the temperament dimension of positive affect and peer relations, the extant empirical literature in this area is comparatively sparse. In terms of peer *interactions*, there is some evidence to suggest that exuberant children are less socially withdrawn when presented with opportunities for peer engagement (Fox et al., 2001). For example, Spinrad and colleagues (2004) reported that observed solitary activity among preschool children during free play was associated with low levels of positive affect. Similarly, Degnan and colleagues (2011) recently reported that temperamentally exuberant toddlers (identified via observational assessments) were less socially reticent than comparison children when observed during dyadic peer interactions at age 5 years. In contrast, children higher in positive affect tend to have more positive social interactions in the peer group (Denham, McKinley, Couchoud, & Holt, 1990; Lengua, 2002; Skarpness & Carson, 1987). For example, Denham and colleagues (1990) reported that the expression of positive affect (e.g., happiness) when interacting with their peers was associated with higher ratings of child social competence.

However, it should be noted that exuberance is not always associated with positive peer behaviors and outcomes in childhood. Children who are unable to regulate competently the expression of their positive emotions may pose problems in the peer group (Kochanska, Murray, & Harlan, 2000). Indeed, results from a few studies have demonstrated links between excessive positive emotionality/exuberance and indices of impulsivity, aggression, and externalizing problems (e.g., Berdan, Keane, & Calkins, 2008; Oldehinkel, Hartman, de Winter, Veenstra, & Ormel, 2004; Putnam & Stifter, 2005; Rothbart et al., 2001).

With regard to children's peer *relationships*, positive affect has been associated with the formation and maintenance of friendships (Park, Lay, & Ramsay, 1993; Sroufe, Schork, Motti, Lawroski, & LaFreniere, 1984) and the number of friendships children form (Mobley & Pullis, 1991). Finally, there is also at least some evidence to suggest that children's positive affect is predictive of popularity and acceptance in the broader peer *group* (Sroufe et al., 1984).

Overall, the temperament dimension of positive affect does appear to play a positive role in successfully facilitating social interactions, friendships, and peer acceptance. However, there is also some evidence to suggest that in terms of this trait, it is also possible to have "too much of a good thing." In particular, it appears that the combination of high exuberance and low effortful control/self-regulation may put children at risk for externalizing problems (Stifter et al., 2008). On the other hand, "too little of a good thing" can also be problematic. Low positive affect is a well-established risk factor in the etiology of depression (Clark, Watson, & Mineka, 1994; Hammen & Rudolph, 2003).

Attention, Effortful Control, and Self-Regulation

The final cluster of temperamental traits that has been substantially linked to children's peer relations pertains to the regulation and management of attention. *Effortful control* reflects the functioning of the self-regulatory executive attention system (Rothbart, Sheese, & Posner, 2007) that enables children to inhibit a dominant response and/or perform a subdominant response, detect and monitor errors, and engage in planning (Rothbart & Bates, 2006; see Rueda, Chapter 8, this volume). Related terms include *inhibitory control* and *persistence*, as well as (the lack of) *impulsivity* (Zenter & Bates, 2008). The skills involved in effortful control (and related aspects of attention) include the ability to shift and focus attention, inhibit maladaptive and impulsive behaviors, engage in adaptive behaviors, down-regulate negative emotions, and enhance positive emotions (Derryberry & Rothbart, 1997; Rothbart & Bates, 2006). Such skills are necessary in order to process and integrate information from multiple sources, plan effectively, and modulate behaviors and emotions in response to internal and external stimuli (Eisenberg, Hofer, & Vaughn, 2007; Eisenberg et al., 2009).

Effortful control has also been postulated as an important contributor toward adaptive social functioning and competent social interactions in the peer group (Eisenberg et al., 2007). For example, children who modulate their attention in response to an emotionally arousing situation are able to inhibit their impulsive behaviors, which allows them to acquire and assess information from other sources. This contributes toward a better understanding of the situation, which in turn aids in planning and executing an adaptive response that might serve to facilitate social interactions (Eisenberg et al., 2007; Rothbart & Derryberry, 2002). In support of this view, Raver, Blackburn, Bancroft, and Torp (1999) found that preschoolers who controlled their attention through the use of self-distraction during a delay-of-gratification task were reported by teachers and peers to be more socially competent. Moreover, children who use more effective emotion-regulating strategies to cope with a stressful event tend to be more sensitive to emotion-related information, which helps to provide a better understanding of their own and others' emotions (Eisenberg et al., 2007). In turn, children's abilities to better understand their own and their peers' emotions appear to mediate relations between emotion regulation and indices of competent social interactions (e.g., Izard, Schultz, Fine, Youngstrom, & Ackerman, 1999–2000).

In accordance with these conceptual links, a plethora of research has examined associations between effortful control and aspects of peer relations. In terms of peer *interactions*, effortful control and attentional self-regulation have been positively related to children's prosocial behavior, social skills, and social competence with peers across the childhood years (Eisenberg et al., 2000; Eisenberg, Guthrie, et al., 1997; Skarpness & Carson, 1987; Spinrad et al., 2006; Sterry et al., 2010). For example, Prior, Sanson, Smart, and Oberklaid (2000) reported that task orientation (i.e., attentional self-regulation) at age 5–6 years was a strong predictor of children's social skills at age 11–12 years.

Fabes and colleagues (1999) reported that children rated by teachers as high in effortful control were observed to interact with their peers in a prosocial manner (e.g., helping a friend, showing affection). Similarly, children high in effortful control have been observed in peer interactions to be cooperative, to use more negotiating skills during a conflict, and to display less negative emotion with peers (David & Murphy, 2007; Fantuzzo, Sekino, & Cohen, 2004). In contrast, children lower in attention and effortful control (i.e., children who are more impulsive) are prone to aggressive and disruptive behaviors with peers (Eisenberg et al., 2000, 2004; Trentacosta & Shaw, 2009).

In terms of peer *relationships*, relatively few studies have specifically examined the contribution of effortful control to children's friendships (e.g., Walden et al., 1999). Gleason and colleagues (2005) reported that children rated as impulsive were nominated *most* frequently by their peers as friends. In interpreting this unexpected finding, the authors speculated that children who lacked inhibitory control but were not disruptive in their impulsivity might be viewed as socially attractive by peers. However, impulsivity can also lead to difficulties in forming and maintaining friendships (Jensen-Campbell & Malcolm, 2007).

In terms of status within the larger peer *group*, children with high levels of effortful control, attention, and self-regulation tend to be more liked, accepted, and popular with peers and experience less peer rejection

(Eisenberg, Guthrie, et al., 1997; Eisenberg, Pidada, & Liew, 2001; Gunnar, Sebanc, Tout, Donzella, & van Dulmen, 2003; Wilson, 2006). For example, in a series of studies, Eisenberg and colleagues (e.g., Eisenberg et al., 1993; Eisenberg, Fabes, Nyman, Bernzweig, & Pinuelas, 1994; Fabes & Eisenberg, 1992) found that children who were better able to cope adaptively with peer provocations (i.e., by shifting their attention to a nonprovoking stimuli or seeking help from adults) were rated as popular by their teachers. As well, in a longitudinal study of boys from low-income families, Trentacosta and Shaw (2009) reported that difficulties in controlling attention during a delay-of-gratification task in preschool significantly predicted the experience of peer rejection in early adolescence. Finally, there is also some evidence to suggest that children who score lower in effortful control and are more impulsive may also be more likely to experience victimization at the hands of peers (Hanish, Eisenberg, et al., 2004; Jensen-Campbell & Malcolm, 2007).

Thus, children with higher levels of effortful control tend to engage in more socially competent behaviors and therefore experience more positive social interactions with their peers. Perhaps as a result, children who are better able to redirect their attention and control their impulsiveness are better liked by their peers and experience less peer rejection. However, it should also be noted that effortful control (and its related constructs) may also play an important *protective* role for children who score high in other temperamental traits associated with poor peer relations (Eisenberg et al., 2007; Sanson et al., 2004). For example, a growing number of studies has demonstrated that effortful control and self-regulation attenuate/exacerbate relations between negative emotionality, frustration, and anger-proneness and children's social behaviors, social competence, and social acceptance (e.g., Belsky, Friedman, & Hsieh, 2001; Calkins et al., 1999; Eisenberg et al., 1993, 2000; Eisenberg, Fabes, Murphy, et al., 1996). Accordingly, this makes this temperamental trait particularly relevant for the development of targeted early interventions (e.g., Campbell-Sills & Barlow, 2007; Izard et al., 2008; Mullin & Hinshaw, 2007).

Future Directions for Temperament and Peer Relations Research

Despite the growing number of empirical studies exploring links between child temperament and peer relations, there are still many areas that warrant additional research attention. In this final section, we highlight some unanswered questions and make a few suggestions for future research directions.

Other Temperamental Characteristics

This review has focused on the four most "relevant" clusters of child temperament, as they pertain to children's peer relations. However, researchers have also explored associations between other dimensions of children's temperament and aspects of peer relations. For example, given its strong conceptual pertinence in this domain, it is perhaps surprising that there have not been more empirical studies of the link between children's peer relations and *sociability* (Cheek & Buss, 1981; Plomin & Rowe, 1977). Sociability reflects the desire to associate with others, which is not equivalent to "low shyness" (see Schmidt & Buss, 2010). Children high in sociability tend to have more positive interactions and relationships with peers, and are well liked (e.g., Eisenberg, Cameron, Tryon, & Dodez, 1981; Pike & Atzaba-Poria, 2003; Stocker & Dunn, 1990). In contrast, links between *unsociability* and peer-related outcomes are less clear (Coplan & Weeks, 2010b). Some researchers have suggested that a preference for solitude is relatively benign, particularly in early childhood (e.g., Asendorpf & Meier, 1993; Harrist, Zaia, Bates, Dodge, & Pettit, 1997; Rubin, 1982). However, results from some studies suggest that even in early childhood, unsociable children may be prone to peer exclusion and rejection (Coplan et al., 2004; Coplan & Weeks, 2010a).

In terms of other traits, temperamental positive *activity* (see Strelau & Zawadzki, Chapter 5, this volume) has been associated with positive and socially competent interactions with peers (Billman & McDevitt, 1980; Skarpness & Carson, 1987), positive friendship quality (Pike & Atzaba-Poria, 2003), and peer acceptance (Sterry et al., 2010). There has also been growing interest in the trait of *agreeableness* (see Knafo & Israel, Chapter 9, this volume), which appears to be related to affiliative and prosocial tendencies (e.g., Graziano, 1994), as well as peer acceptance and friendships (e.g., Gazelle, 2008; Jensen-Campbell et al., 2002).

Along with considering additional, specific temperamental characteristics, research on peer relations would also benefit from the consideration of broader personality traits. Although temperament has generally been conceptualized as a "building block" for the later development of personality, the exact nature of the link between temperament and personality is still the subject of some debate (McAdams & Olson, 2010; see Shiner & Caspi, Chapter 24, this volume). For example, temperamental characteristics do not typically share one-to-one correspondence with personality traits. Moreover, one personality trait (e.g., extraversion) may reflect the combination of several temperament (e.g., sociability, positive affect) and "nontemperament" components (e.g., social potency, desire for social attention) (Ashton, Lee, & Paunonen, 2002). Greater conceptual clarity of the structure of temperament and its later manifestations in personality traits will aid our understanding of how these constructs might differentially impact upon children's peer relations.

Age and Gender Effects

Perhaps not surprisingly, a large majority of the studies reviewed in this chapter has focused on links between temperament and peer relations in early childhood. Accordingly, there is a need to explore further the contribution of child temperament to children's peer experiences in middle and later childhood, adolescence, and into adulthood. Moreover, true *developmental* models need to be developed that consider the changing form and functions of both child temperament and peer relations across age, and how these developmental progressions might influence the associations between these constructs. For example, it has been argued that temperamental shyness and unsociability might become increasingly associated with peer rejection in later childhood because socially withdrawn behaviors increasingly become negatively salient to the peer group during this age period (Younger et al., 1993). As well, there is a need for additional long-term longitudinal studies that allow exploration of the associations between childhood temperament and aspects of peer relations (including romantic relationships) in adolescence and adulthood (e.g., Asendorpf et al., 2008; Caspi et al., 1988; Shiner, 2000; Shiner, Masten, & Roberts, 2003).

It will also be important for future researchers to consider more actively the role of child gender (Else-Quest, Hyde, Goldsmith, & Van Hulle, 2006; see Else-Quest, Chapter 23, this volume), particularly as a potential moderator of the links between temperamental traits and peer relationship outcomes (e.g., Gleason et al., 2005; Hanish, Eisenberg, et al., 2004; Sterry et al., 2010). For example, there is some evidence to suggest that anger is more strongly negatively related to social competence and prosocial behaviors among boys than among girls (Diener & Kim, 2004; Jones, Eisenberg, Fabes, & MacKinnon, 2002). As well, perhaps because it violates gender stereotypes regarding assertion and dominance, temperamental shyness appears to be more strongly associated with peer exclusion and rejection in boys than in girls (e.g., Coplan et al., 2004; Gazelle & Ladd, 2003).

Culture

It is also important to note that the majority of studies cited in this chapter were conducted with children from Western cultures. There is growing research interest in possible cross-cultural differences in temperament (see Chen, Yang, & Fu, Chapter 22, this volume). It will be particularly important for future researchers to continue to consider cultural differences (and similarities) in the implications of different temperamental traits for children's peer relations.

In some instances, there appears to be a high degree of consistency between cultures in the links between a particular temperamental trait and peer-related outcomes. For example, negative emotionality/anger has been positively associated with negative peer-related behaviors and outcomes in Indonesia (Eisenberg et al., 2001) and China (Zhou et al., 2004). In other cases, there are notable cross-cultural differences. For example, in more individualistic cultures where independence, assertiveness, competitiveness are more highly valued and encouraged (e.g., Argentina, Canada, Greece, Italy, the Netherlands, the United States), shyness is positively associated with peer rejection (Casiglia, Lo Coco, & Zappulla, 1998; Cillessen, van IJzendoorn, van Lieshout, & Hartup, 1992; Coplan et al., 2008; Schaughency, Vannatta, Langhinrichsen, Lally, & Seeley, 1992). In contrast, shyness in collectivist China is positively associated with indices of social competence and peer acceptance (e.g., Chen, Cen, Li, & He, 2005; Chen, Rubin, Li, & Li, 1999). It remains to be seen how cultural context may serve to "moderate" links between other temperamental characteristics and children's peer relations.

Complexity of Associations among Variables

Finally, it is important that future researchers continue to consider the potentially complex nature of the associations between temperament and children's peer relations. As mentioned at the outset of this chapter, despite considerable progress, it is likely still the case that most empirical studies in this area only consider linear/direct associations between variables. However, it has become clear that temperament and peer relations can be linked via a combination of indirect, transactional, and interactive associations (Eisenberg et al., 2009; Rothbart & Bates, 2006; Sanson et al., 2004).

For example, in a series of studies, Eisenberg and colleagues have extensively explored additive and interactive effects of aspects of temperamental reactivity (e.g., negative emotionality) and regulation (e.g., effortful control) in the prediction of children's social competence and peer group functioning (Eisenberg et al., 1993, 2000; Eisenberg, Fabes, Murphy, et al., 1996; Eisenberg, Guthrie, et al., 1997). We would assert that the continued exploration of temperament × peer group interactions (and other complex conceptual mechanisms) will serve to strengthen empirical links substantially between temperament and children's peer relations.

Conclusions

It seems clear that from early childhood to adolescence temperament makes a unique, substantive, and integral contribution to the quality and quantity of children's social interactions, friendships, and experiences within the broader peer group. Although a large volume of empirical studies has explored associations between temperamental characteristics and a wide range of peer relations outcomes, it is also evident that there is still much work to be done. Our growing understanding of the complex ways that temperament may be linked to children's peer relations will have direct implications for interventions designed to improve children's socioemotional functioning within the peer group context. Researchers have already begun to utilize child temperament to assist in the identification of children who may be at increased risk for current and future difficulties in the peer group. However, there is pressing need to apply the results of the research reviewed herein to create and adapt intervention programs that are specifically "tailored" to children with different temperamental characteristics. It is anticipated that increasing the "goodness of fit" between characteristics of the target child and the intervention will improve intervention efficacy and serve to promote more strongly positive peer relationships among at-risk children.

Further Reading

Eisenberg, N., Vaughn, J., & Hofer, C. (2009). Temperament, self-regulation, and peer social competence. In K. H. Rubin, W. M. Bukowski, & B. Laursen (Eds.), *Handbook of peer interactions, relationships, and groups* (pp. 473–489). New York: Guilford Press.

Rubin, K. H., Bukowski, W., & Parker, J. G. (2006). Peer interactions, relationships, and groups. In W. Damon, R. M. Lerner, & N. Eisenberg (Eds.), *Handbook of child psychology: Vol. 3. Social, emotional, and personality development* (6th ed., pp. 571–645). New York: Wiley.

Sanson, A., Hemphill, S. A., & Smart, D. (2004). Connections between temperament and social development: A review. *Social Development, 13*, 142–170.

References

Asendorpf, J. B. (2010). Long-term development of shyness: Looking forward and looking backward. In K. H. Rubin & R. J. Coplan (Eds.), *The development of shyness and social withdrawal* (pp. 157–178). New York: Guilford Press.

Asendorpf, J. B., Denissen, J. J. A., & van Aken, M. A. G. (2008). Inhibited and aggressive preschool children at 23 years of age: Personality and social transitions into adulthood. *Developmental Psychology, 44*, 997–1101.

Asendorpf, J. B., & Meier, G. H. (1993). Personality effects on children's speech in everyday life: Sociability-mediated exposure and shyness-mediated reactivity to social situations. *Journal of Personality and Social Psychology, 65*, 1072–1083.

Ashton, M. C., Lee, K., & Paunonen, S. V. (2002). What is the central feature of extraversion?: Social attention versus reward sensitivity. *Journal of Personality and Social Psychology, 83*, 245–252.

Bandura, A., & Walters, R. H. (1963). *Social learning and personality development.* New York: Holt, Rinehart & Watson.

Bates, J. E., Wachs, T. D., & Emde, R. N. (1994). Toward practical uses for biological concepts of temperament. In J. E. Bates & T. D. Wachs (Eds.), *Temperament: Individual differences at the interface of biology and behavior* (pp. 275–306). Washington, DC: American Psychological Association.

Belsky, J., Friedman, S. L., & Hsieh, K.-H. (2001). Testing a core emotion-regulation prediction: Does early attentional persistence moderate the effect of infant negative emotionality on later development? *Child Development, 72*, 123–133.

Berdan, L. E., Keane, S. P., & Calkins, S. D. (2008). Temperament and externalizing behavior: Social preference and perceived acceptance as protective factors. *Developmental Psychology, 44*, 957–968.

Bernt, T. J. (2004). Children's friendships: Shifts over a half-century in perspectives on their development and their effects. *Merrill–Palmer Quarterly, 50*, 206–223.

Billman, J., & McDevitt, S. C. (1980). Convergence of parent and observer ratings of temperament with observations of peer interaction in nursery school. *Child Development, 51*, 395–400.

Bishop, G., Spence, S. H., & McDonald, C. (2003). Can parents and teachers provide a reliable and valid report of behavioral inhibition? *Child Development, 74*, 1899–1917.

Bohlin, G., Hagekull, B., & Anderson, K. (2005). Behavioral inhibition as a precursor of peer social competence in early school age: The interplay with attachment and nonparental conflict. *Merrill–Palmer Quarterly, 51*, 1–19.

Boivin, M., Hymel, S., & Bukowski, W. M. (1995). The roles of social withdrawal, peer rejection, and victimization by peers in predicting loneliness and depressed mood in childhood. *Developmental Psychopathology, 7*, 765–785.

Buss, A. H., & Plomin, R. (1984). *Temperament: Early developing personality traits.* Hillsdale: NJ: Erlbaum.

Cairns, R., & Cairns, B. (1991). Social cognition and social networks: A developmental perspective. In D. Pepler & K. H. Rubin (Eds.), *The development and treatment of childhood aggression* (pp. 249–278). Hillsdale, NJ: Erlbaum.

Calkins, S. D. (1994). Origins and outcomes of individual differences in emotional regulation. *Monographs of the Society for Research in Child Development, 59*, 53–72.

Calkins, S. D., Gill, K. L., Johnson, M. C., & Smith, C. L. (1999). Emotional reactivity and emotional regulation strategies as predictors of social behavior with peers during toddlerhood. *Social Development, 8*, 310–341.

Campbell-Sills, L., & Barlow, D. H. (2007). Incorporating emotion regulation into conceptualizations and treatments of anxiety and mood disorders. In J. J. Gross (Ed.), *Handbook of emotion regulation* (pp. 542–559). New York: Guilford Press.

Casiglia, A. C., Lo Coco, A., & Zappulla, C. (1998). Aspects of social reputation and peer relationships in Italian children: A cross-cultural perspective. *Developmental Psychology, 34*, 723–730.

Caspi, A., Elder, G. H., & Bem, D. J. (1988). Moving away from the world: Life course patterns of shy children. *Developmental Psychology, 24*, 824–831.

Cheek, J. M., & Buss, A. H. (1981). Shyness and sociability. *Journal of Personality and Social Psychology, 41*, 330–339.

Chen, X., Cen, G., Li, D., & He, Y. (2005). Social functioning and adjustment in Chinese children: The imprint of historical time. *Child Development, 76*, 182–195.

Chen, X., DeSouza, A. T., Chen, H., & Wang, L. (2006). Reticent behavior and experiences in peer interactions in Chinese and Canadian children. *Developmental Psychology, 42*, 656–665.

Chen, X., Rubin, K. H., Li, B.-S., & Li, D. (1999). Adolescent outcomes of social functioning in children. *International Journal of Behavioral Development, 23*, 199–223.

Christopher, J. S., Hansen, D. J., & MacMillan, V. M. (1991). Effectiveness of a peer–helper intervention to increase children's social interactions: Generalization, maintenance, and social validity. *Behavior Modification, 15*, 22–50.

Cicchetti, D., & Cohen, D. J. (1995). Perspectives on developmental psychopathology. In D. Cicchetti & D. J. Cohen (Eds.), *Developmental psychopathology* (Vol. 1, pp. 3–16). New York: Wiley.

Cillessen, A. H. N., van IJzendoorn, H. W., van Lieshout, C. F. M., & Hartup, W. W. (1992). Heterogeneity among peer-rejected boys: Subtypes and stabilities. *Child Development, 63*, 893–905.

Clark, L. A., Watson, D., & Mineka, S. (1994).

Temperament, personality, and the mood and anxiety disorders. *Journal of Abnormal Psychology*, 103, 103–116.

Cole, P. M., Michel, M. K., & Teti, L. O. (1994). The development of emotion regulation and dysregulation: A clinical perspective. *Monographs of the Society for Research in Child Development*, 59, 73–102.

Cooley, C. H. (1902). *Human nature and the social order*. New York: Scribner.

Coplan, R. J. (2000). Assessing non-social play in early childhood: Conceptual and methodologicalapproaches. In K. Gitlin-Weiner, A. Sangdrund, & C. Schaefer (Eds.), *Play diagnosis and assessment* (2nd ed., pp. 563–598). New York: Wiley.

Coplan, R. J. (2011). Not just "playing alone": Exploring multiple forms of nonsocial play in childhood. In A. D. Pellegrini (Ed.), *The Oxford handbook of the development of play* (pp. 185–201). New York: Oxford University Press.

Coplan, R. J., Arbeau, K. A., & Armer, M. (2008). Don't fret, be supportive!: Maternal characteristics linking child shyness to psychosocial and school adjustment in kindergarten. *Journal of Abnormal Child Psychology*, 36, 359–371.

Coplan, R. J., DeBow, A., Schneider, B. H., & Graham, A. A. (2009). The social behaviors of inhibited children in and out of preschool. *British Journal of Developmental Psychology*, 27, 891–905.

Coplan, R. J., Girardi, A., Findlay, L. C., & Frohlick, S. L. (2007). Understanding solitude: Young children's attitudes and responses toward hypothetical socially withdrawn peers. *Social Development*, 16, 390–409.

Coplan, R. J., Prakash, K., O'Neil, K., & Armer, M. (2004). Do you "want" to play?: Distinguishing between conflicted shyness and social disinterest in early childhood. *Developmental Psychology*, 40, 244–258.

Coplan, R. J., & Rubin, K. H. (2010). Social withdrawal and shyness in childhood: History, theories, definitions, and assessment. In K. H. Rubin & R. J. Coplan (Eds.), *The development of shyness and social withdrawal in childhood and adolescence* (pp. 3–20). New York: Guilford Press.

Coplan, R. J., Rubin, K. H., Fox, N. A., Calkins, S. D., & Stewart, S. L. (1994). Being alone, playing alone, and acting alone: Distinguishing among reticence and passive and active solitude in young children. *Child Development*, 65, 129–137.

Coplan, R. J., Schneider, B. H., Matheson, A., & Graham, A. (2010). "Play skills" for shy children: Development of a Social Skills Facilitated Play early intervention program for extremely inhibited preschoolers. *Infant and Child Development*, 19, 223–237.

Coplan, R. J., & Weeks, M. (2010a). Unsociability in middle childhood: Conceptualization, assessment, and associations with socio-emotional functioning. *Merrill–Palmer Quarterly*, 56, 105–130.

Coplan, R. J., & Weeks, M. (2010b). Unsociability and the preference for solitude in children. In K. H. Rubin & R. J. Coplan (Eds.), *The development of shyness and social withdrawal* (pp. 64–83). New York: Guilford Press.

David, K. M., & Murphy, B. C. (2007). Interparental conflict and preschoolers' peer relations: The moderating roles of temperament and gender. *Social Development*, 16, 1–20.

Degnan, K. A., Calkins, S. D., Keane, S. P., & Hill-Soderlund, A. (2008). Profiles of disruptive behavior across early childhood: Contributions of frustration reactivity, physiological regulation, and maternal behavior. *Child Development*, 79, 1357–1376.

Degnan, K. A., Hane, A. A., Henderson, H. A., Moas, O. L., Reeb-Sutherland, B. C., & Fox, N. A. (2011). Longitudinal stability of temperamental exuberance and social–emotional outcomes in early childhood. *Developmental Psychology*, 47, 765–780.

Denham, S. A., McKinley, M., Couchoud, E. A., & Holt, R. (1990). Emotional and behavioral predictors of preschool peer ratings. *Child Development*, 61, 1145–1152.

Derryberry, D., & Rothbart, M. K. (1997). Reactive and effortful processes in the organization of temperament. *Development and Psychopathology*, 9, 633–652.

Diener, M. L., & Kim, D. Y. (2004). Maternal and child predictors of preschool children's social competence. *Journal of Applied Developmental Psychology*, 25, 3–24.

Dodge, K. A., Coie, J. D., & Lynam, D. (2006). Aggression and antisocial behavior in youth. In W. Damon & N. Eisenberg (Eds.), *Handbook of child psychology: Vol. 3. Social, emotional, and personality development* (6th ed., pp. 719–788). New York: Wiley.

Dodge, K. A., & Garber, J. (1991). Emotion and social information processing. In J. Garber & K. A. Dodge (Eds.), *The development of emotion regulation and dysregulation* (pp. 159–181). Cambridge, UK: Cambridge University Press.

Dunn, J., & Cutting, A. L. (1999). Understanding others, and individual differences in friendship interactions in young children. *Social Development*, 8, 201–219.

Eisenberg, N., Cameron, E., Tryon, K., & Dodez, R. (1981). Socialization of prosocial behavior in the preschool classroom. *Developmental Psychology*, 17, 773–782.

Eisenberg, N., & Fabes, R. (2006). Emotion regulation and children's socioemotional competence. In B. Lawrence & C. S. Tamir-Lemonda (Eds.), *Child psychology: A handbook of contemporary issues* (2nd ed., pp. 357–381). New York: Psychology Press.

Eisenberg, N., Fabes, R. A., Bernzweig, J., Karbon, M., Poulin, R., & Hanish, L. (1993). The relations of emotionality and regulation to preschoolers' social skills and sociometric status. *Child Development, 64,* 1418–1438.

Eisenberg, N., Fabes, R. A., Guthrie, I. K., Murphy, B. C., Maszk, P., Holmgren, R., et al. (1996). The relations of regulation and emotionality to problem behavior in elementary school children. *Development and Psychopathology, 8,* 141–162.

Eisenberg, N., Fabes, R. A., Guthrie, I. K., & Reiser, M. (2000). Dispositional emotionality and regulation: Their role in predicting quality of social functioning. *Journal of Personality and Social Psychology, 78,* 136–157.

Eisenberg, N., Fabes, R. A., Murphy, B., Karbon, M., Smith, M., & Maszk, P. (1996). The relations of children's dispositional empathy-related responding to their emotionality, regulation, and social functioning. *Developmental Psychology, 32,* 195–209.

Eisenberg, N., Fabes, R. A., Nyman, M., Bernzweig, J., & Pinuelas, A. (1994). The relations of emotionality and regulation to children's anger-related reactions. *Child Development, 65,* 109–128.

Eisenberg, N., Fabes, R. A., Shepard, S. A., Murphy, B. C., Guthrie, I. K., Jones, S., et al. (1997). Contemporaneous and longitudinal prediction of children's social functioning from regulation and emotionality. *Child Development, 68,* 642–664.

Eisenberg, N., Guthrie, I. K., Fabes, R. A., Reiser, M., Murphy, B. C., Holmgren, R., et al. (1997). The relations of regulation and emotionality to resiliency and competent social functioning in elementary school children. *Child Development, 68,* 295–311.

Eisenberg, N., Hofer, C., & Vaughan, J. (2007). Effortful control and its socioemotional consequences. In J. J. Gross (Ed.), *Handbook of emotion regulation* (pp. 287–306). New York: Guilford Press.

Eisenberg, N., Pidada, S., & Liew, J. (2001). The relations of regulation and negative emotionality to Indonesian children's social functioning. *Child Development, 72,* 1747–1763.

Eisenberg, N., Spinrad, T. L., Fabes, R. A., Reiser, M., Cumberland, A., Shepard, S. A., et al. (2004). The relations of effortful control and impulsivity to children's resiliency and adjustment. *Child Development, 75,* 25–46.

Eisenberg, N., Vaughn, J., & Hofer, C. (2009). Temperament, self-regulation, and peer social competence. In K. H. Rubin, W. M. Bukowski, & B. Laursen (Eds.), *Handbook of peer interactions, relationships, and groups* (pp. 473–489). New York: Guilford Press.

Else-Quest, N. M., Hyde, J. S., Goldsmith, H. H., & Van Hulle, C. A. (2006). Gender differences in temperament: A meta-analysis. *Psychological Bulletin, 132,* 33–72.

Fabes, R. A., & Eisenberg, N. (1992). Young children's coping with interpersonal anger. *Child Development, 63,* 116–128.

Fabes, R. A., Eisenberg, N., Jones, S., Smith, M., Guthrie, I., Poulin, R., et al. (1999). Regulation, emotionality, and preschoolers' socially competent peer interactions. *Child Development, 70,* 432–442.

Fantuzzo, J., Sekino, Y., & Cohen, H. L. (2004). An examination of the contributions of interactive peer play to salient classroom competencies for urban Head Start children. *Psychology in the Schools, 41,* 323–336.

Fordham, K., & Stevenson-Hinde, J. (1999). Shyness, friendship quality, and adjustment during middle childhood. *Journal of Child Psychology and Psychiatry, 40,* 757–768.

Fox, N. A., & Henderson, H. A. (1999). Does infancy matter?: Predicting social behavior from infant temperament. *Infant Behavior and Development, 22,* 445–455.

Fox, N. A., Henderson, H. A., Rubin, K. H., Calkins, S. D., & Schmidt, L. A. (2001). Continuity and discontinuity of behavioral inhibition and exuberance: Psychophysiological and behavioral influences across the first four years of life. *Child Development, 72,* 1–21.

Gazelle, H. (2008). Behavioral profiles of anxious solitary children and heterogeneity in peer relations. *Developmental Psychology, 44,* 1604–1624.

Gazelle, H., & Ladd, G. W. (2003). Anxious solitude and peer exclusion: A diathesis–stress model of internalizing trajectories in childhood. *Child Development, 74,* 257–278.

Gazelle, H., & Rudolph, K. D. (2004). Moving toward and away from the world: Social approach and avoidance trajectories in anxious solitary youth. *Child Development, 75,* 829–849.

Gleason, T. R., Gower, A. M., Hohmann, L. M., & Gleason, T. C. (2005). Temperament and friendship in preschool-aged children. *International Journal of Behavioral Development, 29,* 336–344.

Gray, J. A. (1991). The neuropsychology of temperament. In J. Strelau & A. Angleitner (Eds.), *Explorations in temperament: International perspectives on theory and measurement* (pp. 105–128). New York: Plenum Press.

Graziano, W. G. (1994). The development of agreeableness as a dimension of personality. In C. F. Halverson, G. A. Kohnstamm, & R. R. Martin (Eds.), *The developing structure of temperament and personality from infancy to childhood* (pp. 339–354). Hillsdale, NJ: Erlbaum.

Gunnar, M. R., Sebanc, A. M., Tout, K., Donzella, B., & van Dulmen, M. M. (2003). Peer rejection, temperament, and cortisol activity in preschoolers. *Developmental Psychobiology, 43,* 346–358.

Hammen, C., & Rudolph, K. (2003). Childhood depression. In E. J. Mash & R. A. Barkley (Eds.), *Child psychopathology* (2nd ed., pp. 233–278). New York: Guilford Press.

Hanish, L. D., Eisenberg, N., Fabes, R. A., Spinrad, T. L., Ryan, P., & Schmidt, S. (2004). The expression and regulation of negative emotions: Risk factors for young children's peer victimization. *Development and Psychopathology, 16,* 335–353.

Hanish, L. D., Kochenderfer-Ladd, B., Fabes, R. A., Martin, C. L., & Denning, D. (2004). Bullying among young children: The influence of peers and teachers. In D. L. Espelage & S. M. Swearer (Eds.), *Bullying in American schools: A social–ecological perspective on prevention and intervention* (pp. 141–159). Mahwah, NJ: Erlbaum.

Harrist, A. W., Zaia, A. F., Bates, J. E., Dodge, K. A., & Pettit, G. S. (1997). Subtypes of social withdrawal in early childhood: Sociometric status and social-cognitive differences across four years. *Child Development, 68,* 278–294.

Hay, D. F., Payne, A., & Chadwick, A. (2004). Peer relations in childhood. *Journal of Child Psychology and Psychiatry, 45,* 84–108.

Hill, A. L., Degnan, K. A., Calkins, S. D., & Keane, S. P. (2006). Profiles of externalizing behavior problems for boys and girls across preschool: The roles of emotion regulation and inattention. *Developmental Psychology, 42,* 913–928.

Hinde, R. A. (1987). *Individuals, relationships, and culture.* Cambridge, UK: Cambridge University Press.

Izard, C. E. (2009). Emotion theory and research: Highlights, unanswered questions, and emerging issues. *Annual Review of Psychology, 60,* 1–25.

Izard, C. E., King, K. A., Trentacosta, C. J., Morgan, J. K., Laurenceau, J.-P., Krauthamer-Ewing, E. S., et al. (2008). Accelerating the development of emotion competence in Head Start children: Effects of adaptive and maladaptive behavior. *Development and Psychopathology, 20,* 369–397.

Izard, C. E., Schultz, D., Fine, S. E., Youngstrom, E., & Ackerman, B. P. (1999–2000). Temperament, cognitive ability, emotion knowledge, and adaptive social behavior. *Imagination, Cognition, and Personality, 19,* 305–330.

Jensen-Campbell, L. A., & Malcolm, K. T. (2007). The importance of conscientiousness in adolescent interpersonal relationships. *Personality and Social Psychology Bulletin, 33,* 368–383.

Jones, S., Eisenberg, N., Fabes, R. A., & MacKinnon, D. P. (2002) Parents' reactions to elementary school children's negative emotions: Relations to social and emotional functioning at school. *Merrill–Palmer Quarterly, 48,* 133–159.

Kagan, J., Reznick, J. S., Clarke, C., Snidman, S., & Garcia-Coll, C. (1984). Behavioral inhibition to the unfamiliar. *Child Development, 55,* 2212–2225.

Kim, J., & Cicchetti, D. (2010). Longitudinal pathways linking child maltreatment, emotion regulation, peer relations, and psychopathology. *Journal of Child Psychology and Psychiatry, 51,* 706–716.

Kochanska, G., Murray, K. T., & Harlan, E. T. (2000). Effortful control in early childhood: Continuity and change, antecedents, and implications for social development. *Developmental Psychology, 36,* 220–232.

Ladd, G. W. (2006). Peer rejection, aggressive or withdrawn behavior, and psychological maladjustment from ages 5 to 12: An examination of four predictive models. *Child Development, 77,* 822–846.

Ladd, G. W., & Burgess, K. B. (1999). Charting the relationship trajectories of aggressive, withdrawn, and aggressive/withdrawn children during early grade school. *Child Development, 70,* 910–929.

Ladd, G. W., & Golter, B. S. (1988). Parents' management of preschooler's peer relations: Is it related to children's social competence. *Developmental Psychology, 24,* 109–117.

Laible, D., Panfile, T., Eye, J., Carlo, G., & Parker, J. (2010). Emotionality and emotion regulation: A person-centered approach to predicting socioemotional adjustment in young adolescents. *Journal of Research in Personality, 44,* 621–629.

Larson, R., & Richards, M. H. (1991). Daily companionship in late childhood and early adolescence: Changing developmental contexts. *Child Development, 62,* 284–300.

Ledingham, J. E. (1991). Social cognition and aggression. In D. J. Pepler & K. H. Rubin (Eds.), *The development and treatment of childhood aggression* (pp. 279–286). Hillsdale, NJ: Erlbaum.

Lemerise, E., & Arsenio, W. F. (2000). An integrated model of emotion processes and cognition in social information processing. *Child Development, 71,* 107–118.

Lengua, L. J. (2002). The contribution of emotionality and self-regulation to the understanding of children's response to multiple risk. *Child Development, 73,* 144–161.

McAdams, D. P., & Olson, B. D. (2010). Personality development: Continuity and change over the life course. *Annual Review of Psychology, 61,* 517–542.

Mead, G. H. (1934). *Mind, self, and society.* Chicago: University of Chicago Press.

Mobley, C. E., & Pullis, M. E. (1991). Temperament and behavioral adjustment in preschool children. *Early Childhood Research Quarterly, 6,* 577–586.

Mullin, B. C., & Hinshaw, S. P. (2007). Emotion regulation and externalizing disorders in children and adolescents. In J. J. Gross (Ed.), *Handbook of emotion regulation* (pp. 523–541). New York: Guilford Press.

Oh, W., Rubin, K., Bowker, J., Booth-LaForce, C., Rose-Krasnor, L., & Laursen, B. (2008). Trajectories of social withdrawal middle childhood to early adolescence. *Journal of Abnormal Child Psychology, 36*(4), 553–566.

Oldehinkel, A. J., Hartman, C. A., de Winter, A. F., Veenstra, R., & Ormel, J. (2004). Temperament profiles associated with internalizing and externalizing problems in preadolescence. *Development and Psychopathology, 16,* 421–440.

Olweus, D. (1978). *Aggression in the schools: Bullies and whipping boys.* Washington, DC: Wiley.

Park, K. A., Lay, K. L., & Ramsay, L. (1993). Individual differences and developmental changes in preschoolers' friendships. *Developmental Psychology, 29,* 264–270.

Paterson, G., & Sanson, A. (1999). The association of behavioral adjustment to temperament, parenting and family characteristics among 5-year-old children. *Social Development, 8,* 293–309.

Paulussen-Hoogeboom, M. C., Stams, G. J., Hermanns, J. M., & Peetsma, T. T. (2007). Child negative emotionality and parenting from infancy to preschool: A meta-analytic review. *Developmental Psychology, 43,* 438–553.

Pedersen, S., Vitaro, F., Barker, E. D., & Borge, A. I. H. (2007). The timing of middle-childhood peer rejection and friendship: Linking early behavior to early-adolescent adjustment. *Child Development, 78,* 1037–1051.

Pellegrini, A. D., Galda, L., Flor, D., Bartini, M., & Charak, D. (1997). Close relationships, individual differences, and early literacy learning. *Journal of Experimental Child Psychology, 67,* 409–422.

Pérez-Edgar, K., Bar-Haim, Y., McDermott, J. M., Chronis-Tuscano, A., Pine, D. S., & Fox, N. A. (2010). Attention biases to threat and behavioral inhibition in early childhood shape adolescent social withdrawal. *Emotion, 10,* 349–357.

Perren, S., & Alsaker, F. D. (2006). Social behavior and peer relationships of victims, bully-victims, and bullies in kindergarten. *Journal of Child Psychology and Psychiatry, 47,* 45–57.

Perry, D. G., Kusel, S. J., & Perry, L. C. (1988). Victims of peer aggression. *Developmental Psychology, 24,* 807–814.

Piaget, J. (1932). *The moral judgement of the child.* Glencoe, IL: Free Press.

Pike, A., & Atzaba-Poria, N. (2003). Do sibling and friend relationships share the same temperament origins?: A twin study. *Journal of Child Psychology and Psychiatry and Allied Disciplines, 44,* 598–611.

Plomin, R., & Rowe, D. (1977). A twin study of temperament in young children. *Journal of Psychology, 97,* 107–113.

Prior, M., Sanson, A., Smart, D., & Oberklaid, F. (2000). *Pathways from infancy to adolescence: Australian Temperament Project: 1983–2000.* Melbourne: Australian Institute of Family Studies.

Putnam, S. P., & Stifter, C. A. (2005). Behavioral approach–inhibition in toddlers: Prediction from infancy, positive and negative affective components, and relations with behavior problems. *Child Development, 76,* 212–226.

Rapee, R., Kennedy, S., Ingram, M., Edwards, S., & Sweeney, L. (2005). Prevention and early intervention of anxiety disorders in inhibited preschool children. *Journal of Consulting Clinical Psychology, 73,* 488–497.

Raver, C. C., Blackburn, E. K., Bancroft, M., & Torp, N. (1999). Relations between effective emotion self-regulation, attentional control, and low income preschoolers' social competence with peers. *Early Education and Development, 10,* 333–350.

Renshaw, P. D. (1981). The roots of peer interaction research: A historical analysis of the 1930s. In S. R. Asher & J. M. Gottman (Eds.), *The development of children's friendships* (pp. 1–25). New York: Cambridge University Press.

Rimm-Kaufman, S. E., & Kagan, J. (2005). Infant predictors of kindergarten behavior: The contribution of inhibited and uninhibited temperament types. *Behavioral Disorders, 30,* 329–345.

Rothbart, M. K. (1989). Temperament and development. In G. A. Kohnstamm, J. E. Bates, & M. K. Rothbart (Eds.), *Temperament in childhood* (pp. 187–247). New York: Wiley.

Rothbart, M. K., Ahadi, S. A., Hershey, K. L., & Fisher, P. (2001). Investigations of temperament at three to seven years: The Children's Behavior Questionnaire. *Child Development, 72,* 1394–1408.

Rothbart, M. K., & Bates, J. E. (2006). Temperament. In N. W. Damon, R. M. Lerner, & N. Eisenberg (Eds.), *Handbook of child psychology: Vol. 3. Social, emotional and personality development* (6th ed., pp. 99–166). New York: Wiley.

Rothbart, M. K., & Derryberry, D. (2002). Temperament in children. In C. von Hofsten & L. Bäckman (Eds.), *Psychology at the turn of the millennium: Vol. 2. Social, developmental, and clinical perspectives* (pp. 17–35). East Sussex, UK: Psychology Press.

Rothbart, M. K., Sheese, B. E., & Posner, M. I. (2007). Executive attention and effortful control: Linking temperament, brain networks, and genes. *Child Development Perspectives, 1,* 2–7.

Rubin, K. H. (1982). Non-social play in preschoolers: Necessary evil? *Child Development, 53,* 651–657.

Rubin, K. H., Bowker, J., & Gazelle, H. (2010). Social withdrawal in childhood and adolescence:

Peer relationships and social competence. In K. H. Rubin & R. J. Coplan (Eds.), *The development of shyness and social withdrawal* (pp. 131–156). New York: Guilford Press.

Rubin, K. H., Bukowski, W. M., & Laursen, B. (Eds.). (2009). *Handbook of peer interactions, relationships, and groups.* New York: Guilford Press.

Rubin, K. H., Bukowski, W., & Parker, J. G. (2006). Peer interactions, relationships, and groups. In W. Damon, R. M. Lerner, & N. Eisenberg (Eds.), *Handbook of child psychology: Vol. 3. Social, emotional, and personality development* (6th ed., pp. 571–645). New York: Wiley.

Rubin, K. H., Chen, X., McDougall, P., Bowker, A., & McKinnon, J. (1995). The Waterloo Longitudinal Project: Predicting adolescent internalizing and externalizing problems from early and midchildhood. *Developmental Psychopathology, 7,* 751–764.

Rubin, K. H., Coplan, R. J., Fox, N. A., & Calkins, S. D. (1995). Emotionality, emotion regulation, and preschoolers' social adaptation. *Development and Psychopathology, 7,* 49–62.

Rubin, K. H., Daniels-Beirness, T., & Bream, L. (1984). Social isolation and social problem solving: A longitudinal study. *Journal of Consulting and Clinical Psychology, 52,* 17–25.

Rubin, K. H., Hastings, P. D., Stewart, S. L., Henderson, H. A., & Chen, X. (1997). The consistency and concomitants of inhibition: Some of the children all the time. *Child Development, 68,* 467–483.

Rubin, K. H., LeMare, L., & Lollis, S. (1990). Social withdrawal in childhood: Developmental psychopathologies to peer rejection. In S. R. Asher & J. D. Coie (Eds.), *Peer rejection in childhood* (pp. 217–249). New York: Cambridge University Press.

Rubin, K. H., Wojslawowicz, J. C., Rose-Krasnor, L., Booth-LaForce, C., & Burgess, K. B. (2006). The best friendships of shy/withdrawn children: Prevalence, stability, and relationships quality. *Journal of Abnormal Child Psychology, 34,* 143–157.

Rydell, A. M., Thorell, L. B., & Bohlin, G. (2007). Emotion regulation in relation to social functioning: An investigation of child self-reports. *European Journal of Developmental Psychology, 4,* 293–313.

Sanson, A., Hemphill, S. A., & Smart, D. (2004). Connections between temperament and social development: A review. *Social Development, 13,* 142–170.

Sanson, A. V., Smart, D. F., Prior, M., Oberklaid, F., & Pedlow, R. (1994). The structure of temperament from three to seven years: Age, sex and demographic influences. *Merrill–Palmer Quarterly, 40,* 233–252.

Schaughency, E. A., Vannatta, K., Langhinrichsen, J., Lally, C., & Seeley, J. (1992). Correlates of sociometric status in school children in Buenos Aires. *Journal of Abnormal Child Psychology, 20,* 317–326.

Schmidt, L. A., & Buss, A. H. (2010). Understanding shyness: Four questions and four decades of research. In K. H. Rubin & R. J. Coplan (Eds.), *The development of shyness and social withdrawal* (pp. 23–41). New York: Guilford Press.

Schneider, B. (1999). A multi-method exploration of the friendships of children considered socially withdrawn by their peers. *Journal of Abnormal Psychology, 27,* 115–123.

Schneider, B. H. (2009). An observational study of the interactions of socially withdrawn/anxious early adolescents and their friends. *Journal of Child Psychology and Psychiatry, 50,* 799–806.

Schneider, B. H., Richard, J., Younger, A. J., & Freeman, P. (2000). A longitudinal exploration of the continuity of children's social participation and social withdrawal across socioeconomic status levels and social settings. *European Journal of Social Psychology, 30,* 497–519.

Shiner, R. L. (2000). Linking childhood personality with adaptation: Evidence for continuity and change across time into late adolescence. *Journal of Personality and Social Psychology, 78,* 310–325.

Shiner, R. L., Masten, A. S., & Roberts, J. M. (2003). Childhood personality foreshadows adult personality and life outcomes two decades later. *Journal of Personality, 71,* 1145–1170.

Skarpness, L. R., & Carson, D. K. (1987). Correlates of kindergarten adjustment: Temperament and communicative competence. *Early Childhood Research Quarterly, 2,* 367–376.

Spence, S. H., De Young, A., Toon, C., & Bond, S. (2009). Longitudinal examination of the associations between emotional dysregulation, coping responses to peer provocation, and victimisation in children. *Australian Journal of Psychology, 61,* 145–155.

Spinrad, T. C., Eisenberg, N., Cumberland, A., Fabes, R. A., Valiente, C., Shepard, S. A., et al. (2006). Relation of emotion-related regulation of children's social competence: A longitudinal study. *Emotion, 6,* 498–510.

Spinrad, T. C., Eisenberg, N., Harris, E., Hanish, L., Fabes, R. A., Kupanoff, K., et al. (2004). The relation of children's everyday non-social peer play behavior to their emotionality, regulation, and social functioning. *Developmental Psychology, 40,* 67–80.

Sroufe, L. A., Schork, E., Motti, F., Lawroski, N., & LaFreniere, P. (1985). The role of affect in social competence. In C. E. Izard, J. Kagan, & R. B. Zajonc (Eds.), *Emotions, cognition, and behavior* (pp. 289–319). New York: Cambridge University Press.

Sterry, T. W., Reiter-Purtill, J., Gartstein, M. A., Gerhardt, C. A., Vannatta, K., & Noll, R. B. (2010). Temperament and peer acceptance: The role of social behavior. *Merrill–Palmer Quarterly, 56,* 189–219.

Stifter, C. A., Putnam, S., & Jahromi, L. (2008). Exuberant and inhibited toddlers: Stability of temperament and risk for problem behavior. *Development and Psychopathology, 20,* 401–421.

Stocker, C., & Dunn, J. (1990). Sibling relationships in childhood: Links with friendships and peer relationships. *British Journal of Developmental Psychology, 8,* 227–244.

Sullivan, H. S. (1953). *The interpersonal theory of psychiatry.* New York: Norton.

Szewczyk-Sokolowski, M., Bost, K. K., & Wainwright, A. B. (2005). Attachment, temperament, and preschool children's peer acceptance. *Social Development, 14,* 379–397.

Thomas, A., & Chess, S. (1977). *Temperament and development.* New York: Brunner/Mazel.

Trentacosta, C. T., & Shaw, D. S. (2009). Emotional self-regulation, peer rejection and antisocial-behavior: Developmental associations from early childhood to early adolescence. *Journal of Applied Developmental Psychology, 30,* 356–365.

Wachs, T. D., & Kohnstamm, G. A. (2001). *Temperament in context.* Hillsdale, NJ: Erlbaum.

Walden, T., Lemerise, E., & Smith, C. M. (1999). Friendship and popularity in preschool classrooms. *Early Education and Development, 10,* 351–371.

Wichmann, C., Coplan, R. J., & Daniels, T. (2004). The social cognitions of socially withdrawn children. *Social Development, 13,* 377–392.

Wilson, B. J. (2006). The entry behavior of aggressive/rejected children: The contributions of status and temperament. *Social Development, 15,* 463–479.

Younger, A. J., Gentile, C., & Burgess, K. B. (1993). Children's perceptions of social withdrawal: Changes across age. In K. H. Rubin & J. B. Asendorpf (Eds.), *Social withdrawal, inhibition, and shyness in childhood* (pp. 215–235). Hillsdale, NJ: Erlbaum.

Zentner, M., & Bates, J. E. (2008). Child temperament: An integrative review of concepts, research programs, and measures. *European Journal of Developmental Science, 2,* 7–37.

Zhou, Q., Eisenberg, N., Wang, Y., & Reiser, M. (2004). Chinese children's effortful control and dispositional anger/frustration: Relations to parenting styles and children's social functioning. *Developmental Psychology, 40,* 352–366.

CHAPTER 22

Culture and Temperament

Xinyin Chen
Fan Yang
Rui Fu

Cross-cultural research has indicated that children and adults in different societies may differ in social, behavioral, and psychological functioning. For example, children in many non-Western societies, such as Bedouin Arab (Ariel & Sever, 1980), Mayan (Gaskins, 2000), and Kenyan, Mexican, and Indian (Edwards, 2000) societies, tend to engage in less sociodramatic play than Western children. Moreover, during social pretense play, children in some cultural and ethnic groups, such as Korean Americans, display more thematic, daily-life activities (e.g., family role play) and fewer fantasy activities (e.g., actions related to legend or fairy-tale characters) than European American children (e.g., Farver, Kim, & Lee, 1995). There is also evidence that children in China, Korea, Mexico, and Sweden tend to exhibit more cooperative-compliant behaviors and less aggressive and oppositional behaviors than children in North America (e.g., Bergeron & Schneider, 2005; Kagan & Knight, 1981; Orlick, Zhou, & Partington, 1990; Russell, Hart, Robinson, & Olsen, 2003). Finally, researchers have found that Asian children and adolescents appear less sociable than their Western counterparts in social interactions (e.g., Chen, Desouza, Chen, & Wang, 2006; Gong, 1984).

Given this brief background, it would appear important to ask the following questions:

1. Are there cross-cultural differences in early temperamental characteristics that constitute a developmental origin of individual social, behavioral, and psychological functioning?
2. How do adults and children in different cultures perceive, evaluate, and respond to, specific temperamental characteristics? How does culture "define" the meanings of these characteristics?
3. How does a distinct pattern of temperamental development emerge in a particular society or community? What role do cultural factors play in determining the developmental pattern and in regulating temperamental influence on individual development?

In this chapter, we attempt to address these questions. We focus mainly on the fundamental dimensions of temperamental characteristics such as reactivity and self-control and their development in cultural context. We first discuss some conceptual issues and present a theoretical framework concerning the involvement of cultural norms and values in temperamental development. Then, we discuss methodological issues in cross-cultural research on temperament. Next, we review the literature on cross-cultural variations in the display of major temperamental characteristics. We also discuss the functional meanings and developmental patterns of these characteristics in particular societies or communities and the role of socialization, social interaction, and other contextual factors in temperamental development. The chapter concludes with a discussion of future directions in the study of culture and temperament.

Culture, Social Interaction, and Temperament: A Contextual–Developmental Perspective

Cultural influence on human development has been discussed mainly from two broad perspectives. The *socioecological theory* (Bronfenbrenner & Morris, 2006; Super & Harkness, 1986) indicates that culture affects individual attitudes, behaviors, and emotions, mainly as a part of the socioecological environment. The cultural beliefs and values that are endorsed in a society or community may directly guide individual behaviors. In addition, culture may play a role in shaping development through organizing various social settings such as community services and school and day care arrangements. From a different perspective, the *sociocultural theory* (Cole, 1996; Rogoff, 2003; Vygotsky, 1978) focuses on the transmission or internalization of external symbolic systems from the social level to the intrapersonal or psychological level. During development, children master these systems and use them as psychological tools to perform such mental processes as remembering and recalling.

Based on the socioecological and sociocultural perspectives, Chen (2012) and his colleagues (e.g., Chen & French, 2008) have recently proposed a contextual–developmental framework focusing on cultural values of socioemotional characteristics and the mediating role of the social interaction process in cultural influence on individual development (see Figure 22.1 for a depiction of the model). According to this perspective, there exist individual and group differences in early temperament that constitute a major source of individual and group variations in socioemotional and cognitive development. Peers and adults may perceive and evaluate temperamental characteristics in a manner consistent with cultural belief systems in the society. Moreover, adults and peers in different cultures may respond differently to these characteristics and express different attitudes (e.g., acceptance, rejection) toward children who display the characteristics in social interactions. Social evaluations and responses, which are guided by changing cultural norms and values, in turn serve to regulate children's behaviors and, ultimately, developmental patterns. The regulatory function of social interaction may be affected by children's sensitivity to social evaluations, such as attention to evaluations of others, understanding of social cues, and concern about social relationships. With age, children also play an increasingly active role in the social processes through their reactions to social influence and their participation in adoption of existing cultures and construction of new cultures for social evaluation and other peer activities (Chen, 2012).

Consistent with other writings (e.g., Greenfield, Suzuki, & Rothstein-Fisch, 2006), the contextual–developmental perspective focuses on cultural values of social initiative and self-control, two fundamental dimensions of socioemotional functioning (Chen & French, 2008). *Social initiative* refers to the tendency to initiate and maintain social interactions, which is often indicated by reactivity to challenging social situations. Whereas some children may readily engage in potentially challenging interactions, others may experience internal anxiety and fear, leading to exhibition of low levels of social initiative or sociability (Asendorpf, 1990). *Self-control* represents the regulatory ability to modulate behavioral and emotional reactivity, a dimension necessary for maintaining appropriate behavior during social interactions. Different societies emphasize social initiative and norm-based behavioral control in children to different extents. In Western self-oriented or individualistic cultures where acquiring independence and assertive social skills is an important socialization goal, social initiative is viewed as a major indication of

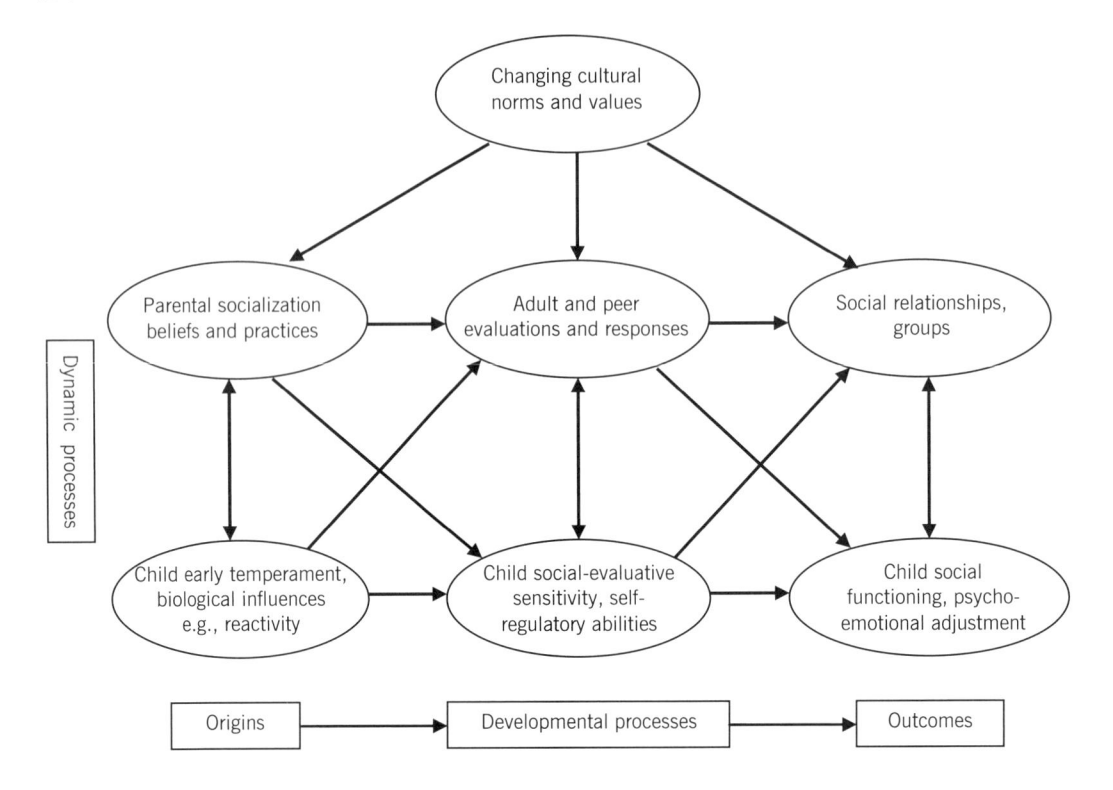

FIGURE 22.1. A contextual–developmental model concerning the mediating role of social interaction in cultural influence on temperamental development. From Chen, Chung, and Hsiao (2009). Copyright 2009 by The Guilford Press. Adapted by permission.

social competence. Although self-regulation and control are perceived as necessary for positive social interactions, individuals are encouraged to maintain a balance between the needs of the self and those of others. Consequently, behavioral control is regarded as less important, especially when it conflicts with the attainment of individual goals (Triandis, 1995). In group-oriented cultures, on the other hand, social initiative may not be highly valued because it may interfere with the harmony and cohesiveness of the group. To maintain interpersonal and group harmony, individuals need to restrain personal desires in an effort to address the needs and interests of others; thus, self-control, particularly effortful control, is more strongly and consistently emphasized. Cultural values of social initiative and self-control may influence specific aspects of socioemotional functioning, including aggression–disruption (high social initiative and low control), shyness–inhibition (low social initiative and adequate control to constrain behavioral and emotional reactivity), and sociable and prosocial-cooperative behaviors (active social initiative with effective control).

The socioecological theory (Bronfenbrenner & Morris, 2006) is concerned mainly with cultural conditions for human development, with relatively little attention to the processes of cultural influence. Whereas the sociocultural theory (Vygotsky, 1978) stresses the socialization role of adults in transmitting culture to the young generation, the theory focuses on the internalization of external symbolic systems as an important aspect of the development of cognitive or mental functions. However, the processes of cultural involvement in development, particularly in socioemotional areas, are more complicated than internalization of cultural systems or learning from senior members of the society. Many cultural norms and values about social behaviors, such as self-control in resource-limited situations and helping others, do not have inherent benefit and thus may not be readily appreciated by children.

Moreover, adult influence becomes more indirect, distal, and perhaps inadequate as children develop greater autonomy with age and engage in more social activities outside the home and classroom. The contextual–developmental perspective (Chen, 2012) highlights the role of social interaction, particularly in the peer group, as a context in mediating the links between culture and socioemotional development. The need for intimate affect and mutual support within friendship and a sense of belonging to the group is the main motivational force that directs children to participate in peer interactions, to attend to peers' social evaluations, and to maintain or modify their behaviors according to peer cultural standards. The mediational processes occur mainly at the group level, including the establishment of group norms, acceptance-based peer evaluations, and peer regulation of children's behaviors.

Methodological Issues in Cross-Cultural Research on Temperament

Cross-cultural research on temperamental characteristics and socioemotional functioning has burgeoned in the past 20 years. The methods that cross-cultural researchers have used in this area include observation; peer evaluation; teacher-, parent- and self-reports; qualitative interviews; and, to a lesser extent, physiological assessment. Each of the methods has its noticeable strengths and weaknesses. Observation, either in the controlled laboratory or naturalistic settings, provides relatively objective information about behavioral manifestations of the underlying temperamental tendency, which allows for direct cross-cultural comparisons. However, maintaining equivalent conditions in different settings, developing culturally sensitive coding systems, training coders to code data reliably from different cultures, and interpreting the results beyond observed variables are often highly challenging tasks for researchers. Peer evaluation is another method that is often highly reliable in assessing children's temperamental characteristics such as shyness–sensitivity (e.g., the Revised Class Play; Chen, Rubin, & Sun, 1992; Masten, Morison, & Pellegrini, 1985). This method is particularly useful for cross-cultural research because it taps the insiders' perspectives of children. However, peer evaluation is used mainly with children from grade 3 or 4 in schools and does not permit cross-cultural comparisons on group mean scores because peer nomination or rating data often need to be standardized within the class. Moreover, peer evaluation focuses on specific behaviors that are evident in social interactions; peers may not be particularly sensitive to many of the complicated temperamental characteristics such as low-intensity emotions and reactions to constraint.

Parent-, teacher-, and self-reports are commonly used in cross-cultural studies because of relatively low costs for data collection and advantages in data organization and analysis. With young children, parental ratings are perhaps the most common, and sometimes the only accessible, method in cross-cultural research. However, there are obvious concerns and limitations in self-report methods, such as culturally specific response biases, the "reference group" effect, and differences in understanding of the items and willingness to reveal personal information to others, which can confound the responses of participants (e.g., Schneider, French, & Chen, 2006). A possible strategy for handling many of the methodological problems is to use a multimethod approach and integrative analysis, which likely reduces potential biases and errors in the data from a single source.

Cross-cultural research relies heavily on comparisons of groups from two or more cultures. This approach can provide interesting findings about similarities and differences between children or adults in different societies, which are important for understanding the role of culture in human development. However, there are many methodological difficulties in making valid inferences from the findings. The difficulties result from various aspects of research, such as selecting representative cultural groups and controlling for confounding factors such as socioeconomic status (Schneider et al., 2006). Moreover, cross-cultural comparisons provide little information about how cultural contexts are involved in the developmental processes.

A major challenge in the cross-cultural study of temperament is the understanding of its cultural meanings. Consistent with the contextual–developmental perspective (Chen, 2012), which emphasizes the role of social interaction in cultural influence on individual behavior, we suggest that researchers examine (1) how temperamental characteristics are associated with social interactions and relationships, particularly in the peer group, and (2) how temperamental characteristics develop (e.g., how they are associated with other culturally relevant variables, what developmental outcomes they lead to) in the culture. An in-depth examination of temperamental characteristics in the context of social interactions helps promote understanding of the functional meaning that the culture ascribes to these characteristics because positive and negative evaluations and responses in interactions are indicators of cultural values and norms that are endorsed in the group. Longitudinal research may significantly promote understanding through tapping into the developmental significance of the characteristics; an examination of antecedents, concomitants, and outcomes (e.g., career achievement, psychopathological symptoms) of temperamental characteristics in the society or community may reveal their adaptive and maladaptive nature from a developmental perspective.

Culture and the Display of Temperament Characteristics

Temperament represents biologically rooted, relatively stable individual tendencies to respond to the environment. Although genetic factors and maturation constitute a foundation for temperamental development, individual experiences play an important role in shaping temperament characteristics (Rothbart & Derryberry, 1981). The experiences in culturally directed socialization and social interaction processes may facilitate or impede the exhibition of temperamental characteristics. The integration of experiences and dispositions eventually determines the development of personality, psychological well-being, and adaptation to the environment (Rothbart & Bates, 2006).

A number of studies have examined cross-cultural similarities and differences in the display of temperamental characteristics in childhood, adolescence, and adulthood. Most of the studies have relied on parental ratings or self-reports, which suffer from the methodological problems discussed earlier, and have produced inconsistent and often perplexing results. Despite the problems and confusions, some interesting cross-cultural differences have emerged among children and adults in Asian, Latino, European, and North American societies. For example, studies based on parental reports (e.g., Gartstein et al., 2006; Knyazev, Zupančič, & Slobodskaya, 2008) indicated that children in some Asian cultures were less expressive of both positive and negative emotions than children in European and North American cultures. In several observational studies, Camras and her colleagues (1998; Camras, Chen, Bakeman, Norris, & Cain, 2006) also found that Chinese infants scored lower than European American infants on the expression of positive and negative emotions, including smiling and disgust. Research on adolescent and adult personality suggested that individuals in Africa (e.g., Nigeria, South Africa), Asia (e.g., China, Korea, Japan), and South America (e.g., Costa Rica) (e.g., Lee, Okazaki, & Yoo, 2006; Oakland, Mogaji, & Dempsey, 2006; Oakland, Mpofu, & Sulkowski, 2007; Oakland, Pretorius, & Lee, 2008) are less extraverted and more introverted than Western individuals, a finding that is largely consistent with the cross-cultural literature on children. Whereas cross-cultural differences in overall expressivity are interesting, according to Chen and French (2008), cultural influence on temperament may be reflected more evidently and systematically on the dimensions of child reactivity and regulation or control in social situations.

Reactivity to Stressful Situations

Child reactivity to stressful or challenging situations is a temperamental characteristic that has pervasive effects on social and emotional development (Kagan, 1997; Rothbart & Bates, 2006). Cross-cultural differences in child negative reactivity in the early years have been found in a number of studies. Hsu, Soong, Stigler, Hong, and Liang (1981), for example, found that Taiwanese parents rated infants as displaying greater negative reactivity than did American parents. Specifically, relative to their American counterparts, Taiwanese infants were rated as more intense and irritable, and less likely to approach the unfamiliar situation. Other researchers (e.g., Ahadi, Rothbart, & Ye, 1993; Gartstein et al., 2006; Porter et al., 2005) also reported that Chinese mothers rated their children as more shy–anxious and fearful in challenging settings than did American parents. Similarly, Japanese, Vietnamese, and Haitian mothers reported high levels of reactivity in their infants (e.g., Pomerleau, Sabatier, & Malcuit, 1998; Prior, Garino, Sanson, & Oberklaid, 1987). In a study of ethnic differences on temperament and psychopathological symptoms using self-report measures, Austin and Chorpita (2004) found that Chinese American, Philipino American, and Japanese American children and adolescents reported higher levels of social anxiety and fear than their European American counterparts.

Consistent with the findings based on parental ratings and self-reports, Asian and Western children have been observed to differ in their reactivity to stressful situations. Rubin and colleagues (2006) found that Korean and Chinese toddlers exhibited more fearful and anxious reactions than Italian and Australian toddlers in novel situations. An intensive analysis of children's behaviors by Chen and colleagues (1998) revealed that Chinese toddlers stayed closer to their mothers and were less likely to explore the environment. When interacting with a stranger, Chinese toddlers displayed more vigilant and anxious behaviors, as reflected in their higher scores on the latency to leave the mother and to touch the toys when they were invited to do so.

There is some evidence that Chinese and Japanese adults and children differ from European Americans in serotonin transporter genetic polymorphisms (5-HTTLPR); cortisol reactivity; and the function of the autonomic nervous system, such as heart rate and heart rate variability in stressful settings (e.g., Kagan, Kearsley, & Zelazo, 1978; Tsai, Hong, & Cheng, 2002). These biological measures are associated with reactivity in Western children (e.g., Kagan, 1997). However, it is unknown whether similar associations exist in Asian children. Thus, one should be careful in interpreting cross-cultural differences in reactivity in terms of biological influences. Disentangling biological and environmental contributions to cross-cultural differences in temperament is an extremely difficult, if not impossible, task. A useful strategy may be to study groups of children that have similar biological backgrounds but different cultural experiences, and groups of children that have different biological backgrounds but similar cultural experiences (e.g., comparing immigrant Chinese, Canadian-born Chinese, and Canadian-born non-Chinese children in Canada; Chen & Tse, 2008, 2010).

Despite the general findings that Asian children tend to display relatively higher reactivity than Western children, several studies revealed mixed results. For example, Freedman and Freedman (1969) found that newborn Asian American infants were calmer and less labile than European American infants. More recently, Kagan and colleagues (1994) reported that Chinese infants were less active, irritable, and vocal than American infants. Chinese infants also cried less often than American infants in several stressful laboratory paradigms. The lower levels of activity and vocalization in Asian infants might be due to their greater anxiety and fear in the stressful situations. A possible reason for the exhibition of fewer explosive emotions such as irritability and crying is that Asian children might regulate, either automatically or effortfully or both, their frustration and distress to a greater extent than do European American children, even in the early years. Further investigation is clearly needed on this issue.

Self-Control

Researchers have found cultural variations in children's self-regulation and control in early childhood. Chinese and East Asian infants are often rated by their mothers as more persistent in orienting than U.S. and other Western infants, and the differences tend to increase with age (Gartstein et al., 2006). Chen and colleagues (2003) found that Chinese toddlers more often than Canadian toddlers maintained their compliant behaviors without adult intervention during a cleanup session, indicating committed and internalized control. Moreover, during a delay task in which the experimenter told the child to wait to play with a packet of attractive crayons until she returned to the room, Chinese toddlers waited for a significantly longer time than Canadian toddlers. Sabbagh, Xu, Carlson, Moses, and Lee (2006) and Oh and Lewis (2008) also found that Chinese and Korean preschoolers performed more competently than their U.S. counterparts on executive function tasks assessing self-control abilities associated with the prefrontal cortex of the brain. It is believed that cultural values of group harmony and behavioral restraint facilitate the early socialization of self-control (e.g., Ho, 1986).

In a cross-cultural study of attention and behavioral control, Brewis, Schmidt, and Casas (2003) observed that Mexican school-age children displayed more inattentive and impulsive behaviors than American children, as indicated by errors they made on several structured tasks. Gartstein, Slobodskaya, and Kinsht (2003) found that Russian infants exhibited lower levels of regulatory functioning than U.S. infants. Interestingly, Gartstein, Peleg, Young, and Slobodskaya (2009) recently reported that infants of Russian families in Israel demonstrated higher regulatory ability and were described by their parents as requiring shorter time to recover from distress compared to Russian infants in the U.S., which might be due to the fact that coping with stress is an inherent component of everyday life in Israel, and that effective regulation, including recovery from minor distress, is critical to adjustment in the Israeli environment. Moreover, for the Russian immigrants in Israel, parental involvement in the Israeli (host) culture was related to higher levels of infants' duration of orienting/persistence of attention, an index of regulatory capacity. The results of these studies indicate the influence of cultural context and acculturation on parental perceptions of infant characteristics, which in turn may have implications for the development of temperament.

In summary, empirical research has revealed relatively consistent cross-cultural variations in major dimensions of temperament, including reactivity to stressful situations and self-control, despite some mixed findings. To understand the cross-cultural variations in these dimensions, it is important to explore how culturally directed socialization and social interaction processes play a role in the development of distinct temperamental characteristics and, more specifically, how cultural values serve as a framework of reference for judging and evaluating temperamental characteristics and to determine their significance for adaptive and maladaptive development.

Cultural Values, Social Attitudes, and Temperament

According to Klein (1991), individuals in different societies may hold different views of ideal temperament of children (e.g., more active, more positive in mood, and higher in adaptability in the U.S. than in Israel). These views constitute a part of the general cultural belief system, which may moderate the development of temperament and the contributions of temperament to the development of social, cognitive, and psychological outcomes. The mechanism for the moderation involves the socialization process, which includes social judgments of, and responses to, specific child characteristics. Consistent with this argument, research findings have shown cross-cultural differences in parental and peer attitudes toward children's temperamental characteristics.

Parental Attitudes and Socialization Practices

Parental attitudes toward children's temperamental characteristics, to a large extent, reflect the demands and values in the society. DeVries and Sameroff (1984) observed that in one of the East African tribes, the "clock time" was not considered important for daily activities. Because of the lack of concern for time, parents tended to focus on infants' present needs, instead of helping the infants to develop regular behaviors, such as feeding and sleeping. As a result, the infants in this tribe had lower scores on the regularity dimension of temperament than their counterparts in other two tribes. Super and colleagues (2008) found that parents in the Netherlands rated their children as significantly more regular than did parents in Australia, Italy, Poland, Spain, Sweden, and the United States because establishing and maintaining a regular and calm schedule for young children is regarded as important in the Dutch culture. In this study, the researchers used parental perceptions of "difficult child" as a criterion to explore cultural meanings of various temperamental characteristics. One of the salient findings was that low approach and adaptability were associated with global difficulty in Italian children, which, as argued by the authors, is consistent with a cultural model of parenting that includes introducing the child to a variety of social situations and encouraging the development of emotionally close relationships starting in early infancy. The results suggest that a child who is temperamentally shy or withdrawn in social situations represents a difficult challenge to parents in Italy. Taken together, the results of the studies by DeVries and Sameroff and Super and colleagues demonstrate from different perspectives that cultural socialization goals and beliefs are related to parental perceptions and evaluations of child temperamental characteristics.

Chen and his colleagues (1998) investigated the relations between parental attitudes and toddlers' reactivity or behavioral inhibition in Canada and China. The results in Canada indicated that child inhibition was positively associated with mothers' negative attitudes toward the child, such as punishment orientation and rejection. However, the trend was the opposite in China: Child inhibition was positively associated with maternal warm and accepting attitudes, and negatively associated with maternal rejection.

Parents in Canada and China also appear to react differently to self-control. Compared with Canadian parents, Chinese parents tend to expect their children to maintain a higher level of control (Chen et al., 2003; Ho, 1986). The greater emphasis of Chinese parents on behavioral control may be attributable in part to the influence of traditional values in the culture, in which children are required to learn the dictates of *li* (propriety)—a set of rules for actions—to cultivate and strengthen innate virtues (Ho, 1986).

In an observational study, Trommsdorff and Friedlmeier (2010) found differences in parenting goals and toddlers' emotion regulation in Japan and in Germany. Compared to the German girls, Japanese girls showed more negative emotional responses to the distress of their playmates, and were more likely to turn to their mothers for comfort. More important, German mothers responded to their children's emotion with less sensitive and contingent behaviors than did Japanese mothers. The authors argued that Japanese mothers regarded helping their children understand others' feelings as an important childrearing goal and thus expected them to respond to the distress of their playmate in an emotional way. In contrast, German mothers might have believed it was desirable for the child to comfort the playmate rather than to react emotionally. Consequently, German mothers perhaps discouraged their children from seeking maternal support by neglecting their emotional reaction.

Keller and colleagues (2004) also found cross-cultural differences in parental attitudes toward children's self-regulation. Rural Cameroonian Nso toddlers displayed more regulated behaviors than Costa Rican toddlers, who in turn had higher regulation scores than Greek toddlers, as indicated by their compliance with maternal requests and prohibitions. Accordingly, Cameroonian Nso mothers scored higher than Costa Rican mothers, who scored higher than middle-class Greek mothers, on a proximal parenting style (body contact, body stimulation) that was believed to facilitate child obedience and regulation. Keller and colleagues argued that whereas behavioral control may be viewed as interfering and infringing on the child's freedom in individualistic cultures, control and compliance are viewed as a duty, an expression of social maturity and competence in group-oriented cultural contexts.

Cole, Tamang, and Shrestha (2006) investigated caregivers' attitudes and reactions to children's anger and undercontrolled behavior in two different villages in Nepal: Brahmans and Tamangs. The results indicated that the majority of active responses (i.e., not ignoring) by Tamang caregivers involve rebuking the angry youngster, whereas most of active responses by Brahman caregivers involve supporting and coaxing the angry child to feel better. Thus, Brahman parents were more likely than Tamang parents to send the message to the child that anger and undercontrol were acceptable. The results seem to be consistent with the cultural orientations; whereas Brahmans are high-caste Hindus, who value hierarchy and dominance, Tamangs value social equality, compassion, modesty, and nonviolence.

In short, parental attitudes and socialization practices are largely indicative of cultural values and requirements of the society. Research on culturally relevant parental attitudes and behaviors, especially in parent–child interactions, is likely to shed light on the role of sociocultural conditions in the development of temperament.

Peer Evaluations and Responses

With age, peer interactions become an increasingly important socialization context for social and cognitive development. During interactions, peers may evaluate and respond to children's socioemotional characteristics and behaviors, and cultural norms and values serve as a guideline for these evaluations and responses. This has been illustrated by a series of studies by Chen and his colleagues (2006) concerning shyness and peer interactions and relationships in Canada and China. In an observational study of peer interactions among 4-year-olds, for example, Chen and colleagues found different peer attitudes in China and Canada toward children who displayed shy and inhibited behaviors. When shy children in Canada attempted to initiate social interaction, peers were likely to make negative responses, such as overt refusal, disagreement, and intentionally ignoring the initiation. However, peers tended to respond in a more positive manner in China by controlling their negative actions and showing approval and support. The passive and wary behaviors displayed by shy children were perceived by peers as incompetent and deviant in Canada, but appropriate or even desirable in China, indicating courteousness and a sign of looking for social engagement. In addition, whereas peers were more likely to make negative or high-power voluntary initiations (e.g., verbal teasing) to shy than to nonshy children in Canada, peers made similar voluntary initiations to shy and nonshy children in China. Therefore, peers were generally forceful and unreceptive in Canada but more supportive and cooperative in China in their interactions with children who displayed shy behavior.

Cultural values are also reflected in general peer attitudes such as acceptance and rejection. There is evidence that shy children seem to experience fewer problems in peer acceptance in societies where assertiveness and autonomy are not valued or encouraged. Eisenberg, Pidada, and Liew (2001) found that shyness in Indonesian school-age children was negatively associated with peer nominations of dislike. Chen, Rubin, and Li (1995) found that shyness was associated with peer rejection in Canadian children, but with peer acceptance in Chinese children. Moreover, as urban China is changing toward a competitive, market-oriented society with the introduction of more individualistic values, children's shyness is increasingly associated with negative peer attitudes. By the early part of the 21st century, as the country became more deeply immersed in a market economy, shy children, unlike their counterparts in the early 1990s, were rejected by peers (Chen, Cen, Li, & He, 2005). An interesting finding is that shyness was positively associated with both peer acceptance and peer rejection in the late 1990s, which seemed to indicate ambivalent attitudes of peers toward shy–inhibited children during a transitional period characterized by mixed traditional Chinese and new Western values.

In summary, research findings have indicated considerable variations in cultural expectations and values of children's social and behavioral qualities. These expectations and values are manifested in adults' and peers' attitudes and responses in interactions, which in turn constitute social environments for the development of children with different temperamental characteristics. Through organizing socialization environments, culture shapes the ways in which temperamental characteristics are expressed in various aspects of development.

Temperament and Adaptive and Maladaptive Development: The Role of Cultural Context

Given the different social attitudes and responses across cultures toward temperamental characteristics such as reactivity and regulation, it is conceivable that they are likely to lead to culturally distinct developmental outcomes. The interaction of culture and temperament in their contributions to social, cognitive, and psychological development is often described as *goodness of fit*—the adjustment of a child in the society depending on how the child's temperament fits cultural requirements (e.g., Lerner & Lerner, 1983). According to the contextual–development perspective (Chen & French, 2008), culturally directed social interaction processes such as evaluations and responses serve to regulate children's behaviors and their developmental patterns. The processes may occur gradually as children attempt to maintain or modify their behaviors or behavioral styles during interactions according to social and cultural expectations and standards.

In North America, for example, the negative peer feedback that shy children receive heightens the pressure to alter their behaviors. Those who fail to do so may experience frustrations and other negative emotions such as loneliness and depression (e.g., Rubin, Coplan, & Bowker, 2009). In contrast, peer approval and support that shy children receive in China inform them that their wary and inhibited behaviors are regarded as acceptable and appropriate. The favorable experience is conducive to the development of self-confidence, which helps shy children display their competencies in social interactions and other areas, such as school performance (Chen, Chen, Li, & Wang, 2009). As social assertiveness has recently become more valued in urban China, children may attempt to adjust their behaviors according to the new expectations.

"Difficult" Temperament and Adjustment

In the Western literature (e.g., Thomas & Chess, 1977), children with difficult temperaments (i.e., children who are less adaptable, more irregular, and more negative in their reactions) are at greater risk than others for developing behavioral and psychological problems. However, this is not necessarily the case in other cultures. A compelling example is the finding that difficult temperament is associated with lower infant mortality among the Masai people of East Africa during a famine (DeVries, 1984). The study revealed that in 1974, when there was a sub-Saharan drought, mortality was lower for infants with a difficult temperament. DeVries (1984) argued that in the harsh environment, infants with a difficult temperament were able to get more maternal attention because of their fussiness, which increased their chances of survival.

In a similar study, Korn and Gannon (1983) examined the relations between temperament and adjustment in 5-year-old boys from European American and Puerto Rican families. They found that difficult temperament tended to lead to adjustment problems in European American, but not in Puerto Rican boys. The authors argued that the Puerto Rican parents responded to child difficulty in a more accommodating way, which reduced the possibility for the boys to develop problems.

Shyness–Inhibition and Adjustment

There is increasing evidence that shyness–inhibition, as vigilant, wary, and anxious reactivity to stressful or challenging social situations (Chen, 2010), predicts different adjustment outcomes in North America, China, and some other nations. In North America, children who are shy and inhibited are likely to develop socioemotional and school difficulties (e.g., Asendorpf, Denissen, & van Aken, 2008; Coplan, Prakash, O'Neil, & Armer, 2004; Rubin, Burgess, & Coplan, 2002). Moreover, when shy–inhibited children realize their difficulties in social functioning, they may develop negative self-perceptions of their social competencies and other internalizing problems, such as depression (e.g., Caspi et al., 2003; Schwartz, Snidman, & Kagan, 1999), although the findings are sometimes inconsistent (e.g., Asendorpf & van Aken, 1994). The results may be related to the emphasis on individual autonomy and assertiveness in Western societies. In societies where autonomy and assertiveness are not so highly valued, shy and inhibited behavior are viewed as less deviant and maladaptive. Eisenberg and colleagues (2001) found that shyness in Indonesian children was negatively associated with social, behavioral, and emotional problems. Kerr, Lambert, and Bem (1996) examined the outcomes of shyness in Swedish society, where shy-reserved behavior is viewed more positively than in North America. The researchers followed a sample of children born in a suburb of Stockholm in the mid-1950s to adulthood, and found that although shyness predicted later marriage and parenthood, it did not affect adulthood occupational stability (as indicated by frequency of job changes), education, or income among Swedish men, which was different from the findings in the United States (e.g., Caspi, Elder, & Bem, 1988). According to Kerr and colleagues, the social welfare and support systems that evolved from the egalitarian values in Sweden ensured that people did not need to be assertive or competitive to achieve career success.

In a longitudinal study in China, Chen, Chen, and colleagues (2009) found that behavioral inhibition in 2-year-olds predicted positive social and school adjustment 5 years later, including cooperative behavior, peer liking, perceived social integration, positive school attitudes, and school competence. Chinese inhibited toddlers displayed more cooperative behaviors and were better adjusted than others in middle childhood.

The positive contribution of shyness–inhibition to social, school, and psychological adjustment has also been found in middle childhood and adolescence in China. Shy Chinese children are more likely than others to achieve leadership status in the school and to perform well in academic areas. Moreover, shy children in China do not feel lonely or depressed, or develop negative perceptions of their competence (Chen et al., 2004). Longitudinal data (Chen, Rubin, Li, & Li, 1999) indicate that shyness in childhood is positively associated with adjustment in adolescence, including teacher-assessed competence, leadership, academic achievement, and self-perceptions of competence. Recent studies in China demonstrate that although shy children in urban areas have started to experience problems in adjustment, such as learning difficulties and depression, as a result of social change (e.g., Chen et al., 2005; Chen, Wang, & Wang, 2009), shy children in rural areas still obtain approval from peers and adults, and achieve social and academic success (Chen & Wang, 2011).

Taken together, the findings from a number of projects suggest that shyness–inhibition in cultures such as China, Indonesia, and Sweden does not necessarily lead to maladaptive development, in contrast to what has been found in North America. In these cultures, shy–inhibited children may not experience evident obstacles in getting involved in social interactions. Engagement in social activities may provide the opportunity for shy–inhibited children to learn norms and skills to behave appropriately in social situations. At the same time, social support and encouragement from others may help shy–inhibited children develop confidence and the ability to establish social relationships, which in turn are beneficial to the development of positive attitudes toward the school and motivation to achieve success in education and career.

Self-Control and Adjustment

Compared with the results concerning shyness–inhibition, there are fewer evident cultural differences in the relations between self-control or regulation and adjustment. Nevertheless, the findings indicate that cultural norms and values may affect the developmental outcome of some aspects or types of self-control. For example, emotion suppression involves the reduction of emotion–expressive behavior while the individual is emotionally aroused (Gross & Levenson, 1997), which represents an active effort to control emotional activities. Butler, Lee, and Gross (2007) found that cultural values may affect the social consequence of emotion suppression. Specifically, habitual suppression was associated with negative emotional experiences in women holding predominantly European values, but not in women holding Asian–European bicultural values. Moreover, emotional suppression for women with European values tended to lead to hostile interactions, whereas women with bicultural values engaged in less hostile interactions when they suppressed their emotions.

Cheung and Park (2010) conducted a study of anger suppression and depression in Asian American and European American students. The results showed that while anger suppression was positively associated with depression in general, the association was significantly weaker in Asian Americans than in European Americans. Moreover, a stronger interdependent self-construal attenuated the relation between anger suppression and depressive symptoms. According to Cheung and Park, for individuals holding

Western values, suppression serves a self-protective function, whereas for individuals who hold more Asian values, suppression may be conducive to achieving prosocial goals. Anger suppression may be one form of emotion regulation that promotes social engagement and psychological well-being for interdependent individuals.

Research results concerning relations between the broad construct of self-control or regulation and internalizing problems in American and Asian cultures are consistent with results found by Butler and colleagues (2007) and Cheung and Park (2010), although the results are clearer in some cultures than in others. Self-control clearly contributes to positive behavioral and psychological adjustment in Chinese children. In a recent study with Chinese children, for example, Eisenberg and colleagues (2007) found that self-control was *negatively* associated with internalizing problems such as symptoms of fearfulness and anxiety. Similarly, Chen, Zhang, Chen, and Li (2012), in a longitudinal study in China, found that self-control, as assessed by performance on delay tasks at age 2 years, negatively predicted self-reported loneliness and depression at 11 years. Children who have the ability to control their behavioral and emotional reactions likely display appropriate behaviors, such as caution and compliance, which are highly valued in group-oriented Chinese society. As a result, the social support these children may receive from others may increase their self-confidence and buffer against the development of negative self-feelings. At the same time, high emphasis on self-control in China may place great pressure on children who have difficulties maintaining their behaviors according to social standards. The stressful experience may trigger in these children negative emotional reactions toward the self and others. Moreover, poorly controlled children may receive frequent negative feedback from adults and peers on their behavior, particularly in the regular public evaluations in Chinese schools, which results in further social dissatisfaction and psychopathological symptoms.

Research findings with American children have been generally mixed (see Klein, Dyson, Kujawa, & Kotov, Chapter 26, this volume). Lonigan and Vasey (2009) found that effortful control moderated the relation between negative affectivity and attentional bias; children with low levels of effortful control and high levels of negative affectivity showed an attentional bias to threat stimuli. However, several studies indicated virtually no associations between effortful control and internalizing behaviors (Eisenberg et al., 2001, 2005; Oosterlaan & Sergeant, 1996). Furthermore, some studies in the United States suggested that self-control tends to be positively associated with internalizing problems (e.g., Murray & Kochanska, 2002), supporting the argument that overcontrol may result in behaviors and emotions of an internalizing nature (Weisz, Sigman, Weiss, & Mosk, 1993). The inconsistent results may be due to different methods used to assess self-control or effortful control. Further research should be conducted before any conclusions can be drawn about cross-cultural similarities or differences in the relations between self-control and internalizing problems.

There seem to be robust links between low self-control and externalizing behaviors in North American children (e.g., Olson, Sameroff, Kerr, Lopez, & Wellman, 2005; see Tackett, Martel, & Kushner, Chapter 27, this volume). Similar relations have been found in many other countries (e.g., Eisenberg, Zhou, Liew, Champion, & Pidada, 2006). Zhou, Lengua, and Wang (2009) reported that low control and high anger–irritability were associated with high externalizing problems in both American and Chinese children. However, the associations were stronger in the Chinese children. The results indicate that self-control has extensive effects on socioemotional and behavioral development in Chinese and perhaps other Asian cultures.

Conclusions and Future Directions

Temperament constitutes an important developmental origin of social, behavioral, and psychological functioning in human beings. Through socialization and social interaction processes, cultural norms and values determine, in part, the exhibition and functional significance of temperament in development. Consequently, the prevalence of specific temperamental characteristics and their relations with social and psychological adjustment may vary across cultures.

Research on culture and temperament has focused on direct or indirect cross-cultural comparisons. Although cross-cultural similarities and differences are interesting, this approach provides little information about the processes in which cultural beliefs and values affect individual development. We have discussed in this chapter the role of social interaction in mediating cultural influence on socioemotional development from a contextual–developmental perspective (Chen, 2012). However, this perspective is largely speculative. Although there is some evidence for the influence of cultural values on social attitudes in peer interaction and for the links between peer evaluations and individual behaviors (e.g., Chen et al., 2006), the general framework remains to be tested in empirical research. Moreover, many issues in the framework need to be further clarified and examined. For example, parenting and parent–child interaction have long been recognized as a main mechanism through which children are socialized according to culturally prescribed developmental goals, particularly in the early years (e.g., Keller et al., 2004; Super & Harkness, 1986). How peer interaction and parent–child interaction affect each other in their joint contributions to child development will be an interesting question. In addition, according to the contextual–developmental perspective (Chen, 2012), cultural influence on individual behavior is a dynamic process in which children play an increasingly active role during development. The active role of children with different temperamental characteristics has received little attention in cross-cultural research. Continuous exploration of children's social interaction in different societies will be necessary to achieve an in-depth understanding of culture and development.

Cross-cultural researchers are often interested in comparing children in Western, self-oriented societies with those in collectivistic, group-oriented societies. It is important to note that international and domestic migrations have made the exposure to different beliefs and lifestyles a part of the experience of children and adults today. Communication and exchange across nations during globalization have created a constantly changing context, with diverse values for people in most societies. Moreover, cultural interaction may lead to the merging, coexistence, and integration of different value systems. It will be interesting to investigate temperament and its developmental significance in these culturally integrated and sophisticated environments.

Further Reading

Chen, X., DeSouza, A. T., Chen, H. C., & Wang, L. (2006). Reticent behavior and experiences in peer interactions in Chinese and Canadian children. *Developmental Psychology, 42*, 656–665.

Cole, P. M., Tamang, B. L., & Shrestha, S. (2006). Cultural variations in the socialization of young children's anger and shame. *Child Development, 77*, 1237–1251.

Keller, H., Yovsi, R., Borke, J., Kartner, J., Jensen, H., & Papaligoura, Z. (2004). Developmental consequences of early parenting experiences: Self-recognition and self-regulation in three cultural communities. *Child Development, 75*, 1745–1760.

References

Ahadi, S. A., Rothbart, M. K., & Ye, R. (1993). Children's temperament in the U.S. and China: Similarities and differences. *European Journal of Personality, 7*, 359–377.

Ariel, S., & Sever, I. (1980). Play in the desert and play in the town: On play activities of Bedouin Arab children. In H. B. Schwartzman (Ed.), *Play and culture* (pp. 164–175). West Point, NY: Leisure Press.

Asendorpf, J. (1990). Beyond social withdrawal: Shyness, unsociability, and peer avoidance. *Human Development, 33*, 250–259.

Asendorpf, J. B., Denissen, J. J. A., & van Aken, M. A. G. (2008). Inhibited and aggressive preschool children at 23 years of age: Personality and social transition into adulthood. *Developmental Psychology, 44*, 997–1011.

Asendorpf, J. B., & van Aken, M. A. G. (1994). Traits and relationship status: Stranger versus peer group inhibition and test intelligence versus peer group competence as early predictors of later self-esteem. *Child Development, 65*, 1786–1798.

Austin, A., & Chorpita, B. (2004). Temperament, anxiety, and depression: Comparisons across five ethnic groups of children. *Journal of Clinical Child and Adolescent Psychology, 33*, 216–226.

Bergeron, N., & Schneider, B. H. (2005). Explaining cross-national differences in peer-directed aggression: A quantitative synthesis. *Aggressive Behavior, 31*, 116–137.

Brewis, A., Schmidt, K. L., & Casas, C. A. S.

(2003). Cross-cultural study of the childhood development of attention and impulse control. *International Journal of Behavioral Development*, 27, 174–182.

Bronfenbrenner, U., & Morris, P. A. (2006). The bioecological model of human development. In W. Damon (Series Ed.) & R. M. Lerner (Vol. Ed.), *Handbook of child psychology: Theoretical models of human development* (Vol. 1, pp. 793–828). New York: Wiley.

Butler, E. A., Lee, T. L., & Gross, J. J. (2007). Emotion regulation and culture: Are the social consequences of emotion suppression culture-specific? *Emotion*, 7, 30–48.

Camras, L. A., Chen, Y., Bakeman, R., Norris, K., & Cain, T. (2006). Culture, ethnicity, and children's facial expressions: A study of European American, mainland Chinese, Chinese American, and adopted Chinese girls. *Emotion*, 6, 103–114.

Camras, L. A., Oster, H., Campos, J., Campos, R., Ujiie, T., Miyake, K., et al. (1998). Production of emotional facial expressions in American, Japanese and Chinese infants. *Developmental Psychology*, 34, 616–628.

Caspi, A., Elder, G. H., Jr., & Bem, D. J. (1988). Moving away from the world: Life-course patterns of shy children. *Developmental Psychology*, 24, 824–831.

Caspi, A., Harrington, H., Milne, B., Amell, J. W., Theodore, R. F., & Moffitt, T. E. (2003). Children's behavioral styles at age 3 are linked to their adult personality traits at age 26. *Journal of Personality*, 71, 495–513.

Chen, X. (2010). Socioemotional development in Chinese children. In M. H. Bond (Ed.), *Handbook of Chinese psychology* (pp. 37–52). Hong Kong: Oxford University Press.

Chen, X. (2012). Culture, peer interaction, and socioemotional development. *Child Development Perspective*, 6, 27–34.

Chen, X., Cen, G., Li, D., & He, Y. (2005). Social functioning and adjustment in Chinese children: The imprint of historical time. *Child Development*, 76, 182–195.

Chen, X., Chen, H., Li, D., & Wang, L. (2009). Early childhood behavioral inhibition and social and school adjustment in Chinese children: A 5-year longitudinal study. *Child Development*, 80, 1692–1704.

Chen, X., Chung, J., & Hsiao, C. (2009). Peer interactions, relationships and groups from a cross-cultural perspective. In K. H. Rubin, W. M. Bukowski, & B. Laursen (Eds.), *Handbook of peer interactions, relationships, and groups* (pp. 432–451). New York: Guilford Press.

Chen, X., DeSouza, A. T., Chen, H. C., & Wang, L. (2006). Reticent behavior and experiences in peer interactions in Chinese and Canadian children. *Developmental Psychology*, 42, 656–665.

Chen, X., & French, D. C. (2008). Children's social competence in cultural context. *Annual Review of Psychology*, 59, 591–616.

Chen, X., Hastings, P. D., Rubin, K. H., Chen, H. C., Cen, G. Z., & Stewart, S. L. (1998). Child-rearing attitudes and behavioral inhibition in Chinese and Canadian toddlers: A cross-cultural study. *Developmental Psychology*, 34, 677–686.

Chen, X., He, Y., De Oliveira, A. M., Lo Coco, A, Zappulla, C., Kaspar, V., et al. (2004). Loneliness and social adaptation in Brazilian, Canadian, Chinese and Italian children. *Child Psychology and Psychiatry and Allied Disciplines*, 45, 1373–1384.

Chen, X., Rubin, K. H., & Li, B. (1995). Social and school adjustment of shy and aggressive children in China. *Development and Psychopathology*, 7, 337–349.

Chen, X., Rubin, K. H., Li, B., & Li, Z. (1999). Adolescent outcomes of social functioning in Chinese children. *International Journal of Behavioral Development*, 23, 199–223.

Chen, X., Rubin, K. H., Liu, M., Chen, H., Wang, L., Li, D., et al. (2003). Compliance in Chinese and Canadian toddlers. *International Journal of Behavioral Development*, 27, 428–436.

Chen, X., Rubin, K. H., & Sun, Y. (1992). Social reputation and peer relationships in Chinese and Canadian children: A cross-cultural study. *Child Development*, 63, 1336–1343.

Chen, X., & Tse, H. C. (2008). Social functioning and adjustment in Canadian-born children with Chinese and European backgrounds. *Developmental Psychology*, 44, 1184–1189.

Chen, X., & Tse, H. C. (2010). Social and psychological adjustment of Chinese Canadian children. *International Journal of Behavioral Development*, 34, 330–338.

Chen, X., & Wang, L. (2011). Shyness–sensitivity and unsociability in rural Chinese children: Relations with social, school, and psychological adjustment. *Child Development*, 82, 1531–1543.

Chen, X., Wang, L., & Wang, Z. (2009). Shyness–sensitivity and social, school, and psychological adjustment in rural migrant and urban children in China. *Child Development*, 80, 1499–1513.

Chen, X., Zhang, G., Chen, H., & Li, D. (2012). Performance on delay tasks in early childhood predicted socioemotional and school adjustment and problems 9 years later: A longitudinal study in Chinese children. *International Perspectives in Psychology: Research, Practice, Consultation*, 1, 3–14.

Cheung, R. Y. M., & Park, I. J. K. (2010). Anger suppression, interdependent self-construal, and depression among Asian American and European American college students. *Cultural Diversity and Ethnic Minority Psychology*, 16, 517–525.

Cole, M. (1996). *Culture in mind*. Cambridge, MA: Harvard University Press.
Cole, P. M., Tamang, B. L., & Shrestha, S. (2006). Cultural variations in the socialization of young children's anger and shame. *Child Development, 77*, 1237–1251.
Coplan, R. J., Prakash, K., O'Neil, K., & Armer, M. (2004). Do you "want" to play?: Distinguishing between conflicted-shyness and social disinterest in early childhood. *Developmental Psychology, 40*, 244–258.
DeVries, M. W. (1984). Temperament and infant mortality among the Masai of East Africa. *American Journal of Psychiatry, 141*, 1189–1194.
DeVries, M. W., & Sameroff, A. J. (1984). Culture and temperament—influences on infant temperament in 3 East-African societies. *American Journal of Orthopsychiatry, 54*, 83–96.
Edwards, C. P. (2000). Children's play in cross-cultural perspective: A new look at the Six Culture Study. *Cross-Cultural Research, 34*, 318–338.
Eisenberg, N., Michalik, N., Spinrad, T. L., Hofer, C., Kupfer, A., Valiente, C., et al. (2007). The relations of effortful control and impulsivity to children's sympathy: A longitudinal study. *Cognitive Development, 22*, 544–567.
Eisenberg, N., Pidada, S., & Liew, J. (2001). The relations of regulation and negative emotionality to Indonesian children's social functioning. *Child Development, 72*, 1747–1763.
Eisenberg, N., Sadovsky, A., Spinrad, T. L., Fabes, R. A., Losoya, S. H., Valiente, C., et al. (2005). The relations of problem behavior status to children's negative emotionality, effortful control, and impulsivity: Concurrent relations and prediction of change. *Developmental Psychology, 41*, 193–211.
Eisenberg, N., Zhou, Q., Liew, J., Champion, C., & Pidada, S. U. (2006). Emotion, emotion-related regulation, and social functioning. In X. Chen, D. C. French, & B. H. Schneider (Eds.), *Peer relationships in cultural context* (pp. 170–197). New York: Cambridge University Press.
Farver, J. M., Kim, Y. K., & Lee, Y. (1995). Cultural differences in Korean- and Anglo-American preschoolers' social interaction and play behaviors. *Child Development, 66*, 1088–1099.
Freedman, D. G., & Freedman, N. A. (1969). Differences in behavior between Chinese-American and European-American newborns. *Nature, 224*, 1227.
Gartstein, M. A., Gonzalez, C., Carranza, J. A., Ahadi, S. A., Ye, R., Rothbart, M. K., et al. (2006). Studying cross-cultural differences in the development of infant temperament: Peoples Republic of China, the United States of America, and Spain. *Child Psychiatry and Human Development, 37*, 145–161.
Gartstein, M. A., Peleg, Y., Young, B. N., & Slobodskaya, H. R. (2009). Infant temperament in Russia, United States of America, and Israel: Differences and similarities between Russian-speaking families. *Child Psychiatry and Human Development, 40*, 241–256.
Gartstein, M. A., Slobodskaya, H. R., & Kinsht, I. A. (2003). Cross-cultural differences in the first year of life: United States of America (U.S.) and Russian. *International Journal of Behavioral Development, 27*, 316–328.
Gaskins, S. (2000). Children's daily activities in a Mayan village: A culturally grounded description. *Cross-Cultural Research, 34*, 375–389.
Gong, Y. (1984). Use of the Eysenck Personality Questionnaire in China. *Personality and Individual Differences, 5*, 431–438.
Greenfield, P. M., Suzuki, L. K., & Rothstein-Fisch, C. (2006). Cultural pathways through human development. In K. A. Renninger & I. E. Sigel (Eds.), *Handbook of child psychology: Vol. 4. Child psychology in practice* (pp. 655–699). New York: Wiley.
Gross, J. J., & Levenson, R. W. (1997). Hiding feelings: The acute effects of inhibiting negative and positive emotion. *Journal of Abnormal Psychology, 106*, 95–103.
Ho, D. Y. F. (1986). Chinese pattern of socialization: A critical review. In M. H. Bond (Ed.), *The psychology of the Chinese people* (pp. 1–37). Hong Kong: Oxford University Press.
Hsu, C., Soong, W., Stigler, J. W., Hong, C., & Liang, C. (1981). The temperamental characteristics of Chinese babies. *Child Development, 52*, 1337–1340.
Kagan, J. (1997). Temperament and the reactions to unfamiliarity. *Child Development, 68*, 139–143.
Kagan, J., Arcus, D., Snidman, N., Wang Y., Hendler, J., & Greene, S. (1994). Reactivity in infants: A cross-national comparison. *Developmental Psychology, 30*, 342–345.
Kagan, J., Kearsley, R. B., & Zelazo, P. R. (1978). *Infancy: Its place in human development*. Cambridge, MA: Harvard University Press.
Kagan, S., & Knight, G. P. (1981). Social motives among Anglo-American and Mexican-American children: Experimental and projective measures. *Journal of Research in Personality, 15*, 93–106.
Keller, H., Yovsi, R., Borke, J., Kartner, J., Jensen, H., & Papaligoura, Z. (2004). Developmental consequences of early parenting experiences: Self-recognition and self-regulation in three cultural communities. *Child Development, 75*, 1745–1760.
Kerr, M., Lambert, W. W., & Bem, D. J. (1996). Life course sequelae of childhood shyness in Sweden: Comparison with the United States. *Developmental Psychology, 32*, 1100–1105.
Klein, H. A. (1991). Temperament and childhood group care adjustment: A cross-cultural com-

parison. *Early Childhood Research Quarterly*, 6, 211–224.

Knyazev, G. G., Zupančič, M., & Slobodskaya, H. R. (2008). Child personality in Slovenia and Russia. Structure and mean level of traits in parent and self-ratings. *Journal of Cross-Cultural Psychology*, 39, 317–334.

Korn, S. J., & Gannon, S. (1983). Temperament, cultural variation and behavior disorder in preschool-children. *Child Psychiatry and Human Development*, 13, 203–212.

Lee, M. R., Okazaki, S., & Yoo, H. C. (2006). Frequency and intensity of social anxiety in Asian Americans and European Americans. *Cultural Diversity and Ethnic Minority Psychology*, 12, 291–305.

Lerner, J. V., & Lerner, R. M. (1983). Temperament and adaptation across life: Theoretical and empirical issues. In P. B. Baltes & O. G. Brim, Jr. (Eds.), *Life-span development and behavior* (Vol. 5, pp. 197–231). New York: Academic Press.

Lonigan, C. J., & Vasey, M. W. (2009). Negative affectivity, effortful control, and attention to threat-relevant stimuli. *Journal of Abnormal Child Psychology*, 37, 387–399.

Masten, A., Morison, P., & Pellegrini, D. (1985). A revised class play method of peer assessment. *Developmental Psychology*, 17, 344–350.

Murray, K. T., & Kochanska, G. (2002). Effortful control: Factor structure and relation to externalizing and internalizing behaviors. *Journal of Abnormal Child Psychology*, 30, 503–514.

Oakland, T., Mogaji, A., & Dempsey, J. (2006). Temperament styles of Nigerian and U.S. children. *Journal of Psychology in Africa*, 16, 27–34.

Oakland, T., Mpofu, E., & Sulkowski, M. (2007). Temperament styles of Zimbabwe and U.S. children. *Canadian Journal of School Psychology*, 21, 139–153.

Oakland, T., Pretorius, J., & Lee, D. H. (2008). Temperament styles of children from South Africa and the United States. *School Psychology International*, 29, 627–639.

Oh, S., & Lewis, C. (2008). Korean preschoolers' advanced inhibitory control and its relation to other executive skills and mental state understanding. *Child Development*, 79, 80–99.

Olson, S. L., Sameroff, A. J., Kerr, D. C. R., Lopez, N. L., & Wellman, H. M. (2005). Developmental foundations of externalizing problems in young children: The role of effortful control. *Development and Psychopathology*, 17, 25–45.

Oosterlaan, J., & Sergeant, J. A. (1996). Inhibition in ADHD, aggressive, and anxious children: A biologically based model of child psychopathology. *Journal of Abnormal Child Psychology*, 24, 19–36.

Orlick, T., Zhou, Q. Y., & Partington, J. (1990). Co-operation and conflict within Chinese and Canadian kindergarten settings. *Canadian Journal of Behavioral Science*, 22, 20–25.

Pomerleau, A., Sabatier, C., & Malcuit, G. (1998). Quebecois, Haitian, and Vietnamese mothers' report of infant temperament. *International Journal of Psychology*, 33, 337–344.

Porter, C. L., Hart, C. H., Yang, C., Robinson, C. C., Olsen, S. F., Zeng, Q., et al. (2005). A comparative study of child temperament and parenting in Beijing, China and the western United States. *International Journal of Behavioral Development*, 29, 541–551.

Prior, M., Garino, E., Sanson, A., & Oberklaid, F. (1987). Ethnic influences on "difficult'" temperament and behavioural problems in infants. *Australian Journal of Psychology*, 39, 163–171.

Rogoff, B. (2003). *The cultural nature of human development*. New York: Oxford University Press.

Rothbart, M. K., & Bates, J. E. (2006). Temperament. In N. Eisenberg (Ed.), *Handbook of child psychology: Vol. 3. Social, emotional, and personality development* (pp. 99–166). New York: Wiley.

Rothbart, M. K., & Derryberry, D. (1981). Development of individual differences in temperament. In M. E. Lamb & A. L. Brown (Eds.), *Advances in developmental psychology* (Vol. 1, pp. 37–86). Hillsdale, NJ: Erlbaum.

Rubin, K. H., Burgess, K. B., & Coplan, R. J. (2002). Social withdrawal and shyness. In P. K. Smith & C. H. Hart (Eds.), *Blackwell handbook of childhood social development* (pp. 330–352). Malden, MA: Blackwell.

Rubin, K. H., Coplan, R. J., & Bowker, J. C. (2009). Social withdrawal in childhood. *Annual Review of Psychology*, 60, 141–171.

Rubin, K. H., Hemphill, S. A., Chen, X., Hastings, P., Sanson, A., Lo Coco, A., et al. (2006). A cross-cultural study of behavioral inhibition in toddlers: East–west–north–south. *International Journal of Behavioral Development*, 30, 219–226.

Russell, A., Hart, C. H., Robinson, C. C., & Olsen, S. F. (2003). Children's sociable and aggressive behavior with peers: A comparison of the U.S. and Australia, and contributions of temperament and parenting styles. *International Journal of Behavioral Development*, 27, 74–86.

Sabbagh, M. A., Xu, F., Carlson, S. M., Moses, L. J., & Lee, K. (2006). The development of executive functioning and theory of mind: A comparison of Chinese and U.S. preschoolers. *Psychological Science*, 17, 74–81.

Schneider, B., French, D., & Chen, X. (2006). Peer relationships in cultural perspective: Methodological reflections. In X. Chen, D. French, & B. Schneider (Eds.), *Peer relationships in cultural context* (pp. 489–500). New York: Cambridge University Press.

Schwartz, C. E., Snidman, N., & Kagan, J. (1999). Adolescent social anxiety as an outcome of inhibit temperament in childhood. *Journal of the American Academy of Child and Adolescent Psychiatry, 38,* 1008–1015.

Super, C. M., Axia, G., Harkness, S., Welles-Nyström, B., Zylicz, P. O., Parmar, P., et al. (2008). Culture, temperament, and the "difficult child": A study of seven Western cultures. *European Journal of Developmental Science, 2,* 136–157.

Super, C. M., & Harkness, S. (1986). The developmental niche: A conceptualization at the interface of child and culture. *International Journal of Behavioral Development, 9,* 545–569.

Thomas, A., & Chess, S. (1977). *Temperament and development.* Oxford, UK: Brunner/Mazel.

Triandis, H. C. (1995). *Individualism and collectivism.* Boulder, CO: Westview Press.

Trommsdorff, G., & Friedlmeier, W. (2010). Preschool girls' distress and mothers' sensitivity in Japan and Germany. *European Journal of Developmental Psychology, 7,* 350–370.

Tsai, S. J., Hong, C. J., & Cheng, C. Y. (2002). Serotonin transporter genetic polymorphisms and harm avoidance in the Chinese. *Psychiatric Genetics, 12,* 165–168.

Vygotsky, L. S. (1978). *Mind in society: The development of higher psychological processes.* Cambridge, MA: Harvard University Press.

Weisz, J. R., Sigman, M., Weiss, B., & Mosk, J. (1993). Parent reports of behavioral and emotional problems among children in Kenya, Thailand, and the United States. *Child Development, 64,* 98–109.

Zhou, Q., Lengua, L. J., & Wang, Y. (2009). The relations of temperament reactivity and effortful control to children's adjustment problems in China and the United States. *Developmental Psychology, 45,* 724–739.

CHAPTER 23

Gender Differences in Temperament

Nicole M. Else-Quest

Questions, assumptions, and stereotypes about psychological gender differences are pervasive within both psychological science and popular culture. At a very basic level, many of these gender differences (e.g., in emotion, motivation, abilities, or psychopathology) implicate temperament directly or indirectly. For example, the ubiquitous stereotype that women are more "emotional" than men involves temperament dimensions of emotional intensity, emotionality, and negative affectivity; concerns about the higher incidence of attention deficit disorder among boys inevitably return to gender differences in the attention regulation traits of persistence and distractibility. While modern child temperament theories have not made strong assertions about gender differences or similarities in temperament, a handful of theories about gender differences in other psychological characteristics (e.g., emotion) have implicated temperament as a contributing factor. In this chapter, I review empirical and new meta-analytic findings on gender differences in mean levels of and variability in dimensions within five basic temperament traits. However, just as important as *if* there are gender differences in temperament is *why* those differences exist; thus, I also discuss a variety of factors that may contribute to these gender gaps. Finally, I describe research within an emerging area of developmental psychology that examines gender as a moderator of temperament effects.

Making Sense of Gendered Patterns in the Vast Temperament Literature

As described in other chapters in this volume, a major challenge in interpreting the enormous and diverse temperament literature lies in the fact that there have been several unique theoretical approaches to the conceptualization and measurement of temperament. Else-Quest, Hyde, Goldsmith, and Van Hulle (2006), in our meta-analysis of gender differences in childhood temperament, focused on the three predominant approaches to temperament that have generated the most data. I briefly describe these approaches here in order to orient the reader and organize the following discussion of where gender differences and similarities are found.

In their behavioral style approach, Thomas and Chess (1977, 1980; Thomas, Chess, Birch, Hertzig, & Korn, 1963) articulated a model of temperament that sought to conceptualize the *how* rather than the *what* or *why* of behavior. They identified nine dimensions of temperament, including activity level, rhythmicity, approach or withdrawal, adaptability, threshold of responsiveness, intensity of reaction, quality of mood, distractibility, and attention span and persistence. In addition, Bates (e.g., Bates, Freeland, & Lounsbury, 1979) built upon this work to include a cluster of behavioral styles that is difficult for a caregiver to manage, known as *difficult temperament*. This cluster includes irregular biological functioning, poor adaptability, high emotionality, high fearfulness, and high frequency of fussing and crying.

The criterial approach of Buss and Plomin (1975) sought to frame temperament as a developmental antecedent to adult personality. It emphasizes the evolved genetic foundation of temperament in its inclusion criteria. Their model comprises four dimensions—Emotionality, Activity, Sociability, and Impulsivity.

The psychobiological approach developed by Rothbart (1981, 1986; Rothbart, Ahadi, & Hershey, 1994) and others (e.g., Goldsmith, 1996) defines temperament as constitutionally based individual differences in reactivity and self-regulation, explicitly including motivation and emotion. Dimensions described by this approach vary, but include, for infants and children, soothability, smiling, shyness, frustration or distress in response to limitations, fear or distress in response to novelty, high- and low-intensity pleasure, attention focusing and shifting, perceptual sensitivity, as well as activity level.

How does one interpret patterns of gender differences in the many dimensions of temperament across these three approaches? It would be inappropriate to aggregate the dimensions from different approaches, in part because the approaches conceptualize temperament and measure temperament dimensions in unique ways. Instead, the dimensions should be analyzed individually but interpreted collectively within major temperament factors. Based on empirical and theoretical considerations, Rothbart and other theorists have recommended a three-factor model including effortful control, negative affectivity, and surgency (e.g., Ahadi, Rothbart, & Ye, 1993; Rothbart, Ahadi, & Evans, 2000; Shiner & Caspi, 2003).

More recently, De Pauw, Mervielde, and Van Leeuwen (2009) conducted a principal components analysis of preschoolers' scores on temperament measures across the three major approaches (Thomas and Chess, Buss and Plomin, and Rothbart) and a measure of the Five-Factor Model of personality. The resulting factors included sociability, conscientiousness, disagreeableness, activity, negative emotionality, and sensory sensitivity.

Similarly, Shiner and DeYoung (in press) described a six-factor model integrating temperament and personality traits. Departing only slightly from the Big Five model of personality, their model includes the factors of surgency/extraversion, negative emotionality/neuroticism, effortful control/conscientiousness, activity, agreeableness, and openness. In the interest of drawing links to the literature on gender differences in adult personality, I have tried to describe the pattern of gender differences in temperament dimensions in the context of the Big Five model and the model proposed by Shiner and DeYoung, informed by the analyses of Rothbart and colleagues (2000) and De Pauw and colleagues (2009).

Empirical Evidence of Gender Differences in Childhood Temperament

Folk psychology or lay theories about gender differences in temperament are well known. Often, parenting books describe boys as more active, and girls as more sociable and better at managing their attention, but also more fearful or shy. In contrast to this "common knowledge" that boys and girls are essentially different, the evidence from modern gender differences research, which emerged in the 1970s with feminist psychology, suggests a more complex picture. In 1974, Eleanor Maccoby and Carol Jacklin provided the first major literature review of gender differences in temperament traits among children. They reported a handful of gender differences—broadly, boys tend to score higher in emotional volatility and activity, but girls develop the ability to manage their negative emotional responses earlier than boys.

It would take over 30 years for the next major review on the topic to appear; in 2006, Else-Quest, Hyde, Goldsmith, and

Van Hulle conducted a meta-analysis of gender differences in temperament, focusing on research with children between age 3 months and 13 years. I focus on these findings in this chapter because they represent both the most recent and the most comprehensive review of data on gender differences in temperament; I also describe a handful of studies published since the meta-analysis. Else-Quest and colleagues aggregated the results from 191 published and unpublished studies from 1960 to 2002, representing $n = 237{,}516$ ratings or observations of temperament. Cohen's (1988) effect size, d, was computed as a measure of the magnitude of gender gaps in temperament, such that negative effect sizes indicate higher scores or ratings for girls and positive effect sizes indicate higher scores or ratings for boys. A total of 1,196 effect sizes were computed for 36 dimensions across the three major theoretical approaches. What follows is a summary of those meta-analytic results, as well as a review of more recent studies examining gender differences in children's temperament and comparable traits in adults.

Activity

Although activity level has typically been considered a dimension within surgency, De Pauw and colleagues (2009) found that it, along with impulsivity, inhibitory control, and high-intensity pleasure, comprises a separate factor. The dimension of activity level can be assessed with traditional questionnaire methods, as well as with actigraphy, which involves mechanical assessment of activity level. The meta-analytic results of Else-Quest and colleagues (2006) regarding the dimension of activity level are largely consistent with previous investigations of the same construct (e.g., Maccoby & Jacklin, 1974), in that males were more active than females, but effects were small. Eaton and Enns (1986) conducted a meta-analysis on gender differences in activity and found that boys were more active than girls by nearly one-half standard deviation.

In terms of developmental changes in the size of gender differences in activity level, Eaton and Enns (1986) reported that gender gaps in activity actually increased in magnitude across childhood. Similarly, moderator analyses of data from Else-Quest and colleagues (2006) indicate that gender differences in activity level grow in magnitude from infancy through middle childhood, then become nonsignificant at preadolescence. Consistent with this developmental shift, Wickel, Eisenmann, and Welk (2009) found, using actigraphy, that gender differences in activity level declined in adolescence. In addition, Feingold (1994) reported that the gender gap in activity level among adults was "trivial," and Costa, Terracciano, and McCrae (2001) found a very small gender difference that favored women ($d = -0.11$).

The positive effect size in high-intensity pleasure indicates that boys derive more pleasure out of high-intensity activities, such as playing sports and being engaged in rough-and-tumble play. This gender gap appears to be stable into adulthood, judging from Costa and colleagues' (2001) meta-analytic findings of gender differences in excitement-seeking among adults ($d = 0.31$). Maccoby (1990, 1998) argued that high-intensity activities are predominant among male peer groups, and that these groups serve to strengthen the gender difference in play styles in childhood. The social environment may reinforce and maintain this gender difference.

Else-Quest and colleagues (2006) found a medium effect size in inhibitory control favoring girls, and a small effect size in impulsivity favoring boys; these findings indicate that girls are better at controlling or inhibiting impulsive behaviors. Booth-LaForce and Oxford (2008) reported small gender differences in inhibitory control at 54 months in the National Institute of Child Health and Human Development (NICHD) Study of Early Child Care and Youth Development. In summary, then, findings within the factor of activity level are consistent in direction, though they vary somewhat in magnitude, and point to a pattern in which boys are more active and impulsive, and more likely to engage in high-intensity activities.

Effortful Control and Conscientiousness

The temperament dimensions reflecting attention regulation (i.e., purposeful shifting and focusing) comprise the factor of conscientiousness identified by De Pauw and colleagues' (2009) analyses. As shown in Table 23.1, Else-Quest and colleagues (2006)

TABLE 23.1. Number of Computed and Estimated Effect Sizes (k), Total Number of Individuals Assessed (n), Weighted Mean Effect Sizes (d), and Variance Ratios (VR) for Gender Differences in Temperament Dimensions within Three Broad Theoretical Approaches

Factor	Dimension	k	n	d	VR
Activity	Activity[a]	80	22,065	0.22**	1.05
	Activity[b]	33	6,791	0.13**	1.06
	Activity[c]	36	5,636	0.23**	1.00
	Approach[c]	17	2,310	−0.04	0.97
	High-intensity pleasure[c]	18	1,953	0.30**	1.00
	Impulsivity[c]	21	2,254	0.18*	0.95
	Inhibitory control[c]	30	3,668	−0.50**	1.10
Conscientiousness/ Effortful Control	Attention[b]	8	2,187	−0.24**	1.08
	Attention focus[c]	30	4,107	−0.15**	1.06
	Attention shifting[c]	12	1,279	−0.31*	1.11
	Distractibility[a]	56	9,745	0.03	1.03
	Interest[c]	6	1,469	0.09	0.97
	Persistence[a]	87	22,430	−0.06*	1.00
Extraversion/ Surgency	Approach[a]	71	15,789	−0.08**	0.94
	Mood[a]	69	16,661	−0.05*	1.07
	Shyness[b]	25	4,720	−0.08*	1.19
	Shyness[c]	23	3,802	−0.03	1.04
	Smiling[c]	27	3,029	0.00	0.94
	Sociability[b]	29	8,632	−0.05	1.04
Neuroticism/ Negative Affectivity	Adaptability[a]	73	11,956	−0.02	1.04
	Anger/frustration[c]	25	3,984	0.03	0.90
	Difficulty[a]	36	9,820	0.11**	1.11
	Difficulty[c]	7	879	0.03	0.86
	Discomfort[c]	15	1,825	−0.17*	0.98
	Distress to limits[c]	20	2,321	0.00	0.95
	Emotionality[b]	35	8,475	0.00	0.94
	Fear[c]	38	4,858	−0.11**	0.93
	Intensity[a]	65	12,304	0.07*	1.07
	Sadness[c]	16	2,314	−0.10	1.18
	Threshold[a]	46	14,254	−0.04	1.03
Openness/ Sensitivity	Low-intensity pleasure[c]	20	3,252	−0.21*	1.14
	Perceptual sensitivity[c]	14	1,757	−0.38**	1.11
	Rhythmicity[a]	56	15,354	0.03	0.86
	Soothability[c]	31	3,410	0.05	0.94

Note. Negative d indicates higher values for girls; positive d indicates higher values for boys; VR > 1.0 indicates greater male variability, whereas VR < 1.0 indicates greater female variability. Data from Else-Quest, Hyde, Goldsmith, and Van Hulle (2006).
[a]Dimension within the behavioral style approach of Thomas and Chess.
[b]Dimension within the criterial approach of Buss and Plomin.
[c]Dimension within the psychobiological approach of Rothbart and Goldsmith.
*$p < .05$; ** $p < .01$.

found that the majority of gender gaps in dimensions within this factor were significant and favored females. These mean-level gender differences are qualified by the finding that most of the dimensions also show greater male variability. Thus, it can be said that compared to boys, girls tend to focus their attention more appropriately, but there are more boys than girls in the extreme tails of the distributions of these traits.

A handful of studies (k = 6) in the meta-analysis analyzed Rothbart's effortful control; dimensions included in this factor are attention shifting and focusing, as well as perceptual sensitivity, interest, and inhibitory control. The average effect size in effortful control across those studies was very large (d = –1.01) and favored girls. While DeBoo and Kolk (2007) found no evidence of gender differences in effortful control among Dutch, Turkish, Moroccan, and mixed-ethnicity children, other, recently published reports are consistent with the findings of Else-Quest and colleagues (2006). For example, Sulik and colleagues (2010) evaluated a variety of behavioral measures of effortful control in a sample of ethnically diverse low-income preschoolers; gender differences in these measures tended to favor girls and most were small in magnitude. Gender differences in effortful control dimensions suggest a robust trend in which boys consistently lag behind girls in traits that are commonly regarded as critical for success in school.

In contrast, the adult personality literature has generally found very small or negligible gender differences in conscientiousness and its constituent facets (e.g., Costa et al., 2001; Feingold, 1994; Schmitt, Realo, Voracek, & Allik, 2008). Costa and colleagues (2001) found that only the facet of competence showed significant gender differences, a small effect favoring men, but that the facets of order, dutifulness, achievement striving, self-discipline, and deliberation were all nonsignificant. This apparent discrepancy may stem from measurement differences, an issue that I address later in this chapter.

Surgency, Positive Affectivity, and Extraversion

Surgency comprises dimensions such as approach, smiling, sociability, and low shyness. As shown in Table 23.1, the dimensions within this factor show only negligible gender differences; that is, effect sizes in all dimensions are smaller than one-tenth of a standard deviation. However, across the handful of studies (k = 9) that analyzed surgency as a factor, the average effect size was medium and favored boys (d = 0.50, $p < .01$); yet those studies included high-intensity pleasure and impulsivity in the factor of surgency, and boys score higher than girls on these traits.

With regard to positive affectivity and smiling, girls and women tend to score higher than boys and men. For example, in their sample of Dutch, Moroccan, Turkish, and mixed-ethnicity children, DeBoo and Kolk (2007) found small-to-medium gender differences in positive affectivity, favoring girls. Similarly, Costa and colleagues (2001) reported that women scored higher than men on positive emotions. Smiling is typically an indicator of positive affect and is a fine-grained trait on the Infant Behavior Questionnaire (Rothbart, 1981, 1986). Two published meta-analyses suggest a pattern in which gender differences in smiling may develop during adolescence. That is, while Hall and Halberstadt (1986) found no gender differences in smiling during childhood, LaFrance, Hecht, and Paluck (2003) found a medium gender difference in smiling (d = –0.41) such that women and adolescent girls smile more. These findings, in combination with the negligible gender difference Else-Quest and colleagues (2006) found in smiling in childhood, suggest that gender differences in smiling may develop in adolescence.

The negligible gender differences in shyness and sociability found by Else-Quest and colleagues (2006) are consistent with Maccoby and Jacklin's (1974) findings. Similarly, Booth-LaForce and Oxford (2008) found negligible gender differences in shyness in their analyses of the NICHD study data for children at ages 6 and 24 months.

In adults, the trait of extraversion (which includes warmth, gregariousness, assertiveness, activity, excitement seeking, and positive emotions) shows inconsistent findings. Mixed patterns of gender differences in extraversion were observed in Costa and colleagues' (2001) meta-analysis, such that women scored higher than men on all facets except assertiveness and excitement seeking (which were higher in men). Also, Schmitt and colleagues' (2008) International Sexuality Description Project (ISDP) sample showed a negligible gender gap (favoring women) in extraversion across 55 countries. Yet some reports have demonstrated higher levels of extraversion among men (Lynn & Martin, 1997). In contrast to the gender similarities seen in childhood shyness and sociability, a gender gap in gregariousness is found with adults. Feingold's (1994) meta-analysis reported that women scored somewhat higher ($d = -0.19$) than men on gregariousness, and Costa and colleagues reported that women scored higher than men on gregariousness and warmth. Thus, it appears that gender differences in some extraversion facets develop or emerge during adolescence or adulthood.

Neuroticism and Negative Affectivity

Rothbart's factor of negative affectivity comprises dimensions such as negative emotionality, sadness, anger, and distress to limits; this is a departure from the facets of adult neuroticism, which include anxiety, depression, and self-consciousness. The pattern of gender differences estimated within the factor of negative affectivity suggests a trend of gender similarities. Across studies ($k = 12$) that analyzed negative affectivity as a factor, $d = 0.00$. Very few effect sizes for gender differences in the dimensions were significant, and the magnitude of those effects was very small. Similarly, Booth-LaForce and Oxford (2008) found negligible gender differences in adaptability in 6-month-olds in the NICHD study. DeBoo and Kolk (2007) reported inconsistent findings of gender differences in negative affectivity; gender differences were small to medium, favoring females, in Dutch and Moroccan samples, but were very small or close to zero in Turkish and mixed-ethnicity samples.

As seen in Table 23.1, childhood gender differences in mood (positive vs. negative in the Thomas-and-Chess approach), anger, and sadness are negligible. Similarly, Booth-LaForce and Oxford (2008) found only negligible gender differences in mood in their analyses of the NICHD study data for children at ages 6 and 24 months. These findings contrast with Costa and colleagues' (2001) findings for adults on the facets of depression and angry hostility, which both showed small gender differences favoring females.

Regarding the dimension of fear, Else-Quest and colleagues (2006) found very small gender differences across 38 studies. These results are similar to the findings of Maccoby and Jacklin's (1974) narrative review, which concluded that boys and girls do not differ in fearfulness. Yet at some point in adolescent or adult development, a gender difference in anxiety develops, such that women are more anxious than men ($d = -0.40$; Costa et al., 2001).

Gender differences in the personality trait of neuroticism in adults are well established, and these differences are reflected in gender ratios in anxiety, depression, and other mood disorders. Meta-analyses of the personality literature have found medium to large gender differences favoring females (Costa et al., 2001; Feingold, 1994), and the ISDP sample showed an average gender gap of $d = -0.40$ across 55 nations (Schmitt et al., 2008; see also Lynn & Martin, 1997).

Sensory Sensitivity and Openness

The personality trait of openness to experience includes facets such as fantasy, aesthetics, feelings, and ideas. De Pauw and colleagues (2009) noted that temperament models generally ignore this trait, despite evidence that at least elements of it (e.g., creativity) are identified in young children. In their analyses, De Pauw and colleagues found evidence of a sixth factor, sensitivity, which includes dimensions such as low-intensity pleasure, perceptual sensitivity, soothability, rhythmicity, and smiling (described earlier as a dimension within surgency). Thus, this factor encompasses sensitivity to changes in the environment and engagement in low-intensity activities (e.g., reading/looking at books). As can be seen in Table 23.1, two of these dimensions show nonsignificant, negligible effect sizes, and two show small-to-medium effect sizes favoring girls. That girls may derive more enjoyment from low-intensity activities dovetails with boys' greater enjoyment in high-intensity activities (described under the activity factor).

The gender difference in perceptual sensitivity indicates that girls are more aware or attuned than boys to details in their environment. This finding is consistent with research demonstrating that women encode life events in more detail than men do (Seidlitz & Diener, 1998). Compared to boys and men, girls and women tend to recall more childhood memories, recall them faster, and recall them from younger ages (Davis, 1999). The gender difference in perceptual sensitivity extends to being aware of and accurately decoding the nonverbal emotional expressions of others in childhood (Bosacki & Moore, 2004) and adulthood (Hall, 1984; Hall & Matsumoto, 2004).

In adults, evidence for gender differences in openness is mixed. For example, Schmitt and colleagues (2008) found only a negligible gender difference ($d = 0.05$) in openness across 55 countries. Across the facets of openness, Costa and colleagues (2001) found that women score significantly higher than men in aesthetics, feelings, and actions, but that men score higher than women in fantasy and ideas; these effects were small in magnitude. There was no significant gender difference in the facet of values.

Agreeableness

The personality trait of agreeableness includes facets such as compliance, tender-mindedness, and altruism, and generally shows small or medium gender differences favoring women (Costa et al., 2001; Feingold, 1994; Schmitt et al., 2008). De Pauw and colleagues (2009) noted that although developmental psychologists study related behaviors such as compliance and empathy in children, they generally do not identify agreeableness as a temperament trait (but see Knafo & Israel, Chapter 9, this volume, for evidence for a temperamental basis of agreeableness). Yet research on gender differences in these behaviors suggests that the gender difference in agreeableness is evident early in life. For example, compared to girls, boys are more aggressive (Archer, 2004; Hyde, 1984) and less empathetic (Eisenberg & Fabes, 1998). These findings are consistent with patterns of higher agreeableness in women.

Measurement Matters

How we measure temperament has implications for the meaning of the patterns of gender differences observed. An important study characteristic that has received much attention in the temperament literature is the source of temperament ratings; that is, researchers have been interested in whether parent reports, teacher reports, and behavioral observations are all valid and accurate temperament assessments (e.g., Achenbach, McConaughy, & Howell, 1987; Goldsmith & Hewitt, 2003; Seifer, 2003). Although a meta-analysis of gender differences in temperament cannot answer that question per se, it can shed light on the debate, insofar as gender differences in temperament are moderated by source of temperament rating. For example, gender differences in distractibility and persistence are larger with teacher reports ($d = 0.27$, $p < .01$, and $d = -0.16$, $p < .01$, respectively) than with parent reports ($d = -0.04$, $p > .05$, and $d = -0.01$, $p > .05$, respectively). A similar trend was seen with effect sizes for activity, both from the behavioral style approach (parent: $d = 0.14$, $p < .01$; teacher: $d = 0.40$, $p < .01$) and from the psychobiological approach (parent: $d = 0.17$, $p < 0.01$; teacher: $d = 0.49$, $p < .01$), as well as with intensity (parent: $d = -0.01$, $p > .05$; teacher: $d = 0.32$, $p < .01$) and rhythmicity (parent: $d = 0.00$, $p > .05$; teacher: $d = 0.37$, $p < .01$). For no dimension was this pattern reversed; that is, if gender differences varied by source of rating, teacher reports consistently yielded larger gender gaps than parent reports. It is most likely the case that these moderator analyses illustrate the context-specific expression of temperament traits, such that children behave differently in different contexts (Achenbach et al., 1987). To some extent, this pattern of results is consistent with Maccoby's (1990, 1998) theorizing that gender differences are largest in peer groups, given that this is the typical context within which teachers observe child behavior and temperament.

Because parents observe their children in a variety of contexts, they may observe less gender differentiation in the behavior of their sons and daughters. Yet because teachers have experience with more children, they observe a greater range of behaviors and have a better sense of behavior norms against which to rate children. In addition, gender gaps in traits such as effortful control are likely very salient to teachers, who are highly attuned to children's ability to regulate attention, to self-control inappropriate behaviors, and to be engaged with low-intensity activities in the classroom. The efforts of teachers to control or manage the behavior of children with low effortful control contribute to and foster a dynamic and reciprocal relationship with the child's temperament. Moreover, depending on the teacher's endorsement of gender stereotypes, he or she may respond differently to boys and girls who display difficulty regulating their attention or behavior in the classroom, potentially exacerbating or mitigating gender gaps. Such a pathway is consistent with Scarr and McCartney's (1983) description of *evocative effects*, in which small gender differences grow as a result of gender role socialization and social interaction. Thus, the source of temperament rating is no small matter to the assessment of gender differences.

The finding that gender gaps in childhood temperament do not parallel those in adult personality may also stem, in part, from the conceptualization and measurement of some traits. Regarding negative affectivity and neuroticism, the meta-analytic findings of Else-Quest and colleagues (2006) stand in contrast to generally consistent reports in the personality literature that men and women differ in the Big Five trait of neuroticism and its facets, such as anxiety, depression, self-consciousness, vulnerability, and impulsiveness. What explains the lack of correspondence between gender gaps in neuroticism and negative affectivity? Insofar as the temperament factor of negative affectivity is a developmental precursor to the personality trait of neuroticism, similar patterns of gender differences would be expected. Yet, neuroticism and negative affectivity are not entirely redundant. While the measurement of neuroticism (as a personality trait) emphasizes internally focused distress, anxiety, and vulnerability, measures of negative affectivity include dimensions such as irritability, fear, and sadness. Similarly, the different patterns found with effortful control in childhood and conscientiousness in adulthood may stem from differences in measurement. While effortful control emphasizes attention regulation, conscientiousness includes facets such as self-discipline and achievement striving. In summary, the lack of correspondence between gender gaps in childhood negative affectivity and effortful control and adult neuroticism and conscientiousness, respectively, appears to be linked to how we conceptualize and measure those traits; of course, this does not rule out developmental change.

In addition, measurement bias is relevant to our discussion of gender differences in temperament, in that gender stereotypes of emotion may bias perceptions or reports of gender differences in temperament. A handful of well-known studies found that adults judge temperament traits in children based on knowledge of the child's gender (e.g., Condry & Condry, 1976), although such findings have not been replicated consistently (Maccoby & Jacklin, 1974; Stern & Karraker, 1989). Similarly, gender stereotypes of emotion may result in contrast or even null effects, such that actual gender differences in temperament are obscured when different raters use shifting standards of temperament (Biernat, 2003, 2005). For example, what a teacher considers "very active" for a boy may differ from what he or she considers "very active" for a girl. In summary, gender stereotypes held by temperament raters—whether they are parents, teachers, or oneself—are wildcards, contributing measurement error to data on gender differences in temperament. For these reasons, it is critical to increase our use of observational measures of temperament and/or use multiple informants in order to obtain "cleaner" temperament data that are more reliable. In summary, how we conceptualize and measure traits can moderate gender differences in temperament. Efforts to improve the validity of temperament measurement are important here, insofar as measurement error—from source of report or bias—contributes to variability in findings of gender differences and similarities.

Potential Causes of Gender Differences in Temperament

What contributes to gender differences in temperament? There are a number of hypothesized causes, ranging from prenatal sexual differentiation to gender role socialization. Here I summarize several potential causes.

Biological Contributions

Given that temperament reflects biological predispositions, it is appropriate to consider the biological contributions to gender differences in temperament. These involve both distal explanations from evolutionary psychology and proximal explanations stemming from brain organization theory. Evolutionary psychologists have argued that it was evolutionarily adaptive (i.e., reproductive fitness was enhanced) for males and females to develop divergent personality traits in response to sexual selection pressures stemming from parental investment (Geary, 2010). For example, given women's greater investment in childrearing, it would be adaptive for women to be nurturant and agreeable. Similarly, higher neuroticism—particularly fearfulness—might be adaptive for women, in that environmental threats ultimately exert greater fitness costs on women than on men, insofar as offspring rarely survive without their mothers (Rakison, 2009). In contrast, risk taking was more adaptive for men, who would be likely to be involved in big game hunting or aggressive behaviors. Thus, evolutionary psychology would predict greater agreeableness and neuroticism in women, but greater impulsivity and risk taking in men; in terms of childhood temperament, we can extrapolate to predict greater fearfulness and agreeableness in girls and greater activity, high-intensity pleasure, and impulsivity in boys. To some extent, these predictions are supported by the temperament data reviewed here.

Of course, environmental constraints can change, thereby changing which traits are adaptive for men and women. For example, human development (i.e., opportunity for economic, educational, and physical well-being) can shape the expression of sex-selected traits, contributing to variability in the magnitude of gender gaps in traits (Schmitt et al., 2008). That is, gender gaps are plastic, such that they are larger when opportunities for role specialization exist (i.e., higher levels of human development) and smaller when environmental conditions require more androgynous temperament profiles. A wealthier and more developed nation can provide us with an environment that fosters more specialization of traits and behaviors, but a poorer and less developed nation does not give us that luxury.

In terms of more proximal explanations for gender gaps in temperament, brain organization theory maintains that prenatal sex hormones exert organizational effects in the sexual differentiation of reproductive as well as brain structures (Jordan-Young, 2010). Specifically, the presence of prenatal testosterone masculinizes structures in boys, and its absence allows feminine structures to develop in girls. Much of the evidence for the brain organization hypothesis comes from research with girls affected by congenital adrenal hyperplasia (CAH), who are exposed to abnormally high levels of adrenal androgens during prenatal development. If prenatal testosterone causes "masculine" temperament and personality traits to develop, girls with CAH should be more masculine than typically developing girls. Indeed, the evidence regarding brain organization theory, while problematic for a number of reasons (Jordan-Young, 2010), generally suggests that girls with CAH are more aggressive, more active, less tender-minded, and less interested in infants (e.g., Mathews, Fane, Conway, Brook, & Hines, 2009; Pasterski et al., 2007). Boys with CAH do not appear to show any deviation from typically developing boys in their traits, probably because negative feedback loops reduce gonadal testosterone secretions in response to abnormally high adrenal secretions.

However, these findings do not necessarily mean that prenatal testosterone causes males to be more active, more aggressive, and less tender-minded than girls. In the absence of experimental data with humans, we cannot make such claims; however, it seems probable that prenatal sexual differentiation plays some role. A stronger case for links between prenatal sex hormones and temperament comes from research showing lower levels of conscientiousness among children with more masculine right 2D:4D digit (finger) length ratios, an index of greater prenatal testosterone exposure (Martel, 2009). Yet in light of findings that prenatal testosterone exposure may be linked to temperament behaviors in boys but not in girls (e.g., Bergman, Glover, Sarkar, Abbott, & O'Connor, 2010; Martel, Gobrogge, Breedlove, & Nigg, 2008), we should consider a more complex model than classic brain organization theory proposes.

Gender Socialization

Many gender development theorists have argued that psychological differences between males and females develop out of gender roles and gender socialization or learning (e.g., Bussey & Bandura, 1999; Eagly & Wood, 1999; Leaper, 2000). Consider how parents' socializing behaviors might exert effects on the development and expression of temperament traits. Insofar as parents socialize their children about how to label and interpret their emotions, gender stereotypes of emotion may be imposed and contribute to the development of gender differences in the more "emotional" temperament traits (e.g., fear, sadness, anger/frustration). Consider the finding that despite minimal gender differences in emotionality, mood, fear, sadness, and anger/frustration, parents talk about emotions more and use more emotion words with daughters than with sons (Brody, 2000; Fivush, Brotman, Buckner, & Goodman, 2000; Flannagan & Perese, 1998). Yet, consistent with gender roles, mothers tend not to talk about anger with daughters (Fivush, 1989). Thus, these types of socializing behaviors have the potential to shape the expression of temperament traits.

Consistent with this developmental process, Leslie Brody (1997, 1999, 2000) theorizes that small gender differences in temperament are at the foundation of gender differences in emotion. She maintains that subtle gender differences in infant temperament traits of activity and sociability elicit different socialization patterns in girls and boys, such that boys are encouraged to manage their arousal and control their emotions, while girls are encouraged to be sociable, empathetic, and emotionally expressive. In this way, small gender differences are exacerbated by parental socialization, and display rules and gender stereotypes of emotion. However, the negligible gender gaps in smiling and sociability found by Else-Quest and colleagues (2006) do not support Brody's theory.

The peer group also contributes to gender socialization and, potentially, the development of gender differences in temperament. Maccoby (1990, 1998) maintained that gender differences in many individual characteristics, such as personality and temperament, are likely to be small except when children are observed in peer groups. She argued that some gender differences in behavior develop as a result of gender segregation in peer interactions. More recently, Zakriski, Wright, and Underwood (2005) argued that gender differences in personality are context-specific patterns of social adaptation more than overall mean-level differences in traits. For example, they reported that girls are not more prosocial than boys, but girls are more likely than boys to be in contexts that elicit prosocial behavior. It is likely that peer groups reinforce and exacerbate gender differences in temperament given that same-gender peer groups tend to differ in their style of interaction (Maccoby, 1990, 1998).

In addition, parents, teachers, peers, and the media all contribute to gender socialization and, thus, may foster gender differences in temperament. These socialization forces may exert particularly strong pressure on individuals to adhere to gender roles *during adolescence* as a part of the gender intensification process. For example, consider the developmental pattern found with smiling, such that gender differences appear to develop during adolescence. At that time, gender intensification may foster a strong motivation in girls to smile (more so than in adolescent boys) in order to obey cultural display rules. This pattern may also be consistent with social learning theories positing that women are taught to smile more, and that smiling is a part of the female role (LaFrance et al., 2003).

Gender Stereotypes

Gender stereotypes may influence the development of gender differences in temperament via multiple pathways, including self-stereotyping. Girls and women have long been stereotyped as generally more emotional than boys and men (Barrett & Bliss-Moreau, 2009; Birnbaum, Nosanchuk, & Crull, 1980; Brody & Hall, 2008; Shields, 2002). Specifically, anger, pride, and contempt are stereotyped as masculine emotions, whereas awe, distress, fear, happiness, love, sadness, shyness, surprise, and sympathy are stereotyped as feminine emotions (Plant,

Hyde, Keltner, & Devine, 2000). Such gender stereotypes provide an important context for gender differences in temperament traits involving emotion (e.g., dimensions within negative affectivity). While the presence of such stereotypes does not confirm or reject the presence of gender differences in corresponding temperament traits, gender stereotypes can be associated with findings of gender differences in temperament in several ways. In some cases, gender stereotypes are highly accurate (Hall & Carter, 1999). Indeed, data indicate that compared to men, women are more emotionally expressive (Kring & Gordon, 1998) and report more sadness (Brody & Hall, 2008). In other cases, gender stereotypes may be exaggerations of small gender differences in temperament. Gender stereotypes of emotion can play a role in gender development, insofar as the expression of gender-stereotyped emotions may be reinforced or punished in the process of gender role socialization. In summary, gender stereotypes probably have a reciprocal causal relationship with gender differences in temperament.

Maturational Effects

A discussion of the potential causes of gender differences in temperament should consider maturational effects. The point at which gender differences appear to emerge or develop over the lifespan can shed light on what contributes to the differences. While males and females are largely similar on negative affectivity dimensions in childhood, they appear to diverge in their levels sometime after age 13 (the upper age limit of samples used in the meta-analysis by Else-Quest et al., 2006). That is, gender differences in neuroticism and negative affectivity generally do not surface until adolescence, when girls begin to display higher levels of traits associated with neuroticism. For example, Baetens, Claes, Willem, Muehlenkamp, and Bijttebier (2011) reported gender differences (favoring girls) in negative affectivity in high schoolers. The emergence of gender differences in negative affectivity could stem from developmental changes in adolescence, such as activational effects of sex hormones (Martel, Klump, Nigg, Breedlove, & Sisk, 2009) or neocortical maturation.

Such patterns of developmental change would be consistent with the widening of the gender gap in self-esteem during adolescence (Kling, Hyde, Showers, & Buswell, 1999), as well as with the emergence of gender differences in depression between ages 13–15 (Hankin et al., 1998). Indeed, such a developmental shift suggests that if the temperament trait of negative affectivity is at the root of depression, as described earlier (Clark, Watson, & Mineka, 1994; Hyde, Mezulis, & Abramson, 2008), gender differences in depression do not develop linearly from gender differences in child temperament. Rather, negative affectivity may serve as a vulnerability factor that, in combination with other vulnerabilities and stressors, contributes to greater depression among adolescent girls and women (Hyde et al., 2008). Similarly, girls and boys may differ in terms of how reactive they are to negative or stressful events (Hankin, Mermelstein, & Roesch, 2007).

To some extent, gender differences in effortful control may reflect a developmental lag on the part of boys. In other words, boys may develop the capacity to regulate their attention a bit later than girls. This would be manifest as gender gaps that exist earlier in childhood but disappear at a later age. Indeed, new moderator analyses indicate that gaps in persistence and attention shifting widen from infancy through middle childhood, but begin to narrow just before puberty, while gaps in other dimensions remain relatively stable.[1] Thus, although some gender differences fluctuate across childhood, most appear temporally stable. Moreover, conscientiousness tends to show negligible or very small gender differences in adulthood (Costa et al., 2001; Feingold, 1994; Schmitt et al., 2008); thus, the explanation of a developmental lag for boys seems plausible. Similarly, maturation of neocortical structures (e.g., the prefrontal cortex) may be linked to changes in the magnitude of this gender gap during adolescence.

Links to Developmental Psychopathology

Empirical and theoretical work in developmental psychopathology provides a context for findings of gender differences in temperament. A number of disorders appear linked to extreme levels on temperament traits, and some of those disorders also show gender differences.

Externalizing Disorders

Consider the gender gap in externalizing disorders, in which males display more antisocial behavior, attention problems, aggressive behavior, and substance abuse than females (Bongers, Koot, van der Ende, & Verhulst, 2003; Lemery, Essex, & Smider, 2002; Nigg, Goldsmith, & Sachek, 2004; Rosenfield, 2000; also see Tackett, Martel, & Kushner, Chapter 27, this volume). The inability to inhibit inappropriate responses and regulate behavior and attention is a central feature of such disorders (Lahey, Moffitt, & Caspi, 2003; Lemery et al., 2002). This pattern of behavior extends to temperament traits such as attention focusing, difficult temperament, anger, and inhibitory control, which are established correlates of externalizing problems (Lemery et al., 2002; Skodol, 2000). That temperament traits are linked to externalizing disorders showing gender differences echoes findings of underlying gender gaps in relevant temperament traits. Moreover, there is some evidence that boys are more likely than girls to possess risk factors for life-course-persistent antisocial behavior—including difficult temperament, hyperactivity, and behavior problems (Moffitt & Caspi, 2001).

Internalizing Disorders

Internalizing disorders such as depression also show gender gaps, and some theoretical perspectives implicate temperament traits in the etiology of those disorders. For example, Clark and colleagues' (1994) tripartite theory of depression argues that temperament traits (specifically, low positive affectivity or surgency and high negative affectivity) moderate one's vulnerability to depression (see Klein, Dyson, Kujawa, & Kotov, Chapter 26, this volume). In light of the well-established finding of gender differences in depression that emerges in adolescence (Costello, Mustillo, Erkanli, Keeler, & Angold, 2003; Hankin et al., 1998; Kessler, 2003), it is logical to investigate gender differences in the childhood traits predicted by the tripartite model to lead to depression (i.e., negative and positive affectivity) (DeBoo & Kolk, 2007; Else-Quest et al., 2006). Similarly, some models of gender differences in depression specify greater emotional reactivity among girls than boys (Hankin et al., 2007), which suggests potential gender differences in dimensions of negative affectivity. Zahn-Waxler, Shirtcliff, and Marceau (2008) reviewed the antecedents to depression and highlighted the potential role of childhood anxiety, which may stem from temperament traits such as approach–withdrawal or, more specifically, fearfulness. Although the links between developmental psychopathology and temperament are varied, these examples provide a developmental context for the gender differences found.

Gender as a Moderator of Temperament Effects

There is considerable evidence suggesting that males and females do not differ in the temporal continuity or stability of temperament (Prinzie & Dekovic, 2008; Schneider, Younger, Smith, & Freeman, 1998). Likewise, data indicate that gender does not moderate changes or trait consistency in temperament (Roberts & DelVecchio, 2000; Roberts, Walton, & Viechtbauer, 2006). In addition, Sulik and colleagues (2010) found gender similarities in the factor structure and loadings in behavioral measures of effortful control. While there appears to be little theoretical reason to suspect that males and females differ in the structure of temperament, is not clear that we can generalize these findings to other temperament factors or measures.

Recently, researchers have made an effort to move beyond the basic question of gender differences in mean levels of traits or behaviors and to examine how developmental processes may differ between males and females; that is, they have explored how gender moderates the links between temperament and later outcomes. The *meaning* of some temperament traits may differ for boys and girls; that is, high or low levels of a trait are not perceived or experienced the same way for boys and girls. Males and females can be similar in their mean levels of a trait but differ in how that trait is linked to other outcomes (e.g., Fabes, Martin, Hanish, Anders, & Madden-Derdich, 2003). Such effects may go undetected by researchers, who, in an attempt to address gender, only examine between-groups differences in means. Here I describe a handful of studies that has addressed the issue of gender as a moderating variable in temperament research. Broadly, such studies demonstrate gender differences in the meaning of temperament dimensions, such that some dimensions present risk differently for boys and girls.

For example, social withdrawal or shyness appears to be more problematic for boys than for girls (Rubin & Coplan, 2004; Stevenson-Hinde & Glover, 1996), insofar as it is linked to adjustment. In examining the life course sequelae of shyness, Caspi, Elder, and Bem (1988) found that, relative to same-gender peers, shy girls tended to follow a traditional life course pattern of marriage and childbearing, but shy boys tended to delay these major life events. Given that shyness is more acceptable, relative to gender roles, for girls than for boys in North American culture (Sadker & Sadker, 1994), peers and parents respond negatively to shyness in boys (Simpson & Stevenson-Hinde, 1985). In this way, gender moderates the effect of shyness on adjustment.

Similarly, the extent to which particular temperament traits serve as risk factors can vary by gender. For example, Rothbart and Bates (1998) proposed that in light of gender similarities in childhood temperament and robust gender differences in psychological adjustment, such as internalizing or externalizing disorders, the developmental or etiological role of temperament in psychopathology might differ for males and females; that is, high or low levels of particular temperament traits may be risk factors for some disorders among males, but for others among females. Consistent with this hypothesis, Rothbart and colleagues (1994) found that whereas negative affectivity predicted the internalization of negative self-conscious emotions and empathy in girls only, it predicted aggression in boys. Thus, a trait such as negative affectivity may play an important role in the development of psychopathology, but do so differently for boys and girls. Similarly, being high in arousability (a composite of emotionality, fearfulness, and impulsivity) is associated with problem behaviors for boys but not girls (Fabes, Shepard, Guthrie, & Martin, 1997).

Fabes and colleagues (2003) found that in the context of young children's same-sex peer interactions, the link between effortful control and social competence in school differs for boys and girls. That is, low effortful control is problematic for the development of social competence, but for boys this effect depends on their interactions in the same-sex peer groups, which are likely to involve dominance and aggressive behaviors. In contrast, for girls, effortful control fosters social competence regardless of their peer group's gender composition.

Suggestions for Future Research

From this review emerge several lines of research regarding gender differences in temperament that warrant further exploration. The first line concerns the degree of *continuity* in gender differences in temperament. For several dimensions, it appears that the magnitude or direction of gender differences changes from childhood temperament to adult personality. Research on the continuity of gender differences in temperament would require more longitudinal temperament research extending from childhood into adolescence and adulthood. In addition, *biological contributions*—especially with regard to the roles of organizational and activational effects of sex hormones and maturation of the prefrontal cortex—should be examined systematically. Continued collaboration among temperament researchers and neuroscientists is important to ensure that this line of research, which is guided by brain organization theory, utilizes appropriate temperament measures (Jordan-Young, 2010). Last, research examining *gender as a moderator* of temperament effects is intriguing but also generally difficult to identify in a literature search, and may involve unrelated theoretical perspectives. A more concerted effort to identify such patterns would expand our understanding of both temperament and gender, and ultimately translate to more effective therapies and interventions for children with temperaments that put them at risk for developmental difficulties.

Conclusions

So, given the many diverse approaches to temperament and their respective dimensions, what can we conclude about gender differences in temperament? While girls tend to score higher than boys on measures of dimensions within conscientiousness/effortful control and openness/sensitivity, gender similarities are the dominant trend in neuroticism/negative affectivity. On the dimensions within activity, boys tend to score higher than girls, but gender similarities are the trend in extraversion/surgency dimensions. Importantly, the majority of effect sizes are small, consistent with the gender similarities hypothesis (Hyde, 2005), which maintains that males and females are similar on most but not all psychological behaviors, traits, and abilities. Thus, male and female distributions overlap considerably, and differences *within* genders tend to be more substantial than differences *between* them. Nonetheless, gender does matter. We have only begun to understand how gender moderates links between temperament and developmental outcomes, but given differences in psychopathology and emotional expression, there is reason to continue investigating such links. A child's gender can shape parent and teacher expectations for and evaluations of the child's behavior, thereby influencing the dynamic relationships between a child's temperament and his or her social environment. Thus, our tendency to seek out gender gaps must be balanced with the recognition that exaggerating or overemphasizing such differences can have negative consequences for the development of both boys and girls.

Note

1. While Else-Quest et al. (2006) were limited in their opportunity for moderator analyses as a result of using a random-effects model, new analyses from the same data, but using a mixed-effects model, are reported here. There has been some debate regarding the assumptions meta-analytic techniques make about the nature of the distribution of effect sizes (e.g., Hedges & Vevea, 1998; Lipsey & Wilson, 2001). Traditionally, meta-analyses have been based on fixed-effects models, which assume that variability among effect sizes is completely systematic and accounted for by the moderators in the analysis. In recent years, some have chosen instead to compute homogeneity statistics using the random-effects model, which assumes that variability among effect sizes is random. Both models are problematic, however: Whereas the fixed-effects model requires untenable statistical assumptions about the homogeneity of the sample of effect sizes (thereby increasing the Type I error rate), the random-effects model enlarges the error term so greatly that it is difficult to find significant moderators (e.g., indicators of gender equity), even with large samples of studies. In this chapter, I have analyzed the data from Else-Quest et al. using the mixed-effects model, which attributes effect size variability to systematic between-study variations, subject-level sampling error, and random effects. The average effect sizes reported here and in the original report do *not* differ; the only substantive difference is that the mixed-effects model permitted moderator analyses and the random-effects model did not.

Further Reading

Blakemore, J. E. O., Berenbaum, S. A., & Liben, L. S. (2009). *Gender development.* New York: Psychology Press.

Else-Quest, N. M., Hyde, J. S., Goldsmith, H. H., & Van Hulle, C. (2006). Gender differences in temperament: A meta-analysis. *Psychological Bulletin, 132,* 33–72.

Jordan-Young, R. M. (2010). *Brainstorm: The flaws in the science of sex differences.* Cambridge, MA: Harvard University Press.

References

Achenbach, T. M., McConaughy, S. H., & Howell, C. T. (1987). Child/adolescent behavioral and emotional problems: Implications of cross-informant correlations for situational specificity. *Psychological Bulletin, 101,* 213–232.

Ahadi, S. A., Rothbart, M. K., & Ye, R. (1993). Children's temperament in the U.S. and China: Similarities and differences. *European Journal of Personality, 7,* 359–378.

Archer, J. (2004). Sex differences in aggression in real-world settings: A meta-analytic review. *Review of General Psychology, 8,* 291–322.

Baetens, I., Claes, L., Willem, L., Muehlenkamp, J., & Bijttebier, P. (2011). The relationship between non-suicidal self-injury and temperament in male and female adolescents based on child- and parent-report. *Personality and Individual Differences, 50,* 527–530.

Barrett, L. F., & Bliss-Moreau, E. (2009). She's emotional. He's having a bad day: Attributional explanations for emotion stereotypes. *Emotion, 9*, 649–658.

Bates, J. E., Freeland, C. A., & Lounsbury, M. L. (1979). Measurement of infant difficultness. *Child Development, 50*, 794–803.

Bergman, K., Glover, V., Sarkar, P., Abbott, D. H., & O'Connor, T. G. (2010). In utero cortisol and testosterone exposure and fear reactivity in infancy. *Hormones and Behavior, 57*, 306–312.

Biernat, M. (2003). Toward a broader view of social stereotyping. *American Psychologist, 58*, 1019–1027.

Biernat, M. (2005). *Standards and expectancies: Contrast and assimilation in judgments of self and others*. New York: Routledge.

Birnbaum, D. W., Nosanchuk, T. A., & Crull, W. L. (1980). Children's stereotypes about sex differences in emotionality. *Sex Roles, 29*, 435–443.

Bongers, I. L., Koot, H. M., van der Ende, J., & Verhulst, F. C. (2003). The normative development of child and adolescent problem behavior. *Journal of Abnormal Psychology, 112*, 179–192.

Booth-LaForce, C., & Oxford, M. L. (2008). Trajectories of social withdrawal from grades 1 to 6: Prediction from early parenting, attachment, and temperament. *Developmental Psychology, 44*, 1298–1313.

Bosacki, S. L., & Moore, C. (2004). Preschoolers' understanding of simple and complex emotions: Links with gender and language. *Sex Roles, 50*, 659–676.

Brody, L. R. (1997). Gender and emotion: Beyond stereotypes. *Journal of Social Issues, 53*, 369–394.

Brody, L. R. (1999). *Gender, emotion, and the family*. Cambridge, MA: Harvard University Press.

Brody, L. R. (2000). The socialization of gender differences in emotional expression: Display rules, infant temperament, and differentiation. In A. H. Fischer (Ed.), *Gender and emotion: Social psychological perspectives* (pp. 24–47). Cambridge, UK: Cambridge University Press.

Brody, L. R., & Hall, J. A. (2008). Gender and emotion in context. In M. Lewis, J. M. Haviland-Jones, & L. Feldman Barrett (Eds.), *Handbook of emotions* (3rd ed., pp. 395–408). New York: Guilford Press.

Buss, A. H., & Plomin, R. (1975). *A temperament theory of personality development*. New York: Wiley.

Bussey, K., & Bandura, A. (1999). Social cognitive theory of gender development and differentiation. *Psychological Review, 106*, 676–713.

Caspi, A., Elder, G. H., Jr., & Bem, D. J. (1988). Moving away from the world: Life-course patterns of shy children. *Developmental Psychology, 24*, 824–831.

Clark, L. A., Watson, D., & Mineka, S. (1994). Temperament, personality, and the mood and anxiety disorders. *Journal of Abnormal Psychology, 103*, 103–116.

Cohen, J. (1988). *Statistical power analysis for the behavioral sciences*. Hillsdale, NJ: Erlbaum.

Condry, J., & Condry, S. (1976). Sex differences: A study of the eye of the beholder. *Child Development, 47*, 812–819.

Costa, P. T., Terracciano, A., & McCrae, R. R. (2001). Gender differences in personality traits across cultures: Robust and surprising findings. *Journal of Personality and Social Psychology, 81*, 322–331.

Costello, E. J., Mustillo, S., Erkanli, A., Keeler, G., & Angold, A. (2003). Prevalence and development of psychiatric disorders in childhood and adolescence. *Archives of General Psychiatry, 60*, 837–844.

Davis, P. J. (1999). Gender differences in autobiographical memory for childhood emotional experiences. *Journal of Personality and Social Psychology, 76*, 498–510.

DeBoo, G. M., & Kolk, A. M. (2007). Ethnic and gender differences in temperament, and the relationship between temperament and depressive and aggressive mood. *Personality and Individual Differences, 43*, 1756–1766.

De Pauw, S. S. W., Mervielde, I., & Van Leeuwen, K. G. (2009). How are traits related to problem behavior in preschoolers?: Similarities and contrasts between temperament and personality. *Journal of Abnormal Child Psychology, 37*, 309–325.

Eagly, A. H., & Wood, W. (1999). The origins of sex differences in human behavior. *American Psychologist, 54*, 408–423.

Eaton, W. O., & Enns, L. R. (1986). Sex differences in motor activity level. *Psychological Bulletin, 100*, 19–28.

Eisenberg, N., & Fabes, R. A. (1998). Prosocial development. In W. Damon & N. Eisenberg (Eds.), *Handbook of child psychology: Vol. 3. Social, emotional, and personality development* (5th ed., pp. 701–778). Hoboken, NJ: Wiley.

Else-Quest, N. M., Hyde, J. S., Goldsmith, H. H., & Van Hulle, C. (2006). Gender differences in temperament: A meta-analysis. *Psychological Bulletin, 132*, 33–72.

Fabes, R. A., Martin, C. L., Hanish, L. D., Anders, M. C., & Madden-Derdich, D. A. (2003). Early school competence: The roles of sex-segregated play and effortful control. *Developmental Psychology, 39*, 848–858.

Fabes, R. A., Shepard, S. A., Guthrie, I. K., & Martin, C. L. (1997). Roles of temperamental arousal and gender-segregated play in young children's social adjustment. *Developmental Psychology, 33*, 693–702.

Feingold, A. (1994). Gender differences in personality: A meta-analysis. *Psychological Bulletin, 116,* 429–456.

Fivush, R. (1989). Exploring sex differences in the emotional content of mother–child conversations about the past. *Sex Roles, 20,* 675–691.

Fivush, R., Brotman, M. A., Buckner, J. P., & Goodman, S. H. (2000). Gender differences in parent–child emotion narratives. *Sex Roles, 42,* 233–253.

Flannagan, D., & Perese, S. (1998). Emotional references in mother–daughter and mother–son dyads' conversations about school. *Sex Roles, 39,* 353–367.

Geary, D. C. (2010). *Male, female: The evolution of human sex differences* (2nd ed.). Washington, DC: American Psychological Association.

Goldsmith, H. H. (1996). Studying temperament via construction of the Toddler Behavior Assessment Questionnaire. *Child Development, 67,* 218–235.

Goldsmith, H. H., & Hewitt, E. C. (2003). Validity of parental report of temperament: Distinctions and needed research. *Infant Behavior and Development, 26,* 108–111.

Hall, J. A. (1984). *Nonverbal sex differences: Communication accuracy and expressive style.* Baltimore: Johns Hopkins University Press.

Hall, J. A., & Carter, J. D. (1999). Gender-stereotype accuracy as an individual difference. *Journal of Personality and Social Psychology, 77,* 350–359.

Hall, J. A., & Halberstadt, A. G. (1986). Smiling and gazing. In J. S. Hyde & M. C. Linn (Eds.), *The psychology of gender: Advances through meta-analysis* (pp. 136–158). Baltimore: John Hopkins University Press.

Hall, J. A., & Matsumoto, D. (2004). Gender differences in judgments of multiple emotions from facial expressions. *Emotion, 4,* 201–206.

Hankin, B. L., Abramson, L., Moffitt, T., Silva, P., McGee, R., & Angell, K. (1998). Development of depression from preadolescence to young adulthood: Emerging gender differences in a 10-year longitudinal study. *Journal of Abnormal Psychology, 107,* 128–140.

Hankin, B. L., Mermelstein, R., & Roesch, L. (2007). Sex differences in adolescent depression: Stress exposure and reactivity models. *Child Development, 78,* 279–295.

Hedges, L. V., & Vevea, J. L. (1998). Fixed- and random-effects models in meta-analysis. *Psychological Methods, 3,* 486–504.

Hyde, J. S. (1984). How large are gender differences in aggression?: A developmental meta-analysis. *Developmental Psychology, 20,* 722–736.

Hyde, J. S. (2005). The gender similarities hypothesis. *American Psychologist, 60,* 581–592.

Hyde, J. S., Mezulis, A. H., & Abramson, L. Y. (2008). The ABCs of depression: Integrating affective, biological, and cognitive models to explain the emergence of the gender difference in depression. *Psychological Review, 115,* 291–313.

Jordan-Young, R. M. (2010). *Brainstorm: The flaws in the science of sex differences.* Cambridge, MA: Harvard University Press.

Kessler, R. (2003). Epidemiology of women and depression. *Journal of Affective Disorders, 74,* 5–13.

Kling, K. C., Hyde, J. S., Showers, C. J., & Buswell, B. N. (1999). Gender differences in self-esteem: A meta-analysis. *Psychological Bulletin, 125,* 470–500.

Kring, A. M., & Gordon, A. H. (1998). Sex differences in emotion: Expression, experience, and physiology. *Journal of Personality and Social Psychology, 74,* 686–703.

LaFrance, M., Hecht, M. A., & Paluck, E. L. (2003). The contingent smile: A meta-analysis of sex differences in smiling. *Psychological Bulletin, 129,* 305–334.

Lahey, B. B., Moffitt, T. E., & Caspi, A. (Eds.). (2003). *Causes of conduct disorder and juvenile delinquency.* New York: Guilford Press.

Leaper, C. (2000). Gender, affiliation, and the interactive context of parent–child play. *Developmental Psychology, 36,* 381–393.

Lemery, K. S., Essex, M. J., & Smider, N. A. (2002). Revealing the relation between temperament and behavior problem symptoms by eliminating measurement confounding: Expert ratings and factor analyses. *Child Development, 73,* 867–882.

Lipsey, M. W., & Wilson, D. B. (2001). *Practical meta-analysis.* Thousand Oaks, CA: Sage.

Lynn, R., & Martin, T. (1997). Gender differences in extraversion, neuroticism, and psychoticism in 37 nations. *Journal of Social Psychology, 137,* 369–373.

Maccoby, E. E. (1990). Gender and relationships: A developmental account. *American Psychologist, 45,* 513–520.

Maccoby, E. E. (1998). *The two sexes: Growing up apart, coming together.* Cambridge, MA: Harvard University Press.

Maccoby, E. E., & Jacklin, C. N. (1974). *The psychology of sex differences.* Stanford, CA: Stanford University Press.

Martel, M. M. (2009). Conscientiousness as a mediator of the association between masculinized finger-length ratios and attention-deficit/hyperactivity disorder (ADHD). *Journal of Child Psychology and Psychiatry, 50,* 790–798.

Martel, M. M., Gobrogge, K. L., Breedlove, S. M., & Nigg, J. T. (2008). Masculinized finger-length ratios of boys, but not girls, are associated with attention-deficit/hyperactivity disorder. *Behavioral Neuroscience, 122,* 273–281.

Martel, M. M., Klump, K., Nigg, J. T., Breedlove, S. M., & Sisk, C. L. (2009). Potential hormonal mechanisms of attention-deficit/hyperactivity disorder and major depressive disorder: A new perspective. *Hormones and Behavior, 55,* 465–479.

Mathews, G. A., Fane, B. A., Conway, G. S., Brook, C. G. D., & Hines, M. (2009). Personality and congenital hyperplasia: Possible effects of prenatal androgen exposure. *Hormones and Behavior, 55,* 285–291.

Moffitt, T. E., & Caspi, A. (2001). Childhood predictors differentiate life-course persistent and adolescence-limited antisocial pathways among males and females. *Development and Psychopathology, 13,* 355–375.

Nigg, J. T., Goldsmith, H. H., & Sachek, J. (2004). Temperament and attention-deficit/hyperactivity disorder: Preliminary convergence across child temperament and adult personality data may aid a multi-pathway model. *Journal of Clinical Child and Adolescent Psychology, 33,* 42–53.

Pasterski, V. L., Hindmarsch, P., Geffner, M., Brook, C., Brain, C., & Hines, M. (2007). Increased aggression and activity level in 3- to 11-year-old girls with congenital adrenal hyperplasia (CAH). *Hormones and Behavior, 52,* 368–374.

Plant, E. A., Hyde, J. S., Keltner, D., & Devine, P. G. (2000). The gender stereotyping of emotions. *Psychology of Women Quarterly, 24,* 81–92.

Prinzie, P., & Dekovic, M. (2008). Continuity and change of childhood personality characteristics through the lens of teachers. *Personality and Individual Differences, 45,* 82–88.

Rakison, D. H. (2009). Does women's greater fear of snakes and spiders originate in infancy? *Evolution and Human Behavior, 30,* 438–444.

Roberts, B. W., & DelVecchio, W. F. (2000). The rank-order consistency of personality traits from childhood to old age: A quantitative review of longitudinal studies. *Psychological Bulletin, 126,* 3–25.

Roberts, B. W., Walton, K. E., & Viechtbauer, W. (2006). Patterns of mean-level change in personality traits across the life course: A meta-analysis of longitudinal studies. *Psychological Bulletin, 132,* 1–25.

Rosenfield, S. (2000). Gender and dimensions of the self. In E. Frank (Ed.), *Gender and its effects on psychopathology* (pp. 23–36). Washington, DC: American Psychiatric Press.

Rothbart, M. K. (1981). Measurement of temperament in infancy. *Child Development, 52,* 569–578.

Rothbart, M. K. (1986). Longitudinal observation of infant temperament. *Developmental Psychology, 22,* 356–365.

Rothbart, M. K., Ahadi, S. A., & Evans, D. E. (2000). Temperament and personality: Origins and outcomes. *Journal of Personality and Social Psychology, 78,* 122–135.

Rothbart, M. K., Ahadi, S. A., & Hershey, K. L. (1994). Temperament and social behavior in childhood. *Merrill–Palmer Quarterly, 40,* 21–39.

Rothbart, M. K., & Bates, J. (1998). Temperament. In N. Eisenberg (Ed.) & P. H. Mussen (Series Ed.), *Handbook of child psychology: Vol. 3. Social, emotional, and personality development* (pp. 105–176). New York: Wiley.

Rubin, K. H., & Coplan, R. J. (2004). Paying attention to and not neglecting social withdrawal and social isolation. *Merrill–Palmer Quarterly, 50,* 506–534.

Sadker, M., & Sadker, D. (1994). *Failing at fairness: How America's schools cheat girls.* New York: Scribner.

Scarr, S., & McCartney, K. (1983). How people make their own environments: A theory of genotype–environment effects. *Child Development, 54,* 424–435.

Schmitt, D. P., Realo, A., Voracek, M., & Allik, J. (2008). Why can't a man be more like a woman?: Sex differences in Big Five personality traits across 55 cultures. *Journal of Personality and Social Psychology, 94,* 168–182.

Schneider, B. H., Younger, A. J., Smith, T., & Freeman, P. (1998). A longitudinal exploration of the cross-context stability of social withdrawal in early adolescence. *Journal of Early Adolescence, 18,* 734–396.

Seidlitz, L., & Diener, E. (1998). Sex differences in the recall of affective experiences. *Journal of Personality and Social Psychology, 74,* 262–271.

Seifer, R. (2003). Twin studies, biases of parents, and biases of researchers. *Infant Behavior and Development, 26,* 115–117.

Shields, S. A. (2002). *Speaking from the heart: Gender and the social meaning of emotion.* Cambridge, UK: Cambridge University Press.

Shiner, R., & Caspi, A. (2003). Personality differences in childhood and adolescence: Measurement, development, and consequences. *Journal of Child Psychology and Psychiatry, 44,* 2–32.

Shiner, R., & DeYoung, C. G. (in press). The structure of temperament and personality traits: A developmental perspective. In P. Zelazo (Ed.), *Oxford handbook of developmental psychology.* New York: Oxford University Press.

Simpson, A. E., & Stevenson-Hinde, J. (1985). Temperamental characteristics of three- to four-year-old boys and girls and child–family interactions. *Journal of Child Psychology and Psychiatry, 26,* 43–53.

Skodol, A. E. (2000). Gender-specific etiologies for antisocial and borderline personality disorders? In E. Frank (Ed.), *Gender and its effects on psychopathology* (pp. 37–58). Washington, DC: American Psychiatric Press.

Stern, M., & Karraker, K. H. (1989). Sex stereotyping of infants: A review of gender labeling studies. *Sex Roles, 20,* 501–522.

Stevenson-Hinde, J., & Glover, A. (1996). Shy girls and boys: A new look. *Journal of Child Psychology and Psychiatry, 37,* 181–187.

Sulik, M., Huerta, S., Zerr, A. A., Eisenberg, N., Spinrad, T. L., Valiente, C., et al. (2010). The factor structure of effortful control and measurement invariance across ethnicity and sex in a high-risk sample. *Journal of Psychopathology Behavioral Assessment, 32,* 8–22.

Thomas, A., & Chess, S. (1977). *Temperament and development.* Oxford, UK: Brunner/Mazel.

Thomas, A., & Chess, S. (1980). *The dynamics of psychological development.* New York: Brunner/Mazel.

Thomas, A., Chess, S., Birch, H. G., Hertzig, M. E., & Korn, S. (1963). *Behavioral individuality in early childhood.* New York: New York University Press.

Wickel, E. E., Eisenmann, J. C., & Welk, G. J. (2009). Maturity-related variation in moderate-to-vigorous physical activity among 9–14 year olds. *Journal of Physical Activity and Health, 6,* 597–605.

Zahn-Waxler, C., Shirtcliff, E. A., & Marceau, K. (2008). Disorders of childhood and adolescence: Gender and psychopathology. *Annual Review of Clinical Psychology, 4,* 275–303.

Zakriski, A. L., Wright, J. C., & Underwood, M. K. (2005). Gender similarities and differences in children's social behavior: Finding personality in contextualized patterns of adaptation. *Journal of Personality and Social Psychology, 88,* 844–855.

CHAPTER 24

Temperament and the Development of Personality Traits, Adaptations, and Narratives

Rebecca L. Shiner
Avshalom Caspi

In the first two decades of life, individual differences in the human personality expand in a remarkable fashion. Infants display individual differences in their typical emotions and behaviors, including their predispositions toward negative and positive emotions and their early capacities for self-regulation. As infants move into later childhood, this relatively small set of individual differences broadens rapidly; children's repertoires of behaviors grow increasingly complex as children develop physically, cognitively, socially, and emotionally. By the elementary school years and continuing into adolescence, youth vary markedly from one another in many different ways: their typical emotions; their capacities for empathy, self-control, and imagination; their goals and expectations; their views of relationships and themselves; their ways of coping with stress and adversity; and their emerging identities and stories about who they are. In short, by the adolescent years, children have richly differentiated and complex *personalities*.

In this chapter, we offer a framework for the role of children's temperament traits in their personality development. We consider temperament traits to be early-emerging basic dispositions in the domains of activity, affectivity, and self-regulation (Goldsmith et al., 1987). These temperament dispositions are the products of complex interactions among genetic, biological, and environmental factors across time (Shiner et al., 2012). In contrast, personality encompasses a broader range of more complex individual differences in thinking, feeling, and behaving. Temperament traits emerge in infancy and early childhood, prior to the development of other aspects of personality. Because of their early appearance and significant impact on children's experiences of the world, temperament traits have the potential to shape children's personality development in profound ways. This chapter offers a theoretical model for conceptualizing the role of temperament traits in personality development, and we illustrate this model using current research examples of relevant processes.

Because personality encompasses such a complex set of individual differences, it is important to begin with a taxonomy that organizes those personality differences into a system. In this chapter, we use a taxonomy developed by McAdams and colleagues (McAdams & Olson, 2010; McAdams & Pals, 2006). This model divides personality into three broad domains. First, the *dis-*

positional signature includes the traits that people express in their behaviors, thoughts, and emotions with some consistency across situations and over time. These include the Big Five traits, along with other stable and consistent tendencies. Second, *characteristic adaptations* include "a wide range of motivational, social-cognitive, and developmental adaptations" that are specific to a particular time, place, or role (McAdams & Pals, 2006, p. 208). These characteristic adaptations differ from traits in that their instantiation is more specific to particular life contexts. For example, youth vary in their goals and their sense of self-efficacy in particular domains of their lives (e.g., academics, friendships). Third, by adolescence people begin to form *personal narratives*, stories about their lives that help them to make sense out of their identities over time. These narratives are unique to each person but can be studied empirically in terms of their common features across individuals. Children's temperament traits are relevant to the development of all three levels of personality.

This chapter addresses the role of temperament in personality development in six sections. First, we present a conceptual model for understanding the interplay between temperament traits and the broader range of personality differences that people exhibit from childhood through adulthood. Second, we describe the processes through which temperament influences personality over time. Third, we assess research on the relationship between temperament and personality traits, and review what is known about the stability of such traits. In the fourth and fifth sections, we describe current work on childhood and adolescent characteristic adaptations and personal narratives, respectively, and offer some illustrations of how temperament may or may not shape these domains of personality. We conclude with suggestions for research into this relatively new but potentially rich area of investigation.

The Role of Temperament in Personality Development

In Figure 24.1, we outline the potential role of temperament in the development of personality and of life outcomes. Temperament traits are placed at the start of this model to indicate that temperamental differences emerge before other individual differences in personality, during the first year of life (Rothbart & Bates, 2006). Three overarching temperament trait dimensions capture many of children's important individual differences from infancy (Gartstein & Rothbart, 2003) through childhood (Rothbart, Ahadi, Hershey, & Fisher, 2001). *Surgency* (sometimes called Positive Emotionality) taps children's tendencies toward sociability, positive emotions, and their eagerness in approaching potentially pleasurable activities. *Negative Emotionality* measures children's general tendencies toward a wide range of negative emotions. Even in infancy, however, this trait can be separated into two related but distinct components: more internalizing negative emotions (fear, withdrawal, sadness) and more externalizing negative emotions (anger, irritability, frustration) (Caspi & Shiner, 2006; Rothbart & Bates, 2006). *Effortful Control* reflects children's emerging behavioral constraint and regulation, including the ability to sustain attention and persist at tasks. Individual differences in these traits appear prior to the development of other early-emerging aspects of personality, such as the formation of attachment representations, which are under construction during infancy (Johnson, Dweck, & Chen, 2007).

It is important to emphasize that although temperament is placed at the beginning of this conceptual model, we do not mean to imply that temperament itself does not develop. Sometimes temperament is conceptualized in a nondevelopmental fashion, as if it were merely a *cause* of various outcomes but not a product of development itself (Sroufe, 2009). Recent empirical work has made clear that this is a very limited view of temperament traits. At birth, infants' temperament traits have already been influenced by prenatal experiences (Huizink, Chapter 15, this volume), and parenting predicts change and continuity in temperament traits (Bates, Schermerhorn, & Petersen, Chapter 20, and van IJzendoorn & Bakermans-Kranenburg, Chapter 19, this volume). Some new work has found preliminary evidence for possible gene × environment interactions influencing children's temperament traits as well, such as Negative Emotionality (Hayden et

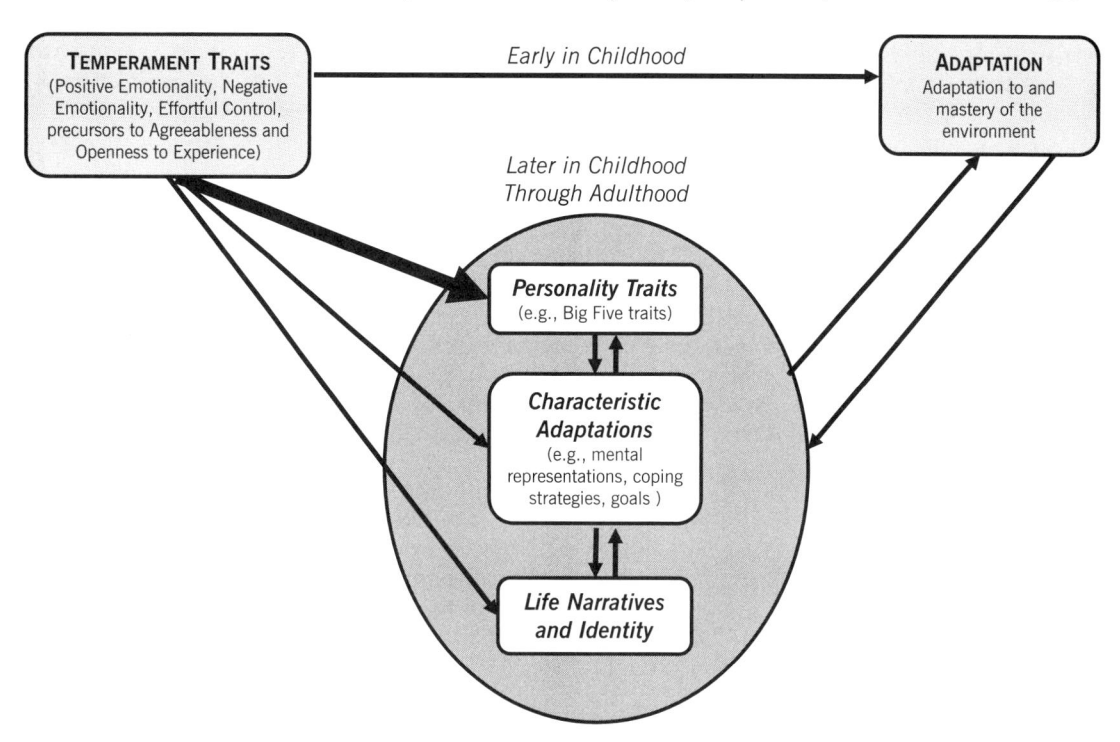

FIGURE 24.1. A conceptual model for the role of temperament traits in the development of personality and adaptation.

al., 2011), self-regulation (Kochanska, Philibert, & Barry, 2009), and sensation seeking (Sheese, Voelker, Rothbart, & Posner, 2007). Even though temperamental differences emerge early, they continue to be modified over time.

Temperament traits shape children's typical emotions, motivations, behaviors, and the ways that they engage the environment; we describe these processes more fully in the next section. Because of the broad and deep impact of temperament on children's experience of the world, temperament is likely to affect the development of all levels of personality. We have depicted the influence of temperament traits on personality traits, characteristic adaptations, and life narratives and identity in Figure 24.1 through the arrows linking temperament with these later-developing aspects of personality. The three aspects of personality are encircled together to convey that they are part of an interacting personality system. The arrow linking temperament with personality traits is larger to indicate that there is a more direct link between temperament and personality traits than between temperament and the other aspects of personality functioning. As we argue later, temperament and personality traits are likely to reflect individual differences in the same basic biological systems, modified through experience. In contrast, the impact of temperament traits on the development of other aspects of personality is likely to be smaller and more indirect. As McAdams and Pals (2006) have suggested, both characteristic adaptations and narrative identity are influenced by traits, but they are likely to be shaped by many other processes as well, including life experiences that are largely or entirely separate from individuals' traits.

Just as temperament traits influence personality development, they shape important outcomes for children. As Allport (1937, p. 342) noted, traits are "*modi vivendi*, ultimately deriving their significance from the role they play in advancing adaptation within, and mastery of, the personal environment." In Figure 24.1, temperament is depicted as a direct source of influence on children's early adaptation, for example, their relationships with parents and caregivers (Bates et al., Chapter 20, and van IJzendoorn & Bakermans-Kranenburg, Chapter 19, this volume), peer relationships (Coplan & Bullock, Chapter 21, this volume), school functioning (Duckworth & Allred, Chapter 30, this volume), health (Hampson & Vollrath, Chapter 28, this volume), and psychopathology (Klein, Dyson, Kujawa, & Kotov, Chapter 26, and Tackett, Martel, & Kushner, Chapter 27, this volume). Figure 24.1 also illustrates that, later in childhood, children's personality traits and characteristic adaptations have affected many of their outcomes, and in adolescence their emerging life narratives may begin to exert an influence. In addition, these newer aspects of personality interact with traits in shaping individuals' adaptive functioning. For example, children who are behaviorally inhibited (a temperament trait) and have an insecure attachment to their mothers (a characteristic adaptation) experience increases in cortisol in the face of novelty, whereas inhibited children with secure maternal attachments do not (Nachmias, Gunnar, Mangelsdorf, Parritz, & Buss, 1996). Thus, children's traits, both alone and in interaction with other aspects of personality, play an important role in shaping adaptation.

Although temperament traits initially affect the development of other aspects of children's personalities and life outcomes, the relationship between temperament and other aspects of personality likely becomes bidirectional over time. In other words, other personality characteristics may influence the expression of individuals' traits. Figure 24.1 represents the multiple aspects of personality in interaction by placing bidirectional arrows between each level of personality. For example, as young people begin to develop goals for themselves, they may learn to override trait-based tendencies in order to pursue their goals more effectively (Little, 2008). An adolescent scoring high on Negative Emotionality may learn to manage these emotions better because of striving toward a goal of being an effective student or school leader. Other, less deliberate processes may also take place, as children's and adolescents' self-concepts, expectations, and coping styles begin to alter the expression of their traits. In a similar fashion, the relationship between traits and adaptation likely becomes bidirectional over time, as depicted in Figure 24.1 by the bidirectional arrows between the personality system and adaptation; individuals' relative success or difficulty in mastering the environment may shape their traits. For example, there is some evidence that children's mastery of important tasks in childhood—the cultivation of positive peer relationships, academic attainment, and rule-abiding conduct—predicts decreases in Negative Emotionality from childhood through late adolescence (Shiner, Masten, & Tellegen, 2002). As noted, traits themselves are malleable, and other aspects of personality and adaptation are likely to be one important source of change over time.

The Processes through Which Temperament Shapes Personality Development

In this section, we describe a number of processes through which an initial temperamental disposition is elaborated so that it increasingly organizes emotion, thought, and action over time. We propose that, through these basic processes, temperament traits come to be elaborated into personality traits, as well as to have more indirect effects on other aspects of personality—both characteristic adaptations and narrative identities—and on adaptation. We describe four processes in the order of their hypothesized emergence and offer current empirical examples for each one; the four processes and hypothetical examples of each are presented in Table 24.1. Learning processes and environmental elicitation are hypothesized to influence the course of personality development already in the first few months of life; environmental construal can influence personality development only following the emergence of necessary cognitive functions in early and middle childhood; and environmental selection and manipulation generally require the emergence of self-regulatory functions in childhood and are likely to become particularly important as youth move into adolescence.

The first process refers to learning. Specifically, temperament differences influence several learning mechanisms, including children's proclivities toward positive and negative reinforcement, punishment, discrimination learning, and extinction in

TABLE 24.1. Processes through Which Early Temperament Shapes the Development of Later Personality and Adaptation

Process	Definition	Example
Learning processes	Temperament shapes the child's experience of classical and operant conditioning.	Toddlers with high activity level may find more physically arousing situations to be positively reinforcing.
Environmental elicitation	Temperament shapes the response of adults and peers to the child.	Children with high Positive Emotionality may evoke greater positive engagement from caregivers.
Environmental construal	Temperament shapes the ways that children interpret the environment and their experiences.	Children with high Effortful Control may interpret stressful situations as benign occasions for solving problems.
Environmental selection	Temperament shapes children's choices about their day-to-day environments.	Children with high Negative Emotionality may attempt to avoid threatening situations.

the face of different experiences. Rothbart (2011) suggests that temperament provides a "meaning structure" for experience even before language develops; whether a child experiences an event as positive or negative will be shaped by his or her emotional dispositions. For example, an infant's perception of intense sensory stimulation as positive or negative will depend in part on the child's temperament. An example of learning processes in somewhat older children comes from Kochanska and Aksan's (2006) theoretical and empirical model of conscience development. In this model, children's temperamental fearfulness shapes their susceptibility to learning processes. Because more fearful children are susceptible to feeling negative emotions following a transgression (i.e., their emotions "punish" them following transgressions), they avoid such situations and more easily develop an internalized conscience. A complementary example comes from research on *behavioral inhibition*, a temperament type characterized by sensitivity to novelty and withdrawal in the face of such novelty (Kagan & Fox, 2006). In a longitudinal study of children who displayed high or low behavioral inhibition across the early childhood and elementary school years, the behaviorally inhibited children later showed heightened attentional bias to threat (Pérez-Edgar et al., 2010); this type of child thus seems to show a particular learning bias for negative stimuli. As we describe later, Negative Emotionality more generally may involve individual differences in an avoidance system that is sensitive to potential threats. The implication from these examples is that different individuals should learn different things from common experiences.

The second process is *environmental elicitation*. Temperament differences elicit different reactions from the environment and influence how other people react to children, beginning in the first few months of life (Bates et al., Chapter 20, this volume). For example, Effortful Control in toddlers and preschoolers predicts maternal teaching strategies, such that higher Effortful Control positively predicts more use of cognitive assistance and less use of directive strategies among mothers over time (Eisenberg et al., 2010). It appears that children's capacities for self-regulation affect their mothers' strategies, such that greater Effortful Control evokes more positive maternal strategies. The evocative effects of children's temperaments extend beyond the family environment to other caregivers, teachers, and peers; in turn, the responses that children evoke from others are likely to be internalized as part of children's emerging self-concepts. Temperament characteristics elicit not only behaviors on the part of others but also expectations. Adults have implicit theories about developmental trajectories that they associate with particular temperament attributes. As such, children's temperament-based behaviors may elicit expectancy-based reactions from adult caregivers (Graziano, Jensen-Campbell, & Sullivan-Logan, 1998).

The third process is *environmental construal*. With the emergence of belief systems and expectations, temperament differences also begin to influence how environmental experiences are construed, thus shaping each person's "effective experience" of the environment. In other words, the child's more automatic ways of making meaning become elaborated into more complex cognitions as language skills develop (Rothbart, 2011). Research about the construal process stems from the cognitive tradition in personality psychology that emphasizes each person's subjective experience and unique perception of the world. This research focuses on what people "do" mentally (Mischel & Shoda, 2010), demonstrating that social information processing—including attention, encoding, retrieval, and interpretation—is a selective process shaped by individual differences in temperament and personality (Derryberry & Tucker, 2006). For example, individual differences in children's Positive and Negative Emotionality shape the cues they notice in the environment, the goals that are salient to them, and the types of potential responses they generate (Lemerise & Arsenio, 2000). Children who score high on Positive Emotionality, for example, may construe loud, busy social situations as exciting opportunities for making new friends, whereas children with a lower score on this trait may instead interpret such situations as being chaotic and overwhelming.

The fourth process is *environmental selection and manipulation*. As children's self-regulatory competencies increase with age, they begin to make choices and display preferences that may reinforce and sustain their characteristics. Processes of environmental selection become increasingly important across the years from childhood to adulthood. Even among very young children, temperament is likely to shape the spheres they occupy within the environments chosen for them by adults (e.g., fearful, inhibited toddlers may avoid interactions with other children in child care). As children move into middle childhood and adolescence, they are given greater freedom to choose the environments in which they spend their time. Children's peer relationships are an important arena in which temperament shapes their selection of experiences. For example, more socially anxious youth tend to select fewer friends, and the ones they do select tend to be more socially anxious themselves; over time, such friendships promote greater social anxiety (Van Zalk, Van Zalk, Kerr, & Stattin, 2011). Once the self-concept is firmly established, and with the development of more sophisticated self-regulatory capacities, individuals begin to alter, modify, and manipulate the environments in which they find themselves, in ways that are consistent with their own personalities (Buss, 1987). These processes may become particularly important as children become more skilled in regulating their own behavior and more insightful into the causes of others' behaviors.

Why would temperament traits have such a broad impact on individuals' interactions with the environment? A number of researchers have argued that both temperament and personality traits may be more elaborated forms of basic behavioral systems that have been selected through evolution and are shaped by individuals' life experiences (MacDonald, Chapter 14, this volume; Nettle, 2006). A number of biological systems are relevant for personality functioning and crucial for human survival. Although these biological systems are part of the human makeup, people vary in the strength of such systems, and their life experiences create further variations in the expression of the underlying systems; the resulting variations may be expressed through individual differences in temperament or personality traits. The following are examples of such biological systems and the traits through which they may be expressed: systems supporting the detection of rewards (Surgency/Extraversion), the detection of threats (Negative Emotionality/Neuroticism), achievement of social dominance (Surgency/Extraversion), striving after long-term goals (Effortful Control/Conscientiousness), nurturance of the young (Agreeableness), aggression toward others (low Agreeableness), and exploration of new environments (Openness to Experience).

If, indeed, temperament and personality traits represent variations in these basic biological systems, traits should shape individuals' motivations and interactions with the environment in pervasive ways. For example, Gray (1982) has argued that Positive Emotionality or Extraversion may reflect a behavioral approach or activation system (Pickering & Gray, 1999) that activates approach and exploratory behavior when there are signals of potential reward. This perspective would help to explain why this trait is associated with strong reinforcement from rewards, vigorous engagement in social situations, positive construal of situations, and selection into more exciting contexts (Shiner & DeYoung, in press). As expressions of biological systems that direct and motivate behavior, traits should be expected to shape learning processes, typical ways of engaging the environment, and the interpretation of experiences.

From Temperament to Personality Traits

Points of Convergence between Temperament and Personality Traits

In this section, we describe the relationship between temperament traits and later developing personality traits. In the McAdams and Pals (2006) model, the earliest emerging aspects of the broader personality system consist of people's general tendencies to behave, think, and feel in relatively consistent ways across situations and across time—in other words, traits. Historically, child temperament and adult personality have been studied as distinct sets of individual differences, with child temperament comprising more narrowly defined consistencies that appear earlier in life, and personality comprising a broader range of consistencies that emerge later in life. However, if we restrict our consideration of personality to traits rather than characteristic adaptations or narratives, then temperament and personality traits have much in common (for similar arguments that personality traits in adulthood are, in essence, temperamental traits, see Caspi & Shiner, 2006; Clark & Watson, 2008; McCrae et al., 2000; Rothbart, 2011; Zentner & Bates, 2008). In this section, we focus on the Big Five personality traits (John, Naumann, & Soto, 2008) because they capture many of the most important variations in personality traits and they have received the most research attention over the past several decades. The links between temperament and other personality traits (e.g., optimism) are likely to be less direct and thus smaller in magnitude.

Evidence from behavior genetics, comparative psychology, and structural research all point to the possibility that child temperament traits become elaborated into the Big Five personality traits over time. First, both sets of individual differences are shaped by heredity and by the environment (Krueger & Johnson, 2008; Saudino & Wang, Chapter 16, this volume). Sometimes laypeople and psychologists assume that traits start out as largely heritable in origin and gradually come to be more influenced by the environment as children have more life experiences. This model has turned out to be incorrect, in that both types of traits are moderately heritable and shaped by environmental experiences. Temperament traits in childhood and the Big Five personality traits in adulthood also follow an interesting pattern: Stability in individuals' temperament and personality traits seems to derive from genetic influences, whereas changes in these traits are influenced by both genetic and environmental factors (Krueger & Johnson, 2008; Saudino & Wang, Chapter 16, this volume).

Second, animals display individual differences in behavior that mirror most of the major temperament dimensions in childhood and Big Five personality trait dimensions in adults (Weinstein, Capitanio, & Gosling, 2008). Only Effortful Control, or Conscientiousness, is not widely evident in other species, although it can be assessed in chimpanzees. If traits do represent variations in basic biological systems, as suggested earlier, it makes sense that similar individual differences can be identified in rudimentary form in other animal species.

Third, temperament traits and personality traits show both stability and change over time (Roberts & DelVecchio, 2000). Sometimes personality traits are wrongly viewed as being highly stable and very nearly unchangeable (Sameroff, 2008), whereas temperament is seen as being more malleable. Roberts and DelVecchio's (2000) meta-analysis of studies examining the stability of temperament and personality traits did find that traits become increasingly stable over the life course. The following estimated cross-time population correlations for dispositional measures were obtained for childhood and adolescence: 0–2.9 years = 0.35; 3–5.9 years = 0.52; 6–11.9 years = 0.45; and 12.0–17.9 years = 0.47. These results suggest that individual differences show more modest continuity during infancy and toddlerhood, then a rather large increase in stability during the preschool years. This level of stability is maintained through the young adult years. Traits do not become more highly stable until the 50s. Thus, although later in life stability is higher for personality traits than for temperament, the stability of temperament traits earlier in life is not strikingly different from the stability of personality traits in the early adult years (see Zentner & Shiner, Chapter 32, this volume).

Fourth, a final point of convergence between temperament traits and the Big Five personality traits is their very similar structure and content, as we review shortly. Historically, research on the structure of child temperament and adult personality traits proceeded in two distinct traditions; despite this, the two lines of research have converged on two similar sets of traits. This suggests the possibility of a close link between temperament and personality traits: Temperament traits that are part of each individual's genetic heritage accumulate response strength through their repeated reinforcement, and become elaborated into cognitive and affective representations that are quickly and frequently activated—that is, into personality traits.

Temperament and the Big Five Traits in Childhood: Commonalities in Structure and Content and Continuity over Time

Over the last decade and a half, substantial progress has been made in identifying the structure of children's personality traits. There is now convincing evidence that, at least by the school years (and, most likely, earlier), children's personality traits are structured much like adults' traits. Work on the structure of adult personality has converged on a five-trait model known variously as the Big Five model or the Five-Factor Model (John et al., 2008). These traits include *Extraversion*, *Neuroticism*, *Conscientiousness*, *Agreeableness*, and *Openness to Experience/Intellect*. Like adults, children and adolescents differ along this same basic set of traits. A five-factor structure of children's traits has been found in studies with different reporters (parents, teachers, and older children and adolescents) and in both questionnaire and Q-sort measures (Shiner & DeYoung, in press). Although some studies obtaining a five-factor structure in childhood have employed measures prestructured to reflect the Big Five traits, other studies have found the same structure in measures designed simply to tap a broad range of personality traits in childhood (e.g., Digman & Takemoto-Chock, 1981; John, Caspi, Robins, Moffitt, & Stouthamer-Loeber, 1994). Remarkably, when children as young as 5 years old rate their personalities in the context of a interview with puppets, they can provide coherent, differentiated reports on the Big Five traits (Measelle, John, Ablow, Cowan, & Cowan, 2005). A recent study of children and adolescents ages 10 to 20 demonstrated that youth's personality self-reports increasingly conform to a Big Five factor structure with age (Soto, John, Gosling, & Potter, 2008).

Taken together, these studies provide a promising starting point for a taxonomy of children's personality traits. In the following sections, we describe each of the Big Five traits in childhood and adolescence, and review what is known about differences and similarities between these traits and the likely temperament traits that precede them.

Positive Emotionality/Extraversion

Extraversion measures children's tendencies to be vigorously, actively, and surgently engaged with the world around them. Extraverted children and adolescents are described as sociable, expressive, high-spirited, lively, socially potent, physically active, and energetic, whereas more introverted children are described as shy, reserved, and lethargic. Infants and young children vary in their expression of positive emotions, such as pleasure, joy in social interactions, and laughter, and, as noted previously, this trait is often called *Surgency* (Rothbart & Bates, 2006) or Positive Emotionality (Putnam, Chapter 6, this volume). From preschool age onward, children display variations in a broader Extraversion trait (De Pauw, Mervielde, & Van Leeuwen, 2009). By preschool age, this trait includes at least three major components (Olino, Klein, Durbin, Hayden, & Buckley, 2005): children's *positive emotions*, such as joy and enthusiasm; their *sociability*, meaning their motivation to engage and interact with others; and their eagerness to *approach* rewarding situations. One difference between temperament measures of Surgency and child personality measures of Extraversion is that Extraversion includes children's tendencies to be assertive leaders among their peers (Shiner & DeYoung, in press). As noted earlier, the overarching trait appears to reflect individual differences in a biologically based approach system that activates behavior to seek rewards (DeYoung & Gray, 2009). Robust evidence exists for the continuity of markers of Extraversion from early to later in childhood. Early positive emotions (especially high-intensity positive emotions), sociability, and positive activity level in early childhood all predict later childhood Extraversion (Caspi & Shiner, 2006), and Positive Emotionality itself is moderately stable from toddlerhood through the preschool years, then through middle childhood (Neppl, Donnellan, Scaramella, Widaman, & Spilman, 2010).

Negative Emotionality/Neuroticism

Just as children vary in their predisposition toward positive emotions, they vary in their susceptibility to negative emotions and general distress, a trait termed *Neuroticism*. Neuroticism shows clear conceptual overlap with the temperamental trait of Negative Emotionality, and the traits are related empirically (De Pauw et al., 2009; Digman & Shmelyov, 1996). Children and adolescents who score high on Neuroticism are described as anxious, vulnerable, tense, easily frightened, "falling apart" under stress, guilt-prone, moody, low in frustration tolerance, and insecure in relationships with others. In contrast, children who score low on this trait are self-assured, emotionally stable, and calm. Thus, the childhood trait of Neuroticism overlaps considerably with Negative Emotionality in its focus on a wide range of negative emotions. Neuroticism, however, includes components that only become expressed as children develop greater awareness of themselves and the capacity to think about the future (e.g., insecurity, jealousy, fear of failing, concern about acceptance). As noted previously, the overarching trait appears to reflect individual differences in a biologically based withdrawal system that motivates behavior to avoid threats (DeYoung & Gray, 2009). Neuroticism and its related components (fear, irritability/anger) in childhood are predicted by earlier childhood markers of negative emotions (Caspi & Shiner, 2006; Durbin, Hayden, Klein, & Olino, 2007; Shiner & DeYoung, in press), and Negative Emotionality is already moderately to strongly stable from the toddler years to the preschool years, and from the preschool years, through middle childhood (Neppl et al., 2010).

A temperamental tendency termed *inhibition to the unfamiliar* or *behavioral inhibition* has been identified by Kagan and colleagues (Kagan, Chapter 4, this volume; Kagan & Fox, 2006). As noted earlier, behavioral inhibition involves the tendency to withdraw and express fear in the face of stressful novel situations (Fox, Henderson, Marshall, Nichols, & Ghera, 2005). Inhibition shows itself in infancy through motor reactivity and distress, and later in childhood through reticent, withdrawn behavior in response to novelty (Kagan, 2008); the tendency is typically measured as a personality type rather than as a continuous trait. Despite in-depth research on this trait, it remains unclear how this tendency relates to other measures of fear and Negative Emotionality (Hane, Fox, Henderson, & Marshall, 2008). More detailed work is needed to clarify the relationship among the constructs of behavioral inhibition, fear, and Negative Emotionality, especially given that this trait seems to have important long-term implications for development (Kagan, Chapter 4, this volume).

Effortful Control/Conscientiousness

Conscientiousness reflects children's individual differences in self-control in large part as control is used in service of constraining impulses and striving to meet standards. Highly Conscientious children and adolescents are described as being responsible, attentive, persistent, orderly and neat, planful; possessing high standards; and thinking before acting. Low Conscientiousness manifests itself in more careless, impulsive, and distractible behavior. Individual differences in self-regulation emerge in infancy and early childhood in the form of temperamental Effortful Control (Rothbart & Bates, 2006; Rueda, Chapter 8, this volume). Empirically, Conscientiousness is associated with measures of Effortful Control (Halverson et al., 2003). In a multimeasure study of preschool-age children, Conscientiousness formed a factor along with temperament measures of attention focusing, persistence, and the capacity to inhibit behavior (De Pauw et al., 2009). Both traits capture children's capacities for self-control, including their abilities to persist at tasks and to be planful, cautious, deliberate and controlled in their actions. Temperament models tend to emphasize attention and impulse control, whereas childhood Conscientiousness measures include traits that children do not exhibit until the preschool period, such as orderliness, dependability, and motivation to strive for high standards. Although little is known about the antecedents of Conscientiousness as measured in the Big Five research, the antecedents of Effortful Control include the early ability to focus attention and persist at tasks (Shiner & DeYoung, in press). The trait itself is highly stable by the preschool years (Kochanska & Knaack, 2003), and from the preschool years through middle childhood (Neppl et al., 2010).

Agreeableness

Two personality traits in Big Five research are not explicitly included in most temperament models: Agreeableness and Openness to Experience (sometimes called Intellect). *Agreeableness* involves differences in self-regulation in the service of maintaining positive relationships with others (Graziano, Habashi, Sheese, & Tobin, 2007). Highly Agreeable children are characterized as warm, considerate, empathic, generous, gentle, protective of others, and kind, whereas highly disagreeable children are characterized as aggressive, rude, spiteful, stubborn, bossy, cynical, and manipulative. Agreeableness also includes children's willingness to accommodate others' needs and wishes. In a recent study examining parents' ratings of the temperament and personality traits of their preschool children, an Agreeableness factor clearly emerged, suggesting that this trait can be measured coherently by at least preschool age (De Pauw et al., 2009); the trait included typical markers of Agreeableness (high altruism and compliance and low egocentrism and willfulness), as well as temperamental measures of inflexibility and angry, irritable reactions to challenging situations. As noted earlier, children's Negative Emotionality includes a component reflecting outer-directed, hostile emotions such as anger, frustration, and irritability (Deater-Deckard & Wang, Chapter 7, this volume; Rothbart & Bates, 2006; Shiner & DeYoung, in press). Agreeableness and its components in childhood are predicted negatively by early differences in high-intensity irritability and frustration, and positively by early attention and self-control (Caspi & Shiner, 2006), suggesting that this trait may emerge in part from the irritability/anger aspect of Negative Emotionality. Rothbart and Posner (2006) have argued for a biologically based Affiliativeness system that may underlie children's differences in prosocial and aggressive behaviors. Similarly, Knafo and Israel (Chapter 9, this volume) have demonstrated that children show stable, genetically influenced differences in empathy and prosocial behavior by the toddler and preschool years. Thus, serious consideration should be given to Agreeableness as a temperament trait that manifests itself in children's early differences in empathy and prosocial behavior, as well as in low levels of hostility and irritability.

Openness to Experience/Intellect

Although the final Big Five trait—*Openness to Experience* or *Intellect*—was not as well-supported empirically in some earlier studies (Caspi & Shiner, 2006), there is now better evidence that this trait is an important aspect of children's individuality when it is measured carefully, even as early as preschool age (De Pauw et al., 2009; Shiner & DeYoung, in press). Children who score high on this trait are described as eager and quick to learn, clever, knowledgeable, perceptive, imaginative, curious, and original, whereas children who score low on this trait exhibit lower levels of fantasy, creativity, and interests. Some additional markers of Openness/Intellect in children are enthusiastic involvement in extracurricular activities, eagerness to take on creative and intellectual work, imaginativeness in play, confidence, and adaptability in the face of uncertainty (Abe, 2005; Goldberg, 2001; Shiner & Masten, 2012). The developmental precursors of Openness/Intellect are not well understood, but there are three interesting potential antecedents: high-intensity positive emotions, curiosity and eager exploration of new situations, and sensitivity to internal and external sensory stimulation (Shiner & DeYoung, in press). Although the early manifestations of Openness/Intellect are poorly understood, this trait warrants greater attention in childhood research. Openness/Intellect is important for the development of individuals' values and political beliefs, their academic and creative achievement (Caspi & Shiner, 2006), and resilient functioning in the face of adversity (Shiner & Masten, 2012), and it is therefore worth measuring in childhood.

Temperament and Characteristic Adaptations

Characteristic Adaptations Defined and Linked with Temperament

A second aspect of children's emerging individuality is what McAdams and Pals (2006) call *characteristic adaptations*: "a wide range of motivational, social-cognitive, and developmental adaptations, contextualized in time, place, and/or social role" (p. 208). Compared to traits, these aspects of personality are more specific to particular life contexts, such as a particular developmental phase, social role, or domain of functioning. For example, a school-age girl may be pursuing one set of goals in terms of her academic work (e.g., to be a strong student) and another in terms of her relationships with peers (e.g., to find close friendships and to be well liked by peers). Even within the domain of intimate relationships, she may have different goals depending on her role as friend, child, or student. As an adolescent, her goals will likely shift to new ones, such as the pursuit of college, a sense of identity, or romantic relationships. A variety of characteristic adaptations have received research attention in childhood and adolescence; youth vary significantly in their styles of cognition, motivation, and emotion across many areas of their lives (Pomerantz & Thompson, 2008).

Unlike traits, this broad domain of personality lacks a clear-cut taxonomy. However, it is still possible to delineate important general categories of characteristic adaptations, including perception, thinking, motivation, strategies, and emotions (Funder, 2007). People differ in their *perceptions* of the world, meaning the ways that they take in information from the environment. People also vary in their ways of *thinking* about various aspects of their lives (e.g., their values, mental representations, interpretive biases, and views of the self). People differ in their typical *motivation*—what they desire and strive for and what they avoid—in different domains of life. People also employ different *strategies* for handling daily events and more long-term challenges. And, finally, people experience and express *emotions* in varied ways across many areas of their lives. These psychological processes have been explored in a number of different traditions in the study of personality, including Freudian and neo-Freudian perspectives, humanistic and existential traditions, and social-cognitive frameworks (Funder, 2007; McAdams & Pals, 2006).

Because these aspects of personality are so varied and complex, different characteristic adaptations are likely to emerge as aspects of personality at different points in development. Some of the characteristic adaptations derive from children's emotional experiences and characteristic means of handling those emotions, or from their experiences in early relationships (e.g., attachment); these may arise early. In contrast, other characteristic adaptations depend on the development of more complex cognitive skills. By middle childhood, children can better engage in planning because they can think more flexibly and imagine future scenarios (Lightfoot, Cole, & Cole, 2009). They can also think increasingly about how to think (i.e., engage in meta-cognition), which enables them to solve problems in more complex ways (Flavell, 2007). Consequently, children's goals, strategies, and cognitions are likely to become more complex and important in this phase of life. By adolescence, youth begin to think even more abstractly (Lightfoot et al., 2009), and can therefore develop more long-term, future-oriented goals. Thus, characteristic adaptations become more complex over development, just as traits do.

As noted earlier in our theoretical model of the role of traits in personality development, temperament traits influence the characteristic adaptations that children develop, albeit in a less direct fashion than they influence personality traits. All four of the processes through which temperament shapes experiences—effects on learning processes, interpretation of the environment, evocation of responses, and environmental selection—are likely to be involved as temperament shapes emerging perceptions, cognitions, motivations, and strategies. Temperament's effects on interpretation of the environment may be especially important, in that so many characteristic adaptations involve perceptual and cognitive processes. It is important to emphasize, however, that in most cases the impact of temperament on characteristic adaptations is likely to be modest. Even in research on adults, the associations between the Big Five traits and daily strivings (Romero, Villar, Luengo, & Gomez-Fraguela, 2009) and major life goals (Roberts & Robins, 2000) are relatively modest. Because characteristic adaptations are more context-specific, they may be shaped by contextual factors that are unrelated to traits.

Empirical Examples of Links between Temperament and Characteristic Adaptations: Coping Styles and Cognitive Biases

In this section, to illustrate current work on the influence of temperament traits on characteristic adaptations, we review research on temperament and two important characteristic adaptations: coping strategies and cognitive biases.

Coping Strategies

Children develop different *coping strategies* for handling stresses, and they use a variety of strategies, depending on the particular situations they are facing (Seiffge-Krenke, Aunola, & Nurmi, 2009; see also Lengua & Wachs, Chapter 25, this volume). Like adults, children and adolescents use both *engagement* strategies (approach-oriented, active strategies for handling stressors, such as problem solving, support seeking, and distraction) and *disengagement* strategies (avoidance-oriented attempts at distancing themselves from the stressors such as withdrawal, denial, substance abuse) (Compas, Connor-Smith, Saltzman, Thomsen, & Wadsworth, 2001; Connor-Smith, Compas, Wadsworth, Thomsen, & Saltzman, 2000;). Children and adolescents' repertoires of coping strategies develop over time. Among preschool- and school-age children, the predominant forms of coping are support seeking, problem solving, escape, and distraction (Skinner & Zimmer-Gembeck, 2007). As children move into adolescence, their coping strategies become more complex and cognitively advanced. Although some of these new strategies enable better coping (e.g., cognitive restructuring), other strategies are self-defeating (e.g., rumination, aggression, blaming others). In general, however, although the negative strategy of withdrawal increases during early adolescence, youth increasingly use the more mature strategies of engagement and internal cognitive coping across the adolescent years (Seiffge-Krenke et al., 2009).

Not surprisingly, children's temperament traits are associated with their capacities for coping with daily stress. As articulated by Derryberry, Reed, and Pilkenton-Taylor (2003), temperament itself may be viewed as an early version of coping: The positive reactivity associated with Positive Emotionality and negative reactivity associated with Negative Emotionality are both adaptive means of responding to and coping with rewarding and potentially threatening situations, respectively, and Effortful Control offers a more direct means of self-regulation in response to stress. A meta-analysis (Connor-Smith & Flachsbart, 2007) explored the relations between temperament and personality traits, and particular coping styles in youth and adults; temperament and personality traits were categorized together into the Big Five traits. In general, the associations between traits and coping were modest in magnitude. Extraversion was associated with numerous markers of engagement coping, Neuroticism with numerous markers of disengagement coping and high expression of negative emotions, and Conscientiousness with problem solving and cognitive restructuring. These three traits had the most robust links with coping. Interestingly, the authors found that traits were more strongly related to coping strategies in younger samples than in older ones, perhaps because children have less well-developed strategies that they can use to overcome their temperamental responses to stress. Traits related to self-regulation seem to be especially important for children's developing coping skills (Buckner, Mezzacappa, & Beardslee, 2009). There is some evidence, for example, that Effortful Control may lead to diminished behavior problems, mediated in part by Effortful Control's positive impact on engagement coping and dampening of involuntary responses to stress (Valiente, Lemery-Chalfant, & Swanson, 2009). Despite the evidence for these modest effects of traits on coping, it is important to recognize that both traits and coping contribute independently to life outcomes, and both play important, separate roles in managing stress (Carver & Connor-Smith, 2010).

Cognitive Biases

Cognitive biases are one example of a more general category of *mental representations*—the many ways that children and adolescents perceive and think about their experiences of themselves, other people, life events, and their more general environment. Mental representations may be consistently accompanied by particular sets of emotions that are evoked when the mental representation operates (Izard, Stark, Trentacosta, & Schultz, 2008). These mental representations are a primary means through which children's earlier experiences are brought forward into the present (Dweck & London, 2004). Children and adolescents display a very wide range of mental representations, particularly as they get older and develop more complex cognitive skills. For example, children vary in their attachment representations (Fraley & Shaver, 2008; Johnson et al., 2007); feelings of alienation from others and assumptions about whether peers have hostile intentions (Leff et al., 2006); and beliefs about what they can offer to others (Rudolph, Hammen, & Burge, 1995) and the malleability of their own behavior (Molden & Dweck, 2006). In fact, mental representations are one of the most thoroughly studied aspects of children's developing personalities.

Children vary in their typical styles of interpreting negative experiences. Some children tend to perceive threats and long-standing problems in such situations, and others tend to have more benign interpretations (Lonigan, Vasey, Phillips, & Hazen, 2004). Children's cognitive biases for interpreting negative experiences are an especially important type of mental representation because of their relevance for the development of psychopathology. Such biases are robustly associated with the development of depression and anxiety in adults (Mathews & MacLeod, 2005), and are therefore of great interest to researchers trying to understand the origins of internalizing disorders in young people.

A recent empirical example of such construal processes involves the development of *depressogenic cognitive biases*—tendencies to interpret situations in a hopeless or pessimistic manner. In a study examining children's Positive Emotionality and Negative Emotionality at age 3 and their cognitive styles at age 7 (Hayden, Klein, Durbin, & Olino, 2006), early Positive Emotionality (but not Negative Emotionality) predicted a later tendency to interpret an ambiguous social situation in a hopeless manner and to see the causes of positive life events in a less positive way. Although that study did not find an association between early Negative Emotionality and depressogenic cognitive biases, other studies have documented such links. Children's early tendencies toward Negative Emotionality interact with their negative life experiences to predict a negative attributional style for explaining life events in middle childhood (Mezulis, Hyde, & Abramson, 2006). Higher Negative Emotionality in adolescence likewise predicts higher tendencies toward a ruminative response to negative life events, but only among adolescents with lower levels of Effortful Control (Verstraeten, Vasey, Raes, & Bijttebier, 2009). Negative Emotionality may also undermine positive coping strategies by causing children to perceive more situations as threatening (Lengua, Sandler, West, Wolchik, & Curran, 1999). Taken together, these studies suggest that both Positive and Negative Emotionality may influence the development of depressogenic cognitive biases in conjunction with particular negative life experiences, or together with lower levels of self-regulation.

Taken together, these two lines of research—on temperament's effects on coping and cognitive biases—suggest that children with different traits may develop different coping strategies and interpretive styles to draw from in times of stress. Research on temperament's effects on other characteristic adaptations is likely to yield equally valuable insights into the development of these more context-specific aspects of personality.

Temperament and Narrative Identity

The final domain included in McAdams and colleagues' (McAdams & Olson, 2010; McAdams & Pals, 2006) personality taxonomy is one that becomes increasingly salient as youth move into adolescence and early adulthood, namely, personal narratives. Personal narratives help young people to articulate and develop a clear identity. As Erikson (1950) pointed out more than half a century ago, an important developmental task for adolescents in modern Western cultures is the development of a coherent sense of identity. This sense of identity emerges from adolescents' attempts to understand and define who they are as people, including their overarching sense of their goals, values, meaning, and direction. According to McAdams and colleagues, the main vehicle through which identity develops is narratives. In other words, *narrative identity* emerges as youth and adults reflect on their lives as evolving stories. People look back on their previous experiences and weave these together into a narrative that connects current identity with specific memories and recurrent themes.

Recent work has begun to identify some of the important normative developmental patterns seen in children's, adolescents', and adults' narratives. By the middle of elementary school, children typically can tell a narrative about a single event in a coherent fashion, and their ability to develop a coherent life narrative continues to improve over the later elementary school and adolescent years (Bohn & Berntsen, 2008). In a recent cross-sectional study, young people ages 8, 12, 16, and 20 were asked to narrate their life stories (Habermas & de Silveira, 2008). With age, life stories were increasingly coherent in terms of the participants' abilities to link experiences across time, to trace causal associations among experiences, and to articulate overarching themes. Indicators of coherence were relatively uncommon among the youngest participants and were considerably more common among the 12-year-olds. In adolescence, youth begin to incorporate other important aspects of identity into their sense of who they are in a broader context—their cultural, ethnic, and group identity (Schwartz, Zamboanga, & Weisskirch, 2008). By adulthood, there are many individual differences apparent in life narratives. Adult narratives vary in their narrative coherence and complexity; reflection of growth and meaning; general themes; high points, low points, and turning points; expression of motives; handling of negative experiences; and inclusion of positive and negative emotions (McAdams, 2008). These individual differences have important implications for adults' coping, well-being, and development (McAdams, 2008).

As with characteristic adaptations, temperament and later personality traits seem likely to have an impact on adolescents' evolving narrative identities. Again, this is likely to occur through the processes described previously, but particularly through the impact of traits on interpretation or meaning making. Nelson (2010) has described the importance of meaning making in personality development: "What is retained from an experience, either as general knowledge or as individual memory, is what has meaning for the individual child. Meaning is thus made through the history of the individual's past experience, and this meaning, in turn, affects what may be experienced in future encounters" (p. 44). Children can make meaning of experiences, particularly negative experiences, in more limited ways (Fivush, Sales, & Bohanek, 2008). However, there is a sharp increase in the capacity for making individual interpretations of narrated life events in adolescence (Pasupathi & Wainryb, 2010), which suggests that traits may have more of an impact on individual differences in narratives in adolescence.

Currently, research on individual differences in adolescent narrative identity is relatively limited and, to the best of our knowledge, researchers have not yet examined the effect of temperament or personality traits on narrative identity development in childhood and adolescence. However, two lines of evidence suggest that traits may play at least some role in narrative identity development. First, a small number of studies have examined the links between children's temperament traits and variations in parents' narratives styles. By preschool age, children already work with their parents to co-construct retellings of past experiences (Nelson & Fivush, 2004), which may provide a foundation for later narrative development. Parents typically encourage their children to tell autobiographical stories, and together children and their parents discuss their diverging recollections about events. Parents of less sociable and active children use a more repetitive narrative style (Lewis, 1999). Parents are also more likely to have more emotion-focused conversations about past events if they see their children as higher in Effortful Control (Bird, Reese, & Tripp, 2006), or if they perceive their children as low on temperamental difficulty, and if they themselves are not hostile in their parenting style (Bost, Choi, & Wong, 2010). Thus, children's temperament traits may shape the kinds of stories that their parents tend to share with them.

Second, the adult literature on traits and narratives has documented associations between personality traits and individual differences in narratives. In a study in which adult life narratives were coded, all of the Big Five traits except Conscientiousness were associated with trait-relevant themes and self-descriptions in the narratives (Raggatt, 2006). For example, the two interpersonal traits of Extraversion and Agreeableness had different narrative correlates: Extraversion was associated with narratives highlighting personal strength, activity, optimism, and positive emotions, whereas Agreeableness was associated with narratives focused on love, nurturing, and family ties. In a longitudinal study of college students, students who scored higher on Extraversion, Conscientiousness, and Openness at the start of college were more likely as seniors to tell complex, coherent, meaning-making narratives about personality change during their college years (Lodi-Smith, Geise, Roberts, & Robins, 2009). This research with adults suggests that although the links between traits and narratives are relatively modest, the associations are conceptually coherent and interesting. New work on the role of temperament and personality traits in parent–child storytelling and narrative development will help to shed light on the role of traits in the emergence of narrative identity.

Conclusion and Future Directions

Youth clearly display a broad range of personality characteristics: Children's and adolescents' differences range from their personality traits to their typical motivations, to coping strategies and mental representations, to their life narratives. Because temperamental differences emerge so early in life and have such significant effects on children's lived experiences in the world, temperament traits have the potential to play an important role in the development of all of these personality differences. We have argued in this chapter that temperament traits develop into the broader Big Five traits over time, but temperament traits are likely to have a more indirect influence on characteristic adaptations and narrative identities as well. Several overarching questions will be particularly important to address in exploring the role of temperament in personality development across these broad domains of personality.

First, more work needs to be done to uncover the pathways through which temperament traits are transformed into broader personality traits over time. Personality traits, as measured in childhood, include some important components that their temperament counterparts lack: Extraversion includes assertiveness; Neuroticism includes insecurity, jealousy, fear of failing, and concern about acceptance; and Conscientiousness includes orderliness, dependability, and achievement motivation. These new components of each trait derive from new cognitive and social capacities that children develop after infancy. We have suggested in this chapter that temperament traits may shape the emergence of these more complex components by shaping children's experiences. But, perhaps personality traits are broader in content simply because biological maturation and expanding experiences permit the expression of new facets of the same basic underlying traits. Temperament research could be enhanced by measuring traits more broadly as children get older, and exploring the processes through which these newer aspects emerge. In addition, future work should more seriously consider the possibility that Agreeableness/Affiliativeness and Openness/Intellect are temperament traits with their own early manifestations. Rather than closing the canon on the list of temperament traits, the field should remain open to the possibility that there are temperamental traits that have yet to be fully explored.

Second, there remain significant gaps in our understanding of the influence of temperament traits on characteristic adaptations and narratives. We have described the state of research on two particular characteristic adaptations—coping strategies and negative cognitive biases—but many other characteristic adaptations could be studied in relation to temperament as well. Children vary in their goals in different domains, for example, their social strivings for dominance, intimacy, and popularity with peers (Kiefer & Ryan, 2008), and their goals for academic and occupational attainment (Massey, Gebhardt, & Garnefski, 2008). Youth also vary substantially in their self-concepts (Harter, 2006) and values (Daniel et al., 2012), and in the many mental representations described previously in the chapter. All of these characteristic adaptations are potentially fruitful areas for study in relation to temperament, as is the development of narratives.

Finally, the investigation of personality development would be deepened by research that examines youth in a broader range of real-world contexts. Children and adolescents around the globe experience many day-to-day challenges, and young people's responses to these challenges are shaped by their temperament and personality characteristics (Lengua & Wachs, Chapter 25, this volume). For example, a recent study found that children's standing on all of the Big Five traits except for Extraversion predicted their attainment of resilient adult outcomes despite their exposure to significant adversity in childhood and adolescence (Shiner & Masten, 2012). Children's emerging personalities likewise are affected by the diverse experiences they face (Lengua & Wachs, Chapter 25, this volume). Extreme adversity, including significant poverty, may have negative effects on personality development, including children's emerging capacity for self-regulation (Blair, 2010; Hart, Atkins, & Matsuba, 2008). Although there is some work investigating personality development in the context of real-life contexts, other important social, cultural, and global changes in children's lives have received relatively little attention, including immigration, war, violence, illness, and abuse (Belfer, 2008). Because characteristic adaptations and narratives are more context-specific than traits, it will be especially important to explore how children's life experiences shape those personality characteristics (e.g., the life goals that children develop, and the stories they tell about their difficult experiences). By pinpointing how children's personalities both shape and are shaped by their experiences, it will be possible to help children with a range of temperament traits to flourish across diverse contexts.

Further Reading

McAdams, D. P., & Olson, B. D. (2010). Personality development: Continuity and change over the life course. *Annual Review of Psychology*, 61, 517–542.

Rothbart, M. K. (2011). *Becoming who we are: Temperament and personality in development.* New York: Guilford Press.

Shiner, R. L., & DeYoung, C. G. (in press). The structure of temperament and personality traits: A developmental perspective. In P. D. Zelazo (Ed.), *The Oxford handbook of developmental psychology.* New York: Oxford University Press.

References

Abe, J. A. (2005). The predictive validity of the five-factor model of personality with preschool-age children: A nine year follow-up study. *Journal of Research in Personality*, 39, 423–442.

Allport, G. W. (1937). *Personality: A psychological interpretation.* New York: Holt.

Belfer, M. L. (2008). Child and adolescent mental disorders: The magnitude of the problem across the globe. *Journal of Child Psychology and Psychiatry*, 49(3), 226–236.

Bird, A., Reese, E., & Tripp, G. (2006). Parent–child talk about past emotional events: Associations with child temperament and goodness-of-fit. *Journal of Cognition and Development*, 7, 189–210.

Blair, C. (2010). Stress and the development of self-regulation in context. *Child Development Perspectives*, 4(3), 181–188.

Bohn, A., & Berntsen, D. (2008). Life story development in childhood: The development of life story abilities and the acquisition of cultural life scripts from late middle childhood to adolescence. *Developmental Psychology*, 44(4), 1135–1147.

Bost, K. K., Choi, E., & Wong, M. S. (2010). Narrative structure and emotional references in parent–child reminiscing: Associations with child gender, temperament, and the quality of parent–child interactions. *Early Child Development and Care, 180*(1 & 2), 139–156.

Buckner, J. C., Mezzacappa, E., & Beardslee, W. R. (2009). Self-regulation and its relations to adaptive functioning in low-income youths. *American Journal of Orthopsychiatry, 79*(1), 19–30.

Buss, D. M. (1987). Selection, evocation, and manipulation. *Journal of Personality and Social Psychology, 53*, 1214–1221.

Carver, C. S., & Connor-Smith, J. (2010). Personality and coping. *Annual Review of Psychology, 61*, 679–704.

Caspi, A., & Shiner, R. L. (2006). Personality development. In W. Damon & R. Lerner (Series Eds.) & N. Eisenberg (Vol. Ed.), *Handbook of child psychology: Vol. 3. Social, emotional, and personality development* (6th ed., pp. 300–365). New York: Wiley.

Clark, L. A., & Watson, D. (2008). Temperament: An organizing paradigm for trait psychology. In O. P. John, R. W. Robins, & L. A. Pervin (Eds.), *Handbook of personality: Theory and research* (3rd ed., pp. 265–286). New York: Guilford Press.

Compas, B. E., Connor-Smith, J. K., Saltzman, H., Thomsen, A. H., & Wadsworth, M. E. (2001). Coping with stress during childhood and adolescence: Progress, problems, and potential in theory and research. *Psychological Bulletin, 127*, 87–127.

Connor-Smith, J. K., Compas, B. E., Wadsworth, M. E., Thomsen, A. H., & Saltzman, H. (2000). Response to stress: Measurement of coping and reactivity in children and adolescents. *Journal of Consulting and Clinical Psychology, 68*, 976–992.

Connor-Smith, J. K., & Flachsbart, C. (2007). Relations between personality and coping: A meta-analysis. *Journal of Personality and Social Psychology, 93*(6), 1080–1107.

Daniel, E., Benish-Weisman, M., Schiefer, D., Mollering, A., Boehnke, K., & Knafo, A. (2012). Value differentiation in adolescence: The role of age and cultural complexity. *Child Development, 83*(1), 322–336.

De Pauw, S. S. W., Mervielde, I., & Van Leeuwen, K. G. (2009). How are traits related to problem behavior in preschool children?: Similarities and contrasts between temperament and personality. *Journal of Abnormal Child Psychology, 37*, 309–325.

Derryberry, D., Reed, M. A., & Pilkenton-Taylor, C. (2003). Temperament and coping: Advantages of an individual differences perspective. *Development and Psychopathology, 15*, 1049–1066.

Derryberry, D., & Tucker, D. M. (2006). Motivation, self-regulation, and self-organization. In D. Cicchetti & D. J. Cohen (Eds.), *Developmental psychopathology: Vol. 2. Developmental neuroscience* (2nd ed., pp. 502–532). New York: Wiley.

DeYoung, C. G., & Gray, J. R. (2009). Personality neuroscience: Explaining individual differences in affect, behavior, and cognition. In P. J. Corr & G. Matthews (Eds.), *Cambridge handbook of personality* (pp. 323–346). New York: Cambridge University Press.

Digman, J. M., & Shmelyov, A. G. (1996). The structure of temperament and personality in Russian children. *Journal of Personality and Social Psychology, 71*, 341–351.

Digman, J. M., & Takemoto-Chock, N. K. (1981). Factors in the natural language of personality: Re-analysis, comparison, and interpretation of six major studies. *Multivariate Behavioral Research, 16*, 149–170.

Durbin, C. E., Hayden, E. P., Klein, D. N., & Olino, T. M. (2007). Stability of laboratory-assessed temperamental emotionality traits from ages 3 to 7. *Emotion, 7*, 388–399.

Dweck, C. S., & London, B. (2004). The role of mental representation in social development. *Merrill–Palmer Quarterly, 50*, 428–444.

Eisenberg, N., Vidmar, M., Spinrad, T. L., Eggum, N. D., Edwards, A., Gaertner, B., et al. (2010). Mothers' teaching strategies and children's effortful control: A longitudinal study. *Developmental Psychology, 46*(5), 1294–1308.

Erikson, E. H. (1950). *Childhood and society*. New York: Norton.

Fivush, R., Sales, J. M., & Bohanek, J. G. (2008). Meaning making in mothers' and children's narratives of emotional events. *Memory, 16*(6), 579–594.

Flavell, J. H. (2007). Theory-of-mind development: Retrospect and prospect. In G. W. Ladd (Ed.), *Appraising the human developmental sciences* (pp. 38–55). Landscapes of Childhood series. Detroit, MI: Wayne State University Press.

Fox, N. A., Henderson, H. A., Marshall, P. J., Nichols, K. E., & Ghera, M. M. (2005). Behavioral inhibition: Linking biology and behavior within a developmental framework. *Annual Review of Psychology, 56*, 235–262.

Fraley, R. C., & Shaver, P. R. (2008). Attachment theory and its place in contemporary personality theory and research. In O. P. John, R. W. Robins, & Pervin, L. A. (Eds.), *Handbook of personality: Theory and research* (3rd ed., pp. 518–541). New York: Guilford Press.

Funder, D. C. (2007). *The personality puzzle* (4th ed.). New York: Norton.

Gartstein, M. A., & Rothbart, M. K. (2003). Studying infant temperament via the Revised Infant Behavior Questionnaire. *Infant Behavior and Development, 26*, 64–86.

Goldberg, L. R. (2001). Analyses of Digman's child-personality data: Derivation of Big Five factor scores from each of six samples. *Journal of Personality, 69,* 709–743.

Goldsmith, H. H., Buss, A. H., Plomin, R., Rothbart, M. K., Thomas, A., Chess, S., et al. (1987). Roundtable: What is temperament?: Four approaches. *Child Development, 58,* 505–529.

Gray, J. A. (1982). *The neuropsychology of anxiety: An enquiry into the functions of the septohippocampal system.* New York: Oxford University Press.

Graziano, W. G., Habashi, M. M., Sheese, B. E., & Tobin, R. M. (2007). Agreeableness, empathy, and helping: A person × situation perspective. *Journal of Personality and Social Psychology, 93,* 583–599.

Graziano, W. G., Jensen-Campbell, L. A., & Sullivan-Logan, G. (1998). Temperament, activity, and expectations for later personality development. *Journal of Personality and Social Psychology, 74,* 1266–1277.

Habermas, T., & de Silveira, C. (2008). The development of global coherence in life narratives across adolescence: Temporal, causal, and thematic aspects. *Developmental Psychology, 44,* 707–721.

Halverson, C. F., Havill, V. L., Deal, J., Baker, S. R., Victor, J. B., Pavlopoulos, V., et al. (2003). Personality structure as derived from parental ratings of free descriptions of children: The Inventory of Child Individual Differences. *Journal of Personality, 71,* 995–1026.

Hane, A. A., Fox, N. A., Henderson, H. A., & Marshall, P. J. (2008). Behavioral reactivity and approach–withdrawal bias in infancy. *Developmental Psychology, 44,* 1491–1496.

Hart, D., Atkins, R., & Matsuba, M. K. (2008). The association of neighborhood poverty with personality change in childhood. *Journal of Personality and Social Psychology, 94*(6), 1048–1061.

Harter, S. (2006). The self. In W. Damon & R. Lerner (Series Eds.) & N. Eisenberg (Vol. Ed.), *Handbook of child psychology: Vol. 3. Social, emotional, and personality development* (6th ed., pp. 505–570). New York: Wiley.

Hayden, E. P., Klein, D. N., Dougherty, L. R., Olino, T. M., Dyson, M. W., Durbin, C. E., et al. (2011). The role of brain-derived neurotrophic factor genotype, parental depression, and relationship discord in predicting early-emerging negative emotionality. *Psychological Science, 21,* 1678–1685.

Hayden, E. P., Klein, D. N., Durbin, C. E., & Olino, T. M. (2006). Positive emotionality at age 3 predicts cognitive styles in 7-year-old children. *Development and Psychopathology, 18,* 409–423.

Izard, C., Stark, K., Trentacosta, C., & Schultz, D. (2008). Beyond emotion regulation: Emotion utilization and adaptive functioning. *Child Development Perspectives, 2*(3), 156–163.

John, O. P., Caspi, A., Robins, R. W., Moffitt, T. E., & Stouthamer-Loeber, M. (1994). The "Little Five": Exploring the five-factor model of personality in adolescent boys. *Child Development, 65,* 160–178.

John, O. P., Naumann, L. P., & Soto, C. J. (2008). Paradigm shift to the integrative Big Five trait taxonomy: History, measurement, and conceptual issues. In O. P. John, R. W. Robins, & L. A. Pervin (Eds.), *Handbook of personality: Theory and research* (3rd ed., pp. 114–158). New York: Guilford Press.

Johnson, S. C., Dweck, C. S., & Chen, F. S. (2007). Evidence for infants' internal working models of attachment. *Psychological Science, 18,* 501–502.

Kagan, J. (2008). The biological contributions to temperaments and emotions. *European Journal of Developmental Science, 2,* 38–51.

Kagan, J., & Fox, N. A. (2006). Biology, culture, and temperamental biases. In N. Eisenberg (Ed.), *Handbook of child psychology* (Vol. 3, pp. 167–225). Hoboken, NJ: Wiley.

Kiefer, S. M., & Ryan, A. M. (2008). Striving for social dominance over peers: The implications for academic achievement during early adolescence. *Journal of Educational Psychology, 100,* 417–428.

Kochanska, G., & Aksan, N. (2006). Children's conscience and self-regulation. *Journal of Personality, 74*(6), 1587–1617.

Kochanska, G., & Knaack, A. (2003). Effortful control as a personality characteristic of young children: Antecedents, correlates, and consequences. *Journal of Personality, 71,* 1087–1112.

Kochanska, G., Philibert, R. A., & Barry, R. A. (2009). Interplay of genes and early mother–child relationship in the development of self-regulation from toddler to preschool age. *Journal of Child Psychology and Psychiatry, 50*(11), 1331–1338.

Krueger, R. F., & Johnson, W. (2008). Behavioral genetics and personality: A new look at the integration of nature and nurture. In O. P. John, R. W. Robins, & L. A. Pervin (Eds.), *Handbook of personality: Theory and research* (3rd ed., pp. 287–310). New York: Guilford Press.

Leff, S. S., Crick, N. R., Angelucci, J., Haye, K., Jaward, A. F., Grossman, M., et al. (2006). Social cognition in context: Validating a cartoon-based attributional measure for urban girls. *Child Development, 77,* 1351–1358.

Lemerise, E. A., & Arsenio, W. F. (2000). An integrated model of emotion processes and cognition in social information processing. *Child Development, 71,* 107–118.

Lengua, L. J., Sandler, I. N., West, S. G., Wolchik,

S. A., & Curran, P. J. (1999). Emotionality and self-regulation, threat appraisal, and coping in children of divorce. *Development and Psychopathology, 11*, 15–37.

Lewis, K. D. (1999). Maternal style in reminiscing: Relations to child individual differences. *Cognitive Development, 14*, 381–399.

Lightfoot, C., Cole, M., & Cole, S. R. (2009). *The development of children* (6th ed.). New York: Worth.

Little, B. R. (2008). Personal projects and free traits: Personality and motivation reconsidered. *Social and Personality Compass, 2*(3), 1235–1254.

Lodi-Smith, J., Geise, A. C., Roberts, B. W., & Robins, R. W. (2009). Narrating personality change. *Journal of Personality and Social Psychology, 96*(3), 679–689.

Lonigan, C. J., Vasey, M. W., Phillips, B. M., & Hazen, R. A. (2004). Temperament, anxiety, and the processing of threat-relevant stimuli. *journal of Clinical Child and Adolescent Psychology, 33*(1), 8–20.

Massey, E. K., Gebhardt, W. A., & Garnefski, N. (2008). Adolescent goal content and pursuit: A review of the literature from the past 16 years. *Developmental Review, 28*, 421–460.

Mathews, A., & MacLeod, C. (2005). Cognitive vulnerability to emotional disorders. *Annual Review of Clinical Psychology, 1*, 167–195.

McAdams, D. P. (2008). Personal narratives and the life story. In O. P. John, R. W. Robins, & L. A. Pervin (Eds.), *Handbook of personality: Theory and research* (3rd ed., p. 242–262). New York: Guilford Press.

McAdams, D. P., & Olson, B. D. (2010). Personality development: Continuity and change over the life course. *Annual Review of Psychology, 61*, 517–542.

McAdams, D. P., & Pals, J. L. (2006). A new Big Five: Fundamental principles for an integrative science of personality. *American Psychologist, 61*, 204–217.

McCrae, R. R., Costa, P. T., Jr., Ostendorf, F., Angleitner, A., Hřebíčková, M., Avia, M. D., et al. (2000). Nature over nurture: Temperament, personality, and life span development. *Journal of Personality and Social Psychology, 78*, 173–186.

Measelle, J., John, O. P., Ablow, J., Cowan, P. A., & Cowan, C. P. (2005). Can children provide coherent, stable, and valid self-reports on the Big Five dimensions? *Journal of Personality and Social Psychology, 89*, 90–106.

Mezulis, A. H., Hyde, J. S., & Abramson, L. Y. (2006). The developmental origins of cognitive vulnerability to depression: Temperament, parenting, and negative life events in childhood as contributors to negative cognitive style. *Developmental Psychology, 42*, 1012–1025.

Mischel, W., & Shoda, Y. (2010). The situated person. In B. Mesquita, L. Feldman Barrett, & E. R. Smith (Eds.), *The mind in context* (pp. 149–173). New York: Guilford Press.

Molden, D. C., & Dweck, C. S. (2006). Finding "meaning" in psychology: A lay theories approach to self-regulation, social perception, and social development. *American Psychologist, 61*, 192–203.

Nachmias, M., Gunnar, M., Mangelsdorf, S., Parritz, R. H., & Buss, K. (1996). Behavioral inhibition and stress reactivity: The moderating role of attachment security. *Child Development, 67*, 508–522.

Nelson, K. (2010). Developmental narratives of the experiencing child. *Child Development Perspectives, 4*(1), 42–47.

Nelson, K., & Fivush, R. (2004). The emergence of autobiographical memory: A social cultural developmental theory. *Psychological Review, 111*, 486–511.

Neppl, T. K., Donnellan, M. B., Scaramella, L. V., Widaman, K. F., & Spilman, S. K. (2010). Differential stability of temperament and personality from toddlerhood to middle childhood. *Journal of Research in Personality, 44*, 386–396.

Nettle, D. (2006). The evolution of personality variation in humans and other animals. *American Psychologist, 61*, 622–631.

Olino, T. M., Klein, D. N., Durbin, C. E., Hayden, E. P., & Buckley, M. E. (2005). The structure of extraversion in preschool aged children. *Personality and Individual Differences, 39*, 481–492.

Pasupathi, M., & Wainryb, D. (2010). On telling the whole story: Facts and interpretations in autobiographical memory narratives from childhood through midadolescence. *Developmental Psychology, 46*(3), 735–746.

Pérez-Edgar, K., McDermott, J. M., Pine, D. S., Bar-Haim, Y., Chronis-Tuscano, A., & Fox, N. A. (2010). Attention biases to threat and behavioral inhibition in early childhood shape adolescent social withdrawal. *Emotion, 10*(3), 349–357.

Pickering, A. D., & Gray, J. A. (1999). The neuroscience of personality. In L. A. Pervin & O. P. John (Eds.), *Handbook of personality: Theory and research* (2nd ed., pp. 277–299). New York: Guilford Press.

Pomerantz, E. M., & Thompson, R. A. (2008). Parents' role in children's personality development: The psychological resource principle. In O. P. John, R. W. Robins, & L. A. Pervin (Eds.), *Handbook of personality: Theory and research* (3rd ed., pp. 351–374). New York: Guilford Press.

Raggatt, P. (2006). Putting the Five-Factor Model into context: Evidence linking Big Five traits to narrative identity. *Journal of Personality, 74*(5), 1321–1347.

Roberts, B. W., & DelVecchio, W. F. (2000). The

rank-order consistency of personality traits from childhood to old age: A quantitative review of longitudinal studies. *Psychological Bulletin, 126*, 25–30.

Roberts, B. W., & Robins, R. W. (2000). Broad dispositions, broad aspirations: The intersection of personality traits and major life goals. *Personality and Social Psychology Bulletin, 26*, 1284–1296.

Romero, E., Villar, P., Luengo, M. A., & Gomez-Fraguela, J. A. (2009). Traits, personal strivings, and well-being. *Journal of Research in Personality, 43*, 535–546.

Rothbart, M. K. (2011). *Becoming who we are: Temperament and personality in development*. New York: Guilford Press.

Rothbart, M. K., Ahadi, S. A., Hershey, K. L., & Fisher, P. (2001). Investigation of temperament at three to seven years: The Children's Behavior Questionnaire. *Child Development, 72*, 1394–1408.

Rothbart, M. K., & Bates, J. E. (2006). Temperament. In W. Damon & R. Lerner (Series Eds.) & N. Eisenberg (Vol. Ed.), *Handbook of child psychology: Vol. 3. Social, emotional, and personality development* (6th ed., pp. 99–166). New York: Wiley.

Rothbart, M. K., & Posner, M. I. (2006). Temperament, attention, and developmental psychopathology. In D. Cicchetti & D. J. Cohen (Eds.), *Developmental psychopathology: Vol. 2. Developmental neuroscience* (2nd ed., pp. 465–450). Hoboken, NJ: Wiley.

Rudolph, K. D., Hammen, C., & Burge, D. (1995). Cognitive representations of self-family, and peers in school-age children—Links with social competence and sociometric status. *Child Development, 66*, 1385–1402.

Sameroff, A. (2008). The developmentalist's gag reflex. *Developments, 51*(3), 3.

Schwartz, S. J., Zamboanga, B. L., & Weisskirch, R. S. (2008). Broadening the study of the self: Integrating the study of personal identity and cultural identity. *Social and Personality Psychology Compass, 2*, 635–651.

Seiffge-Krenke, E., Aunola, K., & Nurmi, J.-E. (2009). Changes in stress perception and coping during adolescence: The role of situational and personal factors. *Child Development, 80*(1), 259–279.

Sheese, B. E., Voelker, P. M., Rothbart, M. K., & Posner, M. I. (2007). Parenting quality interacts with genetic variation in dopamine receptor D4 to influence temperament in early childhood. *Development and Psychopathology, 19*, 1039–1046.

Shiner, R. L., Buss, K. A., McClowry, S. G., Putnam, S. P., Saudino, K. J., & Zentner, M. (2012). What is temperament *now*?: Assessing progress in temperament research on the twenty-fifth anniversary of Goldsmith et al. (1987). *Child Development Perspectives*.

Shiner, R. L., & DeYoung, C. G. (in press). The structure of temperament and personality traits: A developmental perspective. In P. D. Zelazo (Ed.), *The Oxford handbook of developmental psychology*. New York: Oxford University Press.

Shiner, R. L., & Masten, A. S. (2012). Childhood personality as a harbinger of competence and resilience in adulthood. *Development and Psychopathology, 24*(2), 507–528.

Shiner, R. L., Masten, A. S., & Tellegen, A. (2002). A developmental perspective on personality in emerging adulthood: Childhood antecedents and concurrent adaptation. *Journal of Personality and Social Psychology, 83*, 1165–1177.

Skinner, E. A., & Zimmer-Gembeck, M. J. (2007). The development of coping. *Annual Review of Psychology, 58*, 199–144.

Soto, C. J., John, O. P., Gosling, S. D., & Potter, J. (2008). The developmental psychometrics of Big Five self-reports: Acquiescence, factor structure, coherence, and differentiation from ages 10 to 20. *Journal of Personality and Social Psychology, 94*, 718–737.

Sroufe, L. A. (2009). The concept of development in developmental psychopathology. *Child Development Perspectives, 3*(3), 178–183.

Valiente, C., Lemery-Chalfant, K., & Swanson, J. (2009). Children's responses to daily social stressors: Relations with parenting, children's effortful control, and adjustment. *Journal of Child Psychology and Psychiatry, 50*(6), 707–717.

Van Zalk, N., Van Zalk, M., Kerr, M., & Stattin, H. (2011). Social anxiety as a basis for friendship selection and socialization in adolescents' social networks. *Journal of Personality, 79*(3), 499–525.

Verstraeten, K., Vasey, M. W., Raes, F., & Bijttebier, P. (2009). Temperament and risk for depressive symptoms in adolescence: Mediation by rumination and moderation by effortful control. *Journal of Abnormal Child Psychology, 37*, 439–461.

Weinstein, T. A. R., Capitanio, J. P., & Gosling, S. D. (2008). Personality in animals. In O. P. John, R. W. Robins, & L. A. Pervin (Eds.), *Handbook of personality: Theory and research* (3rd ed., pp. 328–348). New York: Guilford Press.

Zentner, M., & Bates, J. E. (2008). Child temperament. *European Journal of Developmental Science, 2*, 2–37.

PART VI

CLINICAL PERSPECTIVES ON TEMPERAMENT

CHAPTER 25

Temperament and Risk
Resilient and Vulnerable Responses to Adversity

Liliana J. Lengua
Theodore D. Wachs

In a bioecological model it is posited that individuals develop within multiple contexts, and that development is affected by transactions and interactions of factors at many levels, including distal and proximal influences (Bronfenbrenner & Morris, 1998). Distal factors, such as cultural-, socioeconomic-, and community-level influences provide the contexts in which proximal factors, such as family relationships and parenting, influence individual development. Risk factors present at these varying contextual levels can result in children developing cognitive, social–emotional or behavioral problems. However, individual-level factors also play a critical role, both directly by contributing to developmental outcomes, and indirectly by filtering or altering the impact of contextual risk on development. One essential individual difference factor is temperament, which is a key contributor to children's vulnerable or resilient responses to the experience of adversity or risk.

The conceptual model shown in Figure 25.1, on which this chapter is based, posits that risk and promotive factors shape the biological underpinnings and behavioral manifestations of temperament. In turn, temperament influences the degree to which a child is exposed to risk and promotive factors, and contributes to the likelihood of children developing problems. Temperament also moderates experiences of adversity or risk. For example, individual differences in sensitivity to threat, affective arousal in the face of stress, and capacity for regulating cognitive, emotional, and behavioral responses to stress can either increase or decrease the impact of other risk factors, thus contributing to the likelihood of vulnerable or resilient outcomes. This chapter first provides a brief overview of the conceptual frameworks of risk, resilience, and temperament employed in our discussion. We then present evidence for risk and promotive factors shaping temperament, the role of temperament in influencing exposure to risk and promotive factors, and the moderating effects of temperament on experiences of adversity or risk.

A Conceptual Framework for Risk and Promotive Influences and Resilience

Developmental risks refer to biological (e.g., toxins, malnutrition) and psychosocial (e.g., abusive parenting, family stress) influences that are known to compromise children's cognitive, social–emotional, or

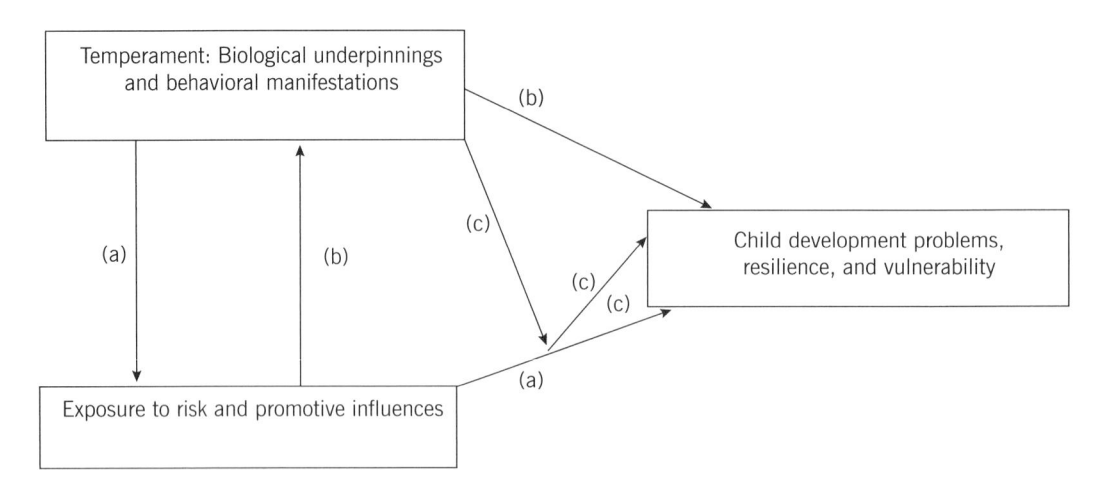

FIGURE 25.1. Links among temperament, risk and promotive influences, child problems, resilience, and vulnerability. (a) Relation of temperament to child outcomes mediated by risk or promotive influences. (b) Relation of risk and promotive influences to child outcomes mediated by child temperament. (c) Relation of risk and promotive influences to child outcomes moderated by child temperament.

physical–neural development (Krishnakumar & Black, 2002; Sameroff, Gutman, & Peck, 2003). The link between risk exposure and development is not straightforward, with risk factors operating in a probabilistic manner. Exposure to a developmental risk increases the likelihood of, but does not guarantee, compromised development. For example, even though early institutional rearing is a known risk factor for reduced cognitive and social–emotional competence, a surprisingly high proportion of children experiencing prolonged institutional rearing show essentially normal development (Rutter et al., 2010). The developmental impact of risk factors depends on (1) the level of the child's exposure to the risk (dosage); (2) whether the child is also exposed to other risks (cumulative risks); (3) the context within which the risk occurs (e.g., culture, social class); (4) whether the child encounters protective influences that can reduce the likelihood of adverse consequences when he or she is exposed to risks; and (5) individual differences in vulnerability to risk (Masten & Obradovic, 2006; Wachs, 2000).

Promotive or protective factors reduce the impact of risk (Sameroff, Bartko, Baldwin, Baldwin, & Seifer, 1998). *Protective factors* support development for children exposed to significant developmental risks, whereas *promotive factors* enhance development regardless of risk status. For simplicity's sake, unless exposure to specific risk conditions is clearly documented, we use the term *promotive* to refer to both protective and promotive influences. Promotive factors may be extrinsic to the child (e.g., high-quality rearing environment) or may involve individual child characteristics such as temperament. As with risk factors, promotive influences also operate in a probabilistic fashion, increasing the likelihood of more optimal development.

Resilience in children results from the interplay between risk and promotive factors. *Resilience* refers to healthy or successful functioning within the context of significant adversity or risk (Luthar, Cicchetti, & Becker, 2000). Children's successful functioning in the face of risk can be conceptualized as the absence of adjustment problems or psychopathology, the presence of social or emotional competence or self-esteem, or the mastery of appropriate developmental tasks (Kim-Cohen, Moffitt, Caspi, & Taylor, 2004; Masten & Obradovic, 2006).

A Temperament Framework

Temperament is defined as the physiological basis for individual differences in reactivity and self-regulation, including motivation, affect, activity, and attention characteristics. These individual differences are biologically based, present early in life and are relatively stable, yet shaped by experience (Rothbart & Bates, 2006). *Reactivity* refers to responsiveness to change in the external and internal environments. It includes physiological and emotional reactions related to both negative and positive affect. Dimensions of *negative reactivity* include frustration (anger, irritability) and fear (inhibition, withdrawal). Dimensions of *positive reactivity* include approach, pleasure, smiling, and laughter. *Self-regulation* refers to executive control processes and behaviors that operate to modulate physiological, affective, or behavioral reactivity. Self-regulation includes attention focusing, attention shifting, and inhibitory control, which comprise the construct of effortful control (Rothbart, Ahadi, Hershey, & Fisher, 2001).

Despite temperament's heritability and stability, experience plays a role in shaping the expression of temperament (Rothbart & Bates, 2006). Fundamentally, temperament represents characteristics present early in life that shape and are shaped within the context of social and environmental interactions (Shiner & Caspi, 2003), and that result in differential responsiveness to socialization experiences (Wachs, 2000). Thus, temperament serves as a mediator or moderator of experiences of adversity or risk. In this chapter we emphasize Rothbart's conceptual framework, though we also reference other conceptual models of temperament that have been examined as predictors of children's vulnerability or resilience, such as difficult temperament.

Developmental Risks Shape Individual Differences in Temperament

Other chapters in this volume review the role of "normative" biological (Saudino & Wang, Chapter 16; White, Lamm, Helfinstein, & Fox, Chapter 17; Depue & Fu, Chapter 18) and psychosocial influences (Bates, Schermerhorn, & Petersen, Chapter 20; Chen, Yang, & Fu, Chapter 22) upon individual differences in temperament. In this chapter we focus on the contributions of biological and psychosocial risks to temperament. As shown in Figure 25.1 exposure to developmental risk factors can directly impact the biological roots of temperament (e.g., the brain; Hackman, Farah, & Meaney, 2010), or psychosocial factors linked to individual differences in the developmental course or behavioral manifestations of temperament (Henderson & Wachs, 2007). Biological or psychosocial risks that are most consistently linked to individual differences in temperament are highlighted below.

Biological Risk Factors

Prenatal Biological Risks

Associations between substance abuse during pregnancy and infant temperament, and mechanisms underlying such associations, are documented by Huizink (Chapter 15, this volume). In terms of other prenatal teratogens a few studies have investigated relations between temperament and prenatal exposure to environmental toxins such as lead or methylmercury (Gump et al., 2008; Jacobson, Jacobson, & Humphrey, 1990; Myers et al., 2003). Given the small body of findings, no firm conclusions can be drawn on links between prenatal exposure to environmental toxins and postnatal temperament.

There is a small literature on temperament patterns in preterm or small for gestational age (SGA) infants. While some studies have shown greater negative affect in low birthweight (LBW) infants compared to normal birthweight infants (Pesonen, Raikkonen, Kajantie, et al., 2006; Pesonen, Raikkonen, Strandberg, & Jarvenpaa, 2006), other studies have reported no group differences (Gorman, Lourie, & Choudhury, 2001; Olafsen et al., 2008). Differences in results may reflect the presence of other biomedical problems that can covary with preterm birth (e.g., intraventricular hemorrhage). Research has indicated an increased risk of difficult temperament or lower adaptability for preterm or SGA infants with additional early biomedical risks (Hwang, Soong, & Liao, 2009; Larroque et al., 2005). Relations between LBW and subsequent infant negative affect also can be moderated by the quality of the postnatal rearing environment (Gorman et al., 2001).

Research also has related pre- or neonatal iron deficiency to lower infant alertness, soothability, and self-regulation, and increased negative emotionality (Vaughn, Brown, & Carter, 1986; Wachs, Kanashiro, & Gurkas, 2008; Wachs, Pollitt, Cueto, Jacoby, & Creed-Kanashiro, 2005). Prenatal iron deficiency has also been shown to be related to lower alertness and self-regulation during the preschool years (Tamura et al., 2002). This pattern of findings likely reflects the influence of iron on early brain development (Georgieff, 2007).

Postnatal Biological Risks

Higher levels of body lead in infancy are associated with higher levels of withdrawal (Mendelsohn et al., 1998; Wasserman, Staghezza-Jaramillo, Shrout, Popovac, & Graziano, 1998) and lower levels of emotion regulation (Mendelsohn et al., 1998) and activity (Padich, Dietrich, & Pearson, 1985). Higher body lead levels during the toddler and preschool years also are related to higher levels of physiological stress reactivity (cortisol) at 9 years (Gump et al., 2008) and to lower teacher ratings of sociability (Hubbs-Tait, Kennedy, Droke, Belanger, & Parker, 2007). The effects of exposure to environmental lead may be cumulative (Wasserman et al., 1998). Adverse temperament consequences may reflect early lead exposure disrupting emotion-related metabolic pathways, such as those involving glutamate metabolism (Hubbs-Tait, Nation, Krebs, & Bellinger, 2005).

Multiple studies have shown significant reductions in reactivity, emotional control, sociability, attention, and activity level plus increased distractibility and fear in undernourished compared to more adequately nourished infants (e.g., Baker-Henningham, Hamadani, Huda, & Grantham-McGregor, 2009; Meeks-Gardner, Grantham-McGregor, Himes, & Chang, 1999; Pollitt, Saco-Pollitt, Jahari, Husaini, & Huang, 2000). Infant and toddler iron deficiency is linked to lower activity level, positive affect, and reactivity, and higher inhibition and negative emotionality (Lozoff et al., 2006; Thomas, Grant, & Aubuchon-Endsley, 2009). Currently only a few studies are available linking temperament to postnatal deficits in other nutrients, such as B vitamins (Rahmanifar et al., 1993) or zinc (Ashworth, Morris, Lira, & Grantham-McGregor, 1998). Nutritionally driven impairments in brain development and function (Lecours, Mandujano, & Romero, 2001; Lozoff et al., 2006), involving systems such as the hippocampus and dopamine receptors (Henderson & Wachs, 2007), likely underlie associations between nutrition and temperament.

Psychosocial Risk Factors

Stress

Huizink (Chapter 15, this volume) has provided a detailed review of the infrahuman and human research literature on the association between prenatal stress and postnatal temperament. Paralleling prenatal findings, higher postnatal maternal cortisol levels (as a measure of stress) were positively related to fear in breastfed infants but unrelated to fear in formula fed infants (Glynn et al., 2007). Similarly, self-reported maternal stress concurrently predicted higher infant fear and negative reactivity at 6 months of age (Pesonen, Raikkonen, Strandberg, & Jarvenpaa, 2005) and higher negative affect and lower attention focusing and soothability at 5½ years of age (Pesonen et al., 2007). Stressful family risk conditions have also been related to temperament. Higher levels of parental alcoholism and personality disorder assessed when children were preschoolers predicted poorer reactive control, lower resiliency, and higher negative emotionality in childhood and adolescence (Martel et al., 2009). In addition, higher levels of home chaos have been linked to lower infant adaptability and higher infant negative mood (Matheny & Phillips, 2001; Wachs, 1988), and to higher levels of child impulsivity in preschool (Corapci, 2008).

Maternal Depression

Huot, Brennan, Stowe, Plotsky, and Walker (2004) reported that infants of prenatally depressed mothers had higher levels of negative affect and stress reactivity. Postnatal maternal depression also has been linked to infant negative emotionality (Galler, Harrison, Ramsey, Butler, & Forde, 2004; McGrath, Records, & Rice, 2008), lower infant adaptability and approach (Galler et al., 2004) and higher intensity (Hanington, Ramchandani, & Stein, 2010). Maternal depression has also been associated with lower positive emotionality in preschool children (Durbin, Klein, Hayden, Buckley, & Moerk, 2005) and higher negative emotionality in childhood (Bouma, Omel, Verhulst, & Odlehinkel, 2008). In interpreting these findings a critical question is whether depression biases maternal reports of temperament. However, a similar pattern of results is found when temperament is assessed using objective temperament measures (Feldman et al., 2009; Olino, Klein, Dyson, & Rose, 2010) or physiological measures of reactivity, such as offspring cortisol (Murray, Halligan, Goodyer, & Herbert, 2010), which suggests that the temperament–depression association is not due solely to shared measurement variance. Because some studies have concurrent measurements, there is a question of whether problematic infant temperament is a cause or a consequence of maternal depression. Although the question of directionality remains an issue, available evidence suggests that the transmission is primarily from mother to child (Durbin et al., 2005; Hanington et al., 2010; Olino et al., 2010).

Summary

Exposure to biological and psychosocial risk factors such as pre- and postnatal stress, environmental lead, nutritional deficiencies, and maternal depression can alter the nature and course of temperament. Links between biological risk factors and temperament may be mediated through their impact on brain development and brain function. However, particularly for psychosocial risks, it is important to recognize the potential importance of a transactional relation, wherein temperament both shapes and is shaped by environmental influences.

The Influence of Temperament on Adjustment, Vulnerability, or Resiliency

As shown in Figure 25.1 temperament is expected to contribute to individual adjustment, vulnerability, or resilience in at least three ways. First, temperament may *indirectly* influence outcomes through increasing the child's exposure to risk or promotive factors. Second, there may be *direct effects* whereby individual differences in temperament, either in isolation or in combination with other risk factors, independently impact adjustment. Third, temperament may act as a *moderator*, either mitigating or exacerbating the impact of risk factors upon development.

Individual Differences in Temperament Increase Exposure to Risk or Promotive Influences

Individual differences in temperament may have indirect effects on children's adjustment by increasing the probability of exposure to developmental risk or promotive influences (also see Hampson & Vollrath, Chapter 28, this volume). There are several potential mechanisms through which individual differences in temperament can result in differential exposure to risk or promotive influences. One such potential mechanism is *reactive covariance* (also called environmental elicitation; Shiner & Caspi, 2003), which involves differential treatment of children with different individual characteristics (Wachs, 2006). In this mechanism, children are more likely to encounter psychosocial risks when their temperament evokes more critical, conflicted, or harsh interactions with parents, peers, or caregivers. In contrast, a greater likelihood of exposure to promotive influences would occur when children have temperament characteristics that elicit more positive and supportive interpersonal relationships from others.

A second potential mechanism is *active covariance* (also called environmental selection; Shiner & Caspi, 2003), wherein children with different individual temperament characteristics selectively gravitate to environments that are compatible with their characteristics. Through this process, children's temperament influences their selection of environments, experiences, or peers that either increase or reduce their exposure to risk or promotive influences (Wachs, 2006).

A third mechanism involving indirect processes is *multistage mediation*, wherein individual temperament characteristics result in cognitive or behavioral consequences that in turn are associated with increased exposure to risk or promotive influences, or to increased or decreased likelihood of adjustment problems. Evidence for each of these mechanisms is reviewed below.

Reactive Covariance

Perhaps the most dramatic example of the operation of positive reactive covariance processes involves children raised in highly depriving institutions. Even in such circumstances, children who are higher in friendliness (sociability) or positive emotionality are more likely to receive what little extra attention institutional caregivers are able to give (Chisholm, 1988; Vorria et al., 2003). A less extreme example is seen when children's temperament characteristics, such as negative reactivity or poor self-regulation, elicit negative parenting, which is a developmental risk factor. While findings on the reactive effects of child easy–difficult temperament upon parenting are not always consistent, there is solid evidence linking child fear/inhibition, frustration, and self-regulation to parenting (see Bates et al., Chapter 20, this volume). Reactive covariance processes may also underlie the link between low self-regulation and reduced levels of social support (Buckner, Mezzacappa, & Beardslee, 2009). Inconsistent findings may reflect the impact of other influences that can moderate relations between child temperament and parenting, such as the mother's level of stress reactivity (Ispa, Fine, & Thornburg, 2002) or self-efficacy beliefs (Corapci & Wachs, 2002). It also is important to recognize that child temperament characteristics that evoke positive or negative reactions from caregivers may vary across cultures (Chen et al., Chapter 22, this volume). Furthermore, there is ambiguity in some studies with regard to the question of directionality, namely, whether parenting → temperament or temperament → parenting.

Active Covariance

While far less evidence is available, results from a few studies suggest that temperament may influence children's selection of environmental circumstances that expose them to greater or lower levels of risk. Specifically, high-intensity pleasure and lower effortful control are related to a greater probability of deviant peer affiliations (Creemers et al., 2010), and low self-regulation increases the likelihood of children experiencing negative life events (Buckner et al., 2009; King, Molina, & Chassin, 2008; Sobolewski, Strelau, & Zawadzki, 2001).

Multistage Mediation

An excellent example of multistage meditation involves evidence linking temperament to sleep problems in infancy and early childhood. As shown in Figure 25.2, a number of studies have reported that infants with lower levels of adaptability and rhythmicity and higher levels of negative mood or difficultness are at increased risk for a variety of sleep disturbances. In turn, infant sleep disturbances increase the probability of occurrence of a variety of additional psychosocial risk factors for infants and their families. Although evidence supports a link between temperament, sleep problems, and additional risk exposure, one issue of concern is the direction of causality (i.e., whether certain types of temperament influence infant sleep, or whether infants with more disturbed sleep patterns are more at risk for certain types of temperament).

Another example of the operation of multistage meditation occurs when temperament differences predispose children to utilize specific appraisal, coping, or emotion regulation strategies to deal with stress. The type of coping used can lead to either vulnerable or resilient responses (Compas, Connor-Smith, & Jaser, 2004). For example, under stress conditions, children high in fearfulness or inhibition are more likely to practice avoidant coping strategies, including repression, wishful thinking, expression of negative emotions, and seeking proximity to adults (Lengua & Long, 2002; Parritz, 1996). In contrast, under stress, children high in self-regulation are better able to redirect their attention as needed (Lonigan, Vasey, Phillips, & Hazen, 2004), are more likely to use active coping approaches (Buckner et al., 2009; Lengua & Long, 2002), and to respond in adaptive and flexible ways (Frick & Morris, 2004; Lengua & Sandler, 1996). Children who are high in positive emotionality, approach, and activity level are more likely to use active coping strategies to deal with stress, whereas children low in these temperament dimensions are more likely to use avoidant strategies (Carson & Bittner, 2001; Lengua et al., 1999;

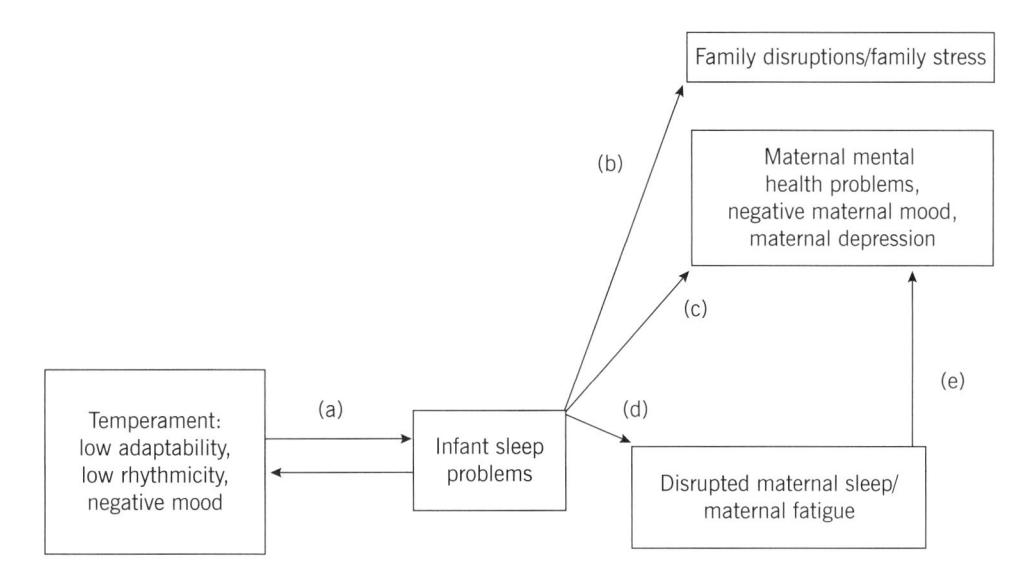

FIGURE 25.2. Model linking temperament, sleep problems and risk exposure. Supporting references for Path *a* (infant sleep assessed by maternal report [DeLeon & Karraker, 2007; Novosad, Freudigman, & Thoman, 1999; Morrell & Stelle, 2003]; by objective measures such as the actigraph [Scher et al., 1992; Spruyt, Aitken, So, Charlton, Adamson, & Horne, 2008]); Path *b* (Bates et al., 2002; Morrell & Steele, 2003); Path *c* (Fehlings et al., 2001; Fiese et al., 2007; Gregory, Eley, O'Connor, Rijsdijk, & Plomin, 2005); Path *d* (Boergers et al., 2007; Meltzer & Mindell, 2007); Path *e* (Meltzer & Mindell, 2007).

Lengua & Long, 2002). Children who use more active, flexible coping strategies when faced with stress are more likely to successfully manage stress, thus experiencing fewer adjustment problems.

Indirect multistage mediation processes linking temperament to maternal feeding practices also may underlie links between temperament and child obesity, while associations between temperament and child safety practices may underlie links between temperament and accident risk (see Hampson & Vollrath, Chapter 28, this volume). Similarly, there is evidence that young children with lower self-regulation are at an increased risk of poor school readiness, which is a known risk factor in reducing the chances of later school success (Blair & Diamond, 2008).

Summary: Temperament Indirect Effects

Available evidence links individual differences in temperament to differential exposure to risk or promotive factors. Indirect models involving reactive covariance and multistage mediation are likely mechanisms underlying these associations. However, it is important to recognize that in a number of temperament–risk associations it is not clear what underlying mechanisms are involved. In such situations it may be important to look for potential third causes, such as genes or neurotransmitters common to both risk and temperament, as suggested by both Bates and colleagues and Hampson and Vollrath (Chapters 20 and 28, respectively, this volume).

Temperament as a Direct Risk

As documented in previous reviews (Nigg; 2006; Rothbart & Bates, 2006) and by Klein, Dyson, Kujawa, and Kotov (Chapter 26, this volume) and Tackett, Martel, and Kushner (Chapter 27, this volume), temperament directly predicts children's adjustment problems and competencies. Findings generally indicate that several temperament characteristics directly increase the likelihood of psychopathology emerging and contribute to specific symptom presentation. When additively combined with other risk or promotive factors, temperament also adds unique prediction of adjustment. For example, individual differences in temperament serve as a unique risk or promotive influence over and above the effect of cumulative risk (Corapci, 2008; Lengua, 2002), maternal depression (Gartstein & Bateman, 2008), and harsh discipline (Leve, Kim, & Pears, 2005). Evidence linking specific temperament dimensions to vulnerable or resilient responses to adversity is presented in the following sections.

Easy–Difficult Temperament

Significant effects of easy or difficult temperament as a predictor of child outcomes often emerge, over and above the effects of other demographic, maternal, and family risk factors (Kilmer, Cowen, & Wyman, 2001; Kyrios & Prior, 1990; Martinez-Torteya, Bogat, von Eye, & Levendosky, 2009; Werner & Smith, 1992; Wyman, Cowen, Work, & Parker, 1991). These findings suggest independent or additive effects of easy or difficult temperament, which contribute unique variance to children's resilient or vulnerable outcomes. This conclusion is also supported by longitudinal evidence that difficult temperament in children is partially mediated by the relation between parental depression and subsequent offspring depression (Bruder-Costello et al., 2007). It is interesting that in one study, easy temperament was related to a lower likelihood of children being nonresilient or vulnerable but not related to a greater likelihood of children being categorized as competent (Martinez-Torteya et al., 2009), whereas, in another study, easygoing temperament distinguished children with higher social competence (Smith & Prior, 1995). Thus, whether easy temperament serves a promotive function is unclear. Clarification is needed on temperament's role in predicting positive adjustment outcomes.

Although there is value to examining temperament as a cluster of characteristics that compose the easy–difficult dimension, there is also value in examining the role of specific temperament dimensions in contributing to vulnerability or resilience. Reactivity and self-regulation might operate differently in relation to risk (e.g., Lengua, 2002), and the components defining reactivity might operate differently from each other. For example, fear and frustration are posited to stem from different neurobiological systems and may operate differently in relation to adjustment outcomes. Fearfulness appears to encourage more warm and supportive parenting (Lengua, 2006), to make children easier to discipline, and to predict more compliance in toddlers (Kochanska, Coy, & Murray, 2001; van der Mark, Bakermans-Kranenburg, & van IJzendoorn, 2002). Fearfulness also is related to a lower likelihood of antisocial problems (van der Laan, Veenstra, Bogaerts, Verhulst, & Ormel, 2010) and better social competence (Bush, Lengua, & Colder, 2010). In contrast, frustration appears to encourage more negative parenting and predict more behavioral and emotional problems (Lengua & Kovacs, 2005; Rothbart & Bates, 2006). Below we discuss studies that have examined specific temperament dimensions.

Negative Emotionality

Negative emotionality predicts behavioral, emotional, and social problems in the face of adversity (Lengua, 2002), differentiates stress-resilient and stress-affected children (Mathiesen & Prior, 2006), and does so over and above the effects of other factors such as parenting, family, and contextual risk (Kilmer et al., 2001, Lengua, 2002; Li-Grining, Votruba-Drzal, Bachman, & Chase-Lansdale, 2006). Components of negative emotionality, particularly frustration and fear, also have been examined in relation to risk. Frustration is a risk factor for conduct problems and lower social competence (Eisenberg et al., 2004; Lengua, 2003), and predicts adjustment over and above the effects of cumulative risk, neighborhood risk, and parenting (Bush et al., 2010; Lengua, 2006; Olson, Sameroff, Kerr, Lopez, & Wellman, 2005; van der Laan et al., 2010). Fear or inhibition is a risk factor for anxiety problems (Leve et al., 2005; Muris, 2006; Nigg, 2006), with evidence of direct relations to adjustment outcomes over and above the effects of neighborhood risk and low family income (Bush et al., 2010; Lengua, 2006).

Surgency

Surgency is a superordinate factor of temperament comprised of approach, sensation seeking, activity level, impulsivity, and positive emotionality (Rothbart et al., 2001). Several studies have demonstrated direct effects for temperament dimensions related to surgency. In one study, *outgoing temperament*, defined as confidence and eagerness in approaching novel situations, predicted cognitive or academic resilience but not behavioral resilience (Kim-Cohen et al., 2004). Similarly, higher approach distinguished adolescents in residential institutions who were categorized as resilient compared to those with conduct problems (Losel & Bliesener, 1994). In these two studies, higher approach was promotive. However, in another study, surgency appeared to increase vulnerability. Specifically, for children categorized as being serious, minor, or nondelinquents, low surgency predicted nondelinquency, whereas high surgency predicted higher delinquency, over and above the effects of other risk factors (van der Laan et al., 2010). This contradictory pattern of relations across studies suggests that further clarification and differentiation of the construct of surgency is needed, particularly as it relates to positive emotionality.

Positive Emotionality

Although positive emotionality stems from approach or activation systems and is a component of surgency (Rothbart & Bates, 2006), when it is operationalized as smiling, laughter, positive mood, or cheerfulness, positive emotionality operates differently than other indicators of surgency. Positive emotionality is related to higher well-being and social competence (Lengua, 2003), while low positive affect and reduced reward responsiveness are associated with depression (Dennis, 2007; Muris, 2006; Watson, Gamez, & Simms, 2005). In addition, positive emotionality demonstrated additive effects, in that it predicted higher child social competence and self-esteem, over and above the effects of cumulative contextual risk, and also differentiated resilient from vulnerable children (Lengua, 2002).

Self-Regulation

Evidence for the contribution of self-regulation or effortful control in children's resilient or vulnerable responses to stress is mounting. In general, high effortful control has promotive effects, whereas low effortful control is a risk factor (Martel et al., 2009; van der Laan et al., 2010). Effortful control is related to lower internalizing and externalizing problems, and higher social competence, empathy, conscience development, and self-esteem (e.g., Kochanska, 1995; Kochanska, Murray, & Harlan, 2000; Lengua, 2006; Lengua, Honorado, & Bush, 2007; Murray & Kochanska, 2002; Olson et al., 2005; Spinrad et al., 2006; Valiente et al., 2004). Direct effects of self-regulation or effortful control on developmental outcomes and adjustment have been demonstrated with children from low-income/high-risk families (Brody, Dorsey, Forehand, & Armistead, 2002; Buckner, Mezzacappa, & Beardslee, 2003; Li-Grining et al., 2006; Mendez, Fantuzzo, & Cichetti, 2002), over and above the effects of other family and sociodemographic risk factors (Kyrios & Prior, 1990; Lengua, 2002, 2006; Loukas & Roalson, 2006; Miller-Lewis et al., 2006; Olson et al., 2005: van der Laan et al., 2010).

Supportive findings are also seen in studies where self-regulation mediated the effects of other risk factors. For example, the relation of exposure to cumulative risk with child behavior problems was partially mediated by the child's level of adaptability (Ackerman, Izard, Schoff, Youngstrom, & Kogos, 1999). Also, effortful control at 8 years mediated the relations of LBW and head circumference to hyperactivity and behavior problems assessed at 8 years (Schlotz, Jones, Godfrey, & Phillips, 2008).

Summary: Temperament Direct Effects

Temperament is an important additional risk factor to consider when attempting to understand children's response to adversity. Studies have documented the direct contribution of temperament reactivity (fear, frustration) and self-regulation (effortful control) to children's behavior problems, vulnerability, and resilience, over and above the effects of other risk factors.

Temperament as a Moderator of the Effects of Other Risk Factors

As shown in Figure 25.1 temperament can have moderating effects, increasing or decreasing an individual's vulnerability in the face of risk. Several conceptual models for the moderating effects of temperament have been proposed. One early model was *goodness of fit*, which posited that children's adjustment depended on the congruence (fit) of the child's temperament with the predominant characteristics of the child's context, including caregiver interactive styles, values, goals, or cultural demands (Lerner & Lerner, 1994; Thomas & Chess, 1977). This model implies that a particular context or experience could have beneficial effects for one child and detrimental effects for another depending on goodness or poorness of fit. While goodness of fit is an appealing conceptual model, empirical support for this model has been tenuous (Wachs, 2005).

The *differential reactivity* model proposes that children with different individual characteristics vary in their reactivity to the same environmental stressors or supports (Wachs, 1992). For example, higher levels of negative emotionality or difficult temperament characteristics can increase children's vulnerability in the face of adversity through increased reactivity to environmental stressors or decreased reactivity to environmental supports. Conversely, self-regulation or easy temperament can render children relatively resilient in the presence of risk through muted responses to environmental stressors or enhanced responses to environmental supports. Differential reactivity is consistent with diathesis–stress models, in that children with a given temperament risk factor demonstrate greater problems in the presence of stress than do children without that temperament risk factor who experience the same level of stress. It is also consistent with vulnerability models, wherein children with temperament risk factors demonstrate greater adjustment problems regardless of the presence of contextual risk, whereas the level of problems in children without the temperament risk depends on the level of risk exposure.

A subsequent variation of the differential reactivity model is the *differential susceptibility* or *biological sensitivity to context* model (Ellis & Boyce, 2008). As discussed by van IJzendoorn and Bakermans-Kranenburg (Chapter 19, this volume), the core prediction of the differential susceptibility model is that individuals who are high in reactivity are highly susceptible to either risk or promotive influences. In contrast, individuals who are low in reactivity are less affected by either risk or promotive influences. Thus, highly reactive children demonstrate poorer adjustment in negative contexts but better adjustment in positive contexts relative to individuals who are low in reactivity. van IJzendoorn and Bakermans-Kranenburg (Chapter 19, this volume) cite a number of studies in support of the validity of the differential susceptibility model. However, other studies showing increased resilience in response to stress of children with less reactive or easy temperaments are more consistent with the differential reactivity model (Smith & Prior, 1995; Werner & Smith, 1982; Wills, Sandy, Yaeger, & Shinar, 2001). This mixed pattern of findings may reflect actual differences in underlying processes or may result from methodological challenges in comparing models.

Comparison of the differential reactivity and differential susceptibility models requires systematic evaluation of children with contrasting temperaments across contrasting risk versus promotive contexts. At present many of the available studies do not systematically make this comparison, and as such are not directly applicable to model testing. In addition, the combination of statistically significant temperament × risk/support interactions *plus* nonsignificant associations between temperament and risk/support are both necessary to demonstrate the operation of either differential reactivity (Wachs, 1992) or differential susceptibility (van IJzendoorn & Bakermans-Kranenburg, Chapter 19, this volume). When interactions are not directly tested it is difficult to determine whether the contributions of temperament are additive or interactive. However, tests for interactions are highly sensitive to statistical power, which depends, in good part, on sample size (Cronbach, 1991). In studies with small samples it is difficult to determine whether a nonsignificant interaction term means a lack of moderation by temperament or a lack of power. Conceptually, interpreting temperament × risk interactions as evidence for moderation implies that children with different temperaments are reacting differently to the same level of risks or supports. However, if children with different temperaments are actually encountering different levels or types of risks or supports, then we cannot assume that our findings reflect differential reactivity or susceptibility. In this latter case a more parsimonious interpretation would involve temperament-driven reactive covariance. Keeping both models and these methodological issues in mind, we turn to findings on the moderation of risk and promotive influences by individual differences in specific dimensions of child temperament.

Easy–Difficult Temperament

Difficult temperament is expected to impact children's vulnerability or resilience by increasing their sensitivity to adversity or stress, by constraining their stress responses to be inflexible and maladaptive, and by taxing parental caregiving abilities (Davies & Windle, 2001). With some exceptions (e.g., Rosenthal, Wilson, & Futch, 2009), easy–difficult temperament measures consistently distinguish children's responses to adversity or risk and discriminate between children classified as either stress-resilient or stress-affected (Wachs, 2006; Werner & Smith, 1982; Wyman et al., 1991). Overall, children with easy temperaments are more likely to show resilience under stress (Rende & Plomin, 1992; Rutter & Quinton, 1984; Smith & Prior, 1995; Wertlieb, Weigel, Springer, & Feldstein, 1987; Wills et al., 2001), whereas children with difficult temperaments are more likely to be vulnerable when they experience risk conditions including family conflict, adversity, and parental substance use (Guerin, Gottfried, Oliver, & Thomas, 2003; Maziade et al., 1985; Ramos, Guerin, Gottfried, Bathurst, & Oliver, 2005; Sanson, Oberklaid, Pedlow, & Prior, 1991; Tschann, Kaiser, Chesney, Alkon, & Boyce, 1996; Whiteside-Mansell, Bradley, Casey, Fussell, & Conners-Burrow, 2009). However, there is also evidence that the previous pattern of moderating effects of easy–difficult temperament may vary depending on context. As shown by Pluess and Belsky (2009), when child care quality was low, children with a difficult temperament showed higher levels of behavior problems and reduced levels of social competence, but when child care quality was high, children with difficult temperament showed reduced levels of behavior problems and higher social competence.

Negative Emotionality

With some exceptions (e.g., Lengua, 2002), evidence indicates that negative emotionality interacts with risk or adversity to predict adjustment outcomes. For example, negative emotionality amplified the effects of maternal employment transitions on children's behavior problems (Li-Grining et al., 2006). Similarly, the impact of nonstandard maternal work schedules on toddler externalizing and internalizing problems was greater for children who were high in reactivity (Daniel, Grzywacz, Leerkes, Tucker, & Han, 2009).

As noted earlier, negative emotionality is composed of frustration (or irritability) and fear (or inhibition). Very few studies have examined interactions of frustration or irritability with other risk factors, although, as documented earlier, frustration predicts adjustment over and above the effects of other risk factors. One study that examined the interaction between neighborhood risk and irritability found that children high in irritability showed lower social competence regardless of level of neighborhood risk, whereas low-irritability children's social competence depended on level of neighborhood risk, consistent with a vulnerability model (Bush et al., 2010).

While studies have examined moderating effects of fear, the overall pattern of findings is complicated. For example, lower infant fearfulness predicted lower internalizing problems during middle childhood for children experiencing a high-risk neighborhood (Colder, Lengua, Fite, Mott, & Bush, 2006). However, in middle childhood, higher fear predicted higher levels of internalizing regardless of level of neighborhood risk, whereas with lower fear, level of neighborhood risk was associated with level of internalizing problems (Bush et al., 2010). Interestingly, in the same study, higher fear was also related to higher social competence for children in low-risk neighborhoods, but levels of social competence decreased as neighborhood risk increased (Bush et al., 2010). These findings reflect the possibility that fearfulness may be protective in a high-risk neighborhood if it reduces youth exposure to deviant peers, risky behaviors, or dangerous situations, suggestive of a goodness-of-fit model. However, consistent with methodological issues discussed earlier, these findings could result from fearful children's different neighborhood environment rather than a moderating effect of temperament.

Low approach, which might reflect inhibition, was found to predict greater social withdrawal in children except when families were high in conflict, in which case children demonstrated average levels of social withdrawal regardless of their level of approach (Tschann et al., 1996). Such complexities again suggest the possibility of multiple moderators. For example, low shyness at age 5 interacted with harsh discipline at age 5 to predict 17-year-olds' externalizing problems and increases in externalizing problems from ages 5–17 years for girls but not for boys (Leve et al., 2005). Evidence also indicates that while young children who receive less sensitive or responsive care are more likely to show elevated cortisol, this association is particularly strong for children who are high in fear (Gunnar & Donzella, 2002). In summary, fear may operate as a vulnerability or a protective factor, depending on the outcome assessed, the contextual risk factor examined, or the presence of other potential moderators.

Positive Emotionality

At present, very few studies have examined positive affect as a moderator of other risk factors. In one study, positive affect showed additive effects on resilience but did not interact with cumulative risk to predict adjustment (Lengua, 2002). In another study, infant low-positive affect interacted with poor-quality neighborhood to predict greater increases in internalizing problems during middle childhood compared to high-positive affect (Colder et al., 2006). A third study examined promotive temperament, which combined positive affect and task orientation. Promotive temperament was related to lower initial levels of youth substance use and moderated the relations of parent–child conflict and peer and parental substance use to adolescent substance use, such that adolescents higher in promotive temperament were less adversely affected by these risk factors (Wills et al., 2001). Overall, positive affect appears to have a protective effect, mitigating the effects of risk exposure.

Self-Regulation or Effortful Control

Temperament characteristics related to self-regulation, such as flexibility (Losel & Bliesener, 1994; Rutter, 1993), persistence (Mathiesen & Prior, 2006), and effortful control (Lengua, 2002), have been shown to differentiate children identified as resilient or vulnerable. Self-regulation has also been shown to moderate the effects of risk. For example, there is evidence that the detrimental impact of societal violence upon the adjustment of young Kenyan children was significantly greater for children with lower emotional self-regulation than for those with better self-regulation (Kithakye, Morris, Terranova, & Myers, 2010). In addition, task orientation, related to the attention regulation component of effortful control, has been shown to moderate the effects of marital discord (Davies & Windle, 2001) and parent–child conflict (Wills et al., 2001), such that the adverse effects of risk were buffered by higher task orientation. Flexibility might also reflect children's self-regulation and has been shown to buffer the effects of family stress on behavior problems in 3-year-olds (Earls, 1984, cited in Wills et al., 2001). Exposure to indices of risk such as low socioeconomic status (SES) (Veenstra, Oldehinkel, De Winter, Lindenberg, & Ormel, 2006) or maternal and environmental risk variables (Lengua, 2002; Lengua, Bush, Long, Kovacs, & Trancik, 2008) in preadolescent children was related to adjustment problems for children low in effortful control but unrelated to problems for children higher in effortful control. Effortful control moderated the effect of maternal employment transitions on young children's academic and social competence and behavior problems, demonstrating protective effects (Li-Grining et al., 2006). Although some tests of interactions have not shown a protective effect (Olson et al., 2005), the overall pattern of findings indicates that self-regulation, or dimensions of self-regulation such as effortful control, interact with risk, such that higher self-regulation is protective.

Summary: Temperament as a Moderator

The overall pattern of findings indicates that easy–difficult temperament, negative emotionality, and self-regulation emerge as significant moderators of children's responses to risk exposure. At present, less evidence exists for other temperament characteristics, such as positive affect and surgency. Although self-regulation predominantly demonstrates protective effects, interactions of risk with negative emotionality are consistent with a variety of models, including both differential reactivity and differential susceptibility. While there is evidence for temperament acting as a moderator of risk, the specific mechanisms of these interactions are not always clear and present an important direction for future research.

Future Research Directions on Temperament and Risk

Risk Influences Individual Differences in Temperament

It is clear that biological risk factors, such as environmental lead exposure, postnatal malnutrition or iron deficiency, and psychosocial risk factors (e.g., postnatal family stress and maternal depression), can influence the development and behavioral manifestations of temperament. However, more evidence is needed with regard to the impact of other biological risks, such as prenatal exposure to environmental toxins, LBW, prenatal maternal depression, and nutritional deficiencies other than malnutrition or iron deficiency (e.g., B vitamin or zinc deficiency). For psychosocial risk factors, evidence is needed with regard to causality: Are specific patterns of infant temperament a cause or a consequence of increased risk, or is the relation bidirectional? Finally, given evidence on the neural consequences of exposure to toxins, stress, parental depression, or inadequate iron intake, it is very likely that links between risk exposure and temperament are mediated by brain development and brain function. This emphasizes a need for additional research to determine which specific biological and psychosocial risks influence brain function or areas of brain development that are closely related to individual differences in temperament.

Temperament Influences Individual Differences in Risk Exposure and Responses

Studies reviewed here document that individual differences in certain dimensions of temperament evoke more harsh or negative parenting, or elicit more supportive behavior from parents, teachers, and peers. Other studies show that certain temperament characteristics can increase or decrease children's exposure to psychosocial risk factors such as family or life stressors. However, not all studies document such a pattern of association. This may reflect our use of oversimplified models that assume a direct link between temperament and risk exposure. In future research it will be important to identify and integrate potential contextual moderators of this link, including specific caregiver and cultural characteristics. In addition, as noted earlier, directionality is an issue with regard to the nature of links between temperament and infant sleep problems, maternal depression, and parenting. This ambiguity emphasizes the need for longitudinal studies and advanced quantitative methods that can be brought to bear on questions of direction of effects between risk exposure and temperament.

It has also been hypothesized that temperament can influence the nature and degree of "niche seeking," such as the selection of peers and situations that can increase or decrease exposure to an adverse context. At present there is a dearth of research on temperament and active covariance processes, particularly with regard to the question of which temperament dimensions influence selection into what types of context. This also is an important topic where more research is needed. Finally, particularly relevant to our understanding of multiple-mediation processes would be additional research on the mechanisms through which temperament predisposes children to specific appraisal, coping, or emotion regulation strategies.

Temperament Functions as a Direct Risk Factor

As discussed earlier, individual differences in some temperament dimensions can function as risk or promotive factors, either in isolation or over and above the impact of other risk or promotive factors. From the evidence reviewed, children high in negative affect or difficult temperament tend to have higher adjustment problems regardless of their level of risk exposure, but when exposed to risk, their problems can be more pronounced. Evidence also indicates that there may be value in separating out components of negative affectivity or difficult temperament as they might operate differently in some cases. For example, fearfulness appears to confer both risk and promotive effects. Fear increases the risk for internalizing problems, particularly anxiety, in response to risk but also reduces the risk for antisocial behaviors and may predict greater social competence. Comprehensive models encompassing these complex outcomes need to be developed.

There is less research available on whether temperament promotes positive or adaptive outcomes. Evidence reviewed does show that self-regulation or effortful control operates as a vulnerability factor when it is low and a promotive factor when it is high. The evidence for promotive effects of effortful control has led to increased examination of effortful control in the context of disadvantage or adversity. Understanding the effects of adversity on developing effortful control is an important next step in this area of research. In addition, only limited attention has been given to other, potentially promotive aspects of temperament, such as positive emotionality. This emphasizes the need for future research to include both positive and negative indicators of adjustment and to test whether positive emotionality has both protective and promotive effects in the context of adversity. Furthermore, as discussed below, future research needs to utilize more complex models that include multiple intervening steps in the pathways linking risk or promotive dimensions of temperament to developmental outcomes.

Temperament as a Moderator of Risk

Evidence reviewed in this chapter also documents that certain dimensions of temperament accentuate or attenuate the impact of risk factors. However, studies have not uncovered the underlying processes involved. A critical direction for future research is to elucidate the mechanisms by which temperament exacerbates or mitigates the impact of adversity or stress.

In addition to identifying general moderating mechanisms, investigation also is needed on more narrowly focused domain-specific models of processes underlying the moderating effects of temperament for specific outcome domains. One such domain-specific model is the effect of temperament on the emergence of cognitive vulnerabilities for psychopathology, such as attribution biases, dysfunctional attitudes, negative cognitive styles, and rumination (Halvorsen et al., 2009; Hankin et al., 2009; Hayden, Klein, Durbin, & Olino, 2006). It will be important to go beyond direct linkages to identify mechanisms through which temperament interacts with stress or risk in accounting for the emergence of cognitive vulnerabilities. For example, Mezulis, Hyde, and Abramson (2006) demonstrated that withdrawal negativity, which included temperament fearfulness, sadness, distress to novelty, and sensitivity, interacted with negative life events to predict a greater likelihood of demonstrating negative cognitive styles that present a risk for depression. More studies of this type are needed.

It will also be important to understand how self-regulation or effortful control interacts with reactivity to predict cognitive vulnerabilities, as the effects of negative affect might be mitigated by higher effortful control. In one study effortful control was shown to moderate the relations of both negative affectivity and positive affectivity to depressive symptoms, as well as to mediate the relation of negative affect to rumination in predicting depressive symptoms, particularly for youth low in effortful control (Verstraeten, Vasey, Raes, & Bijttebier, 2009). Studies examining moderated mediation are models for understanding the complicated processes that account for the vulnerability or resilience to psychopathology afforded by certain temperament characteristics.

Developmental Timing of Risk

Evidence of the role of temperament in individuals' responses to adversity exists at most developmental stages, from infancy though adolescence. However, the issue of developmental timing of risk exposure is important for studies on both the impact of risk exposure on subsequent temperament and the impact of temperament on children's adjustment. For example, there is ample evidence that low income or poverty is related to lower effortful control (Evans & English, 2002; Hughes, Ensor, Wilson, & Graham, 2010; Lengua, 2002, 2006; Li-Grining, 2006; Mezzacappa, 2004), and that effortful control is protective in relation to risk associated with low income (Lengua, 2002; Veenstra et al., 2006). However, studies also have shown that low income might predict smaller increases in effortful control during the preschool years, when effortful control is developing dramatically (Lengua et al., 2007), but may not be related to developmental changes during the preadolescent period (King, Lengua, & Monohan, in press). This timing effect may reflect the rapid developmental increase in effortful control in the preschool years. Given evidence that the impact of risk on different central nervous system areas depends, in part, on timing of risk exposure (Fox, Levitt, & Nelson, 2010), these findings also suggest that the developmental timing of risk exposure might have different implications for different neural–temperament systems. Fruitful directions for future research are to increase our understanding of the effects of developmental timing of experiences of risk and to examine the interplay among brain development, risk, and temperament at specific time periods.

The Role of Multiple Pathways and Moderators

Much of the current research on temperament and risk involves a single stage, searching for direct links in risk → temperament, temperament → risk, and temperament as risk → developmental outcomes. However, single-stage strategies may not reflect the complexity of pathways linking temperament, risk, and development. Pathways between temperament, risk, and developmental outcomes may involve multiple intervening steps, as seen in Figure 25.2. Alternatively, links between temperament and risk may be moderated by nontemperament variables such as cognitive vulnerabilities (Verstraeten et al., 2009), maternal beliefs, or home chaos (Corapci & Wachs, 2002). Particularly when results are inconsistent, it will be important for future research to consider nontemperament variables that can serve either as intervening steps between temperament and outcome or as moderators of the relation between temperament and risk. Multistage models also may be useful in clarifying the nature of links between surgency and resilience or vulnerability. Similarly, it will be important to look for variables, such as the postnatal rearing environment, that could moderate the association between LBW and temperament.

Clinical Implications

An important aspect of clinical work involves using individual patterns of temperament to identify children at risk for various developmental problems (see Klein et al., Chapter 26, and Tackett et al., Chapter 27, this volume). However, there is very little information on whether individual differences in temperament may influence how children at risk react to clinical interventions. It has been hypothesized that children with a difficult temperament may be more resistant to efforts to promote better child sleep patterns (Hayes, Parker, Sallinen, & Davare, 2001), or that children with a temperament pattern characterized by high-intensity negative moods may be more resistant to treatment for obesity (Carey, Hegvik, & McDevitt, 1988). However, within the framework of the differential susceptibility hypothesis, such children may benefit more if they do accept treatment. Evidence on this issue would be important both theoretically and in terms of tailoring interventions to match child characteristics.

Conclusion

Across a variety of approaches to conceptualizing and operationalizing temperament, across risk factors, and across outcomes, evidence points to temperament being shaped by exposure to risk, contributing to children's exposure to risk, directly predicting adjustment, and moderating the impact of risk and promotive influences upon development. At this point, the direct and moderating effects of temperament have the greatest support and are increasingly articulated for specific dimensions of temperament. However, we need to know far more about the interplay of temperament, risk, and promotive influences. What is needed are comprehensive, large-scale, longitudinal studies derived from a bioecological model of development, which include a comprehensive assessment of multiple specific dimensions of temperament and risk, and promotive factors. The goal of such research would be to uncover the specific processes through which temperament contributes to children's vulnerable or resilient responses to adversity.

Further Reading

Lengua, L. J. (2009). Effortful control in the context of socioeconomic and psychosocial risk. *APA Psychological Science Agenda*, 23(1). Available at www.apa.org/science/about/psa/2009/01/lengua.aspx.

Luthar, S. (2006). Resilience in development: A synthesis of research across 5 decades. In D. Cicchetti & D. Cohen (Eds.), *Developmental psychopathology: Vol. 3. Risk, disorder and adaptation* (2nd ed., pp. 739–795). Hoboken, NJ: Wiley.

Wachs, T. D. (2006). Contributions of temperament to buffering and sensitization processes in children's development. *Annals of the New York Academy of Sciences*, 1094, 28–39.

References

Ackerman, B., Izard, C., Schoff, K., Youngstrom, E., & Kogos, J. (1999). Contextual risk, caregiver emotionality and the problem behaviors of six and seven-year-old children from economically disadvantaged families. *Child Development*, 70, 1415–1427.

Ashworth, A., Morris, S., Lira, P., & Grantham-McGregor, S. (1998). Zinc supplementation, mental development and behaviour in low birth weight term infants in northeast Brazil. *European Journal of Clinical Nutrition*, 52, 223–227.

Baker-Henningham, H., Hamadani, J., Huda, S., & Grantham-McGregor, S. (2009). Undernourished children have different temperaments than better-nourished children in rural Bangladesh. *Journal of Nutrition*, 139, 1765–1771.

Bates, J., Viken, R., Alexander, D., Beyers, J., & Stockton, L. (2002). Sleep and adjustment in preschool children: Sleep diary reports by mothers relate to behavior reports by teachers. *Child Development*, 73, 62–74.

Blair, C., & Diamond, A. (2008). Biological processes in prevention and intervention: The promotion of self-regulation as a means of preventing school failure. *Development and Psychopathology*, 20, 899–911.

Boergers, J., Hart, C., Owens, J., & Streisand, R. (2007). Child sleep disorders: Associations with parental sleep deprivation and daytime sleepiness. *Journal of Family Psychology*, 21, 88–94.

Bouma, E. M. C., Ormel, J., Verhulst, F. C., & Oldehinkel, A. J. (2008). Stressful life events and depressive problems in early adolescent boys and girls: The influence of parental depression, temperament and family environment. *Journal of Affective Disorders*, 105, 185–193.

Brody, G., Dorsey, S., Forehand, R., & Armistead, L. (2002). Unique and protective contributions of parenting and classroom processes to the adjustment of African American children living in single-parent families. *Child Development*, 73, 274–286

Bronfenbrenner, U., & Morris, P. (1998). The ecology of developmental processes. In W. Damon & R. Lerner (Eds.), *Handbook of child psychology* (5th ed., Vol. 1, pp. 992–1028). New York: Wiley.

Bruder-Costello, B., Warner, V., Talati, A., Nomura, Y., Bruder, G., & Weissman, M. (2007). Temperament among offspring at high and low risk for depression. *Psychiatry Research*, 153, 145–151.

Buckner, J. C., Mezzacappa, E., & Beardslee, W. R. (2003). Characteristics of resilient youths living in poverty: The role of self-regulatory processes. *Development and Psychopathology*, 15, 139–162.

Buckner, J. C., Mezzacappa, E., & Beardslee, W. R. (2009). Self-regulation and its relations to adaptive functioning in low income youths. *American Journal of Orthopsychiatry*, 79, 19–30.

Bush, N., Lengua, L. J., & Colder, C. R. (2010). Temperament as a moderator of neighborhood effects: Predicting children's adjustment. *Journal of Applied Developmental Psychology*, 31, 351–361.

Carey, W., Hegvik, R., & McDevitt, S. (1988). Temperamental factors associated with rapid weight gain and obesity in middle childhood. *Journal of Developmental and Behavioral Pediatrics*, 9, 194–198.

Carson, D., & Bittner, M. (2001) Temperament and school-aged children's coping abilities and responses to stress. *Journal of Genetic Psychology*, 155, 289–302.

Chisholm, K. (1988). A three year follow-up of attachment and indiscriminate friendliness in children adopted from Romanian orphanages. *Child Development*, 69, 1092–1106.

Colder, C. R., Lengua, L. J., Fite, P. J., Mott, J. A., & Bush, N. R. (2006). Temperament in context: Infant temperament moderates the relationship between perceived neighborhood quality and behavior problems. *Journal of Applied Developmental Psychology*, 27, 456–467.

Compas, B., Connor-Smith, J., & Jaser, S. (2004). Temperament, stress reactivity, and coping:

implications for depression in childhood and adolescence. *Journal of Clinical Child and Adolescent Psychology, 33*, 21–31.

Corapci, F. (2008). The role of child temperament on Head Start preschoolers social competence in the context of cumulative risk. *Journal of Applied Developmental Psychology, 29*, 1–16.

Corapci, F., & Wachs, T. D. (2002). Does parental mood or efficacy mediate the influence of environmental chaos upon parenting behavior? *Merrill–Palmer Quarterly, 48*, 182–201.

Creemers, H. E., Dijkstra, J. K., Vollebergh, W. A. M., Ormel, J., Verhulst, F. C., & Huizink, A. C. (2010). Predicting life-time and regular cannabis use during adolescence: The roles of temperament and peer substance use: The TRAILS study. *Addiction, 105*, 699–708.

Cronbach, L. (1991). Emerging views on methodology. In T. D. Wachs & R. Plomin (Eds.), *Conceptualization and measurement of organism–environment interaction* (pp. 87–104). Washington, DC: American Psychological Association.

Daniel, S., Grzywacz, J., Leerkes, E., Tucker, J., & Han, W. (2009). Non-standard maternal work schedules during infancy: Implications for children's early behavior problems. *Infant Behavior and Development, 32*, 195–207.

Davies, P., & Windle, M. (2001). Interparental discord and adolescent adjustment trajectories: The potentiating and protective role of intrapersonal attributes. *Child Development, 72*, 1163–1178.

DeLeon, C., & Karraker, K. (2007). Intrinsic and extrinsic factors associated with night waking in 9-month old infants. *Infant Behavior and Development, 30*, 596–605.

Dennis, T. (2007). Interactions between emotion regulation strategies and affective style: Implications for trait anxiety versus depressed mood. *Motivation and Emotion, 31*, 200–207.

Durbin, C., Klein, D., Hayden, E., Buckley, M., & Moerk, K. (2005). Temperamental emotionality in preschoolers and parental mood disorders. *Journal of Abnormal Psychology, 114*, 28–37.

Eisenberg, N., Spinrad, T. L., Fabes, R. A., Reiser, M., Cumberland, A., Shepard, S. A., et al. (2004). The relations of effortful control and impulsivity to children's resiliency and adjustment. *Child Development, 75*, 25–46.

Ellis, B. J., & Boyce, W. T. (2008). Biological sensitivity to context. *Current Directions in Psychological Science, 17*, 183–187.

Evans, G. W., & English, K. (2002). The environment of poverty: Multiple stressor exposure, psychophysiological stress, and socioemotional adjustment. *Child Development, 73*, 1238–1248.

Fehlings, D., Weiss, S., & Stephens, D. (2001). Frequent night awakenings in infants and preschool children referred to a sleep disorders clinic: The role of non-adaptive sleep associations. *Children's Health Care, 30*, 43–55.

Feldman, R., Granat, A., Pariente, C., Kanety, H., Kuint, J., & Gilboa-Schechtman, E. (2009). Maternal depression and anxiety across the postpartum year and infant social engagement, fear regulation, and stress reactivity. *Journal of the American Academy of Child and Adolescent Psychiatry, 48*, 919–927.

Fiese, B., Winter, M., Anbar, R., & Sliwinski, M. (2007). Nighttime waking in children with Asthma: An exploratory study of daily fluctuations in family climate. *Journal of Family Psychology, 21*, 95–103.

Fox, S. E., Levitt, P., & Nelson, C. A. (2010). How the timing and quality of early experiences influence the development of brain architecture. *Child Development, 81*, 28–40.

Frick, P., & Morris, A. (2004). Temperament and developmental pathways to conduct problems. *Journal of Clinical Child and Adolescent Psychology, 33*, 54–68.

Galler, J., Harrison, R., Ramsey, F., Butler, S., & Forde, V. (2004). Postpartum maternal mood, feeding practices and infant temperament in Barbados. *Infant Behavior and Development, 27*, 267–287.

Gartstein, M. A., & Bateman, A. E. (2008). Early manifestations of childhood depression: Influences of infant temperament and parental depressive symptoms. *Infant and Child Development, 17*, 223–248.

Georgieff, M. (2007). Nutrition and the developing brain: Nutrient priorities and measurement. *American Journal of Clinical Nutrition, 85*(Suppl. 2), 614s–620s.

Glynn, L., Davis, E., Schetter, C., Chicz-DeMet, A., Hobel, C., & Sandman, C. (2007). Postnatal maternal cortisol levels predict temperament in healthy breastfed infants. *Early Human Development, 83*, 675–681.

Gorman, K., Lourie, A., & Choudhury, N. (2001). Differential patterns of development: The interaction of birth weight, temperament, and maternal behavior. *Journal of Developmental and Behavioral Pediatrics, 22*, 366–375.

Gregory, A., Eley, T., O'Connor, T., Rijsdijk, F., & Plomin, R. (2005). Family influences on the association between sleep problems and anxiety in a large sample of pre-school aged twins. *Personality and Individual Differences, 39*, 1337–1348.

Guerin, D., Gottfried, A., Oliver, P., & Thomas, C. (2003). *Temperament: Infancy through adolescence.* New York: Kluwer Academic Press.

Gump, B., Stewart, P., Reihman, J., Lonky, E., Darvill, T., Parsons, P., et al. (2008). Low-level prenatal and postnatal blood lead exposure and adrenocortical responses to acute stress in children. *Environmental Health Perspectives, 116*, 249–255.

Gunnar, M., & Donzella, B. (2002). Social regulation of the cortisol levels in early human development. *Psychoneuroendocrinology, 27,* 199–220.

Hackman, D., Farah, M., & Meaney, M. (2010). Socioeconomic status and the brain: Mechanistic insights from human and animal research. *Nature Reviews Neuroscience, 11,* 651–659.

Halvorsen, M., Wang, C. E., Richter, J., Myrland, I., Pedersen, S. K., Eisemann, M., et al. (2009). Early maladaptive schemas, temperament and character traits in clinically depressed and previously depressed subjects. *Clinical Psychology and Psychotherapy, 16,* 394–407.

Hanington, L., Ramchandani, P., & Stein, A. (2010). Parental depression and child temperament: Assessing child to parent effects in a longitudinal population study. *Infant Behavior and Development, 33,* 88–95.

Hankin, B. L., Oppenheimer, C., Jenness, J., Barrocas, A., Shapero, B. G., & Goldband, J. (2009). Developmental origins of cognitive vulnerabilities to depression: Review of processes contributing to stability and change across time. *Journal of Clinical Psychology, 65,* 1327–1338.

Hayden, E. P., Klein, D. N., Durbin, C. E., & Olino, T. M. (2006). Positive emotionality at age 3 predicts cognitive styles in 7-year-old children. *Development and Psychopathology, 18,* 409–423.

Hayes, M., Parker, K., Sallinen, B., & Davare, A. (2001). Bedsharing, temperament and sleep disturbance in early childhood. *Sleep, 24,* 657–662.

Henderson, H., & Wachs, T. D. (2007). Temperament theory and the study of cognition–emotion interactions across development. *Developmental Review, 27,* 396–427.

Hubbs-Tait, L., Kennedy, T., Droke, E., Belanger, D., & Parker, J. (2007). Zinc, iron and lead: Relations to Head Start children's cognitive scores and teacher's rating of behavior. *Journal of the American Dietetic Association, 107,* 128–133.

Hubbs-Tait, L., Nation, J., Krebs, N., & Bellinger, D. (2005). Neurotoxicants, micronutrients, and social environments: Individual and combined effects on children's development. *Psychological Science in the Public Interest, 6*(3), 57–121.

Hughes, C., Ensor, R., Wilson, A., & Graham, A. (2010). Tracking executive function across the transition to school: A latent variable approach. *Developmental Neuropsychology, 35,* 20–36.

Huot, R. L., Brennan, P. A., Stowe, Z. N., Plotsky, P. M., & Walker, E. F. (2004). Negative affect in offspring of depressed mothers is predicted by infant cortisol levels at 6 months and maternal depression during pregnancy, but not postpartum. In R. Yehuda & B. McEwen (Eds.), *Biobehavioral stress response: Protective and damaging effects* (pp. 234–236). New York: New York Academy of Sciences Press.

Hwang, A., Soong, W., & Liao, H. (2009). Influences of biological risk at birth and temperament on development at toddler and preschool ages. *Child: Care, Health and Development, 35,* 817–825.

Ispa, J., Fine, M., & Thornburg, K. (2002). Maternal personality as a moderator of relations between difficult infant temperament and attachment security in low-income families. *Infant Mental Health Journal, 23,* 130–144.

Jacobson, J., Jacobson, S., & Humphrey, H. (1990). Effects of exposure to PCBs and related compounds on growth and activity in children. *Neurotoxicology and Teratology, 12,* 319–326.

Kilmer, R. P., Cowen, E. L., & Wyman, P. A. (2001). A micro-level analysis of developmental, parenting, and family milieu variables that differentiate stress-resilient and stress-affected children. *Journal of Community Psychology, 29,* 391–416.

Kim-Cohen, J., Moffitt, T. E., Caspi, A., & Taylor, A. (2004). Genetic and environmental processes in young children's resilience and vulnerability to socioeconomic deprivation. *Child Development, 75,* 651–668.

King, K. J., Lengua, L. J., & Monohan, K. (in press). Individual differences in the development of self-regulation during pre-adolescence: Connections to context and adjustment. *Journal of Abnormal Child Psychology.*

King, K. M., Molina, B. S. G., & Chassin, L. (2008). A state–trait model of negative life event occurrence in adolescence: Predictors of stability in the occurrence of stressors. *Journal of Clinical Child and Adolescent Psychology, 37,* 848–859.

Kithakye, M., Morris, A., Terranova, M., & Myers, S. (2010). The Kenyan political conflict and children's adjustment. *Child Development, 81,* 1114–1128.

Kochanska, G. (1995). Children's temperament, mothers' discipline, and security of attachment: Multiple pathways to emerging internalization. *Child Development, 66,* 597–615.

Kochanska, G., Coy, K., & Murray, K. (2001). The development of self-regulation in the first four years of life. *Child Development, 72,* 1091–1111.

Kochanska, G., Murray, K., & Harlan, E. (2000). Effortful control in early childhood: Continuity and change, antecedents and implications for social development. *Developmental Psychology, 36,* 220–232.

Krishnakumar, A., & Black, M. (2002). Longitudinal predictors of competence among African-American children: The role of distal and proximal risk factors. *Journal of Applied Developmental Psychology, 23,* 237–266.

Kyrios, M., & Prior, M. (1990). Temperament, stress and family factors in behavioural adjustment of 3-5-year-old children. *International Journal of Behavioral Development, 13,* 67–93.

Larroque, B., Tich, S., Guedeney, A., Marchand,

L., Burguet, A., & the Epipage Study Group. (2005). Temperament at 9 months of very preterm infants born at less than 29 weeks gestation: The Epipage Study. *Developmental and Behavioral Pediatrics, 26,* 48–55.

Lecours, A., Mandujano, M., & Romero, G. (2001). Ontogeny of brain and cognition: Relevance to nutrition research. *Nutrition Reviews, 59*(Suppl.), s7–s11.

Lengua, L. J. (2002). The contribution of emotionality and self-regulation to the understanding of children's response to multiple risk. *Child Development, 73,* 144–161.

Lengua, L. J. (2003). Associations among emotionality, self-regulation, adjustment problems and positive adjustment in middle childhood. *Journal of Applied Developmental Psychology, 24,* 595–618.

Lengua, L. J. (2006). Growth in temperament and parenting as predictors of adjustment during children's transition to adolescence. *Developmental Psychology, 42,* 819–832.

Lengua, L. J., Bush, N. R., Long, A. C., Kovacs, E. A., & Trancik, A. M. (2008). Effortful control as a moderator of the relation between contextual risk factors and growth in adjustment problems. *Development and Psychopathology, 20,* 509–528.

Lengua, L. J., Honorado, E., & Bush, N. (2007). Cumulative risk and parenting as predictors of effortful control and social competence in preschool children. *Journal of Applied Developmental Psychology, 28,* 40–55.

Lengua, L. J., & Kovacs, E. A. (2005). Bidirectional associations between temperament and parenting, and the prediction of adjustment problems in middle childhood. *Journal of Applied Developmental Psychology, 26,* 21–38.

Lengua, L. J., & Long, A. C. (2002). The role of emotionality and self-regulation in the appraisal-coping process: Tests of direct and moderating effects. *Journal of Applied Developmental Psychology, 23,* 471–493.

Lengua, L. J., & Sandler, I. N. (1996). Self-regulation as a moderator of the relation between coping and symptomatology in children of divorce. *Journal of Abnormal Child Psychology, 24,* 681–701.

Lerner, J. V., & Lerner, R. M. (1994). Explorations of the goodness-of-fit model in early adolescence. In W. B. Carey & S. McDevitt (Eds.), *Prevention and early intervention: Individual differences as risk factors for the mental health of children: A festschrift for Stella Chess and Alexander Thomas* (pp. 161–169). Philadelphia: Brunner/Mazel.

Leve, L., Kim, H., & Pears, K. (2005). Childhood temperament and family environment as predictors of internalizing and externalizing trajectories from ages 5–17. *Journal of Abnormal Child Psychology, 33,* 505–520.

Li-Grining, C. (2006). Effortful control among low-income preschoolers in three cities: Stability, change, and individual differences. *Developmental Psychology, 43,* 208–222.

Li-Grining, C. P., Votruba-Drzal, E., Bachman, H. J., & Chase-Lansdale, L. (2006). Are certain preschoolers at risk in the era of welfare reform?: The moderating role of children's temperament. *Children and Youth Services Review, 28,* 1102–1123.

Lonigan, C., Vasey, M. W., Phillips, B. M., & Hazen, R. A. (2004). Temperament, anxiety, and the processing of threat-relevant stimuli. *Journal of Clinical Child and Adolescent Psychology, 33,* 8–20.

Losel, F., & Bliesener, T. (1994). Some high-risk adolescents do not develop conduct problems: A study of protective factors. *International Journal of Behavioral Development, 17,* 753–777.

Loukas, A., & Roalson, L. A. (2006). Family environment, effortful control, and adjustment among European American and Latino early adolescents. *Journal of Early Adolescence, 26,* 432–455.

Lozoff, B., Beard, J., Connor, J., Felt, B., Georgieff, M., & Schallert, T. (2006). Long-lasting neural and behavioral effects of iron deficiency in infancy. *Nutrition Reviews, 64*(Suppl.), s34–s43.

Luthar, S., Cicchetti, D., & Becker, B. (2000). The construct of resilience: A critical evaluation and guidelines for future work. *Child Development, 71,* 543–562.

Martel, M., Pierce, L., Nigg, J., Jester, J., Adams, K., Puttler, L., et al. (2009). Temperament pathways to childhood disruptive behavior and adolescent substance abuse: Testing a cascade model. *Journal of Abnormal Child Psychology, 37,* 363–373.

Martinez-Torteya, C., Bogat, G. A., von Eye, A., & Levendosky, A. A. (2009). Resilience among children exposed to domestic violence: The role of risk and protective factors. *Child Development, 80,* 562–577.

Masten, A., & Obradovic, J. (2006). Competence and resilience in development. *Annals of the New York Academy of Sciences, 1094,* 13–27.

Matheny, A., & Phillips, K. (2001). Temperament and context: Correlates of home environment with temperament continuity and change, newborn to 30 months. In T. D. Wachs & G. Kohnstamm (Eds.), *Temperament in context* (pp. 81–102). Mahwah, NJ: Erlbaum.

Mathiesen, K., & Prior, M. (2006). The impact of temperament factors and family functioning on resilience processes from infancy to school age. *European Journal of Developmental Psychology, 3,* 357–387.

Maziade, M., Caperaa, P., Laplante, B., Boudreault, M., Thivierge, J., Cote, R., et al. (1985). Value of difficult temperament among 7-year-olds in the general population for predicting psychiatric diagnosis at age 12. *American Journal of Psychiatry, 142,* 943–946.

McGrath, J., Records, K., & Rice, M. (2008). Maternal depression and infant temperament characteristics. *Infant Behavior and Development, 31,* 71–80.

Meeks-Gardner, J., Grantham-McGregor, S., Himes, J., & Chang, S. (1999). Behaviour and development of stunted and non-stunted Jamaican children. *Journal of Child Psychology and Psychiatry, 40,* 819–827.

Meltzer, L., & Mindell, J. (2007). Relationship between child sleep disturbances and maternal sleep, mood and parenting stress: A pilot study. *Journal of Family Psychology, 21,* 67–73.

Mendelsohn, A., Dreyer, B., Fierman, A., Rosen, C., Legano, L., Kruger, H., et al. (1998). Low-level lead exposure and behavior in early childhood. *Pediatrics, 101,* 464–465.

Mendez, J., Fantuzzo, J., & Cicchetti, D. (2002). Profiles of social competence among low-income African American preschool children. *Child Development, 73,* 1085–1100.

Mezulis, A. H., Hyde, J. S., & Abramson, L. Y. (2006). The developmental origins of cognitive vulnerability to depression: Temperament, parenting, and negative life events in childhood as contributors to negative cognitive style. *Developmental Psychology, 42,* 1012–1025.

Mezzacappa, E. (2004). Alerting, orienting, and executive attention: Developmental properties and sociodemographic correlates in an epidemiological sample of young, urban children. *Child Development, 75,* 1373–1386.

Miller-Lewis, L. R., Baghurst, P. A., Sawyer, M. G., Prior, M. R., Clark, J. J., Arney, F. M., et al. (2006). Early childhood externalizing behavior problems: Child, parenting, and family-related predictors over time. *Journal of Abnormal Child Psychology, 34,* 891–906.

Morrell, J., & Steele, H. (2003). The role of attachment security, temperament, maternal perception and care-giving behavior in persistent infant sleeping problems. *Infant Mental Health Journal, 24,* 447–468.

Muris, P. (2006). The pathogenesis of childhood anxiety disorders: Considerations from a developmental psychopathology perspective. *International Journal of Behavioral Development, 30,* 5–11.

Murray, K., & Kochanska, G. (2002). Effortful control: Factor structure and relation to externalizing and internalizing behaviors. *Journal of Abnormal Child Psychology, 30,* 503–514.

Murray, L., Halligan, S., Goodyer, I., & Herbert, J. (2010). Disturbances in early parenting of depressed mothers and cortisol secretion in offspring: A preliminary study. *Journal of Affective Disorders, 122,* 218–223.

Myers, G., Davidson, P., Cox, C., Shamlaye, C., Palumbo, D., Cerrichiari, E., et al. (2003). Prenatal methylmercury exposure from ocean fish consumption in the Seychelles Child Development Study. *Lancet, 361,* 1686–1692.

Nigg, J. T. (2006). Temperament and developmental psychopathology. *Journal of Child Psychology and Psychiatry, 47,* 395–422.

Novosad, C., Freudigman, K., & Thoman, E. (1999). Sleep patterns in newborns and temperament at eight months: A preliminary study. *Journal of Developmental and Behavioral Pediatrics, 20,* 99–105.

Olafsen, K., Kaaresen, P., Handegard, B., Ulvund, S., Dahl, L., & Renning, J. (2008). Maternal ratings of infant regulatory competence from 6 to 12 months: Influence of perceived stress, birthweight and intervention: A randomized controlled trial. *Infant Behavior and Development, 31,* 408–421.

Olino, T., Klein, D., Dyson, M., & Rose, S. (2010). Temperament emotionality in preschool-aged children and depressive disorders in parents: Associations in a large community sample. *Journal of Abnormal Psychology, 119,* 468–478.

Olson, S. L., Sameroff, A. J., Kerr, D. C. R., Lopez, N. L., & Wellman, H. M. (2005). Developmental foundations of externalizing problems in young children: The role of effortful control. *Development and Psychopathology, 17,* 25–45.

Padich, R., Dietrich, K., & Pearson, D. (1985). Attention activity level on lead exposure at 18 months. *Environmental Research, 38,* 137–143.

Parritz, R. (1996). A descriptive analysis of toddler coping in challenging circumstances. *Infant Behavior and Development, 19,* 171–180.

Pesonen, A., Raikkonen, K., Heinonen, K., Komsi, N., Jarvenpaa, A., & Strandberg, E. (2007). A transactional model of temperamental development: Evidence of a relationship between child temperament and maternal stress over five years. *Social Development, 17,* 326–340.

Pesonen, A., Raikkonen, K., Kajantie, E., Heinonen, K., Strandberg, T., & Jarvenpaa, A. (2006). Fetal programming of temperamental negative affectivity among children born healthy at term. *Developmental Psychobiology, 48,* 633–643.

Pesonen, A., Raikkonen, K., Strandberg, T., & Jarvenpaa, A. (2005). Continuity of maternal stress from the pre-to the postnatal period: Associations with infants' positive, negative and overall emotional reactivity. *Infant Behavior and Development, 28,* 36–47.

Pesonen, A., Raikkonen, K., Strandberg, T., & Jarvenpaa, A. (2006). Do gestational age and weight for gestational age predict concordance in parental perceptions of infant temperament? *Journal of Pediatric Psychology, 31,* 331–336.

Pluess, M., & Belsky, J. (2009). Differential susceptibility to rearing experience: The case of childcare. *Journal of Child Psychology and Psychiatry, 50*, 396–404.

Pollitt, E., Saco-Pollitt, C., Jahari, A., Husaini, M., & Huang, J. (2000). Effects of an energy and micronutrient supplement on mental development and behaviour under natural conditions in undernourished children in Indonesia. *European Journal of Clinical Nutrition, 54*(Suppl.), s80–s90.

Rahmanifar, A., Kirksey, A., Wachs, T. D., McCabe, G., Bishry, Z., Galal, O., et al. (1993). Diet during lactation associated with infant behavior and caregiver infant interaction in a semirural Egyptian village. *Journal of Nutrition, 123*, 164–175.

Ramos, M. C., Guerin, D. W., Gottfried, A. W., Bathurst, K., & Oliver, P. H. (2005). Family conflict and children's behavior problems: The moderating role of child temperament. *Structural Equations Modeling, 12*, 278–298.

Rende, R., & Plomin, R. (1992). Relations between first grade stress, temperament, and behavior problems. *Journal of Applied Developmental Psychology, 13*, 435–446.

Rosenthal, B. S., Wilson, W. C., & Futch, F. A. (2009). Trauma, protection and distress in late adolescence: A multi-determinant approach. *Adolescence, 44*, 693–703.

Rothbart, M., Ahadi, S., Hershey, K., & Fisher, P. (2001). Investigations of temperament at three to seven years: The Children's Behavior Questionnaire. *Child Development, 72*, 1394–1408.

Rothbart, M., & Bates, J. (2006). Temperament. In N. Eisenberg, N. Damon, & R. Lerner (Eds.), *Handbook of child psychology: Vol. 3. Social, emotional, and personality development* (6th ed., pp. 99–166). Hoboken, NJ: Wiley.

Rutter, M. (1993). Developmental psychopathology as a research perspective. In D. Magnusson & P. Casaer (Eds.), *Longitudinal research on individual development* (pp. 127–152). Cambridge, UK: Cambridge University Press.

Rutter, M., & Quinton, D. (1984). Parental psychiatric disorder: Effects on children. *Psychological Medicine, 14*, 853–880.

Rutter, M., Sonuga-Barke, E., Beckett, C., Castle, J., Kreppner, J., Kumsta, R., et al. (2010). Deprivation-specific psychological patterns: Effects of institutional deprivation. *Monographs of the Society for Research in Child Development, 75*, 1–20.

Sameroff, A., Bartko, W., Baldwin, A., Baldwin, C., & Seifer, R. (1998). Family and social influences on the development of competence. In M. Lewis & C. Feiring (Eds.), *Families, risk and competence* (pp. 161–186). Mahwah, NJ: Erlbaum.

Sameroff, A., Gutman, L., & Peck, S. (2003). Adaptation among youths facing multiple risks: Prospective research findings. In S. Luthar (Ed.), *Resilience and vulnerability: Adaptation in the context of childhood adversities* (pp. 364–391). New York: Cambridge University Press.

Sanson, A., Oberklaid, F., Pedlow, R., & Prior, M. (1991). Risk indicators: Assessment of infancy predictors of pre-school behavioural maladjustment. *Journal of Child Psychology and Psychiatry, 32*, 609–626.

Scher, A., Epstein, R., Sadeh, A., Tirosh, E., & Lavie, P. (1992). Toddlers sleep and temperament: Reporting bias or a valid link?: A research note. *Journal of Child Psychology and Psychiatry, 33*, 1249–1254.

Schlotz, W., Jones, A., Godfrey, K., & Phillips, D. (2008). Effortful control mediates associations of fetal growth with hyperactivity and behavioural problems in 7-to 9-year-old children. *Journal of Child Psychology and Psychiatry, 49*, 1228–1236.

Shiner, R., & Caspi, A. (2003). Personality differences in childhood and adolescence: Measurement, development, and consequences. *Journal of Child Psychology and Psychiatry, 44*, 2–32.

Smith, J., & Prior, M. (1995). Temperament and stress resilience in school-age children: A within-families study. *Journal of the American Academy of Child and Adolescent Psychiatry, 34*(2), 168–179.

Sobolewski, A., Strelau, J., & Zawadzki, B. (2001). The temperamental determinants of stressors as life changes. *European Psychologist, 6*, 287–295.

Spinrad, T. L., Eisenberg, N., Cumberland, A., Fabes, R. A., Valiente, C., Shepard, S. A., et al. (2006). Relation of emotion-related regulation to children's social competence: A longitudinal study. *Emotion, 6*, 498–510.

Spruyt, K., Aitken, R., So, K., Charlton, M., Adamson, T., & Horne, R. (2008). Relationship between sleep/wake patterns, temperament and overall development in term infants over the first year of life *Early Human Development, 84*, 289–296.

Thomas, D., Grant, S., & Aubuchon-Endsley, N. (2009). The role of iron in neurocognitive development. *Developmental Neuropsychology, 34*, 196–222.

Tamura, T., Goldenberg, R. L., Hou, J., Johnston, K. E., Cliver, S. P., Ramey, S. L., et al. (2002). Cord serum ferritin concentrations and mental and psychomotor development of children at five years of age. *Obstetrical and Gynecological Survey, 57*(8), 493–494.

Thomas, A., & Chess, S. (1977). *Temperament and development.* New York: Brunner/Mazel.

Tschann, J. M., Kaiser, P., Chesney, M. A., Alkon, A., & Boyce, W. T. (1996). Resilience and vulnerability among preschool children: Family functioning, temperament, and behavior problems. *Journal of the American Academy of Child and Adolescent Psychiatry, 35*, 184–192.

Valiente, C., Eisenberg, N., Fabes, R. A., Shepard, S. A., Cumberland, A., & Losoya, S. H. (2004). Prediction of children's empathy-related responding from their effortful control and parents' expressivity. *Developmental Psychology, 40*, 911–926.

van der Laan, A. M., Veenstra, R., Bogaerts, S., Verhulst, F. C., & Ormel, J. (2010). Serious, minor and non-delinquents in early adolescence: The impact of cumulative risk and promotive factors. *Journal of Abnormal Child Psychology, 38*, 339–351.

van der Mark, I., Bakermans-Kranenburg, M., & van IJzendoorn, M. (2002). The role of parenting, attachment, and temperamental fearfulness in the prediction of compliance in toddler girls. *British Journal of Developmental Psychology, 20*, 361–378.

Vaughn, J., Brown, J., & Carter, J. P. (1986). The effects of maternal anemia on infant behavior. *Journal of the National Medical Association, 78*, 963–968.

Veenstra, R., Oldehinkel, A. J., De Winter, A. F., Lindenberg, S., & Ormel, J. (2006). Temperament, environment, and antisocial behavior in a population sample of preadolescent boys and girls. *International Journal of Behavioral Development, 30*, 422–432.

Verstraeten, K., Vasey, M. W., Raes, F., & Bijttebier, P. (2009). Temperament and risk for depressive symptoms in adolescence: Mediation by rumination and moderation by effortful control. *Journal of Abnormal Child Psychology, 37*, 349–361.

Vorria, P., Papaligoura, Z., Dunn, J., van IJzendoorn, M., Steele, M., Kontopoulou, A., et al. (2003). Early experiences and attachment relationships of Greek infants raised in residential group care. *Journal of Child Psychology and Psychiatry, 44*, 1208–1220.

Wachs, T. D. (1988). Relevance of physical environment influences for toddler temperament. *Infant Behavior and Development, 11*, 431–445.

Wachs, T. D. (1992). *The nature of nurture.* Newbury Park, CA: Sage.

Wachs, T. D. (2000). *Necessary but not sufficient: The respective roles of single and multiple influences on human development.* Washington, DC: American Psychological Association Press.

Wachs, T. D. (2005). Person–environment "fit" and\ individual development. In D. Teti (Ed.), *Handbook of research methods in developmental science* (pp. 443–466). Oxford, UK: Blackwell.

Wachs T. D. (2006). Contributions of temperament to buffering and sensitization processes in children's development. *Annals of the New York Academy of Sciences, 1094*, 28–39.

Wachs, T. D., Kanashiro, H., & Gurkas, P. (2008). Intra-individual variability in infancy: Structure, stability and nutritional correlates. *Developmental Psychobiology, 50*, 217–231.

Wachs, T. D., Pollitt, E., Cueto, S., Jacoby, E., & Creed-Kanashiro, H. (2005). Relation of neonatal iron status to individual variability in neonatal temperament. *Developmental Psychobiology, 46*, 141–153.

Wasserman, G., Staghezza-Jaramillo, B., Shrout, P., Popovac, D., & Graziano, J. (1998). The effect of lead exposure on behavior problems in preschool children. *American Journal of Public Health, 88*, 481–486.

Watson, D., Gamez, W., & Simms, L. (2005). Basic dimensions of temperament and their relation to anxiety and depression: A symptom-based perspective. *Journal of Research in Personality, 39*, 46–66.

Werner, E., & Smith, R. (1982). *Vulnerable but invincible: A longitudinal study of resilient children and youth.* New York: McGraw-Hill.

Werner, E., & Smith, R. (1992). *Overcoming the odds.* Ithaca, NY: Cornell University Press.

Wertlieb, O., Weigel, C., Springer, T., & Feldstein, M. (1987). Temperament as a moderator of children's stressful experiences. *American Journal of Orthopsychiatry, 57*, 234–245.

Whiteside-Mansell, L., Bradley, R. H., Casey, P., Fussell, J., & Conners-Burrow, N. (2009). Triple risk: Do difficult temperament and family conflict increase the likelihood of behavioral maladjustment in children born low birth weight and preterm? *Journal of Pediatric Psychology, 34*, 396–405.

Wills, T. A., Sandy, J. M., Yaeger, A., & Shinar, O. (2001). Family risk factors and adolescent substance use: Moderation effects for temperament dimensions. *Developmental Psychology, 37*, 283–297.

Wyman, P. A., Cowen, E. L., Work, W. C., & Parker, G. R. (1991). Developmental and family milieu correlates of resilience in urban children who have experienced major life stress. *American Journal of Community Psychology, 19*, 405–426.

CHAPTER 26

Temperament and Internalizing Disorders

Daniel N. Klein
Margaret W. Dyson
Autumn J. Kujawa
Roman Kotov

The hypothesis that temperament is linked to psychopathology can be traced to antiquity, when Hippocrates, and later Galen, argued that particular "humors" were responsible for specific temperament types and forms of psychopathology. In this chapter, we focus on the depressive and anxiety disorders, which collectively are referred to as the *internalizing disorders*. We review the major conceptual models that have been proposed to explain associations between temperament and internalizing psychopathology, comment on important conceptual and methodological issues, selectively review the empirical literature on temperament and the internalizing disorders, discuss mediators and moderators of the relation between temperament and internalizing disorders, and consider the role of temperament in treatment.

Understanding the associations between temperament and the internalizing disorders has a number of potentially important implications for clinical research and practice. First, temperament traits associated with emotional experience, expression, and regulation may be intermediate phenotypes that provide more tractable targets for genetic and neurobiological research than do psychiatric diagnoses (Canli, 2008). Second, temperament may be useful in identifying more homogeneous subgroups of depressive and anxiety disorders that differ in developmental trajectories and etiological influences (e.g., Akiskal, 1983). Third, tracing the pathways between temperament and internalizing disorders can help elucidate more proximal processes involved in the development of psychopathology (Klein, Dougherty, Laptook, & Olino, 2008). Fourth, temperament may be useful in tailoring treatment (Zinbarg, Uliaszek, & Adler, 2008) and predicting treatment response (Quilty, De Fruyt, et al., 2008). Fifth, temperament traits may provide a means to identify at-risk individuals who could benefit from prevention and early intervention efforts (Kovacs & Lopez-Duran, 2010). Finally, there is substantial comorbidity among internalizing disorders and between internalizing disorders and other forms of psychopathology. Some temperament traits, such as neuroticism, are associated with multiple psychiatric conditions. Thus, temperament could help explain patterns of comorbidity and point toward more etiologically relevant classification systems (Brown & Barlow, 2009; Clark, 2005).

Historically, theorists have distinguished between the constructs of temperament and personality traits. The former term typically refers to biologically based, early-emerging, relatively stable individual differences in emotion and its regulation; the latter term has been used to incorporate both temperament and the subsequent influence of socialization processes. However, this distinction has increasingly been abandoned in light of the large body of evidence that has accumulated indicating that personality traits have all the characteristics of temperament, including strong genetic and biological bases and substantial stability over the lifespan (Kandler et al., 2010; Watson, Kotov, & Gamez, 2006). Hence, the terms temperament and personality traits are now often used interchangeably (Caspi & Shiner, 2006; Clark & Watson, 1999).

A variety of temperament classifications have been proposed over the last century, but in recent years there is a growing convergence between models of temperament and the "Big Three" and "Big Five" models from the adult personality literature (Caspi & Shiner, 2006; De Pauw & Mervielde, 2010; see Mervielde & De Pauw, Chapter 2, and Shiner & Caspi, Chapter 24, this volume). Thus, there is growing consensus that temperament can be described using between three and five broad dimensions, each of which includes a number of finer-grained facets (Caspi & Shiner, 2006; De Pauw & Mervielde, 2010; Rothbart & Bates, 2006).

The three dimensions on which there is the widest agreement are the Big Three traits of Neuroticism (or Negative Emotionality [N/NE]), Extraversion (also referred to as Surgency and Positive Emotionality [E/PE]), and Disinhibition (vs. constraint; often referred to as Effortful Control [EC] in younger children). NE refers to a disposition to experience negative emotions, such as fear, anxiety, sadness, and anger; PE reflects a disposition to positive emotions, such as exuberance and joy, high reward sensitivity, and sociability; Disinhibition refers to the tendency to behave impulsively and recklessly, as opposed to being planful and cautious. In the Big Five, Disinhibition is replaced, in part, by Conscientiousness, which refers to being careful, dependable, self-disciplined, and dutiful. Disinhibition (as well as NE) is also correlated with the fourth Big Five dimension, Agreeableness (vs. antagonism), which reflects friendliness, cooperativeness, and kindness (Clark & Watson, 1999). Finally, the Big Five includes Openness to Experience, which encompasses intellectual curiosity, imaginativeness, and esthetic sensitivity. Openness is independent of the Big Three dimensions and has generally not been assessed in younger children (Caspi & Shiner, 2006; De Pauw & Mervielde, 2010).

In addition to these traits, which are conceptualized as continuous dimensions, a categorical construct, behavioral inhibition (BI), has also received considerable attention in the child temperament literature. BI refers to wariness, fear, and low exploration in novel situations (Fox, Henderson, Marshall, Nichols, & Ghera, 2005; Kagan, Snidman, Kahn, & Towsley, 2007). From the perspective of the Big Three, it combines aspects of N/NE (fear and anxiety), low E/PE (low approach), and constraint (Klein, Kotov, & Bufferd, 2011).

In this chapter, we examine the relations of the internalizing disorders with the Big Three and Big Five traits and BI. Following the literature, we emphasize N/NE and E/PE.

Nature of the Relations between Temperament and Internalizing Disorders

A variety of models of the relation between temperament and psychopathology have been proposed (e.g., Krueger & Tackett, 2003). They include the following: (1) Temperament and psychopathology have common causes; (2) temperament traits and mental disorders form a continuous spectrum; (3) temperament traits are precursors of mental disorders; (4) temperament predisposes to developing psychopathology; (5) temperament has pathoplastic effects on psychopathology; (6) temperament features are state-dependent concomitants of psychiatric symptoms; and (7) temperament features are consequences (or scars) of psychopathology. The distinctions between some of these accounts are subtle, and other models are plausible. However, these seven models provide a useful conceptual framework (for a more detailed discussion, see Klein et al., 2011).

These models can be divided into three groups. The first three models (common cause, continuum/spectrum, and precursor) view temperament and psychopathology as having similar causal influences, but do not see one domain as having a causal influence on the other. The fourth and fifth models (predisposition and pathoplasty) hold that temperament has causal effects on the onset or maintenance of psychopathology. The sixth and seventh models (concomitants and consequences) view psychopathology as having a causal influence on temperament.

The *common cause model* views temperament and mental disorders as distinct entities that arise from the same, or at least an overlapping, set of etiological processes. From this perspective, temperament and psychopathology are not directly related; rather, the association is due to a shared third variable.

The *continuum/spectrum model* emphasizes the conceptual overlap between temperament and psychopathology, and argues for a fundamental continuity between them. A mental disorder is thought to identify individuals who have the most extreme scores on a relevant trait. Like the common cause model, the continuum/spectrum model assumes that temperament and psychopathology arise from a similar, if not identical, set of causal factors. However, the continuum/spectrum model goes further in positing that the association between the trait and disorder should be fairly specific, as they are on the same continuum. Moreover, this association is expected to be nonlinear, so that almost nobody below the definitional threshold on the trait has the diagnosis but nearly everyone above the threshold meets the criteria.

The *precursor model* views temperament as an early manifestation or *formes frustes* of mental disorders. Like the common cause and continuum/spectrum accounts, the precursor model posits that temperament and psychopathology are caused by similar etiological factors. Also, like the continuum/spectrum account, it implies considerable phenomenological similarity between the relevant trait and disorder. However, the precursor model differs from both of these other models in that it assumes a particular developmental sequence, with the temperament traits being evident prior to the onset of psychopathology. In other words, both the common cause and continuum/spectrum models assume a fixed clinical expression as traits or disorder, whereas the precursor model implies escalation from traits to disorder within individuals over time.

The common cause, continuum/spectrum, and precursor models do not posit causal relations between temperament and mental disorders. In contrast, the *predisposition model* holds that temperament plays a causal role in the onset of psychopathology. However, the predisposition model overlaps with the precursor model in that both propose that the relevant traits are evident prior to the onset of disorder. The major difference between these two accounts is that the precursor model assumes that temperament and psychopathology derive from the same set of etiological processes, whereas the predisposition model posits that the processes that underlie temperament differ from those that lead to psychopathology. Thus, the predisposition account implies a complex interplay among risk factors involving moderation and/or mediation, and this is what distinguishes it from the precursor model. The most common example—the diathesis–stress model—conceptualizes temperament as the diathesis and stress as a moderator that precipitates the onset of psychopathology. Alternatively, stress may be a mediator, so that temperament vulnerability leads to negative experiences (e.g., interpersonal rejection, job loss), which in turn increase the probability of developing psychopathology. A second difference between these models is that the predisposition model does not assume any phenomenological links between temperament traits and psychopathology. Consequently, the predisposing trait may not have any phenotypic similarity to the disorder. In practice, the common cause, continuum/spectrum, precursor, and predisposition models have been very difficult to distinguish (see Klein et al., 2011, for a more detailed discussion).

The *pathoplasty model* is similar to the predisposition model in that it also views temperament as having a causal influence on psychopathology. However, rather than contributing to the onset of mental disorders, the pathoplasty model posits that temperament influences the expression of the disorder after onset. This influence can include the severity or pattern of symptomatology, course, and response to treatment.

The final two models also assume that there is a causal relation between temperament and psychopathology. However, these models reverse the direction of causality. In the *concomitants (or state-dependent) model*, assessments of temperament are colored, or distorted, by psychiatric symptoms. This model implies that temperament returns to its baseline form after recovery from the episode. In contrast, the *consequences (or scar) model* holds that the disorder has an enduring effect on temperament, such that changes in temperament persist after recovery.

Conceptual and Methodological Issues

A number of conceptual and methodological issues must be considered in evaluating the relation between temperament and internalizing disorders, including (1) the dynamic nature of temperament; (2) etiological heterogeneity, equifinality, and multifinality in the internalizing disorders; and (3) the assessment of temperament and psychopathology.

Dynamic Nature of Temperament

Temperament is not static, but rather develops over the lifespan and changes in response to maturation and life circumstances (Fraley & Roberts, 2005; Rothbart & Bates, 2006). For example, although the rank-order stability of most traits is in the moderate range, it increases over the course of development (Roberts & DelVecchio, 2000). In addition, mean levels of Conscientiousness, Agreeableness, and some facets of E/PE increase, and levels of N/NE decrease, over time, particularly in young adulthood (Roberts, Walton, & Viechtbauer, 2006). A number of processes contribute to temperament stability and change. For example, genes are a major influence on stability (see Saudino & Wang, Chapter 16, this volume; Kandler et al., 2010). In addition, people often select, create, and construe environments in ways that reinforce and maintain their initial trait dispositions (Caspi & Shiner, 2006). However, both genes and life events can also contribute to changes in temperament (Fraley & Roberts, 2005; Kandler et al., 2010; Saudino & Wang, Chapter 16, this volume).

Models of temperament–psychopathology relations can be expanded to recognize the malleability of traits (e.g., Ormel, Oldehinkel, & Brilman, 2001). For example, one can posit dynamic models in which early temperament defines the baseline level of risk, but subsequent experiences modify trait liability to psychopathology (see Klein et al., 2011, for a more detailed discussion). In a dynamic predisposition model, negative life experiences influence not only disorder onset but also levels of trait vulnerability. This increase in temperamental liability may then lead to additional life stress. If this vicious cycle is not interrupted, trait liability continues to increase, and at some point, a negative life event may overwhelm coping capabilities and trigger the onset of disorder.

Dynamic models offer richer and more complete accounts of the role of temperament in the development of internalizing psychopathology (Klein et al., 2011). Moreover, it is important to recognize that internalizing disorders have been linked to multiple traits (as reviewed below), and it is likely that different temperament dimensions contribute through different pathways.

Etiological Heterogeneity, Equifinality, and Multifinality

The depressive and anxiety disorders are almost certainly etiologically heterogeneous, reflecting the convergence of multiple causal influences and developmental pathways (i.e., *equifinality*). Hence, it is likely that the role of temperament traits and, as suggested earlier, the applicability of different models of the relation between temperament and psychopathology differ for different disorders and disorder subtypes. A major challenge in elucidating the influence of temperament on the development of internalizing psychopathology is to parse the heterogeneity of these disorders. As temperament is likely to play a greater role in some cases of a particular disorder, while other etiological factors have a stronger influence in other cases with the same disorder, failure to take equifinality into account may obscure important temperament–psychopathology associations. Conversely, temperament may provide a basis for identifying more homogeneous subgroups within the internalizing disorders.

Temperament traits also appear to have influences that cut across traditional diagnostic boundaries (an example of *multifinality*). Indeed, temperament may be a "third variable" that explains broad patterns of comorbidity. For example, recent hierarchical models of classification posit that trait dispositions such as N/NE account for the much of the variance in associations among the internalizing disorders, as well as much of the overlap between internalizing and externalizing disorders (Clark, 2005; Watson et al., 2006). Thus, in order to understand the influence of temperament on psychopathology, traditional diagnostic categories may not be the optimal dependent variables.

Assessment of Temperament

Temperament can be assessed using a variety of methods, including self-report inventories, semi-structured interviews, informants' reports, and observations in naturalistic settings and the laboratory. Unfortunately, most of the literature examining the association between temperament and internalizing disorders, especially in older youth and adults, has assessed traits via self-report. This is potentially problematic because self-reports of temperament can be complicated by current mood state, limited insight, response styles, and the difficulty of distinguishing traits from the effects of stable environmental contexts (Chmielewski & Watson, 2009). In addition, when the same individual provides information on both temperament and psychopathology, as is often the case, common method variance can inflate associations. Hence, there is a need for greater use of informant report and observational measures in this area.

In this chapter we focus on studies using self-report and observational measures of temperament; the former represents the bulk of the extant literature, the latter provides the strongest methodological contrast. Convergence between these maximally different methods affords the greatest confidence in the findings. Due to space limitations, we do not review the sparser literature examining associations of parent- and teacher-reports of temperament with internalizing disorders. However, the results of these studies are generally consistent with the self-report and observational literature.

A second issue concerns the overlap between some temperament constructs and psychopathology (Lahey, 2004). This is problematic from both a methodological and a conceptual perspective. With respect to methods, some items on temperament scales are very similar to items on measures of depressive and anxiety symptoms. This is particularly troublesome for N/NE (Ormel, Rosmalen, & Farmer, 2004). Item overlap inflates associations between measures of temperament and psychopathology. This may be partially mitigated by the fact that temperament and symptom scales often have different time frames, with trait scales reflecting long-standing patterns and symptom measures tapping more recent experiences (e.g., the past week or month). Thus, the degree to which item overlap threatens the validity of temperament–psychopathology research depends, at least in part, on the duration/chronicity of the disorders of interest.

From a conceptual perspective, there is considerable overlap between the cardinal features of some temperament traits and some psychiatric disorders (e.g., BI and anxiety disorders; Rapee & Coplan, 2010). This raises questions about whether temperament and psychopathology are really different constructs. The extent to which this is a concern depends on one's model of temperament–psychopathology relations (Klein et al., 2011). From the continuum/spectrum framework, some temperament traits and internalizing disorders are variants of the same phenomenon, so the two constructs should overlap. In contrast, the predisposition model views temperament and internalizing psychopathology as distinct domains, so from this perspective it is important to define and assess these sets of constructs as independently as possible.

Temperament and Depressive Disorders

Studies Using Self-Reports of Temperament

In light of the assessment issues discussed earlier, we review studies using self-reports and observational measures of temperament separately. There is a large and rich literature on self-reported temperament and depression in adults, adolescents, and older children (Klein et al., 2008, 2011). Given the depth of this literature, we focus on studies that use depressive diagnoses rather than symptom scales.

Cross-Sectional Associations

In a very influential body of work, Clark and Watson (1999) have posited that depressive disorders are characterized by high levels of N/NE and low levels of E/PE. A large number of cross-sectional studies have evaluated these relations, as well as the links between depression and the other Big Five dimensions. Kotov, Gamez, Schmidt, and Watson (2010) recently reported a meta-analysis of this literature, and found that major depressive disorder (MDD) was associated with very high N/NE (Cohen's $d = 1.33$) and low Conscientiousness ($d = -0.90$). The link to low E/PE was more modest ($d = -0.62$). However, this probably masks stronger effects at the facet level, as there is growing evidence that the affective component E/PE (positive affect) is much more strongly associated with depression than the interpersonal component (e.g., sociability) (Watson & Naragon-Gainey, 2010). Associations with Agreeableness and Openness were both small and nonsignificant.

Dysthymic disorder exhibited stronger links to N/NE ($d = 1.93$), E/PE ($d = -1.47$), and conscientiousness ($d = -1.24$). This is not surprising, as dysthymic disorder is thought to be more trait-like than MDD, and a greater contribution from temperament might be expected.

Longitudinal and Twin Studies

A variety of methods and designs have been used to try to understand the nature of the relation between temperament and depressive disorders. These include examining temperament in individuals during and after remission from a depressive episode; comparing temperament before and after the occurrence of an initial depressive episode; assessing temperament in a cohort of never-depressed individuals and following them to determine who develops depression; examining the relations between personality and depression in same-sex monozygotic and dizygotic twins; and assessing temperament in a sample of depressed individuals and following them to examine the course of depression. In this section, we focus on N/NE and E/PE, as few longitudinal studies have examined the other Big Five traits.

One of the best approaches to testing the concomitants (mood state) model is by assessing temperament when individuals are experiencing a MDD episode and again, after they have remitted. Studies have consistently found that individuals with MDD report higher levels of N/NE when they are depressed than when not depressed (Hirschfeld et al., 1983; Kendler, Neale, Kessler, Heath, & Eaves, 1993; Ormel, Oldehinklel, & Vollebergh, 2004). In contrast, the evidence for mood state effects on E/PE is weaker and less consistent (De Fruyt, Van Leeuwen, Bagby, Rolland, & Rouillon, 2006; Kendler et al., 1993; Morey et al., 2010). However, the influence of mood state on temperament should not be overstated. Even though levels of N/NE decline significantly after remission from a depressive episode (i.e., absolute stability), individuals' relative positions with respect to levels of N/NE (i.e., rank-order stability) tend to be moderately well preserved (De Fruyt et al., 2006; Morey et al., 2010).

A related design has been used to test the consequences (or "scar") hypothesis. This involves comparing temperament measures in depressed individuals before and after a MDD episode. The results of these studies have been inconsistent. Kendler and colleagues reported increases in N/NE (but not E/PE) after a depressive episode in two separate samples (Fanous, Neale, Aggen, & Kendler, 2007; Kendler et al., 1993); however, other studies have found that N/NE and E/PE do not change from before to after a MDD episode (e.g., Ormel, Oldehinkel, et al., 2004; Shea et al., 1996). Importantly, the studies reporting scarring used less stringent criteria for recovery and shorter follow-ups, suggesting that the findings may be due to residual symptoms and/or that the scars dissipate over time.

The most direct approach to testing the precursor and predisposition models is to conduct prospective studies of temperament in never-depressed participants to determine whether these traits predict the subsequent onset of depressive disorders. Several studies using large community samples have reported that higher levels of N/NE predict the onset of first lifetime MDD episodes (de Graaf, Bijl, Ravelli, Smit, & Vollenbergh, 2002; Fanous et al., 2007; Kendler et al., 1993; Kendler, Gatz, Gardner, & Pedersen, 2006; Ormel, Oldhehinkel, et al., 2004). Although there is some evidence that E/PE predicts the first onset of MDD (Kendler et al., 2006; Rorsman, Grasbeck, Hagnell, Isberg, & Otterbeck, 1993), it is much weaker, and several studies have failed to find an association (Fanous et al., 2007; Hirschfeld et al., 1989; Kendler et al., 1993). However, these studies have not distinguished between the affective and interpersonal aspects of E/PE; as noted earlier, the former are much more strongly linked to depression than the latter (Watson & Naragon-Gainey, 2010).

Twin studies provide a particularly useful approach to testing the common cause, continuum/spectrum, and precursor models. These studies indicate that there are substantial associations between the genetic liabilities for N/NE and MDD, but only weak associations between the liabilities for E/PE and MDD (Fanous et al., 2007; Kendler et al., 1993, 2006).

Finally, to test the pathoplasty model, a number of studies have assessed temperament during MDD episodes and followed the individuals to examine their course and outcome. These studies indicate that higher N/NE and lower E/PE predict a poorer course, although the findings for E/PE are somewhat weaker (Duggan, Lee, & Murray, 1990; Klein et al., 2011). While these findings are consistent with the pathoplasty model, these data cannot exclude the possibility that extreme traits are a marker for a more severe or etiologically distinct group (Klein et al., 2011).

Clinical Traits

Separate from work in the field of temperament and personality, clinical researchers have identified a number of trait-like characteristics that are hypothesized to reflect dispositions to depression. Three of the best-studied traits are ruminative response style, self-criticism, and dependency. These traits are similar in scope to personality facets, and their stability is comparable to that of a typical personality dimension (e.g., Kasch, Klein, & Lara, 2001; Zuroff, Mongrain, & Santor, 2004). Factor analytic studies have shown that these traits can be subsumed within N/NE (Watson et al., 2006). Most of this work has been done with adults, but there is growing interest in these traits in children and adolescents (Abela & Hankin, 2008).

Ruminative response style is a tendency to dwell on sad mood and thoughts. It is correlated with concurrent depressive symptoms, but has a much weaker relation with anxiety symptoms (Nolen-Hoeksema, Wisco, & Lyubomirsky, 2008). Rumination is associated with increases in depressive symptoms over time in youth and adults, and predicts the onset of MDD in adults (Abela & Hankin, 2008; Nolen-Hoeksema et al., 2008).

Blatt's (1974) theory of depression focuses on two trait vulnerabilities: *self-criticism* (an inclination to feelings of guilt and failure stemming from unrealistically high expectations for oneself) and *dependency* (a disposition to feelings of helplessness and fears of abandonment resulting from a preoccupation with relationships). These constructs are similar, although not identical, to Beck's (1983) constructs of autonomy and sociotropy. Studies indicate that the link between dependency and depressive disorders is modest and nonspecific, whereas self-criticism has been established as a stronger and more specific factor in these conditions (see review by Zuroff et al., 2004). Self-criticism, and to a lesser extent dependency, predict future increases in depressive symptoms in youth and adults (Abela & Hankin, 2008; Zuroff et al., 2004). In addition, there is evidence that dependency predicts the subsequent onset of MDD in older, but not younger, adults (Hirschfeld et al., 1989; Rohde, Lewinsohn, & Seeley, 1990). The concomitants and pathoplasty models have also received empirical support (Zuroff et al., 2004). Finally, there is some research indicating that dependency may increase as a function of depressive episodes (consequences model) in youth but not adults (Rohde et al., 1990, 1994; Shea et al., 1996).

Studies Using Observational Measures of Temperament

A number of researchers have used observational measures to examine temperament in the young children of parents with depressive disorders. As parental diagnosis can be regarded as a marker of risk for depression, these studies are most relevant to the precursor and predisposition models, but they also have some bearing on the common cause and continuum/spectrum models.

In a community sample of 100 three-year-olds, Durbin, Klein, Hayden, Buckley, and Moerk (2005) found that maternal history of depressive disorders was associated with child low E/PE in emotion-eliciting laboratory tasks. Importantly, this effect was limited to the affective and motivational, rather than the interpersonal, components of E/PE. Maternal depression was not associated with N/NE or BI. Follow-ups of this sample indicated that low E/PE at age 3 predicted depressive cognitive biases at age 7 (Hayden, Klein, Durbin, & Olino, 2006) and parent-reported depression at age 10 (Dougherty, Klein, Durbin, Hayden, & Olino, 2010).

In a subsequent study with a much larger sample of preschoolers, Olino, Klein, Dyson, Rose, and Durbin (2010) found that parental depression was associated with significantly elevated levels of N/NE and BI in children. However, these effects were qualified by interactions with child E/PE. At high and moderate levels of child PE, higher levels of N/NE and BI were each associated with higher rates of parental depression. Conversely, at low levels of child NE, low PE was associated with higher rates of parental depression. These results suggest that children of depressed parents may exhibit diminished E/PE or elevated N/NE and BI. In this latter sample, low E/PE was also associated with elevated levels of cortisol shortly after awakening, an index of hypothalamic–pituitary–adrenal axis dysregulation that has been shown to predict MDD in adolescents and adults (Dougherty, Klein, Olino, Dyson, & Rose, 2009).

Several other groups have reported mixed findings regarding the link between parental depression and child BI. Kochanska (1991) found that young children of mothers with unipolar depression did not differ on BI from children of nondepressed controls; however, there was a difference when only mothers with recent symptoms were considered. In two studies, Rosenbaum and colleagues (1988, 2000) reported that the young children of parents with a history of MDD and panic disorder had significantly higher rates of BI than children of parents with no history of mood or anxiety disorders. However, in both studies, children of parents with MDD alone did not differ from either the comorbid or the control group.

Finally, in accordance with the precursor and predisposition models, there is some direct evidence that observational assessments of child temperament predict the development of depressive disorders in adulthood. Caspi, Moffitt, Newman, and Silva (1996) reported that children who were rated as socially reticent, inhibited, and easily upset at age 3 had elevated rates of depressive (but not anxiety or substance use) disorders at age 21. In addition, van Os, Jones, Lewis, Wadsworth, and Murray (1997) found that physicians' ratings of behavioral apathy at ages 6, 7, and 11 predicted chronic depression in middle adulthood.

In summary, there are robust cross-sectional associations between depressive disorders and self-reports of N/NE, E/PE, and Conscientiousness, and clinical traits such as rumination and self-criticism in older youth and adults. This work is complemented by observational studies of temperament in young children, some (but not all) of which report associations of N/NE, E/PE, and BI with parental depression and other risk markers for depressive disorders. The nature of the relation between temperament and depression appears to be complex, with evidence supporting mood state effects, pathoplastic influences on the course of depression, shared genetic influences, and the prediction of onset of first lifetime depressive episodes. These data are particularly strong for N/NE, and are consistent with the concomitants/state, pathoplasty, common cause, and predisposition models. In contrast, there is little evidence that depressive episodes produce enduring changes in most temperament traits (the scar/consequences model).

Temperament and Anxiety Disorders

Studies Using Self-Reports of Temperament

Consistent with Clark and Watson's (1999) influential model, most cross-sectional studies have reported links between anxiety disorders/symptoms and N/NE (e.g., Bienvenu et al., 2001; Brown, Chorpita, & Barlow, 1998; Trull & Sher, 1994; Weinstock & Whisman, 2006). However, a number of studies have also shown that low E/PE correlates with anxiety disorders, particularly social phobia and, in some studies, generalized anxiety disorder (GAD) (e.g., Bienvenu et al., 2001; Brown et al., 1998; Trull & Sher, 1994).

In Kotov and colleagues' (2010) comprehensive meta-analysis, N/NE had strong links with all of the anxiety disorders. The largest effect sizes were with posttraumatic stress disorder (PTSD; $d = 2.25$), obsessive–compulsive disorder (OCD; $d = 2.07$), GAD ($d = 1.96$), and panic disorder ($d = 1.92$). Specific phobia exhibited the smallest, albeit still substantial, association ($d = 0.92$). The effect sizes for the relations with E/PE were also all significant, with the exception of specific phobia ($d = -0.20$). Social phobia ($d = -1.31$) exhibited the largest effect size, followed by OCD ($d = -1.12$), panic disorder ($d = -1.07$), GAD ($d = -1.02$), and agoraphobia ($d = -0.98$). However, similar to the work on depression, these findings may obscure a pattern of relatively greater specificity at the facet level. Thus, although social phobia is modestly associated with low positive affect, its correlations with the interpersonal components of E/PE are much larger (Watson & Naragon-Gainey, 2010). In addition, while almost all anxiety disorders exhibit reduced levels of positive affect, the magnitude of these associations is much smaller than it is for MDD (Watson & Naragon-Gainey, 2010).

Kotov and colleagues (2010) also found strong associations with Conscientiousness, and these were evident across all the anxiety disorders, with effect sizes ranging from -0.67 to -1.13. In contrast, almost none of the associations with Agreeableness and Openness were significant.

The links between low Conscientiousness and anxiety and depressive disorders have not received much attention in the literature. One possible explanation, discussed further below, is that Conscientiousness reflects self-regulatory skills that can be used to modulate or compensate for elevated or reduced levels of NE and PE. Hence, consistent with dynamic models of the relations between temperament and psychopathology outlined earlier, individuals with good self-regulatory skills may be able to maintain a high level of functioning despite having extreme levels of temperamental emotionality, and may therefore be less prone to generate life stressors and difficulties that could precipitate the onset or recurrence of anxiety and depressive disorders. Alternatively, the associations between Conscientiousness and internalizing disorders could simply reflect the functional impairment caused by psychopathology.

Unlike the depression literature, few studies have tested explanatory models of the nature of the relation between temperament and anxiety (Pagura, Cox, & Enns, 2009). There is some evidence that temperament scores are more deviant in individuals with panic disorder during periods of panic attacks than in remission, raising the possibility that the temperamental abnormalities associated with anxiety disorders at least partially reflect mood state effects (Reich, Noyes, Hirschfeld, Coryell, & O'Gorman, 1987). In addition, shared genes account for a substantial proportion of the association between N/NE and GAD, panic, agoraphobia, and social and specific phobias (Hettema, Neale, Myers, Prescott, & Kendler, 2006), which is consistent with the common cause, continuum/spectrum, and precursor models.

In addition to the Big Five dimensions, several narrower traits have been posited to contribute to anxiety disorders. *Anxiety sensitivity* (AS) and *negative evaluation sensitivity* (NES) are the most widely studied of these traits, and both show some degree of specificity in their associations with anxiety disorders. AS refers to the fear of bodily sensations, which are misinterpreted as dangerous and threatening, and is hypothesized to have a specific link with panic disorder (Reiss & McNally, 1985); NES is characterized by exaggerated fear of being evaluated by others, and is thought to be specifically associated with social phobia (Fenigstein, Scheier, & Buss, 1975). Both traits overlap with N/NE and can be viewed as facets of this higher-order dimension (Watson et al., 2006).

Two recent meta-analyses not only confirmed the strong cross-sectional association between AS and panic disorder but also found strong associations with PTSD and GAD (Naragon-Gainey, 2010; Olatunji & Wolitzky-Taylor, 2009). In contrast, AS had much weaker relations with the other anxiety disorders and depression. A number of prospective studies of AS have also found that this trait predicts the development of panic attacks (e.g., Schmidt, Lerew, & Jackson, 1999), as well as anxiety disorders in general (Schmidt, Zvolensky, & Maner, 2006). There is less research on NES, but several studies have supported the hypothesis of a strong link with social phobia (e.g., Ball, Otto, Pollack, Uccello, & Rosenbaum, 1995).

Taken together, this literature suggests that it may be possible to construct a unique temperament profile for each anxiety disorder (Pagura et al., 2009). Kotov, Wilson, Robles, and Schmidt (2007) tested a model positing that N/NE is associated with all anxiety disorders; low E/PE is correlated with social phobia, and to a lesser extent, with GAD; AS is most strongly related to panic disorder but is also linked to social phobia, PTSD, and GAD; and NES is a unique factor in social phobia. Using an undergraduate sample, they found significant support for this model. Thus, there has been significant progress in delineating some of the temperament factors that are associated with anxiety disorders. However, as noted earlier, research using longitudinal, twin, and other informative designs is needed to tease apart the various explanatory models discussed earlier in this chapter.

Studies Using Observational Measures of Temperament

Observational studies of temperament and anxiety disorders have focused on BI in young children (Kagan et al., 2007). Differentiating BI from anxiety disorders/symptoms is often challenging, as these constructs share a number of similarities (Degnan, Almas, & Fox, 2010; Rapee & Coplan, 2010). For instance, several of the core features of BI (e.g., fearful affect, social withdrawal, and vigilance) are also characteristic of several types of anxiety disorders. However, BI does not overlap entirely with any one particular anxiety disorder. Thus, despite being highly related, some investigators (e.g., Rapee & Coplan, 2010) argue that BI and anxiety represent distinct constructs.

A number of studies have examined BI in the children of parents with anxiety disorders, primarily focusing on parents with panic disorder. These studies have generally followed Kagan's original work in this area by assessing BI using laboratory paradigms designed to elicit relevant behaviors. Most of these studies revealed increased rates of BI in offspring (e.g., Rosenbaum et al., 1988, 2000).

A number of prospective longitudinal studies of children have used observational measures of BI. These studies have generally found that BI predicts subsequent anxiety disorders in later childhood and adolescence (e.g., Biederman et al., 1993; Chronis-Tuscano et al., 2009; Hirshfeld-Becker et al., 2008). Of the various anxiety disorders, BI is most associated with later social phobia. However, there are conflicting findings about whether BI also predicts other types of anxiety disorder (e.g., Biederman et al., 1993; Hirshfeld-Becker et al., 2008). Interestingly, Caspi and colleagues (1996) found that BI in early childhood predicted MDD and suicide attempts, but not anxiety disorders in early adulthood. However, Caspi and colleagues defined and assessed BI differently than other studies, rating children's behavior during tasks that were not specifically designed to elicit BI, and categorizing children on the basis of a cluster analysis of a broad range of behaviors rather than using a priori codes targeting BI from Kagan's original work. While most of the longitudinal studies are consistent with BI as a precursor or predisposing factor for later anxiety disorders, few ruled out the possibility that the children were already suffering from anxiety disorder at the time of the initial assessment (Rapee, Schniering, & Hudson, 2009). As anxiety disorders are often evident in early childhood, the temporal direction of the association between BI and anxiety disorders has not been firmly established.

While BI exhibits a familial relationship with panic disorder and predicts the subsequent development of anxiety disorders, particularly social phobia, given the inconsistencies in the literature we cannot rule out the alternative hypothesis that BI is a general risk factor, similar to N/NE, for internalizing disorders (Rapee, Schniering, & Hudson, 2009). Moreover, the association between BI and anxiety disorders is modest (Degnan et al., 2010; Hirschfeld-Becker et al., 2008), and there appear to be other pathways to anxiety disorders that do not include an inhibited temperament (Prior, Smart, Sanson, & Oberklaid, 2000). While the relation between BI and anxiety disorders may be underestimated due to measurement error, it is also plausible that this association is moderated by other variables, as discussed below.

In summary, cross-sectional studies of older youth and adults indicate that anxiety is associated with self-reports of high N/NE and low Conscientiousness. It is also related to low E/PE, although this appears primarily to be due to facets reflecting social behavior rather than exuberant mood and reward sensitivity. The narrower trait of AS is associated with panic disorder, GAD, and PTSD, and predicts the development of panic attacks and possibly other anxiety disorders. Observational studies of younger children indicate that BI predicts subsequent social phobia. Few studies have explored the nature of the relation between anxiety and temperament. However, there is evidence that anxiety influences self-reports of N/NE (concomitants/state model), that N/NE and many anxiety disorders share some genetic influences (common cause, continuum/spectrum, and precursor models), and AS and BI are associated with later anxiety disorders (precursor and predisposition models).

Temperament and Depression–Anxiety Comorbidity

There is extensive comorbidity between depressive and anxiety disorders (e.g., Kessler et al., 2005). This has led a number of investigators to hypothesize that some temperament traits, particularly N/NE, are a risk factor for both groups of disorders and may therefore explain their high co-occurrence (e.g., Clark, 2005; Watson et al., 2006).

A number of studies have provided support for this conjecture, showing that N/NE accounts for much of the shared variance between depressive and anxiety disorders (e.g., Bienvenu et al., 2001; Brown & Barlow, 2009; Kotov et al., 2007). In addition, several twin studies have examined whether comorbidity between depressive and anxiety disorders can be explained by genetic influences that are also shared with N/NE (Hettema et al., 2006; Kendler, Gardner, Gatz, & Pedersen, 2007). These studies indicate that not only does N/NE account for some of the comorbidity between depressive disorders and anxiety disorders, but this is because individual differences in all three constructs are attributable to some of the same genes.

Mediators and Moderators of the Temperament–Internalizing Disorders Association

As temperament refers to early-emerging patterns of emotional reactivity and regulation, and internalizing disorders often do not develop until adolescence and adulthood, it is likely that intervening processes mediate temperament-internalizing psychopathology associations. Moreover, as discussed earlier, the relations between temperament and internalizing disorders are probably characterized by both equifinality and multifinality. Hence, there are also likely to be factors that moderate the relations between temperament and internalizing psychopathology (Klein et al., 2008).

Mediators

Although research in this area is limited, in this section we consider several variables that may play mediating roles in the association between temperament and internalizing disorders: interpersonal difficulties, cognitive biases, coping, and neuroendocrine stress reactivity.

Interpersonal Difficulties and Stressors

Temperament plays a large role in social development by directly influencing behavior across social contexts, which has an impact on peer relationships and social support systems (Sanson, Hemphill, & Smart, 2004; also see Coplan & Bullock, Chapter 21, this volume). Certain temperamental styles have been associated with negative social outcomes. For example, BI is related to social withdrawal, which in turn is linked to lower social competence and peer rejection (Rubin, Coplan, & Bowker, 2009). In addition, inhibited preschoolers have been shown to have lower levels of social support as young adults (Newman, Caspi, Moffitt, & Silva, 1997).

Interpersonal difficulties in turn predict internalizing psychopathology. Interpersonal problems, such as social isolation and limited acceptance from peers, in early childhood have been linked to internalizing problems later in childhood (e.g., Hymel, Rubin, Rowden, & LeMare, 1990). In addition, relational victimization and negative interactions in close friendships have been shown to predict both social anxiety and depression among adolescents (La Greca & Harrison, 2005). Few studies have directly examined interpersonal difficulties and stressors as a mediator of temperament-internalizing disorders associations. One important exception, however, is a recent study of adolescents by Wetter and Hankin (2009). In this study, low social support mediated the relationship between low E/PE and subsequent depressive symptoms. In addition, dependent stressors (i.e., at least partially due to the participants' behavior), which are generally of an interpersonal nature, partially mediated the relationship between N/NE and depressive symptoms (Wetter & Hankin, 2009). Thus, this study suggests that temperament predisposes children to interpersonal difficulties, which, in turn, leads to internalizing symptoms.

Cognitive Biases

High N/NE, low E/PE, and high BI have all been linked to maladaptive cognitive and attentional processes. For example, higher N/NE appears to be linked to more negative biases in memory retrieval and judgment making (Rusting, 1999). Low E/PE among 3-year-olds has been shown to predict helplessness and decreased recall of positive self-descriptive adjectives in later childhood (Hayden et al., 2006). In addition, several temperament dimensions, including BI and the combination of high N/NE and low effortful control (EC), have been linked to attentional biases toward threatening stimuli (Lonigan & Vasey, 2009; Pérez-Edgar et al., 2010).

Biases in attention, memory and interpretation have also been found across internalizing disorders and may be vulnerability markers that precede the onset of psychopathology (Mathews & MacLeod, 2005). Attentional biases toward threatening stimuli have been observed in both anxious children and adults, and are hypothesized to play a causal role in the development of anxiety disorders (Bar-Haim, Lamy, Pergamin, Bakermans-Kranenburg, & van IJzendoorn, 2007). Similarly, negative cognitive styles have been shown to predict both the onset and recurrence of depression (Alloy et al., 2006).

Although the evidence is limited, there is some suggestive support for the hypothesis that cognitive biases mediate the association between temperament and later internalizing psychopathology. For example, Nolan, Roberts, and Gotlib (1998) reported that rumination mediated the effect of N/NE on changes in depression severity in college students. Verstraeten, Vasey, Raes, and Bijttebier (2009) reported similar findings in young adolescents, although this effect was particularly pronounced for youth with lower EC.

It is likely that the links between temperament and internalizing disorders are complex, and some variables may play both mediating and moderating roles. For example, a recent study found that attentional biases to threat interacted with childhood BI in predicting social withdrawal in adolescence (Pérez-Edgar et al., 2010), suggesting that at least some cognitive factors may also moderate the effects of temperament on internalizing symptoms. Thus, it appears that maladaptive information-processing styles may serve as both mediators and moderators in the relationship between temperament and internalizing disorders.

Neuroendocrine Dysregulation

A number of temperament dimensions have been associated with dysregulation of the hypothalamic–pituitary–adrenal (HPA) axis, a neuroendocrine system that contributes to regulating responses to stress. The HPA axis is widely believed to play a central role in both depressive and anxiety disorders (Arborelius, Owens, Plotsky, & Nemeroff, 1999). In addition, the temperament traits of N/NE, E/PE, and BI have all been linked to variations in a number of HPA axis parameters. Currently, some of the most interesting findings involve abnormalities in cortisol levels shortly after awakening. Thus, a number of studies have reported that low E/PE is associated with elevated morning cortisol in both children and adults (Chida & Steptoe, 2009; Dougherty et al., 2009). In addition, a growing number of studies have found that elevated morning cortisol levels in never-depressed youth predict the subsequent onset of depressive disorders (e.g., Adam et al., 2010). Given that elevated morning cortisol is linked to temperament and appears to precede the onset of psychopathology, it is plausible that it mediates the association between temperament and internalizing disorders.

Moderators

A number of variables may moderate the associations between temperament and internalizing psychopathology. These include sex, interpersonal stress, parental personality and psychopathology, parenting, and other temperament dimensions (Klein et al., 2008).

Sex

Depressive disorders and most anxiety disorders are approximately two times more common in females than in males (Kessler et al., 2005). Little research has directly addressed whether the association between temperament and internalizing disorders differs between males and females, but there is growing evidence of gender differences in the temperament traits associated with internalizing problems. Among children, girls tend to exhibit greater fearfulness and less surgency than boys, and N/NE is higher in adult women compared to men (Else-Quest, Hyde, Goldsmith, & Van Hulle, 2006; also see Else-Quest, Chapter 23, this volume). Moreover, environmental factors may differentially moderate the relation between temperament and psychopathology for males and females. For example, both parental and peer rejection have been shown to interact with gender and temperament in predicting depressive symptoms, such that girls high in NE are particularly sensitive to rejection (Brendgen, Wanner, Morin, & Vitaro, 2005; Oldehinkel, Veenstra, Ormel, de Winter, & Verhulst, 2006). Thus, gender may moderate the associations between temperament and psychopathology, and these interactions may themselves be further moderated by environmental influences.

Life Stressors and Difficulties

As noted earlier, some mediators may also function as moderators. Life stress is a prime candidate for playing multiple roles, as it could serve both to trigger the onset of an episode of depression or anxiety and to amplify the effects of other risk factors (see the earlier discussion of dynamic models). We summarized evidence earlier that suggests interpersonal problems may mediate the association between temperament and internalizing symptoms. There are also data indicating that life stressors and interpersonal difficulties moderate this association. For example, in a large community sample of adults, Kendler, Kuhn, and Prescott (2004) found that life stress moderated the effects of N/NE on the subsequent onset of a MDD episode, such that individuals with elevated N/NE scores had a greater risk for depression if they also experienced greater stress. In Brendgen and colleagues' (2005) study of young adolescents, peer rejection was related to a pattern of increasing depressive symptoms for girls with elevated N/NE in childhood. Finally, Wetter and Hankin (2009) found a significant interaction between E/PE and supportive relationships on depressive symptoms, indicating that the stress associated with low social support may have a particularly powerful impact on adolescents with low E/PE. Thus, life stress may serve as both a mediator and a moderator of the association between temperament and internalizing disorders.

Parental Personality and Psychopathology

Parental personality and psychopathology may also moderate the association between child temperament and internalizing symptoms. For example, when mothers are high in N/NE or depressive symptoms, infants high in negative reactivity (a precursor of BI) are likely to show more social wariness in childhood; however, this relationship is not apparent for mothers low in NE and depression (Degnan, Henderson, Fox, & Rubin, 2008). In addition, children high in BI are significantly more likely to develop social anxiety compared to children low in BI when one or more of their parents have a history of panic disorder (Biederman et al., 2001). These findings suggest that the relationship between temperament and internalizing disorders may be particularly strong among children of parents high in NE or with a history of internalizing symptoms themselves.

Parenting and Parental Behavior

There is also evidence that parenting moderates the effects of temperament. For example, permissive parenting seems to moderate the effects of BI, such that internalizing problems in early childhood are greatest among children with high BI and permissive parents (Williams et al., 2009). Parental overprotection, low warmth, and rejection also appear to moderate the effects of fearfulness and some other facets of N/NE (e.g., frustration), such that these parental behaviors are more strongly associated with depressive symptoms among children with higher levels of these traits (Oldehinkel et al., 2006). Finally, there is evidence that parental behavior also moderates the effects of E/PE on internalizing psychopathology. For example, parental rejection was found to be more strongly related to depressive symptoms following divorce for children low in E/PE compared to those high in E/PE (Lengua, Wolchik, Sandler, & West, 2000).

Some aspects of parenting behavior may serve both as mediators and moderators. For example, while permissiveness and overprotection appear to moderate the effects of BI on later anxiety symptoms, they may also serve as mediators, as child fearfulness tends to elicit overprotective and intrusive parenting, which limits children's exposure to fear-eliciting contexts, and then serves to maintain the child's fearfulness (Kiel & Buss, 2010). Thus, parenting style appears to moderate the link between temperament and internalizing disorders, but it may also play a mediating role.

Interactions between Temperament Traits

Additive models of temperament may underestimate traits' contribution to the development of internalizing psychopathology. Rather, some temperament traits may moderate the effects of other traits. Some studies have found that N/NE and E/PE interact in predicting depressive symptoms, such that individuals with both high N/NE and low E/PE having the greatest symptoms (Dougherty, Klein, Durbin, Hayden, & Olino, 2010; Gershuny & Sher, 1998; Joiner & Lonigan, 2000; Wetter & Hankin, 2009). In addition, there is evidence suggesting that EC moderates the relations between E/PE, N/NE, and internalizing problems (Rothbart & Bates, 2006). Thus, individuals low in EC but high in N/NE or low in E/PE exhibit the highest levels of depressive symptoms (Verstraeten et al., 2009). By the same token, higher EC reduces the risk of internalizing symptoms in youth with elevated levels of N/NE (Oldehinkel, Hartman, Ferdinand, Verhulst, & Ormel, 2007).

EC, however, is a heterogeneous construct, and *higher* levels of some aspects of EC may interact with temperament to *increase* risk for psychopathology. For example, enhanced response monitoring appears to increase the risk of anxiety disorders in adolescents with a history of high BI (McDermott et al., 2009). In addition, while higher levels of attention shifting appear to reduce risk of anxiety for children with high BI, increased inhibitory control may actually *increase* risk in combination with high BI (White, McDermott, Degnan, Henderson, & Fox, 2011). Thus, interactions between temperament traits appear to moderate associations with internalizing disorders, but the nature of the interaction may vary depending on the specific construct assessed.

Implications for Treatment

There is growing interest in the role of temperament in the treatment of internalizing disorders in adults and youth. Important questions include whether (1) temperament can predict treatment outcome and aid in treatment selection; (2) current treatments influence temperament; and (3) change in temperament mediates the effects of treatment. Most of this work has focused on the treatment of depressive disorders in adults, but there has also been some research examining the effects of treatment on BI and anxiety disorders in children.

Although there are some null findings, N/NE generally predicts a poorer response to treatment for MDD (Kennedy, Farvolden, Cohen, Bagby, & Costa, 2005; Tang et al., 2009). There is also evidence that higher E/PE is associated with a better response;

however, the findings are less consistent (Kennedy et al., 2005; Tang et al., 2009). In one of the largest studies to date, Quilty, De Fruyt, and colleagues (2008) examined the ability of the Big Five traits to predict response to combined pharmacotherapy and psychotherapy in depressed outpatients. They found that lower N/NE and Conscientiousness independently predicted poorer outcomes, and that both effects were moderated by E/PE, such that patients with low E/PE and high N/NE and patients with low Conscientiousness and low E/PE were least likely to respond. There is also evidence that temperament traits may be useful in treatment selection. For example, Bagby and colleagues (2008) reported that patients with high levels of N/NE or low levels of some facets of Agreeableness responded better to antidepressant medication than to psychotherapy.

A number of studies have reported that pharmacological and psychosocial interventions that are effective in treating depression also influence temperament, for example, reducing levels of N/NE and increasing levels of E/PE (e.g., De Fruyt et al., 2006; Quilty, De Fruyt, et al., 2008; Zinbarg et al., 2008). This raises the possibility that these changes are simply concomitants of the change in depression. However, several studies have found that treatment-related changes in temperament are not fully accounted for by changes in depressive symptoms (De Fruyt et al., 2006; Tang et al., 2009). If the changes in temperament are not due to symptom change, it is conceivable that these changes mediate the effects of treatment on symptoms. Quilty, Meusel, and Bagby (2008) tested a mediation model in MDD and found that N/NE mediated the effects of pharmacotherapy in reducing depressive symptoms.

As noted earlier, few studies have examined the role of temperament in treating anxiety disorders. Some studies have reported that higher levels of N/NE predict a poor response to treatment for anxiety disorders (e.g., Chavira et al., 2009). Rapee, Kennedy, Ingram, Edwards, and Sweeney (2010) tested an early intervention program for preventing anxiety disorders in children with high BI. After 3 years, significantly fewer children whose parents received the group cognitive-behavioral intervention met criteria for an anxiety disorder compared to a no-intervention comparison group. However, the groups did not differ on change in parent-reports or laboratory observations of BI. Thus, the effect of the cognitive-behavioral parent intervention on child anxiety disorder did not appear to be mediated by its effects on child BI.

Thus, a growing literature suggests that temperament may have a useful role in the treatment of internalizing disorders. However, further research is needed on the prognostic utility of specific temperament dimensions and patterns of dimensions, particularly for anxiety disorders in youth, and the value of temperament in choosing between treatment options.

Conclusions

The literature on temperament and the internalizing disorders is large but uneven. Research on temperament relative to depressive disorders is much more extensive than that on temperament and anxiety disorders. Nonetheless, it is possible to draw a number of conclusions. First, the broad traits of N/NE, E/PE, and Conscientiousness have moderate-to-large cross-sectional associations with both depressive and anxiety disorders. Second, there is greater specificity when considering narrower constructs. For example, the affective component of E/PE, rumination, and self-criticism appear to have relatively specific relations with depressive disorder, and BI and AS have relatively specific associations with some anxiety disorders. Third, reports of some traits, particularly N/NE, are influenced by clinical state. However, state effects cannot fully account for the associations between temperament and depression (nor probably anxiety). Fourth, shared etiological factors (e.g., genes) account for a portion of the associations of N/NE with both depressive and anxiety disorders, supporting the common cause and continuum/spectrum models. In addition, shared genetic influences account for a significant portion of the comorbidity between these disorders. Fifth, some traits, particularly N/NE, predict the subsequent onset of depressive disorders. However, it is unclear at this point whether they are best conceptualized as precursors or predispositions, and analogous research on anxiety disorders is limited. Nonetheless, temperament traits may be a promising approach to identifying young children at risk for internalizing disorders. Sixth, there is evidence suggesting that other traits, such as low E/PE and low Conscientiousness/EC, may moderate the relationship between N/NE and internalizing psychopathology. Seventh, it appears unlikely that depressive episodes produce enduring changes in most temperament traits. Comparable data for anxiety disorders are not available. Finally, N/NE, and to a lesser degree E/PE, predicts, and may influence, the course and treatment response of internalizing disorders.

At least six issues should be considered in future research on the relations between temperament and the internalizing disorders. First, most research on temperament and internalizing disorders has focused on the broad traits of N/NE and E/PE. There is a need for further work on Conscientiousness and on lower levels in the trait hierarchy (i.e., facets). Second, there is a critical need for prospective, longitudinal studies, particularly in anxiety disorders. As the internalizing disorders often have an early onset, it is important to begin these studies at a young enough age to establish the temporal relation between temperament and the onset of psychopathology, and to trace the developmental pathways between them. Third, few studies have examined whether the role of temperament in internalizing psychopathology differs as a function of development. There are some hints that it may (e.g., Hirschfeld et al., 1989; Rohde et al., 1990, 1994); hence, this requires further exploration. Fourth, most of the work in this area has treated temperament as static. However, temperament changes over the course of development, and future studies must begin to consider the complex temperament–environment transactions that can influence predispositions and trajectories for internalizing disorders. In addition, as understanding of environmental and other influences on gene expression (*epigenetics*) grows, it will be important to explore epigenetic effects on temperament and their relation to depressive and anxiety disorders. Fifth, to the extent that temperament is a precursor of, or predisposition to, the development of internalizing disorders, there is a need for more systematic research to identify the moderating factors and mediating processes involved in these pathways. Finally, self-reports have borne the brunt of most research in this area and made important contributions. However, like all methods, they have limitations and cannot be applied in all contexts (e.g., young children). Thus, there is a need for further work using complementary methods such as informant reports and observations in naturalistic and laboratory settings. Temperament occupies a central place in the complex network of influences affecting internalizing disorders, and elucidating these questions should significantly advance understanding of the development, prevention, and treatment of these highly prevalent and impairing conditions.

Further Reading

Clark L. A. (2005). Temperament as a unifying basis for personality and psychopathology. *Journal of Abnormal Psychology, 114*, 505–521.

Klein, D. N., Kotov, R., & Bufferd, S. J. (2011). Personality and depression: Explanatory models and review of the evidence. *Annual Review of Clinical Psychology, 7*, 269–295.

Pagura, J., Cox, B. J., & Enns, M. W. (2009). Personality factors in the anxiety disorders. In M. M. Antony & M. B. Stein (Eds.), *Oxford handbook of anxiety and related disorders* (pp. 190–206). New York: Oxford University Press.

References

Abela, J. R. Z., & Hankin, B. L. (2008). Cognitive vulnerability to depression in children and adolescents: A developmental psychopathology perspective. In J. R. Z. Abela & B. L. Hankin (Eds.), *Handbook of depression in children and adolescents* (pp. 35–78). New York: Guilford Press.

Adam, E. K., Doane, L. D., Zinbarg, R. E., Mineka, S., Craske, M. G., & Griffith, J. W. (2010). Prospective prediction of major depressive disorder from cortisol awakening responses in adolescence. *Psychoneuroendocrinology, 35*, 921–931.

Akiskal, H. S. (1983). Dysthymic disorder: Psychopathology of proposed chronic depressive subtypes. *American Journal of Psychiatry, 140*, 11–20.

Alloy, L. B., Abramson, L. Y., Whitehouse, W. G., Hogan, M. E., Panzarella, C., & Rose, D. T. (2006). Prospective incidence of first onsets and recurrences of depression in individuals at high and low cognitive risk for depression. *Journal of Abnormal Psychology, 115*, 145–156.

Arborelius, L., Owens, M. J., Plotsky, P. M., & Nemeroff, C. B. (1999). The role of corticotropin-releasing factor in depression and anxiety disorders. *Journal of Endocrinology, 160,* 1–12.

Bagby, R. M., Quilty, L. C., Segal, Z. V., McBride, C. C., Kennedy, S. H., & Costa, P. T. (2008). Personality and differential treatment response in major depression: A randomized controlled trial comparing cognitive-behavioural therapy and pharmacotherapy. *Canadian Journal of Psychiatry, 53,* 361–370.

Ball, S. G., Otto, M. W., Pollack, M. H., Uccello, R., & Rosenbaum, J. F. (1995). Differentiating social phobias and panic disorder: A test of core beliefs. *Cognitive Therapy and Research, 19,* 473–481.

Bar-Haim, Y., Lamy, D., Pergamin, L., Bakermans-Kranenburg, M. J., & van IJzendoorn, M. H. (2007). Threat-related attentional bias in anxious and nonanxious individuals: A meta-analytic study. *Psychological Bulletin, 133,* 1–24.

Beck, A. T. (1983). Cognitive therapy of depression: New approaches. In P. Clayton & J. Barrett (Eds.), *Treatment of depression: Old and new approaches* (pp. 265–290). New York: Raven Press.

Biederman, J., Hirshfeld-Becker, D. R., Rosenbaum, J. F., Hérot, C., Friedman, D., Snidman, N., et al. (2001). Further evidence of association between behavioral inhibition and social anxiety in children. *American Journal of Psychiatry, 158,* 1673–1679.

Biederman, J., Rosenbaum, J. F., Bolduc-Murphy, E. A., Faraone, S. V., Chaloff, J., Hirshfeld, D. R., et al. (1993). A 3-year follow-up of children with and without behavioral inhibition. *Journal of the American Academy of Child and Adolescent Psychiatry, 32,* 814–821.

Bienvenu, O. J., Nestadt, G., Samuels, J. F., Costa, P. T., Howard, W. T., & Eaton, M. W. (2001). Phobic, panic and major depressive disorders and the five-factor model of personality. *Journal of Nervous and Mental Disease, 189,* 154–161.

Blatt, S. J. (1974). Levels of object representation in anaclitic and introjective depression. *Psychoanalytic Study of the Child, 29,* 107–157.

Brendgen, M., Wanner, B., Morin, A. J. S., & Vitaro, F. (2005). Relations with parents and with peers, temperament, and trajectories of depressed mood during early adolescence. *Journal of Abnormal Child Psychology, 33,* 579–594.

Brown, T. A., & Barlow, D. H. (2009). A proposal for a dimensional classification system based on the shared features of the DSM-IV anxiety and mood disorders: Implications for assessment and treatment. *Psychological Assessment, 21,* 256–271.

Brown, T. A., Chorpita, B. F., & Barlow, D. H. (1998). Structural relationships among dimensions of the DSM-IV anxiety and mood disorders and dimensions of negative affect, positive affect, and autonomic arousal. *Journal of Abnormal Psychology, 107,* 179–192.

Canli, T. (2008). Toward a neurogenetic theory of neuroticism. *Annals of the New York Academy of Sciences, 1129,* 153–174.

Caspi, A., Moffitt, T. E., Newman, D. L., & Silva, P. A. (1996). Behavioral observations at age 3 years predict adult psychiatric disorders: Longitudinal evidence form a birth cohort. *Archives of General Psychiatry, 53,* 1033–1039.

Caspi, A., & Shiner, R. L. (2006). Personality development. In W. Damon, R. Lerner, & N. Eisenberg (Eds.), *Handbook of child psychology: Vol. 3. Social, emotional, and personality development* (6th ed., pp. 300–364) New York: Wiley.

Chavira, D. A., Stein, M. B., Golinelli, D., Sherbourne, C. D., Craske, M. G., Sullivan, G., et al. (2009). Predictors of clinical improvement in a randomized effectiveness trial for primary care patients with panic disorder. *Journal of Nervous and Mental Disease, 197,* 715–721.

Chida, Y., & Steptoe, A. (2009). Cortisol awakening response and psychosocial factors: A systematic review and meta-analysis. *Biological Psychology, 80,* 265–278.

Chmielewski, M., & Watson, D. (2009). What is being assessed and why it matters: The impact of transient error on trait research. *Journal of Personality and Social Psychology, 97,* 186–202.

Chronis-Tuscano, A., Degnan, K. A., Pine, D. S., Pérez-Edgar, K., Henderson, H. A., Diaz, Y., et al. (2009). Stable early maternal report of behavioral inhibition predicts lifetime social anxiety disorder in adolescence. *Journal of the American Academy of Child and Adolescent Psychiatry, 48,* 928–935.

Clark, L. A. (2005). Temperament as a unifying basis for personality and psychopathology. *Journal of Abnormal Psychology, 114,* 505–521.

Clark, L. A., & Watson, D. (1999). Temperament: A new paradigm for trait psychology. In L. A. Pervin & O. P. John (Eds.), *Handbook of personality* (2nd ed., pp. 399–423). New York: Guilford Press.

De Fruyt, F., Van Leeuwen, K., Bagby, R. M., Rolland, J., & Rouillon, F. (2006). Assessing and interpreting personality change and continuity in patients treated for major depression. *Psychological Assessment, 18,* 71–80.

de Graaf, R., Bijl, R. V., Ravelli, A., Smit, F., & Vollenbergh, W. A. M. (2002). Predictors of first incidence of DSM-III-R psychiatric disorders in the general population: Findings from the Netherlands Mental Health Survey and Incidence Study. *Acta Psychiatrica Scandinavica, 106,* 303–313.

De Pauw, S. S. W., & Mervielde, I. (2010). Temperament, personality and developmental psychopathology: A review based on the conceptual dimensions underlying childhood traits. *Child Psychiatry and Human Development, 41,* 313–329.

Degnan, K. A., Almas, A. N., & Fox, N. A. (2010). Temperament and the environment in the etiology of childhood anxiety. *Journal of Child Psychiatry and Psychiatry, 51,* 497–517.

Degnan, K. A., Henderson, H. A., Fox, N. A., & Rubin, K. H. (2008). Predicting social wariness in middle childhood: The moderating roles of childcare history, maternal personality and maternal behavior. *Social Development, 17,* 471–487.

Dougherty, L. R., Klein, D. N., Durbin, C. E., Hayden, E. P., & Olino, T. M. (2010). Temperamental positive and negative emotionality and children's depressive symptoms: A longitudinal prospective study from age three to age ten. *Journal of Social and Clinical Psychology, 29,* 462–488.

Dougherty, L. R., Klein, D. N., Olino, T. M., Dyson, M., & Rose, S. (2009). Increased waking salivary cortisol and depression risk in preschoolers: The role of maternal history of melancholic depression and early child temperament. *Journal of Child Psychology and Psychiatry, 50,* 1495–1503.

Duggan, C. F., Lee, A. S., & Murray, R. M. (1990). Does personality predict long-term outcome in depression? *British Journal of Psychiatry, 157,* 19–24.

Durbin, C. E., Klein, D. N., Hayden, E. P., Buckley, M. E., & Moerk, K. C. (2005). Temperamental emotionality in preschoolers and parental mood disorders. *Journal of Abnormal Psychology, 114,* 28–37.

Else-Quest, N. M., Hyde, J. S., Goldsmith, H. H., & Van Hulle, C. A. (2006). Gender differences in temperament: A meta-analysis. *Psychological Bulletin, 132,* 33–72.

Fanous, A. H., Neale, M. C., Aggen, S. H., & Kendler, K. S. (2007). A longitudinal study of personality and major depression in a population-based sample of male twins. *Psychological Medicine, 37,* 1163–1172.

Fenigstein, A., Scheier, M. F., & Buss, A. H. (1975). Public and private self-consciousness: Assessment and theory. *Journal of Consulting and Clinical Psychology, 43,* 522–527.

Fox, N. A., Henderson, H. A., Marshall, P. J., Nichols, K. E., & Ghera, M. M. (2005). Behavioral Inhibition: Linking biology and behavior within a developmental framework. *Annual Review of Psychology, 56,* 235–262.

Fraley, R. C., & Roberts, B. W. (2005). Patterns of continuity: A dynamic model for conceptualizing the stability of individual differences in psychological constructs across the life course. *Psychological Review, 112,* 60–74.

Gershuny, B. S., & Sher, K. J. (1998). The relation between personality and anxiety: Findings from a 3-year prospective study. *Journal of Abnormal Psychology, 107,* 252–262.

Hayden, E. P., Klein, D. N., Durbin, C. E., & Olino, T. M. (2006). Positive emotionality at age 3 predicts cognitive styles in 7-year-old children. *Development and Psychopathology, 18,* 409–423.

Hettema, J. M., Neale, M. C., Myers, J. M., Prescott, C. A., & Kendler, K. S. (2006). A population-based twin study of the relationship between neuroticism and internalizing disorders. *American Journal of Psychiatry, 163,* 857–864.

Hirschfeld, R. M. A., Klerman, G. L., Clayton, P. J., Keller, M. B., McDonald-Scott, P., & Larkin, B. H. (1983). Assessing personality: Effects of the depressive state on trait measurement. *American Journal of Psychiatry, 140,* 695–699.

Hirschfeld, R. M. A., Klerman, G. L., Lavori, P., Keller, M. B., Griffith, P., & Coryell, W. (1989). Premorbid personality assessments of first onset of major depression. *Archives of General Psychiatry, 46,* 345–350.

Hirshfeld-Becker, D. R., Micco, J., Henin, A., Bloomfield, A., Biederman, J., & Rosenbaum, J. (2008). Behavioral inhibition. *Depression and Anxiety, 25,* 357–367.

Hymel, S., Rubin, K. H., Rowden, L., & LeMare, L. (1990). Children's peer relationships: Longitudinal prediction of internalizing and externalizing problems from middle to late childhood. *Child Development, 61,* 2004–2021.

Joiner, T. E., & Lonigan, C. J. (2000). Tripartite model of depression and anxiety in youth psychiatric inpatients: Relations with diagnostic status and future symptoms. *Journal of Clinical Child Psychology, 29,* 372–382.

Kagan, J., Snidman, N., Kahn, V., & Towsley, S. (2007). The preservation of two infant temperaments into adolescence. *Monographs of the Society for Research on Child Development, 72,* 1–95.

Kandler, C., Bleidorn, W., Riemann, R., Spinath, F. M., Thiel, W., & Angleitner, A. (2010). Sources of cumulative continuity in personality: A longitudinal multiple-rater twin study. *Journal of Personality and Social Psychology, 98,* 995–1008.

Kasch, K. L., Klein, D. N., & Lara, M. E. (2001). A construct validation study of the Response Styles Questionnaire Rumination scale in participants with a recent-onset major depressive episode. *Psychological Assessment, 13,* 375–383.

Kendler, K. S., Gardner, C. O., Gatz, M., & Pedersen, N. L. (2007). The sources of comorbidity between major depression and generalized anxiety disorder in a Swedish national twin sample. *Psychological Medicine, 37,* 453–462.

Kendler, K. S., Gatz, M., Gardner, C. O., & Pedersen, N. L. (2006). Personality and major depression. *Archives of General Psychiatry, 63,* 1113–1120.

Kendler, K. S., Kuhn, J., & Prescott, C. A. (2004). The interrelationship of neuroticism, sex, and stressful life events in the prediction of episodes of major depression. *American Journal of Psychiatry, 161,* 631–636.

Kendler, K. S., Neale, M. C., Kessler, R. C., Heath, A. C., & Eaves, L. J. (1993). A longitudinal twin study of personality and major depression in women. *Archives of General Psychiatry, 50,* 853–862.

Kennedy, S. H., Farvolden, P., Cohen, N. L., Bagby, R. M., & Costa, P. T. (2005). The impact of personality on the pharmacological treatment of depression. In M. Rosenbluth, S. H. Kennedy, & R. M. Bagby (Eds.), *Depression and personality* (pp. 97–119). Arlington, VA: American Psychiatric Publishing.

Kessler, R. C., Berguland, P., Demler, O., Jin, R., Merikangas, K. R., & Walters, E. E. (2005). Lifetime prevalence and age-of-onset distributions of DSM Distributions of the DSM-IV disorders in the National Comorbidity Survey Replication. *Archives of General Psychiatry, 62,* 593–602.

Kiel, E. J., & Buss, K. A. (2010). Maternal accuracy and behavior in anticipating children's responses to novelty: Relations to fearful temperament and implications for anxiety development. *Social Development, 19,* 304–325.

Klein, D. N., Dougherty, L. R., Laptook, R. S., & Olino, T. M. (2008). Temperament and risk for mood disorders in adolescents. In N. Allen & L. Sheeber (Eds.), *Adolescent emotional development and the emergence of depressive disorders* (pp. 238–261). Cambridge, UK: Cambridge University Press.

Klein, D. N., Kotov, R., & Bufferd, S. J. (2011). Personality and depression: Explanatory models and review of the evidence. *Annual Review of Clinical Psychology, 7,* 269–295.

Kochanska, G. (1991). Patterns of inhibition to the unfamiliar in children of normal and affectively ill mothers. *Child Development, 62,* 250–263.

Kotov, R., Gamez, W., Schmidt, F. L., & Watson, D. (2010). Linking "Big Five" personality traits to anxiety, depressive, and substance use disorders: A meta-analysis. *Psychological Bulletin, 136,* 768–821.

Kotov, R., Wilson, D., Robles, J., & Schmidt, N. B. (2007). Personality traits and anxiety symptoms: The multilevel trait predictor model. *Behaviour Research and Therapy, 45,* 1485–1503.

Kovacs, M., & Lopez-Duran, N. (2010). Prodromal symptoms and atypical affectivity as predictors of major depression in juveniles: Implications for prevention. *Journal of Child Psychology and Psychiatry, 51,* 472–496.

Krueger, R. F., & Tackett, J. L. (2003). Personality and psychopathology: Working toward the bigger picture. *Journal of Personality Disorders, 17,* 109–128.

La Greca, A. M., & Harrison, H. M. (2005). Adolescent peer relations, friendships, and romantic relationships: Do they predict social anxiety and depression? *Journal of Clinical Child and Adolescent Psychology, 34,* 49–61.

Lahey, B. B. (2004). Commentary: Role of temperament in developmental models of psychopathology. *Journal of Clinical Child and Adolescent Psychology, 33,* 88–93.

Lengua, L. J., Wolchik, S. A., Sandler, I. N., & West, S. G. (2000). The additive and interactive effects of parenting and temperament in predicting problems of children of divorce. *Journal of Clinical Child Psychology, 29,* 232–244.

Lonigan, C. J., & Vasey, M. W. (2009). Negative affectivity, effortful control, and attention to threat-relevant stimuli. *Journal of Abnormal Child Psychology, 37,* 387–399.

Mathews, A., & MacLeod, C. (2005). Cognitive vulnerability to emotional disorders. *Annual Review of Clinical Psychology, 1,* 167–195.

McDermott, J. M., Pérez-Edgar, K., Henderson, H. A., Chronis-Tuscano, A., Pine, D. S., & Fox, N. A. (2009). A history of childhood behavioral inhibition and enhanced response monitoring in adolescence are linked to clinical anxiety. *Biological Psychiatry, 65*(5), 445–448.

Morey, L. C., Shea, M. T., Markowitz, J. C., Stout, R. L., Hopwood, C. J., Gunderson, J. G., et al. (2010). State effects of major depression on the assessment of personality and personality disorder. *American Journal of Psychiatry, 167,* 528–535.

Naragon-Gainey, K. (2010). Meta-analysis of the relations of anxiety sensitivity to the depressive and anxiety disorders. *Psychological Bulletin, 136,* 128–150.

Newman, D. L., Caspi, A., Moffitt, T. E., & Silva, P. A. (1997). Antecedents of adult interpersonal functioning: Effects of individual differences in age 3 temperament. *Developmental Psychology, 33,* 206–217.

Nolan, S. A., Roberts, J. E., & Gotlib, I. H. (1998). Neuroticism and ruminative response style as predictors of change in depressive symptomatology. *Cognitive Therapy and Research, 22,* 445–455.

Nolen-Hoeksema, S., Wisco, B.E., & Lyubomirsky, S. (2008). Rethinking rumination. *Perspectives in Psychological Science, 3,* 400–424.

Olatunji, B. O., & Wolitzky-Taylor, K. B. (2009). Anxiety sensitivity and the anxiety disorders: A meta-analytic review and synthesis. *Psychological Bulletin, 135,* 974–999.

Oldehinkel, A. J., Hartman, C. A., Ferdinand, R. F., Verhulst, F. C., & Ormel, J. (2007). Effortful control as modifier of the association between negative emotionality and adolescents' mental health problems. *Development and Psychopathology, 19,* 523–539.

Oldehinkel, A. J., Veenstra, R., Ormel, J., de Winter, A. F., & Verhulst, F. C. (2006). Temperament, parenting, and depressive symptoms in a population sample of preadolescents. *Journal of Child Psychology and Psychiatry, 47,* 684–695.

Olino, T. M., Klein, D. N., Dyson, M. W., Rose, S. A., & Durbin, C. E. (2010). Temperamental emotionality in preschool-aged children and depressive disorders in parents: Associations in a large community sample. *Journal of Abnormal Psychology, 119,* 468–478.

Ormel, J., Oldehinkel, A. J., & Brilman, E. I. (2001). The interplay and ecological continuity of neuroticism, difficulties, and life events in the etiology of major and subsyndromal, first and recurrent depressive episodes in later life. *American Journal of Psychiatry, 158,* 885–891.

Ormel, J., Oldehinkel, A. J., & Vollebergh, W. (2004). Vulnerability before, during, and after a major depressive episode. *Archives of General Psychiatry, 61,* 990–996.

Ormel, J., Rosmalen, J., & Farmer, A. (2004). Neuroticism: A non-informative marker of vulnerability to psychopathology. *Social Psychiatry and Psychiatric Epidemiology, 39,* 906–912.

Pagura, J., Cox, B. J., & Enns, M. W. (2009). Personality factors in the anxiety disorders. In M. M. Antony & M. B. Stein (Eds.), *Oxford handbook of anxiety and related disorders* (pp. 190–206). New York: Oxford University Press.

Pérez-Edgar, K., Bar-Haim, Y., McDermott, J. M., Chronis-Tuscano, A., Pine, D. S., & Fox, N. A. (2010). Attention biases to threat and behavioral inhibition in early childhood shape adolescent social withdrawal. *Emotion, 10,* 349–357.

Prior, M., Smart, D., Sanson, A., & Oberklaid, F. (2000). Does shy–inhibited temperament in childhood lead to anxiety problems in adolescence? *Journal of the American Academy of Child and Adolescent Psychiatry, 39,* 461–468.

Quilty, L. C., De Fruyt, F., Rolland, J. P., Kennedy, S. H., Rouillon, P. F., & Bagby, R. M. (2008). Dimensional personality traits and treatment outcome in patients with major depressive disorder. *Journal of Affective Disorder, 108,* 241–250.

Quilty, L. C., Meusel, L. C., & Bagby, R. M. (2008). Neuroticism as a mediator of treatment response to SSRIs in major depression. *Journal of Affective Disorders, 111,* 67–71.

Rapee, R. M., & Coplan, R. J. (2010). Conceptual relations between anxiety disorder and fearful temperament. *New Directions for Child and Adolescent Development, 127,* 17–31.

Rapee, R. M., Kennedy, S., Ingram, M., Edwards, S. L., & Sweeney, L. (2010). Altering the trajectory of anxiety in at-risk young children. *American Journal of Psychiatry, 167,* 1518–1525.

Rapee, R. M., Schniering, C. A., & Hudson, J. L. (2009). Anxiety disorders during childhood and adolescence: Origins and treatment. *Annual Review of Clinical Psychology, 5,* 311–341.

Reich, J., Noyes, R., Hirschfeld, R., Coryell, W., & O'Gorman, T. (1987). State and personality in depressed and panic patients. *American Journal of Psychiatry, 144,* 181–187.

Reiss, S., & McNally, R. J. (1985). Expectancy model of fear. In S. Reiss & R. R. Bootzin (Eds.), *Theoretical issues in behavior therapy* (pp. 107–121). San Diego, CA: Academic Press.

Roberts, B. W., & DelVecchio, W. F. (2000). The rank-order consistency of personality from childhood to old age: A quantitative review of longitudinal studies. *Psychological Bulletin, 136,* 3–25.

Roberts, B. W., Walton, K. E., & Viechtbauer, W. (2006). Patterns of mean-level change in personality traits across the life course: A meta-analysis of longitudinal studies. *Psychological Bulletin, 132,* 1–25.

Rohde, P., Lewinsohn, P. M., & Seeley, J. R. (1990). Are people changed by the experience of having an episode of depression?: A further test of the scar hypothesis. *Journal of Abnormal Psychology, 99,* 264–271.

Rohde, P., Lewinsohn, P. M., & Seeley, J. R. (1994). Are adolescents changed by an episode of major depression? *Journal of the American Academy of Child and Adolescent Psychiatry, 33,* 1289–1298.

Rorsman, B., Grasbeck, A., Hagnell, O., Isberg, P.-E., & Otterbeck, L. (1993). Premorbid personality traits and psychometric background factors in depression: The Ludby Study 1957–1972. *Neuropsychobiology, 27,* 72–79.

Rosenbaum, J. F., Biederman, J., Gersten, M., Hirschfeld, D. R., Meminger, S. R., & Herman, J. B., et al. (1988). Behavioral inhibition in children of parents with panic disorder and agoraphobia: A controlled study. *Archives of General Psychiatry, 45,* 463–470.

Rosenbaum, J. F., Biederman, J., Hirshfeld-Becker, D. R., Kagan, J., Snidman, N., Friedman, D., et al. (2000). A controlled study of behavioral inhibition in children of parents with panic disorder and depression. *American Journal of Psychiatry, 157,* 2002–2010.

Rothbart, M. K., & Bates, J. E. (2006). Temperament in children's development. In W. Damon, R. Lerner, & N. Eisenberg (Eds.), *Handbook of child psychology: Vol. 3. Social, emotional, and personality development* (6th ed., pp. 99–1660). New York: Wiley.

Rubin, K. H., Coplan, R. J., & Bowker, J. C. (2009). Social withdrawal in childhood. *Annual Review of Psychology, 60,* 141–171.

Rusting, C. L. (1999). Interactive effects of personality and mood on emotion-congruent memory and judgment. *Journal of Personality and Social Psychology, 77,* 1073–1086.

Sanson, A., Hemphill, S. A., & Smart, D. (2004). Connections between temperament and social development: A review. *Social Development, 13,* 142–170.

Schmidt, N. B., Lerew, D. R., & Jackson, R. J. (1999). Prospective evaluation of anxiety sensitivity in the pathogensis of panic: Replication and extension. *Journal of Abnormal Psychology, 108,* 532–537.

Schmidt, N. B., Zvolensky, M. J., & Maner, J. K. (2006). Anxiety sensitivity: Prospective prediction of panic attacks and Axis I pathology. *Journal of Psychiatric Research, 40,* 691–699.

Shea, M. T., Leon, A. C., Mueller, T. I., Solomon, D. A., Warshaw, M. G., & Keller, M. B. (1996). Does major depression result in lasting personality change? *American Journal of Psychiatry, 153,* 1404–1410.

Tang, T. Z., DeRubeis, R. J., Hollon, S. D., Amsterdam, J., Shelton, R., & Schalet, B. (2009). Personality change during depression treatment: A placebo-controlled trial. *Archives of General Psychiatry, 66,* 1322–1330.

Trull, T. J., & Sher, K. J. (1994). Relationship between the five-factor model of personality and Axis I disorders in nonclinical sample. *Journal of Abnormal Psychology, 103,* 350–360.

Van Os, J., Jones, P., Lewis, G., Wadsworth, M., & Murray, R. (1997). Developmental precursors of affective illness in a general population birth cohort. *Archives of General Psychiatry, 54,* 625–631.

Verstraeten, K., Vasey, M. W., Raes, F., & Bijttebier, P. (2009). Temperament and risk for depressive symptoms in adolescence: Mediation by rumination and moderation by effortful control. *Journal of Abnormal Child Psychology, 37,* 349–361.

Watson, D., Kotov, R., & Gamez, W. (2006). Basic dimensions of temperament in relation to personality and psychopathology. In R. F. Krueger & J. L. Tackett (Eds.), *Personality and psychopathology* (pp. 7–38). New York: Guilford Press.

Watson, D., & Naragon-Gainey, K. (2010). On the specificity of positive emotional dysfunction in psychopathology: Evidence from the mood and anxiety disorders and schizophrenia/schizotypy. *Clinical Psychology Review, 30,* 839–848.

Weinstock, L. M., & Whisman, M. A. (2006). Neuroticism as a common feature of the depressive and anxiety disorders: A test of the Revised Integrative Hierarchical Model in a national sample. *Journal of Abnormal Psychology, 115,* 68–74.

Wetter, E. K., & Hankin, B. L. (2009). Mediational pathways through which positive and negative emotionality contribute to anhedonic symptoms of depression: A prospective study of adolescents. *Journal of Abnormal Child Psychology, 37,* 507–520.

White, L., McDermott, J., Degnan, K., Henderson, H., & Fox, N. (2011). Behavioral inhibition and anxiety: The moderating roles of inhibitory control and attention shifting. *Journal of Abnormal Child Psychology, 5,* 735–747.

Williams, L. R., Degnan, K. A., Pérez-Edgar, K. E., Henderson, H. A., Rubin, K. H., Pine, D. S., et al. (2009). Impact of behavioral inhibition and parenting style on internalizing and externalizing problems from early childhood through adolescence. *Journal of Abnormal Child Psychology, 51,* 497–519.

Zinbarg, R. E., Uliaszek, A. A., & Adler, J. M. (2008). The role of personality in psychotherapy for anxiety and depression. *Journal of Personality, 76,* 1649–1688.

Zuroff, D. C., Mongrain, M., & Santor, D. A. (2004). Conceptualizing and measuring personality vulnerability to depression: Comment on Coyne and Whiffen (1995). *Psychological Bulletin, 130,* 489–511.

Chapter 27

Temperament, Externalizing Disorders, and Attention-Deficit/Hyperactivity Disorder

Jennifer L. Tackett
Michelle M. Martel
Shauna C. Kushner

Child psychopathology has long been characterized by differentiating internalizing problems (e.g., mood and anxiety symptoms) from externalizing problems (e.g., conduct and attentional problems). Externalizing disorders covary with one another in large part due to shared temperamental features, particularly the trait of disinhibition (Nigg, 2006; Tackett, 2006, 2010). We begin this chapter by defining externalizing problems, with a focus on problems in childhood and adolescence. We then discuss empirical connections between temperamental traits and externalizing problems, review proposed theoretical models for explaining these links, and discuss dynamic conceptualizations of these relationships as they interact with the environment. Throughout this chapter, we draw largely from a trait perspective of temperament, incorporating other research (including research on personality traits) when relevant. This growing area of research has provided strong evidence that characterological differences, such as personality and temperament, provide a psychologically rich backdrop against which psychopathology can be better understood.

Defining Externalizing Disorders

Conduct Disorder and Oppositional Defiant Disorder

Within the literature on externalizing psychopathology, clinically significant and recurrent oppositional/defiant, aggressive, and rule-breaking behaviors are subsumed under two syndromes classified in DSM-IV-TR: conduct disorder (CD) and oppositional defiant disorder (ODD) (American Psychiatric Association, 2000). CD represents more severe behavioral manifestations of antisocial behavior, including bullying or threatening others, using a weapon, and physical cruelty to animals. In the current version of DSM, CD can further be distinguished into subtypes according to whether symptoms arise in childhood (i.e., prior to 10 years of age) or in adolescence. Age of onset is associated with different patterns of symptoms, with childhood-onset being associated with more aggressive behaviors, and adolescent-onset being associated with more delinquent, rule-breaking behaviors (Lahey et al., 1999; Zoccolillo, 1993). The prevalence of CD has been estimated as being between 6 and 16% for males and between 2 and 9% for females (American Psychiatric Association, 2000; Nock, Kazdin, Hiripi, & Kessler, 2006).

ODD consists of problematic acting-out behaviors that are of lower severity and often represent more pervasive interpersonal patterns of behavior than seen in the diagnostic criteria for CD. ODD symptoms include deliberate attempts to annoy others, frequent arguments with adults, and holding grudges. Unlike CD and attention-deficit/hyperactivity disorder (ADHD), DSM-IV-TR does not include subtypes for ODD. In general, ODD has received the least research attention of these disorders, despite being quite common in the general population. The estimated lifetime prevalence of ODD is between 2 and 16% for males and 2 and 9% for females (American Psychiatric Association, 2000; Nock, Kazdin, Hiripi, & Kessler, 2007).

Attention-Deficit/Hyperactivity Disorder

ADHD is a childhood disruptive behavior disorder characterized by excessive inattention–disorganization (e.g., often fails to give close attention to details" or "makes careless mistakes in schoolwork, work, or other activities") and/or hyperactivity–impulsivity (e.g., "often fidgets with hands or feet," "squirms in seat," or "often has difficulty awaiting turn"; American Psychiatric Association, 2000). Due to the disorder's behavioral heterogeneity, ADHD is further divided into three subtypes (i.e., predominantly inattentive, predominantly hyperactive–impulsive, and combined) in DSM-IV (American Psychiatric Association, 2000); however, these subtypes have not been well validated (Lahey, Pelham, Loney, Lee, & Willcutt, 2005). Thus, the current conceptualization of ADHD focuses on multiple pathways to the disorder (e.g., Nigg, Goldsmith, & Sachek, 2004; Sonuga-Barke, 2005). The disorder has a 5% prevalence rate in childhood, with boys being approximately three times more likely to be diagnosed than girls (American Psychiatric Association, 2000). ADHD is commonly comorbid with other childhood disruptive behavior disorders such as ODD and CD (American Psychiatric Association, 2000). ADHD exhibits a relatively chronic course, with only slightly lower prevalence rates in adulthood than in childhood (Faraone, Biederman, & Mick, 2006; Kessler et al., 2006), and it follows a developmental trajectory of difficulties with impulse control arising as early as preschool, followed by difficulties with attention that become most prominent around school entry (Olson, 1996). ADHD is highly impairing and is associated with increased accident rates and injuries, as well as deficits in cognition, language, adaptive functioning, motor development, emotion, school performance, task performance, neuropsychological executive functioning, and peer status (Barkley, 2006). Due to its early development and prominent behavioral characteristics, ADHD is often considered to be a trait-like characteristic (Braaten & Rosen, 1997; Nigg, Blaskey, Huang-Pollock, & John, 2002), and recent research suggests that ADHD is best conceptualized as a dimensional trait rather than a categorical diagnostic category (Haslam et al., 2006; Levy, Hay, McStephen, Wood, & Waldman, 1997).

Other Externalizing Constructs

The domain of externalizing behaviors has often subsumed additional behaviors, including substance use, inappropriate sexual behavior, and eating problems characterized by impulsivity such as bulimia nervosa (Krueger, Markon, Patrick, Benning, & Kramer, 2007; Tackett, 2006). Substance use is frequently considered an externalizing problem in both youth and adult samples, and includes problematic use of nicotine and alcohol, as well as illicit drug use. Recent examinations of the broader externalizing domain in both child and adult populations have included the construct of *relational aggression* (Baker, Jacobson, Raine, Lozano, & Bezdjian, 2007; Krueger et al., 2007). Relational aggression includes behaviors intended to damage the victim's social status or interpersonal relationships (Crick & Grotpeter, 1995). There is currently some debate over whether relational aggression reflects developmentally normative behaviors or psychopathology (Tackett, Waldman, & Lahey, 2009). Relational aggression does show substantial connections with psychopathology (Card, Stucky, Sawalani, & Little, 2008), and some evidence supports grouping it with externalizing problems given that it exhibits stronger connections to externalizing than to internalizing problems (Tackett & Ostrov, 2010). Finally, it is important to consider early manifestations of personality disorders that would likely fall under the externalizing domain. Although much less often studied, characteristics reflecting emotion dysregulation, self-harm, narcissism, and callousness may represent early phenotypes of Cluster B personality disorders such as borderline, narcissistic, and antisocial personality disorders (Tackett, Balsis, Oltmanns, & Krueger, 2009). It is important to include such constructs in our representation of externalizing disorders at younger ages, in order to encourage future research and assessment to examine broader links with temperamental characteristics early in life.

Externalizing-Relevant Temperamental Traits

A number of traits have been associated with externalizing problems, particularly traits reflecting self-regulatory capacity and the experience of negative emotions (Tackett, 2006). Major taxonomies of temperament and personality are often hierarchical in nature; higher-order traits represent broader domains of individual differences, whereas lower-order domains represent more narrowly defined characteristics, of which the higher-order domains are typically composed. For example, the broader trait of constraint may be defined by multiple facets, including orderliness, harm avoidance, behavioral control, and traditionalism (Tellegen & Waller, 2001). This distinction is particularly important because different levels of the hierarchy may hold different sources of utility. For example, higher-order traits may be more conducive to examination of general risk factors, such as genetic and psychobiological influences (Baker et al., 2007; Dick et al., 2008); lower-order traits, on the other hand, may be better predictors of specific behavioral outcomes (Eisenberg et al., 2004). Both higher- and lower-order traits have been identified in relation to youth externalizing disorders, although these have often been measured using different taxonomical approaches, instruments, and methods.

Effortful control is the primary higher-order trait that has most often linked to externalizing problems across the lifespan (Eisenberg, Spinrad, & Eggum, 2010; Nigg, 2006; Tackett, 2006, 2010). Effortful Control has approximate analogues in other temperament/personality models, such as Conscientiousness and Constraint. Effortful Control/Conscientiousness is a broad trait that reflects characteristics such as impulsivity, norm-governed behavior, and intrapersonal self-regulation. The other higher-order trait that is often connected with externalizing problems at younger ages is Negative Emotionality/Neuroticism (Eisenberg et al., 2010; Nigg, 2006; Tackett, 2006, 2010), which typically includes a propensity to experience negative affect (e.g., sadness, anxiety, and irritability). One important trait for understanding adult externalizing disorders is Agreeableness, which often does not have a direct analogue in child temperament/personality models (Tackett et al., in press). Importantly, some aspects of Agreeableness (e.g., compliance) tend to covary with Effortful Control, whereas other aspects of Agreeableness (e.g., antagonism) tend to covary with Negative Emotionality in childhood. The extent to which Agreeableness comes to represent an important, distinct personality trait in understanding externalizing disorders may emerge as a development phenomenon during the transition to adolescence.

Overall patterns for lower-order traits in relation to externalizing problems are harder to identify because the traits under investigation often differ depending on the temperament/personality taxonomy utilized. One important lower-order construct for externalizing pathology is callous–unemotional traits, which have been connected to both temperament and personality models (Essau, Sasagaw, & Frick, 2006; Frick & Sheffield-Morris, 2004), and show substantial links with severe antisocial behavior (see Moffitt et al., 2008, for a review). Callous–unemotional traits index characteristics such as lack of empathy, caring, and emotional response. Similar to the overall pattern for externalizing problems, callous–unemotional traits tend to show strong negative associations with Agreeableness and Conscientiousness;

however, contrary to overall externalizing problems, these traits tend to show negligible associations with Neuroticism (Essau et al., 2006). It is important for researchers to develop a common language regarding lower-order temperament characteristics in order to understand better their relation to a variety of behavioral outcomes, including externalizing problems. We next turn to a discussion of how such traits relate to externalizing disorders and problem behaviors.

Broad Models of the Externalizing Psychopathology/Temperament Relationship

Several different models have been proposed to explain the relations between dispositional characteristics and psychopathology (see Tackett, 2006, for a review). The pathoplasty/exacerbation model explains the effect that temperament traits may have on an emerging or manifest psychological disorder, regardless of whether those traits played a causal role in disorder emergence. For example, premorbid temperament may alter the particular symptom constellation that emerges or the course or severity of the disorder, all of which might be explained by the pathoplasty/exacerbation model. The complication/scar model, on the other hand, implies that the presence or history of a psychological disorder may scar the underlying temperament—such that the disorder causes some change in the individual's premorbid temperament. These models have received little empirical attention at any age, but particularly little for temperament–psychopathology links in younger populations. Some research has suggested that temperamental characteristics related to fearfulness/inhibition might serve as a resiliency factor for antisocial behavior by predicting better prognosis in comparison to antisocial children with lower levels of fearful/inhibited traits (Tackett, 2006). This relationship is a nice example of the pathoplasty/exacerbation model.

The two models that have received moderate empirical attention in younger age groups are the vulnerability and spectrum models. In the vulnerability model, early temperament acts as a risk factor for later disorder. An important implied aspect of the vulnerability model is that temperament and psychopathology are distinct psychological phenomena that act upon one another; that is, temperamental traits may *cause* psychopathology, and these constructs are considered nonoverlapping. The spectrum model, on the other hand, positions temperament and psychopathology as quantitatively related on the same dimension. According to a spectrum perspective, general causal factors may influence both temperament and related disorder manifestations, with the difference between the two being one of degree rather than one of kind. In other words, psychopathology can be conceptualized as a severe manifestation of a temperament trait (or constellation of traits).

It is important to emphasize that many studies supporting a vulnerability perspective cannot rule out a potential spectrum explanation (Tackett, 2006). That is, an early temperament trait may significantly predict later disorder because it is a risk factor for the disorder, but the possibility that the early temperament trait and later disorder are different manifestations of the same underlying phenomenon may also explain basic longitudinal connections. The strongest test of the spectrum model comes from studies that measure hypothesized underlying common causes to test directly whether they explain these relations or whether temperament can actually be considered a distinct risk factor for the disorder. Since most work has used a vulnerability or spectrum model, our review emphasizes these approaches and is organized around these approaches as they have been applied to each type of psychopathology. It is important to note that the following studies are organized largely based on the implicit or explicit frameworks utilized by the authors of the research summarized. Those studies summarized under vulnerability models typically utilize a standard risk–outcome framework, with temperament conceptualized as one of many potential risk factors directly influencing psychopathology development. Those studies summarized under spectrum models further aim directly to disentangle a simplified risk-based perspective by investigating common causes and/or psychometric evidence suggesting a quantitative, rather than qualitative, relationship between temperament and psychopathology constructs.

Vulnerability Models of CD/ODD

The supposition that temperament–personality characteristics may serve as vulnerability factors for developing CD and ODD is supported by numerous empirical investigations (see Figure 27.1). A large body of research has implicated temperamental–personality characteristics related to self-regulation as predispositional factors for CD and ODD. Even in typically developing children, lower effortful control predicts later increases in disruptive behavior, especially for children who are less guilt prone (Kochanska, Barry, Jimenez, Hollatz, & Woodard, 2009). Furthermore, high levels of child guilt and effortful control appear to protect against the later development of disruptive behavior problems (Kochanska et al., 2009). Several studies have provided support for the capacity of early impulsivity (e.g., Farrington & West, 1993; Henry, Caspi, Moffitt, & Silva, 1996; White, Bates, & Buyske, 2001), novelty seeking (Barnow, Lucht, & Freyberger, 2005; Hiramura et al., 2010; Raine, Reynolds, Venables, Mednick, & Farrington, 1998; Sigvardsson, Bohman, & Cloninger, 1987), low deliberation (Miller, Lynam, & Leukefeld, 2003), and low harm avoidance (Hiramura et al., 2010; Sigvardsson et al., 1987; White et al., 2001) for predicting antisocial behavior later in development. Additional studies have demonstrated a general association between low Conscientiousness and CD/delinquency (Anderson, Tapert, Moadab, Crowley, & Brown, 2007; John, Caspi, Robins, Moffitt, & Stouthamer-Loeber, 1994). Similarly, the self-regulatory construct of behavioral disinhibition has also been shown to predict delinquency and related externalizing problems in adolescence (Hirshfeld-Becker et al., 2007; Pitzer, Esser, Schmidt, & Laucht, 2009; White et al., 2001) and young adulthood (Caspi, Moffitt, Newman, & Silva, 1996).

Self-regulatory traits also show discriminant validity in their ability to distinguish both disorder subtypes and patterns of comorbidity. For example, lack of control and low constraint have been identified as specific predictors of early-onset persistent CD relative to adolescent onset, supporting the age of onset distinction as embedded in DSM-IV-TR (Moffitt, Caspi, Dickson, Silva, & Stanton, 1996; Taylor & Iacono, 2007). In terms of comorbidity profiles, disinhibition has been shown to distinguish comorbid ODD and internalizing disorders in middle childhood from pure cases of ODD (Hirshfeld-Becker et al., 2007). In a similar vein, low constraint has distinguished comorbid CD and ADHD from pure samples of CD and ADHD, such that comorbid cases demonstrate the lowest levels of constraint (Cukrowicz, Taylor, Schatschneider, & Iacono, 2006). These findings suggest that self-regulatory temperament traits hold predictive utility for CD and ODD but go beyond these simple associations to further discriminate subtypes and comorbid groups within these diagnostic categories.

Negative affect and several related temperamental–personality dimensions (e.g., anger, irritability, emotionality) have been associated with CD/ODD and related constructs of antisocial behavior (e.g., Burke, Hipwell, & Loeber, 2010; Gjone & Stevenson, 1997; Guerin, Gottfried, & Thomas, 1997; Lahey et al., 2008; Lemery, Essex, & Smider, 2002; Miller et al., 2003; Stringaris, Maughan, & Goodman, 2010). Emotionality is particularly effective in predicting comorbid profiles, including relative risk for comorbid ODD and internalizing disorders (Burke et al., 2010; Stringaris et al., 2010), as well as comorbid CD and ADHD (Cukrowicz et al., 2006). This work suggests that negative emotionality may represent a general underlying vulnerability for psychopathology, even across internalizing–externalizing categorization.

Although negative affect and its facets have typically been positively related to CD/ODD, the related dimension of fearfulness

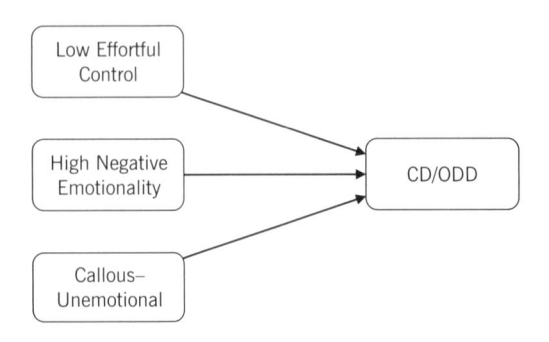

FIGURE 27.1. Trait associations with CD and ODD.

displays an inverse association. Specifically, low fearfulness in early life has been shown to predict later CD/ODD and aggression (Calkins, Blandon, Williford, & Keane, 2007; Cimbora & McIntosh, 2003; Raine et al., 1998; Shaw, Lacourse, & Nagin, 2005). These findings, however, are consistent with the observed association between low harm avoidance and later antisocial behavior (Sigvardsson et al., 1987; White et al., 2001). Fearfulness has also been negatively associated with the more antisocial features of psychopathy (Dolan & Rennie, 2007), and may therefore be better conceptualized as a callous–unemotional trait. Further research is required to tease apart the interrelations of these associations.

A separate body of research has focused on psychopathic personality dimensions, such as callous–unemotional traits, which have been shown to predict greater frequency, variety, severity, and chronicity of conduct problems and antisocial behavior (Frick, Cornell, Barry, Bodin, & Dane, 2003; Lynam, 1997; Lynam, Miller, Vachon, Loeber, & Stouthamer-Loeber, 2009; Rowe et al., 2010; Silverthorn, Frick, & Reynolds, 2001). In the prediction of externalizing personality disorders, temperamental traits such as high stimulation seeking/sociability and low fearfulness at age 3 predict adult psychopathy (Glenn, Raine, Venables, & Mednick, 2007), whereas emotional lability and low frustration tolerance in childhood predict adult borderline characteristics (Zanarini, Frankenburg, Hennen, Reich, & Silk, 2005). Surprisingly, few studies have examined agreeableness in relation to CD/ODD, although the results from those few have demonstrated associations between low Agreeableness and aggressive behaviors (Anderson et al., 2007) delinquency (John et al., 1994), and antisocial behavior in early adulthood (Miller et al., 2003).

Vulnerability Models of ADHD

Dispositional traits have also been investigated in relation to ADHD (see Figure 27.2). Across cross-sectional samples of children and adults with ADHD, wherein ADHD symptoms and traits were measured concurrently, the temperament and personality traits of low Effortful Control/Conscientiousness, high Negative Emotionality/Neuroticism, high Surgency/Extraversion, and low Agreeableness are significantly associated with ADHD (Martel & Nigg, 2006; Nigg, John, et al., 2002). In these cross-sectional samples of children and adults with ADHD, low Effortful Control/Conscientiousness appears to be more specifically associated with inattentive ADHD symptoms, whereas low Agreeableness and possibly high Extraversion are more associated with hyperactive–impulsive ADHD symptoms (Martel & Nigg, 2006; Martel, Nigg, & von Eye, 2009; Nigg, John, et al., 2002). In regard to ADHD comorbidity, high Neuroticism appears to increase risk for comorbid internalizing and externalizing psychopathology in children with ADHD, while low Agreeableness may specifically increase risk for comorbid externalizing disorders in children with ADHD (Cukrowicz et al., 2006; De Pauw & Mervielde, 2010). Although these associations hold across cross-sectional samples of children and adults with ADHD, longitudinal examination of these associations remains limited and will be important for clarification of the relationship between traits and ADHD (Martel, 2009). One longitudinal study of children with ADHD found that childhood remitting ADHD is related to low levels of control or Conscientiousness, perhaps in line with Shaw and colleagues' (2007) finding that some children with ADHD are characterized by later maturation of the prefrontal cortex. However, ADHD that persists into

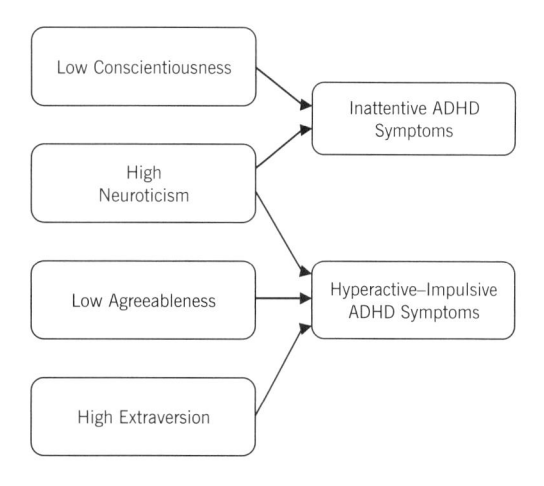

FIGURE 27.2. Trait associations with ADHD symptom domains.

adolescence is additionally characterized by increased Neuroticism and decreased Agreeableness (Miller, Miller, Newcorn, & Halperin, 2008). Furthermore, a study of infants at familial risk for ADHD demonstrated that the temperament traits of high activity level, high anger, and low attentional and Effortful Control distinguish children at high risk for ADHD as early as 7 months of age, suggesting the early manifestation of a characteristic temperament trait profile consistent with vulnerability model predictions (Auerbach et al., 2008). The potential for genetic contributions in such studies again raises the difficulty in distinguishing between vulnerability and spectrum models, to which we turn next.

Spectrum Models of CD/ODD

True tests of a spectrum association are more challenging, as they most often include measurement of "third variables" that are hypothesized to account for observed associations between personality and psychopathology. Thus, researchers have conducted fewer investigations of the viability of spectrum models than of the vulnerability model to explain the relationship between temperamental–personality dimensions and CD/ODD. One study provided support for the spectrum model using a psychometric approach. van Leeuwen, Mervielde, De Clercq, and De Fruyt (2007) provided psychometric support for a spectrum model of trait-externalizing behavior relations in a heterogeneous clinical sample, as compared to a nonreferred community sample of children. In this study, the authors found mean-level differences in personality traits between the clinical and community samples; however, interactions between personality traits (specifically, benevolence and conscientiousness) and parenting predictive of externalizing problems operated in a similar fashion in both the clinical and community samples (van Leeuwen et al., 2007). Such evidence supports a dimensional rather than qualitative distinction between personality traits in the normal and clinical ranges.

The bulk of studies evaluating the spectrum model of trait-externalizing relations have examined whether shared heritability factors influence both CD/ODD and related traits, such as behavioral disinhibition, negative affect, and callous–unemotional traits. To date, multiple studies in childhood and adolescence have found support for shared genetic influences on the traits of Conscientiousness/constraint and/or Negative Emotionality with CD/ODD-related externalizing problems. For instance, Krueger and colleagues (2002) found support for a biometric model of concurrent substance dependence, antisocial behavior, and disinhibitory personality traits, suggesting that this co-occurrence is largely due to a shared underlying genetic factor. A study of older adolescent twins revealed that impulsive antisociality, a factor characterized by Negative Emotionality and low behavioral constraint, was associated with a shared genetic risk for externalizing problems (Blonigen, Hicks, Krueger, Patrick, & Iacono, 2005). In a longitudinal twin study, the covariance of emotionality and aggressive behavior in childhood and adolescence was accounted for by shared genetic influences (Gjone & Stevenson, 1997). In a separate twin study spanning infancy and early childhood, shared genetic influences accounted for the covariance of Negative Emotionality and externalizing problems (Schmitz et al., 1999). More recently, Singh and Waldman (2010) observed nonadditive genetic influences for Negative Emotionality and CD. Such evidence suggests that shared genetic influences may underlie the association between temperamental traits and externalizing problems, thus supporting for the spectrum model.

Shared etiological influences via Negative Emotionality are not specific to externalizing disorders, however. A recent twin study found that genetic influences on comorbidity of CD and MDD in male children and adolescents was entirely mediated by genetic influences on Negative Emotionality (Tackett, Waldman, Van Hulle, & Lahey, 2011). Thus, some core components of a spectrum conceptualization may be generalizable across types of psychopathology.

Other investigations have examined evidence for a spectrum association between callous–unemotional traits and antisocial behavior in children and adolescents. Results from a twin study of psychopathy revealed that the association between callous–unemotional traits and antisocial behavior in childhood was primarily due to shared genetic influence (Viding, Blair, Moffitt, & Plomin, 2005). A subsequent study suggests that the heritability of antisocial behavior is greater among children with callous–unemotional traits than among those without callous–unemotional traits, and that this difference was even more pronounced after controlling for hyperactive symptoms (Viding, Jones, Frick, Moffitt, & Plomin, 2008).

Moving beyond genetic factors as potential "third variables" supporting a spectrum model, other endogenous factors may also have provided evidence of spectrum associations for youth antisocial behavior. Research has demonstrated that certain psychophysiological functions (e.g., autonomic arousal) have been associated with the covariance of disruptive behavior disorders and several temperamental–personality dimensions, such as Negative Emotionality and Disinhibition (Beauchaine, 2001; Beauchaine, Katkin, Strassberg, & Snarr, 2001). A recent review of aggression, psychopathy, and brain imaging studies has provided support for shared frontal and temporal lobe dysfunctions in violent antisocial behavior and psychopathy, although further investigations are needed to examine limbic structures that have previously been linked to psychopathic personality (Wahlund & Kristiansson, 2009). In addition, reduced activity in the anterior cingulate cortex in response to negative affective pictures was predicted by novelty-seeking in boys with CD versus healthy controls (Stadler et al., 2007). These results provide encouragement for future studies of the shared genetic, psychophysiological, and neurological factors underlying temperamental–personality dimensions and CD/ODD that might provide support for a spectrum explanation.

Spectrum Model of ADHD

Although behavioral genetics research and taxometric research utilizing epidemiological samples suggests that ADHD is best characterized as a continuous dimension (vs. a categorical diagnosis; Haslam et al., 2006; Sherman, Iacono, & McGue, 1997), few articles to date have provided a test of the spectrum hypothesis of trait and ADHD relations. De Pauw and Mervielde (2010) examined the spectrum hypothesis of trait and ADHD relations, as formulated by Van Leeuwen and colleagues (2007). De Pauw and Mervielde (2010) evaluated mean levels, psychometric properties, and nomological network differences of temperament and personality traits measured via the Buss–Plomin and Rothbart temperament models and Big Five personality model in community and clinical (i.e., ADHD) groups of children. Study results indicated significant differences between groups in the means and variances of traits. Specifically, children with ADHD exhibited significantly lower means and variances of Conscientiousness/Effortful Control and higher means and variances of Negative Emotionality/Affect. In contrast, there were few significant group differences in the reliability, factorial structure, and covariance structures of the traits between the clinical and nonclinical groups. Since the nonclinical and clinical ADHD groups differed primarily in the mean levels of different temperament and personality traits, without corresponding differences in psychometric properties or nomological structure, this provides preliminary support for the spectrum hypothesis of trait-ADHD relations (De Pauw & Mervielde, 2010).

A second study evaluated the spectrum model of trait associations with ADHD by examining whether Conscientiousness and Neuroticism mediated associations between molecular genetic risk (i.e., *DRD4*, *DAT1*, and *ADRA2A* genes) and ADHD (Martel, Nikolas, Jernigan, Friderici, & Nigg, 2010). Low Conscientiousness mediated associations between genetic risk and inattentive ADHD symptoms, whereas high Neuroticism mediated associations between genetic risk and ADHD and ODD symptoms (Martel et al., 2010). Since traits explained significant variance between genetic risk and ADHD, these results support the spectrum model of associations between traits and ADHD. Thus, preliminary work to date provides support for the spectrum model, but more work in this area is needed.

Temperament, Externalizing Problems, and Environmental Factors

Currently, individual-difference researchers have a better understanding of the impact of individual differences on development *in context*. Individual differences, such as temperamental traits, can have an impact on the environmental factors to which children are exposed. Similarly, environmental factors can impact the development of temperament. Furthermore, temperamental and environmental factors can interact with one another, such as the differential outcomes that may occur when a socially inhibited child is put into a busy, bustling social setting versus an extraverted child placed in the same environment. For these reasons, it is important to consider some of the major research areas in which environmental factors have been examined. Specifically, we discuss parenting as an environmental factor that can shape and be shaped by child temperament, psychobiological and genetic underpinnings of temperament in interaction with environmental factors, and the importance of environmental influence when considering the potential for psychological treatments to act with and effect child temperament.

Parenting

Parenting style and a number of related family-level dimensions have been shown to interact with temperamental–personality traits to influence their relationship with later externalizing problems (also see Bates, Schermerhorn, & Petersen, Chapter 20, this volume). Multiple longitudinal studies have confirmed the moderating role of child Negative Emotionality in the association between child care quality and later externalizing problems. For instance, a longitudinal study of child care quality revealed an association between long hours in nonparental care and externalizing problems at 2½ years among youth identified as easily frustrated at 6 months, but not among infants in other types of nonparental care (Crockenberg & Leerkes, 2005). One study found that more negative mothering in the second and third years of life was associated with higher externalizing behavior problems in highly negative infants, and less negative fathering in the second and third years and more positive fathering in the second year was related to more inhibition at age 3 in highly negative infants, whereas parenting did not significantly predict externalizing or inhibition in infants with low Negative Emotionality (Belsky, Hsieh, & Crnic, 1998). The use of corporal punishment (i.e., spanking) predicted later conduct problems in infants characterized by low fussiness and low positive affect, but not in infants with higher levels of these traits (Lahey et al., 2008). In addition, negative emotionality in childhood and difficult temperament in infancy moderated the influence of family conflict on externalizing problems (Ramos, Guerin, Gottfried, Bathurst, & Oliver, 2005; Whiteside-Mansell, Bradley, Casey, Fussell, & Conners-Burrow, 2009). These findings highlight the moderating impact of parenting on the associations between early temperamental traits and later externalizing problems.

Some studies have looked at particular dimensions of parenting behavior in interaction with temperamental traits. For example, De Clercq, Van Leeuwen, De Fruyt, Van Hiel, and Mervielde (2008) found that negative control by parents interacted with the child's disagreeableness and emotional instability to predict externalizing problems. Specifically, children with higher levels of disagreeableness and emotional instability seemed to be more susceptible to the influence of negative control on externalizing outcomes than children who scored lower on those traits. In another study, parental negative reinforcement of child aggression, affect dysregulation, and irritability in an observed family interaction reliably predicted boys' later antisocial behavior (Snyder, Schrepferman, & St. Peter, 1997). In contrast, low maternal responsiveness (e.g., frequency of verbal communication to child, physical displays of affection, expressing interest in toys/activities, monitoring, maintaining safe play environment) predicted conduct problems in children with low fearfulness (Lahey et al., 2008), which is consistent with other reports that fearfulness negatively predicts CD/ODD (Calkins et al., 2007; Cimbora & McIntosh, 2003; Raine et al., 1998; Shaw et al., 2005).

Research on aspects of socialization and conscience development is particularly relevant for the study of externalizing problems and attempts to improve prevention and intervention efforts aimed at these disorders. Temperament moderates parenting effects on socialization, conscience development, and externalizing behavior problems (Dadds & Salmon, 2003; Eisenberg et al., 2010). Child anger moderates the relationship between maternal responsiveness in infancy and children's later receptive cooperation (Kochanska, Aksan, & Carlson, 2005). For highly anger-prone children, parental responsiveness has a positive effect on children's receptive cooperation with their parents. These lines of study point to fruitful directions for future research examining the role of temperament in prevention of externalizing problems.

Although fearfulness and behavioral inhibition are not typically associated with externalizing problems, research on these traits also holds important clues for better understanding of temperament–parenting interactions in the development of youth externalizing problems. Child fearfulness moderates the link between parenting and successful socialization (Kochanska, Aksan, & Joy, 2007). For relatively fearless children, mother–child positive relationship, maternal responsiveness, and secure attachment predict future successful socialization outcomes, including conscience development (Kochanska, 1995, 1997; Kochanska et al., 2007). For relatively fearful children, fathers' power assertion predicts poor socialization outcomes, while maternal gentle discipline promotes conscience development (Kochanska, 1995, 1997; Kochanska et al., 2007). Another study examined the interaction of parenting and child inhibition in the development of guilt and empathy (Cornell & Frick, 2007). Children rated by teachers as behaviorally inhibited exhibited higher levels of parent-reported guilt and empathy than uninhibited children, regardless of parenting. For uninhibited children, greater inconsistency in parenting was associated with lower levels of guilt and empathy, whereas authoritarian parenting was associated with higher levels of guilt. Furthermore, parent personality also impacts parenting and subsequent child outcomes. For example, mothers high in negative emotionality and disagreeableness reported more power-assertive and less nurturing parenting, and indicated that their children were more defiant and angry, while mothers high in constraint report more positive outcomes (Kochanska, Clark, & Goldman, 1997). Thus, these studies suggest that child fearfulness, behavior inhibition, and possibly parent personality may be good candidates for individualization of treatment for childhood externalizing problems.

A much smaller literature has investigated temperament–parenting interactions for externalizing personality disorders, although some studies have looked at psychopathy-relevant callous–unemotional traits and borderline personality disorder (BPD). For example, effects of parenting on conduct problems appear to depend on child levels of callous–unemotional traits. In one study, ineffective parenting was associated with conduct problems only when callous–unemotional traits in children were low (Wootton, Frick, Chelton, & Silverthorn, 1997). Children high in callous–unemotional traits exhibited high conduct problems, regardless of the type of parenting received. Some related findings have emerged for BPD as well. Increased risk for BPD may emerge from an interaction between temperamental stress reactivity in the child and problematic attachment (Gunderson & Lyons-Ruth, 2008).

Psychobiological and Genetic Interactions with Environment

A number of psychobiological and genetic factors have been shown to impact the association between temperamental–personality traits and externalizing problems (see Figure 27.3; Tackett & Krueger, 2011). As researchers increasingly try to understand the mechanisms by which basic biological building blocks influence eventual behavior, intermediary phenotypes—such as temperament—represent an important potential key toward outlining these mechanisms. Because temperamental traits are biologically based and evidenced from very early in life, one likely mechanistic pathway is that biological influences, such as genes, influence individual propensity for certain temperament traits that then shape resultant externalizing problems. Thus, a full understanding of the effect of basic biological mechanisms on psychopathology is likely to be strengthened by incorporating such findings into our knowledge of temperamental trait development. Here, we discuss work that likely has implications for both temperamental traits already identified in this chapter (Negative Emotionality, Effortful Control/Conscientiousness) and externalizing problems specifically.

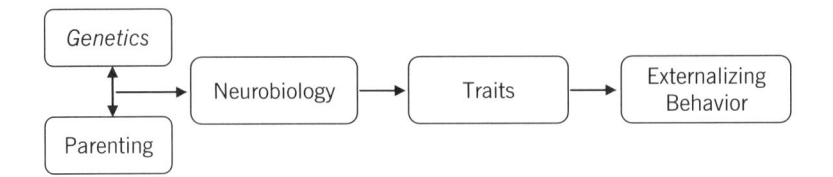

FIGURE 27.3. Schematic of possible gene × environment interaction pathways to traits and externalizing behavior.

For example, perinatal and birth complications and cognitive dysfunction (e.g., diminished vocabulary, deficits in executive functioning) have been shown to interact with social risk factors (e.g., harsh disciplinary style, maternal permissiveness, inadequate parenting, low socioeconomic status [SES]) in the prediction of early-onset persistent aggression in boys and girls, and adolescent-onset aggression in boys only (Brennan, Hall, Bor, Najman, & Williams, 2003). Overall, studies investigating the relationship between neurobiological factors underlying the development of CD and ODD have been limited. One proposed theory suggests that disruptive behavior disorders may result from the interaction of low fear of punishment and physiological underactivity in the hypothalamic–pituitary–adrenal axis and serotonergic system (van Goozen & Fairchild, 2006). Other research found that youth with early-onset CD demonstrated higher activation in the left side of the amygdala during the presentation of negative pictures when compared with controls (Herpetz et al., 2008). Such work highlights the possibility of underlying psychobiological mechanisms showing differential responsivity to the environment.

Results from multiple twin studies suggest that externalizing behavior is moderately to highly heritable, often with negligible shared environmental effects (Button, Lau, Maughan, & Eley, 2008; Hicks, Krueger, Iacono, McGue, & Patrick, 2004). Hicks and colleagues (2004) proposed that vulnerabilities for specific externalizing disorders may be largely due to environmental factors. A study of the genetic factors underlying psychopathic personality traits and externalizing revealed evidence for the influence of gender: Specifically, the psychopathic trait impulsive antisociality was genetically linked with externalizing psychopathology only in 17-year-old males, not in their female counterparts (Blonigen et al., 2005). Increased environmental adversity, such as poor academic performance, affiliation with deviant peer groups, harsh discipline, poor parental monitoring, and stressful life events, was associated with a heightened genetic risk for externalizing disorders (Hicks, South, Dirago, Iacono, & McGue, 2009). Externalizing behaviors, such as substance use and rule breaking, were more influenced by genetic factors in youth from urban settings, whereas shared environmental factors were more important among boys from rural settings (Legrand, Keyes, McGue, Iacono, & Krueger, 2008). Some studies of familial risk also support the role of gene × environment interactions in the development of externalizing problems. For example, Buschgens and colleagues (2009) observed small interaction effects for familial risk and prenatal and perinatal risk factors (e.g., birthweight under 4.5 kilograms, maternal smoking during pregnancy, and complications during pregnancy and labor), on externalizing behaviors in preadolescence. Specifically, maternal prenatal smoking more strongly predicted inattention and hyperactivity/impulsivity in children without familial risk than in children with familial risk. Furthermore, severe pregnancy and delivery complications more strongly predicted aggression among children without familial risk than for children with familial risk.

Several genetic polymorphisms have been implicated in the association between temperamental–personality dimensions and externalizing problems. The presence of a dopamine D4 receptor (*DRD4*) 7-repeat polymorphism increased the risk of oppositional and aggressive behaviors in preschoolers exposed to maternal insensitivity (Bakermans-Kranenburg & van IJzendoorn, 2006). Similarly, Bakermans-Kranenburg, van IJzendoorn, Pijlman, Mesman, and Juffer (2008) demonstrated that an intervention geared to promote positive parenting and sensitive discipline had the largest effect on reducing externalizing behaviors in children with the *DRD4* 7-repeat allele (see van IJzendoorn & Bakermans-Kranenburg, Chapter 19, this volume, for other work on this genetic polymorphism). The *DRD4* 7-repeat allele also predicted children's sensitivity to parenting, such that children with the allele who were exposed to lower-quality parenting were more likely to show higher levels of sensation seeking (Sheese, Voelker, Rothbart, & Posner, 2007). Again, such work suggests that molecular genetic influences may act on broader phenotypes, such as temperament, which interact with environmental risk to increase the chance of specific problematic behavioral outcomes.

It is likely, however, that several genetic polymorphisms are involved in the development of CD and ODD. For example, in an examination of the roles of *DRD4* and a dopamine D2 receptor (*DRD2*), neither polymorphism demonstrated significant independent effects on CD or antisocial behaviors; rather, there was evidence of a gene–gene interaction between *DRD4* and *DRD2*, whereby symptoms of CD were more likely among youth with both the A-1 and 7-repeat alleles (Beaver et al., 2007). There is also genetic support underlying the life-course-persistent versus adolescent onset subtypes of CD. Specifically, the *GABRA2* gene was associated with youth exhibiting persistent, elevated externalizing problems, which increased the likelihood of a life-course-persistent trajectory with each additional copy of the minor allele (Dick et al., 2009). More recently, Sakai and colleagues (2010) observed that a single nucleotide polymorphism in the *GABRA2* gene was associated with CD, but not ADHD, in a sample of adolescent patients in a substance abuse treatment program. There is evidence supporting the role of the gene *CHRM2* contributing to a general externalizing phenotype, comprising substance use disorders, CD, antisocial personality disorder, novelty seeking, and general externalizing behaviors (Dick et al., 2008). The authors concluded that this region on chromosome 7 may predispose individuals to disinhibitory behaviors. A polymorphism in the gene encoding monoamine oxidase A (MAO-A) has been suggested to moderate children's sensitivity to maltreatment, contributing to the development of later antisocial behavior in males (Caspi et al., 2002). Subsequent studies, however, have revealed conflicting evidence, suggesting a need for further replication of this finding in order to understand this mechanism better (Prom-Wormley et al., 2009; Young et al., 2006). Recent research on specific genetic influences has offered some support for generalized mechanisms of risk influencing relevant temperamental traits, as well as specific externalizing problems. This represents an exciting area of future research.

Treatment Studies

Although temperament has been conceptualized as moderately stable, changes can occur. A discussion of environmental influences is especially relevant for treatment, as evidence of environmental influence offers great potential for identification of external mechanisms of change to incorporate into prevention and intervention efforts. For example, preschoolers were rated by their mothers as having a more flexible temperament, measured via the Flexibility–Inflexibility scale from the Short Temperament Scale for Children, following behavioral treatment (i.e., parent–child interaction therapy), compared to before treatment (Nixon, 2001). Callous–unemotional traits decreased over the course of a parent training intervention for a subset of a clinical sample of children with conduct problems (Hawes & Dadds, 2007). However, post hoc analyses indicated that boys with the most stable high callous–unemotional traits had the worst outcomes (Hawes & Dadds, 2007). Treatment studies have also addressed attention; for example, 5 days of attention training appears to improve executive attention, particularly for those children with more Extraversion and less Effortful Control (Rueda, Rothbart, McCandliss, Saccomanno, & Posner, 2005). Overall, findings have not been conclusive regarding long-term gains, but research does suggest that interventions can improve aspects of executive function and emotion regulation, which should lead to improvements in externalizing problems (Eisenberg et al., 2010). Taken together, such findings suggest important areas for closer research attention to identify those mechanisms most likely to promote adaptive temperament change, which should also lead to better externalizing outcomes in youth.

Conclusions and Future Directions

In summary, temperamental characteristics show robust relations to externalizing problems across the lifespan. Traits indexing self-regulatory control and disinhibition seem to form a core component of externalizing problems, largely accounting for the substantial comorbidity seen among these problems. A growing body of evidence supports a spectrum conceptualization of temperament and externalizing disorders, such that disinhibition likely shares common genetic end environmental causes, as well as psychobiological correlates, with externalizing problems. Parenting appears to play an important role in the development of externalizing problems, although it seems to interact with the child's temperament to affect behavioral change. Recent research has increasingly turned to a person × environment perspective in investigating causal factors.

There have been many limitations to further understanding the relations between temperament and externalizing in childhood and adolescence. The lag in development of a comprehensive, psychometrically sound assessment tool for use in middle childhood and early adolescence has certainly impeded research in this domain (Tackett, Krueger, Iacono, & McGue, 2008). With recent advances in measuring dispositional characteristics across the lifespan comes opportunity to incorporate these measures in studies of externalizing psychopathology. It is particularly encouraging that Conscientiousness/Constraint—likely the most important trait for externalizing psychopathology—is reliably and validly measured by parent-report in childhood and shows the best prediction of later self-reports of the trait (Tackett et al., 2008). It is important for future studies on externalizing psychopathology to include age-appropriate measures of temperamental traits, particularly longitudinal studies and investigations measuring genetic and psychobiological causes and correlates.

Such research is needed in order to begin to tease apart competing models for explaining temperament–psychopathology relations, as well as the development of psychopathology more generally.

Consistent with much current work in developmental psychology, an understanding of temperament and externalizing problems must take a dynamic approach to understanding the individual in context and across time. Identification of critical developmental periods may help longitudinal research to hone in on those developmental phases that are most in need of closer examination. For example, in the development of personality disorders, three critical developmental periods have been identified: infancy–toddlerhood, middle childhood–early adolescence, and late adolescence–early adulthood (Tackett, Balsis, et al., 2009). Importantly, each of these periods relates to highly salient changes in the child's interpersonal environment. Personality disorders are centrally defined by dysregulated or disrupted interpersonal relationships, so taken together, these begin to form a coherent developmental narrative of early vulnerability factors, critical developmental periods for the interaction of vulnerability and stress, and the resultant manifestation of disorder. Critical developmental periods for specific types of externalizing behavior must be more clearly defined in order to focus research better on risk trajectories and maladaptive outcomes in this domain. Such a dynamic conceptualization of person × situation, gene × environment, and diathesis × stress will lead to a more comprehensive understanding of the development of externalizing disorders in our children and youth.

Further Readings

Eisenberg, N., Spinrad, T. L., & Eggum, N. D. (2010). Emotion-related self-regulation and its relation to children's maladjustment. *Annual Review of Clinical Psychology, 6*, 495–525.

Nigg, J. T. (2006). Temperament and developmental psychopathology. *Journal of Child Psychology and Psychiatry, 47*, 395–422.

Tackett, J. L. (2006). Evaluating models of the personality–psychopathology relationship in children and adolescents. *Clinical Psychology Review, 26*, 584–599.

References

American Psychiatric Association. (2000). *Diagnostic and statistical manual of mental disorders* (4th ed., text rev.). Washington, DC: Author.

Anderson, K. G., Tapert, S., Moadab, I., Crowley, T. J., & Brown, S. A. (2007). Personality risk profile for conduct disorder and substance use disorders in youth. *Addictive Behaviors, 32*, 2377–2382.

Auerbach, J. G., Berger, A., Atzaba-Poria, N., Arbelle, S., Cypin, N., Friedman, A., et al. (2008). Temperament at 7, 12, and 25 months in children at familial risk for ADHD. *Infant and Child Development, 17*(4), 321–338.

Baker, L. A., Jacobson, K. C., Raine, A., Lozano, D. I., & Bezdjian, S. (2007). Genetic and environmental bases of childhood antisocial behavior: A multi-informant twin study. *Journal of Abnormal Psychology, 116*(2), 219–235.

Bakermans-Kranenburg, M. J., & van IJzendoorn, M. H. (2006). Gene–environment interaction of the dopamine D4 receptor (DRD4) and observed maternal insensitivity predicting externalizing behavior in preschoolers. *Developmental Psychobiology, 48*, 406–409.

Bakermans-Kranenburg, M. J., van IJzendoorn, M. H., Pijlman, F. T. A., Mesman, J., & Juffer, F. (2008). Experimental evidence for differential susceptibility: Dopamine D4 receptor polymorphism (DRD4 VNTR) moderates intervention effects on toddlers' externalizing behavior in a randomized controlled trial. *Developmental Psychology, 44*(1), 293–300.

Barkley, R. A. (2006). *Attention-deficit/hyperactivity disorder: A handbook for diagnosis and treatment* (3rd ed.). New York: Guilford Press.

Barnow, S., Lucht, M., & Freyberger, H. J. (2005). Correlates of aggressive and delinquent conduct problems in adolescence. *Aggressive Behavior, 31*, 24–39.

Beauchaine, T. (2001). Vagal tone, development, and Gray's motivational theory: Toward an integrated model of autonomic nervous system functioning in psychopathology. *Development and Psychopathology, 13*, 183–214.

Beauchaine, T. P., Katkin, E. S., Strassberg, Z., & Snarr, J. (2001). Disinhibitory psychopathology in male adolescents: Discriminating conduct disorder from attention-deficit/hyperactivity disorder through concurrent assessment of multiple autonomic states. *Journal of Abnormal Psychology, 110*(4), 610–624.

Beaver, K. M., Wright, J. P., DeLisi, M., Walsh, A., Vaughn, M. G., Boisvert, D., et al. (2007). A gene × gene interaction between DRD2 and DRD4 is associated with conduct disorder and antisocial behavior in males. *Behavioral and Brain Functions, 3*, 30.

Belsky, J., Hsieh, K., & Crnic, K. (1998). Mothering, fathering, and infant negativity as antecedents of boys' externalizing problems and inhibition at age 3 years: Differential susceptibility to rearing experience? *Development and Psychopathology, 10*, 301–319.

Blonigen, D. M., Hicks, B. M., Krueger, R. F., Patrick, C. J., & Iacono, W. G. (2005). Psychopathic personality traits: Heritability and genetic overlap with internalizing and externalizing psychopathology. *Psychological Medicine, 35*, 637–648.

Braaten, E. B., & Rosen, L. A. (1997). Emotional reactions in adults with symptoms of attention deficit hyperactivity disorder. *Personality and Individual Differences, 22*(3), 355–361.

Brennan, P. A., Hall, J., Bor, W., Najman, J. M., & Williams, G. (2003). Integrating biological and social processes in relation to early-onset persistent aggression in boys and girls. *Developmental Psychology, 39*(2), 309–323.

Burke, J. D., Hipwell, A. E., & Loeber, R. (2010). Dimensions of oppositional defiant disorder as predictors of depression and conduct disorder in preadolescent girls. *Journal of the American Academy of Child and Adolescent Psychiatry, 49*(5), 484–492.

Buschgens, C. J. M., Swinkels, S. H. N., van Aken, M. A. G., Ormel, J., Verhulst, F. C., & Buitelaar, J. K. (2009). Externalizing behaviors in preadolescents: Familial risk to externalizing behaviors, prenatal and perinatal risks, and their interactions. *European Child and Adolescent Psychiatry, 18*, 65–74.

Button, T. M., Lau, J. Y., Maughan, B., & Eley, T. C. (2008). Parental punitive discipline, negative life events and gene–environment interplay in the development of externalizing behavior. *Psychological Medicine, 38*(1), 29–39.

Calkins, S. D., Blandon, A. Y., Williford, A. P., & Keane, S. P. (2007). Biological, behavioral, and relational levels of resilience in the context of risk for early childhood behavior problems. *Development and Psychopathology, 19*(3), 675–700.

Card, N. A., Stucky, B. D., Sawalani, G. M., & Little, T. D. (2008). Direct and indirect aggression during childhood and adolescence: A meta-analytic review of gender differences, intercorrelations, and relations to maladjustment. *Child Development, 79*(5), 1185–1229.

Caspi, A., McClay, J., Moffitt, T. E., Mill, J., Martin, J., Craig, I. W., et al. (2002). Role of genotype in the cycle of violence in maltreated children. *Science, 297*, 851–854.

Caspi, A., Moffitt, T. E., Newman, D. L., & Silva, P. A. (1996). Behavioral observations at age 3 years predict adult psychiatric disorders: Longitudinal evidence from a birth cohort. *Archives of General Psychiatry, 53*(11), 1033–1039.

Cimbora, D. M., & McIntosh, D. N. (2003). Emotional responses to antisocial acts in adolescent males with conduct disorder: A link to affective morality. *Journal of Clinical Child and Adolescent Psychology, 32*(2), 296–301.

Cornell, A. H., & Frick, P. J. (2007). The moderating effects of parenting styles in the association between behavioral inhibition and parent-reported guilt and empathy in preschool children. *Journal of Clinical Child and Adolescent Psychology, 36*(3), 305–318.

Crick, N. R., & Grotpeter, J. K. (1995). Relational aggression, gender, and social-psychological adjustment. *Child Development, 66*(3), 710–722.

Crockenberg, S. C., & Leerkes, E. M. (2005). Infant temperament moderates associations between child care type and quantity and externalizing and internalizing behaviors at 2½. *Infant Behavior and Development, 28*(1), 20–35.

Cukrowicz, K. C., Taylor, J., Schatschneider, C., & Iacono, W. G. (2006). Personality differences in children and adolescents with attention-deficit/hyperactivity disorder, conduct disorder, and controls. *Journal of Child Psychology and Psychiatry, 47*(2), 151–159.

Dadds, M. R., & Salmon, K. (2003). Punishment insensitivity and parenting: Temperament and learning as interacting risks for antisocial behavior. *Clinical Child and Family Psychology Review, 6*(2), 69–86.

De Clercq, B., Van Leeuwen, K., De Fruyt, F., Van Hiel, A., & Mervielde, I. (2008). Maladaptive personality traits and psychopathology in childhood and adolescence: The moderating effect of parenting. *Journal of Personality, 76*(2), 357–383.

De Pauw, S. S. W., & Mervielde, I. (2010). The role of temperament and personality in problem behaviors of children with ADHD. *Journal of Abnormal Child Psychology, 39*(2), 277–291.

Dick, D. M., Aliev, F., Wang, J. C., Grucza, R. A., Schuckit, M., Kuperman, S., et al. (2008). Using dimensional models of externalizing psychopathology to aid in gene identification. *Archives of General Psychiatry, 65*(3), 310–318.

Dick, D. M., Latendresse, S. J., Lansford, J. E., Budde, J. P., Goate, A., Dodge, K. A., et al. (2009). Role of GABRA2 in trajectories of externalizing behavior across development and evidence of moderation by parental monitoring. *Archives of General Psychiatry, 66*(6), 649–657.

Dolan, M. C., & Rennie, C. E. (2007). Is juvenile psychopathy associated with low anxiety and fear in conduct-disordered male offenders? *Journal of Anxiety Disorders, 21*(8), 1028–1038.

Eisenberg, N., Spinrad, T. L., & Eggum, N. D. (2010). Emotion-related self-regulation and its relation to children's maladjustment. *Annual Review of Clinical Psychology, 6*, 495–525.

Eisenberg, N., Spinrad, T. L., Fabes, R. A., Reiser, M., Cumberland, A., Shepard, S. A., et al. (2004). The relations of effortful control and impulsivity to children's resiliency and adjustment. *Child Development, 75*(1), 25–46.

Essau, C. A., Sasagaw, S., & Frick, P. J. (2006). Callous–unemotional traits in a community sample of adolescents. *Assessment, 13*(4), 454–469.

Faraone, S. V., Biederman, J., & Mick, E. (2006). The age-dependent decline of attention deficit hyperactivity disorder: A meta-analysis of follow-up studies. *Psychological Medicine, 36*(2), 159–165.

Farrington, D. P., & West, D. J. (1993). Criminal, penal and life histories of chronic offenders: Risk and protective factors and early identification. *Criminal Behaviour and Mental Health, 3*(4), 492?523.

Frick, P. J., Cornell, A. H., Barry, C. T., Bodin, S. D., & Dane, H. E. (2003). Callous–unemotional traits and conduct problems in the prediction of conduct problem severity, aggression, and self-report of delinquency. *Journal of Abnormal Child Psychology, 31*(4), 457–470.

Frick, P. J., & Sheffield-Morris, A. (2004). Temperament and developmental pathways to conduct problems. *Journal of Clinical Child and Adolescent Psychology, 33*(1), 54–68.

Gjone, H., & Stevenson, J. (1997). A longitudinal twin study of temperament and behavior problems: Common genetic or environmental influences? *Journal of the American Academy of Child and Adolescent Psychiatry, 36*(10), 1448–1456.

Glenn, A. L., Raine, A., Venables, P. H., & Mednick, S. A. (2007). Early temperamental and psychophysiological precursors of adult psychopathic personality. *Journal of Abnormal Psychology, 116*(3), 508–518.

Guerin, D. W., Gottfried, A. W., & Thomas, C. W. (1997). Difficult temperament and behaviour problems: A longitudinal study from 1.5 to 12 years. *International Journal of Behavioral Development, 21*(1), 71–90.

Gunderson, J. G., & Lyons-Ruth, K. (2008). BPD's interpersonal hypersensitivity phenotype: A gene–environment–developmental model. *Journal of Personality Disorders, 22*(1), 22–41.

Haslam, N., Williams, B., Prior, M., Haslam, R., Graetz, B., & Sawyer, M. (2006). The latent structure of attention-deficit/hyperactivity disorder: A taxometric analysis. *Australian and New Zealand Journal of Psychiatry, 40*(8), 639–647.

Hawes, D. J., & Dadds, M. R. (2007). Stability and malleability of callous–unemotional traits during treatment for childhood conduct problems. *Journal of Clinical Child and Adolescent Psychology, 36*(3), 347–355.

Henry, B., Caspi, A., Moffitt, T. E., & Silva, P. A.

(1996). Temperamental and familial predictors of violent and nonviolent criminal convictions: Age 3 to age 18. *Developmental Psychology, 32*(4), 614–623.

Herpetz, S. C., Huebner, T., Marx, I., Vloet, T. D., Fink, G. R., Stoecker, T., et al. (2008). Emotional processing in male adolescents with childhood-onset conduct disorder. *Journal of Child Psychology and Psychiatry, 49*(7), 781–791.

Hicks, B. M., Krueger, R. F., Iacono, W. G., McGue, M., & Patrick, C. J. (2004). Family transmission and heritability of externalizing disorders: A twin-family study. *Archives of General Psychiatry, 61*(9), 922–928.

Hicks, B. M., South, S. C., Dirago, A. C., Iacono, W. G., & McGue, M. (2009). Environmental adversity and increasing genetic risk for externalizing disorders. *Archives of General Psychiatry, 66*(6), 640–648.

Hiramura, H., Uji, M., Shikai, N., Chen, Z., Matsuoka, N., & Kitamura, T. (2010). Understanding externalizing behavior from children's personality and parenting characteristics. *Psychiatry Research, 175*(1–2), 142–147.

Hirshfeld-Becker, D. R., Biederman, J., Henin, A., Faraone, S. V., Micco, J. A., van Grondelle, A., et al. (2007). Clinical outcomes of laboratory-observed preschool behavioral disinhibition at five-year follow-up. *Biological Psychiatry, 62*(6), 565–572.

John, O. P., Caspi, A., Robins, R. W., Moffitt, T. E., & Stouthamer-Loeber, M. (1994). The "little five": Exploring the nomological network of the five-factor model of personality in adolescent boys. *Child Development, 65*(1), 160–178.

Kessler, R. C., Adler, L., Barkley, R., Biederman, J., Conners, C. K., Demler, O., et al. (2006). The prevalence and correlates of adult ADHD in the United States: Results from the National Comorbidity Survey Replication. *American Journal of Psychiatry, 163*(4), 716–723.

Kochanska, G. (1995). Children's temperament, mothers' discipline, and security of attachment: Multiple pathways to emerging internalization. *Child Development, 66*(3), 597–615.

Kochanska, G. (1997). Multiple pathways to conscience for children with different temperaments: From toddlerhood to age 5. *Developmental Psychology, 33*(2), 228–240.

Kochanska, G., Aksan, N., & Carlson, J. J. (2005). Temperament, relationships, and young children's receptive cooperation with their parents. *Developmental Psychology, 41*(4), 648–660.

Kochanska, G., Aksan, N., & Joy, M. E. (2007). Children's fearfulness as a moderator of parenting in early socialization: Two longitudinal studies. *Developmental Psychology, 43*(1), 222–237.

Kochanska, G., Barry, R. A., Jimenez, A. L., Hollatz, A. L., & Woodard, J. (2009). Guilt and effortful control: Two mechanisms that prevent disruptive developmental trajectories. *Journal of Personality and Social Psychology, 97*(2), 322–333.

Kochanska, G., Clark, L. A., & Goldman, M. S. (1997). Implications of mothers' personality for their parenting and their young children's developmental outcomes. *Journal of Personality, 65*(2), 387–420.

Krueger, R. F., Hicks, B. M., Patrick, C. J., Carlson, S. R., Iacono, W. G., & McGue, M. (2002). Etiologic connections among substance dependence, antisocial behavior, and personality: Modeling the externalizing spectrum. *Journal of Abnormal Psychology, 111*(3), 411–424.

Krueger, R. F., Markon, K. E., Patrick, C. J., Benning, S. D., & Kramer, M. D. (2007). Linking antisocial behavior, substance use, and personality: An integrative quantitative model of the adult externalizing spectrum. *Journal of Abnormal Psychology, 116*(4), 645–666.

Lahey, B. B., Goodman, S. H., Walkman, I. D., Bird, H., Canino, G., Jensen, P., et al. (1999). Relation of age of onset to the type and severity of child and adolescent conduct problems. *Journal of Abnormal Child Psychology, 27*(4), 247–260.

Lahey, B. B., Pelham, W. E., Loney, J., Lee, S. S., & Willcutt, E. (2005). Instability of the DSM-IV subtypes of ADHD from preschool through elementary school. *Archives of General Psychiatry, 62*(8), 896–902.

Lahey, B. B., Van Hulle, C. A., Keenan, K., Rathouz, P. J., D'Onofrio, B. M., Rodgers, J. L., et al. (2008). Temperament and parenting during the first year of life predict future child conduct problems. *Journal of Abnormal Child Psychology, 36*(8), 1139–1158.

Legrand, L. N., Keyes, M., McGue, M., Iacono, W. G., & Krueger, R. F. (2008). Rural environments reduce the genetic influence on adolescent substance use and rule-breaking behavior. *Psychological Medicine, 38*(9), 1341–1350.

Lemery, K. S., Essex, M. J., & Smider, N. A. (2002). Revealing the relation between temperament and behavior problem symptoms by eliminating measurement confounding: Expert ratings and factor analyses. *Child Development, 73*(3), 867–882.

Levy, F., Hay, D. A., McStephen, M., Wood, C. H., & Waldman, I. (1997). Attention-deficit/hyperactivity disorder: A category or a continuum?: Genetic analysis of a large-scale twin study. *American Academy of Child and Adolescent Psychiatry, 36*(6), 737–744.

Lynam, D. R. (1997). Pursuing the psychopath: Capturing the fledgling psychopath in a nomological net. *Journal of Abnormal Psychology, 106*(3), 425–438.

Lynam, D. R., Miller, D. J., Vachon, D., Loeber, R.,

& Stouthamer-Loeber, M. (2009). Psychopathy in adolescence predicts official reports of offending in adulthood. *Youth Violence and Juvenile Justice, 7*(3), 189–207.

Martel, M. M. (2009). A new perspective on attention-deficit/hyperactivity disorder: Emotion dysregulation and trait models. *Journal of Child Psychology and Psychiatry, 50*(9), 1042–1051.

Martel, M. M., & Nigg, J. T. (2006). Child ADHD and personality/temperament traits of reactive and effortful control, resiliency, and emotionality. *Journal of Child Psychology and Psychiatry, 47*(11), 1175–1183.

Martel, M. M., Nigg, J. T., & von Eye, A. (2009). How do trait dimensions map onto ADHD symptom domains? *Journal of Abnormal Child Psychology, 37*(3), 337–348.

Martel, M. M., Nikolas, M., Jernigan, K., Friderici, K., & Nigg, J. T. (2010). Personality mediation of genetic effects on attention-deficit/hyperactivity disorder. *Journal of Abnormal Child Psychology, 38*(5), 633–643.

Miller, C. J., Miller, S. R., Newcorn, J. H., & Halperin, J. M. (2008). Personality characteristics associated with persistent ADHD in late adolescence. *Journal of Abnormal Child Psychology, 36*(2), 165–173.

Miller, J. D., Lynam, D., & Leukefeld, C. (2003). Examining antisocial behavior through the lens of the five factor model of personality. *Aggressive Behavior, 29*(6), 497–514.

Moffitt, T. E., Arseneault, L., Jaffee, S. R., Kim-Cohen, J., Koenen, K. C., Odgers, C. L., et al. (2008). Research review: DSM-V conduct disorder: Research needs for an evidence base. *Journal of Child Psychology and Psychiatry, 49*(1), 3–33.

Moffitt, T. E., Caspi, A., Dickson, N., Silva, P., & Stanton, W. (1996). Childhood-onset versus adolescent-onset antisocial conduct problems in males: Natural history from ages 3 to 18 years. *Development and Psychopathology, 8*(2), 399–424.

Nigg, J. T. (2006). Temperament and developmental psychopathology. *Journal of Child Psychology and Psychiatry, 47*(3–4), 395–422.

Nigg, J. T., Blaskey, L., Huang-Pollock, C., & John, O. (2002). ADHD symptoms and personality traits: Is ADHD an extreme personality trait? *The ADHD Report, 10*(5), 6–11.

Nigg, J. T., Goldsmith, H. H., & Sachek, J. (2004). Temperament and attention deficit hyperactivity disorder: The development of a multiple pathway model. *Journal of Clinical Child and Adolescent Psychology, 33*(1), 42–53.

Nigg, J. T., John, O. P., Blaskey, L. G., Huang-Pollock, C. L., Willcutt, E. G, Hinshaw, S. P., et al. (2002). Big Five dimensions and ADHD symptoms: Links between personality traits and clinical symptoms. *Journal of Personality and Social Psychology, 83*(2), 451–469.

Nixon, R. D. V. (2001). Changes in hyperactivity and temperament in behaviourally disturbed preschoolers after parent–child interaction therapy (PCIT). *Behaviour Change, 18*(3), 168–176.

Nock, M. K., Kazdin, A. E., Hiripi, E., & Kessler, K. C. (2006). Prevalence, subtypes, and correlates of DSM-IV conduct disorder in the National Comorbidity Survey Replication. *Psychological Medicine, 36*(5), 699–710.

Nock, M. K., Kazdin, A. E., Hiripi, E., & Kessler, K. C. (2007). Lifetime prevalence, correlates, and persistence of oppositional defiant disorder: Results from the National Comorbidity Survey Replication. *Journal of Child Psychology and Psychiatry, 48*(7), 701–713.

Olson, S. (1996). Developmental perspectives. In S. Sandberg (Ed.), *Hyperactivity and attention disorders of childhood* (2nd ed., pp. 242–289). New York: Cambridge University.

Pitzer, M., Esser, G., Schmidt, M. H., & Laucht, M. (2009). Temperamental predictors of externalizing problems among boys and girls: A longitudinal study in a high-risk sample from ages 3 months to 15 years. *European Archives of Psychiatry and Clinical Neuroscience, 259*(8), 459–458.

Prom-Wormley, E. C., Eaves, L. J., Foley, D. L., Gardner, C. O., Archer, K. J., Wormley, B. K., et al. (2009). Monoamine oxidase A and childhood adversity as risk factors for conduct disorder in females. *Psychological Medicine, 39*(4), 579–590.

Raine, A., Reynolds, C., Venables, P. H., Mednick, S. A., & Farrington, D. P. (1998). Fearlessness, stimulation-seeking, and large body size at age 3 years as early predispositions to childhood aggression at age 11 years. *Archives of General Psychiatry, 55*(8), 745–751.

Ramos, M. C., Guerin, D. W., Gottfried, A. W., Bathurst, K., & Oliver, P. H. (2005). Family conflict and children's behavior problems: The moderating role of child temperament. *Structural Equation Modeling, 12*(2), 278–298.

Rowe, R., Maughan, B., Moran, P., Ford, T., Briskman, J., & Goodman, R. (2010). The role of callous unemotional traits in the diagnosis of conduct disorder. *Journal of Child Psychology and Psychiatry, 51*(6), 688–695.

Rueda, M. R., Rothbart, M. K., McCandliss, B. D., Saccomanno, L., & Posner, M. I. (2005). Training, maturation, and genetic influences on the development of executive attention. *Proceedings of the National Academy of Sciences USA, 102*(41), 14931–14936.

Sakai, J. T., Stallings, M. C., Crowley, T. J., Gelhorn, H. L., McQueen, M. B., & Ehringer, M. A. (2010). Test of association between

GABRA2 (SNP rs279871) and adolescent conduct/alcohol use disorders utilizing a sample of clinic referred youth with serious substance and conduct problems, controls and available first degree relatives. *Drug and Alcohol Dependence*, *106*(2–3), 199–203.

Schmitz, S., Fulker, D. W., Plomin, R., Zahn-Waxler, C., Emde, R. N., & DeFries, J. C. (1999). Temperament and problem behaviour during early childhood. *International Journal of Behavioral Development*, *23*(2), 333–355.

Shaw, D. S., Lacourse, E., & Nagin, D. S. (2005). Developmental trajectories of conduct problems and hyperactivity from ages 2 to 10. *Journal of Child Psychology and Psychiatry*, *46*(9), 931–942.

Shaw, P., Eckstrand, K., Sharp, W., Blumenthal, J., Lerch, J. P., Greenstein, D., et al. (2007). Attention-deficit/hyperactivity disorder is characterized by a delay in cortical maturation. *Proceedings of the National Academy of Sciences USA*, *104*(49), 19649–19654.

Sheese, B. E., Voelker, P. M., Rothbart, M. K., & Posner, M. I. (2007). Parenting quality interacts with genetic variation in dopamine receptor D4 to influence temperament in early childhood. *Development and Psychopathology*, *19*(4), 1039–1046.

Sherman, D. K., Iacono, W. G., & McGue, M. K. (1997). Attention-deficit hyperactivity disorder dimensions: A twin study of inattention and impulsivity-hyperactivity. *Journal of the American Academy of Child and Adolescent Psychiatry*, *36*(6), 745–753.

Sigvardsson, S., Bohman, M., & Cloninger, C. R. (1987). Structure and stability of childhood personality: Prediction of later social adjustment. *Journal of Child Psychology and Psychiatry and Allied Disciplines*, *28*(6), 929–946.

Silverthorn, P., Frick, P. J., & Reynolds, R. (2001). Timing and onset and correlates of severe conduct problems in adjudicated girls and boys. *Journal of Psychopathology and Behavioral Assessment*, *23*(3), 171–181.

Singh, A. L., & Waldman, I. D. (2010). The etiology of associations between negative emotionality and childhood externalizing disorders. *Journal of Abnormal Psychology*, *119*(2), 376–388.

Snyder, J., Schrepferman, L., & St. Peter, C. (1997). Origins of antisocial behavior: Negative reinforcement and affect dysregulation of behavior as socialization mechanisms in family interaction. *Behavior Modification*, *21*(2), 187–215.

Sonuga-Barke, E. J. S. (2005). Causal models of attention-deficit/hyperactivity disorder: From common simple deficits to multiple developmental pathways. *Biological Psychiatry*, *57*(11), 1231–1238.

Stadler, C., Sterzer, P., Schmeck, K., Krebs, A., Kleinschmidt, A., & Poustka, F. (2007). Reduced anterior cingulate activation in aggressive children and adolescents during affective stimulation: Associations with temperament traits. *Journal of Psychiatric Research*, *41*(5), 410–417.

Stringaris, A., Maughan, B., & Goodman, R. (2010). What's in a disruptive disorder?: Temperamental antecedents of oppositional defiant disorder: Findings from the Avon Longitudinal Study. *Journal of the American Academy of Child and Adolescent Psychiatry*, *49*(5), 474–483.

Tackett, J. L. (2006). Evaluating models of the personality–psychopathology relationship in children and adolescents. *Clinical Psychology Review*, *26*(5), 584–599.

Tackett, J. L. (2010). Toward an externalizing spectrum in DSM-V: Incorporating developmental concerns. *Child Development Perspectives*, *4*(3), 161–167.

Tackett, J. L., Balsis, S., Oltmanns, T. F., & Krueger, R. F. (2009). A unifying perspective on personality pathology across the life span: Developmental considerations for the fifth edition of the *Diagnostic and Statistical Manual of Mental Disorders*. *Development and Psychopathology*, *21*(3), 687–713.

Tackett, J. L., & Krueger, R. F. (2011). Dispositional influences on human aggression. In P. R. Shaver & M. Mikulincer (Eds.), *Human aggression and violence: Causes, manifestations, and consequences* (pp. 89–104). Washington, DC: American Psychological Association.

Tackett, J. L., Krueger, R. F., Iacono, W. G., & McGue, M. (2008). Personality in middle childhood: A hierarchical structure and longitudinal connections with personality in late adolescence. *Journal of Research in Personality*, *42*(6), 1456–1462.

Tackett, J. L., & Ostrov, J. M. (2010). Measuring relational aggression in middle childhood in a multi-informant multi-method study. *Journal of Psychopathology and Behavioral Assessment*, *32*(4), 490–500.

Tackett, J. L., Slobodskaya, H., Mar, R. A., Deal, J., Halverson, C. F., Jr., Baker, S. R., et al. (in press). The hierarchical structure of childhood personality in five countries: Continuity from early childhood to early adolescence. *Journal of Personality*.

Tackett, J. L., Waldman, I. D., & Lahey, B. B. (2009). Etiology and measurement of relational aggression: A multi-informant behavior genetic investigation. *Journal of Abnormal Psychology*, *118*(4), 722–733.

Tackett, J. L., Waldman, I. D., Van Hulle, C. A., & Lahey, B. B. (2011). Shared genetic influences on negative emotionality and major depression/conduct disorder comorbidity. *Journal of the*

American Academy of Child and Adolescent Psychiatry, 50(8), 818–827.
Taylor, J., & Iacono, W. G. (2007). Personality trait differences in boys and girls with clinical or sub-clinical diagnoses of conduct disorder versus antisocial personality disorder. *Journal of Adolescence, 30*(4), 537–547.
Tellegen, A., & Waller, N. G. (2001). *Exploring personality through test construction: Development of the multidimensional personality questionnaire*. Minneapolis: University of Minnesota Press.
van Goozen, S. H. M., & Fairchild, G. (2006). Neuroendocrine and neurotransmitter correlates in children with antisocial behavior. *Hormones and Behavior, 50*(4), 647–654.
van Leeuwen, K., Mervielde, I., De Clercq, B. J., & De Fruyt, F. (2007). Extending the spectrum idea: Child personality, parenting and psychopathology. *European Journal of Personality, 21*(1), 63–89.
Viding, E., Blair, R. J. R., Moffitt, T. E., & Plomin, R. (2005). Evidence for substantial genetic risk for psychopathy in 7-year-olds. *Journal of Child Psychology and Psychiatry, 46*(6), 592–597.
Viding, E., Jones, A. P., Frick, P. J., Moffitt, T. E., & Plomin, R. (2008). Heritability of antisocial behavior at 9: Do callous–unemotional traits matter? *Developmental Science, 11*(1), 17–22.
Wahlund, K., & Kristiansson, M. (2009). Aggression, psychopathy and brain imaging—Review and future recommendations. *International Journal of Law and Psychiatry, 32*(4), 266–271.

White, H. R., Bates, M. E., & Buyske, S. (2001). Adolescence-limited versus persistent delinquency: Extending Moffitt's hypothesis into adulthood. *Journal of Abnormal Psychology, 110*(4), 600–609.
Whiteside-Mansell, L., Bradley, R. H., Casey, P. H., Fussell, J. J., & Conners-Burrow, N. A. (2009). Triple risk: Do difficult temperament and family conflict increase the likelihood of behavioural maladjustment in children born low birth weight and preterm? *Journal of Pediatric Psychology, 34*(4), 396–405.
Wootton, J. M., Frick, P. J., Chelton, K. K., & Silverthorn, P. (1997). Ineffective parenting and childhood conduct problems: The moderating role of callous–unemotional traits. *Journal of Consulting and Clinical Psychology, 65*(2), 301–308.
Young, S. E., Smolen, A., Hewitt, J. K., Haberstick, B. C., Stallings, M. C., Corley, R. P., et al. (2006). Interaction between MAO-A genotype and maltreatment in the risk for conduct disorder: Failure to confirm in adolescent patients. *American Journal of Psychiatry, 163*(6), 1019–1025.
Zanarini, M. C., Frankenburg, F. R., Hennen, J., Reich, D. B., & Silk, K. R. (2005). The McLean Study of Adult Development (MSAD): Overview and implications of the first six years of prospective follow-up. *Journal of Personality Disorders, 19*(5), 505–523.
Zoccolillo, M. (1993). Gender and the development of conduct disorder. *Development and Psychopathology, 5*(1–2), 65–78.

CHAPTER 28

Temperament and Physical Health over the Lifespan

Sarah E. Hampson
Margarete E. Vollrath

In this chapter, we examine the influence of temperament and personality on physical health outcomes across the lifespan from infancy to old age. Well-being is maximized when we experience good physical health, satisfying interpersonal relationships, and accomplishment in our chosen fields of endeavor. Health is fundamental to well-being, but we tend to take it for granted until we get sick; then we ask, why me? Parts of the complex answer to this question lie in genetic vulnerabilities, environmental adversities, and exposure to infectious agents or violence. Another piece of this puzzle is the role played by the nature of our individuality: our temperament. In this chapter we take a journey through the lifespan, examining the relation between temperament and present and future health.

As described in depth by other chapters in this handbook, inherited biological differences in combination with environmental influences give rise to individual variation in reactivity and self-regulation called *temperament*. Temperament *traits* refer to emotional reactions, approach, avoidance, and attentional tendencies that show consistency across situations and over time (Rothbart, 2011). Temperamental differences can be observed from very early in life (Rothbart, 1989); infants and young children can be distinguished in terms of quite specific temperamental traits, including activity level, positive and negative emotions, sociability versus withdrawal, irritability, biological rhythmicity, and persistence (Caspi & Shiner, 2006). In spite of remarkable changes in their manifestation, temperamental traits are relatively stable and predictive of adult personality (Caspi, 2000). Adult temperament is usually described with fewer dimensions than infant and child temperament, and can be captured by the three broad dimensions of Positive and Negative Emotionality and Effortful Control. Adult temperament and personality traits are closely related and can be mapped onto each other (Caspi & Shiner, 2006; Evans & Rothbart, 2007; Shiner & DeYoung, in press). The most widely accepted model of adult personality traits today is the Five-Factor Model (McCrae & Costa, 2008) and the very similar Big Five taxonomy (John, Naumann, & Soto, 2008), both comprising five broad trait dimensions of Extraversion, Agreeableness, Conscientiousness, Emotional Stability, and Intellect/Openness to Experience. The alignment of specific temperament and personality traits is discussed at various points later in the chapter, and we use the broad terms *temperament* and *personality* interchangeably.

There are a number of benefits of considering research on temperament and physical health from a lifespan perspective. Physical health is a process, not a fixed entity. One's current health reflects past health history and is an indicator of future health status. Therefore, physical health is ideally studied in the context of the life course. At any one point in time, we can freeze the frame and measure a person's heart rate, blood pressure, blood glucose level, and so forth, and use this information to diagnose disease and implement treatment. Yet we also know that many chronic diseases have origins that can be traced back to much earlier points in the lifespan, even to experiences in the womb (Barker, 1995). Prevention, as they say, is better than cure. The more we can learn about early disease processes, in particular, why some people show early vulnerabilities to a later disease whereas others do not, the better we will be at prevention.

A lifespan perspective emphasizes change more than stability. Some aspects of temperament and personality change more than others over the life course. Moreover, the influence of temperament on health may change depending on the life stage, and change in temperament itself may be associated with change in health outcomes. There are also reciprocal relations between health and personality: physical health influences temperament and personality, and vice versa. Lifespan methodology includes cross-sectional and longitudinal designs (short and long term), although longitudinal research is better suited to investigating change and reciprocal relations between temperament and health, and provides more convincing support for causal relations. The goal of this research is to understand what causes ill health, yet we must always remain cautious about inferring causality from observational studies, even when examining prospective associations and controlling for confounding variables.

As we shall see, there is by now a substantial body of research documenting associations between temperament and physical health. As the field advances, research is addressing the mechanisms that account for these associations. A lifespan perspective directs attention to these mechanisms as they unfold over time, which demands more sophisticated models and methods than those for cross-sectional or short-term prospective studies of processes (Hampson & Friedman, 2008). In this chapter, by focusing on findings relating temperament and personality measured at an earlier life stage on health outcomes assessed at a later stage, we hope to learn more about lifespan models relating personality to health.

Mechanisms to account for associations between personality and health are chiefly of four kinds: biological, behavioral, cognitive, and social (see Table 28.1). From a lifespan perspective, these mechanisms refer to dynamic pathways moving through time. They are not mutually exclusive, and any given trait–health association is likely best explained by some combination of them. Biological mechanisms (e.g., stress-and-disease models) describe personality influences in terms of their hypothesized impact on processes in various body systems, such as the cardiovascular system, the hypothalamic–pituitary–adrenal system, and immune functioning. Behavioral mechanisms (e.g., health–behavior models) are mediational: The association between traits and health outcomes is explained in terms of hypothesized health-damaging or health-protective behavioral mediators such as smoking or physical activity. Cognitive mechanisms are also mediational but hypothesize that traits influence health through their effects on intervening thoughts or cognitions, such as perseverating on negative thoughts, or broadening versus narrowing of attention. Social mechanisms (e.g., coping and health) seek to explain trait influences in terms of their effects on garnering and benefiting from social relationships. In addition, third-variable models are always a possibility; that is, some other variable may account for both the personality trait and the health outcome in question, rendering the association between the two spurious rather than causal. Where the third variable is a common gene or set of genes resulting in more than one phenotypic outcome, this phenomenon is known in psychobiology as *pleiotropy*. We discuss these mechanisms and their variants in more detail throughout the chapter.

For present purposes, we have grouped the developmental periods that make up the lifespan into two stages: infancy, childhood, and adolescence; and adulthood and old age. Within these periods, we examine the rela-

TABLE 28.1. Examples of Hypotheses Derived from Mechanisms by Which Temperament Influences Health Outcomes

Mechanisms	Processes	Hypotheses for children	Hypotheses for adults
Biological	Stress reactions, BIS/BAS	Internalizing is associated with more experienced stress and dysregulation of the immune response.	Positive affect is associated with better immune function and less susceptibility to the cold virus.
Behavioral	Health behaviors	Preference for healthy food mediates the relation between Externalizing and overweight.	High Conscientiousness is associated with health-enhancing behaviors and better health.
Cognitive	Executive functioning	Positive Emotionality is associated with overestimation of physical activities and more injuries.	High Conscientiousness is associated with better executive functioning and impulse control.
Social	Social relationships, social support	Mothers of children high on Externalizing feed them less healthful diets.	High Neuroticism is associated with evoking more negative interpersonal events and experiencing more distress.
Pleiotropy (i.e., a common underlying cause for different phenotypic outcomes)	Genetics	The central dopamine system underlies both the regulation of weight and the regulation of emotions.	A common genetic basis may contribute to both Positive Emotionality and resistance to disease.

Note. BIS, behavioral inhibition system; BAS, behavioral activation system.

tions between temperament and physical health, both concurrently and prospectively, although with greater emphasis on longitudinal studies. Within each of these main sections, research is organized by three broad dimensions of temperament: Positive Emotionality, Internalizing, and Externalizing traits for children; and Positive Emotionality, Negative Emotionality, and Effortful Control for adults. Associations with physical health are examined for various temperament and personality traits subsumed by these broad dimensions. The chapter ends with overall conclusions and directions for future research.

Temperament and Physical Health in Infancy, Childhood, and Adolescence

There are at least three important reasons for seeking a better understanding of the ways in which temperament influences physical health during the formative years of infancy, childhood, and adolescence. First, childhood and adolescence are stages of life during which health-related habits, such as exercise and dietary patterns, are shaped and may become deeply ingrained. Second, lifestyle-related disorders such as obesity and elements of the metabolic syndrome, a precursor of coronary heart disease and Type 2 diabetes, are now being observed with increasing frequency in childhood and adolescence. Third, temperament-related behaviors constitute a major risk factor for unintentional injuries—the leading cause of death and disabilities in childhood (Centers for Disease Control and Prevention, 2008).

In selecting the studies to highlight in this review, we applied two criteria. We favored population studies over patient studies because of complicating factors such as comorbidity with psychopathology and other limitations on generalizability that are associated with patient samples. We also relied predominantly on prospective studies in which the onset of somatic disease or the occurrence of injuries was measured at some time interval after the assessment of child temperament. These designs support more confident inferences of temperamental influences on disease and injury rather than vice versa, although they must still be interpreted with due caution.

When reviewing studies on temperament and somatic health in infants, children, and adolescents, we were struck by the wide range of constructs that have been used to assess individual differences for these age groups, drawing from temperament, personality, behavior problems, and psychopathology. To organize these diverse constructs, we relied initially on the taxonomic framework provided by Shiner and Caspi (Caspi & Shiner, 2006; Shiner, 1998). Their framework maps the plethora of childhood temperament measures onto four of the Big Five personality domains: Extraversion or Positive Emotionality, Neuroticism or Negative Emotionality, Agreeableness, and Conscientiousness. However, to integrate better the research relating internalizing and externalizing child behavior problems to health, it was necessary to further reduce the number of trait domains to three: Positive Emotionality traits, Internalizing traits, and Externalizing traits. Positive Emotionality traits roughly correspond to the domain of Extraversion and its various more specific traits, such as sociability and activity. Internalizing traits correspond to the domain of Negative Emotionality or Neuroticism, save for the anger/hostility component. Externalizing problems constitute an amalgam of the domains of low Agreeableness and low Conscientiousness (De Pauw, Mervielde, & van Leeuwen, 2009; Krueger et al., 2011).

Positive Emotionality Traits

Differences in Positive Emotionality and activity manifest themselves early in infancy, through smiling and laughter, showing signs of pleasure, and vigorous bodily activity. In early and middle childhood, children high in Positive Emotionality are sociable and outgoing: They enjoy being with other children and adults, and they are energetic, enthusiastic, and active. Indeed, motor activity is such an easily discernable and dominant trait in infants and children that it is considered a separate construct in many temperament models (Buss & Plomin, 1984; De Pauw et al., 2009). Even if activity and hyperactivity overlap empirically, they are distinct conceptually, primarily because hyperactive children are characterized by lack of persistence. Therefore, findings pertaining to hyperactivity are reported under the rubric of externalizing traits.

Although traits belonging to the domain of Positive Emotionality are socially desirable and correlate with happiness and good mental health (DeNeve & Cooper, 1998), they can jeopardize an individual's somatic health. Cross-sectional studies show higher injury risk for children who are impulsive, active, optimistic, and energetic (Plumert & Schwebel, 1997; Vollrath, Landolt, & Ribi, 2003). These findings are bolstered by a longitudinal study documenting that children with high Positive Emotionality tend to have more lifetime injuries (Schwebel & Plumert, 1999).

On the other hand, Positive Emotionality in childhood appears to be protective for other aspects of physical health. In infants, high levels of activity appear to protect against weight gain and fatness (Slining, Adair, Goldman, Borja, & Bentley, 2009). Similar findings have been documented for older children and over longer periods. A study following children and adolescents for 3 years showed that mental vitality and activity predicted lower body mass index (BMI), and positive emotionality predicted lower risk for other precursors of the metabolic syndrome: high blood pressure, insulin resistance, and high waist-to-hip ratio (Ravaja & Keltikangas-Järvinen, 1995). Moreover, Hampson, Goldberg, Vogt, and Dubanoski (2007) found that Extraversion in children predicted better health status 40 years later, defined as a combination of better self-rated health, lower weight, and better functional status.

Mechanisms

A biological mechanism underlying the active and sociable behavior of children high in Positive Emotionality has been spelled out in Gray's reinforcement sensitivity theory (Gray, 1987), which holds that human behavior is governed by two neurobiological motivational systems that determine an individual's sensitivity to reward and punishment, respectively. Sensitivity to reward is determined by the strength of the behavioral approach system. Individuals who are sensitive to reward are more strongly motivated to seek and find opportunities for hedonic experiences. Confronted with adversity, for example, they recognize the potential for positive outcomes. This in turn has protective effects on physical health by reducing physiological arousal and feelings of stress. For example, children high in Positive Emotionality experiencing their parents' divorce felt less threatened by the situation and used more positive cognitive restructuring as a coping strategy (Lengua, Sandler, West, Wolchik, & Curran, 1999).

Both cognitive and behavioral mechanisms mediating the association between Positive Emotionality traits and injury proneness in children have been proposed. A cognitive mechanism associated both with Positive Emotionality and injury proneness is the tendency to overestimate one's physical abilities compared with the demands of the situation (Schwebel & Plumert, 1999). Behavioral mechanisms relating Positive Emotionality to injury proneness stem from these children's tendency to seek new, thrilling experiences by engaging in a greater variety of activities, ultimately resulting in greater exposure to hazardous situations (Schwebel & Barton, 2006).

At the same time, high levels of activity can have protective effects on health. High levels of physical activity and engagement in sports, for example, entail greater caloric output in children and can thus protect them from becoming overweight (Anderson, Bandini, Dietz, & Must, 2004).

Internalizing Traits

This group of traits includes the disposition to experience and express negative emotions such as anxiety and depression, to be shy and withdrawn, emotionally unstable and to have low self-esteem.

Whether traits from the Internalizing spectrum assessed in childhood predict mortality has been debated extensively, but a recent study added compelling evidence. This prospective study that followed a large British cohort from birth to age 46 found that teacher-rated internalizing behavior increased later mortality risk (Jokela, Ferrie, & Kivimäki, 2009). At the same time, the study documented that Internalizing traits had protective effects on health, decreasing the risk of unintentional injuries in adolescence and adulthood (Jokela, Power, & Kivimäki, 2009). However, the latter is contradicted by findings from Rowe, Simonoff, and Silberg (2007), who showed that childhood overanxiousness predicted a higher risk for injury involvement.

The evidence relating Internalizing traits in childhood to concurrent and later morbidity is mixed and depends on the disease under study. With respect to general morbidity, findings from a study following over 500 children into adulthood showed that being more distress prone as a child predicted worse self-reported health and more illnesses as an adult (Kubzansky, Martin, & Buka, 2009). There is also evidence that Internalizing traits are associated with diseases with childhood onset. Asthma, allergies, and eczemas are among the most common diseases in childhood and are related to traits of the Internalizing spectrum, such as anxiety and depression (Feldman, Ortega, Koinis-Mitchell, Kuo, & Canino, 2010; Katon et al., 2007; Lien, 2008; McQuaid, Kopel, & Nassau, 2001). However, the causal direction of this association is unclear. Whereas some researchers consider Internalizing problems to be a consequence of having asthma or similar disorders, others argue that Internalizing temperamental traits precede asthma (Lilljeqvist, Smorvik, & Faleide, 2002). Most of the longitudinal studies on this topic have examined rather small samples (Klinnert et al., 2001; Lilljeqvist et al., 2002), but a more recent prospective study following more than 5,000 children from ages 5–14 years clearly established that Internalizing problems in that sample were a consequence of asthma and not vice versa (Alati et al., 2005).

Childhood obesity is another disease whose prevalence is increasing at an alarming pace worldwide. In adults, there is a reciprocal association between depression and obesity, where depression both precedes and supersedes obesity (Luppino et al., 2010). In contrast, in infancy and early childhood, the association between Internalizing traits and weight in population studies has been inconsistent (Bradley et al., 2008; Datar, 2004; Garthus-Niegel, Hagtvet, & Vollrath, 2010; Sawyer et al., 2006). The association becomes more clear-cut when longer follow-up periods are examined, for instance, when children and adolescents are followed into adulthood. In these studies, it appears that Internalizing problems or depression in childhood or adolescence increase the risk for overweight in adulthood (Hasler et al., 2004; Richardson et al., 2003).

Mechanisms

Internalizing traits such as anxiety, shyness, depression, and withdrawal have been conceptualized within the framework of the behavioral inhibition system. Persons with a strong behavioral inhibition system are sensitive to cues of punishment and nonreward. Confronted with novel stimuli, their tendency to avoid punishment leads to behavioral inhibition, tense arousal, and increased attention. The behavioral inhibition system may be considered both as a cognitive and a physiological system (Gray & McNaughton, 2000). The cognitive aspects of the behavioral inhibition system can have both protective and damaging effects on health. On the cognitive level, increased attention to symptoms of ill health ensuing from high behavioral inhibition may not only facilitate early disease detection but also lead to poor treatment adherence, as any sign of disease deterioration may arouse overwhelming fear and thus avoidance behavior. Physiologically, high sensitivity to punishment leads to greater vulnerability and greater autonomic arousal in reaction to stress. Stress, in turn, is associated with dysregulation of immune responses, which play a role in chronic inflammatory conditions such as asthma and allergies (Priftis, Papadimitriou, Nicolaidou, & Chrousos, 2009). At the same time, the causal pathway between stress and disease is bidirectional, as any chronic disease can function as a chronic stressor, and has been shown to be associated with symptoms of anxiety and depression (Lavigne & Faier-Routman, 1992).

The link between Internalizing traits and obesity may be mediated by biological, behavioral, and social mediators. There is increasing evidence that sweet and fatty foods improve mood and reduce the effects of stress via brain opioidergic and dopaminergic pathways, and some researchers propose that there are parallels between overeating and the consumption of addictive substances (Davis & Carter, 2009; Gibson, 2006). A third variable explanation that has also been put forward claims that the central dopamine system underlies the regulation of both weight and emotions (Yasuno et al., 2001). On a behavioral level, a cross-sectional association between internalizing traits and higher consumption of sweets and sweet drinks has recently been demonstrated in a population study of 18-month-olds (Vollrath, Tonstad, Rothbart, & Hampson, 2011). Another study showed that adolescents' Neuroticism was related to emotional eating, that is, eating when upset or distressed (Heaven, Mulligan, Merrilees, Woods, & Fairooz, 2001). At the same time, the reverse causal pathway should not be dismissed, as obesity is considered unattractive and socially undesirable, which can result in bullying and social exclusion of obese children (Janssen, Craig, Boyce, & Pickett, 2004). Indeed, rejection of obese children by their peers occurs as early as age 3 years (Cramer & Steinwert, 1998).

Externalizing Traits

The Externalizing spectrum includes traits capturing the tendency to act without forethought, such as impulsiveness and poor self-control; traits capturing negative emotions, such as irritability, anger, and aggression; traits reflecting lack of attentional focus and hyperactivity; and traits capturing poor adjustment to external demands, such as conduct problems and defiance (Caspi & Shiner, 2006). In adults Externalizing problems overlap with the Big Five personality domains of low Conscientiousness and low Agreeableness (De Pauw et al., 2009; Krueger et al., 2011).

Externalizing traits are associated with a host of negative health outcomes, as well as mortality. A landmark study in the United States following 11-year-olds for over 65 years showed lower mortality among children with the highest scores on Conscientiousness, but a particular cause of death for those dying early could not be identified (Friedman et al., 1993). In a similar vein, a large British cohort study showed that Externalizing behaviors in 11-year-olds increased the risk for mortality across both adolescence and young and middle adulthood. By the age of 46, a twofold mortality risk for those in the highest quartile of Externalizing problems was observed (Jokela, Ferrie, & Kiwimäki, 2009).

Externalizing traits in children and adolescents are associated with nonfatal unintentional injuries (Schwebel, 2004; Vollrath et al., 2003). Longitudinal studies following toddlers into early childhood (Schwebel & Plumert, 1999; Soubhi, 2004), children into adolescence (Rowe et al., 2007), and schoolchildren across adolescence into middle adulthood (Jokela, Power, & Kiwimäki, 2009) documented that Externalizing traits preceded the injuries. Soubhi (2004) showed that childhood Externalizing traits interacted with neighborhood socioeconomic disadvantage. That is, children with externalizing traits from neighborhoods characterized by poor housing conditions, incomplete families, and lack of cohesion among neighbors were at increased risk of injury.

Traits from the Externalizing spectrum in childhood are also associated with diseases and somatic risk factors for disease. A Finnish study showed that in children and adolescents, hostility, hyperactivity, aggression, and anger predicted metabolic syndrome precursors over a 3-year follow-up period (Ravaja & Keltikangas-Järvinen, 1995). Moreover, hyperactivity in children predicted adult carotid artery media thickness, a risk factor for cardiovascular disease, 21 years later (Keltikangas-Järvinen, Pulkki-Råback, Puttonen, Viikari, & Raitakari, 2006). Likewise, a 3-year follow-up study in healthy adolescents demonstrated that trait anger predicted higher waist-to-hip ratios, whereas hostility predicted greater arterial stiffness (Midei & Matthews, 2009).

Clear associations between childhood Externalizing traits and subsequent greater weight have been demonstrated as well. A recent longitudinal study showed that boys with shorter attention span and girls with difficult temperament as 1-year-olds had greater increases in standardized weight and were more likely to be overweight at the age of 6 years (Faith & Hittner, 2010). Associations of Externalizing traits in childhood with higher weight or overweight in adulthood have also been demonstrated in several longitudinal studies: One of these studies showed that childhood anger and aggression predicted higher BMI in adulthood (Pulkki-Råback, Elovainio, Kivimäki, Raitakari, & Keltikangas-Järvinen, 2005), and another study showed that conduct disorder predicted elevated BMI and obesity in adulthood (Pine, Cohen, Brook, & Coplan, 1997). Finally, yet another study showed that the effect of low childhood Conscientiousness on adult BMI applied only to women, not to men (Hampson, Goldberg, Vogt, & Dubanoski, 2006).

Mechanisms

Lack of self-control, inhibition, responsibility and rule compliance entail a wide range of uninhibited and reckless behavior, exposing the child to a variety of health risks. With respect to injury proneness, studies reviewed by Schwebel and Barton (2006) showed that impulsive, uninhibited children take more chances in traffic situations and are less willing to adopt safe behaviors, such as wearing bicycle helmets. Moreover, impulsive children tend to have impulsive parents who are less effective at monitoring their children's behavior systematically.

With respect to overweight and the metabolic syndrome, diet, eating behavior, and exercise are important mediators. Children and adolescents with Externalizing traits are less likely to attend to satiety cues and have a tendency to overeat and to prefer sweet and fatty foods to more healthy ones (Davis, Strachan, & Berkson, 2004; Oddy et al., 2009; Verbeken, Braet, Claus, Nederkoorn, & Oosterlaan, 2009). Indeed, the association between Externalizing traits and a preference for sweet taste has been shown to emerge in infancy (Vollrath et al., 2011).

Social mechanisms mediating the Externalizing–feeding relationship involve maternal feeding style, as well as dietary choices of the mothers on behalf of their children. Mothers may overfeed children who are acting out in a misguided effort to calm them or to curb their emotional reactions (Faith & Hittner, 2010). Alternatively, they may restrict children's consumption of sweets once they become overweight, provoking angry and defiant reactions that ultimately result in even greater consumption of sweets (Francis, Hofer, & Birch, 2001). Moreover, children with Externalizing traits are more likely to have mothers with high Negative Emotionality, who also tend to feed their children less healthy diets (Hampson, Tonstad, Irgens, Meltzer, & Vollrath, 2010; Ystrom, Barker, & Vollrath, 2012; Ystrom, Niegel, & Vollrath, 2009).

A third variable explanation for the relation between appetitive behaviors, including drug abuse, and Externalizing traits has been proposed as well: Externalizing traits and the regulation of pleasurable experiences are both governed by the dopaminergic system (Krueger, Markon, Patrick, Benning, & Kramer, 2007).

Methodological Challenges

Conducting studies on the association between child temperament and later physical health is challenging in several ways. The onset of many of the health outcomes that researchers want to predict, such as coronary heart disease or Type 2 diabetes, occurs long after childhood. Observation periods spanning several decades are necessary, entailing the risk of serious attrition to the sample and complicating the chain of associations with many intervening variables. Causal directions are not easy to determine, as somatic disease also influences temperament and mental health, so reciprocal relations over time are highly likely. Moreover, even prospective studies can give no definite answers with respect to causality because unmeasured third variables such as biological dispositions give rise to both temperament and disease. Child temperament is less stable than adult temperament, which poses a challenge when prediction over the lifespan is the goal. The diversity of childhood temperament constructs that have been studied, and the poor psychometric properties of some of the measures, makes it difficult to compare findings and build a cumulative knowledge base. Last, the health risks posed by temperament traits over the lifespan should also be evaluated in the context of the multiplicity of environmental risk factors present even before birth, within the fetal environment.

Temperament and Physical Health in Adulthood and Old Age

By adulthood, personality has developed from its roots in early temperament into a hierarchical organization of numerous specific behaviors and narrow traits subsumed by fewer but broader trait dimensions (Eysenck, 1947; Roberts & Wood, 2006). Three broad temperament dimensions in adulthood capture the five broad groups of adult personality traits as follows: Positive Emotionality includes Extraversion traits; Negative Emotionality includes Neuroticism traits; and Effortful Control includes Conscientiousness traits (Clark & Watson, 2008). Agreeableness traits are more difficult to locate in a temperament framework, but we have chosen to include traits reflecting low Agreeableness as part of Negative Emotionality. Until very recently, Openness to Experience has been viewed as distinct from temperament, so we have chosen not to include studies of Openness and health in this chapter.

Although the basic organizational structure of adult personality traits remains stable, normative developmental changes continue across the lifespan. For example, people tend to become more agreeable, conscientious and emotionally stable in adulthood, and decline in the sociability component of Extraversion and Openness (Roberts, Wood, & Caspi, 2008). These changes have implications for health. For example, increasing Conscientiousness may result in adults being more likely than adolescents to engage in health-protective behaviors and avoid health-damaging ones. Despite these normative maturational trends, individual variability in personality change over time may also be an important predictor of health outcomes (Mroczek & Spiro, 2003, 2007). Reciprocal associations between adult temperament or personality and health are likely: Personality change occurs in response to life events, such as marriage and parenthood, and may also change in response to the experience of injury and disease.

Positive Emotionality

Some people are more likely than others to experience positive emotions, and this trait-like tendency is referred to as Positive Emotionality or Positive Affectivity. Adult Positive Emotionality corresponds well to its counterpart in children. Positive Emotionality has been very broadly defined to include constructs such as self-esteem, optimism, mastery, and extraversion, as well as the tendency to experience positive emotions. These various dispositions share a common underlying core of approach temperament, which orients behavior and attention toward positive stimuli (Elliot & Thrash, 2010; Rothbart, 2011). The personality trait of Extraversion–Introversion contrasts people who are described as sociable, energetic, and dominant with ones who are reserved, withdrawn, and submissive (John & Srivastava, 1999). It is closely aligned with the temperament of Positive Emotionality or positive affect (Clark & Watson, 2008; John et al., 2008; Rothbart, 2011).

Adults who are more extraverted experience greater happiness, and subjective and existential well-being than those inclined to introversion, and those who tend to experience positive emotions also tend to enjoy better health. Until the rise of positive psychology (Lopez & Snyder, 2009), studies of the relation between Positive Emotionality and health were less common than studies of Negative Emotionality. However, there is now such an accumulation of research on Positive Emotionality and health that there are several meta-analytic and narrative reviews on the subject. In these reviews, Positive Emotionality is defined broadly to encompass both short-term and more trait-like tendencies to experience positive emotional states (Chida & Steptoe, 2008; Howell, Kern, & Lyubomirsky, 2007; Ong, 2010; Pressman & Cohen, 2005; Steptoe, Dockray, & Wardle, 2009).

The tendency to experience positive emotions is associated with longevity, particularly among community samples of older individuals (Pressman & Cohen, 2005). For example, in a prospective study of 185 Catholic nuns, Danner, Snowdon, and Friesen (2001) found an association between positive emotional content of written autobiographies at age 22 and longevity six decades later, after controlling for age and education. There was a 2.5-fold difference in the risk of dying for those in the lowest versus the highest quartiles of positive emotional expression in their writing. A recent meta-analytic review of positive psychological well-being and mortality confirmed the association between Positive Emotionality and lower mortality risk in both initially healthy adult samples and samples with preexisting conditions, and also established that this association was independent of negative affect (Chida & Steptoe, 2008).

Cross-sectional studies of positive affect and physical illness suggest that people with physical illness have less positive affect, and the more illnesses they have, the less their experience of positive emotion (Pressman & Cohen, 2005). These studies are open to interpretation: Illness may reduce Positive Emotionality, and Positive Emotionality may reduce the likelihood of illness. More significantly, positive affect is associated prospectively with subsequent better health and less illness. For example, Davidson, Mostofsky, and Whang (2010) showed that positive affect was associated with reduced incidence of cardiovascular disease over a 10-year follow-up in a population-based sample. Negative Emotionality (depression, hostility, and anxiety), was also associated with increased risk of cardiovascular disease, confirming the importance of treating Positive and Negative Emotionality as separate dimensions, and demonstrating the effects of one independent of the other. Positive affect is also associated with better self-reported health, less pain, and fewer symptoms (Pressman & Cohen, 2005). However, these subjective findings are less compelling because they may be due to the influence of positive affect on how people regard their health rather than their objective health status.

Extraversion

There is not a substantial body of evidence demonstrating consistent relations between the adult personality trait of Extraversion and positive health outcomes. This may due to Extraversion having both advantages and disadvantages for health and survival (Nettle, 2006). Insofar as extraverts are more sociable and active they should derive health benefits from larger and more diverse social networks and perceived social support. On the other hand, their reward sensitivity and approach temperament may have negative consequences for health, for example, as a result of risk taking. For extraverts who survive to old age, their higher Extraversion appears to be beneficial. In a community sample of men and women 65 years and older, high Extraversion was associated with a 21% decrease in risk of death over an average 6-year follow-up (Wilson et al., 2005).

Optimism

The trait of *Optimism* is the tendency to have positive expectations about the future (Carver, Scheier, Miller, & Fulford, 2009). Although it is associated with better subjective health outcomes (Steptoe, Wright, Kunz-Ebrecht, & Iliffe, 2006), its association with objectively measured physical outcomes is less consistent. Findings for the beneficial effects of Optimism in the short to medium term include faster recovery from medical interventions such as coronary artery bypass graft surgery (Scheier et al., 1999). Similarly, more optimistic head and neck cancer patients had a greater chance of 1-year survival (Allison, Guichard, Fung, & Gilain, 2003), and women who were more optimistic showed less progression of carotid artery disease than did those who were chronically pessimistic (Räikkönen, Matthews, Sutton-Tyrrell, & Kuller, 2004). Some studies also show longer-term effects of Optimism. In an 8-year follow-up of initially disease-free women, Tindle and colleagues (2009) observed lower rates of coronary heart disease and all-cause mortality among the most optimistic women.

These findings typically survive controlling for sociodemographic and other risk factors associated with optimism. Studies such as these suggest that optimism has a protective effect through its association with slower disease processes. The cross-sectional association between optimism and lower levels of inflammation supports this view (Roy et al., 2010) because inflammation is an early indicator of developing cardiovascular disease. However, there is also a body of evidence relating optimism to poorer immune functioning, with negative consequences for diseases such as HIV and some cancers (Segerstrom, 2005). In some cases, optimists' persistence under difficult circumstances may work to their disadvantage, exacerbating negative health effects through impaired immune functioning. Optimism, like Extraversion, has both advantages and disadvantages for health.

Mechanisms

Establishing a causal relation between Positive Emotionality and health is challenging because the association between feeling good and feeling well is undoubtedly bidirectional. It is also important to establish that the findings for Positive Emotionality are not just the inverse of those for negative emotion, but are independent effects. Although not identified so far, there could be a pleiotropic process at work, that is, a common genetic basis contributing to both Positive Emotionality and resistance to disease (Steptoe et al., 2009). There is some support for an association between traits related to positive affect and several health behaviors, such as more physical activity, less smoking and alcohol use, and more healthy diet (Grant, Wardle, & Steptoe, 2009). In studies controlling for these health behaviors, it is common for the association between Positive Emotionality and health outcomes to remain significant, suggesting that other mechanisms are involved (Ong, 2010). Positive affect is associated with more effective immune function and less inflammation, after researchers control for negative affect and other covariates. For example, Cohen, Alper, Doyle, Treanor, and Turner (2006) related subjects' positive emotional style (averaged daily reports of emotional states over 2 weeks) to incidence of clinically diagnosed colds and symptom reports after being infected with a cold virus. Those with a more positive emotional style were less likely to develop a cold or to report symptoms, even after researchers controlled for numerous demographic factors and closely related traits such as Extraversion.

An incident of extreme positive emotion can cause intense physiological arousal resulting in negative health consequences, even triggering a heart attack. However, more typically, positive emotions are associated with beneficial physiological effects, including dampening of arousal and lower levels of stress hormones. In older adults (age 60 and over), positive affect has been related to lower (i.e., healthier) cortisol levels (Steptoe, O'Donnell, Badrick, Kumari, & Marmot, 2008), and adults with higher positive affect have reduced (i.e., healthier) cardiovascular reactivity both in daily monitoring studies and in laboratory studies involving a challenge (Steptoe et al., 2009).

A cognitive mechanism for the benefits of positive emotions has been proposed by Fredrickson (2001). Positive emotions broaden attentional focus, whereas negative emotions narrow it. Broad attentional focus produces cognitive flexibility and creativity, which builds intellectual and social coping resources; broadening and narrowing of attentional focus may occur without conscious emotional experience (Friedman & Förster, 2010). Through these mechanisms, positive emotions may even undo the effects of negative emotions (Tugade, Fredrickson, & Feldman Barrett, 2004).

Social support is another mechanism by which Positive Emotionality may influence health outcomes. It is particularly important among older adults for maintaining independence, and Positive Emotionality is associated with more active coping in middle-aged adults (e.g., seeking out social support), independent of negative affect and other covariates (Steptoe, O'Donnell, Marmot, & Wardle, 2008). Interventions to increase Positive Emotionality, for example by loving-kindness meditation, may result in greater social support and its associated benefits for health (Fredrickson, Cohn, Coffey, Pek, & Finkel, 2008).

Negative Emotionality

Adult *negative emotionality* refers to the extent to which a person experiences the world as distressing, problematic, and threatening (Clark & Watson, 2008). The broad trait of Neuroticism is the chronic tendency for some individuals to experience more negative thoughts and feelings than others, to be emotionally unstable and insecure. In contrast to those who are emotionally stable, more neurotic individuals are described as prone to worry, anxiety, moodiness, irritability, and depression (Costa & McCrae, 1992; John & Srivistava, 1999). Neuroticism is closely aligned with the temperament trait Negative Emotionality (Clark & Watson, 2008; Evans & Rothbart, 2007; John et al., 2008) and with the neurological behavioral inhibition system (Gray & McNaughton, 2000). Greater neurobiological sensitivity to negative events results in greater behavioral orientation and attention to them (Canli, 2006; Elliot & Thrash, 2010; H. J. Eysenck & M. W. Eysenck, 1985; Gray & McNaughton, 2000).

In many respects, adult Negative Emotionality corresponds to childhood internalizing temperament. However, in childhood, some aspects of Negative Emotionality, such as anger, are best captured by the Externalizing dimension. Indeed, anger, quarrelsomeness, and hostility are difficult to locate in trait structures because they relate both to high Neuroticism and low Agreeableness (Caspi & Shiner, 2006). In particular, it is difficult to reconcile anger-related traits as part of avoidance temperament. However, for adolescents and adults, Negative Emotionality appears to encompass both the Internalizing and Externalizing negative emotions; hence, we have included these traits under Negative Emotionality here (Neiss, Stevenson, Legrand, Iacono, & Sedikides, 2009).

High levels of Negative Emotionality sound unhealthy by definition, and indeed there is a substantial body of evidence associating the tendency to experience negative emotions with ill health. However, such research is beset by a major challenge: separating the effects of perceived from actual ill health. Measures of Negative Emotionality, particularly measures of trait Neuroticism may predict subjective distress but not more objective measures of disease (Costa & McCrae, 1985; Feldman, Cohen, Doyle, Skoner, & Gwaltney, 1999; Watson & Pennebaker, 1989). More neurotic individuals may have heightened sensitivity to changes in their health that precede clinically observable symptoms of disease, or they may interpret normal bodily sensations as causes of concern. Nevertheless, there is a substantial body of evidence that goes beyond such artifactual effects, showing prospective associations between Negative Emotionality and mortality, physical disease (particularly cardiovascular disease), and pain (Charles, Gatz, Kato, & Pedersen, 2008; Friedman & Booth-Kewley, 1987; Suls & Bunde, 2005).

Negative Emotionality/Affectivity and Neuroticism

Mortality is incontrovertibly an objective outcome. A number of studies have associated higher levels of Neuroticism with reduced longevity in adult community samples (Roberts, Kuncel, Shiner, Caspi, & Goldberg, 2007; Shipley, Weiss, Der, Taylor, & Deary, 2007; Terracciano, Lockenhoff, Zonderman, Ferrucci, & Costa, 2008; Wilson, Bienias, Mendes de Leon, Evans, & Bennet, 2003; Wilson et al., 2005), and shorter survival time in those already ill

(Christensen, Ehlers, Raichle, & Lawton, 2002). A landmark study by Mroczek and Spiro (2007) related Neuroticism assessed over a 12-year period in old age to mortality, and found that men with high and more rapidly increasing Neuroticism had the highest mortality risk. However, some studies have not observed an association between Negative Emotionality or Neuroticism and mortality (e.g., Almada et al., 1991). Furthermore, in the Terman Lifecycle Study, Neuroticism measured in early adulthood predicted higher mortality for women but decreased mortality risk for men (Friedman, Kern, & Reynolds, 2010). These conflicting findings indicate that the relation between Negative Emotionality and health outcomes in adulthood is not straightforward. The heightened attention and sensitivity to negative stimuli that characterize Negative Emotionality may also have protective effects for health, and a challenge for future research is to understand the conditions that result in health-protective versus health-damaging effects of this aspect of temperament.

Adult Negative Emotionality, in the form of the overlapping constructs of anger, hostility, anxiety, and depression, predicts cardiovascular disease among initially healthy populations and, to a lesser extent, disease progression among those with cardiovascular disease (Smith, Glazer, Ruiz, & Gallo, 2004; Suls & Bunde, 2005). The evidence for hostility and anger was less consistent, particularly for disease progression. The overlap among these various Negative Emotionality traits indicates that it may be more worthwhile to investigate a broad temperament of negative affect in relation to cardiovascular disease, instead of making distinctions among the various narrower traits. In contrast, others have demonstrated the benefits of drilling down to more specific associations between aspects of negative affect and cardiovascular disease. In a prospective study of adult men and women ranging widely in age, Hakkula, Konttinen, Laatikainen, Kawachi, and Uutela (2010) investigated cynical hostility, anger in, anger out, and anger control as risk factors for later onset of cardiovascular disease. Cynical hostility and low anger control predicted fatal and nonfatal cardiovascular disease, whereas anger in and anger out did not.

Adult Negative Emotionality has been associated with risk factors for cardiovascular disease such as hypertension, higher BMI and weight gain, and smoking (Brummett et al., 2006; Faith, Flint, Fairburn, Goodwin, & Allison, 2001; Whiteman, 2006; Whiteman, Deary, & Fowkes, 2000; Zhange et al., 2005). Another risk factor is the night-to-day blood pressure ratio: Greater cardiovascular risk is associated with less of a nighttime decline. This variable was been associated with low life purpose and high hostility in a sample of men and women with cardiovascular disease, largely independent of various measures of sleep quality (Mezick et al., 2010). Middle-aged women who were more depressed, tense, and angry at baseline were at increased risk of developing the metabolic syndrome, itself a major risk factor for cardiovascular disease and diabetes, during the 7–8 years of follow-up (Räikkönen, Matthews, & Kuller, 2002; Räikkönen et al., 2004). In this same study, those with metabolic syndrome at baseline were more likely to be angry and anxious at follow-up, illustrating the bidirectional nature of the relations between Negative Emotionality and disease over time. Similarly, the association between depression and obesity is also reciprocal. As noted earlier, a meta-analysis of longitudinal studies demonstrated that depression predicts the development of obesity, and that obesity increases the risk for depression (Luppino et al., 2010).

There is increasing interest in relating temperament traits to early indicators of disease as a way of studying the influence of temperament on the long-term course of cardiovascular and other diseases. Carotid artery intimal media thickening, a subclinical indicator of atherosclerosis, has been related cross-sectionally to hopelessness, independent of depression and other risk factors. For example, women with higher levels of hopelessness had more clinically significant thickening (Whipple et al., 2009). Prospective studies linking Negative Emotionality to disease progression are even more interesting. For example, Player, King, Mainous, and Geesey (2007) showed that trait anger was associated with the progression from hypertension to incident coronary heart disease in middle-aged men.

Research on the association between negative affectivity and cancer has produced inconsistent findings (Augustine, Larsen, Walker, & Fisher, 2008). There are numerous methodological challenges to this work, including the appropriate population to study: For example, associations may differ for at-risk populations such as smokers or the obese. However, Augustine and colleagues (2008) demonstrated that lung cancer patients at the same stage of the disease, but with higher levels of negative affect, had received surgery at a younger age than those with lower negative affect, suggesting that they developed the disease sooner.

Pessimism

Pessimism is an aspect of Negative Emotionality that, in some studies, relates to health independently from optimism. In the Harvard Study of Adult Development, pessimistic explanatory style assessed at age 25 predicted poor health at ages 45–60, controlling for physical and mental health at age 25 (Peterson, Seligman, & Vaillant, 1988). In adults ages 30–59, pessimism independently predicted mortality from cancer 8 months later (Schulz, Bookwala, Knapp, Scheier, & Williamson, 1996), and pessimism was associated with increased mortality risk over a 30-year follow-up of self-referred general medical patients (Maruta, Colligan, Malinchoc, & Offord, 2000).

Mechanisms

The processes by which Negative Emotionality is associated with physical illness include biological mechanisms involving psychophysiological reactivity and impaired recovery to stress; social mechanisms (e.g., hostile people creating hostile environments for themselves); and health–behavior mechanisms that relate Negative Emotionality to health-damaging behaviors such as tobacco use (Smith et al., 2004). Evidence for third variable models demonstrates that these mechanisms are complicated to unravel. For example, increased central nervous system serotonin function was associated with a more favorable profile of temperament, psychosocial, metabolic, and cardiovascular measures (Williams et al., 2010). It can be revealing to compare the influence of more than one mechanism in the same study. For example, Bolger and Schilling (1991) investigated both reactivity and evocative mechanisms in their investigation into why neurotic people experience more distress. In a daily diary study, they demonstrated that neurotic people experience more stressful situations, suggesting that they created (evoked) more stress for themselves than non-neurotic people. However, the greater part of their distress was explained by their stronger reactions to such events confirming the importance of the heightened physiological reactivity associated with Neuroticism (Suls & Martin, 2005).

The physiological mechanisms by which depression is related to cardiovascular disease include autonomic nervous system dysfunction and inflammation. Depression among participants in the Cardiovascular Health Study (age 65 and older) was associated with both heart rate variability (an indicator of autonomic nervous system dysfunction) and inflammation, and increased risk of dying from cardiovascular disease over a 13-year follow-up period (Kop et al., 2010). However, the association between depression and cardiovascular mortality was only partially explained by these mechanisms. It is also interesting that interventions to reduce depression among patients with cardiovascular disease do not appear to have marked beneficial effects on cardiovascular outcomes, indicating that the causal relation between depression and cardiovascular disease is far from straightforward (Honig et al., 2007). Nevertheless, laboratory studies that induce negative affect show adverse effects on the immune system, cortisol, and cardiovascular functioning (e.g., Tsuboi et al., 2008) and negative affect experienced during a typical day is associated with increased ambulatory heart rate (Daly, Delaney, Doran, Harmon, & MacLachlan, 2010).

Effortful Control and Conscientiousness

Positive and Negative Emotionality and their associated personality traits of Extraversion and Neuroticism are complemented by a third aspect of adult temperament and personality, that of Effortful Control, constraint, or self-regulation (Carver, 2005; Clark & Watson, 2008; Elliot & Thrash, 2010; Evans & Rothbart, 2007; Rothbart, 2011). Effortful Control traits develop later in childhood and may have their roots in infant traits such as soothability (Caspi & Shiner, 2006; Rothbart, 2011). The personality trait of Conscientiousness closely corresponds to the temperament trait Effortful Control, and describes individual differences in adherence to socially prescribed rules and norms for impulse control, in being task- and goal-directed, and in being able to delay gratification (John & Srivastava, 1999). This dimension distinguishes people who are orderly, industrious, and planful from those who are undisciplined, lazy, and unreliable. Effortful Control requires mental capacity to regulate other systems and is associated with attentional networks in the brain (Nigg, 2000; Rothbart, 2007; Rothbart & Rueda, 2005). In addition to intentional, goal-based Effortful Control, self-regulation results from reactive, automatic inhibition, which may also be a component of Conscientiousness (Eisenberg et al., 2004; Nigg, 2000; Rothbart & Ahadi, 1994). To the extent that maintaining good physical health is a function of goal-directed behavior, a person's level of Effortful Control should be important. Research into the relation between the personality trait of Conscientiousness and health outcomes indicates this to be the case.

Conscientiousness

In the Terman Lifecycle Study, Conscientiousness measured in early adulthood predicted lower mortality risk (Friedman et al., 2010). As we saw earlier, in that same sample, Conscientiousness measured in childhood predicted lower risk of mortality across the lifespan (Friedman et al., 1993). Prior to these groundbreaking findings, this aspect of personality and temperament had not been seriously considered with regard to health outcomes. The association between Conscientiousness and longevity has now been established as a replicable, generalizable finding (Kern & Friedman, 2008). For example, in the Edinburgh Artery Study, a prospective study of a community sample of men and women, men who were less conscientious were more likely to die from any cause over a 7-year follow-up (Whiteman, 2006). Weiss and Costa (2005) observed protective effects of high Conscientiousness on mortality over a 5-year follow-up in old age. In a study of men and women in the Catholic clergy, the 5-year risk of mortality was halved for those with high versus low Conscientiousness scores assessed at age 75, controlling for the effects of the other traits and physical health (Wilson, Mendes de Leon, Bienias, Evans, & Bennett, 2004). From a lifespan perspective, these enduring effects of Conscientiousness in adulthood and old age are particularly interesting. Less conscientious individuals are more likely to die at all ages (Friedman et al., 1995; Martin, Friedman & Schwartz, 2007). By old age, therefore, survivors are likely to be relatively conscientious; yet even at these relatively high levels, variability in conscientiousness measured at an earlier point in time is still important for longevity.

Studies have also related low Conscientiousness to morbidity. Obesity is a morbid condition that is a risk factor for cardiovascular disease, Type 2 diabetes, and various cancers. Adults tend to gain weight at midlife, putting them at risk for becoming obese. In the North Carolina Alumni Heart Study, midlife weight gain measured at four time points over 14 years was larger among men and women who were less conscientious (Brummett et al., 2006). Conscientiousness has been shown to be associated with slower disease progression, which is important from a lifespan perspective. For example, renal patients low on Conscientiousness were more likely to have died 4 years later, as were those high on Neuroticism, after controlling for age and diabetic status (Christensen et al., 2002). Conscientiousness may have a moderating effect on other personality traits. People with high Conscientiousness may be able to apply appropriate Effortful Control to overcome the disadvantages of, say, low Agreeableness or high Neuroticism. For example, Brickman, Yount, Blaney, Rothberg, and De-Nour (1996) compared renal deterioration time in adult diabetes patients grouped by their scores on Neuroticism and Conscientiousness. The combination of moderate Neuroticism and high Conscientiousness was most protective against renal deterioration. The moderating effect of Conscientiousness on other traits should be examined in future studies.

Mechanisms

Health behavior models are commonly invoked to explain the effects of Conscientiousness on physical health. It is well established that more conscientious people engage in more health-enhancing behaviors and fewer health-damaging ones (Bogg &

Roberts, 2004). Therefore, it is reasonable to hypothesize that because conscientious people take better care of themselves, they are less likely to become ill and more likely to live longer. However, there are surprisingly few tests of this mediation model in prospective studies with objective measures of health, and those that have been conducted typically show that health behaviors can only partially account for the effects of Conscientiousness. For example, in the Terman Lifecycle Study, smoking and alcohol use did not fully account for the association between Conscientiousness and longevity. Similarly, Hampson and colleagues (2006, 2007) found that the effect of childhood Conscientiousness on adult self-rated health was only partly mediated by health behaviors performed in adulthood. Accordingly, the effects of third variables on Conscientiousness and health cannot be ruled out, and other mechanisms for the effects of constructs related to Effortful Control should be investigated.

There is growing interest in cognitive models of Effortful Control. Constructs tapping impulsivity versus Effortful Control form a broad latent construct of Disinhibition (Bogg & Finn, 2010). Many health-damaging behaviors, such as smoking or drinking alcohol to excess, require the ability to refrain from disinhibited, impulsive behavior. Edmonds, Bogg, and Roberts (2009) found that laboratory and self-report measures of impulsivity contributed independently to the prediction of health behaviors, suggesting that the effects of Disinhibition were not mediated by executive functioning deficits. Further research would be valuable to investigate the role of individual differences in cognitive competencies in relation to health behaviors that require the ability to override automatic responses (Suchy, 2009; Williams & Thayer, 2009). The possibility that Effortful Control can be trained and that this can have a lasting impact on the brain offers exciting possibilities for the development of interventions to modify trait Conscientiousness (Posner & Rothbart, 2007).

Conclusions

Although there are many theoretical and methodological challenges to drawing conclusions about the influence of temperament on physical health over the lifespan, based on the research we have reviewed, we see a coherent pattern of findings emerging. For both children and adults, Positive Emotionality is a mixed blessing. Positive Emotionality is associated with better health outcomes over the short and long term, but positive emotionality is also associated with risk taking and injuries, with sometimes fatal consequences. There are beneficial physical effects of Positive Emotionality, such as enhanced immune function and reduced stress responses, but the approach motivation associated with Positive Emotionality can have disastrous consequences. Later in adulthood, Positive Emotionality seems to be more consistently associated with better health. With few exceptions, Negative Emotionality in adults, and both Internalizing and Externalizing in children, are related to poor health outcomes through multiple pathways including behavioral and physiological mechanisms. However, there may be some health advantages from the protective effects of avoidance temperament and sensitivity to punishment. Increased vigilance to threat cues may protect against injury and increase preventive behaviors. In contrast, Effortful Control, particularly the trait of Conscientiousness assessed in children and adults, is consistently related to better health outcomes. Pathways through health behavior mechanisms only provide a partial explanation for the benefits associated with Conscientiousness.

These findings must be evaluated in terms of the methodological challenges and complexities of this field. These include the importance of isolating the effects of one aspect of temperament or personality independent of the others (e.g., Negative Emotionality independent of low Positive Emotionality), and independent of other determinants of health. Emotionality may color our perceptions of health, rendering subjective outcomes suspect, yet how well we feel is an important part of our overall health and well-being. Reciprocal relations between temperament and health complicate matters further, particularly when considered from a lifespan perspective. Despite the many challenges, the accumulation of evidence from a body of well-conducted studies is such that from an epidemiological perspective, the case for the influence of temperament on physical health has been made. Furthermore, the increasing knowledge of the mechanisms by which temperament is associated with health is opening up new avenues for intervention.

Future Directions

Given the compelling epidemiological evidence, the possibility of intervening to promote health-enhancing personality traits is gaining currency (Moffitt et al., 2011). From a lifespan perspective, the influence of temperament or personality on physical health occurs through a chain of causality from early life to death (Ben-Shlomo & Kuh, 2002; Kuh, Ben-Shlomo, Lynch, Hallqvist, & Power, 2003). Parenting interventions may be influential early in the chain to deflect children from an unhealthy path, at a time when temperament may be more amenable to change. Indeed, the broader socialization and education process is itself an intervention that promotes physical health, as well as other desirable life outcomes. An alternative to intervening directly on temperament or personality traits is to focus on the behaviors associated with them. For example, patients with low Conscientiousness need more support and guidance to adhere to a treatment regimen than do patients with high Conscientiousness. This approach suggests targeting particular individuals for intervention, or tailoring interventions to particular individuals, based on a personality assessment. Now that relatively brief yet valid measures of personality are available (Gosling, Rentfrow, & Swann, 2003; Woods & Hampson, 2005), adding a personality assessment as part of a doctor's visit is realistic and could be incorporated into the concept of personalized medicine (Hamburg & Collins, 2010). Randomized controlled trials of interventions to improve physical health outcomes or to prevent disease onset by changing personality traits would also provide compelling tests of causal relations between traits and health to complement epidemiological studies (Howe, Reiss, & Yuh, 2002).

We have emphasized the value of longitudinal studies throughout this chapter. Observational studies that separate the measurement of temperament and health in time permit more confident causal inferences to be made. Longitudinal studies are also preferable for the study of mechanisms of effects that unfold over time. Experimental (or quasi-experimental) studies provide the most compelling evidence of causal associations between personality and health, but they are rare in this field. Future research that includes experimental designs to test hypotheses about specific mechanisms within a longitudinal study would be very valuable.

A lifespan perspective emphasizes change, and with multiple assessments over time it is possible using latent growth modeling techniques to study temperament or personality and health outcomes as trajectories with normative trends and individual variation (Mroczek, 2007). Such designs are valuable for studying the mechanisms by which personality influences health because they permit the modeling of change over time. Any single longitudinal study will have specific limitations (e.g., of sample, measures, or life stage), and future research should take advantage of developments in integrative data analysis techniques that enable data from different studies to be combined (Hofer & Piccinin, 2009).

A challenge for either conceptually or empirically integrating longitudinal studies of temperament and health over different stages of the lifespan is the continuity of temperament and personality trait constructs over time. For example, if "sociability" can be observed in infants, children, and adults, but the behaviors associated with this trait are different for each age group, is it justified to assume the construct is the same across time? We encountered this problem in the organization of this chapter. It was not possible to use the same broad organizational framework for temperament to research for both children and adults. Theoretical developments that resolve issues of construct continuity across development will enable us to draw stronger conclusions about the influence of temperament on health outcomes.

Other directions for future research include the study of joint effects of more than one aspect of temperament or personality, for example, is the combination of high Negative Emotionality and low Effortful Control particularly detrimental for health? As knowledge of genetic influences on temperament and health increases, so will our understanding of so-called "third variable" models. Finally, there is much more to be learned about the mechanisms through which temperament is associated with health from a lifespan perspective.

In conclusion, we opened this chapter by proposing that part of the answer to the question of who gets sick lies in an individual's temperament and personality, and we have now seen ample evidence to support this claim across the lifespan. Temperament is associated with physical health, and there are biological, social, cognitive, and behavioral mechanisms that account for this association. Future theoretical and methodological developments concerning the study of temperament and health over the lifespan will enrich our understanding of these complex relations.

Acknowledgment

Preparation of this chapter was supported in part by Grant No. AG20048 from the National Institute on Aging to Sarah E. Hampson.

Further Reading

Friedman, H. S., Kern, M. L., & Reynolds, C. A. (2010). Personality and health, subjective well-being, and longevity. *Journal of Personality, 78*, 179–215.

Hampson, S. E. (2012). Personality processes: Mechanisms by which personality traits "get outside the skin." *Annual Review of Psychology, 63*, 315–339.

Moffitt, T. E., Arseneault, L., Belsky, D., Dickson, N., Hancox, R. J., Harrington, H., et al. (2011). A gradient of childhood self-control predicts health, wealth, and public safety. *Proceedings of the National Academy of Sciences, 108*, 2693–2698.

References

Alati, R., O'Callaghan, M., Najman, J. M., Williams, G. M., Bor, W., & Lawlor, D. A. (2005). Asthma and internalizing behavior problems in adolescence: A longitudinal study. *Psychosomatic Medicine, 67*(3), 462–470.

Allison, P. J., Guichard, C., Fung, K., & Gilain, L. (2003). Dispositional optimism predicts survival status one year after diagnosis in head and neck cancer patients. *Journal of Clinical Oncology, 21*, 543–548.

Almada, S. J., Zonderman, A. B., Shekelle, R. B., Dyer, A. R., Daviglus, M. L., Costa, P. T., Jr., et al. (1991). Neuroticism and cynicism and risk of death in middle-aged men: The Western Electric Study. *Psychosomatic Medicine, 53*, 165–175.

Anderson, S. E., Bandini, L. G., Dietz, W. H., & Must, A. (2004). Relationship between temperament, nonresting energy expenditure, body composition, and physical activity in girls. *International Journal of Obesity, 28*(2), 300–306.

Augustine, A. A., Larsen, R. J., Walker, M. S., & Fisher, E. B. (2008). Personality predictors of the time course for lung cancer onset. *Journal of Research in Personality, 42*, 1448–1455.

Barker, D. J. P. (1995). Fetal origins of coronary heart disease. *British Medical Journal, 311*, 171–174.

Ben-Shlomo, Y., & Kuh, D. (2002). A life course approach to chronic disease epidemiology: Conceptual models, empirical challenges and interdisciplinary perspectives. *International Journal of Epidemiology, 31*, 285–293.

Bogg, T., & Finn, P. R. (2010). A self-regulatory model of behavioral disinhibition in late adolescence: Integrating personality traits, externalizing psychopathology, and cognitive capacity. *Journal of Personality, 78*, 441–470.

Bogg, T., & Roberts, B. W. (2004). Conscientiousness and health-related behaviors: A meta-analysis of the leading behavioral contributors to mortality. *Psychological Bulletin, 130*, 887–919.

Bolger, N., & Schilling, E. A. (1991). Personality and the problems of everyday life: The role of neuroticism in exposure and reactivity to daily stressors. *Journal of Personality, 59*, 355–386.

Bradley, R. H., Houts, R., Nader, P. R., O'Brien, M., Belsky, J., & Crosnoe, R. (2008). The relationship between body mass index and behavior in children. *Journal of Pediatrics, 153*(5), 629–634.

Brickman, A. L., Yount, S. E., Blaney, N. T., Rothberg, S. T., & De-Nour, A. K. (1996). Personality traits and long-term health status: The influence of neuroticism and conscientiousness on renal deterioration in Type-1 diabetes. *Psychosomatics: Journal of Consultation Liaison Psychiatry, 37*, 459–468.

Brummett, B. H., Babyak, M. A., Williams, R. B., Barefoot, J. C., Costa, P. T., Jr., & Siegler, I. C. (2006). NEO Personality domains and gender predict levels and trends in body mass index over 14 years during midlife. *Journal of Research in Personality, 40*, 222–236.

Buss, A. H., & Plomin, R. (1984). *Temperament: Early developing personality traits.* Hillsdale, NJ: Erlbaum.

Canli, T. (Ed.). (2006). *Biology of personality and individual differences.* New York: Guilford Press.

Carver, C. S. (2005). Impulse and constraint: Perspectives from personality psychology, convergence with theory in other areas, and potential for integration. *Personality and Social Psychology Review, 9*, 312–333.

Carver, C. S., Scheier, M. F., Miller, C. J., & Fulford, D. (2009). Optimism. In C. R. Snyder & S. J. Lopez (Eds.), *Oxford handbook of positive psychology* (2nd ed., pp. 303–311). New York: Oxford University Press.

Caspi, A. (2000). The child is father of the man: Personality continuities from childhood to adulthood. *Journal of Personality and Social Psychology, 78*(1), 158–172.

Caspi, A., & Shiner, R. L. (2006). Personality development. In W. Damon & R. Lerner (Series Eds.) & N. Eisenberg (Vol. Ed.), *Handbook of child psychology: Vol. 3. Social, emotional, and personality development* (6th ed., pp. 300–365). New York: Wiley.

Centers for Disease Control and Prevention. (2008). *CDC Childhood Injury Report: Patterns of unintentional injuries among 0–19 Year Olds in the United States, 2000–2006.* Atlanta: U.S. Department of Health and Human Services.

Charles, S. T., Gatz, M., Kato, K., & Pedersen, N. L. (2008). Physical health twenty-five years later: The predictive ability of neuroticism. *Health Psychology, 27*, 369–378.

Chida, Y., & Steptoe, A. (2008). Positive psychological well-being and mortality: A quantitative review of prospective observational studies. *Psychosomatic Medicine, 70*, 741–756.

Christensen, A. J., Ehlers, S. L., Raichle, K. A., & Lawton, W. J. (2002). Patient personality predicts mortality in chronic renal insufficiency: A four-year prospective examination. *Health Psychology, 21*, 315–320.

Clark, L. A., & Watson, D. (2008). Temperament: An organizing paradigm for trait psychology. In O. P. John, R. W. Robins, & L. A. Pervin (Eds.), *Handbook of personality: Theory and research* (3rd ed., pp. 265–286). New York: Guilford Press.

Cohen, S., Alper, C. M., Doyle, W. J., Treanor, J. J., & Turner, R. B. (2006). Positive emotional style predicts resistance to illness after experimental exposure to rhinovirus or influenza A virus. *Psychosomatic Medicine, 68*, 809–815.

Costa, P. T., Jr., & McCrae, R. R. (1985). Hypochondriasis, neuroticism, and aging: When are somatic complaints unfounded? *American Psychologist, 40*, 19–28.

Costa, P. T., Jr., & McCrae, R. R. (1992). *NEO PI-R professional manual.* Odessa, FL: Psychological Assessment Resources.

Cramer, P., & Steinwert, T. (1998). Thin is good, fat is bad: How early does it begin? *Journal of Applied Developmental Psychology, 19*, 429–451.

Daly, M., Delaney, L., Doran, P. P., Harmon, C., & MacLachlan, M. (2010). Naturalistic monitoring of the affect–heart rate relationship: A day reconstruction study. *Health Psychology, 29*, 186–195.

Danner, D. D., Snowdon, D. A., & Friesen, W. V. (2001). Positive emotions in early life and longevity: Findings from the nun study. *Journal of Personality and Social Psychology, 80*, 804–813.

Datar, A. (2004). Childhood overweight and parent- and teacher-reported behavior problems. *Archives of Pediatric and Adolescent Medicine, 158*, 804–810.

Davidson, K. W., Mostofsky, E., & Whang, W. (2010). Don't worry, be happy: Positive affect and reduced 10-year incident coronary heart disease: The Canadian Nova Scotia Health Survey. *European Heart Journal, 31*, 1065–1070.

Davis, C., & Carter, J. C. (2009). Compulsive overeating as an addiction disorder: A review of theory and evidence. *Appetite, 53*(1), 1–8.

Davis, C., Strachan, S., & Berkson, M. (2004). Sensitivity to reward: Implications for overeating and overweight. *Appetite, 42*, 131–138.

DeNeve, K. M., & Cooper, H. (1998). The happy personality: A meta-analysis of 137 personality traits and subjective well-being. *Psychological Bulletin, 124*(2), 197–229.

De Pauw, S. S. W., Mervielde, I., & van Leeuwen, K. G. (2009). How are traits related to problem behavior in preschoolers?: Similarities and contrasts between temperament and personality. *Journal of Abnormal Child Psychology, 37*(3), 309–325.

Edmonds, G. W., Bogg, T., & Roberts, B. W. (2009). Are personality and behavioral measures of impulse control convergent or distinct predictors of health behaviors? *Journal of Research in Personality, 43*, 806–814.

Eisenberg, N., Spinrad, T. L., Fabes, R. A., Reiser, M., Cumberland, A., Shepard, S. A., et al. (2004). The relations of effortful control and impulsivity to children's resiliency and adjustment. *Child Development, 75*, 25–46.

Elliot, A. J., & Thrash, T. M. (2010). Approach and avoidance temperament as basic dimensions of personality. *Journal of Personality, 78*, 865–906.

Evans, D. E., & Rothbart, M. K. (2007). Development of a model for adult temperament. *Journal of Research in Personality, 41*, 868–888.

Eysenck, H. J. (1947). *Dimensions of personality.* London: Routledge & Kegan Paul.

Eysenck, H. J., & Eysenck, M. W. (1985). *Personality and individual differences: A natural science approach.* New York: Plenum Press.

Faith, M. S., Flint, J., Fairburn, C. G., Goodwin, G. M., & Allison, D. B. (2001). Gender differences in the relationship between personality dimensions and relative body weight. *Obesity Research, 9*, 647–650.

Faith, M. S., & Hittner, J. B. (2010). Infant temperament and eating style predict change in standardized weight status and obesity risk at 6 years of age. *International Journal of Obesity, 34*(10), 1515–1523.

Feldman, J. M., Ortega, A. N., Koinis-Mitchell, D., Kuo, A. A., & Canino, G. (2010). Child and family psychiatric and psychological factors associated with child physical health problems: Results from the Boricua Youth Study. *Journal of Nervous and Mental Disease, 198*(4), 272–279.

Feldman, P., Cohen, S., Doyle, W. J., Skoner, D. P., & Gwaltney, J. M. (1999). The impact of personality on the reporting of unfounded symptoms and illness. *Journal of Personality and Social Psychology, 77*, 370–378.

Francis, L. A., Hofer, S. M., & Birch, L. L. (2001). Predictors of maternal child-feeding style: Maternal and child characteristics. *Appetite, 37*(3), 231–243.

Fredrickson, B. L. (2001). The role of positive emotions in positive psychology: The broaden-and-build theory of positive emotions. *American Psychologist, 56*, 218–226.

Fredrickson, B. L., Cohn, M. A., Coffey, K. A., Pek, J., & Finkel, S. M. (2008). Open hearts build lives: Positive emotions, induced through loving-kindness meditation, build consequential personal resources. *Journal of Personality and Social Psychology, 95*, 1045–1062.

Friedman, H. S., & Booth-Kewley, S. (1987). The "disease-prone personality": A meta-analytic view of the construct. *American Psychologist, 42*, 539–555.

Friedman, H. S., Kern, M. L., & Reynolds, C. A. (2010). Personality and health, subjective well being, and longevity. *Journal of Personality, 78*, 179–215.

Friedman, H. S., Tucker, J., Schwartz, J. E., Martin, L. R., Tomlinson-Keasey, C., Wingard, D., et al. (1995). Childhood conscientiousness and longevity: Health behaviors and cause of death. *Journal of Personality and Social Psychology, 68*, 696–703.

Friedman, H. S., Tucker, J., Tomlinson-Keasey, C., Schwartz, J., Wingard, D., & Criqui, M. H. (1993). Does childhood personality predict longevity? *Journal of Personality and Social Psychology, 65*, 176–185.

Friedman, R. S., & Förster, J. (2010). Implicit affective cues and attentional tuning: An integrative review. *Psychological Bulletin, 136*, 875–893.

Garthus-Niegel, S., Hagtvet, K. A., & Vollrath, M. E. (2010). A prospective study of weight development and behavior problems in toddlers: The Norwegian Mother and Child Cohort Study. *BMC Public Health, 10*, 626.

Gibson, E. L. (2006). Emotional influences on food choice: Sensory, physiological and psychological pathways. *Physiological Behavior, 89*(1), 53–61.

Gosling, S. D., Rentfrow, P. J., & Swann, W. B., Jr. (2003). A very brief measure of the Big-Five personality domains. *Journal of Research in Personality, 37*, 504–528.

Grant, N., Wardle, J., & Steptoe, A. (2009). The relationship between life satisfaction and health behaviour: A cross-cultural analysis of young adults. *International Journal of Behavioral Medicine, 16*, 159–168.

Gray, J. A. (1987). *The psychology of fear and stress*. Cambridge, UK: Cambridge University Press.

Gray, J. A., & McNaughton, N. (2000). *The neuropsychology of anxiety: An enquiry into the functions of the septo-hippocampal system* (2nd ed.). New York: Oxford University Press.

Hakkula, A., Konttinen, H., Laatikainen, T., Kawachi, I., & Uutela, A. (2010). Hostility, anger control, and anger expression as predictors of cardiovascular disease. *Psychosomatic Medicine, 72*, 556–562.

Hamburg, M. A., & Collins, F. S. (2010). The path to personalized medicine. *New England Journal of Medicine, 363*, 301–304.

Hampson, S. E., & Friedman, H. S. (2008). Personality and health: A lifespan perspective. In O. P. John, R. W. Robins, & L. A. Pervin (Eds.), *The handbook of personality: Theory and research* (3rd ed., pp. 770–794). New York: Guilford Press.

Hampson, S. E., Goldberg, L. R., Vogt, T. M., & Dubanoski, J. P. (2006). Forty years on: Teachers' assessments of children's personality traits predict self-reported health behaviors and outcomes at midlife. *Health Psychology, 25*, 57–64.

Hampson, S. E., Goldberg, L. R., Vogt, T. M., & Dubanoski, J. P. (2007). Mechanisms by which childhood personality traits influence adult health status: Educational attainment and healthy behaviors. *Health Psychology, 26*, 121–125.

Hampson, S. E., Tonstad, S., Irgens, L. M., Meltzer, H. M., & Vollrath, M. E. (2010). Mothers' negative affectivity during pregnancy and food choices for their infants. *International Journal of Obesity, 34*(2), 327–331.

Hasler, G., Pine, D. S., Gamma, A., Milos, G., Ajdacic, V., Eich, D., et al. (2004). The associations between psychopathology and being overweight: A 20-year prospective study. *Psychological Medicine, 34*, 1047–1057.

Heaven, P. C. L., Mulligan, K., Merrilees, R., Woods, T., & Fairooz, Y. (2001). Neuroticism and conscientiousness as predictors of emotional, external, and restrained eating behaviors. *International Journal of Eating Disorders, 30*(2), 161–166.

Hofer, S. M., & Piccinin, A. M. (2009) Integrative data analysis through coordination of measurement and analysis protocol across independent longitudinal studies. *Psychological Methods, 14*, 150–164.

Honig, A., Kuyper, A. M., Schene, A. H., van Melle,

J. P., de Jonge, P., Tulner, D. M., et al. (2007). Treatment of post-myocardial infarction depressive disorder: A randomized, placebo-controlled trial with mirtazapine. *Psychosomatic Medicine, 69,* 606–613.

Howe, G. W., Reiss, D., & Yuh, J. (2002). Can prevention trials test theories of etiology? *Development and Psychopathology, 14,* 673–694.

Howell, R. T., Kern, M. L., & Lyubomirsky, S. (2007). Health benefits: Meta-analytically determining the impact of well-being on objective health outcomes. *Health Psychology Review, 1,* 83–136.

Janssen, I., Craig, W. M., Boyce, W. F., & Pickett, W. (2004). Associations between overweight and obesity with bullying behaviors in school-aged children. *Pediatrics, 113*(5), 1187–1194.

John, O. P., Naumann, L. P., & Soto, C. J. (2008). Paradigm shift to the integrative Big Five trait taxonomy: History, measurement, and conceptual issues. In O. P. John, R. W. Robins, & L. A. Pervin (Eds.), *Handbook of personality: Theory and research* (3rd ed., pp. 114–158). New York: Guilford Press.

John, O. P., & Srivastava, S. (1999). The Big Five trait taxonomy: History, measurement, and theoretical perspectives. In L. A. Pervin & O. P. John (Eds.), *Handbook of personality: Theory and research* (2nd ed., pp. 102–138). New York: Guilford Press.

Jokela, M., Ferrie, J., & Kivimäki, M. (2009). Childhood problem behaviors and death by midlife: The British National Child Development Study. *Journal of the American Academy of Child and Adolescent Psychiatry, 48*(1), 19–24.

Jokela, M., Power, C., & Kivimäki, M. (2009). Childhood problem behaviors and injury risk over the life course. *Journal of Child Psychology and Psychiatry, 50*(12), 1541–1549.

Katon, W., Lozano, P., Russo, J., McCauley, E., Richardson, L., & Bush, T. (2007). The prevalence of DSM-IV anxiety and depressive disorders in youth with asthma compared with controls. *Journal of Adolescent Health, 41*(5), 455–463.

Keltikangas-Järvinen, L., Pulkki-Råback, L., Puttonen, S., Viikari, J., & Raitakari, O. T. (2006). Childhood hyperactivity as a predictor of carotid artery intima media thickness over a period of 21 years: The Cardiovascular Risk in Young Finns Study. *Psychosomatic Medicine, 68*(4), 509–516.

Kern, M. L., & Friedman, H. S. (2008). Do conscientious individuals live longer?: A quantitative review. *Health Psychology, 27,* 505–512.

Klinnert, M. D., Nelson, H. S., Price, M. R., Adinoff, A. D., Leung, D. Y. M., & Mrazek, D. A. (2001). Onset and persistence of childhood asthma: Predictors from infancy. *Pediatrics, 108*(4), E69.

Kop, W. J., Stein, P. K., Tracy, R. P., Barzilay, J. I., Schulz, R., & Gottdiener, J. S. (2010). Autonomic nervous system dysfunction and inflammation contribute to the increased cardiovascular mortality risk associated with depression. *Psychosomatic Medicine, 72,* 626–635.

Krueger, R. F., Eaton, N. R., Clark, L. A., Watson, D., Markon, K. E., Derringer, J., et al. (2011). Deriving an empirical structure for personality pathology for DSM-V. *Journal of Personality Disorders, 25*(2), 170–191.

Krueger, R. F., Markon, K. E., Patrick, C. J., Benning, S. D., & Kramer, M. D. (2007). Linking antisocial behavior, substance use, and personality: An integrative quantitative model of the adult externalizing spectrum. *Journal of Abnormal Psychology, 116*(4), 645–666.

Kubzansky, L. D., Martin, L. T., & Buka, S. L. (2009). Early manifestations of personality and adult health: A life course perspective. *Health Psychology, 28*(3), 364–372.

Kuh, D., Ben-Shlomo, Y., Lynch, J., Hallqvist, J., & Power, C. (2003). Life course epidemiology. *Journal of Epidemiology and Community Health, 57,* 778–783.

Lavigne, J. V., & Faier-Routman, J. (1992). Psychological adjustment to pediatric physical disorders: A meta-analytic review. *Journal of Pediatric Psychology, 17*(2), 133–157.

Lengua, L. J., Sandler, I. N., West, S. G., Wolchik, S. A., & Curran, P. J. (1999). Emotionality and self-regulation, threat appraisal, and coping in children of divorce. *Development and Psychopathology, 11*(1), 15–37.

Lien, L. (2008). The association between mental health problems and inflammatory conditions across gender and immigrant status: A population-based cross-sectional study among 10th-grade students. *Scandinavian Journal of Public Health, 36*(4), 353–360.

Lilljeqvist, A. C., Smorvik, D., & Faleide, A. O. (2002). Temperamental differences between healthy, asthmatic, and allergic children before onset of illness: A longitudinal prospective study of asthma development. *Journal of Genetic Psychology, 163*(2), 219–227.

Lopez, S. J., & Snyder, C. R. (Eds.). (2009). *Handbook of positive psychology* (2nd ed.). Oxford, UK: Oxford University Press.

Luppino, F. S., de Wit, L. M., Bouvy, P. F., Stijnen, T., Cuijpers, P., Penninx, B. W., et al. (2010). Overweight, obesity, and depression: A systematic review and meta-analysis of longitudinal studies. *Archives of General Psychiatry, 67,* 220–229.

Martin, L. R., Friedman, H. S., & Schwartz, J. E. (2007). Personality and mortality risk across the lifespan: The importance of conscientiousness as a biopsychosocial attribute. *Health Psychology, 26,* 428–436.

Maruta, T., Colligan, R. C., Malinchoc, M., & Offord, K. P. (2000). Optimists vs. pessimists: Survival rate among medical patients over a

30-year period. *Mayo Clinic Proceedings, 75,* 140–143.

McCrae, R. R., & Costa, P. T., Jr. (2008). The five-factor theory of personality. In O. P. John, R. W. Robins, & L. A. Pervin (Eds.), *Handbook of personality: Theory and research* (3rd ed., pp. 159–181). New York: Guilford Press.

McQuaid, E. L., Kopel, S. J., & Nassau, J. H. (2001). Behavioral adjustment in children with asthma: A meta-analysis. *Journal of Developmental and Behavioral Pediatrics, 22*(6), 430–439.

Mezick, E. J., Matthews, K. A., Hall, M., Kamarck, T. W., Buysse, D. J., Owens, J. F., et al. (2010). Low life purpose and high hostility are related to an attenuated decline in nocturnal blood pressure. *Health Psychology, 29,* 196–204.

Midei, A. J., & Matthews, K. A. (2009). Social relationships and negative emotional traits are associated with central adiposity and arterial stiffness in healthy adolescents. *Health Psychology, 28*(3), 347–353.

Moffitt, T. E., Arseneault, L., Belsky, D., Dickson, N., Hancox, R. J., Harrington, H., et al. (2011). A gradient of childhood self-control predicts health, wealth, and public safety. *Proceedings of the National Academy of Sciences, 108,* 2693–2698.

Mroczek, D. K. (2007). The analysis of longitudinal data in personality research. In R. W. Robins, R. C. Fraley & R. F. Krueger (Eds.), *Handbook of research methods in personality psychology* (pp. 543–556). New York: Guilford Press.

Mroczek, D. K., & Spiro, A. (2003). Modeling intraindividual change in personality traits: Findings from the normative aging study. *Journals of Gerontology: Psychological Sciences, 58,* 153–165.

Mroczek, D. K., & Spiro, A. (2007). Personality change influences mortality in older men. *Psychological Science, 18,* 371–376.

Neiss, M. B., Stevenson, J., Legrand, L., Iacono, W. G., & Sedikides, C. (2009). Self-esteem, negative emotionality, and depression as a common temperamental core: A study of mid-adolescent twin girls. *Journal of Personality, 77,* 327–346.

Nettle, D. (2006). The evolution of personality variation in humans and other animals. *American Psychologist, 6,* 622–631.

Nigg, J. T. (2000). On inhibition/disinhibition in developmental psychopathology: Views from cognitive and personality psychology as a working inhibition taxonomy. *Psychological Bulletin, 126,* 220–246.

Oddy, W. H., Robinson, M., Ambrosini, G. L., O'Sullivan, T. A., de Klerk, N. H., Beilin, L. J., et al. (2009). The association between dietary patterns and mental health in early adolescence. *Preventive Medicine, 49*(1), 39–44.

Ong, A. D. (2010). Pathways linking positive emotion and health later in life. *Current Directions in Psychological Science, 19,* 358–362.

Peterson, C., Seligman, M. E. P., & Vaillant, G. E. (1988). Pessimistic explanatory style is a risk factor for physical illness: A thirty-five-year longitudinal study. *Journal of Personality and Social Psychology, 55,* 23–27.

Pine, D. S., Cohen, P., Brook, J. S., & Coplan, J. D. (1997). Psychiatric symptoms in adolescence as predictors of obesity in early adulthood: A longitudinal study. *American Journal of Public Health, 87*(8), 1303–1310.

Player, M. S., King, D. E., Mainous, A. G., III, & Geesey, M. E. (2007). Psychosocial factors and progression from prehypertension to hypertension or coronary heart disease. *Annals of Family Medicine, 5,* 403–411.

Plumert, J. M., & Schwebel, D. C. (1997). Social and temperamental influences on children's overestimation of their physical abilities: Links to accidental injuries. *Journal of Experimental Child Psychology, 67*(3), 317–337.

Posner, M. I., & Rothbart, M. K. (2007). *Educating the human brain.* Washington DC: American Psychological Association.

Pressman, S. D., & Cohen, S. (2005). Does positive affect influence health? *Psychological Bulletin, 131,* 925–971.

Priftis, K. N., Papadimitriou, A., Nicolaidou, P., & Chrousos, G. P. (2009). Dysregulation of the stress response in asthmatic children. *Allergy, 64*(1), 18–31.

Pulkki-Råback, L., Elovainio, M., Kivimäki, M., Raitakari, O. T., & Keltikangas-Järvinen, L. (2005). Temperament in childhood predicts body mass in adulthood: the Cardiovascular Risk in Young Finns Study. *Health Psychology, 24*(3), 307–315.

Räikkönen, K., Matthews, K. A., & Kuller, L. H. (2002). The relationship between psychological risk attributes and the metabolic syndrome in healthy women: Antecedent or consequence? *Metabolism, 51,* 1537–1577.

Räikkönen, K., Matthews, K. A., Sutton-Tyrrell, K., & Kuller, L. H. (2004). Trait anger and the metabolic syndrome predict progression of carotid atherosclerosis in healthy middle-aged women. *Psychosomatic Medicine, 66,* 903–908.

Ravaja, N., & Keltikangas-Järvinen, L. (1995). Temperament and metabolic syndrome precursors in children—a 3-year follow-up. *Preventive Medicine, 24*(5), 518–527.

Richardson, L. P., Davis, R., Poulton, R., McCauley, E., Moffitt, T. E., Caspi, A., et al. (2003). A longitudinal evaluation of adolescent depression and adult obesity. *Archives of Pediatrics and Adolescent Medicine, 157*(8), 739–745.

Roberts, B. W., Kuncel, N., Shiner, R., Caspi, A., & Goldberg, L. R. (2007). The power of personality: The comparative validity of personality traits, socio-economic status, and cognitive ability for predicting important life outcomes. *Perspectives in Psychological Science, 2,* 313–345.

Roberts, B. W., & Wood, D. (2006). Personality development in the context of the neo-socioanalytic model of personality. In D. Mroczek & T. Little (Eds.), *Handbook of personality development* (pp. 11–39). Mahwah, NJ: Erlbaum.

Roberts, B. W., Wood, D., & Caspi, A. (2008). The development of personality traits in adulthood. In O. P. John, R. W. Robins, & L. A. Pervin (Eds.), *Handbook of personality: Theory and research* (3rd ed., pp. 375–398). New York: Guilford Press.

Rothbart, M. K. (1989). Temperament in childhood: A framework. In G. A. Kohnstamm, J. E. Bates, & M. K. Rothbart (Eds.), *Temperament in childhood* (pp. 59–75). Chichester, UK: Wiley.

Rothbart, M. K. (2007). Temperament, development, and personality. *Current Directions in Psychological Science, 16*, 207–212.

Rothbart, M. K. (2011). *Becoming who we are: Temperament and personality in development.* New York: Guilford Press.

Rothbart, M. K., & Ahadi, S. A. (1994). Temperament and the development of personality. *Journal of Abnormal Psychology, 103*, 55–66.

Rothbart, M. K., & Rueda, M. R. (2005). The development of effortful control. In U. Mayr, E. Awh, & S. W. Keele (Eds.), *Developing individuality in the human brain: A tribute to Michael I. Posner* (pp. 167–188). Washington, DC: American Psychological Association.

Rowe, R., Simonoff, E., & Silberg, J. L. (2007). Psychopathology, temperament and unintentional injury: Cross-sectional and longitudinal relationships. *Journal of Child Psychology and Psychiatry, 48*(1), 71–79.

Roy, B., Diez-Roux, A. V., Seeman, T., Ranjit, N., Shea, S., & Cushman, M. (2010). Association of optimism and pessimism with inflammation and hemostasis in the Multi-Ethnic Study of Atherosclerosis (MESA). *Psychosomatic Medicine, 72*, 134–140.

Sawyer, M. G., Miller-Lewis, L., Guy, S., Wake, M., Canterford, L., & Carlin, J. B. (2006). Is there a relationship between overweight and obesity and mental health problems in 4- to 5-year-old Australian children? *Ambulatory Pediatrics, 6*(6), 306–311.

Scheier, M. F., Matthews, K. A., Owens, J. F., Schulz, R., Bridges, M. W., Magovern, G. J., et al. (1999). Optimism and rehospitalization following coronary artery bypass graft surgery. *Archives of Internal Medicine, 159*, 829–835.

Schulz, R., Bookwala, J., Knapp, J. E., Scheier, M., & Williamson, G. M. (1996). Pessimism, age, and cancer mortality. *Psychology and Aging, 11*, 304–309.

Schwebel, D. C. (2004). Temperamental risk factors for children's unintentional injury: The role of impulsivity and inhibitory control. *Personality and Individual Differences, 37*, 567–578.

Schwebel, D. C., & Barton, B. K. (2006). Temperament and children's unintentional injuries. In M. E. Vollrath (Ed.), *Handbook of personality and health* (pp. 51–72). Chichester, UK: Wiley.

Schwebel, D. C., & Plumert, J. M. (1999). Longitudinal and concurrent relations among temperament, ability estimation, and injury proneness. *Child Development, 70*(3), 700–712.

Segerstrom, S. C. (2005). Optimism and immunity: Do positive thoughts always lead to positive effects? *Brain, Behavior, and Immunity, 19*, 195–200.

Shiner, R. L. (1998). How shall we speak of children's personalities in middle childhood?: A preliminary taxonomy. *Psychological Bulletin, 124*(3), 308–332.

Shiner, R. L., & DeYoung, C. G. (in press). The structure of temperament and personality traits: A developmental perspective. In *Oxford handbook of developmental psychology*. New York: Oxford University Press.

Shipley, B. A., Weiss, A., Der, G., Taylor, M. D., & Deary, I. J. (2007). Neuroticism, extraversion, and mortality in the UK Health and Lifestyle Survey: A 21-year prospective cohort study. *Psychosomatic Medicine, 69*, 923–931.

Slining, M. M., Adair, L., Goldman, B. D., Borja, J., & Bentley, M. (2009). Infant temperament contributes to early infant growth: A prospective cohort of African American infants. *International Journal of Behavioral Nutrition and Physical Activity, 6*, 51.

Smith, T. W., Glazer, K., Ruiz, J. M., & Gallo, L. C. (2004). Hostility, anger, aggressiveness and coronary heart disease: An interpersonal perspective on personality, emotion and health. *Journal of Personality, 72*, 1217–1270.

Soubhi, H. (2004). The social context of childhood injury in Canada: Integration of the NLSCY findings. *American Journal of Health Behavior, 28*, S38–S50.

Steptoe, A., Dockray, S., & Wardle, J. (2009). Positive affect and psychobiological processes relevant to health. *Journal of Personality, 77*, 1747–1775.

Steptoe, A., O'Donnell, K., Badrick, E., Kumari, M., & Marmot, M. (2008). Neuroendocrine and inflammatory factors associated with positive affect in healthy men and women: Whitehall II Study. *American Journal of Epidemiology, 167*, 96–102.

Steptoe, A., O'Donnell, K., Marmot, M., & Wardle, J. (2008). Positive affect and psychosocial processes relevant to health. *British Journal of Psychology, 99*, 211–217.

Steptoe, A., Wright, C., Kunz-Ebrecht, S. R., & Iliffe, S. (2006). Dispositional optimism and health behaviour in community dwelling older people: Associations with healthy ageing. *British Journal of Health Psychology, 11*, 71–84.

Suchy, Y. (2009). Executive functioning: Overview, assessment, and research issues for non-neuropsychologists. *Annals of Behavioral Medicine*, 37, 106–116.

Suls, J., & Bunde, J. (2005). Anger, anxiety, and depression as risk factors for cardiovascular disease: The problems and implications of overlapping affective dispositions. *Psychological Bulletin*, 131, 260–300.

Suls, J., & Martin, R. (2005). The daily life of the garden-variety neurotic: Reactivity, stress exposure, mood spillover, and maladaptive coping. *Journal of Personality*, 73, 1–25.

Terracciano, A., Lockenhoff, C. E., Zonderman, A. B., Ferrucci, L., & Costa, P. T., Jr. (2008). Personality predictors of longevity: Activity, emotional stability, and conscientiousness. *Psychosomatic Medicine*, 70, 621–627.

Tindle, H. A., Chang, Y.-F., Kuller, L. H., Manson, J. E., Robinson, J. G., Rosal, M. C., et al. (2009). Optimism, cynical hostility, and incident coronary heart disease and mortality in the Women's Health Initiative. *Circulation*, 120, 656–662.

Tsuboi, H., Hamer, M., Tanaka, G., Takagi, K., Kinae, N., & Steptoe, A. (2008). Responses of ultra-weak chemiluminescence and secretory IgA in saliva to the induction of angry and depressive moods. *Brain, Behavior, and Immunity*, 22, 209–214.

Tugade, M. M., Fredrickson, B. L., & Feldman Barrett, L. (2004). Psychological resilience and emotional granularity: Examining the benefits of positive emotions on coping and health. *Journal of Personality*, 72, 1161–1190.

Verbeken, S., Braet, C., Claus, L., Nederkoorn, C., & Oosterlaan, J. (2009). Childhood obesity and impulsivity: An investigation with performance-based measures. *Behaviour Change*, 26(3), 153–167.

Vollrath, M., Landolt, M. A., & Ribi, K. (2003). Personality of children with accident-related injuries. *European Journal of Personality*, 17, 299–307.

Vollrath, M. E., Tonstad, S., Rothbart, M. K., & Hampson, S. E. (2011). Infant temperament is associated with potentially obesogenic diet at 18 months. *International Journal of Pediatric Obesity*, 6, 408–414.

Watson, D., & Pennebaker, J. W. (1989). Health complaints, stress, and distress: Exploring the central role of negative affectivity. *Psychological Review*, 96, 234–254.

Weiss, A., & Costa, P. T., Jr. (2005). Domain and facet personality predictors of all-cause mortality among Medicare patients aged 65 to 100. *Psychosomatic Medicine*, 67, 724–733.

Whipple, M. O., Lewis, T. T., Sutton-Tyrrell, K., Matthews, K. A., Barinas-Mitchell, E., Powell, L. H., et al. (2009). Hopelessness, depressive symptoms, and carotid atherosclerosis in women: The Study of Women's Health Across the Nation (SWAN) heart study. *Stroke*, 40, 3166–3172.

Whiteman, M. C. (2006). Personality, cardiovascular disease and public health. In M. Vollrath (Ed.), *Handbook of personality and health* (pp. 13–34). Chichester, UK: Wiley.

Whiteman, M. C., Deary, I. J., & Fowkes, F. G. R. (2000). Personality and social predictors of atherosclerotic progression: Edinburgh Artery Study. *Psychosomatic Medicine*, 62, 703–714.

Williams, P. G., & Thayer, J. F. (2009). Executive functioning and health: Introduction to the special series. *Annals of Behavioral Medicine*, 37, 101–105.

Williams, R. B., Surwit, R. S., Siegler, I. C., Ashley-Koch, A. E., Collins, A. L., Helms, M. J., et al. (2010). Central nervous system serotonin and clustering of hostility, psychosocial, metabolic, and cardiovascular endophenotypes in men. *Psychosomatic Medicine*, 72, 601–607.

Wilson R. S., Bienias, J. L., Mendes de Leon, C. F., Evans, D. A., & Bennett, D. A. (2003). Negative affect and mortality in older persons. *American Journal of Epidemiology*, 158, 827–835.

Wilson, R. S., Krueger, K. R., Gu, L., Bienias, J. L., Mendes de Leon, C. F., & Evans, D. A. (2005). Neuroticism, extraversion, and mortality in a defined population of older persons. *Psychosomatic Medicine*, 67, 841–845.

Wilson, R. S., Mendes de Leon, C. F., Bienias, J. L., Evans, D. A., & Bennett, D. A. (2004). Personality and mortality in old age. *Journals of Gerontology B: Psychological Sciences*, 59, 110–116.

Woods, S. A., & Hampson, S. E. (2005). Measuring the Big Five with single items using a bipolar response scale. *European Journal of Personality*, 19, 373–390.

Yasuno, F., Suhara, T., Sudo, Y., Yamamoto, M., Inoue, M., Okubo, Y., et al. (2001). Relation among dopamine D(2) receptor binding, obesity and personality in normal human subjects. *Neuroscience Letters*, 300(1), 59–61.

Ystrom, E., Barker, M., & Vollrath, M. E. (2012). Impact of mothers' negative affectivity, parental locus of control and child-feeding practices on dietary patterns of 3-year-old children: The MoBa Cohort Study. *Maternal and Child Nutrition*, 8(1), 103–114.

Ystrom, E., Niegel, S., & Vollrath, M. E. (2009). The impact of maternal negative affectivity on dietary patterns of 18-month-old children in the Norwegian Mother and Child Cohort Study. *Maternal and Child Nutrition*, 5(3), 234–242.

Zhange, J., Niaura, R., Todaro, J. F., McCaffery J. M., Shen, B., Spiro, A., III., et al. (2005). Suppressed hostility predicted hypertension incidence among middle-aged men: The Normative Aging Study. *Journal of Behavioral Medicine*, 28(5), 443–453.

Part VII

Applied Perspectives on Temperament

CHAPTER 29

Temperament-Based Intervention
Reconceptualized from a Response-to-Intervention Framework

Sandee Graham McClowry
Ashleigh Collins

A successful behavioral intervention follows a predictable theory, practice, and research spiral that recurs over and over—gaining depth and breadth at each iteration. Typically, first the pioneers—the gifted visionaries—introduce a novel approach for resolving a long-standing clinical problem. Their unique perspective often gains widespread excitement in both the clinical and the research realms. Researchers study the clinical pathways hypothesized by the practitioners to differentiate further the theory first advanced by the pioneers. Simultaneously, educators formulate the pioneers' proposed strategies into a body of knowledge that can be taught to other practitioners. Then, a second generation of practitioner/scientists creates behavioral interventions that are standardized and tested for their efficacy. Prevention and clinical trials identify intervention outcomes, and the findings either support the underlying theory and its related constructs or contribute to their refinement. In a circular fashion, the efficacy trials lead to the implementation of the behavioral interventions by practitioners, who also adapt them for other populations and settings. The adaptations of the interventions also are tested for their efficacy.

Temperament-based intervention has been engaged in this theory, practice, and research spiral for more than 60 years. Our purpose in this chapter is to provide an overview of temperament-based intervention for practitioner/scientists and clinician/educators who are developing or conducting temperament-based interventions. First, the history of temperament-based intervention is reviewed. Second, two tools useful for developing and implementing behavioral interventions are explained: response to intervention (RTI) and theory of change. Third, three empirically supported temperament-based interventions, each representing one of the RTI tiers, are presented. Finally, recommendations for further advancements in temperament-based intervention are offered.

The History of Temperament-Based Intervention

The gifted visionaries who pioneered temperament-based intervention were the husband and wife psychiatrist team of Stella Chess and Alexander Thomas (1986). Based on their astute clinical and personal observations in the early 1950s, they asserted that children were active participants in their own development, not products of their environment. Their perspective was a vast departure from the prevailing psychoanalytic and behaviorist theories of the time that contended mothers were to blame for children's behavioral disorders. In contrast, Chess and Thomas and their colleagues (Thomas, Chess, Birch, Hertzig, & Korn, 1963) began studying how children varied in their own reaction patterns to parental caregiving and other aspects of their environment. They later called the reaction patterns "temperament."

By 1956, Chess and Thomas were conducting the New York Longitudinal Study (NYLS) to examine how temperament influences children's adaptation to their environments. Chess and Thomas identified dimensions of child temperament and common typologies. They also examined, based on a goodness-of-fit framework, how interpersonal and environmental conditions lead to children's adjustment or maladjustment. *Adaptation*, they asserted, occurred when the expectations, demands, and opportunities of the environment were compatible with a child's temperament (Chess & Thomas, 1986). Conversely, *maladaptation* is likely to occur when there is dissonance between a child and the environment. The compatibility between a child and the environment is referred to as a *goodness of fit*, and the dissonance between a child and the environment is referred to as a *poorness of fit*.

Practitioners and educators appreciated the NYLS findings for providing a research-derived taxonomy that resonated with their experiences working with children, families, and schools. Researchers, too, were intrigued by the concept of childhood temperament. As a result, the temperament field grew exponentially—clinically and scientifically. Although a comprehensive review of temperament research is beyond the scope of this chapter, notable findings are presented to demonstrate how they informed temperament-based intervention.

A major contribution to the development of temperament-based interventions has been the identification of children at risk for developing behavioral problems and other negative developmental outcomes. Chess and Thomas (1984) identified a "difficult" temperament that comprised intense negative mood, high withdrawal in reaction to new situations, slow adaptation to changes in the environment, and irregularity in biological functioning. Although the temperament profile has been associated with behavioral problems (Chess & Thomas, 1984; Maziade et al., 1990), the term *difficult* is controversial for a number of reasons (Rothbart, 2011). Temperament characteristics regarded as difficult in one context may be advantageous in another. *Difficult* also can be pejorative, especially when applied to a child whose caregivers may perceive him or her positively. Moreover, temperaments regarded as difficult to manage by some caregivers can be more effectively handled by others. Although *difficult temperament* is still used by some practitioners (Turecki & Tonner, 1999), others have substituted other terms. For instance, educator Kurcinka (2006) calls such children "spirited," and practitioner/scientist McClowry (2003) has relabeled a similar temperament typology as "high maintenance."

The characteristics that define temperamentally at-risk children have been examined from other perspectives as well. Kagan and his colleagues (Kagan, Reznick, & Snidman, 1988) focus on the temperament of children who are inhibited. They (Kagan, Snidman, Zentner, & Peterson, 1999) found that temperamentally inhibited children were three times more likely to develop anxiety symptoms by age 7 than their less inhibited peers.

From a neurobiological perspective, Rothbart and her colleagues (Rothbart & Derryberry, 1981; Rothbart, Sheese, & Posner, 2007) identify other temperament differences. Effortful control emerges in the toddler and preschool years. It is related to many aspects of self-regulation, such as the development of conscience (Kochanska & Knaack, 2003), delay of gratification, empathy, adjustment, social competence, and cognitive and academic performance (Eisenberg, Smith, Sadovsky, & Spinrad, 2004). Children with temperamental tendencies low in effortful control are at risk for poor self-regulation.

Regardless of the perspective taken, the goodness-of-fit model encourages researchers and interventionists to appraise children's temperament characteristics within the context of the environment. A number of studies have identified how caregiver interactions have differential effects depending on a child's temperament. For example, cautious children need only a gentle request before they comply, while fearless children require firmer parental control (Kochanska, 1997). Children who are highly resistant to control need even more assertive parental disciplinary actions (Bates, 2001). Moreover, appropriate parental responsiveness to a child's distress enhances his or her ability to regulate positive and negative affects (Davidov & Grusec, 2006).

Within the classroom, teacher responsiveness to student temperaments also is associated with positive outcomes. Students with caring and responsive teachers have higher reading, math, and end-of-year student achievement than those with less responsive teachers (Brock, Nishida, Chiong, Grimm, & Rimm-Kaufman, 2008; Rimm-Kaufman & Chiu, 2007). Likewise, students at risk for low academic achievement because of temperaments low in attention and high in activity achieve at higher academic levels when they have emotionally supportive teachers (Hamre & Pianta, 2005; Rudasill, Gallagher, & White, 2010).

The goodness-of-fit model continues to influence temperament-based intervention today. A number of books by practitioners and educators offer temperament-based guidance to parents (Carey, 2004; Kurcinka, 2006; McClowry, 2003; Neville & Johnson, 1997; Turecki & Tonner, 1999), teachers (Keogh, 2003), and other clinicians (Carey & McDevitt, 1995). Like other components of temperament theory, however, goodness of fit has evolved. De Pauw and Mervielde (2010) have expanded the model to incorporate the impact of emotions and motivation on children's expression of temperament. McClowry, Rodriguez, and Koslowitz (2008) reexamined the goodness-of-fit model in light of recent studies that indicate children's emotional and self-regulation can be malleable. They recommend that, as children get older, optimally responsive caregiving enhances children's ability to self-regulate their emotions, behaviors, and attention when they encounter a temperamentally challenging circumstance.

Still, after more than 60 years of incorporating the lessons learned from temperament theory, research, and practice, the general goals of temperament-based interventions have remained the same. Temperament-based intervention aims to cultivate environments conducive to child adjustment by (1) assisting parents, teachers, and other caregivers in understanding how a child's temperament influences his or her behavior; (2) fostering responsivity in child–caregiver interactions that improve or repair the dyadic relationship; (3) teaching caregivers strategies that reduce child behavior problems and/or enhance social competency; and (4) assisting children in using strategies that enhance their own self-regulation.

A major policy-driven movement, however, is changing temperament-based intervention. Like the current imperative in public health, medicine, education, and many other fields, temperament-based interventions need to demonstrate efficacy in achieving their intended effects (Cook, 2007; No Child Left Behind, 2002; Slavin, 2002). Although substantial progress has been made in the last two decades in producing evidence-based interventions that support the adjustment of children (Durlak, Weissberg, Dymnicki, Taylor, & Schellinger, 2011; Greenberg, Domitrovich, & Bumbarger, 2001), too few temperament-based interventions exist.

Fortunately, a number of tools are available to assist temperament-based interventionists and researchers to develop, conduct, evaluate, and refine their programs. This chapter explains two of these tools: RTI and theory of change. An RTI framework matches the needs of the targeted population to ensure that an appropriate level of intervention is provided. A theory of change explicates the pathways taken to achieve the intended intervention outcomes. After further explanation of these tools, we describe their application in three temperament-based interventions. The interventions were developed by a second generation of temperament practitioner/scientists. Each draws heavily on the work of the temperament pioneers, as well as the existing body of literature. Although the interventions occur at different levels of development, each continues to evolve while simultaneously gathering evidence to support its efficacy.

Response to Intervention

RTI is a framework established to ensure that developmentally appropriate child outcomes are achieved (Fox, Carta, Strain, Dunlap, & Hemmeter, 2010; Stecker, Fuchs, & Fuchs, 2008). The framework begins with the use of standardized tools to assess a child's performance. If a discrepancy exists between what is developmentally appropriate and the child's actual performance, evidence-based intervention is implemented (Joyce, 2010; Stecker et al., 2008). The initial assessment is then repeated and used to monitor a child's progress throughout the course of the intervention. RTI has significantly reduced the number of children who require more intensive levels of support (Fletcher et al., 1994; Fuchs, Mock, Morgan, & Young, 2003; Reynolds & Shaywitz, 2009; Torgesen, 2009). Although RTI was initially developed as a system to support academic performance, it also is relevant for the social–emotional development of children (Fletcher et al., 1994; Kovaleski, 2003; Sailor, Doolittle, Bradley, & Danielson, 2009; Sugai, Horner, & Gresham, 2002).

RTI has three tiers. The focus of Tier 1 RTI is on prevention and is similar to a "universal" intervention as defined by the Institute of Medicine's continuum of prevention care (Mrazek & Haggerty, 1994). When applied specifically to social–emotional development, positive behavior support programs are offered proactively to foster the social skills of all the students in a school or other setting. The goal of such programs is to enhance social skills and to ameliorate behavioral deficits before they rise to a diagnostic level (Fox et al., 2010; Joyce, 2010; Mrazek & Haggerty, 1994; Sugai et al., 2002). Tier 1 interventions are expected to meet the needs of 80–90% of children effectively (Vaughn, Wanzek, Linan-Thompson, & Murray, 2007).

Children who are unresponsive to Tier 1 services are identified as being in need of additional support. RTI's Tier 2 targets the subset of 5–10% of children at high risk for social–emotional behavioral disorders because they have been nonresponsive to Tier 1 intervention or because they already demonstrate symptomatology. From a prevention framework, these programs are called "selective" because they are directed at the specific emotional or behavioral problems of children (Mrazek & Haggerty, 1994). Tier 2 interventions are conducted with children in small groups.

Between 1 and 5% of children require Tier 3 services because the previous levels of interventions were unsuccessful in eliminating their behavioral problems (Joyce, 2010). Tier 3 of RTI includes "indicated" programs or treatments (Mrazek & Haggerty, 1994) for children with complex, severe, or multifaceted behavioral disorders. Such children typically require interventions or treatments delivered individually or in groups smaller than those of Tier 2 interventions.

The RTI framework can assist interventionists in developing, adapting, or implementing temperament-based programs that match the needs of intended participants. Explicating a theory of change is another tool that can assist temperament interventionists in formulating and testing the efficacy of their program or treatment.

Theory of Change

A theory of change articulates a conceptual framework that explains the development, refinement, and evaluation of an intervention. Often depicted graphically by a logic model, a theory of change explains how an intervention is intended to operate and what outcomes are anticipated (Connell & Klem, 2000; Izzo, Connell, Gambone, & Bradshaw, 2004). Although logic models are depicted in a variety of formats, they usually explicate several components (Connell & Klem, 2000; W. K. Kellogg Foundation, 2004): *assumptions* derived from the literature and/or a community needs assessment; *participants and resources* (e.g., human capital, time, financial support, organizational commitment and community participation); the *intervention* and its related activities (i.e., the number of sessions and how the intervention is conducted); and the *outputs*, the products and mediators leading to the intended proximal or distal outcomes.

Having a logic model that graphically depicts the theory of change can facilitate communication among the intervention developers, program staff, funding sources, and targeted participants. The theory of change and logic model offers a succinct explanation of the intervention resources, approaches, and outcomes. In addition to clarifying the pathways an intended intervention logic model can assist community stakeholders in assessing whether the intervention is developmentally, culturally, and clinically appropriate—all of which are critical components to ensuring that intervention design and implementation achieve intended outcomes.

The temperament field is producing interventions that have been manualized and are amassing empirical support. In the following section, three temperament-based interventions are presented. Each exemplifies one of the tiers of RTI. First the development of intervention is explained. Then the intervention is presented and its empirical support is reported. A logic model derived from its theory of change is illustrated. Lessons learned and future plans also are discussed.

A Tier 1 Temperament-Based Intervention

As a Tier 1 temperament-based intervention, *INSIGHTS into Children's Temperament* offers a general, social–emotional program for all students in primary grades. INSIGHTS partners with urban elementary school students, their parents, and their teachers.

Development of the Intervention

INSIGHTS into Children's Temperament was developed in response to the concerns of parents and teachers regarding children's behavior in urban, public elementary schools. Using an iterative method based on temperament theory, research, and clinical practice, the INSIGHTS curriculum was crafted and recrafted in partnership with the school's parents, teachers, administrators, and community members (McClowry & Galehouse, 2002; McClowry et al., 1996). Originally, INSIGHTS was intended to be only a parenting program. Sandee McClowry and nurse colleague Pamela Galehouse met weekly with parents to discuss child temperament and behavior management strategies. Reviewing videotaped parent–child interactions provided a deeper understanding of parent–child interactions.

Soon after, classroom observations were conducted, and the teachers were invited to attend a couple of afterschool meetings. The teachers were enthusiastic about the content of the parent program and insisted they have a parallel program. The intervention was soon expanded to include not only a teacher component but also a classroom component for children.

During its development, four questions contributed to the development of INSIGHTS:

1. How can temperament theory and research be presented in a way that informs the stakeholders?
2. What interactional processes among children, parents, and teachers enhance goodness of fit?
3. What are the practical strategies that assist parents and teachers in being both responsive and skilled in child management strategies?
4. What strategies enhance children's self-regulation?

The stakeholders evaluated the intervention as it was developed. Parents and teachers reviewed the curriculum materials and identified any parts that were unclear. They pointed out the child management strategies that were unrealistic given the children's school and home contexts. The parents and teachers also identified aspects of the program that were culturally insensitive. For example, some of the adult program participants expressed concern with the religious connotations associated with the word *praise*. Based on their suggestions, curricular references to *praise* were changed to *recognition* or *acknowledgment*.

In addition to integrating feedback from the program stakeholders, research studies examined the psychometrics of relevant instrumentation, particularly as it pertained to the targeted population (McClowry & Galehouse, 2002; McClowry, Halverson, & Sanson, 2003). The feasibility of the intervention approaches was also examined (McClowry & Galehouse, 2002). Creation of media and other visual curriculum materials was based on empirical studies (McClowry, 2002a, 2002b), and a qualitative study explored the cultural appropriateness of INSIGHTS for African American families (Yearwood & McClowry, 2006, 2008). Finally, after acquiring funding from the National Institutes of Health, INSIGHTS was tested in a prevention trial.

Description of the Intervention

With the major tenets of temperament as its theoretical foundation (McClowry, 2003), INSIGHTS provides parents and teachers of primary grade students with a framework for appreciating and supporting the temperamental differences of children. Caregivers are taught how to recognize a child's temperament, reframe their perceptions to acknowledge the child's strengths, and respond effectively with strategies that gain the child's compliance. Understanding a child's temperament is intended to assist parents and teachers in determining the ideal combination of warmth and discipline strategies for specific types of child temperaments. The program also assists parents and teachers in enhancing goodness of fit by replacing counterproductive responses with those that foster children's social competency.

The parent and teacher programs have three parts. In Part 1, "The *3 R's* of Child Management: Recognize, Reframe, and Respond," participants are taught to *recognize* the unique qualities that children exhibit as an expression of their temperament. *Intentionality*, the belief that a child consciously misbehaves, is reduced when participants recognize that reactions to specific situations are related to a child's temperament. Participants are encouraged to *reframe* their perceptions, with the understanding that every temperament has strengths and areas of concern. They also learn that while temperament is not easily amenable to change, parent and teacher *responses* can, in turn, influence the behavior of children.

Recognition and acceptance of a child's temperament, however, does not imply permissiveness. In Part 2, "Gaining Compliance," temperament-based management strategies are implemented to improve child behavior. Parents and teachers are assisted in identifying and implementing effective child management strategies that are matched to specific child temperaments. For example, while time-out can be effective with many children, it can be counterproductive for a child who is low in task persistence and would prefer to be removed from an assignment than focus on it for an extended time frame. Instead parents and teachers are encouraged to assist the child in extending his attentional tendencies by dividing the assignment into manageable components and provide recognition when each segment is completed.

Finally, Part 3, "Fostering Self-Regulation," focuses on strategies that support children in becoming more socially competent, especially when encountering situations that are temperamentally challenging. For example, parents and teachers are encouraged to assess the level of difficulty involved in a situation for the child. If the situation is manageable with support, then the adult is encouraged to scaffold the child's situational encounter, while applying strategies that gently stretch the child's emotional, attentional, and behavioral repertoire.

The content of the parent and teacher programs are delivered during 2-hour, weekly sessions, over a 10-week period. Trained facilitators use a manualized curriculum to conduct the sessions that include didactic content, professionally produced videotaped vignettes, session handouts, and group discussion. Four children, with common temperament profiles—social/eager to try, cautious/slow to warm, industrious, and high maintenance (McClowry, 2002a, 2002b)—are featured, interacting in the vignettes with their parents, teachers, and peers.

During the same 10-week period, the children are involved in a 45-minute classroom component. During the first 4 weeks, the facilitators introduce the children to one of the four puppets that represent the temperament typologies: Fredrico the Friendly is social and eager to try; Coretta the Cautious is shy; Hilary the Hard Worker is industrious; and Gregory the Grumpy is high maintenance (McClowry, 2002a, 2002b). The children are taught that, based on one's temperament, some situations are easy and others may be challenging for individuals. Using a stoplight, child are taught to problem-solve daily dilemmas using three steps: "Stop: Recognize a Dilemma," "Caution: Think and Plan," and "Go: Try It Out." Workbook sheets, videos, books, and vocabulary flashcards also reinforce session content.

Empirical Support for the Intervention

To date, the efficacy of INSIGHTS has been tested in three prevention trials. The primary focus of the first prevention study was to reduce child behavior problems. Study participants included 148 first- and second-grade children and their parents. The children were in 46 classrooms in six demographically similar urban schools. Their teachers also participated. The race/ethnicity of the children included 89% black; 9% Hispanic, nonblack; and 2% racially mixed. None of the children were receiving any medications for behavioral problems. Four schools hosted the INSIGHTS intervention, and two schools had a Read Aloud afterschool program as an attention control condition.

A repeated-measures multivariate analysis of variance showed that the children in INSIGHTS had a significantly greater decline in behavior problems at home compared to the children in the Read Aloud program (McClowry, Snow, & Tamis-LeMonda, 2005). INSIGHTS was even more efficacious than the control Read Aloud program in reducing the behavior problems of children at diagnostic levels for attention-deficit/hyperactivity disorder, oppositional defiant disorder, and/or conduct disorder.

Classroom effects were also examined. INSIGHTS, compared to the Read Aloud program, was successful in reducing the attentional difficulties and overt aggression of boys. In addition, the teachers in INSIGHTS reported feeling more efficacious in handling the emotional–oppositional behavior, attentional difficulties, and covert discipline of their male students (McClowry, Snow, Tamis-LeMonda, & Rodriguez, 2010). The teachers also perceived their male students more positively, compared to those in the Read Aloud program.

Parent and teacher graduates of the program inspired a second prevention trial of INSIGHTS. The parents and teachers recommended combining their workshop sessions to enhance their communication and collaboration in resolving child behavior problems. As a result, in the second study, two versions of INSIGHTS were compared—a *parallel* model in which 10 workshops for parents and teachers were conducted separately, and a *collaborative* model, in which five of the workshops were conducted jointly with parents and teachers, and five were conducted separately (O'Connor, Rodriguez, Cappella, Morris, & McClowry, 2012). Curriculum content was added to the collaborative model to enhance the social competencies of the adult participants and to foster comparable social skills in children. The social competencies included listening, empathy, giving recognition, assertiveness, cooperation, problem solving, controlling one's temper, and conflict resolution.

The participants in this study included 202 parents and children from 82 general education, elementary classrooms in 11 urban schools. The race/ethnicity of the children was as follows: 54% percent were black, non-Hispanic; 44% were Hispanic, nonblack; and 2% were racially mixed.

Individual growth modeling showed that children in both models demonstrated a decrease in disruptive behavior problems over the course of the intervention. At the end of the intervention, however, children in the collaborative model had a greater reduction in disruptive behavior than their peers in the parallel model. Effects varied as a function of child temperament. Children in the collaborative model with high-maintenance temperaments (high in negative reactivity and activity, but low in task persistence) had faster rates of decline in disruptive behaviors than their peers in the parallel model with the same temperament type. In fact, at the end of the intervention, there were no significant differences in the disruptive behavior of the children with high-maintenance temperaments and those who were industrious (high in task persistence and low in negative reactivity and activity) in the collaborative model. Follow-up tests of mediation revealed changes in the parents' sense of competence. Compared to those in the parallel version, parents in the collaborative model reported increased parenting competence over the course of the intervention, which, in turn, was related to lower levels of their children's disruptive behavior.

Currently, the efficacy of INSIGHTS is being tested in a group-randomized study in 22 elementary schools. The outcomes of this study, as depicted in the logic model shown in Figure 29.1, are related to children's academic context and achievement. The study

Assumptions

Every child desires to be understood and cherished.

Temperament influences child behavior, social interactions, and reactions to life situations.

Social–emotional adjustment is enhanced when there is a goodness of fit—a match between the child's temperament and the environment.

Responsive parents and teachers match their management strategies to a child's temperament.

Resources

Partnering schools

Participating teachers, parents, and children

Facilitators

Developmentally and culturally appropriate intervention materials

Intervention

INSIGHTS for:
Teachers
Parents
Children

Mediators and Their Outputs

Teacher/Classroom Environment:
↑ Classroom climate
↑ Teacher efficacy

Parental Involvement:
↑ Parent efficacy
↑ Parent participation

Proximal Outcomes: Academic Learning Context

Student Classroom Behavior:
↓ Aggression
↑ Engagement
↑ Attentiveness

Impact/Distal Outcomes

↑ Academic achievement

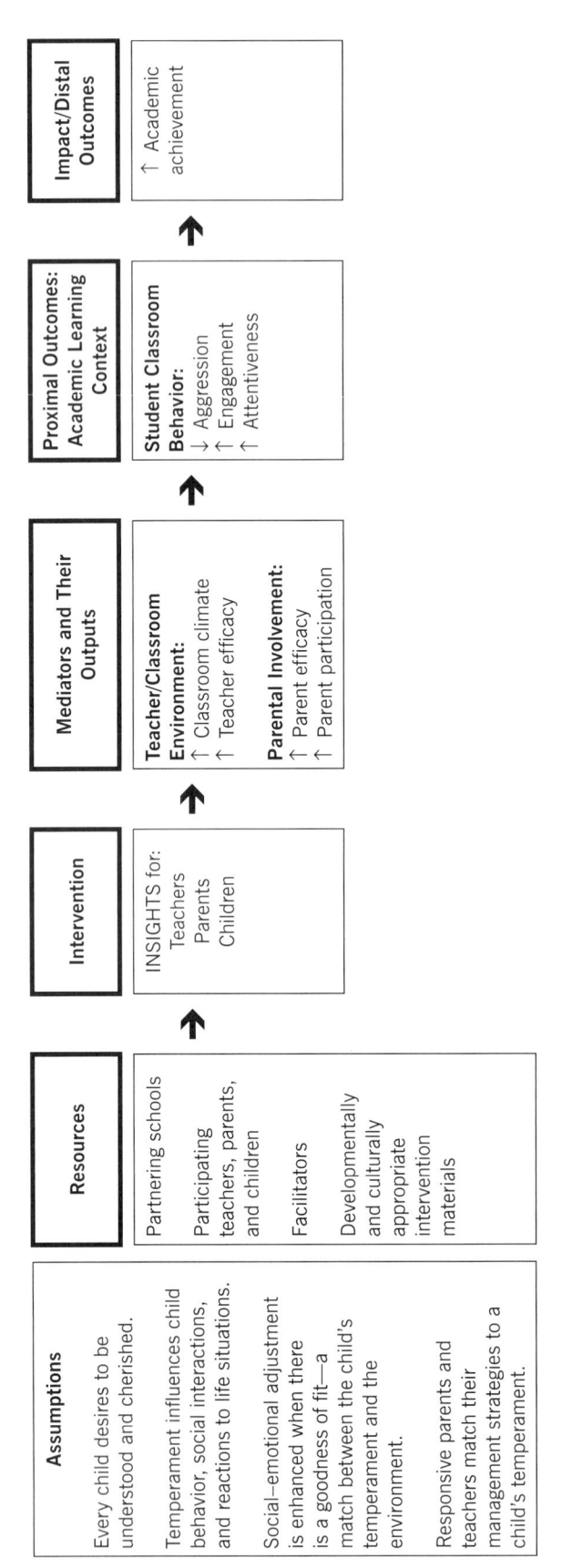

FIGURE 29.1. Logic model for INSIGHTS for Children's Temperament.

is funded by the Institute of Education Sciences (McClowry, O'Connor, & Cappella, 2008).

Logic Model

The current study tests the efficacy of INSIGHTS compared to a supplemental reading program. Proximal outcomes include enhancing the academic learning context via improvements to students' classroom behavior or the mediated effects of improved classroom environment and parental involvement that result from teachers' and parents' program participation. Partnering schools, teachers, parents, and students serve as both the program's resources and participants. Trained facilitators, using developmentally and culturally appropriate curriculum materials, also are program resources.

Lessons Learned

As is evident in the aforementioned development of INSIGHTS, the intervention underwent many revisions. Knowledge gained from the literature, preliminary studies, and the wisdom acquired from a clinical background informed the creative aspects of INSIGHTS development. Part of the interventions development can be attributed to the generous involvement of the community stakeholders and team members who contributed ideas and assessed the cultural appropriateness of the program. The challenges of acquiring funding provided a great opportunity to revise the program! The critiques by INSIGHTS grant application reviewers were, in hindsight, vital to fine-tuning the intervention and the protocol to test its efficacy. Openness to criticism and suggestions from our grant reviewers, program stakeholders, and the many, many team members further enhanced the intervention.

Future Plans

One of INSIGHTS' future plans came, again, at the initiation of the stakeholders. Latino parent leaders and teachers from a partnering school requested that the program be adapted to accommodate the growing number of monolingual, Spanish-speaking Latino parents. When a number of hurdles were presented to them, they enthusiastically volunteered their help in creating a Spanish-language version of INSIGHTS. The parents and teachers have kept their promise, and research team members are in the process of fulfilling their request.

Other goals include extending the intervention beyond the primary grades to a schoolwide model and disseminating the content in other formats, such as professional development for school personnel and instruction provided to parenting groups. A train-the-trainer model teaches facilitators how to conduct the program in their own communities. More details about these initiatives are available at the INSIGHTS website: *www.insightsintervention.com*.

A Tier 2 Temperament-Based Intervention

A Tier 2 temperament-based intervention is appropriately directed at children who are temperamentally at risk for emotional or behavioral disorders, or who exhibit early symptoms of related disorders. Rapee and his colleagues (Rapee & Jacobs, 2002; Rapee, Lyneham, & Schniering, 2006) developed *Cool Little Kids*, a targeted Tier 2 temperament-based intervention that focuses on the prevention of anxiety disorders among children with temperaments high in inhibition.

Development of the Intervention

An extensive body of literature has reported that children with inhibited temperaments are at risk for developing symptoms of anxiety and depression (Cole, Pecke, Martin, Truglio, & Seroczynski, 1998; Kagan, Snidman, Arcus, & Resnick, 1994; Last, Perrin, Hersen, & Kazdin, 1996). The risk for internalizing behaviors is exacerbated when a temperamentally inhibited child has a parent(s) with an anxiety disorder (Hudson & Rapee, 2004).

Although efficacious treatments for adult anxiety disorders exist (Hunot, Churchill, Silva de Lima, & Teixeira, 2007), few empirically supported prevention programs are available for young children. Only one reported study (LaFreniere & Capuano, 1997) focuses on preventing anxiety/withdrawal among preschool children. The intervention was successful in enhancing the children's social skills and reducing maternal control but did not change the children's anxiety or withdrawal symptoms. In addition, the intervention is lengthy and expensive.

Concerned about the sustainability of such a costly and time-intensive approach, Rapee and his colleagues (Kennedy, Rapee, & Edwards, 2009; Rapee & Jacobs, 2002; Rapee, Kennedy, Ingram, Edwards, & Sweeney, 2005) aimed to develop a minimally intrusive, low-cost intervention intended to prevent child anxiety disorders in inhibited preschool children by enhancing parenting skills. The intervention was an adaptation of the Cool Kids program that Rapee and his colleagues developed for anxiety management in older children (Rapee et al., 2006).

Description of the Intervention

The Cool Little Kids program is for parents who have preschool children with inhibited temperaments. The program teaches parents how to reduce their children's anxiety by using exposure hierarchies, in which a feared event or situation is broken down incrementally into manageable steps. Although the initial step is the least distressful, each subsequent one is increasingly more frightening, until eventually the child reaches the final, feared event. The rationale for gradually moving to the feared event is to make the child increasingly more comfortable so that he or she can deal with the situation without undue distress. Parents are concurrently taught to reduce the urge to prevent their children from greater independent discovery of the world. Parents also are taught how to model courageous coping though the use of realistic self-talk.

The Cool Little Kids program has three parts: (1) information about the nature of anxiety and its development; (2) techniques for teaching their children how to manage anxiety; and (3) strategies to help parents manage their own anxiety. The curriculum of the sessions is as follows:

- Session 1. Psychoeducation covering the nature of inhibition, anxiety, and risk factors for anxiety.
- Session 2. Parenting strategies, especially those related to inhibited behaviors. Reducing overprotection and anxious modeling and rewarding confident child behaviors.
- Session 3. Introduction to graded exposure. Learning how to build hierarchies for a child's fears and avoidance, and developing goals for the coming weeks.
- Session 4. Troubleshooting exposure and discussing difficulties encountered when implementing the program strategies. Cognitive restructuring of the parents' own fears and worries.
- Session 5. Continued application and troubleshooting of exposure. Additional practice and discussion of parents' cognitive restructuring.
- Session 6. Troubleshooting of exposure and parents' cognitive restructuring. Setting future goals and discussion of future "risk" periods.

Cool Little Kids is conducted in six to eight 90-minute sessions, with groups of no more than six parents. A clinical psychologist with extensive experience treating anxious children conducts the sessions. Parents receive a workbook and homework so that they can practice the skills they are taught. A booster telephone call is conducted 1 month after the completion of the program to reinforce program content and to troubleshoot any problems that the parents may have encountered.

Empirical Support for the Intervention

The empirical support for the Cool Little Kids program has been examined in three studies. In a pilot study (Rapee & Jacobs, 2002), parents of preschool children whose temperaments were high in inhibition were invited to participate. Mothers of seven temperamentally inhibited 4-year-old boys attended six psychoeducational sessions during a 9-week period. Although the small sample size was not adequate for assessing the efficacy of the intervention, it did indicate that the mothers perceived their children as less withdrawn after attending the program.

In the second study (Rapee et al., 2005), the parents of 146 Australian temperamentally inhibited preschool children were the participants. At baseline, 90% of the children met the criteria for an anxiety disorder. The parents were randomly assigned to the Cool Little Kids program or a monitoring condition for 1 year, during which they received no treatment.

Mediational analyses used structural equation modeling to examine the program effects. Children whose parents attended Cool Little Kids, compared to the monitoring group, had a significant reduction in anxiety disorders over the 1-year duration of the intervention. The differences between the groups were examined again after 3 years (Rapee, Kennedy, Ingram, Edwards, & Sweeney, 2010). The children whose parents attended Cool Little Kids continued to have fewer anxiety symptoms and disorders.

Kennedy and colleagues (2009) focused their third study on children observed to have high levels of behavioral inhibition on a laboratory measure and also parents with anxiety disorders. The participants included 71 parents of preschool children from middle- to upper-middle-class Anglo-Celtic families. Half of the parents were randomly assigned to Cool Little Kids and the others were placed on a waitlist for 6 months.

Repeated-measures analysis of variance demonstrated that after the intervention, significantly fewer children whose parents were in Cool Little Kids had anxiety disorders compared to those on the waitlist. Although there were no significant differences in parental reports of the children's anxiety or in the parent's own symptoms of anxiety in either group, the preschool children of the parents in Cool Little Kids, compared to children on the waitlist, showed significant reductions in their laboratory-observed inhibition, including changes in their speech speed, proximity to their mothers, and level of interaction with unfamiliar adults.

Logic Model

As shown in Figure 29.2, the logic model for the Cool Little Kids program depicts the reduction of child anxiety disorders as a distal outcome by reducing anxiety and inhibition symptoms and by increasing the social skills of preschool children. The effects of the intervention are mediated by the enhancement of parental skills and children's coping skills. Trained facilitators from the community conduct the program with small groups of parents.

Lessons Learned

A number of measurement issues are embedded in conducting a Tier 2 temperament-based preventive intervention. In general, instrumentation to differentiate reliably temperament, early symptomatology, and low levels of the relevant disorder are lacking (Durbin, 2010). Not surprisingly, Kennedy and colleagues (2009) found it challenging to differentiate between children temperamentally at risk and those already at a diagnostic level of disorder. It is particularly difficult when the target population includes young children and the disorder is an internalizing one (Durbin, 2010).

Future Plans

Rapee and his colleagues are conducting a longitudinal study following the 146 children in the 2005 study, who are now approximately 15 years of age. The purpose of the study is to examine the long-term outcomes of the intervention.

Another, larger study is underway to test further the efficacy of the Cool Little Kids program (Bayer, Rapee, Hiscock, Ukoumunne, Mihalopoulos, & Wake, 2011). The study includes 500 inhibited 3- to 5-year-old children recruited through community sampling at preschools and early childhood centers. Trained facilitators will run the program at the various community locations. Continued testing of the Cool Little Kids program is likely to provide additional evidence to support early temperament-based parental intervention in preventing child anxiety.

A Tier 3 Temperament-Based Intervention

Children who are not responsive to Tier 1 or Tier 2 interventions are referred to Tier 3 programs. As a Tier 3 temperament-based intervention, *STORIES* is a more intensive, individualized treatment for students who exhibit high levels of aggressive behavior.

Development of the Intervention

Children with temperaments that are high in negative reactivity are at risk for devel-

Assumptions	Resources	Intervention	Mediators and Their Outputs	Proximal Outcomes	Impact/Distal Outcomes
Temperamentally shy children tend to be anxious and withdrawn in social situations.	Small groups of parents with anxiety symptoms and temperamentally shy children	The *Cool Little Kids* parent education program	↑ Effective parental responsiveness	**Preschool child** ↓ Anxiety symptoms	↓ Child anxiety disorders
Inhibited shy child behavior can elicit overprotection from anxious parents.	Trained facilitators from the community		↓ Parental anxiety	↓ Inhibition symptoms	
Parental anxiety exacerbates child anxiety symptoms.			↓ Parental negative thinking	↑ Social skills	
Effective parental responsiveness can reduce children's symptoms of anxiety.			↓ Parent overprotection		
Parent education can prevent preschool children's symptoms of anxiety from developing into anxiety disorders.			↑ Child coping		

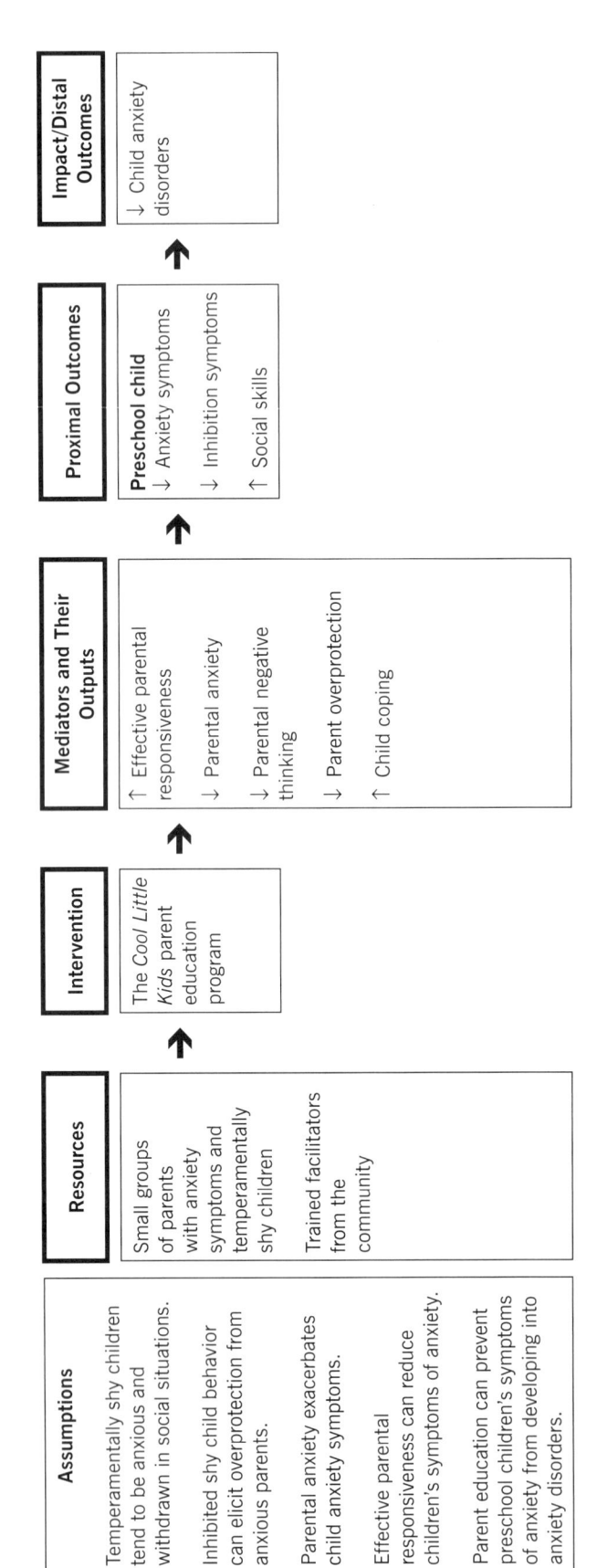

FIGURE 29.2. Logic model for the Cool Little Kids Program.

oping disruptive disorders, which interferes in their ability to process social cues accurately (Izard, Stark, Trentacosta, & Schultz, 2008). Such children often attribute erroneous and negative interpretations to others' expressive behavior. STORIES (Structure/Themes/Open Communication/Reflection/Individuality/Experiential Learning/Social Problem Solving) focuses on students with identified emotional disabilities, including aggressive behavior and related deficits in social-information processing and problem solving. School psychologists Teglasi, Rahill, and Rothman (2007) developed the intervention for elementary school students whose emotional disabilities compromise their academic progress and require them to receive specialized behavioral services. Ultimately, STORIES seeks to improve the emotional regulation of such students.

Description of the Intervention

Activities in STORIES are intended to enhance empathy skills by helping children with emotional disabilities understand how individual perceptions and responses vary. STORIES is conducted over 25 weeks with groups of three to seven children. Each session lasts 40–45 minutes and is conducted by two trained group leaders who are school psychologists.

During intervention sessions, group leaders read stories to the children about everyday events. For example, in "A Peaceful Warrior," a student is bullied at his new school but is supported by a friend. Consistent with temperament theory, the reactions of each person in the story are explored. The group leader explores with the children how the bully, victim, and bystanders have different views, feelings, and reactions to the same event. The children discuss what the different characters are feeling; identify the characters' goals and intentions; and discuss whether the characters are accomplishing their goals by their actions and how they monitor their behaviors.

STORIES encourages the children to reorganize the way they process social information in their own lives. The group leader asks the children to evaluate their reactions to the characters and plots, and to reflect on how the moral of the story is related to the children's experiences. The children also are encouraged to recall times when their behavior has been automatic and lacking self-regulation. More effective problem-solving strategies are role-played in the group.

Empirical Support for the Intervention

A pilot study was conducted with students from fourth and fifth-grade classrooms in two urban elementary schools (Teglasi & Rothman, 2001). All but two of the 54 participating children were African American. Although the students were in regular education classrooms, their teachers reported that, in general, the children exhibited high levels of aggression. School personnel identified some students as being highly aggressive.

Half of the students participated in STORIES in the fall. The rest of the students were on a waitlist to receive the intervention in the spring. Each group of students in STORIES comprised four to six students, including one or two highly aggressive children.

Repeated-measures analysis of variance demonstrated that after participation in STORIES in the fall, overall, the aggressive behavior of the children decreased compared to that of children who had not yet received the intervention. There was, however, an unexpected differential effect. The children identified as highly aggressive increased their externalizing behavior over time, while the unidentified students decreased in aggression.

Close examination of the pilot data suggested variations in the children's responses within the unidentified and aggressive groups of students. Some children in the highly aggressive group improved, while some students in the unidentified group became more aggressive. The small number of participants, however, did not provide enough power to test adequately the efficacy of the program, so an additional pilot study was conducted.

The second pilot study (Rahill & Teglasi, 2003) examined the effects of STORIES on children with identified emotional, but not intellectual, disabilities. The sample included 82 children in grades 2 through 6 in four special education centers. Eighty-five percent of the children were male. The race/

ethnicity of the children was: 25% African American; 10% Hispanic American, non-black; and 65% European American, non-Hispanic.

The participating children were assigned to one of three conditions: (1) STORIES, (2) a skillstreaming program (McGinnis & Goldstein, 1997) that teaches nine steps to enhance social skills, or (3) nonspecific counseling sessions. All of the groups met for 40–45 minutes for 25 weeks. Multivariate analysis of covariance demonstrated that after the intervention, the children who participated in STORIES had significantly fewer behavior problems than those in the skillstreaming program. Their behavior, however, was not significantly different than those in the nonspecific counseling group. Multiple regression was used to evaluate the changes over the course of the interventions in the cognitive processing skills of the children in STORIES compared to those in the skillstreaming program. Children in STORIES showed greater gains in cognitive processing at the end of the intervention than children in the skillstreaming program.

Logic Model

As depicted in the logic model in Figure 29.3, the intended distal outcome of STORIES is to treat children with aggressive disorders so that they learn to engage in socially appropriate behavior. The more proximal outcomes are to enhance students' empathy skills and feelings of recognition, and to decrease aggressive behavior. The outcomes are mediated by enhancing the cognitive processing skills of the children. School psychologists conducts STORIES with very small groups of children with emotional disabilities.

Lessons Learned

The results from the second pilot study supported that STORIES enhanced the cognitive processing of students with identified emotional disorders. Because the sample sizes in the pilot studies were small, they did not adequately evaluate the efficacy of the intervention. Thus, additional research is warranted to evaluate the efficacy of STORIES as a temperament-based, Tier 3 intervention.

Future Plans

STORIES developers have considered extending the length of the intervention because children qualifying for Tier 3 services often demonstrate wide variations in their behavioral responses to intervention and typically require lengthy treatment (Quinn, Kavale, Mathur, Rutherford, & Forness, 1999). Adding teacher and parent components also is planned because comprehensive interventions are often more effective in reducing disruptive behaviors than those that target just the child (Greenberg et al., 2001; Webster-Stratton, Reid, & Stoolmiller, 2008). Testing the efficacy of STORIES with a randomized clinical trial is an important next step.

Recommendations for Future Advances in Temperament-Based Intervention

Each of the three temperament-based interventions presented in this chapter represents one of the tiers of the RTI framework. INSIGHTS into Children's Temperament provides a Tier 1, social–emotional intervention supporting the development of primary grade children in urban schools. The Cool Little Kids program offers a Tier 2 intervention to prevent anxiety disorders in preschool children with temperaments high in inhibition, by teaching their parents how to model effective coping strategies. A Tier 3 intervention, the STORIES program, uses a story-based curriculum to develop and strengthen empathy skills in elementary school students with emotional disabilities.

Recommendations for Practice

These temperament-based interventions and others described in McClowry, Rodriguez, and colleagues (2008) lead to recommendations for practice and research that can further advance temperament-based intervention. Enough evidence already exists to support the dissemination of temperament-based interventions in a variety of formats and locations. The next generation of practitioners/scientists can contribute to the ongoing temperament theory, research, and practice spiral by capitalizing on the lessons already learned.

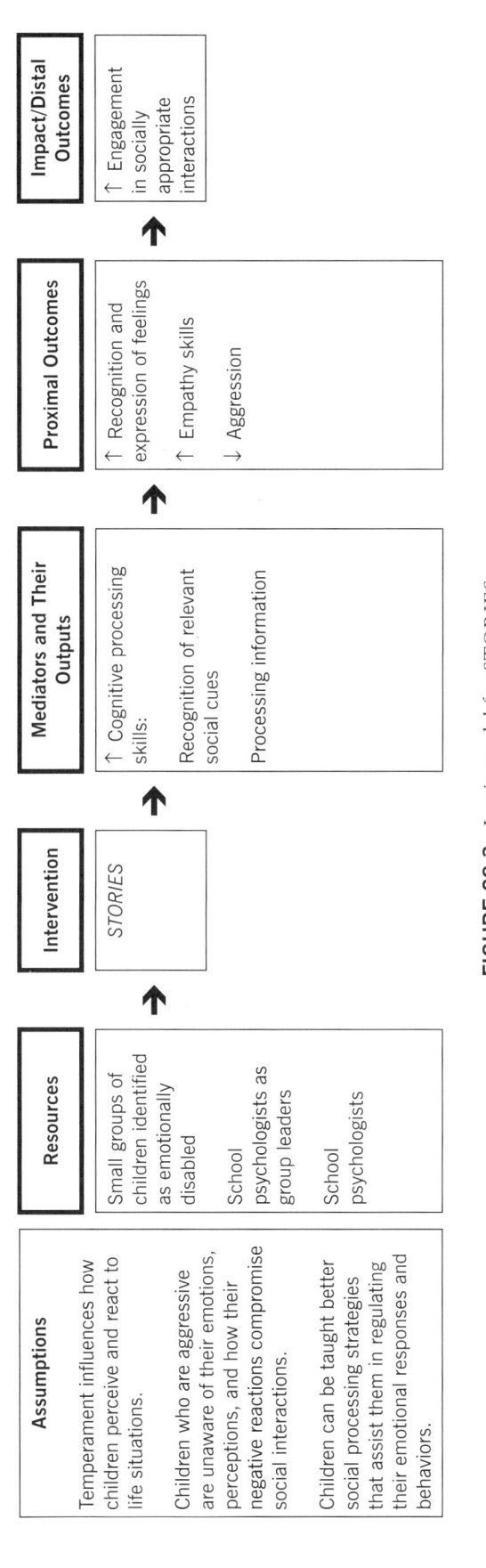

Assumptions	Resources	Intervention	Mediators and Their Outputs	Proximal Outcomes	Impact/Distal Outcomes
Temperament influences how children perceive and react to life situations. Children who are aggressive are unaware of their emotions, perceptions, and how their negative reactions compromise social interactions. Children can be taught better social processing strategies that assist them in regulating their emotional responses and behaviors.	Small groups of children identified as emotionally disabled School psychologists as group leaders School psychologists	STORIES	↑ Cognitive processing skills: Recognition of relevant social cues Processing information	↑ Recognition and expression of feelings ↑ Empathy skills ↓ Aggression	↑ Engagement in socially appropriate interactions

FIGURE 29.3. Logic model for STORIES.

Use of the RTI framework for developing and adapting temperament-based interventions is recommended. RTI can assist interventionists in clarifying the focus of the intervention, addressing anticipated problems, and finding the appropriate target population. Specifying a theory of change and a logic model can help clarify necessary resources, intervention components, and intended outcomes or outputs. It can also facilitate collaboration between the intervention team and the stakeholders. Additional strategies for involving stakeholders in developing and adapting temperament-based intervention, with an emphasis on adapting existing interventions for different cultural groups, are discussed in McClowry, Rodriguez, and colleagues (2008).

Temperament-based interventions can occur in myriad creative ways. Rather than being stand-alone programs, temperament-based interventions can supplement existing child development initiatives (Pelco & Reed-Victor, 2003). Federally supported programs such as Head Start could benefit by adding temperament-based content to the services they offer to parents. Teaching modules and other educational tools, such as videos, could be developed for parents and for the staff at Head Start and other preschool programs. Foster and adoptive parents also are likely to find temperament-based intervention helpful for their families in transition.

Schools are ideal locations for comprehensive temperament-based intervention that involve children and their parents and teachers. Many school districts already encourage their schools to have positive behavior programs aimed at enhancing the social development of their students. The RTI framework could offer a schoolwide model for integrating three tiers of temperament-based intervention.

Multi-level temperament-based interventions could be conducted in private practices and community centers. If well coordinated, the intensity of individual or family temperament-based intervention can be stepped up or down as needed, similar to the three tiers of the RTI framework. Salloum (2010) explains that the advantages of "stepped" services are greater accessibility and flexibility, maximized use of resources, and reduced costs. Possible types of temperament-based services include bibliotherapy, telephone advice, computer-based therapy, group sessions or workshops, and individualized treatment.

Recommendations for Research

Temperament-based interventions would certainly benefit from additional prevention and clinical trials that test their efficacy. After all, experimental designs are regarded as producing the highest level of scientific evidence (Cook, 2007). To address implementation feasibility, school- and community center–based intervention studies often use quasi-experimental methods (Shadish, Cook, & Campbell, 2002). Applying such rigorous designs to efficacy trials will advance knowledge of the psychological underpinnings of temperament-based interventions.

Lingering research questions demonstrate the ongoing need for a practice, theory, and research spiral. Construct validity studies have the potential to differentiate between temperament, psychological symptomatology, and mental health disorders (Durbin, 2010; McClowry et al., in press). Identification of moderating and mediating factors in intervention studies would provide important clinical insights into the participants who fail to respond to an intervention. The replication of efficacy studies would be advantageous in examining whether intervention effects can be reproduced in other communities and under different circumstances. Additionally, since the distal impact of behavioral interventions is often stronger than its proximal impact (Greenberg et al., 2001), the long-term effects of temperament-based interventions should be explored.

Social psychology pioneer Kurt Lewin said, "If you want to truly understand something, try to change it." Using the goodness-of-fit model, implementing it, and studying intervention efficacy has proved invaluable in advancing temperament-based intervention. Over the next 60 years, the temperament theory, practice, and research spiral will generate further support that temperament-based intervention can be efficacious when conducted across a range of settings—homes, schools, and clinical environments.

Further Reading

Chess, S., & Thomas, A. (1999). *Goodness of fit: Clinical applications from infancy through adult life*. Philadelphia: Brunner/Mazel.

Fox, L., Carta, J., Strain, P., Dunlap, G., & Hemmeter, M. (2010). Response to intervention and the pyramid model. *Infants and Young Children*, 23(1), 3–13.

McClowry, S. G., Koslowitz, R., & Rodriguez, E. T. (2008). Temperament-based intervention: Re-examining goodness of fit. *European Journal of Developmental Science*, 2, 120–135.

References

Bates, J. E. (2001). Adjustment style in childhood as a product of parenting and temperament. In T. D. Wachs & G. A. Kohnstamm (Eds.), *Temperament in context* (pp. 61–79). Mahwah, NJ: Erlbaum.

Bayer, J. K., Rapee, R. M., Hiscock, H., Ukoumunne, O. C., Mihalopoulos, C., & Wake, M. (2011). Translational research to prevent internalizing problems in early childhood. *Depression and Anxiety*, 28, 50–57.

Brock, L., Nishida, T., Chiong, C., Grimm, K., & Rimm-Kaufman, S. (2008). Children's perceptions of the classroom environment and social and academic performance: A longitudinal analysis of the contribution of the Responsive Classroom approach. *Journal of School Psychology*, 46(2), 129–149.

Carey, W. (2004). *Understanding your child's temperament*. Bloomington, IN: Xlibris.

Carey, W. B., & McDevitt, S. C. (1995). *Coping with children's temperament: A guide for professionals*. New York: Basic Books.

Chess, S., & Thomas, A. (1984). Genesis and evolution of behavioral disorders: From infancy to early adult life. *American Journal of Psychiatry*, 141(1), 1–9.

Chess, S., & Thomas, A. (1986). *Temperament in clinical practice*. New York: Guilford Press.

Cole, D., Pecke, L., Martin, J., Truglio, R., & Seroczynski, A. (1998). A longitudinal look at the relation between depression and anxiety in children and adolescents. *Journal of Consulting and Clinical Psychology*, 66, 451–460.

Connell, J. P., & Klem, A. M. (2000). You can get there from here: Using a theory of change approach to plan urban education reform. *Journal of Educational and Psychological Consultation*, 11(1), 93–120.

Cook, T. (2007). Randomized experiments in education: Assessing the objections to doing them. *Economics of Innovation and New Technology*, 16(5), 331–355.

Davidov, M., & Grusec, J. E. (2006). Untangling the links of parental responsiveness to distress and warmth to child outcomes. *Child Development*, 77(1), 44–58.

De Pauw, S., & Mervielde, I. (2010). Temperament, personality and developmental psychopathology: A review based on the conceptual dimensions underlying childhood traits. *Child Psychiatry and Human Development*, 41(3), 313–329.

Durbin, C. E. (2010). Modeling temperamental risk for internalizing psychopathology using developmentally sensitive laboratory paradigms. *Child Development Perspectives*, 4(3), 168–173.

Durlak, J. A., Weissberg, R. P., Dymnicki, A. B., Taylor, R. D., & Schellinger, K. B. (2011). The impact of enhancing students' social and emotional learning: A meta-analysis of school-based universal interventions. *Child Development*, 82, 405–432.

Eisenberg, N., Smith, C. L., Sadovsky, A., & Spinrad, T. L. (2004). Effortful control: Relations with emotion regulation, adjustment, and socialization in childhood. In R. F. Baumeister & K. D. Vohs (Eds.), *Handbook of self-regulation: Research, theory, and applications* (pp. 259–282). New York: Guilford Press.

Fletcher, J., Shaywitz, S., Shankweller, D., Katz, L., Liberman, I., Stuebing, K., et al. (1994). Cognitive profiles of reading disability: Comparisons of discrepancy and low achievement definitions. *Journal of Education Psychology*, 86(1), 6–23.

Fox, L., Carta, J., Strain, P., Dunlap, G., & Hemmeter, M. (2010). Response to intervention and the pyramid model. *Infants and Young Children*, 23(1), 3–13.

Fuchs, D., Mock, D., Morgan, P. L., & Young, C. L. (2003). Responsiveness-to-intervention: Definitions, evidence, and implications for the learning disabilities construct. *Learning Disabilities Research and Practice*, 18(3), 157–171.

Greenberg, M. T., Domitrovich, C., & Bumbarger, B. (2001). The prevention of mental disorder in school-aged children: Current state of the field. *Prevention and Treatment*, 4(1).

Hamre, B. K., & Pianta, R. C. (2005). Can instructional and emotional support in the first-grade classroom make a difference for children at risk of school failure? *Child Development*, 76(5), 949–967.

Hudson, J. L., & Rapee, R. M. (2004). From anxious temperament to disorder: An etiological model of generalized anxiety disorder. In R. G. Heimberg, C. L. Turk, & D. S. Mennin (Eds.), *Generalized anxiety disorder: Advances in research and practice* (pp. 51–76). New York: Guilford Press.

Hunot, V., Churchill, R., Silva de Lima, M., & Teixeira, V. (2007). Psychological therapies for generalized anxiety disorder. *Cochrane Database of Systematic Reviews*, Issue 1 (Article

No. CD001848), DOI: 10.1002/14651858. CD001848.pub4.

Izard, C., Stark, K., Trentacosta, C., & Schultz, D. (2008). Beyond emotion regulation: Emotion utilization and adaptive functioning. *Child Development Perspectives*, 2(3), 156–163.

Izzo, C. V., Connell, J. P., Gambone, M. A., & Bradshaw, C. P. (2004). Understanding and improving youth development initiatives through evaluation. In S. F. Hamilton & M. A. Hamilton (Eds.), *Youth development handbook: Coming of age in American communities* (pp. 301–326). Thousand Oaks, CA: Sage.

Joyce, D. (2010). *Essentials of temperament assessment*. Hoboken, NJ: Wiley.

Kagan, J., Reznick, J., & Snidman, N. (1988). Biological bases of childhood shyness. *Science*, 240, 167–171.

Kagan, J., Snidman, N., Arcus, D., & Resnick, J. S. (1994). *Galen's prophecy: Temperament in human nature*. New York: Basic Books.

Kagan, J., Snidman, N., Zentner, M., & Peterson, E. (1999). Infant temperament and anxious symptoms in school age children. *Development and Psychopathology*, 11(2), 209–224.

Kennedy, S., Rapee, R., & Edwards, S. (2009). A selective intervention program for inhibited preschool-aged children of parents with an anxiety disorder: Effects on current anxiety disorders and temperament. *Journal of the American Academy of Child and Adolescent Psychiatry*, 48(6), 602–609.

Keogh, B. (2003). *Temperament in the classroom: Understanding individual differences*. Baltimore: Brookes.

Kochanska, G. (1997). Mutually responsive orientation between mothers and their young children: Implications for early socialization. *Child Development*, 68, 94–112.

Kochanska, G., & Knaack, A. (2003). Effortful control as a personality characteristic of young children: Antecedents, correlates, and consequences. *Journal of Personality*, 71(6), 1087–1112.

Kovaleski, J. F. (2003). The three tier model for identifying learning disabilities: Critical program features and system issues. Retrieved from *www.coe.iup.edu/kovaleski/nrcld_article.doc*.

Kurcinka, M. (2006). *Raising your spirited child: A guide for parents whose child is more intense, sensitive, perceptive, persistent, and energetic* (rev. ed.). New York: HarperCollins.

LaFreniere, P., & Capuano, F. (1997). Preventive intervention as a means of clarifying direction of effects in socialization: Anxious–withdrawn preschoolers case. *Development and Psychopathology*, 9, 551–564.

Last, C., Perrin, S., Hersen, M., & Kazdin, A. (1996). A prospective study of childhood anxiety disorders. *Journal of the American Academy of Child and Adolescent Psychiatry*, 35, 1505–1510.

Maziade, M., Caron, C., Cote, R., Merette, C., Bernier, H., Laplante, B., et al. (1990). Psychiatric status of adolescents who had extreme temperaments at age 7. *American Journal of Psychiatry*, 147, 1531–1536.

McClowry, S. G. (2002a). The temperament profiles of school-age children. *Journal of Pediatric Nursing*, 17, 3–10.

McClowry, S. G. (2002b). Transforming temperament profile statistics into puppets and other visual media. *Journal of Pediatric Nursing*, 17, 11–17.

McClowry, S. G. (2003). *Your child's unique temperament: Insights and strategies for responsive parenting*. Champaign, IL: Research Press.

McClowry, S. G., & Galehouse, P. (2002). A pilot study conducted to plan a temperament-based parenting program for inner city families. *Journal of Child and Adolescent Psychiatric Mental Health Nursing*, 15, 97–105.

McClowry, S. G., Galehouse, P., Hartnagle, W., Kaufman, H., Just, B., Moed, R., et al. (1996). A comprehensive school-based clinic: University and community partnership. *Journal of Society of Pediatric Nurses*, 1, 19–26.

McClowry, S. G., Halverson, C. F., & Sanson, A. (2003). A re-examination of the validity and reliability of the School-Age Temperament Inventory. *Nursing Research*, 52, 176–182.

McClowry, S. G., O'Connor, E., & Cappella, E. (2008). *Testing the efficacy of INSIGHTS in enhancing the academic learning context* (Grant No. R305A080512). Washington, DC: Institute of Education Sciences.

McClowry, S. G., Rodriguez, E. T., & Koslowitz, R. (2008). Temperament-based intervention: Re-examining goodness of fit. *European Journal of Developmental Science*, 2(1–2), 120–135.

McClowry, S. G., Rodriguez, E. T., Tamis-LeMonda, C. S., Spellmann, M. E., Carlson, A., & Snow, D. L. (in press). Teacher/student interactions and classroom behavior: The role of student temperament and gender. *Journal of Research in Childhood Education*.

McClowry, S. G., Snow, D. L., & Tamis-LeMonda, C. S. (2005). An evaluation of the effects of INSIGHTS on the behavior of inner city primary school children. *Journal of Primary Prevention*, 26, 567–584.

McClowry, S. G., Snow, D. L., Tamis-LeMonda, C. S., & Rodriguez, E. T. (2010). Testing the efficacy of INSIGHTS on student disruptive behavior, classroom management, and student competence in inner city primary grades. *School Mental Health*, 2, 23–35.

McGinnis, E., & Goldstein, A. (1997). *Skillstreaming the elementary school child: New strategies and perspectives for teaching prosocial skills* (rev. ed.). Champagne, IL: Research Press.

Mrazek, P., & Haggerty, R. (1994). *Reducing risks for mental disorders: Frontiers for preventive intervention research.* Washington, DC: Institute of Medicine, Committee on Prevention of Mental Disorders.

Neville, H., & Johnson, D. C. (1997). *Temperament tools: Working with your child's inborn traits.* Seattle, WA: Parenting Press.

No Child Left Behind (NCLB) Act of 2001, Public Law No. 107-110, § 115, Stat. 1425 (2002).

O'Connor, E. E., Rodriguez, E. T., Cappella, E., Morris, J. G., & McClowry, S. G. (2012). Child disruptive behavior and parenting efficacy: A comparison of the effects of two models of INSIGHTS. *Journal of Community Psychology, 40,* 555–572.

Pelco, L. E., & Reed-Victor, E. (2003). Understanding and supporting differences in child temperament: Strategies for early childhood. *Young Exceptional Children, 6*(3), 2–11.

Quinn, M., Kavale, K., Mathur, S., Rutherford, R., & Forness, S. (1999). A meta-analysis of social skill intervention for students with emotional or behavioral disorders. *Journal of Emotional and Behavioral Disorders, 7*(1), 54–64.

Rahill, S., & Teglasi, H. (2003). Processes and outcomes of story based and skill-based social competency programs for children with emotional disabilities. *Journal of School Psychology, 41,* 413–429.

Rapee, R., & Jacobs, D. (2002). The reduction of temperamental risk for anxiety in withdrawn Preschoolers: A pilot study. *Behavioural and Cognitive Psychotherapy, 30,* 211–215.

Rapee, R., Kennedy, S., Ingram, M., Edwards, S., & Sweeney, L. (2005). Prevention and early intervention of anxiety disorders in inhibited preschool children. *Journal of Consulting and Clinical Psychology, 73*(3), 488–497.

Rapee, R. M., Kennedy, S., Ingram, M., Edwards, S. L., & Sweeney, L. (2010). Altering the trajectory of anxiety in at-risk young children. *American Journal of Psychiatry, 167,* 1518–1525.

Rapee, R. M., Lyneham, H. J., & Schniering, C. A. (2006). *The cool kids child and adolescent anxiety program therapist manual.* Sydney: Centre for Emotional Health, Macquaire University.

Reynolds, C., & Shaywitz, S. (2009). Response to intervention: Ready or not?: Or, from wait-to-fail to watch-them-fail. *School Psychology Quarterly, 24*(2), 130–149.

Rimm-Kaufman, S. E., & Chiu, Y.-J. I. (2007). Promoting social and academic competence in the classroom: An intervention study examining the contribution of the *Responsive Classroom* approach. *Psychology in the Schools, 44*(4), 397–413.

Rothbart, M. K. (2011). *Becoming who we are: Temperament and personality in development.* New York: Guilford Press.

Rothbart, M. K., & Derryberry, D. (1981). Development of individual differences in temperament. In M. E. Lamb & A. L. Brown (Eds.), *Advances in developmental psychology* (Vol. 1, pp. 37–86). Hillsdale, NJ: Erlbaum.

Rothbart, M. K., Sheese, B. E., & Posner, M. I. (2007). Executive attention and effortful control: Linking temperament, brain networks, and genes. *Child Development Perspectives, 1*(1), 2–7.

Rudasill, K. M., Gallagher, K., & White, J. M. (2010). Temperamental attention and activity, classroom emotional support, and academic achievement in third grade. *Journal of School Psychology, 489*(2), 113–134.

Sailor, W., Doolittle, J., Bradley, R., & Danielson, L. (2009). Response to intervention and positive behavior support. In W. Sailor, G. Dunlop, G. Sugai, & R. Horner (Eds.), *Handbook of positive behavior support* (Vol. 4., 729–753). New York: Springer.

Salloum, A. (2010). Minimal therapist-assisted cognitive-behavioral therapy interventions in stepped care for childhood anxiety. *Professional Psychology: Research and Practice, 41,* 41–47.

Shadish, W., Cook, T., & Campbell, D. (2002). *Experimental and quasi-experimental designs for generalized causal inference.* Boston: Houghton-Mifflin.

Slavin, R. (2002). Evidence-based education policies: Transforming educational practice and research. *Educational Researcher, 31*(7), 15–21.

Stecker, P., Fuchs, D., & Fuchs, L. (2008). Progress monitoring as essential practice within response to intervention. *Rural Special Education Quarterly, 27*(4), 10–17.

Sugai, G., Horner, R. H., & Gresham, F. (2002). Behaviorally effective school environments. In M. R. Shinn, G. Stoner, & H. M. Walker (Eds.), *Interventions for academic and behavior problems: Preventive and remedial approaches* (pp. 315–350). Silver Spring, MD: National Association of School Psychologists.

Teglasi, H., Rahill, S., & Rothman, L. (2007). A story guided peer group intervention for reducing bullying and victimization in schools. In J. E. Zins, M. J. Elisas, & C. A. Maher (Eds.), *Bullying, victimization, and peer harassment: A handbook of prevention and intervention* (pp. 219–237). New York: Haworth Press.

Teglasi, H., & Rothman, L. (2001). STORIES: A classroom-based program to reduce aggressive behavior. *Journal of School Psychology, 39,* 71–94.

Thomas, A., Chess, S., Birch, H., Hertzig, M., & Korn, S. (1963). *Behavioral individuality in early childhood.* New York: New York University Press.

Torgesen, J. K. (2009). The response to intervention instructional model: Some outcomes from a large-scale implementation in reading first schools. *Child Development Perspectives, 3*(1), 38–40.

Turecki, S., & Tonner, L. (2000). *The difficult child: Expanded and revised edition.* New York: Bantam.

Vaughn, S., Wanzek, J., Linan-Thompson, S., & Murray, C. (2007). Monitoring response to supplemental services for students at risk for reading difficulties: High and low responders. In S. R. Jimerson, M. K. Burns, & A. M. Van Der Heyden (Eds.), *Handbook of response to intervention* (Vol. 3, pp. 234–243). New York: Springer.

Webster-Stratton, M., Reid, M., & Stoolmiller, M. (2008). Preventing conduct problems and improving school readiness: Evaluation of the Incredible Years Teacher and Child Training Programs in high-risk schools. *Journal of Child Psychology and Psychiatry, 49*(5), 471–488.

W. K. Kellogg Foundation. (2004). *Using logic models to bring together planning, evaluation and action: Logic model development guide.* Battle Creek, MI: Author.

Yearwood, E., & McClowry, S. G. (2006). Duality in context: The process of preparedness in communicating with at-risk children. *Journal of Family Nursing, 12,* 38–55.

Yearwood, E., & McClowry, S. G. (2008). Home is for caring, school is for learning: Qualitative data from child graduates of INSIGHTS. *Journal of Child and Adolescent Psychiatric Nursing, 21,* 238–245.

CHAPTER 30

Temperament in the Classroom

Angela Lee Duckworth
Kelly M. Allred

Some students fare better than others, even when researchers control for family background, school curriculum, and teacher quality. Variance in academic performance that persists when situational variables are held constant suggests that whether students fail or thrive depends on not only circumstance but also relatively stable individual differences in how children respond to circumstance. More academically talented children, for instance, generally outperform their less able peers. Indeed, *general intelligence*, defined as the "ability to understand complex ideas, to adapt effectively to the environment, to learn from experience, to engage in various forms of reasoning, to overcome obstacles by taking thought" (Neisser et al., 1996, p. 77), has a monotonic, positive relationship with academic performance, even at the extreme right-tail of the population (Gottfredson, 2004; Lubinski, 2009). Much less is known about how traits unrelated to general intelligence influence academic outcomes.

This chapter addresses several related questions: What insights can be gleaned from historical interest in the role of temperament in the classroom? What does recent empirical research say about the specific dimensions of temperament most important to successful academic performance? In particular, which aspects of temperament most strongly influence school readiness, academic achievement, and educational attainment? What factors mediate and moderate associations between temperament and academic outcomes? What progress has been made in deliberately cultivating aspects of temperament that matter most to success in school? And, finally, for researchers keenly interested in better understanding how and why temperament influences academic success, in which direction does future progress lie?

Temperament and Personality

We use the term *temperament* to refer to individual differences in behaving, feeling, and thinking that are relatively stable across time and situation and reflect "the relatively enduring biological makeup of the organism, influenced over time by heredity, maturation, and experience" (Rothbart & Rueda, 2005, p. 167). Our conception of temperament overlaps considerably with the construct of personality, but temperament, typically studied much earlier in the life course, is presumably shaped more by hereditary than by environmental influences, reflecting basic biological processes more so than do the elaborated cognitive structures (e.g., goals, values, coping styles, schemas, metacognitive strategies) that form the basis of adult personality. Whereas the classical trait perspective holds that traits are *perfectly* stable over time, it is now well recognized that temperament and personality traits do change. In fact, both mean-level and rank-order change in traits across the life course, despite substantial stability, is the rule rather than the exception (Roberts & DelVecchio, 2000; Roberts, Walton, & Viechtbauer, 2006). Introverts do not become extraverts overnight, yet the cumulative effects of experience on temperament do leave their mark, and as we discuss toward the end of this chapter, there is evidence that specific aspects of temperament can be deliberately cultivated through direct intervention.

Because formal schooling is a project that extends, for many individuals, well into early adulthood, many relevant studies employ measures of personality rather than temperament. The bridging of measurement systems for temperament and personality traits—which should permit synthesis of findings across the developmental span from preschool to adulthood—is challenging for at least four reasons. First, the behavioral expression of a trait may qualitatively change during development: Sensation seeking at age 4 may manifest in jumping from the top of stairs, at 17 in driving over the speed limit and experimenting with cigarettes, and in adulthood as risky and promiscuous sexual behavior. Second, certain dimensions of behavior, such as motor activity or regularity in sleeping and eating habits, demonstrate more between-individual variability earlier in life than later, whereas more complex dimensions of behavior, such as conventionality and organization, do not emerge until later in the life course. Indeed, increasing complexity of individual differences over the life course in behaving, feeling, and thinking has led many researchers to conceive of temperament as the rudimentary building blocks from which more intricate structures, with life experience, gradually evolve. Third, the latent psychological processes that give rise to overt manifestations of temperament and personality are not directly observable, and while these latent processes may be constant across situation, their expression and activation surely vary in response to situational cues that may change markedly from childhood to adulthood.

A fourth challenge to linking temperament to personality is the lack of a consensual taxonomy for temperament traits. In contrast, there is reasonable agreement among personality researchers that a five-factor organization—Conscientiousness, Openness to Experience, Emotional Stability, Agreeableness, and Extraversion—describes personality traits at the broadest level of abstraction. The five-factor structure (often referred to as the *Big Five*) has also been identified in middle childhood and early adolescence (John, Caspi, Robins, Moffitt, & Stouthamer-Loeber, 1994; Soto, John, Gosling, & Potter, 2008), and both theoretical arguments and a limited body of empirical evidence have linked the Big Five factors to specific temperament traits (De Pauw & Mervielde, 2010; Evans & Rothbart, 2007).

Of particular relevance to academic performance, *effortful control*, the temperament factor conceptualized by Rothbart and colleagues as "the ability to inhibit a dominant response to perform a subdominant response, to detect errors, and to engage in planning ... a major form of self-regulation... children's ability to control reactions to stress, maintain focused attention, and interpret mental states in themselves and others" (Rothbart & Rueda, 2005, p. 169), is closely related, both conceptually and empirically, to Big Five Conscientiousness (Rothbart, Ahadi, & Evans, 2000). In contrast to reactive (i.e., automatic, involuntary) dimensions of temperament (e.g., surgency, negative affectivity, behavioral inhibition), effortful control is intentional and voluntary. Indeed, the core function of effortful control seems to be goal-directed self-regulation of more reactive behavioral, attentional, and affective processes (Eisenberg, Smith, Sadovsky, & Spinrad, 2004). Generally not observed by caregivers until the toddler and preschool years, effortful control becomes more coherent (i.e., stable across situation and time) throughout early development (Kochanska & Knaack, 2003) and, generally, more pronounced throughout childhood and beyond

(Rothbart, 2007). Because effortful control allows for flexible and deliberate inhibition over reactive tendencies, it is not surprising that effortful control predicts a range of positive developmental outcomes, including compliance, morality and conscience, and social competence (see Eisenberg et al., 2004, for a review).

The most commonly measured facets of effortful control include the ability to control attention, inhibit impulses, and initiate subdominant actions in flexible and adaptive ways (Rothbart, Sheese, & Posner, 2007). Recent theorizing by leaders in effortful control research suggests that these competencies depend on a well-functioning executive attention network, whose function is to monitor and resolve conflicts between other brain networks (Rothbart & Rueda, 2005). Laboratory research studies employing a variety of so-called *executive function* tasks requiring control of attention and inhibition of prepotent impulses, and/or working memory, demonstrate reliable associations between task performance and caregiver ratings of effortful control (Duckworth & Kern, 2011), and independent measures of these two constructs demonstrate similar developmental trajectories, increasing monotonically through childhood (Best & Miller, 2010). Nevertheless, effortful control and executive function are not identical, interchangeable constructs: Correlations between effortful control and executive function are quite modest in magnitude (Duckworth & Kern, 2011), working memory is a facet of the latter but not the former (Liew, 2012), and each provides independent predictive validity for academic outcomes (Blair & Razza, 2007).

Historical Interest in Temperament and Academic Performance

The notion that temperament in general, and aspects of effortful control in particular, play an important role in the classroom is not new. In a series of lectures addressed to Boston schoolteachers, William James (1899), opined that in "schoolroom work" there is inevitably "a large mass of material that must be dull and unexciting" (pp. 104–105). Furthermore, "there is unquestionably a great native variety among individuals in the type of their attention. Some of us are naturally scatter-brained, and others follow easily a train of connected thoughts without temptation to swerve aside to other subjects" (p. 112). It follows, James argued, that a dispositional advantage in the capacity for sustained attention is tremendously beneficial in the classroom: "Our acts of voluntary attention, brief and fitful as they are, are nevertheless momentous and critical, determining us, as they do, to higher or lower destinies. The exercise of voluntary attention in the schoolroom must therefore be counted one of the most important points of training that takes place there" (p. 189).

Ironically, pioneers of intelligence testing were among the first to recognize the importance of self-regulation to academic performance. Alfred Binet (Binet & Simon, 1916), architect of the first modern intelligence test, noted that performance in school

> admits of other things than intelligence; to succeed in his studies, one must have qualities which depend especially on attention, will, and character; for example a certain docility, a regularity of habits, and especially continuity of effort. A child, even if intelligent, will learn little in class if he never listens, if he spends his time in playing tricks, in giggling, in playing truant. (p. 254)

At about the same time, Charles Spearman, best known for his work on the factor structure of intelligence, and his student Edward Webb undertook studies of "character" because of "the urgency of its practical application to all the business of life" (Spearman, 1927; Webb, 1915, p. 1). Spearman and Webb applied an early form of factor analysis to teacher ratings of several samples of male students, concluding that many positive aspects of character form a positive manifold, loading on a single factor that Spearman and Webb chose to call "persistence of motives," meaning "consistency of action resulting from deliberate volition, or will." They dubbed the factor *w* for will and emphasized its independence from *g*, the factor for general intelligence (Webb, 1915, p. 60).

David Wechsler (1943), who several decades later helped usher intelligence testing into widespread clinical and educational practice, made similar observations about the unfortunate neglect of "non-intellective" factors that, in conjunction with general intelligence, determine intelligent behavior. In reviewing his own extensive data, Wechsler (1950) came to two conclusions:

> First, that factors other than intellectual contribute to achievement in areas where, as in the case of learning, intellectual factors have until recently been considered uniquely determinate, and, second, that these other factors have to do with functions and abilities hitherto considered traits of personality. Among those partially identified so far are factors relating primarily to the conative functions like *drive, persistence, will, and perseverance*, or in some instances, to aspects of temperament that pertain to *interests and achievement*. (p. 81, emphasis added)

Despite exhortations from prominent figures in the intelligence literature, the study of temperament and its role in academic achievement languished for much of the 20th century. Happily, there has been a renaissance of theoretical and empirical interest in the role of temperament and personality in determining success in and beyond school (Borghans, Duckworth, Heckman, & ter Weel, 2008; Duckworth & Seligman, 2005; Roberts, Kuncel, Shiner, Caspi, & Goldberg, 2007).

Dimensions of Academic Performance

Academic performance has at least three distinct dimensions: school readiness, academic achievement, and educational attainment.[1] *School readiness* refers to preparation for success in kindergarten and has been used, broadly, to encompass the physical, social, emotional, and cognitive resources that young children require to thrive in their first years of formal schooling. *Academic achievement* refers to mastery of material presented in school and is typically measured by course grades or standardized achievement test scores. *Educational attainment* refers to the quantity of formal education completed (e.g., graduation from high school, cumulative years of education). Put simply, readiness refers to *how prepared* a child is to embark upon the challenge of formal education, achievement refers to *how well* a student performs when in school, and attainment refers to *how much* education a student ultimately attains. Both the quantity and quality of formal education predict long-term outcomes. For instance, years of schooling and graduation from high school both predict earnings, employment, and health in adulthood (Hanushek & Woessmann, 2008; Sum et al., 2007). Likewise, standardized achievement tests and teacher-assigned course grades predict the same outcomes (Currie & Thomas, 2001; Kuncel, Hezlett, & Ones, 2004; Sackett, Borneman, & Connelly, 2008).

School Readiness

The transition to formal schooling, typically in kindergarten for U.S. schoolchildren, marks a dramatic change in the way young children spend time, expectations for self-regulation and compliance with authority, and consequences for their meeting these expectations. There is now considerable evidence that aspects of effortful control, more so than other temperament traits, set children up for success during this transition. Martin (1989) was among the first to demonstrate, in a series of small-sample studies, that teacher and parent ratings of early childhood persistence, (low) distractibility, and (low) activity prospectively predict both course grades and standardized achievement test scores in the first years of primary school. More recently, in a sample of preschool children from low-income homes, parent and teacher ratings of effortful control accounted for unique variance in standardized achievement test scores in kindergarten, even after researchers controlled for general intelligence (Blair & Razza, 2007). In a cross-sectional study of a comparable sample of low-income preschoolers, ratings of children's resilience, including capacity for self-control and adaptive engagement with their environment, based on structured interviews with preschool teachers, were associated with performance on individually administered tests of children's knowledge of colors, letters, numbers, sizes, comparisons, and shapes (Munis, Greenfield, Henderson, & George, 2007). Similarly, teacher and parent ratings of kindergartners' effortful control predicted performance on standardized achievement tests 6 months later, and this association held when researchers controlled for both verbal intelligence and family socioeconomic status (Valiente, Lemery-Chalfant, Swanson, & Reiser, 2010). Likewise, performance at the start of kindergarten on the Head-Toes-Knees-Shoulders (HTKS) task, which requires young children to perform the opposite of a dominant response (e.g., to touch their heads when the experimenter says "Touch your toes") (Ponitz et al., 2008), correlates positively with parent ratings of attentional focusing and inhibitory control, and predicts higher levels of academic achievement in the spring, as well as better teacher-rated classroom self-regulation (McClelland et al., 2007).

Suggestive evidence points to effortful control as being more critical than social competence for success in the classroom. For instance, in a representative sample of Baltimore first graders, teacher ratings of attention span–restlessness, but not cooperation–compliance, predicted both course grades and standardized achievement test scores 4 years later (Alexander, Entwisle, & Dauber, 1993). Likewise, in a longitudinal study of French children, preschool teacher ratings of children's attention, but not conduct problems, unsociability, or hyperactivity, independently predicted performance on reading tasks in first grade (Giannopulu, Escolano, Cusin, Citeau, & Dellatolas, 2008). Similarly, Schoen and Nagle (1994) found that kindergarten children rated by their teachers as showing superior attention span and persistence on learning tasks scored higher on a standardized test of school readiness, whereas teacher ratings of adaptability in novel social situations and emotional intensity did not incrementally predict school readiness. Perhaps most definitively, a meta-analysis by Duncan and colleagues (2007) in which effects from six large, longitudinal datasets were synthesized, determined that attention skills at the beginning of formal schooling, measured variously by task and questionnaire measures, prospectively predicted math and reading achievement test scores years later, even when researchers controlled for math and reading skills at school entry, but there was no evidence for the predictive validity of either externalizing or internalizing behaviors.

Course Grades in Primary, Secondary, and Postsecondary Education

Once children have transitioned to primary school, traits conceptually related to effortful control continue to predict academic achievement, particularly as assessed by higher report card grades. Poropat (2009) completed a definitive meta-analysis of Big Five personality factors and course grades, in which cumulative sample sizes ranged to over 70,000. As shown in Figure 30.1, in primary school, all five personality factors are related to report card grades, though the cross-sectional associations between course grades and the personality factors of Emotional Stability and Extraversion are markedly weaker than those between course grades and Conscientiousness, Openness to Experience, and Agreeableness.

As children progress through secondary and postsecondary education, associations between individual differences and course grades markedly diminish, with the notable exception of Conscientiousness, whose association with course grades incrementally *increases* as students progress to higher levels of education. Interestingly, associations between course grades and cognitive ability decline markedly over the same period, a pattern consistent with the speculation of intelligence researchers (e.g., Jensen, 1980) that diminishing predictive validity estimates reflect increasing restriction on range. If, indeed, students who do poorly in their courses selectively drop out of research samples and, as a consequence, the traits that determine course grade performance are progressively restricted in terms of variance in the population, then range-corrected associations between course grades and Conscientiousness, which do not shrink, are in fact stronger at more advanced levels of education than observed correlations suggest.

Why might traits related to Conscientiousness and effortful control matter more and more to earning high marks from teachers as students progress through the formal education system? One plausible explanation is that the task demands of formal schooling change as students mature. Compared to primary school students, older students are expected to spend more hours studying and completing homework outside the classroom, to regulate their attention indepen-

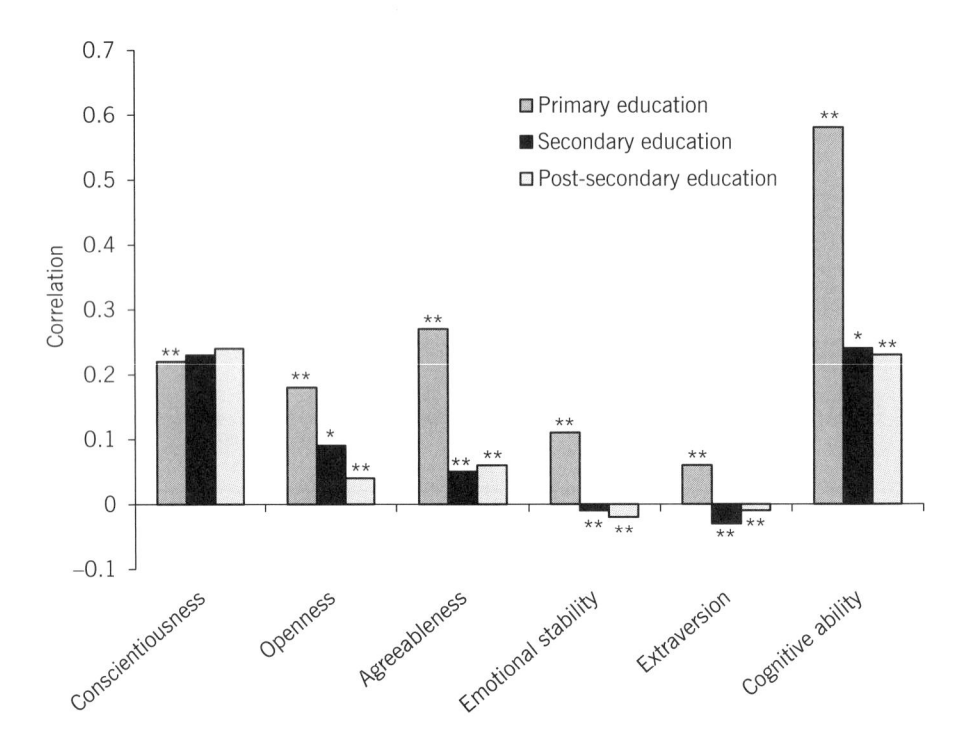

FIGURE 30.1. Associations between Big Five personality factors and course grades by level of education. Associations are reported in a meta-analysis by Poropat (2009). Estimated correlations with Big Five personality factors control for cognitive ability and are corrected for scale reliability.

dently while in the classroom, and to otherwise take responsibility for their learning with decreasing support from teachers (Zimmerman, 2002).

A handful of prospective, longitudinal studies have confirmed the predictive validity of more narrowly defined temperament and personality traits for later course grades, while controlling for baseline course grades. In general, these prospective studies support the conclusions of more numerous, less rigorously controlled studies. For instance, effortful control predicted report card grades when controlling for baseline grades in a sample of Chinese primary school children (Zhou, Main, & Wang, 2010). Similarly, self-control predicted final report card grades, when researchers controlled for first marking period grades, as well as general intelligence, in a sample of American middle school students (Duckworth & Seligman, 2005). Likewise, within-individual changes in self-control predicted subsequent within-individual changes in report card grades over a 4-year period in a different sample of American middle school students (Duckworth, Tsukayama, & May, 2010).

Overlap—and Divergence— between Course Grades and Standardized Achievement Tests

In addition to course grades, effortful control predicts performance on standardized achievement tests (SATs). For instance, in a sample of over 1,000 children from 55 schools, teacher ratings of inattention at the beginning of the fourth grade predicted SAT scores at the end of the school year (Finn, Pannozzo, & Voelkl, 1995). Even more impressive because more than a decade separated the measurement of temperament and test performance, the number of seconds 4-year old children delayed gratification in order to receive a preferred treat predicted their performance on the SAT college admission test more than a decade later (Mischel, Shoda, & Rodriguez, 1989). In a separate sample of older children, adaptive attentional strategies (e.g., not staring at the treat, which, if consumed immediately, forfeits the preferred but delayed treat) had a direct, positive effect on delay behavior, underscoring the importance of attention regulation to voluntary regulation of behavior in the presence of temptations (Rodriguez, Mischel, & Shoda, 1989).

Course grades and standardized test scores are generally highly correlated (Willingham, Pollack, & Lewis, 2002), but the former may be more sensitive to individual differences in traits related to effortful control. In two longitudinal, prospective studies of middle school students, IQ predicted changes in standardized achievement test scores over time better than did self-control, whereas self-control predicted changes in report card grades over time better than did IQ (Duckworth, Quinn, & Tsukayama, 2012). These findings are consistent with those of Willingham and colleagues (2002), who examined data from N = 8,454 high school seniors in the National Education Longitudinal Study (NELS). Conscientious behaviors, including attending class regularly and promptly, participating in class activities, completing work on time, and avoiding drug and gang activity, were more strongly associated with course grades than with SAT scores. Likewise, Oliver, Guerin, and Gottfried (2007) found that parent- and self-report ratings of distractibility and persistence at age 16 predicted high school and college course grades, but not SAT test scores, and several cross-sectional studies of college students have shown that Big Five Conscientiousness is more strongly associated with grade point average (GPA) than with SAT scores (Conard, 2005; Noftle & Robins, 2007; Wolfe & Johnson, 1995).

Interestingly, Bowen, Chingos, and McPherson (2009) found that cumulative high school GPA predicts class rank and successful graduation dramatically better than do SAT/American College Testing (ACT) scores. In an analysis of about 80,000 University of California students followed over 4 years, Geiser and Santelices (2007) reached the same conclusion. Bowen and colleagues have speculated that aspects of Conscientiousness seem *differentially* essential to earning strong course grades because of what is required of students to earn them:

> [High school grades] reveal qualities of motivation and perseverance—as well as the presence of good study habits and time management skills. . . . Getting good grades in high school, however demanding (or not) the high school, is evidence that a student consistently met a standard of performance. (p. 124)

Indeed, it seems likely that effortful control enables students to regulate impulses and urges that conflict with teacher-endorsed goals and standard.

Graduation from High School

Whereas course grades and SATs reflect the *quality* of academic performance, the *quantity* of education students obtain is also an important predictor of later life outcomes. Unfortunately, about 1 in 4 American students drops out of formal schooling before receiving a high school diploma (Heckman & LaFontaine, 2007). Research on the General Educational Development (GED) testing program suggests that many high school dropouts are sufficiently intelligent to graduate with their classmates, and that aspects of temperament may contribute to their failure to complete high school training. The GED was originally designed to certify veterans who interrupted their high school education to serve in World War II. Since its inception, the GED has evolved into a second-chance program for high school dropouts to certify they have mastered the same skills and knowledge as typical high school graduates. GED recipients have the same measured intelligence as high school graduates who do not attend college, but when measured ability is controlled for, GED recipients have lower hourly wages and annual earnings, and attain fewer years of education, suggesting they may "lack the abilities to think ahead, to persist in tasks, or to adapt to their environments (Heckman & Rubinstein, 2001, p. 146). Indeed, several prospective studies have found that personality traits related to Big Five Conscientiousness (e.g., self-control, distractibility) and Big Five Neuroticism (e.g., external locus of control) predict successful graduation from high school (Bowman & Matthews, 1960; Gough, 1964; Hathaway, Reynolds, & Monachesi, 1969; Janosz, LeBlanc, Boulerice, & Tremblay, 1997; Kelly & Veldman, 1964; Whisenton & Lorre, 1970).

Only a handful of longitudinal studies has examined the predictive validity of temperament traits measured very early in life for graduation from high school. Overall, these studies have identified either attentional control or (lack of) aggression as predictors of high school graduation. Duncan and Magnuson (2011) found that parent ratings of persistent behavior problems, but not persistent attention problems, measured across middle childhood uniquely predicted high school completion and college attendance. Likewise, Fergusson and Horwood (1998) found that teacher and parent ratings of conduct problems at age 8 (inversely) predicted high school completion at age 18. Conversely, Vitaro, Brendgen, Larose, and Tremblay (2005) examined individuals in a population-based sample of Quebec children (N = 4,340) and found that kindergarten teacher ratings of hyperactivity–inattention (inversely) predicted completion of high school *better* than did aggressiveness–opposition.

Cumulative Lifetime Years of Education

While related, the number of years an individual pursues formal schooling and whether he or she graduates from high school are distinct outcomes. In the United States, for example, about 68% of students accumulate additional years of schooling beyond high school. Two published studies using large, representative samples have examined cross-sectional relationships between Big Five factors and years of education. Goldberg, Sweeney, Merenda, and Hughes (1998) found in a representative sample (N = 3,629) of American working adults ages 18–75 that Openness to Experience (r = .31) was most strongly associated with years of education, whereas associations with Conscientiousness (r = .12), Agreeableness (r = –.08), Extraversion (r = –.04), and Neuroticism (r = –.03) were more modest. Van Eijck and de Graaf (2004) reported a similar pattern of associations in a nationally representative sample (N = 2,029) of Dutch adults ages 18–70. Specifically, when controlling for gender, age, father's education, mother's education, and father's occupational status, years of schooling was most strongly associated with Openness to Experience (β = .14). Associations with Emotional Stability (β = .09), Extraversion (β = –.07), Agreeableness (β = –.07) and Conscientiousness (β = .05) were more modest.

Unfortunately, neither Goldberg and colleagues (1998) nor Van Eijck and de Graaf (2004) controlled for cognitive ability in their analyses. Because Openness to Experience is the only Big Five factor with moderate associations with general intelligence (r = .33 in a meta-analysis; Ackerman & Heggestad, 1997), and intelligence is itself robustly associated with years of education (r = .5, Neisser et al., 1996), unadjusted associations between Openness to Experience and years of education in these studies may have been confounded by associations with cognitive ability. For this chapter, therefore, we conducted a cross-sectional analysis of data collected in the Health and Retirement Study. Specifically, we used a structural equation model to assess associations between latent Big Five personality factors and years of education. Among American adults (N = 9,646) from this nationally representative sample, Openness to Experience (β = .16, p < .001) was the only personality trait positively correlated with years of education when Big Five personality factors and cognitive ability, as well as gender, ethnicity, and age, were entered as predictors in the same model.

In summary, traits related to Big Five Openness to Experience seem particularly important in determining how many years individuals spend in school over their lifetimes but, as illustrated in Figure 30.1, seem to play a diminishing role in how well students meet their course requirements as they progress through school. We suggest that enjoyment of learning for its own sake may get students to show up to school but it does not mean that students execute all of the tasks necessary to achieve high grades in those courses. Consistent with this supposition, Openness to Experience is the best Big Five predictor of school attendance among middle and high school students (Lounsbury, Steel, Loveland, & Gibson, 2004). Moreover, a longitudinal study of high school students showed that when researchers controlled for cognitive ability, students' intrinsic motivation while studying a particular academic subject predicted the difficulty level of courses in that subject over 4 years of high school (Wong & Csikszentmihalyi, 1991) but *not* course grades in that subject. In the same study, Conscientiousness, measured using a self-report questionnaire, did not consistently predict course difficulty, but it was the best personality predictor of course grades.

Mediation: Quality-Adjusted Learning Hours

As summarized in this chapter, a growing body of empirical evidence has established the relevance of temperament traits for various academic outcomes. Most notably, effortful control and its facets have emerged as the most robust predictors of the broadest range of academic outcomes, including school readiness; course grades in primary, secondary, and postsecondary school; and graduation from high school. Why? Aristotle's observation of the learning process offers one clue: "The roots of education are bitter, but the fruit is sweet." Indeed, even gifted and talented American high school students dislike homework and studying (Wong & Csikszentmihalyi, 1991). More generally, the tasks requirements of formal schooling—including not only homework and independent studying but also paying attention to the teacher rather than joking with classmates, practicing skills repeatedly to the point of fluency, showing up to school rather than playing hooky—yield long-term rewards at the expense of short-term comfort and pleasure. Likewise, the social nature of the formal classroom setting suggests that relationships with peers and teachers affect the quality of a student's learning experience, and maintaining positive social relationships requires suppression of impulses (the impulse to tell off a teacher or classmate in a moment of anger, the impulse to interrupt a fellow classmate in discussion, etc.) whose discharge may provide immediate relief but lead to long-term regret.

Figure 30.2 summarizes our theoretical model relating effortful control to course grades at all levels of schooling. We suggest that the proximal causal variable linking effortful control to course grades is *quality-adjusted learning hours* (QALH), a variable that encompasses both the quality and quantity of learning experiences.[2] Our model is similar to that proposed by Eisenberg,

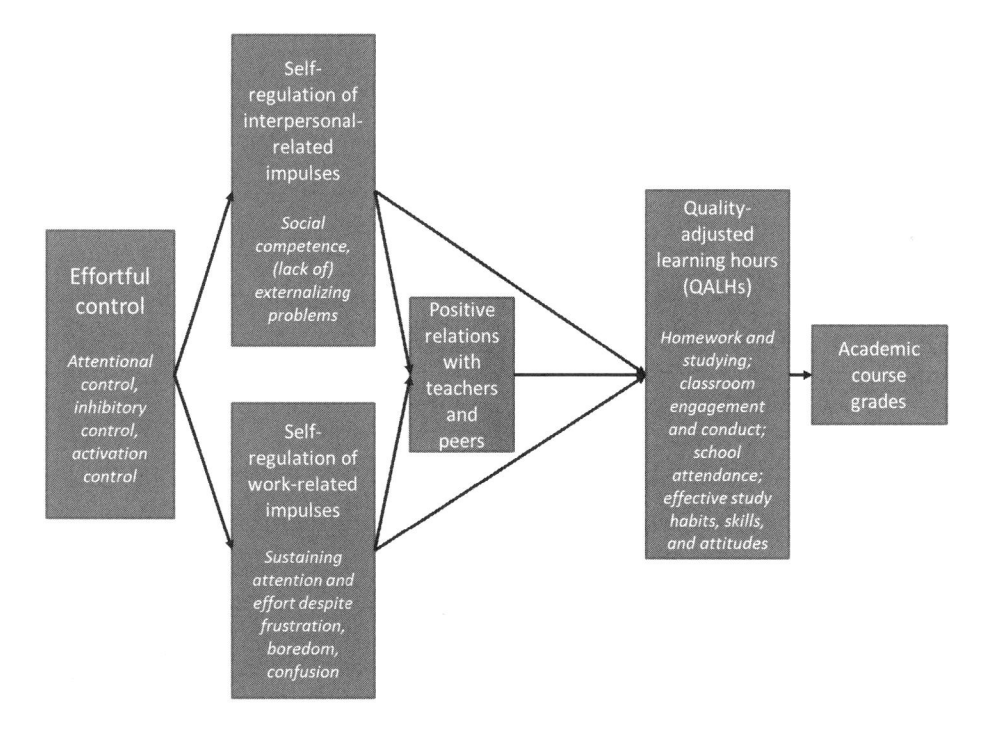

FIGURE 30.2. Theoretical model relating effortful control to academic course grades.

Valiente, and Eggum (2010), which highlights the importance of social competence, and also Zimmerman and Kitsantas (2005), which places special emphasis on diverse self-regulatory strategies that optimize performance in preparation, execution, and later reflection of learning opportunities. In the interest of simplicity, our model omits grade level, gender, and other demographic variables, in addition to general intelligence, school motivation, and other individual differences that are no doubt important to school achievement. Likewise, we have omitted recursive pathways, though we recognize that virtuous and vicious cycles are almost certainly at play in determining trajectories of course grades for students from kindergarten to college (Tsukayama, 2012; see also Houts, Caspi, Pianta, Arseneault, & Moffitt, 2010). Finally, we have not specified the relative weights of causal pathways, nor have we indicated how the relative importance of causal antecedents might vary with student, teacher, or school characteristics.

No single investigation has tested all of the proposed relationships in Figure 30.2. Nevertheless, extant empirical evidence is consistent with our suppositions. For instance, Tsukayama, Duckworth, and Kim (2011) found that trait-level self-control in middle school students is associated with the regulation of both interpersonal-related and work-related impulses. In a separate sample of middle school students, Duckworth and colleagues (2012) used a cross-lagged model to establish that a composite measure of control over both interpersonal-related and work-related impulses predicted changes in course grades from fall to spring, and that changes in course grades were mediated by midyear changes in homework completion and classroom behavior. In a sample of primary school children, Valiente, Lemery-Chalfant, Swanson, and Reiser (2008) found that teacher–child relationships, social competence, and classroom participation partially mediated the prospective association between effortful control and change in GPA from the beginning to the end of the school year. Similarly, in a 6-year longitudinal study, Valiente and colleagues (2011) found that social functioning (e.g., social competence and lower levels of externalizing problems) fully mediated the relationship between effortful control at 73 months and report card grades at 12 years. In a sample of Chinese primary school children, Zhou, Main, and Wang (2010) showed that effortful control predicted GPA in fifth and sixth grade, controlling for baseline GPA, and that social competence mediated this relationship. Veenstra, Lindenberg, Tinga, and Ormel (2010) found that 11-year-old children who were lower in self-control were more likely to be persistently truant from school, an association mediated by poor social bonds with teachers, parents, and peers. Rudasill and Rimm-Kaufman (2009) found that effortful control measured at 54 months in the National Institute of Child Health and Human Development (NICHD) Study of Early Child Care and Youth Development (SECCYD) sample predicted teacher–child relationship quality in first grade. In a sample of 3- to 5-year-olds from low-income backgrounds, Silva and colleagues (2011) showed that teacher- and parent-reported effortful control in the fall predicted school liking in the spring, and that this relationship was mediated by teacher–child relationship quality. Finally, Birch and Ladd (1997) have shown in cross-sectional analyses that teacher–child relationship quality in kindergarten is associated with positive school engagement and academic performance. Among college students, there is evidence that effective study habits (e.g., frequency of studying sessions, review of material) and attitudes (e.g., a positive attitude toward education), which are associated with Big Five Conscientiousness, predict college grades over and above college admissions tests (Credé & Kuncel, 2008). As well, the salutary, causal role of studying on college GPA has been confirmed in quasi-experimental analyses that minimize the possibility of third-variable confounds (Stinebrickner & Stinebrickner, 2007).

School-Based Interventions

The salutary effects of effortful control, and evidence that rank-order and mean-level change are possible, raise the question: What can schools and teachers do to encourage its development? Several promising advances in this direction are worth highlighting and, collectively, provide convincing evidence for the benefits of supportive, thoughtfully designed educational environments.

Three multifaceted preschool curricula have demonstrated salutary effects on effortful control and school readiness in random-assignment studies. The oldest of these, the Montessori program, is an educational approach developed over a century ago, whose implementation, while somewhat variable across schools, characteristically features multiage classrooms, student-chosen learning activities carried out with minimal instruction from teachers, and long periods of time designated for uninterrupted pursuit of these activities. Children who attend a Montessori school have been shown to perform better on tasks of executive function and on achievement tests than children who lost the lottery to go to the Montessori and therefore were at other schools (Lillard & Else-Quest, 2006). More recently, *Tools of the Mind*, a Vygotskian preschool and early primary school program, has been shown in random-assignment studies to improve performance on executive function tasks and classroom behavior (Barnett et al., 2008; Diamond, Barnett, Thomas, & Munro, 2007). Key principles of the Tools of the Mind curriculum include scaffolding student development from regulation-by-others to self-regulation, mental tools (i.e., strategies) to help children gain control of their behavior, reflective and metacognitive thinking, practice of self-regulation via developmentally appropriate games and activities, and increasingly complex and extended social imaginary play (Bodrova & Leong, 2007). Finally, a recent cluster-randomized trial showed that the *Chicago School Readiness Project*, which provides preschool teachers with training in a variety of strategies for managing classrooms effectively and encouraging children to regulate their behavior, improves effortful control in low-income children, and that these improvements partially mediate gains in school readiness (Raver et al., 2011).

Econometric analyses suggest that early investment in children should be followed by complementary investment later in development, in order to maximize long-term benefits to children and to society (Heckman, 2006). Happily, social and emotional learning (SEL) programs, typically designed for implementation in primary school but sometimes targeting older children, have been shown to improve academic course grades ($d = 0.33$) and standardized achievement tests scores ($d = 0.27$) in a meta-analysis of controlled studies involving over 270,000 children in kindergarten through college (Durlak, Weissberg, Dymnicki, Taylor, & Schellinger, 2011).

An excellent exemplar of the SEL approach, the *Promoting Alternative Thinking Strategies* (PATHS) curriculum, teaches self-control, emotional awareness, and social problem-solving skills (Bierman et al., 2010). The PATHS curriculum is multifaceted, with an explicit commitment to fostering skills that support each other. For instance, emotional awareness (e.g., recognizing the internal and external cues of affect) is understood as essential to social problem solving (e.g., sustaining friendships, peacefully resolving conflicts with classmates). Teachers trained to deliver the PATHS curriculum guide students through skills-building activities and also reinforce the same lessons throughout the school day. A recent random-assignment, longitudinal study demonstrated that the PATHS curriculum reduces teacher and peer ratings of aggression, improves teacher and peer ratings of prosocial behavior, and improves teacher ratings of academic engagement (Bierman et al., 2010). There is some evidence that improvements in inhibitory control partially mediate the benefits of PATHS on behavioral outcomes (Riggs, Greenberg, Kusche, & Pentz, 2006). Likewise, a randomized controlled trial of a preschool version of PATHS showed that the intervention improved both performance on an executive function task and experimenter ratings of children's capacity to sustain attention during the testing session, and these gains partially mediated benefits of the intervention on school readiness (Bierman, Nix, Greenberg, Blair, & Domitrovich, 2008).

It is important to note that not all implementations of SEL programming are successful: Seven SEL programs, including PATHS, studied in a multisite, longitudinal, random-assignment study were not found to improve social and emotional competence, behavior, or academic achievement outcomes among primary school students when considered together or individually by program (Social and Character Development Research Consortium, 2010). Thus, additional research is needed to elucidate moderating factors that influence the efficacy of SEL programs, including baseline characteristics of students, teachers, and schools, as well as implementation integrity and dosage.

Beyond direct intervention, emotional support in the classroom has been shown to protect children with low effortful control from poor academic outcomes. For instance, children identified as being at risk, based on demographic characteristics and prior attention and behavior problems, who are placed in warm, relaxed, and well-managed first-grade classrooms develop positive relationships with their teachers and perform as well on standardized achievement tests as their low-risk peers (Hamre & Pianta, 2005). Likewise, classroom emotional support moderates the association between poor attention regulation just before school entry and achievement test scores in third grade: Individual differences in attentional control influence achievement more in classrooms with lower emotional support (Rudasill, Gallagher, & White, 2010). A similar study in which effortful control was measured using an executive function task (tracing a figure as slowly and accurately as possible) showed that positive student–teacher relationships served as a compensatory factor, such that children with low task accuracy performed as well as their counterparts if paired with a positive and supportive teacher (Liew, Chen, & Hughes, 2010). Therefore, professional development opportunities that help teachers create generally positive classroom environments should yield downstream benefits for their students (Jennings & Greenberg, 2009; Zins, Elias, & Greenberg, 2007).

More targeted intervention efforts delivered to individual children can also improve aspects of effortful control. For instance, Rueda, Rothbart, McCandliss, Saccomanno, and Posner (2005) designed a set of computer exercises to train attention in children between 4 and 6 years of age. Children in the intervention group improved in performance on computer tasks of attention relative to children who instead watched interactive videos for a comparable amount of time. Similarly, Stevens, Fanning, Coch, Sanders, and Neville (2008) designed a 6-week computerized intervention and showed that it can improve selective auditory attention (i.e., the ability to attend to a target auditory signal in the face of an irrelevant, distracting auditory signal). Tominey and McClelland (2011) developed physical games to improve self-regulation in preschool children and have demonstrated that such exercises can improve performance on the HTKS self-regulation task for children who, at baseline, perform poorly on the HTKS.

Interventions that teach children metacognitive strategies, such as goal setting and planning, can also improve self-regulatory competence and, in turn, academic outcomes. The technique of mental contrasting with implementation intentions (MCII), for example, first developed as a self-regulatory strategy for adults, has also been shown to help children and adolescents. For instance, in a random-assignment study of high school students preparing for college entrance examinations, students were instructed to contrast mentally the positive benefits of studying (e.g., "I'll have a better chance of getting into my top-choice college") with obstacles that stood in the way of this study goal (e.g., "My little sister bothers me when I try to study"), then to make a plan to obviate these obstacles (e.g., "If my little sister bothers me, then I will study in my bedroom with the door closed") (Duckworth, Grant, Loew, Oettingen, & Gollwitzer, 2011). Compared to students in a placebo-control condition who wrote a practice essay for the college entrance exam, students who learned MCII completed over 60% more questions in study materials provided to students in both conditions. Likewise, in a random-assignment study at an urban middle school, fifth-grade students taught MCII improved their report card grades and school attendance relative to students in a placebo-control condition (Duckworth, Gollwitzer, Kirby, & Oettingen, 2012). Children as young as preschool age demonstrate superior self-control when using plans to avoid distraction and temptation (Mischel & Patterson, 1976, 1978; Patterson & Mischel, 1975, 1976), suggesting that the metacognitive strategy of planning might be introduced to children in the earliest years of formal education.

Any review of school-based interventions to foster positive dimensions of temperament would be incomplete without mention of exercise and play. Aerobic exercise has been shown to improve attention and performance on SATs in preadolescent children (Hillman et al., 2009). The robust findings linking physical activity to attention and other aspects of self-control suggest that eliminating gym class to make room for formal academic instruction may, paradoxically, reduce self-control (Hillman, Erickson, & Kramer, 2008). Play, and in particular, pretend (i.e., imaginary) play with others facilitates the development of a wide array of self-regulation skills (Berk, Mann, & Ogan, 2006; Saltz, Dixon, & Johnson, 1977; D. G. Singer & J. L. Singer, 1990; J. L. Singer & D. G. Singer, 2006). Like gym class, recess is often considered to be of secondary importance to academic objectives, but reducing opportunities for children to make up stories, exercise their imaginations and their bodies, and resolve conflicts without help from adults may ultimately impair the normative development of effortful control (Panksepp, 2007).

Directions for Future Research

Early psychologists speculated that differences in temperament can help or hinder performance in—and beyond—the classroom. Extant empirical evidence supports this commonsense conjecture, pointing in particular to aspects of effortful control as supportive of children's educational attainment and achievement. Nevertheless, further investigation is needed to establish which facets of effortful control are most important to academic success. Moreover, longitudinal studies in which likely confounds (e.g., baseline academic performance and socioeconomic status) are precisely measured and statistically controlled are still the exception rather than the rule. Finally, additional multivariate research is needed to confirm that effortful control, rather than some other correlated dimension of temperament, is indeed causally influencing school performance.

In parallel to increasingly fecund research literature on temperament and academic outcomes, public interest in dimensions of human individuality other than general intelligence is growing. An editorial in the *New York Times* suggested that, as a society, we devote more resources to "the moral and psychological traits that are at the heart of actual success" (Brooks, 2006). The positive effects of direct interventions, as well as supportive classrooms and teachers, suggest that such investment should indeed pay considerable societal dividends, not only by improving academic outcomes overall but also by reducing the achievement gap separating disadvantaged children from their wealthier counterparts, who tend to be better at delaying gratification (Evans & Rosenbaum, 2008) and demonstrating superior selective attention (Stevens, Lauinger, & Neville, 2009).

In what direction should research on temperament and academic performance proceed? Over a century ago, addressing local schoolteachers, William James (1899) observed that the science of psychology and the art of education are complementary: "The teacher's attitude toward the child, being concrete and ethical, is positively opposed to the psychological observer's, which is abstract and analytic" (p. 13). Accordingly, we suggest that psychologists collaborate more intimately with educators—sharing insights, debating intuitions, thinking creatively and drawing from respective knowledge bases— to develop multifaceted interventions aimed at durably changing behavior and, in turn, objectively measuring academic outcomes. In such translational research studies, theoretically predicted mechanisms of change (e.g., homework completion, school attendance, classroom participation) and moderators (e.g., baseline temperament, school quality, demographic factors) should be precisely assessed over time, so that we can begin to fill in details of the undoubtedly complex causal story relating temperament to outcomes. In tandem, short-term, controlled field and laboratory experiments should be undertaken, providing a less expensive, more flexible complement to large-scale intervention research and a means of efficiently investigating the "active ingredients" of behavior change. In summary, we see the royal road to progress as one that is inherently interdisciplinary, rife with challenges, and open to as yet unimagined possibilities.

Notes

1. Prosocial behavior, including kindness and consideration of others, and compliance with classroom rules, has long been an explicit goal of formal education, particularly in primary school (Dewey, 1909; Franklin, 1747), and, indeed, prosocial classroom behavior predicts life outcomes even when researchers control for course

grades and standardized achievement tests (Segal, in press). However, considering prosocial behavior as an outcome raises concerns about tautology (i.e., that ratings of temperament based in part on observed behavior in the classroom are then used to predict an outcome based on the same criteria). Thus, our narrow focus in this review is the empirical evidence linking aspects of temperament to school readiness, academic achievement, and educational attainment.

2. Our conception of QALH was inspired by the analogous construct in the public health literature, quality-adjusted life years (QALY).

Further Reading

Diamond, A. (2010). The evidence base for improving school outcomes by addressing the whole child and by addressing skills and attitudes, not just content. *Early Education and Development, 21,* 780–793.

Liew, J. (2012). Effortful control, executive functions, and education: Bringing self-regulatory and social-emotional competencies to the table. *Child Development Perspectives, 6,* 105–111.

Poropat, A. E. (2009). A meta-analysis of the five-factor model of personality and academic performance. *Psychological Bulletin, 135,* 322–338.

References

Ackerman, P. L., & Heggestad, E. D. (1997). Intelligence, personality, and interests: Evidence for overlapping traits. *Psychological Bulletin, 121,* 219–245.

Alexander, K. L., Entwisle, D. R., & Dauber, S. L. (1993). First-grade classroom behavior: Its short- and long-term consequences for school performance. *Child Development, 64,* 801–814.

Barnett, W. S., Jung, K., Yarosz, D. J., Thomas, J., Hornbeck, A., Stechuk, R., et al. (2008). Educational effects of the Tools of the Mind curriculum: A randomized trial. *Early Childhood Research Quarterly, 23,* 299–313.

Berk, L. E., Mann, T. D., & Ogan, A. T. (2006). *Make-believe play: Wellspring for development of self-regulation.* New York: Oxford University Press.

Best, J. R., & Miller, P. H. (2010). A developmental perspective on executive function. *Child Development, 81,* 1641–1660.

Bierman, K. L., Coie, J. D., Dodge, K. A., Greenberg, M. T., Lochman, J. E., McMahon, R. J., et al.(2010). The effects of a multiyear universal social–emotional learning program: The role of student and school characteristics. *Journal of Consulting and Clinical Psychology, 78,* 156–168.

Bierman, L. E., Nix, R. L., Greenberg, M. T., Blair, C., & Domitrovich, C. E. (2008). Executive functions and school readiness intervention: Impact, moderation, and mediation in the Head Start REDI program. *Development and Psychopathology, 20,* 821–843.

Binet, A., & Simon, T. (1916). *The development of intelligence in children (the Binet-Simon Scale).* Baltimore: Williams & Wilkins.

Birch, S. H., & Ladd, G. W. (1997). The teacher–child relationship and children's early school adjustment. *Journal of School Psychology, 35,* 61–79.

Blair, C., & Razza, R. P. (2007). Relating effortful control, executive function, and false belief understanding to emerging math and literacy ability in kindergarten. *Child Development, 78,* 647–663.

Bodrova, E., & Leong, D. J. (2007). *Tools of the Mind: The Vygotskian approach to early childhood education* (2nd ed.). Upper Saddle River, NJ: Pearson Education.

Borghans, L., Duckworth, A. L., Heckman, J. J., & ter Weel, B. (2008). The economics and psychology of personality traits. *Journal of Human Resources, 43,* 972–1059.

Bowen, W. G., Chingos, M. M., & McPherson, M. S. (2009). Test scores and high school grades as predictors. In *Crossing the finish line: Completing college at America's public universities* (pp. 112–133). Princeton, NJ: Princeton University Press.

Bowman, P. C., & Matthews, C. V. (1960). Motivations of youth for leaving school (Project No. 200). Washington, DC: U.S. Office of Education Cooperative Research Program.

Brooks, D. (2006, May 7). Marshmallows and public policy. *New York Times,* p. A13.

Conard, M. A. (2005). Aptitude is not enough: How personality and behavior predict academic performance. *Journal of Research in Personality, 40,* 339–346.

Credé, M., & Kuncel, N. R. (2008). Study habits, skills, and attitudes: The third pillar supporting collegiate academic performance. *Perspectives on Psychological Science, 3,* 425–453.

Currie, J., & Thomas, D. (2001). Early test scores, school quality and SES: Long run effects on wage and employment outcomes. *Worker Wellbeing in a Changing Labor Market, 20,* 103–132.

De Pauw, S. S. W., & Mervielde, I. (2010). Temperament, personality, and developmental psychopathology: A review based on the conceptual dimensions underlying childhood traits. *Child Psychiatry and Human Development, 41,* 313–329.

Dewey, J. (1909). *Moral principles in education.* Boston: Houghton Mifflin.

Diamond, A., Barnett, W. S., Thomas, J., & Munro, S. (2007). Preschool program improves cognitive control. *Science, 318,* 1387–1388.

Duckworth, A. L., Gollwitzer, A., Kirby, T., & Oettingen, G. (2012). *From fantasy to action: Mental contrasting with implementation intentions (MCII) improves report card grades and school attendance among disadvantaged children.* Manuscript submitted for preparation.

Duckworth, A. L., Grant, H., Loew, B., Oettingen, G., & Gollwitzer, P. M. (2011). Self-regulation strategies improve self-discipline in adolescents: Benefits of mental contrasting and implementation intention. *Educational Psychology, 31,* 17–26.

Duckworth, A. L., & Kern, M. (2011). A meta-analysis of the convergent validity of self-control measures. *Journal of Research in Personality, 45,* 259–268.

Duckworth, A. L., Quinn, P. D., & Tsukayama, E. (2012). What No Child Left Behind leaves behind: The roles of IQ and self-control in predicting standardized achievement test scores and report card grades. *Journal of Educational Psychology, 104,* 439–451.

Duckworth, A. L., & Seligman, M. E. P. (2005). Self-discipline outdoes IQ in predicting academic performance of adolescents. *Psychological Science, 16,* 939–944.

Duckworth, A. L., Tsukayama, E., & May, H. (2010). Establishing causality using longitudinal hierarchical linear modeling: An illustration predicting achievement from self-control. *Social Psychology and Personality Science, 1,* 311–317.

Duncan, G. J., Dowsett, C. J., Claessens, A., Mugnuson, K., Huston, A. C., Klebanov, P., et al. (2007). School readiness and later achievement. *Developmental Psychology, 43,* 1428–1446.

Duncan, G. J., & Magnuson, K. (2011). The nature and impact of early achievement skills, attention skills, and behavior problems. In G. Duncan & R. Murnane (Eds.), *Wither opportunity?: Rising inequality, schools, and children's life chances* (pp. 47–70). New York: Russell Sage Foundation.

Durlak, J. A., Weissberg, R. P., Dymnicki, A. B., Taylor, R. D., & Schellinger, K. (2011). The impact of enhancing students' social and emotional learning: A meta-analysis of school-based universal interventions. *Child Development, 82,* 405–432.

Eisenberg, N., Smith, C. L., Sadovsky, A., & Spinrad, T. (2004). Effortful control: Relations with emotion regulation, adjustment and socialization in childhood. In R. Baumeister & K. D. Vohs (Eds.), *Handbook of self-regulation: Research, theory, and applications* (pp. 259–282). New York: Guilford Press.

Eisenberg, N., Valiente, C., & Eggum, N. D. (2010). Self-regulation and school readiness. *Early Education and Development, 21,* 681–698.

Evans, D. E., & Rothbart, M. K. (2007). Developing a model for adult temperament. *Journal of Research in Personality, 41,* 868–888.

Evans, G. W., & Rosenbaum, J. (2008). Self-regulation and the income-achievement gap. *Early Childhood Research Quarterly, 23,* 504–514.

Fergusson, D. M., & Horwood, L. J. (1998). Early conduct problems and later life opportunities. *Journal of Child Psychology and Psychiatry, 39,* 1097–1108.

Finn, J. D., Pannozzo, G. M., & Voelkl, K. E. (1995). Disruptive and inattentive–withdrawn behavior and achievement among fourth graders. *Elementary School Journal, 95,* 421–434.

Franklin, B. (1747). *Proposal relating to the education of youth in Pensilvania.* Philadelphia: University of Pennsylvania Press.

Geiser, S., & Santelices, M. V. (2007). Validity of high school grades in predicting student success beyond the freshman year: High-school record vs. standardized tests as indicators of four-year college outcomes. *Research and Occasional Paper Series from the Center for Studies in Higher Education at the University of California, Berkeley, CSHE 2007 (CSHE.6.07).* Retrieved from http://cshe.berkeley.edu/publications/publications.php?id=265.

Giannopulu, I., Escolano, S., Cusin, F., Citeau, H., & Dellatolas, G. (2008). Teachers' reporting of behavioural problems and cognitive academic performances in children aged 5–7 years. *British Journal of Educational Psychology, 78,* 127–147.

Goldberg, L. R., Sweeney, D., Merenda, P. F., & Hughes, J. E., Jr. (1998). Demographic variables and personality: The effects of gender, age, education, and ethnic/racial status on self-descriptions of personality attributes. *Personality and Individual Differences, 24,* 393–403.

Gottfredson, L. S. (2004). Schools and the g factor. *Wilson Quarterly, 28,* 34–35.

Gough, H. G. (1964). Graduation from high school as predicted by CPI. *Psychology in the Schools, 3,* 208–216.

Hamre, B. K., & Pianta, R. C. (2005). Can instructional and emotional support in the first-grade classroom make a difference for children at risk of school failure? *Child Development, 76,* 949–967.

Hanushek, E. A., & Woessmann, L. (2008). The role of cognitive skills in economic development. *Journal of Economic Literature, 46,* 607–668.

Hathaway, S. R., Reynolds, P. C., & Monachesi, E. D. (1969). Follow-up of the later careers and lives of 1,000 boys who dropped out of high school. *Journal of Consulting and Clinical Psychology, 33,* 370–380.

Heckman, J. J. (2006). Skill formation and the economics of investing in disadvantaged children. *Science, 312,* 1900–1902.

Heckman, J. J., & LaFontaine, P. A. (2007). *The American high school graduation rate: Trends and levels* (Discussion Paper No. 3216). Bonn, Germany: Institute for the Study of Labor.

Heckman, J. J., & Rubinstein, Y. (2001). The importance of noncognitive skills: Lessons from the GED testing program. *American Economic Review, 91*, 145–149.

Hillman, C. H., Erickson, K. I., & Kramer, A. F. (2008). Be smart, exercise your heart: Exercise effects on brain and cognition. *Nature Reviews Neuroscience, 9*, 58–65.

Hillman, C. H., Pontifex, M. B., Raine, L. B., Castelli, D. M., Hall, E. E., & Kramer, A. F. (2009). The effect of acute treadmill walking on cognitive control and academic achievement in preadolescent children. *Neuroscience, 159*, 1044–1054.

Houts, R. M., Caspi, A., Pianta, R. C., Arseneault, L., & Moffitt, T. E. (2010). The challenging pupil in the classroom: The effect of the child on the teacher. *Psychological Science, 21*, 1802–1810.

James, W. (1899). *Talks to teachers on psychology; and to students on some of life's ideals*. New York: Holt.

Janosz, M., LeBlanc, M., Boulerice, B., & Tremblay, R. E. (1997). Disentangling the weight of school dropout predictors: A test on two longitudinal samples. *Journal of Youth and Adolescence, 26*, 733–762.

Jennings, P. A., & Greenberg, M. T. (2009). The prosocial classroom: Teacher social and emotional competence in relation to student and classroom outcomes. *Review of Educational Research, 79*, 491–525.

Jensen, A. R. (1980). *Bias in mental testing*. New York: Free Press.

John, O. P., Caspi, A., Robins, R. W., Moffitt, T. E., & Stouthamer-Loeber, M. (1994). The "little five": Exploring the nomological network of the five-factor model of personality in adolescent boys. *Child Development, 65*, 160–178.

Kelly, F. J., & Veldman, D. J. (1964). Delinquency and school dropout behavior as a function of impulsivity and nondominant values. *Journal of Abnormal and Social Psychology, 69*, 190–194.

Kochanska, G., & Knaack, A. (2003). Effortful control as a personality characteristic of young children: Antecedents, correlates, and consequences. *Journal of Personality. 71*, 1087–1112.

Kuncel, N. R., Hezlett, S. A., & Ones, D. S. (2004). Academic performance, career potential, creativity, and job performance: Can one construct predict them all? *Journal of Personality and Social Psychology, 86*, 148–161.

Liew, J. (2012). Effortful control, executive functions, and education: Bringing self-regulatory and social–emotional competencies to the table. *Child Development Perspectives, 6*, 105–111.

Liew, J., Chen, Q., & Hughes, J. N. (2010). Child effortful control, teacher–student relationships, and achievement in academically at-risk children: Additive and interactive effects. *Early Child Research Quarterly, 25*, 51–64.

Lillard, A., & Else-Quest, N. (2006). Evaluating Montessori education. *Science, 313*, 1893–1894.

Lounsbury, J. W., Steel, R. P., Loveland, J. M., & Gibson, L. W. (2004). An investigation of personality traits in relation to adolescent school absenteeism. *Journal of Youth and Adolescence, 33*, 457–466.

Lubinski, D. (2009). Exceptional cognitive ability: The phenotype. *Behavior Genetics, 39*, 350–358.

Martin, R. P. (1989). Activity level, distractibility, and persistence: Critical characteristics in early schooling. In G. A. Kohnstamm, J. E. Bates, & M. K. Rothbart (Eds.), *Temperament in childhood* (pp. 451–461). Chichester, UK: Wiley.

McClelland, M. M., Cameron, C. E., Connor, C. M., Farris, C. L., Jewkes, A. M., & Morrison, F. J. (2007). Links between behavioral regulation and preschoolers' literacy, vocabulary, and math skills. *Developmental Psychology, 43*, 947–959.

Mischel, W., & Patterson, C. J. (1976). Substantive and structural elements of effective plans for self-control. *Journal of Personality and Social Psychology, 34*, 942–950.

Mischel, W., & Patterson, C. J. (1978). Effective plans for self-control in children. *Minnesota Symposia on Child Psychology, 11*, 199–230.

Mischel, W., Shoda, Y., & Rodriguez, M. L. (1989). Delay of gratification in children. *Science, 244*, 933–938.

Munis, P., Greenfield, D. B., Henderson, H. A., & George, J. L. (2007). Development and validation of the Preschool Temperament Classification System for use with teachers. *Early Childhood Research Quarterly, 22*, 440–450.

Neisser, U., Boodoo, G., Bouchard, T. J., Jr., Boykin, A. W., Brody, N., Ceci, S. J., et al. (1996). Intelligence: Knowns and unknowns. *American Psychologist, 51*, 77–101.

Noftle, E. E., & Robins, R. W. (2007). Personality predictors of academic outcomes: Big Five correlates of GPA and SAT scores. *Journal of Personality and Social Psychology, 93*, 116–130.

Oliver, P. H., Guerin, D. W., & Gottfried, A. W. (2007). Temperamental task orientation: Relation to high school and college educational accomplishments. *Learning and Individual Differences, 17*, 220–230.

Panksepp, J. (2007). Can play diminish ADHD and facilitate the construction of the social brain? *Journal of the Canadian Academy of Child and Adolescent Psychiatry, 16*, 57–66.

Patterson, C. J., & Mischel, W. (1975). Plans to resist distraction. *Developmental Psychology, 11*, 369–378.

Patterson, C. J., & Mischel, W. (1976). Effects of temptation-inhibiting and task-facilitating plans on self-control. *Journal of Personality and Social Psychology, 33,* 209–217.

Ponitz, C. C., McClelland, M. M., Jewkes, A. M., Connor, C. M., Farris, C. L., & Morrison, F. J. (2008). Touch your toes!: Developing a direct measure of behavioral regulation in early childhood. *Early Childhood Research Quarterly, 23,* 141–158.

Poropat, A. E. (2009). A meta-analysis of the five-factor model of personality and academic performance. *Psychological Bulletin, 135,* 322–338.

Raver, C. C., Jones, S. M., Li-Grining, C. P., Zhai, F., Bub, K., & Pressler, E. (2011). CSRP's impact on low-income preschoolers' pre-academic skills: Self-regulation as a mediating mechanism. *Child Development, 82,* 362–378.

Riggs, N. R., Greenberg, M. T., Kusche, C. A., & Pentz, M. A. (2006). The mediational role of neurocognition in the behavioral outcomes of a social-emotional prevention program in elementary school students: Effects of the PATHS curriculum. *Prevention Science, 7,* 91–102.

Roberts, B. W., & DelVecchio, W. F. (2000). The rank-order consistency of personality traits from childhood to old age: A quantitative review of longitudinal studies. *Psychological Bulletin, 126,* 3–25.

Roberts, B. W., Kuncel, N. R., Shiner, R., Caspi, A., & Goldberg, L. R. (2007). The power of personality: The comparative validity of personality traits, socioeconomic status, and cognitive ability for predicting important life outcomes. *Perspectives on Psychological Science, 2,* 313–345.

Roberts, B. W., Walton, K. E., & Viechtbauer, W. (2006). Patterns of mean-level change in personality traits across the life course: A meta-analysis of longitudinal studies. *Psychological Bulletin, 132,* 1–25.

Rodriguez, M. L., Mischel, W., & Shoda, Y. (1989). Cognitive person variables in the delay of gratification of older children at risk. *Journal of Personality and Social Psychology, 57,* 358–367.

Rothbart, M. K. (2007). Temperament, development, and personality. *Current Directions in Psychological Science, 14,* 207–212.

Rothbart, M. K., Ahadi, S. A., & Evans, D. E. (2000). Temperament and personality: Origins and outcomes. *Journal of Personality and Social Psychology, 78,* 122–135.

Rothbart, M. K., & Rueda, M. R. (2005). The development of effortful control. In U. Mayr, E. Awh, & S. W. Keele (Eds.), *Developing individuality in the human brain* (pp. 167–188). Washington, DC: American Psychological Association.

Rothbart, M. K., Sheese, B. E., & Posner, M. I. (2007). Executive attention and effortful control: Linking temperament, brain networks, and genes. *Child Development Perspectives, 1,* 2–7.

Rudasill, K. M., Gallagher, K. C., & White, J. M. (2010). Temperamental attention and activity, classroom emotional support, and academic achievement in third grade. *Journal of School Psychology, 48,* 113–134.

Rudasill, K. M., & Rimm-Kaufman, S. E. (2009). Teacher–child relationship quality: The roles of child temperament and teacher–child interactions. *Early Childhood Research Quarterly, 24,* 107–120.

Rueda, M. R., Rothbart, M. K., McCandliss, B. D., Saccomanno, L., & Posner, M. I. (2005). Training, maturation, and genetic influences on the development of executive attention. *Proceedings of the National Academy of Sciences, 102,* 14931–14936.

Sackett, P. R., Borneman, M. J., & Connelly, B. S. (2008). High stakes testing in higher education and employment: Appraising the evidence for validity and fairness. *American Psychologist, 63,* 215–227.

Saltz, E., Dixon, D., & Johnson, J. (1977). Training disadvantaged preschoolers on various fantasy activities: Effects on cognitive functioning and impulse control. *Child Development, 48,* 367–380.

Schoen, M. J., & Nagle, R. J. (1994). Prediction of school readiness from kindergarten temperament scores. *Journal of School Psychology, 32,* 135–147.

Segal, C. (in press). Misbehavior, education, and labor market outcomes. *Journal of the European Economic Association.*

Silva, K. M., Spinrad, T. L., Eisenberg, N., Sulik, M. J., Valiente, C., Huerta, S., et al. (2011). Relations of children's effortful control and teacher–child relationship quality in a low-income sample. *Early Education and Development, 22,* 411–433.

Singer, D. G., & Singer, J. L. (1990). Cognitive and emotional growth through play. In *The house of make-believe: Children's play and the developing imagination* (pp. 117–152). Cambridge, MA: Harvard University Press.

Singer, J. L., & Singer, D. G. (2006). Preschoolers' imaginative play as precursor of narrative consciousness. *Imagination, Cognition and Personality, 25,* 97–117.

Social and Character Development Research Consortium. (2010). *Efficacy of schoolwide programs to promote social and character development and reduce problem behavior in elementary school children.* Retrieved from http://ies.ed.gov/ncer/pubs/20112001/pdf/20112001.pdf.

Soto, C. J., John, O. P., Gosling, S. D., & Potter, J. (2008). The developmental psychometrics of Big Five self-reports: Acquiescence, factor structure, coherence, and differentiation from ages 10 to 20. *Journal of Personality and Social Psychology, 94,* 718–737.

Spearman, C. (1927). *The abilities of man: Their*

nature and measurement. New York: Macmillan.
Stevens, C., Fanning, J., Coch, D., Sanders, L., & Neville, H. (2008). Neural mechanisms of selective auditory attention are enhanced by computerized training: Electrophysiological evidence from language-impaired and typically developing children. *Brain Research, 1205,* 55–69.
Stevens, C., Lauinger, B., & Neville, H. (2009). Differences in the neural mechanisms of selective attention in children from different socioeconomic backgrounds: An event-related brain potential study. *Developmental Science, 12,* 634–646.
Stinebrickner, R., & Stinebrickner, T. R. (2007). The causal effect of studying on academic performance. *The B. E. Journal of Economic Analysis and Policy, 8*(1), 1–53.
Sum, A., Khatiwada, I., McLaughlin, J., Tobar, P., Mortroni, J., & Palma, S. (2007). *An assessment of the labor market, income, health, social, civic and fiscal consequences of dropping out of high school.* Boston: Center for Labor Market Studies, Northeastern University.
Tominey, S. L., & McClelland, M. M. (2011). Red light, purple light: Findings from a randomized trial using circle time games to improve behavioral self-regulation in preschool. *Early Education and Development, 22,* 489–519.
Tsukayama, E. (2012). *Virtuous cycles of skill: Psychological mechanisms of self-productivity.* Manuscript in preparation.
Tsukayama, E., Duckworth, A. L., & Kim, B. E. (2011). *Domain specific impulsivity in school-age children.* Manuscript in preparation.
Valiente, C., Eisenberg, N., Haugen, R., Spinrad, T. L., Hofer, C., Liew, J., et al. (2011). Children's effortful control and academic achievement: Mediation through school functioning. *Early Education and Development, 22,* 411–433.
Valiente, C., Lemery-Chalfant, K., & Swanson, J., & Reiser, M. (2010). Prediction of kindergartners' academic achievement from their effortful control and emotionality: Evidence for direct and moderated relations. *Jounal of Educational Psychology, 102*(3), 550–560.
Valiente, C., Lemery-Chalfant, K., Swanson, J., & Reiser, M. (2008). Prediction of children's academic competence from their effortful control, relationships, and classroom participation. *Journal of Educational Psychology, 100,* 67–77.
Van Eijck, K., & de Graaf, P. M. (2004). The Big Five at school: The impact of personality on educational attainment. *Netherlands Journal of Social Sciences, 41,* 24–42.
Veenstra, R., Lindenberg, S., Tinga, F., & Ormel, J. (2010). Truancy in late elementary and early secondary education: The influence of social bonds and self-control. *International Journal of Behavioral Development, 34,* 302–310.
Vitaro, F., Brendgen, M., Larose, S., & Tremblay, R. E. (2005). Kindergarten disruptive behaviors, protective factors, and educational achievement by early adulthood. *Journal of Educational Psychology, 97,* 617–629.
Webb, E. (1915). *Character and intelligence: An attempt at an exact study of character.* Cambridge, UK: Cambridge University Press.
Wechsler, D. (1943). Non-intellective factors in general intelligence. *Journal of Abnormal and Social Psychology, 38,* 101–103.
Wechsler, D. (1950). Cognitive, conative, and nonintellective intelligence. *American Psychologist, 5,* 78–83.
Whisenton, J. T., & Lorre, M. R. (1970). A comparison of the values, needs, and aspirations of school leavers with those of non-school leavers. *Journal of Negro Education, 39,* 325–332.
Willingham, W. W., Pollack, J. M., & Lewis, C. (2002). Grades and test scores: Accounting for observed differences. *Journal of Educational Measurement, 39,* 1–37.
Wolfe, R. N., & Johnson, S. D. (1995). Personality as a predictor of college performance. *Educational and Psychological Measurement, 55,* 177–185.
Wong, M. M., & Csikszentmihalyi, M. (1991). Motivation and academic achievement: The effects of personality traits and the duality of experience. *Journal of Personality, 59,* 539–574.
Zhou, Q., Main, A., & Wang, Y. (2010). The relations of temperamental effortful control and anger/frustration to Chinese children's academic achievement and social adjustment: A longitudinal study. *Journal of Educational Psychology, 102,* 180–196.
Zimmerman, B. J. (2002). Achieving self-regulation: The trial and triumph of adolescence. In F. Pajares & T. Urdan (Eds.), *Academic motivation of adolescents* (pp. 1–27). Greenwich, CT: Information Age.
Zimmerman, B. J., & Kitsantas, A. (2005). The hidden dimension of personal competence: Self-regulated learning and practice. In A. J. Elliot & C. S. Dweck (Eds.), *Handbook of competence and motivation* (pp. 509–526). New York: Guilford Press.
Zins, J. E., Elias, M. J., & Greenberg, M. T. (2007). School practices to build social–emotional competence as the foundation of academic and life success. In R. Bar-On, J. G. Maree, & M. J. Elias (Eds.), *Educating people to be emotionally intelligent* (pp. 79–94). Westport, CT: Praeger.

Chapter 31

Temperament in Psychotherapy
Reflections on Clinical Practice with the Trait of Sensitivity

Elaine N. Aron

This chapter differs substantially from the rest of this volume in three ways. First, it transitions to the application of a "temperament perspective" (Kristal, 2005) to psychotherapy, mainly with adults. Second, since there is almost nothing written on this subject (beyond a few studies of personality and outcome), this chapter also differs in that much of it is based on my own clinical experience (E. Aron, 2010). Third, rather than making generalizations that would need to apply to all temperament traits, the clinical examples are of working with one particular trait, sensitivity, which is discussed in an early section. The chapter's goal is to offer readers some thoughts on how temperament can be integrated into clinical practice, which includes (1) assessing for temperament, (2) adapting treatment to temperament, and (3) using knowledge of temperament to improve general functioning specifically in the work place and close relationships. It also suggests a number of areas for future research.

The Importance of Considering Temperament for Successful Psychotherapy

Why is temperament important for successful treatment of adult clients? First, it exists as a prominent feature of every individual from birth, and while it is widely studied in children, children do become adults and still have temperaments when they enter psychotherapy. The fact that it can be more difficult in adults to sort out genetic factors from environment and history makes temperament no less critical in understanding clients' backgrounds; temperament may be a primary causative factor of some clients' symptoms, as well as another source of leverage in creating change.

In practice, very little consideration seems to be given to temperament in the context of psychotherapy. Understandably, some therapists have found a temperament or nature (vs. nurture) perspective to be discouraging, as it could be taken to imply that change will be difficult or impossible, that the nurture of therapy will be irrelevant, and the attempt to heal the past, pointless. Most have heard that there is a "gene–environment interaction," but genetics can still seem to act like a limit on change, a limit that is associated with unpalatable assumptions and values, such as "Psychologically troubled people, like the poor, will always be with us" (if one rules out selective breeding), so why try to change that? An emphasis on nurture, however, can lean too far the opposite way, such that anyone could do anything with the right opportunities in childhood or the right therapy in adulthood. This approach pushes temperament into the closet and can potentially waste time and lower clients' self-esteem because ignoring temperament may lead to inappropriate goals and treatments.

The work on differential susceptibility (e.g., Belsky & Pluess, 2009; van IJzendoorn & Bakermans-Kranenburg, Chapter 19, this volume) may be the solution to this conundrum, in that it suggests that some temperament traits make nurture more, not less, relevant. When children with certain early appearing at-risk behaviors or genes are raised in a supportive home or participate in an intervention to improve their home or school environment, they often benefit more than those without the at-risk factor, suggesting a greater susceptibility to the effects of their surroundings rather than mere vulnerability. There is at least one study of this in adults: Parents with at-risk genes when under stress parent less sensitively, but with fewer daily stressors they parent more sensitively (van IJzendoorn, Bakermans-Kranenburg, & Mesman, 2008). Several studies with college students provide additional evidence for differential susceptibility (E. Aron, Aron, & Davies, 2005; Liss, Timmel, Baxley, & Killingsworth, 2005; Taylor et al., 2006). Not only does the susceptibility perspective bring nurture back into the picture along with temperament, but it may lead to the discovery that individuals carrying certain alleles gain more than others from psychotherapy that helps them, for example, to deal with stress.

Whatever future research reveals, bringing temperament into the open rather than ignoring it surely provides more understanding and opportunities to change problem behaviors. Almost any behavior (as opposed to the underlying processes) associated with a temperament trait can probably be modified by environment and interventions, but understanding must precede intervention. In a familiar example, when children do not sit still in school, the usual approach is to give a warning, followed by punishment. However, children born with a high activity level have more difficulty sitting still, which calls for a quite different intervention—more frequent breaks (Kristal, 2005). It seems clear that therapists can use knowledge of temperament in similar ways to fit interventions to temperament.

Improves Assessment and Reduces Misdiagnoses

This simple example of temperament wisdom, allowing active children more exercise time during school hours, can also avoid an escalation of behaviors that appear to be attention-deficit/hyperactivity disorder (ADHD) or oppositional defiant disorder (Kristal, 2005). Similarly, not pressuring temperamentally sensitive children to speak up in class before they are ready can avoid diagnoses of depression or anxiety. In adults, too, a "poor fit" between temperament and environment can be a major underlying issue, perhaps even with something as simple as activity level. An active person with no words for this normal difference could spend years trying to adapt to a desk job with decreasing success and health, all the while observing others for whom it is easy, and feeling more and more flawed. Adults who have been increasingly horrified and ashamed by attempting to speak up in front of others are often diagnosed with social phobia, an anxiety disorder, but a temperament trait of sensitivity often lies behind that. Their problem may still meet the diagnostic criteria, but client and therapist understand the problem and can approach it quite differently if an assessment reveals a broader underlying sensitivity that leads to overarousal in highly stimulating performance situations and then secondarily to anxiety about performing when past one's optimal level of arousal.

Adult clients might be more likely than schoolchildren to have true diagnosable disorders given the longer amount of time for these to develop. On the other hand, if adult clients have rarely experienced a good fit throughout their lives, finding a better fit in therapy, then understanding their temperament and finding a better fit in various other places in their lives may rapidly reduce criteria to below disorder level. As discussed later in this chapter, when a diagnosis from the *Diagnostic and Statistical Manual of Mental Disorders* (DSM; American Psychiatric Association, 1994) is needed, temperament matters. Temperament traits can potentially (1) be misdiagnosed as disorders (or, on the other hand, be so much the focus that disorders are overlooked); (2) create a vulnerability to certain disorders, so that the therapist must consider whether the level of precipitating environmental factors might be enough to tilt toward diagnosing the disorder in those with a vulnerability, but not in those without it; and (3) cause a disorder to appear differently—depression may be hidden by a conscientious style in one person, or appear less as sadness and more as agitation or irritability in another.

Builds Therapeutic Alliance

"Looking for temperament" can provide a good beginning and a touchstone for a strong therapeutic alliance throughout the work. Acknowledging a person's temperament is in a sense acknowledging that person's most basic self. Even close others may have missed it or seen it as something else, perhaps something weak or needing to be changed. Providing a neutral name for the trait, then accepting it and praising its positive side and how the client has coped in situations when it was a disadvantage can help build a strong alliance.

For example, a client begins to cry (or blush, tremble, perspire, etc.) early in the first session, before any material has been communicated. The client looks uncomfortable and perhaps ashamed, maybe saying, "I don't know why I'm crying like this." The therapist has many working hypotheses to test, but one might be, and perhaps be appropriate to mention, a predisposition to tears (associated for example with high sensitivity; E. Aron & Aron, 1997). If the hypothesis is correct, there can be immediate relief. "Oh yes, I've been doing this all my life. It's worse with people I hardly know. It's so embarrassing." The tears may prove to be due to something else, but for the moment the client feels best understood in this way, and an important trait may have been uncovered. Tears still have meaning. Indeed, if they come easily and often, they can become a valuable signal that an important issue has been broached. The client may benefit greatly by realizing "This is just how I am," and may come to see his or her temperament, including crying easily, as simply a normal variation in human personality. At some point, the therapeutic work may focus on ways to help the client handle these tearful moments when around others, but perhaps more important is the bond that can last throughout the work by helping the client feel deeply understood in the first session. The therapist saw this hidden but essential reason for what had previously seemed to be shameful.

Enhances Objective Self-Esteem

By discussing temperament early in the work, therapists have the opportunity to give clients a positive perspective on what previously they had only seen as a flaw, but that, in fact, bestows equal benefits, depending on the situation. The therapist might say about the tears, "I think that crying easily can be a form of emotional leadership—sometimes others may feel like crying and need to cry, and you break the ice, almost literally." Or a therapist mentions a client's persistence since childhood (Kristal, 2005; Thomas & Chess, 1997). "Persistent? I've always been told I was just stubborn. But you're right, I was born this way and it's gotten me a long ways in life." This boost in self-esteem can buffer the client later, when the therapist must point out problem behaviors with fewer redeeming values.

Sometimes a temperament perspective for individuals and especially couples provides a no-blame explanation for some of their difficulties. "So he needs more time to himself, and I'm the type that has to get out and do new things or go nuts. We've been fighting about this all our lives. But you're saying we're just different in that way. Born different." Similarly, therapist and client may be able to reframe, partially or completely, a number of past "failures." For example, the trait of low flexibility from the list of Thomas and Chess (1997) can lie behind repeated job losses. "So when my jumpy boss keeps changing what we're supposed to be doing, or moves us from job to job on a moment's notice, I resent it even more than the others because I'm just somebody who needs more time to transition from one thing to the next. Yeah, I've always been that way." The solution may be for the client to learn to control herself better and blame supervisors less by seeing that they are people under their own pressures, but perhaps she can also stop seeing herself as a loser because her anger has led to the loss of three jobs.

May Shorten Treatment

Because knowledge of temperament can lead to more realistic outcome goals, as well as a better working alliance and improved self-esteem, treatment may be briefer—indeed, sometimes very brief, in that it will be little more than temperament counseling. The presenting problem can be solved and future ones avoided if the underlying need was for the client to adopt behaviors and lifestyles that create congruence between temperament and environment. More complicated issues can still be better understood and treated when temperament is kept in mind. A person with a history of sexual abuse, for example, may have been the target or been more affected by the abuse because of temperament. The key is that by keeping temperament traits as working hypotheses, both therapist and client can develop a better sense of what can be changed and what cannot, and even should not, be changed.

Reduces the Effects of Minority Status

Some traits, or at least extreme levels of traits, are relatively uncommon, so that they are in a statistical sense not normal and therefore, to some, abnormal. Furthermore, certain traits are deemed undesirable in a given culture, family, or subculture, such as a profession. We all have temperaments, but as Margaret Mead eloquently observed, certain traits in certain cultures are encouraged "in every thread of the social fabric—in the care of the young child, the games the children play, the songs the people sing, the political organization, the religious observance, the art and the philosophy" (1935, p. 284). Other traits are ignored, discouraged, or even shunned. A trait viewed in this way may only be seen for its negative effects, such as shyness or "troublemaking," and parents, teachers, and later partners or friends may try to wipe these out for the individual's own benefit, so that he or she will "fit in better." Although parents across cultures agree to a surprising extent about what makes a child "difficult," there are also important cultural differences regarding which traits parents see as problematic (Super et al., 2008), and these judgments surely have an affect across the lifespan.

Because of their temperament, some clients experience being a member of a minority, whether they recognize it or not, and are subjected to negative stereotypes, some of which will inevitably be internalized. In these cases, the research on stereotype threat (Steele, Spencer, & Aronson, 2002; Taylor & Walton, 2011) is quite relevant, in that clients may both learn and perform less successfully than they are capable of, due to their identity as a certain negatively stereotyped type of person. This negative stereotyping may well apply in not only academic and professional situations but also social ones. Exploring the ramifications of having been a member of a minority in this sense, of having an unusual or less culturally desirable temperament, is another way that attending to temperament can uncover and resolve serious issues.

The Example Temperament Trait: Research on Sensitivity

Because this chapter uses for its examples the temperament trait of sensitivity, this section provides a brief summary of the theory and research and behind it, especially the concept of sensory processing sensitivity (SPS; E. Aron & A. Aron, 1997) unrelated to "sensory processing disorder" (e.g., Bundy, Shia, Qi, & Miller, 2007), but also other traits related to SPS in varying degrees.

Evolutionary Function and Genetic Basis of SPS

SPS, measured with the 27-item Highly Sensitive Person (HSP) Scale (E. Aron & A. Aron, 1997), refers to a tendency to process stimulation more thoroughly, which is facilitated by stronger emotional reactions. It can be viewed as the manifestation in humans of one of two strategies (although the trait may in fact be a dimension) that have evolved in at least 100 species (for a review of the model and research, see E. Aron, A. Aron, & Jagiellowicz, in press). The more sensitive strategy relative to others is to be more responsive to cues in the environment (Sih & Bell, 2008; Wolf, Van Doorn, & Weissing, 2008). Sensitivity is a negative-frequency-dependent trait in that, if the majority had access to the benefits created by the trait, the competition for the benefits would result in few or no benefits for any; for example, when only a few people know a shortcut for getting around a traffic jam, it remains a timesaver, but when more people know the route it does not save anyone time. Sensitivity, sometimes termed *responsivity* in biology, has also been shown in mathematical and computer models (Wolf et al., 2011) to be a necessary trait for other consistent behaviors or traits to evolve, in that, for example, an individual benefits from being trustworthy or cooperative only if someone else notices and responds.

According to the SPS model (E. Aron, A. Aron, & Jagiellowicz, in press), the negative-frequency-dependent form of responsivity/sensitivity is expressed in humans largely as a deeper (in the sense of Craik & Lockhart, 1972) cognitive processing of stimuli that is facilitated by a heightened emotional reactivity to both positive and negative stimuli. Sensitivity to the environment can be expressed in a number of other ways besides cognitive recognition—for example, sensitivity of the immune system (Boyce et al., 1995) or a faster startle response and greater sensitivity to pain (E. Aron & A. Aron, 1997). But given the general importance of cognition in the evolution of humans, depth of processing seems likely to be a central feature of the human responsivity strategy, and the role of strong affect is in keeping with the view that emotion frequently facilitates learning and memory (Baumeister, Vohs, DeWall, & Zhang, 2007). Similar processes that involve the intertwining of reactivity and behaviors suggesting something like depth of processing as an inherited personality difference have been found in nonhuman animals (e.g., rodents: Koolhaas et al., 1999; fish: Schjolden & Winberg, 2007; birds: Groothuis & Carere, 2005).

Clearly in the SPS model, sensitivity is a genetically determined trait. Thus far it has been tentatively associated with both the serotonin (Licht, Mortensen, & Knudsen, 2011) and dopamine systems (Chen et al., 2011). The short (s) allele of the serotonin transporter gene has been inconsistently associated with depression, perhaps because that is not its main function. In some studies, s-allele carriers with poor childhoods and stressful lives who are more likely to be depressed are with a better environment actually less likely to be depressed than others (e.g., Taylor et al. 2006). Similarly, those with high SPS and poor childhoods are more likely to be depressed, but without such childhoods they are no more likely than others to be depressed (E. Aron et al., 2005; Liss et al., 2005); a crossover interaction was produced experimentally (E. Aron et al., 2005, Study 4). Studies of s-allele carriers have pointed to certain clear benefits of this variation as a result of the combining of emotional reactivity and depth of processing (Homberg & Lesch, 2011). For example, Roiser, Rogers, Cook, and Sahakian (2006) found that s-allele carriers in a gambling-based decision-making task outperformed others, evidencing heightened emotional risk aversion when there was a low probability of winning, but risk seeking when there was a high probability; in addition, s-allele carriers took substantially longer to reflect before making difficult choices. They also performed better on a delayed-pattern recognition task and a task requiring recognizing letters in mirrored versus normal form. Rhesus monkeys also have an s-allele for the serotonin transporter gene, and carriers evidence similar "broadly superior performance" (Jedema et al., 2009, p. 519) on a variety of decision-making tasks.

The study of dopamine genes (Chen et al., 2011) involved a very different method of looking at essentially all the genes with polymorphisms (98) that affect the dopamine system, to see which, if any, were associated with SPS, which Chen and colleagues (2011) chose to study because it is "deeply rooted in the nervous system," (p. 1). Of the 98, a set of 10 genes predicted 15% of the variance (a medium to high correlation with the scale; the authors point out that this is much higher than the variance found in most genetic studies of most personality traits). An additional 2% of the variance was contributed by stressful life events, which is a relatively small environmental contribution. Dividing the genes by the subsystems of dopamine synthesis, degradation/transport, receptor and modulation, the last two made the most significant contribution.

Together these studies provide strong evidence that SPS is indeed an inherited temperament trait.

Neuroimaging Studies

Neuroimaging studies using functional magnetic resonance imaging (fMRI) have yielded findings consistent with the view that those high in SPS process information more thoroughly and have stronger emotional reactions. Those scoring high on the HSP Scale, when performing a task involving subtle visual discriminations, have increased brain activation in areas associated with secondary (as opposed to initial) perceptual processing, especially when attending to subtle stimuli (Jagiellowicz et al., 2011). Another fMRI study (A. Aron et al., 2010) looked at a well-known perceptual processing bias: Given a task of recalling the relative size of a line to a surrounding box (a task in which the relation of one thing to its surrounding is key) it was already known (Hedden, Ketay, Aron, Markus, & Gabrieli, 2008) that the general population of an individualistic culture has more difficulty and therefore more activation of attention areas when doing this task. At the same time, given a task of recalling the absolute length of a line regardless of the size of the surrounding box (a task in which the object is the focus and the context has to be ignored), the general population of a collectivist culture has more difficulty and thus more attentional activation. What A. Aron and colleagues (2010) found was that sensitive subjects in both cultures required equal amounts of attentional activation regardless of their culture.

Regarding emotional reactivity and SPS, a study linking perceptual processing to emotion (Acevedo, Aron, & Aron, 2010) found that when viewing photos of happy or sad strangers versus neutral faces, and doing the same with happy and sad photos of romantic partners, in all comparisons those scoring high on the HSP Scale showed increased activation in the same perceptual areas as the two previous studies (A. Aron et al., 2010; Jagiellowicz et al., 2011) as well as activation in areas associated with mirror neurons and in the insula across all conditions. The insula is thought to integrate emotional and sensory input in the service of the overall moment-to-moment experience of subjective awareness (Craig, 2009) and may prove to be the "seat" of SPS. These three neuroimaging studies suggest that there are clear differences in the processing of perceptual and emotional stimulation in those scoring high on the HSP Scale, and that it measures an important temperament variable.

Relation to Other Temperament and Personality Constructs

Aspects of a sensitive or responsive strategy have long been observed behaviorally. The difficulty in studying this pattern has been the lack of certainty about the underlying reason for a particular behavior. For example, when for reasons of temperament a child pauses before entering a room, this could be due to any of a number of proposed traits: fearfulness; inhibitedness; harm avoidance; a withdrawing or negative temperament; or a strategy of responsiveness, SPS, leading the child to pause to observe first.

Several traits discussed in this section have been put forth as the main reason for some of the various behaviors one would also expect to arise from SPS (greater sensitivity to sensory stimuli, enhanced cognitive processing of stimuli, taking longer to decide, better decisions, strong emotional reactions, etc.) and clinicians will want to be aware of these.

Developmental Sensitivity

Several lines of research have focused on a form of sensitivity that directly affects development, although it may extend beyond childhood (see van IJzendoorn & Bakermans-Kranenburg, Chapter 19, this volume). Boyce and Ellis (2005) have provided a biological marker, reactivity of the nervous system, for sensitivity in children, as well as a theory about its origins in a more general infant plasticity or "biological sensitivity to context." As already discussed, Belsky and Pluess (2009) reviewed research, mostly with children, supporting a pattern of several at-risk traits and genes leading to negative outcomes in poor environments but better than average positive outcomes in good environments. They hypothesized that developmental outcomes are linked to sensitivity to the environment, including rewards and punishments, that is due to central nervous system differences. This susceptibility to the environment may be broader than SPS, however, in that the crossover interaction pattern holds for children at risk for being angry and impulsive, as well as those who are more typically sensitive (e.g., cautious about risk, sensitive to others' feelings, bothered by noise). The example in this chapter, SPS, is limited to this second group.

Low Stimulus Threshold

A low threshold of response to stimuli (Thomas & Chess, 1997) has been another observable behavior that in the SPS model is usually, but not always, the result of an underlying trait of sensitivity. In this tradition, Rothbart, Ahadi, and Evans (2000) expanded the idea of sensitivity to stimuli to include Orienting Sensitivity. Evans and Rothbart (2007), in developing the Adult Temperament Questionnaire (ATQ), conceptualize it as "noticing peripheral stimuli with emotional relevance" (p. 883), as evidenced by two of the three subscales, Emotional Reactions to Low-Intensity Stimuli and General Perceptual Sensitivity (the third is Associative Sensitivity, involving spontaneous, nonstandard experiences such as visual images during resting). Evans and Rothbart see sensory discomfort as an aspect of negative affect and separate from orienting sensitivity; the SPS model (E. Aron & A. Aron, 1997) sees sensory discomfort as a typical concomitant of sensitivity. However, a low sensory threshold leading to sensory discomfort, when isolated from an underlying depth of processing, may be quite separate from SPS, a feature of poor processing, such as in autistic spectrum disorders, or as an expression of negative affect having an entirely environmental origin. Hence, although a low sensory threshold and sensory discomfort are easily observed by themselves, they may or may not indicate SPS.

Inhibition of Behavior

The inhibition of behavior in a novel situation can be seen as a fear reaction (Kagan, 1994), and the initial conception of the behavioral inhibition system (BIS) was based on brain systems affected by drugs known to reduce anxiety. However, Gray and others (Amodio, Master, Yee, & Taylor, 2008; McNaughton & Gray, 2000) now view the BIS as inhibiting behavior in order to mediate between approach and fear reactions (e.g., reward areas, as well as fear areas, of the brain in "inhibited" adolescents are more easily activated; Bar-Haim et al., 2009). To decide on whether to activate an approach or a fear response, the BIS must process all stimuli, not simply threats. A trait involving a stronger BIS would mean one that processes stimuli even more thoroughly, often, but not always, leading to a longer or greater inhibition of behavior. Of course, inhibiting behavior may also be attributed to many other reasons, for example, an insecure attachment style (Seifer, Schiller, Sameroff, Resnick, & Riordan, 1996). An insecure attachment style can also interact with SPS (in Gray's terms, a strong BIS) such that a person high in SPS, whether secure or insecure, might always pause to observe before entering a new situation due to a heightened alertness of an emotional nature (e.g., desire to inspect for the best opportunity, concern), but if the individual also has an insecure attachment system, a novel situation is more likely to be perceived as a threat (Nachmias, Gunnar, Mangelsdorf, Parritz, & Buss, 1996). Clinicians often meet with clients who appear to be or describe themselves as fearful, shy, or inhibited, and the exact cause of this needs to be assessed with temperament in mind.

Introversion–Extraversion, Neuroticism, and Other Five-Factor Traits

Regarding Introversion, it is very interesting that 20 years ago sensitivity was considered the definitive indicator of introversion as it was then defined and measured, as arousability, using the Eysenck Personality Inventory (Stelmack, 1997). Presently the Big Five/Five-Factor Model conceptualizes and measures Introversion as lack of positive affect. If SPS is associated with stronger emotions, then stronger positive emotions would lead to a correlation with Extraversion (as found by Evans & Rothbart, 2007) and stronger negative emotions with Neuroticism. Indeed, correlations between the HSP Scale and measures of Introversion vary widely (E.

Aron & A. Aron [1997] performed complex analyses to sort out the relationship with SPS) according to whether they focus on arousability (Eysenck Personality Inventory, significant correlations of .19 to .29 in various samples) or affect and sociability (Big Five model, nonsignificant correlation).

Two studies have compared the HSP Scale to all of the scales in the Five-Factor Model. E. Aron and A. Aron (1997), using the John, Donahue, and Kentle Big Five Inventory (1992), and Smolewska, McCabe, and Woody (2004), using the NEO Personality Inventory and Five-Factor Inventory (NEO-FFI; Costa & McCrae, 1992), found no significant correlation with Introversion, Agreeableness, or Conscientiousness. Smolewska and colleagues reported a significant (.19) correlation with Openness (the ATQ's Orienting Sensitivity correlates .65; Evans & Rothbart, 2007). In those two studies there was, however, a strong correlation (.41 and .46, respectively) with five-factor Neuroticism, as would be expected. The problem for researchers and clinicians alike is sorting out the causes of this negative affect given that history also plays a role. Two studies (E. Aron et al., 2005, reporting three replications; Liss et al., 2005) found negative affect to be moderated by negative parental environment in childhood, such that those scoring high on the HSP Scale who had good childhoods actually evidenced no more negative affect than those without the trait. (In Study 4 [E. Aron et al., 2005] the effect of those high on this trait being more emotionally affected than others by self-significant events was demonstrated experimentally.) This is also in keeping with the already mentioned research reviewed by Belsky and Pluess (2009) and by van IJzendoorn and Bakermans-Kranenburg (Chapter 19, in this volume), some of which finds that sensitive individuals (sometimes designated fearful, inhibited, reactive, carrying the serotonin transporter [5-HTTP] risk allele) when raised in supportive environments or in the context of clinical or social interventions evidence less negative affect than those without the trait.

This is not to say that a sensitive child or adult raised in a supportive environment will have no difficulties; rather, their negative responses to truly negative experiences will still typically be stronger. For example, regardless of the quality of a sensitive person's general past and present environments, witnessing a suicide or murder will almost certainly produce a stronger emotional reaction, and posttraumatic stress disorder (PTSD) may be a more common result (a question needing research). Those high in SPS will also still have problems with goodness of fit, and need to balance adapting to others along with not living as others do in many ways. There are also the problems that result from being in a numerical minority, with a trait not always in favor within the culture. But sensitivity does not seem reducible to either Introversion or Neuroticism, or to any other five-factor trait.

Assessing Temperament

Assessing for temperament in adults is not as difficult as it might seem. The first step is having a versatile list of traits in mind that have been validated by research and the therapist's expanding experience with temperament. These can overlap and be at different levels; the goal is clinical utility not theoretical purity. Many temperament counselors (e.g., Kristal, 2005) have used the reliable list from Thomas and Chess (1997) to good effect for years with children, and Kristal (2005) reports the five most frequently observed combinations seen in children in clinical settings. These very useful lists of traits can be looked for in adult clients when taking their history, as questions related to temperament in childhood may indicate much not about only their childhood but also about who they are now. But the Thomas-and-Chess traits are not necessarily visible or the best way to think of adult temperament, since they miss conceptualizations of traits based more on processes, genetic polymorphisms, or our deepening understanding of cognition and the brain, which are the aspects of traits that probably tend to persist throughout life. For this purpose, one might turn to Evans and Rothbart's (2007) list of adult temperament traits. The Big Five/Five-Factor Model traits, although these probably do not represent temperament traits per se, are so familiar to some, especially Introversion–Extraversion, that these may be part of the list a clinician keeps in mind, along with sensation seeking, effortful control, and others that seem useful.

It is also useful to be familiar, if possible, with different trait descriptors of the same set of behaviors. For example, in the case of SPS, the closest Thomas and Chess description behaviorally might be the slow-to-warm-up child, characterized by withdrawing, low sensory threshold, and low adaptability. This snapshot can be a useful template, even though it is based on behaviors observable in childhood. There is no reason, however, not to keep in mind slow-to-warm-up, SPS, Orienting Sensitivity, Openness to Experience, and facets of both Introversion and Extraversion when thinking about sensitivity in a particular client or discussing it with him or her. None of these terms is written in stone; our terminology is still evolving.

Information from History

A possible temperament trait can become a working hypothesis from the outset during a clinical history taking. The client's education or employment, for example, and how that has worked out, all begin to reveal temperament. A person who has begun a business or actively invests in the stock market is probably a risk taker. Have the risks been successful? Were they taken easily or with agony? Circumstances and traits are constantly interacting, so it helps to think like Sherlock Holmes. If a client were high in SPS, for example, he or she would probably invest very shrewdly only when highly confident of the results, and still worry. When these clients are low in self-confidence, however, they will be low risk-takers and probably not begin businesses or invest heavily. A high sensation seeker, on the other hand, will probably love these lines of work.

As one moves on to marital status, has there been risk taking in relationships? Has this been impulsive or well considered, successful or not? If the person avoids relationships, does the history suggest reasons for this, such as an avoidant attachment style, or could it be that high SPS has led to the person being overly aware of another's flaws or taking almost too seriously the responsibilities involved in a commitment? If the client chose to have no children or only one, could the reason be a sensitive person's wish to avoid overstimulation?

Another way to think of the search for temperament's contribution is that it is a process of "partialing out" the effects of history in order to see what remains. If the client has experienced a trauma, is the reaction to that type of trauma similar to that of most people? If the person is depressed, anxious, abusing substances, or whatever, do circumstances and history seem to warrant it? If not, how might temperament be playing a role? Is the drug use part of sensation seeking or is it self-medicating? In a similar statistical vein, one can look for how a given temperament trait might interact with environment to produce behaviors. For example, in some cultures or environments, those high in SPS might be more likely to be a target of bullying; in others, perhaps they are less often the target. Even when looking at early attachment trauma, one can ask how that might have interacted with or been filtered through the lens of a certain temperament.

Moving into taking the history, again, a temperament hypothesis can be pursued with questions about clients' childhoods. How did parents or teachers describe them? Did anyone speak directly about their temperament or behavior from birth? When an odd behavior is mentioned—"I was always hiding under beds"—the therapist can explore both environmental and temperament explanations without being wedded to either category. When taking the relationship history, questions about how others view them currently can be revealing. "My friends say I'm too shy" or "My wife says I'm 'high maintenance.'" Follow-up questions can ferret out the reasons. When the client reports only negative views from others, temperament may be revealed by asking, "If you are so high maintenance, I wonder if you can imagine why she married you?" or why he or she is still married. A sensitive husband might reply, "Well, she does say I've always listened well." Another type might say, "I guess she 'maintains' me the way I expect because she knows I'm a good provider."

Because a therapist's experience of a temperament trait is mostly based on clients who have diverse problems or are in stressful circumstances that have interacted with a given trait, one way mentally to partial out the effect of clients' major stress or trauma from the "pure" trait is to have an image of how the trait appears in individuals with relatively fewer life difficulties. Sometimes this can be done by constructing a composite picture of the trait from people one knows personally who have the trait but are functioning unusually well. For example, the initial phase of research on SPS (E. Aron & A. Aron, 1997) involved interviews with a nonclinical sample of 39 persons of varying ages and occupations, most of whom did not have special difficulties. At the other extreme from typical clients, this sample included a man who was a widely published scientist, the chair of his academic department, popular and well traveled, happily married, and successful as an artist (described by E. Aron [1996], with some details altered to protect confidentiality). He was beloved as a child and his sensitivity was considered a gift. His preference to read rather than play with the other boys was encouraged. He had known about this trait his entire life and knew he was a member of a minority, but he was very happy with it. His main complaint was that he was easily overstimulated, so that he might not sleep after an intense day, and he had turned down career opportunities that would have been too stressful. He reported having deep emotions that occasionally led to depression and knew he could take things "too hard," but had learned to handle his emotions. He had enjoyed and gained from a psychoanalysis of many years.

Looking for neutral and positive aspects of a trait in clients, however troubled they may be by it or by other things, helps in deciding whether it is present. Perhaps they have put it to good use in a career or with friends. A sensitive client who has had strong emotional reactions to negative events or traumas throughout life should also have had strong positive reactions to some events.

Assessing Broadly

Traits are by definition stable across time and found across many contexts. In any hypothesis testing about the presence of a trait, it is helpful to have a sense of a wide variety of ways that it would manifest. That is, what are the basic indicators, broadly found, and if any were missing, would that disprove the hypothesis? In the case of SPS, one can use the acronym DOES (E. Aron, 2010) to remember the characteristics that probably should be found somewhere in a person's life in order to conclude this trait is present. First would be signs of D for depth of processing (in a sense, the basis for the other three). Signs of D might mean having given special thought to the meaning of life, even at a young age, along with concern about world events, vivid dreams, a high level of creativity or appreciation of the arts, and conscientiousness (having considered more the consequences of one's actions). Of course, all of these could be present without SPS, but these are some evidence.

Another sign of D would be taking longer to make a decision or spending more time planning one's life. Of course, a problem with decision making could be due instead to or exist along with inner conflicts or a decision "trauma" (after an extremely difficult or regretted decision). But decision difficulties or slowness should be found broadly, and the decisions should have frequently resulted in better outcomes. A possible line of questioning might be, "When you and a friend are deciding on something to do, do you often have a sense of what will work best, and are you usually right? And if you don't mention it because your friend wants to do something else, what usually happens? Do you turn out to be right?" Sensitive clients with low self-esteem are usually surprised to realize that often they do decide well, even if slowly.

Second, O, being easily overaroused, is often behind the presenting problem with SPS. Processing the subtleties of a situation usually means that sensitive clients caught in environments where there are high levels of other stimuli or too much information coming at once will complain of feeling overwhelmed, "stressed out," or "burned out." They are more prone to insomnia and stress-related illnesses. Anyone around persons with this trait are also usually most aware of this aspect, in that they avoid stimulating situations (parties, shopping malls, meeting strangers, etc.), want to stop an activity before others, or pack less stimulation into a day (e.g., they do not go out in the evenings during the week; when on vacation, after a day of sightseeing they want to spend the evening in their hotel room), and generally want more time alone than others want to give them. Spouses who come home from work and do not participate in family life are sometimes high in SPS. Being easily overaroused also affects performance, such as timed tests or being observed during training on the job. Of course, being easily stressed by too much going on at once can also be a sign of a stressful history or of an environment that would be too much for anyone, so by itself, O is also not an indicator of high SPS. Again, it is the presence of most or all DOES characteristics that best validates the hypothesis.

Third, E, emotional reactivity, is in response to both positive and negative experiences. Of course, if the sensitive client has had a very difficult past, negative affect will predominate. Other signs of E are crying or laughing easily, elation, almost manic excitement when involved in creative projects (but without risk taking), being highly affected by seeing violence even in television or movies, anguish over the suffering of others, being "touchy" or "too" sensitive to criticism, and avoiding much of life because one is so easily affected by everything. Again, high emotional reactivity without the other aspects does not indicate SPS.

Finally, S, sensory sensitivity, is often what first comes to mind with the word *sensitive*. If asked, these clients immediately acknowledge that they are aware of subtleties in their environment (birds singing, the need to change a room's lighting) and also unusually bothered by noise, irritating odors, scratchy fabrics, and much more. They are usually more sensitive to pain, which can lead to avoiding activities such as rough sports, without being aware of why. They also report unusual sensory pleasure if asked, and often especially appreciate being in nature. Many are particularly aware of stimuli to one sense. However, sensory discomfort or perseveration with one sense can also indicate neurological problems such as autism spectrum disorders. Once again, one aspect without the others may indicate something else entirely.

Paper-and-Pencil Self-Reports

Self-report measures of temperament can be useful, such as the ATQ (Evans & Rothbart, 2007) or a measure of the Big Five personality traits, although some of the terms (e.g., Neuroticism, Negative Affectivity, or Low Agreeableness, Conscientiousness and Openness to Experience) have to be translated into gentler terms. However, the assets and liabilities of such measures both derive from the fact that they are usually developed to support hypotheses about the structure of human personality, and the purity with which a trait is presented may leave out the nuances of a clinical presentation. Like any paper-and-pencil measure, personality or temperament scales or inventories should not be the sole basis for a clinical decision.

With the proper amount of caution, however, these measures are helpful at least in that they present therapist and client with an organized list of situations they may not have thought of and help them establish how broadly a behavioral characteristic is occurring. For example, the HSP (E. Aron & A. Aron, 1997) is a set of items one might have found answers to already in the process of an assessment, but a glance at the list could remind the therapist of other questions that would be worth asking. "Are you especially affected by hunger?" By pain? Caffeine? Now I'm curious. What about movies with lots of violence and gore? Do you enjoy them or avoid them?"

An additional consideration here and throughout a temperament assessment is that not only do cultures have preferences about temperament traits, as noted earlier, but they also have preferences about those each gender should display. When there is a mismatch, an innate behavioral style is more likely to be hidden or change in its manifestation. For example, although every individual item on the HSP Scale is uncorrelated with gender, men (at least North American men) score lower when answering the entire set, which may suggest a defensiveness due to culture, that is a fear of being seen as feminine or weak. Hence, with men, one may learn more by not giving the scale, and by not asking at one time too many direct questions about sensitivity.

Taking into Account the Interaction of Contrasting Traits

A fine-tuning of the evidence for a temperament hypothesis about a client would involve considering whether two highly contrasting but independent traits are present, and if so, how they would interact and appear behaviorally or symptomologically. The classic temperament example is a child who is both distractible and persistent. Such children look up often from what they are doing, responding to the slightest perturbation, but are more likely to return to their task rather than be drawn away by the new stimuli.

In the case of SPS, a contrasting but independent trait is high sensation seeking. Those scoring high on the HSP Scale can sometimes also score high on measures of sensation seeking if high risk items or wordings are replaced by ones without risk of harm. (See such a scale in E. Aron [2000, p. 17]; e.g., "I rarely watch a movie twice"; "If I see something unusual I will go out of my way to check it out"; and "I prefer friends who are unpredictable." A similar adaptation in the Evans and Rothbart [2007] ATQ is the High-Intensity Pleasure scale within the broader construct of Surgency/Extraversion.) Individuals with these contrasting traits often have difficulty finding friends, partners, and careers that suit both aspects, and when they are happily employed, the two traits are often noticeable side by side. For example, individuals high on both SPS and sensation seeking are often employed as news reporters and interviewers, in which their sensitivity helps them uncover the best stories, while the constant change satisfies their sensation seeking. They can appear self-destructive, in that they are continually exhausting themselves due to their own choices. It can also leave them vulnerable to trauma. For example, one of these individuals, a news reporter, had a severe PTSD reaction to a terrorist bombing she witnessed while on vacation and was the first to report internationally. Her spouse, a photographer and not sensitive, was largely unaffected and even a bit delighted by the career opportunity. The event precipitated a career, marital, and health crisis, as well as the PTSD itself. After carefully reviewing her history and the stresses in her life, it became clear that this was largely a temperament issue.

Those with the sensation seeking and SPS combination really serve two masters and may actually be showing considerable skill handling this innate conflict. Recognizing their quandary is an important first step in treatment.

Similarly, while SPS has a low but significant correlation with some measures of social introversion (E. Aron & A. Aron, 1997), many are social extraverts. They will have a large circle of friends and enjoy social gatherings and meeting strangers. Their sensitivity is noticeable however, first, in their admission that they need more down-time than most extraverts. They also may appear to have "poor boundaries," in that they are inclined to voice publicly their deepest thoughts, then be embarrassed or have hurt feelings because of how others react. Usually their history reveals reasons for their Extraversion (e.g., growing up in a close community, including neighborhoods in large cities or extended families; adapting to social pressure).

Temperament and DSM

When a DSM diagnosis is needed, obviously clinicians employing a temperament perspective do not want to confuse temperament and disorder in an assessment. It helps to remember, first, that every case of major depressive disorder or general anxiety disorder, every person with a substance abuse problem or having a psychotic episode, everyone dealing with dementia or PTSD, is still a person with an innate temperament pattern. Looking around and under symptoms for these normal predispositions, then seeing how a disorder might be filtered through temperament should lead to better diagnosis and treatment.

Second, the central DSM criterion is clinically significant impairment or distress, and that should remain after having discussed temperament issues that could in themselves be creating distress only because they are not understood. For example, I have seen clients' panic disorder and agoraphobia fail to meet criteria for that diagnosis after they understand that their first panic attack was due to overstimulation. Likewise, when responses to life events are reframed in terms of temperament, anxiety and depression that were due to low self-esteem may be so positively affected that the clients no longer meet the criteria for diagnosis. Here one also wants to take into account internalized cultural prejudices that certain traits or aspects of them are in themselves an impairment or cause of distress (e.g., sensitivity in men is weak), perhaps by being distressful to others.

Third, behaviors and problems characteristic of a temperament trait would have been present before most precipitating factors of the DSM condition. In the case of PTSD or other anxiety disorders, nonsensitive clients may describe being hypervigilant and having poor sleep, but only since the trauma or the beginning of stressful situations in their lives. That is, the client can recall a time without the disorder. When environmental factors such as poverty or neglect have been present from the beginning of life, it can be more difficult to distinguish nature from nurture, but the very fact that these are present requires considering whether temperament increased or decreased vulnerability.

Regarding SPS specifically, it is helpful to delay or revisit a diagnosis. In the first few sessions, sensitive persons may be far from their normal behavior, since beginning psychotherapy can be highly stimulating for anyone, but more so for sensitive clients. Sensitive persons can also be overly aware of or exceptionally conscientiousness about reporting symptoms and flaws that may later appear to be not so significant. On the other hand, some sensitive clients, especially those with personality disorders, may present as functioning better than they are, in that they have used their sensitivity to adapt to the expectations of others, which also can contribute to a better outcome.

Axis I Diagnoses

Proceeding through the DSM list, this and the following section use SPS as an example of how a trait can interact with disorders. It is based only on personal clinical observations. Page numbers refer to DSM-IV. (For a more complete discussion of SPS and DSM diagnoses, see E. Aron, 2010.)

Innate sensitivity, especially when mixed with shyness, has been sometimes viewed as the mildest form of autism (e.g., Ratey & Johnson, 1997). However, distress from sensory stimulation is not listed in DSM-IV criteria for what are now being called autistic spectrum disorders. It appears only in the autistic disorder description, as "odd responses to sensory stimuli" (pp. 67–68), including a high threshold to pain, not a low one. Inconsistency seems to be the main feature of these odd responses, such as focusing on certain stimuli while ignoring others. Otherwise, none of the criteria for autism or Asperger's disorder would likely be met by a highly sensitive adult or child as defined here, mainly because fMRI studies indicate that those high in SPS are unusually responsive to social cues and, when in a familiar social environment, can be quite skilled at social interaction. Highly sensitive men who have chosen a lifestyle or career that allows them to avoid social rejection also may have been told or decided on their own that they might have Asperger's, so careful attention must be given to clients' empathy with the therapist and how they describe their relationships with others.

Attention-deficit/hyperactivity disorder (ADHD) or attention deficit disorder (ADD) are confused surprisingly often with high sensitivity, but when not overstimulated, those high in SPS lack the major DSM characteristics of this disorder. In particular, in a quiet environment, those high in SPS have no difficulty focusing their attention. However, sensitive persons, like anyone else, may avoid or fail at tasks requiring focus or following directions if they have failed at these in the past. The original cause, however, would have been not a general inability to focus but a specific difficulty with overarousal. Sensitive persons sometimes do not realize how much they must practice and prepare in order to overcome the often debilitating levels of arousal that accompany tests, performances, and other evaluated tasks. After a failure, they are even more overaroused by expecting failure the next time; thus, they almost surely avoid such tasks or are unable to focus when they try. Whether sensitive persons can also have "true" ADHD remains to be determined by research.

Regarding depression, a misdiagnosis can occur if therapists do not appreciate that the highly sensitive are going to "ruminate" or process negative events more deeply. They will be more affected by losses, separations, defeats, and failures. Simply listening to others' troubles or reading news articles may leave them depressed and anxious. They may also have what, compared to others, is a pessimistic view of the future of the world or of their own abilities, but this pessimism may well be accurate, as in the case of depressive realism (Alloy & Abramson, 1979). However, again, a poor parenting environment in childhood is known to lead more often to diagnosable depression in sensitive persons (E. Aron et al., 2005; Liss et al., 2005). Furthermore, anxiety or sadness about something appropriate, such as grief after a death, may turn more easily into diagnosable depression.

Depressed clients high in SPS may appear to be functioning all right because of their ability to manage their persona and their desire to be conscientious and carry on as needed. The more important criteria may be subjective states reported in therapy, such as worthlessness, emptiness, or unending sadness. Fatigue, loss of focus, or anhedonia may also be present but covered up. Those living with the client who have seen the person during a previous episode may be best able to recognize a recurrence.

Regarding anxiety disorders, most sensitive persons report anxiety (Liss et al., 2005). Many have also probably had something like a panic attack, in that they have had moments of feeling overwhelmed and being all too aware of and frightened by their body being on the edge of what DSM describes: pounding or palpitating heart, sweating, shaking, feeling unable to breathe, dizziness or numbness, as well as sometimes feeling unreal, detached, or afraid of losing control, dying, or going crazy. The first time usually occurs in youth, for example, when taking a recreational drug, attending a rock concert, or performing in public. The question will be whether these recur even after providing this explanation and meet the criteria for diagnosis.

As for social phobia, DSM criteria are somewhat vague anyway, in that almost everyone has had, at some point in life, bouts of "marked and persistent fear" (American Psychiatric Association, 1994, p. 416) of being scrutinized and humiliated that they knew to be excessive, was impairing their functioning, and invariably occurred in the feared social situation. Sensitive persons are even more aware than others that people do scrutinize each other. Due to their emotional reactivity, in these situations they may be even more aroused than others, which impairs their response and causes them to feel even more scrutinized. All of this becomes a disorder only when they are utterly powerless to overcome their fear in almost all situations.

As with social phobia, DSM criteria for generalized anxiety are highly dependent on defining *excessive* ("excessive anxiety and worry . . . occurring more days than not for at least 6 months," p. 435). Paying attention, for example, to where the emergency exits are in hotels, theaters, or planes might seem like excessive worry until there is a fire. DSM symptoms such as feeling on edge, easily fatigued, having trouble concentrating or having one's mind go blank, irritability, muscle tension, and sleep disturbance are all common life occurrences for highly sensitive persons when simply overstimulated. As always, the issue is degree of impairment after a discussion of the client's temperament and an opportunity to observe the person for several sessions.

Axis II Diagnoses

Personality disorders are similar to temperament in that both are "an enduring pattern of inner experience and behavior" that can sometimes seem to deviate "markedly from the expectations of the individual's culture," be "pervasive and inflexible . . . stable over time," and lead to "distress and impairment" (p. 629) when there is a bad fit between client and environment. Of course, temperament traits are present along with personality disorders, as well as occasionally being mistaken for them. Those most easily confused with high sensitivity are those that sensitive persons are also mostly likely to develop: avoidant, schizoid, borderline, dependent, and obsessive–compulsive disorders. In addition, regarding the other personality disorders, the highly sensitive can *seem* paranoid when they describe subtle motivations in others that most people do not notice; schizotypal due to their unusual perceptions or spiritual proclivities; narcissistic because of their greater "self-absorption" or any real giftedness they may have; and histrionic in their intense emotional reactions. Decisions about an Axis II diagnosis involve an assessment of distress and impairment of normal functioning, and with clients having unusual temperaments should probably be delayed until after they have adjusted their lifestyle, self-expectations, and self-esteem through therapy to be consistent with their traits (or it is clear that they cannot, so that the distress and impairment remain).

Treatment with Temperament in Mind

The concept of goodness of fit can be useful in thinking about temperament in the context of treatment. At the outset, and perhaps throughout, an important part of any treatment can be providing clients with the experience of a good fit in the therapy environment, by the therapist making a point of adapting to the client. This might especially be the case when clients have rarely, if ever, experienced this before. Besides helping a client simply feel more comfortable, it displays an appreciation and respect for a client's unique disposition.

Sometimes goodness of fit applies more to helping clients provide this for themselves by making lifestyle changes or altering their behavior within their relationships. The therapist might choose to provide a good fit or adapt more to the client at first, and later expect the client to do more of the adapting, as practice for what is needed outside of sessions. However, this will vary according to need rather than being a simple progression. As with children, one can think about an adult client's developmental age or stage. When functioning is still poor, or problems go back to childhood insecurity (including parents who provided a very poor fit), continued and consistent adapting to the client can build security—indeed, it may be crucial to it.

Adapting to the Client's Temperament

Goodness of fit (or even teaching a client to accommodate to others) cannot occur until the therapist respects the client's temperament traits as intrinsically valuable, important parts of the person. As with parent and child, goodness of fit in therapy probably does not depend on similarity so much as paying close attention to what is required to bring out the client's best and discussing this when it is useful to do so.

Regarding clients with high SPS, perhaps the most important adaptation is in the "volume" of speech—not only its loudness but also the level of directness, brusqueness, or confrontation. Kochanska and Thompson (1997), in observing how moral development occurs in childhood according to temperament, discussed the importance of an optimal level of arousal for internalizing moral lessons. Punishment or the threat of it may be necessary to get the attention of the average child, but it is far too overarousing for the sensitive ones. With too much arousal, what is remembered is the punishment rather than the principle. Kochanska's research (summarized in Kochanska & Thompson, 1997) found that with "fearful" or sensitive children (e.g., those more likely to notice flaws in toys), gentle discipline deemphasizing power works best. The same can easily be said for highly sensitive clients. Too much or too little arousal probably generally interferes with their absorbing the lessons to be gained in therapy. They are more likely to gain from low-arousing hints, suggestions, affirmations, reflection of feelings, insightful interpretations (when these sound like theories being tested by presenting a possibility, not judgments), and questions that probe gently in a way that implies all answers are equally interesting and valuable. Not "*What* were you thinking when you did that?" so much as "I'm curious—if you can recall—what were you thinking the moment when you made that decision?"

Goodness of fit is also in the details of the first meeting and its setting. For example, sensitive types will like waiting rooms or offices with soft lights and muted colors, light classical music or none at all, subtle artwork, no clutter, and perhaps the opportunity to serve themselves tea. Their opposites might like bright lights; artwork depicting athletics, entertainment, or travel; and coffee. Nothing will suit everyone, but medical office blandness sends its own message. Perhaps it is best that furniture and artwork reflect one's professional philosophy and personality, allowing the clients to begin to sense for themselves whether this will be a good fit.

In the first minutes of the first session a client high in SPS will probably sense a great deal, consciously or not, about the therapist. Indeed, in private practice this may start even before meeting, with the voice on the message machine and the manner in which initial arrangements are made. At this point, not knowing the client's temperament, the therapist cannot adapt very much, although, like the client, the therapist can begin to assess and even treat through messages and ways of handling details. The sensitive client with low self-esteem might accept office practices without question, perhaps not asking about a sliding scale even when clearly needing it or questioning a strict policy about missed sessions. The therapist might have to probe about how the client's needs will be met, not just the therapist's. A time convenient for the therapist, for example, could cause a sensitive client to drive an extra hour in traffic, but being low in self-esteem, the client says nothing. Sensitive types with more self-esteem might ask politely about all the details that might affect them, negotiating when something is a problem for them, but not challenging the reasons for policies. In all cases, one can begin both to provide a good fit and to explore temperament traits openly: "It seems you are an unusually thoughtful and certainly agreeable person, and I appreciate that, but let's be sure you have also thought enough about your own needs" or "You seem to be a details person—I'm going to enjoy going over my office policies with you when we meet in person because I suspect you will be paying attention and ask questions before signing anything—a good way to be."

Retention and Termination

As the work proceeds, therapists may want to discuss and rediscuss the length of therapy. Often this is determined by other factors—finances, insurance, or the form of therapy—but temperament is a factor here as well. In particular, sensitive clients are likely to form strong attachments due to their emotional reactivity, and should be informed and reminded about the probable number of sessions. Sensitive clients also may require more sessions than others, perhaps needing more time to feel safe and to sort through their often complicated, subtle thoughts and feelings. If they are rushed or anxious about ending before they feel ready, it may only increase the time needed to achieve results. Sensitive persons also may choose to stay in therapy longer, enjoying the deep reflection and discussion that can occur in therapy, as well as the kindness, attention, and good fit.

Whatever the planned number of sessions, it is best to probe for and be very accepting of any desire for more, then to discuss why a client might want or need more time than others. This way a client does not feel overly needy or fear being in therapy forever because of not understanding why he or she is so inclined to continue.

On the other hand, sensitive clients can quit unexpectedly after going on for weeks, months, or even years without a word of complaint because in fact they felt they were not being helped but could not say it. Therapists need to ask these clients frequently whether the work seems to be meeting their needs and how it might be improved. Helping them admit when they are being disappointed may be the very breakthrough they need.

Helping Clients Develop a Temperament-Appropriate Lifestyle

Besides the goodness of fit with the therapist and therapeutic environment, the temperament aspect of therapy may require helping clients find the right fit in lifestyle, living environment, career, and social relationships. For any temperament, a major issue is degree of stimulation. One's life can be overstimulating, too much in the fast lane with not enough down-time, or one can be so withdrawn from the world that one is under stimulated and bored. We need stimulation much as we need food, and not having the right amount can lead to many symptoms (e.g., substance abuse, marital affairs, acting out, anxiety, depression) that are not usually seen as being due to too much or too little stimulation.

As clients decide on changes that would improve their lives, the therapist has to consider whether these are realistic changes and how to react to failures to achieve them. It can help to frame any outcome as simply information: "I'll be very interested to see if you can speak to at least one stranger a day, but if you can't for some reason, we'll just treat that as information. More grist for the mill. So whenever you hit a roadblock, try to make note of what else was going on at the time and what you were feeling or thinking."

More follows about making temperament-related changes both in work and relationships.

Treating the Effects of Temperament Prejudice

As discussed earlier, some clients feel the effects of negative stereotypes within their culture or subculture regarding a trait of theirs. It may be unpopular or viewed as abnormal, too extreme, or a sign of weakness if they cannot control it, so they feel they have a deep inner flaw to hide, contributing to defensive behaviors such as withdrawal or impressing others by going to the opposite extreme such as high risk taking. Reframing will need to be consistent and repeated many times. It is also valuable to point out explicitly the role of culture (without giving too much of a sense of having been victimized). For example, a study (Chen, Rubin, & Sun, 1992) comparing sensitive children in Canada and China, found that in China they were among the most popular as seen by their peers, and in North America they were among the least popular (although apparently China is increasingly like Canada; Chen, He, Cen, & Li, 2005; see Chen, Yang, & Fu, Chapter 22, this volume). This type of factual evidence can be valuable to share with some sensitive clients.

Research on treating the effects of stereotype threat indicates that promoting a positive attitude ("I can do this") does not help as much as working on the negative stereotype of the trait that the client has internalized (Forbes & Schmader, 2010); although value affirmations (thinking about one's deepest values—family, spirituality, helping others, productivity, creativity, etc.) do appear to have an effect (Taylor & Walton, 2011). Since it may be true that a temperament trait actually does make some situations more difficult, the best approach might be to focus on the fact that the trait is an advantage in many situations, especially those that are most important to the client, and to plan ways to counter any real disadvantage in performance situations, perhaps by extra preparation. Then the client can know, "I can do this because I have taken my temperament into account—it's a huge advantage in the situations that matter to me, like my volunteer work, but in this case I have to plan for its effects."

If reframing and a cultural perspective do not help with an internalized negative stereotype of a trait, a deeper exploration of the core worthlessness is needed. Such feelings are often the product of a few comments heard early in life from important others or an interaction of temperament with emotional schemas due to past social and attachment traumas, and are better altered after sufficient trust has been generated for the defenses to drop and the sense of worthlessness to be even more openly felt. A goal might be that the client can answer affirmatively if asked, "If you could choose whether to be born with this trait, would you?"

Temperament and Work

Temperament is often behind problems in the workplace. While vocational counselors, career counselors, coaches, and the like may take "type" or preference into account, they more often focus only on abilities and learning to overcome emotional obstacles. A therapist rather than a coach or vocational counselor is needed when difficulties arise, and these require a careful sorting out of the variables of temperament and history. "Minority" temperaments in particular can play a role in conflict at work or frequent job changes because others may not know or care to adapt to the needs of an unusual person, and the client may not know how to evaluate and act on a temperament problem or seek a better fit elsewhere.

Career Choice

If clients are considering a career choice or change, taking temperament into account often involves a simultaneous narrowing and broadening of possibilities. The narrowing involves acknowledging that even if a person has a talent in a certain area, the emotional and motivational aspects of temperament may preclude certain choices. For example, a very active, stimulus-seeking, extraverted person may also be good at careful data analysis, but if the job requires sitting in front of a monitor all day without many breaks, trouble may lie ahead. The broadening involves noticing careers that do fit aspects of a person's temperament that perhaps have been ignored by past advisors who focused more on the client's talents.

A clinical example of this was V., a highly sensitive person who was having intense alternating bouts of anxiety and depression, with only a very vague sense of the reason. Since he was very young, his parents had given him a choice—law school or medical school. He was their firstborn, "very smart," and noticing his sensitivity and that he was not very "aggressive," his parents had wanted him to have a profession with guaranteed status and income. V. had conscientiously done as his parents wished, choosing law because he was "good at learning details and I wasn't sure about me and blood and cadavers." But after 1 year of law school he had dropped out and taken up accounting. Not sure why, we explored his experience in law school and found that, basically, he was shocked by what he saw as the ruthless competitiveness of his fellow students. Being good at math, he quickly enrolled in an accounting program in order to work in his family's business. The decision had only increased his anxiety and depression, however. He was vaguely afraid that it was also a mistake, and he could not bear to face having made two costly wrong choices. Yet he dreamed of "the walls closing in" and was agonized by the thought that he "would never make a difference in the world" beyond his family.

In therapy V. began to understand the role of his sensitivity in all of this and to open up to the many careers that might take advantage of it. Sensitive people have proven to be especially suited to teaching, consulting, the arts, scientific research; some forms of medicine and healing; and working with plants, animals, infants, and older adults. They can actually enjoy almost any career if they do it in a way that suits their temperament, although they appear even more than others to need to find their work meaningful. Also, as in the case of V., they need to be especially careful not to rely too much on the advice of well-meaning others, and to slow down a decision process in order to gather information and reflect on their own values. This also provides the opportunity to learn to approach a problem in a way that takes advantage of their reflective temperament. Above all, they have to accept that difficult decisions are that way because there are uncertainties involved. These mean that mistakes are bound to happen—something that they, by nature, particularly try hard to avoid.

Workplace Issues

Given the hours one spends at work, a good fit between the work environment and temperament is obviously important. Activity level, need for excitement or stimulation, need for social contact, and many other temperament-related factors can lead to a good or bad fit, to job satisfaction or job misery. Highly sensitive clients in particular may complain of physical and emotional stressors at work that others seem not to notice (although everyone's performance and health may be affected)—for example, long hours or long commutes, frequent deadlines that require overtime, micromanaging, poor lighting or ventilation, bad odors, too much noise, open floor plans, and cubicles without soundproofing. Therapist and client have to explore whether the client is in a position to complain, and if so, how to propose a change that will clearly benefit the organization as well as him- or herself. Clients who are valued employees (sensitive employees often are, but do not realize it unless asked to think about it) and can speak in terms of profit, not simply their own special needs, can make a persuasive case. Otherwise, the focus may need to be on adapting or changing jobs. Some jobs are definitely emotionally and physically unhealthy, and helping a client see that and make a safe change can be very important.

Often the problem for sensitive clients is the social or emotional climate. They thrive on praise and wither under even offhand criticisms that others would hardly notice. Sometimes they are able to convey their need for positive feedback and have that well received; other times, they may be able to adapt with the therapist's help. A few report harassment, including bullying. A hindrance in all workplace situations is that many sensitive clients have felt like and, of course, actually been victims in the past, and this issue may need to be addressed first, before they can think strategically about how to solve a workplace problem and take action in a way that will not open them to further abuse.

Often sensitive clients struggle in meetings because they see problems or the long-term consequences of decisions being made, but if they speak up they are viewed as naysayers. If they hold back, their reticence is often sensed, or they feel they have put themselves "off the team." Offering too many creative solutions carries other risks in some environments. Overall, they need to be encouraged to use their sensitivity to analyze the best strategy rather than feel helpless or be passive.

Some sensitive clients struggle in management positions. They are usually popular in these roles, being thoughtful of others' needs and less inclined to misuse their power, but they have to learn to turn up their volume loud enough to be heard by their less sensitive staff and to tolerate criticism from above and below.

All in all, they are often happiest in small businesses that value their quiet presence and encourage their creative contributions, and where they have some control over their working conditions. Many choose self-employment, enabling them to work shorter hours, "doing less and accomplishing more," without others to criticize them or try to please.

Couple Psychotherapy with a Temperament Perspective

A temperament perspective is profoundly important for relationship choice and maintenance. For example, in a twin study, McGue and Lykken (1996) found that 53% of the variance in divorce risk was attributable to the genetic contribution of one spouse. In a follow-up twin study, Jockin, McGue, and Lykken (1996) measured personality traits known to be somewhat heritable. Positive Emotionality and Negative Emotionality were positively related to divorce rate; Constraint was related negatively. In this study, some heritable trait contributed to 30% of the divorce risk in women and 42% of the risk in men.

The negative effects of Positive Emotionality are probably attributable to reward-oriented impulsivity and high sensation seeking, since both, along with Extraversion, are related to dopamine levels (Canli, 2006). Persons high in sensation seeking are known to be more easily bored in a relationship and more likely to have an affair (Seto, Lalumiere, & Quinsey, 1995). As for the role of Negative Emotionality, it probably arises through the interaction already described: Something innate, some form of sensitivity, interacts with a difficult past, something not innate, leading to chronic negative emotionality, which is known to be the largest single predictor of low marital satisfaction (Karney & Bradbury, 1997). The trait linked to lower divorce, Constraint, would often be an aspect of innate sensitivity, as sensitive persons tend to reflect long and hard before leaving a relationship.

However, these findings do not demonstrate that *any* gene *has to cause* divorce. Just as medically certain innate conditions become dangerous if not recognized soon after birth but otherwise are easily treated, innate traits are threats mostly because partners do not recognize each other's unchangeable aspects, so that they can make the right adaptations.

I have added the HSP Scale to a series of relationship studies conducted for other purposes and employing standard relationship quality measures. Looking at samples totaling about 600 college students and about 200 married adults from the surrounding Long Island community, there has been no direct correlation with sensitivity on relationship success, satisfaction, closeness, and intimacy after partialing out Neuroticism, but couples in which both were sensitive were slightly more satisfied than couples who were dissimilar on this trait (E. Aron, 2004).

When Seeing One Member of the Couple

Although most of what follows assumes that partners are being seen together, relationship problems are just as frequently discussed in individual therapy, creating special temperament-related issues. As a general rule, when informing clients in individual therapy about their temperament, the therapist should warn them that those close to them may not be as pleased as they are about these new discoveries. Rather, it can be quite threatening and convey a feeling that the bond is weaker because the two are now less similar and therefore more separate than before. The news also signals change, usually to improve conditions for the one claiming a special trait. For example, armed with temperament constructs, a client might say during a conflict, "I can't do that, I'm too sensitive" or "I'm just the type who has to move on after awhile." The shift of relative status can be abrupt, especially when a client has been the "identified patient." Suddenly science has deemed the client as normal and having verifiable needs. Through the individual client, the therapist can encourage the two to consider, whenever the subject comes up, what they gain from the other's temperament, the advantages of being in a relationship with someone different rather than similar (e.g., a wider range of behaviors and resources), and also the many other ways that they are actually quite similar.

Temperament is also relevant in individual therapy when it is a client's partner who has a "minority" temperament. These clients may need as much or more support in accepting and adapting to the "special" partner, as well as standing up for their own way of being.

As for sensitive clients specifically, when they are talking about partner problems in individual therapy, because of their emotional intensity they tend to feel strongly in this area, too. They may be so distressed about the relationship in the moment that they seem to be describing hell. Or they may describe it as perfect, being too afraid to open it up to discussion because they feel they overestimate their need for the other. They may feel intense guilt about complaining, viewing love as a virtue that must be maintained whatever the partner does. They often benefit from a definition of love that emphasizes responsiveness: *Each* wanting to know the other, to be near the other in some sense, and to meet the other's needs as much *as possible*, while not ignoring their own, and, when needs conflict, negotiating this as equals and with deep concern for each other.

When the Two Have Dissimilar Temperaments

When partners' temperaments are highly contrasting, before looking for solutions to their temperament-related conflicts, it can help to encourage clients to grieve what they cannot have in this relationship because of the other's temperament. For example, sensitive persons are more easily bored than others in a close relationship. They are no less eager to do interesting, "exciting" activities; the main difference is that they are particularly bored when there is a lack of meaningful conversation in a close relationship, even after controlling for general relationship satisfaction (E. Aron, Aron, Jagiellowicz, & Tomlinson, 2010), so a nonsensitive partner can be especially disappointing to them in conversations. Meanwhile that partner must face, for example, that the sensitive one may never enjoy travel in developing countries, attending large sporting events, or going to shopping malls during the holidays.

The grief can be eased by suggesting that there may be friends or relatives who could meet these needs instead, and again, that they remember what they gain because of their partner's different temperament. The therapist might say:

"Temperament is always a package deal, in that we have to accept the good and the bad sides of a trait, whether in ourselves or another, and the bad side may only be that we can't have the A and not-A. Often, too, what attracts us at first becomes an annoyance in other ways later. If you'd fallen in love with him because of his intensity—the way he blurted out 'I love you' on the third date—it would mean that he probably would not have been quite as calm as you would like. If you had fallen in love with him because he made it clear that he would pursue you to the ends of the earth, you may have found this persistence less attractive in an argument. To have in the same person both intensity and calmness or both persistence and flexibility—usually it doesn't happen. Only in the movies do we see men who are unfazed by anything yet highly sensitive and gentle around women, or women who are always game for any kind of adventure, rough and ready, yet perfectly attuned and perfectly sensitive to another's needs."

Once they accept the consequences of their differences, the two can often come up with creative solutions to what have been long-standing conflicts. For example, visiting a new city, one partner can hit the streets and start exploring while the sensitive one rests. Then the explorer can show the other the best sights later. Or taking two cars to an event allows the sensitive partner to leave sooner. When a sensitive partner takes some "down-time," he or she can reassure the other, "It's nothing to do with you—I love you dearly—I just need a little solitude again." They can also begin to take advantage of and praise each other's strengths rather than feeling inferior or competitive: "Sure, go check it out—I know you're better at those things than I am."

Conflict Resolution

Conflict resolution requires fairness and equality, but all temperaments are not equal in their reaction to conflict. Some mind conflict less than others, even feeling, it seems, that a good argument now and then adds a touch of excitement to the relationship. Such partners are often more successful at getting their way because they are not as overaroused. They keep their heads and argue well, so that in contrast to the other, they are more powerful—that is, influential. When subjects in experiments are made to feel more powerful, they tend to become more focused on their own goals, to move more quickly to achieve them, and to pay less attention to the characteristics of others compared to those given less power (Keltner, Gruenfeld, & Anderson, 2003). In relationships, too, one partner can feel more powerful than the other at certain times or all the time, for whatever reason, and thus tend to be less considerate of the other without realizing why. Often it appears as a sense that one partner does not respect the other. Focusing on the reason for issues of power being present is helpful. If the issue is not who is earning more, temperament (and attitudes toward a particular temperament) is often behind the power differential and its effects.

Those with minority temperaments, especially those who are highly sensitive, may feel, look, and act less powerful, and thus avoid conflict or give in. This is not intrinsically so or always the case. They can also strategize more effectively and may need to be reminded of that. But for highly sensitive clients, direct conflict is usually more upsetting and overstimulating. They are more conscientious, less competitive, more likely to see all sides to a conflict, and more prone to recognize how others will suffer if their needs are not met. Their partners can learn to take advantage of this, even unintentionally. On the other hand, sometimes it is the less sensitive partner who does not speak up out of fear of hurting the more "delicate" feelings of the sensitive partner or being attacked by a person very capable of knowing just what to say that hurts most. Obviously when temperament has bestowed more power on one partner, for whatever reason, it is an obstacle to fair conflict resolution.

In conflict resolution training, the therapist needs to see that the less powerful partner, often the more sensitive one, recognizes and speaks up about his or her preferences. This may require some assertiveness training: "In this way of resolving conflicts, you will listen carefully to your partner for 15 minutes, which I know you are good at, and then when it is your turn, you must speak out about your own needs and feelings, and I want you to give some thought to this and not just go along with your partner because it seems to be so important to her." The clinician can also ask partners to think of a scale that for each "want" weighs how important it is that each of them have it, and how bad it would feel not to receive it. Sometimes less sensitive partners actually care very little about something they are fighting for quite effectively, while it is something their sensitive partner desperately wants.

Differences in conflict resolution styles due to temperament need to be highlighted repeatedly, along with how each gains from the other's style in other settings:

"So you like how Jack, being more sensitive, listens better than you, sees the whole picture, and from what he tells you about a situation, you can step in and do what has to be done. So naturally when you argue, you are bolder and more decisive than Jack. That means your task is to hold back, listen to him, and not take a stand so quickly. Jack has to stop seeing the whole picture and focus on his own needs for once. Otherwise you may 'resolve' things too soon, which means they are not really resolved at all."

"Time-outs" when things have become too tense is another tool these couples in particular need. Gottman, Driver, and Tabares (2002) recommend that partners check their own pulses, and if either pulse is over 100, they need to back off for at least 20 minutes and think about something else. This objective measure is also useful for demonstrating to partners the physiological underpinnings of their different temperaments.

Therapists can also appeal to the more sensitive partner's strong ethical sense: "If you don't stand up for yourself, you are almost inviting Jean to take advantage of you." Both parties can also be warned that, ultimately, the partner not being heard will almost certainly resort to passive–aggressive behaviors or simply leave when the opportunity comes along.

Sexuality

Temperament has to play a substantial role in sexual preferences and practices. In perhaps the first study of the role of temperament in sexuality (E. Aron, 2000, 2004), subscribers to a newsletter for sensitive people responded anonymously to a mailed questionnaire and also gave it to a nonsensitive friend, to be mailed separately. These anonymous questionnaires included items about sexual experiences, current practices, problems, and preferences, as well as a short-form of the HSP Scale. Based on 450 respondents, there were four main results for both genders after statistically controlling for negative affectivity (Neuroticism) and traumatic events in childhood. First, there was a near-zero difference between the sensitive and nonsensitive in overall satisfaction with their sex lives and reports of sexual problems. Second, sensitive persons were substantially more likely to report that sex for them had a "sense of mystery and power." Third, sensitive participants were less sexually responsive to explicit sexual cues, such as pornography, and less interested in having variety in their sexual practices. Fourth, they were more sensitive to stimulation during sex, even to the point of it being painful or of needing to stop for a break, and more bothered by slight sounds or "off" smells and more easily distracted. In addition, sensitive women were more cautious about their choice of partner and more concerned about any negative consequences for both, and they had had fewer negative sexual experiences.

Children and Psychotherapy

When a child needs help, something in the parenting is not containing the problem because of family stress or dysfunction or the parents not knowing how to deal with a child's unusual temperament, or something else. Whatever the cause, the possibility that temperament also is a factor always needs to be considered. We know now how much upbringing can affect certain temperaments for better or worse—here is a real opportunity for prevention.

Before seeing a child alone for psychotherapy, Kristal (2005) recommends in most cases that the therapist begin with a temperament assessment and try temperament counseling with the parents alone. Children often sense that seeing the therapist means something is wrong with them, which they are prone to believe anyway as soon as something is not right at home. When a child does need individual therapy, having completed a temperament assessment helps therapists adapt their work to the child, much as this chapter suggests be done with adults.

Clearly temperament plays a large role in many children's problems, especially when parents are not providing a good fit, perhaps trying to raise one child as they have successfully raised others or as their parents raised them, or following the ideas in parenting guides that work well for the majority of children but not always for those with minority temperaments. Explaining the role of temperament in their child's issues and the positive aspects of a problematic trait can have the immediate positive effect of helping the parents to stop blaming themselves or the child. When they put into practice the suggestions that would make a better fit, sometimes the most serious behavior problems end entirely, making parents more amenable to working on other issues, such as the effect of a divorce.

Some parents (and teachers even more so) think at the outset that tailoring their behavior to a child's peculiar needs is too much work, or that having failed so far, they will fail at this, too. They secretly may also be very angry with their child or be too conditioned to react negatively to the child's behavior. Therapists need to watch for and treat parents' stress around their child's temperament-related behaviors.

Regarding sensitive children in particular, *The Highly Sensitive Child* (E. Aron, 2002) contains suggestions for both parents and therapists, and attempts to correct problems such as overprotecting or pushing children too hard in an effort to overcome or cure them of what appears to be a weakness.

Fathers especially can be disappointed about a highly sensitive boy and leave him to his mother to raise. These fathers need to hear about the strengths to be found in a sensitive son—which may be a story of their own secret strengths as well. Very often the most rejecting fathers are themselves highly sensitive and have hidden it, feeling especially negative about it. Meanwhile, the sensitive son may have become the confidant of the mother. Zeff (2010), writing for the parents of these boys, interviewed 30 self-identified sensitive men in five countries. He found that the same trait manifested quite differently according to their culture's view of men with that trait, and his work can help to provide parents with a positive image of the normal sensitive male, separate from culture.

Suggestions for Research

I hope that future volumes of this handbook will have chapters on temperament and psychotherapy that review many relevant studies rather than being largely based, as this one is, on the experience of a few temperament-informed adult psychotherapists. This research needs to be in at least three areas. First, the research on temperament itself could focus more on biological and cognitive processes underlying behaviors, "styles," and symptoms, so that these can be addressed to achieve broader effects and to avoid inappropriate treatment goals.

Second, this chapter has assumed that therapy outcomes are improved by both the therapist and the client being more knowledgeable about the client's temperament, but that needs to be better studied, including the best type of information (e.g., discussion, books, self-report inventories, genetic testing) and the timing of its introduction (e.g., initially or as needed). It will be important to look at not only the effects on outcome but also the immediate effects of this information on the client and the therapy process (e.g., when it leads to breakthroughs or to distress, how it affects the client's view of the therapist and the reverse, whether therapists develop expectations about outcome based on temperament and can this limit outcome). It will also be useful to know how this information actually alters, for example, clients' self-attributions, self-esteem, affect regulation, and coping methods. There is also the issue of how and when this information should be shared with others in the client's social environment (family, work, friendship network) and the impact of doing so.

Third, there are many questions to be answered about how various temperament traits affect the therapy process and outcomes. For example, are those with a given temperament trait (those high in sensation seeking, distractibility, sensitivity, etc.) more prone than others to change therapists or leave therapy, to benefit most from brief or long therapy, or to gain from "homework"? What best motivates temperamentally different clients, and what "volume" holds their attention, keeping them in their optimal level of arousal? What is the effect of a therapist's and client's temperaments being closely matched or complementary, and does adapting treatment matter more with some temperament traits than others? For example, it would be valuable to know whether highly sensitive clients actually do have poorer outcomes when therapists do not adapt to their trait. Especially important would be to watch for crossover interactions with therapist skill, looking to see whether sensitive individuals are made worse by "bad" therapy and improve more than others in "good" therapy. Indeed, there is the question of whether different forms of therapy are more effective (for one preliminary study, see Joyce et al., 2007) or preferred according to temperament. It would also be important to know whether, if given a choice, individuals would choose the method, style, length, and so forth, of therapy that best suits their temperament, and whether being able to make a temperament-informed choice in itself improves outcome.

Finally, knowing the impact on both client and therapist of their culture's view of a given minority trait and how best to deal with the effects of negative stereotypes regarding temperament traits would be extremely valuable. More cross-cultural research in particular would help client and therapist maintain a broader, more objective perspective regarding an unusual trait—that it has advantages and disadvantages according to situations, but cultures differ in the emphasis they give to these advantages and disadvantages.

Conclusion

The temperament perspective for psychotherapists can be summed up as assess, appreciate, and attune. Assessing means being able to recognize temperament within the maze of life experiences, which is not always easy. Appreciating means seeing the potential value of a trait for the individual and for society. This is often helped by understanding the trait's evolutionary function—that is, why the trait is still with us in our gene pool. Attuning is always an important skill, but it can be more difficult when clients' words and actions come from an underlying temperament-related process that is not the same as the therapist's. Therapists are trained to have a multicultural perspective, but not a multitemperament perspective.

It is a continual surprise that although these "three A's of temperament work" are not a central part of clinical training; it seems that it is up to therapists to train themselves and their colleagues. The briefest possible course might be as follows: "For me, a temperament perspective helps me understand my clients, build a strong alliance with them, and raise their self-esteem, so that they appreciate their strengths and accept their natural limits, and all that means they can choose the partner, career, and life style for which they are best suited." When therapists make temperament important, they promote a world in which people assume less that others are seeing the world exactly as they are. Families will know better how to raise each of their children, and organizations will make better use of human resources.

Furthermore, thinking specifically about high sensitivity, no doubt we all would benefit from more respect being given to those who especially reflect about the consequences of actions before they are taken and care very strongly about the outcomes. Therapists are crucial for helping these more responsive, reflective individuals to gain that respect, another gift that comes with taking a temperament perspective.

Further Reading

Aron, E. (2010). *Psychotherapy and the highly sensitive person.* New York: Routledge.
Aron, E., Aron, A., & Jagiellowicz, J. (in press). Sensory processing sensitivity: A review in the light of the evolution of biological responsivity. *Personality and Social Psychology Review.*
Kristal, J. (2005). *The temperament perspective.* New York: Brookes.

References

Acevedo, B., Aron, A., & Aron, E. (2010, August). Sensory processing sensitivity and neural responses to strangers emotional states. In A. Aron (Chair), High sensitivity, a personality/temperament trait: Lifting the shadow of psychopathology. Symposium presented at the annual meeting of the American Psychological Association, San Diego, CA.
Alloy, L. B., & Abramson, L. Y. (1979). Judgment of contingency in depressed and nondepressed students: Sadder but wiser? *Journal of Experimental Psychology, 108,* 441–485.
American Psychiatric Association. (1994). *Diagnostic and statistical manual of mental disorders* (4th ed.). Washington, DC: Author.
Amodio, M. D., Master, L. S., Yee, M. C., & Taylor, E. S. (2008). Neurocognitive components of the behavioral inhibition and activation systems: Implications for theories of self-regulation. *Psychophysiology, 45,* 11–19.
Aron, A., Ketay, S., Hedden, T., Aron, E. N., Markus, H. R., & Gabrieli, J. D. E. (2010). Temperament trait of sensory processing sensitivity moderates cultural differences in neural response. *Social Cognitive and Affective Neuroscience, 5*(2–3), 219–226.
Aron, E. (1996). *The highly sensitive person.* New York: Carol.
Aron, E. (2010). *Psychotherapy and highly sensitive person: Improving outcomes for that minority of people who are the majority of clients.* New York: Routledge.
Aron, E. (2000). *The highly sensitive person in love.* New York: Broadway Books.
Aron, E. (2002). *The highly sensitive child.* New York: Broadway Books.
Aron, E. (2004). The impact of adult temperament on closeness and intimacy. In D. Mashek & A. Aron (Eds.), *Handbook of closeness and intimacy* (pp. 267–283). Mahwah, NJ: Erlbaum.
Aron, E., & Aron, A. (1997). Sensory-processing sensitivity and its relation to introversion and emotionality. *Journal of Personality and Social Psychology, 73,* 345–368.
Aron, E., Aron, A., & Davies, K. M. (2005). Adult shyness: The interaction of temperamental sensitivity and an adverse childhood environment. *Personality and Social Psychology Bulletin, 31,* 181–197.
Aron, E., Aron, A., & Jagiellowicz, J. (in press). Sensory processing sensitivity: A review in the light of the evolution of biological responsivity. *Personality and Social Psychology Review.*
Aron, E. N., Aron, A., Jagiellowicz, J., & Tomlinson, J. (2010, July). *Sensory processing sensitivity is associated with boredom in close relationships.* Paper presented at the International Association for Relationship Research Conference, Herzliya, Israel.
Bar-Haim, Y., Fox, N. A., Benson, B., Guyer, A. E., Williams, A., Nelson, E. E., et al. (2009). Neural correlates of reward processing in adolescents with a history of inhibited temperament. *Psychological Science, 20,* 1009–1018.

Baumeister, R. F., Vohs, K. D., DeWall, N. C., & Zhang, L. (2007). How emotion shapes behavior: Feedback, anticipation, and reflection, rather than direct causation. *Personality and Social Psychology Review*, 11(2), 167–203.

Belsky, J., & Pluess, M. (2009). Beyond diathesis–stress: Differential susceptibility to environmental influences. *Psychological Bulletin*, 135, 885–908.

Boyce, T. W., Chesney, M., Alkon, A., Tschann, M. J., Adams, S., Chesterman, B., et al. (1995). Psychobiologic reactivity to stress and childhood respiratory illness: Results of two prospective studies. *Psychosomatic Medicine*, 57, 411–422.

Boyce, W. T., & Ellis, B. J., (2005). Biological sensitivity to context: I. An evolutionary–developmental theory of the origins and functions of stress reactivity. *Development and Psychopathology*, 17, 271–301.

Bundy, A. C., Shia, S., Qi, L., & Miller, L. J. (2007). How does sensory processing dysfunction affect play? *American Journal of Occupational Therapy*, 61, 201–208.

Canli, T. (2006). Genomic imaging of extraversion. In T. Canli (Ed.), *Biology of personality and individual differences* (pp. 93–115). New York: Guilford Press.

Chen, C., Chen, C., Moyzis, R., Stern, H., He, Q., Li, H., et al. (2011). Contributions of dopamine-related genes and environmental factors to highly sensitive personality: A multi-step neuronal system-level approach. *PLoS ONE*, 6, e21636.

Chen, X., He, Y., Cen, G., & Li, D. (2005). Social functioning and adjustment in Chinese children: The imprint of historical time. *Child Development*, 76(1), 182–195.

Chen, X., Rubin, K., & Sun, Y. (1992). Social reputation and peer relationships in Chinese and Canadian children: A cross-cultural study. *Child Development*, 63, 1336–1343.

Costa, P. T., & McCrae, R. R. (1992). *Revised NEO Personality Inventory and NEO Five Factor Inventory professional manual*. Odessa, FL: Psychological Assessment Resources.

Craig, A. D. (2009). How do you feel—now?: The anterior insula and human awareness. *Nature Reviews Neuroscience*, 10, 59–70.

Craik, F., & Lockhart, R. (1972). Levels of processing: A framework for memory research. *Journal of Verbal Learning and Verbal Behavior*, 11, 671–684.

Evans, D. E., & Rothbart, M. K. (2007). Development of a model for adult temperament. *Journal of Research in Personality*, 73, 868–888.

Forbes, C., & Schmader, T. (2010). Retraining attitudes and stereotypes to affect motivation and cognitive capacity under stereotype threat. *Journal of Personality and Social Psychology*, 99, 740–754.

Gottman, J., Driver, J., & Tabares, A. (2002). Building the sound marital house: An empirically-derived couple therapy. In A. S. Gurman & N. S. Jacobson (Eds.), *Clinical handbook of couple therapy* (3rd ed., pp. 373–399). Guilford Press.

Groothuis, T. G. G., & Carere, C. (2005). Avian personalities: Characterization and epigenesis. *Neuroscience and Biobehavioral Reviews*, 29, 137–150.

Hedden, T., Ketay, S., Aron, A., Markus, H., & Gabrieli, J. D. E. (2008). Cultural influences on neural substrates of attentional control. *Psychological Science*, 19, 13–17.

Homberg, R. J., & Lesch, K. P. (2011). Looking on the bright side of Serotonin transporter gene variation. *Biological Psychiatry*, 69, 513–519.

Jagiellowicz, J., Xu, X., Aron, A., Aron, E., Cao, G., Feng, T., et al. (2011) The trait of sensory processing sensitivity and neural responses to changes in visual scenes. *Social Cognitive and Affective Neuroscience*, 6(1), 38–47.

Jedema, H. P., Gianaros, P. J., Greer, P. J., Kerr, D. D., Liu, S., Higley, J. D., et al. (2009). Cognitive impact of genetic variation of the serotonin transporter in primates is associated with differences in brain morphology rather than serotonin neurotransmission. *Molecular Psychiatry*, 15, 512–522.

Jockin, V., McGue, M., & Lykken, D. T. (1996). Personality and divorce: A genetic analysis. *Journal of Personality and Social Psychology*, 71(2), 288–299.

John, O. P., Donahue, E. M., & Kentle, R. L. (1992). The "Big Five" Inventory—Versions 4a and 54 [Technical Report]. Berkeley, CA: Institute of Personality Assessment and Research.

Joyce, P. R., McKenzie, J. M., Carter, J. D., Luty, S. E., Frampton, C. M. A., & Multer, R. T. (2007). Temperament, character and personality disorders as predictors of response to interpersonal psychotherapy and cognitive-behavioural therapy for depression. *British Journal of Psychiatry*, 190, 503–508.

Kagan, J. (1994). *Galen's prophecy: Temperament in human nature*. New York: Basic Books.

Karney, B. R., & Bradbury, T. N. (1997). Neuroticism, marital interaction, and the trajectory of marital satisfaction. *Journal of Personality and Social Psychology*, 72, 1075–1092.

Keltner, D., Gruenfeld, D., & Anderson, C. (2003). *Power, approach, and inhibition*. Washington, DC: American Psychological Association.

Kochanska, G., & Thompson, R. A. (1997). The emergence and development of conscience in toddlerhood and early childhood. In J. E. Grusec & L. Kuczynski (Eds.), *Handbook of parenting and the transmission of values* (pp. 53–77). New York: Wiley.

Koolhaas, J. M., Korte, S. M., De Boer, S. F., Van Der Vegt, B. J., Van Reenen, C. G., Hopster,

H., et al. (1999). Coping styles in animals: Current status in behavior and stress–physiology. *Neuroscience and Biobehavioral Reviews, 23*, 925–935.

Kristal, J. (2005). *The temperament perspective: Working with children's behavioral styles.* Baltimore: Brookes.

Mead, M. (1935). *Sex and temperament in three primitive societies.* New York: Morrow.

Licht, C., Mortensen, E. L., & Knudsen, G. M. (2011). Association between sensory processing sensitivity and the serotonin transporter polymorphism 5-HTTLPR short/short genotype. *Biological Psychiatry, 69*(Suppl.).

Liss, M., Timmel, L., Baxley, K., & Killingsworth, P. (2005). Sensory processing sensitivity and its relation to parental bonding, anxiety, and depression. *Personality and Individual Differences, 39*, 1429–1439.

McGue, M., & Lykken, D. (1996). Personality and divorce: A genetic analysis. *Journal of Personality and Social Psychology, 71*, 288–299.

McNaughton, N., & Gray, J. A. (2000). Anxiolytic action on the behavioural inhibition system implies multiple types of arousal contribute to anxiety. *Journal of Affective Disorders, 61*, 161–176.

Nachmias, M., Gunnar, M., Mangelsdorf, S., Parritz, R. H., & Buss, K. (1996). Behavioral inhibition and stress reactivity: The moderating role of attachment security. *Child Development, 67*, 508–522.

Ratey, J., & Johnson, C. (1997). *Shadow syndromes: The mild forms of major depressive disorders that sabotage us.* New York: Random House.

Roiser, J. P., Rogers, R. D., Cook, L. I., & Sahakian, B. J. (2006). The effect of polymorphism at the serotonin transporter gene on decision-making, memory and executive function in ecstasy users and controls. *Psychopharmacology, 188*, 213–227.

Rothbart, M. K., Ahadi, S. A., & Evans, D. E. (2000). Temperament and personality: Origins and outcomes. *Journal of Personality and Social Psychology, 78*, 122–135.

Schjolden, J., & Winberg, S. (2007). Genetically determined variation in stress responsiveness in rainbow trout: Behavior and neurobiology. *Brain Behavior and Evolution, 70*(4), 227–238.

Seifer, R., Schiller, M., Sameroff, A. J., Resnick, S., & Riordan, K. (1996). Attachment, maternal sensitivity, and infant temperament during the first year of life. *Developmental Psychology, 32*, 12–25.

Seto, M. C., Lalumiere, M. L., & Quinsey, V. L. (1995). Sensation seeking and males' sexual strategy. *Personality and Individual Differences, 19*, 669–675.

Sih, A., & Bell, A. M. (2008). Insights for behavioral ecology from behavioral syndromes. *Advances in the Study of Behavior, 38*, 227–281.

Smolewska, K. A., McCabe, S. B., & Woody, E. Z. (2004). A psychometric evaluation of the highly sensitive person scale: The components of sensory-processing sensitivity and their relation to the BIS/BAS and "Big Five." *Personality and Individual Differences, 40*, 1269–1279.

Steele, C. M., Spencer, S. J., & Aronson, J. (2002). Contending with group image: The psychology of stereotype and social identity threat. *Advances in Experimental Social Psychology, 34*, 379–440.

Stelmack, R. M. (1997). Toward a paradigm in personality: Comment on Eysenck's view. *Journal of Personality and Social Psychology, 73*, 1238–1241.

Super, C. M., Axia, G., Harkness, S., Welles-Nystrom, B., Zylicz, P. O., Parmar, P., et al. (2008). Culture, temperament, and the "difficult child:" A study in seven Western cultures. *European Journal of Developmental Science, 2*, 136–157.

Taylor, E. S., Way, M. B., Welch, T. W., Hilmert, J. C., Lehman, J. B., & Eisenberger, I. N. (2006). Early family environment, current adversity, the serotonin transporter promoter polymorphism, and depressive symptomatology. *Biological Reviews, 60*, 671–676.

Taylor, V. J., & Walton, G. M. (2011). Stereotype threat undermines academic learning. *Personality and Social Psychology Bulletin, 37*, 1055–1067.

Thomas, A., & Chess, S. (1977). *Temperament and development.* New York: Brunner/Mazel.

van IJzendoorn, M. H., Bakermans-Kranenburg, M. J., & Mesman, J. (2008). Dopamine system genes associated with parenting in the context of daily hassles. *Genes, Brain, and Behavior, 7*, 403–410.

Wolf, M., Van Doorn, S., & Weissing, F. J. (2008). Evolutionary emergence of responsive and unresponsive personalities. *Proceedings of the National Academy of Sciences, 105*(41), 15825–15830.

Wolf, M., Van Doorn, G. S., & Weissing, F. J. (2011). On the coevolution of social responsiveness and behavioural consistency. *Proceedings of the Royal Society B: Biological Sciences, 278*, 440–448.

Zeff, T. (2010). *The strong sensitive boy.* San Ramon, CA: Prana.

Part VIII

Integration and Outlook

CHAPTER 32

Fifty Years of Progress in Temperament Research
A Synthesis of Major Themes, Findings, and Challenges and a Look Forward

Marcel Zentner
Rebecca L. Shiner

As modern-era research on temperament approaches its 50th anniversary, it is worth remembering some of the forces that propelled temperament into the mainstream of research in psychology, psychiatry, neuroscience, and genetics. Broadly, the emergence of modern temperament research owes to two strands of study with somewhat different goals and emphases. One strand has its origin in child psychology and psychiatry. As described by Rothbart (Chapter 1, this volume), precursors of this tradition included Gesell (1928), Shirley (1933), Bergman and Escalona (1949; Escalona, 1968), and Meili (1957). However, the systematic study of infant and child temperament was not to take off until Thomas and Chess launched their highly influential New York Longitudinal Study, first extensively described 50 years ago in *Behavioral Individuality in Early Childhood* (Thomas, Chess, Birch, Hertzig, & Korn, 1963).

Somewhat paradoxically, the authors initially did not see themselves as temperament researchers. Rather, they set out to study "primary reaction patterns" that could be seen in infants. Their interest was in studying the implications of individual differences in these early patterns for normal and abnormal psychological development, and in exploring the clinical benefits of seeing the child as an autonomous agent (rather than merely as a reflection of parental influences). It was only later that the researchers adopted the term *temperament*. With its background in child psychiatry and pediatrics, this work paved the way for developmentally oriented work on temperament—an almost entirely new genre of temperament research (Rothbart, Chapter 1, this volume). The second strand had more in common with traditional temperament research, notably in its interest in the hereditary, constitutional, neurobiological, and evolutionary origins of temperament. As described in detail by Zuckerman (Chapter 3, this volume), this strand owed much to the foundational contributions of, among others, Kretschmer (1925), Sheldon and Stevens (1942), Diamond (1957), Eysenck (1967), Gray (1973), Zuckerman (1979), and Strelau (1983).

In 1975, A. H. Buss and Plomin provided an influential blend of these two largely unrelated strands of research (Buss & Plomin, 1975; see also Rowe & Plomin, 1977). Placing research on the heritability and biology of adult temperament and the study of child temperament under one roof galvanized the field and helped to forge the identity of the field of temperament as it is known today.

The first works describing and reviewing the results of this modern era of temperament research appeared toward the late 1980s and early 1990s (Carey & McDevitt, 1989; Goldsmith et al., 1987; Kohnstamm, 1986; Kohnstamm, Bates, & Rothbart, 1989; Plomin & Dunn, 1986; Strelau & Angleitner, 1991).

Since that time, temperament research has seen an unprecedented expansion, owing in part to its relevance across disciplines, including neuroscience, psychiatry, behavioral and molecular genetics, pediatrics, psychopharmacology, prevention science, counseling, and school psychology. Figure 32.1 illustrates this dramatic growth of temperament-related publications between 1970 and 2010, relative to the growth in publications on attachment and personality. The figure plots the percentage of growth in number of publications, in 5-year intervals, relative to the year 1970. Although the number of publications across the whole time period is higher for attachment (863 to 4,624) and personality (2,509 to 7,479) than it is for temperament (38 to 867), what is striking about the growth in temperament-related publications is its exponential nature. It is clear from this chart that an integrative volume on the current state of research in temperament was long overdue. In what follows, we attempt to provide an integrative view of some of the most important developments described in the previous 31 chapters. Specifically, our overview revolves around five major themes that relate to the meaning, structure, etiology, development, and applications of temperament. We trace progress across these areas, highlight key findings, discuss challenges, and point to possible solutions, as well as future developments.

The Meaning of Temperament

How tricky it can be to define psychological constructs as if they were quasi-material entities is illustrated by a recent survey, in which 33 world authorities in emotion research responded to a request to define the construct of emotion. The degree of consensus was disappointing (Izard, 2007). An alternative, and possibly more effective approach, is to define a construct by what the field intends to study. Temperament can be characterized as a field engaged in a comprehensive, concerted effort to identify early appearing, enduring behavioral phenotypes with a presumed biological basis; to examine their role in psychological development; and to explore their relevance for treatment. In the modern era, biological predispositions are increasingly described in terms of neurogenetic mechanisms (e.g., serotonin

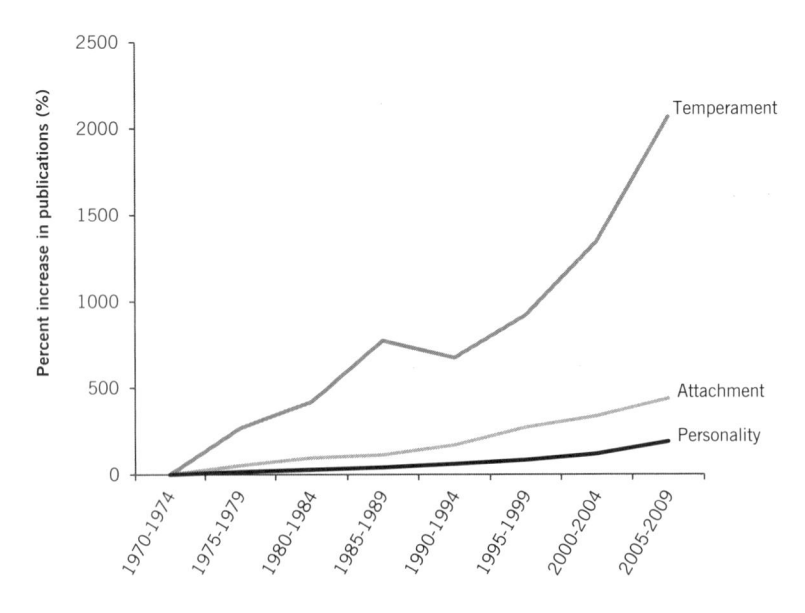

FIGURE 32.1. Increase in percentage of publications with temperament, attachment, and personality in their titles between 1970 and 2010, retrieved from the Web of Science.

[5-HT] transporter allele), but it is recognized that these can be environmentally influenced (e.g., a mother's substance abuse during pregnancy). Indeed, it is now clear that environmentally induced or mediated experiences in the prenatal and postnatal phase that shape gene expression and neural pathways eventually get "under the skin"; that is, they become biologically embedded, forging a neuroaffective signature that contributes to the maintenance of the behavioral characteristics studied under the heading of temperament.

The contemporary view of temperament differs from most temperament conceptions entertained before 1960 in both its strong developmental orientation and its neurobiological sophistication. The strong interest in studying the appearance of temperament in the opening years of life stems from the assumption that infancy and toddlerhood may represent key periods for the appearance and stabilization of temperament. Indeed, traits broadly relating to affect, activity, and attention show marked temporal stability from about age 3, often extending well into adolescence and adulthood. Adult outcomes of early childhood temperament include adult personality traits, psychopathology, and school achievement (see the section "Temperament and Development," later in this chapter).

In their attempt to particularize the constitutional aspect of temperament, Kretschmer (1925) and Sheldon and Stevens (1942) had little choice but to rely on morphology. Russian and Eastern European temperament scholars paid more attention to possible neural correlates of temperament. However, with the limited access to the brain at the time, some of their tenets related to what Skinner (1938) referred to as the "conceptual nervous system"—a nervous system more hypothetical than real. In the meantime, game-changing advances in genetics and neuroimaging have given a completely new meaning to the "biological" or "constitutional" component of temperament (e.g., Bogdan, Carré, & Hariri, in press; Smith, 2012). Taken together, developmental and neurobiological research suggests that temperament is a neurobehavioral and neuroaffective foundation with far-reaching implications for individuals' life-course patterns.

This dual emphasis of current temperament research and concepts on early development and neuroscience sets it apart from personality, which has always referred to a broader range of individual differences in later periods of development, or from attachment, with its focus on early interpersonal experience. However, this volume points to several interconnections across these areas. In the wake of advances in personality trait taxonomies, including the three-factor model (e.g., Tellegen, 1985) and the Five-Factor Model (Goldberg, 1990), personality psychologists have become increasingly interested in the biological signatures and the early childhood manifestations of these higher-order traits (see Mervielde & De Pauw, Chapter 2, and Shiner & Caspi, Chapter 24, this volume).

There is nonetheless an important difference between research on child temperament and investigations into the appearance of broad personality factors. The former endorsed a bottom-up approach, focusing on individual differences that can be observed across infancy and toddlerhood, such as individual differences in circumscribed responses to novelty, vocalizing and smiling, attentional focusing, ability to delay gratification, vigor, and duration of motor movement. The latter adopted a top-down approach in looking for early signs of broad personality traits (Lamb, Chuang, Wessels, Broberg, & Hwang, 2002). These differences notwithstanding, a certain measure of integration has been achieved in recent years (Rothbart, 2011; Shiner & DeYoung, in press).

Most attachment researchers, in turn, acknowledge today that attachment security cannot be monotonically attributed to parental beliefs (e.g., internal working models) or behaviors (e.g., maternal sensitivity). Rather, the relationship patterns that emerge between parents and children are more appropriately conceptualized as outcomes of a complex interplay among genetic predispositions, infant temperament, and parenting, as discussed by van IJzendoorn and Bakermans-Kranenburg (Chapter 19, this volume). Conversely, temperament researchers have come to realize that there is no such thing as a purely biological trait, and that the role of temperamental dispositions in psychological development depends on their interactions with a host of environmental variables (Bates, Schermerhorn, & Petersen, Chapter 20, and Lengua & Wachs, Chapter

25, this volume). The developments traced in these latter three chapters of this volume mark a welcome departure from the quasi-ideological battle between two seemingly irreconcilable views of early psychological development that separated temperament and attachment research for several decades.

The Structure of Temperament

Research on the structure of temperament strives to identify basic temperament dimensions and types. Compared to the typological tradition, with its ancient Greco-Roman roots, research on temperament dimensions is much more recent, in part due to its roots in psychometrics (Rothbart, Chapter 1, this volume). Influenced by the pioneering work of Heymans and Wiersma (1906), this line of work endorsed a multidimensional view of temperament, yet this was not a forgone direction to take. Indeed, in popular parlance, *temperament* is often referred to as a unidimensional quality that people have more or less of, not unlike intelligence or self-esteem. Thus, in several languages, individuals are characterized as differing in *amount* of temperament. If having met a new person, someone exclaims "Quel tempérament!" in French, this is generally understood as an expression of admiration for the person's vitality, vigor, and strength of will, salted with connotations of potential moodiness, willfulness, or intensity. This same meaning of temperament is also found in German, Italian, Spanish, and English, although English variants of the term place a stronger emphasis on capriciousness and volatility (e.g., *temperamental* and *temper*).

An illustrative embodiment of a person "full of temperament" may be seen in Carmen, the protagonist of Bizet's famous opera (Figure 32.2). It is hard to fathom what would happen if Carmen were to be miraculously transported into one of today's temperament laboratories. It is certain, however, that she would not be seen as "scoring high on temperament." Rather, Carmen would be seen as scoring high on different dimensions instead. In terms of the three higher-order temperament traits described by Rothbart (Chapter 1, this volume) and Zuckerman (Chapter 3, this volume), Carmen's energy and enthusiasm would earn her high scores on positive emotionality; her moodiness and intensity, high scores on negative emotionality; and her willpower, high scores on effortful control. Thus, Carmen's temperament would stand out for its cross-dimensional potency—a high-voltage phenomenon worthy of study to those in search of a general personality factor (e.g., Muzek, 2007).

FIGURE 32.2. "Full of temperament": Carmen. Photograph by Bill Cooper. Reprinted by permission.

Temperament Dimensions

Research on temperament dimensions has predominantly relied on factor analysis, sometimes in combination with behavioral observations guided by a theoretical rationale about the nature of temperament. Not surprisingly, this led to competing models of the dimensional structure of temperament that hampered progress in temperament research. Yet the differences in the number and type of dimensions have recently been found to be more apparent than real. Thus, Zentner and Bates (2008) found that a taxonomy based on six temperament dimensions could serve as an integrative model for most dimensions and scales of child temperament. The research described by Mervielde and De Pauw (Chapter 2, this volume) takes this work a step further by analyzing the structure of child temperament traits across questionnaires from the models of Rothbart (2011), Buss and Plomin (1975), and Thomas and Chess (1977). The authors found that the questionnaires converged on a set of traits, similar to those identified by Zentner and Bates (2008).

There is now also a higher level of integration regarding adult temperament, as described by Zuckerman (Chapter 3, this volume). To an extent, the childhood traits converge with the adult temperament traits. Traits with the broadest support across ages and models are discussed in detail in a series of chapters: behavioral inhibition (Kagan, Chapter 4, this volume); activity (Strelau & Zawadzki, Chapter 5, this volume); positive emotionality (Putnam, Chapter 6, this volume); anger and irritability (Deater-Deckard & Wang, Chapter 7, this volume); effortful control (Rueda, Chapter 8, this volume); and empathy and prosocial traits (Knafo & Israel, Chapter 9, this volume). Further convergence is emerging in studies with animals, in which most of these temperament characteristics have been found, as described in Barr, Chapter 13, this volume. Table 32.1 provides an overview of these dimensions, including some closely related variants.

As a caveat, it is important to keep in mind that some of the traits have more research on record than others to commend them as basic temperament traits. Thus, compared with most other characteristics, the status of empathy and sensory sensitivity as distinct temperament dimensions is less well established by research. However, we also need to look forward. Thus, we found empathy to be intriguing enough to be included in Part II of this handbook with a dedicated chapter. Sensory sensitivity is touched upon

TABLE 32.1. An Integrative Taxonomic Map of Temperament Traits

Super-factors	Basic traits	Capsule definitions	Related dimensions
Negative Emotionality (Neuroticism)	Behavioral inhibition Trait anxiety	Inhibition of behavior in response to novel unfamiliar people and situations	Fearfulness, harm avoidance, anxious temperament
	Anger	Aggressive or irritated behavior in response to painful and/or frustrating input	Irritability, frustration
Positive Emotionality (Extraversion)	High-intensity pleasure	Propensity to positive emotions, including pleasure, positive anticipation, and excitement in social interaction	Exuberance, hyperthymia, sensation seeking, high-intensity pleasure
	Low-intensity pleasure	Ability to experience delight in response to sensuous gratification and comfort	Consummatory hedonia, low-intensity pleasure
	Activity level	Frequency, briskness, and vigor of motor movement; intolerance to enforced idleness	Briskness, tempo
Effortful Control (Constraint)	Attention/persistence	Capacity for attentional focusing and control as basis for persistence	Self-control, willpower, impulsivity (−), undercontrol (−)
	Inhibitory control	Ability to inhibit a dominant response and/or activate a subdominant response, to plan, and to detect errors	Delay of gratification
	Sensory sensitivity	Amount of stimulation needed to evoke a sensory response (e.g., tactile, olfactory, gustatory)	Perceptual sensitivity, threshold, high sensitivity, sensory defensiveness
	Empathy/affiliativeness	Disposition to recognize and value salient social cues as a basis for affiliative reward	Cuddliness, kindness, reward dependence

by Mervielde and De Pauw (Chapter 2, this volume) and Aron (Chapter 31, this volume) and will be briefly discussed at the end of this section.

Although the traits in Table 32.1 have been studied with different methodologies, including questionnaire/interview approaches (Gartstein, Bridgett, & Low, Chapter 10, this volume), objective behavioral approaches (Goldsmith & Gagne, Chapter 11, this volume), and neuroscience-based approaches (Calkins & Swingler, Chapter 12, this volume), much of the evidence in their support has come from questionnaire ratings subjected to factor analysis. The latter tends to promote a vision of temperament consisting of broad, context-independent factors, whereas behavioral and physiological methods more often lead to greater focus on specific, context-dependent facets of temperament. Although the two foci are different, they are not incompatible if one looks at temperament as a hierarchically organized structure. Thus, specific behaviors or lower-level facets of temperament traits tend to covary, and the covariation among those traits can be condensed into higher-order factors with greater breadth by means of data reduction techniques (Shiner & DeYoung, in press). Most of the traits compiled in Table 32.1 represent higher-order factors, or families of temperament characteristics, rather than highly specific temperament dispositions.

Broad traits are taxonomically useful because they provide a structure for organizing, integrating, and comparing diffuse empirical findings obtained through a bewildering array of measures and concepts, often carrying different names but measuring constructs with considerable overlap (Caspi, 1998). However, broad constructs may not always represent the best level of analysis for research in temperament. One limitation of overarching temperament constructs is that important predictive relationships may be lost. For example, impulse control in toddlers has been found to predict good performance in most executive function–related tasks at age 17 years, but underperformance in some (Friedman, Miyake, Robinson, & Hewitt, 2011). Another risk is that broad traits may obscure temperament's neural etiology (see Kagan, Chapter 4, and Goldsmith & Gagne, Chapter 11, this volume). Thus, the factor positive emotionality almost certainly includes at least two subfacets with differing neurobiological underpinnings. These are sometimes referred to as low- versus high-intensity pleasure (Rothbart, 2011) or as appetitive versus consummatory hedonia (Putnam, Chapter 6, and Depue & Fu, Chapter 18, this volume). However, even this distinction probably fails to capture the richness of dispositional positive affect. Goldsmith and Gagne (Chapter 11, this volume) make several suggestions about how a greater particularization of positive emotionality may be achieved, for example, by drawing on models that focus on positive emotion (Shiota, Keltner, & John, 2006).

Within the context of the higher-order traits, researchers have attempted to examine the extent of relatedness or organization of the traits. For example, activity is sometimes seen as a ramification of surgency or extraversion. Mervielde and De Pauw (Chapter 2, this volume) found that activity is an important, separate temperament dimension until about middle childhood, at which point it tends to fuse with extraversion. In contrast, according to Strelau's model, activity level preserves a status as an independent temperament characteristic through adulthood (Strelau & Zawadzki, Chapter 5, this volume). Other adult temperament models, with origins in dimensional models of mood and emotion, have also frequently posited an independent activity-like dimension, labeled activation or arousal (Mehrabian, 1996; Thayer, Newman, & McClain, 1994; see also Clark & Watson, 2008). The situation is clearer with negative emotionality, which is generally found to ramify into behavioral inhibition and anger, and possibly sadness, although the latter has only begun to be looked at from a temperament perspective (Klein, Dyson, Kujawa, & Kotov, Chapter 26, this volume).

All of the traits discussed thus far have an obvious emotive component. The important role of emotion across most temperament traits was noted long ago (Allport, 1937; Goldsmith & Campos, 1982), and continues to be emphasized in current-day conceptions of temperament (Goldsmith & Gagne, Chapter 11, this volume). In contrast, effortful control represents a more recent but increasingly consequential area of research on "regulatory" aspects of temperament, including concepts such as "self-control," "inhibitory control," "persistence," "constraint," or "willpower" (in this volume, see Rothbart, Chapter 1; Rueda, Chapter 8; White, Lamm, Helfinstein, & Fox, Chapter 17; Depue & Fu, Chapter 18). Empirically, effortful control and its affiliates are highly inversely correlated with impulsivity, suggesting that effortful control is, in effect, impulse control. Some authors make a distinction between the two. In the latter view, impulsivity is a heterogeneous characteristic, possibly the result of a temperament × temperament interaction. Thus, impulsivity may be seen as the expression of an accelerator (positive emotionality) that is not contained in an appropriate breaking system (inhibitory control). However, since it is at present unclear whether impulsivity is anything more (or less) than the reverse of effortful control, we subsume it under constraint in Table 32.1.

Although there is consensus that effortful control and its affiliates comprise a basic dimension of temperament, several authors have noted its peculiarity relative to other temperamental traits (e.g., Carver, 2005). For example, it does not seem to have an obvious link to an emotional or motivational system and it is also a relatively late-emerging temperament characteristic, not fully expressed until about the third year of life. One view is that constraint acts as a superordinate disposition that determines the probability of elicitation of the affective traits and their neurochemical bases, such as the dopaminergic circuitry underlying incentive-motivated behavior and positive affect (e.g., corticotropin-releasing hormone [CRH] in the potentiation of anxiety, µORs in the mediation of affiliative reward; see Depue & Fu, Chapter 18, this volume). It has been suggested that this disposition may be linked to serotonergic functioning, but evidence is conflicting (e.g., Carver, Johnson, & Joormann, 2008). The understanding of effortful control as a superordinate system to emotive temperaments is consistent with Rothbart's view that effortful control modulates behavioral manifestations of the lower-level incentive and threat sensitivities (Rothbart & Derryberry, 1981). A question rarely addressed, however, is what would make control *effortful*? From a biological, mechanistic point of view, some individuals would be predisposed to act planfully and control impulses naturally and, indeed, *effortlessly*. What may be effortful, then, is the training required to strengthen this temperament. As suggested by Baumeister, self-control or "willpower" may operate like a muscle: fatigued by overuse and strengthened with practice (Baumeister & Tierney, 2012).

Another intriguing feature of effortful control is its affinity with skills traditionally catalogued under the heading cognition. Initially, temperament and cognitive functioning (as summarily represented in IQ scores) were seen as clearly separate, nonoverlapping constructs. However, as shown by Rueda (Chapter 8, this volume), temperamental and cognitive control may have a common origin in the executive attention network—a neurocognitive system involved in the regulation and coordination of action in novel or challenging situations, in the detection and correction of errors, and in the suppression of habitual (or automatic) responses. In this view, the executive attention network is seen as a neural substrate supporting constraint or effortful control, as well as more traditionally cognitive skills such as working memory (Posner & Rothbart, 2007). A number of findings are consistent with this view. Succeeding in an impulse control task during toddlerhood significantly predicted higher IQ scores at age 16 (Friedman et al., 2011). Limitations in working memory have been found to relate to adult introversion, albeit in a complex way (Lieberman & Rosenthal, 2001). Resistance to interference in the classical Stroop color-naming task (a form of inhibitory control) has been shown to correlate substantially with measures of personality, and with resiliency in girls and control in boys (Block, 2005). As research on control advances, the nature of constraint, including its independence from or interdependence with the emotive temperaments, as well as its connectedness with cognitive functioning, should lead to more clarity as to how constraint or effortful control may be best conceptualized.

Compared with the preceding characteristics, empathy and other traits relating to the recognition of social cues and affiliative reward have been considered from a temperament perspective only in recent years (Knafo & Israel, Chapter 9, and Depue & Fu, Chapter 18, this volume); thus, they are less established by research. In contrast, sensory sensitivity is relatively well studied but has proved difficult to characterize and classify. Possibly this is because it seems to include two separate, though possibly related facets, namely, (1) sensitivity to aversive stimuli such as loud noises or scratchy clothes, which are captured in the sensory discomfort construct (Kochanska, Coy, Tjebkes, & Husarek, 1998; Rothbart, 2011); and (2) the ability to react to sensory stimuli of low stimulative value, captured by the notion of perceptual sensitivity (Goldsmith, 1996; Rothbart, 2011), which has been allocated to effortful control by Rothbart. The commonalities between perceptual sensitivity and effortful control may not be immediately obvious. However, they are easier to understand if one looks at their possible common basis in the capacity for error detection, a function of the executive attention network that involves the anterior cingulate and other frontal brain areas (Posner & Rothbart, 2007). Related constructs such as threshold (Thomas & Chess, 1977), sensory defensiveness (Goldsmith, Van Hulle, Arneson, Schreiber, & Gernsbacher, 2006), or high sensitivity (Aron, 1996) probably represent mixtures of both aspects of sensitivity (Aron, Chapter 31, this volume; see also Zentner & Bates, 2008).

Temperament Types

Like the heroine of Bizet's opera, people can be characterized in terms of a mixture or pattern of several temperamental attributes. For example, some preschoolers with high levels of anger score low in self-control, whereas other children with high levels of anger have high concomitant levels of control. To researchers accustomed to thinking in dimensional terms, the example of the high-anger, high-control child may seem somewhat incongruous because when questionnaire measures are factor-analyzed, there is a moderately negative relationship between the anger and control dimensions, as there is between negative emotionality and effortful control (Deater-Deckard & Wang, Chapter 7, and Rueda, Chapter 8, this volume). Yet dispositional anger and willpower can be entrenched in one and the same individual, as in the case of authoritarian personalities (Altemeyer, 1998). Thus, implications of a given temperament trait are not monotonic; rather, they depend on the presence of other attributes in an individual's temperament profile.

That the connection between a temperament trait and psychosocial adjustment can be lessened or strengthened through the presence or absence of other temperamental attributes is shown in several examples from the recent literature. Notably, when the developmental trajectories of children high in temperamental negative emotionality and low in effortful control are compared with children who are high in both, well-regulated and prosocial behaviors are more prevalent among the latter (e.g., Eisenberg, Smith, & Spinrad, 2011; Rothbart & Bates, 2006; Verstraeten, Vasey, Raes, & Bijttebier, 2009). In turn, behaviorally inhibited children high in inhibitory control may be at increased risk for developing anxiety disorders (White, McDermott, Degnan, Henderson, & Fox, 2011). Still other studies found that a high level of negative emotionality predisposes to depressive symptoms, in particular when it is coupled with low positive emotionality (Klein et al., Chapter 26, this volume).

Although not conceived as such, research on temperament types is, in effect, a natural extension of work on temperament × temperament interactions. The number of possible combinations of temperamental attributes being incalculable, it makes sense to discern "typical" combinations, that is, those occurring with above average frequency. The literature on temperamental types has a long history dating back to Galen and earlier, as described by Rothbart (Chapter 1, this volume) and Kagan (Chapter 4, this volume). Yet modern-era temperament typologies are very different from those expounded in works such as Kretschmer's *Physique and Character* (1925) or Sheldon and Stevens's *The Varieties of Temperament* (1942). The focus on morphology or body build has been relinquished and supplanted with an emphasis on the early identification and developmental significance of temperament constellations. This was evident from Thomas and Chess's (1977) threefold temperament typology that distinguished between difficult, slow to warm up, and easy children. More recently, a related triadic scheme has identified undercontrolled, overcontrolled, and resilient children (e.g., Asendorpf &

van Aken, 1999; Caspi & Silva, 1995; Hart, Burock, London, Atkins, & Bonilla-Santiago, 2005). On the basis of these studies, the three types can be described with the following distinctive attributes:

Undercontrolled child: willful, restless, inattentive, impulsive, and emotionally volatile
Overcontrolled child: shy, compliant, quiet, and self-critical
Resilient child: self-confident, able to concentrate, self-reliant, cooperative, and open

Because the more recent studies on types were based on samples of preschoolers or older children, the infant precursors to these three types remain to be elucidated. It is not clear, however, how temperament typologies ought to be derived during infancy. Kagan (Chapter 4, this volume) has described one model of infant types focused on variations in behavioral inhibition. Kagan's identification of infant temperament types was based on the assumption that amygdalar hyperreactivity might play a pivotal role in determining behavioral inhibition. A combination of previous research and behavioral observations led him to hypothesize that motor unrest and crying might be two potential early infancy markers of amygdalar hyperreactivity. In his work, he found that about 20% of 4-month-old infants react irritably to the unexpected appearance of unfamiliar visual, auditory, or olfactory stimuli, whereas about 40% of the infants reacted without signs of distress (Kagan & Snidman, 2004). As described in detail by Kagan (Chapter 4, this volume), the developmental pathways of the two types in early infancy differed in several respects, including behavioral, emotional, psychophysiological, and neurobiological characteristics (see also White et al., Chapter 17, this volume).

Future research on temperament types faces intriguing questions. While it is relatively straightforward to identify types from questionnaire ratings by means of cluster or inverse factor analysis, there are at present no established procedures for identifying early infancy temperament types or developmentally meaningful temperament × temperament interactions. *Taxometrics*—a set of statistical procedures used to determine whether the latent structure of a construct is continuous or categorical (i.e., *taxonic*; Schmidt, Kotov, & Joiner, 2004)—can be used to examine whether quantitative indices of a phenotype are subtended by qualitative latent structure. Kagan and colleagues found that this was the case for high- and low-reactive infants (Woodward, Lenzenberger, Kagan, Snidman, & Arcus, 2000). However, the technique can only confirm, not identify, types.

A further question that has been raised particularly by advocates of a dimensional approach is the added value of types over dimensions. In other words, if researchers were to endorse exclusively a dimensional approach, would this prevent them from gaining important insights into the nature of temperament and its implications for psychological development and adjustment? In part, the answer to this question depends on how types are defined. In a recent follow-up of preschoolers from the Munich Logic Study, only the upper 8% in terms of preschool inhibition exhibited internalizing problems at age 23 years. If the outcomes were analyzed with respect to inhibition in the upper 15% of the preschoolers, most of the effects vanished (Asendorpf, Denissen, & van Aken, 2008). This finding does suggest that ignoring extreme groups may come at a cost, perhaps precisely because individuals at the extreme ends of a distribution share a number of attributes that are not shared by individuals at less extreme ends. Furthermore, the growing evidence on temperament × temperament interactions indicates that prediction and understanding can sometimes be improved by looking at combinations of temperamental attributes, rather than at temperament dimensions in isolation.

Finally, it has also been noted that the merits of typological approaches cannot be described on statistical grounds exclusively (e.g., amount of variance explained) and that some of the advantages of typologies result from a more natural and genuinely psychological way of studying individuals such as the practice of conceptualizing the latter as persons rather than variables (Caspi, Roberts, & Shiner, 2005; Hart, Atkins, & Fegley, 2003). In summary, then, both dimensional and typological approaches offer unique advantages for furthering our understanding of the structure of temperament.

The Etiology of Temperament: Nature and Nurture

Etiology, that is, the study of causation or origination of phenomena, has been a particularly challenging area of temperament research. At the dawn of modern-era research on temperament, Thomas and Chess (1977) described several possible causes of the temperamental features they observed in young children, notably prenatal, postnatal, and genetic influences. In doing so, they acknowledged the importance of both inherited and environmentally induced pre-, peri-, and postnatal factors in shaping a child's temperament. However, research on temperament's etiology was not one of their research priorities. The interest in etiology became apparent in several articles and volumes, published in the late 1980s, that focused on heritability estimates for temperament traits, as derived from behavior genetic studies (Kohnstamm et al., 1989; Plomin & Dunn, 1986).

Since then, several key developments have significantly expanded our insights into the origin of temperamental differences: research on prenatal precursors of temperament differences, refinement of behavior genetic methods, the application of molecular genetic research to the study of temperament, and research on the neurobiological structures and processes associated with temperament. Perhaps most important, there is now a clearer understanding of the ways in which postnatal environmental factors impinge on temperamental predispositions, whether neurogenetically or prenatally determined.

Behavior Genetics of Temperament

Advances in behavioral or quantitative genetics have allowed researchers to move beyond simple heritability estimates of temperament to address more sophisticated questions. Somewhat paradoxically, one of the richest contributions of behavior genetics has been in particularizing environmental influences on temperament, such as the relative contribution of the shared and nonshared environment on various temperament traits. More important, behavior genetics methodology, such as longitudinal quantitative genetic analyses that explore genetic and environmental contributions to phenotypic continuity and change across age, can now examine more complex questions than was possible in the past. For example, recent findings on the genetics of temperament allow for the possibility that certain traits may be expressed or muted only later in life, conceivably up to old age, either through new genes turning on, or as a result of gene × environment interactions precipitated by incisive life events (Saudino & Wang, Chapter 16, this volume).

These methods inform us about developmental processes by assessing the extent to which genetic and environmental effects on a trait persist across age, and whether new genetic and environmental influences emerge across time. Studies of early temperament typically find that stability is due to genetic factors, and change is largely environmental; however, for some dimensions, there is also evidence of genetic contributions to developmental change, as detailed in Saudino and Wang (Chapter 16, this volume). Increasing evidence suggests that the link between temperament and behavior problems is in part driven by genetic influences (Klein et al., Chapter 26, and Tackett, Martel, & Kushner, Chapter 27, this volume). These findings are important because they suggest that temperament may convey a genetic risk for maladaptive outcomes and point to temperament dimensions as possible endophenotypes for clinical disorders.

Recent work on gene × environment interactions and correlations has led to an important insight, namely, that the environments children experience (e.g., parenting) partly reflect genetically influenced temperaments, indicating genotype–environment correlations. This work has allowed researchers to look at outcomes typically attributed to environmental factors in a different light. For example, prevailing wisdom has it that divorce causes children's disruptive behavior. Yet, Block, Block, and Gjerde (1986) found that male toddlers' restless and impulsive behavior preceded parental divorce by many years. A possible interpretation of this finding in terms of genotype–environment correlations is that the boys' behavior, with the stresses on family life it entails, could have been a cause rather than a consequence of divorce. Despite progress in behavior genetics methodology, several methodological problems that stand in the way of further progress include measure- and context-specific effects (Saudino & Wang, Chapter 16, this volume).

Neurogenetics of Temperament

Behavior genetics, however advanced, has the limitation that it cannot identify specific genes that may be responsible for individual differences in temperament. This gap in our knowledge is now being progressively filled by molecular genetics. The excitement around this area of research is understandable because it opens up the possibility of specifying the genetic material that codes for individual differences in both neurochemistry and temperament. Indeed, using the allelic association strategy described by Saudino and Wang (Chapter 16, this volume), researchers have been able to identify certain polymorphisms that appear to play a role in the etiology of temperament. Even so, the variance in temperaments explained by allelic variation is scarcely impressive. There are several reasons for this circumstance.

First, temperament is a complex behavioral phenotype, unlike circumscribed developmental disabilities, such as *trisomy*, which results from having three copies of chromosome 18 in each cell in the body instead of the usual two copies. The extra genetic material disrupts the normal course of development, causing the characteristic features of trisomy 18. In cases such as these, a genetic variant explains a large portion of the variance in the behavior phenotype, but temperament researchers face a more sobering situation in which many genes explain a modest part of the variance in phenotypic features.

Second, the neural structures and mechanisms subserving temperament are more likely to involve brain circuitries than specific brain areas or receptor densities at given brain sites. Although there is evidence to suggest a role for the amygdala in behavioral inhibition and trait anxiety (see Kagan, Chapter 4, and Depue & Fu, Chapter 18, this volume), a hyperresponsive amygdala may have different temperamental expressions, depending on its connectivity to other areas. For example, several studies suggest that the prefrontal cortex, particularly the anterior cingulate cortex (ACC), has a role in suppressing the amygdala's natural response in negatively valenced situations (White et al., Chapter 17, this volume). Consistent with this work, it has been found that heightened amygdala activation relates to trait anxiety chiefly in those individuals with weak connections between the prefrontal cortex and the amygdala. In individuals with strong connections, the prefrontal cortex seems to suppress amygdala activation successfully following an upsetting experience or emotion, thereby facilitating recovery from it (Kim & Whalen, 2009). Thus, the circuitry modulating amygdala reactivity via inhibitory feedback from the prefrontal cortex during times of emotional stress may play a critical role in trait anxiety. A behavioral parallel to this interaction may be seen in the previously discussed finding that children high in negative reactivity are more likely to suffer negative consequences when they are also low in effortful control.

Third, the understanding of genetic effects on temperament remains incomplete as long as the specific neural functions that mediate these effects are not known. As described in Part IV of this volume, there is now mounting evidence that functional polymorphisms are implicated in temperamental differences. On the other hand, there is increasing evidence that neurobiological structures and neurochemical signaling pathways are implicated in temperamental differences. Some examples include a role for the amygdala and possibly also for the bed nucleus of the stria terminalis (BNST) in behavioral inhibition and trait anxiety, with 5-HT and CRH playing an important role on the level of neurochemical transmission. The prefrontal and anterior cingulate cortex have been shown to play a role in attentional and emotional control, and there is also a certain consensus that the ventral striatum is involved in exuberance, with DA being one of the key neurotransmittors regulating activation in this brain site (White et al., Chapter 17, and Depue & Fu, Chapter 18, this volume).

Yet, what remains unclear is how alleles or functional polymorphisms impart on temperament through their effect on neurochemistry and neuroanatomy. Modeling of such interconnectivities might specify, for example, how the HTR1A-1019G allele influences trait anxiety by modulating 5-HT synaptic autoreceptor expression in the amygdala (see, e.g., Bodgan et al., in press; Hariri, 2009). Elaborating a comprehensive neuroscientific theory of temperament will require advances in instrumentation. At present, the detailed dynamics of neural processes, including neurotransmitter activity, remains hidden from the scanner and can be inferred only indirectly. This could change in a few years, when several promising techniques, such as hyperpolarization with parahydrogen (Adams et al., 2009), will have sufficiently progressed to let researchers measure the dynamics of neural activity with unprecedented precision (see Smith, 2012, for a review of these techniques). Technical innovations in neuroimaging combined with the refinement of temperament measures will enhance our understanding of the neurogenetics of temperament.

Acquired Biology and the Role of Epigenetics

By the time temperament can be reliably assessed as a relatively enduring trait, the development of neural circuitries subtending temperament has not simply executed a genetic script: It has also been shaped by experience. As has become increasingly clear in recent years, the brain is sensitive to both adversity and opportunity, resulting in changes to metabolic, endocrine, and neuroregulatory pathways, especially in a period of high brain plasticity such as infancy. As we now know, these processes start before birth in response to factors such as maternal stress, depression, or substance abuse, with potential "programming" effects on the brain, such as a hyperresponsiveness of the hypothalamus–pituitary–adrenal (HPA) axis (Huizink, Chapter 15, this volume). In the postnatal period, nutritional deficiencies, environmental lead, and parental neglect can all affect the infant's brain and alter the nature and course of temperament (Lengua & Wachs, Chapter 25, this volume).

What is more, the genetic activity itself may be altered as a result of postnatal influences. Such alterations are currently being intensely investigated across disciplines under the heading of *epigenetics*—the study of changes in gene activity that occur without any changes in the structure of the gene's DNA. After birth, the transduction of environmental influences into neurochemical and neurobiological signatures can work through epigenesis. For example, Meaney (2010) found that the gene encoding the corticosteroid receptor in rats carries different epigenetic marks, or modifications, in the brains of the offspring of negligent compared with nurturant mothers. As a result, the gene is less active in the neglected offspring, lessening the corticoid receptors that reduce stress responses, even in rats with high corticosteriod receptor DNA. In humans, the glucocorticoid receptor gene has shown increased methylation in human cord-blood DNA from newborns of depressed or anxious mothers (Oberlander et al., 2008).

Thus, in the postnatal period, exogenous life events can modulate gene expression of structural proteins, receptors, and signaling molecules, thereby establishing a basic neural foundation underlying the type of emotional behavior we call temperament. Indeed, there is accumulating evidence to suggest that the neurobiological legacy forged by these early processes can have long-lasting effects (Halligan, Herbert, Goodyer, & Murray, 2007; Heim, Newport, Mletzko, Miller, & Nemeroff, 2008; McGowan et al., 2009), thereby contributing to the stability of temperamental qualities that is typically observed after about age 3, as we shall see next.

Temperament and Development

An understanding of the role of temperament in development was hampered for a long time because of the scarcity of large-scale longitudinal studies extending from birth to adulthood (e.g., Kagan & Zentner, 1996). Over the past decade, a few such studies have sufficiently matured to give researchers the opportunity to examine adolescent and adult outcomes of early childhood temperament. Because previous chapters have extensively covered short- to medium-term longitudinal studies describing outcomes of early temperament (in this volume, see Shiner & Caspi, Chapter 24; Lengua & Wachs, Chapter 25; Klein et al., Chapter 26; Tackett et al., Chapter 27), the emphasis in this concluding chapter is on long-term longitudinal studies describing adolescent and adult outcomes of early temperament. When we say "early temperament," we mean temperament assessed in infancy and toddlerhood up until age 3.

Most of the evidence for the predictive power of early childhood temperament has been found for two traits, or syndromes, on which this review focuses. The first temperament component broadly relates to impaired impulse control and includes constructs such as "temperamental difficulty," "undercontrol," impulsivity, and inattention. These constructs are not identical, to be sure, but they share important features (Duckworth & Kern, 2011). The second temperament component relates to behavioral inhibition and related dimensions, such as fearfulness and social anxiety. Tables 32.2a and 32.2b list prospective longitudinal studies relating to adolescent and/or adult outcomes of both types of infant and/or toddler temperament. The majority of studies assessed early temperament based on examiner observations and/or objective behavioral coding; exceptions are the New York Longitudinal Study, the Fullerton Longitudinal Study, and the Uppsala Longitudinal Study, in which same and cross-informant questionnaire ratings were used to assess infant temperament. We should note that Tables 32.2a and 32.2b list but a few notable predictor and outcome variables. For more complete information on design and methodology, the reader is referred to the references listed in the right-hand columns of these tables.

Connections between Early Childhood Temperament and Adolescent/Adult Outcomes

Long-Term Outcomes of Impulse Control

The *Dunedin Multidisciplinary Health and Development Study* followed a cohort of slightly over 1,000 children from birth to the age of 32 years. Among its many measures was an assessment of the degree of self-control in 3-year-old children. The study showed that preschool degree of self-control predicted physical health, substance dependence, personal finances, and criminal offending outcomes at age 32 years (Moffitt et al., 2011). Because results are by far more trustworthy if they replicate across studies (Ledgerwood & Sherman, 2012), it is worth noting that similar findings have emerged from another important long-term longitudinal study, the *Mauritius Child and Health Study*, in which children's temperamental attributes at age 3 were rated by examiners on the island of Mauritius. It provides additional evidence that low levels of fearfulness and inhibition, and high levels of stimulation seeking, are a risk for the subsequent development of a psychopathic personality in adulthood (Glenn, Raine, Venables, & Mednick, 2007).

Comparable findings emerged from another classic long-term study, the *Block and Block Longitudinal Project* (Block, 1993, 2006), which had a smaller sample but included a rich set of assessments. Participants were recruited in preschool while attending either a parent cooperative or a university-run nursery school. The sample members were assessed at various ages, beginning at age 3 and including assessments at ages 14, 18, and 23. At each age, participants were seen on multiple occasions, by multiple observers, and rated on overcontrol, undercontrol, and resiliency as they completed a wide variety of tasks. The most relevant dimension in the present context is undercontrol, an expression for "unbridled impulsivity" (Block & Kremen, 1996, p. 351). There was a significant degree of continuity with respect to undercontrol from ages 3 to 23 years (Block, 2006). In addition, undercontrolled 3-year-old children, whose most salient traits include impulsivity and inattention, were at a higher risk to develop a variety of externalizing problem outcomes, including drug abuse and narcissism, across adolescence and young adulthood (Block, 1993; Carlson & Gjerde, 2009). Because narcissism shares some features with antisocial personality, this outcome is somewhat comparable with findings from the Dunedin and Mauritius studies.

In the *Colorado Longitudinal Twin Study*, over 600 toddlers were measured at their homes at ages 14, 20, 24, and 36 months on a "don't touch a toy" prohibition task (Friedman et al., 2011). On the basis of latent class growth analysis, the toddlers were allocated to one of two groups: high control or low control. At age 17, participants were measured on a battery of nine computerized executive function tasks administered in the laboratory. The two groups differed significantly and sizably on overall executive function performance at age 17.

The *Fullerton Longitudinal Study*, launched in 1979, chronicled the development of 109 children and their families from infancy through age 17 years by using same and cross-informant ratings (Guerin, Gottfried, Oliver, & Thomas, 2003). Infant temperament was measured through parental ratings on the Infant Characteristics Questionnaire (Bates, Freeland, & Lounsbury, 1979) and, at age 17 years, participants pro-

TABLE 32.2a. Temperamental Factors Predicting Adolescent and Adult Personality and Psychopathology: Impulsivity/Inattention

Longitudinal study	Infant/toddler temperament	Adolescent/adult outcome	Key references
Dunedin Multidisciplinary Health and Development Study	Undercontrol/impulsivity, 3 years	Elevated suicide risk Alienation, hostility Criminal offending, substance dependence 18, 26, and 32 years, respectively	Caspi et al. (1996) Caspi et al. (2003) Moffitt et al. (2011)
Mauritius Child Health Project	Fearlessness, disinhibition, 3 years	Psychopathy	Glenn et al. (2007)
Block & Block Longitudinal Project	Ego-undercontrol, 3 years	Ego-undercontrol, 14, 18, and 23 years	Block (2006)
		Narcissism, 23 years	Carlson & Gjerde (2009)
Colorado Longitudinal Twin Study	Impulse control, 18–36 months	Executive functions, IQ, 16–17 years	Friedman et al. (2011)
Mannheim Longitudinal Study	Attentional deficits, 3 months	Novelty seeking, 16 years	Laucht et al. (2006)
Fullerton Longitudinal Study	Temperamental difficulty, 18 months	Externalizing and internalizing behaviors, intelligence (–), 17 years	Guerin et al. (2003)
New York Longitudinal Study	Temperamental difficulty, 3 years	Maladjustment, 18–24 years	Thomas & Chess (1986)

vided self-ratings on the Youth Self-Report. "Difficult" infant temperament (fussy, unadaptable) predicted modest but significant amounts of variance in both externalizing and internalizing behavior problems at age 17 years. Interestingly, and in line with the findings from the Colorado Study, difficult infant temperament was also predictive of diminished intellectual functioning and school achievement in late adolescence (Guerin et al., 2003).

Similar findings emerged from the *New York Longitudinal Study*, which followed 133 children from early infancy to early adulthood. Notably, toddler temperamental difficulty, a combination of negative mood, slow adaptability, and highly intense reactions, as inferred from interviews with parents, was reported to be significantly related to interview ratings of adult maladjustment, a generic outcome variable including negative self-evaluation and problems in scholastic and social functioning (Thomas & Chess, 1986). Three additional long-term studies starting somewhat later than age 3 also showed that preschoolers' impaired impulse control predicted an aggressive–externalizing personality in adulthood (Asendorpf et al., 2008; Deal, Halverson, Havill, & Martin, 2005; Mischel et al., 2011).

Long-Term Outcomes of Behavioral Inhibition

Some of the long-term connections of infancy and toddler behavioral inhibition and related constructs emerged from the studies just reviewed, which had also measured inhibition and shyness at age 3. Thus, in the Dunedin Study, inhibited children reported more harm avoidance and less social potency and positive emotionality at both ages 18 and 26, and at age 26 they were described by informants as less extraverted (Caspi et al., 2003). The inhibited children were also more likely to be depressed and had more often attempted suicide compared with the well-adjusted children (Caspi et al., 1996). In a recent follow-up of the *Uppsala Longitudinal Study*, significant correlations emerged between toddler shyness and adult social anxiety, as well as depressive symptoms, at age 21 years (Bohlin & Hagekull, 2009).

The most extensive evidence for the early appearance and long-term implications of this temperamental disposition comes from the *Harvard Longitudinal Study*. The early infancy assessments and the inclusion of a wide array of psychophysiological and neurobiological measurements make this work particularly interesting. Some infants show high levels of negative reactivity to unknown objects, people, or locations, typically expressed by an increase in motor activity and negative affect, such as crying. This pattern of reactivity is related to behavioral inhibition and anxious behavior later in childhood and adolescence (Kagan, Chapter 4, this volume). Of note is also the predictive relationship between behavioral inhibition assessed in toddlerhood by maternal ratings and social anxiety disorder found in a related study by Fox and colleagues (Chronis-Tuscano et al., 2009; in this volume, see White et al., Chapter 17; Klein et al., Chapter 26).

Weight is added to these findings from an unlikely source. In 1950, the Swiss psychologist Richard Meili launched the *Bernese Longitudinal Study* to examine infancy origins of later personality differences. He began by studying 3- to 4-month-old infants' responses to unfamiliar stimuli, such as a black ball swung in front of an infant's visual field (Meili, 1957). After having infants' behaviors filmed and coded from record on 4 separate days, he found the reactivity to novel objects to be relatively stable (Pulver, 1959). In one of the few passages of his work ever translated into English, he summarized his findings as follows: "[I] discovered a difference between responses to an object in children between three and four months of age; some after initial inhibition rapidly resumed a calm expression, relaxed and sometimes smiled; others remained tense, moved irritably and began to cry" (Meili, 1963/1968, p. 245). He interpreted the infants' reactions in terms of differences in the ease of processing novel objects—a dimension Meili (1957) deemed to be "characterologically relevant." On this assumption, he followed these children into adolescence. He found moderate-to-high correlations between tenseness between 3 and 4 months, and multiple inhibition and shyness measures at ages 7 and 15 years (Meili & Meili-Dworetzki, 1972).

Taken collectively, the long-term studies reviewed here indicate that two traits appearing in infancy and toddlerhood, impulsivity/inattention and behavioral inhibition, are predictive of outcomes extending well into adolescence and adulthood. Crucially, links have been documented repeatedly by independent investigators working in different time periods, across different geographic locations, and using different methodologies within and across studies.

TABLE 32.2b. Temperamental Factors Predicting Adolescent and Adult Personality and Psychopathology: Inhibition/Fearfulness

Longitudinal study	Infant/toddler temperament	Adolescent/adult outcome	Key references
Harvard Longitudinal Study	High reactivity, 4 months	Trait anxiety, 15 years; Amygdala hyperresponsiveness, 21 years	Kagan et al. (2007); Schwartz et al. (in press)
Bernese Longitudinal Study	Infant irritability, 3 to 4 months	Shyness, 15 years	Meili & Meili-Dworetzki (1972)
Uppsala Longitudinal Study	Shyness, 20 months	Social anxiety, depressive symptoms, 21 years	Bohlin & Hagekull (2009)
Dunedin Multidisciplinary Health and Development Study	Inhibition, 3 years	Depression, 18 years; Harm avoidance, indecision, 26 years	Caspi et al. (1996); Caspi et al. (2003)

Mechanisms Underlying the Links between Early Temperament and Adult Outcomes

An important question for researchers is how to interpret the previously reported empirical connections both quantitatively and qualitatively. Although the connections are statistically significant, well replicated, and quite impressive given the long time intervals, the effect sizes are modest. Thus, the links need to be cast in probabilistic terms. Impulsive, undercontrolled toddlers can develop in many different ways, but some ways are more likely than others. This fact is easier to understand today than it was 20 years ago, thanks to novel insights into the processes underpinning stability and change.

A particularly important finding to emerge from behavioral genetics research is that genetic factors contribute substantially to measures of the environments of individuals, as detailed by Saudino and Wang (Chapter 16, this volume). Because environments have no DNA, the most plausible interpretation is that genetically influenced traits frame and shape the environments in their own image, as it were. How this is possible is fleshed out by Shiner and Caspi (Chapter 24, this volume), who discuss several processes through which temperament can shape environments in its own image. Through *environmental elicitation*, a child's temperament shapes the responses he or she evokes from adults and peers, and those reactions may in turn reinforce the child's temperament. Coplan and Bullock (Chapter 21, this volume) review the ways that children's temperament traits predict the responses of their peers toward them. *Environmental selection* describes a process through which a child seeks out an environment that is consistent with his or her temperament. Thus, a child with high levels of attention and self-control may choose to spend time reading and learning about new topics, and those activities may further strengthen the child's capacities for attention and self-regulation.

Environmental construal relates to temperament imposing a "meaning structure" on events (Rothbart, 2011). Depending on their temperaments, young children interpret and experience similar environments in profoundly different ways from birth. This may happen through a selective perceptual bias that gives more salience to certain components of the environment compared with others, or through a different interpretation of the same components of the environment. Thus, as opposed to the low-reactive infant, the high-reactive infant tends to focus on the threatening components of his or her environment. Because perceiving the world as a threatening place exacerbates the initial disposition to fearful reactions, this can only operate to reinforce the temperamental bias.

Although these processes go a long way in explaining why, in numerous cases, there is a certain inertia to temperament, temperament determines neither the environment nor the child's development. Three relatively recent lines of research help us to understand why a range of different outcomes is possible given the identical temperament. First, interactions between temperament dispositions and contextual factors can strengthen or weaken a child's temperament qualities, thereby promoting varied positive or negative adjustment outcomes (Bates et al., Chapter 20, and Lengua & Wachs, Chapter 25, this volume). Within the context of normal development, Kochanska's research on moral and conscience development has shown that the same parenting practices that promote the development of children's moral integrity and sense of justice in one type of child are unhelpful for another type of child. Thus, fearful children develop internalized self-controls best when they have mothers who use gentle child disciplinary strategies, whereas fearless children develop best with mothers who are warm and responsive, yet firmer in their interactions (Kochanska & Aksan, 2006).

Second, as described by van IJzendoorn and Bakermans-Kranenburg (Chapter 19, this volume), research has found certain temperamental dispositions to be particularly susceptible to environmental influences. This finding is generally referred to as *differential susceptibility*, which is not simply another expression for vulnerability. Rather, it denotes temperamental dispositions that confer particularly negative development in response to bad environments, but also exceptionally positive development in response to good environments. On the other extreme are temperamental qualities that appear to make children psychologically less permeable to environmental effects. These children will be protected from adverse environments but may in turn benefit less from enriching ones. These two different types of children have been poetically characterized as *orchid* and *dandelion* children, as discussed by van IJzendoorn and Bakermans-Kranenburg (Chapter 19, this volume). This new line of research raises the intriguing possibility that mutability or immutability in response to events may be a feature of temperament itself.

Third, the child's environment transcends the family. It includes the powerful sibling and peer context (Coplan & Bullock, Chapter 21, this volume). On a broader level, the context is woven from norms, laws, values, beliefs, customs, and traditions that define an entire cultural context. Chen, Yang, and Fu (Chapter 22, this volume) discuss how these cultural components of the environment can interact with the child's temperament. Peers and adults tend to perceive, evaluate, and respond to a child's temperamental characteristics through the lenses of their culture's value system. Such evaluations and responses affect the child's self-concept and behaviors, thereby affecting developmental patterns. For example, in Canadian samples, inhibition was found to evoke negative maternal attitudes and reactions, such as punishment orientation and rejection. However, the trend was the opposite in China, where inhibition was associated with warm and accepting maternal attitudes. Similarly, Canadian peers saw the subdued behaviors of inhibited children as deficient, but Chinese peers looked at them in a positive way, as signs of courteousness and readiness for social engagement. Consistent with these results, a recent study demonstrated that the same genotype—a serotonin receptor polymorphism (5-HTR1A)—is associated with different cognitive styles in Korea and in the United States (holistic vs. analytic), thus adding weight to the notion that the same genotype may have different, sometimes contrasting, phenotypic expressions depending on the context (Kim et al., 2010). Other factors that interact with temperament are social class and gender. Although interactions between temperament and low income or poverty are discussed by Lengua and Wachs (Chapter 25, this volume), and the literature on temperament and gender is reviewed by Else-Quest (Chapter 23, this volume), these domains deserve more attention in the future.

In summary, developmental work on temperament has greatly expanded our understanding of social, emotional, and personality development. Initially, the most perceptible shift was from an emphasis on the parent and other environmental factors to the child. More recently, however, the environment has resurfaced as an important factor in child development, albeit in a form that is very different from the one-size-fits-all understanding of the effects of parenting proclaimed in the 1960s and 1970s (e.g., Baumrind, 1967). This contemporary understanding of parenting and other environmental influences has more in common with the emergence of personalized medicine, that is, the customization of health care that involves tailoring practices to the individual patient by use of genetic or other information.

Temperament Research in the Public Interest

This volume provides strong evidence for the role of temperament in shaping risks for school failure (Duckworth & Allred, Chapter 30, this volume), depressive and anxiety symptoms (Klein et al., Chapter 26, this volume), and behavior problems, including serious antisocial behavior (Tackett et al., Chapter 27, this volume). In recognition of these findings and the fact that temperamental risk factors can be assessed as early as the second and third years of life, the field has come to appreciate the implications of its findings for prevention, intervention, and policymaking. As forcefully put by Moffitt and colleagues in their study on life outcomes of early impulsivity:

> It was possible to disentangle the effects of children's self-control from effects of variation in the children's intelligence, social class, and home lives of their families, thereby singling out self-control as a clear target for intervention policy. Joining earlier longitudinal follow-ups . . . , our findings imply that innovative policies that put self-control center stage might reduce a panoply of costs that now heavily burden citizens and governments. Differences between children in self-control predicted their adult outcomes approximately as well as low

intelligence and low social class origins, which are known to be extremely difficult to improve through intervention. (2011, p. 2697)

The idea of relying on certain behavioral markers for the purposes of screening and intervention is not new, of course. There is a copious literature on the possibilities for identifying at-risk children early in life, in particular those at risk for developing externalizing problems because they are hard to overlook (e.g., Conduct Problems Prevention Research Group, 2011). However, as we show next, temperament research has much to offer to this time-honored tradition of preventive science and practice.

Temperament in Childhood Prevention and Intervention

Temperament research offers at least four ways of strengthening current practices in prevention and intervention. First, most approaches to prevention and intervention target children during school age, although some programs have moved their initial assessments back to preschool. The move from school age back to preschool age or kindergarten recognizes that early intervention is key to the prevention of behavior disorders, particularly externalizing behaviors. The assessment procedures resulting from recent research on temperament can be applied to children of a younger age, including toddlers. The possibility of identifying at-risk behavioral patterns earlier than has been customary has the potential of making prevention more effective. Thus, the research described in this handbook gives a new meaning to what "early intervention" can be.

Second, temperament concepts and measures cover a relatively broad spectrum of traits, ranging from dispositional anger and fear to impairments in persistence and attention. These traits are relevant to both social functioning and academic competence, outcomes that have tended to be targeted separately. Thus, whereas behavioral inhibition carries a greater risk for predisposing children to low self-esteem and impaired social functioning (Coplan & Bullock, Chapter 21, this volume), effortful control and its affiliated constructs of constraint and self-control bear quite directly on behaviors required for scholastic achievement (Duckworth & Allred, Chapter 30, this volume). In other words, temperament concepts and measures not only provide the possibility of an earlier at-risk assessment compared with other screening tools, but also lend themselves to a more comprehensive screening of behavioral risk factors.

Third, early childhood temperament, though modestly predictive of later behavior problems, refers to variations within the normal range. Thus, temperament concepts avoid the overtly diagnostic or even pathologizing vocabulary that is characteristic of widely used screening tools. Interventions can capitalize on the benign vocabulary offered by temperament research and theory, and can frame its programs in terms of, for example, enhancing "character literacy" rather than preventing psychopathology or violence. Although this may seem like a minor change in labeling, it could go a long way toward ensuring parents' and teachers' acceptance of a given prevention or intervention. Few parents like to see their child as a potential criminal or depressive, whereas most parents would agree that character building is as important as passing exams. More important, avoiding unfavorable labeling of a child may prevent parents, teachers, counselors, and other child professionals from building up negative expectations that may end in self-fulfilling prophecies.

Fourth, the field of child temperament tends to spur personalized interventions, that is, practices that are tailored to the individual child's behavioral phenotype, as described by McClowry and Collins (Chapter 29, this volume). This development marks a departure from one-size-fits-all approaches that are characteristic of many prevention programs. Although certain practices and exercises can be effectively applied to all children, preventive science can ill afford to ignore the fact that what helps certain children may be unhelpful or even counterproductive for others. This development has an interesting parallel with the recent advent of personalized medicine. Knowing which genes are involved in a particular patient's disease can allow treatments to be deployed with greater precision. Thus, targeted therapies aimed at specific cancer-causing mutations, including Gleevec (imatinib) for chronic myelogenous leukemia and

Herceptin (trastuzumab) for some types of breast cancer, have been highly successful. Relatedly, a better understanding of which temperamental dispositions are involved in a given behavior disorder should allow clinicians to deploy prevention tools and treatments with greater effectiveness.

In summary, there are many ways in which the research covered in this handbook could enrich early intervention and prevention programs, thus making a difference for children's scholastic achievement and mental health. However, to build a bridge between basic research on temperament and practice effectively, more needs to be done. One problem is that despite the large number of temperament measures described in Part III of the handbook, hardly any instruments have been normed and standardized. This limits their usefulness as screening tools for purposes of prevention and intervention, although they can be readily used in temperament research. There are currently few temperament inventories with relatively extensive norms ($N > 1,000$). One is the Revised Temperament Assessment Battery for Children (TABC-R), which has norms from a U.S. sample (Martin & Bridger, 1999). It measures negative emotionality, activity, and persistence (based on New York Longitudinal Study concepts), from which composite scores of inhibition and impulsivity can be derived. Another instrument is the Integrative Child Temperament Inventory (ICTI), a 30-item measure of frustration, behavioral inhibition, attention/persistence, activity, and sensory sensitivity. It has been normed for use in Germany (Zentner & Ihrig, 2010), the United States, and the United Kingdom (Zentner & Wang, in press).

Yet even the most sensitive diagnostic tools are of limited value if they cannot be matched with putting in place effective interventions in the case of a risk diagnosis. McClowry and Collins (Chapter 29, this volume), Duckworth and Allred (Chapter 30, this volume), and Aron (Chapter 31, this volume) all describe a range of such possible interventions, showing how much the field has moved beyond the parent guidance originally envisaged by Chess and Thomas (1986; see also Carey & McDevitt, 1989). Even so, the integration of temperament concepts into intervention practices still leaves much room for improvement. At present, only very few temperament-inclusive interventions have demonstrated efficacy in reducing problem behaviors and enhancing adaptation in a variety of settings. One is the Cool Little Kids program for temperamentally inhibited preschool children (Kennedy, Rapee, & Edwards, 2009). Coplan, Schneider, Matheson, and Graham (2010) recently introduced an intervention called "Play Skills," also designed for very inhibited preschoolers, and reported promising results. INSIGHTS into Children's Temperament (McClowry, Snow, Tamis-LeMonda, & Rodriguez, 2010) is a more comprehensive intervention program based on an assessment of the child's entire temperamental profile; this intervention has been shown to be effective in two randomized controlled trials (see McClowry & Collins, Chapter 29, this volume).

An important point to keep in mind is that rather than being stand-alone programs, temperament-based interventions can be integrated into existing child development initiatives. In part, this is already happening, albeit somewhat unknowingly and invisibly. For example, several interventions enhance children's self-control and other self-regulatory abilities, which are facets of effortful control (Rueda, Chapter 8, this volume). Indeed, Duckworth and Allred (Chapter 30, this volume) ask with good reason: "The salutary effects of effortful control, and evidence that rank-order and mean-level change are possible, raise the question, what can schools and teachers do to encourage its development?" These authors describe several programs of prevention and intervention, such as Tools of the Mind, PATHS, and the Chicago School Readiness Program, which have shown good results in reducing problem behaviors related to deficits in effortful control. Also, forms of training, such as computerized and noncomputerized games, have been shown to improve the executive functions of preschoolers and school-age children (Diamond & Lee, 2011; see also Rueda, Chapter 8, and Goldsmith & Gagne, Chapter 11, this volume). In addition, there is growing interest in using classmates to deliver targeted group or school-wide programs that teach and encourage more effective coping with anger and aggression (Deater-Deckard & Wang, Chapter 7, this volume). Finally, temperament-inclusive interventions could also play a significant role in preventing health problems such as obesity (Hampson & Vollrath, Chapter 28, this volume).

Thus, there is clearly scope for improving the level of integration between the temperament and intervention literature. One advantage of bridging the two is that intervention could start earlier than is presently the case. For example, behavioral inhibition and deficits in effortful control are risk factors that can be discerned and measured as early as in toddlerhood (in this volume, see Kagan, Chapter 4; Rueda, Chapter 8; Gartstein et al., Chapter, 10; Goldsmith & Gagne, Chapter 11). This is important in the light of evidence showing that temperament predicts performance in reading and numerical tasks (e.g., Coplan, Barber, & Lagace-Seguin, 1999; Fuhs, Wyant, & Day, 2011). Thus, current temperament concepts can facilitate the deployment of interventions at an age when the relatively high degree of brain and behavioral plasticity makes successful outcomes more likely.

Temperament in Psychotherapy

C. G. Jung's views in *Psychological Types* (1923) triggered Freud's scorn (see Paskaukas, 1995, p. 424), but are consistent with current thinking about applications of temperament research and personalized interventions more generally. An extravert needs action and company to feel well, but being forced constantly to socialize, attend parties and office functions, and be deprived of a measure of solitude will likely throw an introverted type out of balance. In and of itself, this notion is hardly original. What makes it controversial is its clash with current-day Western ideals for gregariousness and a general preference for action over contemplation. Indeed, most parents, teachers, psychotherapists, and psychiatrists would risk being accused of acting irresponsibly were they to encourage children or patients to cut down on socializing and make time for extensive periods of solitude.

Easily overlooked, however, is that the desirability of extraversion is variable across cultural context and historical period. In 19th-century England, restraint and a measure of eccentricity passed as signs of class and nobility. The legendary character Phileas Fogg, before attempting to circumnavigate the world in 80 days (Verne, 1874), lived a happy life as a bachelor, carrying out his daily activities with mathematical precision in London's Savile Row. Even in the contemporary reader, the character does not arouse serious psychiatric suspicions because there is an appreciation for the fit between the person and his time. More important, and as discussed by Chen and colleagues (Chapter 22, this volume), to keep to oneself is considered normal, and sometimes even a desirable sign of wisdom in other cultural contexts.

Another example is self-control, whose virtues are currently emphasized and contrasted with the perils of impulsivity (Baumeister & Tierney, 2012). Although self-control has been demonstrably linked to several positive outcomes, in certain contexts, it may also impose certain limitations on exploratory and creative behavior (Block, 2006). Steve Jobs, for many an epitome of entrepreneurial creativity, experimented with drugs in his youth, drove a car without a license plate, and was notoriously emotional in his handling of employees (Isaacson, 2011)—hardly signs of the kind of self-control that preventive programs strive to promote in children.

Even neuroticism had its ups and downs. The author of a recent *New York Times* essay looks back at a time when "being neurotic meant something more than merely being anxious. . . . It meant being interesting (if sometimes exasperating) at a time when psychoanalysis reigned in intellectual circles and Woody Allen reigned in movie houses" (Carey, 2012). MacDonald (Chapter 14, this volume) takes an evolutionary approach to understanding the costs and benefits associated with various temperamental characteristics. The concept of *fluctuating selection* posits that both ends of any of the basic temperamental dimensions were "selected" because each end is associated with both evolutionary costs and fitness benefits, depending on environmental circumstances. Thus, it is only through the preservation of variation in temperament that evolutionary fitness can be maintained (see also K. Akiskal & Akiskal, 2005).

Although the kinds of temperamental traits that make life harder or easier vary according to cultural and historical contexts, the clinical benefits of this realization are limited. No time machine can transport a patient into an epoch that might have provided a better fit to his or her temperament. And although people do occasionally relocate to places that suit their temperament better than the previous one, this is not often practicable. As a consequence, when temperament gets in the way of social or professional functioning, means for enhancing behavioral flexibility will be the most sensible choice. This can be achieved through the previously described intervention programs or other established forms of psychotherapy.

Aron (Chapter 31, this volume) offers a number of suggestions for ways that clinicians can address patients' varied temperaments effectively in the context of therapy. She argues that a temperament perspective offers significant advantages to treatment: It may improve assessment, reduce misdiagnosis, help build a therapeutic alliance, improve the efficiency of treatment, and nurture patients' self-esteem by helping them to value their individual differences. Another important recognition has been that temperament can predict which type of psychotherapy will be most effective (Klein et al., Chapter 26, this volume). Thus, for example, in a study of psychotherapy of depression by Joyce and colleagues (2007), the higher patients scored on harm avoidance, the more they benefited from interpersonal therapy (vs. cognitive-behavioral therapy), whereas persistence was associated with a more positive response to cognitive-behavioral therapy (see Table 32.3). Another study found that people with some temperament and personality characteristics seem to respond better to pharmacotherapy compared with psychotherapy (Bagby et al., 2008). Taken together, these findings suggest that temperament could play a useful role in guiding treatment selection.

Temperament, Biological Psychiatry, and Neuropsychopharmacology

Temperament was never far from the interests of biological psychiatry and neuropsychopharmacology. This strand evolved somewhat separately from the study of temperament and psychopathology covered in this volume by Lengua and Wachs (Chapter 25), Klein et al. (Chapter 26), and Tackett et al. (Chapter 27), and may be traced to Kretschmer on one hand, and Axelrod and other eminent neuropsychopharmacologists on the other (Healy, 2002). For example, drawing on Kretschmer's (1925) notion that endogenous psychoses are exaggerated forms of normal temperament, Akiskal views temperament as the earliest clinically observable phenotypic expressions of an underlying genetic diathesis for mood disorder distinctions (H. Akiskal & Akiskal, 1992). He distinguishes five major "subaffective temperaments": cyclothymic, dysthymic, hyperthymic, irritable, and anxious (H. Akiskal, Akiskal, Haykal, Manning, & Connor, 2005). This conception of temperament as a subclinical phenotype is related to the continuum/spectrum framework of temperament–psychopathology links discussed by Klein and colleagues (Chapter 26). The psychiatric approach to temperament also has a stronger emphasis on psychopharmacology. Although both strands look at the role of temperament in psychopathology, the connections between the two strands are not as strong as they might be. Yet, a tighter connection between these domains would have obvious advantages.

First, several temperament measures used in psychiatric research, such as those developed by Akiskal and Cloninger, overlap considerably with the mainstream temperament concepts and measures discussed in Part II (see Table 32.1; Zuckerman, Chapter 3, this volume). A taxonomic integration of these models could make research on temperament and psychopathology more cumulative and incremental. Thus, the serotonin transporter allele(s) has been linked to "cyclothy-

TABLE 32.3. Correlation of Temperament with Percentage Improvement, by Therapy

Temperament	Correlation (r) IPT	CBT
Novelty seeking	.22*	.09
Harm avoidance	.37***	−.17
Persistence	.06	.18
Reward dependence	.24	.22*

Note. Based on Joyce et al. (2007). CBT, cognitive-behavioral therapy; IPT, interpersonal psychotherapy.
*$p < .05$; $p < .01$; ***$p < .001$.

mic" and "anxious" temperament (Rihmer, Akiskal, Rihmer, & Akiskal, 2010), "harm avoidance" (Wu et al., 2010), and "neuroticism" (see Depue & Fu, Chapter 18, this volume). In effect, these findings likely represent variants of one and the same relationship. Yet use of different terminologies creates the appearance of three different types of results—an instantiation of the *jangle fallacy*, that is, the obfuscation of similarity in constructs and results by the use of different terms (Block, 1995).

Second, a temperament diagnosis could help to predict which patients will respond best to a given psychotropic agent. Currently, the edge that psychotropic agents have over placebos in treating anxiety, depression, impulsivity, or rigidity is scarcely impressive (e.g., Kirsch, Deacon, Huedo-Medina, Moore, & Johnson, 2008). One reason is that psychotropic medication efficacy has been shown to vary widely from patient to patient (Simon & Perlis, 2010). Understanding and predicting that variation could have considerable benefits for both doctors and patients. The current recommendation in psychiatry is to try a given drug first, then to switch to another compound if there is no response or side effects occur. If the second drug fails, a third one might be tried, and so on. The inability to match a patient with a drug often sends both the doctor and patient on a protracted odyssey until a compound that works is found.

There are several hypotheses about individuals differential responsiveness to antidepressive and antipsychotic agents, including purely metabolic ones (Simon & Perlis, 2010). But there is also recognition that individuals may respond differentially because of different neuroaffective bases of their personalities. For example, Joyce, Mulder, and Cloninger (1994) showed that people with certain temperament profiles were more likely to respond to drugs acting on the serotonin system, whereas others responded to drugs acting on the norepinephrine system. More recently, Phan, Lee, and Coccaro (2011) found that patients' scores on harm avoidance predicted effectiveness of selective serotonin reuptake inhibitors (SSRIs) in treating depression. Thus, as a proxy for the neural basis of personality, temperament concepts could help clinicians to find the effective compound for a given individual right away. To be sure, the evidence for the differential effectiveness of drugs, depending on the temperamental characteristics of patients, is in its infancy.

Finally, the rapid progress in our understanding of brain–temperament relationships might ultimately facilitate the development of targeted psychotropic drugs. For example, some recent findings suggest that axonal disintegration may play an important role in trait anxiety because the former tends to disrupt connectivity across brain sites involved in anxiety regulation (Westlye, Bjørnebekk, Grydeland, Fjell, & Walhovd, 2011). Thus, compounds that can halt or reverse axonal neuropathology might also have an anxiolytic effect. In summary, as we enter into the new era of personalized pharmacotherapy (Gurwitz, Lunshof, & Altman, 2006), a tighter integration of temperament research in psychopharmacology and in biological and molecular psychiatry seems an obvious step to take.

Some Caveats Regarding Temperament-Inclusive Interventions

Although there are clear advantages of integrating temperament research, measures, and concepts into current forms of prevention, intervention, and treatment, there is also a certain potential for misuse. First, interventionists should be mindful of interventions' dependence on value systems, as pointed out before. Furthermore, although temperament could play a salutary role in psychiatry, and perhaps in medicine more generally, the concept of temperament should not itself be medicalized. Although most readers of this volume will appreciate that calling a trait, such as impulsivity, *temperament* does not imply a clear-cut biological etiology, in popular parlance, the term often stands informally for behavioral tendencies with a neural or genetic cause, such as a chemical imbalance in the brain. From here it is only a small step to the claim that because temperament is a result of chemical imbalances or badly routed synapses, the behaviors can only be rectified by pharmacological intervention. Capitalizing on this informal (and incorrect) use of the term *temperament*, interest groups such as drug companies would only be too happy to see temperament concepts spreading across the helping professions, thus broadening the market for their lines of product.

Another sensitive area is jurisdiction. The obvious worry is that temperament concepts, wrongly understood as implying biological determinism, could be misused to exculpate individuals for criminal offenses or other harmful actions. In this view, some unfortunate individuals act the way nature intends them to act. Indeed, this view may wrongly suggest that these individuals should themselves be seen as helpless victims of a temperament generated by a brain malfunction, such as a deficiency of positively charged sodium ions along the membranes of axons in the prefrontal cortex or the nucleus accumbens (see Gazzaniga, 2011, for a recent discussion of problems in using biological determinism in the courtroom).

Conclusion

Overseeing the incredibly rich, diverse, and rigorous research compiled in this volume has been a heartening experience. Even so, one can see that research on temperament is very much a work in progress. As noted by Pavlov long ago, there is a proper sequence to research priorities that cannot be circumvented: "From the very beginning of your work, school yourselves to severe gradualness in the accumulation of knowledge.... Never begin the subsequent without mastering the preceding" (1936, p. 369). Before attempting to crack the code of temperament's ultimate workings, the field had first to establish a system for describing, characterizing, and classifying the phenomenon of interest. This work has in itself been fruitful, leading to a comprehensive system for the classification and measurement of normal individual differences in emotive and regulatory behaviors, currently unmatched by any other conceptual or assessment instrumentarium for the period of infancy and toddlerhood (Parts II and III, this volume). In parallel, it began to gradually expand its research into the antecedents and consequences of temperamental qualities showing that individual differences in temperament have appreciable predictive validity regarding personality, psychopathology, and interpersonal functioning, as well as health and occupational achievement, as is detailed in Parts V and VI of this volume. From this foundation, the field is now in a better position to embrace Pavlov's second piece of advice: "[T]ry not to stay on the surface of the facts.... Try to penetrate to the secret of their occurrence, persistently search for the laws which govern them" (p. 369). The new developments traced in this handbook show that this is now happening.

Because the focus of the volume is inherently developmental, we have not singled out the role of temperament in specific age periods (infancy, childhood, adolescence, adulthood). Thus, the chapters in Part II delineate basic temperament traits across the lifespan, from infancy to adulthood. Moreover, this volume has two chapters specifically devoted to temperament in adults (Zuckerman, Chapter 3; Depue & Yu, Chapter 18). Even so, not all areas in adult temperament research have equally been covered, and more could have been added on models relating to affective styles (Davidson, 2000), the behavioral inhibition and activation systems in temperament (Carver, 2005), or other two-dimensional models of temperament (Clark & Watson, 2008). Similarly, infancy's somewhat special role in temperament research has been touched upon in many chapters of this volume. Still, it may deserve more special treatment, especially with respect to uses of temperament concepts in pediatrics.

Finally, although this volume addressed links between temperament and developmental psychopathology in Klein and colleagues, Chapter 26, and Tackett and colleagues, Chapter 27, a previous section in this chapter has pointed to other ways in which temperament concepts and measures could be profitably integrated into biological psychiatry and psychopharmacology. A chapter dedicated specifically to these latter areas would undoubtedly enrich this volume and contribute to bridging the current gap between temperament research in biological psychiatry and psychopharmacology on the one hand, and research on temperament in clinical psychology and developmental psychopathology on the other.

So much for the "known unknowns." The "unknown unknowns" are, by definition, unknown. There is little doubt that these unknowns will be brought to our attention. This we can only welcome and embrace. Incongruous findings or secluded research initiatives have often acted as a source of creativity and progress. Several chapters in this volume point to currently neglected questions, whose examination may enrich the area in important and unexpected ways. Despite its incompleteness, we hope that the new level of integration achieved with this volume is substantial enough to spur the research insights and alliances required to meet the challenges that lie ahead.

Acknowledgments

We wish to thank Kirby Deater-Deckard, Jerome Kagan, Daniel Klein, and Mary Rothbart for their valuable comments on previous versions of this chapter.

References

Adams, R. W., Aguilar, J. A., Atkinson, K. D., Cowley, M. J., Elliott, P. I., Duckett, S. B., et al. (2009). Reversible interactions with parahydrogen enhance NMR sensitivity by polarization transfer. *Science, 323,* 1708–1711.

Akiskal, H., & Akiskal, K. (1992). Cyclothymic, hyperthymic, and depressive temperaments as subaffective variants of mood disorders. *American Psychiatric Press Review of Psychiatry, 11,* 43–62.

Akiskal H., Akiskal, K., Haykal, R. F., Manning, J. S., & Connor, P. (2005). TEMPS-A: Progress towards validation of a self-rated clinical version of the Temperament Evaluation of the Memphis, Pisa, Paris, and San Diego Autoquestionnaire. *Journal of Affective Disorders, 85,* 3–16.

Akiskal, K., & Akiskal, H. (2005). The theoretical underpinnings of affective temperaments: Implications for evolutionary foundations of bipolar disorder and human nature. *Journal of Affective Disorders, 85,* 231–239.

Allport, G. W. (1937). *Personality: A psychological interpretation.* New York: Holt.

Altemeyer, B. (1998). The other "authoritarian personality." *Advances in Experimental Social Psychology, 30,* 47–91.

Aron, E. (1996). *The highly sensitive person: How to thrive when the world overwhelms you.* New York: Birch Lane Press.

Asendorpf, J. B., Denissen, J., & van Aken, M. (2008). Inhibited and aggressive preschool children at 23 years of age: Personality and social transitions into adulthood. *Developmental Psychology, 44,* 997–1011.

Asendorpf, J. B., & van Aken, M. A. (1999). Resilient, overcontrolled, and undercontrolled personality prototypes in children: Replicability, predictive power, and the trait-type issue. *Journal of Personality and Social Psychology, 77,* 815–832.

Bagby, R. M., Quilty, L. C., Segal, Z. V., McBride, C. C., Kennedy, S. H., & Costa, P. T. (2008). Personality and differential treatment response in major depression: A randomized controlled trial comparing cognitive-behavioral therapy and pharmacotherapy. *Canadian Journal of Psychiatry, 53,* 361–370.

Bates, J. E., Freeland, C. A. B., & Lounsbury, M. L. (1979). Measurement of infant difficulties. *Child Development, 50,* 794–803.

Baumeister, R. F., & Tierney, J. (2012). *Willpower: Rediscovering our greatest strength.* London: Allen Lane.

Baumrind, D. (1967). Child care practices anteceding three patterns of preschool behavior. *Genetic Psychology Monographs, 75,* 43–88.

Bergman, P., & Escalona, S. (1949). Unusual sensitivities in very young children. *Psychoanalytic Study of the Child, 3–4,* 333–352.

Block, J. (1993). Studying personality the long way. In D. C. Funder, R. D. Parke, C. Tomlinson-Keasey, & K. Widaman (Eds.), *Studying lives through time: Personality and development* (pp. 9–41). Washington, DC: American Psychological Association.

Block, J. (1995). A contrarian view of the five-factor approach to personality description. *Psychological Bulletin, 117,* 187–215.

Block, J. (2005). The Stroop effect and its relation to personality. *Personality and Individual Differences, 38,* 735–746.

Block, J. (2006). Venturing a 30-year longitudinal study. *American Psychologist, 61,* 315–327.

Block, J., & Kremen, A. M. (1996). IQ and ego-resiliency: Conceptual and empirical connections and separateness. *Journal of Personality and Social Psychology, 70,* 349–361.

Block, J. H., Block, J., & Gjerde, P. J. (1986). The personality of children prior to divorce: A prospective study. *Child Development, 57,* 827–840.

Bodgan, R., Carré, J. M., & Hariri, A. (in press). Toward a mechanistic understanding of how variability in neurobiology shapes individual differences in behavior. *Current Topics in Behavioral Neurosciences.*

Bohlin, G., & Hagekull, B. (2009). Socio-emotional development: From infancy to young adulthood. *Scandinavian Journal of Psychology, 50,* 592–601.

Buss, A. H., & Plomin, R. (1975). *A temperament theory of personality development.* New York: Wiley.

Carey, B. (2012, April 1). Where have all the neurotics gone? *New York Times,* p. SR1.

Carey, W. B., & McDevitt, S. C. (1989). *Clinical and educational applications of temperament research.* Amsterdam/Lisse: Swets & Zeitlinger.

Carlson, K. S., & Gjerde, P. F. (2009). Preschool personality antecedents of narcissism in adolescence and young adulthood: A 20-year longitudinal study. *Journal of Research in Personality, 43*, 570–578.

Carver, C. (2005). Impulse and constraint: Perspectives from personality psychology, convergence with theory in other areas, and potential for integration. *Personality and Social Psychology Review, 9*, 312–333.

Carver, C. S., Johnson, S. L., & Joormann, J. (2008). Serotonergic function, two-mode models of self-regulation, and vulnerability to depression: What depression has in common with impulsive aggression. *Psychological Bulletin, 134*, 912–943.

Caspi, A. (1998). Personality development across the life course. In W. Damon (Series Ed.) & N. Eisenberg (Vol. Ed.), *Handbook of child psychology: Vol. 3. Social, emotional, and personality development* (pp. 311–388). New York: Wiley.

Caspi, A., Harrington, H., Milne, B., Amell, J. W., Theodore, R. F., & Moffitt, T. E. (2003). Children's behavioral styles at age 3 are linked to their adult personality traits at age 26. *Journal of Personality, 71*, 495–513.

Caspi, A., Moffitt, T. E., Newman, D. L., & Silva, P. (1996). Behavioral observations at age 3 years predict adult psychiatric disorders: Longitudinal evidence from a birth cohort. *Archives of General Psychiatry, 53*, 1033–1039.

Caspi, A., Roberts, B. W., & Shiner, R. L. (2005). Personality development: Stability and change. *Annual Review of Psychology, 56*, 453–484.

Caspi, A., & Silva, P. A. (1995). Temperamental qualities at age three predict personality traits in young adulthood: Longitudinal evidence from a birth cohort. *Child Development, 66*, 486–498.

Chess, S., & Thomas, A. (1986). *Temperament in clinical practice*. New York: Guilford Press.

Chronis-Tuscano, A., Degnan, K. A., Pine, D. S., Pérez-Edgar, K., Henderson, H. A., Diaz, Y., et al. (2009). Stable early maternal report of behavioral inhibition predicts lifetime social anxiety disorder in adolescence. *Journal of the American Academy of Child and Adolescent Psychiatry, 48*, 928–935.

Clark, L. A., & Watson, D. (2008). Temperament: An organizing paradigm for trait psychology. In O. P. John, R. W. Robins, & L. A. Pervin (Eds.), *Handbook of personality: Theory and research* (3rd ed., pp. 265–286). New York: Guilford Press.

Conduct Problems Prevention Research Group. (2011). The effects of the Fast Track preventive intervention on the development of conduct disorder across childhood. *Child Development, 82*, 331–345.

Coplan, R. J., Barber, A. M., & Lagace-Seguin, D. G. (1999). The role of child temperament as a predictor of early literacy and numeracy skills in preschoolers. *Early Childhood Research Quarterly, 14*, 537–553.

Coplan, R. J., Schneider, B. H., Matheson, A., & Graham, A. (2010). "Play skills" for shy children: Development of a Social Skills Facilitated Play early intervention program for extremely inhibited preschoolers. *Infant and Child Development, 19*, 223–237.

Davidson, R. J. (2000). Affective style, psychopathology, and resilience: Brain mechanisms and plasticity. *American Psychologist, 55*, 1196–1214.

Deal, J., Halverson, C., Havill, V., & Martin, R. P. (2005). Temperament factors as long-term predictors of young adult personality. *Merrill–Palmer Quarterly, 51*, 315–334.

Diamond, A., & Lee, K. (2011). Interventions shown to aid executive function development in children 4 to 12 years old. *Science, 333*, 959–964.

Diamond, S. (1957). *Personality and temperament*. New York: Harper.

Duckworth, A. L., & Kern, M. L. (2011). A meta-analysis of the convergent validity of self-control measures. *Journal of Research in Personality, 35*, 259–268.

Eisenberg, N., Smith, C. L., & Spinrad, T. L. (2011). Effortful control: Relations with emotion regulation, adjustment, and socialization in childhood. In K. D. Vohs & R. F. Baumeister (Eds.), *Handbook of self-regulation: Research, theory, and applications* (2nd ed., pp. 263–283). New York: Guilford Press.

Escalona, S. K. (1968). *The roots of individuality. Normal patterns of development in infancy*. Chicago: Aldine.

Eysenck, H. J. (1967). *The biological basis of personality*. Springfield, IL: Thomas.

Friedman, N. P., Miyake, A., Robinson, J. L., & Hewitt, J. K. (2011). Developmental trajectories in toddlers' self-restraint predict individual differences in executive functions 14 years later: A behavioral genetic analysis. *Developmental Psychology, 47*, 1410–1430.

Fuhs, M. W., Wyant, A., & Day, J. (2011). Unique contributions of impulsivity and inhibition to prereading skills in preschoolers at head start. *Journal of Research in Childhood Education, 25*, 145–159.

Gazzaniga, M. S. (2011). *Who's in charge?: Free will and the science of the brain*. New York: HarperCollins.

Gesell, A. (1928). *Infancy and human growth*. New York: Macmillan.

Glenn, A. L., Raine, A., Venables, P. H., & Mednick, S. A. (2007). Early temperamental and psychophysiological precursors of adult psychopathic personality. *Journal of Abnormal Psychology, 116*, 508–518.

Goldberg, L. R. (1990). An alternative description

of personality: The Big-Five factor structure. *Journal of Personality and Social Psychology, 59,* 1216–1229.

Goldsmith, H. H. (1996). Studying temperament via construction of the Toddler Behavior Assessment Questionnaire. *Child Development, 67,* 218–235.

Goldsmith, H. H., Buss, A. H., Plomin, R., Rothbart, M. K., Thomas, A., Chess, S., et al. (1987). Roundtable: What is temperament? Four approaches. *Child Development, 58,* 505–529.

Goldsmith, H. H., & Campos, J. J. (1982). Toward a theory of infant temperament. In R. N. Emde & R. J. Harmon (Eds.), *The development of attachment and affiliative systems* (pp. 161–193). New York: Plenum Press.

Goldsmith, H. H., Van Hulle, C. A., Arneson, C. L., Schreiber, J. E., & Gernsbacher, M. A. (2006). A population-based twin study of parentally reported tactile and auditory defensiveness in young children. *Journal of Abnormal Child Psychology, 34,* 378–392.

Gray, J. A. (1973). Causal theories of personality and how to test them. In J. R. Royce (Ed.), *Multivariate analysis and psychological theory* (pp. 409–463). New York: Academic Press.

Guerin, D. W., Gottfried, A. W., Oliver, P. H., & Thomas, C. W. (2003). *Temperament: Infancy through adolescence.* New York: Kluwer Academic.

Gurwitz, D., Lunshof, J. E., & Altman, R. B. (2006). From pharmacogenetics to personalized medicine: A vital need for educating health professionals and the community. *Pharmacogenomics, 5,* 571–579.

Halligan, S. L., Herbert, J., Goodyer, I., & Murray, L. (2007). Disturbances in morning cortisol secretion in association with maternal postnatal depression predict subsequent depressive symptomatology in adolescents. *Biological Psychiatry, 62,* 40–46.

Hariri, A. R. (2009). The neurobiology of individual differences in complex behavioral traits. *Annual Review of Neuroscience, 32,* 225–247.

Hart, D., Atkins, R., & Fegley, S. (2003). Personality and development in childhood: A person-centered approached. *Monographs of the Society for Research in Child Development, 68*(1, Serial No. 272).

Hart, D., Burock, D., London, D., Atkins, R., & Bonilla-Santiago, G. (2005). The relation of personality types to physiology, behavioural and cognitive processes. *European Journal of Personality, 19,* 391–407.

Healy, D. (2002). *The creation of psychopharmacology.* Cambridge, MA: Harvard University Press.

Heim, C., Newport, J. D., Mletzko T., Miller, A. H., & Nemeroff, C. B. (2008). The link between childhood trauma and depression: Insights from HPA axis studies in humans. *Psychoneuroendocrinology, 33,* 693–710.

Heymans, G., & Wiersma, E. D. (1906). Beiträge zur speziellen Psychologie auf Grund einer Massenuntersuchung [Contributions to differential psychology from a mass study]. *Zeitschrift für Psychologie, 43,* 81–127.

Isaacson, W. (2011). *Steve Jobs.* New York: Simon & Schuster.

Izard, C. E. (2007). Basic emotions, natural kinds, emotion schemas, and a new paradigm. *Perspectives on Psychological Science, 2,* 260–280.

Joyce, P. R., McKenzie, J. M., Carter, J. D., Rae, A., Luty, S. E., Frampton, C. M., et al. (2007). Temperament, character and personality disorders as predictors of response to interpersonal psychotherapy and cognitive-behavioural therapy for depression. *British Journal of Psychiatry, 190,* 503–508.

Joyce, P. R., Mulder, R. T., & Cloninger, C. R. (1994). Temperament predicts clomipramine and dopamine response in major depression. *Journal of Affective Disorders, 30*(1), 35–46.

Jung, C. G. (1923). *Psychological types* (G. Baynes, Trans.). New York: Harcourt Brace.

Kagan, J., & Snidman, N. (2004). *The long shadow of temperament.* Cambridge, MA: Harvard University Press.

Kagan, J., Snidman, N., Kahn, V., & Towsley, S. (2007). The preservation of two infant temperaments through adolescence. *Monographs of the Society for Research in Child Development, 72*(Serial No. 287)

Kagan, J., & Zentner, M. R. (1996). Early childhood predictors of adult psychopathology. *Harvard Review of Psychiatry, 3,* 341–350.

Kennedy, S., Rapee, R., & Edwards, S. (2009). A selective intervention program for inhibited preschool-aged children of parents with an anxiety disorder: Effects on current anxiety disorders and temperament. *Journal of the American Academy of Child and Adolescent Psychiatry, 48,* 602–609.

Kim, H. S., Sherman, D. K., Taylor, S. E., Sasaki, J. Y., Chu, T. Q., Ryu, C., et al. (2010). Culture, serotonin receptor polymorphism and locus of attention. *Social Cognition and Affective Neuroscience, 5,* 212–218.

Kim, M. J., & Whalen, P. J. (2009). The structural integrity of an amygdala–prefrontal pathway predicts trait anxiety. *Journal of Neuroscience, 29,* 11614–11618.

Kirsch, I., Deacon, B., Huedo-Medina, T. B., Moore, T. J., & Johnson, B. T. (2008). Initial severity and antidepressant benefits: A meta-analysis of data submitted to the Food and Drug Administration. *PLoS Medicine, 5,* e45.

Kochanska, G., & Aksan, N. (2006). Children's conscience and self-regulation. *Journal of Personality, 74,* 1587–1617.

Kochanska, G., Coy, K. C., Tjebkes, C. T., & Husarek, S. (1998). Individual differences in emotionality in infancy. *Child Development*, 69, 375–390.

Kohnstamm, G. A. (Ed.). (1986). *Temperament discussed: Temperament and development in infancy and childhood*. Lisse, The Netherlands: Swets & Zeitlinger.

Kohnstamm, G. A., Bates, J., & Rothbart, M. K. (Eds.). (1989). *Temperament in childhood*. New York: Wiley.

Kretschmer, E. (1925). *Physique and character*. New York: Harcourt Brace.

Lamb, M. E., Chuang, S. S., Wessels, H., Broberg, A. G., & Hwang, C. P. (2002). Emergence and construct validation of the Big Five factors in early childhood: A longitudinal analysis of their ontogeny in Sweden. *Child Development*, 73, 1517–1524.

Laucht, M., Becker, K., & Schmidt, M. H. (2006). Visual exploratory behaviour in infancy and novelty seeking in adolescence: Two developmentally specific phenotypes of DRD4? *Journal of Child Psychology and Psychiatry*, 47, 1143–1151.

Ledgerwood, A., & Sherman, J. W. (2012). Short, sweet, and problematic? The rise of the short report in psychological science. *Perspectives on Psychological Science*, 7, 60–66.

Lieberman, M., & Rosenthal, R. (2001). Why introverts can't always tell who likes them: Multitasking and nonverbal decoding. *Journal of Personality and Social Psychology*, 80, 294–310.

Martin, R. P., & Bridger, R. (1999). *The Temperament Assessment Battery for Children—Revised (TABC-R)*. Athens, GA: School Psychology Clinic.

McClowry, S. G., Snow, D. L., Tamis-LeMonda, C. S., & Rodriguez, E. T. (2010). Testing the efficacy of INSIGHTS on student disruptive behavior, classroom management, and student competence in inner city primary grades. *School Mental Health*, 2, 23–35.

McGowan, P. O., Sasaki, A., D'Alessio, A. C., Dymov, S., Labonté, B., Szyf, M., et al. (2009). Epigenetic regulation of the glucocorticoid receptor in human brain associates with childhood abuse. *Nature Neuroscience*, 12(3), 342–348.

Meaney, M. J. (2010). Epigenetics and the biological definition of gene × environment interactions. *Child Development*, 81, 41–79.

Mehrabian, A. (1996). Pleasure–arousal–dominance: A general framework for describing and measuring individual differences in temperament. *Current Psychology*, 14, 261–292.

Meili, R. (1957). *Anfänge der Charakterentwicklung* [Beginnings of character development]. Bern: Huber.

Meili, R. (1968). The structure of personality (A. Spillmann, Trans.). In J. Nuttin, P. Fraisse, & R. Meili (Eds.), *Motivation, emotion and personality*. London: Routledge & Kegan Paul. (Original work published 1963)

Meili, R., & Meili-Dworetzki, G. (1972). *Grundlagen individueller Persönlichkeitsunterschiede* [Foundations of individual differences in personality]. Bern: Huber.

Mischel, W., Ayduk, O., Berman, M. G., Casey, B. J., Gotlib, I. H., Jonides, J., et al. (2011). "Willpower" over the life span: Decomposing self-regulation. *Social Cognitive and Affective Neuroscience*, 6, 252–256.

Moffitt, T. E., Arseneault, L., Belsky, D., Dickson, N., Hancox, R. J., Harrington, H., et al. (2011). A gradient of childhood self-control predicts health, wealth, and public safety. *Proceedings of the National Academy of Sciences*, 108, 2693–2698.

Muzek, J. (2007). A general factor of personality: Evidence for the Big One in the five-factor model. *Journal of Research in Personality*, 41, 1213–1233.

Oberlander, T. F., Weinberg, J., Papsdorf, M., Grunau, R., Misri, S., & Devlin, A. M. (2008). Prenatal exposure to maternal depression, neonatal methylation of human glucocorticoid receptor gene (NR3C1) and infant cortisol stress response. *Epigenetics*, 3, 97–106.

Paskaukas, A. R. (1995). *The complete correspondence of Sigmund Freud and Ernest Jones, 1908–1939*. Cambridge, MA: Belknap Press.

Pavlov, I. (1936, April 17). Bequest of Pavlov to the academic youth of his country. *Science*, 83 (2155), 369.

Phan, K. L., Lee, R., & Coccaro, E. F. (2011). Personality predictors of antiaggressive response to fluoxetine: Inverse association with neuroticism and harm avoidance. *Internationl Clinical Psychopharmacology*, 26, 278–283.

Plomin, R., & Dunn, J. (1986). *The study of temperament: Changes, continuities, and challenges*. Hillsdale, NJ: Erlbaum.

Posner, M. I., & Rothbart, M. K. (2007). Research on attention networks as a model for the integration of psychological science. *Annual Review of Psychology*, 58, 1–23.

Pulver, U. (1959). Untersuchung zur Irritierbarkeit bei Säuglingen [A study on irritability in infants]. *Schweizerische Zeitschrift für Psychologie*, 18, 18–33.

Rihmer, Z., Akiskal, K., Rihmer, A., & Akiskal, H. (2010). Current research on affective temperaments. *Current Opinion in Psychiatry*, 23, 12–18.

Rothbart, M. K. (2011). *Becoming who we are: Temperament and personality in development*. New York: Guilford Press.

Rothbart, M. K., & Bates, J. E. (2006). Temperament. In W. Damon & R. Lerner (Series Eds.) & N. Eisenberg (Vol. Ed.), *Handbook of child psychology: Vol. 3. Social, emotional, and personality development* (6th ed., pp. 99–166). New York: Wiley.

Rothbart, M. K., & Derryberry, D. (1981). Development of individual differences in temperament. In M. E. Lamb & A. L. Brown (Eds.), *Advances in developmental psychology* (Vol. 1, pp. 37–86). Hillsdale, NJ: Erlbaum.

Rowe, D. C., & Plomin, R. (1977). Temperament in early childhood. *Journal of Personality Assessment, 41*, 150–156.

Schmidt, N. B., Kotov, R., & Joiner, T. (2004). *Taxometrics: Toward a new diagnostic scheme for psychopathology*. Washington, DC: American Psychological Association.

Schwartz, C. E., Kunwar, P. S., Greve, D. N., Kagan, J., Snidman, N. C., & Bloch, R. B. (in press). A phenotype of early infancy predicts reactivity of the amygdala in male adults. *Molecular Psychiatry*.

Sheldon, W. H., & Stevens, S. S. (1942). *The varieties of human temperament*. New York: Harper & Row.

Shiner, R. L., & DeYoung, C. G. (in press). The structure of temperament and personality traits: A developmental perspective. In P. Zelazo (Ed.), *Oxford handbook of developmental psychology*. New York, NY: Oxford University Press.

Shiota, M. N., Keltner, D., & John, O. P. (2006). Positive emotion dispositions differentially associated with Big Five personality and attachment style. *Journal of Positive Psychology, 1*, 61–71.

Shirley, M. (1933). *The first two years: Vol. 3. Personality manifestations*. Minneapolis: University of Minnesota Press.

Simon, G. E., & Perlis, R. H. (2010). Personalized medicine for depression: Can we match patients with treatments? *American Journal of Psychiatry, 167*, 1445–1455.

Skinner, B. F. (1938). *The behavior of organisms: An experimental analysis*. New York: Appleton–Century–Crofts.

Smith, K. (2012). fMRI 2.0. *Nature, 484*, 24–26.

Strelau, J. (1983). *Temperament, personality, activity*. London: Academic Press.

Strelau, J., & Angleitner, A. (Eds.). (1991). *Explorations in temperament: Individual perspectives on theory and measurement*. New York: Plenum Press.

Tellegen, A. (1985). Structures of mood and personality and their relevance to assessing anxiety, with an emphasis on self-report. In A. H. Tuma & J. D. Maser (Eds.), *Anxiety and the anxiety disorders* (pp. 681–706). Hillsdale, NJ: Erlbaum.

Thayer, R. E., Newman, J. R., & McClain, T. M. (1994). Self-regulation of mood: Strategies for changing a bad mood, raising energy, and reducing tension. *Journal of Personality and Social Psychology, 67*, 910–925.

Thomas, A., & Chess, S. (1977). *Temperament and development*. New York: New York University Press.

Thomas, A., & Chess, S. (1986). The New York Longitudinal Study: From infancy to early adult life. In R. Plomin & J. Dunn (Eds.), *The study of temperament: Changes, continuities, and challenges* (pp. 39–52). Hillsdale, NJ: Erlbaum.

Thomas, A., Chess, S., Birch, H. G., Hertzig, M. E., & Korn, S. (1963). *Behavioral individuality in early childhood*. New York: New York University Press.

Verne, J. (1874). *Around the world in eighty days* (G. Towle, Trans.). Boston: Osgood & Company.

Verstraeten, K., Vasey, M. W., Raes, F., & Bijttebier, P. (2009). Temperament and risk for depressive symptoms in adolescence: Mediation by rumination and moderation by effortful control. *Journal of Abnormal Child Psychology, 37*, 349–361.

Westlye, L. T., Bjørnebekk, A., Grydeland, H., Fjell, A. M., & Walhovd, K. B. (2011). Linking an anxiety-related personality trait to brain white matter microstructure: Diffusion tensor imaging and harm avoidance. *Archives of General Psychiatry, 68*, 369–377.

White, L. K., McDermott, J. M., Degnan, K. A., Henderson, H. A., & Fox, N. A. (2011). Behavioral inhibition and anxiety: The moderating roles of inhibitory control and attention shifting. *Journal of Abnormal Psychology, 39*(5), 735–747.

Woodward, S., Lenzenberger, M., Kagan, J., Snidman, N., & Arcus, D. (2000). Taxonic structure of infant reactivity: Evidence from a taxometric perspective. *Psychological Science, 11*, 296–301.

Wu, I. T., Lee, I. H., Yeh, T. L., Chen, K. C., Chen, P. S., Yao, W. J., et al. (2010). The association between the harm avoidance subscale of the Tridimensional Personality Questionnaire and serotonin transporter availability in the brainstem of male volunteers. *Psychiatry Research, 181*, 241–244.

Zentner, M., & Bates, J. E. (2008). Child temperament: An integrative review of concepts, research programs, and measures. *European Journal of Developmental Science, 2*, 7–37.

Zentner, M., & Ihrig, L. (2010). *Inventar zur integrativen Erfassung des Kind-Temperaments* [Inventory for the integrative assessment of child temperament] (IKT) *manual*. Berne: Huber.

Zentner, M., & Wang, F. (in press). *The Integrative Child Temperament Inventory (ICTI) manual*. Oxford, UK: Hogrefe.

Zuckerman, M. (1979). *Sensation seeking: Beyond the optimal level of arousal*. Hillsdale, NJ: Erlbaum.

Author Index

Abbott, D. H., 298, 301, 487
Abe, J. A., 507
Abela, J. R. Z., 547
Abler, B., 130, 350, 351, 382, 383
Ablow, J., 504
Ablow, J. C., 186, 191
Abramson, L., 116
Abramson, L. Y., 489, 509, 532, 657
Abreu-Villaca, Y., 303
Acevedo, B., 650
Achenbach, T. M., 88, 199, 485
Ackerman, B., 527
Ackerman, B. P., 451
Ackerman, P. L., 634
Adair, L., 584
Adam, E. K., 553
Adamec, R. E., 73
Adams, C. M., 351
Adams, R. W., 684
Adamson, T., 525
Adelson, J., 282
Adler, J. M., 541
Adler, N. E., 436
Adolphs, R., 79, 224
Adriani, W., 351
Afonso, D., 298
Aggen, S. H., 546
Aggleton, J. P., 349
Ahadi, S. A., 12, 13, 14, 26, 27, 84, 86, 107, 108, 109, 111, 114, 128, 146, 147, 157, 173, 184, 190, 191, 278, 283, 234, 448, 467, 480, 498, 521, 594, 628, 651
Ainsworth, M. D., 404, 406, 408, 409
Aitken, R., 525
Akimova, E., 377, 378
Akiskal, H., 692, 693, 694

Akiskal, H. S., 189, 190, 198, 541
Akiskal, K., 692, 693, 694
Akiskal, K. K., 198
Aksan, N., 15, 16, 109, 157, 173, 216, 220, 230, 415, 434, 501, 571, 688
Alati, R., 305, 585
Albert, F. W., 255
Aldrich, N., 131
Alessandri, S. M., 111, 125
Alexander, A. L., 349
Alexander, K. L., 631
Alkon, A., 529
Allan, S., 133
Allen, A. M., 303
Allen, B., 128
Allen, J., 231
Allen, J. J. B., 113, 234, 235
Allen, W., 692
Allik, J., 483
Allison, D. B., 592
Allison, P. J., 590
Alloy, L., 116
Alloy, L. B., 552, 657
Allport, G. W., 4, 146, 151, 499, 678
Allred, K. M., 12, 136, 500, 627, 689, 690, 691
Almada, S. J., 592
Almas, A. N., 550
Alonso, S. J., 298, 299
Alper, C. M., 590
Alpert, J., 135
Alsaker, F. D., 447
Altemeyer, B., 680
Althoff, R. R., 196
Altman, R. B., 694
Aluja, A., 48, 51, 53, 91
Alwin, J., 111, 191, 238

Ambady, N., 133
Amelang, M., 45
Amodio, M. D., 651
Anders, M. C., 491
Anderson, C., 665
Anderson, C. A., 289
Anderson, J. D., 191
Anderson, J. R., 171
Anderson, K., 447
Anderson, K. G., 566, 567
Anderson, P., 353
Anderson, S. E., 585
Andersson, A., 415
Ando, J., 317
Andrews, C., 383
Angleitner, A., 7, 22, 26, 58, 91, 95, 190, 192, 674
Angold, A., 490
Anisman, H., 372
Ansorge, M., 376, 377
Aoki, J., 324, 325
Apfelbach, R., 370
Apter, A., 52
Arbeau, K. A., 446
Arbelle, S., 322, 324
Arbisi, P., 382
Arborelius, L., 552
Archer, J., 52, 131, 134, 276, 286, 485
Arcus, D., 73, 77, 434, 615, 681
Arenberg, D., 46
Arevalo, R., 298
Arias, B., 329
Ariel, S., 462
Armer, M., 110, 446, 471
Armistead, L., 527
Armstrong, J. M., 416
Arneson, C. L., 680

Arnow, B. A., 197
Aron, A., 280, 281, 351, 354, 417, 646, 647, 648, 649, 650, 651, 652, 654, 655, 656, 664
Aron, E., 417, 419, 646, 647, 648, 649, 650, 651, 652, 654, 655, 656, 657, 663, 666, 680
Aron, E. N., 10, 280, 281, 417, 419, 645, 664, 678, 680, 691, 693
Aronson, J., 648
Arseneault, L., 636
Arsenio, W., 126, 133
Arsenio, W. F., 448, 502
Asbury, K., 320
Asendorpf, J. B., 22, 34, 73, 193, 331, 431, 447, 452, 453, 463, 471, 680, 681, 686
Asensio, A. B., 136
Asherson, P., 87, 303, 317, 318, 332
Ashton, M. C., 453
Ashworth, A., 522
Asmussen, L., 128
Aston-Jones, G., 371, 373
Atkins, M. S., 195
Atkins, R., 512, 681
Attia, J., 321
Atzaba-Poria, N., 449, 452
Atzil, S., 281
Aubuchon-Endsley, N., 522
Auerbach, J., 112
Auerbach, J. G., 131, 321, 322, 323, 324, 360, 377, 568
Augustine, A. A., 592, 593
Aunola, K., 508
Austin, A., 467
Ávila, C., 53
Axelrod, R., 168
Ayduk, O., 126
Ayer, L., 196
Azzaro, A. J., 298

Baas, J. M., 76
Bachevalier, J., 72
Bachman, H. J., 526
Bachner-Melman, R., 173
Bade, U., 200
Badrick, E., 590
Baetens, I., 489
Bagby, R. M., 546, 554, 555, 693
Bailey, B. A., 196
Bailey, D. B., 191
Bailey, J. N., 264
Bakeman, R., 466
Baker, E. H., 191
Baker, L. A., 317, 563, 564
Baker-Henningham, H., 522
Bakermans-Kranenburg, M. J., 12, 14, 47, 60, 132, 154, 369, 378, 387, 403, 406, 408, 409, 410, 411, 412, 413, 414, 415, 416, 417, 418, 419, 420, 498, 500, 526, 528, 552, 572, 573, 646, 650, 652, 675, 688, 689
Bakow, H. A., 215
Baldessarini, R. J., 356
Baldwin, A., 520
Baldwin, A. L., 168
Baldwin, C., 520

Baldwin, C. P., 168
Balka, E., 134
Ball, S. G., 550
Balleyguier, G., 7
Balsis, S., 564, 574
Banaschewski, T., 333
Bancroft, M., 158, 451
Bandini, L. G., 585
Bandura, A., 125, 443, 488
Bantelmann, J., 58, 190
Barbaranelli, C., 208
Barber, A. M., 692
Barber, B. K., 425
Barch, D. M., 149, 353
Bardo, M. T., 51
Barglow, P., 300
Bar-Haim, Y., 350, 357, 360, 361, 552, 651
Barker, D. J., 297, 298
Barker, D. J. P., 582
Barker, E. D., 447
Barker, M., 588
Barkley, R. A., 214, 563
Barlow, D., 116
Barlow, D. H., 370, 452, 541, 548–549, 551
Barnett, W. S., 161, 637
Barnow, S., 566
Baron-Cohen, S., 169
Barr, C., 387
Barr, C. S., 4, 60, 251, 256, 260, 261, 263, 264, 265, 266, 267, 275, 278, 279, 281, 284
Barratt, E. S., 50
Barrett, L. C., 219
Barrett, L. F., 488
Barrett, P., 91
Barrett, P. T., 53
Barry, C. T., 567
Barry, R. A., 154, 157, 336, 499, 566
Bar-Tal, D., 171
Bartels, A., 281, 286
Bartels, M., 131, 332
Barten, S., 9
Barth, R. P., 306
Bartini, M., 449
Bartko, W., 520
Barton, B. K., 585, 587
Bateman, A. E., 526
Bates, J., 112, 114, 184, 186, 521, 525, 526, 527, 674
Bates, J. E., 3, 4, 10, 12, 14, 15, 16, 21, 22, 27, 84, 90, 105, 107, 109, 113, 125, 126, 127, 129, 130, 132, 136, 145, 146, 148, 149, 159, 169, 170, 174, 183, 185, 193, 195, 198, 199, 211, 213, 218, 229, 230, 240, 251, 273, 278, 279, 280, 281, 284, 286, 288, 300, 378, 405, 412, 419, 425, 426, 427, 428, 429, 430, 432, 433, 434, 435, 436, 437, 442, 444, 445, 449, 450, 451, 452, 454, 466, 480, 491, 498, 500, 501, 503, 504, 506, 521, 524, 525, 542, 544, 554, 570, 609, 675, 676, 677, 680, 685, 688
Bates, M. E., 566
Bathurst, K., 529, 570

Batson, C. D., 169, 171–172, 175
Battaglia, M., 322, 324, 352
Baud, P., 131
Baudonnière, P.-M., 331
Bauer, E. P., 373
Baumeister, R. F., 10, 156, 649, 679, 692
Baumrind, D., 431, 689
Baxley, K., 646
Bayer, J. K., 617
Bayles, K., 218, 426, 427
Bayley, N., 215
Beardslee, W. R., 509, 524, 527
Beauchaine, T., 232, 233, 569
Beauducel, A., 44, 53
Beauregard, M., 153, 353
Beaver, K. M., 573
Becerra, L., 351
Becher, M., 303
Beck, A. T., 547
Beck, S., 377
Becker, B., 520
Becker, K., 308, 323, 333
Beckmann, D., 200, 430
Belanger, D., 522
Belfer, M. L., 512
Belin, D., 382
Bell, A. M., 649
Bell, G., 274
Bell, I., 44
Bell, L., 192
Bell, M. A., 126, 235, 349
Bell, R. Q., 431
Bellgrove, M. A., 154
Belmaker, R. H., 49
Belova, M. A., 79
Belsky, J., 105, 110, 114, 281, 377, 403, 404, 408, 409, 410, 411, 413, 414, 415, 419, 429, 430, 431, 433, 434, 452, 529, 570, 646, 650, 652
Bem, D. J., 447, 471, 472, 491
Benediktsson, R., 299
Benenson, J. F., 169, 171
Benga, O., 171
Benham, G., 280, 281
Benish-Weisman, M., 173, 174
Benjamin, J., 49, 264, 321, 360
Bennett, A. J., 263, 266
Bennett, D. A., 591, 594
Bennett, P. C., 253
Benning, S. D., 563, 588
Ben-Shlomo, Y., 596
Bentley, M., 584
Ben-Zion, I. Z., 49
Berard, J., 266
Berdan, L., 115, 241
Berdan, L. E., 450
Berenson, K., 126
Bergeman, C., 130
Berger, A., 154, 155
Bergeron, N., 462
Bergman, D., 8
Bergman, K., 301, 302, 309, 487
Bergman, P., 673
Berk, L. E., 639
Berkson, M., 587
Berlin, L., 109

Berndt, T. J., 282
Bernier, A., 160, 428, 432
Bernieri, F., 330
Berns, G. S., 351
Bernstein, I. H., 184, 199
Bernstein, M., 193
Bernston, G., 233
Bernt, T. J., 447
Berntsen, D., 510
Bernzweig, J., 157, 444, 452
Berridge, C. W., 257
Berridge, K. C., 361, 383
Berry, J. W., 169
Berus, A. V., 45
Besevegis, E., 22
Besson, C., 113
Best, J. R., 629
Bethea, C. L., 262, 263
Betzig, L., 276
Beveridge, M., 301
Bevilacqua, L., 261
Beythmarom, R., 351
Bezdjian, S., 317, 563
Bhanji, J., 382, 393
Bhatnagar, S., 264
Bhatt, M., 79
Biederman, J., 31, 550, 553, 563
Bienias, J. L., 591, 594
Bienvenu, O. J., 548, 549, 551
Bierman, K. L., 637
Bierman, L. E., 637
Biernat, M., 486
Bijl, R. V., 547
Bijttebier, P., 489, 509, 532, 552, 680
Billman, J., 452
Binder, E. B., 373
Binet, A., 629
Birch, H., 70, 229, 608
Birch, H. G., 9, 211, 229, 479, 673
Birch, L. L., 587
Birch, S. H., 636
Bird, A., 511
Birkle, D. L., 298
Birnbaum, D. W., 488
Birns, B., 9
Birring, S. S., 52, 134
Birru, S., 301
Bishop, G., 187, 193, 447
Bishop, S., 349, 350, 357
Bittner, M., 524
Bizarro, L., 303
Bjork, J. M., 351
Bjørnebekk, A., 694
Black, M., 520
Blackburn, E. K., 158, 451
Blackford, J. U., 78
Blackson, T., 135
Blair, C., 159, 238, 239, 414, 512, 525, 629, 630, 637
Blair, R. J., 353
Blair, R. J. R., 158, 569
Blake, C. S., 136
Blanchard-Fields, F., 129
Blandon, A. Y., 567
Blaney, N. T., 594
Blasi, G., 154, 356
Blaskey, L., 563

Blatt, S. J., 547
Blehar, M. C., 404
Bliesener, T., 527, 530
Blijlevens, P., 114
Bliss-Moreau, E., 488
Block, J., 129, 193, 679, 682, 685, 686, 692, 694
Block, J. H., 129, 193, 682
Blonigen, D. M., 128, 129, 130, 568, 572
Bloom, P., 168
Bodgan, R., 675, 683
Bodin, S. D., 567
Bodrova, E., 637
Boer, F., 25
Boergers, J., 525
Boes, A. D., 77
Bogaerts, S., 526
Bogat, G. A., 526
Bogg, T., 594, 595
Bohanek, J. G., 510
Bohlin, G., 86, 109, 115, 160, 185, 186, 415, 447, 687
Bohman, M., 566
Bohn, A., 510
Boileau, I., 383
Boivin, M., 334, 429, 446, 447
Boker, S., 174
Bokhorst, C. L., 406, 417
Bolger, N., 593
Boncori, L., 98, 100
Bond, A., 130
Bond, C., 265, 387
Bond, S., 449
Bongers, I. L., 490
Bonilla-Santiago, G., 681
Bons, T. A., 277
Book, A. S., 134
Bookwala, J., 593
Boomsma, D. I., 48, 76, 130, 131, 332
Booth-Kewley, S., 591
Booth-LaForce, C., 447, 481, 483, 484
Bor, W., 572
Borge, A. I. H., 447
Borghans, L., 630
Borja, J., 584
Borkenau, P., 91
Borneman, M. J., 630
Bornett-Gauci, H. L., 254
Bornstein, M. H., 160, 218, 425
Borsook, D., 351
Bosacki, S. L., 485
Bost, K. K., 408, 449, 511
Both, C., 274
Both, L., 77
Botvin, G. J., 135
Botvinick, M., 153
Botvinick, M. M., 149, 353
Bouchard, T. J., 275
Bouchard, T. J., Jr., 48, 56
Bouissou, M.-F., 253
Boulerice, B., 633–634
Bouma, E. M. C., 523
Bourgouin, P., 153, 353
Boutin, P., 89
Bowen, W. G., 633
Bowker, A., 447

Bowker, J., 446
Bowker, J. C., 471, 551
Bowlby, J., 4, 261, 281, 404
Bowman, P. C., 633
Boyce, T. W., 649
Boyce, W. F., 586
Boyce, W. T., 233, 403, 410, 416, 419, 436, 528, 529, 650
Braaten, E. B., 563
Bradbury, T. N., 663
Bradley, C. F., 300
Bradley, R., 610
Bradley, R. H., 160, 415, 434, 529, 570, 585
Bradshaw, C. P., 610
Bradwejn, J., 253
Braet, C., 587
Brake, W., 384
Brammer, M., 353
Branchey, M., 133
Brand, S. R., 300, 302
Brandt, M. E., 50
Branje, S., 114
Braungart, J. M., 317, 319, 330, 335
Braungart-Rieker, J. M., 128, 430
Braver, T. S., 149, 353
Brazelton, T., 125
Brazelton, T. B., 214, 215
Bream, L., 447
Breedlove, S. M., 487, 489
Breese, C. R., 301
Breidenthal, S. E., 264
Breiter, H. C., 351
Brendgen, M., 553, 634
Brennan, P., 52
Brennan, P. A., 522, 572
Breslau, N., 308
Brett, M., 349
Brewis, A., 468
Briand, L., 154
Brickman, A. L., 594
Bridger, R., 86, 193, 691
Bridger, W., 9
Bridges, D., 175
Bridgett, D. J., 15, 126, 183, 185, 195, 432, 678
Briggs, S., 22, 185, 219
Briggs-Gowan, M. J., 199
Brigham, J., 135
Brilman, E. I., 544
Broberg, A. G., 675
Brock, L., 609
Brocke, B., 44, 50, 322
Brody, G., 527
Brody, G. H., 89
Brody, L. R., 488, 489
Broeren, S., 193
Bronfenbrenner, U., 463, 464, 519
Bronson, G. W., 348
Brook, C., 279
Brook, C. G. D., 487
Brook, D. W., 304
Brook, J., 135
Brook, J. S., 134, 304, 587
Brooks, D., 306, 639
Brotman, M. A., 488
Broughton, R., 282

Brown, J., 522
Brown, K., 195
Brown, R. M., 153
Brown, S. A., 566
Brown, T., 116
Brown, T. A., 541, 548, 549, 551
Brown, W. A., 126
Brozdinsky, L. K., 193
Brozoski, T. J., 153
Bruce, J., 156, 238
Bruder, G. E., 76
Bruder-Costello, B., 526
Bruderer, C., 254
Bruhis, S., 134
Brumbach, B. H., 277
Brummett, B. H., 592, 594
Bruno, K. J., 259
Bryant, K., 135
Buckhalt, J. A., 240
Buckholtz, J. W., 265, 321, 382, 383
Buckingham, J., 384
Buckley, M., 523
Buckley, M. E., 505, 548
Buckner, J. C., 509, 524, 527
Buckner, J. P., 488
Bufferd, S. J., 542
Bugental, D. B., 425
Buhle, J., 353
Buhrmester, D., 282
Buhs, E. S., 158
Buitelaar, J. K., 297, 301
Buka, S. L., 307, 585
Bukowski, W., 442, 443, 446, 447, 448, 449
Bulbena, A., 76
Bull, R., 159
Bullock, A., 12, 133, 442, 500, 551, 688, 689, 690
Bumbarger, B., 609
Bunde, J., 591, 592
Bundy, A. C., 648
Bunge, S. A., 153, 353, 354, 355
Bunzeck, N., 382
Burge, D., 509
Burgess, K. B., 435, 447, 471
Burk, C., 390
Burk, L. R., 416
Burke, J. D., 566
Burke, M., 89
Burkett, J. P., 261, 281
Burock, D., 681
Burrowes, B. D., 132
Burt, C., 107
Burt, C. L., 7
Bus, A. G., 417
Buschgens, C. J. M., 572
Bush, G., 152, 353
Bush, N., 526, 527, 529
Bush, N. R., 436, 529, 530
Bushman, B. J., 289
Buss, A., 124
Buss, A. H., 21, 25, 26, 29, 32, 41, 42, 51, 84, 85, 86, 90, 95, 105, 125, 173, 187, 189, 193, 196, 229, 230, 251, 330, 442, 446, 452, 480, 482, 549, 569, 584, 673, 676
Buss, D. M., 273, 274, 282, 502

Buss, K., 409, 500, 651
Buss, K. A., 26, 30, 84, 112, 190, 221, 230, 233, 235, 240, 317, 319, 353, 417, 426, 554
Bussey, K., 488
Bussing, R., 192
Buswell, B. N., 489
Butler, E., 133
Butler, E. A., 472, 473
Butler, S., 522
Butterfield, E. L., 76
Button, T. M., 309, 572
Buur, H., 219
Buydens-Branchey, L., 133
Buyske, S., 566
Byrne, E. A., 231

Cabib, S., 259
Cadwell, J., 187, 191
Cahill, S. P., 135
Cain, T., 466
Cairns, B., 448
Cairns, R., 448
Calder, A. A., 299
Caldewell, K. K. A., 303
Calhoun, V. D., 355
Calkins, S. D., 15, 69, 70, 73, 105, 110, 113, 115, 125, 126, 213, 229, 230, 231, 232, 233, 234, 235, 238, 240, 241, 278, 348, 349, 353, 409, 435, 446, 448, 449, 450, 567, 570, 678
Camac, C., 42
Camerer, C. F., 79
Cameron, A., 299
Cameron, D., 232
Cameron, E., 169, 452
Campbell, D., 622
Campbell, K. B., 44
Campbell, L., 350
Campbell, S., 132
Campbell-Sills, L., 452
Campos, J., 105, 111
Campos, J. J., 21, 23, 30, 32, 36, 42, 84, 85, 112, 212, 215, 216, 230, 319, 417, 426, 678
Camras, L. A., 466
Canfield, R. L., 300
Canino, G., 585
Canli, T., 356, 370, 374, 375, 377, 383, 388, 389, 391, 393, 541, 591, 663
Canzoniero, A., 129
Capaldi, D. M., 195
Capitanio, J. P., 256, 503
Cappella, E., 613, 615
Capuano, F., 414, 615
Card, J. A., 230
Card, N. A., 563
Carelli, R. M., 384
Carere, C., 274, 649
Carey, B., 692
Carey, G., 116
Carey, W., 86, 105, 533, 609
Carey, W. B., 5, 24, 86, 96, 184, 185, 186, 187, 188, 191, 193, 199, 609, 674, 691
Carlo, G., 170, 171, 173, 448

Carlson, E., 404
Carlson, G., 73, 110
Carlson, J. J., 571
Carlson, K. S., 685, 686
Carlson, M. D., 128
Carlson, S. M., 155, 157, 159, 160, 428, 468
Caron, C., 89
Caron, M. G., 321
Carpenter, L. L., 374
Carr, T. S., 52
Carranza, J. A., 87, 151
Carré, J. M., 675
Carrigan, P. M., 43
Carson, D., 524
Carson, D. K., 450, 451, 452
Carstensen, L. L., 128
Carta, J., 610
Carter, A. S., 199, 332
Carter, C., 156
Carter, C. S., 149, 153, 353, 354, 355, 356
Carter, J. D., 489
Carter, J. P., 522
Caruso, J. C., 283, 586
Carver, C. S., 53, 107, 108, 111, 113, 189, 195, 197, 321, 377, 388, 389, 509, 590, 593, 679, 695
Casas, C. A. S., 468
Caserás, X., 53
Cases, O., 369
Casey, B., 156
Casey, B. J., 283, 351, 352, 353, 354, 355, 356, 357, 358
Casey, P., 529
Casey, P. H., 570
Casiglia, A. C., 454
Caspers, K., 412
Caspi, A., 3, 22, 42, 46, 47, 51, 52, 56, 72, 107, 108, 109, 117, 125, 127, 128, 209, 229, 263, 264, 265, 283, 332, 334, 369, 376, 405, 412, 419, 447, 453, 471, 472, 480, 490, 491, 497, 498, 503, 504, 505, 506, 507, 520, 521, 523, 542, 544, 548, 550, 551, 566, 573, 581, 584, 586, 588, 591, 593, 628, 630, 636, 675, 678, 681, 684, 686, 687, 688
Cassidy, J., 408, 414
Castellanos, F. X., 88
Castellanos, M. A., 171
Casten, R. J., 188, 195
Castle, J., 171
Catron, T. F., 115, 188, 194, 195
Cattell, E. B., 46
Cauffman, E., 351
Cen, G., 454, 470, 661
Chadwick, A., 443
Chakrabarti, B., 172
Chambers, A., 231
Chamove, A. S., 256
Champagne, D., 379, 380
Champagne, F., 384
Champion, C., 223, 473
Champoux, M., 263, 266, 376
Chang, L., 133
Chang, S., 522

Chaouloff, F., 257
Chapman, E., 282
Chappie, T. A., 360
Charak, D., 449
Charles, S. T., 128, 591
Charlesworth, W. R., 279
Charlton, M., 525
Charney, D. S., 264
Charng, H. W., 169
Charnov, E. L., 276
Chase-Lansdale, L., 526
Chassin, L., 435, 524
Chavira, D. A., 555
Chawla, S., 213, 320
Checa, P., 151, 158, 159, 160
Checkley, S., 45
Cheek, J. M., 25, 452
Chelton, K. K., 571
Chen, C., 132, 649
Chen, F. S., 498
Chen, H., 75, 447, 471, 473
Chen, H. C., 462
Chen, K., 46
Chen, Q., 160, 638
Chen, Q. L., 171
Chen, S. H., 428
Chen, X., 12, 13, 75, 133, 428, 446,
  447, 453, 454, 462, 463, 464,
  465, 466, 467, 469, 470, 471,
  472, 473, 474, 521, 524, 661,
  689, 692
Chen, Y., 466
Cheng, C. Y., 467
Cherry, S. S., 219, 318, 319, 330, 331
Cherry, E. C., 44
Chesney, M. A., 529
Chess, S., 9, 10, 23, 24, 25, 32, 34, 35,
  36, 41, 42, 70, 83, 84, 85, 86, 87,
  88, 89, 90, 98, 105, 127, 145,
  187, 191, 192, 193, 195, 196,
  211, 223, 229, 251, 298, 404,
  405, 442, 444, 448, 471, 479,
  480, 482, 484, 528, 607, 608,
  647, 648, 651, 652, 673, 676,
  680, 682, 686, 691
Cheung, R. Y. M., 472, 473
Chew, K. H., 185
Chiavegatto, S., 79
Chida, Y., 553, 589
Chingos, M. M., 633
Chiong, C., 609
Chiou, H.-H., 89
Chisholm, K., 524
Chiu, Y.-J. I., 609
Chmielewski, M., 545
Choi, E., 511
Choi, M. J., 328
Chong, R. Y., 266
Chorpita, B., 116, 467
Chorpita, B. F., 195, 548
Choudhury, N., 521
Christ, S., 158
Christakis, N. A., 416
Christensen, A. J., 592, 594
Christopher, J. S., 448
Christopherson, E. R., 280
Chronis-Tuscano, A., 348, 350, 357,
  361, 550, 687
Chrousos, G. P., 264, 586

Chu, A., 133
Chuang, S. S., 675
Chung, J., 464
Churchill, R., 615
Chynoweth, J., 303
Cialdini, R. B., 175
Cicchetti, D., 410, 445, 449, 520, 527
Cicchetti, P., 349
Cillessen, A. H. N., 454
Cimbora, D. M., 567, 570
Cipriano, E. A., 160, 232
Citeau, H., 631
Clara, I., 75
Clark, L. A., 108, 112, 116, 117, 189,
  197, 199, 280, 285, 289, 427,
  450, 489, 490, 503, 541, 542,
  545, 546, 548, 551, 571, 588,
  589, 591, 593, 678, 695
Clark, R. D., 191
Clarke, A. R., 194
Clarke, A. S., 298
Clarke, C., 31, 231, 446
Claus, L., 587
Claxton, L. J., 157
Clements, A. D., 196
Cliff, N., 283
Clohessy, A. B., 155
Cloninger, C. R., 8, 41, 42, 49, 56, 57,
  58, 59, 95, 189, 194, 196, 197,
  251, 321, 368, 566, 694
Coan, J., 116
Coan, J. A., 224, 234, 235
Coccaro, E. F., 52, 130, 134, 374, 388,
  389, 391, 694
Coch, D., 160, 638
Cochran, A., 237
Coe, C. L., 238, 298, 299
Coffey, K. A., 591
Coghill, D., 333
Cohen, D. J., 319, 445
Cohen, H. L., 451
Cohen, J., 90, 196, 481
Cohen, J. D., 149, 153, 353, 354, 357,
  371, 373, 382
Cohen, J. R., 351
Cohen, N. L., 554
Cohen, P., 126, 134, 135, 587
Cohen, S., 589, 590, 591
Cohn, J. F., 234
Cohn, M. A., 105, 591
Coie, J. D., 132, 134, 449
Colder, C. R., 526, 529, 530
Cole, D., 615
Cole, D. A., 129
Cole, M., 463, 507
Cole, P. M., 448, 469
Cole, S. R., 507
Cole-Love, A. S., 88, 192
Coleman, T. 303
Coleman, B., 77
Collaer, M. L., 279
Colligan, R. C., 593
Collin, V. T., 115
Collins, A., 10, 136, 607, 613
Collins, F. S., 596
Collins, P., 259, 382, 690, 691

Collins, P. F., 43, 54, 55, 285, 286,
  368, 380, 381, 382, 384, 385,
  388, 390, 391
Collins, W. A., 404, 425
Colombo, J. A., 12
Cómbita, L. M., 160
Comings, D. E., 131
Como, P. G., 50
Compas, B. E., 508, 524
Comrey, A. L., 199
Conard, M. A., 633
Condry, J., 486
Condry, S., 486
Congdon, E., 383
Connell, J. P., 610
Connelly, B. S., 630
Conner, P. D., 198
Conner, T. S., 131
Conners-Burrow, N., 529, 570
Connor, P., 693
Connor-Smith, J., 508, 509, 524
Constantion, J. N., 188, 194
Conture, E. G., 191
Conway, A., 357
Conway, G. S., 279, 487
Cook, C. L., 130
Cook, L. I., 649
Cook, T., 609, 622
Cooley, C. H., 442
Cools, R., 388, 389
Cooper, A. J., 370
Cooper, B., 676
Cooper, H., 584
Cooper, J. C., 351
Copeland, W. E., 261, 265, 266
Coplan, J. D., 374, 587
Coplan, R. J., 12, 69, 73, 77, 110, 115,
  133, 427, 428, 442, 446, 447,
  448, 452, 453, 454, 471, 491,
  500, 545, 550, 551, 688, 689,
  690, 691, 692
Corapci, F., 522, 524, 526, 533
Corley, R., 73, 319
Corley, R. P., 215, 318
Cornell, A. H., 435, 567, 571
Cornoldi, C., 159
Corr, P. J., 45, 53, 54, 370
Cortes, J. B., 6
Corwyn, R. F., 415, 434
Coryell, W., 549
Cosmides, L., 274, 275
Costa, P. T., 22, 58, 107, 189, 281,
  285, 286, 481, 483, 484, 485,
  489, 554, 652
Costa, P. T., Jr., 42, 43, 45, 46, 47, 48,
  55, 56, 90, 91, 129, 189, 196,
  197, 198, 283, 581, 591, 594
Costa, R. M., 384
Costello, E. J., 490
Costigan, K. A., 133, 184
Cote, K. A., 235
Cote, R., 89
Couchoud, E. A., 117, 450
Couper, D. J., 136
Cousins, M. M., 303
Coventry, W. L., 317
Cowan, C. P., 504
Cowan, P. A., 504

Cowan, R., 135
Cowen, E. L., 526
Cox, B., 75
Cox, B. J., 549
Cox-Fuenzalida, L.-E., 44
Coy, K., 526
Coy, K. C., 15, 185, 213, 680
Craig, A., 386
Craig, A. D., 650
Craig, I., 376
Craig, W. M., 586
Craiger, J. P., 168
Craik, F., 649
Cramer, P., 586
Craske, M. G., 350
Cratton, A., 384
Cratty, M. S., 298
Crawford, F. C., 49, 352
Crawford, J. R., 197
Crea, T. M., 306, 308
Credé, M., 636
Creed-Kanashiro, H., 522
Creemers, H. E., 524
Cremers, H. R., 358
Crichton, L., 185
Crick, N. R., 563
Crnic, K., 105, 110, 410, 433, 570
Crockenberg, S., 427, 432
Crockenberg, S. B., 407, 414
Crockenberg, S. C., 419, 570
Crockett, L. J., 170
Croft, C. M., 407
Cronbach, L., 528
Crottaz-Herbette, S., 153
Crowley, T. J., 566
Crull, W. L., 488
Csikszentmihalyi, M., 635
Cubells, J., 387
Cueto, S., 522
Cugini, C., 134
Cukrowicz, K. C., 566, 567
Cummings, E. M., 12, 425
Cunningham, C. C., 22, 192, 199
Curran, P. J., 509, 585
Currie, J., 630
Cushing, B., 387
Cusin, F., 631
Cutting, A. L., 449
Cyphers, L. H., 319, 330
Czeschlik, T., 194, 199

Dabbs, J. M., Jr., 52
Dadds, M. R., 426, 570, 573
Dagher, A., 384
Dahl, R. E., 355, 357
Dahlen, E. R., 133
Dahlof, L. G., 298
Daitzman, R. J., 51
Dalley, J., 384, 389
Dalley, J. W., 382
Daly, M., 276, 279, 593
Damasio, A. R., 224
D'Amato, F., 387
D'Amato, F. R., 265
Dane, H. E., 567
Daniel, E., 512
Daniel, S., 529

Daniels, D., 320
Daniels, T., 446
Daniels-Beirness, T., 447
Danielson, L., 610
Danner, D. D., 117, 589
D'Ardenne, K., 382
Darley, J. M., 175
Darwin, C., 21, 252, 259, 404
Darwin, C. R., 124
Datar, A., 585
Dauber, S. L., 631
Davare, A., 533
Davey, M., 117
David, A. S., 224
David, C. F., 197
David, K. M., 451
Davidov, M., 171, 609
Davidson, K. W., 589
Davidson, M. C., 156
Davidson, R., 371
Davidson, R. A., 50
Davidson, R. J., 73, 75, 108, 217, 223, 224, 233, 234, 235, 256, 278, 279, 349, 357, 373, 695
Davies, K. M., 417, 646
Davies, L., 171
Davies, P., 529, 530
Davies, P. L., 158, 355, 356
Davis, C., 586, 587
Davis, E. P., 156, 238, 239, 301, 302, 368
Davis, M., 347, 370, 371, 374
Davis, P. J., 485
Davis-Stober, C. P., 151, 156
Daw, N., 350, 351
Dawes, C. T., 416
Dawson, G., 287
Day, A., 131
Day, J., 692
Day, J. J., 384
Dayan, P., 351
De Bolle, M., 208
De Clercq, B., 22, 568, 570
De Dreu, C. K. W., 172
de Fonseca, F. R., 303
De Fruyt, F., 22, 85, 208, 541, 546, 555, 568, 570
de Gelder, B., 393
de Geus, E. J. C., 48, 76
de Graaf, P. M., 634
de Graaf, R., 547
de Haan, A. D., 435
de Haan, M., 238, 239
de Jong, G., 274
de la Torre, A. J., 303
De Liberto, S., 159
De Luca, A., 322, 323, 324, 332
de Medina, P. G., 301
De Pascalis, V., 44
De Pauw, S. S. W., 9, 16, 21, 22, 23, 28, 31, 34, 58, 84, 85, 88, 90, 95, 125, 126, 184, 193, 198, 199, 211, 223, 229, 251, 278, 300, 405, 480, 481, 484, 485, 504, 505, 506, 542, 567, 569, 584, 586, 609, 628, 675, 676, 678
De Ross, J., 76
De Schipper, J. C., 413

de Silveira, C., 510
de Waal, F. B. M., 168, 169, 171, 175
de Weerth, C., 301, 302
de Winter, A. F., 114, 157, 450, 530, 553
De Wolff, M. S., 408, 430
De Young, A., 449
Deacon, B., 694
Deal, J., 686
Deal, J. E., 208, 429
Dearing, E., 411
Deary, I. J., 591, 592
Deater-Deckard, K., 10, 14, 124, 126, 127, 128, 131, 132, 134, 135, 173, 199, 257, 317, 319, 320, 332, 334, 405, 412, 413, 433, 448, 506, 677, 680, 691, 696
DeBoo, G. M., 483, 484, 490
DeBow, A., 73, 446
Decety, J., 171, 172
Dedmon, S. E., 232, 233
Deffenbacher, J., 126, 131, 135, 136
DeFries, J. C., 172, 317, 318, 330, 334
DeGangi, G., 232, 233
Degnan, K., 241, 554
Degnan, K. A., 230, 238, 347, 348, 357, 358, 426, 435, 436, 449, 450, 550, 553, 680
Dehaene, S., 154
Deiner, E., 286
Dekovic, M., 160, 428, 434, 435, 490
Delaney, L., 593
DeLeon, C., 525
Delgado, M. R., 351
Dellatolas, G., 631
Deller, M., 386
Dellu, F., 50
DelVecchio, W. F., 129, 490, 503, 544, 628
Demetriou, H., 171
Deminiere, J. M., 298
Dempsey, J., 466
Den Boer, J. A., 321
DeNeve, K. M., 584
Denham, S. A., 117, 414, 450
Denissen, J. J. A., 274, 447, 471, 681
Denning, D., 449
Dennis, T., 111, 428, 527
Dennis, T. A., 109, 114, 117, 353, 357
Denollet, J., 222
De-Nour, A. K., 594
Denson, T. F., 130
Depue, R. A., 8, 9, 14, 43, 47, 51, 54, 55, 60, 108, 112, 113, 130, 131, 171, 210, 256, 259, 261, 273, 278, 279, 280, 281, 285, 286, 287, 322, 350, 351, 352, 368, 370, 374, 380, 381, 382, 383, 384, 385, 386, 387, 388, 389, 390, 391, 521, 678, 679, 683, 694, 695
Der, G., 591
Derringer, J., 49
Derryberry, D., 9, 14, 27, 41, 84, 100, 107, 109, 110, 111, 115, 145, 147, 185, 196, 230, 251, 278, 347, 352, 353, 357, 450, 451, 466, 502, 508, 608, 679
DeSouza, A. T., 447, 462

DeThorne, L. S., 128, 317
Deussing, J., 373
Devine, P. G., 489
Devinsky, O., 353
DeVries, M. W., 405, 468, 469, 471
DeWall, N. C., 649
Dewey, J., 639
DeWolff, M. W. E., 406
DeYoung, C. G., 172, 283, 480, 503, 504, 505, 506, 507, 581, 675, 678
Diamond, A., 12, 154, 155, 160, 353, 525, 637, 691
Diamond, D., 371
Diamond, S., 5, 170, 251, 252, 253, 254, 255, 261, 673
Dibble, E., 319
Dick, D. M., 564, 573
Dickstein, S., 200
Diego, M., 133
Diener, E., 133, 278, 280, 288, 485
Diener, M. L., 449, 453
Dietrich, K., 522
Dietz, W. H., 585
Diez, J. L., 136
DiFranza, J. R., 303
DiGirolamo, G. J., 147
Digiuseppe, R., 136
Digman, J. M., 26, 107, 108, 111, 283, 504, 505
Ding, Y.-C., 132, 154
Dingemanse, N. J., 257, 274, 275, 278
Diorio, J., 309
DiPietro, J., 133, 184, 232
Dirago, A. C., 572
Dishion, T. J., 437
Dixon, D., 639
Dmitrieva, J., 132
Dockray, S., 589
Dodez, R., 452
Dodge, K. A., 126, 133, 134, 412, 413, 430, 433, 436, 437, 448, 449, 452
Doelger, L., 153, 317
Dolan, C. V., 353
Dolan, M. C., 567
Dolan, R. J., 158, 172, 350, 351, 353, 382
Dolezal, S., 129
Dollar, J. M., 232
Dollinger, S. J., 283
Domes, G., 386
Domitrovich, C. E., 609, 637
Dommett, E., 72
Donahue, E. M., 652
Donaldson, Z. R., 172, 386
Donlevy, M., 76
Donnellan, M. B., 505
D'Onofrio, B. M., 306, 307, 308, 309
Donohew, R. L., 51
Donzella, B., 111, 115, 191, 233, 237, 238, 239, 426, 452, 530
Doobay, A. F., 109
Doolittle, J., 610
Doran, P. P., 593
Dorsey, S., 527
Dougherty, D. M., 214
Dougherty, L. R., 114, 116, 541, 548, 553, 554

Doussard-Roosevelt, J. A., 232
Douvan, E. A., 282
Downey, G., 126
Doyle, W. J., 590, 591
Drabant, E. M., 326
Dragan, W. L., 323, 324
Draper, P., 281
Drent, P. A., 274
Drent, P. J., 274
Drevets, W. C., 152, 382
Drew, D., 89
Drew, K. D., 117
Drew, N., 131
Dribin, A. E., 240
Driscoll, C. D., 303
Driscoll, P., 50
Driver, J., 665
Drobny, H., 136
Droke, E., 522
Dubanoski, J. P., 584, 587
Duberstein, K. J., 253
Duckworth, A. L., 12, 136, 500, 627, 629, 630, 632, 633, 636, 638, 685, 689, 690, 691
Ducrest, A. L., 77
Dudukovic, N. M., 354
Duffy, D. L., 254
Dugas, M. J., 74
Duggan, C. F., 547
DuHamel, K., 88
Dumenci, L., 196
Duncan, G. J., 161, 631, 634
Duncan, I. J. H., 254
Duncan, J., 159, 349
Dunlap, G., 610
Dunn, A. J., 257
Dunn, J., 320, 449, 452, 674, 682
Durbin, C. E., 110, 114, 216, 217, 218, 221, 505, 509, 523, 532, 548, 554, 617, 622
Durkee, A., 51, 124, 125
Durlak, J. A., 609, 637
Durrant, C., 419
Durston, S., 156, 356
Durvarci, S., 373
Duzel, E., 351, 382
Dvoskin, R. L., 256, 260, 266
Dweck, C. S., 498, 509
Dwyer, K. M., 435
Dyck, M. J., 197
Dye, D. A., 189, 198
Dymnicki, A. B., 609, 637
Dyrenforth, P. S., 107
Dyson, M. W., 7, 16, 73, 110, 115, 135, 216, 332, 473, 490, 500, 523, 525, 541, 548, 680

Eagly, A. H., 279, 488
Eaker, D. G., 117
Earls, F., 191, 530
Eaton, K. L., 132
Eaton, W., 26
Eaton, W. O., 83, 87, 213, 279, 317, 481
Eaves, L. J., 46, 306, 546
Ebbinghaus, H., 6
Eber, H. W., 46
Ebstein, R., 131, 321, 322, 360, 377

Ebstein, R. P., 49, 170, 172, 173, 264, 322, 323, 324, 325, 327
Ebsworthy, G., 350
Eddie, H. J., 130
Edelbrock, C. S., 88
Edmonds, G. W., 595
Edmundson, M., 169
Edwards, C. P., 462
Edwards, C. R., 299
Edwards, D. H., 259
Edwards, J. H., 321
Edwards, K., 126
Edwards, S., 448, 616, 691
Edwards, S. L., 555, 616, 617
Eens, M., 274
Egan, B. M., 136
Egeland, B., 185, 300, 404
Eggum, N. D., 564, 636
Egner, T., 153
Ehlers, S. L., 592
Ehlert, U., 239
Ehrhardt, A. A., 279
Eid, M., 133
Eiden, R. D., 133
Eisenberg, N., 15, 132, 147, 157, 158, 168, 169, 170, 171, 173, 175, 191, 214, 223, 232, 430, 432, 443, 444, 448, 449, 451, 452, 453, 454, 470, 471, 473, 485, 501, 526, 564, 570, 573, 594, 608, 628, 629, 635, 680
Eisenberg, N. A., 117
Eisenberger, N., 388
Eisenberger, N. I., 388
Eisenberger, N. L., 265
Eisenbud, L., 232
Eisenmann, J. C., 481
Ekelund, J., 323
Ekman, P., 12, 30, 111, 133, 224
El Marroun, H. E., 305, 308
Elberger, A. J., 303
Eldar, S., 350
Elder, G. H., 447
Elder, G. H., Jr., 472, 491
Eley, T. C., 172, 525, 572
El-Faddagh, M., 308
Elfenbein, H. A., 133
El-Gabalawy, R., 75
Elger, C., 131
Elias, M. J., 638
Elkovitch, N., 427
Elliot, A. J., 107, 117, 589, 591, 593
Ellis, B. J., 403, 410, 411, 417, 528, 650
Ellis, L. K., 14, 15, 27, 29, 107, 146, 147, 157, 188, 195, 196
Ellis, M., 289
Elovainio, M., 587
Else-Quest, N. M., 13, 15, 85, 114, 131, 279, 286, 287, 453, 479, 480, 481, 482, 483, 484, 486, 488, 489, 490, 492, 553, 637, 689
El-Sheikh, M., 132, 233, 240
Embretson, S. E., 222
Emde, R. N., 169, 450
Emons, W. H., 222
Endres, T., 370
Eng, P. M., 136
Engebretson, T. O., 126

Engel, S. M., 300
Engfer, A., 430
England, B. G., 238
English, K., 533
Enns, L. R., 87, 481
Enns, M. W., 549
Ensor, R., 533
Entwisle, D. R., 631
Epstein, S., 199, 219
Erath, S. A., 240
Erhard, H. W., 253
Erickson, K. I., 639
Eriksen, B. A., 151
Eriksen, C. W., 151
Erikson, E. H., 510
Erk, S., 130, 350, 382
Erkanli, A., 490
Ernst, M., 301, 303, 304, 351, 357
Ersland, L., 72
Escalona, S. K., 8, 211, 673
Escolano, S., 631
Espy, K. A., 304
Essau, C. A., 564, 565
Esser, G., 308, 566
Essex, M. J., 30, 73, 184, 209, 216, 220, 416, 419, 490, 566
Estevez, A. F., 151
Etkin, A., 153, 349
Evans, D., 3, 7, 14, 283
Evans, D. A., 591, 594
Evans, D. E., 22, 27, 107, 108, 127, 146, 147, 184, 189, 196, 198, 281, 283, 284, 286, 287, 480, 581, 591, 593, 628, 651, 652, 655, 656
Evans, G. W., 533, 639
Evans, L., 309
Everitt, B. J., 382, 417
Eye, J., 448
Eysenck, H. J., 6, 7, 8, 42, 43, 44, 45, 46, 47, 48, 51, 52, 53, 54, 55, 57, 59, 90, 91, 146, 172, 256, 288, 289, 368, 369, 588, 591, 673
Eysenck, M. W., 6, 42, 43, 45, 46, 90, 91, 591
Eysenck, S. B. G., 42, 43, 45, 48, 57, 91

Fabes, R. A., 157, 169, 171, 232, 444, 448, 449, 451, 452, 453, 454, 485, 491
Fagot, B., 429, 430
Fagot, B. I., 88, 191
Fahrenberg, J., 45
Fahy, T., 224
Faier-Routman, J., 586
Fair, D. A., 156, 355
Fairbanks, L. A., 257, 260, 261, 264
Fairburn, C. G., 592
Fairchild, G., 572
Fairooz, Y., 586
Faith, M. S., 587, 592
Faleide, A. O., 585
Falkenstein, M., 158
Fan, J., 147, 151, 152, 153, 214, 353, 356
Fan, X., 259
Fane, B. A., 279, 487
Fang, H., 304

Fanning, J., 160, 638
Fanous, A. H., 546, 547
Fanselow, M. S., 265
Fantuzzo, J., 451, 527
Farah, M. J., 160, 521
Faraone, S. V., 563
Farber, E., 300
Farmer, A., 545
Farmer, R. F., 196, 197
Farou, M., 377
Faroy, M., 131, 321, 322, 323, 324, 360
Farrington, D. P., 566
Farver, J. M., 462
Farvolden, P., 554
Faulk, D. M., 50
Fava, M., 135
Fazel, A., 303
Fegley, S., 681
Fehlings, D., 525
Fehr, E., 171, 173
Feij, J. A., 50
Feiler, A. R., 43
Feingold, A., 481, 483, 484, 485, 489
Feldman, J. M., 585
Feldman, P., 591
Feldman, R., 114, 281, 415, 523
Feldman Barrett, L., 591
Feldstein, M., 529
Fendt, M., 370
Fenigstein, A., 549
Fenton, G. W., 52
Fenwick B. B. C., 52
Fera, F., 354
Ferdinand, R. F., 554
Fergusson, D. M., 634
Ferreira, A. J., 297, 300
Ferrie, J., 585, 587
Ferrucci, L., 591
Fiebach, C. J., 131
Field, T., 133, 194, 200
Fielding, J., 330
Fields, H., 388
Fiese, B., 525
Fiez, J. A., 351
Figner, B., 351
Figueredo, A. J., 277, 283, 284
Finch, C., 299
Findlay, L. C., 447
Fine, M., 524
Fine, S. E., 451
Finegan, J. A., 193
Fink, B., 51
Finkel, S. M., 591
Finn, J. D., 632
Finn, P. R., 595
Fischbacher, U., 171, 172
Fish, M., 114, 409, 429
Fisher, E. B., 592
Fisher, P., 12, 27, 86, 109, 128, 147, 190, 278, 448, 498, 521
Fisher, P. M., 378
Fisk, N. M., 299
Fiskerstrand, C. E., 266
Fissell, C., 351
Fissell, K., 153
Fite, P. J., 529
Fitz, S., 374

Fitzgerald, D. A., 134
Fitzgerald, M., 132
Fitzmaurice, G., 136
Fivush, R., 488, 510, 511
Fjell, A. M., 694
Flachsbart, C., 508
Flannagan, D., 488
Flavell, J. H., 507
Fleming, A. S., 386, 387
Fletcher, J., 610
Flinn, M. V., 238
Flint, J., 383, 419, 592
Flombaum, J. I., 152, 153, 353
Flor, D., 449
Flores, J., 371
Florio, P., 299
Floyd, F. J., 199
Foa, E. B., 135
Foley, M., 88
Fong, G. W., 351
Forbes, C., 661
Forbes, E. E., 383
Forde, V., 522
Fordham, K., 447
Forehand, R., 527
Forget-Dubois, N., 334
Forness, S., 620
Förster, J., 591
Fortuna, K., 416
Fortunao, C. K., 240
Fossella, J., 153, 154, 356
Fowkes, F. G. R., 592
Fowler, J. H., 416
Fox, A., 373
Fox, A. S., 73
Fox, G., 426
Fox, L., 610
Fox, N. A., 3, 9, 69, 70, 71, 73, 75, 76, 105, 110, 112, 113, 115, 173, 210, 213, 217, 230, 231, 232, 234, 235, 236, 240, 256, 278, 279, 287, 322, 336, 347, 348, 349, 353, 356, 357, 358, 361, 403, 408, 409, 426, 433, 446, 450, 501, 505, 521, 542, 550, 553, 554, 679, 680, 687
Fox, S., 133, 368, 376
Fox, S. E., 533
Frady, R. I., 52
Fraley, R. C., 317, 407, 509, 544
Francis, D. D., 309
Francis, L. A., 587
Franke, B., 333
Frankel, K. A., 429, 430
Frankenburg, F. R., 567
Franklin, B., 639
Franzen, P. L., 156
Fraundorf, S. H., 155, 353
Fredrickson, B. L., 105, 590, 591
Freedman, D. G., 467
Freedman, N. A., 467
Freeland, C. A. B., 105, 125, 127, 184, 186, 218, 405, 480, 685
Freeman, H. D., 256, 274, 278, 279, 289
Freeman, P., 446, 490
Freifeld, T. R., 168
French, D. C., 463, 465, 466, 471

Freud, S., 692
Freudigman, K., 525
Freyberger, H. J., 566
Frick, P. J., 184, 289, 435, 524, 564, 567, 569, 571
Fricke, R. A., 259
Friderici, K., 569
Fried, P. A., 298, 304
Friedel, S., 336
Frieder, B., 299
Friedlmeier, W., 469
Friedman, H. S., 134, 135, 582, 586, 591, 592, 594
Friedman, M., 136
Friedman, N. P., 678, 679, 685, 686
Friedman, R. S., 591
Friedman, S. L., 452
Fries, M. E., 9
Friesen, W. V., 12, 30, 117, 133, 589
Friesenborg, A. E., 427
Frith, C. C., 158
Frith, C. D., 172, 353
Fritzsche, B. A., 168
Frodl, T., 376
Froger, N., 262
Frohlick, S. L., 447
Frye, C., 224
Fu, R., 9, 12, 14, 43, 47, 60, 108, 112, 113, 130, 131, 133, 171, 210, 256, 259, 261, 273, 278, 279, 280, 281, 286, 287, 322, 350, 351, 352, 368, 453, 462, 521, 661, 678, 679, 683, 689, 694, 695
Fuchs, D., 610
Fuchs, L., 610
Fuchs, L. S., 159
Fuentes, L. J., 151
Fuhs, M. W., 692
Fujimoto, K., 261
Fulford, D., 590
Fulker, D. W., 48, 172, 317, 318, 319
Fulkner, D. W., 317
Fullard, W., 24, 32, 86, 105, 186, 188, 191, 195
Funder, D. C., 507
Fung, K., 590
Fuqua, D. R., 131
Furby, L., 351
Fureix, C., 254
Furman, W., 282
Fussell, J., 529
Fussell, J. J., 570
Futch, F. A., 529

Gable, P., 117
Gable, P. A., 287
Gabrieli, J. D. E., 153, 353, 354, 650
Gaddis, L. R., 89, 117
Gade-Andavolu, R., 327
Gaertner, B. M., 214
Gagne, J. R., 15, 84, 126, 130, 209, 211, 213, 216, 217, 218, 219, 220, 223, 225, 317, 319, 320, 330, 332, 678, 691, 692
Galambos, N. L., 128
Galda, L., 449
Gale, A., 44

Galehouse, P., 611
Gallagher, K. C., 117, 199, 415, 434, 609, 638
Gallegos, R. A., 386
Galler, J., 522
Gallo, L. C., 135, 592
Galvan, A., 351, 352, 360
Gambone, M. A., 610
Gamez, W., 527, 542, 546
Gandour, M. J., 215
Ganiban, J. M., 317, 330, 331, 332, 334, 335, 336, 426, 431
Gannon, S., 471
Gansle, K. A., 136
Garber, J., 448
Garcia-Coll, C., 31, 32, 69, 70, 193, 197, 231, 446
Gardener, H., 307
Gardner, C. O., 547, 551
Garey, J., 280
Garino, E., 186, 186, 467
Garnefski, N., 512
Garpenstrand, H., 326
Garthus-Niegel, S., 585
Gartstein, M. A., 14, 15, 27, 28, 86, 87, 109, 110, 111, 114, 126, 128, 146, 147, 183, 185, 186, 191, 196, 199, 219, 466, 467, 468, 498, 526, 678, 692
Garvan, C. W., 192
Gaskins, S., 462
Gasman, I., 26
Gaspar, P., 369, 376, 377, 378
Gatti, F. M., 6
Gatz, M., 547, 551, 591
Gaughan, J. M., 218
Gauvin, M., 429, 430
Gavin, W. J., 355
Gazelle, H., 444, 446, 447, 448, 453
Gazzaniga, 695
Ge, X., 46, 425
Geangu, E., 171
Geary, D. C., 487
Gebhardt, C., 323, 325
Gebhardt, W. A., 512
Geesey, M. E., 592
Gehlbach, L., 154
Geijer, T., 131
Geise, A. C., 511
Gelernter, J., 387
Gelhorn, H., 222
Geller, V., 321, 323, 324, 360
Genazzani, A. R., 299
Gentile, C., 447
George, C. J., 234
George, J. L., 630
Georgieff, M., 522
Geracioti, T., 374
Geracioti, T. D., 374
Gerardi-Caulton, G., 15, 147, 151, 191, 353
Gerbion, M., 134
Gernsbacher, M. A., 680
Gershuny, B. S., 554
Gerstadt, C. L., 150, 353
Gerstle, J. E., 52
Gesell, A., 8, 673

Ghera, M. M., 71, 133, 217, 505, 542
Giancola, P. R., 192
Giannopulu, I., 631
Gibbons, J., 105, 348
Gibbs, M. V., 22, 192, 199
Gibson, E. L., 586
Gibson, L. W., 634
Giedd, J., 353
Giedd, J. N., 368
Giegling, I., 131
Gietl, A., 131
Gilain, L., 590
Gilbert, P., 133
Gilissen, R., 415
Gilkeson, J. A., 253
Gill, K. L., 448
Gillespie, N. A., 58, 194
Gillespie, S., 374
Gillies, G., 384
Gilliland, F., 44
Gilman, S. E., 307, 308, 309
Gingrich, J., 376
Ginsburg, H. J., 280
Girardi, A., 447
Gitau, R., 299
Gjerde, P. F., 685, 686
Gjerde, P. J., 682
Gjone, H., 333, 566, 568
Gladstone, G., 189, 197
Glancy, G., 136
Glaser, D., 426
Glazer, K., 135, 592
Gleason, T. C., 449
Gleason, T. R., 449, 451, 453
Glenn, A. L., 567, 685, 686
Glernter, J., 376
Glickstein, S. B., 321
Glocker, M. L., 351
Glover, A., 491
Glover, G., 352
Glover, V., 299, 301, 309, 487
Glueck, E., 6
Glueck, S., 6
Glynn, L., 522
Gobrogge, K. L., 487
Godfrey, K., 527
Goh, C., 266
Gold, P. W., 234, 264
Goldberg, L. R., 22, 46, 196, 197, 283, 507, 584, 587, 591, 630, 634, 675
Golding, J., 301
Goldman, B. D., 584
Goldman, D., 261, 264, 265
Goldman, M. S., 571
Goldman, P. S., 153
Goldner, I., 173
Goldsmith, H., 73, 105, 111, 114, 130
Goldsmith, H. H., 15, 21, 22, 23, 26, 30, 32, 36, 42, 84, 85, 86, 87, 108, 112, 125, 126, 148, 150, 153, 169, 173, 185, 187, 190, 193, 209, 212, 213, 215, 216, 217, 219, 220, 223, 224, 225, 230, 233, 278, 279, 317, 318, 319, 333, 353, 407, 416, 417, 426, 429, 431, 453, 479, 480, 482, 485, 490, 497, 553, 563, 674, 678, 680, 691, 692

Goldstein, A., 620
Goldstein, S., 194
Gollan, J., 374
Gollwitzer, A., 638
Gollwitzer, P. M., 638
Golter, B. S., 442
Gomez, M., 304
Gomez-Fraguela, J. A., 508
Gonda, X., 324, 325, 352
Gong, Y., 462
Gonzalez, C., 87, 151
Gonzalez, R. G., 351
Goodenough, W. H., 13
Goodman, R., 173, 195, 566
Goodman, S. H., 488
Goodnight, J. A., 426, 437
Goodwin, G. M., 592
Goodyer, I., 523, 684
Gorbounova, O., 303
Gordis, E. B., 240
Gordon, A. H., 489
Gordon, B., 191
Gordon, I., 114
Gorman, B. S., 136
Gorman, K., 521
Gorodetsky, E., 360
Gorrindo, T., 135
Gortmaker, S. L., 72
Gorwood, P., 332
Gosling, S. D., 171, 256, 274, 278, 279, 284, 286, 289, 503, 504, 596, 628
Gotlib, I. H., 197, 552
Gottesman, I. I., 319, 333
Gottfredson, L. S., 627
Gottfried, A. W., 15, 529, 566, 570, 633, 685
Gottman, J., 232, 233, 665
Gough, H. G., 633
Gould, T. D., 333
Gower, A. M., 449
Graham, A., 448, 533, 691
Graham, A. A., 73, 446
Grandin, T., 260
Grandjean, D., 130
Granger, D., 238
Granger, D. A., 240
Grant, H., 638
Grant, N., 590
Grant, S., 522
Grant, W., 111
Grantham-McGregor, S., 522
Grasbeck, A., 547
Grawe, J. M., 319
Gray, E. A., 131
Gray, J., 6, 70
Gray, J. A., 7, 8, 9, 15, 27, 42, 44, 45, 52, 53, 54, 56, 57, 59, 60, 93, 107, 111, 151, 197, 277, 278, 279, 368, 370, 503, 584, 586, 591, 651, 673
Gray, J. R., 505
Graziano, J., 522
Graziano, P. A., 233, 241
Graziano, W. G., 108, 114, 115, 117, 168, 171, 173, 453, 502, 506
Greenbaum, C. W., 415
Greenberg, M. T., 609, 620, 622, 637, 638

Greenberger, E., 132
Greenfield, D. B., 630
Greenfield, P. M., 463
Greenspan, S. I., 232
Gregory, A., 525
Gregory, A. M., 172
Gresham, F., 610
Griffith, W. H., 302
Grillon, C., 76
Grimm, K., 609
Grimm, V. E., 299
Gritsenko, I., 173
Grob, A., 133, 286
Groeneveld, M. G., 415
Groenewegen, H. J., 282
Groothuis, T. G. G., 649
Gross, C., 377
Gross, E., 376, 378, 379, 380
Gross, J. J., 129, 130, 153, 223, 353, 354, 357, 472
Grossmann, T., 287
Grotpeter, J. K., 563
Gruber, C., 72
Gruber, J., 108, 116
Gruenfeld, D., 665
Gruner, R., 72
Grusec, J. E., 425, 609
Grydeland, H., 694
Grzywacz, J., 529
Guay, F., 159
Guerin, C. W., 15
Guerin, D. W., 529, 566, 570, 633, 685, 686
Guichard, C., 590
Guidash, K. M., 190
Guilford, J. P., 43, 90
Guilford, J. S., 90, 91, 92
Gump, B., 521, 522
Gundersen, H., 72
Gunderson, J. G., 571
Guner, B., 217
Guner, B. M., 71
Gunnar, M. R., 109, 111, 112, 113, 115, 191, 233, 237, 238, 239, 409, 426, 452, 500, 530, 651
Gunthert, K. C., 376
Guo, S., 306
Gurkas, P., 522
Gurwitz, D., 694
Gustavsson, J. P., 208
Guthrie, I. K., 449, 451, 452, 454, 491
Gutman, D. A., 298
Gutman, L., 520
Gutteling, B. M., 301, 302
Guyer, A. E., 360
Gwaltney, J. M., 591
Gwynn, E. P., 239

Habashi, M. M., 168, 506
Haber, J. R., 306
Habermas, T., 510
Habib, K., 373
Hackman, D., 160, 521
Hadwin, J. A., 76
Hagekull, B., 86, 185, 186, 415, 447, 687
Haggerty, R., 610

Hagino, N., 303
Haglin, C., 298
Hagnell, O., 547
Hagtvet, K. A., 585
Haier, R. J., 45
Hajcak, G., 357
Hakamata, Y., 326
Hakkula, A., 592
Halberstadt, A. G., 132, 483
Haley, T., 136
Hall, J., 572
Hall, J. A., 483, 485, 488, 489
Halligan, S., 523, 684
Hallowell, A. I., 75
Hallqvist, J., 596
Halperin, J. M., 193, 568
Halverson, C., 107, 686
Halverson, C. F., 22, 129, 208, 429, 506, 611
Halverson, C. F., Jr., 9, 22
Halvorsen, M., 532
Ham, B. J., 324, 325, 327, 328
Hamadani, J., 522
Hamann, S., 354
Hamburg, M. A., 596
Hamdaoui, A., 51
Hamer, D., 264
Hamer, D. H., 236, 325
Hamilton, L. C., 411
Hamilton, W. D., 171
Hamlin, J. K., 168
Hammen, C., 450, 509
Hamon, M., 262
Hampson, S. E., 6, 135, 332, 500, 523, 525, 581, 582, 584, 586, 587, 588, 595, 596, 597, 692
Hamre, B. K., 609, 638
Hamre, K. M., 303
Hamrin, V., 136
Han, W., 529
Hane, A. A., 71, 113, 217, 403, 409, 505
Hane, N. A., 349
Hanington, L., 522, 523
Hanish, L. D., 444, 449, 452, 453, 491
Hankin, B. L., 116, 489, 490, 532, 547, 552, 554
Hanley, C., 6
Hansen, D. J., 448
Hanushek, E. A., 630
Happaney, K. R., 149
Harbaugh, W. T., 171
Hard, E., 298
Hardin, M., 357
Hare, T. A., 283, 352, 357, 358, 360
Hargett-Beck, M. Q., 191
Hariri, A., 16, 675
Hariri, A. R., 263, 352, 354, 356, 357, 358, 374, 375, 382, 683
Harker, L., 117
Harkness, S., 463, 474
Harlan, E. T., 15, 145, 214, 282, 432, 450, 527
Harlow, H. F., 256, 404
Harman, C., 154
Harmon, C., 593
Harmon-Jones, C., 287

Author Index

Harmon-Jones, E., 108, 111, 113, 116, 117, 130, 287
Harms, P., 128
Harold, G. T., 431
Harrington, N. G., 51
Harris, D., 117
Harris, M. J., 330
Harris, V., 115, 195
Harris, V. S., 188, 194
Harrison, H. M., 552
Harrison, R., 522
Harrist, A. W., 452
Hart, C. H., 173, 462
Hart, D., 512, 681
Hart, J., 238
Hart, S., 200
Harter, S., 512
Hartman, C. A., 29, 114, 157, 450, 554
Hartmann, A. M., 131
Hartup, W. W., 454
Hashemi, B., 194
Hashimoto, R., 326
Haslam, N., 563
Hasler, G., 586
Hastings, P. D., 175, 428, 431, 435, 446
Hathaway, S. R., 633
Hatton, D. D., 191
Hausberger, M., 254
Hauser, K. F., 301
Haverkock, A., 200
Havill, V., 22, 159, 686
Hawes, D. J., 426, 573
Hawley, P., 125
Hay, D. A., 563
Hay, D. F., 171, 443
Hayden, E. P., 110, 113, 114, 116, 217, 219, 322, 324, 498, 505, 509, 523, 532, 548, 552, 554
Hayden, L. C., 195, 200
Hayes, M., 533
Haykal, R. F., 198, 693
Hazeltine, E., 155
Hazen, R. A., 509, 524
He, J., 111, 113
He, Y., 454, 470, 661
Healey, D. M., 193
Healy, D., 693
Heath, A. C., 58, 194, 317, 546
Heatherton, T., 388
Heaven, P. C. L., 586
Hebb, D. O., 44, 70
Hebebrand, J., 336
Hecht, M. A., 483
Heckman, J. J., 630, 633
Hedden, T., 650
Hedges, L. V., 492
Heffelfinger, A. K., 238
Hegeman, I. M., 71
Heggestad, E. D., 634
Hegvik, R. L., 24, 86, 188, 193, 194, 533
Heider, K., 133
Heim, C., 237, 684
Heiman, N., 317
Heimer, L., 371
Heinrichs, M., 172, 386
Heir, T., 71

Hejjas, K., 264
Held, B. S., 118
Helfinstein, S. M., 9, 70, 112, 210, 234, 256, 279, 322, 347, 357, 360, 361, 521, 679
Heller, W., 278, 288
Hellstrom-Lindahl, E., 303
Hemmeter, M., 610
Hemphill, S. A., 158, 443, 551
Hen, R., 376, 378, 379, 380
Henderson, H., 521, 522, 554
Henderson, H. A., 70, 110, 113, 234, 235, 240, 278, 348, 349, 353, 357, 358, 426, 428, 446, 450, 505, 542, 553, 630, 680
Hendler, T., 281
Hendricks, A. A. J., 208
Hennen, J., 567
Hennig, J., 51, 356, 390
Henrich, C., 125
Henriksen, S. J., 386
Henry, B., 566
Henry, J. D., 128, 197
Henson, R. K., 184, 199
Herald, S. L., 158
Herbert, J., 523, 684
Herbsman, C. R., 132
Herbst, J. H., 58, 197, 323, 325
Hermanns, J. M. A., 24, 427, 429, 448
Hernandez-Reif, M., 133
Heron, J., 301
Herpetz, S. C., 572
Herrmann, M., 133
Herry, C., 72, 79
Hersen, M., 615
Hersey, K. L., 147
Hershey, K., 12, 147, 190, 230, 521
Hershey, K. L., 27, 86, 107, 109, 110, 111, 114, 128, 157, 173, 278, 448, 480, 498
Hertzig, M., 229, 608
Hertzig, M. E., 9, 70, 479, 673
Hesketh, T., 12
Hess, E. J., 259
Hesse, E., 408
Hetherington, E. M., 26, 317, 425
Hettema, J. M., 549, 551
Heuer, H., 155
Heuven, H. C. M., 254
Hewitt, E. C., 485
Hewitt, J. K., 317, 678
Heymans, G., 7, 83, 90, 93, 100, 676
Hezlett, S. A., 630
Hibbeln, J. R., 133
Hicks, B. M., 108, 128, 172, 568, 572
Higham, J. P., 265
Higley, J. D., 52, 253, 257, 261, 263
Hill, A., 231
Hill, A. L., 449
Hillman, C. H., 638, 639
Hill-Soderlund, A. L., 128, 430, 435, 449
Himes, J., 522
Hinde, R. A., 4, 10, 11, 12, 13, 16, 261, 443, 444
Hines, M., 279, 487
Hinney, A., 336

Hinshaw, S. P., 452
Hinton, D., 75
Hinton, S., 75
Hintsanen, M., 92
Hipwell, A. E., 566
Hiramura, H., 566
Hiripi, E., 563
Hirsch, J., 153
Hirschfeld, R. M. A., 546, 547, 549, 556
Hirshfeld-Becker, D. R., 550, 566
Hiscock, H., 617
Hittner, J. B., 587
Ho, D. Y. F., 468, 469
Hodge, S., 159
Hodgson, D. M., 184
Hoekstra, R. A., 131
Hofer, C., 443, 451
Hofer, S. M., 317, 587, 596
Hoffheimer, J. A., 232
Hoffman, M., 171
Hoffman, M. L., 169
Hogan, A. M., 76
Hohmann, L. M., 449
Hohnsbein, J., 158
Holbrook, J., 117
Holker, L., 350
Hollatz, A. L., 157, 566
Holmboe, K., 323, 324
Holmes, A., 263, 356
Holsboer, F., 264
Holt, R., 117, 450
Homberg, J. R., 266
Homberg, R. J., 649
Homel, P., 218
Hommer, D., 351
Hong, C., 466
Hong, C. J., 467
Hong, M., 109
Hong, Y. J., 353
Hongwanishkul, D., 149
Honig, A., 593
Honorado, E., 527
Honsberger, M. J., 353
Hood, J., 193
Hooe, E. S., 116, 197
Hoormann, J., 158
Hornack, J., 383
Horne, R., 525
Horner, R. H., 610
Hornowska, E., 96
Horwood, L. J., 634
Hosie, J. A., 128
Houpt, K. A., 261
Houts, R. M., 636
Howe, G. W., 596
Howell, C. T., 485
Howell, D. N., 306
Howell, R. T., 589
Howells, K., 131
Howrigan, D., 283
Hsiao, C., 464
Hsieh, K., 105, 410, 570
Hsieh, K.-H., 433, 452
Hsu, C., 466
Hsu, M., 79
Hu, S., 264

Hu, X. Z., 266
Huang, J., 522
Huang, L. Z., 302
Huang, Y. Y., 261
Huang-Pollock, C., 563
Hubbard, J. A., 128, 134
Hubbs-Tait, L., 522
Hubert, N. C., 215
Huda, S., 522
Hudson, J. L., 550, 615
Hudziak, J. J., 196, 332
Huedo-Medina, T. B., 694
Huffman, L. C., 232, 233
Hugdahl, K., 72
Hughes, C., 533
Hughes, J. E., Jr., 634
Hughes, J. N., 160, 638
Huizinga, M., 353
Huizink, A. C., 15, 60, 133, 297, 298, 299, 300, 301, 302, 304, 305, 498, 521, 522, 684
Humphrey, H., 521
Humphreys, A. P., 279
Hundt, W., 264
Hunot, V., 615
Huot, R. L., 522
Hur, Y.-M., 48, 130, 172, 275, 277, 317
Husaini, M., 522
Husarek, S. J., 185, 680
Hutchison, K. E., 266
Hutchison, M. D., 253
Huttunen, M., 24
Hwang, A., 521
Hwang, C. P., 675
Hwang, J., 110, 117, 191, 210
Hyde, J., 114
Hyde, J. S., 85, 131, 279, 453, 479, 480, 482, 485, 489, 492, 509, 532, 553
Hymel, S., 446, 552

Iacono, L., 377
Iacono, W. G., 112, 128, 333, 335, 336, 566, 568, 569, 572, 574, 591
Ihrig, L., 691
Ikemoto, S., 383
Ikonomidou, C., 303
Iliffe, S., 590
Ilott, N., 323
Ingram, M., 448, 555, 616, 617
Inoue, H., 327
Inoue, K., 261, 281
Inouye, J., 26, 283
Insel, T. R., 281, 386
Irgens, L. M., 588
Irwing, P., 277, 283
Isaacson, W., 692
Isabella, R., 114, 409
Isabella, R. A., 429
Isberg, P.-E., 547
Isen, J. D., 317
Ishii, G., 327
Ispa, J., 524
Israel, S., 10, 168, 169, 170, 172, 452, 485, 506, 677
Itoh, K., 327
Ivashenko, O. V., 45
Ivorra, J. L., 323, 324, 329, 336

Ivry, R. B., 155
Iwata, J., 349
Izard, C., 509, 527, 619
Izard, C. E., 450, 451, 452, 674
Izzo, C. V., 610

Jaber, M., 321
Jacklin, C. N., 480, 481, 483, 484, 486
Jackson, D. C., 223, 235
Jackson, R. J., 550
Jacob, T., 306
Jacobs, D., 615, 616
Jacobs, M., 71
Jacobson, J., 521
Jacobson, K. C., 563
Jacobson, S., 521
Jacoby, E., 522
Jacques, T. Y., 15, 148, 191, 214
Jaddoe, V. W., 407
Jaferi, A., 264
Jagiellowicz, J., 649, 650, 664
Jahari, A., 522
Jahn, A. L., 375
Jahromi, L., 115, 450
Jain, A., 231, 232
James, W., 147, 629, 639
Jang, K. L., 51
Janosz, M., 633
Janson, H., 433
Janssen, I., 586
Jarvenpaa, A., 521, 522
Jaser, S., 524
Jedema, H. P., 649
Jehle, J., 153
Jenkins, J., 132
Jenkins, J. M., 132
Jennings, P. A., 638
Jensen, A. R., 631
Jensen-Campbell, L. A., 117, 449, 451, 452, 453, 502
Jernigan, K., 569
Jimenez, A. L., 566
Jimenez, N. B., 157
Jobs, S., 692
Jockin, V., 663
Joffe, L. S., 300
Johansen, J., 388
John, B., 172
John, O. P., 112, 171, 196, 283, 284, 286, 503, 504, 563, 566, 567, 581, 589, 591, 594, 628, 652, 678
Johnson, A. M., 43, 45
Johnson, B. T., 694
Johnson, C., 304, 383, 657
Johnson, D. C., 609
Johnson, E. A., 298
Johnson, E. H., 136
Johnson, J., 639
Johnson, J. H., 191
Johnson, M. C., 125, 448
Johnson, M. O., 105, 348
Johnson, P., 374
Johnson, S. C., 498, 509
Johnson, S. D., 633
Johnson, S. L., 108, 116, 377, 679
Johnson, T. R. B., 184
Johnson, W., 112, 335, 336, 503

Johnstone, T., 349
Joiner, T., 681
Joiner, T. E., 554
Joireman, J., 42, 53, 55
Jokela, M., 336, 585, 587
Jolly, J. B., 197
Jones, A., 527
Jones, A. P., 569
Jones, N. A., 349
Jones, P., 548
Jones, R. M., 283, 351, 357
Jones, S., 125, 453
Jonkman, L. M., 156
Joo, Y. H., 324, 325
Joormann, J., 377, 679
Jordan-Young, R. M., 487, 491
Jorgensen, M. J., 261, 264
Jorm, A. F., 322, 324, 326, 327, 332
Joy, M. E., 415, 434, 571
Joyce, D., 85, 610
Joyce, P. R., 667, 693, 694
Juffer, F., 14, 403, 408, 414, 573
Julius, S., 136
Jung, C. G., 110, 692
Junger, M., 434

Kaczmarek, M., 95
Kafry, D., 107
Kagan, J., 3, 5, 6, 7, 9, 10, 14, 16, 23, 25, 31, 32, 42, 69, 70, 71, 72, 73, 74, 76, 77, 78, 105, 110, 173, 183, 184, 193, 197, 200, 211, 213, 230, 231, 233, 234, 235, 236, 237, 238, 239, 251, 256, 257, 263, 279, 319, 347, 348, 349, 361, 375, 403, 404, 405, 406, 409, 419, 433, 446, 447, 466, 467, 471, 501, 505, 542, 550, 608, 615, 651, 677, 678, 680, 681, 683, 684, 687, 692, 696
Kagan, S., 462
Kahana, M., 131, 322, 360, 377
Kahn, V., 70, 230, 542
Kaiser, E., 351
Kaiser, P., 529
Kaiser, S., 298
Kajantie, E., 521
Kalin, N. H., 73, 223, 233, 235, 256, 257, 263, 264, 298, 371, 373, 375
Kamata, M., 328
Kammerer, H., 350, 382
Kamphaus, R. W., 88, 159
Kanashiro, H., 522
Kandel, E. R., 153
Kandler, C., 542, 544
Kang, J. I., 131
Kang, N. J., 126
Kanske, P., 14, 16, 147
Kant, I., 5, 6, 13, 15
Kaplan, J. R., 261
Kaplan, L. A., 309
Kaplan, N., 408
Karalis, K. P., 299
Karbon, M., 232, 444
Karney, B. R., 663
Karraker, K., 486, 525
Karrass, J., 115, 128, 195, 430
Karreman, A., 160, 428

Kasch, K. L., 197, 547
Kasckow, J., 374
Kasckow, J. W., 374
Kasper, S., 377
Kassinove, H., 136
Katkin, E. S., 233, 569
Kato, K., 591
Katon, W., 585
Katz-Newman, R., 191
Kaufman, E., 71
Kavale, K., 620
Kavoussi, R., 130
Kawachi, I., 136, 592
Kazama, A. M., 72
Kazantseva, A. V., 324, 325, 326
Kazdin, A., 615
Kazdin, A. E., 563
Keane, S., 115
Keane, S. P., 233, 241, 435, 449, 450, 567
Kearsley, R. B., 467
Keele, S. W., 155
Keeler, G., 490
Keeling, L. J., 254
Kegel, C. A. T., 417
Keiley, M. K., 430
Keller, H., 469, 474
Keller, L., 77
Keller, M. C., 317
Kellett, J., 76
Kelley, A., 371
Kelley, K., 415, 434
Kelley, W., 370, 388
Kellison, I., 192
Kelly, A. M., 355
Kelly, E. M., 191
Kelly, F. J., 634
Kelly, M., 131
Keltikangas-Järvinen, L., 323, 326, 336, 584, 587
Keltner, D., 112, 117, 489, 665, 678
Kempenaers, B., 274
Kendler, K. S., 71, 546, 547, 549, 551, 553
Kennedy, A. E., 431, 432
Kennedy, B. C., 261
Kennedy, H. G., 124
Kennedy, J. L., 384
Kennedy, S., 448, 555, 616, 617, 691
Kennedy, S. H., 554, 555
Kennedy, T., 522
Kent, P., 372
Kentle, R. L., 652
Keogh, B. K., 187, 191, 609
Kern, M. L., 134, 589, 592, 594, 629, 685
Kerns, J. G., 353
Kerr, D. C. R., 157, 473, 526
Kerr, M., 13, 128, 135, 471, 472, 502
Kertes, D. A., 428
Keshavan, M., 368
Kessen, W., 8
Kessler, K. C., 563
Kessler, R. C., 490, 546, 551, 553, 563
Ketay, S., 650
Keyes, M., 572
Kiebel, S. J., 172

Kiefer, S. M., 512
Kieffer, B. L., 260, 265, 387
Kiehl, K. A., 158, 355
Kiel, E. J., 221, 554
Kieling, C., 71
Kieras, J. E., 147, 353
Kiers, H., 42
Kiesler, D. J., 281
Killingsworth, P., 646
Kilmer, R. P., 526
Kim, B. E., 636
Kim, C. H., 323, 324, 325, 326
Kim, D. Y., 449, 453
Kim, G., 115, 195
Kim, H., 349, 526
Kim, J., 128, 129, 134, 135, 371, 449
Kim, M. J., 683, 689
Kim, S. H., 354
Kim, S. J., 131, 323, 324, 325, 326
Kim, S. Y., 324, 325, 326
Kim, Y. K., 462
Kim, Y. S., 323, 324, 325, 326
Kim-Cohen, J., 520, 527
King, D. E., 592
King, J., 283
King, J. E., 253, 284
King, K., 133
King, K. J., 533
King, K. M., 435, 524
King, M., 132
Kinnally, E. L., 263
Kinney, L., 235
Kinsht, I. A., 468
Kirby, T., 638
Kirsch, I., 694
Kirschbaum, C., 239
Kistner, J. A., 197
Kithakye, M., 530
Kitsantas, A., 636
Kittilsen, S., 77
Kivimäki, M., 585, 587
Klein, D., 523
Klein, D. E., 216
Klein, D. N., 7, 16, 73, 110, 114, 115, 135, 217, 332, 473, 490, 500, 505, 509, 525, 532, 533, 541, 542, 543, 544, 545, 546, 547, 548, 551, 553, 554, 678, 680, 682, 684, 687, 689, 693, 695, 696
Klein, H. A., 468
Klein, M. H., 73
Klein, T. A., 417
Klein, Z., 279
Klein Velderman, M., 403, 414, 416
Klem, A. M., 610
Klimecki, O., 169
Kline, J. P., 113
Kling, K. C., 489
Klingberg, T., 160
Klinnert, M. D., 30, 585
Kloppel, S., 131
Klump, K., 489
Knaack, A., 214, 282, 283, 506, 608, 628
Knafo, A., 10, 168, 169, 170, 171, 172, 173, 174, 175, 176, 218, 257, 281, 452, 485, 506, 677, 679

Knapp, J. E., 593
Knight, G. P., 462
Knopik, V. S., 301, 303, 304, 305, 306, 308, 309
Knudsen, G. M., 649
Knutson, B., 351, 382, 383, 393
Knyazev, G. G., 45, 466
Kobiella, A., 72
Kochanska, G., 8, 15, 16, 109, 111, 112, 114, 115, 118, 132, 145, 148, 149, 150, 154, 155, 157, 161, 185, 191, 213, 214, 282, 283, 336, 408, 414, 415, 427, 428, 429, 430, 432, 434, 436, 437, 450, 473, 499, 501, 506, 526, 527, 548, 566, 571, 608, 609, 628, 659, 680, 688
Kochenderfer-Ladd, B., 449
Koenig, A. L., 15, 148, 191, 214
Koenigs, M., 77
Kogos, J., 527
Kohnstamm, G. A., 9, 22, 129, 442, 674, 682
Koinis-Mitchell, D., 585
Kolb, B., 282
Kolk, A. M., 483, 484, 490
Komsi, N., 109
Konrad, K., 355
Konttinen, H., 592
Koob, G. F., 257
Koolhaas, J. M., 255, 275, 649
Koopmans, J. R., 48
Koot, H. M., 490
Kop, W. J., 593
Kopel, S. J., 585
Kopp, C., 352, 353
Kopp, C. B., 426
Korn, S., 9, 90, 196, 229, 471, 479, 608, 673
Korner, A., 9
Korsmit, M., 386
Korte, S. M., 255, 263, 264, 275
Kosfeld, M., 172
Koslowitz, R., 609
Kotchoubey, B., 72
Kotov, R., 7, 16, 115, 135, 332, 473, 490, 500, 525, 541, 542, 546, 549, 550, 551, 553, 680, 681
Kottler, J., 71
Kouros, C. D., 12
Kovacs, E. A., 114, 429, 430, 431, 526, 530
Kovacs, M., 234, 541
Kovaleski, J. F., 610
Kovecses, Z., 133
Kraemer, G. W., 263, 386
Krafchuck, E., 219
Krafchuk, E. E., 215
Kraft, M., 42, 53, 55
Krahn, H. J., 128
Kramer, A. F., 639
Kramer, K., 387
Kramer, M. D., 588
Kramer, T., 197
Kranzler, H., 387
Krasner, S., 126
Krause, E. J., 261
Krawczak, M., 266

Krebs, N., 522
Krebs, R. M., 351
Kremen, A. M., 685
Kretschmer, E., 6, 673, 675, 680, 693
Kring, A. M., 489
Kringelbach, M., 383
Krishnakumar, A., 520
Krishnan, R. R., 131
Kristal, J., 645, 646, 647, 652, 666
Kristiansson, M., 569
Krueger, R. F., 108, 112, 128, 172, 283, 285, 335, 336, 370, 503, 542, 563, 564, 568, 571, 572, 574, 584, 586, 588
Krueger, W. K., 111, 191, 238
Kubiak, P., 373
Kubinyi, E., 254, 264
Kubzansky, L. D., 136, 585
Kuh, D., 596
Kuhlman, D. M., 42, 43, 47, 48, 53, 55
Kuhlman, M., 48, 91
Kuhn, J., 553
Kühn, K. U., 327
Kujawa, A. J., 7, 16, 115, 135, 332, 473, 490, 500, 525, 541, 680
Kuller, L. H., 136, 590, 592
Kumakiri, C., 324, 325
Kumar, A., 379
Kumari, M., 590
Kumari, V., 45
Kuncel, N. R., 591, 630, 636
Kuntsi, J., 87, 317, 318
Kunz, K., 156
Kunz-Ebrecht, S. R., 590
Kuo, A. A., 585
Kuppens, P., 126
Kurcinka, M., 609
Kusanagi, 191
Kusche, C. A., 637
Kusel, S. J., 447
Kushner, S. C., 7, 134, 332, 473, 490, 500, 525, 562, 682
Kusumi, I., 327
Kyrios, M., 526, 527

La Gasse, L., 72
La Greca, A. M., 552
Laatikainen, T., 592
Lacourse, E., 567
Lad, H. V., 72
Ladd, C. O., 374
Ladd, G. W., 158, 442, 444, 447, 448, 453, 636
Ladouceur, C. D., 355, 356, 357
Lafenêtre, P., 257
LaFontaine, P. A., 633
LaFrance, M., 483, 488
LaFreniere, P. J., 279, 414, 450, 615
Lagace-Seguin, D. G., 692
Lahey, B. B., 433, 434, 490, 545, 562, 563, 566, 568, 570
Lahvis, G. P., 171, 261
Laible, D., 448
Laible, D. J., 173
Lakatos, K., 322, 323, 324
Lakatos, M., 383

Lally, C., 454
Lalumiere, M. L., 663
Lamb, M. E., 408, 675
Lambert, C., 76
Lambert, W. W., 471
Lamm, C., 9, 70, 112, 156, 171, 210, 234, 256, 279, 322, 347, 353, 354, 355, 356, 357, 521, 679
Lamy, D., 552
Landolt, M. A., 584
Lane, S. K., 238
Lanfumey, L., 262
Lang, S., 72
Lange, L. A., 427
Langford, D. J., 171
Langhinrichsen, J., 454
Lang-Takoc, E., 282
Lansade, L., 253
Lanzenberger, R. R., 377, 378
Laptook, R. S., 73, 110, 541
Lara, M. E., 547
Larose, S., 634
Larroque, B., 521
Larsen, R. J., 278, 280, 288, 592
Larsen, S. A., 266
Larson, G. J., 5
Larson, M. C., 237, 238
Larson, R., 128, 442
Larsson, K., 298
Last, C., 615
Latané, B., 175
Latzman, R. D., 427, 428
Lau, J. Y., 572
Laucht, M., 308, 566, 686
Lauinger, B., 160, 639
Laurent, J., 197
Laursen, B., 442
Laviola, G., 309, 351
Laviolette, S. R., 386
Law, K. L., 304
Lawrence, A. D., 349
Lawroski, N., 450
Lawson, E., 232
Lawton, W. J., 592
Lay, K. L., 450
Le, K., 107
Le Gall, A., 7
Le Moal, M., 50, 257
Le Scolan, N., 254
Le Senne, R., 7
Leaper, C., 488
Leary, M., 133
LeBlanc, M., 633
Lecours, A., 522
Ledgerwood, A., 685
Ledingham, J. E., 448
LeDoux, J. E., 279, 347, 349, 371
Lee, A. S., 547
Lee, B. C., 325, 326, 328
Lee, C., 266
Lee, C. L., 430
Lee, D. H., 466
Lee, H. J., 323, 325
Lee, H. S., 323, 324, 325, 326
Lee, J. W., 303

Lee, K., 453, 468, 691
Lee, L., 12
Lee, M. R., 466
Lee, R., 374, 694
Lee, S. S., 563
Lee, T. L., 472
Lee, W. S., 149
Lee, Y., 374, 462
Leenders, F., 24
Leerkes, E. M., 185, 419, 529, 570
Leff, S. S., 509
Legrand, L. N., 333, 572, 591
Lehman, E. B., 190
Lehnart, J., 426
Lehtimaki, T., 336
Leibenluft, E., 126, 135
Leiser, T., 171
Leitch, M., 211
Lejuez, C. W., 414
LeMare, L., 445, 552
Lemerise, E., 126, 133, 448, 449
Lemerise, E. A., 502
Lemery, K. S., 23, 26, 30, 31, 84, 112, 148, 184, 190, 209, 216, 230, 317, 318, 319, 333, 407, 417, 426, 490, 566
Lemery-Chalfant, K., 153, 173, 223, 230, 317, 319, 332, 509, 631, 636
Lemola, S., 133
Lengua, L. J., 7, 16, 114, 115, 116, 133, 160, 300, 332, 378, 410, 413, 429, 430, 431, 433, 434, 435, 450, 473, 509, 512, 519, 524, 526, 527, 529, 530, 533, 554, 585, 675, 684, 688, 689, 693
Lenroot, R. K., 77
Lenzenweger, M. F., 388, 681
Leon, A., 382
Leon, C. F. M., 126
Leonardo, A., 376, 379, 380
Leong, D. J., 637
Lerew, D. R., 550
Leri, F., 371
Lerner, J. V., 471, 528
Lerner, R. M., 6, 89, 91, 95, 188, 192, 194, 195, 199, 471, 528
Lesch, K.-P., 263, 266, 360, 374, 375, 377, 383, 388, 389, 391, 649
LeScolan, N., 254
Lesimple, C., 254
Letsch, E. A., 49, 352
Leue, A., 53
Leukefeld, C., 566
Leve, L., 526, 530
Levendosky, A. A., 526
Levenson, R. W., 133, 231, 472
Levesque, J., 153, 353, 354
Levin, E. D., 303
Levine, J., 131, 322, 360, 377
Levine, S., 238
Levita, L., 351
Levitt, P., 153, 368, 533
Levy, F., 563
Lew, R. A., 303
Lewin, K., 622
Lewinsohn, P. M., 547

Lewis, C., 468, 633
Lewis, D. A., 356
Lewis, G., 132, 419, 548
Lewis, K. D., 511
Lewis, M., 111, 124, 126, 128, 129
Lewis, M. D., 156, 353, 354, 355, 357
Lewis, M. W., 125
Lewis, N. K. C., 6
Lewis, T., 169
Ley, J. M., 253
Leyton, M., 382
Lezer, S., 323, 324
Li, B., 470, 472
Li, B.-S., 454
Li, D., 75, 454, 470, 471, 473, 661
Li, I., 89
Li, Q., 262
Li, Z., 472
Liang, C., 466
Liao, H., 521
Liberzon, I., 224
Licht, C., 649
Lieberman, M., 388, 679
Lien, L., 585
Liew, J., 160, 452, 470, 473, 629, 638
Lifford, K. J., 431
Light, S. N., 169, 170, 171, 175, 224
Light Häusermann, J. H., 172
Lightfoot, C., 507
Li-Grining, C. P., 526, 527, 529, 530, 533
Lillard, A., 637
Lilljeqvist, A. C., 585
Lim, M. M., 386
Linan-Thompson, S., 610
Lindell, S., 263, 265, 266, 267
Linden, W., 135
Lindenberg, S., 530, 636
Lindhagen, K., 86, 185, 186
Lindqvist, S., 160
Linnet, K. M., 304
Linnoila, M., 52, 257
Linting, M., 415
Lipina, S. J., 12
Lipsey, M. W., 492
Lipsitt, L. P., 72
Lira, A., 376
Lira, P., 522
Lisonbee, J. A., 239
Liss, M., 646, 649, 652, 657, 658
Liston, C., 355, 356
Little, B. B., 303
Little, B. R., 500
Little, T., 125
Little, T. D., 563
Liu, L., 12
Liu, Q., 386
Liu, X., 302
Liu, Z.-H., 383
Lloyd, A. S., 254
Lo Coco, A., 454
Lockenhoff, C. E., 591
Lockhart, R., 649
Lodi-Smith, J., 511
Loeber, R., 566, 567
Loehlin, J. C., 87, 334
Loew, B., 638

Lofthouse, N., 430
Logan, G. D., 214
Lollis, S., 445
London, B., 509
London, D., 681
Loney, J., 563
Long, A. C., 524, 525, 530
Longley, S., 23, 148, 216, 318, 407
Lonigan, C. J., 116, 197, 350, 473, 509, 524, 552, 554
Lopez, J. F., 263
Lopez, N. L., 157, 473, 526
Lopez, S. J., 589
Lopez-Duran, N., 541
Lorenz, J. G., 252
Lorre, M. R., 634
Losel, F., 527, 530
Louilot, A., 113
Loukas, A., 527
Lounsbury, A. L., 218
Lounsbury, J. W., 208, 634
Lounsbury, M. L., 105, 125, 127, 184, 186, 405, 480, 685
Lourie, A., 521
Lovejoy, E. A., 266
Loveland, J. M., 634
Low, C., 15, 126, 183, 678
Lowe, J. R., 169
Lozano, D. I., 563
Lozoff, B., 522
Lubinski, D., 627
Luby, J. L., 188, 196
Lucas, R. E., 107, 286
Lucht, M., 566
Luciana, M., 214, 382
Ludwig, J., 161
Luengo, M. A., 508
Luijk, M. P. C. M., 407
Lukas, J. H., 50
Lumsden, J., 52
Luna, B., 353, 354, 355
Lundin, M. C., 254
Lunshof, J. E., 694
Luo, X., 266
Lupien, S. J., 237
Luppino, F. S., 585, 592
Lusk, D., 274
Luthar, S., 520
Luther, J., 135
Luu, P., 152, 353
Lykken, D. T., 56, 274, 663
Lynam, D., 134, 449, 566, 567
Lynch, J., 596
Lynch, K. B., 135
Lyneham, H. J., 615
Lynn, R., 484
Lyons-Ruth, K., 571
Lyoo, I. K., 196
Lytton, H., 319
Lyubomirsky, S., 547, 589

Ma, X.-H., 377
Ma, Y., 223
Maccari, S., 309
Maccoby, E. E., 425, 480, 481, 483, 484, 485, 486, 488

MacDonald, A. W., III, 354
MacDonald, K., 109, 274
MacDonald, K. B., 4, 60, 260, 273, 274, 279, 281, 282, 283, 285, 286, 288, 289, 405, 502, 692
Macey, D., 373
Machado, C. J., 72
Mackenzie, C., 75
Mackinlay, R. J., 351
MacKinnon, D. P., 453
Mackler, J. S., 230
MacLachlan, M., 593
MacLean, P. D., 289
MacLeod, C., 350, 509, 552
MacMillan, V. M., 448
Macri, S., 351
Madden-Derdich, D. A., 491
Maercker, A., 135
Maes, H., 174
Magnuson, K., 634
Mahadeo, M., 135
Main, A., 428, 632, 636
Main, M., 408
Mainous, A. G., III, 592
Maisel, B., 431
Majdandzic, M., 23, 28, 114
Majeski, S. A., 115
Majzoub, J. A., 299
Malaiyandi, V., 308
Malcolm, K. T., 449, 451, 452
Malcuit, G., 467
Malhotra, A. K., 352
Malinchoc, M., 593
Malouff, J. M., 98
Mandujano, M., 522
Maner, J. K., 550
Mangelsdorf, S., 219, 409, 500, 651
Mann, J. J., 261
Mann, T. D., 639
Manning, J. S., 198, 693
Mannoury La Cour, C., 262
Manuck, S. B., 261, 390
Maor, G. I., 299
Mar, A. C., 382
Marceau, K., 490
Marcoen, A., 301, 302
Marinelli, M., 382
Markon, K. E., 283, 284, 285, 286, 287, 289, 370, 563, 588
Markovitz, J., 136
Markus, H., 650
Marmion, J., 87, 185, 219
Marmot, M., 590, 591
Maroteaux, L., 369
Marsh, D. M., 214
Marsh, R., 355
Marshall, P. J., 113, 349, 408, 409, 505, 542
Marshall, T. R., 105, 213, 349
Marsicano, G., 257
Martel, M. M., 7, 134, 332, 427, 473, 487, 489, 490, 500, 522, 525, 527, 562, 567, 569, 682
Martin, C. L., 449, 491
Martin, J., 615
Martin, J. A., 425

Martin, J. E., 254
Martin, L. R., 594
Martin, L. T., 585
Martin, N., 172
Martin, N. G., 46, 58, 194, 317
Martin, R., 126, 129, 159, 593
Martin, R. C., 133
Martin, R. P., 9, 24, 86, 89, 107, 117, 129, 187, 192, 193, 630, 686, 691
Martin, T., 484
Martinez-Torteya, C., 526
Maruta, T., 593
Marzillier, J. S., 76
Mascolo, M. F., 12, 13
Mashburn, A. J., 159
Massey, E. K., 512
Masten, A. S., 117, 410, 453, 465, 500, 507, 512, 520
Master, L. S., 651
Matheny, A., 522
Matheny, A. P., 318, 319, 330
Matheny, A. P., Jr., 215
Mather, M., 128
Matheson, A., 448, 691
Mathews, A., 509, 552
Mathews, G. A., 279, 282, 487
Mathias, C. W., 52, 214
Mathiesen, K., 526, 530
Mathiesen, K. S., 26, 433
Mathur, S., 620
Matlina, E., 299
Matsuba, M. K., 512
Matsumoto, D., 485
Matsumoto, Y., 328
Matsuzawa, T., 171
Mattay, V. S., 354
Matthews, C. V., 633
Matthews, G., 45
Matthews, K. A., 136, 587, 590, 592
Maughan, B., 566, 572
Mauss, I., 130, 133
May, H., 632
Mayo, W., 50
Mayr, U., 155, 171, 172
Maziade, M., 89, 529, 608
Mazzanti, C., 261, 263
McAdams, D. P., 453, 497, 498, 499, 503, 507, 510
McArthur, S., 384
McAuliffe, M. D., 134
McBride-Chang, C., 133
McCabe, S. B., 280, 652
McCallum, K., 196
McCandliss, B. D., 152, 153, 214, 353, 573, 638
McCartney, K., 330, 486
McClain, T. M., 678
McClearn, G. E., 172, 317
McClellan, J., 132
McClelland, M. M., 631, 638
McCloskey, M. S., 134
McClowry, S. G., 10, 86, 88, 136, 188, 607, 608, 609, 611, 612, 613, 615, 620, 622, 690, 691
McClure, S. M., 382
McConaughy, S. H., 485

McCracken, J. T., 264
McCrae, R. R., 3, 13, 22, 42, 43, 45, 46, 47, 48, 55, 56, 58, 91, 107, 129, 189, 196, 197, 198, 281, 283, 285, 286, 481, 503, 581, 591, 652
McCulloch, J., 153
McCulloch, M. C., 153
McDermott, J. M., 350, 353, 356, 357, 358, 360, 361, 554, 680
McDevitt, S., 105, 186, 188, 193, 533
McDevitt, S. C., 24, 86, 184, 185, 186, 187, 191, 199, 452, 609, 674, 691
McDonald, A., 371
McDonald, C., 187, 193, 447
McDonald, N., 357
McDouball, P. T., 257
McDougall, P, 447
McEwen, B. S., 237, 255, 264, 275, 299
McFadyen-Ketchum, S., 240
McGinnis, E., 620
McGowan, P. O., 684
McGrath, J., 215, 522
McGrath, J. J., 233
McGreevy, P., 253
McGrogan, C., 253
McGue, M., 56, 108, 172, 274, 569, 572, 574, 663
McGuffin, P., 71, 172, 309, 317, 321, 419
McGuire, S., 317
McGuire, S. M., 26
McIntosh, D. E., 88, 192
McIntosh, D. N., 567, 570
McIntosh, J., 372
McKeen, N. A., 87
McKinley, M., 117, 450
McKinnon, J., 447
McLinn, C. M., 171
McNab, F., 160
McNally, R. J., 549
McNaughton, N., 53, 54, 370, 586, 591, 651
McPherson, M. S., 633
McQuaid, E. L., 585
McStephen, M., 563
Mead, G. H., 442
Mead, M., 648
Meaney, M., 369, 376, 378, 379, 380, 384, 521, 684
Meaney, M. J., 309, 374, 403, 409
Measelle, J. R., 186, 191, 504
Mechelen, I., 126
Mednick, S. A., 52, 566, 567, 685
Medoff-Cooper, B., 86, 186
Meehl, P. E., 111, 116, 211
Meeks-Gardner, J., 522
Meesters, C., 28, 114, 188, 195
Mehlman, P. T., 257, 276
Mehrabian, A., 678
Meier, G. H., 447, 452
Meijer, R. R., 222
Meilahn, E. M., 136
Meili, R., 7, 673, 687
Meili-Dworetzki, G., 7, 687
Melamed, S., 134
Melega, W. P., 261

Melke, J., 327
Meltzer, H. M., 588
Meltzer, L., 525
Mendelsohn, A., 522
Mendes de Leon, C. F., 591, 594
Mendez, J., 527
Mendlowicz, M. V., 190, 198
Menon, V., 153
Merali, Z., 372, 373
Merenda, P. F., 634
Mereu, G., 303
Mermelstein, R., 489
Merrilees, R., 586
Mertesacker, B., 200, 430
Mervielde, I., 9, 16, 21, 22, 34, 37, 58, 84, 85, 125, 126, 184, 193, 198, 199, 208, 211, 223, 229, 251, 278, 300, 405, 480, 504, 542, 567, 568, 569, 570, 584, 609, 628, 675, 676, 678
Mesman, J., 14, 413, 416, 417, 434, 573, 646
Messick, S., 199
Meusel, L. C., 555
Meyer-Lindenberg, A., 173, 265, 374
Mezick, E. J., 592
Mezulis, A. H., 489, 509, 532
Mezzacappa, E., 509, 524, 527, 533
Mezzich, A. C., 192
Mian, N. D., 199
Michael, K., 50
Michaud, D., 372
Michel, A., 322
Michel, M. K., 448
Mick, E., 563
Midei, A. J., 587
Miers, A., 135, 136
Mihalopoulos, C., 617
Miklósi, Á., 254
Miller, A. H., 684
Miller, C. J., 321, 388, 389, 568, 590
Miller, D. J., 567
Miller, E. K., 353, 354, 357
Miller, G., 274
Miller, G. M., 260, 265, 266
Miller, J. D., 566, 567
Miller, L. J., 648
Miller, M. W., 303
Miller, P. H., 629
Miller, S. M., 280
Miller, S. R., 568
Miller-Lewis, L. R., 527
Mills-Koonce, W. R., 241
Milnamow, M., 195
Milne, A. B., 128
Milner, C. E., 235
Milovchevich, D., 131
Milstin, J., 76
Mindell, J., 525
Mineka, S., 450, 489
Minelli, A., 327
Mischel, W., 150, 175, 502, 632, 633, 638, 686
Miskovic, V., 74, 76, 77, 232, 234
Missale, C., 321
Mitchell, J. T., 115, 116
Mitsuyasu, H., 323

Mittelman, M., 90, 196
Miyake, A., 678
Mize, J., 239, 240
Mletzko T., 684
Moadab, I., 566
Mobbs, D., 131
Mobley, C. E., 450
Mock, D., 610
Moerk, K., 523
Moerk, K. C., 548
Moffitt, T. E., 14, 42, 129, 263, 283, 352, 376, 412, 490, 504, 520, 548, 551, 564, 566, 569, 596, 628, 636, 685, 686, 687, 689
Mogaji, A., 466
Molden, D. C., 509
Moles, A., 265, 387
Molina, B. S. G., 524
Moller, H. J., 131
Molto, J., 53
Monachesi, E. D., 633
Mongrain, M., 547
Monk, C., 309
Monk, C. S., 349, 350, 358, 360
Monohan, K., 533
Montag, C., 131, 327
Montague, P. R., 351
Moolchan, E. T., 301
Moore, C., 485
Moore, G., 233, 241, 242, 303
Moore, G. A., 426
Moore, T. J., 694
Moretti, M., 134
Morey, L. C., 546
Morgan, B. E., 130
Morgan, P. L., 610
Morin, A. J. S., 553
Morison, P., 465
Morley-Fletcher, S., 309, 351
Morrell, J., 413, 525
Morrell, M. J., 353
Morrill, A., 137
Morris, A., 524, 530
Morris, A. S., 147
Morris, J. G., 613
Morris, J. S., 158, 353
Morris, P., 519
Morris, P. A., 463, 464
Morris, S., 522
Morrison, S. E., 79
Morrone-Strupinsky, J., 108, 112, 113, 286, 368, 380, 381, 383, 386, 391
Morrow, M. T., 134
Mortensen, E. L., 649
Moseley, M., 89
Moses, L. J., 157, 468
Mosk, J., 473
Moskal, J., 277, 278
Moskowitz, D. S., 126, 131
Mosley, M., 117
Moss, H., 135
Mostofsky, E., 589
Mott, J. A., 529
Motti, F., 450
Moukheiber, A., 74
Mousavi, M., 303

Mpofu, E., 466
Mrazek, D. A., 30, 319
Mrazek, P., 610
Mroczek, D. K., 588, 592, 596
Muehlenkamp, J., 489
Mulder, E. J., 297, 301, 304, 305
Mulder, R. T., 694
Mullen, M., 31
Mulligan, K., 586
Mullin, B. C., 452
Mullineaux, P. Y., 127, 128, 130, 131, 199, 317, 319, 320
Mullola, S., 193
Munafo, M. R., 352, 383, 419
Munis, P., 630
Munro, S., 161, 637
Muris, P., 28, 114, 188, 193, 195, 526, 527
Murphy, A. Z., 261, 281
Murphy, B., 452, 454
Murphy, B. C., 451
Murphy, D. L., 321, 377
Murray, C., 610
Murray, K., 148, 191, 214, 526, 527
Murray, K. T., 15, 145, 149, 213, 214, 282, 432, 450, 473
Murray, L., 413, 523, 684
Murray, N., 129
Murray, R., 548
Murray, R. M., 547
Murtaugh, T. T., 50
Must, A., 585
Mustillo, S., 490
Muzek, J., 676
Myamlin, V. V., 45
Myers, G., 521
Myers, J. M., 71, 549
Myers, S., 530
Myowa-Yamakoshi, M., 171
Myrtek, M., 45

Nachmias, M., 409, 500, 651
Nader, M., 373
Naerde, A., 189, 196, 197
Nagin, D. S., 567
Nagle, R. J., 193, 631
Najman, J. M., 572
Nakamura, Y., 327
Nam, J. Y., 377
Namkoong, K., 131
Nandy, A. S., 130
Nappi, C., 299
Naragon-Gainey, K., 75, 546, 547, 549
Nassau, J. H., 585
Nater, U. M., 239
Nation, J., 522
Naumann, L. P., 503, 581
Navarro, M., 303
Neale, M. C., 71, 172, 174, 333, 546, 549
Neave, N., 51
Nebylitsyn, V. D., 6
Nederkoorn, C., 587
Needham, J., 5
Neiderhiser, J. M., 317, 334, 426
Neiss, M. B., 333, 591
Neisser, U., 627, 634

Nelson, B., 159
Nelson, C., 214
Nelson, C. A., 156, 368, 533
Nelson, E. E., 73, 376
Nelson, K., 510, 511
Nelson, R. J., 79
Nemanov, L., 173
Nemeroff, C. B., 298, 373, 552, 684
Nemeroff, S., 374
Neppl, T. K., 505, 506
Nesin, A. E., 132
Nesselroade, J. R., 192, 329
Nestler, E., 379
Netter, P., 51, 390
Nettle, D., 274, 502, 589
Neumann, I. D., 260, 263, 264
Neville, H., 160, 609, 638, 639
Newberry, B. H., 7, 95
Newcomer, J. W., 238
Newcorn, J. H., 568
Newman, D. L., 42, 548, 551, 566, 687
Newman, J. L., 131
Newman, J. P., 278
Newman, J. R., 274, 678
Newman, T. K., 261, 263, 264, 265, 266, 267
Newport, J. D., 684
Neyer, F. J., 426
Nias, D. K. B., 172
Niaura, R. S., 126
Niccols, A., 193
Nichols, K. E., 505, 542
Nichols, T. R., 135
Nicolaidou, P., 586
Nie, Z., 373
Niegel, S., 588
Nieto, F. J., 135
Nigg, J. T., 108, 115, 487, 489, 490, 525, 526, 562, 563, 564, 567, 569, 594
Nikolas, M., 569
Nishida, T., 609
Nix, R. L., 637
Nixon, R. D. V., 573
Noble, E. P., 323, 325
Nock, M. K., 563
Noftle, E. E., 633
Nolan, S. A., 552
Nolen-Hoeksema, S., 547
Noll, D. C., 351
Nordberg, A., 303
Norman, W. T., 46
Normandeau, S., 159
Norris, K., 466
Northam, E., 192
Northcut, T., 136
Nosanchuk, T. A., 488
Novaco, R. W., 124, 134
Novosad, C., 525
Nowak, M. A., 168, 171
Noyes, R., 549
Nugent, J. K., 215
Nugent, K., 71, 125
Nugier, A., 133
Nunez, P. L., 234
Nunnally, J. C., 184, 199

Nurmi, J.-E., 508
Nusslock, R., 116, 118
Nutley, S. B., 160
Nyman, E. S., 323, 325
Nyman, M., 157, 452
Nystrom, L. E., 153, 351, 382

Oakes, T. R., 73, 373
Oakland, T., 466
Oberklaid, F., 86, 107, 147, 186, 192, 448, 451, 467, 529, 551
Oberlander, T. F., 684
Obradovic, J., 410, 436, 520
O'Brien, W. H., 233
Ochsner, K. N., 129, 153, 353, 354, 357
O'Connell, S. M., 171
O'Connor, E., 615
O'Connor, E. E., 613
O'Connor, L. E., 169
O'Connor, T., 525
O'Connor, T. G., 301, 302, 309, 407, 487
O'Day, D. H., 386
Oddo, S., 77
Oddy, W. H., 587
Odludas, Y., 153
O'Doherty, J., 383
O'Donnell, K., 590, 591
Oetting, E., 135
Oettingen, G., 638
Offord, K. P., 593
Ogan, A. T., 639
O'Gorman, J. G., 44
O'Gorman, T., 549
Ogunseitan, O., 132
Oh, S., 468
Oh, W., 447
O'Hearn, K., 353
Okazaki, S., 466
Oki, H., 254
Okkenhaug, J. J., 74
Okuyama, Y., 323
Olafsen, K., 521
Olatunji, B. O., 549
Olausson, H., 386
Oldehinkel, A. J., 114, 157, 450, 523, 530, 544, 546, 547, 553, 554
O'Leary, K. D., 136
Olejnik, S., 89
Oler, J., 373
Olesen, P. J., 160
Olino, T., 523
Olino, T. M., 73, 110, 114, 216, 217, 505, 509, 532, 541, 548, 554
Oliver, P., 529
Oliver, P. H., 15, 529, 570, 633, 685
Olmstead, M. C., 260, 265
Olsen, J. A., 425
Olsen, L., 266
Olsen, S. F., 173, 462
Olson, B. D., 453, 497, 510
Olson, S., 563
Olson, S. L., 10, 149, 157, 427, 473, 526, 527, 530
Olsson, C. A., 376, 377
Oltmanns, T. F., 564
Olweus, D., 134, 447, 449

Onaga, E., 89
O'Neil, K., 110, 446, 471
Ones, D. S., 630
Ong, A. D., 589, 590
Oniszczenko, W., 86, 94, 95, 96, 192, 323, 324
Ono, Y., 323
Oosterlaan, J., 473, 587
Orendi, J. L., 354, 355
Orf, L. A., 283
Orlebeke, J. F., 50
Orlick, T., 462
Ormel, J., 114, 157, 450, 523, 526, 530, 544, 545, 546, 547, 553, 554, 636
Ortega, A. N., 585
Orth, U., 135
Ortiz, J., 288
Osborne, M. L., 195
Osgood, M., 168
Ostendorf, F., 22
Osterweil, Z., 282
Ostrov, J. M., 564
Oswald, L., 384
Ott, U., 356
Otterbeck, L., 547
Ottinger, D. R., 300
Otto, M. W., 550
Ouagazzal, A. M., 260
Overall, K. L., 254, 257, 260
Owen, M. J., 132, 321
Owens, E. B., 427, 429
Owens, M. J., 552
Oxford, M. L., 481, 483, 484

Paciello, M., 134
Padich, R., 522
Padmanabhan, A., 353
Page, A. C., 98
Pagnoni, G., 351
Pagura, J., 549, 550
Palermo, M., 192
Palisin, H., 194
Palmero, F., 136
Pals, J. L., 497, 498, 499, 503, 507, 510
Paluck, E. L., 483
Pandiella, N. M., 301
Paneth, N., 308
Panfile, T. M., 173, 448
Pang, G., 266
Panksepp, J., 8, 171, 261, 277, 278, 280, 281, 286, 388, 389, 639
Pannozzo, G. M., 632
Papadimitriou, A., 586
Papp, L. M., 12
Parade, S. H., 185
Pardo, S. T., 426
Pare, D., 373
Parent, C., 309
Park, I. J. K., 472, 473
Park, K. A., 450
Park, S. Y., 110
Parke, R. D., 279
Parker, E. H., 128
Parker, G., 189, 197
Parker, G. R., 526

Parker, J., 448, 522
Parker, J. D. A., 115, 116
Parker, J. G., 442
Parker, K., 533
Parker, S. W., 239
Parritz, R. H., 409, 500, 524, 651
Partington, J., 462
Pascoe, J., 169
Paskaukas, A. R., 692
Passolunghi, M. C., 159
Pasterski, V. L., 279, 487
Pasupathi, M., 510
Paterson, A. D., 384
Paterson, G., 449
Paton, J. J., 79
Patrick, C. J., 563, 568, 572, 588
Patterson, C. J., 638
Patterson, G. R., 437
Pauli-Pott, U., 200, 336, 430, 431
Paulussen-Hoogeboom, M. C., 427, 428, 429, 448, 449
Pauly, J. R., 301
Pauly, T. H., 301
Paunonen, S. V., 208, 453
Paus, T., 368, 393
Pavlov, I., 44, 695
Payne, A., 443
Pearlson, G. D., 355
Pears, K., 526
Pearson, D., 522
Pearson, E., 232
Peck, S., 520
Pecke, L., 615
Pedersen, N. L., 547, 551, 591
Pedersen, S., 447
Pedersen, W. C., 130
Pedlow, R., 107, 147, 448, 529
Peeke, L., 129
Peetsma, T. T. D., 427, 429, 448
Peirson, A. R., 321
Pek, J., 591
Pelco, L. E., 622
Peled, M., 134
Peleg, Y., 468
Pelham, W. E., 563
Pellegrini, A. D., 449
Pellegrini, D., 465
Pellowski, M. W., 191
Pendry, P., 239
Penke, L., 274
Pennebaker, J. W., 591
Penner, L. A., 168, 173
Penney, S. J., 109
Pentz, M. A., 637
Peraza, D. M., 153
Perese, S., 488
Pérez-Edgar, K., 236, 349, 350, 352, 353, 357, 360, 361, 444, 501, 552
Pergamin, L., 552
Perine, J., 136
Perkins, A. M., 370
Perlis, R., 135
Perlis, R. H., 694
Perlstein, W. M., 50
Perren, S., 447
Perrett, D. I., 158, 353

Perrin, S., 615
Perry, D. G., 447
Perry, L. C., 447
Pesonen, A., 521, 522
Peters, D. A., 298
Peters, R., 238
Petersen, I. T., 12, 132, 378, 425, 498, 521, 570, 675
Petersen, S. E., 147, 152
Peters-Martin, P., 215
Peterson, B. S., 280
Peterson, C., 287, 593
Peterson, E., 31, 73, 211, 608
Petraglia, F., 299
Petrill, S. A., 127, 134, 199, 317, 319, 320, 332
Petrovic, P., 131
Pettit, G. S., 126, 412, 426, 427, 430, 433, 434, 435, 436, 437, 452
Pezawas, L., 357, 375, 376
Pfaff, D. W., 280
Pfeifer, M., 108, 110, 217, 278
Phan, K. L., 224, 694
Phan, L., 134
Philibert, R., 412
Philibert, R. A., 154, 336, 499
Philips, K., 318, 319
Phillips, B. M., 116, 509, 524
Phillips, D., 527
Phillips, D. A., 161
Phillips, K., 319, 522
Phillips, L., 76
Phillips, L. H., 128, 129
Phillips, M. L., 224
Phillips, N., 281
Piaget, J., 443
Pianta, R. C., 159, 609, 636, 638
Piatigorsky, A., 71
Piazza, P. V., 50
Piccinin, A. M., 596
Pickering, A. D., 53, 503
Pickett, W., 586
Pidada, S., 452, 470, 473
Pierce, S., 238
Pierre, J. S., 254
Pijlman, F. T. A., 14, 417, 573
Pike, A., 320, 449, 452
Piliavin, J. A., 169
Pilkenton-Taylor, C., 508
Pillemer, K., 426
Pine, D., 135
Pine, D. S., 126, 357, 587
Pinuelas, A., 157, 452
Piquero, A., 52
Pitzer, M., 566
Plant, E. A., 488
Player, M. S., 592
Plikuhn, M., 426
Plomin, R., 21, 25, 26, 29, 32, 41, 42, 84, 85, 86, 90, 91, 95, 105, 125, 170, 172, 173, 174, 187, 189, 193, 194, 196, 229, 230, 251, 316, 317, 318, 320, 321, 329, 330, 334, 335, 431, 442, 452, 480, 482, 525, 529, 569, 584, 673, 674, 676, 682
Plotsky, P. M., 309, 374, 522, 552

Plude, D. J., 232
Pluess, M., 324, 336, 415, 419, 434, 529, 646, 650, 652
Plumert, J. M., 584, 585, 587
Polak-Toste, C. P., 71, 109, 112, 113, 217
Pollack, J. M., 633
Pollack, M. H., 550
Pollak, S. D., 223
Pollitt, E., 522
Pomerantz, E. M., 507
Pomerleau, A., 467
Ponitz, C. C., 631
Popovac, D., 522
Popp, T. K., 428, 431
Porges, S. W., 231, 232, 233
Poropat, A. E., 631, 632
Porrino, L., 373
Portales, A. L., 232
Porter, C. L., 467
Posner, J., 280, 288
Posner, M. I., 3, 14, 15, 16, 17, 27, 41, 84, 113, 126, 128, 129, 147, 148, 149, 151, 152, 153, 154, 155, 156, 157, 161, 210, 214, 236, 282, 332, 336, 347, 352, 353, 356, 360, 409, 451, 499, 506, 573, 595, 608, 629, 638, 679, 680
Posthuma, D., 76
Potegal, M., 130, 131
Potempa, G., 303
Potter, J., 286, 504, 628
Pottig, M., 264
Poulin, R., 444
Pourtois, G., 130
Power, C., 585, 587, 596
Prakash, K., 110, 446, 471
Prescott, A., 23, 148, 216, 318
Prescott, C. A., 549, 553
Presley, R., 24, 107, 192
Pressman, S. D., 589
Preston, S. D., 175
Pretorius, J., 466
Priftis, K. N., 586
Prinzie, P., 435, 490
Prior, M., 86, 107, 147, 186, 192, 448, 451, 467, 526, 527, 528, 529, 530, 551
Pritchard, W. S., 50
Prom-Wormley, E. C., 573
Propper, C., 233, 241, 426
Prudhomme-White, B., 237
Pruessner, J., 384
Przybeck, T. R., 56, 95, 194, 196
Puglisi-Allegra, S., 259
Pulkki-Råback, L., 587
Pullis, M. E., 187, 191, 450
Pulver, U., 687
Purper-Ouakil, D., 332
Puskar, K. R., 136
Putnam, S. P., 10, 14, 16, 27, 28, 86, 105, 107, 108, 109, 110, 111, 112, 114, 115, 116, 125, 127, 128, 129, 146, 173, 186, 191, 257, 278, 450, 677, 678
Puttonen, S., 587

Qi, L., 648
Qiang, M., 303
Quay, H. C., 114, 288
Quilty, L. C., 541, 555
Quinkert, A. W., 280, 284
Quinn, J. P., 266
Quinn, M., 620
Quinn, P. D., 633
Quinsey, V. L., 134, 663
Quinton, D., 529

Rabinovitz, B., 193
Radke-Yarrow, M., 132
Radmore, N., 169
Radomska, A., 86, 94
Raes, F., 509, 532, 552, 680
Raggatt, P., 511
Rahill, S., 619
Raichle, K. A., 592
Raichle, M. E., 152
Räikkönen, K., 521, 522, 590, 592
Raine, A., 52, 125, 288, 317, 563, 566, 567, 685
Raitakari, O. T., 587
Rajkowski, J., 373
Rakison, D. H., 487
Ramchandani, P., 522
Rammsayer, T. H., 44, 45
Ramos, M. C., 529, 570
Ramsay, D. S., 111
Ramsay, L., 450
Ramsden, S. R., 128
Ramsey, F., 522
Randall, B. A., 170
Rapee, R., 448, 615, 616, 691
Rapee, R. M., 545, 550, 555, 615, 616, 617
Rasmussen, H. B., 266
Ratey, J., 657
Rauch, S. L., 78, 236, 349
Ravaja, N., 584, 587
Ravelli, A., 547
Raver, C. C., 158, 451, 637
Raviv, A., 171
Rawitch, A. B., 303
Ray, L. A., 266
Raz, A., 214, 353
Razza, R. P., 159, 629, 630
Rea, M., 309
Reader, S. M., 257
Réale, D., 257, 274, 275, 278
Realo, A., 483
Rebert, C. S., 299
Rebollo, I., 130
Records, K., 522
Redmond, D. E., Jr., 57
Reeb, B. C., 349
Reeb-Sutherland, B. C., 350, 357
Reed, M., 150
Reed, M. A., 508
Reed-Victor, E., 622
Reese, E., 511
Reeves, D., 22, 192, 199
Reich, D. B., 567
Reich, J., 549
Reichel, M., 427

Reid, J. B., 437
Reid, M., 620
Reilly, H. H., 318
Reilly, J., 23, 148, 216, 407
Reiner, I., 323
Reis, D. J., 349
Reise, S. P., 222
Reiser, M., 132, 448, 449, 631, 636
Reisner, I. R., 261
Reiss, D., 26, 317, 426, 596
Reiss, S., 549
Reist, C., 261
Rende, R., 529
Rennie, C. E., 567
Renshaw, P. D., 442
Rentfrow, P. J., 596
Renthal, D., 379
Rescorla, L. A., 199
Resnick, J. S., 251, 615
Resnick, S., 651
Rettew, D. C., 196
Reuter, M., 131, 327, 356, 390
Reynolds, C., 566, 610
Reynolds, C. A., 134, 592
Reynolds, C. R., 88
Reynolds, P. C., 633
Reynolds, R., 567
Reynolds, S. M., 361
Reznick, J., 608
Reznick, J. S., 25, 31, 32, 69, 71, 73, 105, 193, 231, 279, 319, 348, 446
Rhee, S. H., 170, 332, 333
Rhoades, K. A., 428
Riad, J. F., 52
Ribi, K., 584
Ricciuti, A. E., 407
Rice, F., 307, 308, 309
Rice, M., 522
Richard, J., 446
Richards, J. E., 232
Richards, M. H., 442
Richardson, L. P., 586
Richard-Yris, M., 254
Rickman, M., 108, 217, 278
Ricon, T., 350
Ridd, M. J., 46
Ridge, B., 436
Rieffe, C., 135
Riemann, R., 91, 95, 192
Riese, M. L., 215, 330
Rieser-Danner, L. A., 22, 185, 213, 219
Rietveld, M. J. H., 332
Riggs, N. R., 637
Rihmer, A., 694
Rihmer, Z., 694
Rijsdijk, F., 172, 318, 525
Riksen-Walraven, J. M., 30
Riley, E. P., 303
Riley, W. T., 135
Rimm, E., 136
Rimm-Kaufman, S. E., 73, 446, 447, 609, 636
Riordan, K., 651
Riordan, L., 184
Risch, N., 419
Rjimen, F., 126
Roalson, L. A., 527

Robbins, T., 389
Robbins, T. W., 382, 388, 417
Roberts, A. C., 388
Roberts, B. W., 128, 129, 209, 369, 490, 503, 508, 511, 544, 588, 591, 595, 628, 630, 681
Roberts, J. E., 552
Roberts, J. M., 453
Roberts, N., 133
Robins, R. W., 283, 504, 508, 511, 566, 628, 633
Robinson, C., 173
Robinson, C. C., 462
Robinson, J., 169, 170, 175
Robinson, J. L., 73, 215, 218, 319, 678
Robinson, M., 130
Robinson, M. D., 126, 129
Robinson, M. L., 301
Robinson, S. W., 321
Robles, J., 550
Rodaros, D., 371
Rodriguez, E. T., 609, 613, 620, 622, 691
Rodriguez, M., 298
Rodriguez, M. L., 632, 633
Rodriguez-Bailon, R., 151
Roed, I. S., 51
Roesch, L., 489
Roesch, S. C., 170
Roff, D., 276
Rogers, H., 87, 317
Rogers, R. D., 649
Rogoff, B., 463
Rohde, P., 547, 556
Rohleder, N., 239
Roiser, J. P., 649
Roisman, G. I., 317, 407
Roitfarb, M., 200
Roitman, M. F., 384
Rolland, J., 546
Rolls, E., 383
Romano, L. J., 134
Romero, E., 508
Romero, G., 522
Romero, T., 171
Romero-Canyas, R., 126
Ronald, A., 170
Ronquillo, J., 130
Rorsman, B., 547
Rose, S., 523
Rose, S. A., 548
Rose-Krasnor, L., 447
Rosen, H., 299
Rosen, J. B., 238
Rosen, L. A., 563
Rosenbaum, J., 639
Rosenbaum, J. F., 548, 550
Rosenberg, A., 77
Rosenberg, D. R., 356
Rosenberg, L. T., 238
Rosenfield, S., 490
Rosenman, R., 136
Rosenstock, E. G., 73
Rosenthal, B. S., 529
Rosenthal, R., 679
Rosmalen, J., 545
Ross, D., 125

Ross, S. A., 125
Rosvold, H. E., 153
Roth, T., 386
Rothbart, M., 234, 521, 525, 526, 527
Rothbart, M. K., 3, 4, 6, 7, 9, 10, 11, 12, 13, 14, 15, 16, 21, 22, 23, 26, 27, 28, 29, 30, 36, 41, 42, 71, 84, 85, 86, 87, 93, 100, 105, 107, 108, 109, 110, 111, 113, 114, 115, 117, 125, 126, 127, 128, 129, 130, 132, 145, 146, 147, 148, 149, 150, 151, 152, 153, 154, 155, 156, 157, 159, 160, 161, 173, 183, 184, 185, 186, 188, 189, 190, 191, 193, 194, 195, 196, 198, 199, 210, 211, 213, 215, 216, 218, 223, 224, 229, 230, 236, 240, 251, 273, 278, 279, 280, 281, 282, 283, 284, 286, 287, 288, 332, 336, 347, 348, 352, 353, 356, 357, 360, 361, 388, 391, 405, 409, 425, 426, 427, 428, 433, 442, 444, 445, 448, 450, 451, 454, 466, 467, 480, 482, 483, 491, 498, 499, 501, 502, 503, 504, 506, 542, 544, 554, 569, 573, 581, 586, 589, 591, 593, 594, 595, 608, 627, 628, 629, 638, 651, 652, 655, 656, 673, 674, 675, 676, 678, 679, 680, 688, 696
Rothbaum, F., 433
Rothberg, S. T., 594
Roth-Hanania, R., 171
Rothman, L., 619
Rothstein-Fisch, C., 463
Rottenberg, J., 197
Rouillon, F., 546
Roulin, A., 77
Rovine, M., 408
Rowan, K., 427
Rowden, L., 552
Rowe, D., 452
Rowe, D. C., 86, 187, 193, 194, 673
Rowe, R., 567, 587
Roy, B., 590
Roysamb, E., 196
Rozanov, V., 131
Rubia, K., 353, 355
Rubin, K., 234, 661
Rubin, K. H., 69, 70, 73, 77, 110, 115, 234, 278, 348, 428, 431, 435, 442, 443, 445, 446, 447, 448, 449, 450, 452, 454, 465, 467, 470, 471, 472, 491, 551, 552, 553
Rubinstein, Y., 633
Rubio, P., 303
Ruch, W., 58, 190
Rudasill, K. M., 117, 199, 609, 636, 638
Rudolph, K. D., 448, 450, 509
Rueda, M. R., 10, 12, 14, 15, 128, 129, 145, 146, 147, 148, 149, 151, 152, 153, 156, 158, 159, 160, 173, 214, 257, 282, 325, 348, 352, 353, 355, 388, 391, 451, 506, 573, 594, 627, 628, 629, 638, 677, 679, 680, 691, 692
Ruf, H. T., 223, 230
Ruff, H. A., 154
Ruiz, J. M., 135, 592

Rujescu, D., 131, 390
Rusalov, V. M., 7
Rushton, J. P., 170, 172, 277, 283
Russell, A., 173, 462
Russell, J. A., 280, 288
Russell, V. A., 259
Rusting, C. L., 552
Rutherford, E., 350
Rutherford, R., 620
Rutter, M., 9, 520, 529
Ruys, K., 125
Ryan, A. M., 512
Rydell, A., 109, 111, 115
Rydell, A. M., 449
Rymeski, B. A., 261

Sabatier, C., 467
Sabbagh, M. A., 468
Sabol, S. Z., 264
Saccomanno, L., 153, 573, 638
Sachek, J., 108, 490, 563
Sachser, N., 298
Sackett, G. P., 299
Sackett, P. R., 630
Saco-Pollitt, C., 522
Sadahiro, R., 329
Sadker, D., 491
Sadker, M., 491
Sadovsky, A., 15, 608, 628
Saetre, P., 73, 254
Sagi, A., 171
Sahakian, B. J., 649
Sahuque, L., 373
Sailor, W., 610
Saini, M. A., 136
Saiz, P. A., 324, 325, 327
Sakai, J. T., 573
Sales, J. M., 510
Sallinen, B., 533
Salloum, A., 622
Salmon, K., 570
Salo, J., 326
Saltz, E., 639
Saltzman, H., 508
Salzman, C. D., 79
Sameroff, A. J., 10, 157, 200, 215, 219, 409, 425, 426, 468, 469, 473, 503, 520, 526, 651
Samochowiec, J., 46, 265, 324, 325, 326, 328
Sanchez, M. M., 374
Sander, D., 130, 133
Sanders, L., 160, 638
Sanders, M. J., 265
Sandler, I. N., 115, 433, 509, 524, 554, 585
Sandman, C. A., 368
Sandy, J. M., 528
Sanford, C. P., 135
Sanson, A. V., 86, 107, 147, 158, 186, 192, 443, 448, 449, 451, 452, 454, 467, 529, 551, 611
Santesso, D. L., 158, 235, 356
Santor, D. A., 547
Santucci, A. K., 231
Sapolsky, R., 378, 379
Sapolsky, R. M., 264, 299

Sarafino, E. P., 191
Sarinopolous, I., 74
Sarkar, P., 301, 309, 487
Sasagaw, S., 564
Saucier, G., 287, 289
Saudino, K. J., 14, 15, 16, 26, 83, 87, 98, 130, 131, 170, 172, 213, 219, 235, 261, 305, 306, 315, 317, 318, 319, 320, 321, 330, 331, 332, 334, 335, 352, 407, 426, 431, 433, 503, 521, 544, 682, 683, 688
Saulsman, L. M., 98
Savage, D. D., 303
Savaki, H. E., 153
Sawalani, G. M., 563
Sawyer, M. G., 585
Saxton, P. M., 50
Scafidi, F., 194
Scanlon, M. B., 282
Scaramella, L. V., 505
Scarr, S., 330, 486
Scerif, G., 159
Schachar, R. J., 214
Schatschneider, C., 566
Schaughency, E. A., 88, 191, 454
Scheier, L. M., 188, 195
Scheier, M., 593
Scheier, M. F., 549, 590
Schellinger, K., 637
Schellinger, K. B., 609
Scher, A., 525
Scherag, S., 333
Scherer, K., 126
Schermerhorn, A. C., 12, 132, 378, 425, 426, 498, 521, 570, 675
Schiff, N. D., 280
Schiller, M., 651
Schillera, M., 200
Schilling, E. A., 593
Schilling, E. M., 149
Schinka, J. A., 49, 352
Schjerlderup-Ebbe, T., 255
Schjolden, J., 649
Schlotz, W., 527
Schmader, T., 661
Schmauss, C., 321
Schmidt, F. L., 546
Schmidt, K. L., 468
Schmidt, L., 76
Schmidt, L. A., 70, 110, 158, 232, 234, 235, 236, 238, 278, 324, 348, 356, 446, 450, 452
Schmidt, M. H., 308, 566
Schmidt, N. B., 550, 681
Schmidt, N. L., 223, 230
Schmidtke, J., 266
Schmitt, D. P., 282, 483, 484, 485, 487, 489
Schmitz, S., 317, 332, 333, 568
Schneider, B. H., 73, 446, 447, 448, 462, 465, 490, 691
Schneider, M. L., 263, 298, 299
Schneider, R. H., 136
Schneider, S. M. R., 277
Schneider, T., 303
Schneirla, T. C., 41
Schniering, C. A., 550, 615

Schoen, M. J., 193, 631
Schoff, K., 527
Schoppe, S. J., 219
Schore, A. N., 426
Schork, E., 450
Schork, N. J., 376
Schosser, A., 325, 326, 327
Schott, B. H., 351, 382
Schreiber, J. E., 680
Schrepferman, L., 570
Schuengel, C., 406
Schulkin, J., 238
Schultz, D., 451, 509, 619
Schultz, W., 351, 382
Schulz, R., 593
Schutte, N. S., 98
Schutter, D. J. L. G., 130
Schwandt, M. L., 256, 260, 261, 263, 265, 266, 267
Schwartz, C. E., 31, 77, 78, 236, 237, 349, 471, 687
Schwartz, D., 133
Schwartz, J. E., 594
Schwartz, S., 130
Schwartz, S. J., 510
Schwebel, D. C., 584, 585, 587
Scott, B., 280
Scourfield, J., 172
Sebanc, A. M., 115, 239, 452
Sechrist, J., 426
Seckl, J. R., 299
Sedikides, C., 333, 591
Seeley, J., 454
Seeley, J. R., 547
Segal, C., 640
Segal, N. L., 56
Segalowitz, S. J., 158, 353, 355, 356
Segerstrom, S. C., 590
Seghier, M., 130
Seidler, F. J., 303
Seidlitz, L., 485
Seifer, R., 200, 219, 300, 485, 520, 651
Seiffge-Krenke, E., 508
Seiger, A., 303
Sekino, Y., 451
Seligman, M. E. P., 593, 630, 632
Sell, A. 275
Sellers, E. M., 308
Senior, C., 224
Sergeant, J. A., 473
Seroczynski, A., 130, 615
Serpell, J. A., 254
Servatius, R., 373
Seto, M. C., 663
Settle, J. E., 416
Sever, I., 462
Sewell, J., 86, 186
Sexton, K. A., 74
Seymour, B., 350, 351
Shadish, W., 622
Shammah-Lagnado, S., 371
Shannon, C., 257, 263, 266
Shannon, D., 184
Shao, L., 286
Shapiro, J., 134
Shapka, J., 132
Shaver, P. R., 408, 509

Shaw, D. S., 427, 449, 451, 452, 567, 570
Shaw, P., 567
Shaywitz, S., 610
Shea, A. K., 303
Shea, M. T., 546, 547
Shechter, M., 134
Sheeber, L. B., 191
Sheese, B. E., 9, 14, 113, 147, 153, 154, 155, 168, 223, 230, 323, 324, 325, 326, 328, 332, 336, 352, 353, 356, 360, 409, 451, 499, 506, 573, 608, 629
Sheffield Morris, A., 564
Shekhar, A., 374
Sheldon, W. H., 6, 673, 675, 680
Shelton, S. E., 73, 256, 257, 371, 373
Shen, L., 192
Shen, P.-S., 89
Shepard, S. A., 491
Sher, K. J., 549, 554
Sherman, D. K., 569
Sherman, J. W., 685
Sherman, L. J., 414
Shi, C., 371
Shia, S., 648
Shibuya, N., 329
Shih, J. C., 46
Shimizu, E., 328
Shin, L. M., 78, 236, 349
Shin, R., 383
Shinar, O., 528
Shiner, R. L., 3, 9, 22, 108, 117, 125, 209, 229, 332, 334, 369, 405, 453, 480, 497, 498, 500, 503, 504, 505, 506, 507, 512, 521, 523, 542, 544, 581, 584, 586, 591, 593, 630, 673, 675, 678, 681, 684, 688
Shinwell, E., 323, 324
Shiota, M. N., 112, 678
Shipley, B. A., 591
Shipman, K. L., 132
Shiptley, M., 373
Shiraishi, H., 326
Shirley, M., 8, 673
Shirtcliff, E. A., 490
Shmelyov, A. G., 505
Shoda, Y., 175, 502, 632, 633
Showers, C. J., 489
Shrestha, S., 469
Shrout, P., 522
Shulkin, J., 234
Shumsky, J. S., 153
Siegel, J., 50
Siegman, A. W., 126, 136
Siever, L., 388, 389, 391
Sigelman, J., 130, 287
Sigman, M., 473
Sigvardsson, S., 566, 567
Sih, A., 649
Silberg, J. L., 306, 317
Silk, K. R., 567
Silva, P., 548, 687
Silva, P. A., 42, 72, 127, 551, 566, 681
Silva de Lima, M., 615
Silverthorn, P., 567, 571
Siman-Tov, I., 175

Simmons, J. E., 300
Simms, L., 527
Simms, L. J., 199
Simon, G. E., 694
Simon, H., 50
Simon, T., 629
Simonds, J., 146, 147, 151, 157, 353
Simons, R. F., 50, 357
Simpson, A. E., 491
Simpson, D. B., 131
Simpson, J. A., 404
Singer, D. G., 639
Singer, J. L., 639
Singer, T., 169, 171, 172, 175, 351
Singh, A. L., 568
Singh, D., 274
Sirota, A. D., 126
Sisk, C. L., 489
Sisson, D. G., 50
Sjoberg, R. L., 265
Skarpness, L. R., 450, 451, 452
Skinner, B. F., 675
Skinner, E. A., 508
Skinner, M., 191
Skodol, A. E., 490
Skoner, D. P., 591
Skre, I., 74
Slattery, M. J., 73
Slavin, R., 609
Slikker, W., Jr., 303
Slining, M. M., 584
Slobodskaya, H. R., 45, 466, 468
Slotkin, T. A., 303
Slowiaczek, L., 118
Sluyter, F., 131
Smart, D., 158, 443, 451, 551
Smart, D. F., 107, 147, 448
Smider, N. A., 30, 184, 490, 566
Smillie, L. D., 53, 54
Smit, D. J. A., 76
Smit, F., 547
Smith, A. B., 353
Smith, B. D., 50
Smith, C. L., 15, 428, 448, 608, 628, 680
Smith, C. M., 449
Smith, G. D., 305
Smith, H., 373
Smith, J., 526, 528, 529
Smith, K., 675, 684
Smith, M. J., 254
Smith, P. K., 279
Smith, R., 526, 528, 529
Smith, T., 490
Smith, T. W., 126, 135, 136, 592, 593
Smolewska, K. A., 280, 281, 652
Smoller, J. W., 263, 328
Smorvik, D., 585
Snarr, J., 233, 569
Snidman, N., 25, 31, 70, 71, 73, 76, 105, 184, 211, 230, 231, 251, 279, 348, 471, 542, 608, 615, 681
Snidman, S., 446
Snieder, H., 131
Snow, D. L., 613, 691
Snowdon, D. A., 117, 589
Snyder, C. R., 589

Snyder, J., 132, 570
Snyder, K., 156
So, K., 525
Sobolewski, A., 524
Soeby, K., 266
Sokoloff, L., 153
Sokolowski, M., 131
Sol, D., 257
Solomon, B., 109
Solomon, E., 126
Solomon, R. M., 136
Somerville, L., 349, 351, 370, 371, 372, 373, 388
Sommer, T., 153, 214, 356
Sonuga-Barke, E. J. S., 563
Soong, W., 466, 521
Sora, I., 387
Sorenson, A. M., 132
Sorenson, E. R., 12
Soto, C. J., 503, 504, 581, 628
Soubhi, H., 587
Soubrie, P., 51
South, S., 335
South, S. C., 112, 336, 572
Southwick, S. M., 264
Souza, G. G., 76
Spangler, G., 323
Sparks, J. A., 301
Spearman, C., 629
Specht, K., 72
Spector, P. E., 133
Spence, S. H., 187, 193, 447, 449
Spencer, S. J., 648
Spiegel, L. L., 261, 281
Spielberger, C. D., 126
Spilman, S. K., 505
Spinath, F. M., 26, 91
Spinelli, S., 263, 266
Spinrad, T., 15, 169, 628
Spinrad, T. C., 450, 451, 527
Spinrad, T. L., 214, 223, 239, 428, 564, 608, 680
Spiro, A., 192, 588, 592
Spitzer, M., 350, 382
Spoont, M., 380, 388, 389, 390, 391
Spring, K., 264
Springer, T., 529
Spruyt, K., 525
Srivastava, S., 283, 286, 589, 591, 594
Sroufe, L. A., 403, 404, 407, 408, 409, 450, 498
St. Peter, C., 570
Stadler, C., 569
Stadlmayr, W., 133
Staghezza-Jaramillo, B., 522
Stahl, D., 171
Stallings, M. C., 317
Stamperdahl, J., 436
Stams, G. J., 427, 429, 448
Stanford, M. S., 52
Stanga, Z., 134
Stanley, M., 261
Stansbury, K., 238
Stanwood, G. D., 153
Stapel, D., 125
Stapp, 304
Stark, K., 509, 619

Stark, K. H., 136
Starzyk, K. B., 134
Stattin, H., 502
Stearns, S., 276
Stecker, P., 610
Steel, R. P., 634
Steele, C. M., 648
Steele, H., 525
Steffan, V. J., 279
Steier, A., 190
Stein, A., 522
Stein, M. B., 376
Steinberg, L., 281, 351, 425
Steinberg, T., 173
Steiner, M., 303
Steinwert, T., 586
Stelmack, R. M., 44, 45, 651
Stemmler, G., 130
Stenger, V. A., 354
Stephens, D. W., 171
Steptoe, A., 553, 589, 590, 591
Stern, M., 486
Sterry, T. W., 443, 452, 453
Stevens, C., 160, 638, 639
Stevens, J. R., 171
Stevens, M. C., 355
Stevens, S. S., 6, 673, 675, 680
Stevenson, J., 330, 333, 566, 568, 591
Stevenson-Hinde, J., 409, 447, 491
Stewart, J., 371
Stewart, S. L., 69, 73, 428, 446
Stieben, J., 353
Stifter, C. A., 110, 111, 112, 114, 115, 116, 160, 231, 232, 233, 234, 450
Stigler, J. W., 466
Stimson, C., 171
Stinebrickner, T. R., 636
Stiver, D. J., 169
Stocker, C., 452
Stolerman, I. P., 303
Stolz, H. E., 425
Stoneman, Z., 89
Stonnington, C., 131
Stoolmiller, M., 132, 620
Stopp, C., 304
Stouthamer-Loeber, M., 283, 566, 567, 628
Stowe, Z. N., 522
Strachan, S., 587
Strain, P., 610
Strandberg, T., 521, 522
Strassberg, Z., 233, 569
Streiner, D. L., 184, 199
Streissguth, A. P., 303
Strelau, J., 6, 7, 10, 15, 21, 41, 42, 58, 59, 83, 85, 90, 91, 92, 93, 94, 95, 96, 97, 98, 100, 126, 128, 130, 132, 173, 184, 190, 192, 211, 257, 280, 288, 347, 452, 524, 673, 674, 677, 678
Striano, T., 171
Stright, A. D., 415, 434
Stringaris, A., 126, 566
Strobel, A., 322, 323
Strome, E. M., 264
Stroop, J. R., 151
Stuber, G. D., 384
Stucky, B. D., 563

Stupica, B., 414
Suarez, E. C., 131
Suchy, Y., 595
Suess, P. E., 232, 233
Sugai, G., 610
Sugden, K., 376
Sugiyama, H., 303
Suh, E. M., 286
Suitor, J. J., 426
Sukhodolsky, D. G., 136
Sulik, M., 483, 490
Sulik, M. J., 149, 150
Sulkowski, M., 466
Sullivan, H. S., 443
Sullivan, M. W., 111, 125
Sullivan, R., 386
Sullivan-Logan, G., 502
Suls, J., 591, 592, 593
Sum, A., 630
Sun, Y., 465, 661
Sundet, J. M., 74
Sunohara, G. A., 384
Suomi, S., 417
Suomi, S. J., 52, 253, 257
Super, C. M., 13, 24, 463, 468, 469, 474, 648
Susman, E. J., 240
Sutherland, R. J., 303
Sutton-Tyrrell, K., 590
Suzuki, A., 324, 325, 328
Suzuki, L. K., 463
Svrakic, D. M., 56, 95, 194, 196
Swann, W. B., Jr., 596
Swanson, J., 154, 509, 631, 636
Sweeney, D., 634
Sweeney, J. A., 353, 354
Sweeney, L., 448, 555, 616
Swenson, L. P., 306
Swickert, R. J., 44
Swingler, M. M., 15, 126, 229, 678
Switzer, G., 232
Szekely, A., 322, 323, 324, 325
Székely, E., 407
Szewczyk-Sokolowski, M., 449

Tabares, A., 665
Tackett, J. L., 7, 21, 134, 332, 473, 490, 500, 525, 533, 542, 562, 563, 564, 565, 568, 571, 574, 682, 684, 689, 693, 695
Tafrate, R. C., 136
Takahashi, L. K., 298, 299
Takahashi, N., 326
Takahashi, Y., 431
Takemoto-Chock, N. K., 283, 504
Talge, N. M., 233
Tamang, B. L., 469
Tambs, K., 26, 74, 196
Tamietto, M., 393
Tamis-LeMonda, C. S., 613, 691
Tamura, T., 522
Tang, T. Z., 554, 555
Tang, Y., 153, 353
Tangney, J., 128
Tankersley, D., 171
Tannock, R., 214
Tapert, S., 566

Taraldson, B. J., 185
Tarazi, F. I., 356
Tarter, R. E., 88, 135
Tasche, K. G., 44
Tate, C. A., 303
Tatsuoko, M. M., 46
Tavecchio, L. W. C., 413
Taylor, A., 376, 520
Taylor, E., 353
Taylor, E. S., 646, 649, 651
Taylor, J., 566
Taylor, M. D., 591
Taylor, R. D., 609, 637
Taylor, S., 376
Taylor, S. E., 114, 265, 375, 388
Taylor, S. F., 224
Taylor, V. J., 648, 661
Tees, M. T., 300, 302
Teglasi, H., 88, 92, 619
Teixeira, J. M., 299
Teixeira, V., 615
Tellegen, A., 42, 55, 56, 106, 108, 110, 111, 112, 117, 189, 197, 198, 370, 387, 500, 564, 675
Tenenbaum, H., 131
Tennes, J. M., 6
Tenney, A., 6
Teplov, B. M., 6
ter Weel, B., 630
Terracciano, A., 481, 591
Terranova, M., 530
Terwogt, M., 135
Tessitore, A., 354
Teta, P., 42, 55
Teti, L. O., 448
Thapar, A., 309, 431
Thayer, J. F., 595
Thayer, R. E., 678
Theobald, D., 389
Thivierge, J., 89
Thoman, E., 525
Thomas, A., 9, 10, 23, 24, 25, 32, 34, 35, 36, 41, 42, 70, 83, 84, 85, 86, 87, 88, 89, 90, 98, 105, 127, 145, 187, 188, 191, 192, 193, 195, 196, 211, 223, 229, 251, 298, 404, 405, 442, 444, 448, 471, 479, 480, 482, 484, 528, 607, 608, 647, 651, 652, 673, 676, 680, 682, 686, 691
Thomas, C., 15, 529
Thomas, C. W., 566, 685
Thomas, D., 522, 630
Thomas, J., 161, 637
Thomas, K. M., 152, 156, 353
Thomason, M. E., 354
Thompson, L. A., 127, 134, 199, 317, 319, 320, 332
Thompson, R. A., 230, 408, 507, 659
Thomsen, A. H., 508
Thorell, L. B., 115, 160
Thornburg, K., 524
Thornquist, M., 42
Thorsteinsson, E. B., 98
Thrash, T. M., 107, 117, 589, 591, 593
Thurstone, L. L., 90
Tibbetts, S., 52
Tierney, J., 679, 692

Tikkanen, R., 265
Timmel, L., 646
Tinbergen, J. M., 274
Tindle, H. A., 590
Tinga, F., 636
Tjebkes, C. T., 680
Tjebkes, T. L., 185
Tobena, A., 53
Tobin, R. M., 108, 114, 115, 168, 506
Todd, R. M., 353
Tomarken, A. J., 235
Tomasello, M., 171
Tomasini, E. C., 356
Tomincy, S. L., 638
Tomlinson, J., 664
Tonner, L., 608, 609
Tonstad, S., 586, 588
Tooby, J., 274, 275
Toon, C., 449
Torgersen, A. M., 330
Torgesen, J. K., 610
Torp, N., 158, 451
Torrubia, R., 51, 53, 55
Tost, H., 173, 329
Tottenham, N., 239, 356
Tout, K., 115, 238, 239, 452
Towsley, S., 70, 230, 542
Trainor, R., 353
Trainor, R. J., 354, 355
Trancik, A. M., 530
Tranel, D., 79, 224
Trapnell, P. D., 278, 281, 282, 285, 286
Treanor, J. J., 590
Trefilov, A., 266
Treiber, F. A., 131, 135
Tremblay, R. E., 634
Trentacosta, C. T., 449, 451, 452, 509, 619
Triandis, H. C., 464
Trickett, P. K., 240
Tripp, G., 511
Trivedi, M., 135
Trivedi, R., 131
Trivers, R. L., 171, 276
Trofimova, I., 7
Trommsdorff, G., 469
Troyer, D., 232
Truglio, R., 615
Trull, T. J., 189, 281, 549
Trut, L. M., 77
Tryon, F., 169
Tryon, K., 452
Tsai, S. J., 467
Tsankova, S., 379
Tschann, J. M., 529, 530
Tse, H. C., 467
Tsetsenis, T., 377
Tsuboi, H., 593
Tsuchimine, S., 323, 326
Tsukayama, E., 632, 633, 636
Tucker, D. M., 154, 502
Tucker, J., 529
Tugade, M. M., 591
Turcsán, B., 254
Turecki, S., 608, 609
Turner, B., 276, 282
Turner, E. K., 300

Turner, R. B., 590
Tuscher, O., 131
Tyler, L. A., 303
Tyndale, R. F., 308
Tyroler, H. A., 136
Tzur, G., 154

Uccello, R., 550
Uher, R., 71, 263, 419
Uhl, G. R., 387
Ukoumunne, O. C., 617
Ulbricht, J., 317, 334, 426
Uliaszek, A. A., 541
Underwood, M. K., 132, 488
Uno, H., 299
Useda, J. D., 189
Usher, B., 175
Uutela, A., 592
Uylings, H. B. M., 282

Vaccaro, D., 88
Vachon, D., 567
Vaglenova, J., 301, 302
Vahip, S., 189
Vaidya, C. J., 354
Vaidya, J., 108
Vaillant, G. E., 593
Vaish, A., 287
Vaitl, D., 356
Valentino, K., 195
Valentino, R., 373
Valiente, C., 157, 173, 509, 527, 631, 636
Vallender, E. J., 265, 266
Van Aken, C., 434
van Aken, M. A. G., 114, 160, 428, 431, 434, 447, 471, 681
van Baal, G. C. M., 48
Van Bakel, H. J. A., 30
van Beijsterveldt, C. E. M., 332
Van Beveren, T. T., 303
Van de Vijver, F. J. R., 94
van den Berg, L., 254
Van den Berg, S. M., 253, 254, 260
Van den Bergh, B. R., 300, 301, 302
van den Boom, D. C., 23, 28, 114, 406, 414
Van den Oever, M., 387
van der Ende, J., 490
van der Kooy, D., 386
van der Laan, A. M., 526, 527
van der Mark, I., 526
van der Molen, M. W., 353
van der Veer, R., 415
van der Vlugt, E., 24
Van Doorn, S., 649
van Dulmen, M. M. H., 115, 239, 452
Van Eijck, K., 634
Van Gestel, S., 323, 324, 325, 326
van Goozen, S. H. M., 572
van Hees, Y., 301
Van Hiel, A., 570
van Honk, J., 130, 131, 134
Van Hulle, C., 114, 169, 170, 279, 479, 481, 482
Van Hulle, C. A., 85, 216, 220, 453, 553, 568, 680

van IJzendoorn, H. W., 454
van IJzendoorn, M. H., 12, 14, 47, 60, 132, 154, 369, 378, 387, 403, 406, 408, 409, 410, 411, 412, 413, 414, 415, 416, 417, 418, 419, 420, 430, 498, 500, 526, 528, 552, 572, 573, 646, 650, 652, 675, 688, 689
Van Lange, P. A. M., 169
Van Leeuwen, K. G., 22, 85, 184, 278, 480, 504, 546, 568, 569, 570, 584
Van Leijenhorst, L., 351
van Lieshout, C. F. M., 114, 454
van Noordwijk, A. J., 274
Van Oers, K., 274, 275, 278
van Os, J., 548
van Tijen, N., 24
van Tuijl, C., 160, 428
van Veen, V., 156, 353, 354, 356
Van Zalk, M., 502
Van Zalk, N., 502
van Zeijl, J., 413, 415
Vandegeest, K. A., 15, 148, 214
Vandergeest, K. A., 191
Vannatta, K., 454
Vanyukov, M. M., 239
Vardaris, R. M., 303
Vas, J., 264
Vasey, M. W., 350, 473, 509, 524, 532, 552, 680
Vásquez, G., 277
Vaughan, J., 451
Vaughn, B. E., 185, 300, 302, 406, 408
Vaughn, J., 443, 522
Vaughn, S., 610
Vazire, S., 128
Vecchio, T. D., 136
Veenema, A. H., 260, 263, 264
Veenstra, R., 114, 157, 450, 526, 530, 533, 553, 636
Vega-Lahr, N., 194
Veldman, D. J., 634
Velicer, W. F., 191
Venables, P. H., 566, 567, 685
Vendlinski, M. K., 84, 130, 209
Venter, J. C., 152, 316
Ventura, R., 259
Verbeken, S., 587
Verhoeven, M., 434
Verhulst, F. C., 490, 523, 526, 553, 554
Vermeer, H. J., 415
Verne, J., 692
Vernon, P. A., 43
Verstraeten, K., 509, 532, 533, 552, 554, 680
Verweij, K. J. H., 132
Vevea, J. L., 492
Viding, E., 169, 569
Viechtbauer, W., 490, 544, 628
Viikari, J., 587
Villar, P., 508
Virkkunen, M., 131
Visser, G. H., 301
Vitaro, F., 447, 553, 634
Voelker, P. M., 14, 113, 154, 332, 336, 352, 356, 409, 499, 573
Voelkl, K. E., 632
Vogt, B. A., 353

Vogt, T. M., 584, 587
Vohs, K. D., 10, 156, 649
Volavka, J., 52
Volbrecht, M. M., 173
Volkow, N., 382
Vollebergh, W., 546
Vollenbergh, W. A. M., 547
Vollrath, M. E., 6, 135, 332, 500, 523, 525, 581, 584, 585, 586, 587, 588, 692
von Borstel, U. U. K., 254
von Eye, A., 526, 567
Vondra, J. I., 427
Voracek, M., 483
Vorhees, C. V., 298
Vorria, P., 524
Voss, H., 352
Votruba-Drzal, E., 526
Vu, R., 261
Vuga, M., 76, 234, 235
Vygotsky, L. S., 463, 464
Vythilingam, M, 264

Wachs, T. D., 7, 8, 16, 112, 114, 133, 215, 300, 332, 357, 378, 410, 413, 426, 442, 449, 512, 519, 520, 521, 522, 523, 524, 528, 529, 533, 675, 684, 688, 689, 693
Wadsworth, M., 548
Wadsworth, M. E., 508
Wager, T, 224
Wahlund, K., 569
Wainryb, D., 510
Wainwright, A. B., 449
Wainwright, L., 199
Wake, M., 617
Wakshlak, A., 299
Walden, T., 115, 195, 449, 451
Walden, T. A., 188, 194, 195
Waldman, I. D., 332, 563, 568
Walhovd, K. B., 694
Walker, E. F., 522
Walker, M. S., 592
Walker, R. N., 6
Wall, S., 404
Waller, N. G., 55, 56, 198, 370, 564
Wallon, H., 7
Walter, H., 130, 172, 350, 382
Walter, M., 351
Walters, L. H., 117
Walters, R. H., 443
Walton, G. M., 648, 661
Walton, K. E., 490, 544, 628
Wan, C. K., 126
Wang, D. A., 386
Wang, F., 691
Wang, J., 266
Wang, L., 75, 447, 462, 471, 472
Wang, M., 14, 15, 16, 130, 172, 213, 235, 261, 305, 306, 315, 352, 407, 426, 503, 521, 544, 682, 683, 688
Wang, M. W., 303
Wang, X., 131
Wang, Y., 114, 132, 448, 473, 632, 636
Wang, Z., 10, 14, 124, 173, 257, 266, 281, 387, 405, 448, 472, 506, 677, 680, 691

Wanna, S. Y., 190
Wanner, B., 553
Wanzek, J., 610
Ward, H. E., 298
Ward, I. L., 298
Wardle, J., 589, 590, 591
Warkentin, V., 331
Warneken, F., 171
Washington, R. A., 153
Wasserman, D., 131
Wasserman, G., 522
Wasserman, J., 131
Watamura, S. E., 238
Waters, A. M., 350
Waters, E., 404, 406
Watson, D., 106, 108, 110, 111, 112, 116, 117, 126, 189, 197, 199, 280, 283, 285, 289, 370, 450, 489, 503, 527, 542, 545, 546, 547, 548, 549, 551, 588, 589, 591, 593, 678, 695
Way, B. M., 265, 266, 375, 388
Weaver, I., 309, 379
Webb, E., 7, 629
Weber, B., 131
Weber, E. U., 351
Webster-Stratton, M., 620
Wechsler, D., 629, 630
Weeks, M., 452
Wehr, A., 322
Weigel, C., 529
Weinberger, D., 374
Weinberger, D. R., 16, 354
Weinstein, T. A. R., 503
Weinstock, L. M., 549
Weinstock, M., 299
Weisaeth, L., 71
Weiss, A., 591, 594
Weiss, B., 473
Weissberg, R. P., 609, 637
Weisskirch, R. S., 510
Weissing, F. J., 649
Weissman, M. M., 280
Weisz, D. J., 303
Weisz, J., 298
Weisz, J. R., 433, 473
Weitzman, M., 133
Welk, G. J., 481
Wellman, H. M., 157, 526
Wendland, J. R., 263, 264, 265
Wenig, F., 51
Wenner, C. J., 283
Wentzel, M. N., 117
Werge, T., 266
Werner, E., 526, 528, 529
Wertlieb, O., 529
Wertz, A. E., 213, 320
Wessels, H., 675
West, D. J., 566
West, J. R., 303
West, S. G., 115, 433, 509, 554, 585
Westdorp, A., 351
West-Eberhard, M. J., 273
Westenberg, P. M., 26
Westerberg, H., 160
Westergaard, G. C., 257
Westernberg, H. G., 321
Westlye, L. T., 694

Wetter, E. K., 116, 552, 554
Wetzel, R. D., 95
Whalen, P., 370
Whalen, P. J., 349, 683
Whang, W., 589
Wharton, T. A., 350
Wheeler, R. E., 235
Wheelwright, S., 169
Whipple, M. O., 592
Whipple, N., 160, 428
Whisenton, J. T., 634
Whisman, M. A., 549
White, F., 382
White, H. R., 566, 567
White, J. D., 88
White, J. M., 117, 199, 609, 638
White, L., 554
White, L. K., 9, 14, 60, 70, 112, 129, 130, 155, 210, 213, 234, 236, 256, 261, 279, 287, 322, 347, 353, 357, 358, 361, 521, 679, 680, 681, 683, 687
White, T. L., 53, 107, 189, 195, 197, 370, 374
Whiteman, M., 134, 304
Whiteman, M. C., 592, 594
Whiteside-Mansell, L., 529, 570
Whitson, S., 233
Whittle, S., 14, 16, 147, 153
Wichmann, C., 446
Wickel, E. E., 481
Widaman, K. F., 199, 256, 505
Widiger, T. A., 169, 281
Wiebe, S. A., 304
Wiersma, E. D., 7, 90, 93, 100, 676
Wiese, D., 108
Wiggins, J. S., 278, 281, 282, 285, 286
Wightman, R. M., 384
Wilhelm, K., 376
Wilkening, F., 351
Wilkinson, R. G., 254
Wilkowski, B. M., 126, 129, 130
Willcutt, E., 563
Willem, L., 489
Willerman, L., 330
Williams, G., 572
Williams, J. E., 135
Williams, L. M., 130
Williams, L. R., 435, 554
Williams, P. G., 595
Williams, R., 136
Williams, R. B., 593
Williamson, D. E., 257
Williamson, G. M., 593
Williford, A. P., 567
Willingham, W. W., 633
Willis-Owen, S. A., 383
Wills, T. A., 88, 89, 528, 529, 530
Wilson, A., 533
Wilson, B., 232, 233
Wilson, D., 550
Wilson, D. B., 492
Wilson, E. O., 278
Wilson, G. D., 43, 45, 53
Wilson, K. G., 44
Wilson, M., 132
Wilson, M. A., 276, 279

Wilson, R. S., 215, 589, 594
Wilson, W. C., 529
Wilson R. S., 591
Wimmer, G. E., 384
Winberg, S., 649
Windle, M., 88, 91, 95, 188, 192, 194, 195, 199, 529, 530
Wing, R. R., 136
Wingfield, J. C., 255, 275
Wingrove, J., 130
Winkler, A. M., 77
Winslow, J. T., 281
Winstanley, C., 389, 391
Winston, J. S., 172
Winzer-Serhan, U. H., 302
Wisco, B.E., 547
Wise, R., 351
Wisenbaker, J., 24
Wittmann, B., 350, 351, 382
Wittwer, D. J., 298
Woessmann, L., 630
Wojslawowicz, J. C., 447, 448
Wolchik, S. A., 115, 433, 509, 554, 585
Wolf, H., 91
Wolf, J. M., 239
Wolf, M., 649
Wolfe, R. N., 633
Wolitzky-Taylor, K. B., 549
Wong, J. C., 261
Wong, M. M., 635
Wong, M. S., 511
Wong, M. T. H., 52
Wood, A. C., 87, 91, 317, 318, 333
Wood, B. R., 232
Wood, C. H., 563
Wood, D., 128, 588
Wood, W., 488
Woodard, J., 157, 566
Woodhouse, S. S., 414
Woods, M. G., 135
Woods, S. A., 596
Woods, S. W., 71
Woods, T., 586
Woodward, A., 287
Woodward, S., 681
Woody, E. Z., 280, 652
Woolf, P., 9
Wootton, J. M., 571
Work, W. C., 526
Worlein, J. M., 299
Wranik, T., 126
Wright, A., 118
Wright, C., 590
Wright, C. E., 78
Wright, C. I., 236, 349
Wright, J. C., 488

Wright, P. H., 282
Wu, F. C. W., 52, 134
Wu, I. T., 694
Wu, Y., 153, 356
Wundt, W., 84
Wurst, W., 373
Wyant, A., 692
Wyman, P. A., 526, 529
Wynn, K., 155, 168

Xie, G., 174
Xing, Z. W., 12
Xu, F., 468
Xu, J., 192
Xu, Z. A., 303

Yaeger, A., 528
Yalcin, B., 383
Yamagata, S., 317
Yamamoto, M., 132
Yaman, A., 413
Yamano, E., 328
Yamasue, H., 327
Yang, F., 12, 133, 453, 462, 521, 661, 689
Yang, J. W., 131
Yasui-Furukori, N., 327
Yasuno, F., 586
Ye, R., 13, 147, 191, 234, 467, 480
Ye, R. M., 108
Yearwood, E., 612
Yee, M. C., 651
Yeh, S. R., 259
Yehuda, R., 300
Yerkes, A. W., 251
Yerkes, R. M., 251
Yingling, D., 135
Yirmiya, N., 415
Yoo, H. C., 466
Yosida, M., 5
Young, B. N., 468
Young, C. L., 610
Young, G., 383
Young, L. J., 172, 261, 281, 386
Young, S. E., 317, 573
Young, S. K., 173
Younger, A. J., 446, 447, 453, 490
Youngstrom, E., 451, 527
Yount, S. E., 594
Ystrom, E., 588
Yu, A. P., 279
Yuh, J., 596

Zacher, J., 193
Zagoory-Sharon, O., 114
Zahn-Waxler, C., 169, 170, 171, 172, 173, 175, 490

Zaia, A. F., 452
Zak, P. J., 172
Zakriski, A. L., 488
Zald, D., 382, 383, 388, 389
Zald, P. H., 78
Zalsman, G., 52
Zamboanga, B. L., 510
Zammit, S., 132
Zanarini, M. C., 567
Zapfe, J. A., 87, 213, 318, 319
Zappulla, C., 454
Zawadzki, B., 7, 10, 15, 41, 42, 58, 59, 83, 91, 94, 95, 96, 97, 98, 173, 190, 192, 211, 257, 452, 524, 677, 678
Zeff, T., 666
Zeidner, M., 134
Zeki, S., 281, 286
Zelazo, P. D., 149, 156, 353, 354
Zelazo, P. R., 467
Zeman, J., 132
Zentner, M., 3, 4, 6, 7, 9, 21, 22, 31, 73, 84, 90, 125, 136, 169, 170, 174, 211, 230, 251, 300, 405, 419, 450, 451, 503, 608, 673, 676, 677, 680, 684, 691
Zerjal, T., 276
Zhang, D., 387
Zhang, G., 473
Zhang, J., 192
Zhang, L., 649
Zhang, T. Y., 309
Zhange, J., 592
Zhou, M., 376
Zhou, Q., 114, 115, 116, 132, 170, 428, 433, 448, 453, 473, 632, 636
Zhou, Q. Y., 462
Zhuravlev, A. B., 45
Zimmer-Gembeck, M. J., 350, 508
Zimmerman, B. J., 632, 636
Zimmerman, W. S., 90
Zimmermann, U., 264
Zinbarg, R. E., 541, 555
Zink, C. F., 351
Zins, J. E., 638
Zoccolillo, M., 562
Zohar, A. H., 173
Zonderman, A. B., 58, 197, 591
Zubieta, J.-K., 387
Zuckerman, M., 8, 9, 41, 42, 43, 44, 45, 46, 47, 48, 49, 50, 51, 53, 54, 55, 56, 59, 60, 91, 92, 95, 107, 110, 111, 114, 125, 251, 256, 278, 279, 286, 388, 389, 673, 676, 677, 693, 695
Zupančič, M., 466
Zuroff, D. C., 547
Zvolensky, M. J., 550

Subject Index

Page numbers followed by *f* indicate figure, *t* indicate table

"A not B" task, 155
A118G polymorphism, 388
Academic performance. *See also*
    Classroom environment; Teacher
    responsiveness
  achievement, 630, 631–633, 632*f*
  culture and, 472
  dimensions of, 630
  educational attainment, 630,
    633–635
  effortful control and, 58–59
  future research directions, 639
  history of interest in temperament in,
    629–630
  INSIGHTS into Children's
    Temperament intervention,
    613–615, 614*f*
  interactions between temperament
    and parenting and, 436
  overview, 627–629
  peer relationships and, 444*f*
  positive emotionality and, 106*f*, 117
  prefrontal executive control adaptive
    space and, 283
  quality-adjusted learning hours and,
    635–636, 635*f*
  school readiness, 630–631
  school-based interventions and,
    636–639
  self- and other-report measures and,
    199
  temperament research and, 689–695,
    693*t*
Acceptance, 445*f*
ACE gene, 328*t*
Achievement, 381, 630, 631–633, 632*f*.
    See also Academic performance

Activation control, 150*t*, 635*f*
Active covariance, 523, 524
Active engagement, 220*t*
Active GE correlations, 334
Activity
  adult temperament and, 90–92
  Alternative Five system and, 48
  animal models and, 255–257, 258*f*, 259
  behavioral assessment and, 213
  behavioral styles approach and, 24
  comparing adult and child
    temperament traits and, 41–42
  critical approach and, 25–26, 26*t*
  Formal Characteristics of Behavior—
    Temperament Inventory (FCB-TI)
    and, 59
  gender differences in temperament
    and, 481, 482*t*, 487
  genetic factors and, 317
  health and, 584
  infant and children, 83–90, 86*t*
  molecular genetic research, 322
  overview, 48, 83, 98, 100
  peer relationships and, 452–453
  regulative theory of temperament
    and, 92–98, 93*f*, 96*f*, 97*t*
  Western Europe schools and, 7
  See also Activity level; Approach;
    Emotionality, activity, and
    sociability (EAS)
Activity level
  genetic factors and, 333
  molecular genetic research, 323*t*,
    324*t*, 326*t*
  overview, 84, 676–680, 677*t*
  risk factors and, 522
  See also Activity

Adaptive processes
  activity and, 84, 91–92
  behavioral styles approach and, 24
  culture and, 469
  developmental processes and, 12
  evolution and, 273
  genetic factors and, 317
  history of temperament-based
    intervention and, 608
  molecular genetic research, 322, 324*t*
  overview, 9–10
  role of temperament traits in the
    development of personality and,
    499*f*
  See also Characteristic adaptations;
    Reactivity; Self-regulation
Adaptive spaces
  evolution and, 277–289, 283*f*, 285*f*
  fitting to the results of factor-analytic
    studies, 284–289, 285*f*
  nurturance and pair-bonding
    adaptive space, 281–282
  orienting sensitivity adaptive space,
    283–284
  overview, 289–290, 290*f*
  prefrontal executive control adaptive
    space, 282–283, 283*f*
  reactivity/affect intensity adaptive
    space and, 280–281
  See also Evolution
Addiction, 54–55. *See also* Substance
  use
Additive models, 554
Adjustment
  activity and, 88
  culture and, 464*f*, 470–473
  health and, 586–588

727

Subject Index

Adjustment *(cont.)*
  history of temperament-based intervention and, 608
  interactions between temperament and parenting and, 435–436
  moderating role of temperament and, 527–531
  peer relationships and, 444f
  risk factors and, 523–531, 525f
Adolescent Personal Style Inventory, 208
Adolescent Temperament Questionnaire (ADTQ), 188t, 195
Adolescents
  anger, irritability, and frustration and, 128–130, 136
  behavioral inhibition and, 77–79
  brain functioning and, 77–79
  change in temperament and, 332
  characteristic adaptations and, 507
  childhood temperament and, 685–687, 686t, 687t
  culture and, 472
  effortful control and, 156, 158
  gender differences in temperament and, 488, 489
  genetic factors and, 317
  health and, 583–588
  interactions between temperamental reactivity and regulation, 358–359
  interpersonal difficulties and, 552
  kindness and, 171
  list of measures across the lifespan, 188t
  long-term outcomes of impulse control and, 685–687, 686t, 687t
  peer relationships and, 449
  positive emotionality and, 107
  prefrontal executive control adaptive space and, 282–283, 283f
  psychobiological measures and, 233
  reactivity and, 351–352
  self- and other-report measures and, 195–196
  striatum and the development of fearful temperament and, 359–360
  from temperament to personality traits and, 504–507
Adoption studies, 305–306, 309. *See also* Twin studies
ADRA2A gene, 131
Adrenal androgens, 487–488
Adrenal cortex, 371–374
Adrenocorticotropic hormone (ACTH), 262–263, 263–264, 372f
Adult Measure of Behavioral Inhibition (AMBI), 189t, 197
Adult temperament
  activity and, 90–92
  Alternative Five system, 47–52, 50f
  anger, irritability, and frustration and, 128–130, 136
  attachment and, 416–418
  Big Five model and, 46–47
  Big Three System and, 42–46
  childhood temperament and, 685–687, 686t, 687t

Cloninger's three-factor model and, 56–58
compared to child temperament, 41–42
comparison models of temperament and, 55, 55f, 60, 60t
effortful control and, 156
gender differences in temperament and, 489
genetic factors and, 317
Gray's theory and, 52–55, 54f
health and, 583t, 588–593
list of measures across the lifespan, 188t–190t
long-term outcomes of impulse control and, 685–687, 686t, 687t
neurobiological factors and, 391–393, 392f
overview, 41
positive emotionality and, 107
self- and other-report measures and, 196–198
Strelau's regulative theory of temperament and, 58–60
Tellegen's three-factor model and, 55–56
from temperament to personality traits and, 504–507
Adult Temperament Questionnaire (ATQ)
  anger, irritability, and frustration and, 127–128
  effortful control and, 146t
  overview, 189t, 196
  positive emotionality and, 108
  sensory processing sensitivity (SPS) and, 651, 655
Affect, 130, 280–281, 288, 369–370, 389
Affect–Approach, 110
Affectional system, 281–282, 425
Affective styles, 695
Affiliative system
  adaptive spaces and, 284
  animal models and, 255–257, 261
  evolution and, 281
  overview, 27, 676–680, 677t
  positive emotionality and, 106f, 108
  self- and other-report measures and, 195
  See also Prosocial behavior
Age
  activity and, 95
  anger, irritability, and frustration and, 128–130
  change in temperament and, 329–333
  gender differences in temperament and, 489
  peer relationships and, 453
  positive emotionality and, 109
  prefrontal executive control adaptive space and, 282–283, 283f
  See also Developmental processes
Agency, 106f
Agentic (active), 55–56

Aggression
  adaptive spaces and, 286, 287, 288–289
  Alternative Five system and, 48, 51–52
  anger interventions and, 136
  animal models and, 254, 254–255, 255–257
  biological factors in, 130–132
  comparing adult and child temperament traits and, 42
  culture and, 464
  educational attainment and, 634
  effortful control and, 157
  evolution and, 276–277, 278
  externalizing disorders and, 570
  gender differences in temperament and, 487, 490
  health and, 134–135, 135f, 586–588
  irritability and, 405
  moderating role of temperament and, 413
  overview, 125t, 563–564, 676–680, 677t
  peer relationships and, 449
  positive emotionality and, 114–115
  prenatal substance use, 308t
  psychoticism and, 46
  self- and other-report measures and, 195
  STORIES intervention, 617, 619–620, 621f
Aggression Scale: Relational, Reactive, Instrumental, 125t
Aggression–Hostility, 42, 48, 51–52
Aggressive Negative Emotionality, 289, 290f
Agonistic/Highly Aggressive, 256–257
Agoraphobia, 116, 279–280, 549, 656–658. *See also* Anxiety disorders
Agreeableness
  academic performance and, 628–629, 631–633, 632f
  adaptive spaces and, 284, 285, 286, 290f
  aggression and, 51–52
  anxiety disorders and, 549
  Big Five model and, 46–47
  developmental processes and, 544
  externalizing disorders and, 564, 567f
  gender differences in temperament and, 485, 487
  health and, 584, 586–588
  kindness and, 172
  narrative identity and, 511
  neurobiological factors and, 385–387
  neurogenetic and experiential processes and, 369
  peer relationships and, 452–453
  personality and, 499f, 504, 506
  positive emotionality and, 106f, 107, 108, 116
  prosocial behavior and, 173
  psychopathology and, 542
  self- and other-report measures and, 198

Subject Index

Alcohol use
  activity and, 88–89
  animal studies on prenatal substance use, 301–304
  conscientiousness and, 595
  overview, 563–564
  prenatal substance use, 307
  See also Substance use
Allelic association
  etiology of temperament and, 683
  molecular genetic research, 321
  neuroticism and, 374–377, 375f
  sensory processing sensitivity (SPS) and, 649
Alpha-amylase activity, 237–240
Alternative Five system
  comparing adult and child temperament traits and, 42
  comparison of adult models of temperament and, 55, 55f, 60, 60t
  overview, 47–52, 50f
  See also Five-Factor Model
Altruism, 169, 485. *See also* Kindness
Altruistic personality, 168. *See also* Kindness
Amorphous typology, 7
Amygdala
  aggression and, 52
  anger, irritability, and frustration and, 130, 134
  behavioral inhibition and, 72–73, 75–76, 76, 77, 78
  behavioral inhibition model and, 32
  overview, 348
  psychobiological measures and, 236–237
  reactivity and, 78–79, 349, 357–359, 371, 376–377
Anger
  adaptive spaces and, 287
  animal models and, 258f, 259–260
  behavioral assessment and, 220t
  biological factors in, 130–132
  comparing adult and child temperament traits and, 42
  constructs and measures of, 124–128, 125t, 127f
  culture and, 472–473
  developmental processes and, 128–130
  externalizing disorders and, 570–571
  genetic factors and, 332–333
  health and, 134–136, 135f, 586–588, 591–593
  overview, 124, 125t, 136–137, 676–680, 677t
  parenting and, 428, 430, 431
  peer relationships and, 445f, 448–449
  positive emotionality and, 110–111
  socialization and the environment and, 132–134
Animal models
  adaptive spaces and, 284
  alcohol use disorders and, 265–267
  anxiety/stress reactivity and, 370–371, 378–379
  attachment and, 403
  behavioral inhibition and, 73
  biological measures of behavioral inhibition and, 77
  dopamine functioning and, 384
  effortful control and, 356
  evolutionary theory of sex and, 276–277
  fearfulness and aggression and, 254
  genetic factors and, 265–267
  neurobiological factors and, 255–261, 258f, 356
  overview, 251–253, 252t, 267
  pair-bonding and, 281–282
  prenatal period and, 298–300, 301–304, 309
  sensory processing sensitivity (SPS) and, 649
  social bonding and, 386
  variations in temperament within and across species, 254–255
Anterior attentional system, 27
Anterior cingulate cortex (ACC)
  anxiety/stress reactivity and, 375–376, 375f, 378
  behavioral assessment and, 210
  developmental processes and, 355–356
  effortful control and, 152–153, 154–155, 158, 353–356
  etiology of temperament and, 683
  externalizing disorders and, 569
  interactions between temperamental reactivity and regulation, 357–359, 357f
  social rejection sensitivity and, 388
Anthropology (Kant, 1789/2006), 5–6
Antidepressants, 75–76, 377, 555, 694. *See also* Medication
Antisocial behavior, 46, 134, 308t, 444f, 445f
Antisocial personality disorder, 98, 99t
Anxiety
  activity and, 98, 99t
  adult temperament and, 391–393, 392f
  animal models and, 253, 256–257
  comorbidity of with depressive disorders, 551
  culture and, 467, 473
  diagnosis and, 657–658
  gender differences in temperament and, 484
  genetic factors and, 333
  health and, 585–586, 586, 592
  human studies on prenatal stress, 300–301, 302t
  molecular genetic research, 321–322
  neurobiological, genetic, and experiential factors in, 370–380, 372f, 375f, 381f
  neuroticism and, 369–370
  overview, 676–680, 677t
  peer relationships and, 446
  positive emotionality and, 116
  psychobiological measures and, 234–235
  reactivity and, 74–75, 78–79, 358, 358–359
  risk factors and, 532
  sensory processing sensitivity (SPS) and, 651
  from temperament to personality traits and, 505
  See also Anxiety disorders
Anxiety disorders
  anger, irritability, and frustration and, 134–135
  assessment and, 656–658
  Cool Little Kids intervention, 615–616
  diagnosis and, 658
  gender and, 279–280
  mediators and moderators of temperament and, 551–554
  overview, 548–551
  treatment and, 554–555
  See also Anxiety; Internalizing disorders
Anxiety sensitivity (AS), 549–550, 551
APOE gene, 326t
Appraisal mechanisms, 126, 130, 524–525
Approach
  activity and, 95
  adaptive spaces and, 288
  anger, irritability, and frustration and, 130
  behavioral assessment and, 220t
  behavioral styles approach and, 24
  comparing adult and child temperament traits and, 41–42
  culture and, 469
  evolution and, 275–276, 278
  gender differences in temperament and, 482t, 483–484
  molecular genetic research, 323t, 324t, 325t, 327t
  neurobiological factors and, 350
  overview, 9–10
  peer relationships and, 446–448, 449–450
  positive emotionality and, 106–108, 111
  prefrontal executive control adaptive space and, 282–283
  psychobiological measures and, 235
  reactivity and, 111
  reactivity/affect intensity and, 280–281
  from temperament to personality traits and, 505
  withdrawal and, 24, 110, 235
  See also Sensation seeking
Arousal
  activity and, 93–94, 93f
  aggression and, 52
  animal models and, 259
  attachment and, 409
  behavioral inhibition model and, 32
  DOES acronym and, 645–646
  extraversion and, 44
  Gray's theory of adult temperament and, 52–55, 54f

Subject Index

Arousal *(cont.)*
  health and, 586, 590
  overview, 69
  psychobiological measures and, 231
  reactivity and, 280–281, 348–349
  sensation seeking and, 49–51, 50f
Arrogance, 253
Arrogant/Unassuming, 285
Assertiveness, 381
Assessment
  activity and, 94–95
  challenges to, 221–225
  children and, 666
  client history and, 653–654
  gender differences in temperament and, 485–486
  importance of considering temperament for, 646–647
  internalizing disorders and, 545–551
  intervention and, 690–691
  psychopathology and, 545
  psychotherapy and, 652–661
  research of temperament assessment, 212–225, 217f, 220t
  of temperament in animals, 252–253, 252t
  See also Behavioral assessment; Diagnosis; Measurement
Attached state, 256–257
Attachment
  academic performance and, 635f
  animal models and, 261
  characteristic adaptations and, 509–510
  diathesis–stress and, 410
  differential susceptibility and, 410–412, 411f, 412f, 415–418
  evolution and, 281
  genotype–environment interactions (G x E) and, 336
  moderating models, 409–410, 410f, 412–418
  oblique point of view, 408–409
  orthogonal constructs of, 407–408
  overview, 403–407, 675–676
  pair-bonding and, 281
  parenting and, 426
  research and, 224, 418–419
Attachment Q-Sort, 406–407
Attachment security, 159–160, 408, 414–415, 426
Attention deficit disorder (ADD), 657. *See also* Attention-deficit/hyperactivity disorder (ADHD)
Attention Network Test (ANT), 214, 236
Attentional biases, 552
Attentional functioning, 15, 173, 317
Attention-deficit/hyperactivity disorder (ADHD)
  activity and, 88
  anxiety/stress reactivity and, 377
  attachment and, 418
  diagnosis and, 657
  genetic factors and, 154, 333, 573
  human studies on prenatal substance use, 304–305

  overview, 563
  positive emotionality and, 115–116
  prenatal period and, 306, 307–308, 308t, 309
  psychotherapy and, 646
  spectrum models of, 569
  vulnerability models of, 567–568, 567f
  See also Externalizing disorders; Psychopathology
Attention-related processes
  academic performance and, 629–630
  adult temperament and, 392f
  anger, irritability, and frustration and, 126, 127–128, 127f, 129
  animal studies on prenatal substance use, 302–303
  behavioral assessment and, 210, 214
  culture and, 468
  educational attainment and, 634
  effortful control and, 146, 150t, 158–159
  evolution and, 275
  externalizing disorders and, 567–568, 567f, 573
  gender differences in temperament and, 490
  genetic factors and, 333, 334–335
  health and, 586–588
  high- and low-reactive infants and, 74
  internalizing disorders and, 552
  molecular genetic research, 322, 323t, 324t, 325t, 326t, 327t
  multistage mediation and, 524–525
  overview, 676–680, 677t
  peer relationships and, 450–452
  psychobiological approach and, 26–29, 28t, 29t, 231–232, 233
  risk factors and, 522
  self- and other-report measures and, 192–193
Attributions, 126, 445f
Augmenting pattern, 50
Autonomic nervous system (ANS), 231, 233, 373
Autonomy support, 160
Autoreceptor control, 382–383, 383f
Avoidance
  avoidant trait, 73–75
  multistage mediation and, 524–525
  neurobiological factors and, 350
  overview, 676–680, 677t
  striatum and the development of fearful temperament and, 360
Avoidant personality disorder, 98, 100t
Axonal neuropathy, 695

Baby Behavior Questionnaire (BBQ), 85, 86t, 186t
Basolateral area, 72, 371–374, 391–393
Bayley III, 215
Bayley Scales of Infant Development, 215
Bayley's Infant Behavior Record (IBR), 215
BDNF gene, 327t

Bed nucleus of the stria terminalis (BNST)
  adult temperament and, 391–393
  anxiety/stress reactivity and, 371–374, 372f, 375–377, 378–380, 381f
  etiology of temperament and, 683
Behavior
  behavioral mechanisms, 583t
  measurement and, 16
  moral development and, 14–15
  peer relationships and, 444
  personality and, 3–4
  problems with, 413
  regulation of, 146
Behavior Assessment System for Children (BASC), 88
Behavioral Activation Scale (BAS), 189t, 195, 197
Behavioral activation system (BAS), 106f, 107, 116
Behavioral Approach, 286, 288
Behavioral approach adaptive space (BAAS)
  evolutionary theory of sex and, 276–277
  orienting sensitivity adaptive space and, 283–284
  overview, 275, 278, 284, 290f
  See also Adaptive spaces
Behavioral approach system (BAS)
  anger, irritability, and frustration and, 130
  evolution and, 277–278
  Gray's theory of adult temperament and, 53–55, 54f
  prefrontal executive control adaptive space and, 282–283
Behavioral assessment
  challenges to, 221–225
  historical and theoretical contexts for, 211–212
  overview, 209–210, 210t
  research of temperament assessment, 212–225, 217f, 220t
  See also Assessment; Laboratory observations; Measurement
Behavioral dyscontrol, 254
Behavioral genetics
  animal models and, 261–265, 262f
  attachment and, 406–407
  externalizing disorders and, 569
  overview, 682
  personality and, 503
  See also Genetic factors
Behavioral inhibition
  animal models and, 257, 259
  attachment and, 409, 416
  biological measures of, 75–77
  brain functioning and, 77–78
  cognitive biases and, 552
  empathy and, 173
  externalizing disorders and, 568, 571
  genetic factors and, 317
  health and, 586
  HPA axis and, 552–553
  internalizing disorders and, 548, 550–551

Subject Index

long-term outcomes of, 686–687
molecular genetic research, 321–322, 328t
neurochemical basis of, 352
overview, 31–32, 69–71, 79, 347–348, 676–680, 677t
patterns, 78–79
peer relationships and, 446–448
processes through which temperament shapes personality development, 501
psychobiological measures and, 231
psychopathology and, 542
self- and other-report measures and, 193
sensory processing sensitivity (SPS) and, 651
striatum and the development of fearful temperament and, 359–360
from temperament to personality traits and, 505
See also Behavioral inhibition system (BIS); Inhibition
Behavioral Inhibition Questionnaire (BIQ), 193
Behavioral Inhibition Questionnaire (BIQ)—Parent Report Version, 187t
Behavioral Inhibition Questionnaire (BIQ)—Teacher Report Version, 187t
Behavioral Inhibition Scale (BIS), 189t, 195, 197
Behavioral inhibition system (BIS)
Cloninger's three-factor model and, 57
comparing adult and child temperament traits and, 42
Gray's theory of adult temperament and, 53–55, 54f
overview, 70, 279
positive emotionality and, 107
self- and other-report measures and, 200
See also Behavioral inhibition; Inhibition
Behavioral intervention. *See* Intervention
Behavioral Style Questionnaire (BSQ)
activity and, 85, 86t
behavioral styles approach and, 23–25, 25t
overview, 187t, 191
Behavioral styles approach, 23–25, 25t, 479–480
Behavioral tasks, 148–149, 150t, 155–156. *See also individual assessments*; Measurement
Behavioral teratology, 297–298
Behavioral withdrawal adaptive space, 279–280, 290f. *See also* Withdrawal tendencies
Berkeley Puppet Interview (BPI), 186t, 191
Bernese Longitudinal Study, 687, 687t
Beta-endorphin release, 386

Bias
assessment and, 224
characteristic adaptations and, 508–510
high- and low-reactive infants and, 74
internalizing disorders and, 552
measurement and, 183
Bidirectional processes, 412, 415–417, 445
Bielefeld–Warsaw Twin Project, 95–96, 96f
Big Five model
academic performance and, 628–629
activity and, 90, 91, 95, 100
adult models of temperament and, 42, 55, 55f, 60, 60t
assessment and, 224
attachment and, 417
characteristic adaptations and, 508–509
gender differences in temperament and, 480
health and, 584
internalizing disorders and, 555
overview, 3–4, 46–47, 511
positive emotionality and, 107, 108
psychopathology and, 542
psychotherapy and, 652–653
role of temperament traits in the development of personality and, 499f
self- and other-report measures and, 197–198
from temperament traits to, 503–507
See also Five-Factor Model
Big Five Questionnaire—Children, 208
Big Three System
comparing adult and child temperament traits and, 42
comparison of adult models of temperament and, 55, 55f, 60, 60t
overview, 42–46
psychopathology and, 542
See also Three-factor model
Biochemistry, 50–51, 50f, 52
Bioecological model, 519, 533–534
Biological factors
aggression and, 52
Alternative Five system and, 47–52, 50f
anger, irritability, and frustration and, 130–132, 134
animal studies on prenatal stress and, 299–300
attachment and, 410–411
behavioral assessment and, 210
behavioral inhibition and, 32, 75–77
Big Five model and, 47
Big Three System and, 42–43
Cloninger's three-factor model and, 56–57
culture and, 464f
effortful control and, 151–154, 679
etiology of temperament and, 682–684
externalizing disorders and, 569, 571–573, 572f

gender differences in temperament and, 487–488, 491
Gray's theory of adult temperament and, 52–55, 54f
health and, 583t
history of temperament-based intervention and, 608
internalizing disorders and, 552–553
kindness and, 171–173
meaning of temperament and, 674–675
medication and, 693–694
overview, 7–8, 10–12, 11f, 347–348, 360
pair-bonding and, 281–282
parenting and, 432
positive emotionality and, 112–114
processes through which temperament shapes personality development, 502–503
psychobiological measures and, 223–242
risk factors and, 519–520, 520f, 521–522, 528–529
sensation seeking and, 50–51, 50f
See also Brain functioning; Genetic factors; Neurobiological model; Neurological factors; Psychobiological approach
Biological sensitivity to context model, 528–529
Birth, 52, 133
Bivariate heritability, 174, 174f
Block and Block Longitudinal Project, 686t
Blood oxygenation level–dependent (BOLD) signal, 78–79
Bold state, 256–257, 286
Bonding, social, 281–282, 385–387
Borderline personality disorder, 98, 99t
Brain functioning
activity and, 93–94, 93f
adaptive spaces and, 287, 288
aggression and, 52
anger, irritability, and frustration and, 129, 134
animal studies on prenatal stress and, 299–300
anxiety/stress reactivity and, 370–380, 372f, 375f, 381f
behavioral assessment and, 210
behavioral inhibition and, 32, 71–75, 77–78
Cloninger's three-factor model and, 56–57
effortful control and, 152–153
externalizing disorders and, 569
extraversion and, 44–45
gender differences in temperament and, 487–488
high- and low-reactive infants, 71–75
kindness and, 171–173
neuroticism and, 45
overview, 10–12, 11f, 368–369
pair-bonding and, 281–282
positive emotionality and, 106f
prenatal period and, 298

732 Subject Index

Brain functioning *(cont.)*
  psychobiological measures and, 234–240
  sensory processing sensitivity (SPS) and, 650
  See also Neurobiological model; Neurological factors
Brain imaging, 234–240
Briskness, 58, 93–94, 93*f*, 676–680, 677*t*
Broad measures, 16. *See also* Measurement
Broad traits, 565, 676–680, 677*t*

California Child Q-Sort, 193
Callousness, 566*f*, 568, 573
Cambridge Neuropsychological Test Automated Battery (CANTAB), 214
Candidate gene approach, 321
Caractérologie, French school of, 7
Cardiac measures, 230–234, 241
Career choice, 661–663
Caregiving
  attachment and, 404–405, 407–410, 410*f*
  externalizing disorders and, 570–571
  INSIGHTS into Children's Temperament intervention, 612
  psychobiological measures and, 241–242
  See also Parenting
Carey Infant Temperament Questionnaire, 300
Case-crossover design, 306–307
Catechol-O-methyltransferase (COMT) gene. *See* COMT gene
Central amygdala (Ce), 371, 372*f*
Central corticotropin-releasing hormone, 371–374, 372*f*, 375*f*
Central nervous system
  anger, irritability, and frustration and, 130
  animal models and, 260–261
  constraint/conscientiousness and, 388–391, 389*f*, 390*f*
  prenatal period and, 298
  sensation seeking and, 50–51, 50*f*
Cerebrospinal fluid (CSF), 264
Change, theory of, 610–611. *See also* Stability of traits
Change in temperament, 329–333, 503–504, 544
Characteristic adaptations, 498, 507–510, 511–512
Chicago School Readiness Project, 637, 691
Child Behavior Checklist (CBC), 88, 199, 302*t*, 305, 415
Child Behavior Questionnaire (CBQ), 194
Child Behavior Questionnaire: Frustration/Anger, 125*t*
Child Rating Scale of Aggression, 195
Child temperament models
  activity and, 83–90, 86*t*, 100
  behavioral inhibition model and, 31–32
  behavioral styles approach and, 23–25, 25*t*
  compared to adult temperament, 41–42
  critical approach and, 25–26, 26*t*
  emotion regulation model and, 27–29, 28*t*, 29*t*, 30–31
  overview, 21–22, 22*t*, 35–37
  similarities and differences among, 32–35, 33*t*
Childhood
  anger, irritability, and frustration and, 127, 128–130, 136
  behavioral assessment and, 213
  behavioral inhibition and, 31–32, 70
  behavioral styles approach and, 23–25, 25*t*
  connection between adolescent/adult outcomes and, 685–687, 686*t*, 687*t*
  constitutional psychology and, 6
  critical approach and, 25–26, 26*t*
  effortful control and, 147–151, 150*t*, 154–156, 158, 160
  emotion regulation model and, 27–29, 28*t*, 29*t*, 30–31, 432–437
  genetic factors and, 317, 332–333
  health and, 583–588, 583*t*
  kindness and, 171
  long-term outcomes of impulse control and, 685–687, 686*t*, 687*t*
  models of temperament and, 23–32, 25*t*, 26*t*, 28*t*, 29*t*
  moral development and, 14–15
  narrative identity and, 510–511
  overview, 211
  parenting and, 425–437
  positive emotionality and, 107, 108–112
  psychobiological measures and, 231–234, 240–242
  psychotherapy and, 666–667
  reactivity and, 357–358
  research on temperament and, 8–9
  self- and other-report measures and, 186*t*–188*t*, 190–196
  structure of temperament and, 22–23, 35–37
  from temperament to personality traits and, 504–507
  See also Adolescents; Infancy; Preschoolers; Toddlers
Childhood obesity, 585–586, 587
Children-of-twins design, 306, 309
Children's Behavior Questionnaire (CBQ)
  activity and, 85, 86*t*
  anger, irritability, and frustration and, 127–128
  effortful control and, 146*t*, 149
  overview, 12–13, 13–14, 28, 32–35, 33*t*, 36–37, 190–191
  psychobiological approach and, 27–29, 28*t*
CHRNA4 gene, 328*t*, 332
Cigarette use
  activity and, 88–89
  animal studies on prenatal substance use, 303
  conscientiousness and, 595
  human studies on prenatal substance use, 304
  overview, 563–564
  prenatal period and, 307–308, 309
  See also Substance use
Circumplex model, 282
Classification system, 541–542
Classroom environment
  history of temperament-based intervention and, 509
  INSIGHTS into Children's Temperament intervention, 611–615, 614*f*
  overview, 627–629
  school-based interventions and, 636–639
  See also Academic performance; Environment
Clustering approaches, 127
Cognitive functioning
  academic performance and, 631–633, 632*f*
  anger, irritability, and frustration and, 129, 130
  biases in, 508–510, 552
  evolution and, 275
  health and, 583*t*
  parenting and, 425–426
Cognitive styles, 552
Colorado Childhood Temperament Inventory (CCTI), 85, 86*t*, 187*t*, 193, 193–194
Colorado Longitudinal Twin Study, 685–686, 686*t*
Common cause model, 543–544
Community, as a distal factor, 519
Comorbidity, 541, 574
Compassion, 169. *See also* Kindness
COMT gene
  anger, irritability, and frustration and, 131, 132
  anxiety/stress reactivity and, 376–377, 381*f*
  attachment and, 407, 416–418
  change in temperament and, 332
  effortful control and, 154, 356
  molecular genetic research, 326*t*
Concomitants model, 544
Conditioning, 53–54, 383–384
Conduct disorders (CD)
  genetic factors and, 573
  overview, 652–653
  parenting and, 570–571
  psychobiological measures and, 233
  spectrum models of, 568–569
  vulnerability models of, 566–567, 566*f*
  See also Conduct problems; Externalizing disorders; Psychopathology
Conduct problems, 308*t*, 332–333, 634. *See also* Conduct disorders (CD)
Conflict, 151, 152*f*, 445*f*, 664–665
Congenital adrenal hyperplasia (CAH), 487–488
Conscientiousness
  academic performance and, 628–629, 631–633, 632*f*
  adaptive spaces and, 284, 290*f*

Big Five model and, 46–47
comparing adult and child
  temperament traits and, 42
developmental processes and, 544
DOES acronym and, 645
educational attainment and,
  633–634, 635
externalizing disorders and, 564,
  567f
gender differences in temperament
  and, 481, 482t, 483
health and, 584, 586–588, 588,
  593–595, 595–596
internalizing disorders and, 549, 551,
  555–556
neurogenetic and experiential
  processes and, 369
overview, 581
positive emotionality and, 107, 108
prefrontal executive control adaptive
  space and, 283
psychopathology and, 542
reactivity/affect intensity and, 281
self- and other-report measures and,
  198
Tellegen's three-factor model, 55–56
from temperament to personality
  traits and, 504, 505–506
Consequences model, 544
Consistency of traits, 170
Constraint, 676–680
Constraint factor
externalizing disorders and, 564
health and, 593–595
overview, 677t
Tellegen's three-factor model, 55–56
Constraint with Psychoticism, 55–56
Constraint/Conscientiousness, 369,
  388–391, 389f, 390f, 593–595
Consummatory affiliative reward,
  391–393, 392f
Context-specific effects, 318–319
Contextual–developmental perspective
adaptive and maladaptive
  development and, 471
cross-cultural research and, 466
culture and, 463–465, 464f, 473–474
Continuity in temperament, 330–332.
  See also Change in temperament;
  Stability of traits
Continuous performance task (CPT),
  214
Continuum/spectrum model, 543–544
Control, 425, 427, 427–428, 467–468
Cool Little Kids intervention, 618f,
  620, 691
Cooperativeness, 56–57
Coping methods
anger interventions and, 136
characteristic adaptations and,
  508–510
cultural factors in, 12–13
multistage mediation and, 524–525
psychobiological measures and, 233,
  240
role of temperament traits in the
  development of personality and,
  499f

Copy number polymorphisms (CNPs),
  321
Cortical systems, 77, 113, 130
Corticomedial nucleus, 72
Corticotropin-releasing hormone
  (CRH)
adult temperament and, 391
animal models and, 256–257, 257,
  262f, 263–264
anxiety/stress reactivity and, 371–
  374, 372f, 375f, 378–380, 381f
behavioral inhibition model and, 32
dopamine functioning and, 385f
etiology of temperament and, 683
molecular genetic research, 328t
overview, 679
Cortisol
anxiety/stress reactivity and,
  371–374
attachment and, 409
culture and, 467
human studies on prenatal stress,
  301
prenatal period and, 302t
psychobiological measures and,
  237–240
reactivity and, 348–349
Couple psychotherapy, 663–666. See
  also Psychotherapy
CRH gene. See Corticotropin-releasing
  hormone (CRH)
CRH-R1, 373–374
Critical approach, 25–26, 26t
Cross-cultural research
anger, irritability, and frustration
  and, 133
future directions in, 473–474
methodological issues in, 465–466
overview, 12–13, 462–463
See also Culture
Cross-sectional associations, 546
Crown–Crisp Index, Anxiety Scale,
  302t
Cuddliness, 676–680, 677t
Culture
activity and, 94–95
adaptive and maladaptive
  development and, 470–473
anger, irritability, and frustration
  and, 133
behavioral inhibition and, 75
contextual–developmental
  perspective of, 463–465, 464f
display of temperament
  characteristics, 466–468
as a distal factor, 519
future research directions, 473–474
INSIGHTS into Children's
  Temperament intervention,
  611–612
kindness and, 170–171
moderating role of temperament
  and, 413
overview, 12–13, 462–463, 473–474
peer relationships and, 453–454
values and social attitudes and,
  468–470
See also Cross-cultural research

Curious/Bold, 256–257
Curriculum, 611–615, 614f
CYP17 gene, 328t
CYP19 gene, 328t
CYP2C19 gene, 327t

Dandelion children, 410–411, 689
DARPP-32 gene, 131
DBH gene, 328t
Defensive or fearful motivational
  system, 27
Delay, 150t. See also Gratification delay
Delinquency, 566. See also Conduct
  disorders (CD); Oppositional
  defiant disorder (ODD)
Dependency, 547, 658
Dependent personality disorder, 100t
Depression
activity and, 98, 99t
anger, irritability, and frustration
  and, 134–135
anxiety/stress reactivity and, 377
assessment and, 656–658
biological measures of, 75–76
comorbidity of with anxiety
  disorders, 551
culture and, 471–472, 472
diagnosis and, 657–658
evolution and, 279
gender differences in temperament
  and, 484, 489
genetic factors and, 333, 419
health and, 585–586, 592
interactions between temperamental
  reactivity and regulation, 358–359
interpersonal difficulties and, 552
mediators and moderators of
  temperament and, 551–554
molecular genetic research, 321–322
overview, 545–548
positive emotionality and, 106f, 116
reactive adolescents and, 78–79
risk factors and, 522–523, 526
self- and other-report measures and,
  195
treatment and, 554–555
See also Internalizing disorders;
  Psychopathology
Depressogenic cognitive biases, 509
Depth of processing, 645
Desire, 381
Destructive behaviors, 114–115
Developmental processes
adaptive and maladaptive
  development and, 470–473
anger, irritability, and frustration
  and, 128–130, 132–134
change in temperament and,
  329–333
culture and, 463–465, 464f, 470–473
dynamic nature of temperament
  and, 544
effortful control and, 154–156,
  157–158, 160, 355–356, 356–359,
  357f
externalizing disorders and, 574
gender differences in temperament
  and, 488, 489–490

Developmental processes (cont.)
  genetic factors and, 317, 332–333
  health and, 582
  history of temperament-based intervention and, 607–608
  individual differences and, 369
  internalizing disorders and, 556
  kindness and, 170
  list of measures across the lifespan, 186t–190t
  neurobiological factors and, 351–352
  overview, 4–5, 10–12, 11f, 684–689, 686t, 687t, 695
  parenting and, 425–437, 432–437
  peer relationships and, 443–444, 453
  processes through which temperament shapes personality development, 500–503, 501t
  reactivity and, 73–75, 351–352, 356–359, 357f
  risk factors and, 519–520, 520f, 532–533
  role of temperament traits in the development of personality and, 498–500, 499f
  sensory processing sensitivity (SPS) and, 650–651
  socioemotional development, 157–158
Developmental risks, 519–520, 520f. See also Risk factors
Developmental theories, 84
Diagnosis, 333, 646–647, 656–658, 690–691. See also Assessment; Externalizing disorders; *individual diagnoses*; Internalizing disorders; Psychopathology
Diagnostic and Statistical Manual of Mental Disorders (DSM), 647, 656–658
Diagnostic and Statistical Manual of Mental Disorders (DSM-IV-TR), 563, 566
Diagnostic and Statistical Manual of Mental Disorders, fourth edition (DSM-IV), 198, 279
Diathesis–stress, 410, 528, 543–544
Diet, 133–134, 587–588, 590
Differential reactivity, 528–529
Differential susceptibility paradigm
  attachment and, 410–412, 411f, 412f
  bidirectional differential susceptibility, 415–417
  links between early temperament and adult outcomes and, 688–689
  overview, 403, 418–419
  psychotherapy and, 646
  risk factors and, 528–529
Differentiated measures, 16. See also Measurement
Difficult child typology
  activity and, 89–90
  adaptive and maladaptive development and, 471
  culture and, 468–469, 471
  interactions between temperament and parenting and, 432–435

moderating role of temperament and, 413, 529
overview, 24, 211, 405
parenting and, 427–428, 429–431
peer relationships and, 448–449
risk factors and, 526, 529
self- and other-report measures and, 184–185
Difficult temperament, 125t, 127, 480, 608
Dimensions, 210t, 676–680, 677t
Dimensions of Temperament Survey (DOTS), 188t, 192, 199
Dimensions of Temperament Survey—Adult Self-Report (DOTS-ASR), 192
Dimensions of Temperament Survey—Child Self-Report (DOTS-CSR), 192
Dimensions of Temperament Survey—Revised (DOTS-R), 188t, 192, 195
Disagreeable Disinhibition, 284–285, 285f, 286, 287, 289
Discipline, 159–160, 415, 435, 436
Discomfort, 127–128, 127f
Disinhibition
  adaptive spaces and, 284–285, 285f, 289
  animal studies on prenatal substance use, 302–303
  attachment and, 416
  externalizing disorders and, 568
  neurochemical basis of, 352
  psychopathology and, 542
Disposition, 125–126
Dispositional anger, 125–126, 130–132, 134–136. See also Anger
Dispositional signature, 497–498
Disruption, 464
Distal factors, 519
Distractibility, 24
Divorce risk, 663
DNA
  anger, irritability, and frustration and, 131–132
  anxiety/stress reactivity and, 379
  assessment and, 224
  genotype–environment correlations (GEr) and, 334
  molecular genetic research, 321
  sensation seeking and, 49
DOES acronym, 654–655
Dogs, 252–253, 252t, 260–261. See also Animal models
Domain, 210t
Dominance, 260, 278, 286. See also Aggression
Dominance/Sensation Seeking, 278, 285, 286, 290f
Dopamine (DA) projection system, 382–383
Dopamine D4 receptor (DRD4)
  anger, irritability, and frustration and, 131
  animal models and, 262f, 264
  attachment and, 407, 410–411, 416–418, 419

  change in temperament and, 332
  developmental outcomes and, 333
  effortful control and, 153, 356
  externalizing disorders and, 572–573
  genotype–environment interactions (G x E) and, 336
  molecular genetic research, 322, 323t–324t, 325t
  overview, 14
  positive emotionality and, 112–113
  psychobiological measures and, 235–236
  reactivity and, 352
  sensation seeking and, 49
Dopamine system
  adult temperament and, 391
  anger, irritability, and frustration and, 131
  animal studies on prenatal stress and, 299–300
  attachment and, 407, 410–411, 416–418
  behavioral assessment and, 210
  behavioral inhibition and, 32, 72–73
  Cloninger's three-factor model and, 56–57
  effortful control and, 153, 356
  etiology of temperament and, 683
  externalizing disorders and, 572–573
  extraversion and, 382–385, 383f
  interactions between temperamental reactivity and regulation, 357f
  molecular genetic research, 321–322
  positive emotionality and, 106f, 112–113
  psychobiological measures and, 235–236
  sensation seeking and, 49, 50–51, 50f
  sensory processing sensitivity (SPS) and, 649–650
  social bonding and, 386
Dopamine transporter 1 (DAT1), 153–154, 308, 325t–326t, 333
Dopamine transporter (DAT), 384, 385f
Dopamine-beta-hydroxylase (DBH), 50–51, 50f
Dorsal region of the ACC (dACC), 130, 388
Dorsolateral prefrontal cortex (DLPFC), 153
Dot-probe task, 359
Double risk model, 413
Doves, 254–255. See also Animal models
DRD2, 407
Drive, 107
Dropping out of highschool, 633–634. See also Academic performance
Drug use, 88–89. See also Substance use
Dual-risk model, 413
Dunedin Multidisciplinary Health and Development Study, 686t, 687t
Dysregulation, 448–449
Dysthymia, 99t, 546. See also Internalizing disorders

EAAT2 gene, 328t
Eagerness, 527

Subject Index

Early Adolescent Temperament Questionnaire—Revised (EATQ-R)
  effortful control and, 146t
  overview, 32–35, 33t, 188t, 195
  psychobiological approach and, 27–29, 28t
Early Adult Questionnaire (EAQ), 188t, 196
Early Adult Temperament Questionnaire, 90–91
Early adversity, 384, 385f
Early childhood, 32–34, 33t. *See also* Childhood
Early Childhood Behavior Questionnaire (ECBQ), 146t, 186t, 191
Early Infancy Temperament Questionnaire (EITQ), 85, 86t, 186t, 302t
Early Infant and Toddler Temperament Questionnaires, 300
Early positive mutuality, 159–160
EAS Temperament Survey (EAS-TS)
  activity and, 85, 86t, 90–91, 95
  kindness and, 173–174
  overview, 26, 26t, 32–35, 33t, 36–37
EASI model, 25–26, 26t
EASI Questionnaire: Emotionality, 125t
EASI-III Questionnaire, 187t, 193–194
Easy child typology
  moderating role of temperament and, 529
  overview, 24, 211, 405
  risk factors and, 526, 529
Eating disorders, 98, 99t, 116, 563–564
Ectomorphic components, 6, 76–77
Education, 596
Educational attainment, 630, 633–636, 635f
Effect size, 317
Effective experience, 8–9
Effortful control
  academic performance and, 628–629, 630, 635f
  adaptive spaces and, 284
  anger, irritability, and frustration and, 127–128, 127f, 129
  animal models and, 260–261
  behavioral assessment and, 213–214
  biological factors in, 151–154
  characteristic adaptations and, 508–509
  cognitive biases and, 552
  definition of, 145–147
  developmental processes and, 154–156, 355–356
  evolution and, 282–283
  externalizing disorders and, 564, 566f, 567, 573
  gender differences in temperament and, 481, 482t, 483
  genetic factors and, 317, 333
  health and, 593–595, 595
  interactions between temperament and parenting and, 435–436
  measurement and, 147–151, 150t, 152f, 195

molecular genetic research, 323t, 325t, 328t
moral development and, 14–15
narrative identity and, 511
neurobiological factors and, 352–356
overview, 9–10, 145, 146t, 161, 581, 676–680, 677t
parenting and, 428–429
peer relationships and, 444f, 445f, 450–452
positive emotionality and, 108–109
prefrontal executive control adaptive space and, 282–283
processes through which temperament shapes personality development, 501–502
promoting, 159–161
psychobiological approach and, 27, 233
reactivity and, 356–359, 357f
risk factors and, 530, 532
role of temperament traits in the development of personality and, 498, 499f
school-based interventions and, 636
self-regulation and, 156–159
from temperament to personality traits and, 505–506
Western Europe schools and, 7
See also Self-regulation
Effortful Control/Conscientiousness, 288
EGF gene, 326t
Elation, 381
Electroencephalographic (EEG) wave patterns
  animal models and, 256–257
  attachment and, 409
  behavioral assessment and, 213, 224
  behavioral inhibition and, 75–76
  extraversion and, 44
  neuroticism and, 45
  overview, 69, 349
  positive emotionality and, 113
  psychobiological measures and, 234–240
Electromyogram (EMG) eyeblink response, 45
Emotion regulation
  behavioral assessment and, 223
  multistage mediation and, 524–525
  overview, 30–31
  psychobiological approach and, 230
  risk factors and, 522
  self- and other-report measures and, 194–195
See also Self-regulation
Emotional reactivity
  activity and, 93–94, 93f, 97t, 99t–100t
  DOES acronym and, 655
  Formal Characteristics of Behavior—Temperament Inventory (FCB-TI) and, 59
  peer relationships and, 448–449
  sensory processing sensitivity (SPS) and, 650
See also Reactivity

Emotional stability, 581, 628–629, 631–633, 632f
Emotional Stability–Instability, 7–8. *See also* Neuroticism
Emotionality
  comparing adult and child temperament traits and, 42
  critical approach and, 25–26, 26t
  emotion regulation model and, 27–29
  genetic factors and, 317
  high- and low-reactive infants and, 74–75
  overview, 7–8
  psychobiological approach and, 26–29, 28t, 29t, 231–232
  self- and other-report measures and, 194–195
  Western Europe schools and, 7
See also Negative emotionality/affectivity; Neuroticism; Positive emotionality/affectivity
Emotionality, activity, and sociability (EAS), 84. *See also* Activity; Emotionality; Sociability
Emotionality, Activity, and Sociability Temperament Survey for Adults (EAS), 189t, 196–197
Emotional/motivational system, 368–369
Emotion-centered theory of temperament, 84
Emotions, 3–5, 84–85
Empathy
  adaptive spaces and, 286
  animal models and, 255–257, 261
  effortful control and, 157
  externalizing disorders and, 571
  overlap of with other temperament dimensions, 174f
  overview, 168, 169, 173–175, 676–680, 677t
See also Kindness
Endomorphic components, 6
Endophenotypes, 333, 374–377, 375f, 392f
Endorphins, 50f, 51, 386
Endurance, 59, 93–94, 93f
Engagement, 220t, 508
Enthusiasm, 381
Environment
  activity and, 95–96, 96f
  adult temperament and, 392f, 393
  anger, irritability, and frustration and, 126, 132–134
  animal models and, 254–255
  anxiety/stress reactivity and, 378–380, 381f
  attachment and, 405–407, 417–418, 419
  behavioral assessment and, 213
  change in temperament and, 329–333
  developmental processes and, 10–12, 498–499, 499f, 544
  differential susceptibility and, 411–412, 411f, 412f

Environment *(cont.)*
    dopamine functioning and, 384, 385*f*
    evolution and, 273
    externalizing disorders and, 569–574, 572*f*
    extraversion and, 385
    gender differences in temperament and, 487
    genetic factors and, 112, 316, 319–320, 336–337, 417–418, 419
    history of temperament-based intervention and, 607–608
    interactions between temperamental reactivity and regulation, 356–359, 357*f*
    interface between nature and nurture, 333–336
    internalizing disorders and, 553
    links between early temperament and adult outcomes and, 688–689
    meaning of temperament and, 674–675
    moderating role of temperament and, 412–418
    parenting and, 431
    peer relationships and, 446
    prenatal period and, 308
    processes through which temperament shapes personality development, 500–503, 501*t*
    psychobiological measures and, 232–233, 240–241
    reactive covariance, 523
    school-based interventions and, 636–639
    sensory processing sensitivity (SPS) and, 649
Environment of evolutionary adaptedness (EEA), 273. *See also* Adaptive processes; Environment; Evolution
Environmental construal, 500–503, 501*t*, 688–689
Environmental elicitation, 500–503, 501*t*, 688–689
Environmental selection, 688–689
Environmental selection and manipulation, 500–503, 501*t*
Epigenetics, 368–369, 379, 556, 684
Error-related negativity (ERN), 158, 356, 358
ESR1 gene, 327*t*
Etiological heterogeneity, 544–545
Etiology of temperament, 682–684
Event-related potential (ERP)
    behavioral inhibition and, 76
    developmental processes and, 355–356
    effortful control and, 156, 159, 160, 355–356
    extraversion and, 44
Evocative effects of behavior, 425–426
Evoked potentials (EPs), 44–45, 50
Evolution
    adaptive spaces, 277–289, 283*f*, 285*f*
    animal models and, 261
    attachment and, 261, 405

evolutionary theory of sex, 276–277
gender differences in temperament and, 487–488
individual differences and, 273–274
overview, 4–5, 273, 289–290, 290*f*
sensory processing sensitivity (SPS) and, 648–650
social rejection sensitivity and, 388
top-down perspective, 274–276
See also Adaptive spaces
Excitation, 58–60, 95
Excitement
    extraversion and, 381
    overview, 676–680, 677*t*
    peer relationships and, 449–450
    positive emotionality and, 112
Excitement seeking, 42, 287. *See also* Impulsive sensation seeking; Novelty seeking
Exclusion, 445*f*
Executive attention, 147, 153
Executive control, 289, 290*f*
Executive functions
    effortful control and, 14, 160
    health and, 583*t*
    moral development and, 15
    parenting and, 428–429
    psychobiological approach and, 27
Exercise, 638–639
Exophenotype, 392*f*
Experiences, 70–71. *See also* Life experiences
Experiential processes
    adult temperament and, 392*f*
    anxiety/stress reactivity and, 370–380, 372*f*, 375*f*, 381*f*
    individual differences and, 369
    Social Closeness/Agreeableness and, 386–387
Exploration-avoidance, 257
External demands, 586–588
Externalizing
    attachment and, 415
    differential susceptibility and, 411–412, 411*f*, 412*f*
    genetic factors and, 332–333
    health and, 584, 586–588, 591–593, 595
    moderating role of temperament and, 413
    peer relationships and, 444*f*
    positive emotionality and, 106*f*, 114–115
    prenatal substance use, 308*t*
    See also Externalizing disorders
Externalizing disorders
    environmental factors and, 569–574, 572*f*
    gender differences in temperament and, 490
    overview, 562–564, 574
    temperament models and, 564–574, 566*f*, 567*f*, 572*f*
    treatment and, 573–574
    See also Externalizing; *individual diagnoses*; Psychopathology

Extraversion
    academic performance and, 628–629, 631–633, 632*f*
    activity and, 91, 95, 98
    adaptive spaces and, 284, 285, 286, 290*f*
    adult temperament and, 391–393, 392*f*
    Alternative Five system and, 48
    animal models and, 255–257
    Big Five model and, 46–47
    Big Three System and, 43–45
    comparing adult and child temperament traits and, 41–42
    evolution and, 278
    externalizing disorders and, 567–568, 567*f*, 573
    gender differences in temperament and, 482*t*, 483–484
    genetic factors and, 112
    health and, 584, 586–588, 589
    measurement and, 184
    narrative identity and, 511
    neurobiological model and, 380–385, 383*f*, 385*f*
    neurogenetic and experiential processes and, 369
    orienting sensitivity adaptive space and, 283–284
    overview, 676–680, 677*t*
    peer relationships and, 449–450
    positive emotionality and, 106*f*, 107, 108, 111
    processes through which temperament shapes personality development, 503
    psychopathology and, 542
    psychophysiology of, 44–45
    psychotherapy and, 663
    self- and other-report measures and, 197–198
    sensation seeking and, 50–51, 50*f*
    sensory processing sensitivity (SPS) and, 651–652
    Tellegen's three-factor model, 55–56
    from temperament to personality traits and, 504–505
    Western Europe schools and, 7
    See also Positive emotionality/affectivity; Surgency
Extraversion–Introversion, 43
Extraversion–Surgency, 108
Exuberance
    evolution and, 278
    overview, 347–348, 676–680, 677*t*
    peer relationships and, 449–450
    positive emotionality and, 108, 111–112, 113, 115
Eye color, 76–77
Eyeblink response, 45
Eysenck Personality Inventory (EPI), 43
Eysenck's Big Three System. *See* Big Three System
Eysenk Personality Questionnaire (EPQ), 43–45
Eysenk Personality Questionnaire—Revised (EPQ-R), 91, 95

Factor analysis, 256–257, 287–288, 678
Factor analysis model
  adaptive spaces and, 284–289, 285f
  anger, irritability, and frustration and, 127–128, 127f
  temperament dimensions and, 676–680, 677t
Family factors
  adult temperament and, 392f
  anger, irritability, and frustration and, 132–134
  attachment and, 406–407, 407–410, 410f
  culture and, 13
  developmental processes and, 11–12, 11f
  externalizing disorders and, 572
  genetic factors and, 319–320
  genotype–environment correlations (GEr) and, 334–335
  narrative identity and, 511
  processes through which temperament shapes personality development, 501–502
  See also Environment; Genetic factors; Parenting
Fear
  anger, irritability, and frustration and, 127–128, 127f
  behavioral assessment and, 220t
  defensive or fearful motivational system, 27
  genetic factors and, 333
  Gray's theory of adult temperament and, 52–55, 54f
  high- and low-reactive infants and, 74–75
  interactions between temperamental reactivity and regulation, 357
  neuroticism and, 370
  parenting and, 427–428, 430
  peer relationships and, 445f, 446–448
  positive emotionality and, 110
  risk factors and, 526, 529–530
  sensory processing sensitivity (SPS) and, 651
  See also Fearfulness
Fearfulness
  animal models and, 254–257, 259
  attachment and, 407, 415–416, 418–419
  comparing adult and child temperament traits and, 42
  culture and, 467, 473
  evolution and, 279–280
  externalizing disorders and, 570–571
  gender and, 279–280, 487
  interactions between temperament and parenting and, 434–435
  interactions between temperamental reactivity and regulation, 358
  internalizing disorders and, 553
  neurobiological factors and, 349
  overview, 676–680, 677t
  parenting and, 430
  positive emotionality and, 106f

risk factors and, 532
striatum and, 359–360
See also Fear
Fear-induced aggression, 260. See also Aggression
Fetal alcohol syndrome (FAS), 298
Fetal development, 297. See also Pregnancy; Prenatal period
Fight–flight system, 27, 54–55
Fight–flight–freezing (FFF) response, 54–55, 54f, 233
Five Factor Nonverbal Personality Questionnaire, 208
5-HT
  adult temperament and, 391
  anxiety/stress reactivity and, 374–377, 375f, 377–378, 379–380, 381f
  constraint/conscientiousness and, 389–391
  etiology of temperament and, 683
  meaning of temperament and, 674–675
  See also Serontonin system
5-HT1A receptor, 377–378, 380, 390–391
5-HTR1A, 689
5-HTR2A gene, 327t
5-HTR2C gene, 327t
5-HTR3A gene, 327t
5-HTT
  animal models and, 266
  anxiety/stress reactivity and, 374–377, 375f, 381f
  attachment and, 407
  interactions between temperamental reactivity and regulation, 357–358, 359
  molecular genetic research, 322, 324t–325t
  reactivity and, 352
5-HTTLPR
  animal models and, 266
  attachment and, 419
  change in temperament and, 332
  culture and, 467
  developmental outcomes and, 333
  genotype–environment interactions (G x E) and, 336
  molecular genetic research, 322
5-HTTP, 652
5-HTTPR gene, 154
5-hydroxyindoleacetic acid (5-HIAA), 52, 257, 260–261, 264
Five-Factor Model
  academic performance and, 628–629
  adaptive spaces and, 284–289, 285f
  behavioral assessment and, 223–224
  child temperament models and, 22
  comparing adult and child temperament traits and, 41–42
  evolution and, 275, 276, 277, 278
  gender differences in temperament and, 480
  overview, 3–4, 675
  psychopathology and, 542

psychotherapy and, 652–653
reactivity/affect intensity and, 280–281
self- and other-report measures and, 197–198
sensory processing sensitivity (SPS) and, 651–652
See also Alternative Five system; Big Five model
Five-Factor Personality Inventory, 208
FKBP5 gene, 329t
Flanker task, 152f, 156, 160, 236
Flexibility, 221, 530, 573
Fluctuating selection, 692
Focused Attention/Conflict, 150t
For-better-and-for-worse predictions, 412, 415–417
Forebrain neural development, 369
Formal Characteristics of Behavior—Temperament Inventory (FCB-TI), 58–60, 91, 94, 95, 190t
Four-factor model, 284–285
Freezing behavior, 54–55, 54f, 233
Friendships, 444f, 445f, 449, 552. See also Peer relationships
Frontal activation, 234–235
Frontal cortical asymmetry, 106f
Frustration
  academic performance and, 635f
  biological factors in, 130–132
  constructs and measures of, 124–128, 125t, 127f
  developmental processes and, 128–130
  genetic factors and, 332–333
  health and functioning and, 134–136, 135f
  interactions between temperament and parenting and, 435
  irritability and, 405
  overview, 124, 125t, 136–137, 676–680, 677t
  parenting and, 428, 430, 431
  peer relationships and, 448–449
  positive emotionality and, 106f, 110–111
  risk factors and, 526, 529–530
  socialization and the environment and, 132–134
  from temperament to personality traits and, 505
Frustrative and aggressive behavior system, 27
Fullerton Longitudinal Study, 685–686, 686t
Fun seeking, 107
Functional magnetic resonance imaging (fMRI)
  diagnosis and, 657
  effortful control and, 154
  overview, 350–351
  psychobiological measures and, 236–237
  sensory processing sensitivity (SPS) and, 650
Functional significance, 87–90
Functioning, 134–136, 135f

GABRA2 gene, 573
GABRA6 gene, 329t
Game theory, 254–255
Gamma-aminobutyric acid (GABA), 32, 50–51, 50f, 257
GCH1 gene, 329t
Gender
  activity and, 95
  anger, irritability, and frustration and, 131
  evolution and, 276–277, 279
  future research directions, 491
  gender differences in temperament and, 490
  kindness and, 174f
  as a moderator of temperamental effects, 490–491
  negative reactivity and, 429
  overview, 492
  pair-bonding and, 281–282
  peer relationships and, 453
  positive emotionality and, 113–114
  See also Gender differences; Sex
Gender differences
  causes of, 486–489
  developmental psychopathology and, 489–490
  future research directions, 491
  internalizing disorders and, 553
  maturational effects, 489
  measurement and, 485–486
  overview, 479–486, 482t, 492
  See also Gender
Gene–exposure interactions, 307–308
General Educational Development (GED), 633–634. *See also* Academic performance
General intelligence, 627. *See also* Academic performance; Intellect
Generalized anxiety disorder (GAD), 98, 99t, 549–550, 551. *See also* Anxiety disorders
Generosity, 169. *See also* Kindness
Genetic factors
  activity and, 84, 85, 95–96, 96f
  aggression and, 51–52
  alcohol use disorders and, 265–267
  anger, irritability, and frustration and, 130–132, 134
  animal models and, 257, 261–265, 262f, 265–267
  anxiety/stress reactivity and, 370–380, 372f, 375f, 381f
  attachment and, 406–407, 410–411, 416–418, 419
  behavioral assessment and, 213
  behavioral inhibition and, 70–71
  Big Five model and, 47
  change in temperament and, 329–333
  culture and, 467
  developmental processes and, 332–333, 544
  effortful control and, 153–154, 679
  etiology of temperament and, 682–684
  evolution and, 275, 279

experience and, 14
externalizing disorders and, 569, 571–573, 572f
extraversion and, 43–44
health and, 583t
human studies on prenatal substance use, 304–305
interactions between temperament and parenting and, 432–437
interface between nature and nurture, 333–336
internalizing disorders and, 556
kindness and, 172–173, 174f
links between early temperament and adult outcomes and, 689
meaning of temperament and, 674–675
measurement and, 16
motor activity and, 87
neuroticism and, 45
overview, 4–5, 69, 315–329, 323t–329t, 336–337
parenting and, 425–426, 431
personality and, 503
positive emotionality and, 112–113
prenatal period and, 298, 306, 307–308
psychoticism and, 46
sensation seeking and, 48–49
sensory processing sensitivity (SPS) and, 648–650, 652
Social Closeness/Agreeableness and, 386–387
Strelau's regulative theory of temperament and, 59–60
from temperament to personality traits and, 503–507
See also Biological factors; Twin studies
Genetic polymorphisms. *See* Polymorphisms
Genomewide association (GWAS), 131–132, 407
Genotype–environment correlations (GEr), 334–335. *See also* Environment; Genetic factors; Genotype–environment interactions (G x E)
Genotype–environment interactions (G x E)
  attachment and, 417–418, 419
  etiology of temperament and, 682
  externalizing disorders and, 571–573, 572f
  overview, 335–336
  role of temperament traits in the development of personality and, 498–499
  See also Environment; Genetic factors
Glucocorticoid (GC), 237–240, 299–300, 371
Glucocorticoid receptor (GR), 384, 385f
Glutamate transporter systems, 322
Glutamatergic, 322
Goals, 334–335, 499f
Gonadal hormones, 50f, 51

Go/no-go tasks, 214, 354, 359
Goodness-of-fit concept
  activity and, 87–88
  culture and, 470–471
  history of temperament-based intervention and, 608–609
  intervention and, 622
  overview, 23–24, 405
  peer relationships and, 444, 454
  psychotherapy and, 658–660
  risk factors and, 528
GR gene, 379–380
Grades, 631–633, 632f, 636
Gratification delay, 150t, 214, 467–468, 676–680, 677t
Gray matter, 376–377
Gray's theory of adult temperament, 52–55, 54f, 60, 60t
Gregarious/Aloof, 285
GRIK3 gene, 327t
Gross motor movement, 235
Guilford–Zimmerman Temperament Survey (GZTS), 90, 92
Guilt
  adult temperament and, 391–393, 392f
  effortful control and, 157
  externalizing disorders and, 571
  reactivity/affect intensity and, 281
Guinea pigs, 298–299. *See also* Animal models

Habitual behavior, 350
Hard to soothe, 448–449
Harm avoidance
  activity and, 95
  animal models and, 256–257
  Cloninger's three-factor model and, 56–57
  genetic factors and, 317, 321–322, 323t, 325t, 326t, 327t, 328t, w329t
  medication and, 694
  overview, 676–680, 677t
  psychotherapy and, 693t
  See also Negative emotionality/affectivity
Harvard Longitudinal Study, 687, 687t
"Hawk-dove game", 254–255. *See also* Animal models
Hawks, 254–255. *See also* Animal models
Head Start program, 161
Head–Toes–Knees–Shoulders (HTKS) task, 631, 638
Health
  activity and, 96–98, 97t, 99t–100t
  in adulthood and old age, 588–593
  anger, irritability, and frustration and, 134–136, 135f
  behaviors associated with, 583t, 590, 594–595
  educational attainment and, 634
  effortful control and, 146t, 593–595
  future research directions, 596–597
  in infancy, childhood, and adolescence, 583–588

Subject Index

overview, 581–583, 583t, 595–597
prenatal period and, 297–298
See also Illness; Well-being
Heart rate, 231–232, 232–234, 241, 409
Hedonic pursuits, 107, 676–680, 677t
Helplessness, 116
Hierarchical Personality Inventory for Children, 208
High activity levels, 98. *See also* Activity level
High sensitivity, 676–680, 677t
High-intensity pleasure, 278, 676–680, 677t
Highly Sensitive Person (HSP) Scale, 648, 650, 651–652, 655, 663
High-maintenance concept, 608. *See also* Difficult temperament
Highschool graduation, 633–634. *See also* Academic performance
Hinde's model of human development, 10–12, 11f
Hippocampus, 76, 153, 376–377, 379–380, 393
Histrionic personality disorder, 98, 99t
Home observations, 218–222, 220t. *See also* Behavioral assessment; Observational methods of measurement
Horses, 252–253, 252t. *See also* Animal models
Hostility
  adaptive spaces and, 288–289
  attributions of, 126
  comparing adult and child temperament traits and, 42
  health and, 567, 592
  peer relationships and, 448–449
  reactivity/affect intensity and, 281
  See also Aggression
Hostility Inventory, 125t
How I Feel (HIF), 188t, 194–195
HP5 Inventory, 208
HPA axis. *See* Hypothalamic–pituitary–adrenocortical (HPA) axis
HTTLPR, 263
Huntington's disease gene, 131
Hyperactivity problems
  anxiety/stress reactivity and, 377
  educational attainment and, 634
  genetic factors and, 332–333
  health and, 584, 586–588
  See also Attention-deficit/hyperactivity disorder (ADHD)
Hyperpolarization with parahydrogen, 684
Hyperthymia, 676–680, 677t
Hypomania, 99t
Hypothalamic–pituitary–adrenocortical (HPA) axis
  animal models and, 263–264, 299–300
  behavioral inhibition and, 72
  internalizing disorders and, 552–553
  prenatal period and, 299–300, 301
  psychobiological measures and, 237–240
Hypothalamus, 77, 237

Identity, 499f, 510–511. *See also* Narrative identity
Illness, 135–136. *See also* Health
Immune responses, 586. *See also* Health
Impulse control. *See also* Impulsive sensation seeking; Impulsivity
  animal models and, 255–257, 260–261
  long-term outcomes of, 685–687, 686t, 687t
  parenting and, 426
Impulsive sensation seeking
  adult temperament and, 41–42, 53–54
  overview, 48, 50–51, 50f
  See also Approach; Impulsivity; Sensation seeking
Impulsivity
  adaptive spaces and, 286
  animal models and, 254, 255–257, 258f, 260–261
  comparing adult and child temperament traits and, 41–42
  critical approach and, 25–26, 26t
  effortful control and, 158
  evolution and, 278
  externalizing disorders and, 567–568, 567f
  extraversion and, 381
  genetic factors and, 333
  Gray's theory of adult temperament and, 54–55
  health and, 586–588
  molecular genetic research, 321–322, 322, 323t, 324t, 325t, 325t–326t, 326t, 327t, 328t, 329t
  overview, 563–564, 676–680, 677t
  peer relationships and, 450–452
  psychopathology and, 542
  psychoticism and, 46
  See also Impulse control; Impulsive sensation seeking
In vitro fertilization (IVF), 307
Incentive motivation, 210t, 382–383, 391–393, 392f
Inclusion criteria for child temperament, 21–22, 22t
Individual differences
  activity and, 95–96, 96f
  aggression and, 134–135, 135f
  anger, irritability, and frustration and, 126–127, 129
  animal models and, 255
  anxiety/stress reactivity and, 379
  attachment and, 404
  behavioral assessment and, 224
  behavioral inhibition and, 70–71, 279
  child temperament models and, 21–22, 22t, 35–37
  effortful control and, 161
  evolution and, 273–274, 281
  externalizing disorders and, 569–574, 572f
  extraversion and, 383–384
  genetic factors and, 317, 332
  high- and low-reactive infants, 71–75

kindness and, 169, 169–170, 172
medication and, 694
narrative identity and, 510–511
neurogenetic and experiential processes in the development of, 369
overview, 10, 368–369, 497–498
pair-bonding and, 281
personality and, 3–4
positive emotionality and, 118
psychobiological approach and, 26–29, 28t, 29t, 231, 233
risk factors and, 521–523, 523–525, 525f, 531
Infancy
  activity and, 83–90, 86t
  anger and, 111, 128–130
  attachment and, 407–410, 410f
  behavioral assessment and, 213, 215, 216
  behavioral inhibition and, 71–75
  biological measures of behavioral inhibition and, 75–77
  effortful control and, 146–147, 148, 154–155, 352–353
  genetic factors and, 317, 334–335, 335–336
  health and, 583–588
  human studies on prenatal stress, 300–301, 302t
  kindness and, 171
  moderating role of temperament and, 412–418
  overview, 211
  parenting and, 425–437
  positive emotionality and, 107, 108–112
  risk factors and, 521–522
  self- and other-report measures, 184–185, 186t
Infant Behavior Questionnaire (IBQ)
  activity and, 86t
  effortful control and, 146t, 147, 148
  human studies on prenatal stress, 300
  overview, 185, 186t, 218
  positive emotionality and, 105
  smiling and, 483
Infant Behavior Questionnaire—Revised (IBQ-R), 86t, 185, 186t, 223–224
Infant Behavior Record (IBR), 215
Infant Characteristics Questionnaire (ICQ), 125t, 184–185, 186t, 218, 300, 301
Infant Health and Development Program, 414
Infant Temperament Questionnaire (ITQ), 185, 186t, 302t
Inferior parietal region, 376–377
Information processing, 4–5, 130
Inhibited children classification, 42
Inhibition
  academic performance and, 635f
  adjustment and, 470–472
  animal models and, 257, 258f, 259
  attachment and, 409, 416, 418–419
  behavioral assessment and, 213

Inhibition *(cont.)*
  behavioral inhibition model and, 31–32
  comparing adult and child temperament traits and, 42
  critical approach and, 25–26, 26t
  culture and, 471–472
  effortful control and, 150t, 155
  externalizing disorders and, 571
  history of temperament-based intervention and, 608
  molecular genetic research, 328t
  neurochemical basis of, 352
  overview, 405
  parenting and, 427–428, 430
  peer relationships and, 446–448
  positive emotionality and, 110, 113
  processes through which temperament shapes personality development, 501
  risk factors and, 526, 529–530
  sensory processing sensitivity (SPS) and, 651
  Strelau's regulative theory of temperament and, 58–60
  striatum and the development of fearful temperament and, 360
  from temperament to personality traits and, 505
  See also Behavioral inhibition
Inhibition/Activation Control, 150t
Inhibitory control
  academic performance and, 635f
  anger, irritability, and frustration and, 127–128, 127f
  behavioral assessment and, 213–214, 220t
  effortful control and, 146
  genetic factors and, 317
  overview, 676–680, 677t
  parenting and, 428–429
  peer relationships and, 450–452
Inhibitory tendencies, 9–10. *See also* Withdrawal tendencies
Insecure attachment, 336, 408–409. *See also* Attachment
INSIGHTS into Children's Temperament intervention, 611–615, 614f, 620, 691
Integrative Child Temperament Inventory (ICTI), 691
Intellect, 504, 506–507, 581, 627. *See also* Academic performance; Intelligence testing; Openness to experiences
Intelligence testing, 629, 632–633. *See also* Academic performance; Intellect
Intensity of reaction, 9, 24, 84–85, 93–94, 93f, 280–281. *See also* Reactivity
Interaction effects, 426, 444
Internalizing disorders. *See also* Anxiety disorders; Depression; *individual diagnoses*; Internalizing problems; Psychopathology
  anxiety disorders, 548–551
  conceptual and methodological issues, 544–545

  depression and, 545–548, 551
  gender differences in temperament and, 490
  mediators and moderators of temperament and, 551–554
  overview, 541–544, 555–556
  relations between temperament and, 542–544
  treatment and, 554–555
Internalizing problems, 116, 444f, 471–472, 529–530. *See also* Internalizing disorders
Internalizing traits, 584, 585–586, 591–593, 595
Interpersonal Adjective Scale—Big Five version (IAS-R-B5), 281–282
Interpersonal difficulties, 551–552. *See also* Social skills
Interpretation, 126, 509, 552
Intervention
  anger, irritability, and frustration and, 136
  Cool Little Kids intervention, 615–617, 618f
  effortful control and, 159–161
  externalizing disorders and, 573–574
  future recommendations for, 620, 622
  history of, 607–609
  INSIGHTS into Children's Temperament intervention, 611–615, 614f
  internalizing disorders and, 554–555
  overview, 607
  response to intervention (RTI) framework, 610
  risk factors and, 533
  school-based, 636–639
  STORIES intervention, 617, 619–620, 621f
  temperament research and, 690–693, 693t
  theory of change and, 610–611
  See also Psychotherapy
Interview approaches, 211–212
Intimacy, 282, 445f
Introversion, 281. *See also* Introversion–Extraversion dimension
Introversion–Extraversion dimension
  Gray's theory of adult temperament and, 52–55, 54f
  overview, 7–8
  psychotherapy and, 652–653
  sensory processing sensitivity (SPS) and, 651–652
  See also Extraversion; Introversion
Inventory of Children's Individual Differences, 208
Inventory of Children's Individual Differences—Short Version, 208
Irritability
  animal models and, 259–260
  attachment and, 418–419
  biological factors in, 130–132
  constructs and measures of, 124–128, 125t, 127f

  developmental processes and, 128–130
  health and, 134–136, 135f, 586–588
  moderating role of temperament and, 414
  overview, 124, 125t, 136–137, 405, 676–680, 677t
  peer relationships and, 448–449
  risk factors and, 529–530
  socialization and the environment and, 132–134
Irritability and Emotional Susceptibility Scales, 125t
Irritable aggression, 27, 260. *See also* Aggression
Item response theory (IRT), 222

Junior Temperament and Character Inventory (JTCI), 188t, 194, 195–196, 197

Kindness
  biological factors in, 171–173
  measurement and, 169–170
  overlap of with other temperament dimensions, 173–174, 174f
  overview, 168–173, 174–175, 676–680, 677t
  phylogenetic origins, 170–171
  stability and consistency of, 170
  See also Empathy
K-style reproductive style, 277

Lability, 389
Laboratory observations, 183, 212–213. *See also* Behavioral assessment; Measurement
Laboratory Temperament Assessment Battery (Lab-TAB)
  activity and, 87
  attachment and, 409
  effortful control and, 148
  genetic factors and, 318
  home observations, 218–222, 220t
  overview, 216–219, 217f
  positive emotionality and, 109, 110, 113, 114
  prenatal period and, 302t
Laboratory Temperament Assessment Battery—Preschool Version (Lab-TAB), 407
L-allele, 374–377, 375f
Late childhood, 35. *See also* Childhood
Latency of reaction, 9. *See also* Reactivity
Lateral hypothalamus (LH), 372f, 373
Lateral prefrontal areas, 152–153
Laughter, 112, 114–115, 584
Leadership, 472
Learning processes, 500–503, 501t
Life experiences
  behavioral inhibition and, 70–71
  developmental processes and, 4–5
  dopamine functioning and, 384, 385f
  genetic factors and, 14
  internalizing disorders and, 553
  See also Experiences

Lifespan perspective, 582, 596–597. *See also* Developmental processes
Liking, 381
Limbic system
  behavioral assessment and, 210
  externalizing disorders and, 569
  interactions between temperamental reactivity and regulation, 357f
  prefrontal executive control adaptive space and, 283, 283f
Locus coeruleus (LC), 373
Longevity, 589, 591–592. *See also* Health
Longitudinal Israeli Study of Twins (LIST), 173–174
Longitudinal research design, 582, 596
Louisville Twin Study, 215
Love. *See* Nurturance/Love
Low stimulus threshold, 651
Low-intensity pleasure, 127–128, 127f, 676–680, 677t

MacArthur Longitudinal Twin Study, 215–216, 330–332
Magnetic resonance imaging (MRI), 236–237
Major depressive disorder (MDD), 546–547. *See also* Depression; Internalizing disorders; Psychopathology
Mania
  activity and, 98, 99t
  Gray's theory of adult temperament and, 54–55
  positive emotionality and, 106f, 116
Mannheim Longitudinal Study, 686t
Marijuana use, 88–89, 303–304. *See also* Substance use
Marital problems, 663–666
Marker tasks, 149, 151, 152f. *See also individual assessments;* Measurement
Maternal depression, 522–523. *See also* Depression
Maternal negativity, 335
Maternal responsiveness, 570–571
Maternal sensitivity
  attachment and, 414–415
  difficult temperament and, 427–428
  effortful control and, 159–160
  prenatal period and, 309
  psychobiological measures and, 241–242
  See also Parenting
Maternal warmth, 336. *See also* Warmth
Mauritius Child Health Project, 686t
Measurement
  activity and, 85–87, 86t
  anger, irritability, and frustration and, 126–128, 127f
  Big Three System and, 43
  cross-cultural research and, 465–466
  effortful control and, 147–151, 150t, 152f
  extraversion and, 43–44, 44–45
  gender differences in temperament and, 485–486

genetic factors and, 318
inhibition and, 32, 75–78
internalizing disorders and, 545–551
kindness and, 169–170
list of measures across the lifespan, 186t–190t
overview, 15–16
personality measurements, 208
prenatal period and, 302t
psychobiological approach and, 229–242
psychopathology and, 545
research of temperament assessment, 212–225, 217f, 220t
self-regulation and, 428
temperament scales, 12–14
See also Assessment; Behavioral assessment; *individual measurement tools;* Laboratory observations; Observational methods of measurement; Other-report measures; Questionnaires; Self-report measures
Measure-specific effects, 317–318
Medial orbitofrontal cortex, 134
Medication
  anxiety/stress reactivity and, 377
  depression and, 75–76
  internalizing disorders and, 555
  temperament research and, 693–694
Memory
  adult temperament and, 392f
  anger, irritability, and frustration and, 129, 130
  internalizing disorders and, 552
  parenting and, 428
Mental contrasting with implementation intentions (MCII), 638
Mental disorders, 97–98, 99t–100t, 199, 224. *See also individual diagnoses;* Psychopathology
Mental representations, 499f, 509–510
Middle childhood
  characteristic adaptations and, 507
  genetic factors and, 317, 332–333
  interactions between temperamental reactivity and regulation, 358
  positive reactivity and, 429
  temperament models and, 34–35, 36–37
  See also Childhood
Middle Childhood Temperament Questionnaire (MCTQ)
  activity and, 85, 86t
  behavioral styles approach and, 23–25, 25t
  overview, 188t, 193, 194
Mind-mindedness, 159–160
Minnesota Separated Twin Studies, 55–56
Modeling, 426, 683
Moderating models, 409–410, 410f, 529–530, 532
Molecular genetic level
  anger, irritability, and frustration and, 130–132
  attachment and, 406–407

genotype–environment interactions (G x E) and, 336
measurement and, 16
molecular genetic research, 320–329, 323t–329t
overview, 315, 336–337
sensation seeking and, 49
See also Genetic factors
Monkeys
  alcohol use disorders and, 266–267
  anxiety/stress reactivity and, 378–379
  assessment of temperament in, 252–253, 252t
  effortful control and, 261
  fearfulness and, 279–280
  genetic factors and, 262–263, 263–264, 265, 266–267
  neurobiological factors and, 256–257
  overview, 267
  reactivity/affect intensity and, 280–281
  See also Animal models
Monoamine oxidase (MAO), 50–51, 50f
Monoamine oxidase type A (MAOA)
  aggression and, 52
  animal models and, 262f, 264–265
  Big Five model and, 47
  Big Three System and, 46
  effortful control and, 153, 356
  externalizing disorders and, 573
  molecular genetic research, 326t
Mood disorders, 134–135. *See also* Anxiety disorders; Depression
Mortality, 135–136, 594. *See also* Health
Motivation
  adult temperament and, 391–393, 392f
  anger, irritability, and frustration and, 130
  evolution and, 275, 278
  extraversion and, 381
  health and, 584–585
  positive emotionality and, 107–108, 111, 113, 117
  psychobiological approach and, 26–29, 28t, 29t
  risk factors and, 520–521
Motor activity, 87, 235, 628
Multidimensional approaches, 214–218, 217f
Multidimensional Personality Questionnaire (MPQ), 56, 198
Multifinality, 544–545
Multi-Language Seven Questionnaire, 287
Multilevel modeling (MLM) statistical approach, 221
Multiple pathways, 533
Multistage mediation, 523, 524–525
Mu-opiate receptor (mu-OR) family, 386, 388, 391

N2, 353–354, 358
Narcissistic personality disorder, 98, 100t

Subject Index

Narrative identity, 498, 499f, 510–511
National Institute of Child Health and Human Development (NICHD)
  academic performance and, 636
  gender differences in temperament and, 481
  interactions between temperament and parenting and, 434
  overview, 415
  smiling and, 483
Negative Affectivity/Neuroticism, 129–130
Negative Emotionality with Neuroticism, 55–56
Negative emotionality/affectivity
  adaptive spaces and, 284–285, 285f, 287, 289
  anger, irritability, and frustration and, 127–128, 127f, 129–130
  behavioral assessment and, 217–218
  characteristic adaptations and, 508–509
  cognitive biases and, 552
  comparing adult and child temperament traits and, 42
  depression–anxiety comorbidity, 551
  developmental processes and, 498–499, 499f, 544
  evolution and, 279
  externalizing disorders and, 564, 566f, 568
  frustration and, 110
  gender differences in temperament and, 482t, 484
  genetic factors and, 333
  genotype–environment interactions (G × E) and, 335
  health and, 584, 586–588, 591–593, 595
  HPA axis and, 552–553
  internalizing disorders and, 548, 549, 551
  measurement and, 184
  moderating role of temperament and, 529–530
  molecular genetic research, 322, 323t, 324t, 328t
  overview, 7–8, 369–370, 581, 676–680, 677t
  parenting and, 425
  peer relationships and, 444f, 445f, 448–449
  positive emotionality and, 110
  psychopathology and, 542, 545
  psychotherapy and, 663
  risk factors and, 526, 529–530
  self- and other-report measures and, 194–195, 197–198
  sensory processing sensitivity (SPS) and, 651–652
  Tellegen's three-factor model, 55–56
  from temperament to personality traits and, 505
  Western Europe schools and, 7
  See also Harm avoidance; Neuroticism

Negative evaluation sensitivity (NES), 549–550
Negative reactivity, 348–352, 429–431, 432–435, 521. See also Negative emotionality/affectivity; Reactivity
Negativity bias, 287
Neglect, 445f
NEO Five-Factor Inventory (NEO-FFI), 95
NEO Personality Inventory
  adaptive spaces and, 285
  Alternative Five system and, 48
  comparison of adult models of temperament and, 55, 55f
  extraversion and, 43–44
  sensory processing sensitivity (SPS) and, 652
NEO Personality Inventory and Five-Factor Inventory (NEO-FFI), 652
Neonatal Behavioral Assessment Scale (NBAS), 125t, 214–215
NEO-Personality Inventory—Revised (NEO-PIR), 189t
Nerve growth factor-inducible protein A (NGFI-A), 381f
Nervous processes, 7, 58–60, 95
Nervous system, 77, 231
NET gene, 328t
Network of kindness, 168–169. See also Kindness
Neural network, 152–153
Neurobiological model
  adult temperament and, 391–393, 392f
  animal models and, 255–261, 258f
  anxiety/stress reactivity and, 370–380, 372f, 375f, 381f
  constraint/conscientiousness and, 388–391, 389f, 390f
  developmental processes and, 355–356
  effortful control and, 352–356, 356–359, 357f
  externalizing disorders and, 569
  extraversion and, 380–385, 383f, 385f
  history of temperament-based intervention and, 608
  interactions between temperamental reactivity and regulation, 356–359, 357f
  neuroticism and, 369–380, 372f, 375f, 381f
  overview, 347–348, 360, 368–369
  positive emotionality and, 107–108
  reactivity and, 348–352, 356–359, 357f, 390f
  Social Closeness/Agreeableness and, 385–387
  social rejection sensitivity and, 387–388
  striatum and the development of fearful temperament and, 359–360
  See also Biological factors; Brain functioning; Neurogenetic factors

Neurochemistry
  adult temperament and, 391–393, 392f
  effortful control and, 356
  interactions between temperamental reactivity and regulation, 356–359, 357f
  neuroticism and, 369–380, 372f, 375f, 381f
  overview, 347–348, 360, 368–369
  reactivity and, 352
  striatum and the development of fearful temperament and, 359–360
  See also Biological factors
Neuroendocrine dysregulation, 552–553
Neurogenetic factors
  anxiety/stress reactivity and, 380
  etiology of temperament and, 683–684
  extraversion and, 385
  individual differences and, 369
  overview, 368–369
  See also Neurobiological model
Neuroimaging
  effortful control and, 354
  interactions between temperamental reactivity and regulation, 357–358, 358–359
  overview, 16, 349–350
  sensory processing sensitivity (SPS) and, 650
Neurological factors, 71–75, 171–173, 281–282. See also Biological factors; Brain functioning; Psychobiological approach
Neuropsychopharmacology, 693–694. See also Medication
Neuroscience, 10–12, 11f, 210, 211–212, 223
Neuroticism
  activity and, 91
  adaptive spaces and, 284, 287, 289, 290f
  adult temperament and, 391–393, 392f
  Alternative Five system and, 48
  anger, irritability, and frustration and, 129–130
  Big Five model and, 46–47
  Big Three System and, 43, 45
  comparing adult and child temperament traits and, 42
  externalizing disorders and, 564, 567–568, 567f
  frustration and, 110
  gender differences in temperament and, 482t, 484
  health and, 584, 591–593
  measurement and, 184
  neurobiological model and, 369–380, 372f, 375f, 381f
  neurogenetic and experiential processes and, 369
  overview, 7–8, 676–680, 677t
  psychopathology and, 542

reactivity/affect intensity and, 280–281
self- and other-report measures and, 197–198
sensation seeking and, 50–51, 51f
sensory processing sensitivity (SPS) and, 651–652
Tellegen's three-factor model, 55–56
from temperament to personality traits and, 504, 505
See also Emotionality; Negative emotionality/affectivity
Neuroticism–Anxiety (N-Anx), 48
Neurotransmitters, 130, 210, 280, 299–300, 321–322
New York Longitudinal Study (NYLS)
attachment and, 404–405
history of temperament-based intervention and, 608
long-term outcomes of impulse control and, 686t
overview, 23–24, 196, 211
research on temperament in childhood and, 9
self- and other-report measures and, 184–185, 198–199
Nicotine use
animal studies on prenatal substance use, 303
conscientiousness and, 595
human studies on prenatal substance use, 304
overview, 563–564
prenatal period and, 307–308, 309
See also Cigarette use
Nicotinic acetylcholine receptor alpha-4 subunit gene (CHRNA4). *See* CHRNA4 gene
Nomothetic processes, 4–5
Nonaggressive Negative Emotionality, 289, 290f
Non-approach-based constructs, 108–109
Nonparental care, 415–416. *See also* Caregiving
Nonshared Environment Adolescent Development (NEAD) project, 316–320
Nonshared environmental variance, 316, 319–320
Noradrenaline transporter (NET), 322
Norepinephrine
anger, irritability, and frustration and, 131
behavioral inhibition model and, 32
medication and, 694
reactivity and, 348–349
sensation seeking and, 50f
Norms, culture and, 464–465, 464f
Novelty seeking
activity and, 95
animal models and, 255–257
Cloninger's three-factor model and, 56–57
comparing adult and child temperament traits and, 41–42
externalizing disorders and, 569

genetic factors and, 317, 322, 323t, 324t, 325t, 325t–326t, 326t, 327t, 328t, 329t, 333
peer relationships and, 449–450
psychotherapy and, 693, 693t
sensation seeking and, 51
See also Approach
Nucleus accumbens (NAcc), 382–383, 384
Nurturance, 27, 281–282, 284, 286, 425. *See also* Nurturance/Love
Nurturance adaptive space, 290f
Nurturance and pair-bonding adaptive space, 281–282, 284, 289, 290f
Nurturance/Love
adaptive spaces and, 285, 286, 290f
pair-bonding and, 281–282
reactivity/affect intensity and, 281
Nutrition, 133–134, 522

Obesity, 585–586, 587, 594
Oblique point of view, 408–409
Observational methods of measurement
gender differences in temperament and, 485–486
home observations, 218–222, 220t
internalizing disorders and, 547–548, 550–551
overview, 183
self-regulation and, 428
See also Laboratory observations; Measurement
Obsessive–compulsive disorder, 99t, 224, 549. *See also* Anxiety disorders
Obsessive–compulsive personality disorder, 98, 100t
Old age, 588–593
Openness to experiences
academic performance and, 628–629, 631–633, 632f
adaptive spaces and, 284–285, 290f
attachment and, 417, 418–419
Big Five model and, 46–47
educational attainment and, 634–635
gender differences in temperament and, 482t, 484–485
health and, 588
narrative identity and, 511
orienting sensitivity adaptive space and, 283–284
overview, 581
positive emotionality and, 107
psychopathology and, 542
role of temperament traits in the development of personality and, 499f
self- and other-report measures and, 198
Tellegen's three-factor model, 55–56
from temperament to personality traits and, 504, 506–507
Opiates, 386. *See also* Mu-opiate receptor family
Opioids, 32

Opioid receptors, 281–282
Oppositional defiant disorder (ODD)
genetic factors and, 573
overview, 652–653
parenting and, 570–571
spectrum models of, 568–569
vulnerability models of, 566–567, 566f
See also Externalizing disorders; Psychopathology
OPRM1, 262f, 265, 266
Optimal levels of arousal, 44
Optimism, 54–55, 590
Orbitofrontal cortex (OFC)
anger, irritability, and frustration and, 129, 134
effortful control and, 153
evolution and, 282
psychobiological measures and, 237
Orchid children, 410–411, 689
Orienting response, 49–51, 50f, 147
Orienting sensitivity adaptive space, 283–284, 290f
Orthogonal constructs, 407–408
Other-report measures
adolescents, 195–196
adult temperament and, 196–198
behavioral assessment and, 211
cross-cultural research and, 465–466
gender differences in temperament and, 485–486
infancy and, 184–185, 186t
list of measures across the lifespan, 186t–190t
overview, 183–184, 198–200
personality measurements, 208
school-age children, 194–195
toddler/preschool age, 190–194
See also Measurement; Questionnaires
Overarousal, 645–646
Overcontrolled child classification, 681
OXTR gene, 329t, 407
Oxytocin, 281–282, 386, 407

Pain-induced aggression, 260. *See also* Aggression
Pair-bonding, 281–282, 284, 286
Panic attacks, 76–77, 78–79, 99t, 656–658
Panic disorder, 279–280, 549. *See also* Anxiety disorders
Paragiganticocellularis (Pgi), 372f, 373
Parahippocampal gyrus, 76
Parameter, 210t
Paranoid personality disorder, 99t
Paraventricular nucleus of the hypothalamus (PVN), 371–374, 372f
Parent Temperament Questionnaire (PTQ), 85, 86t, 90–91, 187t, 191
Parental depression, 548
Parental Inhibition Questionnaire, 193
Parental psychopathology, 553–554
Parental substance use, 133. *See also* Substance use

Parent–child relationship
  culture and, 474
  effortful control and, 159–160
  genotype–environment interactions (G × E) and, 335
  interactions between temperament and parenting and, 436
  risk factors and, 530
  See also Parenting
Parent–infant interaction, 241–242
Parenting
  aggression and, 52
  anger, irritability, and frustration and, 132–134
  attachment and, 407–410, 410f, 411–412, 412f
  children and psychotherapy and, 666–667
  Cool Little Kids intervention, 615–617, 618f
  culture and, 468–470, 474
  differential susceptibility and, 411–412, 412f
  directional studies, 429–432
  effortful control and, 159–160
  externalizing disorders and, 570–571, 574
  gender differences in temperament and, 487, 488
  genetic factors and, 319–320, 334–336
  health and, 596
  INSIGHTS into Children's Temperament intervention, 612
  interactions between temperament and, 432–437
  internalizing disorders and, 553–554
  moderating role of temperament and, 412–418
  narrative identity and, 511
  nondirectional association studies, 426–429
  overview, 425–426, 436–437
  psychobiological measures and, 241–242
  psychotherapy and, 646
  risk factors and, 524–525
  Western Europe schools and, 7
  See also Caregiving; Family factors; Maternal sensitivity; Parent–child relationship; Warmth
Parent-Report MCTQ, 194
Parent-report measures, 185. See also Measurement; Other-report measures
Parents, 109, 200, 336. See also Parenting
Passivity, 470
Pathoplasty model, 543–544, 547
PATHS (Promoting Alternative Thinking Strategies) curriculum, 637–638, 691
Pavlovian Temperament Survey (PTS), 95
Pavlov's model of temperament, 6–7
Peak intensity of reaction, 9. See also Reactivity

Peer groups, 449, 450, 488
Peer rejection
  culture and, 470
  effortful control and, 158, 451–452
  internalizing disorders and, 553
  peer relationships and, 444f
  See also Peer relationships
Peer relationships
  academic performance and, 635f
  anger, irritability, and frustration and, 133
  culture and, 463–464, 464f, 470, 474
  effortful control and, 158
  future research directions, 452–454
  gender differences in temperament and, 488
  internalizing disorders and, 552
  links between temperament and, 443–452, 444f, 445f
  overview, 442–443, 454
  positive emotionality and, 116–117
  positive peer relations, 106f
  psychobiological measures and, 231
  risk factors and, 530
  social rejection sensitivity and, 387–388
  See also Peer rejection
PEN theory, 91. See also Extraversion; Neuroticism; Psychoticism
Perceived competence, 445f
Perception
  adult temperament and, 392f
  anger, irritability, and frustration and, 126, 130
  evolution and, 275
  peer relationships and, 445f
  sensitivity and, 127–128, 127f, 676–680, 677t
Peripheral glucocorticoid, 371, 378–380, 381f
Perservation, 58–59, 93–94, 93f
Persistence
  behavioral assessment and, 220t
  Cloninger's three-factor model and, 56–57
  effortful control and, 150t
  extraversion and, 381
  genetic factors and, 322, 323t, 324t, 325t, 326t, 327t, 333, 334–335
  overview, 676–680, 677t
  peer relationships and, 450–452
  psychotherapy and, 693, 693t
Personal narratives, 498, 499f, 510–511
Personality
  academic performance and, 627–629
  activity and, 95
  adaptive spaces and, 290f
  animal models and, 254
  assessment and, 184, 208, 209, 223–224, 224, 240
  characteristic adaptations and, 507–510
  child temperament models and, 22
  eye color and, 76–77
  narrative identity and, 510–511
  neuroticism and, 45

  overview, 3–4, 41, 497–498, 511–512
  prefrontal executive control adaptive space and, 283
  research on temperament in childhood and, 8–9
  role of temperament traits in the development of, 498–500, 499f, 500–503, 501t, 503–507
  Strelau's regulative theory of temperament and, 59
Personality disorders, 97–98, 99t–100t, 574, 658. See also Mental disorders; Psychopathology
Personality Testing and Assessment Anxiety scale, 302t
Personalized medicine, 690–691
Pessimism, 593
Pharmacotherapy. See Medication
Phenotype and affective system, 369–370, 380–381, 385–386
Phenyletahnolamine-N-methyltransferase (PNMT), 322
Phlegmatic typology, 5, 7
Phobias
  activity and, 98, 99t
  diagnosis and, 658
  overview, 549
  positive emotionality and, 116
  See also Anxiety disorders
Phylogenetic origins, 170–171
Physical health. See Health
Physical illness, 135–136. See also Health
Pleasure
  evolution and, 278
  extraversion and, 381
  health and, 584
  overview, 676–680, 677t
  peer relationships and, 449–450
Pleiotropy, 582, 583t
PNMT gene, 328t
Polymorphisms
  adult temperament and, 391, 392f
  anxiety/stress reactivity and, 374–377, 375f
  culture and, 467
  etiology of temperament and, 683
  externalizing disorders and, 572–573
  extraversion and, 383
  links between early temperament and adult outcomes and, 689
  molecular genetic research, 321
  social rejection sensitivity and, 388
Poorness of fit, 608. See also Goodness-of-fit concept
Popularity, 444f, 451–452
Positive and Negative Affect Schedule (PANAS), 189t, 197–198
Positive Emotionality with Extraversion, 55–56
Positive emotionality/affectivity
  adaptive spaces and, 284, 285f, 287, 288
  adult temperament and, 391–393, 392f
  animal models and, 258f, 259

approach and, 106–108, 106f
behavioral assessment and, 217–218
biological factors in, 112–114
characteristic adaptations and, 508–509
cognitive biases and, 552
developmental processes and, 544
extraversion and, 381
fear and inhibition and, 110
frustration and, 110–111
gender differences in temperament and, 483–484
genetic factors and, 112–113, 317
genotype–environment interactions (G x E) and, 335
health and, 584–585, 588–591, 595
HPA axis and, 552–553
internalizing disorders and, 548, 549, 551
measurement and, 184
molecular genetic research, 324t, 326t
non-approach and, 106f, 108–109
outcomes associated with, 114–117
overview, 105–112, 106f, 117–118, 581, 676–680, 677t
parenting and, 425
peer relationships and, 444f, 445f, 449–450
personality development and, 499f, 503
positive emotionality and, 107
psychopathology and, 542
psychotherapy and, 663
risk factors and, 527, 530
self- and other-report measures and, 194–195, 197–198
self-control and, 109
Tellegen's three-factor model, 55–56
from temperament to personality traits and, 504–505
See also Extraversion; Surgency
Positive empathy, 170. *See also* Empathy
Positive expression, 220t
Positive involvement, 425
Positive peer relations, 106f. *See also* Peer relationships
Positive reactivity, 427, 429, 432, 521. *See also* Reactivity
Positive self-descriptors, 116
Positron emission tomographic (PET) studies, 52
Posner's model of attention, 152–153
Postnatal period, 368–369, 522
Posttraumatic stress disorder (PTSD)
assessment and, 656–658
human studies on prenatal stress, 300
overview, 549–550, 551
positive emotionality and, 116
prenatal period and, 302t
sensory processing sensitivity (SPS) and, 652
See also Anxiety disorders
Precursor model, 543–544
Prediction, 74–75, 78–79
Predispositional model, 543–544

Preejection period (PEP), 233–234
Prefrontal cortex
aggression and, 52
anger, irritability, and frustration and, 130
anxiety/stress reactivity and, 376–377
behavioral inhibition and, 75–76, 77
developmental processes and, 355–356
effortful control and, 153, 155, 353–356
interactions between temperamental reactivity and regulation, 357–359, 357f
prefrontal executive control adaptive space and, 282–283, 283f
psychobiological measures and, 234–235, 237
Prefrontal executive control adaptive space, 282–283, 283f, 290f
Prefrontal inhibitory mechanisms, 210
Pregnancy
aggression and, 52
anger, irritability, and frustration and, 133
animal studies on prenatal stress, 298–300
risk factors and, 521–522
See also Prenatal period
Prejudice, psychotherapy and, 660–661
Prenatal period
animal models and, 298–300, 301–304
gender differences in temperament and, 487–488
human studies on, 300–301, 302t, 304–305
overview, 297, 308–310
programming and, 297–298
risk factors and, 521–522
stress and, 298–301
substance use and, 301–308, 308t
See also Pregnancy
Prenatal substance use
anger, irritability, and frustration and, 133
animal studies on prenatal substance use, 301–304
causal and noncausal factors, 305–308, 308t
overview, 297, 298, 308–310
risk factors and, 521–522
See also Substance use
Preschool Characteristics Questionnaire, 193
Preschool Laboratory Temperament Assessment Battery (PS Lab-TAB), 30
Preschool Temperament and Character Inventory (psTCI), 188t, 194
Preschoolers
attachment and, 407
Cool Little Kids intervention, 615–616
effortful control and, 160–161
genetic factors and, 317

narrative identity and, 511
self- and other-report measures and, 186t–188t, 190–194
See also Childhood
Prevention, 582, 610, 615–616, 690–692
Primates, nonhuman. *See* Animal models; Monkeys
Promotive factors
conceptual framework for, 519–520, 520f
future research directions, 531–533
influence of temperament on, 523–525, 525f
moderating role of temperament and, 527–531
overview, 519, 533–534
temperament framework and, 520–521
See also Resilience
Prosocial behavior
academic performance and, 639n–640n
animal models and, 261
measurement and, 169–170
overlap of with other temperament dimensions, 174f
overview, 168, 169, 173–174, 174–175
stability and consistency of, 170
See also Affiliative system; Kindness; Social skills
Protective factors, 520, 531–533. *See also* Promotive factors
Provocation, 126
Proximal factors, 519
Psychiatric diagnoses, 224, 267
Psychiatry, 673, 674, 693, 694, 695
Psychobiological approach
Alternative Five system and, 47–52, 50f
externalizing disorders and, 571–573, 572f
future directions in, 240–242
gender differences in temperament and, 480
measurement and, 229–242
overview, 26–29, 28t, 29t
sensation seeking and, 49–51, 50f
See also Biological factors; Brain functioning; Neurological factors
Psychobiological measures, 229–242. *See also* Measurement
Psychopathology
anger, irritability, and frustration and, 133–134, 135f
assessment and, 224
Big Three System and, 46
gender differences in temperament and, 489–490
genetic factors and, 333
overview, 695
prenatal period and, 298
self- and other-report measures and, 199
temperament research and, 690–695, 693t

Psychopathology *(cont.)*
  treatment and, 554–555
  See also Externalizing disorders;
    individual diagnoses;
    Internalizing disorders; Mental
    disorders
Psychophysiological factors, 44–45,
    45, 52
Psychosis, 656–658. *See also*
    Psychopathology
Psychosocial risk factors, 522–523. *See
    also* Risk factors
Psychotherapy
  assessing for temperament and,
    652–661
  children and, 666–667
  couple psychotherapy, 663–666
  future research directions, 667
  importance of considering
    temperament for, 645–648
  overview, 645, 667–668
  sensitivity and, 648–652
  with temperament in mind, 658–661,
    692–693, 693t
  workplace problems and, 661–663
  See also Intervention
Psychoticism, 43, 45–46, 55–56, 91
Psychoticism–Impulsive Unsocialized
    Sensation Seeking (P-ImpUSS),
    50–51, 51f
Punishment, 53–55, 54f, 359–360, 435,
    584–585, 586

Quality-adjusted learning hours,
    635–636, 635f. *See also* Academic
    performance
Quantitative genetics research,
    315–320. *See also* Genetic factors;
    Research in general
Quantitative trait loci (QTLs), 321
Quasi-experimental design, 306–307,
    596
Questionnaires
  adaptive spaces and, 287–288
  behavioral assessment and, 209–210
  bias and, 224
  cross-cultural research and, 465–466
  effortful control and, 147–148, 153
  gender differences in temperament
    and, 485–486
  kindness and, 169–170
  list of measures across the lifespan,
    186t–190t
  overview, 198–200, 211–212
  self-regulation and, 428
  See also individual questionnaires;
    Measurement; Other-report
    measures; Self-report measures

Rational three-factor model, 56–58
Reaction time, 151
Reactive aggression, 288–289
Reactive covariance, 523, 524
Reactive fear, 9–10
Reactive/evocative GE correlations, 334
Reactive–Proactive Aggression
    Questionnaire, 125t

Reactivity
  activity and, 84, 93–94, 93f, 97t
  adaptive spaces and, 288
  anger, irritability, and frustration
    and, 134
  animal models and, 256–257
  attachment and, 403, 410–411,
    418–419
  behavioral assessment and, 213, 223
  behavioral inhibition and, 71–75,
    77–78
  biological measures of behavioral
    inhibition and, 75–77
  brain functioning and, 77–78
  cultural factors in, 12–13
  culture and, 464f, 466–467
  effortful control and, 147, 158,
    356–359, 357f
  evolution and, 280–281
  genetic factors and, 317
  high- and low-reactive infants, 71–75
  interactions between temperament
    and parenting and, 432–435
  molecular genetic research, 324t,
    325t, 327t, 329t
  neurobiological factors and,
    348–352, 351–352, 390f
  neurochemical basis of, 352
  neuroticism and, 369–370
  overview, 9, 211, 581
  parenting and, 427–428, 429–431
  peer relationships and, 444
  positive emotionality and, 111
  psychobiological approach and,
    26–29, 28t, 29t, 232–233, 236
  risk factors and, 520–521, 521
  Strelau's regulative theory of
    temperament and, 58–60
Reactivity/affect intensity adaptive
    space, 280–281, 286–287, 288,
    290f
Reciprocity, 171. *See also* Kindness
Regularity, 24
Regulative theory of temperament (RTT)
  activity and, 92–98, 93f, 96f, 97t,
    100
  overview, 58–60
  See also Effortful control
Regulatory Capacity/Effortful Control,
    108–109
Regulatory tendencies
  activity and, 88
  behavioral assessment and, 223
  culture and, 463
  genetic factors and, 317
  overview, 9–10
  peer relationships and, 444
Reinforcement sensitivity theory (RST),
    53
Rejection, peer. *See* Peer rejection
Relational aggression, 563–564. *See
    also* Aggression
Relationships with peers. *See* Peer
    relationships
Research in general
  assessment and, 212–225, 217f, 220t
  attachment and, 224

developmental processes and,
    684–689, 686t, 687t
  etiology of temperament and,
    682–684
  longitudinal research design, 582, 596
  meaning of temperament and,
    674–676
  molecular genetic research, 320–329,
    323t–329t
  overview, 8–9, 673–674, 674f
  in the public interest, 689–695, 693t
  quantitative genetics research,
    315–320. *See also* Genetic factors
  structure of temperament and,
    676–681, 676f, 677t
  See also Cross-cultural research
Resilience
  conceptual framework for, 519–520,
    520f
  moderating role of temperament and,
    523–531, 525f, 527–531
  overview, 519, 681
  positive emotionality and, 114
  temperament framework and,
    520–521
  See also Promotive factors
Resource allocation strategies, 276–277
Respiratory sinus arrhythmia (RSA),
    231–232
Response to intervention (RTI)
  framework. *See also* Intervention
  Cool Little Kids intervention,
    615–617, 618f
  future recommendations for, 620,
    622
  INSIGHTS into Children's
    Temperament intervention,
    611–615, 614f
  overview, 609, 610
  STORIES intervention, 617,
    619–620, 621f
Responsiveness, 159–160, 425,
    570–571, 648–652
Retrospective Measure of Behavioral
    Inhibition (RMBI), 189t, 197
Revised Child Anxiety and Depression
    Scale, 195
Revised Dimensions of Temperament
    Questionnaire (DOTS-R), 88–89,
    91, 95
Revised Infant Temperament
    Questionnaire (RITQ), 85, 86t,
    186t
Revised Infant Temperament
    Questionnaire—Short Form
    (SITQ), 85, 86t
Revised NEO Personality Inventory
    (NEO-PI-R), 91, 198
Revised Temperament Assessment
    Battery for Children (TABC-R),
    691
Rewards and reward dependence
  animal models and, 255–257
  Cloninger's three-factor model and,
    56–57
  developmental processes and,
    351–352

extraversion and, 382–383, 383–384
genetic factors and, 317, 323t, 325t, 326t, 327t, 328t, 329t
neurobiological factors and, 351
overview, 281–282, 287–288, 676–680, 677t
positive emotionality and, 107
psychotherapy and, 693, 693t
reward seeking behavior, 358–359
sensitivity and, 53–55, 54f, 278, 286, 584–585, 586
striatum and the development of fearful temperament and, 359–360
Reward-seeking approach behaviors, 130
RGS2 gene, 328t
Rigidity, 389
Risk factors
conceptual framework for, 519–520, 520f
externalizing traits and, 587
future research directions, 531–533
individual differences and, 521–523
influence of temperament on, 523–531, 525f, 532
optimism and, 590
overview, 519, 533–534
psychotherapy and, 646
temperament framework and, 520–521, 689–695, 693t
See also Vulnerability factor
Risk taking
academic performance and, 628
adaptive spaces and, 286
animal models and, 256–257
developmental processes and, 351–352
evolutionary theory of sex and, 277
gender differences in temperament and, 487
psychopathology and, 542
Rodents
anxiety/stress reactivity and, 378–379
assessment of temperament in, 252–253, 252t
attachment and, 403
dopamine functioning and, 384
genetic factors and, 263–264
prenatal period and, 299, 303, 309
social bonding and, 386
See also Animal models
Rothbart Scales, 27–29, 28t
R-style reproductive style, 277
Rumination, 77, 126, 547

Sadness
anger, irritability, and frustration and, 127–128, 127f
behavioral assessment and, 220t
evolution and, 279
reactivity/affect intensity and, 281
Salivary alpha-amylase (sAA), 239–240
Schedule for Nonadaptive and Adaptive Personality (SNAP), 285
Schizoid personality disorder, 98, 99t

Schizophrenia, 99t
Schizotypal personality disorder, 98, 99t
School achievement. see Academic performance
School Age Temperament Inventory (SATI), 188t
School readiness, 630–631, 638. See also Academic performance
School-age children, 194–195. See also Childhood
School-Age Temperament Inventory (SATI), 86t, 88
Secure attachment, 159–160, 408, 414–415, 426. See also Attachment
SEEKING system, 277–278
Selective serontonin reuptake inhibitors (SSRIs), 377, 694. See also Medication
Self-consciousness, 446, 484
Self-control
adjustment and, 472–473
behavioral assessment and, 214
culture and, 463–464, 467–468, 472–473
effortful control and, 14
health and, 586–588
overview, 676–680, 677t
positive emotionality and, 106f, 109
psychobiological measures and, 231
Self-criticism, 547
Self-directiveness, 56–57
Self-distraction, 158–159
Self-efficacy, 381
Self-esteem, 158, 333, 646, 647–648, 656–658
Self-regulation
academic performance and, 635f
aggression and, 134
anger, irritability, and frustration and, 129–130
behavioral assessment and, 223
characteristic adaptations and, 508–509
culture and, 12–13, 464f, 467–468
effortful control and, 14, 156–159
emotion regulation model and, 27–29
externalizing disorders and, 564, 566
genotype–environment interactions (G x E) and, 336
health and, 593–595
interactions between temperament and parenting and, 435–436
neurobiological factors and, 352–356
overview, 9, 9–10, 581
parenting and, 425, 428–429, 431–432
peer relationships and, 444, 450–452
processes through which temperament shapes personality development, 501–502
psychobiological approach and, 26–29, 28t, 29t, 231–232
risk factors and, 520–521, 527, 530
role of temperament traits in the development of personality and, 499

See also Effortful control
Self-report measures
adult temperament and, 195–196, 196–198
cross-cultural research and, 465–466
effortful control and, 147–148, 153
infancy and, 184–185, 186t
internalizing disorders and, 545–547, 548–550
list of measures across the lifespan, 186t–190t
overview, 183–184, 198–200
personality measurements, 208
psychotherapy and, 655
school-age children, 194–195
toddler/preschool age, 190–194
See also individual questionnaires; Measurement; Questionnaires
Self-transcendence, 56–57
Sensation seeking
academic performance and, 628
activity and, 95
adaptive spaces and, 286, 288
Alternative Five system and, 48, 48–51, 50f
animal models and, 255–257
Cloninger's three-factor model and, 56–57
comparing adult and child temperament traits and, 41–42
developmental processes and, 351–352
evolution and, 278–279
genetic factors and, 48–49, 323t, 324t, 325t, 325t–326t, 326t, 327t, 328t, 329t
overview, 676–680, 677t
positive emotionality and, 106f, 107, 110, 111
psychotherapy and, 663
psychoticism and, 46
See also Approach
Sensation Seeking Scale (SSS) Form V, 48–49
Sensitivity
gender differences in temperament and, 482t, 484–485
overview, 676–680, 677t
psychotherapy and, 648–652
Sensitivity to Punishment and Sensitivity to Reward Questionnaire (SPSRQ), 53
Sensitivity to Punishment (SP) scale, 53
Sensory defensiveness, 676–680, 677t
Sensory processing sensitivity (SPS)
activity and, 93–94, 93f
assessment and, 652–661
diagnosis and, 656–658
DOES acronym and, 655
Formal Characteristics of Behavior—Temperament Inventory (FCB-TI) and, 59
gender differences in temperament and, 482t, 484–485
overview, 676–680, 677t
psychotherapy and, 648–652
workplace problems and, 661–663

Separation, 213, 333, 387–388
Serontonin system
  animal models and, 257, 260–261, 299–300
  anxiety/stress reactivity and, 374–377, 375f, 377–378, 381f
  attachment and, 407
  behavioral assessment and, 210, 213
  constraint/conscientiousness and, 389–391
  culture and, 467
  effortful control and, 154, 356
  evolutionary theory of sex and, 277
  interactions between temperamental reactivity and regulation, 357f
  links between early temperament and adult outcomes and, 689
  molecular genetic research, 321–322
  sensory processing sensitivity (SPS) and, 652
Serotonin 1A receptor, 371
Serotonin 1b receptor gene (HTR1B), 131
Serotonin receptor 2A (HTR2A) gene, 336
Serotonin system, 14, 50f, 51, 131
Serotonin transporter (5-HTT), 262f
7-repeat allele of the DRD4 gene
  attachment and, 416–418, 419
  early adversity and, 384
  effortful control and, 154
  externalizing disorders and, 572–573
  overview, 14
  positive emotionality and, 112–113
  reactivity and, 352
Sex
  adaptive spaces and, 285–286
  anger, irritability, and frustration and, 131
  evolution and, 276–277, 279
  gender differences in temperament and, 487–488
  internalizing disorders and, 553
  kindness and, 174f
  pair-bonding and, 281–282
  positive emotionality and, 106f, 113–114
  See also Gender
Sex hormones, 489
Sexual activity, 278–279
Sexuality, 665–666
Shared environmental variance, 316, 319
Short Infant Temperament Questionnaire (SITQ), 186t
Shyness
  adaptive and maladaptive development and, 471
  adjustment and, 470–472
  animal models and, 257
  behavioral assessment and, 220t
  change in temperament and, 331
  culture and, 13, 467, 469, 470, 471, 471–472
  eye color and, 76–77
  gender differences in temperament and, 482t, 483–484, 491

genetic factors and, 317, 320, 333, 336
  health and, 586
  high- and low-reactive infants and, 73–75, 75
  interactions between temperamental reactivity and regulation, 358
  molecular genetic research, 322, 323t, 324t, 325t, 327t
  peer relationships and, 444f, 445f, 446–448, 453
  positive emotionality and, 110
  psychobiological measures and, 238
  risk factors and, 530
  sensory processing sensitivity (SPS) and, 651
Single-nucleotide polymorphisms (SNPs), 49, 264, 266, 376–377
Six-factor model, 480
Sixteen Personality Factor (16PF) test, 46
SLC6A4, 262–263, 262f, 374–377, 375f
Sleep problems, 525f
Slow to warm up typology, 24, 211, 405, 446–448
Smiling
  effortful control and, 157
  gender differences in temperament and, 482t, 483–484
  health and, 584
  positive emotionality and, 114–115
SNAP25 gene, 328t
Sociability
  activity and, 95
  animal models and, 255–257, 258f
  critical approach and, 25–26, 26t
  gender differences in temperament and, 482t, 483–484
  genetic factors and, 317, 320
  molecular genetic research, 326t
  overview, 41
  peer relationships and, 452
  positive emotionality and, 110
  risk factors and, 522
  See also Emotionality, activity, and sociability (EAS)
Sociability (Sy), 48
Social and emotional learning (SEL) programs, 637–638
Social anxiety, 74–75, 391–393, 392f, 552. See also Anxiety
Social anxiety disorder (SAD), 377–378
Social attitudes, 468–470
Social behaviors, 425–426
Social bonding, 281–282, 385–387
Social Closeness/Agreeableness, 369, 385–387, 391–393, 392f
Social competence, 449
Social development, 158
Social dominance, 381
Social environment, 126
Social fear, 446–448
Social initiative, 463–464
Social interactions, 676–680, 677t
Social learning theories, 443
Social mechanisms, 583t
Social motivations, 445f

Social phobia, 76–77, 116, 549, 658. See also Anxiety disorders
Social Rejection Sensitivity, 369, 387–388
Social skills
  academic performance and, 635f
  adult temperament and, 392f
  culture and, 463–464, 464f
  effortful control and, 157–158
  internalizing disorders and, 551–552
  parenting and, 425–426
  peer relationships and, 443–444
  positive emotionality and, 116–117
Social support, 298–299, 445f, 473, 583t. See also Peer relationships
Social-cognitive processes, 445f
Social-Emotional and Adaptive Behavior Questionnaire, 215
Socialization
  anger, irritability, and frustration and, 132–134
  culture and, 464f, 466, 468–470
  gender differences in temperament and, 488
  health and, 596
  moral development and, 15
  overview, 12–13
  psychoticism and, 46
  risk factors and, 521
Sociocultural theory, 11f, 12, 463–465, 464f
Socioecological theory, 463–465, 464f
Socioeconomic-status (SES), 414, 427, 519, 530
Socioemotional development, 157–158, 474. See also Developmental processes
Somatic diseases, 6, 97, 97t, 583–588. See also Health
Spectrum model, 565, 568–569
Spirited children, 608. See also Difficult temperament
Stability of traits, 170, 330–332, 503–507, 544, 628. See also Change in temperament
Standardized achievement tests, 632–633, 638–639. See also Academic performance
State-dependent model, 544
State–Trait Anxiety Inventory, 302t
State–Trait Anxiety Inventory for Children (STAIC), 302t
Stereotypes, 485–486, 488–489, 660–661
Stimulus, 93–94, 93f
Stop-signal task, 214
STORIES intervention, 617, 619–620, 621f
Strange Situation, 224, 404, 406–407
Stranger Approach Episode, 407
Strelau Temperament Inventory (STI), 58–60
Strelau Temperament Inventory—Revised Short Form (STI-RS), 190t
Strelau Temperament Inventory—Revised (STI-R), 190t

Subject Index

Strelau's regulative theory of temperament, 58–60, 60
Strength of Excitation, 58–60
Strength of Inhibition, 58–60
Strengths and Difficulties Questionnaire, 195, 302*t*
Stress
 animal models and, 262–263
 attachment and, 404, 409
 culture and, 466–467
 Gray's theory of adult temperament and, 52–55, 54*f*
 health and, 583*t*, 586, 586–588
 internalizing disorders and, 551–552, 553
 multistage mediation and, 524–525
 neurobiological, genetic, and experiential factors in, 370–380, 372*f*, 375*f*, 381*f*
 neuroticism and, 369–370
 prenatal period and, 298–301, 309–310
 risk factors and, 522
 from temperament to personality traits and, 505
Stress-induced aggression, 260. *See also* Aggression
Striatum, 350–351, 351–352, 359–360, 683
Striving, 381
Stroop task, 236, 679
Structural equation modeling, 221
Structural magnetic resonance imaging (sMRI), 236–237
Structure of temperament
 child temperament models and, 22–23
 overview, 10, 676–681, 676*f*, 677*t*
 personality and, 503
Structured Temperament Interview (STI), 88
Study of Early Child Care and Youth Development (SECCYD), 636
Subaffective temperament, 693
Substance use
 activity and, 88–89
 anger, irritability, and frustration and, 133, 135
 animal models and, 265–267, 301–304
 assessment and, 656–658
 conscientiousness and, 595
 gender differences in temperament and, 490
 genetic factors and, 265–267
 interactions between temperament and parenting and, 435
 overview, 563–564
 prenatal period and, 133, 301–308, 308*t*
 risk factors and, 521–522, 530
 substance abuse disorders, 46, 134–135
 See also Parental substance use; Prenatal substance use
Superior temporal sulcus regions, 130

Surgency
 gender differences in temperament and, 481, 482*t*, 483–484
 measurement and, 184
 molecular genetic research, 325*t*
 peer relationships and, 449–450
 positive emotionality and, 106*f*, 107, 108, 111, 115
 psychopathology and, 542
 risk factors and, 526–527
 role of temperament traits in the development of personality and, 498
 self- and other-report measures and, 195
 from temperament to personality traits and, 504–505
Surgency/Extraversion, 278
Susceptibility factor, 412, 413–415, 646. *See also* Risk factors
Sustained attention, 233. *See also* Attention-related processes
Sympathetic arousal, 348–349
Sympathetic nervous system, 77, 231, 239–240
Sympathy, 169. *See also* Kindness

T-703G SNP, 389–391
Task Orientation, 334–335
Task Persistence, 24, 193
Taxometrics, 681
Taxonomy of temperament. *See* Structure of temperament
TBX 19 gene, 131
Teacher Rating Form (TRF), 302*t*
Teacher responsiveness, 509. *See also* Academic performance
Teacher Temperament Questionnaire Short Form (STTQ), 187*t*
Teacher Temperament Questionnaire (TTQ), 85, 86*t*, 187*t*, 191, 193
Teachers, 631, 635*f*
Tellegen's three-factor model, 55–56, 60, 60*t*
Temperament, defining
 academic performance and, 627–629
 overview, 9–10, 21–22, 22*t*, 210*t*, 368–369, 581, 674–676
 psychobiological approach and, 229–230
 risk factors and, 520–521
Temperament, longitudinal studies on
 impulsivity, undercontrol of, 686
 inhibition, fearfulness, 687
 overview, 685–687
Temperament, types of, 71–75, 680–681
Temperament and Character Inventory (TCI)
 activity and, 95
 Cloninger's three-factor model and, 57
 overview, 189*t*, 194, 195–196, 197
Temperament and Character Inventory—Revised (TCI-R), 197
Temperament Assessment Battery for Children (TABC), 85, 86*t*, 88, 89, 192–193

Temperament Assessment Battery for Children (TABC)—Parent Report Version, 187*t*
Temperament Assessment Battery for Children (TABC)—Teacher Report Version, 187*t*
Temperament Assessment Battery for Children—Revised (TABC-R), 193
Temperament Assessment Battery—Revised (TAB-R), 86*t*
Temperament Evaluation of the Memphis, Pisa, Paris, and San Diego Autoquestionnaire (TEMPS-A), 189*t*, 198
Temperament Evaluation of the Memphis, Pisa, Paris, and San Diego Autoquestionnaire—Short Form (TEMPS-A Short), 190*t*
Temperament in Middle Childhood Questionnaire (TMCQ), 146*t*
Temperament Inventory for Children (TIC), 86*t*, 94–95
Temperament Laboratory Assessment (TLA), 87
Temperament risk factor (TRF), 96–98, 97*t*
Temperament scales, 12–14, 126–128, 127*f*. *See also individual scales*; Measurement
Temperamental regulation. *See* Effortful control; Self-regulation
Temperament-based intervention. *See* Intervention
Tender-mindedness, 485, 487
Terman Lifecycle Study, 594
Termination from treatment, 660. *See also* Psychotherapy
Test for Axial Evaluation and Interview Applications (TALEIA-400A), 98
Testosterone
 anger, irritability, and frustration and, 131, 134
 evolution and, 279
 gender differences in temperament and, 487–488
 sensation seeking and, 50*f*, 51
TFAP2B gene, 329*t*
TH gene, 329*t*
Theory of change, 610–611
Therapeutic alliance, 647
Therapy. *See* Psychotherapy
Threat response system, 256–257, 348–349, 445*f*
Three Giant Factors, 91
Three-factor model
 adaptive spaces and, 284–285
 Cloninger's three-factor model, 56–58
 comparison of adult models of temperament and, 60, 60*t*
 overview, 55–56, 56–58, 60, 60*t*, 675
 parenting and, 425
 Tellegen's three-factor model and, 55–56
 See also Big Three System

Threshold of Response, 24, 676–680, 677t
Tiered approach to intervention
  Cool Little Kids intervention, 615–617, 618f
  future research directions, 620, 622
  INSIGHTS into Children's Temperament intervention, 611–615, 614f
  response to intervention (RTI) framework, 610
  STORIES intervention, 617, 619–620, 621f
  See also Intervention
Toddler Behavior Assessment Questionnaire (TBAQ)
  activity and, 85, 86t
  Anger Proneness, 125t
  Frustration/Anger, 125t
  overview, 30–31, 32–35, 33t, 36–37, 187t, 190
Toddler Behavior Questionnaire (TBQ), 186t
Toddler Temperament Scale (TTS)
  activity and, 85, 86t
  behavioral inhibition model and, 32
  behavioral styles approach and, 23–25, 25t
  overview, 32–34, 33t, 36–37, 186t, 191–192
Toddlers
  anger, irritability, and frustration and, 128–130
  behavioral assessment and, 213, 216
  effortful control and, 148, 155–156
  genetic factors and, 317, 332–333, 335–336
  kindness and, 171
  positive emotionality and, 107, 108–112
  psychobiological measures and, 232–233
  reactivity and, 358, 429
  self- and other-report measures and, 186t–188t, 190–194
Tools of the Mind curriculum, 637, 691
TPH2 gene, 327t
Trait, 3–4, 41, 273–274, 581, 655–656. See also Personality
Transactional model, 426–429, 445, 445f
Treatment. See Intervention; Psychotherapy
Tripartite theory of depression, 490

Tryptophan hydroxylase 1 (THP1) gene, 336
Tryptophan hydroxylase (THP2) gene, 389–391
Twin studies
  activity and, 84, 91, 95–96, 96f
  anger, irritability, and frustration and, 127–128, 130–131
  attachment and, 406–407
  behavioral assessment and, 215–216
  change in temperament and, 330–332
  effortful control and, 153–154
  externalizing disorders and, 572–573
  genetic factors and, 320, 333, 335
  internalizing disorders and, 546–547
  kindness and, 170, 172, 173–174
  long-term outcomes of impulse control and, 685–687, 686t, 687t
  overview, 316–317
  parenting and, 426
  prenatal substance use, 306, 309
  See also Adolescents; Genetic factors
Tyrosine hydroxylase (TPH2), 381f

Uncertainty, 74–75
Unconscious Disinhibition, 284–285, 285f, 289
Undercontrolled children classification, 42, 676–680, 677t, 681
Unemotional traits, 566f, 568, 573
Uppsala Longitudinal Study, 687t

Vagal suppression, 436
Vagal tone (Vna), 231–234, 241, 432
Val158Met, 407
Values, 13, 464–465, 464f, 468–470
Variable number of tandem repeats (VNTR), 266, 321, 322, 336
Vasopressin, 386
Ventral tegmental area (VTA), 350–351, 382–383, 384, 386
Ventromedial prefrontal cortex, 77, 237
Venturesomeness, 42
Vetrolateral temporal region, 376–377
Victimization, 444f, 449
Video-Feedback Intervention to Promote Positive Parenting (VIPP), 414–415
Visual sequence task, 155
VTA DA-NAcc pathway, 382–383
Vulnerability factor
  attachment and, 412, 413
  externalizing disorders and, 565, 566–568, 566f, 567f

  future research directions, 531–533
  influence of temperament on, 523–531, 525f
  moderating role of temperament and, 527–531
  overview, 519–520, 520f
  See also Risk factors

Warmth
  adaptive spaces and, 287
  difficult temperament and, 427–428
  effortful control and, 159–160
  fear/inhibition and, 427–428
  genotype-environment interactions (G x E) and, 336
  negative reactivity and, 429–431
  parenting and, 425, 427, 436–437
  positive reactivity and, 429
Well-adjusted children classification, 42
Well-being, 444f, 527, 581. See also Health
Willpower, 14, 57, 676–680, 677t
Withdrawal tendencies
  activity and, 95
  adaptive spaces and, 286–287, 288
  behavioral inhibition model and, 32
  behavioral styles approach and, 24
  culture and, 469
  evolution and, 279–280
  gender differences in temperament and, 491
  molecular genetic research, 322, 323t, 324t, 325t, 327t
  overview, 9–10, 41–42
  peer relationships and, 446–447
  psychobiological measures and, 235
  risk factors and, 522
  striatum and the development of fearful temperament and, 360
  See also Inhibitory tendencies
Working memory, 392f, 428, 679
Workplace, 661–663
Worry, 74–75

Young male syndrome, 276

Zuckerman–Kuhlman Personality Questionnaire (ZKPQ), 48, 55, 55f, 91
Zuckerman–Kuhlman–Aluja Personality Questionnaire (ZKA-PQ), 48